American Film History

The Editors

Cynthia Lucia is Professor of English and Director of Film and Media Studies at Rider University. She is author of *Framing Female Lawyers: Women on Trial in Film* (2005) and writes for *Cineaste* film magazine, where she has served on the editorial board for more than two decades. Her most recent research includes essays that appear in *A Companion to Woody Allen* (Wiley-Blackwell, 2013), *Modern British Drama on Screen* (2014), and *Law, Culture and Visual Studies* (2014).

Roy Grundmann is Associate Professor of Film Studies at Boston University. He is the author of *Andy Warhol's Blow Job* (2003) and the editor of *A Companion to Michael Haneke* (Wiley-Blackwell, 2010). He is Contributing Editor of *Cineaste* and has published essays in a range of prestigious anthologies and journals, including *GLQ, Cineaste, Continuum, The Velvet Light Trap,* and *Millennium Film Journal.* He has curated retrospectives on Michael Haneke, Andy Warhol, and Matthias Müller.

Art Simon is Professor of Film Studies at Montclair State University. He is the author of *Dangerous Knowledge: The JFK Assassination in Art and Film* (2nd edition, 2013). He has curated two film exhibitions for the Solomon Guggenheim Museum in New York City and his work has been published in the edited collection *"Un-American" Hollywood: Politics and Film in the Blacklist Era* (2007) and in the journal *American Jewish History.*

Together they are the editors of the four-volume collection *The Wiley-Blackwell History of American Film* (2012) and *American Film History: Selected Readings, Origins to 1960* (2016), both published by Wiley-Blackwell.

American Film History

Selected Readings, 1960 to the Present

Edited by

Cynthia Lucia, Roy Grundmann, and Art Simon

WILEY Blackwell

This edition first published 2016

Registered Office: John Wiley & Sons Ltd, The Atrium, Southern Gate, Chichester, West Sussex, PO19 8SQ, UK

Editorial Offices: 350 Main Street, Malden, MA 02148-5020, USA
9600 Garsington Road, Oxford, OX4 2DQ, UK
The Atrium, Southern Gate, Chichester, West Sussex, PO19 8SQ, UK

For details of our global editorial offices, for customer services, and for information about how to apply for permission to reuse the copyright material in this book please see our website at www.wiley.com/wiley-blackwell.

Library of Congress Cataloging-in-Publication Data is available for this title

9781118475126 (paperback)

A catalogue record for this book is available from the British Library.

Cover image: Top: Jon Voight and Dustin Hoffman in *Midnight Cowboy*, 1969 (dir. John Schlesinger), photo: United Artists/The Kobal Collection. Bottom: John Turturro and Spike Lee in *Do the Right Thing*, 1989 (dir. Spike Lee), photo: Universal/The Kobal Collection.

Set in 10/12pt BemboStd by Aptara Inc., New Delhi, India
Printed in Singapore by C.O.S. Printers Pte Ltd

1 2016

Contents

Volume II: 1960 to the Present

Part III 1991 to the Present

Also available as part of this series

Volume I: Origins to 1960

Part II 1929–1945

Additional online resources such as sample syllabi, which include suggested readings and filmographies for both general and specialized courses, are available at www.wiley.com.

Acknowledgments

These volumes would not have been possible without the outstanding research and scholarship of our respected cinema and media colleagues whose essays appear on these pages. We thank them, along with other scholars whose advice has been invaluable along the way. We are deeply grateful to Wiley-Blackwell editor Jayne Fargnoli, who was instrumental in helping initiate this project and whose continued support and advice have been crucial. We also thank the highly professional and supportive Wiley-Blackwell editorial team, including Julia Kirk, Mary Hall, Mark Graney, Annie Jackson, Brigitte Lee Messenger, and so many others who have devoted their time and effort to designing these volumes. We also are grateful to Colin Root, Robert Ribera, Virginia Myhaver, and Nicholas Forster of Boston University who assisted in completing the four volume hardcover edition from which this two-volume paperback edition is drawn. And there are so many others – both colleagues and students – at Rider University, Boston University, and Montclair State University to whom we owe our thanks. We also acknowledge the support of Rider University summer fellowships and research leaves that were instrumental in helping us complete both the hardcover and paperback editions.

We deeply appreciate the support of our families and friends through the years we've spent on this project, without whom we could not have sustained our efforts. We remain forever grateful to Barbara Berger, Isaac Simon and Tillie Simon; Mark Hennessey; and Ray Lucia for their love, patience, and support.

We especially want to acknowledge Robert Sklar. Bob's contribution to these volumes goes well beyond the two essays that appear here. His mentorship, scholarship, and friendship meant so much to us over the years. It is with great respect and gratitude that we dedicate these volumes to his memory.

The Editors

Preface

In many ways, this project began in the classroom. When organizing American film history courses, often taught over two semesters, we encountered the recurring problem of how best to select readings for our students. A strong narrative history seemed essential and several of these are available. But because of their scope and synthesis, these texts do not have space for lengthy discussions of important events, film cycles, or artists. We wanted to create a collection of essays that would provide such in-depth discussions. We also wanted original treatments of "bread-and-butter topics" – the rise of the star system, the place of specific genres like the musical and gangster film, the operations of classical-era studios and their executives – as well as less frequently discussed topics. As a means of introducing new areas of inquiry into our courses and the larger field of film scholarship, we especially wanted essays that would cover film production on the margins, such as the avant-garde and documentary, and films made by and on topics associated with underrepresented groups – whether women, African-Americans, Asian-Americans, or gays and lesbians. Although we gladly reprinted several important essays, we mostly asked scholars to contribute new work, extending arguments they had made elsewhere or tackling entirely new areas. The result was *The Wiley-Blackwell History of American Film*, published in 2012, in four-volume hardback and online editions.

The book in front of you is part of a two-volume paperback collection of essays selected from the four-volume hardback/online edition. New material has been added, including expanded introductions and brief overviews of individual essays, designed to guide students by highlighting key concepts and separately listing "additional terms, names, and concepts" of importance. Overviews also reference related essays in the paperback and hardback/online editions,[1] encouraging readers to expand their understanding and further their research. Professors adopting this paperback volume(s) also will have access to pedagogically oriented materials online, including sample syllabi for survey courses in American film history and syllabi using these volumes to create more focused "special topics" courses.

With the classroom in mind, new and expanded introductions address historical time periods marked by each section division. These introductions, it must be noted however, do not pretend to be all-inclusive treatments of their particular periods nor do they systematically survey every essay within each volume – that task is performed by the overviews accompanying individual essays. Rather, the introductions function as a type of establishing long shot, a perspective on some of the more significant events, individuals, films, and developments in a given era, with collected essays providing closer, more detailed views. We also acknowledge that lines of demarcation from section to section, period to period, should always be understood as permeable, never rigid. As such, we do discuss films in the introductory essays that, from time to time, cross these flexible boundary lines.

As with every such collection, and with narrative accounts of film history, we were forced to make difficult decisions about those topics and essays from the 2012 edition that we would include or omit. Undoubtedly, readers will wonder about the inclusion of some subjects and the absence of others. This is perhaps particularly the case when it comes to individual artists. There are essays here devoted to Griffith, Capra, and Wilder but not to Ford, Hawks, and Hitchcock. All historians are painfully aware of who and what gets left out. Moreover, the essays focusing on individuals certainly favor directors over screenwriters or cinematographers. On the other hand, the critical importance of the star is addressed in several essays, many of which simultaneously take up the issue of genre. Our choices grew from the desire to create volumes that could most usefully be integrated into American film history courses as they typically are taught. Although our expanded introductions aim to fill in gaps, we acknowledge that more than a few gaps do, inevitably, remain.

Two approaches to American film history have guided the best work in the field over the past

30 years. The first is a cultural history approach offering an account that combines attention to the industry and its development with a focus on the political and cultural events central to US history in the late nineteenth, twentieth, and twenty-first centuries. A second approach undertakes a far more intensive study of the film industry's production, distribution, and exhibition strategies, tracing the emergence of a "classical" language and recording the shifting authorial forces within the industry. This has been accompanied by important work inside studio archives and with the professional/personal papers of key artists. In writing a history of American film, both approaches are indispensable.

With the 2012 *Wiley-Blackwell History of American Film* and this two-volume edition, we have sought to add a third, vital component – one that pays closer attention to the films themselves. Because the best narrative American film histories have limited space for elaborate, close readings of the films they reference,[2] we believe there is room in historical studies for attention to the relationship between representational or formal strategies of specific films and their narrative or thematic concerns. At the same time, we recognize that a call to include close reading in historical analysis is not without its problems. The wider historical picture can sometimes get lost in studies too focused on one film or a narrow selection of films. Furthermore, interpretive claims about a film do not lend themselves to the type of verification offered by work that draws significantly on archival sources. Still, we believe that close reading is an essential activity and makes a significant contribution. Although the essays published here adopt a "selected topics" approach, we believe they strike a rewarding balance between close readings that contribute to and those that complement the cultural history and history of industry approaches to American film history.

It is commonplace by now to understand cinema not as simple reflection but rather as a form of mediation that produces a perspective on, but by no means a transparent window onto, the world – a world it also simultaneously helps to construct. The relationship between the cinema and the world it represents travels a nuanced route that first passes through the conventions and pressures of the film industry itself. As Robert Sklar has argued in his seminal text *Movie-Made America: A Cultural History of American Movies*,

> We need to be wary of postulating a direct correspondence between society and cinema or condemning its absence. Film subjects and forms are as likely – more likely – to be determined by the institutional and cultural dynamics of motion picture production than by the most frenetic of social upheavals.[3]

With this in mind, we have found it useful to think in terms of groups or clusters of films, closely examining patterns or cycles that form a cinematic landscape. Such clusters or groupings, whether folk musicals of the 1930s and 1940s or comic Westerns of the 1960s, form a coherent field that past audiences had encountered over a relatively concentrated period of time. Essays built along such lines can serve the needs of scholars, students, and teachers who may have time to see or show only one film in class. The significance of that single film hopefully will be illuminated when placed in dialogue with other films with which it is grouped in any one of our essays.

Not all of the essays published here, however, cover clusters of films. Industry practices, significant moments of experimentation, and various modes of documentary and independent filmmaking also are considered, some as parts of larger cycles and some not. Indeed, the scope of these volumes and the larger 2012 collection permits us to place, side by side, a variety of approaches to American film history. We are pleased to showcase the varied methods employed and the range of material now being examined by film historians. We also are gratified to publish the work of so many people in our field, from senior, well-established scholars to those whose important work has garnered attention over the past several years.

Our hope is that, in moving through each volume in a relatively methodical fashion, students and scholars will discover a rich collage that will open new lines of inquiry and contribute to an ever-expanding knowledge of American film history.

The Editors

Notes

1. University libraries and individuals can get information about accessing the online edition at: http://onlinelibrary.wiley.com/book/10.1002/9780470671153

2. We do not mean so much the type of formal analysis of systems offered in a work like David Bordwell, Janet Staiger, and Kristen Thompson's *The Classical Hollywood Cinema* (1985) with its analysis that theorizes an entire mode of production, but, rather, historical writing that includes interpretive claims about the function of specific techniques – mise-en-scène, camerawork, lighting, editing, etc. – as deployed in a film or set of films.
3. Robert Sklar, *Movie-Made America: A Cultural History of American Movies*. Revised and updated. New York: Vintage Books (1994), p. 322.

Part I

1960–1975

1

Setting the Stage
American Film History, 1960–1975

Profound changes rocked American cinema in the second half of the twentieth century, many of which reflected new directions in the history of the nation. A number of these developments occurred or, at least, got under way in the 1960s. By mid-decade, the anxiety that American society had initially kept at bay through a spirit of hope and renewal fully came to the fore, and forces of social and moral cohesion rapidly gave way to tendencies of questioning and confusion. From social rebellion and economic inequality there emerged an impulse toward cultural experimentation that also affected American films, but that, in the late 1970s and 1980s, would give way again to more conservative tendencies, as American politics shifted to the right and the US film industry reconsolidated and eventually reorganized itself on a global scale.

Film Industry Decline and Transformation

The old studio system of five majors (MGM, RKO, Warner Bros., Paramount, and Twentieth Century-Fox), vertically integrated with their own theaters guaranteeing certain exhibition of their films, and three minor studios that did not own theaters (Columbia, Universal, United Artists) had been in place for over 30 years. By the early 1960s this system was largely defunct, its remnants subject to a series of mergers, acquisitions, and restructurings that would install a new generation of leaders at the top of the industry. Their predecessors, the legendary moguls, had run Hollywood as the nation's main purveyor of mass entertainment by defining movie-going as first and foremost a family affair. The new crop faced a dramatically shrinking audience base resulting from demographic shifts brought on by suburbanization and a widening generation gap. During the 1960s, when the nuclear family grew less stable, the industry survived, in part, by targeting the youth market, while not losing sight, for a time at least, of its general audience. And while the relative stability of the classical era had yielded long tenures for studio bosses, enabling them to impart their artistic imprimatur, from the 1960s forward, heads of production became cogs within sprawling corporate structures. In this climate, the rare producers able to flourish long enough to develop a creative oeuvre were semi-independent makers of B-movies, like Roger Corman, and, more recently, writer-director-producers epitomized by Steven Spielberg, whose tycoon status signals a different order of independence.

Hollywood in the 1960s not only found itself in search of a product and an audience, but the industry was also saddled with growing doubt as to how

American Film History: Selected Readings, 1960 to the Present, First Edition. Edited by Cynthia Lucia, Roy Grundmann, and Art Simon.

American it indeed was. By 1966, 30 percent of American films were independently produced and 50 percent were so-called runaway productions – films made in Italy, Spain, and other European countries that beckoned with cheap, non-unionized labor. By that time, also, the effects of the 1948 Paramount Decree, which forced the studios to divest their ownership of theaters, loosened Hollywood's stranglehold on the domestic market. Beginning in the 1950s, exhibitors' burgeoning independence had opened the door to foreign imports. Between 1958 and 1968, the number of foreign films in US distribution would gradually exceed the number of domestic productions (Cook 2004, 427). While in 1955 television was Hollywood's only serious competitor on the media market, ten years later American viewers had an unprecedented array of choices. They could buy a movie ticket to *The Sound of Music* or stay home and watch the *Ed Sullivan Show*; they could (fairly easily) see François Truffaut's *Jules and Jim* (1963) or seek out numerous other examples of what would become known as the golden age of European art cinema – or, starting in the mid-1960s, they could catch the rising tide of third world films. If they were not keen on reading subtitles, their options included artistically ambitious independent films by such directors as John Cassavetes or quirky, independently made horror and exploitation flicks by the likes of George A. Romero and Russ Meyer. Or they could seek out innovative documentaries made in direct cinema style, or avant-garde films like Andy Warhol's *The Chelsea Girls* (1966), which had made the leap from urban underground venues and college film societies into commercial exhibition.

In order to minimize risk, studios began to strike international financing deals that shifted their role to co-producer or distributor of internationally made films, exposing the industry to a wave of foreign talent and new artistic influences. Filmmakers like John Schlesinger and Roman Polanski would parlay their new wave cachet into international careers and relocate to the US. Others, like Michelangelo Antonioni and UK-based American expatriate Stanley Kubrick, directed projects that, while financed by Hollywood, were shot overseas. A new generation of American directors, including Arthur Penn, Sidney Lumet, and John Frankenheimer, who had come from television and also were attuned to foreign film, would also help broaden the aesthetics of American films to a significant degree. The so-called "movie brats" of the late 1960s and early 1970s, the first generation of directors trained in film school, including Martin Scorsese, Francis Ford Coppola, and Brian De Palma, would extend this trend.

By the early 1970s, Hollywood had assimilated stylistic elements from numerous outside sources. The pre-credit sequence it took from television. The long take – while already present in 1940s prestige productions and 1950s widescreen cinema – was extended further through emerging auteurs influenced by European art cinema, independent documentaries, and the avant-garde. These cinemas also helped trigger the opposite trend in Hollywood – the acceleration of cutting and the fragmentation of the image into split screens, multiple slivers (showcased in the credit sequence of *The Thomas Crown Affair*, 1968), or collage-type arrays (as featured in the famous "Pusher Man" sequence from the 1972 blaxploitation film *Superfly*). Finally, the prominence of new wave cinemas inspired a loosening of Hollywood continuity editing conventions. Individualists like Sam Peckinpah, who pioneered slow motion, and Hal Ashby, who popularized the use of telephoto lenses, further broadened the formal palette of studio releases.

When Hollywood staged a return to classical topics and treatments during the Reagan era, some of these devices would be toned down. What ultimately characterizes the era from the late 1960s to the present, however, is the studios' openness to using most any formal and narrative technique, provided it can be placed in the service of contemporary Hollywood storytelling. Since the 1990s, especially, the increased accessibility of filmmaking equipment (brought about by the digital revolution), the diversification of exhibition outlets (generated by the internet and convergence culture), and the emergence of new generations of auteurs (like Steven Soderbergh, Gus Van Sant, Baz Luhrmann, Todd Haynes, Joss Whedon, and Guillermo del Toro, who work on a global scale and cross over between big studio and indie productions, as well as between film and television) have generated a more elastic, globalized film aesthetic for a youth audience weaned on graphic novels, YouTube, and cellphone movies.

Cold War Anxiety

Even before the emergence of the late 1960s counterculture and its wide-ranging critique of American institutions, filmmakers challenged the long-standing political consensus that had underwritten the Cold War.[1] After over half a century in which the movies had lent their support to American military campaigns, celebrating the GIs and the officers who led them, a cluster of films released between 1962 and 1964 no longer marched in step with the Pentagon. *Dr. Strangelove or: How I Learned to Stop Worrying and Love the Bomb* (1964) and *Fail-Safe* (1964) told essentially the same story, the former through black humor and the latter through straight drama. Both questioned the hydrogen bomb as a peacekeeping device and argued that the technology of destruction threatened humanity's power to control it. Although *Fail-Safe* ended with a powerfully frightening montage of freeze frames showing people on the streets just before nuclear detonation – vividly illustrating a population at the mercy of the nuclear age – it was *Dr. Strangelove's* absurdist satire and its eerily incongruent ending – as bombs explode to the song "We'll Meet Again" – that would resonate for decades after its release. Here, citizens are totally absent as the buffoons in charge of their safety channel their own sexual fears and fantasies into a race toward the apocalypse. *Seven Days in May* (1964) imagined a *coup d'état* planned within the Joint Chiefs to stop the President on the verge of signing a treaty with the Soviets. Even more shocking, if ideologically less coherent, as R. Barton Palmer argues in Volume I of this series, was *The Manchurian Candidate* (1962), a returning veteran story at its cruelest, in which Raymond Shaw, falsely decorated a Korean War hero, is brainwashed to become a communist assassin. Caught in the crossfire between Red China and the US, sacrificed by his power hungry mother, and forced to kill his wife, Shaw embodies the myriad suicidal and twisted psycho-sexual impulses woven into Cold War thinking.

Gender Roles and Sexual Mores in Early 1960s Hollywood

During the 1960s, the movies' representation of gender and sexuality underwent dramatic changes, particularly in regard to Hollywood's portrayal of women. Initially, however, change seemed slow to come, as Hollywood's star machinery reflected 1950s ideals of beauty and morality. The reigning box office star from 1959 to 1963 was Doris Day, whose persona in a string of popular, old-fashioned comedies combined Cold War ideals of feminine virtue and propriety with increasingly progressive attitudes towards female independence. In contrast to the best screwball comedies of the 1930s, in which a man and a woman meet, fall in love, separate, and then "remarry" as true equals, in Day's films marriage was not merely the default mode of heterosexual partnership. It became the idealized goal of her protagonists who, in their mid- to late thirties, were afraid of missing the boat that would carry them into the connubial haven of motherhood and domesticity. Glossy Madison Avenue settings in *Pillow Talk* (1959) and *That Touch of Mink* (1961) function as a backdrop for Day's smartly coutured female professionals, as she conveys her characters' conflicted feelings about acting on or reining in her carnal desires with comic verve – all indicative of pressure on Hollywood to acknowledge, however timidly, American women's increasing sexual agency.

Fear of female sexual independence also played itself out in a number of early 1960s dramas about prostitutes: the Hollywood prestige film *Butterfield 8* (1960) starring Elizabeth Taylor, the quirky overseas production *Never on Sunday* (1960) shot by grey-listed Hollywood director Jules Dassin, and two of Billy Wilder's satirical comedies, *Irma La Douce* (1962) and *Kiss Me, Stupid* (1964). Sex for sale served as a displaced arena for exploring various facets of America's uneasy relation to female sexual agency, while ultimately conforming to the logic of a deeply puritanical and patriarchal culture. In best Academy Awards tradition, *Butterfield 8* depicts the prostitute as a tragic, doomed figure whose choice of profession is rooted in an unhappy childhood. *Never on Sunday* and *Irma La Douce* draw on the stereotype of the hooker with a heart of gold, though both are social satires, with left-winger Dassin exploring what happens when prostitutes organize and Wilder lampooning the role of the state in upholding bourgeois mores. *Kiss Me, Stupid* is more abrasive in its indictment of male greed and hypocrisy, as Robert Sklar argues in his essay on Wilder in Volume I of this edition. Perhaps not surprisingly, the film's zany plot – revolving around a small-town composer's scheme of trafficking women to trick a Las Vegas crooner into buying one of his songs – was widely panned as offensively tawdry. As these films indicate, Hollywood was willing to entertain the notion of female sexual agency only if the woman ultimately was punished or the story was moved off-shore to exotic locations and couched within comedy's more outlandishly carnivalesque conventions.

"A Jumpin' Jackpot of Melody": The Musical in the 1960s

In their efforts to domesticate the sexual revolution, the studios were eager to manipulate genre conventions, and none more so than those of the musical. A case in point is MGM's cannibalization of Elvis Presley, whose anarchic musical talent and erotic charge were wasted in dozens of mediocre musical comedies during the 1960s. Even the mildly self-reflexive *Viva Las Vegas!* (1963), one of Presley's better films, heeds mainstream mores by turning his Rusty, a daring race car driver with a musical streak, into an old-fashioned romantic suitor of his sweetheart (Ann-Margret). The film reflects the contradictions of its time by straddling various musical subgenres. Backstage conventions serve to exploit the couple's sexual magnetism in steamy yet safely contained stage rehearsals and show numbers, while off stage the romance plot unfolds with the help of fluidly integrated serenades. Added to the formula are elements of the folk musical and action-packed car racing and crash sequences. Touted by its trailer as "A Jumpin' Jackpot of Melody," *Viva Las Vegas!* is exemplary of how Hollywood, by 1963, extended its time-honored strategy of blending various genres into the musical (Altman 1999), having become so uncertain of its target audience that it tried to be all things to all people.

The trajectory of the musical during this period poignantly illustrates that, despite babies of the earlier boom having grown up to be among the nation's most sophisticated and regular of moviegoers, and the youth market having become an increasingly important demographic, Hollywood still often aimed at a general audience. Family fare remained popular through such vehicles as *Mary Poppins* (1964) and *The Sound of Music* (1965). Industry attempts to recreate that film's overwhelming success failed, however, in such hopelessly old-fashioned yet high-budget extravaganzas as *Dr. Dolittle* (1967), *Camelot* (1967), *Chitty Chitty Bang Bang* (1968), *Star!* (1968), *Paint Your Wagon* (1969), *Darling Lili* (1970), and *On a Clear Day You Can See Forever* (1970) (Cook 2000, 496). The reasons for such failures in the post-studio era are multiple, as Karen Backstein argues in this volume.

As America's musical tastes greatly expanded in the post-war period, especially under the influence of rock 'n roll and rhythm and blues, the repertoire of Hollywood music adapted as well. While a growing number of films incorporated songs by new and emerging artists – Simon and Garfunkel for *The Graduate* (1967), Leonard Cohen for *McCabe & Mrs. Miller* (1971), Isaac Hayes for *Shaft* (1971), and, of course, a small catalog of rock hits for *Easy Rider* (1969) – there remained an important place for traditional scores, especially given the later box office success of futuristic or spectacle cinema. Among those whose music crossed over into popular listenership, but were best known for the movies, was Henry Mancini. After a year at Juilliard and World War II service, Mancini went to work at Universal where he created the stunning music for Orson Welles's *Touch of Evil* (1958). Best known, perhaps, for the soundtrack to Blake Edwards's comedy *The Pink Panther* (1963), the Mancini sound became attached to the early 1960s, with sophisticated scores tinged with sadness, as those written for *Breakfast at Tiffany's* (1961) and *Days of Wine and Roses* (1962).

Gender, Race, and the American Family

Hollywood had been furnishing sober, at times ominous, assessments of the state of the American family even before the inception of suburbia. In the 1960s, however, when the family was far less stable, surprisingly few films dealt with this subject. One reason was the decline of the melodrama – a genre traditionally focused on the family. Peaking in popularity with such films as *Written on the Wind* (1957), *Cat on a Hot Tin Roof* (1958), and *Home from the Hill* (1960), 1950s-style depictions of family strife would appear overwrought just a few years later. Stories involving sex and social mores, as featured in such films as *Peyton Place* (1957) that, upon release, were considered daring and controversial, by the mid-1960s found themselves serialized for television. The family dramas that did get made in the early and mid-1960s were just as claustrophobic as their precursors, but they were filmed in a more realistic style that no longer relied quite so heavily on melodramatic excess and overly ornate mise-en-scène. Adult themes, however, continued to function as a signifier for realism in these films, even as directors like Otto Preminger and Elia Kazan raised the bar on what "adult" would come to mean. As had been the case in the previous decade (and, to a certain extent, before World War II), the industry continued to look to the Broadway stage for adult source material, reaffirming the link between American film and American theater throughout the 1960s.

Kazan had been one of Hollywood's top directors in the 1950s with such adult dramas as *A Streetcar Named Desire* (1951), *On the Waterfront* (1954), *East of Eden* (1955), and *A Face in the Crowd* (1957) – several of which had led to clashes with censors. His 1961 *Splendor in the Grass*, set in late 1920s rural Kansas, is a story about two teenage lovers whose relationship is stifled by a poisonous climate of materialism, sexual repression, and family hypocrisy. Written by William Inge, whose 1950s plays on small town sexual mores, *Picnic* (1955) and *Bus Stop* (1956), became Hollywood box office hits, the film dealt with such issues as premarital sex, rape, abortion, and society's double standards concerning male and female promiscuity. As Cynthia Lucia points out in Volume I of this edition, such issues were just as prevalent in early 1960s America of John F. Kennedy as they were in 1929 – both moments in history on the cusp of sweeping change. *Splendor in the Grass*, like many 1960s family dramas, reflects Hollywood's own anxieties about changing perspectives on gender and sexuality.

Although Hollywood made fewer family dramas during this period, it expanded the scope of the genre by incorporating the issue of race in films like *A Raisin in the Sun* (1961), which depicts a black working-class family's internal and external struggles as they aspire to leave their inner city apartment and move to a white suburb. Made independently by Broadway and TV producers David Susskind and Philip Rose for Columbia Pictures, *A Raisin in the Sun* was, of course, a white production. The studio, however, did allow black playwright Lorraine Hansberry to write the script (under tight supervision), adapting her own 1959 New York Drama Critics' Circle Award-winning Broadway play, which skillfully combined an indictment of racism with so called "cross-over issues" concerning education, entrepreneurship, and home ownership. The film got made, in large part, because of Hollywood's interest in filmed literature and in the rising African-American star Sidney Poitier (Reid 1993, 58).

For black-themed treatments in Hollywood, Poitier's popularity proved a blessing and a curse. He became the first black superstar in American film, but the success of his vehicles hinged on stripping his characters of any political dimension. The formula was at its peak in the biggest – and, as it would turn out, the final – hit of Poitier's career, *Guess Who's Coming to Dinner* (1967), a mixed-race family film in which a white family's liberal ideals are put to the test when their daughter announces that she intends to marry a black man. While hugely popular, the film deeply divided the black community given Hollywood's knee-jerk attempt to ennoble and whitewash Poitier's character – an overachiever and paragon of moral virtue embodying a stereotype Poitier often was forced to play. Although the Civil Rights Movement was at the forefront of national attention in the early 1960s, the studios limited their treatment of race to fewer than a handful of dramas, many of which featured mostly white casts, as true of many Poitier films.

It fell to independent cinema to furnish overtly political stories of black families and black struggle, although these films still were made by white filmmakers. Paul Young and Michael Roehmer's nuanced and gripping drama, *Nothing But a Man* (1963), tells the story of Duff, a railroad worker in the deeply racist South, who struggles to overcome racism and economic adversity in order to found his own family. While the film was poorly distributed, it launched the career of its male lead, Ivan Dixon, who ten years later directed *The Spook Who Sat by the Door* (1973), a film both serious and satirical about the history of the civil rights struggle. These films, as Alex Lykidis discusses in this volume, provide enlightening bookends to the civil rights era.

If Hollywood's adaptation of Hansberry's drama indicated that the industry was becoming interested in black-themed plays, the playwright most popular with studios up until the early 1960s was Tennessee Williams, whose dramas about dysfunctional and taboo aspects of white southern family life had generated solid box office. In 1962, however, a new play signaled a changing of the guard. *Who's Afraid of Virginia Woolf?* by the then unknown Edward Albee upped the ante with its unsympathetic, at times absurdist, portrait of the combative marriage of a middle-aged couple, George and Martha. With a nod to Williams's legacy, Albee's play references the older playwright's 1947 drama *A Streetcar Named Desire.* Although *Streetcar* concludes with the birth of a child, however, *Virginia Woolf* ends with the death of a child – a child that was never more than a fantasy functioning as both tonic and glue for a marriage founded on lies, denial, and false hopes. This same toxic combination dramatically alters the marriage of *Streetcar*'s young couple, the Kowalskis (with Stella Kowalski choosing to stay with her husband even after learning that he raped her sister). As bookends to the baby boom years, both plays represent American families devolving from dysfunction into horror story. Warner Bros. adapted both into highly acclaimed and commercially successful films. The 1951 Williams adaptation, produced under the watchful eye of the still intact Production Code, changed the play's ending, forcing Stella to leave her brutish, rapacious husband. The film thus suppresses the true meaning of Stella's acquiescence in the play, which penetrates the sheen of morality and emotional commitment to reveal the family as an institution driven by practicality and accommodation aimed at securing material comfort and economic stability. With the Production Code all but buried, the costly, high-profile 1966 adaptation of *Virginia Woolf*, by contrast, placed such hypocrisy front and center. The horror of middle-class family morality heavily informed Elizabeth Taylor's Oscar-winning performance as Martha, a character who, like Poitier's Walter Young in *A Raisin in the Sun* and Ivan Dixon's Duff Anderson in *Nothing But a Man*, takes the frustrations of her stunted existence out on her family rather than society. While Walter and Duff's anger must be seen in the context of the Civil Rights Movement, Martha's rage gained resonance with the publication of Betty Friedan's 1963 bestseller, *The Feminine Mystique*, arguing that beneath the façade of married middle-class existence, American women were roiled by unhappiness and frustration. Soon, the facts unearthed by Friedan seeped into an increasing number of films debunking the myth of a "consensus society," including Arthur Penn's 1965 tale of small town violence, *The Chase* – a film as notable for its coterie of unhappy, promiscuous housewives as for its study of male paranoia and violence and that, in many ways, may be regarded as a sequel of sorts to Kazan's stinging depiction in *Splendor in the Grass*.

The Family According to Alfred Hitchcock

Perhaps no director furnished more disturbing portraits of the American family during this period than Alfred Hitchcock. Adapted from a pulp novel and filmed in black and white on a low budget, *Psycho* (1960) – the story of disturbed serial killer Norman Bates (Anthony Perkins), who, after killing his mother, adopts her personality and dresses in her clothes when stabbing his female victims – became a box office hit and now is regarded as a modernist masterpiece. While Hitchcock's understanding of the American family as locus of horrific crimes dates back to the immediate post-war era with *Shadow of a Doubt* (1948) and while the intersection of horror and crime already characterized his Gothic dramas *Rebecca* (1940) and *Suspicion* (1942), it was Hitchcock's late work that both rediscovered and elevated the psychological thriller by demonstrating its suitability for telling critically inflected stories about deep disturbances rooted in family.

If *Psycho* anticipated developments in the horror film (it is now widely considered a precursor to the slasher sub-genre, with the 1974 classic, *The Texas Chain Saw Massacre*, in its own way, very much a family film), Hitchcock's next effort, *The Birds* (1963), on first glance looks back at the genre's 1950s preoccupation with monstrous creatures, in this case, swarms of birds bringing death and destruction to a coastal town in northern California. Yet, more significantly, as mundane inhabitants of our natural world whose behavior remains unexplained, the birds allegorically embody the abysses of the modern age. They thus function as a narrative framework for probing the state of the family – as true also, in a different setting, of the source story by Daphne du Maurier. Intimations of failed relationships, hints at female homoeroticism, constant reminders of an absent, deceased father, and, most of all, the birds' attacks on the town's children convey a deep, multi-layered skepticism as to whether the very concept of family is capable of surviving or, for that matter, worth saving. As in so many of Hitchcock's films, the cast of characters includes attractive women who, because they know too much (to cite an argument by feminist critic Tania Modleski, 1988), cause male anxiety, for which they are punished in one or another way. *The Birds* also extends the Hitchcockian tradition of a domineering mother who attempts to wield influence over a long line of male protagonists and antagonists. Although *Psycho* attributes Norman's pathology at least partially to the abusive effects of maternal power, *The Birds* shifts emphasis by depicting the mother's possessive behavior primarily as a symptom of her inhabiting a role she did not choose – that of family matriarch expected to uphold patriarchal structures.

In *Marnie* (1964), the mother is once again key to what, within limits, may be regarded as an indictment of patriarchy. Here, mother and daughter are two parts of a broken family whose story the film uncovers by tracing the behavior of the daughter, Marnie ("Tippi" Hedren) – a thief with fake identities, a deep distrust of men, and a phobic response to the color red – to a traumatic childhood episode in which she killed a client of her then prostitute mother. The secret is uncovered through "therapy" undertaken by a man (Sean Connery) who forces Marnie to marry him and then rapes her, thus rendering the film problematic, if perhaps also more realistic, as its narrative becomes complicated through characters' mixed motives. These qualities link Hitchcock's 1960s horror-inflected family dramas to films of the European art cinema, even as they made his films less popular with mass audiences. After flocking to *Psycho*, audiences were confused by *The Birds*, all but shunned *Marnie*, and showed little more interest in his cold war spy thrillers *Torn Curtain* (1965) and *Topaz* (1968).

With no musical score, *The Birds* relies heavily on atmospheric sound design, on which composer Bernard Herrmann was a key consultant. Herrmann's contributions to Hitchcock's films cannot be underestimated. His scores range from the screeching violins of *Psycho*'s shower sequence – an aural assault on the audience matching the violent knife-stabbing assault on the body of Marion Crane – to the persistent, insistent chords of urgency that drive Marnie simultaneously forward into her schemes and backward into her own entrapping psyche. Most notably, Herrmann masterfully tempers the lush Wagnerian romanticism of *Vertigo*'s musical score (1958) – in which longing and unrequited desire pulse palpably at key moments – with haunting minor-key melodies that darkly hint at the inevitable deceptions lurking beneath the ideal surface of voyeuristically-inspired attraction.

The Star System in Transition

If horror infused several subcategories of the American family film in the 1960s, it was Elizabeth Taylor's mid-decade transformation in *Virginia Woolf* from 1950s glamour goddess and nervy heroine of Williams adaptations into a middle-aged harridan that would foreground yet another facet of horror – what critics have called "the horror of personality" (Derry 1974). The trope was showcased to great popularity in a string of Gothic family dramas about murderous, diabolical spinsters, which included *What Ever Happened to Baby Jane?* (1962), starring Bette Davis and Joan Crawford; *Hush ... Hush, Sweet Charlotte* (1964), starring Bette Davis and Olivia de Havilland; and *Strait-Jacket* (1964), starring Joan Crawford. While the frightening and freakish nature of characterization and casting placed these films in the horror tradition, the fact that the horrors generated by spinster rage hailed from psychological trauma and emotional frustration rather than Transylvania or outer space illustrated nothing so much as the abiding influence of the melodrama. It seems apposite that the stars of this new brand of horror were Bette Davis and Joan Crawford, two great actresses of the studio era who shrewdly recycled their respective star personas – each closely shaped by the woman's film – for the twilight phase of their careers.

Whether it suffused a low-brow shocker or was performed in the register of prestige drama, the horror of personality heavily drew on camp, an act of recycling an outdated artifact or style to ironic effect and a phenomenon that in the 1960s became influential on all arts. Despite all their differences, what 1960s superstars such as Taylor and Burton had in common with faded Hollywood greats like Crawford and Davis was that, in a decade of rapidly evolving tastes dictated by youth culture, their styles quickly became outdated, which made them subject to recycling. Crawford and Davis's horror vehicles shrewdly referenced their stars' old movies, while Taylor and Burton allowed their movie roles to become conflated with their widely publicized real-life relationship. While camp has multiple facets and implications, its presence in Hollywood films of the 1960s was a portent that the star system was about to undergo a sea change. The days of stars created by the studios were numbered, with successive generations of thespians including Susan Hayward, Lana Turner, Ava

Gardner, Doris Day, Rita Hayworth, Kim Novak, and Janet Leigh bound for retirement, while others, like Davis, Crawford, Olivia de Havilland, and Gene Tierney were enjoying a comeback (however short-lived), and still others, like Barbara Stanwyck, had transitioned to television.

While many of their successors possessed beauty, none of them would become goddesses. And while some had blond hair, none were archetypal blondes like Marilyn Monroe, whose untimely death in 1962 widely signified the death of old Hollywood. Male actors were affected in a similar way, though the movies proved more forgiving of aging male stars. If Montgomery Clift suffered a similarly tragic, premature death as Marilyn Monroe, Paul Newman and Marlon Brando never lost their superstar status after experiencing mid-1960s career slumps (Newman rebounded at the box office with *Butch Cassidy and the Sundance Kid*, 1969, and went on to play leading roles in the 1970s). Burt Lancaster skillfully picked roles that enabled him to showcase both his imposing physique and his acting talent. In many ways the most successful male star of the 1960s, Lancaster turned in memorable performances in many of the decade's high-profile films, including Luchino Visconti's internationally produced art film *The Leopard* (1963) and the Hollywood prestige films *Elmer Gantry* (1960), *Judgment at Nuremberg* (1961), *Birdman of Alcatraz* (1962), *Seven Days in May*, and *The Swimmer* (1968). By contrast, Rock Hudson's career as a leading man in movies came to an end during this period, though he was able to transition to television, while John Wayne, Henry Fonda, and William Holden garnered attractive roles into the 1970s, continuing to hold their own against the new generation of stars that included Warren Beatty, Robert Redford, Dustin Hoffman, and Steve McQueen.

The generational turnover was paralleled by the shifting status of the star in the industry. Already the 1950s had seen a change in ground rules "from the studios who owned stars to the stars who owned the picture," as David Cook points out (1994, 427), by virtue of the rising power of talent agencies that packaged movie deals sealed by star power (a development

Figure 1.1 The enraged Martha (Elizabeth Taylor) and the heavy-drinking George (Richard Burton), in Mike Nichols's *Who's Afraid of Virginia Woolf?* (1966, producer Warner Bros. Entertainment), are not quite the perfect Production Code couple.

signaled by the 1962 takeover of Universal by Lew Wasserman's powerful talent agency MCA). Freed from long-term contracts and now often receiving a percentage of the profits, stars, by the early 1960s, had more power than ever before, but were also more vulnerable to the marketplace. No one experienced this more acutely than Taylor and Burton, who, after starring in *Cleopatra* (1963), *The Sandpiper* (1965), and *Who's Afraid of Virginia Woolf?* (1966), were arguably the biggest movie stars in the world, but who complained about a dearth of good parts after pricing themselves out of the market – which, however, in no way diminished their status as global celebrities.

Thus, the 1960s not only witnessed a generational changeover with regard to stars but also an ironic bifurcation of the very concept of movie stardom. On the one hand, the industry during this decade produced a sizable number of films that self-consciously thematized the commoditization of personality and presented stardom in a critical, even skeptical light – whether in dramas like *Two Weeks in Another Town* (1962) and *The Legend of Lyla Clare* (1968), in horror films like *What Ever Happened to Baby Jane?*, or in musicals such as *Gypsy* (1962), *Inside Daisy Clover* (1965), *Star!*, and *Funny Girl* (1968). On the other hand, as Taylor and Burton demonstrate, the concept of movie stardom was eclipsed by another concept – global celebrity – for which starring in movies was no longer as central a requirement. While this shift may have placed traditional movie stardom at a remote distance for the performers who would rise to prominence in the years of the New Hollywood, it also arguably freed them up to express with greater conviction their interest in and commitment to acting as a craft. With the exception, of course, of Raquel Welch – a throwback to the Hollywood sexpot.

A New Immorality

In the course of the 1960s, studios became increasingly unwilling to compromise the integrity of controversial but promising properties of the kind Warner Bros. had on its hands with *Virginia Woolf*. Preparing for the film's release, the studio requested an exemption from the Production Code Administration, offering to release it with announcements on theater lobby placards warning audiences that the film was not suitable for children and that anyone under 18 would not be admitted without parental accompaniment. The PCA agreed because it already was working on its own new classification system that *Virginia Woolf* could help catalyze (Leff & Simmons 1990, 258–265). *Virginia Woolf*'s chipping away at the Code more seriously extended the challenges that director Otto Preminger had earlier posed in releasing *The Moon Is Blue* (1953) and *The Man with the Golden Arm* (1955) without a seal of approval. In 1968, the Motion Picture Association of America (MPAA) announced that motion pictures would now be reviewed by a new Code and Rating Administration (CRA) that would apply a set of audience-advisory ratings: G for films acceptable to all audiences, M for films appropriate for adults and mature youth, R for films with "theme, content and treatment, [that] should not be presented to persons under 16 unless accompanied by parent or adult guardian" (Maltby 2003, 599). The CRA also established an X rating for films that did not qualify for a Code seal of approval and to which no one under 18 would be permitted admission. In 1970, the R rating was broadened and the operative age for restriction was raised from 16 to 17. The new ratings guided parents about movie content but also served as a continued form of industry self-censorship and as a marketing device for distributors.

Films that contained nudity and explicit representations of violence – and an ever-growing body of films included both – were generally cut to the measure of an R rating. On the other hand, the X rating came to designate films produced in a realm beyond the boundaries of the MPAA in which the explicit representations of sex earned the title "hard core." That realm had its own long history, as Eric Schaefer points out in this volume, one that ran parallel with and, at times, entered the margins of the mainstream. In the post-war period, the sex-exploitation film achieved both profits and wider popularity in the work of Russ Meyer, whose first film, *The Immoral Mr. Teas*, was produced in 1959 for $24,000. Fifteen years later, his *Super Vixens*, made for a little less than $220,000 grossed in excess of $16 million (Donahue 1987, 243). Against the backdrop of the New Hollywood and its somber projections of diminished personal power, Meyer's films were fantasies of abundance, a sexual world with few limits.

But Meyer's films were only the most conspicuous examples of a wave of relatively low-budget productions that would swell in the 1960s and climax in the 1970s. Built around various exploitation formulas, these films traded on Gothic horror, youth cycles about beach parties and motorcycle gangs, and soft-core voyeurism featuring stewardesses and cheerleaders. By 1970, close to 900 theaters exhibited some form of "sexploitation" cinema and a quarter of these were drive-ins (*Report* 1970, 97). Heir to the 1950s B-film, American International Pictures (AIP) was the most prolific producer of independent exploitation movies and its most influential figure was Roger Corman. Corman's forte was cheap thrills that sacrificed narrative complexity for action and a production mode that quickly moved projects from script to screen in order to cash in on movies addressing popular trends – whether in horror flicks such as *The Raven* (1963), an atmospheric Edgar Allan Poe adaptation, or films with a strong subcultural appeal, such as *The Wild Angels* (1966), a biker film precursor, of sorts, to the phenomenally successful *Easy Rider*, which was initially developed at AIP. With a keen eye on youth culture, music, and sex, another AIP product, *Wild in the Streets* (1968), about the rise and fall of a crypto-fascist rock singer-turned-president, worked as both a teen exploitation film and a political satire capitalizing on America's obsession with youth and middle-class perceptions and projections of countercultural hedonism.

For the most part, films produced by AIP or its low-budget contemporaries flew under the critical radar. Hard core, on the other hand, did not. *Deep Throat* (1972), shot by Gerard Damiano in six days in January 1972 for under $25,000, forced explicit cinema into the national consciousness, as Linda Williams explains in the hardcover/online edition. The film would rank eleventh in box office grosses for 1973. Damiano would follow up the next year with *The Devil in Miss Jones* (1973) which would rank seventh. The exhibition of *Deep Throat* brought charges of obscenity and a very public 11-day trial resulting in a $3 million judgment against its exhibitor. Yet, despite the judge's pronouncement that the film was "indisputably obscene by any measurement," *Deep Throat* played in 70 cities over an 18-month period (Turan & Zito 1974, 145). Ultimately, the XXX cinema, as it came to be known, was more licentious than liberating. The formal economy of hard core, its close-ups of genitals in action and its claustrophobic living-room-as-studio interiors, for the most part drew much greater attention to the body than the body politic. In its above-ground popularity, *Deep Throat* represented a moment of middle-class transgression for a population negotiating a shift in social mores. While hard-core cinema would migrate rather quickly to home video, it would remain, after 1973, an extremely lucrative component of movie-making, one with its own star system and fan base.

The Avant-garde

While the institutional and formal conventions of commercial movie-making lend themselves to a more coherent chronicle, the array of forms, philosophies, and artists that compose the avant-garde resists any brief overview. Still, some of the most important contours can be articulated, but only after two essential questions are addressed. First, as several historians of the avant-garde have argued, experimental cinema is no less embedded in economic and social factors than the products of Hollywood. Nor does it exist in some parallel realm totally isolated from the commercial cinema. While artists like Stan Brakhage and Paul Sharits created films in a language radically different from the mainstream, others such as Kenneth Anger, Bruce Conner, and George Kuchar entered into a critical, sometimes comic, dialogue with popular culture and the Hollywood cinema. Second, the post-war avant-garde, like its ancestors of an earlier era, developed not as a random set of personal experiments but with the assistance of an institutional structure of theaters, magazines, and distributors.

The exhibition component of that structure was initially set in New York and San Francisco. In New York City, the most important site of exhibition would be Cinema 16, founded in 1947 by Amos Vogel, who operated it until its end in 1963 (James 1992, 6). In 1962, Jonas Mekas, émigré filmmaker and champion of what some were now calling the New American Cinema, established the Film-Makers' Cooperative, which would become a crucial source for the distribution of experimental films. Around the same time, filmmaker Bruce Baillie began a series of informal screenings of experimental films at his home in Canyon, California, and Chick Strand founded *Canyon Cinemanews*, a journal in support of the emerging West Coast avant-garde scene. In 1967, a group of Bay Area filmmakers, including Bruce Conner, Larry Jordan, and Ben Nelson, founded Canyon Cinema, a filmmaker-run distribution company. This infrastructure for the circulation of experimental film was accompanied by an emerging critical discourse, most notably in the pages of *Film Culture*, a magazine founded in 1955. Here, filmmakers and scholars of the avant-garde published manifestos, critical dialogues, and trenchant reviews for an experimental film audience that had begun to spread beyond New York and San Francisco to the nation's museums and college campuses. This audience absorbed a body of work remarkable for its aesthetic diversity, with no single impulse that could claim priority.

While this aesthetic diversity had adhered to the avant-garde scene since the late 1940s, by the late 1950s and early 1960s, it had become part of a broader rejection of cultural and artistic hierarchies. This mentality reached critical mass with the "New Sensibility," whose proponents commended the new avant-garde for leaving behind the seriousness of the 1950s with its distinctions between "high" and "low," as it sought to blur the boundaries between art, science, and pop culture. In this new atmosphere a song by the Beatles was deemed as edifying and as worthy of discussion as a painting by Jasper Johns (Ross 1989, 141). No longer looking to Europe for models of legitimacy, the 1960s avant-garde was thoroughly American, reflecting youthful open-mindedness and self-assurance. As such, it also had a privileged place in the democratic vision of the Kennedy administration, which projected a vibrant, rejuvenated America. By establishing the arts at the center of American life, however, the White House embraced high art and the arts establishment, legitimizing the competitive Cold War posture of "America First" – whether in space or culture. Ironically, then, the White House's top-down arts initiatives were nothing if not European in their inflection and practice. Despite an apparent spirit of renewal, the concrete benefits of cultural institution building operated at a remove from such liminal artistic spheres as the downtown Greenwich Village art scene and the film avant-garde.

This scene became the creative center of much of what was touted as the new arts in the 1960s. As Sally Banes has argued, its numerous overlapping, sometimes rivaling networks of artists were forming the multifaceted base of an alternative, newly bohemian culture (Banes 1993, 35). Wildly experimental and sexually libertarian, it enacted the radical notions of community that were merely talked about in other places, practicing the very democracy the established scene merely aspired to, and, with its championing of women's roles and the emphasis on play, bringing about the fusion of art and politics that in other spheres of American life would remain consigned to the realm of theory.

The "underground" component of American experimental film, which Jared Rapfogel discusses in Volume I, is remarkable both for its sexual diversity and its formal eclecticism. Its most penetrating works combine both personal and social address, oftentimes within the same film. In *Fireworks* (1947) and *Scorpio Rising* (1963), Kenneth Anger projected the complicated relationship among (homo)sexuality, subjectivity, and the artifacts of popular culture. Images of the naked body were projected by the underground well before it was permissible in above-ground culture. In 1963, underground performance artist and filmmaker Jack Smith created a scandal when his 16mm film *Flaming Creatures* was confiscated by the NYPD. The film depicted an orgiastic rooftop gathering of drag queens flaunting their genitals. Barbara Rubin's *Christmas on Earth* (1964) presented a New York apartment orgy through dual projections of overlapping images. What followed later in the decade were both serious meditations on sexuality, such as Carolee Schneemann's densely layered *Fuses* (1967), and playful, impoverished melodramas like *Hold Me While I'm Naked* (1966) and *The Devil's Cleavage* (1973) by George Kuchar. Collage aesthetics were likewise a staple of the underground, with its most important practitioner in Bruce Conner. Stitching together found footage from virtually every genre – Hollywood, educational films, ethnographic cinema, softcore porn, newsreels – Conner created dynamic montages that followed the culture's own fixations on technologies of violence and the illicit image. Indeed, underground film got its name not only because it existed beyond or beneath the scrutiny of mainstream culture but also because it traded in many of its taboo subjects.

One significant cluster of avant-garde films, despite their profound differences, can be understood through the principle of reinvention, that is, the shaping of cinema. For Stan Brakhage, the most prolific of experimental film artists, the project was nothing less than the reconstruction of vision, the creation of a new way of seeing not mediated by language but produced through the camera-eye. In the opening paragraph of his book, *Metaphors on Vision*, Brakhage poses a series of questions that became chapter and verse to students of the avant-garde: "How many colors are there in a field of grass to the crawling baby unaware of 'Green'? How many rainbows can light create for the untutored eye?" (Brakhage 1976, 1). In literally hundreds of films free from the constraints of narrative and spoken language, Brakhage sought the cinematic revisualization and thus reconceptualization of nature, family, and myth.

Another cluster of films to gesture toward reinvention was the so-called structural film. In the work of Michael Snow, Ken Jacobs, Paul Sharits, Ernie Gehr, and Hollis Frampton, the cinema emerges cleansed of everything but its essential structures. P. Adams Sitney, the most influential commentator on the avant-garde during the 1960s and 1970s, identifies four primary characteristics of structural film – the fixed frame, the flicker effect, loop printing, and re-photography off the screen (Sitney 1979, 370). What places the accent on reconstruction is the tendency of some structural filmmakers to apply their experiments to pieces of early cinema – most notably Ken Jacobs's 115 minute re-photography of *Tom, Tom, the Piper's Son* (1969), a 1905 Biograph short, and Ernie Gehr's *Eureka* (1974), a radical expansion of another 1905 film shot from a trolley moving down Market Street in San Francisco. The vast majority of structural films, however, did not rework fragments of early cinema but rather pursued what the earliest filmmakers had pursued – an interest in the apparatus itself. Just as film pioneers had created a new spectator, so, too, did structural filmmakers invite, some would say provoke, even sophisticated viewers into new, occasionally uncomfortable positions. In *Wavelength* (1967), Michael Snow, for instance, presents a 45-minute gradual zoom, parsed out through multiple cuts, across a SoHo loft. In *nostalgia* (1971), Hollis Frampton deliberates on photography, memory, and loss. But unlike the elongated temporality in these films, Paul Sharits engineered a style of flicker and assault. His *T*O*U*C*H*I*N*G* (1969) and *Razor Blades* (1965–1968), the latter a dual projector film, bounced bright colors and still images off the screen in violent bursts.

The films of Bruce Baillie weave together multiple strands of the avant-garde. In *All My Life* (1966) he contemplates the panning camera in a trip over flowers and bushes set to the voice of Ella Fitzgerald. Part structural film, part postcard from a beautiful summer day, *All My Life* underscores the home movie potential of experimental film. In *Castro Street* (1966), Baillie uses multiple exposures and smooth camera movement to create a colorfully fluid, at times ghostly mosaic of trains and industry along a rail line in California. And in *Mass for the Dakota Sioux* (1963–1964) and *Quixote* (1964–1968), Baillie created films that are part travel journal and part political treatise, merging collage, diary, and documentary in a single text.

When pop artist Andy Warhol turned to the cinema in 1963 he, too, sought a reinvention, but one in stark contrast to most other avant-garde filmmakers. Warhol's re-creation was of the industrial cinema, now transported to his mid-town Manhattan Factory, complete with an alternate star system, screen tests (of which he made approximately 500) and a mode of collaborative production in which, after 1968, Warhol moved from director to brand name. His monumental films *Empire* (1964) and *Sleep* (1963) proffered a reinvention through distillation, reducing cinema to the fixed frame and the long take. In fact, if motion had been the first fascination for the Lumière brothers as the medium's original attraction, Warhol chose to reshape film history with stasis – 321 minutes of John Giorno asleep or 485 minutes of the Empire State Building. Through a string of films that were teasingly erotic (*Blow Job*, 1964; *The Nude Restaurant*, 1967; *Lonesome Cowboys*, 1967; *Bike Boy*, 1967), if rarely graphic (*Couch*, 1965; *Blue Movie*, 1968), Warhol also gave new dimension to sexual representation, ironically referencing mainstream conventions and pushing them to new limits (see Grundmann 2003). Finally, Warhol, in the mid- to late 1960s, was at the center of a new development referred to as expanded cinema. Through his experiments with double-screen projection for *Inner and Outer Space* (1965) and *The Chelsea Girls* (1966), as well as his multi-media light and performance show, *The Exploding Plastic Inevitable* (*EPI*) (1967), Warhol expanded the notion of cinema to include various technologies (among them video recordings and TV monitors), multiple film projectors, light shows, and live music performances by The Velvet Underground. Other artists, like filmmaker Stan Vanderbeek and abstract animators John and James Whitney, used fledgling computer technologies for their experiments with expanded cinema (Grundmann 2004, 48).

Independent Fiction and Nonfiction Film

In 1969, Hollywood released *Midnight Cowboy*, a film about a male prostitute walking the streets of Manhattan in rodeo attire. Based on a 1965 novel, its style heavily courted resemblance to Warhol's 1967 cycle of sexploitation films, with a key scene in a Factory-type setting. Warhol, who had pioneered the depiction of male prostitution with his 1965 underground film *My Hustler* (rereleased in an extended version as part of the 1967 cycle), realized he and his Factory had been cannibalized by Hollywood. Instead of accepting a courtesy offer to appear in *Midnight Cowboy*, Warhol followed the advice of his assistant, Paul Morrissey, that the Factory should issue its own narrative feature about a male hustler. The result was *Flesh* (1969), whose genesis, historically speaking, is a textbook case of independent cinema forming the dialectical synthesis of Hollywood and the avant-garde. Like *My Hustler* but in contrast to *Midnight Cowboy*, *Flesh* takes place outside the system of mainstream morality; like *Midnight Cowboy* but unlike *My Hustler*, *Flesh* is fully scripted and was conceived for theatrical distribution and exhibition. It not only marked Warhol's transition to producer, but it also launched the filmmaking career of Morrissey, who became a respectable director in his own right on the flourishing independent scene – shaped mainly, but not exclusively, by white male artists like Woody Allen, John Sayles, and, of course, John Cassavetes.

Cassavetes, for many years, was the most prominent filmmaker to chart a path for narrative cinema outside of Hollywood. From his late 1950s interracial debut feature, *Shadows* (1959), to his 1970s dramas about the complexity of interpersonal relationships, Cassavetes consistently countered Hollywood's standardized approaches to scripted narrative with his own brand of cinema, the most prominent features of which were intimate camera work and improvised acting. Films such as *Faces* (1968), *A Woman Under the Influence* (1974), and *Opening Night* (1977) teased out performances of historic status from Cassavetes's wife and lead actor, Gena Rowlands. But to grant Cassavetes pioneer status is to ignore that the very concept of independent film significantly predates him, going back to the birth of the Hollywood industry, which itself had been founded as a confederacy of former outsiders, and against which the early indies would come to define themselves. Whether defined institutionally or in artistic-aesthetic terms, a history of independent film must begin, at the very latest, with such historic figures as Oscar Micheaux and other makers of so called "race films" in the 1910s and 1920s, as Paula Massood outlines in Volume I of this series, and must continue with a consideration of the New York Shtetl films of the 1930s, before arriving at such landmark films as *Salt of the Earth* (1950), whose independent status is defined not merely by creative sensibility, but also, and most centrally, in starkly political terms. Cassavetes's indie status is further qualified by the fact that he kept one foot firmly planted in the industry as an actor for television and for Hollywood movies, not unlike independent filmmakers Jim McBride (*David Holzman's Diary*, 1968) and Milton Moses Ginsberg (*Coming Apart*, 1969) who had tenuous ties with the industry. By contrast, many of their contemporaries, including black independent filmmaker William Greaves (*Symbiopsychotaxiplasm: Take One*, 1967) and experimental filmmaker Shirley Clarke (*The Cool World*, 1963) had no connections to the industry.

Clarke, to whom we shall return shortly, is instructive also for the ways in which her work and 1960s independent cinema in general blurred the line between narrative and documentary. The most important new step for documentary filmmakers came in the form of the direct cinema movement, a style that eschewed the voiceover narration and explicitly didactic form that had dominated much of nonfiction film during the Depression and war years. New lightweight cameras and portable synchronous sound equipment afforded filmmakers unprecedented mobility and intimacy in their desire to peel away all signs of constructedness and manipulation.

As Charles Warren details in his comprehensive discussion of direct cinema in this volume, many pioneers of direct cinema got their start with Robert Drew and Associates, initial forays facilitated by ABC News as the network sought to fulfill the Federal

Communication Commission's mandate for public affairs programming (Barsam 2001, 212). In the work of D. A. Pennebaker, Richard Leacock, Albert and David Maysles, Joyce Chopra, and Charlotte Zwerin direct cinema documented contemporary political and cultural life, less by analyzing social structures than by profiling significant personalities. In *Primary* (Drew, 1960), *Don't Look Back* (Pennebaker, 1967), and *Meet Marlon Brando* (Maysles, 1965), the direct cinema approach relied on the charisma of its subjects (JFK and Hubert Humphrey, Bob Dylan, and Brando, respectively) as it gained access not found in television news, while *Happy Mother's Day* (Chopra and Leacock, 1963) and *Salesman* (Maysles and Zwerin, 1969) probed the American scene divorced from the glow of celebrity. Also pursuing this latter course was Frederick Wiseman, whose work consistently documented American institutions, carrying broad implications for the culture as a whole. In *High School* (1968), for example, the seemingly successful North East High School in Philadelphia is represented as a semi-authoritarian environment where students are trained in rigid gender roles and rule-following. A school administrator, in the closing scene, reads a letter from a former student now in Vietnam, deeming their education of the boy a success when he describes himself as "just a body doing a job."

Shirley Clark became involved in heated debates with her direct cinema colleagues, with whom she had formed a post-production facility, Filmmakers Inc. (Rabinovitz 1991, 110). Clarke accused her colleagues of creating the *appearance* of reality through "invisible" editing, especially in scenes involving "crisis moment" situations. These documentaries thus created fictional narrative constructs of psychological revelation, according to Clarke, in the guise of unmediated renderings of objective truth (Rabinovitz 1991, 113). Clarke believed that the presence of the camera should be openly acknowledged through interactions between subjects and the filmmaker – as in the work of French cinéma vérité filmmaker Jean Rouch. While Clarke's first feature film, *The Connection* (1962), is a fiction film (about documentary filmmakers filming a group of drug addicts waiting for their heroin delivery), her best-known film, which links her interest in experimental documentary with her interest in race, is *Portrait of Jason* (1967), a classic of direct cinema featuring an extended interview with a black gay man who recounts his experiences working as a servant for wealthy whites.

In the late 1960s when "official" discourse from establishment figures was perceived as misleading or downright dishonest, direct cinema was part of a larger gesture toward authenticity and honesty also found in some nonfiction literature at the time. A documentary political critique more commensurate with, indeed organic to, the counterculture began in December 1967 with the formation of New York Newsreel, a radical filmmaking collective. In a short time, branches of Newsreel opened in Boston, Chicago, Ann Arbor, and San Francisco. Unlike observational direct cinema, Newsreel was avowedly activist, an outgrowth of the New Left, seeking not just to educate but to mobilize viewers around issues of social justice and anti-war protest. Developing guerrilla filmmaking tactics that eschewed critical distance for direct contact and participation with those involved in revolutionary protest, Newsreel debuted with two important 1968 films – *Columbia Revolt* and *Black Panther* (Renov 1987, 23). Like the movement of which it was a part, Newsreel would, in the early 1970s, suffer from factionalism centered on issues of power and representation. As women and people of color demanded greater access to equipment and attention to their concerns, the focus of the various collectives shifted. In San Francisco, this was accelerated by the production of *The Woman's Film* (Louise Alaimo, Judy Smith, and Ellen Sorren) in 1971, and in 1975, the chapter was officially renamed California Newsreel. In 1973, in recognition of the growing centrality of African-American, Latino/a and Asian members, New York Newsreel was renamed Third World Newsreel.

The New Hollywood

As the 1960s drew to a close, Hollywood still seemed loathe to acknowledge a fact of social reality that was openly reflected in all types of American films made outside the industry – that the American film audience could no longer be understood or addressed as a unified population. As the national consensus was torn apart by the struggle over civil rights, the woman's movement, and protest of the war in southeast Asia, the film industry registered the turmoil in highly mediated and indirect ways. Indeed, with exceptions as antithetical as *The Green Berets* (1968) and *Medium Cool* (1969), the commercial cinema largely failed to represent those struggles at the heart of political contestation. In some cases it represented anti-war sentiments in films about other wars – *Catch-22* (1970), set during World War II, *M*A*S*H* (1970), set during the Korean War, and even *Little Big Man* (1970), set during the period leading up to and climaxing in the Battle of Little Big Horn. Frequently, however, the industry's politics were articulated through a revisionist approach to the genres – like the detective film, the Western, and the gangster film – that had lent ideological support to the hegemonic forces in American society.

This translated into what Thomas Elsaesser (1975) termed, "a cinema of pathos," one in which heroes could no longer tame the West, heal the sick, or police the streets. Historian Godfrey Hodgson has suggested that, during this period, Americans

> learned that there was moral ambiguity where they had once thought that the issues of right and wrong were clearest; that their own motives were not above suspicion; and that there seemed little that political action could achieve, however idealistic its intentions, without evoking unforeseen or unwanted action. (Hodgson 1978, 484)

Hodgson's diagnosis is aimed at the late 1960s, of course, but it could also read as an apt description of earlier films noir. Indeed, Hollywood had always made films that registered the nation's anxieties. But now the balance was shifting. Without the old studio system, fewer films were projecting an affirmative attitude. The industry's most respected directors and a generation of stars who had matured outside the studio system gave their energies to films that echoed Hodgson's characterization of America at this time. A loss of certainty and doubts about personal and institutional agency were inscribed across many of their films. In *Midnight Cowboy*, *Five Easy Pieces* (1970), *They Shoot Horses, Don't They?* (1969), *The Hospital* (1971), *The Conversation* (1974), *Dog Day Afternoon* (1975), *Across 110th Street* (1972), and *The Last Picture Show* (1971), to name just a few, protagonists are overwhelmed by economic forces, personal demons, and failed insitutions. Perhaps no single line of dialogue better encapsulates the idea that place overwhelms purpose than the last defeatist line of Polanski's 1974 neo-noir masterpiece: "Come on Jake, it's Chinatown." The heroes of such films, Elsaesser concluded, underscore an "almost physical sense of inconsequential action, of pointlessness and uselessness, a radical skepticism, in short, about the American virtues of ambition, vision, drive" (Elsaesser 1975, 15). For many of these films, narrative closure came in the form of either flight – *The Graduate*, *Serpico* (1973), *Klute* (1971), *Catch-22* (1970), *Five Easy Pieces*, *Two-Lane Blacktop* (1971) – or death – *Easy Rider*, *Cool Hand Luke* (1966), *Electra Glide in Blue* (1973), *The Parallax View* (1974), *They Shoot Horses, Don't They?*, *McCabe & Mrs. Miller*.

As Derek Nystrom's essay in this volume details, the New Hollywood was a complex phenomenon in terms of both the industrial practices and talents it deployed and the contents and styles it generated. It was the product not just of auteurs groomed by television (Altman, Penn, Lumet), but of an even younger generation of filmmakers, the so-called "movie-brats" – Francis Coppola, Peter Bogdanovich, Brian De Palma, Martin Scorsese, many of them film school-trained and a full generation outside of the studio system. But the New Hollywood, despite its modest experiments and sobering vision, cannot be separated from the industry's shifting economic fortunes, rotating set of studio bosses, and the profound recession that hit the movie business from 1969 to 1971. Industry losses have been estimated at $200 million for 1969 alone (Maltby 2003, 175). A series of box-office failures for high-budget films imperilled several companies, while industry-wide overproduction far exceeded audience demand. During these nadir years, studio bosses desperate for solutions took chances by hiring off-beat talent or working out deals with small, artisanal production companies structured around a writer-director-producer (Elasaesser 2004, 53). Some of the films that were products of this collaboration failed to resonate at the box office because their topics and treatments lacked mainstream appeal or because they never achieved proper distribution. Yet the cinema that emerged in the late 1960s and early 1970s showed an unprecedented degree of social seriousness and aesthetic experimentation, leading some to claim that this was the only period in which American films approached art cinema status. While some filmmakers like Jonathan Demme, Mike Nichols, and obviously Scorsese, De Palma, Spielberg, and Lucas, were able to extend their careers into the period of industry reconsolidation of the second New Hollywood (or New Hollywood II, as Nystrom refers to it), others, such as Hal Ashby, Bob Rafelson, Jerry Schatzberg, and Monte Hellman were unable to do so. It is their fates rather than those of the former group that have confirmed for many critics and historians that the New Hollywood – and, by extension, American film of the 1970s – constituted the last great American picture show.[2]

This generally accepted understanding of the New Hollywood benefits, however, from a fuller account of the contemporaneous complexities of the industry, revealing that such assumptions are incomplete on several fronts. Most strikingly, they ignore the experimentation that took place and became "necessary for the 'system' to first adjust and then renew itself" (Elsaesser 2004, 44). One case in point is a film like *Easy Rider*, which lastingly demonstrates the double imperative for any entertainment effort to provide youth appeal through incorporating soundtrack as an integral marketing tool. A second case in point is the work of director-producer Roger Corman, who, while never aspiring to create art, keenly understood the continuum of art and commerce in the 1960s and 1970s. His low-budget production units, sometimes regarded, by Thomas Elsaesser, for instance, as indirect research and development units for the studio system, nevertheless continued testing the margins of permissible onscreen content and provided hands-on apprenticeships to future auteurs. Corman also acted as a distributor of European art films, helping redefine the status of the cult exhibition circuit as both a stage for and mirror of rebellious and transgressive sensibilities (Elsaesser 2004, 51–54). A third case is exemplified by an actor like Jack Nicholson, whose career straddled several periods and cultural frames of reference. Nicholson got his start in Corman's 1960s B-movies and played roles in key films associated with the New Hollywood (*Easy Rider*, *Five Easy Pieces*, *Chinatown*) and international art cinema (*The Passenger*, 1975), before finally taking his place in the pantheon of Hollywood superstars. Key to this transition, which exemplifies the shift from the New Hollywood to the New New Hollywood, was *One Flew Over the Cuckoo's Nest* (1974), a critically acclaimed mental asylum drama in which Nicholson plays a wrongfully committed patient who rouses his fellow inmates to revolt against the cold, uncaring institution. Nicholson's bad boy rebellion is fueled by the energy of the film's source novel, written by Ken Kesey, one of the counterculture's literary icons. At close inspection, however, the film simply adheres to the conventional underdog formula. While the film is directed by edgy Czech New Wave director Miloš Forman, its young co-producer, Michael Douglas, was an up-and-coming TV star who became an icon of 1980s Reaganite cinema.

Another aspect ignored by the swan-song narrative of 1970s American cinema is that the films it produced certainly revised but never erased the tradition of genre filmmaking. As Thomas Elsaesser argues in this volume, no director is more exemplary of this dynamic than Robert Altman who, in his most fruitful years (1969–1975), produced a series of films that, while rarely commercial hits, became textbook studies of genre revisionism. *M*A*S*H* (1970) subverted the war film and had enough mainstream appeal to warrant retooling as a long-running TV satiric sit-com; *McCabe & Mrs. Miller* and *The Long Goodbye* (1973) subverted the Western and film noir respectively. While neither one was commercially successful, both were slightly more extreme (and mildly ironic versions) of mainstream fare of the period. *McCabe* ironically anticipated Redford's star vehicle *Jeremiah Johnson* (1972) and *Goodbye*, in retrospect, might fruitfully be compared with popular TV policier, *Columbo* (first broadcast in 1971 and starring Peter Falk).

It is in this context that 1970s genres must be placed, and none more so than the Western. No genre, arguably, has more concertedly communicated national historical myths. Between 1960 and 1975, the Western was subjected to a penetrating revision. As Teresa Podlesney points out in this volume, the dismantling of the genre was, in part, rendered by comedies (*Cat Ballou*, 1965; *Paint Your Wagon*, 1969) functioning, in her words, as "protracted rituals of debasement," as if the humorous drunken fights that punctuated John Ford's earlier films "have metastasized, threatening the maturity and integrity of the host genre." Dramatic Westerns also rethought the glory of their heroes. If *The Magnificent Seven* (1960) already portrayed the gunman as lonely wanderer rather than ennobled loner, it still sought to recuperate a matinee vision of heroism. By contrast, in *Ride the High Country* (1962), *The Ballad of Cable*

Hogue (1970), and *The Wild Bunch* (1969), Sam Peckinpah depicted aging Westerners – men whose days, to quote Pike Bishop (William Holden) in *The Wild Bunch*, "are closing fast." In the Western, space had been equated with opportunity, a distinct visualization of progress. But in the Westerns of the New Hollywood, the desert setting creates a mise-en-scène of physical limits, an environment as brutal as it is beautiful and an apt background for characters close to the end. More than any other director perhaps, Peckinpah redefined cinematic violence, especially for the Western, discarding it as a tool for justice in order to record, in choreographies of blood, its sheer powers of devastation.

Ethnic Heroes and Independent Women

The Hollywood renaissance was also defined by the reemergence of two figures – the ethnic hero and the independent woman. Given its fascination with urban life, Hollywood had a long history of portraying ethnic Americans – James Cagney's Irish Americans and Edward G. Robinson's Italian Americans both at the heart of the gangster film. In the 1960s, when many productions fled studio artifice and set stories on location in the city, their casts often featured actors who looked more at home in the streets than on a horse. Indeed, the cover of the July 11, 1969 issue of *LIFE* magazine presented a split image featuring drawings of aging Western star John Wayne and a youthful Dustin Hoffman, with the headline: "Dusty and the Duke: A Choice of Heroes." *Midnight Cowboy* had been released that season, and, as Art Simon points out in this volume, Dustin Hoffman's Ratso Rizzo embodied the American dream in reverse, living in a New York that was, contrary to legend, anything but hospitable to the sons of immigrants. Al Pacino joined Hoffman as the most important of the new ethnic stars. In *Serpico* (1973) and *Dog Day Afternoon*, he would play volatile men caught in desperate and threatening circumstances.

But *The Godfather* (1972) and *The Godfather Part II* (1974) projected the most daring image of ethnic America, bringing together three of its most charismatic actors, Brando, Pacino, and Robert De Niro. Indeed, it is *Part II* that roots the Corleone family in American history, juxtaposing Coppola's stunning re-creation of immigrant life – from Ellis Island to Little Italy – with family life under Michael Corleone thousands of miles from New York, now fenced within the family compound in Lake Tahoe. Both films set their sights on the myth of the self-made immigrant, situating him within an urban America defined by violence, corruption, and fear instead of honest hard labor. Indeed, for Michael Corleone, murder and the consolidation of power are the distinguishing aspects of his first-generation citizenship. Textbook lessons are not his version of America. "If history has taught us anything," he tells Tom Hagen (Robert Duvall), "it's that you can kill anyone."

The ethnic persona, however, was not reserved strictly for drama. American film comedy returned to its early sound era roots with the work of Woody Allen, the most important comic auteur since Chaplin. *Take the Money and Run*, released in 1969, marked Allen's directorial debut, inaugurating one of the most accomplished careers in American cinema. Indeed, as a playwright, literary humorist, screenwriter, stand-up comic, actor, and director, Allen stands at the top of the American comic tradition. His early films – *Bananas* (1971), *Sleeper* (1973), *Love and Death* (1975), and the script for *Play It Again, Sam* (1972, directed by Herbert Ross) – continued a legacy of comic outsiders – part coward, part neurotic, part romantic hero – extending back to Eddie Cantor, Groucho Marx, Bob Hope, and Jack Benny. Allen locates his schlemiel persona in a Latin American revolution in *Bananas*, in the distant future in *Sleeper*, and in Czarist Russia in *Love and Death*.

But Allen's comic films reached far beyond this persona with which he became identified. To a remarkable degree, his films, extending into the 1980s, engaged the notion of a media-made identity, the enfolded relationship of culture and self. *Take the Money and Run* and *Zelig* (1983) mine the conventions of documentary, the latter in particular making the case for a seamless interweaving of psychology and cinematic tropes. Whether it is the televised broadcast of a revolution in *Bananas*, the thorough identification with Humphrey Bogart in *Play It Again, Sam*, the slippage between film, dream, and memoir in *Stardust Memories* (1980), the interaction of screen life and real life in *The Purple Rose of Cairo* (1985), or the power of radio in *Radio Days* (1987), Allen has returned again and again to the shaping forces of mass (and often literary) culture on contemporary identity, while also

Figure 1.2 In Herbert Ross's *Play It Again, Sam* (1972, producer Arthur P. Jacobs and writer Woody Allen) film critic Allan (Woody Allen) falls in love with Linda (Diane Keaton), his best friend's wife, and uses Humphrey Bogart's cinematic persona as a role model for romance and self-sacrifice.

romanticizing and earning mainstream acceptance for the neurotic psyche that worked to survive modern urban life.

Survival instincts were also essential to another important cinematic persona of the period – the independent woman. Like the ethnic male hero, she had her ancestry in an earlier Hollywood tradition established by Mae West, Barbara Stanwyck, Katharine Hepburn, and Bette Davis. But informed by second-wave feminism, she was less likely to bend to social mandates about romantic coupling, and she often maintained a cynical awareness of her place within a male-dominated world. Julie Christie, Faye Dunaway, and Jane Fonda created women who consistently possessed a broader vision than their male counterparts. In *McCabe & Mrs. Miller* Christie understands far better than her befuddled lover the momentum of history and the encroaching corporatization of the West. In *Bonnie and Clyde* (1967) Dunaway also sees beyond the narrow perspective of her partner, eulogizing and mythologizing the couple through her poem that is published in a local newspaper. In *Network* (1976) Dunaway's Diana Christensen wields power in a male-dominated industry, understanding – indeed manufacturing – the phenomenon of TV personality Howard Beal. And in *Chinatown* it is Dunaway's character, Evelyn Mulwray, alone, who knows the full truth about the depth of institutional corruption – and that knowledge destroys her.

But it is perhaps Jane Fonda who best embodied the feminist impulse of the period as mediated by Hollywood. Her performance as Anna Reeves, in love with two men, in Arthur Penn's *The Chase* (1966), attested to her capacity to play tough independence. And at the end of the decade, Fonda pulled off one of the most remarkable shifts of on-screen persona in American film history as she moved from the futuristic sex kitten of *Barbarella* in 1968 to the hardened, suicidal Gloria in Sydney Pollack's *They Shoot Horses, Don't They?* one year later. The hint of complaint that always seemed to inform Fonda's voice was given full expression in Gloria. At the heart of Fonda's performance is her seamless movement between angry resistance and cynical submission. In her brutal honesty about the realities of Depression life, she discards social niceties. Closed off from affection, she sees the pain more acutely than her naïve dance partner Robert (Michael Sarrazin). And in a single line that sums up her attitude toward life and the deep skepticism of the New Hollywood, Gloria dismisses all illusions and tells Robert: "Maybe it's just the whole damn world is like Central Casting, they got it all rigged before you show up." Fonda's version of the world-weary independent woman, and the threat she posed, was granted institutional recognition when she was awarded the best actress Oscar for her next role in *Klute* (1971).

While Sidney Poitier had carried the burden of representing the black experience in dramatic films of the 1960s, the early 1970s saw a limited expansion of roles for black performers in vehicles that sharply departed from the stoic determinism of Poitier's characters but that also stood in marked contrast to the pathos of failure that dominated white stories authored by Hollywood. Indeed, the Blaxploitation film – the one genre that consistently offered roles to multiple black actors (Richard Roundtree, Jim Brown, Fred Williamson, Ron O'Neal) – emphasized precisely the black man's hyper-agency. As Ed Guerrero discusses in the hardcover/online edition, however, these films rarely attached that agency to the wider political struggle of the era, choosing, instead, to position their heroes on the fringes of the movement. Blaxploitation's brief heyday ended in the mid-1970s with the emergence of new black stars like Richard Pryor, who were paired with white male leads like Gene Wilder in action-comedy hybrids with cross-over appeal – *Silver Streak* (1976) is one such example.

The anarchic hypermasculinity of Blaxploitation and the alienated meanderings of the New Hollywood are now widely regarded as two alternate expressions of a dominant industry. While languishing, this industry was still very much in place during the early 1970s. To represent these trends as insider/outsider narratives bears certain risks for film historians who choose this course. It bestows on these movements the kind of coherence that they may, in fact, never have possessed as historical occurrences. It also threatens to eclipse other phenomena of a time that we have barely begun to fathom, perhaps because they appear to us in fragments that are inconspicuously scattered in the shade of more palatable eulogies of a bygone America. Among these phenomena we may include the careers of certain filmmakers as well as the stories, histories, and topographies of particular films. Consider the fragile careers of early 1970s women filmmakers like Barbara Loden, whose single filmmaking effort *Wanda* (1970) is a textbook study of the odds that female directors faced even during a period of purported permeability of industry structures, or, for that matter, Elaine May, to whom Hollywood was much less forgiving than it was of her male contemporaries. Consider also that in the years between Sidney Poitier and Blaxploitation, the films of Gordon Parks and Ossie Davis, which were based on urban black literature, appeared. Consider the Gothic themes and settings littering the margins of American mainstream film that often used Southern stories (*The Beguiled*, 1976) and scenarios of rural poverty (*Deliverance*, 1972; *The Texas Chain Saw Massacre*). The rich commentary of these films on class represented a traumatized America already stuck in an amoral swamp, rather than carefully styled acts of moral indignation (*Five Easy Pieces*, 1970; *Network*) or bitter swansongs of craggy masculinity set in the American Southwest (*The Wild Bunch*, *Pat Garrett and Billy the Kid*, 1973). Students of film history cannot afford to neglect these phenomena and are tasked with restoring them to their rightful place in the larger narrative.

Notes

1. Parts of this discussion of the New Hollywood are adapted from a previously published essay: Art Simon. (2000). "La Struttura narrativa del cinema americano, 1960–1980 [The Structure of American Narrative Cinema, 1960–1980]." In Gian Piero Brunetta (ed.), *Storia del cinema mondiale gli Stati Uniti II* (pp. 1635–1684). Turin: Giulio Einaudi.
2. Indeed, this moniker is the title of a valuable collection of essays (Elsaesser, Horwath, & King 2004) that deals with the period in detail. See especially Thomas Elsaesser's introduction, "American Auteur Cinema: The Last – or First – Great Picture Show," for a detailed film-historical deliberation of the many intersecting dynamics of this period.

References

Altman, Rick. (1999). *Film/Genre*. London: British Film Institute.

Banes, Sally. (1993). *Greenwich Village 1963: Avant-garde Performance and the Effervescent Body*. Durham, NC: Duke University Press.

Barsam, Richard. (2001). "The Nonfiction Film." In Paul Monaco (ed.), *The Sixties: 1960–1969* (pp. 198–230). Berkeley: University of California Press.

Brakhage, Stan. (1976). *Metaphors on Vision*. New York: Anthology Film Archives.

Cook, David A. (2000). *Lost Illusions: American Cinema in the Shadow of Watergate and Vietnam 1970–1979*. Berkeley: University of California Press.

Cook, David A. (2004). *A History of Narrative Film*. New York: W. W. Norton & Company.

Derry, Charles. (1974). "The Horror of Personality." *Cinefantastique*, 3.3 (Fall), 15–27.

Donahue, S.M. (1987). *American Film Distribution*. Ann Arbor: University of Michigan Press.

Elsaesser, Thomas. (1975). "The Pathos of Failure: American Cinema in the 70s." *Monogram*, 6, 13–19.

Elsaesser, Thomas. (2004). "American Auteur Cinema: The Last – or First – Great Picture Show." In Thomas Elsaesser, Alexander Horwath, & Noel King (eds.), *The Last Great American Picture Show: New Hollywood Cinema in the 1970s* (pp. 37–69). Amsterdam: Amsterdam University Press.

Grundmann, Roy. (2003). *Andy Warhol's Blow Job*. Philadelphia: Temple University Press.

Grundmann, Roy. (2004). "Masters of Ceremony: Media Demonstration as Performance in Three Instances of Expanded Cinema." *The Velvet Light Trap*, 54 (Fall), 48–64.

Hodgson, Godfrey. (1978). *America in Our Time*. New York: Vintage Books.

James, David (ed.). (1992). *To Free the Cinema: Jonas Mekas and the New York Underground*. Princeton: Princeton University Press.

Leff, Leonard J. & Simmons, Jerold L. (1990). *The Dame in the Kimono: Hollywood, Censorship, and the Production Code from the 1920s to the 1960s*. New York: Doubleday.

Maltby, Richard. (2003). *Hollywood Cinema*. 2nd edn. Malden, MA: Blackwell Publishing.

Modleski, Tania. (1988). *The Women Who Knew Too Much: Hitchcock and Feminist Theory*. New York: Routledge.

Rabinovitz, Lauren. (1991). *Points of Resistance: Women, Power and Politics in the New York Avant-garde Cinema, 1943–71*. Urbana: University of Illinois Press.

Reid, Mark A. (1993). *Redefining Black Film*. Berkeley: University of California Press.

Renov, Michael. (1987). "Newsreel Old and New." *Film Quarterly*, 41.1 (Autumn), 20–33.

Report of the Commission on Obscenity and Pornography. (1971). New York: Random House.

Ross, Andrew. (1989). *No Respect: Intellectuals and Popular Culture*. New York: Routledge.

Sitney, P. Adams. (1979). *Visionary Film: The American Avant-Garde 1943–1978*. Oxford: Oxford University Press.

Turan, Kenneth & Stephen Zito. (1974). *Sinema: American Pornographic Films and the People Who Make Them*. New York: Praeger.

2

Adults Only
Low-Budget Exploitation

Eric Schaefer
Associate Professor, Emerson College, United States

The film industry faced daunting economic challenges with the 1948 **Paramount decision**, forcing studios to divest their ownership of movie theaters in what had been a highly profitable **vertically integrated** system. The **advent of television** posed further difficulties. While one response centered on high-budget cinematic spectacles, another dramatically different response centered on **low-budget exploitation films**. Often shot in black-and-white, these films exposed nudity and sexual subjects impossible for television to broadcast and crucial in defying a weakening **Production Code**. Eric Schaefer examines two tantalizing exploitation genres – **teenpics**, a specialty of **American International Pictures (AIP)**, and the **adults-only feature**, evolving from **nudie-cuties** to **sexual melodramas**. Schaefer argues that, while these films are fixated on the female body, some manage to challenge male viewers invited to examine their own roles in the exploitation of women. Schaefer's essay shares ground with Jared Rapfogel on underground film in Volume I and with Peter Stanfield on teenpics and social problem films and Linda Williams on film pornography in the hardcover/online edition.

Additional terms, names, and concepts: *Burstyn v. Wilson*, Roger Corman, New World Pictures, Russ Meyer, *Roth v. United States*, *Alberts v. California*, *Hiklin* standard, *Jacobellis v. Ohio*, William Rotsler, Adult Film Association of America (AFAA), soft-core sexploitation, hard-core pornography

The years following World War II dealt the Hollywood film industry multiple blows. The Supreme Court's Paramount decision (1948) and the subsequent divorce of the vertically integrated studios' production/distribution arms from their theaters left them staggering, without a guaranteed venue for their productions. Weakly performing theaters were shuttered as American families moved from cities to the expanding suburbs and as television began to dominate time once reserved for movies and radio. In the 15 years from 1946 to 1961, the percentage of television households in the United States went from

American Film History: Selected Readings, 1960 to the Present, First Edition. Edited by Cynthia Lucia, Roy Grundmann, and Art Simon.

virtually zero, to almost 90 percent. The studios had to pull themselves off the ropes to find new ways to attract audiences and to differentiate their product from television. This meant a renewed emphasis on technology (3-D, widescreen, color, stereo sound), as well as an emphasis on cinematic spectacle (e.g., *Around the World in Eighty Days*, 1956; *The Ten Commandments*, 1956; etc.). Still, box office receipts plunged from a record high of almost $1.7 billion in 1946, to an anemic $900 million in 1962.

The pummeling that major studios endured presented opportunities for others outside the system. Stars and directors, who in many instances, had labored at the majors under long-term contracts, were able to create their own production companies. Increasingly, the majors distributed these new, "independent," productions and often supplied financing. Some filmmakers, Otto Preminger and Elia Kazan among them, relied on more adult themes in the wake of the *Burstyn v. Wilson* decision (1952), which gave motion pictures First Amendment protection, and helped relax the grip of the aging Production Code that governed motion picture content. With a more even playing field, theaters were forced into pitched competition for product, and many were required to turn to specialized movies that appealed to niche audiences. Distributors of foreign films found audiences growing progressively more receptive to their fare. This was especially true in big cities and college towns where "art cinemas" began to attract more sophisticated patrons. At the opposite end of the spectrum another sector benefited from these postwar shifts: the low-budget exploitation movie.

"Classical" exploitation films had been around since the late teens.[1] Made on shoestring budgets far lower than even those of "B" movies, and usually dealing with controversial or taboo subjects, they were created on the fringes of the mainstream film industry but played in regular theaters that were unaffiliated with the majors – often to sell-out crowds. Exploitation movies were limited to independent theaters due to provisions of the Production Code that forbade nudity, depictions of drug use, the topic of sex hygiene (general sex education, childbirth, venereal disease, etc.), and other vices. Representative titles include *The Road to Ruin* (1928, remade in 1933), *Reefer Madness* (1936), *The Pace That Kills* (1928, remade in 1935), *Slaves in Bondage* (1937), and *The Devil's Sleep* (1949). The forbidden quality of exploitation films – so-called because they required additional "exploitation" beyond the standard posters and advertising to attract an audience – was their primary selling point. In states and cities that did not have censorship boards or activist police forces and prosecutors, ticket buyers could expect to see images that never appeared in typical Hollywood films, including scenes of childbirth, drug use, and nudity. The films were advertised as, and shown for, "adults only," a key indicator of difference from movies made by the major studios, which were designed to be seen by patrons of all ages. To balance their potential salaciousness and further differentiate themselves from Hollywood movies, exploitation films were also promoted as educational, typically operating as exposés of their difficult subject matter.

During the 1950s the term "exploitation movie" broadened to include almost any low-budget production that was forced to rely on the hard sell, garish advertising and poster art with tantalizing taglines, and was targeted at a specialized market. This included films from companies such as Allied Artists (originally a subsidiary of B-movie stalwart Monogram in 1946 created to make better films), and newer firms like Filmgroup and Headliner. The most successful of the bunch, American International Pictures (AIP), thrived by gearing its films toward the expanding teen audience. But if some companies attempted to develop movies that exploited the emerging youth culture – and often helped to define it – others continued to mine the adults-only territory, even as Hollywood started to take a more mature approach to subject matter and themes. Here I will examine these two competing strains of exploitation movies that existed from the mid-1950s into the 1970s. One was pitched at the teen market and attempted to draw on youngsters who had expendable income; the other lured adults – mostly men – with images of nude women and stories that focused on sexual situations.

AIP and Teenpic Exploitation

In the 1958 *Film Daily Yearbook of Motion Pictures*, Chester B. Bahn, editor of the *Film Daily*, concluded,

> For exhibition, it was a year of increasing stress and apprehension. The challenges were many and varied, and unfortunately there were no easy answers. Indeed, as the

year faded, solutions in the main were still lacking, and the clouds were, if anything, darkening. (1958, 78)

Opposite Bahn's gloomy assessment of theatrical exhibition was a simple, full-page ad for American International Pictures. It featured the company logo at the top, and listed James H. Nicholson as president and Samuel Z. Arkoff as vice-president at the bottom. In the middle were four words in capital letters: "specialists in exploitation features." Nicholson, who had been sales manager for Realart Pictures, met Arkoff, an entertainment lawyer, on opposite sides of a potential lawsuit. They became fast friends and in 1954 formed American Releasing Corporation (soon to be renamed AIP). ARC's first release was *The Fast and the Furious* (1954), made by fledgling producer/director Roger Corman. The film's successful release (a quarter-million gross on a $50,000 investment) cemented a relationship between Corman and AIP that would last for 15 years.

Nicholson and Arkoff built AIP's success on providing exhibitors with favorable terms (letting them keep a larger percentage of the box office receipts than they would with a release from the majors), and providing ready-made double bills. Although theater bookers and owners originally balked at the idea, the success of *The Day the World Ended* and *Phantom from 10,000 Leagues* (both 1955) during a newspaper strike in Detroit proved to be a windfall and led to other dates. As Arkoff related,

> The combination opened on the first Wednesday in January in Los Angeles in six theaters and eight drive-ins, and on the following Tuesday, *Daily Variety* printed the box office receipts for the first half-week. In L.A. alone, our double bill had grossed $140,000. (1992, 47)

AIP's combinations proved to be hits with desperate exhibitors and, as the industry trade magazine *Boxoffice* explained in 1962, "paid off handsomely at the box office" (*Boxoffice* 1962a). Charlie MacDonald, head of a Pennsylvania theater chain, claimed that AIP had "solved many a booking problem" and that "I am happy to say that we have never played an AIP attraction which did not prove profitable to our theaters" (*Boxoffice* 1962b).

In his autobiography, Arkoff explained that he and Nicholson soon discovered that there was money to be made in the teen market:

> TV might have been keeping parents at home, but teenagers needed to get out of the house and be with kids their own age – and parents couldn't wait for them to leave. ... We eventually realized that if we concentrated on movies aimed at the youth market, we might be able to create a lucrative niche for ourselves. (1992, 30)

In addition to Corman, AIP struck deals with other independent producers, such as Herman Cohen and Bert I. Gordon, to insure a steady stream of product. Among their notable double-bills were *I Was a Teenage Werewolf* and *Invasion of the Saucer-Men* (both 1957), *I Was a Teenage Frankenstein* and *Blood of Dracula* (both 1957), *Hot Rod Gang* and *High School Hellcats* (both 1958), and *How to Make a Monster* and *Teenage Caveman* (both 1958).

Arkoff described the AIP production process in their early days:

> Jim [Nicholson] was the best title man I ever knew; he had a talent for coming up with titles that could create excitement on marquees from coast to coast. ... [He] was also terrific at creating the basic concept of an ad, the copy lines, and the type of artwork that would be necessary to make it into one cohesive package.

Lacking big stars, AIP had to rely on "strong titles and catch lines" (1992, 38). Once the title and ad strategies were developed, the material was passed on to Al Kallis, who created the artwork for the campaigns and then tested with the target market. As Arkoff explained, "If the reaction was positive, we moved ahead, creating the story line, commissioning the script, and preparing the actual shooting" (1992, 39). The movies were budgeted at under $100,000, filmed in black-and-white, and shot in less than two weeks; in other words, AIP films were fast and cheap. They featured youthful leads, rock or rhythm and blues soundtracks, and they had a topical edge.

Drag Strip Girl (1957), directed by Edward L. Cahn, was a typical AIP film from the period. The film opens with newly arrived Louise Blake (Fay Spain) racing friends Fred Armstrong (John Ashley) and Jim Donaldson (Steven Terrell) down an L.A. boulevard in their hot rods. Fred straddles the two jalopies (all done with rear-screen projection) for a thrill. A rivalry over Louise emerges between the wealthy Fred and hard-working Jim, who hopes that his talent with engines will help him win a regional sweepstakes race that includes a college scholarship. Fred buys a hot rod in order to compete, defeat Jim, and win Louise. Jim feels used by Louise, and his friendship with Fred sours into a series of fistfights, threats, and challenges. The night before the big race, Fred convinces another kid, Rick, to help him steal Jim's car in advance of the sweepstakes race so he can test it out – only to hit a motorist who is changing a tire. On race day, Louise returns to Jim, contrite, and they both resolve to start over again. At the race Fred continues to try to intimidate Jim, but the police show up at the track looking for a missing hubcap from Jim's car found at the scene of the accident. Louise hops into Jim's rod to finish the competition, and Fred tries to run her off the track. The police stop the race, and Fred, realizing his number is up, attempts to escape by crashing through a gate. The cops haul him and Rick away. The film concludes with Louise and Jim together as Jim plans to attend college.

To please its target audience *Drag Strip Girl* featured a sufficient mixture of action (fights and races), romance, comedy (mostly provided by comedian/impressionist Frank Gorshen as a grease monkey), bouts of dancing to rock 'n' roll records, and a touch of anti-authoritarianism (Louise mouths off to her mother, and the kids give guff to the cops when they show up at their pizza shop hangout). The plot is simple, the characters one-dimensional, and the dialogue calculated. Settings are limited (the pizza joint, the garage where the kids work on their cars, Louise's home, a few exteriors). Like the hot rods in the film, *Drag Strip Girl* may have been a bit of a rough ride, but clocking in at a brisk 69 minutes, it was primarily designed for speed and fun. However, that doesn't mean that AIP lacked sophistication. Hot on the heels of its hits *I Was a Teenage Werewolf* and *I Was a Teenage Frankenstein*, the company turned out *How to Make a Monster* (1958). The film concerned a studio called American International sold to new owners who decide to stop their production of horror movies. This leads the company's crazed makeup man to turn young actors into a real teenage werewolf and Frankenstein to exact his revenge against the new executives. The film was savvy in its recycling of AIP's earlier successes and signature makeup designs, as well as in the way it played on the company's image – all with tongue planted firmly in cheek.

By the early 1960s AIP was diversifying, while still remaining true to its target demographic through its focus on "action, lots of excitement, and kicks and thrills aplenty" (*Boxoffice* 1962a). The company began to import films such as *Alakazam the Great* (Japan, 1960), *Burn, Witch, Burn* (Great Britain, 1962), *Samson and the Seven Miracles of the World* (France/Italy, 1962), and *Goliath and the Sins of Babylon* (Italy, 1963). They also gradually improved production values. In 1960, Corman made *The House of Usher*, a wide-screen, color adaptation of the Edgar Allan Poe short story with Vincent Price. It was the first of a long line of Poe films turned out by AIP that included *The Pit and the Pendulum* (1961), *Tales of Terror* (1961), *The Raven* (1963), and *Masque of the Red Death* (1964), most of which were directed by Corman and featured Price. The films were surprisingly well received by critics, and youthful horror fans made them box office hits. In 1964, Price asserted the films were popular with adults as well, although they may have refused to admit it: "I think that this is because the Poe films are so popular with teenagers or perhaps because of snobbishness – but whatever the reason, a large audience admires these terror classics secretly, even furtively, and go to see them frequently" (1964, 8).

Despite Price's suggestion that AIP had the ability to reach a broader adult audience, the company remained firmly committed to the teen set. This was abundantly clear with the release of *Beach Party* in 1963. The film featured Annette Funicello, the pubescent heartthrob of television's *Mickey Mouse Club* in the late 1950s, and Frankie Avalon, who had already had several hits topping the top-40 charts and appeared in movies such as *The Alamo* (1960) with John Wayne, and AIP's post-apocalyptic *Panic in the Year Zero!* (1962). The duo played Dolores and Frankie, two aging teens who migrate to the beach with their friends for sun, surfing, and fun. The film – almost plotless – revolves around Dolores and Frankie's romantic misunderstandings as both try to gain each other's attention by prompting respective jealousies. Frankie takes up with a buxom barmaid as Dolores spends time with Professor Sutwell, an inept, middle-aged biologist in the Alfred Kinsey mode (Robert Cummings) who is completing a study of teenage sex habits. The narrative is frequently interrupted by songs from Frankie, Annette, and the surf band Dick Dale and the Del Tones; surfing footage;

Figure 2.1 Dolores (Annette Funicello) introduces Professor Sutwell (Robert Cummings) to teen sex habits on the beaches of southern California in William Asher's *Beach Party* (1963, producers James H. Nicholson and Lou Rusoff).

and comic bits by Harvey Lembeck as Eric Von Zipper, the bungling leader of a motorcycle gang, and Morey Amsterdam, the proprietor of Big Daddy's (the kids' beachfront hangout, named for the scruffy figure who sleeps near the door of the joint throughout the film).

What *Beach Party* had going for it was an abundance of clean-cut kids (all white, largely middle-class, and all fairly attractive) in bathing suits, dancing and romancing in a setting that for youth of the early 1960s was close to idyllic – the southern California coast. The movie rode the wave of the surf craze of the early 1960s and provided a visual equivalent to the Beach Boys' "Surfin' Safari" and "Surfin' U.S.A." and Jan and Dean's "Surf City" that blasted from transistor radios and juke boxes around the country. It also contained some modest double-entendre, as well as in-jokes that were becoming an AIP staple. At one point the biologist's assistant (Dorothy Malone, in something of a comedown from her Best Supporting Actress Oscar role for *Written on the Wind*, 1957) tartly observes that his study of teen sex will never get through the mails: "But hang onto the picture rights. American International will snap it right up." At the end of the film the snoozing figure of Big Daddy, from whom the kids have been waiting for "the word," snaps awake and is revealed to be AIP's top draw, Vincent Price. The word he says is "The Pit, and continues, "Bring me my pendulum kiddies, I feel like swinging!" He then promptly falls back to sleep.

Beach Party was shot in widescreen and color, a little confection that was simultaneously sexy and demure. When Frankie first arrives at the beach house that he hopes he will be sharing with Dolores alone, his lascivious intent is obvious. But the couple stumbles onto a group of boys sacked out together on the living room floor, and Frankie then falls into a corresponding group of girls sleeping chastely in the adjacent bedroom. The sexual tension and randy undertone of the film are continually undercut by a clear emphasis on monogamy and marriage. *Beach Party* was, at heart, a slightly sexy film ideal for 13-year-olds. And the formula proved to be a hit for AIP, which over the next several years cranked out *Muscle Beach Party* (1964), *Bikini Beach* (1964), *Pajama Party* (1964), *Beach Blanket Bingo* (1965), *How to Stuff a Wild Bikini* (1965), and *The Ghost in the Invisible Bikini* (1966). As time went on, the bikinis became skimpier, the films became more outlandish, and the target audience became less interested.

Like AIP's earlier cycles, including the rock 'n' roll pictures, the sword and sandal epics, and the Poe movies, the beach party films finally ran out of steam. Meanwhile, the company continued to diversify by producing records and making forays into television. Arkoff and Nicholson produced a series of cheap (even by AIP standards) Texas-based 16mm remakes of some of their 1950s titles that were sold directly to television. They also picked up foreign films for TV syndication. But their core values of producing low-budget, exploitable fare for teens and young adults remained intact. In the mid-1960s Arkoff and Nicholson embraced the harder edge of the counter-culture. Comic bikers like Eric Von Zipper were transformed into existential nomads in the outlaw biker genre. *The Wild Angels* (1966) was the first of the series, directed by Corman. It featured copious footage of Peter Fonda as Heavenly Blues, accompanied by Nancy Sinatra and Bruce Dern, rolling through the California countryside. Little happened in the film, but its dynamite box office led to *Devil's Angels* (1967), *Hell's Angels on Wheels* (1967), among many others. The biker films reached their zenith with *Easy Rider* (1969), produced by Fonda and directed by Dennis Hopper. But by then Arkoff and Nicholson had already deemed the biker genre passé. Columbia put up the financing for that film and reaped the rewards at the box office.

Concurrent with AIP's biker cycle came movies about the generation gap and protest politics such as *Riot on Sunset Strip* (1967) and *Wild in the Streets* (1968), and others that centered on the drug culture, such as *The Trip* (1967) and *Psych-Out* (1968), films short on story but loaded with spectacle in the form of psychedelic imagery. After the release of the first "Blaxploitation" pictures such as *Sweet Sweetback's Baadasssss Song* (1971) and *Shaft* (1971), AIP jumped on the bandwagon with horror riffs including *Blacula* (1972), and following up with films that featured tough, sexy female leads, including an avenging nurse out to bust a drug syndicate in *Coffy* (1973) and a federal agent seeking revenge for the death of her lover in *Foxy Brown* (1974), among others.

In the early 1970s, the market that AIP had dominated was changing. Nicholson left the company, in part due to a messy divorce settlement, and died of a brain tumor in 1972 at age 56. By that time, numerous small competitors had emerged to duke it out with AIP in the drive-in and shrinking neighborhood theater markets. AIP's strongest competition came from Roger Corman, who broke free of its orbit in 1970 to found his own production/distribution company, New World Pictures, in order to have greater control over the release of his films. New World proved to be a powerful rival, and Corman came to be known for nurturing emerging directors, among them Martin Scorsese, Jonathan Demme, and Ron Howard, as well as being one of the few executives to regularly hire female directors. Arkoff ran AIP until 1979, when the company was sold to Filmways. But by then, the video revolution, coupled with the decline of the drive-in and Hollywood's new obsession with big-budget blockbusters, meant the position of AIP and New World as producers and distributors of viable theatrical releases was in sharp decline. Corman sold New World in 1983.

Adults-Only Exploitation Films

The late 1950s saw "classical" exploitation films, much like the classical Hollywood cinema, undergoing substantial changes. Many of the topics that had sustained the classical exploitation for years, including narcotic use and teen pregnancy, become fair game for Hollywood under the revised Production Code and received major studio treatment (e.g., *The Man with the Golden Arm*, 1955; *Blue Denim*, 1957). As the 1960s dawned, sex hygiene was becoming the exclusive province of classroom films rather than theatrical exploitation, which it had been for decades. More and more, adults-only exploitation was focusing on female nudity. Censorship challenges surrounding *The Garden of Eden* (1954), about a young widow who finds fulfillment in a nudist camp, led to court rulings that held that nudity per se was not obscene. A number of films set in nudist camps were made or imported in the mid to late 1950s, joining burlesque movies – which had become popular after World War II – that featured striptease numbers and baggy-pants comedy routines. Along with racier foreign films, often classified as "art films," such as Roger Vadim's *And God Created Woman* (1956) with Brigitte Bardot, exploitation films that focused on sex came to be known as sexploitation, a term used in industry trades at least as early as 1958.

The same lack of product that had caused exhibitors to turn to teenpics during the 1950s pushed other theater operators to turn to art films. Continuing product shortages in the early 1960s, coupled with the realization that many of their patrons were far more interested in bare breasts and sexually oriented stories than in subtlety and subtitles, led some exhibitors to embrace sexploitation. The producer/director most often associated with the advent of sexploitation in the United States, Russ Meyer, mused:

> the public was waiting for something new. I think they were becoming disenchanted with the so-called European sex films, like some of the early Lollobrigida pictures. … So there were a number of secondary art houses that were floundering and they were looking for product. It was this field that we were able to jump into. Once [*The Immoral Mr. Teas*] caught on, it was booked all over the country in these art houses and the picture would just hang in there for a year and play incredibly. (Quoted in Turan & Zito 1974, 11)

David F. Friedman, who toured with sex hygiene exploitation films in the postwar years and went on to become one of the most significant producers of the sexploitation era, echoed Meyer, noting that during the 1950s there were two markets for candid films:

> one for the select, sophisticated white-wine-and-canapés crowd, the other, and much larger one, for the less discriminating, cold-beer-and-greaseburger gang. As diverse as the two audiences were, both were intent, oddly enough, on viewing pictures in which human female epidermis was exposed. (1990, 100)

Individual houses shifted from foreign "art" films to homegrown sexploitation, which, like earlier classical exploitation films, were billed as "adults only."

The early sexploitation era was governed by the Supreme Court's guidelines on obscenity developed in the decision of two companion cases, *Roth v. United States* and *Alberts v. California*. The *Roth* case involved a New York distributor convicted under a federal statute for sending obscene material through the mail; David Alberts was convicted under a California law for publishing pictures of nude or scantily clad women. The Supreme Court's 1957 *Roth–Alberts* decision upheld the original convictions, contending that obscenity did not have protection under the First Amendment, because it is "utterly without redeeming social importance." However, the Court cautioned, "sex and obscenity are not synonymous," essentially reversing the long-standing *Hicklin* standard that considered any material that might "deprave and corrupt those whose minds are open to such immoral influences" to be obscene. Under *Roth*, obscenity could only be determined if "the average person, applying contemporary community standards, [found] the dominant theme of the material taken as a whole appeals to the prurient interest" (quoted in Randall 1968, 56).

By the early 1960s "average persons" were less inclined to find material to be obscene. Behavior during World War II had already proved that there was a disparity between professed standards of morality in the United States and actual practice. Alfred Kinsey's volumes on sexual behavior in the human male and female (1948 and 1953, respectively) added statistical weight and the clout of science to suspicions that Americans did not necessarily practice what they preached when it came to the bedroom, and prompted intense media coverage and significant introspection. All the while there was a growing comfort with a popular culture that was more sexualized, be it on the page in publications like *Playboy*, or on the silver screen.

Many of the theaters that embraced sexploitation were in downtown areas that had fallen on hard times as populations moved to the suburbs. These marginal venues might have been shuttered had they not been able to cater to workingmen, both blue collar and white collar, stealing time on their lunch hour or at the end of the workday. The *Technical Report of the Commission on Obscenity and Pornography* indicated that by 1970 approximately 880, or roughly 15 percent, of all US theaters were regularly exhibiting sexploitation product every week of the year, and roughly double that number – including many drive-ins – played sexploitation films occasionally (Commission 1971, 38). In the era of classical exploitation, running an occasional adults-only film could be, as *Variety* might put it, a "box office hypo." But during the 1960s, playing sexploitation films for exclusively adult audiences became an important survival strategy for many theaters, particularly in the decaying entertainment districts in cities across the country. As the *Independent Film Journal* observed in a 1969 article on "The Sex Exploitation Explosion," "Audiences at urban sex houses in transient locations and downtown areas are predominantly male singles. The audiences are 'not bums' but respectable businessmen 'with wallets' who have the wherewithal to pay the high admission tariffs" (*Independent Film Journal* 1969, 17).

Meyer's *The Immoral Mr. Teas* (1959) is generally credited as the first American film to signal the shift from classical exploitation to sexploitation. As a concatenation of standard burlesque film tropes (nudity and comic sketches), *Mr. Teas* was not terribly original as it followed a beleaguered everyman who, after a dose of nitrous oxide at the dentist's office, gains the ability to see women without their clothes. It may have been as cheaply made as a routine, black-and-white burley movie, yet the cartoonish Eastmancolor visuals and the mock-serious narration filled with double entendres gave *Mr. Teas* a fresh and breezy attitude that seemed new. It became a hit, playing for months on end in many "art houses" around the nation and sparking a raft of imitators. The films that combined female nudity (always above the waist or from the rear) and voyeuristic comic male figures (henpecked husbands, sexless sad-sacks, and dim-witted rubes) came to be known as "nudie-cuties." The nudity in the films was almost invariably nonsexual, involving bathing, dressing, or simply lounging about, but coupled with the suggestive narration, the movies had an erotic appeal.

Not Tonight Henry (1960) was released shortly after *Mr. Teas*. Whether it was made to capitalize on the success of *Teas*, or was already in production when Meyer's film hit the screens is not clear, but it was made by men who were well versed in adults-only filmmaking. *Not Tonight Henry was* written and produced by Ted Paramore, a manufacturer of 8mm nudie films, and Bob Heiderich, and directed by W. Merle Connell, an exploitation veteran who had directed hygiene films such as *Test Tube Babies* (1948), burlesque features such as *Ding Dong* (1951) and *Kiss Me Baby* (1957), and dozens of striptease shorts. The film featured Hank Henry, a comedian who headlined a burlesque revue at Las Vegas's Silver Slipper. Henry, a dead ringer for Rodney Dangerfield, plays a browbeaten husband, Mr X. His situation is analyzed by Dr Finster in a running voiceover done with a Dutch dialect. Finster explains that the reason Mr and Mrs X "don't have any kiddies" is "de transposition of de male and female role in modern marriage vit de female usurping de dominant role!" When Mr X's wife goes out, leaving him at home drying the dinner dishes, he sneaks a beer out of the refrigerator that he's hidden in a milk carton. Finster concludes, "Now here's vat's happened to man. He's become a bottle baby!" The rest of the film follows Mr X as he goes to a bar and daydreams about being various historical or mythical characters: Mark Antony, Napoleon, Captain John Smith, Sampson, and a caveman, among them. The film is littered with undraped women and double entendres. For instance, in the John Smith/Pocahontas episode, Finster remarks: "He's really going to give her something – a poke in the hontas!" Dr Finster's "assistant" Herman, an attractive, topless blonde, pops up on screen periodically to distract him from his narration. The film concludes with Mr X returning home, talking to his goldfish. "You're a big shot in a big bowl. Me, I'm just a mouse." He says he loves his wife, but she's got to stop pushing him around. When his comely wife emerges from the bedroom in negligee he exclaims, "You're gorgeous! You mean I don't have to sleep on the couch?" She replies, "Not tonight, Henry"– a turnabout on the title which one might assume to be a rebuff to a sexual overture.

It is not hard to imagine elements of *Not Tonight Henry* as a sketch on television's *Ed Sullivan Show* or as an episode of a mid-1960s sitcom – only with nudity and leering narration thrown in. But it was exactly the nudity and the double entendres that set the film and other nudie-cuties apart, not only from television, but also from mainstream motion picture entertainment in the early 1960s. They also made the movie a target of censorship. The State Board of Censors in New York demanded that the regional distributor make a number of cuts in *Not Tonight Henry* before they would grant a license to exhibit the film in the Empire State. In his affidavit dated May 18, 1962, appealing the cuts to the New York censors, Ted Paramore asserted that the movie was not made to appeal to prurient interests of the average person "or anyone else." "On the contrary," he stated, "it is a humorous film, spoofing all the professorial studies on the 'war between the sexes.'" Paramore claimed the movie was aligned with *Playboy* "and its numerous imitators." He wrote, "I do not claim that *Not Tonight Henry* is a great film," but

> I do say it is an entertaining film suitable for viewing by the average person. It is an escape film and we all know that with the hydrogen bomb, the atom bomb and the pressures of civilization there is much to escape from. If it can be argued that the film is only light entertainment, all I can say is that it pretends to no greater heights and entertainment serves its purposes too. I am proud of the film *Not Tonight Henry* because it has been able to entertain a vast audience. (Paramore 1962)

While Paramore's estimation of a "vast audience" may have been overstated, nudie-cuties like *The Immoral Mr. Teas, Not Tonight Henry, Tonight for Sure* (1961), and *Kiss Me, Quick!* (1964) did provide an escape for working men from the responsibilities of a job and family. They were a retreat, if only for an hour or two, into a world of adult fantasy in the relative anonymity of a dingy, urban theater.

The nudie-cuties dominated the early sexploitation scene – in part due to their light (if usually sophomoric) touch, their color photography, the attractiveness of the female players, and to their ability to command long runs in theaters. However, from the mid-1950s, a series of grim, sexually charged melodramas were also a part of the adults-only market, some from Europe, and some made in the United States (e.g., *Violated*, 1953; *The Lonely Sex*, 1959). Through the early 1960s these films grew in number. They were similar to nudie-cuties in that they usually cost less than $25,000 to produce, and made use of voiceovers or postdubbed "dialogue" rather than synch-sound. But rather than the Eastmancolor and nudity found in the nudie-cuties, they were in black-and-white and focused on stories of sexual seduction, dissatisfaction, or dysfunction. A number of the films involved girls leaving their homes in the country or small towns, only to find difficulty in the city or in their place in society: *One Naked Night* (1963), *Naughty Dallas* (1964), *Bad Girls Go to Hell* (1965), *A Sweet Sickness* (1965), and *Diary of a Swinger* (1967), among others. *Girl in Trouble* (1963) serves as an archetypal example.

In *Girl in Trouble* (1963), Judy Collins (Tammy Clark) tells her tale in flashback. She had left behind her boyfriend Johnny and her drab life in Springfield. "The life I wanted was somewhere down the road," she says in voiceover, "and like a fool I took the first steps toward destruction." The driver who offers to give her a lift to New Orleans attacks her. She knocks him over the head with a rock and drives on to the Big Easy where she becomes "Jane Smith," eventually landing in a shabby rooming house. Her landlady, Mona, leads her to a job modeling nighties and underwear. She goes to a private modeling session in a hotel where a client rapes her. Next, the ever-helpful Mona finds Jane a job stripping in a joint on Bourbon Street. "Let 'em look, make 'em pay for it," councils the landlady. As Jane auditions for the owner of the club, she says in voiceover, "He inspected me like a buyer in a meat market, a cold dispassionate appraisal of so much live flesh on the hoof. In a way it was a relief. To him I wasn't a girl, I was a commodity." Jane begins work as the "Texas Twister" in the strip club, where she becomes a hit. Johnny, who has been scouring the streets of New Orleans, finally finds his estranged girlfriend at the club. He walks out of the strip joint, disillusioned by the choices his former girlfriend has made. At the boarding house Jane takes an overdose of sleeping pills. She's rushed to a hospital emergency room where her life is saved. As she is being discharged, she pronounces that she has lost her will to live. But Johnny is waiting on the sidewalk outside the hospital for her. She drives off with him, returning, we assume, to their dull but safe lives in Springfield.

Girl in Trouble and films with similar storylines considered the changing roles of women in society, especially with regard to work and self-fulfillment. In the same year that *Girl in Trouble* was released, Betty Friedan's pioneering book *The Feminine Mystique* was published. If Friedan's book, about middle-class American women feeling trapped and a lack of satisfaction in their roles as housewives initiated a discussion among women that ultimately fueled the feminist movement, sexploitation films like *Girl in Trouble, One Naked Night*, and others raised the same issues for a largely male audience. The films frequently showed men conducting themselves like pigs and women suffering as a result of their atrocious behavior. While we cannot discount the fact that some men may have gotten a sexual charge from witnessing the abuse women faced in these films, others may have considered society's inequitable treatment of women and recognized their own culpability.

With the 1964 *Jacobellis v. Ohio* decision, the United States Supreme Court established the principle that "material dealing with sex in a manner that advocates ideas, or that has literary or scientific or artistic value or any other form of social importance, may not be branded as obscenity" and banned (De Grazia & Newman 1982, 264–265). At this point the nudity of nudie-cuties and the sexual melodrama of films like *Girl in Trouble* began to unite. The resulting movies were more explicit than anything that had appeared on public screens to date. As producer/director John Amero explained in 1967:

> Nobody wants nudies anymore, they've had them. So we go in for violence and orgies. Orgies are very big. But we give it to them in small doses – like maybe 15 minutes out of a 90-minute picture – and the rest of the time we bore them with the *worst* stories and the *worst* actors. In this business quality will kill you. You can't *think* low enough. And they come back for more. (Quoted. in Hallowell 1967, 7)

Amero's cynicism was unbridled, and his view of the audience was not just on the border of contempt, it was already into the next county. But he was correct in his assessment that the audience for adults-only sexploitation films was largely made up of regulars who returned week in and week out. One industry observer, in 1969, likened sexploitation films to B-Westerns: "If patrons see three or four, they like them as much as the cowboy pictures of old" (*Independent Film Journal* 1969, 17).

The Agony of Love (1966) was just the type of film that drew those regulars in, with its melodramatic story, and increased quotient of nudity and simulated sexual encounters. It was the first film made by William Rotsler, sexploitation's renaissance man: writer, director, photographer, sometime actor, cartoonist, and chronicler of the sex film scene. In many respects it was typical of the films made at the time – low-budget, shot in black-and-white, featuring location shooting in apartments, office buildings, streets, and the use of nonsynchronous sound. *The Agony of Love* opens with shots of Los Angeles at night. Barbara Thomas (Pat Barrington), an attractive youthful brunette, runs along the sidewalks and through the streets. In voiceover Barbara asks, "How did this happen to me? Why? I had everything. Why me? What's wrong with me?" There is a cut to her walking down a sidewalk in the California sun, getting into a Cadillac convertible and pulling out into traffic. She arrives at her husband's office for a lunch date, but he is too busy to leave. Barbara heads to an apartment she keeps for herself, her voiceover expressing ennui and insecurity: "What good are you? What have you ever done that's worth anything – except on your back?" She lights a cigarette. "You've had everything handed to you. You can even afford to keep this apartment, just to work in. What good are you?" She paces. There is a knock on the door. A dumpy, middle-aged man enters, asking if she's "Brandy." She sticks out her hand and he slaps cash into it. "Now that you've bought me," she asks, "what do you want me to do?" As snappy piano music rises, Barbara screams, "Do it! Do it! Hurt me! Dirty me!" There are close-ups of her facial expressions as they engage in simulated sex. The john sits up, lights a cigarette for himself, and one for her; his doughy hand reaches out to her but she pulls away. She goes into the bathroom, calling herself a whore in the mirror, and gets into the shower. The john sits in bed, smoking, looking concerned as she showers. She slips on her shoes and says, "Just close the door behind you when you leave." Barbara returns home, tosses the money she's received from the assignation into a shoebox, and crawls into bed.

The rest of the film follows Barbara's ambivalent meetings with clients, her husband's indifference, visits to her psychiatrist, her own affair with a beatnik (played by director Rotsler under his pseudonym Shannon Carse), whom she pays for sex, and her troubled dreams in which she fondles and coils herself in an unending string of greenbacks. The film concludes with Barbara in her role as part-time hooker at a party: unknowingly hired by her husband to entertain a high-powered client. There she confronts her shocked husband, who pleads, "Why Barbara, why?" "I like it," she snaps, "because I'm no good, because you're you, because I'm me. Because I'm not good for anything except in bed!" Cut to the shots that opened the film of Barbara running into the street where she is hit by a car. Her husband runs up to her and affirms,

Figure 2.2 "Why, Barbara, why?" implores Barton Thomas (Sam Taylor) when he discovers his wife (Pat Barrington) is a prostitute at the climax of Fatin Abdel Wahab's *The Agony of Love* (1966, producer William Rotsler).

"I love you Barbara." The film ends with a shot of her purse, stuffed with cash, as the bills scatter into the wind. Images of the skyline appear as the credits roll and sirens wail in the background.

The Agony of Love was overt in the way it posed questions about commerce and consumerism and their links to identity. Barbara's repeated question to her johns, "Now that you've bought me, what do you want me to do?" is more a plea for direction and purpose in life than an indication that she is striving to achieve a 100 percent ranking in customer service. While purveying its titillation, which it does in a highly charged fashion given the limitations of the time, *Agony of Love* acknowledges that women in the mid-1960s were largely defined by their gender roles and sexuality and that this had negative results for identity and self-esteem. The film did not offer any solutions, but by drawing attention to the issues, it tapped into contemporary anxieties. In many ways the film is a 1960s equivalent to Maya Deren's avant-garde classic *Meshes of the Afternoon* (1943) – only with beehive hairdos and heavy mascara.

Agony of Love is also interesting in its portrayal of men. Barbara's husband is shown as an indifferent careerist and his chief client is a lecherous creep. Barbara's customers are portrayed as a string of dumpy losers. This characterization in particular was quite common and was frequently alluded to in the titles of the movies (*The Molesters*, 1963; *The Defilers*, 1965), or through questionable behaviors (*Heat of Madness*, 1966; *The Girl Grabbers*, 1968). Men were shown as homely, lonely, square, or disturbed, incapable of connecting with women on any meaningful level. It is no irony that this caricature was the way most sexploitation producers also viewed their regular audience – as a sorry crew whose only authentic sexual outlet was in viewing the tawdry movies that they produced. This characterization helped prompt advertising bans in many newspapers across the country that further marginalized the films (Schaefer 2007).

As the 1960s drew to a close, the number of companies that specialized in the production of sexploitation films expanded. Some, such as American Film Distributors (AFD), Boxoffice International, Distribpix, Entertainment Ventures, Mitam, and Olympic International released as many as a dozen films a year through a series of subdistributors in major cities around the country. Unlike mainstream motion pictures, the barriers to entry in the sexploitation field were fairly low and competition was heated by the late 1960s. Scores of other small companies came and went, producing and releasing a few films before disappearing. Indeed, many a theater-owner who played sexploitation dabbled in production, knocking out a film or two. Exhibition also grew increasingly sophisticated during the period. Companies such as the Art Theater Guild operated some 40 adults-only theaters around the country, while chains like Pussycat dominated the scene in California.

Just as companies like AIP had managed to carve out a profitable niche with teen films, during the 1960s sexploitation films succeeded in monopolizing the adults-only market for a time. If not exactly respectable, sexploitation films were becoming more legitimate, a trend that accelerated as some movies, such as *I, a Woman* (1965) and Russ Meyer's *Vixen* (1968) crossed over into mainstream showcase and suburban theaters. The *Independent Film Journal* noted in "The Sex Exploitation Explosion" in 1969:

> with the invasion of the suburbs, there has been a growth in the distaff audience and an increase in the attendance of couples because of the respectability accompanying increasing permissiveness, the privacy of cars in drive-ins and the move to neighborhood theaters. (*Independent Film Journal* 1969, 17)

The stigma of attending "adults-only" motion pictures declined as they intruded into suburban and neighborhood theaters, and as the "adults-only" tag gave way to an industry-sanctioned ratings system that acknowledged that not every movie made was designed to be seen by viewers of every age.

In 1968 the Motion Picture Association of America (MPAA) scrapped the antiquated Production Code in favor of a system of ratings designed to serve as a guide for parents as to the suitability of films for children. The majors began releasing films that upped the level of screen violence, such as *The Wild Bunch* (1969), but which also dealt with sex with a frankness that would have been impossible a few years earlier, in films such as *The Killing of Sister George* (1968), *Bob & Carol & Ted & Alice* (1969), and *Midnight Cowboy* (1969). The R and the X ratings were not only signals to parents that they might want to keep their children away from certain movies, they also served as an indication that Hollywood was finally growing out of its long adolescence and into maturity. Sexploitation movies, which had dominated the adults-only field, now had to contend with big studios, big budgets, and big stars moving into their traditional territory.

Even more worrisome was the challenge sexploitation producers faced from upstarts using 16mm cameras and projectors. Beginning in 1967, filmmakers in San Francisco began making silent "beaver" films with 16mm cameras. The short movies usually featured a single, naked woman writhing on a bed or couch, with the camera focusing on her genitals. The films were essentially without plot, but far more explicit than anything in conventional 35mm sexploitation. Often shown in small storefront theaters, they began to spread across the country, marquees and advertising promising "Frisco Beaver Gals" to patrons who paid a premium for tickets. Beaver films soon featured variations, such as two women together and then women and men. In 1970, the first hard-core features began to arrive on public screens. Initially disguised as documentaries (*Pornography in Denmark – A New Approach*, *Sexual Freedom in Denmark*), by the summer of that year hard-core narratives such as *Mona* (1970) were turning up in major cities (Schaefer 2002).

Soft-core sexploitation, whether R or X rated, was seen as tamer than hard-core pornography, which became the target of prosecutions in states and communities across the country, and a source of growing public anxiety. Even the makers of sexploitation films worried that the upstart "heat artists" threatened to bring about greater scrutiny and increased prosecutions. In 1969 a group of sexploitation producers, distributors, and exhibitors met in Kansas City to form the Adult Film Association of America (AFAA). The AFAA worked collectively for rights of adults to see adult films, and for the rights of their producers to make, and make a profit on, their movies in the face of harassment by law enforcement and community groups. During its inaugural year, constitutional lawyer Stanley Fleishman prepared a legal kit to help members fight prosecutions. Distributor Sam Chernoff, the first president of the AFAA, explained that they had also prevailed upon some members

> to tone down the contents of their pictures and advertising and we have begun a national campaign to educate the populace and the constituted authorities of the fact that we are in a legal business and can exercise our rights as US citizens to present motion pictures made by adults, for adults. (Chernoff 1969)

The AFAA may have initially counted producers of soft-core movies as their primary membership. But as time passed, and as many of the organization's members shifted to the production of hard-core riding the wave of "porno chic" in the early 1970s, the AFAA focused its attention on the defense of hard-core material, eventually creating an annual erotic film awards ceremony. The adults-only film market had been fundamentally changed by the introduction of the ratings system and the advent of hard-core. Hard-core films sheared away much of the audience that was interested solely in unadulterated sexual spectacle, and the MPAA went to lengths to distance itself from the X rating – the only one it did not protect through copyright. Russ Meyer, who had continued to make soft-core films that were invariably given X ratings (*Beyond the Valley of the Dolls*, 1970; *Supervixens*, 1975) faulted the MPAA for turning its X into "the equivalent of a skull-and-crossbones on a bottle of poison" – essentially for allowing moviegoers to believe that any film rated X was hard-core porn (quoted in Beaupre 1973).

Sexploitation came to be confined to a narrow strip of R-rated territory, frequently referred to as the "hard R," that was dominated by women in prison, teenage hitchhikers, randy nurses, stewardesses, summer school teachers, and horny adolescents-on-the-prowl. Indeed, Corman's New World dominated this market through the late 1970s with films such as *Private Duty Nurses* (1971), *The Big Bird Cage* (1972), *Summer School Teachers* (1974), and *Jokes My Folks Never Told Me* (1978), while other companies, including Boxoffice International, Joseph Brenner Associates, Crown International, Hemisphere Pictures, and Independent International, cranked out similar R-rated sexploitation fare. As was the case with teenpics, the decline of the drive-in, urban renewal that saw grindhouses shuttered and neighborhoods gentrified, and the rise of home video technology conspired to put an end to low-budget theatrical sexploitation as it transitioned to cable television and direct-to-video releases.

In the years following the Paramount decrees, and into the 1970s, low-budget exploitation films provided an alternative to mainstream Hollywood movies for both filmmakers and audiences. Their relatively low barriers to entry made them a jumping off point for producers and distributors, with some of these efforts developing into formidable companies for a time. They also offered audiences access to films that had a particular niche appeal, be it for teens with disposable income wishing to see movies that dealt with their age group, music, and culture, or for adults, who desired entertainment that was more sexually explicit. While hard-core eventually became the sole province of home video, the two strands of theatrical exploitation intersected as the majors discovered the lure of exploitation with films such as *The Blue Lagoon* (1980), *Porky's* (1982), *Private School* (1983), and *Spring Break* (1983). The trend has continued with films like *American Pie* (1999) and *Sex Drive* (2008). And exploitation, through both its youthful focus and its sexual expressiveness, helped to lay the groundwork for racy content of contemporary media – be it in film, on television, or on the internet.

Note

1. For a full history of the form see Schaefer 1999. The term "classical exploitation films" is used to differentiate the movies made during this period from later types of exploitation movies, and because they paralleled the "classical Hollywood cinema" as defined by Bordwell et al., 1985.

References

Arkoff, Samuel Z., with Trubo, Richard. (1992). *Flying Through Hollywood by the Seat of My Pants: From the Man Who Brought You "I Was a Teenage Werewolf" and "Muscle Beach Party."* New York: Birch Lane Press.

Bahn, Chester B. (1958). "Year of Challenge: A Close-up of the Industry in 1957." In Jack Alicoate (ed.), *The 1958*

Film Daily Yearbook of Motion Pictures (pp. 67–107). New York: Film Daily.

Beaupre, Lee. (1973). "Can't Risk Investors Coin Anymore, Russ Meyer Cancels $400,000 'Foxy'; Raps 'Schlock' Films as Spoilsports." *Variety*, July 4.

Bordwell, David, Staiger, Janet, & Thompson, Kristin. (1985). *The Classical Hollywood Cinema*. New York: Columbia University Press.

Boxoffice. (1962a). "AIP Shows Remarkable Advance in 7 Years." January 15, 15.

Boxoffice. (1962b). "Leading Theatermen in Salute to AIP." January 15, 23.

Chernoff, Sam. (1969). "AFAA Formed to Check Irresponsible 'Heat Artists.'" *Independent Film Journal*, October 14, 18.

Commission. (1971). *Technical Report of the Commission on Obscenity and Pornography, Volume III; The Marketplace: The Industry*. Washington, DC: US Government Printing Office.

De Grazia, Edward, & Newman, Roger K. (1982). *Banned Films: Movies, Censors and the First Amendment*. New Providence, NJ: R. R. Bowker.

Friedman, David F., with De Nevi, Don (1990). *A Youth in Babylon: Confessions of a Trash-Film King*. Buffalo, NY: Prometheus Books.

Hallowell, John. (1967). "Making Money for the Goon Trade – Sex! Money! Monotony!" *New York World Journal Tribune*, January 8, 4, 7.

Independent Film Journal. (1969). "The Sex Exploitation Explosion." October 14, 17, 26.

Paramore, Edward E. (1962). Affidavit, Film Censorship Records, File 70264, May 18. New York State Archives, Albany New York.

Price, Vincent. (1964). "Actor's Stance on Pix Biz's Purpose." *Variety*, July 22, 8.

Randall, Richard S. (1968). *Censorship of the Movies: The Social and Political Control of a Mass Medium*. Madison: University of Wisconsin Press.

Schaefer, Eric. (1999). *"Bold! Daring! Shocking! True!" A History of Exploitation Films, 1919–1959*. Durham, NC: Duke University Press.

Schaefer, Eric. (2002). "Gauging a Revolution: 16 mm Film and the Rise of the Pornographic Feature." *Cinema Journal*, 41.3, 3–26.

Schaefer, Eric. (2007). "'Pandering to the 'Goon Trade': Framing the Sexploitation Audience through Advertising." In Jeffrey Sconce (ed.), *Sleaze Artists: Filmmaking at the Margins of Taste, Style, and Politics* (pp. 19–46). Durham, NC: Duke University Press.

Turan, Kenneth, & Zito, Stephen F. (1974). *Sinema: American Pornographic Films and the People Who Make Them*. New York: Praeger.

3

Black Representation in Independent Cinema

From Civil Rights to Black Power

Alex Lykidis

Assistant Professor, Montclair State University, United States

Alex Lykidis reclaims two important works for film history – ***Nothing But a Man*** (1964) and ***The Spook Who Sat by the Door*** (1973), linked by **Ivan Dixon** as featured actor in the first and director of the second. Lykidis situates these films in the context of liberal Hollywood's **integrationist films**, **direct cinema documentaries** on the **Black Panther Party**, the **Blaxploitation** cycle of the early 1970s, and the **Civil Rights** and **Black Power** movements. In the decade between the two films, a transition from nonviolent resistance to "violent participation in revolutionary struggle" is evident. Neither film enjoyed a wide audience, perhaps exemplifying the challenging production and distribution circumstances confronting independent politically themed films. As powerful alternatives to mainstream representations of black identity and politics, these films are, nevertheless, significant predecessors to the **Los Angeles School** of black independent filmmakers who would emerge in the 1970s. This essay shares ground with Janet Cutler on the Los Angeles School in this volume, with Paula Massood on silent African-American cinema in Volume I, and with Ed Guerrero on Blaxploitation and Keith Harris on black crossover films in the hardcover/online edition.

Additional terms, names, and concepts: NAACP, COINTELPRO, Huey P. Newton, Bobby Seale

After World War II, black independent film production waned as black political leaders advocated integration over cultural nationalism, placing utmost importance not on the creation of a viable alternative space for black film culture but rather on improving the level of black participation and the accuracy of black representation in Hollywood cinema. The coordinated actions of the National Association for the Advancement of Colored People (NAACP) and other Civil Rights groups induced Hollywood to incorporate black actors, directors, producers and musicians such as Harry Belafonte and Quincy Jones into the industry, which weakened the pool of talent available for black independents (Cripps 1978,

American Film History: Selected Readings, 1960 to the Present, First Edition. Edited by Cynthia Lucia, Roy Grundmann, and Art Simon.

48). Gladstone Yearwood notes that "as the Civil Rights movement made gains during the 1950s and early 1960s and increasing attention was given to bringing blacks into the mainstream film industry, the black independent film movement underwent a hiatus" (2000, 41).[1] Some postwar black independent films, such as Pierre Chenal's *Native Son* (1951), starring and written by Richard Wright, and Anthony Harvey's *Dutchman* (1967), based on a screenplay by Amiri Baraka, were made outside of the United States and failed to garner the significant attention or support of domestic audiences (Cripps 1978, 47–48). Important black independent documentary filmmakers such as William Greaves and St. Clair Bourne did emerge during this period, but most documentaries about the Civil Rights and Black Power eras were made by white filmmakers, many of whom worked for radical newsreel organizations (Snead 1995, 372).

The relatively higher cost of film production made it difficult for many aspiring black filmmakers to participate in the same way as other artists did in the proliferation of cultural production during the Black Arts movement (James 1989, 177–181). Instead, the period produced notable white-directed films such as John Cassavetes' *Shadows* (1959), Shirley Clarke's *The Cool World* (1963), and Larry Peerce's *One Potato, Two Potato* (1964), all of which sensitively portrayed black themes and characters without recourse to dominant stereotypes, but failed to provide an alternative infrastructure or an identifiable idiom that could inspire imitators or nurture a movement (Yearwood 2000, 39). In the late 1960s, the recognition of black audiences as an economically significant demographic segment led the Hollywood studios to forge closer connections with black independent filmmakers, a phenomenon exemplified by the careers of photographer Gordon Parks, who directed such acclaimed works of black cinema as *The Learning Tree* (1969) and *Shaft* (1971), within the Hollywood studio system, and Melvin Van Peebles, who directed *Watermelon Man* (1970) for Columbia Pictures and then made *Sweet Sweetback's Baadasssss Song* (1971) independently a year later (Guerrero 1993, 83–84).

It was not until the 1970s, with the emergence of the Los Angeles School of filmmakers, including Charles Burnett and Haile Gerima, that black independent cinema entered an era of sustained productivity and widespread critical acclaim, bearing the fruit of earlier developments, such as the entry of black filmmakers into film schools enabled by Civil Rights legislation and the invention of lighter and cheaper 16mm camera equipment that facilitated low-budget filmmaking (Snead 1995, 371).[2] This essay is concerned with the development of black representation in independent cinema in the difficult years preceding the emergence of the Los Angeles School. The focus will be on two films linked by one man, Ivan Dixon, who starred in Michael Roemer's *Nothing But a Man* (1964) and directed *The Spook Who Sat by the Door* (1973), the two films Dixon has identified as the most important accomplishments of his 40-year film career.[3]

Nothing But a Man tells the story of Duff Anderson (Ivan Dixon), a railroad hand stationed in a small town in Alabama, who leaves his job to settle down with Josie (Abbey Lincoln), a level-headed schoolteacher, only to see their new life jeopardized by the racism and anti-union sentiments Duff encounters at his new construction job. After being fired and labeled a troublemaker, Duff suffers through a long period of unemployment and menial jobs, which frays his marital bonds and induces a crisis of confidence. Under these strains, Duff decides to separate from Josie and to visit his alcoholic father (Julius Harris) and his estranged infant son, James Lee, in Birmingham. There, Duff witnesses his father's untimely death, which compels him to return to a pregnant Josie, bringing his son with him, confident that he will be able to take care of his reconstituted family despite the racism and labor exploitation of his surroundings.

The Spook Who Sat by the Door tells the story of Dan Freeman (Lawrence Cook), a man whose intellectual and physical prowess defies the attempts of Central Intelligence Agency officials to prevent their black recruits from passing their examinations and being hired by the agency. Once hired by the CIA, Freeman is relegated to photocopy duties and eventually decides to leave the agency. Upon his return to his native Chicago, he recruits and trains a group of young men from his old neighborhood, many of them former gang members, in the guerrilla warfare he learned at the CIA. Once the training is completed, Freeman leads this group of men, who come to be known as the Black Freedom Fighters of Chicago, in a series of robberies designed to secure cash and ammunition. Group members disperse to major cities across the country to train others in the techniques

Freeman has taught them. The Freedom Fighters begin a national reign of terror against the American government, designed to secure significant concessions for the black community. Freeman and the other members of the group are hounded by the authorities but evade capture. The film ends with an escalation of political violence by the group that forces the President of the United States to declare a state of national emergency.

Nothing But a Man and *The Spook Who Sat by the Door* reflect the political climates of their respective eras. *Nothing But a Man* is set in Alabama where, in 1963, violent protests swept the state following the inaugural speech of Governor George Wallace, during which he declared his support for segregation. In April 1963, Martin Luther King, Jr was arrested at a sit-in in Birmingham, where, five months later, four young girls were murdered in a Baptist church bombing, setting off a new wave of protests and police repression in the state. The racial tensions in Alabama forced Michael Roemer to shoot *Nothing But a Man* in Cape May and Atlantic City, New Jersey, in the tumultuous summer of 1963, during which NAACP field secretary Medgar Evers was murdered in Jackson, Mississippi, and Martin Luther King, Jr delivered his "I Have a Dream" speech on the steps of the nation's capital. The screenplay for the film was written by Roemer and Robert M. Young – Jewish-American documentary filmmakers sympathetic to the Civil Rights struggle – who had earlier collaborated on *Sit-In* (1961), an influential NBC television documentary about efforts to integrate public facilities in Nashville, Tennessee. In 1962, researching the script of *Nothing But a Man*, Roemer and Young revisited their *Sit-In* contacts in Nashville and then embarked on a four-month journey from Tennessee to Alabama, during which time they met with NAACP field secretaries and stayed with black families in the towns they visited. This experience gave them an understanding of the insidious effects of Southern racism on every facet of black life, including the work and family relationships that were to become the focus of *Nothing But a Man* (Dick & Vogel 2005, 58–60; Davidson 2004, 9–10, 14).

The Spook Who Sat by the Door was adapted by Sam Greenlee from his eponymous 1969 novel, released a year after the assassinations of Martin Luther King, Jr and Robert F. Kennedy had fatally wounded the liberal leadership of the Civil Rights Movement, news of the Tet offensive had exposed the horrific scale of American military aggression in Vietnam, and police violence against protesters outside the Democratic Convention in Chicago had provided evidence of the American government's willingness to ruthlessly suppress domestic resistance to its power. Greenlee was influenced by Black Power ideologies of cultural nationalism and violent resistance, which, by 1969, had usurped Civil Rights integrationism and nonviolence at the forefront of black political thought. Greenlee's detailed exegesis of the CIA's counterintelligence operations in *The Spook Who Sat by the Door* was enabled by his military background and government service in Iraq, Indonesia, Pakistan, and Greece for the United States Information Agency (Meyer 1999, 185).

Both *Nothing But a Man* and *The Spook Who Sat by the Door* achieved critical acclaim but only limited distribution. Produced independently for only $160,000, *Nothing But a Man* garnered praise after its showing at the 1964 Venice and New York film festivals, but received only a limited commercial run during which it played in select art house theaters because its distributors deemed it too controversial to be shown in black neighborhoods (Davidson 2004, 3). A few years after the release of *Nothing But a Man*, Ivan Dixon bought the film rights to adapt Sam Greenlee's novel *The Spook Who Sat by the Door*. In 1972, Dixon raised over $600,000 through small donations from members of the black middle class. Production began in 1973, but stopped when funds ran out, leading Dixon to approach United Artists, which agreed to provide finishing funds after Dixon showed them footage selected to disguise the film's radical political content. The distribution deal with United Artists secured a 36-city release and promotional support from the studio. After studio heads saw the completed film, however, they sought to make changes to it and limit their involvement in its release. Under contract, United Artists reluctantly released *The Spook Who Sat by the Door* in September 1973 in New York, where it made an estimated $500,000 in the opening week of its run. But the film's release coincided with the theft of guns from a Compton armory, of explosives from Fort Ord, and the kidnapping of Patty Hearst by the Symbionese Liberation Army, after which United Artists impounded all existing prints of the film and abruptly ended its theatrical run (Berry & Berry 2001, 134–140; Joiner 2003).[4]

The production and distribution challenges faced by the producers of *Nothing But a Man* and *The Spook Who Sat by the Door* reflect the difficulties of black independent filmmaking in the 1960s and early 1970s. Michael Roemer has acknowledged that, ideally, a film like *Nothing But a Man* should have been made by a black director: "Look, the only justification for doing it was that nobody else was telling it" (Davidson 2004, 1). Ivan Dixon's interest in the revolutionary content of *The Spook Who Sat by the Door* was fueled by his frustration with his treatment as an actor by the white-controlled American film industry. "It was my own fantasy. It was how I felt about many things ... [including] the frustration of being in a white industry and being controlled by that."[5] Both films' uncompromising representation of the black experience in America led their distributors to curtail their theatrical runs, condemning the films to relative obscurity until decades later, when they both found an audience through home video distribution (Davidson 2004, 3; Joiner 2003). Hollywood's minimal interest in black-themed films in the early 1960s is reflected by the low-budget independent production of *Nothing But a Man*; whereas Ivan Dixon's deceptive pitch of *The Spook Who Sat by the Door* to United Artists as a Blaxploitation film reflects Hollywood's efforts in the early 1970s to profit from black film audiences by providing them with apolitical fare. By negotiating the exigencies of their industrial contexts, the makers of *Nothing But a Man* and *The Spook Who Sat by the Door* managed to produce two of the period's most significant deviations from mainstream cinematic representations of black culture, identity, and politics.

Integrationism

In the 1930s, New Deal era liberalism swept from Hollywood screens the unabashed racism of Southern genre films such as *The Littlest Rebel* (1935) and *Steamboat Round the Bend* (1935), which featured blackface performances and racial stereotypes like the Zip Coon, Uncle Tom, Sambo, and Buck that originated in nineteenth-century minstrel shows and Southern literature. In their place, Hollywood began cautiously to apply the era's new liberal principles to films about race relations. Films such as *One Mile from Heaven* (1937) and *Rainbow on the River* (1939) featured narratives about white children adopted and raised admirably by black women, their arrangements beset by racist forces hostile to mixed-race families and ultimately destroyed by court decisions that nullified the adoptions (Cripps 1993, 12). It was not until World War II that Hollywood began to make liberal integrationist films which preserved the social proximity between white and black characters through to the end of their narratives.

Three lost patrol films – *Bataan*, *Crash Dive*, and *Sahara* (all released in 1943) – situate a black man within an isolated, otherwise all-white group of soldiers that ends up benefiting in some way from his presence. In *Sahara*, for instance, Tamboul (Rex Ingram), a Sudanese soldier, uses his local knowledge to help a lost Allied tank crew navigate through the desert, and he even intervenes to protect the rights of an Italian prisoner. Tamboul's service to the lost tank crew is meant to invoke black soldiers' military service during World War II, African nations' contributions to the Allied cause, and, most provocatively at the time, black Americans' rightful claims to equality in American society. Such lost patrol films portrayed racial integration positively during a time when unity was considered crucial to winning the war. These positive portrayals of integration were mitigated, however, by the special wartime circumstances that brought black and white characters together in these narratives and by the continued segregation of American armed forces during the war, as well as the exclusion of black characters from most contemporaneous Hollywood films about American civilian life. Nevertheless, lost patrol films constituted an important first phase in the development of the liberal integrationism that would come to dominate Hollywood's depiction of race until the mid-1960s (Cripps 1993, 68–79).[6]

Immediately after the war, the black soldier was replaced by the black civilian in films such as *Home of the Brave* (1949), *Intruder in the Dust* (1949), and *No Way Out* (1950), in which black characters faced prejudice but persevered, educating their white counterparts in the narrative and white audiences about the virtues of integration and the evils of racism. In the 1950s and 1960s, the key figure in liberal integrationist Hollywood films was Sidney Poitier, whose persona came to embody the standards for black integration into white society – unflinching moral probity, selflessness and sacrifice, bourgeois manners and values, and restrained, nonviolent responses to persecution. In *Blackboard Jungle* (1955), *Edge of the City* (1957), and *The Defiant Ones* (1958), Poitier portrays characters who risk or give their lives in order to save white characters from harm. The martyrdom of Poitier's characters predicates racial integration on the willingness of black people to serve white interests (Bogle 1996, 175–176, 180–181). In *Guess Who's Coming to Dinner* (1967), Poitier plays a successful physician – a medical expert working for the United Nations and a candidate for the Nobel Prize – a man of such unassailable credentials that his eventual acceptance by his white fiancée's upper middle-class parents could in no way be interpreted as an indication of white society's growing tolerance toward black people as a whole (Guerrero 1993, 76–78).

Nothing But a Man is an integrationist film if only because it fails to conceive of any viable alternative to integration into dominant society. In the film, those who remain outside of that society, such as Duff's father and abandoned son, are living in a state of destitution. After Duff is blocked from gaining employment by a racist corporate order hostile to his union organizing efforts, he visits Birmingham and it is the squalor of his father and son's surroundings that compels him to return to Josie and give small town life another try. The question in the film is not whether or not to integrate, but rather on what terms. In this regard, while the film fails to address the insufficiencies of integrationism as a political strategy, it does counter the accommodationism with which mainstream integrationist heroes, such as those portrayed by Sidney Poitier, engaged with white society. Throughout *Nothing But a Man*, Duff is defiant against Southern racism and reluctant to submit unequivocally to its unjust social structure. Josie's father, Reverend Dawson (Stanley Greene), is the exemplary integrationist figure in the narrative, tempering his congregants' anger against the system in exchange for minor concessions to the black community from local political leaders. Duff is not willing to keep his head down and follow orders blindly like most of his coworkers at the construction site, nor is he willing to hold his tongue when a racist patron taunts him at the gas station where he works after losing his construction job.

Duff's defiance recalls Ella Baker's description of the developing awareness among many Civil Rights activists of the undesirability of integration into a morally bankrupt society: "Even though the sit-in movement started off primarily as a method of getting in, it led to the concept of questioning whether it was worth trying to get in" (quoted in Bogues 2006, 426). The paradoxical ending of *Nothing But a Man*, during which Duff appears to capitulate to the exigencies of Southern society by returning to live with Josie but then vows vaguely to "make … some trouble in that town," captures the parameters of black political consciousness in the early 1960s: a growing uneasiness with integrationism as a political strategy without a clear sense yet of viable alternatives to it. The vague sentiment of defiance that ends *Nothing But a Man* develops into a coordinated program of action in *The Spook Who Sat by the Door.*

As the film's title suggests, *The Spook Who Sat by the Door* presents a relentlessly ironic vision of the liberal integrationism favored during the Civil Rights era, suggesting that the only benefit of black incorporation into white-controlled, dominant institutions is the attainment of skills and knowledge that can be used to fight the established power structure in American society. Mechanisms of incorporation are lampooned in the first few scenes of the film, in which we discover that a white politician decides to pressure the CIA to accept black recruits only to further his own political career. The CIA training supervisors do everything in their power to ensure that all the black recruits will fail, and despite Freeman's successful completion of CIA training he is relegated to photocopying duties in the third sub-basement of CIA headquarters and only paraded out to give the false impression of racial integration to visiting dignitaries. Freeman's commitment to meet the intellectual and physical challenges posed by CIA training is contrasted to the behavior of other recruits who collude to achieve moderate results in the CIA examinations, figuring that a lack of standout performances will ensure universal acceptance into the agency. By showing two CIA officials secretly listening to a conversation among the recruits – one recruit tells the others: "The word is integration from the top. Now some of us have got to make it. And we're it. You just have to understand the theory of tokenism. Look, they grade on a curve. None of us get too eager. Gentleman's C for everybody, right?" – the film reinforces the notion that in their willingness to accommodate themselves to mediocre expectations, the recruits play into the hands of white society.

The representational history of accommodationism is further lampooned in a later scene when some members of the Freedom Fighters amuse themselves by parodying a trope common to the Hollywood plantation narrative in which former slaves agree to continue working gratis for their former owners in order to help them through the financial challenges of Reconstruction. The principal integrationist figure of the film is Peter Dawson (J. A. Preston), a former Chicago gang leader who has become a police detective. Dawson reminds us of his namesake, Reverend Dawson, in *Nothing But a Man*, in his serving a similar ideological function as suppressor of any discontent in the black community that poses a threat to the status quo. These men use religious doctrine or secular law to manufacture consent for the social order. While Duff and Freeman both confront their respective integrationist antagonists, Freeman ends up killing Dawson in an act of self-defense that is characteristic of the more uncompromising representational politics of *The Spook Who Sat by the Door*. The tension between protagonists and integrationist figures in *Nothing But a Man* and *The Spook Who Sat by the Door* reveals the investment of both films in representing the internal complexity and diversity of the black community – something frequently neglected or polarized in postwar Hollywood cinema.

Community

Black characters in postwar liberal integrationist films such as *Pinky* (1949) and *Lost Boundaries* (1949) typically belong to one of two groups – the working class and the middle class. The working-class characters are frequently darker skinned and display strong ties to the black community and, as a result, are portrayed as uninterested in or unworthy of integration. The middle-class characters are frequently lighter skinned and are portrayed as morally upstanding and dignified, without any apparent personality flaws and, most importantly, disconnected from the black community and its culture as a means of making the case for their integration convincing for white audiences. These films imply that black people need to adopt the bourgeois values and attitudes of white liberals as a prerequisite for social equality and acceptance. For instance, *Lost Boundaries* tells the story of Scott Carter (Mel Ferrer), a light-skinned black doctor who passes as white in order to work at two New England hospitals. The film negatively portrays Carter's childhood home in Harlem, presents a Southern black hospital as racist against light-skinned applicants, predicates Carter's assimilationist ambitions on his bourgeois values and disavowal of Southern black culture, and in its ending sequence emphasizes above all else the racial tolerance shown by Carter's white neighbors after his true racial identity is exposed (Cripps 1993, 219–229).

The trope of situating lone black protagonists within all-white social milieus so prevalent in postwar Hollywood cinema is absent in *Nothing But a Man*. Far from isolating its black protagonist in white society, the film is primarily concerned with Duff's relationship to others within the black community: his coworkers, wife, father, father-in-law, and estranged son. To a certain extent, however, *Nothing But a Man* exhibits an individualism similar to that of liberal integrationist films. Duff appears in almost every scene of the film, so that viewers are sutured into a suffocating identification with him. The characterization of Duff as a restrained, soft-spoken, contemplative figure serves to insulate him from other characters, and thus to further place narrative emphasis on the individual rather than on the community. Unlike films in the Hollywood liberal tradition, however, *Nothing But a Man* problematizes rather than naturalizes its protagonist's feelings of alienation from the black community. Instead of implying that severing one's ties to the black community is a prerequisite to integration into white society, *Nothing But a Man* demonstrates how the bonds that tie black people together are systematically undermined by Southern racism and capitalist exploitation. In the film's narrative, worker collectivity is suppressed by white supervisors who thwart Duff's efforts to unionize his fellow construction workers. The health of Duff's relationship with Josie is jeopardized by the loss of confidence he feels as a result of his unemployment (which is prolonged after a racist incident). And the pressure to survive in white-dominated society creates divisions between those like Reverend Dawson, who choose to comply with the demands of the white power structure, and those like Duff, who refuse to capitulate.

Editing rhythms in *Nothing But a Man* emphasize Duff's feelings of alienation by lingering on his reactions to other characters' words and actions. We see Duff's reactions in extended takes that end with Duff isolated in the frame by camera movement or following the exit of another character. Duff's discomfort with his surroundings is also conveyed through camera angles and blocking that often place him above or below the person with whom he is talking.[7] Two notable exceptions to this height disparity occur during fleeting moments of happiness for Duff: when he is on the open railroad cab with his coworkers at the beginning of the film, and during his courtship with Josie when they are riding in a car together. Duff's alienation is also expressed through tracking shots as he walks outside, with the camera often keeping a greater distance than we might expect, allowing fences or other city structures intermittently to block Duff from our view.

Duff's isolation through framing and editing functions both to individualize his position within the narrative and to problematize Duff's alienation from others in the black community. The ambivalence that results is perhaps most evident in a jarring set of close-ups of Duff's father, when Duff first encounters him in Birmingham, and earlier of Doris (Helene Arrindell), a sex worker Duff runs into at a local bar in the small town where Josie lives. These close-ups of faces, apparently without makeup so that all imperfections are visible, become hard to categorize: Do they convey Duff's fear of economic destitution and immorality or his pity for his father and Doris? Do they constitute a rare instance of immediacy or do they border on grotesquerie? Do they express Duff's suppressed desire for a connection with Doris and his father, or his social distance from them? The absence of easy answers to these questions suggests that *Nothing But a Man* both affirms and subverts the ideological stance of liberal Hollywood cinema that foregrounds individual rather than collective action. On the one hand, Duff's visual isolation from other characters aptly captures the internal complexity and social diversity of the black community which Duff has difficulty negotiating. On the other hand, Duff's visual isolation filters all the complex social dynamics of the black community through the subjectivity of an individual character whose dilemmas and struggles cannot be representative of the totality of black experience.

In *The Spook Who Sat by the Door* individualism is frequently lampooned as the product of the expectations and hypocrisies of a cynical white power structure. Freeman is singled out by the CIA when it accepts him alone from a recruiting class full of gifted black candidates. Media reports about the Freedom Fighters organization focus obsessively on the identity of the group's elusive leader. In one scene, CIA operatives are heard hypothesizing that, given the group's professionalism, a Soviet agent must be its leader. Freeman converts the individual skills he gains during his tenure at the CIA into communal knowledge by training members of his community in the guerrilla tactics he has acquired. Scenes in *The Spook Who Sat by the Door* in which members of the Freedom Fighters perform covert actions while wearing ski masks de-individualizes these characters, making it hard for us to distinguish Freeman from other members of the group.

The visual emphasis on collectivity in *The Spook Who Sat by the Door* is exemplified by a scene of civil unrest that occurs after a black man is shot dead by the Chicago police. As members of the black community gather at the site of the shooting, tempers flare. Police detective Dawson asks Freeman to calm and disperse the crowd, which he does successfully, only to see their anger reignite after the arrival of a policeman with a growling police dog. As violence erupts, we lose track of Freeman and Dawson in a series of alternating long and close shots of the crowd in an uproar. The visual erasure of Freeman in these shots suggests that the discontent felt by members of the black community in Chicago precedes and exceeds his later attempts to incite them toward revolutionary violence. This collective conception of political struggle that transcends the individual character is alluded to in a later scene in which a young National Guardsman is shot by one of the guerrilla fighters. As he lies dying, he asks, "Why me?" to which one of the fighters responds, "'cause it's war." The soldier's understandable impulse to personalize what has happened to him is met by a response that characterizes his shooting as part of a larger, impersonal, and communal struggle.

Yet the representation of collectivity in *The Spook Who Sat by the Door* is mitigated by the film's conventionally heroic characterization of Freeman as the orchestrator of Freedom Fighter activities. A sequence showing the Freedom Fighters robbing a bank is bookended by Freeman's instructions on how to conduct the robbery and by a shot of him inexplicably waiting outside the bank in a car (not the getaway car). In the film's final scene, darkly lit images of Freeman in his apartment making himself a drink are superimposed on a series of images depicting insurrectionary activities undertaken by the Freedom Fighters around the country. The penultimate shot of the film shows Freeman lifting his glass in triumph. The suturing of Freeman into these sequences emphasizes the importance of leadership to black political struggle but it also places narrative emphasis on the individual, reminiscent of Duff's presence in almost every scene of *Nothing But a Man*. And yet both films make it clear that individual actions have consequences for the black community as a whole. In one scene of *The Spook Who Sat by the Door*, Freeman has a meeting with an unnamed woman whom he has befriended (listed in the credits as Dahomey Queen, to which she bears a likeness according to Freeman). When "Dahomey Queen," a former sex worker and current wife of a white CIA official, decides to warn Freeman about the CIA's attempts to destroy the Freedom Fighters, he asks her, "Why are you sticking your neck out?" to which she responds, "I'm black ain't I?" The presence of characters such as Freeman and Dahomey Queen, who develop a growing sense of responsibility to meet the needs of the black community, marks this film as a precursor to such inner-city dramas as *Boyz n the Hood* (1991), *Straight Out of Brooklyn* (1991), and *Juice* (1992) which, as Manthia Diawara states, feature male protagonists surrounded by drugs and gang violence "who grow into men, and develop a politics of caring for the [black] community" (1995, 427). While *Nothing But a Man* and *The Spook Who Sat by the Door* both foreground the ethical responsibilities of individuals to the black community, they differ in their appraisal of the available political responses to white dominance, reflecting the evolving function of violence in black political practice during the 1960s.

Violence

Hollywood liberal integrationist films in the 1950s and 1960s tended to contain their calls for social change within largely symbolic individual acts against white racism and social inequality that failed to capture the collective dynamics of black political struggle. *In the Heat of the Night* (1967) cast Sidney Poitier as Virgil Tibbs, a Philadelphia police detective who becomes involved in a murder investigation in Mississippi. Throughout the investigation, Tibbs faces racist prejudice, especially at the hands of Police Chief Bill Gillespie (Rod Steiger), but he refuses to be cowed or intimidated, going as far as to slap a racist plantation owner who treats him disrespectfully. But Tibbs's principled resistance to such racist treatment fails to illuminate the institutional and structural dynamics of white supremacy or the increasingly politicized and collective responses to it by black activists in the 1960s. As Murray Pomerance notes, "racial tension that was boiling over in America [in the late 1960s] was not about man-to-man confrontations, not a matter of Gillespies barking insidiously at Tibbses and hearing them bark right back" (2008, 182). In *Nothing But a Man*, Duff resembles such liberal integrationist heroes because his defiance of white society remains inchoate and takes self-destructive forms. Duff is mild-mannered and almost aloof throughout most of the narrative. His disarming smile belies his defiance of white racist authority in the narrative, but it also reflects his inability to conceive of a course of action that can truly challenge white dominance. The escalation of violence in American society throughout the 1960s, however, would render the ambivalence of Duff's passive defiance in *Nothing But a Man* no longer tenable.

The period of heightened violence against authorities in the United States began with the urban uprisings in Los Angeles, Cleveland, Newark, and Detroit in 1965–1968. Looting, arson, and assault during these urban protests targeted the economic and political forces that continued to subordinate, marginalize, and disenfranchise the majority of black people in America's inner cities. Signaling a shift from the nonviolence of the Civil Rights era was Stokely Carmichael's adoption of "Black Power" as a rallying cry during the 1966 march that followed the nonfatal shooting of James Meredith, the first African-American admitted to the University of Mississippi, after a protracted legal battle. The escalation of American aggression in Vietnam set off a wave of violent "strikes, teach-ins, rallies, marches, blockades, sit-ins, arson, bombings" in the nation's universities and colleges that intensified in 1970 in reaction to the Nixon administration's secret bombing campaign against Cambodia and the National Guard's murder of four unarmed student protesters at Kent State University (Rhodes 2001, 8–11). During this same period, the FBI and local police waged a violent campaign designed to destroy the Black Panther Party (BPP): In 1967–1969, the police arrested founding BPP leader Huey P. Newton for murder and BPP cofounder Bobby Seale on gun charges, killed BPP activists Bobby Hutton, Mark Clark, and leader of the Chicago BPP Fred Hampton, wounded high-profile BPP member and author Eldridge Cleaver, raided the headquarters of the Los Angeles chapter of the BPP, and firebombed the BPP office in Newark. The FBI, through its COINTELPRO program, infiltrated BPP chapters and incited the murders of BPP members such as Bunchy Carter, John Huggins, and Alex Rackley (Strain 2005, 164–165; Joseph 2006a, 409).[8]

Black power ideology evolved in relation to the escalating violence of American society in the late 1960s. At first, the emphasis was on self-defense, evidenced by the BPP's full name – The Black Panther Party for Self-Defense – which reflected the influence of the self-defense practices of Robert F. Williams, founder of the Black Armed Guard, and The Deacons for Defense and Justice, on Stokely Carmichael, Maulana Keranga, and other early Black Power theorists. Malcolm X's call for black people to take up arms in order to defend themselves against police brutality influenced Huey P. Newton and Bobby Seale as they set up the Ten Point Program that outlined the BPP's objectives and beliefs. The principle of self-defense is clearly articulated in the Program's seventh point which invokes the right to bear arms guaranteed by the Second Amendment and calls for the establishment of self-defense patrols in the black community in order to stop police aggression against black people. In the early days of the BPP, Bobby Seale and Huey P. Newton, given their history of incarceration and harassment by the police, considered the bearing of arms as a necessary defense against the threat of violence by the Oakland Police Department. After Huey P. Newton's arrest for murder in 1967, the BPP became radicalized under the strain of FBI and police attacks on the organization and under the influence of anticolonial, Marxist, and anarchist revolutionary theories, such as Frantz Fanon's notion of violence as a regenerative force for oppressed peoples (see Fanon 1963). BPP leaders' growing awareness of black people as an oppressed group similar to their enslaved and colonized ancestors gave the necessary justification for their eventual advocacy of violence not only as a means of self-defense but also as an offensive tool to be wielded at the service of revolutionary ends. The radicalization of the BPP's position on violence was expressed by Huey P. Newton's call for "self-defense power," defined as the threat or use of violence against the state in order to gain the political leverage necessary to garner concessions that benefit the black community (Strain 2005, 150–163). The shift from self-defensive to offensive theories of violence in BPP ideology is reflected in the differences between *Nothing But a Man* and *The Spook Who Sat by the Door*.

The fact that *Nothing But a Man* concludes with Duff's vague proclamation that he will "make ... some trouble in that town" aptly captures the ambivalence within the black activist community in the early 1960s about the role of violence in political struggle. Throughout *Nothing But a Man*, Duff shows a principled willingness to precipitate his own firing from jobs that require him to be subservient to racist white supervisors. His actions are therefore largely reactive rather than proactive, self-defeating rather than politically effective. Duff risks his employment security in order to attempt to unionize his fellow workers and to rebuff attacks by racist supervisors, coworkers, and customers, thus subjecting himself to repeated ejections from a Southern economic system dominated by anti-union racists. But once outside this system, he finds no recourse other than rejoining the system with a vague pronouncement that he will continue his stance of defiance, thus reflecting the limits of integration as a political strategy in the face of the persistent structural inequalities and institutional exclusions in American society. The emphasis in *Nothing But a Man* on the corrosive effects of Southern racism on Duff's relationship to others in the black community produces an understanding of the way racism acts as a form of psychic and social violence that is internalized by its victims (see Fanon 1994, 109–140). Duff's vague but determined vow of defiance at the end of *Nothing But a Man* serves as a pregnant pause in the history of black cinema that ends with the explicitly oppositional narrative of *The Spook Who Sat by the Door*, wherein the reactive and internalized manifestations of violence of *Nothing But a Man* are externalized, coordinated, and politicized.

Reminiscent of Huey P. Newton's theorization of "self-defense power," Freeman and the other Freedom Fighters in *The Spook Who Sat by the Door* develop a plan of action aimed at destabilizing the American government in order to garner concessions for the black community. The film's conception of violence in terms of revolutionary black nationalism is evidenced by its similarities to Third Cinema, reflecting the significant organizational and intellectual connections between African anticolonial national liberation struggles and the Black Power movement.[9] Freeman's ideological and physical instruction of the Freedom Fighters is presented through a montage sequence that uses dissolves and elliptical editing dynamically to encapsulate guerrilla activities, reminiscent of similar sequences in Gillo Pontecorvo's *The Battle of Algiers* (1966). The use of lighter-skinned Freedom Fighters to carry out a bank robbery in order to evade the attention of the authorities mirrors a similar sequence in *The Battle of Algiers* that depicts passing as a strategy of guerrilla warfare. The satirical representation of the hubris and prejudices of white CIA officials and politicians in *The Spook Who Sat by the Door* resembles the critique of neocolonialist influence and corrupt political elites in Ousmane Sembene's *Xala* (1974), whose narrative features French officials attending Senegalese cabinet meetings with briefcases full of money. While the narrative ellipsis at the end of *The Battle of Algiers* suggests, however obliquely, that the underground guerrilla activities of the FLN (National Liberation Front) in 1957 influenced the spontaneous mass Algerian uprisings in 1960 precipitating the end of French rule, in *The Spook Who Sat by the Door* Freeman ruefully comments on the fact that, despite his organizing efforts, it takes the killing of a small-time drug dealer by the police to ignite mass civil unrest in Chicago. This irony reflects the importance of the symbolic dimensions of violence to the mass mobilizations at the heart of the Black Power movement.

BPP leaders fostered an image of violent defiance against authority by staging symbolically charged protests in which BPP members' militant clothing, mannerisms, and weaponry were placed on public display. These protests functioned as a form of performative violence that enabled the recruitment of new members, fostered pride in the black community, and gave weight to the BPP's revolutionary rhetoric. As Joel P. Rhodes notes: "Handguns, shotguns, carbines, and plenty of ammunition: all were strategic political education tools to mobilize the masses" (2001, 136). The BPP's self-conscious use of political theater and spectacle to advance its agenda was overtaken by the mass media's insatiable desire for images that captured the increasingly violent social antagonisms in American society and the growing polarization of its political discourse (Rhodes 2001, 136–138). The mutually reinforcing dynamics of mass media spectacularization and the BPP's penchant for imagistic self-promotion alienated white segments of the population, precipitated the ruthless state repression of the BPP, and obliterated from public consciousness the BPP's funding of local initiatives such as the "Free Breakfast Program, Free Health Clinics, Clothing and Shoe Programs, and Buses to Prisons Program" (Strain 2005, 166).[10] The representation of the Black Power movement in independent documentaries of the late 1960s and early 1970s reinforced in certain ways the emphasis on image over substance of mass media coverage.

The volatility of political events in the 1960s made quick, inexpensive documentaries in the newsreel tradition an ideal means by which to capture the Black Power movement. Since most black political leaders had neither filmmaking experience nor access to filmmaking equipment, the task fell primarily to white radical documentary filmmakers, many of whom worked within Newsreel documentary organizations in New York, San Francisco, and Los Angeles. Most of the films made about the Black Power movement focused on the BPP – its leaders, rallies, community actions, and platform.[11] The objective of most Black Panther documentaries was to showcase the party leaders' lucid analysis of American capitalism, imperialism, and racism with little intermediation by the filmmakers (James 1989, 183). For instance, in San Francisco Newsreel's *Black Panther* (1968), interviews with Huey P. Newton and Eldridge Cleaver and sound from a speech by Bobby Seale are intercut with footage of police violence, bullet-ridden BPP headquarters, tracking shots of city streets, and BPP members organizing protests in front of government buildings. The sound of the interviews and speech is laid over this footage so that the party platform – its analysis of American society and radical plans for a better future filtered through the personal reflections of its leaders – forms a ubiquitous soundtrack which eschews critical commentary in favor of first-person address. The use of nonsimultaneous sound to establish a dialectical relationship between black political thought and black political activity in *Black Panther* is mirrored in a scene of *The Spook Who Sat by the Door* in which we hear Freeman discussing how to take advantage of white people's unquestioning acceptance of black men in service uniforms in their midst. At the same time we see one of the Freedom Fighters, dressed as a cleaner, stealing the valuable pipe collection of the president of Chicago Edison, as he sits in his office oblivious to the theft.

Despite their attempt at self-effacement, many white documentary filmmakers marked their films with signs of their interest in black culture rather than their active engagement with black political thought, manifested by close framing that lingers excessively on the dress or mannerisms of a black subject or by the care taken to avoid any critical commentary in order to convince audiences of a white filmmaker's objectivity (James 1989, 183).[12] David James, in his discussion of two Black Panther documentaries – Agnes Varda's *Black Panthers: A Report* (1968) and Mike Gray Associates' *The Murder of Fred Hampton* (1971) – argues that these films

> fail to confront the contradictions of the Panther's position, especially as these were duplicated and exaggerated in the sensationalized, reified Panther image constructed in the mass media. ... In their inability to deal with the disparity between the claims of the Panthers' image and their actual political potential, [they] participate in their errors. (1989, 187–188)

The fascination of outsiders with black culture subtly revealed in many Black Panther documentaries is more overtly manifest in a series of white-directed independent films, such as *Shadows*, *The Cool World*, and *Portrait of Jason* (1967), which use a realist long-take style to allow audiences to gaze contemplatively at black subjects. This style sensitively captures the ambiguities of black identity and experience, but also, perhaps inadvertently, cultivates the hip coolness, mysterious detachment, and fashionable disaffection that many white people came to associate with black urban culture in the postwar period.[13]

The Spook Who Sat by the Door, despite its potentially sensational subject matter, emphasizes the ideological and organizational aspects of political struggle rather than the spectacle of political violence. Indeed, there is very little violence in the film and the few scenes that do contain violence – martial arts training, Freeman killing Dawson, Freedom Fighters killing National Guard soldiers – do not feature gratuitous close-ups of blood or gore. This is noteworthy given the increasingly graphic representation of violence in Hollywood cinema after the demise of the Production Code, such as that found in the allegorical Westerns of Sam Peckinpah and the anti-establishment films of Arthur Penn. The martial arts training and National Guard shooting scenes in *The Spook Who Sat by the Door* are depicted through long shots and a fast-paced editing style that emphasize the collective dynamics of the Freedom Fighters' activities rather than the individual, visceral, psychosexual dynamics of violence as in Melvin Van Peebles's *Sweet Sweetback Baadasssss Song* (1971). The representation of violence in *The Spook Who Sat by the Door* emphasizes its figurative rather than its literal significance; violence in the film symbolizes the determination, coordination, and sophistication of political struggle during the Black Power movement. Most of the narrative is taken up by Freeman's recruitment, instruction, and coordination of Chicago men into an efficient political unit; what are stressed are his persuasive powers, political acuity, and leadership skills more than his physical prowess. *The Spook Who Sat by the Door* is less concerned with the spectacular possibilities of violent imagery than with the ability of film language to heighten the political consciousness and effectiveness of the black community. As Ivan Dixon says of the revolutionary violence in the film:

> It really wasn't a real solution. I've got to tell you. It was a fantasy. But it was a fantasy that everybody felt. ... It's just what we have felt after all of the bullshit that we as a people have been put through in this country. (Quoted in Berry & Berry 2002, 140)

What is surprising about *The Spook Who Sat by the Door* is that it lampoons white society's underestimation of black revolutionary potential even though the spectacularization of the BPP in mass media during the late 1960s undoubtedly instilled fear in many white Americans, providing the political impetus that the FBI and local police needed to wage their illegal campaign against the party.[14] The fact that *The Spook Who Sat by the Door* does not address the potentially negative repercussions for black political struggle of guerrilla actions against the asymmetric power of the American state lends further support to figurative rather than literal interpretations of the film's violent subject matter.

The emergence of Blaxploitation as a commercially successful Hollywood genre produced criminalized and individualized representations of the collective dynamics and militancy of the Black Power movement. Blaxploitation films, most of which were made between 1972 and 1974, adopted a common formula: A protagonist who is typically a black pimp or a gangster acts violently to exact revenge on corrupt white officials; the setting is a romanticized version of the inner city, whose inhabitants participate in gratuitous sex and drug use. Blaxploitation narratives are depoliticized, inserting black characters, settings, and culture into gangster film formulas that portray black militancy through the prism of criminality. The politicized, semi-autonomous, and coordinated activities of the black community inspired by the Black Power movement are obscured by the sexual liaisons of Blaxploitation protagonists with white women, their predatory agency in the ghetto – where, as drug dealers or pimps, they function as violent exploiters of other black people – and the distance of their actions from political activism, which is frequently ridiculed in Blaxploitation films (Guerrero 1993, 93–94).[15]

The narrative of *The Spook Who Sat by the Door* repoliticizes black urban space through Freeman's actions to convert members of the Cobras, a Chicago drug gang, into black nationalist revolutionaries. In the film, the violent actions of the Freedom Fighters are framed by Freeman's revolutionary and nationalist rhetoric, which directs the group's actions against the white-controlled state apparatus rather than against others in the black community (notwithstanding Freeman's murder of Dawson in self-defense). While Blaxploitation films frequently construct corrupt white officials as the principal antagonists, *The Spook Who Sat by the Door* depersonalizes the struggle, avoiding the differentiation of white officials in order to emphasize the corruption of the entire political system. The film's systemic scale of analysis reflects the foundational challenges to American political institutions posed by black political struggle in the Civil Rights and Black Power eras.

Freedom

The Civil Rights and Black Power movements did not just challenge the racial hierarchies and social inequalities of American society; they also applied pressure on conventional notions of American political ideals. Black political thought in the 1960s contested liberal conceptions of freedom which define it in purely negative terms as "freedom from" undue influence by the state and others in society, defining it instead as "*freedom in action and in relationship to other human beings*, not a freedom grounded solely in rights" (Bogues 2006, 429). This conception of freedom acknowledges that social antagonisms and economic inequalities set the parameters for free expression and agency in the political realm:

> [The] kind of equality argued for by the Civil Rights Movement went beyond formal political equality and intervened in the economic domain. Thus, the demand for equality could not be organized around only formal procedural rights but necessitated challenges to the structural relationships of the economic system. (Bogues 2006, 429)[16]

The narrative of *Nothing But a Man* reflects this economic conception of freedom. Duff faces racism primarily when he is at work and this racism has severe economic effects, especially when he loses his job as a gas station attendant after a racist incident. In addition, Duff's most significant setback occurs when he is fired for attempting to organize his fellow construction workers. In contrast to his alienation from others in both the black and the white communities, Duff consistently expresses feelings of solidarity for his fellow workers, even inviting his former railroad colleagues over for lunch some time after he has left the railroad for a construction job. The importance of labor politics in *Nothing But a Man* is evident from the film's opening scene, which begins with a long shot of an unidentified man, whom we see from behind as he drills on a railroad track. The sunlight shrouds the man in shadow, so that we see him working without discovering his identity – a wry visualization of alienated labor. This opening shot also establishes the tension between individualism and communalism that informs the class politics of *Nothing But a Man*: Between the legs of the man who is drilling the track (who we later discover is Duff), we see the silhouettes of a group of men working on the track up ahead. The rest of the opening sequence shows these men working together on the tracks. A documentary realism informs this sequence because the forward dynamics of the fictional narrative have not yet been established, the identities of the workers remain unknown, and there is no music to guide our emotions. In the scene, the sounds of machinery are loud and cacophonous, while the dialogue is barely audible. Because the men in this sequence are anonymous and drowned out by the sounds of their environment, their labor power appears to be precarious, foreshadowing the film's later thematization of unemployment, union busting, and racism in the workplace.

The positive notion of freedom, as something forged through action and community, is also captured in *The Spook Who Sat by the Door*. In one scene, Pretty Willie (David Lemieux), a member of the Freedom Fighters guerrilla group, asks Freeman why he has undertaken the training and organization of the group: "What are you in this for? Do you want power? You want revenge, you know? What is it?" Freeman responds, "It's simple, Willie. I just want to be free. How 'bout you?" Freeman's response implicitly equates freedom with action, a conception of freedom that is far from its negative theorization in liberal discourse as freedom from coercion, from the invasive actions of others. The often invisible structural inequalities, social exclusions, and institutional prejudices that define American society are exposed by Freeman's emphasis on coordinated actions against the state as the only means by which to "be free." Just as the racism and union-busting that Duff faces in *Nothing But a Man* point to the fallacy of free-market ideology that claims a worker is free to sell his or her labor in a class-based society, Freeman's equation of freedom with collective action against the system in *The Spook Who Sat by the Door* contests the notion that freedom is possible when one plays by the rules of an unjust society.

Both *Nothing But a Man* and *The Spook Who Sat by the Door* are male-centered narratives that link freedom with masculinity in ways that counter the representation of black manhood in Hollywood cinema. The sexlessness of Sidney Poitier's characters is evident in *The Long Ships* (1964), *A Patch of Blue* (1965), and *Guess Who's Coming to Dinner*, in which Poitier plays, respectively, a Moor who kidnaps a woman but does not touch her because he has made a vow of celibacy, a man who instead of consummating his relationship with a young woman he loves sends her away to a school for the blind, and a man engaged to a woman whom he seems dispassionate about and only kisses once in the course of the narrative (Bogle 1996, 182; Desser 2008, 141–142).

In contrast to the sexlessness of Sidney Poitier's films, *Nothing But a Man*, as evident from the film's title, explicitly concerns itself with the fraught relationship between race, class, and masculinity in American society. The first shot of the film shows Duff drilling a railroad track. The framing of the shot eroticizes his labor, as it directs the viewer's gaze between Duff's legs to the track rolling out in front of him toward the horizon. The drill Duff is operating takes on a phallic significance, alluding to the connection between labor and masculinity. As the narrative progresses, the links between masculinity, class, and race are further articulated. Duff's unemployment causes his romantic relationship with Josie to suffer. The class difference between Josie and Duff manifests itself through Josie's anxiety about pleasing Duff sexually, given her relative sexual inexperience. Ironically, the climax of *Nothing But a Man* sees Duff take responsibility for his son even though he cannot be sure that the boy is biologically his, thus decoupling the film's representation of manhood from sexual teleology. And yet, the close-ups of Doris and Duff's abusive father are surprisingly intimate visual interjections that remind us of the psychosexual dimensions of Duff's efforts to fulfill his ethical responsibilities to those around him.

The acting careers of ex-athletes Jim Brown, Woody Strode, and Fred Williamson ushered in an era in which black sexual prowess and physical strength became acceptable on movie screens. In *The Dirty Dozen* (1967) and *Dark of the Sun* (1968), Jim Brown's physical strength is placed at the service of white interests and thus is relatively unthreatening for white audiences, inverting the old Buck stereotype that associated black sexual and physical prowess with animalistic violence that could not be controlled by white authority (Bogle 1996, 220–222; Guerrero 1993, 78–79). The newfound acceptance of black male physicality was soon channeled into the criminalized and depoliticized narratives of the Blaxploitation genre, and later contained by reactionary white vigilante films such as *Dirty Harry* (1971) and *Death Wish* (1974). *The Spook Who Sat by the Door* is one of the few films from the period that affirmed the connections between masculinity and militancy forged by Black Power politics. The film's heroic characterization of Freeman as intellectually, ethically, and physically superlative provokes audiences to consider the connections between these realms of identity. One effect of this is the politicization of the private realm, evident in the scene in which Freeman tells "Dahomey

Queen" that she reminds him of an African queen – it seems that even the moments before paid sex are used by Freeman for consciousness raising. And yet, the contradictions of Freeman's position as both john and educator in this scene draw our attention to the patriarchal logic that frequently informs the conflation of political and sexual agency in radical political movements.

The male-centered narratives of *Nothing But a Man* and *The Spook Who Sat by the Door* fail to capture the important contributions of female political activists to the Civil Rights and Black Power movements.[17] The inability of these films to conceive of women as central to the struggle, relegating them to supporting/supportive roles as sexual and romantic partners to male protagonists, is as much a function of heteronormativity as it is of sexism, since the potentially queer image of black female revolutionaries, as Kara Keeling has argued, undermines the expectation that women involved in the struggle will remain sexually available to their male counterparts:

> The Black Revolutionary Woman's appearance as masculine breaks down when it enters the so-called private realm of interpersonal relationships with black men, particularly when the terms of those relationships are calibrated to support the domestic realm created through heterosexual arrangements. (2007, 93)

It is female characters in *Nothing But a Man* and *The Spook Who Sat by the Door* – Doris and "Dahomey Queen" – who bear the burden of expressing the figuration of black subordination to white power through the modality of prostitution. The thematization of sexual conquest in both films goes to great lengths to counter the sexlessness of liberal integrationist representations of black manhood, but it fails to acknowledge the challenges to normative constructions of gender and sexuality posed by female participation in black political struggle.[18]

In addition to economic and gendered constructions of freedom, *Nothing But a Man* and *The Spook Who Sat by the Door* also conceive of freedom as a function of black people's ability to establish spaces of relative autonomy from white surveillance and control. The emphasis in these films on liberated spaces outside the hegemonic reach of the white power structure reflects the active role of the American state apparatus, especially its intelligence agencies, in discrediting, disorganizing, and criminalizing the efforts of black political organizations during the Civil Rights and Black Power eras. For instance, the FBI's illegal wiretapping and infiltration of BPP chapters and its incitement, unwarranted prosecutions, and extrajudicial killings of BPP members from 1967 to 1971 were a principal cause of the party's decline (see Churchill & Wall 2002).

Both *Nothing But a Man* and *The Spook Who Sat by the Door* use restricted narration to convey the unnaturalness and invasiveness of white surveillance of the black community. In one scene in *Nothing But a Man*, we see Duff getting dressed alongside his coworkers at the construction site. The scene begins with a medium shot of Duff speaking to a coworker in the showers; then there is an abrupt pan to reveal a white supervisor in medium close-up standing very close to the camera. The supervisor is staring suspiciously at Duff as Duff says, "If they can do it in Birmingham, we should do something around here." There is a cut to a shot of Duff being confronted by the supervisor about whether he is a union man – "What's all this talk about sticking together?" – followed by a cut to a point-of-view shot from Duff's perspective looking at the other workers getting dressed. In this sequence, the appearance of the white supervisor comes as a surprise, revealed in a jarring and abrupt manner through a quick pan. The supervisor's sudden proximity to the camera makes us uncomfortable as does the fact that he had been lurking offscreen in the initial moments of the scene. The point-of-view shot expresses Duff's sense of betrayal and silent accusation of those who informed the supervisor of his attempts to organize them into a union.

This element of surprise – in which the audience is led to believe that the narrative's protagonists are safe from surveillance only to have this illusion shattered suddenly – is also found in two early scenes of *A Spook Who Sat by the Door*. The first scene shows a group of black recruits discussing how to collude in order to undermine the CIA selection process and make sure they all pass. At the end of the scene are two cuts, the first showing the meeting playing on a television, and the second showing white CIA employees looking at and listening to what we assume are the television images that we have just seen. These cuts reveal that the meeting has been under the surveillance of white CIA employees. The editing of this sequence heightens the element of surprise by restricting our

Figure 3.1 White surveillance of the black community is revealed through abrupt pans or cuts in Michael Roemer's *Nothing But a Man* (1964, producers Michael Roemer, Robert Rubin, and Robert M. Young).

knowledge of the surveillance until the end of the scene. In the next scene, we see one of the black recruits walking surreptitiously in a dark room and planting a bomb – we might think that his actions are a protest against the institutional surveillance we have just witnessed – but a cut reveals that this is part of CIA testing of the recruits when we see a white supervisor announce that the recruit we saw earlier has failed the course. The surprise of the supervisor's presence is here amplified by the use of a dissolve to smoothly transition from a long shot of the room in which the recruit has set the bomb to a close-up of the supervisor timing the operation in the adjacent room.

Conclusion

The differences between *Nothing But a Man* and *The Spook Who Sat by the Door* reflect the specificities of cinematic and political practice during the Civil Rights and Black Power eras. Duff's restrained, nonviolent defiance of Southern racism in *Nothing But a Man* contrasts with Freeman's active, violent participation in revolutionary struggle in *The Spook Who Sat by the Door.* The inchoate feelings of frustration smoldering under the surface of the narrative in the earlier film ignite into a coordinated assault on the white power structure in the later film. These differences not only reflect the heightened skepticism toward integrationism and growing importance of performative violence in the Black Power era, but

Figure 3.2 Abrupt pans or cuts also reveal white surveillance of the black community in Ivan Dixon's *The Spook Who Sat by the Door* (1973, producers Ivan Dixon and Sam Greenlee).

they also invoke two heroic types prevalent in modern black literature and film. Duff is an example of the pastoral hero who "succeeds by keeping faith with himself, by remaining the same rather than changing, and by acquiring self-knowledge that eventually reinforces his preference for the small victory of survival with dignity," while Freeman is an example of the urban hero who is "moved to vengeance, prone to violence" (Cripps 1978, 11, 118). *Nothing But a Man* employs an observational style akin to the documentary realism of television news and the "direct cinema" films of Robert Drew, Richard Leacock, and D. A. Pennebaker; whereas *The Spook Who Sat by the Door* uses a satirical and didactic style reminiscent of New Wave and Third Cinema aesthetics. The earlier film's white screenwriter and director testify to the dearth of black independent filmmakers in the early 1960s, while the later film's contentious involvement with United Artists reflects the fraught relationship between Hollywood and black independent cinema in the late 1960s and early 1970s.

The similarities between *Nothing But a Man* and *The Spook Who Sat by the Door* attest to the frequently ignored continuities of black political practice during this period. The movement of Ivan Dixon from lead actor in *Nothing But a Man* to director of *The Spook Who Sat by the Door* parallels the connections between Civil Rights and Black Power organizations typified by the movement of people and ideas from the Student Nonviolent Coordinating Committee (SNCC) to the BPP and the influence of Robert F. Williams's doctrine of self-defense on Huey P. Newton and other BPP leaders. The deviations of the two films from Hollywood conventions of black representation mirror the shared foundational challenges to American political categories of freedom and citizenship waged by the Civil Rights and Black Power movements (Joseph 2006b, 6, 11; Bogues 2006, 424).[19] Attention to the similarities between these films can also help us to understand their shared place in the history of black independent cinema.

Haile Gerima argues that black independent filmmakers should not cater to white audiences' prurient interest in the black experience: "How long can Afro-American artists be travelogue *artists*, taking white America into the underworld, into the worst negative conceptions of black America which happen to titillate and fascinate white America?" (1982, 112). Both *Nothing But a Man* and *The Spook Who Sat by the Door* thematize white surveillance of the black community, emphasizing its unnaturalness and invasiveness in ways that problematize the subject position of the theoretical white viewer. As James Snead notes,

> [many] black independent films since the '60s have the feeling of intimate conversations between filmmaker and audience, and deal with issues within the black community, without special regard for a theoretical white viewer. ... The viewer achieves, in the best of these films, an understanding of a complex black world from within. (1995, 372)

Manthia Diawara concurs with Snead that black independent filmmakers often seek to depict the internal complexity of black communities (1995, 409). Both *Nothing But a Man* and *The Spook Who Sat by the Door* portray communal divisions caused by differences between accommodationism and resistance to white authority and differences in social class, gender, and geography. More importantly, both films differ from Hollywood cinema by presenting alienation from others in the black community as a problem created by the pressures of racism and exploitation rather than as a prerequisite for successful integration into dominant society. Thomas Cripps argues that black independent films frequently use individual characters and storylines to allegorically stand in for the whole of black experience (1978, 10–11). Both *Nothing But a Man* and *The Spook Who Sat by the Door* not only present us with simple narratives rich in allegorical significance, they also foreground the individual's responsibilities to his or her community. More than anything else, it is this insistence on the fundamental ethical relationship between individual actions and communal interest that connects these films to the politics of the Civil Rights and Black Power eras and situates them within the tradition of black independent cinema, during a time in which such filmmaking was rare and imperiled.

Notes

1. Thomas Cripps concurs with Yearwood: "Black movies as a genre moved to the periphery of the industry in [the] twenty years of postwar liberalism ... so little that could be called 'black film' grew out of this period" (1978, 45, 50).

2. The two most celebrated periods of black independent cinema occurred in 1916–1930 and 1974–1984. The first period, in part a response to the unparalleled success of D. W. Griffith's racist epic *The Birth of a Nation* (1915), produced the satirical melodramas of Oscar Micheaux and black-cast, black-themed silent films like *The Scar of Shame* (1927), made for black audiences by white producers such as the Colored Players Company. The second period belonged to the Los Angeles School, the name given to a group of University of California at Los Angeles film school graduates, which included Charles Burnett, Larry Clark, Ben Caldwell, Julie Dash, Haile Gerima, and Billy Woodberry, who made a series of critically acclaimed realist dramas, often about working-class characters. For more on the Los Angeles School, see Masilela 1993.
3. In a May 2006 interview with Reelblack TV, Ivan Dixon stated: "I spent 40-some years in this business and [*Nothing But a Man* was the] one thing that I liked doing. … The rest of the stuff was junk. Well, most of the rest of the stuff. The other thing that I liked doing was *The Spook Who Sat by the Door*, which was my own film." Video interview with Ivan Dixon by Reelblack TV, posted on YouTube on March 30, 2008 at http://www.youtube.com/watch?v=SzAggNO0zMo (accessed March 2011).
4. For more about the production and reception history of *The Spook Who Sat by the Door*, see the documentary by Christine Acham and Clifford Ward, *Infiltrating Hollywood: The Rise and Fall of the Spook Who Sat by the Door* (2011).
5. May 2006 interview with Ivan Dixon by Reelblack TV.
6. Thomas Cripps states that the hero in these films is "a black figure set down in a microcosmic company of whites (who would be the better for his having passed their way). Thus it came to pass that the metaphor of the lone Negro set down in a lost patrol, lifeboat, landing party, became the core of a polyethnic genre that would define a black place in American life for the next generation" (1993, 68).
7. Characters with whom Duff has a height disparity in the frame are James Lee, his son, who is obviously much shorter than he; Reverend Dawson who stands up in one scene while Duff is sitting down; Effie whom we see sitting down as Duff stands; and Duff's father who stands up twice while Duff sits, first at a kitchen table and later at a bar. Duff's social and emotional distance from others is exemplified in the scene in which he visits James Lee in Effie's apartment. As Duff looks into the room where James Lee is playing with other children, James Lee puts a big teddy bear over his face, recalling the moment in Charles Burnett's *Killer of Sheep* (1977) when the daughter of Stan, the film's protagonist, wears a dog mask to shield her from the scrutiny of her parents and, perhaps, the film's audience as well.
8. For more on the COINTELPRO program's campaign against the BPP, see Churchill & Wall 2002.
9. See, for instance, Smith 1999, 65–86; Kelley 2002, 60–109; and Singh 2004, 101–133.
10. Recent studies have unearthed previously neglected political effects of the Black Power movement, showing how the ideologies and organizational capabilities developed by the BPP and other Black Power organizations laid the foundation for important political achievements such as the mayoral victories of Carl Stokes and Richard Hatcher in 1967, Kenneth Gibson in 1970, and the organization of the 1972 National Black Political Convention in Gary, Indiana (Joseph 2006a, 413). For case studies of the local impact of the Black Power movement in Newark and Oakland, see Woodard 1999 and Self 2000. Also see Johnson 2007.
11. The list of documentaries about the Black Power movement made in the late 1960s and early 1970s includes Agnes Varda's *Black Panthers: A Report* (1968), San Francisco Newsreel's *Black Panther* (1968), *Mayday* (1969), *Interview with Bobby Seale* (1969), Leonard Henney's *Black Power, We're Goin' Survive America* (1968), Stewart Bird and Peter Gessner's *Finally Got the News* (1970), Mike Gray Associates' *The Murder of Fred Hampton* (1971), and Third World Newsreel's *Teach Our Children* (1973) and *In the Event Anyone Disappears* (1974). See James 1989, 181–183.
12. For instance, in Videofreex's *Fred Hampton* (1969), handheld camerawork produces canted high and low angle shots and uncomfortably close framing that capture parts of Fred Hampton's face, often in profile, as he speaks. This framing does not seem responsive to what Hampton is saying, but rather manifests a fascination with his appearance and mannerisms that lies outside of and detracts from the film's ostensible subject matter.
13. Thomas Cripps identifies this representational schema as an "*esthétique du cool*" that emphasizes characters' "outward detachment, composed choreographic strides, and self-possessed, enigmatic mask over inner urgency" (1978, 12).
14. After a successful operation to capture a weapons cache from a local military barracks, Freeman assuages the concerns of his associates by assuring them that the authorities would never suspect them of having conducted the raid: "They'll be looking for everyone but us. This took brains and guts, which we don't have right?"
15. David James states: "By presenting the traumas of the ghetto empirically as local criminal issues, Blaxploitation spoke directly to its audience's everyday

experience, but not to what determined it. The genre's conventions ... allowed for a vicarious release of anger in ways that challenged the power of neither the state nor its local institutions" (1989, 190).

16. The awareness of how economic relationships determine social and political inequalities is testament to the influence of Marxism in twentieth-century black political thought. Marxism provides a critical connecting thread between the Civil Rights and Black Power movements, and between black political struggles in the United States and liberation struggles in the Caribbean, Latin America, and Africa. For an account of the influence of Marxism in twentieth-century black political thought, see Robinson 2000 and Kelley 2002, 36–59.
17. See, for instance, Robnett 1997; Williams 2006; Ward 2006; and Houck & Dixon 2009.
18. See, for instance, Springer 2006. The heteronormativity of *The Spook Who Sat by the Door* is made explicit in a scene in which "Dahomey Queen," in response to a question posed by CIA officials, attests unequivocally to Freeman's heterosexuality.
19. For more on Robert F. Williams, see Tyson 2001.

References

Berry, Torriano, & Berry, Venise T. (2002). *The 50 Most Influential Black Films: A Celebration of African-American Talent, Determination and Creativity*. New York: Citadel Press.

Bogle, Donald. (1996). *Toms, Coons, Mulattoes, Mammies, and Bucks: An Interpretive History of Blacks in American Films*. 3rd edn. New York: Continuum.

Bogues, B. Anthony. (2006). "Reflections on African-American Political Thought: The Many Rivers of Freedom." In Lewis Ricardo Gordon & Jane Anna Gordon (eds), *A Companion to African-American Studies* (pp. 417–434). Oxford: Blackwell.

Churchill, Ward, & Wall, Jim Vander. (2002). *Agents of Repression: The FBI's Secret Wars against the Black Panther Party and the American Indian Movement*. Boston: South End Press.

Cripps, Thomas. (1978). *Black Film as Genre*. Bloomington: Indiana University Press.

Cripps, Thomas. (1993). *Making Movies Black: The Hollywood Message Movie from World War II to the Civil Rights Era*. Oxford: Oxford University Press.

Davidson, Jim. (2004). "The Making of *Nothing But a Man*." In *Nothing But a Man* DVD liner notes, released by New Video Group, Inc.

Desser, David. (2008). "1965: Movies and the Color Line." In Barry Keith Grant (ed.), *American Cinema of the 1960s: Themes and Variations* (pp. 130–149). New Brunswick: Rutgers University Press.

Diawara, Manthia. (1995). "Black American Cinema: The New Realism." In Michael T. Martin (ed.), *Cinemas of the Black Diaspora: Diversity, Dependence, and Oppositionality* (pp. 405–427). Detroit: Wayne State University Press.

Dick, Bruce, & Vogel, Mark. (2005). "Demanding Dignity: *Nothing But a Man*." In Leon Lewis (ed.), *Robert M. Young: Essays on the Films* (pp. 58–73). Jefferson, NC: McFarland.

Fanon, Frantz. (1963). *The Wretched of the Earth*. New York: Grove Press.

Fanon, Frantz. (1994). *Black Skin, White Masks*. New York: Grove Press.

Gerima, Haile (1982). "On Independent Cinema." In Gladstone L. Yearwood (ed.), *Black Cinema Aesthetics: Issues in Independent Black Filmmaking* (pp. 106–113). Athens: Ohio University Center for Afro-American Studies.

Guerrero, Ed. (1993). *Framing Blackness: The African American Image in Film*. Philadelphia: Temple University Press.

Houck, Davis W., & Dixon, David E. (eds). (2009). *Women and the Civil Rights Movement, 1954–1965*. Jackson: University Press of Mississippi.

James, David E. (1989). *Allegories of Cinema: American Film in the Sixties*. Princeton: Princeton University Press.

Johnson, Cedric. (2007). *Revolutionaries to Race Leaders: Black Power and the Making of African American Politics*. Minneapolis: University of Minnesota Press.

Joiner, Lotte L. (2003). "After 30 Years a Controversial Film Re-emerges." *The Crisis*, November–December, 41.

Joseph, Peniel E. (2006a). "An Emerging Mosaic: Rewriting Postwar African-American History." In Lewis Ricardo Gordon & Jane Anna Gordon (eds), *A Companion to African-American Studies* (pp. 400–416). Oxford: Blackwell.

Joseph, Peniel E. (2006b). "Toward a Historiography of the Black Power Movement." In Peniel E. Joseph (ed.), *The Black Power Movement: Rethinking the Civil Rights–Black Power Era* (pp. 1–25). New York: Routledge.

Keeling, Kara. (2007). *The Witch's Flight: The Cinematic, the Black Femme and the Image of Common Sense*. Durham, NC: Duke University Press.

Kelley, Robin D. G. (2002). *Freedom Dreams: The Black Radical Imagination*. Boston: Beacon.

Masilela, Ntongela. (1993). "The Los Angeles School of Black Filmmakers." In Manthia Diawara (ed.), *Black American Cinema* (pp. 107–117). New York: Routledge.

Meyer, Adam. (1999). "Sam Greenlee (1930–)." In Emmanuel Sampath Nelson (ed.), *Contemporary African American Novelists: A Bio-Bibliographical Critical Sourcebook* (pp. 185–191). Westport, CT: Greenwood.

Pomerance, Murray. (2008). "1967: Movies and the Specter of Rebellion." In Barry Keith Grant (ed.), *American Cinema of the 1960s: Themes and Variations* (pp. 172–192). New Brunswick: Rutgers University Press.

Rhodes, Joel P. (2001). *The Voice of Violence: Performative Violence as Protest in the Vietnam Era.* Westport, CT: Praeger.

Robinson, Cedric. (2000). *Black Marxism: The Making of the Black Radical Tradition.* Chapel Hill: University of North Carolina Press.

Robnett, Belinda. (1997). *How Long? How Long? African-American Women in the Struggle for Women's Rights.* New York: Oxford University Press.

Self, Robert. (2000). "'To Plan Our Liberation': Black Power and the Politics of Place in Oakland, California, 1965–1977." *Journal of Urban History*, 26.6, 759–792.

Singh, Nikhil Pal. (2004). *Black Is a Country: Race and the Unfinished Struggle for Democracy.* Cambridge, MA: Harvard University Press.

Smith, Jennifer B. (1999). *An International History of the Black Panther Party.* New York: Garland.

Snead, James A. (1995). "Images of Blacks in Black Independent Films: A Brief Survey." In Michael T. Martin (ed.), *Cinemas of the Black Diaspora: Diversity, Dependence, and Oppositionality* (pp. 365–375). Detroit: Wayne State University Press.

Springer, Kimberly. (2006). "Black Feminists Respond to Black Power Masculinism." In Peniel E. Joseph (ed.), *The Black Power Movement: Rethinking the Civil Rights–Black Power Era* (pp. 105–118). New York: Routledge.

Strain, Christopher B. (2005). *Pure Fire: Self-Defense as Activism in the Civil Rights Era.* Athens: University of Georgia Press.

Tyson, Timothy B. (2001). *Radio Free Dixie: Robert F. Williams and the Roots of Black Power.* Chapel Hill: University of North Carolina Press.

Ward, Stephen. (2006). "The Third World Women's Alliance." In Peniel E. Joseph (ed.), *The Black Power Movement: Rethinking the Civil Rights–Black Power Era* (pp. 119–144). New York: Routledge.

Williams, Rhonda Y. (2006). "Black Women, Urban Politics, and Engendering Black Power." In Peniel E. Joseph (ed.), *The Black Power Movement: Rethinking the Civil Rights–Black Power Era* (pp. 79–103). New York: Routledge.

Woodard, Komozi. (1999). *A Nation within a Nation: Amiri Baraka (LeRoi Jones) and Black Power Politics.* Chapel Hill: University of North Carolina Press.

Yearwood, Gladstone L. (2000). *Black Film as Signifying Practice: Cinema, Narration and the African-American Aesthetic Tradition.* Trenton, NJ: Africa World Press.

4

Cinema Direct and Indirect
American Documentary, 1960–1975

Charles Warren
Lecturer, Boston University and Harvard Extension School, United States

With new lightweight 16mm camera and sound equipment in the early 1960s, came the desire among some documentarians to capture reality unobtrusively, as if simply "dropping in" unnoticed. As Charles Warren points out, however, despite the seemingly "objective" and unrehearsed quality of subjects "caught" onscreen by **hand-held cameras**, uneven sound quality, unvarnished black-and-white images, and in some cases "**crisis-structure**" content, **direct cinema documentaries** are highly constructed – from camera placement to editing room selections and structure. Popular musicians, artists and politicians "perform" themselves in **Robert Drew**, **Maysles brothers** and **D. A. Pennebaker** films; everyday people may or may not be doing the same in **Richard Leacock** and **Frederick Wiseman** films. Warren acknowledges genuine interest in the human condition on the part of these modern-day adventurers – capturing the daily routines of celebrities, neighbors next door, and those geographically distant. These filmmakers seek not to mine riches but to unearth tiny fragments of truth through images – a project posing its own set of ideological complications. Warren's essay shares ground with Patricia Aufderheide on post-1999 documentary in this volume and with Paula Rabinowitz on 1930s documentary and Ted Barron on independent cinema in the hardcover/online edition.

Additional terms, names, and concepts: cinéma vérité, Jean Rouch, Robert Flaherty, Joyce Chopra, Emile de Antonio, Peter Davis, Barbara Kopple, voiceover commentary, synchronous sound, rock documentary

"Direct cinema" is a name preferred by certain American filmmakers emerging around 1960, for work they were doing in documentary under new principles and using new techniques. The technical breakthrough was the development of new lightweight equipment that allowed a crew as small as two persons, or even one, to move about freely and relatively unobtrusively, filming in 16mm with synchronous sound recording. The new determination, or basic approach, was to attend to the world with a new

American Film History: Selected Readings, 1960 to the Present, First Edition. Edited by Cynthia Lucia, Roy Grundmann, and Art Simon.

flexibility and even modesty, following what might unfold, walking with the handheld camera and keeping it and the recorder running as long as appropriate, reframing and refocusing without stopping, not planning, not setting up shots, not setting out to teach a moral or make an argument, but just to take an interest, to become *involved* as an observer and to register, record, and relay. Anticipated in part by the Free Cinema movement in Great Britain of the 1950s, direct cinema practitioners in the United States – as Erik Barnouw says of the British – "often poked into places society was inclined to ignore or keep hidden," and they liked to let the material stand with some ambiguity, leaving conclusions to viewers (1983, 231).

The preference for the designation "direct cinema" was in part to make a distinction from "*cinéma vérité*" a term becoming current in the early 1960s for new documentary work in France and Canada in some ways similar to that of the Americans, but in other ways different. Jean Rouch decisively used the term in introducing his important 1960 film *Chronique d'un été* (*Chronicle of a Summer*) – "*cinéma vérité*," "film truth," a French rendering of Dziga Vertov's term from the 1920s, "kino-pravda." *Chronique*, Rouch tells us in voiceover, will be "an experiment in *cinéma vérité*." Filming in Africa or France, Rouch had much in common with the Americans: taking advantage of the new, lightweight synchronous sound cameras and recorders; relishing the long take and the flexibility of following an ongoing action; pushing for a new intimacy with the world, indeed a more direct contact than ever between film and the world. But, as in the voiceover at the start of *Chronique*, Rouch put himself into his films, and not only aurally, but visually. He asked people questions. He provoked people and stirred up situations as he found them, making things happen. The Parisians participating in *Chronique*, as we see over the course of the film, actually have their lives changed by virtue of their involvement with Rouch and his collaborator Edgar Morin in the making of this film "experiment." Film truth is not the truth as film finds it and records it, but a new truth, a *film* truth, which – if one responds to Rouch – can be powerfully revelatory of the actual world, its deeper layers and possibilities. The Americans held to a more purely observational ideal. They avoided voiceover commentary. They did not like to ask questions or draw people out. They sought not to put themselves forward or meddle with situations as they found them. As we shall see, nothing remained pure, and borders were blurred in inevitable and interesting ways. Theoretical debates were sparked in these years about whether the presence of a camera would not inevitably affect what was before it – but the filmmakers never claimed that the camera would have no effect; they simply thought that something was to be gained by trying to be unobtrusive.

In any case, the term "cinéma vérité" came into common parlance in discussing the new American as well as foreign documentary practice of the time. The first extensive study of the American work, Stephen Mamber's in 1974, was titled *Cinema Verite in America* (no French accent marks). And subsequent scholars and critics, as well as the popular press, commonly use the term in talking about the American work of the 1960s, and about a filmmaking style or quality originating there and moving into later work in nonfiction and even fiction filmmaking (the French accents and italicizing of the French words, and even a hyphen in between, come and go). People will watch a long-take passage filmed with a handheld camera somewhere in the bustling world outside the studio, with a rendering of chaotic plausibly ambient sound, and say, "That's very cinéma vérité," or even, "That's very vérité." What is important is not the terminology, or old debates about the possibility of unobtrusive observation, but to try to bear down on what a crucial generation of American documentarists were actually doing, and how what is remarkable and valuable in their work came to evolve and to affect film history.

Drew Associates

The story begins with about 20 films produced by Robert Drew for television broadcast over the years 1960–1963, involving the talents of Richard Leacock, Albert Maysles, D. A. Pennebaker, and other filmmakers. Each film was a collaborative effort supervised by Drew and shaped to make a suitable hour-long television presentation, which, of course, meant use of explanatory voiceover commentary – this varied in quantity and effectiveness from film to film. Drew's background was in photojournalism, working for *Life* magazine in the 1950s, and he brought to the new filmmaking enterprise that photojournalist disposition for open, exploratory reporting, showing America to itself for its own good, in a spirit of education – and occasionally giving an outside perspective, as in *Yanki, No!* (1960), which tours Latin America and relays its hostility toward the US. Drew's sense of mission bears some relation to that of John Grierson, heading the British documentary movement in the 1930s, with his desire both to answer curiosity – allowing film to open up the world – and to improve public understanding, even to help create a more informed electorate. One can feel tension at times in the Drew films between the television/information/news motive and the interest in letting go with the moment, following the quirky and unpredictable, putting understanding aside for the sake of sheer affection for observing the world.[1]

The breakthrough film *Primary* (1960) is still the most well known and widely seen of all the Drew Associates films. Following the 1960 Wisconsin presidential primary campaigns of Hubert Humphrey and John F. Kennedy, the film provides not the analytic understanding of political stakes and strategies that a book can provide, such as Theodore White's *The Making of the President 1960*, but rather the sense of having dropped in on a time and a place. Immediately arresting in the film are shots of the bleak Wisconsin countryside and of town and city streets, of people in their clothes of this era in provincial America, and, closer up, the faces of people, each suggesting a story – farmers who come to hear Humphrey speak; Milwaukee Polish Catholics who come to hear Kennedy – a remarkably young, actively engaged-seeming crowd; and people on the streets who stop to shake a candidate's hand. A primal attraction of film, it can be argued, is to confront a world, to have a world opened up for the viewer. Here in *Primary* is a world and its inhabitants, with much visual detail and also, much of the time, with synchronously recorded sound, with its peculiar feel of giving the breath of life to a scene.

Film, both fiction and documentary, has continually sought ways to get closer to the world and to give viewers a sense of new immediacy in making contact with the world – or with *a* world. The new sense of directness in *Primary* comes with the seeming randomness of the material shot and recorded – throwaway material, even with the candidates, which, once we have a look, shows interest and fascination. Midway through, an especially intense new relation to the world presents itself in the now famous shot, several minutes long, of Kennedy walking through a dense crowd, greeting people, then moving on through a door, down a narrow corridor, up steps, and out onto a stage where he will make a speech – the cameraman, Maysles it turns out, all the time following Kennedy closely with handheld camera a bit higher than head level and looking down on Kennedy's back. One feels in an unprecedented way the presence of the filmmaker in a world we take to be actual. The sense of the filmmaker and camera's presence compounds the sense of the actuality of the world. Somebody not exactly *of* this world is there, so the world must be there. And although the filmmaker follows and observes, he, and the film itself, become almost at one with Kennedy, pressing forward, registering the multiplicity of faces and sounds, poised, coping with it all, enjoying it. The filmmaker and film are at an at least slight distance from the world, but press unusually hard to be at one with it, to share in its spirit. This shot is also presented in abbreviated form at the very beginning of the film, underscoring its declarative value for the whole project.

Hubert and Muriel Humphrey, John and Jacqueline Kennedy, and for a moment Robert Kennedy, all appear in the iconic aspects so familiar over years of images and public appearances on the part of these figures. We see Humphrey napping during a car trip, and Kennedy, tired and rooted to his chair, resting in a bustling hotel room where all are waiting for returns on election night. But even in fatigue, the political people seem all mask, all image. The film chronicles a journey of these special beings into the American heartland with all its awkwardness and unguardedness. Humphrey was from Minnesota and a son of the middle class, but here, like the wealthy northeasterner Kennedy, he seems all front, all rhetoric – the audience of farmers is clearly uneasy with him as he keeps making the effort to break through. In a telling scene, Kennedy, smiling and cooperative but a bit stiff, is posed sitting at a desk for a photographic portrait. Finally there is a surprising cut to a portrait of Humphrey, which turns out to be a poster on the side of a bus. The men are the same, the film seems to say – images, all externalized. Not that *Primary* is cynical. There is sincerity about Humphrey and Kennedy. They stand for something, and voters care about what they stand for and warm up to them, especially to Kennedy. It is just that the film lets us see that political people, beings of a certain kind, journey in a place that is not where they live, and interact with beings quite different from themselves – ordinary

Americans – as part of their calling. To some viewers of the film, especially now, the political people will seem the more familiar, Wisconsin and the Wisconsinites of 1960 the more strange. Such is the power of observational cinema to register, and to allow some play and change in viewer valuation.

The witty cut from a posing Kennedy to the posed poster image of Humphrey – a gesture more like that of a Frederick Wiseman film years down the road – reminds us that *Primary* is a construction, where choices have been made. The film may be very direct at any moment in its contact with reality, but there is certainly an indirection in its offer to give us this primary – even a cross-section of it, or a valid dip into it – over the course of its hour presentation. Selections have been made. Transitions have been contrived. And, after all, even at a given moment, even in a single shot, choices have been made. Where is the camera, and what do the camera and recorder focus on? How long does the shot last? All these things might have been different from what we see and hear in the film as it is, giving a different impression from the one we get here. We hear sound waves remarkably like what we might have heard had we been present at the scene. But we see, after all, black-and-white two-dimensional figures, shadows on a screen. How do such transfigured forms in fact relate to any reality? On the larger and smaller scales we are given fragments. And skepticism could go further, speculating on possible contrivance and manipulation of events being filmed. Skepticism can wither away any filmic representation of reality, just as it can wither away our sense that we have contact, through our senses and mind, with the world about us and with other people. (How do I *know* that I am not dreaming? as philosophers have liked to put it.) But, for the most part, we manage to live in the world and interact and talk with other people. And with film, using judgment and experience – consideration of the many things we see in films of various kinds – we allow that *Primary* and films like it draw us remarkably into a time and place and certain events that we accept as having actually happened.[2]

Drew Associates maintained an interest in political material, as with *The Children Were Watching* (1960), about the New Orleans public school desegregation crisis, giving us a lot of time with the ordinary people involved – parents and children – and their views; or the final Drew film, *Crisis: Behind a Presidential Commitment* (1963), focusing on the forced first admission of black students to the University of Alabama – with Attorney General Robert Kennedy strategizing and talking on the phone with legal and military subordinates in Alabama, and with Governor George Wallace offering resistance. Other films went more into ordinary American life: *On the Pole* (1960) and a sequel, *Eddie* (1961), about race car driver Eddie Sachs and the Indianapolis 500 race; *David* (1961), about a recovering drug addict; *Football* (aka *Mooney vs. Fowle*, 1961), about high school football in Miami; or *Susan Starr* (1962), about a piano competition. Mamber and others have pointed to the "crisis structure" typical of the Drew films, going for a situation where someone – prominent politician, professional, or ordinary person – is put on the spot, put through unusual demands or emotions, and there is suspense as to the outcome. A refreshing change from this, more like later direct cinema work in America, is *On the Road to Button Bay* (1962), about Topeka, Kansas, Girl Scouts preparing for and journeying to a massive Girl Scout meet and campout in Vermont. The film gives us random-seeming, intimate, often amusing scenes with the girls at home, doing Scout work, traveling by train and singing together, going through events in Vermont and coping with the weather and certain tensions that arise. The Scouts and various adults seem quite at ease with the filmmakers, who are there following things dawn to dark and seem to be – one wants to say – living the situation. The film is marred only by an excessive use of voiceover commentary from television personality Garry Moore. *Jane* (1962), following Jane Fonda's preparation for a Broadway play and then the opening night failure, shows an interest in celebrity (besides the politicians) that direct cinema filmmakers will pursue for years to come.

Very powerful and much deserving of revival is the penultimate Drew film, *The Chair* (1962). A black man, Paul Crump, had been sentenced nine years earlier in Chicago to die in the electric chair, for murder. The execution date is just days away, and Crump has been granted a parole board hearing to consider commutation of his sentence to life imprisonment, on the basis of his having been rehabilitated, of his having become an altogether new person. Prison officials, social workers, indeed all who have had contact with Crump during the intervening years, support the plea – only the prosecutorial establishment resists. The film focuses on the tense atmosphere of time running out and on the high drama and formality of the hearing itself. The world that matters here is that of testimony, challenges, and the strict requirements of the law. Everything else is subservient to this: notably the man Paul Crump, whom we see briefly only in two scenes, talking to a publisher's editor about a novel he has written, and meeting reporters after the decision has gone in his favor, both times looking put upon and uncomfortable; Crump's young pro bono lawyer, nervous and obsessed with the case, who weeps openly before the camera after a phone conversation informing him that the local Catholic hierarchy will support Crump (support that is soon rescinded); the prison, with its corridors and many chambers and electric chair, all imposing manifestations of state power, along with a sympathetic and humane warden. The very fragmentary structure of the film, shifting among these realms, serves its sense of lives caught up in institutions and forces greater than themselves. The heart of the film is the hearing room, where people very much of the time in dress and manner, professional and lay, make their points with proper language and formality, while showing a certain human awkwardness. The most exciting moment occurs when stellar attorney Louis Nizer demolishes the uninformed testimony of Crump's original prosecutor, now a judge. The decision goes Crump's way. Justice is served. But what does the film leave us with? Crump, who as a teenager deliberately killed someone during a robbery, has grown up and become somebody new, a writer, a teacher, and an inspiration to other criminal inmates – he helps make the prison a better place. He will not be executed, but he will never leave prison. The film presents its complex view of life under the law, with no excessive verbalizing or moralizing.

Maysles, Pennebaker, and Leacock

Due to the loss of television sponsorship and the desire of the filmmakers involved to pursue their own independent projects, Drew Associates broke up, and Maysles, Leacock, and Pennebaker went on to make the films associated with their respective names. Some of these films are short; some were commissioned by, or sold to, television or private entities. But this body of work consists to a large extent of feature-length films, independently produced and distributed, and aimed at a theatrical audience, if not at the mass and the mainstream. Very remarkably, this work brought documentary into the realm of "movies," each film an event for at least a segment of the moviegoing public, in a way unprecedented in the United States since Robert Flaherty's films decades earlier (*Nanook of the North*, 1922; *Moana*, 1926; *Man of Aran*, 1934) and the New Deal government-sponsored films of Pare Lorentz (*The Plow That Broke the Plains*, 1936; *The River*, 1938). Flaherty and Lorentz, and some occasional government-sponsored work during World War II, such as John Huston's *Battle of San Pietro* (1944) and *Let There Be Light* (1945) (both suppressed), seem exceptions in the course of American film history. But Direct Cinema (as it was coming to be called, often with the words capitalized) was very much a part of the 1960s film scene, when many American viewers took an interest in new kinds of work, such as European films that pushed boundaries in fiction filmmaking (Antonioni, Bergman, the French New Wave), as well as innovative American fiction films (Cassavetes, Arthur Penn, Altman soon to emerge). The documentaries that kept coming seemed one more interesting variety in a diverse film culture. The documentaries influenced fiction filmmaking – or showed a close kinship with it – to the extent that fiction films cultivated a new, casual, observational documentary feel and a new open-endedness in narrative. And these documentaries specifically set a model for later work such as Barbara Kopple's *Harlan County, U.S.A.* (1976) and eventually the films of Errol Morris, Michael Moore, and many others, finding a place in theaters and speaking to a public interested in all kinds of films.

Albert Maysles liked filming, but not editing. He teamed with his brother, David, who recorded sound and oversaw editing. Also very important to the films was the work of editor Charlotte Zwerin and, later on, the participation of Ellen Hovde and Susan Froemke. The Maysles films came from a team, but one with a very unified and focused vision.

Showman (1962), following the activities of film producer Joseph E. Levine, and *What's Happening! The Beatles in the U.S.A.* (1964) are exuberant films, observing and delighting in public figures who enjoy their work and their lives, and meet with great success. Levine seems unfazed even by a challenging encounter with talk show host David Susskind, who praises him for sponsoring De Sica's *Two Women*

(1960), but attacks him for *Hercules* (1959) and debasement of public taste. Both men, arguing, seem to perform for the film a bit. Plainly observant, the film does not take sides. And overall, it simply accepts Levine and finds him interesting to watch, with his charm, crassness, and industriousness. *Showman* itself does not stand apart from the world of *Two Women* or *Hercules*, or Susskind's film production *A Raisin in the Sun* (1961, also discussed), but rather connects with this world, as a different but open and friendly cousin, a new kind of film that is still a film. One dividend of *Showman* is a moment near the end with Kim Novak, where we see that in real life – if that is what it is – she speaks rather like her Madeleine character in Hitchcock's *Vertigo* (1958), but now with some humor and insouciance. She is really more charming here than in her film roles – but, of course, this *is* a film role, of a new kind. This documentary transfigures, and gives space for posing or performing or concealing, but makes its revelations of a new kind – we nowhere else see Levine, or Novak, like *this*, and *this* speaks to who they are.

The interest in celebrities continues with *Meet Marlon Brando* (1965) and *With Love from Truman* (aka *A Visit with Truman Capote*, 1966), and, of course, later with *Gimme Shelter* (1970), featuring the Rolling Stones. The Brando and Capote films are only a half hour each, the first an oddity that got very little distribution, the Capote one made for television. In the Brando film, the Maysles brothers document a series of New York press interviews (one on the street beside Central Park) that Brando gives as part of the promotion campaign for his latest film, *Morituri* (1965). As with all the direct cinema films about performers, we are made aware of the difference between the performer as an actual person and the performer as known only through image and work, and at the same time made aware that the performer – perhaps like all people on film – never ceases to project a certain front. Brando is charming, relaxed, ironic, disparaging of Hollywood, but stays quite aware of the filmmakers and indeed the whole battery of media about him, and puts across a certain deliberate and measured flirtatiousness with young women interviewers – it seems game playing, not really sincere. The film is loose and intimate with him, and catches an intelligence about him and a third dimension, all a little different from the intelligence and depth that come across in his acting roles. Like other direct cinema films – Leacock and Chopra's *A Happy Mother's Day* (1963), about the birth of quintuplets in a small Midwest community, or Pennebaker's *Don't Look Back* (1967), about Bob Dylan – the Brando film stands apart from the media circus that becomes part of its subject matter. Here is a way of reporting more observant, more knowing, more awake, more patient, these films seem to say.

In the Capote film, the writer talks to *Newsweek* reporter Karen Denison – a media person who in this case works in accord with the film – and to the filmmakers themselves, in New York City and on a drive to and inside Capote's eastern Long Island house. He talks about his life and his work, especially the recent bestseller *In Cold Blood*, making his own sort of self-presentation. The Maysles brothers have frequently spoken of being inspired in their own work by *In Cold Blood*, and feeling justified by it. And certainly their films and the whole direct cinema movement are to be associated with the new nonfiction prose of the period coming from such writers as Capote and Norman Mailer, taking a deeper look at America, taking the space needed to do so, taking care with the rendering of detail and with the structuring of a whole presentation. The term "nonfiction novel" became common to designate this work, stressing the *art* of the whole enterprise – a writer's tools of indirection, we might say, for the sake of making newly direct contact with the world and bringing an audience into such contact. It is interesting that Albert and David Maysles felt especially close to Capote and *In Cold Blood*, considering Capote's oddity, his outsider status in almost every realm, his fascination, even identification, with the outlawed, the bizarre, the horrible. The Maysles brothers are giving us a clue to their work. In a close shot at one point in the film, we see Capote inscribe a copy of the book, "with love from Truman" – love, one supposes, for the one who will receive the book, but also suggesting Capote's love *in* the book for what he dispassionately chronicles – the Kansas farm family who have been murdered, the ordinary people and legal system professionals of the Kansas world so remote from Capote's own, the killers themselves, with whom he became intimate in prison visits and whose execution he witnessed.[3]

The Maysles brothers' most significant films are the features *Salesman* (1968), *Gimme Shelter*, and *Grey Gardens* (1975), all extended observational films with no voiceover or other commentary, all concerned with downbeat, disturbing, even violent material, and all bringing charges, from some quarters, of exploitation and a condescending attitude on the part of the filmmakers. *Salesman* deals with door-to-door Bible salesmen working in not very well-off neighborhoods in Massachusetts and Florida; *Gimme Shelter*, with the Rolling Stones concert at Altamont Speedway in California, where a man was killed; and *Grey Gardens*, with the day-to-day life of an eccentric, controlling mother and her middle-aged, apparently mentally ill daughter, living isolated in their run-down, even squalid, Long Island mansion. One can perhaps see the kinship to Capote's temperament in all this. But it is important to note Capote's insistence on affection and his showing of warmth in all his, in a sense, cold and objective account of the world. Albert Maysles, in an interview with James Blue, speaks of filming his subjects with Love (capitalized in the publication) (Beattie 2010, 26). Elsewhere, asked by Robert Phillip Kolker about the term "direct cinema," Maysles says he likes to avoid the issue of "truth" raised by the term "cinema vérité" and remarks, "we go directly to things as they take place" (Beattie 2010, 58). There is a crucial idea here in the merger of an attitude of love with the sense of activity in "going directly to things." Maysles is finding words to characterize his and his brother's *interest* in things and in observing them. What the films give us is not so much truth as the filmmakers' interest in things, and it is an active, going-toward sort of interest, an interest that feels attraction.

Salesman begins in Massachusetts in winter, in bleak urban areas beset with snow and difficult driving conditions, as four men, each on his own, visit working-class and lower middle-class Catholic families who have given their names at church as being possibly interested in a Bible purchase (large, illustrated, ornate), but who mostly balk at the price. The salesmen room together in motels, try to encourage one another, go to sales meetings, and deal with a hard-driving sales manager – an outsider with a mid-Southern accent. One salesman, Paul Brennan, the least successful of the group, becomes the film's center of interest. About a third of the way into the film, all attend a large sales meeting in Chicago and then go on to work in Florida parishes, with little success for Brennan, who looks more and more discouraged and depressed. The Wisconsin of *Primary* looks provincial, but with an openness and a sense of contact with the larger world. *Salesman* is claustrophobic. We feel

Figure 4.1 Paul Brennan thinks about himself in Albert Maysles, David Maysles, and Charlotte Zwerin's *Salesman* (1968, producers and writers Albert Maysles and David Maysles).

confined to the selling mindset of the salesmen and of those above them, and confined in the living rooms of the poor and unaware who squirm and resist the sales pressure. It may be easy for the viewer to condescend to this world and to feel that the film does – some have said so. But the film does not condescend. It is simply there with this world before it, attending, fascinated.

An instance of the going out to what attracts one that Maysles talks about occurs just before the men travel from Massachusetts, which is home, to the Chicago meeting and then on to Florida. Paul Brennan drives through snowy streets. We see him in profile, and through the window beside him the world is a white-gray soft-focus blur – it seems a projection of his discouraged and depressed state of mind. A cutaway to tangled snow-covered tree branches seems to give us something Paul sees, and perhaps underscores that Paul now perceives the world as tangled and bleak. But the shot is quite beautiful, perhaps suggesting that Paul has not lost an eye for beauty. Or perhaps it is the film, and not Paul, that notices the trees, as if wanting to make Paul aware of them, to open him out. In this ambiguous moment there is a fusion of observation, psychic probing, identification, and an offer to help. After some ensuing downbeat discussion of work among the men at their motel, Paul seems finally taken out of himself as he sits and impersonates a customer with an exaggerated Irish accent, becoming more and more fanciful, going on and on, seemingly simply enjoying what he is doing. Maysles slowly moves closer and closer in on Brennan's face – an unusual gesture in the film – as if to get at the mystery, to get closer to, to pay tribute to, this diminutive, weak-chinned, limited man who clearly has imaginative longings in him.

We soon see Paul in a railway station, ready to board the train to Chicago, and then for a time we watch him sitting in the traveling train, right of frame, with a huge window filling the left and center of the image, revealing the passing cityscapes in a series of shots. At first we hear words from a hard and pressing talk by the men's sales manager, perhaps, we may think, taken from the sales meeting we have seen earlier. But then there are cutaways to the meeting to come in Chicago. Paul perhaps remembers, and certainly anticipates, the pressures of these lectures about success and failure. He is thinking about himself, and again Maysles moves in, and this time wavers a little – a *person*, holding a camera with some frailty, is there with Paul, involved with him. The train window with the moving images outside is quite striking, beautiful to contemplate – though the city views are bleak. The window suggests a film screen and being somehow a projection of Paul's thoughts – this pensive man sitting still there before it, looking out a bit. Paul is worried and depressed, but has an energy of imaginative longing in him. Maysles takes an interest in Paul's longing, and suggests it in the movie screen image he finds with the train window. Imagination, thoughts, hopes are like a film. Here *this* film and its subject fuse. And *Salesman* continues the ploy with Paul's arrival in Florida, where we see him driving through Miami Beach and cheerfully talking to himself about what he sees. It is as if he has entered a film, so exotically different from the Massachusetts of winter and failure. Florida is handled as an imaginative expansion for a time, with its new look, some eccentric customers, and the salesmen taking a swim and having breakfast in the open air and play-acting a sales encounter – until Florida, too, turns claustrophobic and signals failure.

Grey Gardens, which in recent years has given rise to a Broadway musical version and a scripted film with actors, originally disturbed many viewers and brought charges of exploitation and cruelty. We spend time with elderly Edith Bouvier Beale and her daughter, also Edith, of questionable mental stability, isolated in their Easthampton, Long Island, grand house and garden, which have become rundown and overgrown. The women and their house have become a scandal to their "Republican," as the daughter calls it, community. They lead an utterly antibourgeois existence, aristocratic in background, bohemian in aspiration, marginal, trapped in their own psychological bubble of remembered frustrations, desire to succeed as performers, and the support they give and harm they cause to each other. The mother, Jacqueline Kennedy Onassis's aunt, had a budding career as a singer and made recordings, all cut off by marriage. The now middle-aged daughter has farfetched hopes to sing and dance in clubs. The women sing and otherwise perform for the film – indeed, they may be said always to be performing, except when they fall into out-of-control recriminations. Early on, the filmmakers show themselves, and do so later to some extent, and often are spoken to by name by the women. The women are not simply being observed but clearly are interacting with the filmmakers, especially the daughter, "Little Edie." The film gives the women a forum for performance, for presenting themselves. Their life becomes being in a film, as does Paul Brennan's life in *Salesman*, or the lives of the figures in Rouch's *Chronicle of a Summer* – and the films, for this, are no less revealing of actual life. People have an imaginative and performative dimension that film can respond to, entering with them onto the new ground of the film, and for that, seeing all the better, and seeing with them, who they really are.

Near the beginning of the film, Little Edie welcomes the filmmakers to the property and shows them parts of the grounds, as she talks eccentrically, manically, about her indeed eccentric costume, her mother, her hopes for the film. Maysles walks about with his camera, panning across a variety of spaces – open, jungle-like, beautiful with dappled light, shadowed and empty and ugly. The camera activity and the images seem to offer a connection with Edie's mysterious mind, its excitements and depressions, its volatility. Writing about Italian Neorealism – certainly an important precursor to direct cinema – Bazin speaks of a needed "tact" on the part of the filmmaker who would point us to reality, saying that artifice is the means of arriving at realism, that the artist "must necessarily choose between what is worth preserving and what should be discarded, and what should not even be considered" (1971, 26). He goes on to say that "what matters is the creative surge, the special way in which the situations are brought to life. ... Surgery could not call for a greater sureness of touch ... cinematographic tact" (1971, 31–32). The words "tact" and "touch" are from the same root, as they are in French, *le tact*. It is up to each viewer to decide whether what we get in *Grey Gardens* is sensationalism or a tactful fusion of film art with a subject that is fully acknowledged, validated, even dignified, in its contact with film.

Gimme Shelter, a few years earlier, had also borne in on disturbing material, the killing that occurred at the Rolling Stones' Altamont concert, and the generally violent, ugly mood of that occasion. The band members watch Altamont footage on an editing table, with the killing elusive and hard to discern. The film has a complex structure, moving from the editing room into the Altamont footage and also to other parts of the band's 1969 tour, to a playback room after a recording session, and to San Francisco attorney Melvin Belli's offices for arranging of the Altamont venue. The film began as a simple documenting of the tour, and after the killing, took that as an organizing event. There is a great deal of musical performance in the film (even by groups other than the Rolling Stones), and the Stones remain themselves, listening to a playback or watching the Altamont footage – Mick Jagger's most let-down moment occurs not offstage but onstage at Altamont when he is clearly alarmed by the mood of the crowd and tries to calm them. *Gimme Shelter* participates in what is virtually a subgenre of direct cinema, the film about rock musicians, especially in performance. The Maysles film about the Beatles was an earlier and joyous example; *Gimme Shelter* is the film of this kind with the sting in it, and is often contrasted with its near contemporary, Michael Wadleigh's three-hour *Woodstock* (1970), documenting in cinema vérité style and in a linear fashion the four-day festival in upstate New York. There is much musical performance in *Woodstock*, but also a rendering of the lived-through day and night experience of the vast numbers camping there for the duration – sex, drugs, toilet cleaning, rain and mud, and withal a remarkable communal feeling and sense of well-being. Woodstock was the great end-of-the-1960s celebration of rock music and countercultural hope. Altamont, following a few months later, was the dose of reality. Communal feeling and joy could not be sustained, and the Maysles brothers were there to film what unexpectedly happened, and went on to fashion a complex, analytical, retrospective film. The difficulty of seeing the killing, which is there on film, seems to figure the perplexity as to where this disruptive violence came from. How could this happen? Where are we now?[4]

Figure 4.2 Bob Dylan performs for the camera, with poet Allen Ginsberg gesturing to the side in D. A. Pennebaker's *Don't Look Back* (1967, producers John Court and Albert Grossman).

After the breakup of Drew Associates, Leacock and Pennebaker formed a company to produce their individual films, and in some cases films on which they worked together, as on *Monterey Pop* (1968), one of the key rock performance films (Albert Maysles and others were also involved in the shooting, all under Pennebaker's supervision). The film is certainly full of good feeling, documenting the three-day 1967 festival at Monterey, California. Onstage performances are captured with great intimacy and flexibility, and music from the performers accompanies intercut footage of the gathering and the offstage activities – so that all is music and its spirit. There is an eclectic mix of performers such as Jefferson Airplane, blues artist Otis Redding, in his first appearance before a large white audience, first American appearances of The Who and Jimi Hendrix, the heretofore little known Janis Joplin emerging with great power, and at the end a long sitar performance by Ravi Shankar, binding East and West with the crowd quite rapt. The festival and the film itself seem to symbolize and in some measure to create the full flowering of the 1960s counterculture. And the film remains, in a sense, to recreate it.

Pennebaker had pursued something similar a bit earlier in *Don't Look Back*, documenting Bob Dylan's 1965 concert tour in England. William Rothman (1997) has discussed this film in scrupulous detail, arguing that it is not so much observational as it is a collaboration between Dylan and Pennebaker to present and advocate a certain human possibility, way of life and, indeed, philosophy. There is plenty of performance footage, with Dylan onstage and with him and others (Joan Baez, Donovan) playing and singing in a hotel room. There is material with Dylan and the rest seemingly unguarded (especially the others), relaxing and partying, or gathering backstage before an appearance. Pennebaker with his camera and recorder seems a familiar and accepted member of the group. Dylan meets with various reporters, giving pointed and sometimes hostile answers to questions, getting carried away and pushing an argument to an uncomfortable extent. He is filmed walking the streets and traveling by train. His rebarbative manager, Albert Grossman, is shown dealing harshly with hotel personnel and negotiating a Dylan television appearance, setting public television off against a private channel. A Dylan song is heard during a trip through the countryside and bleak cityscapes, as if pervading the atmosphere. At the beginning of the film we hear Dylan's "Subterranean Homesick Blues" and watch him standing in a Manhattan alley, not singing, but holding large cards with key words from the lyrics and casting them away one by one as the song proceeds. This sequence suggests that what follows in the bulk of the film is a performance. It is one fusing observational film, music, speech, and behavior, all in the interest of putting across what Dylan's very serious, albeit charming, songs put across: a call to question values and the stances of those who hold to limiting or destructive ones; an openness to those who deserve sympathy, kindness, or help; a call to change – both inner change and change in the ways of the world. Dylan's project entails some roughness, which the film – with its overall look at what goes on during this tour – registers in a way that the charming, moving songs by themselves do not. Dylan has chosen from time to time to work in film. All this work deserves careful attention.

Pennebaker went on to do *Monterey Pop* and a good many more films centered on rock music as it evolved in the 1970s and 1980s, with David Bowie, Depeche Mode, and others. The films are made in the spirit of the music, and want to help to project it, to take it further. Pennebaker has worked a good deal with his wife, Chris Hegedus. Together they made *The War Room* (1993), a widely seen and admired account of strategy and planning during Bill Clinton's first campaign for the presidency, centering on campaign manager James Carville and his way of coping with ongoing events.

Leacock, born in London and raised in the Canary Islands, studied at Harvard and found his way to working as Robert Flaherty's cameraman for *Louisiana Story* (1948), before undertaking some documentary projects of his own in the 1950s and then linking up with Drew. Leacock always defended Flaherty's films and saw them, rightly, as important precursors of what the new documentary movement was trying to do in the 1960s. Flaherty could not flexibly follow ongoing actions with a lightweight camera, nor record synchronous sound – or, in his early films, any sound at all – and Leacock, in his important manifesto, "For an Uncontrolled Cinema" (1961, see Leacock 2000), stressed the importance of sound for new documentary. Moreover, Flaherty set up scenes, created fictional families, and recreated past ways of life in the places he filmed. But he sought – and we feel it in his films – to open himself to the world, to learn from it, and to film and to shape material "without preconception," as he liked to put it. *Nanook of the North*, *Man of Aran*, *Louisiana Story*, and other films have a unique and remarkable sense of place, weather, the drama of the sea, and of actual people living in and coping with specific physical environments, doing the work called for to survive in these places. Flaherty took a strong interest in the world, and took it *as* a filmmaker – this is what Leacock responded to, and what he carried on in his own way over many decades of filming and teaching.

Leacock's best known, because most easily available, film is the 30-minute *A Happy Mother's Day*, made with Joyce Chopra on commission for television broadcast (though the film was broadcast only in reedited form). The film concerns the birth of quintuplets to the Fischer family in Aberdeen, South Dakota, and the reaction of this small city to the event, presenting the family with gifts, a luncheon, and a parade, and taking an interest in ways the town might benefit commercially from what has happened. The film gives a portrait of early 1960s, essentially 1950s, provincial America, and of the not-well-off Fischer family, already large when the quintuplets are born, now trying to cope with the birth and the town's attitude toward it, and with an array of inquisitive media people, including, of course, Leacock and Chopra. The town shows its absurdities, gently handled by the filmmakers. Ed McCurdy provides a sparse voiceover commentary, slightly ironic in tone. We visit the hospital, a Chamber of Commerce meeting, a department store, and the Fischer family farm with its many visitors, and gifts displayed on the lawn. The mother, Mrs Fischer, appears withdrawn and depressed through much of the film, disconcerted by the attention and intrusions, by her husband's attitude in cooperating with it all, and by who knows what else, deep within. She is an intriguing figure, showing sensitivity and awareness and some signs of humor, warming up towards the end of the film.

As with *Don't Look Back*, Rothman (1997) discusses this film in scrupulous detail. He shows how the filmmakers gradually strike a rapport with Mrs Fischer – they are different from the other media, not manipulative, relatively speaking, but appreciative, even loving; and she appreciates this. At the silly and stiff public luncheon near the end, Mrs Fischer gives the camera a little helpless, conspiratorial smile. The filmmakers have arrived in Aberdeen for the "Gypsy Day" parade, and, as Rothman notes, they are in a sense gypsies – outsiders, countercultural, free to roam, odd, we might say, like Capote in Kansas, or like what the Maysles brothers identified with in Capote. This gypsy nature connects with something in Mrs Fischer and draws her out, just as the incongruous notion of Gypsy Day gives this American heartland community something it perversely aspires to.

Leacock was always something of a filmmaker's filmmaker, representing in virtually its purest form an observational unobtrusive way of filming, a willingness to be surprised, a willingness, one might say, to let the world happen. In *A Happy Mother's Day*, essentially a film about a community of a certain time and region and its attitudes, Leacock visits the hospital, where his eye and camera and Chopra's tape recorder are quite taken with the premature infants in their incubators. For a moment their images fill the screen, uncannily gigantic, as we watch and hear their cries and the sound of the sustaining machines – an attestation of primal life, against the grain of the cultural milieu that unfolds more and more. At the end of the formal luncheon scene, almost as a way to escape from it, Leacock turns to an impervious, playful child off to the side, taking us back to the newborns. The film then cuts to children playing rambunctiously on the street, before Leacock begins to walk and turn his camera about to attend to other odd and intriguing, planned and unplanned, aspects of the parade to honor the Fischers.

Leacock made many other films over the years, typically working in collaboration and often shooting on commission – films on the Ku Klux Klan, a convention of police chiefs, Igor Stravinsky, Louise Brooks, and much more – all deserving wider dissemination and more attention than they have received. *A Stravinsky Portrait* (1965) adores the old man's face, energy, and sense of humor, in close low-angle views, and seems to put him and colleagues at ease – orchestra musicians, Pierre Boulez, George Balanchine, Suzanne Farrell, and others – as they work on musical and dance preparations. Here direct cinema lets itself go with and identifies with Stravinsky's musical world as intensely as elsewhere it does with rock stars and the new music and cultural force they represent.

In 1968, Leacock joined Ed Pincus to teach filmmaking at the Massachusetts Institute of Technology, which he continued doing for 20 years, imparting his approach to a series of remarkable younger filmmakers and future teachers – Ross McElwee, Robb Moss, Jeff Kreines, Joel DeMott, Ann Schaetzel, Mark Rance, Mary Jane Doherty, John Gianvito, and others. Pincus had made two strong cinema vérité films about blacks and the Civil Rights Movement in Mississippi, *Black Natchez* (1966) and *Panola* (1970, shot in 1965). And he pioneered the making of one's own life into the subject for direct-cinema film – not the look back and reconstruction of a life (as, for example, in Jerome Hill's experimental *Film Portrait*, 1971), but the filming of one's ongoing relations with family, friends, lovers, one's travels, one's work – all evolving, with the unanticipated continually coming into view. Pincus's three-hour *Diaries: 1971–1976* (1981) is a monument of the form, sketching in the bohemian world centered in Cambridge, Massachusetts, at the time; following the strains on Pincus's marriage as both partners have affairs; showing, specifically, the deleterious effect on his family of Pincus's involvement in filmmaking and teaching, leading to the decision to give up film and retire the family to a Vermont farm. There is a road trip out west, and there is drug experience. *Diaries* is astonishingly direct in its presentation of painful husband/wife quarrels and other intimate material with various people, and in its celebration of life and the youthful disposition to experiment with life. The film has a highly spontaneous feel, of just trying to marshal the camera as well as possible to keep up with events as they unfold. And yet, as with all the best direct cinema, everything seems just right. Camera placement, framing, and editing seem well judged, and the impression grows the more one views the film. Life dictates the filming, but life finds itself in art, becomes art.

Students of Leacock and Pincus went on to make films about their lives and milieus, a leading kind of nonfiction film in the 1980s and beyond. Best known, perhaps, have been the films of Ross McElwee – *Sherman's March* (1986), *Time Indefinite* (1993), *Six O'Clock News* (1997), and others – chronicling Ross's loves and travels, his marriage and the birth of a child, deaths in the family, and other matters as they occur. McElwee, long settled in the Boston area, like so many nonfiction filmmakers is originally from the South, and brings much Southern material into his films – he is a bit of an outsider looking at the North, and, at this point, a bit of an outsider looking at the South. Against the tradition of direct cinema, including Pincus, McElwee writes and speaks elaborate voiceover commentaries. He is seriously meditative – on everyday events and on historical and metaphysical issues – and has a sense of humor and a wry way with words. McElwee's commentaries fuse with the process of day-to-day filming on the part of this man who seems always to carry his camera and recorder, thereby distancing himself from the life about him – something his friends and family comment on – but also showing his profound interest in this life, transfiguring it on film, making it eternal.

Robb Moss's *The Tourist* (1992) deals with his travels as a cinematographer for hire, and at the same time his and his wife's struggle with infertility, and their efforts to have children, all rendered with a reflective voiceover. As with Pincus's *Diaries* and McElwee's films, or indeed Rouch's *Chronicle of a Summer*, filmmaking itself becomes an issue – what it does to those who are filmed and to the world that is filmed, and what it does to the filmmaker. The film about the filmmaker's life, ongoing and with voiceover commentary, took direct cinema strongly in the direction of reflexivity, unprecedented in the American work and bringing the movement back into connection with Rouch, for all the difference in milieu, personality, and tone.

Wiseman and Other Developments

Mamber concludes *Cinema Verite in America* with a chapter on Frederick Wiseman's films of the late 1960s and early 1970s – *Titicut Follies* (1967), *High School* (1968), *Law and Order* (1969), *Hospital* (1970), *Basic Training* (1971), and *Essene* (1972), and Dave Saunders also concludes *Direct Cinema* (2007) with a section on Wiseman. Wiseman was not part of the Drew Associates group, and had no direct connection to the new documentary movement as it had developed up to his time. His background was in law and the teaching of law and social issues. For what turned out to be his first of many films, *Titicut Follies*, he wanted to document the prison/hospital for the criminally insane in Bridgewater, Massachusetts, that he and his students had visited. The problematic treatment of prisoners and the therapy procedures were of concern to him. Wiseman was allowed astonishing access to all aspects of prison life, including prisoner/psychiatrist interviews, and such highly remarkable access has characterized all his work. *Titicut Follies* is a shocking portrait of what looks to be a callous and debased system (more in a moment on Wiseman's point of view). Screenings of the film were banned in Massachusetts for many years, ostensibly out of concern for embarrassment to the prisoners and their families – but the major embarrassment was to the state. Wiseman found a new calling with this film, and has gone on, based in Cambridge, Massachusetts, to make nearly 40 feature-length documentaries, many of the films sponsored by public television and first shown there.

The series constitutes an extraordinary look at American institutions, governmental and private, their promises, day-to-day workings, sights, sounds, and effects – all presented with no commentary, no voiceover of any kind, no interviews, no explanation of background or theory. One simply visits the institution concerned and observes human interactions and exchanges and the many other things that go on. The viewer is given a cross-section of typical activity and procedures, following no particular line of narrative development, getting close to no particular person – though Wiseman loves close views of faces, each suggesting a story and a life history. *High School* concentrates on the intense teaching of conformist values in a suburban Pennsylvania high school during the time of the Vietnam War, when middle-class and well-off boys were subject to the draft. *Law and Order* spends time with the Kansas City, Missouri, police as they make calls coping with domestic violence, purse snatching and armed robbery, drunks on the street, and other matters, in what seems a hopelessly primitive and angry social world. *Hospital* takes us to a New York City emergency room and reveals the difficulties of carrying out follow-up care and communication among the various departments of medical practice. Like the three-hour *Welfare* (1975), this film shows the frustrations and humiliations that a specific institutional system seems to inflict on both its agents and clients. Personal qualities are not really the point. It is the system as such that determines things.

Basic Training does have a narrative line, following a group of troops through the training process from entry to graduation at Fort Knox, Kentucky. We witness the molding, not brutal, but firm, for the cannon fodder of Vietnam. Even the chaplain/counselor, a black man, is part of the process, part of the army system in which military conformity overrides religion and psychiatry. But there is ambiguity about it all. We witness a real metamorphosis of awkward, raw young men who do not know about dental hygiene or how to clean a toilet, as they develop a certain competence, self-discipline, and self-respect. It may not be exactly the metamorphosis one wants to see, but it serves as a figure – if one will read it so – for a metamorphosis that *might* be. One can sense the wonder of metamorphosis itself, on a more abstract plane than the particularities of Fort Knox and the army. Wiseman's characteristic withholding of commentary helps this effect to emerge.

With *Essene*, about a monastery, Wiseman began to look at institutions, usually private, not so much with a critical eye, as with simple fascination. Later films would deal with a well-run zoo, a department store, the American Ballet Theater, the Comédie Française, and the town of Belfast, Maine (at four hours' length) – its schools, industries, natural beauty, and private goings-on. More and more, one senses in Wiseman an affectionate fascination with the world and with filming it, something like that of the earlier direct cinema filmmakers or of Rouch.

Right at the start, Wiseman established a procedure he has kept to, of working with a cameraman whom he guides, of recording sound himself, and of editing and shaping every film from an unusually large body of footage. He always credits himself as "director" as well as editor, and he likes to call his films "reality fictions," insisting that they represent his personal point of view, after rigorous selection, in response to the institutions he turns his attention to, though also insisting that he tries his best to give an honest, informed account.[5] His work really is a cinema of editing, with a distinctive – especially in the early films – ironic/critical character. In *Titicut Follies* Wiseman cuts back and forth between a scene of forced nasal feeding of a prisoner/inmate, and the scene of preparation of the man's corpse. Late in *Law and Order* Wiseman cuts in part of a contemporary campaign speech by Richard Nixon, painting an ideal picture of an America that might be achieved, where law and order prevail, after we have witnessed much evidence of the hopelessly messy, violent, and benighted lives that many Americans live, and of the inability of a more or less good-willed and well-trained police force to make much difference.

Explicitly political nonfiction filmmaking was well developed in this period, notably in the compilation/instructive films of Emile de Antonio, such as *Point of Order* (1964), about unscrupulous anticommunist Senator Joseph McCarthy and the congressional hearings that undid him; *Rush to Judgment* (1967), about the dubious investigation of the John F. Kennedy assassination; *In the Year of the Pig* (1968), about the Vietnam conflict; and *Millhouse: A White Comedy* (1971), about the career of Richard Nixon. Peter Davis, from a television background, made the theatrically successful compilation feature *Hearts and Minds* (1974), about the Vietnam War. Barbara Kopple, who had worked with the Maysles brothers and also with Peter Davis, had a considerable theatrical success with *Harlan County, U.S.A.*, in which she followed a coal miners' strike in Kentucky and broadened the scope to look at a national union election and its aftermath. Kopple recorded sound and credits herself as producer and director. She worked with Hart Perry and other cinematographers, as well as editor Nancy Baker. The film uses archival material on local and union history, and overlays much that we see with folk and workers' songs. But it is the basic and recurring direct cinema approach that gives the film much of its power. Kopple and her crew spend much time in the Appalachian mine village where the strike occurs, and render the atmosphere, colors, daily routines, and outbreaks of violence with intimate handheld shooting, while also recording the chaos of sounds. Kopple wins the confidence of local women, who seem unguarded in allowing her to film a querulous women's political meeting. The camera and recorder are present at a nighttime demonstration where workers are attacked and the operating camera is knocked to the ground as the recorder captures even the filmmakers' cries of distress.

During these years, filmmakers from abroad came to the US and documented what they saw in something of a direct cinema mode. Dušan Makavejev's *WR: Mysteries of the Organism* (1971) presents the life and ideas of psychological and political theorist Wilhelm Reich, who was Viennese but eventually settled in Maine, where he set up an institute. He was later prosecuted by the Food and Drug Administration, and died in 1957 in a Pennsylvania prison. The film uses archival material with explanatory voiceover, eventually developing a fictional story set in Belgrade about contemporary young Reichians. Quite essential are its cinéma vérité sequences, recording contemporaneous American Reichian therapy sessions, individual and group, and observing the more extreme sexually liberated practices of the New York counterculture, whose members display an element of performance for the camera. Chantal Akerman spent considerable time in New York and in 1976 released *News from Home*, where, working with cinematographer Babette Mangolte, she filmed empty Manhattan alleys and busy gathering-place street corners, the Times Square subway station and subway travel from inside moving cars, and views from a car driving on Tenth Avenue, all with ambient sound. About everything there is an empty, alienated mood, coming partly from the filmmaker's choices, of course, but partly – we are made to feel – from what is actually there. At times Akerman's voice fades in, reading letters from her mother back in Brussels; then the voice dissolves away into the sounds of traffic or the subway. Akerman projects the pull, even the burden, of family ties against the adventurous daughter filmmaker who is very directly confronting the buildings, sounds, and mood of New York. In later films, with no commentary or self-presentation, Akerman travels through the American South, where racial issues surface (*Sud (South)*, 1999); and observes activity near and around the Mexico/ Arizona border, where many are dying in the desert while attempting to cross illegally into the United States (*De l'autre côté (From the Other Side)*, 2002). The films are slow, with long takes and often a fixed camera (as in Akerman's fiction films). They give an extraordinary sense of absorption in place, with an attunement to meaning, history, and mood that weigh on everything we contemplate – all quite ordinary, really, even that which has gone wrong and might be changed.

Americans of this era filmed abroad, of course. Wiseman's cameraman on *Titicut Follies*, John Marshall, dedicated his life to studying, filming, and advocating for the !Kung Bushmen of the Kalahari desert in southern Africa. In the 1950s Marshall shot a great deal of material and edited it with Robert Gardner at Harvard University to produce *The Hunters* (1958), an account of a prolonged giraffe hunt, during which Marshall travels with a group of men for many days, camping in various locales, filming ordinary and dramatic activity in loving detail. Sound, consisting of indigenous music and songs, as well as sparse voiceover commentary, was added later.

In 1961, Gardner led a small group to camp for six months in the central highlands of New Guinea among the Dani, at that time a Stone Age culture living in a state of perpetual warfare among themselves, one small territory against another. Of the Americans, Peter Matthiessen produced a writerly nonfiction account of the Dani in *Under the Mountain Wall*, a book akin to the "nonfiction novels" Capote, Mailer, and others would soon be writing on matters American. Karl Heider, who stayed on much longer, produced a professional anthropological study, *The Dugum Dani* (originally a PhD dissertation), published in 1970. Gardner filmed constantly while there, establishing an intimacy with Dani individuals and capturing daily life and work, rituals and amazing battle scenes, that would go to make up *Dead Birds* (1964), one of the most significant of all films about a premodern culture.[6] Gardner did not shoot with synchronous sound, but edited-in appropriate ambient material recorded at his direction by Michael Rockefeller, another member of the group. Gardner established a practice he would continue in later films, shooting his own material, mostly with a handheld camera, in a place where he would spend considerable time, followed by his editing the film back home, laying-in sound recorded by someone else during shooting. For *Dead Birds* Gardner wrote and delivered a fairly full explanatory and meditative voiceover commentary. His words are much sparser for *Rivers of Sand* (1974), about the Hamar and their village life in southwest Ethiopia – though here a Hamar woman repeatedly talks to the camera about her and other women's oppression at the hands of men. And commentary disappears altogether in *Forest of Bliss* (1986), a film about Benares, India, that adopts a day-in-a-life "city symphony" mode harking back to Vertov and Walter Ruttmann. In this Gardner film we are immersed, without explanation, in vivid images and sounds of busy streets, ancient alleys, workshops, temples, ghats on the great river, cremation fires, boats, and people's interaction. Editing choices draw analogies among the many things we see and hear.

Gardner has been drawn again and again to non-Western cultures that he contemplates intensely, allowing the material to come forward and have its say, and in which he recognizes a deep bond or commonality with himself and the world he comes from, a bond he articulates to some degree in words, but more importantly through the images and sounds he records and later selects and arranges. In *Dead Birds* the reality of the foreign world and its bond with Gardner's world is the human penchant to live more intensely through violence. In *Rivers of Sand* it is the self-limiting obsession of male egoism and vanity, with the concomitant oppression of women. In *Forest of Bliss*, the sense of life, even in urban business and distraction, as being involved in cycles of death and rebirth, metamorphosis of physical forms, constant flow and transfiguration.

Documentary filmmakers are perhaps always outsiders, gypsies in a sense, whether contemplating their own familiar worlds, or traveling from the American Northeast to the heartland, or to the far reaches of the globe. They live behind cameras and transfigure the world into film – a very different thing from the world itself. At their best they seek to get close to the world, to render it honestly, to probe and to come to the point of revelation as only film can do. The 1960s and 1970s saw the advent of dramatic new approaches in film for direct access to the world, enabling the world and film to cooperate, or merge. Along with this goes, always, the indirection and incompleteness of shooting and sound recording choices, and of film editing and construction with its emphases and elisions. All goes together in many remarkable films of the time to render an extraordinary *interest* taken in the subject at hand, and overall in the varied and evolving world of these decades.

Notes

1. Dave Saunders in *Direct Cinema* (2007) gives a good account of Drew's background and attitude and of the news aspect of the films, rooted in 1950s journalism.
2. Carl Plantinga's *Representation and Reality in Nonfiction Film* (1997) and Stella Bruzzi's *New Documentary* (2006) (which deals with old documentary as well as new) offer intelligent discussions of how we come to accept what we do accept in documentary film. The relation of film and film viewing to general philosophical skepticism is a concern of Stanley Cavell in *The World Viewed* (1979) and all his subsequent work on film.
3. Joe McElhaney's *Albert Maysles* (2009) stresses the Maysles brothers' outsider status as rooted in their growing up as Jews in a predominately Irish Boston neighborhood with considerable ethnic tension.
4. Saunders' *Direct Cinema* (2007) deals extensively with the downturn in cultural and political hope represented in films from about 1970 on.
5. Wiseman's term gives the title to a good study of him, Thomas Benson and Carolyn Anderson's *Reality Fictions* (2002), which cites the filmmaker's statements about his work. See Thomas Atkins's 1974 interview with Wiseman (1976, 82–84).
6. Gardner gives a full account in his book *Making "Dead Birds"* (2007).

References

Atkins, Thomas R. (ed.). (1976). *Frederick Wiseman*. New York: Monarch Press.

Barnouw, Erik. (1983). *Documentary: A History of the Non-fiction Film*. Revised edn. Oxford: Oxford University Press.

Bazin, André. (1971). *What Is Cinema?* Vol. 2, ed., and trans. Hugh Gray. Berkeley: University of California Press.

Beattie, Keith (ed.). (2010). *Albert and David Maysles Interviews*. Jackson: University of Mississippi Press.

Benson, Thomas, & Anderson, Carolyn. (2002). *Reality Fictions: The Films of Frederick Wiseman*. 2nd edn. Carbondale: Southern Illinois University Press.

Bruzzi, Stella. (2006). *New Documentary: A Critical Introduction*. 2nd edn. London: Routledge.

Cavell, Stanley. (1979). *The World Viewed: Reflections on the Ontology of Film*. Expanded edn. Cambridge, MA: Harvard University Press.

Gardner, Robert. (2007). *Making "Dead Birds": Chronicle of a Film*, ed. Charles Warren. Cambridge, MA: Peabody Museum Press.

Leacock, Richard. (2000). "For an Uncontrolled Cinema." In P. Adams Sitney (ed.), *Film Culture Reader* (pp. 76–78). New York: Cooper Square Press. (Original work published 1961.)

McElhaney, Joe. (2009). *Albert Maysles*. Urbana: University of Illinois Press.

Mamber, Stephen. (1974). *Cinema Verite in America: Studies in Uncontrolled Documentary*. Cambridge, MA: MIT Press.

Plantinga, Carl. (1997). *Rhetoric and Representation in Nonfiction Film*. Cambridge: Cambridge University Press.

Rothman, William. (1997). *Documentary Film Classics*. Cambridge: Cambridge University Press.

Saunders, Dave. (2007). *Direct Cinema: Observational Documentary and the Politics of the Sixties*. London: Wallflower Press.

5

Comedy and the Dismantling of the Hollywood Western

Teresa Podlesney
Lecturer, Keene State College, United States

Few genres have received more critical attention than **the Western** in calibrating its ideological status – whether as a studio product conveying **American expansionist mythology** or as a post-studio critique of that myth. Teresa Podlesney assesses these trajectories through a widely overlooked sub-genre – **the comedic 1960s Western**. Challenging many of the genre's conventions centered on **masculinist sexuality**, these films often pivot around the Westerner as an aging, debased drunkard. Podlesney focuses, in part, on **Lee Marvin** as an overlooked yet essential Western star of the era and provides close readings of ***Cat Ballou***, ***Paint Your Wagon***, and ***The Good Guys and the Bad Guys***. She carefully considers the cinematic image, reminding us that the genre's various ideological impulses always get played within, and not just against, a vast natural and cinematic landscape. Podlesney claims that the 1960s comic Western occupies an important space between the **classical studio Western** and **auteurist revisionist Westerns** produced within the **New Hollywood**. Her essay shares ground with Derek Nystrom on the New Hollywood in this volume, with J. E. Smyth on Hollywood as historian in Volume I and with Kevin Stoehr on the A-Western in the hardcover/ online edition.

Additional terms, names, and concepts: revisionist Western, Andrew McLaglen, Burt Kennedy, John Sturges

In the 1960s, the Western genre was systematically dismantled from within, not by the cynicism of the Italian Western cycle, nor by the revisionist politics of anti-Westerns, but by the spate, indeed, the rash, of Western comedies, many of them directed by Hollywood Western veterans such as John Sturges (*Sergeants 3*, 1962; *The Hallelujah Trail*, 1965), Andrew McLaglen (*McLintock!*, 1963; *The Ballad of Josie*, 1967), and Burt Kennedy (*The Rounders*, 1965; *The War Wagon*, 1967; *Support Your Local Sheriff*, 1969). Hollywood's 1960s comedy Westerns are often protracted rituals of debasement in which Western characters,

American Film History: Selected Readings, 1960 to the Present, First Edition. Edited by Cynthia Lucia, Roy Grundmann, and Art Simon.

contexts, and stars agonizingly perform their schtick in a dollar-store "studio" mise-en-scène that is constantly upstaged and rendered additionally tatty by stunningly photographed Western locations. In the 1960s comedy Westerns, it is as if the little moments played for humor in John Ford's films – the drunken antics of Sergeant Quincannon in *She Wore a Yellow Ribbon* (1949), the fistfight that postpones the wedding in *The Searchers* (1956), the Dodge City sequence in *Cheyenne Autumn* (1964) – have metastasized, threatening the maturity and integrity of the host genre.

That the Western relentlessly laughs at itself during the 1960s, winning box office profits and industry awards for this self-derision, suggests some consensus about the cultural obsolescence of the genre. As Barry Langford states in "Revisiting the 'Revisionist' Western," "by the mid-1960s the episteme of the Western could no longer win assent from a public that was itself increasingly divided and contesting the very values the Western had traditionally promulgated" (2003, 28). Citing the fracturing and recombination of political and cultural landscapes wrought by the movement for Civil Rights, the rise of the New Left and counterculture, and the Vietnam War, Langford suggests that

> we might speak of the emergent terminal crisis of the liberal social and political settlement of the postwar era, a settlement the Western had worked hard to legitimate and a sense of whose incipient dissolution structures the Westerns of the 60s and after. (2003, 28)

What Langford sees as an epistemological "crisis" is certainly constructed as such by the revisionist films he addresses, but the growing irrelevance of the genre is treated with much less gravity in the comedy Westerns of the 1960s, which suggest that the old form's inability to speak to contemporary culture is a sign of its advanced age. The comedy Westerns readily admit that it is long past time to let different stories be told. But, like Hunt Bromley in *The Gunfighter* (1950), Hollywood's "young guns," the revisionists, cannot let the genre go. Following Sam Peckinpah's trail, these men stake their claims to Western territory with vengeance, prerogative, and determination. The so-called anti-, new- or personal-Westerns of the late 1960s, through to the genre's big-screen demise in the mid-1970s, reassemble the sullied myth of the Westerner, saving it from its low-brow comedic debasement like Chance kicking the spittoon from Dude's reach in *Rio Bravo* (1959). While excoriating the Western for its problematic racism and Manifest Destiny rhetoric, the revisionists insistently try to reanimate the moral, often existential, decidedly masculine code at its core. If the German and Italian Westerns had revealed the genre to be fundamentally about form and therefore accessible to any filmmaker regardless of national origin, New Hollywood Westerns reclaim the American-ness of the genre, bolster its defenses against parody and "empty formalism," and make it "mean something" again.

Rehabilitation of the Western in the late 1960s and early 1970s was undertaken in criticism as earnestly as in film production, with an explosion of serious academic publications on the genre: Jim Kitses' *Horizons West* (1969); John Cawelti's *The Sixgun Mystique* (1971); Philip French's *Westerns* (1973); *Focus on the Western*, edited by Jack Nachbar (1974); Will Wright's *Sixguns and Society* (1975); the revision of George Fenin and William Everson's early compendium, *The Western from Silents to Cinerama* (1962), as *The Western from Silents to the Seventies* (1973). In 1973, Richard Slotkin published *Regeneration through Violence*, the first volume of his important three-volume frontier-centered cultural history of the United States. While these texts deployed a variety of methodologies for understanding the Western's long tenure as popular US cultural form, both academy and industry worked from the basic critical paradigm of the auteur at this time, understanding a film's director as responsible for creating its meaning and success. In its US translation from the original French, auteurism read like the individual's triumph over the system's constraints; this framework of intelligibility both encouraged and was able to most enthusiastically make sense of films that were concerned with the struggle of a complex individual living in a marketplace of conformity. For the brief few years when the auteurs of New Hollywood had the run of the shop, they often allegorized their own nominal outsider status in films they produced about misunderstood visionaries and heroic alienation. Explorations of the contemporary individual's ambivalent place in society found uncanny, resonant expression through the topos of the Western.

Writing in 1973, Jack Nachbar explains that "the formula of current Western movies resembles the pellets from a discharged shotgun" (1974, 108). He goes on to say that "in the 1960's and 70's, by spreading into several new directions, Westerns have demonstrated that another aspect of their extraordinary longevity is their capacity to creatively embrace a wide spectrum of ideas and aesthetic constructions" (1974, 111). Recognizing the multiple and conflicting tendencies within the Western genre, Nachbar acknowledges for criticism a situation that had always obtained across the spectrum of Western films. But Nachbar is committed to seeing the Western's polyvocality as a recent historical phenomenon:

> For sixty years, through three wars and a depression, the movies' unified myth of the West was able to satisfactorily articulate the purpose and the worthiness of the American experience … [U]p against the social and political nightmares of the 60's and 70's … that heretofore solid vision has exploded into pieces. (1974, 112)

The sense of living through an exceptional moment in time that characterizes much writing in and about the 1960s partakes of the same tropic structures that gave shape to the imperialist exceptionalism of US economic and geopolitical policy of the decade. In other words, as Robert Ray says of the period, "The Left and Right's shared preoccupation with the frontier account of American history indicates that the potentially convulsive events of 1963–1974 did not cause a complete 'break' in the traditional American mythology" (1985, 256). Understanding "mythology" through the lens of Althusserian ideology, Ray reminds us of the crucial gap between the real and its representations:

> Certainly the sixties abounded in incidents capable of discrediting the traditional American mythology … Because this mythology represented not American experience (historical, social, or geographic) but the culture's collective means of dealing with that experience, it could not be overthrown by events alone. (1985, 251)

If Hollywood's presentations of US experience in the 1960s and 1970s were not as "ideologically fragmented" as Nachbar and many other commentators then and since have claimed, the representations of the preceding decades were neither ideologically simplistic nor coherently "unified." The exciting, radical difference of Westerns from the late 1960s and early 1970s is bought at the expense of assuming the static homogeneity of previous industry products. There is a methodological risk in attempts to corral Western films as a genre when the body of films thus designated is so ample, so rarely seen; when the genre's silent history is largely destroyed; when discussions of its more recent history have until lately been rigidly segregated – with B pictures, programmers, serials, and television Westerns marginalized and disallowed from discussions of major features. As Tag Gallagher says,

> It would be easy to cite apt examples for each period; but it would be just as easy to cite exceptions … [R]ich lodes of ambivalence are overlooked in order to bolster a specious argument that 'classic' westerns are simple and naive. (1986, 209–212)

What Nachbar perceives as the 1960s and 1970s Westerns "exploding into pieces" is more productively engaged as an instantiation in their production of the same thematic that is said to characterize their narrative concerns: a result of the closing off of options or, as Paul Seydor writes of *The Wild Bunch*, "of fixed and limited spaces becoming increasingly crowded, which only multiplies the possibilities for conflict and violence" (1997, 195). With the gradual dismantling of the studio system from 1948 on, and the concomitant reduction in the number of films produced each year, a vast spectrum of Western subject matter was realized through fewer production outlets. Although television initially took up the content of serials and programmers, William Boddy reminds us that the 30-minute Western had disappeared from television altogether by 1961 (1998, 131).[1] Ideas, stars, and plotlines heretofore expressed in a variety of formats crowded together in the destabilized feature marketplace of the 1960s, when television-trained directors vied for projects alongside film school graduates, old-style Hollywood tradesmen, and exploitation entrepreneurs. What makes films from the 1960s and early 1970s *look* so different from what had come before is that the Hollywood system of production was itself in flux at this very same historical moment, after a long period of relative stabilization. David E. James tells us that

> as the site of conflict or arbitration between alternative productive possibilities … all kinds of sixties' film[s] … invite an allegorical reading in which a given filmic trope – a camera style or an editing pattern – is understood as the trace of a social practice. (1989, 14)

To consider the Western genre in terms of biodiversity instead of evolution makes us sensitive to the ways in which the "revisionist" Westerns of the late 1960s and early 1970s bring to the fore concerns which have always been possible to articulate through the form, but had theretofore not been systematically undertaken with such seriousness of purpose, nor resonated with such tangible cultural force. Thomas Schatz asserts, "one of the reasons for a genre's popularity is the sustained significance of the 'problem' that it repeatedly addresses" (1981, 34). One of the "problems" for which Westerns have always potentially provided the expression is how to *resist* progress – despite critics' continuing attempts to unify the genre ideologically as a celebration of progress and Manifest Destiny. Some of the most satisfying Westerns – including John Ford's *Stagecoach* (1939), long offered as a paradigm of the classical Western's ideological clarity – achieve their depth by mining the rich veins of border-crossing antimodernism that riddle the rhetoric of racist progress. Jacques Mauduy and Gérard Henriet have suggested that the Western's "timid denunciations" of capitalism condemned the genre to increasing insignificance (1989, 191–192), but perhaps it is more than the *films'* capitulations that finally put the Western out to pasture. After a last period of sustained, nihilistic articulation of American exceptionalism, Westerns fade from the big screen during the 1970s not just because the world is increasingly sophisticated and urban, nor wholly due to feminist, multiculturalist, or academic ideology critiques. By the yuppie 1980s, big-screen Westerns finally become history because their messages of individual resistance to wage labor, corporate social strictures, and the technologization of the rhythms of private life are as quaint and undesirable as sod houses, manual typewriters, and public baths – and no longer make cultural sense.

Several writers mark 1962 as the year the Western cedes its status as triumphant national myth, recognizing John Ford's sophisticated *The Man Who Shot Liberty Valance* as its eulogy. But it does not take the panorama-shunning, claustrophobic interiors of this austere black-and-white film to mark the end of an era. The metanarrative history lessons of the expansive Cinerama blockbuster *How the West Was Won*, built upon implausible "love" stories, narrated with pompous bluster, and sold through technological gimmickry, render the myth of the frontier *qua* ideology at once so explicit and so trivial as to be almost nonfunctioning: If it were still workable as ideology, one could build a story around it, without having to announce that one was building a story around it. The direct address to the spectator – narrator, titles, didactic lyrics in the musical score – deployed by this and other self-conscious (in the sense of awkward, not modernist) 1960s Westerns lets the viewers know, on the one hand, that Hollywood *knows* that the viewers know they are watching the same thing they have seen dozens of times before. On the other hand, even as these techniques acknowledge the growing cinematic sophistication of the audience, Hollywood stubbornly continues to grind out the same formulas. Coupling direct address with obstinate plot repetition works to manufacture a dubious but increasingly significant function for Hollywood as repository of the historical memory of the United States, a function later naturalized by the opening sequences in *Butch Cassidy and the Sundance Kid* (1969) and *The Shootist* (1976). Didactic direct address also acknowledges Hollywood's service in the post–World War II US campaign to maintain a global hegemony, exporting to hungry foreign markets ideas of American exceptionalism that were beginning to molder on the shelves at home. Indeed, *How the West Was Won* premiered in London in November 1962, four months before it opened in the United States. Taking the long way home, the film road-showed at Cinerama-equipped theaters throughout Europe, Japan, Australia, and New Zealand before its Los Angeles premiere, an early figuration of the increasing importance of foreign markets to Hollywood's fiscal health.

How the West Was Won and Westerns on TV

The last of the three-strip Cinerama films, *How the West Was Won* was important to both makers and viewers in 1962 for providing the experience of going to one of the very few theaters equipped for Cinerama projection and seeing the image in all its panoramic 2.59:1 aspect ratio glory. The story played an inevitable second fiddle to the display of technology. The difficulty of composing for such a large frame – blocking had to compensate for the curvature of the three screens, and the almost half-ton camera had to be set up inches away from actors to achieve medium shots – often resulted in an unintentionally underpopulated mise-en-scène and "wooden" acting. The seemingly sparse arrangements of props and figures lend a certain budget-belying poverty to interiors, an effect magnified when these shots are contrasted with the stupendous landscape photography on location. The individual projection of emotion through close-ups cannot, in such a format, fully capture back the attention of a vision overwhelmed by the plenitude of the US landscape, and so a certain realism of story is reduced (as critics of the film then and since have well noted). A jarring oscillation between natural-key Pantone-subtle landscapes and high-key Technicolor-bright interiors is characteristic of 1960s Westerns. In this anything but seamless editing, one can witness the reluctant transition from studio to location shooting that was occurring at this time. One can also see the struggle between the different approaches to dialogue and character interaction each type of shooting promotes, and can watch, precisely, the disintegration of Hollywood form. As David E. James encourages us to consider, "[a] film's images and sounds never fail to tell the story of how and why they were produced – the story of their mode of production" (1989, 5).

The spectacular nature of *How the West Was Won* – the last of MGM's grand epics, made in the same year as Columbia's release of *Lawrence of Arabia*, second in 1963 US box office receipts only to Twentieth Century-Fox's financially indulgent *Cleopatra* – suggests the Western's calcification from vital, living genre into period spectacle. Fenin and Everson call *How the West Was Won* a "huge Cinerama monster," proof of what was decried by the mid-1960s as the "decadence of the Western" (1973, 360). Robert Ray provides a similar epithet in a more sustained discussion of Hollywood in the 1960s when he refers to the film as an "inflated" genre picture, an example of Hollywood's post–World War II response to the challenge of "adding serious themes to entertainment films" in order to appeal to the fragmented constituencies of a "previously homogenized mass audience" (1985, 149, 143). When stylistically inflated, an "absolutely traditional story [could] seem suddenly 'important' ... [because of] the meticulous care with which everything had been worked out" (1985, 150). Lengthy running times taken up by elaborately stylized action, framing, and mise-en-scène lent structurally formulaic films the inherent gravitas of an epic. Familiar story lines were additionally inflated by an awkward and generally unsuccessful operation of "grafting" onto them serious critiques and topical moral themes. By the mid-1960s, stylistic and thematic generic amplifications played themselves out. Having unintentionally revealed the ideological imperatives of the Hollywood paradigm they were meant to bolster, these tendencies devolve into comedy and camp (1985, 151). From a contemporary perspective, *How the West Was Won* often teeters on the brink of comedy, a result of the combination of Spencer Tracy's grandiose narration rhetoric, the frequently unconvincing performances, and importantly heroic scenarios punily acted out against the overwhelming stretch of a three-screen landscape. After *How the West Was Won* the Western finds it difficult to play its tropes straight, and the comedy Western becomes a significant expression of a waning genre.

It is possible, too, to see the 1960s comedy Western as an intentional attempt to relieve the intensity of the so-called adult Westerns of the 1950s, whose protagonists were increasingly psychologized – some would say to the point of neurosis – in films by directors like Budd Boetticher and Anthony Mann. The self-deprecating humor of 1960s Hollywood Westerns was also an obvious attempt to engage its audiences in their new TV-made viewing position of distanced, postmodern irony. David Cook asserts that a "constant diet of genre-based TV shows and classical Hollywood genre films bred something like contempt for traditional generic conventions, reinforcing a sense that they had become old-fashioned, 'unrealistic,' and culturally irrelevant" (2000, 173). For John Saunders, "the audience's familiarity with the [Western] formula was largely developed through experience of its most banal manifestations, endlessly recycling the basic settings, characters and plots" (2001, 37). Robert Ray reminds us of the popularity of the television series *Maverick* (ABC, 1957–1960), which "managed to spoof every western convention" and parodied the "dozens of straight television westerns" with which it shared the small screen. "By the spring of 1966, on the eve of the self-proclaimed New Hollywood Cinema, parodic versions of traditional genres had become television and movie staples" (1985, 257).

Television had an additional impact on the Western, cutting cinematic vision to the measure of the human form in its domestication of the moving image. Westerns, "which traditionally exploited the harsh visual contrasts and monumental scale of the Western landscape, probably suffered more than other Hollywood genres in their transition to the small screen" (Boddy 1998, 121). While not "about" the land in the sense of an Albert Bierstadt monumental canvas or a Robert Smithson earthwork, many Westerns are about the interactions of individuals in specific geophysical locations, investigation of the landscape often taking the place of exposition of character. With station managers advised, when editing Hollywood movies for television, to cut "all the long shots in which distant objects get lost" (quoted in Boddy 1998, 121), Westerns are reduced to characters and behaviors that are downright laughable when dissociated from their animating locus.

But what is really so funny about the Western in the 1960s? According to *The Hallelujah Trail* (1965), *Cat Ballou* (1965), *Paint Your Wagon* (1969), *The Good Guys and the Bad Guys* (1969), and *True Grit* (1969), which exemplify the tendencies of many films of the decade, it's old men and drunks. Significant as sidekicks throughout the history of the genre, foils who remind us of what even the most reluctant, hard-drinking, aging hero is not, drunks and old men are brought from supporting roles to center screen in Hollywood's 1960s Westerns. This laughable recentering of the Western's focus effects a significant decentering of the masculinist ideology around which the Western as genre purportedly coheres. Explicitly ridiculed by the script and often painfully ridiculous in their performances, drunks and old men embody a fallible, incompetent, misguided, uncontrolled humanity repressed by the rigid and stylized masculinity of Warshow's "classical" straight-shooting Westerner (Warshow 1974). Even when drunks and old men save the day, and they often do, in *Rio Bravo* (1959) fashion, the comic narratives do not bother to recuperate their excessive behaviors and appearances to any "self-contained" (Warshow's term again) ideal of a Western hero. In *Cat Ballou*, for example, Kid Shelleen's most heroic feat is a hilarious minutes-long montage of sobering up to defeat the villain, an encounter which takes a mere fraction of screen time. For the climactic rescue scene at the end of the film, Shelleen is drunk again – yet just as effective in his alcoholic stupor as he was when sober in getting the job done.

Cat Ballou and the Drunken Hero

Lee Marvin won the 1966 Academy Award for Best Actor for his performance as both Kid Shelleen and the villain Tim Strawn in *Cat Ballou*. In *The Western from Silents to Cinerama*, Fenin and Everson call Marvin's portrayal of Shelleen "the last word in the demythologization of the hero … The Western Superman … reduced to a bottle and his dirty red underwear" (1973, 359). Kid Shelleen is the hero of dime novels surreptitiously read by Catherine "Cat" Ballou (Jane Fonda), an Eastern-educated young lady back out West for a postgraduation visit to her father. When her father and his ranch are threatened by land grabbers and neither the handsome, faithful young Indian hand nor Cat's handsome, goofy young Anglo love interest seem to have sufficient sand, Cat sends for Shelleen to come to her father's defense. The audience anticipates the Kid's arrival as anxiously as Cat, but we are perhaps more dismayed when, after all the other passengers have dismounted from the stage, the Kid is unceremoniously dumped out of the luggage boot and lands on the town's dusty main street in a crumpled, motionless heap. The comedic elements of this scene are created by the score's upbeat barn-dance fiddles and the ironic juxtaposition of the lyrics of "The Ballad of Cat Ballou," which tell us "he had the eyes of a killer, the look of a killer, just wild and ornery and mean" as we see Shelleen's scruffy, greasy, unkempt, and unconscious face for the first time. In a recent reassessment of comedy's function in shoring up the conventions of the Western genre, Matthew Turner rejects the film's ability to demythologize: "It plays up the comic possibilities of the genre, but does not deconstruct the genre as later films like *Blazing Saddles* and *Rustlers' Rhapsody* do" (2003, 49). A closer look at the film's textual machinations suggests that it is the prototype for these later deconstructions. If we appreciate the humor created by *Cat Ballou* specifically as parody, the film provides a litmus test of Linda Hutcheon's claims that "parody can indeed be an important formal mechanism for historicizing and politicizing film … Parody points us at once *to* and *beyond* textuality to the ideological formation of the subject by our various cultural discourses" (1990, 126–128).

"The Ballad of Cat Ballou" is sung by the unlikely duo of Nat King Cole and Stubby Kaye, who function like a Greek chorus to the film's action. Dressed in

Figure 5.1 Inebriated abjection: Lee Marvin as Kid Shelleen in Elliot Silverstein's *Cat Ballou* (1965, producer Harold Hecht).

the clothing of period entertainers, in the frame with the other actors but strumming and singing directly for the audience, these troubadours wander the textual border somewhere between the diegesis and the theater, framing the narrative with their humorous lyrics. The film credits the men only as "shouters," but this simple credit opens onto a whole complex history of performance and representation that gives an additional cultural weight to what Bosley Crowther considered an "easy" and unsurprising "lampoon" of Western formulas. "Shouter" is a reference to "coon shouters," vaudeville performers who sang the "coon songs" that enjoyed extraordinary popularity in the US from 1880 to 1920.

> Unlike standard sentimental ballads written by minstrel men E. B. Christy and Stephen Foster, still much beloved to this day, coon songs were recklessly antisentimental tunes written by emerging and prolific black and Jewish composers such as Earnest Hogan, Irving Berlin, Harry von Tilzer (Harry Gumm) and Monroe Rosenfeld. (Lavitt 1999, 255)

Coon songs deployed and promulgated racist stereotypes about the supposed laziness, drunkenness, ignorance, and surfeit sexuality of African-Americans, playing these stereotypes for humor in a vaudeville context in which whole shows were developed around song lyrics. The most popular shouters were usually Jewish women, among them the well-known Sophie Tucker and Fannie Brice, who frequently performed in blackface, continuing a performance of racial otherness from early nineteenth-century minstrel shows

> at a crucial time in American Jewish history when Jews – still tallied as "black" and "oriental" by the US Census – were casting themselves increasingly as ethnic variations of the Caucasian race to describe their contributions to American society as distinct from that of African Americans. (Lavitt 1999, 254)

"When it comes to minstrelsy ... we have experienced what might be termed a cultural blindspot," asserts Kathryn Kalinak in an essay entitled "How the

West was Sung." "[M]any frontier songs are minstrel songs of one sort or another. The diversity of the American frontier has been elided in America's cultural memory, covered over by a powerful frontier mythology that constructs American identity in terms of whiteness" (2001, 173–174). The "shouters" who sing "The Ballad of Cat Ballou" make explicit mockery of that mythology as they construct and reflect upon the performances in the film as performances. Nat King Cole's prominent role as shouter – he is the most elegant and self-possessed presence on-screen – invites us to consider the rest of the performances as performances of whiteness, marking *Cat Ballou* as progenitor to *Blazing Saddles* (1974), the vitriolic culmination of the comedy Western and, until the 1990s, the highest grossing Western of all time.

Both "The Balladof Cat Ballou" and the film are "about" Catherine's transformation into and success as an outlaw. The film begins with an animation of Columbia's torch-holding trademark doffing her robes to reveal herself as the bodacious jean-wearing, gun-slinging Cat. This transformation encapsulates both the increasing importance and concomitant reduction of women in 1960s Hollywood cinema to signifiers of a hypertrophied sexual difference. *Cat Ballou* is made by a studio in transition; Cat's emergence from beneath Columbia's robes explicitly calls attention to the film's transgression of the older, "old-fashioned" mode. As it promises a less "prudish" display of the female form, this unveiling also reveals the heart of exploitation that beats beneath the carefully Coded entertainment cinema. In a production environment in which the declining economic power of the female studio-era star coincides with the rise of self-conscious, personal male auteur directors, women as anything other than sexualized objects, marginal to the narrative, seem to disappear from the screen. "From a woman's point of view," writes Molly Haskell in 1974, "the ten years from, say, 1962 or 1963 have been the most disheartening in screen history. In the roles and prominence accorded women, the decade began unpromisingly, grew steadily worse and at present shows no sign of improving." Haskell presents this as commercial cinema's "backlash" against the "growing strength and demands of women in real life" (1987, 323). Having efficiently marginalized women years earlier in its attempts to leave its melodramatic genesis behind (despite the structuralists' emphasis on the generic necessity of woman as signifier of culture), the Western resentfully incorporated highly sexualized women in the latter part of the 1960s. They were frequently made to pay for their distracting presence in a man's world with rape or extermination, however, as exemplified by *Welcome to Hard Times* (1967), *The Wild Bunch* (1969), and *High Plains Drifter* (1973), to name only a few of the most notorious examples of a pervasive tendency.

Despite the emphasis in *Cat Ballou* on Fonda's curves, Lee Marvin eclipses both Fonda and the magnificent landscape as the spectacular focus of the film. Ignored by genealogies of the Western that trace Clint Eastwood to John Wayne's family tree, Lee Marvin is an emblematic Western actor of the 1960s, and performs a different, diffident type of Hollywood masculinity. In the 1950s and 1960s, from *Bad Day at Black Rock* (1955) and *Seven Men from Now* (1956) to *The Man Who Shot Liberty Valance* (1962), *The Professionals* (1966), *Paint Your Wagon* (1969), and *Monte Walsh* (1970), Marvin made traditional Westerns, comedies, and genre revisions, working with important Western directors such as Budd Boetticher, John Sturges, and John Ford. After his Oscar win for *Cat Ballou* and his box office success with *The Dirty Dozen* (1967), Marvin was in high demand. Although *The Wild Bunch* (1969) was initially written as a star vehicle for Marvin, he turned down the role of Pike in order to make the musical Western *Paint Your Wagon*, for which he was paid $1 million plus percentage – $250,000 more than Paul Newman earned that same year for *Butch Cassidy and the Sundance Kid*.

Marvin's first protracted display of Shelleen's inebriated abjection in *Cat Ballou* verges on the obscene, an indication of just how overwhelmingly containment and self-control characterize our apperception of any hero, even one who drinks. Against a deeply ambivalent cultural framework that occasionally acknowledged the growing problem of alcoholism in serious films like *Days of Wine and Roses* (1962) but preferred a steady weekly date at home with the drunken playboy host of *The Dean Martin Show* (NBC, 1965–1974), the filthy, staggering Shelleen is more than just a parody. Called upon to show Cat and company how well he can shoot, Shelleen delivers a soliloquy on the outmoded function of the gunfighter as he guzzles the whiskey he needs to steady his hand. Two-thirds through the bottle, Shelleen stops talking and hits all the targets in sight, much to the delight of those assembled. But the next sip he takes to celebrate his success renders Shelleen dumb drunk once again. Ripping his pants when he tries to pull a gun from his waistband, Shelleen exposes his stained red underwear, much to Cat's horror, and Marvin finishes playing the scene with his pants around his knees, on the verge of tears. Marvin's performance here is riveting, the pathos of his tooth-stained, chap-lipped, sweaty portrayal unrelieved by any humorous musical score until the very end of the scene, when the villain's ominous four-note motif segues into a woozy instrumental reprise of the "Ballad" as Shelleen awkwardly bends to pick up the discarded whiskey bottle.

Drunken Western protagonists rarely verge on the sustained abjection of Kid Shelleen, although when Rooster Cogburn (John Wayne) falls from his horse in *True Grit* (1969) as he tries to empty his bottle he comes close, wallowing fat and drunk and old on the ground before declaiming that his company will camp there for the night. As with Lee Marvin, the arch-traditionalist Wayne won his only Oscar for his turn at playing a Western souse. Up against Wayne's work in *Red River* (1948), *The Searchers*, *The Man Who Shot Liberty Valance*, and *The Shootist* (1966) – complex and sophisticated character studies all – that Wayne should win an Oscar for what Garry Wills suggests is essentially a scenery-chewing Wallace Beery impression (1997, 286) reminds us not only that the drunk is a compelling cultural manifestation of this time, but that Hollywood's Westerner is more noteworthy in flagrant disarray than when functioning at the top of his ideological form. Despite the status of Western movies as "the single most important American story form of the twentieth century" (Nachbar 1974, 2), "the major genre of the world's major national cinema" (Buscombe 1988, 13), only three Best Actor Oscars have been awarded for work in the genre: to Warner Baxter, in the second Academy Awards presentation in 1930, to Lee Marvin in 1965, and to John Wayne in 1970.

Garry Wills argues that Wayne's "unabashed" portrayal of Rooster Cogburn was the key to recuperating his cultural standing, which had been in decline through the 1960s (1997, 284). In choosing to play the marshal as an old, fat drunk, Wayne made a conscious decision to face his aging head-on; when Wayne got laughs in the film, he got them for playing a funny character, not because he was hobbling through a role written for a 30-year-old. A good deal of what was so funny about 1960s Westerns was their refusal to act their age. Like Wayne, many Western actors, the genre, and the Hollywood paradigm itself were old by the mid-1960s, but for much of the decade

Figure 5.2 The comedic potential of the aging hero: Robert Mitchum and George Kennedy in Burt Kennedy's *The Good Guys and the Bad Guys* (1969, producers Ronald M. Cohen and Dennis Shryack).

the stars and the genre continued to carry on as if they were youngsters. The results could be unintentionally comical, as in *Bandolero!* (1968): While the characters played by Dean Martin and James Stewart are scripted for a few laughs, their aging forms and Andrew McLaglen's direction make mockery of Dino's hopes for kids (with Raquel Welch!) and the men's dream of "a ranch of their own." In *The War Wagon*, a Wayne vehicle directed by Burt Kennedy for Wayne's Batjac Production Company in 1967, a 59-year-old Duke looks shockingly old. Yet the movie displaces the potentially comical effects of his decrepitude by pairing Wayne's Taw Jackson with the visually excessive figure of Lomax, a black-kimono-wearing, hyper-athletic dandy played vigorously by Kirk Douglas, who makes Victor Mature's Doc Holliday look like an extra from *Will Penny* (1968).

The Good Guys and the Bad Guys and the Aging Hero

The comedic potential of the aging hero is the whole point of Kennedy's *The Good Guys and The Bad Guys* (1969); that the film is not particularly funny says as much about the relatively humor-free, "us versus them" reification of a generation gap in the 1960s as it does about Kennedy's direction. After an opening aerial shot of expansive, jaw-dropping landscape – an attention-grabbing staple of the genre after *How the West Was Won* – the camera picks out a lone rider (Robert Mitchum) in the sublime wilderness, and the movie's ballad (another common element of the 1960s Western that continues into the 1970s, combining old-fashioned appeal with the youth market's interest in folk and country singers) commences to set the narrative scene: "As men grow old their footsteps drag / Younger folks start makin' jokes / They'll be laughin' at Marshal Flagg / They'll be laughin' at Marshal Flagg / Laughin', laughin' at Marshal Flagg." This one verse from "The Ballad of Marshal Flagg" amply illustrates the film's mode and tenor. The dialogue is choked with deprecating remarks about Flagg's age, but they are not particularly funny because Mitchum, looking great at 52, is not particularly old. But as he rides his horse past automobiles on the streets of town, Flagg is obviously out of place in Progress. The film, like the culture in which it was produced, works hard to conflate traditional ideas about social arrangements with an individual's physical age. The marshal is forced into retirement by Mayor Wilker (Martin Balsam, playing a smooth-talking lecher who is clearly the prototype for *Blazing Saddles'* Governor Lepetomane) because his ideas are old-fashioned.

Reduced to the role of supporting player in his own gang of outlaws by the volatile young Waco (David Carradine), Flagg's nemesis Big John McKaye is also supposedly over the hill, the brunt of yet more jokes and comments about the infirmity of old age. Played by George Kennedy at the age of 44, McKaye is no geezer, but McKaye and Flagg forge a reluctant alliance when both are marginalized by their respective social groups because of their age. At the end of the film the "old" men save the day, and the joke is on those who doubted them: "A man is young then a man grows old / He knows he's still the man he was / And the folks are proud of everything / Everything the old man does." The recuperation of Marshal Flagg's status in the community cannot entirely deflect the box office implications of the film's ageist discourse: After a long association with the genre, *The Good Guys and The Bad Guys* was Robert Mitchum's last Hollywood Western.

The repeated references to Flagg's age in *The Good Guys and the Bad Guys* expose themselves lewdly as Hollywood's forced discursive positioning of the actor. To make sense of the TV-watching audience's (over)familiarity with the Western genre and its stars, Hollywood writes the spatial paradigms of an exponentially expanding postmodern image culture in the older terms of a linear narrative, coming to the conclusion that actors are too familiar because they've lived too long. This logic also motivates, in reverse, the textual machinations of *Nevada Smith*, a Western drama from 1966. The lead role of biracial Westerner Max Sand is played by Steve McQueen, then a robust 36 years old. McQueen's star persona was crafted from a combination of roles as Westerners and military men, and publicity reports of offscreen derring-do. Audiences would be familiar with him from the CBS Western television series *Wanted: Dead or Alive* (1958–1961), and from his performance as Vin in *The Magnificent Seven* (1960). Dialogue throughout *Nevada Smith* repeatedly insists that we recognize Max as "just a kid"; at one point Brian Keith's character hands Max a dollar and says, "Buy yourself some candy." It should be noted that these lines are not played for laughs. The picture is relentlessly serious, and McQueen performs a gawky adolescent physicality that reaffirms the dialogue's positioning of Sand as not much older than a child. McQueen's relatively short period of stardom, his "newness" on the pop culture scene, enables the filmmakers' belief that they can successfully construct him as "young." The effect of this strategy is unsettling – ultimately lending more complexity to the film's exploration of the revenge motif – and illustrates the difficult processes of reconfiguring traditional entertainment and business practices to account for the baby-boom demographic.

As Hollywood's talent pool was aging, so too were its below-the-line workers. The behind-the-scenes struggle of skilled workers to gain and maintain jobs in a rapidly constricting industry is legible in the production practices of both old and new Hollywood. In his materialist, provocative revision of auteurism and the new Hollywood cinema, Derek Nystrom illustrates how the "generation gap" discourse of the 1960s and 1970s at turns occluded and was defused by class struggle:

> As early as 1965, film professor Robert Gessner of New York University bemoaned the aging population of film industry workers – estimates put the average age at fifty-four – and placed "unions [and] guilds" at the top of his list of forces keeping "American youth … locked out" of the studio gate. (2004, 20)

Emphasizing the age of union crew members, the rhetoric of the new Hollywood auteurs "often played nicely into the hands of capital" (2004, 22) by encouraging end runs around union rules in the name of youth, passion, and creative freedom. Brian De Palma succinctly states the sentiments of the time, deftly conflating the recognition of filmmaking as wage labor with regressive politics:

> Suppose I had a union crew here. All those guys are four hundred years old. I would probably have very little rapport with them on any level … There can't be that kind of feeling on a movie like this. Everybody's committed, politically, because they like the material, in all ways. (Quoted in Nystrom 2004, 21)

The final transition from a sprawling, collapsing genre-driven old Hollywood to a lean auteurist-driven New Hollywood is achieved during the "youth cult boomlet" of 1969–1971, heralded by the box office success of 1969's *Easy Rider*, at once the premiere "counterculture" film and a reworking of the Western genre. Several high-profile Westerns were released in this pivotal year for the genre and the industry: *True Grit*, *Paint Your Wagon*, *Butch Cassidy and the Sundance Kid*, *The Wild Bunch*, and the Western-inflected *Midnight Cowboy*. All but *The Wild Bunch* were on the list of top 10 grossing films of 1969. Of these six films, three presented Western tropes as comedy, and *Midnight Cowboy*, 1970's Oscar winner for best picture and best direction, offered up Jon Voight's wanna-be cowboy rube as a laughable figure before shifting gears into pathos. *The Wild Bunch* and *Easy Rider*, two films that took the Western seriously, are recognized as important historical revisions of the myth of the frontier, illustrating the closing down of options for individual sovereignty in the corporatizing Vietnam-era United States.

Sex and Masculinity in *Paint Your Wagon*

While much has been written about the varying cultural significance of *The Wild Bunch*, *Easy Rider*, *Midnight Cowboy*, and *Butch Cassidy and the Sundance Kid*, *Paint Your Wagon* was roundly panned by reviewers at the time of its release and remains a rather forgotten film. It could not recuperate its $20 million production costs at the time and is often considered a colossal failure, even though it earned close to $15 million in rentals. The film was plagued with troubles from preproduction right through its five-month-long shoot on location in Oregon. It was the last film Joshua Logan ever directed, and Clint Eastwood claims that his experiences on the shoot convinced him of the importance of a lean production style for his own Malpaso company. Eastwood also maintains that the original draft of Paddy Chayefsky's script, rewritten from the 1951 Broadway show, was "kind of a moody piece, very dark" (quoted in Schickel 1996, 213). Richard Schickel speculates that it would be "reasonable" for Eastwood to think, "based on what he had read initially, that this project might revitalize [the musical] as the Leone pictures had done to the Western" (1996, 214). But as Schickel points out, the film is neither a revisionist film nor a "lighthearted entertainment," "veer[ing] constantly, hopelessly, from one tack to the other" (1996, 215).

While Schickel writes disparagingly about the formal failures to which such ambivalent narrative oscillation gives rise (1996, 215, 219, 220–223), we have already seen that such "failures" are productive instantiations of the unstable production practices and cultural conflicts of the period. *Paint Your Wagon* is far more intriguing, then, for what it does do than for the classical narrative seamlessness that it is unable to achieve.

Paint Your Wagon tells the story of how Ben Rumson (Lee Marvin), a drunken old prospector, ends up in a three-way marriage in a California gold-mining camp with his partner, Pardner (Clint Eastwood), and Elizabeth (Jean Seberg), the second wife of a Mormon who auctions her off to the highest bidder on his way through the camp. To make certain that the other men in camp do not get their hands on his woman, Rumson devises a scheme to bring in prostitutes and set up a brothel. The brothel brings wood-framed civilization to No Name City, a conceit repeated later in Altman's lauded New Hollywood *McCabe & Mrs. Miller*, a film that Paul Arthur credits for its "near-Brechtian" materialist vision of progress (2003, 19). In fact, the brothel is a defining generic element in serious and comedic Westerns of the 1960s and 1970s alike. Even G-rated comedies like *Support Your Local Sheriff* (1969) and *Support Your Local Gunfighter* (1971) feature happy brothels or satisfied prostitutes. Instances of what Russell Campbell identifies as the Happy Hooker archetype, the brothels of the post-Production Code 1960s and 1970s Westerns are expressions of "the sexual revolution of the 1960s and the 'philosophy' of sexual freedom promulgated by *Playboy*... the fiction that women revel in being prostitutes and are free to prosper in the job" (2006, 230). But, Campbell continues, "the drawback for patriarchal ideology of the Happy Hooker concept is that it opens up a space for female subjectivity, agency, and independence" (2006, 243). In 1960s and 1970s Westerns, then, "prostitution is depicted favorably only within a specific historical context, and the endorsement is terminated once circumstances change" (2006, 246). For these films, as for US mainstream cinema in general,

> fun as it is, many Happy Hooker films suggest, to indulge fantasies of erotic fulfillment with oversexed ladies of the night, one recognizes at the end that this cannot go on: the prostitute leaves the life; the bordellos are shut down, raided by the cops, burned down, blown up. (2006, 248)

Such is the fate of No Name City's brothel: The entire town is literally swallowed up by the earth, collapsing into a series of subterranean tunnels Rumson and his pals have dug under the saloons to collect gold dust drunkenly spilled through the floorboards each night.

Rated M for mature audiences, the risqué plot of *Paint Your Wagon* seems just another example of a big-budget Hollywood film uncertain of how to position itself in the market, exploiting a relaxed post-Code morality to pump up the box office during a major industry slump. From a queer perspective, however, the ménage à trois at the center of the film is only the most visible aspect of a pervasive third-space rhetoric (Licona 2005) that dissolves many of the rigid oppositions – including that between male and female – customarily recognized as integral to the Western's deep structure. As it moves back and forth between the Western and the musical, between genres of determinate and indeterminate space (Schatz 1981), *Paint Your Wagon* systematically defuses and rejects the provocations to misogyny and violence that the "serious" *Easy Rider* and *The Wild Bunch* instigate and reaffirm, and that will overwhelmingly shape the revisionist approach of the 1970s Westerns.

The story begins with mountain man Rumson going to the aid of Pardner, whose wagon has tumbled over a ridge, killing his brother and seriously wounding Pardner. This act of care on Rumson's part involves him with a wagon train of prospectors who decide to mine at the accident site when the grave of Pardner's brother reveals nuggets of gold. Rumson sets up his tent outside the greater camp, and he cares for Pardner as he recuperates from his injuries. The prospectors paint a sign that welcomes travelers to "No Name City, Population: Male," but the explicit gender homogeneity (marked only slightly by ethnic and racial difference) creates a comfortable domestic solidarity rather than a volatile atmosphere of competition and sexual frustration. It is within this emotional environment of greater social context that the relationship between Rumson and Pardner is rendered as caring, not comedic. Scenes of the men in camp fraternally singing and dancing together are intercut with Rumson and Pardner's relationship as it grows. As they head to town one night so that Rumson can "get boiled," Pardner rides a mule that Rumson, walking, leads. Rumson introduces Pardner to men at several points along the journey: "This is my partner." Once in town, Rumson carries Pardner piggyback into the store-cum-bar, loudly announcing, "This is my partner," and settling him gently on a seat before starting in to drink. Called out by the sound of a band and the announcement of a dance, Rumson hoists Pardner up on his back again, carries him outside, sits him down on a wagon, and jumps enthusiastically into the middle of a large group of men dancing around a bonfire. The film cuts to Pardner's smiling reaction at several instances during this dance number. Because of the welcoming homosocial space within which Pardner's introduction is made, because of the dialogue that prefaces this scene, in which Rumson has explained to Pardner that "if I get melancholy, which can happen, I expect you to be my companion, and to solace me," and because of the manner by which the relationship of the two is physicalized, the willing spectator is invited to understand "partner" in full resonance.

From the outset, *Paint Your Wagon* rejects the framework of interpersonal male violence that we have come to expect from Westerns – even Western comedies – and carefully constructs an alternative social system of respect and equitability in its place. Even when the arrival of a Mormon and his two wives sparks angered discussion about the "fairness" of one man having two of what the other men have none at all, the jealousy is soon defused in the camaraderie of an impromptu auction in which the Mormon's second wife, Elizabeth, will be awarded to the highest bidder. When Rumson drunkenly wins the bid, a loud cheer goes up among the men, who joyfully help Rumson get ready for the wedding ceremony in which Elizabeth and Rumson are pronounced "claimed and filed." While some of the men in camp show interest in Elizabeth, they show it respectfully, and Rumson's jealousy is ridiculed as his own paranoid problem, part of his loner mentality, and not indicative of any real threat to his claim. For her part, although sold to the highest bidder, Elizabeth stands her ground against Rumson's worst instincts, and enters into a sexual relationship with him on her own terms, going to him willingly only after he and the other men build her a proper house to live in. When Elizabeth and Pardner finally, inevitably, fall in love, Elizabeth's suggestion that both men be her husbands is a perfectly plausible scenario that arises organically from the alternative social economy already created by the film. While the film makes sure the viewer knows that the men will take alternate nights sleeping with Elizabeth (this is Hollywood, after all, not Warhol's *Lonesome Cowboys*, 1968), all three live contentedly in their relationship, and the arrangement is acknowledged and respected in the town.

The believability of the alternative social arrangements in *Paint Your Wagon* is reinforced by its spectacle and seemingly paradoxical tendency toward cinematic realism. There is a decided emphasis on authentic detail in the art design, and a naturalistic use of environmental elements in the diegetic sound. The cinematography by William Fraker, who would explore the mundane aspects of Western life in his significant cowboy-realist *Monte Walsh* the following year, achieves a textural depth of color gradation in the gorgeous riverside setting of No Name City. That the three-party marriage is presented by both narrative and cinematic form as "natural" could effectively distance audience members who resist such reimaginings of state-sanctioned marriage. That Rumson and Pardner do not fight over Elizabeth, but rather enjoy the domestic comfort of their shared home, may disappoint viewers who expect Lee Marvin and Clint Eastwood to perform a more conventional form of masculinity. Eastwood was in fact hoping to stretch out of his narrow spaghetti Western type by playing this love story, and he sings his own songs in the film. This may strike viewers as funny, but the film does not intentionally offer Eastwood for laughs. It is after Elizabeth, Rumson, and Pardner come together in marriage, when the interesting alternative visioning of the film is done, that *Paint Your Wagon* devolves into more typical Western comedy, bent on laying the groundwork for the exorbitantly expensive special-effects finale. The three-party marriage does not last, called into question when Elizabeth feels the need to disguise it from a family of snowbound Christian pioneers to whom the three give shelter. The town itself, explicitly plagued more by the aimless indolence of too much prosperity than by any particular moral evil (a new sign reads "No Name City, the Hell-thiest place around, Population: Drunk"), ends up in rubble. But Rumson and the other men leave for a new gold strike at the end of the film, an open frontier that suggests they will recreate their appealing, hard-working community based on noncompetitive interpersonal respect.

Conclusion

Displacement of a rigidly constructed masculinity to the genre's margins reveals that rigid masculinity makes a variety of scenarios dramatic, but, *pace* Jane Tompkins (1992), it is not necessarily what makes them Western. Thomas Schatz's discussion of the Western as a genre of determinate space emphasizes the "attitudinally static male" (1981, 29): If you cannot bend or step aside, you are bound to find yourself in conflict with the dynamic world around you. But if the 1960s comedy Western is still recognizably a Western, rigid masculinity is neither sufficient nor necessary for the constitution of the Western as genre; as more contemporary films like Maggie Greenwald's *The Ballad of Little Jo* (1993) illustrate, the genre is able to accommodate meanings potentially in excess of the ideological construction of "what a man's gotta do." For a short time in the 1960s, this revelation resulted in comedy, but the interlocking social repercussions of a US masculinity in crisis soon became too painful to laugh at.

Consider Robert Altman's highly regarded *McCabe & Mrs. Miller* (1971). In setting and color palette the film is strongly reminiscent of *Paint Your Wagon*, and the two share an emphasis on prostitution as an engine of progress. But to mark *McCabe* as a "serious" "New Hollywood" revision, the sun never shines in Presbyterian church, and Vilmos Zsigmond's long-lens photography and low-ceilinged sets collapse the environment around the protagonists. If *Paint Your Wagon*'s characters can leave behind the mess they have made and start out anew, the claustrophobic mise-en-scène of *McCabe* tells us from the beginning that there is no escape. Staking claim to "authenticity" against the old Hollywood's creaky, coded illusionism, the new Hollywood embraced an aesthetic of location realism. This visual aesthetic imperative demanded an equivalent authenticity from narrative content, and Altman and other genre revisionists undertook to re-present a "real" West that had long been buried under an empire of signs. The resulting historical vision positioned itself as critique: "There is no legitimate way of honoring the figures who created the circumstances that allowed modernity to come to fruition" (Corkin 2004, 216). But it was still and only teleological; stories about the documented past were only interesting if they could allegorize what was clearly understood to be a bankrupt present. The limited options that new Hollywood Westerns rehash are the limits of their purgatorial postmodern present. *McCabe*'s apocalyptic, foreclosed vision of the Western mythos is, however, a triumphant *cinematic* vision: Zsigmond's stunning, obsessive, experimental, modernist, influential cinematography makes the viewer question how she ever considered the West as a space of unfettered movement and limitless expansion. The *cinematography* is the revision: Despite the buffoonery of the protagonist, the story still organizes the diegetic world around him; despite his Chaplinesque drunkenness, McCabe as played by Warren Beatty is still physically attractive; despite the fact that McCabe shoots his final opponent with a tiny little gun, he still hits his mark; despite the business acumen of the loud-mouthed Mrs Miller, the plot is still contoured by the same old heteronormative gender hierarchies, including the wishful presentation of prostitution as a fun job.

The bracing return after *The Wild Bunch* of Western stories not played for laughs adamantly reinscribes a frontier mythos for a new generation of white men determined to be (white) men. As Molly Haskell wrote in 1974,

> What is alarming is not that an old geezer like Sam Peckinpah should wish to bathe his twilight years in the blood of "macho" fantasies ... but that young college-grad writers ... should take up the sexist cudgel so enthusiastically ... inventing new tough-guy and man-to-man fables that are no less pernicious for being comic or self-conscious. (1987, 364–365)

In no uncertain terms, Haskell links the recuperation of the male subject on-screen to the achievements of the women's movement offscreen: "The closer women come to claiming their rights and achieving independence in real life, the more loudly and stridently films tell us it's a man's world" (1987, 363), strengthening Robert Ray's assertion that movies of this and any time "reflected not historical events, but the audience's [and makers'] *relationship* to those events, a relationship decisively shaped by the traditional mythological categories perpetuated by the movies themselves" (1985, 248).

The shifting, contradictory, scattered production practices of the 1960s manufactured dis-integrated Westerns like *Cat Ballou* and *Paint Your Wagon*, in which the laborious efforts involved in constructing a coherent framework of intelligibility were awkwardly on display. Unification of a new Hollywood cinema behind an auteurist paradigm smoothed over the textual aporias in which ideological conflicts had been readily glimpsed. In the "new" American cinema, fracture was pushed to the surface of the text, sublimated as the episodic narrative and the jump cut, just possible elements of personal style.

Note

1. Boddy also reminds us to reject a critical will to homogenize Western content: "Despite the tendency of contemporaneous critics and social commentators to treat the genre monolithically ... the TV Western in the late 1950s and early 1960s presented a wide variety of cowardly, sardonic, mercenary, and reformist protagonists" (1998, 136).

References

Arthur, Paul. (2003). "How the West was Spun: *McCabe and Mrs. Miller* and Genre Revisionism." *Cineaste*, 28.3, 18–20.

Boddy, William. (1998). "'Sixty Million Viewers Can't Be Wrong': The Rise and Fall of the Television Western." In Edward Buscombe & Roberta E. Pearson (eds), *Back in the Saddle Again: New Essays on the Western* (pp. 119–140). London: British Film Institute.

Buscombe, Edward (ed.). (1988). *The BFI Companion to the Western*. New York: Atheneum.

Campbell, Russell. (2006). *Marked Women: Prostitutes and Prostitution in the Cinema*. Madison: University of Wisconsin Press.

Cook, David. (2000). *Lost Illusions: American Cinema in the Shadow of Watergate and Vietnam, 1970–1979*. New York: Scribner's.

Corkin, Stanley. (2004). *Cowboys as Cold Warriors: The Western and US History*. Philadelphia: Temple University Press.

Fenin, George N., & Everson, William K. (1973). *The Western from Silents to the Seventies*. New York: Grossman.

Gallagher, Tag. (1986). "Shootout at the Genre Corral: Problems in the 'Evolution' of the Western." In Barry Keith Grant (ed.), *Film Genre Reader* (pp. 202–216). Austin: University of Texas Press.

Haskell, Molly. (1987). *From Reverence to Rape: The Treatment of Women in the Movies*. 2nd revised edn. Chicago: University of Chicago Press.

Hutcheon, Linda. (1990). "An Epilogue: Postmodern Parody: History, Subjectivity, and Ideology." *Quarterly Review of Film and Video*, 12.1–2, 125–133.

James, David E. (1989). *Allegories of Cinema: American Film in the Sixties*. Princeton: Princeton University Press.

Kalinak, Kathryn. (2001). "How the West Was Sung." In Janet Walker (ed.), *Westerns: Films through History* (pp. 151–176). New York: Routledge.

Langford, Barry. (2003). "Revisiting the 'Revisionist' Western." *Film & History*, 33.2, 26–35.

Lavitt, Pamela Brown. (1999). "First of the Red Hot Mamas: 'Coon Shouting' and the Jewish Ziegfield Girl." *American Jewish History*, 37.4, 253–290.

Licona, Adela C. (2005). "(B)orderlands' Rhetorics and Representations: The Transformative Potential of Feminist Third-Space Scholarship and Zines." *National Women's Studies Association Journal*, 17.2, 104–129.

Mauduy, Jacques, & Henriet, Gérard. (1989). *Géographies du western. Une nation en marche*. Paris: Nathan.

Nachbar, Jack. (1974). "Riding Shotgun: The Scattered Formula in Contemporary Western Movies." In Jack Nachbar (ed.), *Focus on the Western* (pp. 101–112). Englewood Cliffs, NJ: Prentice Hall.

Nystrom, Derek. (2004). "Hard Hats and Movie Brats: Auteurism and the Class Politics of the New Hollywood." *Cinema Journal*, 43.3, 18–41.

Ray, Robert. (1985). *A Certain Tendency of the Hollywood Cinema, 1930–1980*. Princeton: Princeton University Press.

Saunders, John. (2001). *The Western Genre: From Lordsburg to Big Whiskey*. London: Wallflower Press.

Schatz, Thomas. (1981). *Hollywood Genres: Formulas, Filmmaking, and the Studio System*. New York: Random House.

Schickel, Richard. (1996). *Clint Eastwood: A Biography*. New York: Knopf.

Seydor, Paul. (1997). *Peckinpah: The Western Films, a Reconsideration*. Chicago: University of Illinois Press.

Tompkins, Jane. (1992). *West of Everything: The Inner Life of Westerns*. New York: Oxford University Press.

Turner, Matthew. (2003). "Cowboys and Comedy: The Simultaneous Deconstruction and Reinforcement of Generic Conventions in the Western Parody." *Film & History*, 33.2, 48–54.

Warshow, Robert. (1974). "Movie Chronicle: The Westerner" (1962). In Jack Nachbar (ed.), *Focus on the Western* (pp. 45–56). Englewood Cliffs, NJ: Prentice Hall.

Wills, Garry. (1997). *John Wayne's America: The Politics of Celebrity*. New York: Simon & Schuster.

6

The New Hollywood

Derek Nystrom
Associate Professor, McGill University, Canada

As early as 1967, film critics identified a new sensibility in American cinema that challenged traditions of studio era Hollywood and reflected, often in highly mediated ways, the political and cultural upheavals of the period labeled "the Sixties." Derek Nystrom examines the **New Hollywood**, locating the term within film scholarship and synthesizing concerns that were largely aesthetic and ideological with those centered on **industrial practices**, including appeal to a **new, college-educated audience**. Nystrom discusses influences of the **European New Waves**, **direct cinema documentary**, **low-budget exploitation**, and television in shaping New Hollywood visual style and creating media-savvy filmgoers. He also explores "**class performance**" in narratives featuring unmotivated heroes and low-gear plot trajectories, making a strong case for New Hollywood films as fascinating alternatives to the studio era and to **blockbuster spectacles** that would dominate "**New Hollywood II**" after 1976. Nystrom's essay shares ground with Cynthia Lucia on Natalie Wood in Volume I of this series and with Eric Schaefer on low-budget exploitation, Teresa Podlesney on the comic Western, Art Simon on the cinema of urban crisis, and Thomas Elsaesser on *Nashville* in this volume.

Additional terms, names, and concepts: crisis of overproduction, ratings system, conglomerate takeovers, auteurism, structure of feeling, genre revision, "demythologization"

There have been, of course, many New Hollywoods. In an industry whose only constant has been change – technological, economic, and aesthetic – there is an almost perennial invocation of a New Hollywood emerging from the Old. Most obviously, the introduction of sound created a new Hollywood that replaced the old silent cinema. Many film historians would argue that 1948 marked the beginning of another new Hollywood, as that year's Supreme Court Paramount decision required the studios to sell off their theaters and stop other practices that had guaranteed them a near-monopoly over exhibition. Furthermore, as Peter Krämer (1998) has illustrated, various film critics and theorists have announced

American Film History: Selected Readings, 1960 to the Present, First Edition. Edited by Cynthia Lucia, Roy Grundmann, and Art Simon.

different, yet by their terms definitive, breaks in Hollywood's narrational and stylistic modes. For example, André Bazin declared that 1939–1940 marked the turning point during which Hollywood filmmaking superseded its "classical" period and underwent various "baroque" developments, while critics like Parker Tyler and Gilbert Seldes cited 1952–1953 as the moment when Hollywood radically reconfigured the cinematic experience via widescreen and 3-D processes in order to differentiate itself from television. A New Hollywood, it seems, never ceases to be in the process of being born.

But when many scholars and fans talk about the New Hollywood, they are most often referring to the one that stretched roughly from 1967 to 1976 – the so-called "Hollywood Renaissance" bookended by *Bonnie and Clyde* (Arthur Penn, 1967) and *The Graduate* (Mike Nichols, 1967) on one end and *Nashville* (Robert Altman, 1975) and *Taxi Driver* (Martin Scorsese, 1976) on the other. In between came such landmark films as *Midnight Cowboy* (John Schlesinger, 1969), *Easy Rider* (Dennis Hopper, 1969), *The Wild Bunch* (Sam Peckinpah, 1969), *Five Easy Pieces* (Bob Rafelson, 1970), *The Last Picture Show* (Peter Bogdanovich, 1971), *Klute* (Alan Pakula, 1971), *The French Connection* (William Friedkin, 1971), *Deliverance* (John Boorman, 1972), *The Godfather* and *The Godfather Part II* (Francis Ford Coppola, 1972, 1974), *Badlands* (Terrence Malick, 1973), *The Last Detail* (Hal Ashby, 1973), *A Woman Under the Influence* (John Cassavetes, 1974), and *Chinatown* (Roman Polanski, 1974), to name just a few. This period of filmmaking is celebrated by books like Peter Biskind's *Easy Riders, Raging Bulls* (1998) and documentaries like Ted Demme and Richard LaGravenese's *A Decade Under the Influence* (2003), accounts which describe a gifted group of auteurs who crafted a politically subversive and aesthetically challenging body of cinema that has few precedents in the history of mainstream Hollywood film. The New Hollywood seemed more engaged with, and thus more relevant to, the larger social world: it was, David Thomson asserts, "the decade when movies mattered" (2004). And it is this era that is cited by many contemporary self-professed auteurs (and their critical supporters) as a model for their own cinematic practice. Sharon Waxman's *Rebels on the Backlot* (2005), a study of the directors Quentin Tarantino, Steven Soderbergh, David Fincher, Paul Thomas Anderson, David O. Russell, and Spike Jonze, opens by describing these filmmakers as "self-conscious heirs" to such 1970s auteurs as Coppola, Bogdanovich, Scorsese, Ashby, and Altman. James Mottram's account of many of the same contemporary filmmakers, *The Sundance Kids*, begins in a similar fashion. Mottram argues that Soderbergh's *sex, lies, and videotape* (1989) kicked off independent filmmaking in the 1990s and 2000s in much the same way that *Easy Rider* served as the "key in the ignition for 1970s Hollywood" (2006, 7). Even though the "Sundance Kids" owe an equal debt to such 1980s filmic precedents as Jim Jarmusch's *Stranger than Paradise* (1984) and David Lynch's *Blue Velvet* (1986), the privileged point of comparison – and thus highest critical compliment – is the New Hollywood of the early 1970s.

Of course, this New Hollywood is not the one that set the agenda for the way most films are currently made in the United States. *That* New Hollywood, as Thomas Schatz (1993) has persuasively argued, started as the earlier New Hollywood ended; emerging in 1975 with the enormously successful *Jaws* (Steven Spielberg), this second New Hollywood (let's call it New Hollywood II)[1] became firmly established with the even more enormously successful *Star Wars* (George Lucas, 1977). New Hollywood II, in other words, takes as its signal production the contemporary blockbuster – a kind of film oriented less by a classically constructed storyline than an amalgamation of special-effects sequences, opportunities for merchandizing and other product tie-ins, and multiple platforms of reissue and spinoff ("secondary" foreign and home-video markets; sequels and prequels; television, video game, and theme-park ride adaptations; soundtracks; novelizations; and so on). As many critics and filmmakers have observed (and complained), New Hollywood II is largely responsible for killing off New Hollywood I. Thus, when the Tarantinos and Finchers of today claim a lineage with this earlier New Hollywood, they are not merely citing a favored group of filmmakers; they are also aligning themselves with a lost tradition, a set of precursors and modes of filmmaking that constitute a road not taken by US cinema.

There are a number of reasons why this earlier New Hollywood takes such precedence over other New Hollywoods in the critical and popular imagination. First of all, the story of this period is almost always structured by the idea of a break or rupture – a particularly seductive narrative device for marking out a privileged period of filmmaking. And indeed, whether one attends to industry dynamics, audience trends, cinematic aesthetics, or political and social content, the New Hollywood of 1967 to 1976 appears as a striking break with the past. It arises from the ashes of the old studio system; it addresses itself to younger, hipper audiences; it raids the visual and narrative vocabularies of both high and low cultural forms (the European New Waves, but also exploitation films and television); and it depicts and embodies the political and cultural turmoil of the period. Moreover, this New Hollywood's end is marked by another seemingly definitive break, as the rise of the blockbuster extinguishes the experiments and provocations of the period and replaces them with what Andrew Britton (1986) has called "Reaganite entertainment." Even though various strains of revisionist scholarship have by now illustrated the often surprising continuities of New Hollywood I with both the "Old" Hollywood and New Hollywood II, this narrative of historical rupture still often hails critic and fan alike.

Secondly, the *content* of this narrative is similarly attractive: the story of a brief but vibrant efflorescence of Hollywood cinema more oriented to aesthetic, political, and/or personal concerns rather than those of the box office, but which was ultimately crushed by the big-budget spectacles of the modern blockbuster. As I have already indicated, it appeals to contemporary "maverick" filmmakers who wish to define their practices against those now dominant in contemporary filmmaking. For them, the New Hollywood of the late 1960s and early 1970s appears as a last stand against a kind of film whose primary purpose is to facilitate corporate synergy. But this narrative is also one that speaks to a methodological and perhaps even affective divide within film studies as a discipline. The early academic champions of the New Hollywood, such as Thomas Elsaesser and Robin Wood, approached these films with genuine cinephilia, whatever their other theoretical and critical orientations (see Elsaesser 1975; Wood 1986). For these practitioners of film studies – a discipline that, as I note below, essentially came into being in the US just as the New Hollywood emerged – the interest in this period is compelled by the films themselves, by their promise of an art cinema indigenous to Hollywood that would challenge the formal and ideological conventions of the industry. Later work on the period, though – exemplified by the historical investigations of scholars like Peter Krämer, Jon Lewis, and Justin Wyatt – reminds us that Hollywood is an industry, and should be studied as such (see Krämer 2005; Lewis 1998, 2000; and Wyatt 1998). These writers argue that whatever aesthetic innovations are to be found in the films of the late 1960s and early 1970s, they must also be understood as attempts to establish new sources of profitability: to find new audiences using new kinds of film financing and production as well as new strategies of marketing and distribution. A good deal of this critical work demonstrates how the earlier New Hollywood often unwittingly paved the way for the later, blockbuster-oriented New Hollywood. New Hollywood II, in this light, comes to look like an unexpected sequel to New Hollywood I, a sequel where a few of the characters from the original (like George Lucas) remain, but which tells a very different story. For industry-minded critics, then, the Hollywood Renaissance of 1967 to 1976 figures as both an interregnum between different regimes of industrial organization and, surprisingly, a testing ground for the production and marketing strategies that would come to dominate contemporary Hollywood practice. In short, the New Hollywood is a period that attracts the gaze of both film-lover and business historian; it serves as a privileged object of inquiry for the study of cinematic form and corporate policy. If the contemporary auteur is drawn to the New Hollywood as a model for alternative filmmaking (and its attendant cachet), the continuing attraction of film studies to the period can perhaps be explained by the way it invites and responds to two different modes of scholarship, and two divergent spirits of academic inquiry.

Changes in the Film Industry

Both cinephiles and business historians agree, though, that the New Hollywood came into being as a result of a series of dramatic changes in the film industry. Any one of these changes would have been significant on its own; together, they created conditions that nearly demanded experimentation with received cinematic forms and practices. In the first place, the production model that the studios had adopted in the postwar period was beginning to falter. To attract audiences after the Paramount divorcement decrees ended the major studios' control over exhibition, Hollywood offered big-budget, star-laden, widescreen productions of musicals, historical epics, and literary adaptations – in a word, blockbusters. However, in the pursuit of ever larger profits, the studios produced a series of expensive flops (such as Fox's *Dr. Dolittle* (Richard Fleischer, 1967), *Star!* (Robert Wise, 1968), and *Hello, Dolly!* (Gene Kelly, 1969)) that suggested the waning efficacy, and the increasing financial risks, of such a strategy. These failures were exacerbated by other events that raised filmmaking costs and produced a crisis of overproduction. New production and distribution companies emerged in the mid-1960s, which increased competition for – and thus the price of – personnel and cinematic properties, while also adding more films to an already crowded theatrical marketplace. This combination of failing blockbusters and a market swamped with too many (and too expensively made) films led to an industry-wide slump between 1969 and 1971 which saw five of the seven major studios in the red. In the words of the *Los Angeles Times*, the film industry was in "in out and out depression" (quoted in Cook 2000, 9).[2]

As the financial ground trembled underneath the studios' feet, other events conspired to unsettle key structures that had previously given Hollywood a modicum of stability. In November 1968, the Motion Picture Association of America (MPAA) replaced the Production Code, which had set the guidelines for acceptable film content since the early 1930s, with a ratings system. In doing so, the film industry widened the vocabulary of representation available to filmmakers. At the same time, the studios went through what Richard Maltby calls "an upheaval in company ownership more substantial even than that of the early 1930s" (1998, 9). Some of the major studios were taken over by conglomerates: Paramount, for example, by Gulf+Western in 1966, and Warner's by Seven Arts in 1967, and then the Kinney Corporation in 1969. Other studios, such as Twentieth Century-Fox, saw their heads forced out due to the poor performance of their films. The result, then, was a generational changing of the guard, as the studio moguls of the 1930s and 1940s, like Fox's Darryl Zanuck and Paramount's Barney Balaban, were replaced by younger corporate managers who often had little experience in the film industry. The combination of all of these changes – failing production models, financial panic, broader possibilities for cinematic content, and new, untested management – generated a genuinely improvisatory context for filmmaking in Hollywood.

A New Audience and a New Relationship to Cinema

This new context was also shaped by the film industry's shifting relationship to its audiences, as well as the changing nature of these audiences. The switch to a rating system only ratified Hollywood's increasing practice of differentiating its film production in order to address specific viewer demographics. Preeminent among these was the youth market, as the baby boom generation provided a vigorous and reliable group of moviegoers – something that did not go unnoticed as other audiences were abandoning the theaters. Indeed, a 1967 study commissioned by the MPAA revealed that 58 percent of movie tickets were purchased by those between the ages of 16 and 30 (Krämer 2005, 7). The unexpected success in that year of *The Graduate* and *Bonnie and Clyde* served to underline this finding. Young viewers not only turned out in droves to see these films, but they returned to see them again and again. Furthermore, the cultural fault-lines these films revealed were especially striking. *Bonnie and Clyde* was subject to a critical drubbing upon its initial release, most famously from the *New York Times*'s soon-to-retire critic Bosley Crowther, who called the film's "blending of farce with brutal killings … as pointless as it is lacking in taste" (quoted in Cawelti 1973, 22). Yet the film was passionately embraced by young viewers as a politically significant work of art, which pointed to a generational divide that encompassed not just film aesthetics but also political and cultural sensibilities. For the studios, the rise of the New Hollywood was largely motivated by an attempt to appeal to these new sensibilities.

In fact, it would be hard to overestimate just how thoroughly the New Hollywood was affiliated with its young, college-educated audiences. *Time* magazine's December 1967 cover story on "The New Cinema" (illustrated with an image from *Bonnie and Clyde*) suggested that this New Cinema had arisen largely because "cinema has become the favorite art form of the young" (quoted in Krämer 2005, 38). Similarly, *Newsweek*, in its December 1970 cover story on the "New Movies," argued that it was "the needs, tastes and temperaments" of a "new audience" – one that was "demonstrably younger ... better educated [and] more selective" – that had "given birth to a new kind of American movie" (*Newsweek* 1970, 62). *Esquire*'s August 1970 cover feature on the "New Movies" went a step further: it posed the question, "What's the difference between a new movie and an old movie?" and answered "You, reader. *You* are the movie." This "you," according to *Esquire*, was the "young American" who had become both the subject matter and audience for the New Hollywood, which held a "rock-scored ... mirror up to the kids" (Karpel 1970, 59). Of course, many signature films of the New Hollywood cannot be considered "mirror images" of its audience – college-aged filmgoers may perhaps have identified with Michael in *The Godfather*, but his concerns in that film cannot be said to be those of the average 20-year-old in 1972. Furthermore, most of the cycle of "youth cult" films that followed in the wake of *Easy Rider*'s success failed to attract a substantial audience (particularly films depicting campus unrest, such as 1970's *Getting Straight* (Richard Rush), *R.P.M.* (Stanley Kramer), and *The Strawberry Statement* (Stuart Hagmann)). Finally, it is not as if Hollywood totally abandoned the larger, general audience entirely: the top two films at the box office in 1970, after all, were *Love Story* (Arthur Hiller) and *Airport* (George Seaton). Still, it is true that young, college-educated filmgoers constituted the intended and often actual audience of the films that were associated with the New Hollywood.

This audience had developed a different relationship to cinema than those of previous generations of moviegoers. One massive influence shaping this changed perspective was television – or, more precisely, the screening of old Hollywood films on television. Robert Ray argues that the networks' post-1960 development of the "Saturday Night Movie" (and the "Sunday Night Movie," and the "Monday Night Movie," and so on), combined with local stations' broadcast of other syndicated Hollywood films, "turned every household into a private film museum" (1985, 264). The constant replaying of older Hollywood films on television instilled a historical consciousness of classical cinema in the baby boomers, who were, of course, the first generation to be raised with television. One might say that, where the French New Wave got its training in Hollywood film history from Henri Langlois's Cinémathèque Française, the audiences of the New Hollywood got theirs from "The Late Show." But in another way, Ray suggests, this familiarity with Hollywood's past also bred a certain kind of contempt: the steady diet of "weak, forgotten versions" of Hollywood genre films "revealed the ideological mechanism[s]" by which such films operated – and continued to operate (1985, 265). To watch a dated, mediocre version of a Western – one whose underlying racial and national mythologies were likely to appear, to late 1960s eyes, all the more baldly presented – was to see the then-current iteration of the same genre in a new light, as the similarities between the two would expose their shared (and suspicious) political commitments. Television's recirculation of film studio archives, then, produced moviegoers who were steeped in Hollywood film history, and who were perhaps more critically aware of the ideologies that this history had supported. At the very least, this audience was more prepared to recognize certain film conventions *as* conventions, and thus less ready to embrace yet another uninspired recapitulation of them.

This critical relationship to classical Hollywood's past was reinforced by other developments in film culture. The postwar spread of foreign films, particularly those of the European New Waves, offered audiences an alternative to Hollywood's narrative and stylistic paradigms. Barbara Wilinsky notes that 'the number of first-run art houses in the United States increased from approximately 80 in 1950 to 450 in 1963" – a period when the total number of theaters in the US declined by more than 25 percent (2001, 2). Furthermore, by the mid-1960s, the major studios had become distributors of international films (providing them with a much-needed source of revenue), which made the works of the European New Waves available in non-art house cinemas as well (Cook 1996, 920–921). The experience of Vittorio De Sica's neorealist visions of Italy's bombed-out postwar landscape, or Jean-Luc Godard's playful quotations of American film history and scrambling of Hollywood's syntax, or Ingmar Bergman's austere interrogations of both existential dilemmas and the cinematic apparatus itself, inevitably caused viewers to see the average Hollywood production in a much different light. This interest in international cinema (and concomitant reappraisal of Hollywood) was furthered by the development of film studies courses and programs in US universities. The study of film had begun in a piecemeal fashion in the 1950s with isolated courses offered in various English and foreign language departments, but the field exploded by the end of the 1960s. In 1970, the American Film Institute – itself an organization devoted in part to facilitating the study of Hollywood film – published a guide that listed 233 colleges offering courses in film, with 68 degree programs in film and related fields, including 11 that offered PhDs (Groening 2008, 412). The study of film in universities encouraged baby boomer students to treat Hollywood cinema with a certain amount of critical distance, even as it legitimated film as an object of serious inquiry. Indeed, the imprimatur this academic study bestowed upon the movies dovetailed with the highbrow and avant-garde aspirations of European art cinema to heighten desires among young American film audiences for a similarly ambitious home-grown film movement.

Finally, it perhaps goes without saying that the larger social and political context of the period played a hugely important role in shaping the audiences to which the New Hollywood would appeal. At this point, "the Sixties" has become such a media cliché – one that has reduced a series of democratic uprisings and cultural transformations to a cartoonish parade of stoned, foolish long-haired teens and/or angry, self-righteous domestic terrorists (cf. *Forrest Gump* (Robert Zemeckis, 1994)) – that it is difficult to appreciate just how significant the political and cultural changes wrought by those movements were, and how profoundly they shaped the lives and imaginations of those who lived through them. Furthermore, these shopworn representations of the 1960s also threaten to flatten out the very real differences between cultural formations that certainly overlapped, but which each traveled according to its own social and political itinerary: the New Left, the antiwar movement, the black freedom movement, the counterculture, and the emergent women's and gay liberation movements. This is certainly not the place to educe the different trajectories of these groups and their influences on moviegoing. Suffice it to say that the rewriting of various social scripts during the time placed significant pressure on Hollywood to revise its cinematic scripts as well.

It is worth noting, though, that despite their differences, many of the 1960s movements shared a newfound media savviness – a sense that political challenges must be staged for a media gaze if they are to be truly effective: As the slogan went, the whole world is watching. The experience of pursuing social change as a media intervention (among other things) meant that many participants in these movements came to see themselves through movie metaphors. To choose just a few examples: former Students for a Democratic Society (SDS) leader Carl Oglesby complained about two leaders of the Weathermen faction by remarking that they were infected by "this Butch Cassidy and Sundance attitude – they were blessed, they were hexed, they would die young, they would live forever" (quoted in Gitlin 1987, 386). Gerald Long, then SDS member and soon to be Weatherman, wrote in the Old Left paper *Guardian* about *Bonnie and Clyde* a few weeks after it was released, praising the titular couple as "consciousness-raising outlaws," equivalents of "Frantz Fanon and Nguyen Van Troi," who were "just out there doing their thing, the thing they should be doing" (quoted in Hoberman 2003, 178). Neil Buckley responded in *New Left Notes* to Long's analysis by arguing that it gave Hollywood "more ideological credit than it deserved," but he also concurred with Long's premise that current activism was to be imagined via cinematic spectacle: "We are not potential Bonnie and Clydes," Buckley asserted, "we are Bonnie and Clydes" (quoted in Hoberman 2003, 185). The irony, of course, is that *Bonnie and Clyde* is about precisely this process of self-mythologization. As J. Hoberman observes, "From the start, Bonnie and Clyde act as though they are living in a movie" (2003, 174). For many among the New Hollywood's audiences, then, one did not go to the theater for an escape from the social world, but rather to experience that social world through the mediating images onscreen. The revolution might not be televised, but it would nonetheless be cinematic.

A Directors' Cinema

The list of filmmakers who would attempt to answer these desires for a new American cinema is by now quite familiar: Martin Scorsese, Francis Ford Coppola, Robert Altman, Sam Peckinpah, John Cassavetes, Peter Bogdanovich, Bob Rafelson, Arthur Penn, Mike Nichols, William Friedkin, Hal Ashby, Alan Pakula, Stanley Kubrick, Terrence Malick, Brian De Palma, and Paul Schrader, as well as European-born filmmakers working in the US like Roman

Polanski, John Boorman, and John Schlesinger. Of course this list is not exhaustive. If one reviews contemporaneous accounts of the New Hollywood, one will read a lot about such figures as Monte Hellman (*Two-Lane Blacktop*, 1971), Paul Williams (*Out of It*, 1969; *The Revolutionary*, 1970), and Paul Mazursky (*Bob & Carol & Ted & Alice*, 1969; *Alex in Wonderland*, 1970), but with the exception of the recent resurgence of interest in Hellman's career (see Jones 2004), these directors are often relegated to footnotes in current accounts of the period. Mazursky and Michael Ritchie (*The Candidate*, 1972; *Smile*, 1975) are celebrated along with Scorsese, Altman, Coppola, Ashby, and Cassavetes in Diane Jacobs's 1977 book *Hollywood Renaissance*, an early attempt to codify the period as said renaissance. Hellman features significantly in the influential essays written in the 1970s by Thomas Elsaesser and Robin Wood on American films of the period, along with directors Robert Aldrich (*The Dirty Dozen*, 1967; *The Longest Yard*, 1974) and Sydney Pollack (*Jeremiah Johnson*, 1972; *Three Days of the Condor*, 1975), who are now rarely mentioned in accounts of the New Hollywood. Joseph Gelmis's 1970 book *The Film Director as Superstar*, which sought to document the new emergence of directors who exerted a strong artistic vision, offers interviews with now all-but-forgotten figures like Robert Downey (*Putney Swope*, 1969) and Jim McBride (*David Holzman's Diary*, 1967). Dennis Hopper's *Easy Rider* is of course one of the landmarks of the period, but his other directorial effort during the period, *The Last Movie* (1971), has occasioned only intermittent critical interest. Michael Cimino (*Thunderbolt and Lightfoot*, 1974; *The Deer Hunter*, 1978) is most often discussed in connection with the New Hollywood largely because the out-of-control budget and subsequent commercial failure of his 1980 film *Heaven's Gate* is widely regarded as having ended the kind of directorial control on which the New Hollywood thrived. The genre parodies of Mel Brooks (*Blazing Saddles*, 1974; *Young Frankenstein*, 1974) and Woody Allen (*Take the Money and Run*, 1969; *Sleeper*, 1973) – as well as Allen's assimilation of New Wave stylistic devices in his late 1970s films – are in keeping with signal New Hollywood traits, but their names are less frequently cited in connection with the film movement. Finally, what does one do with Steven Spielberg and George Lucas? Spielberg's *Sugarland Express* (1974) and Lucas's *THX-1138* (1971) and *American Graffiti* (1973) are solidly established within the New Hollywood canon, yet the central roles these two filmmakers played in creating New Hollywood II has often meant that their status within New Hollywood I is contested.

The disagreements over who "counts" as part of the New Hollywood suggest that our idea of the "New Hollywood" changes based on the critical agenda informing it – by the particular cinematic features and industrial practices one wishes to champion or interrogate. If one wants to emphasize the youth of the New Hollywood directors, our attention is directed more toward Coppola and Williams than Altman and Peckinpah. If the question concerns the influence of the European New Waves, the answer lies more in Penn's use of Godardian jump cuts and Rafelson's Antonioni-esque anomie than in Spielberg's more classical impulses. The impact of documentary and cinéma vérité style is felt more profoundly in Cassavetes's and Ritchie's work than in that of Nichols. A search for traces of avant-garde cinema in the New Hollywood brings Hopper and McBride closer to the foreground. If one wants to highlight the ways in which New Hollywood I prepared the way for New Hollywood II, Lucas and Spielberg become the primary objects of study – as well as otherwise ignored filmmakers like Tom Laughlin, whose innovations in marketing and distributing his 1971 youth-cult film *Billy Jack* (which he wrote, directed, and starred in, and then re-released himself in 1973) served as a model for later Hollywood blockbusters (Wyatt 1998).

No matter the angle from which the New Hollywood is approached, one thing is clear: The director almost always serves as the privileged figure of inquiry. Where the history of the classical Hollywood period is usually traced via the stories of producers like David O. Selznick and studio moguls like Jack Warner, the story of the New Hollywood is most often oriented by the career trajectories of its auteurs. The term "auteur," of course, comes from François Truffaut's 1954 *Cahiers du Cinéma* essay "Une certaine tendance du cinéma français," which announced "la politique des auteurs," a "policy" or "program of authors" that insisted that a film must be understood to have an author, and that this author is the director. The influential American film critic Andrew Sarris adopted (and mistranslated) this claim as "the auteur theory" and formulated his "pantheon" of American film directors in his book *The American Cinema: Directors and Directions, 1929–1968*. In the hands of critics, the auteur theory was a way to argue for a particular director's success at articulating his or her personal vision or worldview, despite the inherently collaborative and commercial nature of feature filmmaking. In this way, auteurism served to reevaluate various figures of Hollywood cinema, and to insist upon the aesthetic and even spiritual possibilities of this mass cultural form. Perhaps more importantly, though, auteurism's descriptive claims also functioned as a prescriptive manifesto: The director *should* be the author of a film. For the rising directors of the New Hollywood – as for Truffaut and his fellow critics-turned-filmmakers Jean-Luc Godard, Jacques Rivette, Eric Rohmer, and Claude Chabrol – auteurism authorized (as it were) a strong form of directorial control over the conditions of film production and over the final product itself. Granted, few studio executives were persuaded to this model of filmmaking by the rhetorical powers of Truffaut and Sarris. Their experiment with a director-centered cinema – and the New Hollywood can be seen as just such an experiment – derived from the temporary failure of the blockbuster strategy, as well as the desire to appeal to young audiences by hiring new, young (and relatively young) directors. As Timothy Corrigan (1998) has argued, auteurism here functioned as a form of branding, of marking the films with youth-oriented accents. Highlighting the name of the auteur was also a way of attracting audiences who had been taught to be interested in things like a director's "vision" by auteurist film criticism and by auteur-oriented university film studies programs.

Indeed, many of the New Hollywood directors were themselves products of film schools, particularly those at the University of Southern California (whose alumni include Lucas, John Milius (*Dillinger*, 1973), and John Carpenter (*Halloween*, 1978)), the University of California at Los Angeles (Coppola and Paul Schrader (*Blue Collar*, 1978)) and New York University (Scorsese). In addition to acquiring the technical know-how for filmmaking, these "movie brats" also had the opportunity to study many disparate film movements. Like many at the time, they fell under the sway of the models provided by the European New Waves: De Palma wanted to be an "American Godard," and Scorsese's first student short (*What's a Nice Girl Like You Doing in a Place Like This?*, 1963) opens with a two-minute citation of Truffaut's *Jules and Jim* (1962) (Pye & Myles 1979, 141, 192). But it is important to note that they were also significantly drawn to recent developments in documentary filmmaking, especially the cinema vérité work of Frederick Wiseman, Robert Drew, D. A. Pennebaker, and Albert and David Maysles (for whom Scorsese worked as a lighting man) (Pye & Myles 1979, 194). However, many of these filmmakers, including Coppola, Bogdanovich, Scorsese, and Hellman, got their first taste of the business through work in "exploitation" cinema, especially through Roger Corman's productions at American International Pictures (AIP), which specialized in low-budget horror and other youth-oriented genres.

Each of these contexts and influences offered alternative models of filmmaking to that of traditional Hollywood fare, alternatives that these filmmakers would draw on in their New Hollywood productions. The European art cinema's disruption of Hollywood's "invisible" style of narration encouraged a similar, critically self-conscious form of cinematic address in the young American directors. The immediacy of vérité documentary's handheld camerawork and live sound recording offered the New Hollywood a potent set of techniques for signifying a new kind of realism. Their adoption of exploitation cinema's vivid, even lurid use of sex and violence suited the new cinematic freedoms of the post-Production Code era, while its on-the-cheap production style prepared these directors for the small budgets that were one of the New Hollywood's main selling points to the studios. Finally, these modes of film production also encouraged a taste for directorial control – even exploitation cinema, which is infamously focused on the bottom line. Describing his work for Corman, Scorsese reflected that, even though he "wonder[s] how I could possibly think I was independent at the time," he also insisted that "Corman would leave you alone" to make your film (quoted in Pye & Myles 1979, 199).

Many of the other New Hollywood directors got their start in television. Altman, Penn, Peckinpah, Rafelson, Friedkin, Spielberg, Ritchie, Pollack, Brooks, George Roy Hill (*Butch Cassidy and the Sundance Kid*, 1969), and Sidney Lumet (*Dog Day Afternoon*, 1975) all directed television programs before coming to Hollywood. This background, too, affected the production styles and aesthetic vocabulary of New Hollywood cinema. In the first place, the flexibility and economy of television filming were more suited to the location shooting that the New Hollywood utilized almost without exception. Moreover, the visual devices of television, especially the use of the zoom lens, became more prevalent, even ubiquitous, in the films of the New Hollywood. These devices, as many critics have argued, tend to draw attention to the apparatus of filmmaking itself – the zoom lens in particular foregrounds the camera's role in framing space and directing the viewer's eye – which works against the self-effacing practices of traditional Hollywood filmmaking. Television also offered an early home to many New Wave stylistic effects: Robert Ray points out that *The Monkees*, which reveled in jump cuts and narrative non sequiturs (and which was produced and occasionally directed by Rafelson), had been on the air for almost a year before New Hollywood's first big film, *Bonnie and Clyde*, debuted (1985, 294–295). That television proved conducive to narrative as well as visual techniques that drew attention to themselves is not surprising, since the medium has from its inception acknowledged the viewer in its diegesis: news anchors, commercials, and station promotions all directly address the viewer, while characters in situation comedies regularly "break the fourth wall" to offer asides to the audience. This is all in strong contrast, of course, to classical Hollywood cinema, in which characters rarely if ever betray an awareness that they are being watched. Many New Hollywood directors transposed these forms of self-consciousness into their films, sometimes literally: For example, the opening credit sequence to Altman's *Nashville* is a parody of a television commercial for the film (the sequence ends by promising that the film will take place "right before your very eyes without commercial interruption!"). In short, television's more self-reflexive visual and narrative elements provided the New Hollywood with another set of techniques with which to revise cinematic grammar.

Easy Rider, New Hollywood Style, and the Unmotivated Hero

This revision of Hollywood's cinematic grammar is vividly evident in *Easy Rider*, whose small budget and runaway success (it cost less than half a million dollars to make, but earned $19.2 million in rentals) helped convince the major studios to invest in youth-oriented (or youth cult) films (Cook 2000, 71). Furthermore, its production history and stylistic commitments provide a nearly synoptic index of New Hollywood traits. Before it was ultimately made through Raybert Productions and distributed by Columbia, *Easy Rider* was originally developed for the exploitation company AIP by costars Peter Fonda and Dennis Hopper, who would also direct. The film's central characters and plot (such as it is) are also in keeping with the exploitation subgenre of biker film which was developed in earlier AIP-produced, Corman-directed films like *Wild Angels* (1966) and *The Trip* (1967) (both of which starred Fonda). The camerawork makes copious use of television-derived devices like zoom lenses. Meanwhile, the Mardi Gras street sequences, shot in 16mm, operate in a manner similar to cinema vérité. The film's editing and cinematographic strategies, in turn, bear imprints of the French New Wave. The use of flash cuts between shots and the occasional flash forward to the protagonists' violent death recalls the violations of linear time found in Alain Renais's *Hiroshima mon amour* (1959) and *Last Year at Marienbad* (1961), while the film's 360-degree pans bring to mind those from Godard's *Weekend* (1967). These disruptions of Hollywood's traditional organization of time and space reach their apex in the acid trip sequence, which utilizes distorting "fish eye" lenses, unsettling soundscapes, and discontinuous editing to create a sustained, hallucinatory effect. David E. James (1989) and Jonathan Rosenbaum (2004) have further argued that many of these devices are derived from underground, avant-garde American cinema, whose connection to *Easy Rider* they trace through Hopper's involvement in various art world circles.

Through its adoption of such influences, *Easy Rider* exemplified many of the signal features of New Hollywood filmmaking as they are described by Steve Neale in an influential 1976 essay. Neale argued that the New Hollywood's New Wave- and television-derived strategies "destroyed the dramatic and spatiotemporal unity that founded classical mise-en-scène," while traditional Hollywood's "plot-linearity and its corollary, the goal-oriented hero, have been replaced by narrative fragmentation and troubled, introspective protagonists." However, although Neale noted that some New Hollywood films eschewed genre conventions for the sake of "realism," he also observed that this alleged realism still observed "the exigencies of narrative conventions"; meanwhile, many other New Hollywood productions did rely on inherited generic structures, even if these were "invested with an empty nostalgia or a knowing cynicism, or both" (1976, 117–118). Thus, Neale argues that despite the significance of the New Hollywood's violation of many classical and formal practices, these developments did not augur a complete break with them: "the changes in the nature of Hollywood narrative, though real, are on the whole far less radical than they may appear" (1976, 120). Neale's account highlights the fact that there has been critical debate about the extent and significance of the New Hollywood's dissent from narrative and stylistic norms almost since its inception. In other words, just how "new" was the New Hollywood? Furthermore, what was the political resonance of these ostensibly new cinematic forms?

There is a case to be made that *Easy Rider* does indeed violate central conventions of Hollywood storytelling. Take, for example, the film's protagonists: Wyatt, or Captain America (Fonda), and Billy (Hopper). In one sense, these characters have the kind of clearly defined goal that traditionally drives Hollywood narrative: They are travelling to New Orleans for Mardi Gras, a trip enabled by the success of the drug deal which opens the film. Yet the fulfillment of this "goal" does not structure the action or the cause–effect relations of the film's narrative; instead, the film is essentially a picaresque, a series of loosely linked episodes that have little to no necessary relation to the protagonists' intention of attending Mardi Gras. The interpretive disagreements that have attended Wyatt's famously ambiguous lament near the film's end – his declaration that "We blew it" – underline the near-irrelevance of the film's ostensible goal: Since *Easy Rider* never makes clear what is really motivating Billy and Wyatt, any idea of what "it" is (and why they failed at it) is left up almost entirely to the viewer's hermeneutic powers. In this way, the film deviates significantly from the tightly ordered, goal-driven plot of the Old Hollywood.

Thomas Elsaesser has argued that this "combination of the unmotivated hero and the motif of the journey," which he identified in many New Hollywood films (*Two Lane Blacktop*, *Five Easy Pieces*, *The Last Detail*, *California Split* (Robert Altman, 1974) as well as *Easy Rider*), pointed to an implicit critique of the ideological structures that traditional Hollywood has supported. Hollywood narrative's focus on causality, a causality motivated by the protagonist's pursuit of a clearly defined goal, presents a world in which the "conflict, contradiction and contingency" of life is rendered as "order, linearity, and articulated energy" – a world that is thus regarded with "a fundamentally affirmative attitude … a kind of a-priori optimism" generated by "the very structure of the narrative" (Elsaesser 1975, 14). In the emergence of the New Hollywood's unmotivated heroes, who displayed "an almost physical sense of inconsequential action, of pointlessness and uselessness," Elsaesser read "a radical scepticism … about the American virtues of ambition, vision, drive." Yet Elsaesser was also careful to say that the New Hollywood is best considered as a "transitional" cinema, as its directors "seem[ed] a little unsure of how to objectify into narrative" this dissent from dominant ideology. While the "affirmative-consequential model of narrative" appeared to be waning, the films of the New Hollywood were marked more by a withdrawal from traditional plot characteristics than by a clearly articulated set of alternative organizing principles (1975, 15).

Once again, *Easy Rider* is a case in point. The film, with its embrace of drug culture, rock music, and anti-authoritarian attitudes, presents itself as aligned with the counterculture. Its heroes, funded by the underground drug economy, spend the bulk of the film exploring various forms of alternative existence while evading the representatives of a repressive social order. The picaresque, road-movie structure, though, enables the film to resist making a strong affiliation with any one mode of dissident social organization (or cinematic practice). As David E. James observes, the heroes' decision to leave the commune serves as an allegory for the film's larger rejection of genuinely radical cinematic and political modes: "A real endorsement of the commune would have brought the film to a halt right there" (1989, 18). Indeed, the rhythms of the commune sequence are palpably out of step with those of the rest of the film, especially in the hushed prayer scene, whose slow, 360-degree pan across the somber faces of the assembled commune members hints at not just a different experience of cinematic temporality – as the film contemplates an almost static tableau that circles back onto itself – but

Figure 6.1 The camera pans across the faces of commune members in the prayer scene from Dennis Hopper's *Easy Rider* (1969, producer Peter Fonda).

perhaps also a different relationship to the social organization of time.

Time is very much on Wyatt's mind when he chooses to leave: The hitchhiking stranger who led Billy and Wyatt to the commune encourages them to drop acid then and there by saying, "This could be the right place. Your time's running out." Wyatt's reply – "I'm hip about time. But I just gotta go" – signifies the film's abandonment of the cinematic and political possibilities made available by locating itself in another kind of time and place. By adhering to its road-movie ethos, *Easy Rider* remains indebted to the forward drive of classical narrative, even if here this drive is largely unmotivated.

The New Hollywood's Class Performance

It is worth noting that, in a few signal New Hollywood films, this negative formal gesture – this emptying out of the protagonist by depriving him (and it is almost always him) of clear motivation – has an explicit class basis. Benjamin of *The Graduate*, as the film's tagline read, is "a little worried about his future," an anxiety that is largely about his hesitation to enter the world of professional achievement for which his schooling and upbringing have trained him. Bobby of *Five Easy Pieces* has dropped out from his promising career as a classical pianist and lives as an itinerant manual laborer. Even a supporting character like *Easy Rider*'s George (Jack Nicholson) shares Billy and Wyatt's largely motiveless wandering, yet his decision to join them on their journey involves an at least temporary rejection of his professional duties as a lawyer (as well as a rebellion against his father's disapproval of his dissolute ways). The motivation that is troubled or disrupted in these characters, in other words, is that of a middle-class imperative to make good on their lengthy (and often expensive) education by taking up professional occupations. In short, these unmotivated heroes are not merely expressing a general skepticism about American values; they are resisting the specific demands of the professional class that they reproduce the parent generation's class position.

Of course, one must be careful about making, on the basis of a handful of films, too strong a claim for this class thematic, especially given the diversity of the New Hollywood's cinematic output. However, just as the film movement's biggest successes resisted direct representations of their audience, and instead depicted their concerns in mediated ways – *Bonnie and Clyde* rang more true to its audience than the youth-cult pandering *The Strawberry Statement* – one could argue that the New Hollywood's other unmotivated heroes also spoke to this class dilemma, albeit in a displaced manner. After all, the audience for the New Hollywood was not merely younger, but also more affluent and more likely to be college educated – in other words, they were the younger generation of the professional middle class. This generation came of age in the orbit of the (largely middle-class) New Left and counterculture, wherein the former's critique of parent/class institutions as complicit in imperialist foreign policy and racist domestic policy dovetailed with the latter's rejection of career-minded advancement in favor of "dropping out" into alternative lifestyles. As Barbara Ehrenreich (1989) has argued, these combined influences instigated a genuine panic among the parent generation of the class, a fear that their offspring would refuse to assume their "rightful" position as the next generation of government, business, and professional leaders. In this context, the unmotivated heroes of the New Hollywood, even those whose relationship to the youth movements is indirect at best, provided a structure of feeling through which the audiences of the New Hollywood might live out the drama of class reproduction.

In fact, this displaced class dimension helps further explain the sense of hesitancy that Elsaesser identifies in the New Hollywood – its inability to move beyond a critique of previous narrative forms toward the construction of a new cinematic language. For if, as I have been suggesting, the New Hollywood suspicion toward the affirmative, goal-oriented, linear plot includes a subtextual wariness about professional achievement and advancement, the films nonetheless appeal in various ways to its viewers' class prerogatives. Thematically, this was often figured through the hero's meritocratic supremacy over members of the working and ruling classes. For example, *M*A*S*H*'s (Robert Altman, 1970) surgeon-protagonists Hawkeye (Donald Sutherland) and Trapper John (Elliott Gould) continually subvert their military superiors (and their lowly ranked followers) by insisting upon the higher authority of their medical expertise – as "the pros from Dover," as they keep calling themselves. Although Michael Ritchie's *The Candidate* is somewhat critical of its young, idealistic left-liberal protagonist (Robert Redford), the film (and the audience) shares in his knowing mockery of the out-of-touch privilege of his aging Republican opponent (Don Porter) as well as the seemingly bovine nature of the lumpen voting public. If films like these did not offer protagonists who fixed themselves to a central goal in an unambiguous, untroubled way, their heroes did exhibit superior forms of knowledge that enabled them still to claim center stage. In doing so, they exact a certain kind of narrative authority that harmonizes with many forms of traditional Hollywood storytelling – a feature that no doubt contributed to the New Hollywood's hesitancy in entirely jettisoning the narrative structures of the Old Hollywood.

This thematic assertion of the authority of middle-class forms of knowledge was reinforced by the formal strategies of the New Hollywood, especially its embrace of New Wave aesthetics and its accompanying ambitions toward "art." As early as January 1969, Richard Schickel complained in the *New York Times* that, due to the rise of foreign film and the emergence of their American inheritors, "the movies are now High Art"; as a result, films had become "the playthings of The New Class," which is to say, the professional and managerial classes (1969, 34). Whatever critique of middle-class privilege the New Hollywood's protagonists and plot structures offered – and one should not discount these critiques – the films' deployment of art cinema styles and techniques both generated and relied on middle-class forms of cultural capital, the kind acquired in places like university film classes. Furthermore, as I have argued elsewhere (Nystrom 2004), this formal strategy of rewarding middle-class knowledge found its industrial counterpart in the practice of auteurism. The "politique des auteurs" was often marshaled in opposition to studio involvement in the creative process – a defense, if you will, of professional knowledge against capital. In the case of the New Hollywood, this discourse of auteurism was also deployed to check the power of the film unions, so that the industry's professional class could assert its authority against the working class as well. In some cases, the New Hollywood directors went against industry norms and made use of nonunion labor, a practice spearheaded by AIP and later adopted by Brian De Palma and Robert Downey, among others, during their first film projects. In other cases, the New Hollywood directors would make use of rival unions that challenged the jurisdiction of the film unions, a tactic which weakens the bargaining position of both. In fact, one of the first major films to utilize the television-based National Association of Broadcast Engineers and Technicians (NABET) instead of the film industry based International Alliance of Theatrical Stage Employees (IATSE) was the early New Hollywood sensation *Easy Rider*. In all of these ways, the New Hollywood proved itself to be a cinema by and for not just the young, but also the professional middle class.

Genre Revision and *The Conversation*

Many commentators noted *Easy Rider*'s self-conscious invocation of Western generic codes: Wyatt and Billy's names are allusions to the famous Western characters Wyatt Earp and Billy the Kid, and early on Billy jokes that they are "fighting Indians and cowboys at every side"; moreover, an early scene draws an explicit (and belabored) analogy between their motorcycles and horses. These generic markers serve as another sign of the New Hollywood's indebtedness to traditional Hollywood forms. Yet the trajectory of Wyatt and Billy's journey – they travel from west to east, rather than the standard westward voyage – also indicates the film's significant reworking of these traditional elements, which in turn draws our attention to another prominent feature of the New Hollywood: its revision of Hollywood genres. On the one hand, many critics have suggested that this working in and through genre conventions indicates the limitations placed on New Hollywood filmmakers. In comparison to the European New Wave directors, whose industrial contexts allowed them greater freedom to reimagine cinematic narrative entirely, the New Hollywood directors faced a more insistent demand to attract sizable audiences. And genre, of course, serves as an important device toward this end, in that generic stories are always already "presold," appealing to viewers who have demonstrated their interest in previous generic outings. Yet to think of genre as merely a constraint is to downplay the profound interrogations of dominant US ideology enabled by the New Hollywood's engagement with genre. As I noted earlier, the audiences of the New Hollywood were well versed in traditional genres from the education in film history they received from television as well as college film courses. But this education also encouraged a critical perspective on these genres, and created an audience open to the various possibilities of their reworking – as did the political and social context of the period, which challenged many of the dominant ideologies these genres served to support. The New Hollywood's exercises in genre, then, can be seen as the movement's most concerted effort to intervene in the US political imaginary.

John Cawelti (1986) discusses what he calls the "demythologization" that many genre reworkings of the 1970s performed. Films such as *Little Big Man* (Arthur Penn, 1970) and *McCabe & Mrs. Miller* (Robert Altman, 1971) stage the genre's conventions in order to expose their internal contradictions and/or their insufficiency in addressing "real" social and political contexts. *Little Big Man* does this by inverting the moral hierarchy of the traditional Western – it valorizes Native American culture against the deranged violence of General Custer – while *McCabe* offers a hero whose drunken dithering and romantic ineptitude explode the genre's investments in patriarchal mastery. These films lay bare the myths that these generic forms underwrite, and expose them as just that – myths. The Western was a particularly important cinematic territory for such demythologizing impulses: The genre's ur-narrative of Western expansion under the sign of Manifest Destiny offered a troubling analogy with US imperialist misadventures in Southeast Asia, while its racial iconography and celebration of white domination over indigenous populations became increasingly untenable in the wake of the various race-based civil rights movements. The demythologization of the Western offered by New Hollywood films, then, was both shaped by and contributed to the critique of these ideological structures.

This project of demythologization illustrates the political value of the New Hollywood's less aesthetically radical engagement with traditional narrational modes. Consider *The Conversation* (Francis Ford Coppola, 1974), a "paranoid conspiracy" film that drew on the conventions of detective films and film noir. Arguing against the claim that the New Hollywood developed a "postclassical" cinematic style, David Bordwell and Janet Staiger discuss *The Conversation* as an example of the persistence of "character-centered causality" that defines classical Hollywood narration. In the film, Harry Caul (Gene Hackman), a surveillance expert, stumbles upon a possible murder plot during his recording of a couple's conversation, and the film's narrative is structured by his attempt to learn more about and hopefully prevent this murder. Thus, as Bordwell and Staiger note, the film's classical structure is largely articulated through "genre conventions – investigation, threat, and evasion maneuvers" (1985, 375). True, the film complicates these conventions by troubling its hero's motivation and emphasizing his inability to act: Harry's professional goals – providing a clear recording to his employers – conflict with his fear of abetting the murder of the couple, and when the expected murder takes place (albeit in a way Harry did not predict), he is unable to intervene. "The paralytic, drifting protagonist," as Bordwell and Staiger put it, "fits badly into the detective role" (1985, 376). Furthermore, the film imports other art cinema strategies, such as unexpected (and unsignaled) shifts from objective to subjective narration as well as "authorial" commentary. However, Bordwell and Staiger point out that "a puzzle and solution remain firmly at the center of the story": At the end of the film, we know what the real murder plot was, and who was responsible (1985, 377). In contrast, *Blow-Up* (Michelangelo Antonioni, 1966), to which *The Conversation* alludes in multiple ways, presents a "detective puzzle that cannot be solved. The protagonist has only the vaguest suspicions; we have no access to the murder plot, to motives, or to any evidence but the photograph" (1985, 377). Therefore, by "anchor[ing] the film within generic expectations," *The Conversation* – like all New Hollywood films, according to Bordwell and Staiger – adheres firmly to classical Hollywood style, subordinating the more radical innovations of the European New Waves to the requirements of this narrational mode (1985, 377). In this way, the New Hollywood practices the same "process of stylistic assimilation ... seen at work throughout Hollywood's history" (1985, 373).

Bordwell and Staiger's argument is persuasive as far as it goes, but its implication – that New Hollywood cinema provides its viewer with an experience that is not substantially different from that of more classically organized films – bears further scrutiny. Consider *The Conversation*'s famous twist ending: Throughout the film, Harry hears the key line from the couple's taped conversation as "He'd *kill* us if he had the chance," suggesting that the couple is in danger from the corporate director who hired Harry. Yet when he discovers that, in fact, the couple has conspired to kill the director, Harry realizes that the sentence is actually "He'd kill *us* if he had the chance." But Harry's mistake is ours as well – or rather, the film forces us to make the same mistake as Harry. We are encouraged to hear the taped conversation as objectively narrated: Not only are we presented with unsteady, vérité style images of the couple having the conversation (as if they are

Figure 6.2 Harry (Gene Hackman) listens intently to his recording in *The Conversation* (1974, director and producer Francis Ford Coppola).

being surreptitiously recorded by a camera as well), but we also watch Harry isolate this conversation on the tape with a complex array of sound equipment, which would seem to guarantee the veracity of the recording.

The film's ending, though, makes us realize that we were experiencing subjective narration, that the sound we thought we were getting from the machine's neutral recording was in fact Harry's subjective experience of that recording (which is colored particularly by his tenderness toward the woman in the couple). Yet our realization comes, as it does for Harry, too late. We have not only been placed amidst a puzzle, but the film's narration of this puzzle is also revealed to be deliberately unreliable – a revelation that comes only at the film's close. *The Conversation* does more than situate a complexly motivated protagonist with dissipated agency at the center of its detective story; it also causes us to share this sense of dissipated agency by depriving us of the ability to deduce the mystery for ourselves. In so doing, the film not only problematizes the efficacy of individual heroic action that is usually celebrated by the detective genre, but also causes us to inhabit the failure of such individual action as if from the inside. The rug that is pulled out from under Harry slips out from under our feet as well.

This intense, affective experience of genre's insufficiency – and, by extension, the insufficiency of the ideologies that genres support – is only possible in a cinema that engages with such generic structures in a thorough manner. Had *The Conversation* pursued more unambiguously art-cinematic strategies – had it approached more closely the modernist indeterminacy of *Blow-Up* – this critique of traditional generic forms would have been nowhere near as powerful. After all, the international art cinema had generated, by the 1970s, a stable viewing practice of its own. As Bordwell himself argues, the art cinema's deviations from traditional forms of causality usually provoke (in the properly trained viewer) an interpretive strategy that reads such deviations as signs of either "realism" or "authorial expressivity"; the habitual art cinema viewer also knows that "when in doubt, read for maximum ambiguity" (1999, 721). Films like *The Conversation* – or for that matter *Chinatown*, or *McCabe & Mrs. Miller*, or *Pat Garrett and Billy the Kid* (Sam Peckinpah, 1973) – do not signal to the viewer that they should look for maximum ambiguity; their genre conventions instead raise other sets of expectations, ones that are more in line with the "affirmative" worldview supported by these genres. When these expectations are dashed by the demythologizing revisions of New Hollywood cinema, the gaps and absences in such affirmative worldviews are felt in a vivid, palpable manner. The New Hollywood, then, performed its political critiques not in spite of its use of genre conventions, but precisely because of them.[3]

The End of the (First) New Hollywood

One of the many ironies of New Hollywood II's displacement of New Hollywood I is that the new blockbusters achieved their success through a reworking of genre as well. Yet these reworkings proceeded via altogether different modes, those of hybridity and pastiche. For example, *Jaws*, as Thomas Schatz points out, is best characterized as an action film, but it draws elements from the "monster" and "slasher" subgenres of horror, as well as the emerging "buddy" film (1993, 18). *Star Wars*, in addition to its citation of various science fiction traditions, alludes to Westerns, films noir, swashbucklers, war films, even Laurel and Hardy comedies. James Monaco characterized the film as a "black-hole neutron star sucking up everything in its wake. Whole genres of film disappear into it," producing "a compendium of genre entertainment from the past thirty years" (1979, 170). Of course, the effect of such pastiche and hybridity is not the demythologization Cawelti describes. Fredric Jameson's analysis of "the nostalgia film" suggests the politically conservative thrust of these new manipulations of genre. The citation of previous cinematic forms in these films usually convey "'the past' through stylistic connotation" (1991, 19); think, for example, of the mix of Western and noir signifiers that populate the saloon sequence in *Star Wars*. Yet this concatenation of stylistic emblems of different historical periods – the intermingling of the nineteenth-century Wild West with mid-twentieth-century gumshoe ambiance, both situated in a futuristic science fiction context – produces what Jameson calls "a waning of our historicity, of our lived possibility of experiencing history in some active way" (1991, 21).[4] The signifying chain of history, in other words, is disassembled by the code mixing of genre hybridity and pastiche, situating the viewer in an ahistorical, perpetual present. Meanwhile, even the sense of knowingness and mastery offered to the viewer by the blockbuster's promiscuous (and often shorthand) allusions to generic codes serves not as ideology critique, but rather its sublation. Slavoj Žižek (1989) suggests that one of the ways ideology functions in postmodern societies is via "cynical reason" – that is, that people recognize the falsity or incoherence of their society's dominant beliefs, but continue to live by them. As Žižek later puts it, "this is how we are believers today – we make fun of our beliefs, while continuing to practice them" (2002, 71). The knowing adoption of exhausted generic paradigms in films like *Star Wars* and *Raiders of the Lost Ark* (Steven Spielberg, 1981) lead the audience to engage in precisely this sort of cynical reason: We are encouraged to recognize the shopworn nature of the intermingled genre elements dispersed throughout the film, even as they are mobilized to focus our attention on the ruthlessly goal-oriented protagonist, whose individualistic heroic action is valorized by the narrative. We wink at the outmoded generic paces we are put through, even as we eagerly follow their path to the film's affirmative resolutions. In short, New Hollywood II took the deconstructed genres of New Hollywood I and reassembled them into Frankenstein-like hybrids, creations that turned out to serve their (capitalist) masters, both materially and ideologically, in surprisingly docile ways.

Of course, as Schatz explains, the genre hybridity of *Star Wars* and other New Hollywood II blockbusters generated "a purposeful incoherence which actually 'opens' the film to different readings (and readers), allowing for multiple interpretive strategies and thus broadening the potential audience appeal" (1993, 23). With these disparate forms of address, the New Hollywood II blockbuster partially reconstituted the segmented audiences of the postwar period. These broader audiences, along with the New Hollywood II blockbuster's multiplying avenues of revenue – not just sequels and television spinoffs, but also foreign markets, home video, soundtracks and other forms of merchandizing – restored a degree of financial stability to the film industry that had been shaken by the crises of the late 1960s. The window of opportunity that these crises had opened for New Hollywood I thus began to close. Bud Smith, the editor on William Friedkin's 1977 film *Sorcerer*, indicated what this development might have felt like when he described the effect of watching his trailer follow the one for *Star Wars*: "We're fucking being blown off the screen" (quoted. in Biskind 1998, 337).

It is hard to imagine that the Hollywood studios would have survived long on the business model offered by the first New Hollywood; the audiences to which it appealed were too small and too specialized for a relentlessly commercial industry with globe-dominating objectives. Furthermore, since the United States is a superpower in which critical introspection is not a dominant political or intellectual mode, its production of a cinema that engages in a persistent critique of the nation's guiding ideological orientations – even one as limited and partial as the New Hollywood's – is a comparatively rare event. One might say that only massive democratic uprisings in the face of various domestic and foreign policy failures could generate the conditions for such a cinema. But the story of the New Hollywood should not end (as it often does) with the lament that "They don't make 'em that way anymore." Because they do, as anyone who has seen a Todd Haynes film can tell you. What has changed since the end of the first New Hollywood is not the disappearance of American films influenced by art cinematic traditions and political dissent; rather, it is that the major studios no longer pin their box office hopes on such films. For all of its limitations and compromises, the New Hollywood offers a model for a minority, "semipopular" cinema (to borrow a term from rock critic Robert Christgau) – especially since many of the films we now celebrate as part of the New Hollywood were (at best) semipopular in their day. Perhaps the story of the New Hollywood, then, is less a tale of a revolutionary cinema that was crushed by the forces of political and aesthetic reaction; perhaps it is more about the adventures of a semipopular cinema that, due to a series of anomalous political and industrial conjunctures, found itself at center stage for a brief period and tried to make the most of its moment in the spotlight.

Notes

1. King (2002) denotes the "two" New Hollywoods in a similar fashion. I will refer to New Hollywood I and II only when drawing a contrast between the two periods; otherwise, "New Hollywood" will refer to films of the 1967–1976 period.
2. On the state of the film industry in this period, see also Schatz 1993 and Maltby 1998.
3. My argument here is influenced by Todd Berliner's provocative essay (2001), although my conclusions are markedly different from his.
4. *Star Wars* is, strictly speaking, not set in the future, but the mise-en-scène is nonetheless futuristic.

References

Berliner, Todd. (2001). "The Genre Film as Booby Trap: 1970s Genre Bending and *The French Connection*." *Cinema Journal*, 40.3, 25–46.

Biskind, Peter. (1998). *Easy Riders, Raging Bulls: How the Sex-Drugs-and-Rock'n'Roll Generation Saved Hollywood.* New York: Simon & Schuster.

Bordwell, David. (1999). "The Art Cinema as a Mode of Film Practice." In Leo Braudy & Marshall Cohen (eds), *Film Theory and Criticism*, 5th edn (pp. 716–724). New York: Oxford University Press.

Bordwell, David, & Staiger, Janet. (1985). "Since 1960: The Persistence of a Mode of Film Practice." In David Bordwell, Janet Staiger, & Kristin Thompson (eds), *The Classical Hollywood Cinema: Film Style and Mode of Production to 1960* (pp. 367–377). New York: Columbia University Press.

Britton, Andrew. (1986). "Blissing Out: The Politics of Reaganite Entertainment." *Movie*, 31–32, 1–42.

Cawelti, John. (1973). *Focus on Bonnie and Clyde.* Englewood Cliffs, NJ: Prentice Hall.

Cawelti, John. (1986). "*Chinatown* and Generic Transformation in Recent American Films." In Barry Keith Grant (ed.), *Film Genre Reader* (pp. 183–201). Austin: University of Texas Press.

Cook, David A. (1996). *A History of Narrative Film.* 3rd edn. New York: Norton.

Cook, David A. (2000). *History of the American Cinema,* vol. 9: *Lost Illusions: American Cinema in the Shadow of Watergate and Vietnam, 1970–1979.* New York: Scribner's.

Corrigan, Timothy. (1998). "Auteurs and the New Hollywood." In Jon Lewis (ed.), *The New American Cinema* (pp. 38–63). Durham, NC: Duke University Press.

Ehrenreich, Barbara. (1989). *Fear of Falling: The Inner Life of the Middle Class.* New York: HarperCollins.

Elsaesser, Thomas. (1975). "Notes on the Unmotivated Hero: The Pathos of Failure – American Films of the 1970s." *Monogram*, 6, 13–19.

Gelmis, Joseph. (1970). *The Film Director as Superstar.* Garden City, NY: Doubleday.

Gitlin, Todd. (1987). *The Sixties: Years of Hope, Days of Rage.* New York: Bantam.

Groening, Stephen. (2008). "Timeline for a History of Anglophone Film Culture and Film Studies." In Lee Grieveson & Haidee Wasson (eds), *Inventing Film Studies* (pp. 399–418). Durham, NC: Duke University Press.

Hoberman, J. (2003). *The Dream Life: Movies, Media, and the Mythology of the Sixties*. New York: New Press.

Jacobs, Diane. (1977). *Hollywood Renaissance*. New York: A. S. Barnes.

James, David E. (1989). *Allegories of Cinema: American Film in the Sixties*. Princeton, NJ: Princeton University Press.

Jameson, Fredric. (1991). *Postmodernism, or the Cultural Logic of Late Capitalism*. Durham, NC: Duke University Press.

Jones, Kent. (2004). "'The Cylinders Were Whispering My Name': The Films of Monte Hellman." In Thomas Elsaesser, Alexander Horwath, & Noel King (eds), *The Last Great American Picture Show: New Hollywood Cinema in the 1970s* (pp. 165–194). Amsterdam: Amsterdam University Press.

Karpel, Craig. (1970). "The Last Great Show on Earth." *Esquire*, August, 59.

King, Geoff. (2002). *New Hollywood Cinema: An Introduction*. New York: Columbia University Press.

Krämer, Peter. (1998). "Post-Classical Hollywood." In John Hill & Pamela Church Gibson (eds), *The Oxford Guide to Film Studies* (pp. 289–309). New York: Oxford University Press.

Krämer, Peter. (2005). *The New Hollywood: From Bonnie and Clyde to Star Wars*. New York: Wallflower.

Lewis, Jon. (1998). "Money Matters: Hollywood in the Corporate Era." In Jon Lewis (ed.), *The New American Cinema* (pp. 87–121). Durham, NC: Duke University Press.

Lewis, Jon. (2000). *Hollywood vs. Hard Core: How the Struggle over Censorship Saved the Modern Film Industry*. New York: New York University Press.

Maltby, Richard. (1998). "'Nobody Knows Everything': Post-Classical Historiographies and Consolidated Entertainment." In Steve Neale & Murray Smith (eds), *Contemporary Hollywood Cinema* (pp. 21–44). New York: Routledge.

Monaco, James. (1979). *American Film Now: The People, the Power, the Money, the Movies*. New York: Plume.

Mottram, James. (2006). *The Sundance Kids: How the Mavericks Took Back Hollywood*. New York: Faber & Faber.

Neale, Steve. (1976). "New Hollywood Cinema." *Screen*, 17.2, 117–122.

Newsweek. (1970). "The New Movies." December 7, 62–64, 69–72.

Nystrom, Derek. (2004). "Hard Hats and Movie Brats: Auteurism and the Class Politics of the New Hollywood." *Cinema Journal*, 43.3, 18–41.

Pye. Michael, & Myles, Linda. (1979). *The Movie Brats: How the Film Generation Took over Hollywood*. New York: Holt, Rinehart & Winston.

Ray, Robert B. (1985). *A Certain Tendency of the Hollywood Cinema, 1930–1980*. Princeton, NJ: Princeton University Press.

Rosenbaum, Jonathan. (2004). "New Hollywood and the Sixties Melting Pot." In Thomas Elsaesser, Alexander Horwath, & Noel King (eds), *The Last Great American Picture Show: New Hollywood Cinema in the 1970s* (pp. 131–152). Amsterdam: Amsterdam University Press.

Schatz, Thomas. (1993). "The New Hollywood." In Jim Collins, Hilary Radner, & Ava Preacher Collins (eds), *Film Theory Goes to the Movies* (pp. 8–36). New York: Routledge.

Schickel, Richard. (1969). "The Movies Are Now High Art." *New York Times Magazine*, January 5, 32–44.

Thomson, David. (2004). "The Decade When Movies Mattered." In Thomas Elsaesser, Alexander Horwath, & Noel King (eds), *The Last Great American Picture Show: New Hollywood Cinema in the 1970s* (pp. 73–82). Amsterdam: Amsterdam University Press.

Waxman, Sharon. (2005). *Rebels on the Backlot: Six Maverick Directors and How They Conquered the Hollywood Studio System*. New York: HarperCollins.

Wilinsky, Barbara. (2001). *Sure Seaters: The Emergence of Art House Cinema*. Minneapolis: University of Minnesota Press.

Wood, Robin. (1986). *Hollywood from Vietnam to Reagan*. New York: Columbia University Press.

Wyatt, Justin. (1998). "From Roadshowing to Saturation Release: Majors, Independents, and Marketing/Distribution Innovations." In Jon Lewis (ed.), *The New American Cinema* (pp. 64–86). Durham, NC: Duke University Press.

Žižek, Slavoj. (1989). *The Sublime Object of Ideology*. New York: Verso.

Žižek, Slavoj. (2002). *Welcome to the Desert of the Real*. New York: Verso.

7

"One Big Lousy X"
The Cinema of Urban Crisis

Art Simon
Professor, Montclair State University, United States

Art Simon identifies a cycle of **New Hollywood** films representing **urban crisis** and the failure of cinema's most trusted heroes – the **cop** and the **cowboy** – to prevail. Produced between 1968 and 1976, these films feature cops breaking the law in order to enforce it and cowboys transported to the city, finding that their Western-styled **masculinity** takes on a whole new meaning. The traditional **immigrant narrative** also is reversed in ***Midnight Cowboy***, with Ratso Rizzo realizing that New York is the cradle of his nightmares rather than his dreams of upward mobility. Providing close readings of film form and the mise-en-scène of crumbling urban locations, Simon situates *Midnight Cowboy*, ***Coogan's Bluff***, and other films, within the economic turmoil of the film industry. He argues that, whereas the era's most salient political struggles – the **anti-war** and **Civil Rights movements** – were largely absent from American screens, the ungovernable city was omnipresent. Simon's essay shares ground with Derek Nystrom on the New Hollywood, Christine Noll Brinckmann on urban iconography in *Force of Evil*, and Teresa Podlesney on the comic Western in this volume, and with Kevin Stoehr on the A-Western in the hardcover/online edition.

Additional terms, names, and concepts: Hollywood Renaissance, corporate conglomerate, Mayor's Office of Film, Theater and Broadcasting, John Schlesinger, Don Siegel, Hal Ashby, urban road film

In the years between 1968 and 1976, the American cinema reacquainted itself with New York City and found there a compelling image of a society appearing to unravel. It brought some of its best-known genre figures, such as the cowboy and the police detective, and some of the culture's richest tropes, like the struggling immigrant and life on the road, to confront a city on the brink of collapse. But the cowboy who had tamed the West was now no match for the frontier of night and the city's brand of bureaucratic justice. The policeman's badge now identified someone who broke the law as often as, and frequently in the name of, enforcing it. The child of immigrants, for whom New York had always meant economic and

American Film History: Selected Readings, 1960 to the Present, First Edition. Edited by Cynthia Lucia, Roy Grundmann, and Art Simon.

artistic opportunity, as well as a patchwork of supportive ethnic neighborhoods, now found himself a crippled lonely man, hustling the streets of a most unglamorous Times Square. And the road, that symbol of mythical freedom for the Beats as well as bikers, and the path by which the counterculture had imagined an escape from middle-class conformity, would become, in the city, a dense circuitry of streets, home to mad car chases and round-the-clock crimes.

Hollywood Renaissance

If, as some film historians have suggested, American film experienced an artistic renewal during these years, a mature, aesthetically ambitious "renaissance," then a constituent part of this new formation, however brief, was its use of the city to register an array of institutions in decline and genres in revision. New York in particular would be not just an important backdrop for stories told during this time, but a defining figure for a cinema that deeply questioned the power of the protagonist to shape his or her own destiny. This goes beyond cliché about the city operating as a main character. Rather, it functions as a condition of existence, one that limits individual agency and frustrates collective action. This cycle of urban crisis films contributed directly to the New Hollywood by insisting that those from an earlier era who had treated a network of social ills, and had thus acquired the loosely defined status of hero, now either struggled mightily or disappeared altogether amidst the city and its problems. Or as Dr Herman Bok proclaims in *The Hospital* (1971), "We cure nothing, we heal nothing!"

The cinema and the modern American city had, of course, emerged together as the nineteenth century turned into the twentieth, and for the next 75 years, Hollywood as well as the avant-garde would find in New York a welcome partner to explore issues social as well as personal. From *The Musketeers of Pig Alley* (1913) to *The Crowd* (1928), *Manhatta* (1921) to *A Bronx Morning* (1931), *City for Conquest* (1940) to *The Naked City* (1948), *On the Town* (1949) to *The Sweet Smell of Success* (1957), New York had cradled cinematic visions of crime and romance, upward mobility and the arts, lyrical rhythms, architectural visions, and broken dreams. But in the late 1960s, as American filmmakers left studio confinement in unprecedented numbers, what had been the occasional trip to on-location shooting in the city became a defining feature of film production.

Indeed, what filmmakers found in New York could be understood as a reflection of the industry's own fiscal woes. The decade that saw most of the well-known studios absorbed by corporate conglomerates – Universal by MCA in 1962, Paramount by Gulf+Western in 1966, United Artists by TransAmerica in 1967, Warners by Kinney National Service in 1969, and MGM by Kirk Kerkorian that same year – ended with one of the industry's worst economic crises. Losses by the major studios from 1969 to 1971 have been put at 600 million dollars (Cook 2000, 9). On the front side of this crisis, and in some measure responsible for it, were big budget, family oriented spectacles such as *Dr. Dolittle* (1967), *Hello, Dolly!* (1969), and *Chitty Chitty Bang Bang* (1968). On the other side would come family oriented, quasi-cartoon blockbusters such as *Jaws* (1975), *Superman* (1978), and *Star Wars* (1977). Of course, the era hardly falls into a neat periodization. The family audience and industry prosperity did not reenter the picture at precisely the same moment. As Thomas Schatz, among others, has pointed out, the industry began to find its economic footing as early as 1972 with the success of *The Godfather*, followed by *The Sting* (1973), *American Graffiti* (1973), and *The Exorcist* (1973) (Schatz 1993, 16). But the fact remains that full economic health, indeed a new era in film financing and marketing, emerged at roughly the same point at which the cycle of urban crisis films came to an end. Each of the four films mentioned by Schatz points in directions quite different from the urban projections seen by moviegoers during the late 1960s and early 1970s. The highly profitable fantasies that followed, whether in the form of disaster films, science fiction or action-adventure films with comic strip superheroes, presented either singular, catastrophic events or heroes who could, quite literally, save the world. Such formula pictures stood in stark contrast, then, to the seemingly chronic and intractable problems at the heart of films like *Midnight Cowboy* (1969) and *The Hospital* (1971), *Across 110th Street* (1972) and *Born to Win* (1971).

To be sure, other films from the period – *Bonnie and Clyde* (1967), *They Shoot Horses, Don't They?* (1969), *The Last Picture Show* (1971), *Chinatown* (1974) – offered deeply pessimistic views of American society.

But even their critiques were mediated by temporal distance. The 1930s mise-en-scène, from clothing fashions to automobiles, or the Hank Williams sound track of small-town Texas, mediated their critiques and located such pain in the past. But the New York cycle declared "here is where we are now," and framed its mise-en-scène as an extension of, rather than an escape from, urban streets. In fact, these were streets on which a diminishing number of movie theaters sat and several films registered the urban crisis by referring in some way to the shift in film exhibition taking place at the time. As the enclosed shopping mall and its environs became the preferred site of suburban moviegoing, downtown theaters either closed or turned increasingly to adult-oriented cinema. In *Midnight Cowboy*, for example, Joe Buck finds homeless refuge in one all-night theater and turns his first gay trick in another. *Shaft* introduces its title character with a high angle pan of theater marquees. As the camera moves toward the subway exit from which John Shaft will emerge, it moves from mainstream titles – *The Scalphunters* with Burt Lancaster and *Little Fauss and Big Halsy* with Robert Redford – to the type of exploitation fare that would consume ever greater numbers of downtown screens, in this case a double bill of imports – *School for Sex* and *The Wild Females*. The shift in the early 1970s to hard-core exhibition would be represented five years later in *Taxi Driver* (1976), the film with which the New York cycle reached its nightmarish climax. Here, Travis Bickle, certifying his antisocial character, takes Betsy on a date to a triple-X film, telling her he has seen plenty of couples going to such movies.

Many of the films that would restore the industry to box office health toward the late 1970s also carried the comfort of familiarity. That is, to minimize risk, the film industry turned to presold product in the form of best-selling novels and well-known plays. The result, as David Cook has written, meant that the reach of a given property "could be extended through publishing tie-ins, sound-track albums, and ancillary merchandise – with the promise of creating a 'synergy' in which the film built the book, which built the album, which in turn built the film" (Cook 2000, 27). In many cases, ticket buyers for *The Godfather*, *The Exorcist*, or *Jaws* had read the book, and of course viewers were more than intimate with the characters in *Star Trek* (1979) and *Superman*.

Such familiarity hardly greeted viewers of the New York cycle despite the fact that many of its films were based on previously published material. *The Taking of Pelham One Two Three* (1974), *Midnight Cowboy*, *Madigan* (1968, based on *The Commissioner*), *Death Wish* (1974), *Shaft* (1971), *Across 110th Street* (based on *Across 110th*), and *The Panic in Needle Park* (1971) were all drawn from novels, but these were not, for the most part, bestsellers. Filmmakers turned to these titles for their subject matter as much as their bankability. While the films made from these titles certainly profited from their connections to soundtrack sales, *Shaft* in particular, they were just as likely to have synergistic ties to another, decidedly less commercial sphere, namely the surge in sociological literature published at the time that focused on the plight of urban America. While *The Exorcist* may have kindled an interest in the supernatural or *The Godfather* an interest in organized crime, filmgoers could hardly escape the spotlight thrown by the government, the mainstream press, and nonfiction publishing, on the city in crisis. The connection was clear for films like *Serpico* (1973) and *The French Connection* (1971), both based on popular nonfiction books, and Scorsese's tale of life in Little Italy echoed the title of Piri Thomas's memoir *Down These Mean Streets*.

The City in Decline

Throughout the latter half of the 1960s, an urban studies literature emerged that produced a deeply troubling image of the American city while simultaneously outlining an unprecedented agenda for renewal. To many observers, the great American city was now beginning to resemble a cemetery. Between 1970 and 1974, the nation's murder rate increased by 30 percent. The 1970 census revealed that most of the nation's central cities had lost population during the 1960s. Old residential neighborhoods that did not fall prey to the wrecking ball were often simply abandoned. An epidemic of arson swept through urban America during the 1970s and nowhere worse than in New York's South Bronx. "In 1974 alone," notes urban historian Jon Teaford, "there were 12,300 blazes in the district, or an average of 34 a day" (Teaford 1990, 206). With manufacturing jobs declining and corporate offices moving out, cities were faced with a shrinking revenue base and a remaining urban population increasingly in need of social services. The result was a fiscal crisis, and in some cases bankruptcy, for what had once been the country's proudest and most robust cities: New York, St Louis, Cleveland, Chicago, and Philadelphia. Hollywood filmmakers arrived just in time to record the decline, well prepared to give cinematic substance to concerns about racial violence, persistent crime, and elected officials unable to govern. Indeed, conventionally oriented to represent crisis rather than renewal (it was, after all, easier to script problems than solutions within the standard narrative format), filmmakers could use the urban dilemma to join the wider political and cultural voices of the moment. Historians have noted how few films of this period engaged directly with the era's most pressing events – the war in Vietnam and the Civil Rights struggle. The cinema of urban crisis, however, pursued just such a direct engagement, albeit still cut to the measure of Hollywood's genre demands, with a topicality rarely seen in the American cinema. In the process, the sociological literature about urban problems that came from journalists, academics, and government offices sustained a discourse that provided a backstory for virtually every film set in the city, a sense that no matter what story was being told on-screen, it echoed with the national conversation about the city in decline.

This was certainly not the first time the image of an oppressive or uncontrollable city had circulated through American culture. In the post-World War I novels of Edith Wharton, John Dos Passos, Scott Fitzgerald, and Nathanael West, Sidney Bremer has identified the "eternal emptiness of the megalopolis," a fractured psychological space made palpable through the collage techniques and grotesque imagery of literary modernism. "Discontinuity and the failure of cohering urban patterns," Bremer writes, "as well as lost hopes, often mark the distance between the pre- and postwar New York novels, even those written by the same author" (1992, 115). The city as site of alienation remained a potent trope for American authors throughout the twentieth century. What distinguished the city-as-representation in the late 1960s and early 1970s was precisely those forms that had become available to filmmakers by this point – freedom from studio artifice and the Production Code, the assimilation of various strategies borrowed from the avant-garde and European New Waves. And perhaps most significantly, the documentary impulse that was fueling the direct cinema movement. Indeed, it did not require sociologists or novelists to point out what most people could see out their own window or on a drive through downtown streets. In this sense, the New York cycle carried a strong ethnographic charge as it recorded the city at street-level, the mobility of the handheld camera and shooting on location serving to complement those moments at which actor intermingled with the pace and flow of unscripted New York.

The impulse to document as well as fictionalize New York life received valuable assistance from Mayor John Lindsay in June 1966 when he created the Mayor's Office of Film, Theatre and Broadcasting (Sanders 2001, 343). The new office streamlined the process by which filmmakers obtained permits for shooting in the city and also ended the long-standing practice of graft for police work done on film shoots. In December 1969, the *New York Times* reported a record 45 films had been shot, whole or in part, in New York during that year (Weiler 1969). According to James Sanders, 366 films were made in New York during the eight years of the Lindsay mayoralty (2001, 344). Many more would follow during the Beame administration. In addition to the titles already mentioned, films shot entirely or in part in New York during this time include *Klute* (1971), *Coogan's Bluff* (1968), *Mean Streets* (1973), *Dog Day Afternoon* (1975), *The Landlord* (1970), *Cotton Comes to Harlem* (1970), *Super Fly* (1972), *Shaft's Big Score* (1972), *Law and Disorder* (1974), and *Rosemary's Baby* (1968), all of which deployed the city in some way to represent a fractured social structure informed by violence, racial conflict, and crime. Comedies such as *The Out-of-Towners* (1970) and *Little Murders* (1971) explored similar subject matter. In fact, films that focused on a troubled New York made up only a portion, albeit a sizable one, of the many films shot in the city during these years, but it would be the collective image of urban decline that most thoroughly characterized this revival of New York cinema.

The impression was hardly lost on contemporary critics. "With practically no studios for fakery," wrote Pauline Kael, "the movie companies use what's really here, so the New York-made movies have been set in Horror City … a permanent record of the city in breakdown" (1973, 314). A couple of years later, Vincent Canby offered a similar conclusion, telling readers, "New York has become a metaphor for what looks like the last days of American civilization" (1974, 14). But what struck both Kael and Canby as perhaps most significant about this phenomenon was how filmmakers were embracing a setting beyond their control, how the city forced directors to adapt stories or abandon studio comforts so that now, as Canby observed, "character and accumulated incident replace more conventional plots" (Canby 1974, 19). New York, with its own reputation for cultural experimentation, now also became associated with a breakdown of traditional civic authority, appealing to filmmakers who were tempted to break cinematic rules. In other words, filmmakers found in New York a mode of production that often paralleled ideas at the heart of their films. They clearly embraced this new mode, cherishing the surprises that might come with filming beyond the climate-controlled studio set. Within these films, the message was stark: Place frequently overwhelmed purpose, the patterns of urban life, both physical and psychological, channeled desire and thwarted ambitions in unpredictable ways. In fact, this theme went well beyond New York, resonating throughout the period of Hollywood renaissance. Its most succinct summary came in the closing lines, "Come on Jake, it's Chinatown," that conclude Roman Polanski's neo-noir masterpiece. The implication is clear: Despite J. J. Gittes's best efforts, he has returned to the scene of past troubles and learned once again how illusory is his power to control events. Time and again the myth of personal agency was exposed in films of this time, creating what Thomas Elsaesser, in a widely influential piece, called "the pathos of failure" (1975, 15). The idea ran through almost every genre – in the Western with *McCabe & Mrs. Miller* (1971), the historical drama with *They Shoot Horses, Don't They?*, in the cop film with *Electra Glide in Blue* (1973), in the political mystery with *The Parallax View* (1974), and in the auteurist thriller with *The Conversation* (1974).

But nowhere was this idea explored more thoroughly than in the cycle of New York crisis films. Here, as we will see, is where Hollywood's most potent genres got subjected to a penetrating revision. Here was a space in which to represent and ridicule the civic institutions about which people had grown deeply suspicious, but which nonetheless challenged the individual's efforts to bring about meaningful change. And, perhaps most poignantly, here was the place that had functioned in the American imagination as a site of new beginnings, for immigrant and migrant alike, launching a whole generation into economic mobility, but which now signified a people, as well as its neighborhoods, condemned.

Midnight Cowboy

No film is as central to the New York cycle and, indeed, to the era of renaissance, as *Midnight Cowboy*. Reversing the east to west trajectory of the traditional Western, Joe Buck boards an eastbound bus for New York, convinced that his Western wear and cowboy good looks will be irresistibly seductive to rich Park Avenue women. Surrounded in his hotel room by the signs of 1960s masculinity, a *Playboy* style pinup and a poster of Paul Newman from *Hud*, Joe's naive enthusiasm quickly crashes on the rocks of New York reality. His new friend Rico Rizzo puts it to him straight: "No rich lady with any class at all buys that cowboy crap anymore. They're laughing at you on the street." New York's status as a terminus for the Western, a point made somewhat more ambivalently in *Coogan's Bluff*, is inseparable from the film's sexual politics. By the late 1960s, even small-town Texas recognized the cowboy as masquerade. When Joe shows up at the diner to quit his job he is wearing his new green Western shirt, black boots, and hat. "What the hell you doing in that getup?" his boss asks angrily. But it is the city that has totally reversed the values of that getup, retaining the costume but featuring it now as the accoutrement of the gay subculture. Transporting Joe Buck to New York not only deterritorialized the cowboy, to use Kevin Floyd's term, it exposed the Westerner's inability (and, quite literally in one scene, his impotence) to "conquer a daunting, dangerous frontier" (Floyd 2001, 109). For Floyd, *Midnight Cowboy* functions as allegory for "both a late-60s shift in the U.S. sexual imaginary and a contemporaneous crisis of U.S. imperial nationalism" (2001, 103). Reversing the masculine values of the cowboy and impoverishing him in the nation's economic capital, the film can critique the genre's long-standing defense of US (Western) expansionism and the deployment of Western myths in the war in Southeast Asia. Indeed, as Joe Buck wakes up from the nightmare that combines images of rape in Texas with the collapse of buildings in New York, he finds Rico clutching his radio listening to casualty figures from Vietnam.

But while most scholars have understandably focused on the film's sexual politics and its relationship to Hollywood's shifting approach to the Western, I want to turn attention from Joe to his pal Rico (Ratso) Rizzo and his identity as child of immigrants. For New York's association with immigrants has been at the heart of its cinematic signature. Even when Hollywood presented the city as home to gangsters and tenement streets as a dangerous proving ground for city youth, it often depicted immigrant neighborhoods as close-knit communities. In *City for Conquest*, for example, the city serves as inspiration for the Gershwinesque compositions of Edward Kenny. His symphony of the city translates "the sound of the ambulance screaming across Forsyth and Delancey" into the kind of popular art even the old gang can understand. Anatole Litvak's tale of boxer Danny Kenny serves as a cautionary tale for those who would choose personal ambition over the Lower East Side ethic of hard work and close friends. In *City for Conquest*, New York provides the fertile ground for artistic growth and lasting bonds for the children of immigrants. A similar duality had already been figured in *The Jazz Singer*, where New York offers Jack Robin the opportunity to assimilate, to find fortune within American popular entertainment and return to the old neighborhood to sing the Kol Nidre service on Yom Kippur. In *Body and Soul* (1947), Charlie Davis, another child of immigrants, sells his soul for a shot at boxing glory, only to learn that his conscience and his dignity, not to mention his true love, are to be found on the Lower East Side. From Popular Front dramas to backstage musicals, New York was defined as a place of opportunity, sometimes corrupting, as in *Force of Evil* (1948), just as often creative, as in *Forty-Second Street* (1933). By 1952, both tendencies were acknowledged as familiar conventions when they were musically combined, and nostalgically presented, in the Broadway Melody number in *Singin' in the Rain* (1952). The young hoofer imagined by Gene Kelly's Don Lockwood comes to the big city where he is launched up the entertainment ladder – Vaudeville, Burlesque, the Follies, Broadway – gets seduced and dumped by a gangster's moll, only to return to his roots among the people as a "gotta dance" hoofer. New York as a place that recognized genuine talent and launched careers, where artists and criminals cohabitated, was now the Technicolor product of the dream factory.

But in *Midnight Cowboy*, optimism is extinguished and the past is hardly romantic. Contrary to the storied myth of the immigrant who labors up the economic ladder, the life of Dominic Salvatore Rizzo, Rico's father, was spent hunched over in subway tunnels polishing shoes 14 hours a day until he "coughed his lungs out from breathing in that wax every day." The generation that struggled so that its children would have it better is presented here as illiterate and unredeemable. For Rico there is no old neighborhood. While he proudly introduces himself as "from the Bronx" when he meets Joe, he is reviled as Ratso by others living on the margins. There is no family, no community of mourners mentioned when he visits his father's grave during one of the film's most important scenes. Rather, he remembers the dead with his new companion but is quick to lash out when Joe confesses that boneyards give him the creeps. "So split," Rico tells him, "he ain't your goddamn father." The two men walk into one of the city's giant cemeteries and stand over Dominic Rizzo's grave. The preceding montage, cut to the sad melody of Toots Thielman's harmonica, has just set the tone of decline that will accompany Rico for the rest of the film. Freezing in a cold doorway, the two men watch as demolition workers get ever closer to their home, Rico's hovel. Next is a long shot of both men crossing a bridge opposite a billboard that mocks them with the slogan "Steak for every lunch and dinner." Now in the cemetery, Rico makes explicit the connection between his father's failures and the destruction surrounding his own life, the literal tearing down of the city. "He couldn't even write his own name. X, that's what it oughta say on that goddamn headstone, one big lousy X, just like on our dump. Condemned, by order of city hall."

Rico will now slide inevitably toward his own death on a Florida-bound bus. As if to suggest that the cemetery visit was an encounter with his own impending mortality, the following scene in the diner finds Rico engaging Joe in a conversation about life after death. As they leave the underground party with Joe about to finally succeed with a straight sex hustle, Rico falls down a flight of stairs, a certain sign that his health has begun its final downward spiral. The promised city, to use the title of Moses Rischin's ground-breaking book, that had welcomed immigrants from Italy and eastern Europe, was promised no more.

Figure 7.1 Joe and Rico at the grave of Dominic Rizzo in John Schlesinger's *Midnight Cowboy* (1969, producer Jerome Hellman).

Immigrant City

The New York that had nurtured immigrants between 1880 and 1920, however, was not fully eclipsed from American cultural discourse at this time. In fact, the stark image of New York in crisis found in films made between 1968 and 1976 comes into bolder relief when situated next to the emerging historiographic focus, and coincident nostalgia, turned toward the immigrant experience during these very same years. Initiated in 1962 with the publication of Rischin's *The Promised City: New York's Jews 1870–1914*, the efforts of historians to chronicle life on the Jewish Lower East Side gained full stride by mid-decade, first with an exhibition in 1966 at New York's Jewish Museum titled "The Lower East Side: Portal to American Life," and then with the publication of several important books: Ronald Sanders's *The Downtown Jews: Portraits of an Immigrant Generation; A Bintel Brief*, a collection of letters that had first appeared in the pages of the *Daily Forward*; and culminating in 1976 with the publication of Irving Howe's sweeping history, *The World of Our Fathers*.

These are only the seminal titles of a body of literature that combined rigorous historical inquiry and a romantic yearning for a difficult if more spiritually satisfying era. This work resembled something of a reclamation project, fixing the portrait of a neighborhood at just the moment its last vestiges were disappearing. It reestablished, if only in the imagination, a cohesive, Yiddish-speaking community, an old country in the new world, that gave roots to an ever more dispersed and assimilated ethnic minority. In fact, this historical work had been preceded in the early 1960s by the paperback republication of three canonical Lower East Side novels: Abraham Cahan's *The Rise of David Levinsky*, Michael Gold's *Jews without Money*, and Henry Roth's *Call It Sleep*. The cinema would offer its own version of this project in 1975 with the independent production of Joan Micklin Silver's *Hester Street* (1975). This adaptation of Cahan's novella *Yekl* maintained the book's ambivalence abo the new country, but depicted the Lower East Side as a supportive community for Gitl, the young woman trapped in a miserable marriage. Indeed, its optimistic ending suggests that New York is a place where old and new world values might coexist, as Gitl imagines her second husband continuing his studies while thinking about the grocery store they can own and she will run.

Thus, by 1976, these two competing visions of New York had been in circulation for almost a decade. One gestured backward to frame the immigrant story as one of tremendous struggle and, for the most part, ultimate triumph. The other depicted the city as violently disordered, a home to loneliness rather than community. Just as the cowboy could not civilize the city, the city could no longer shelter the ethnic working class. Francis Coppola's *The Godfather Part II* (1974), while not a part of this cycle of crisis films, offered a similar perspective. Its flashbacks to the rise to power of Vito Corleone imagine Little Italy as a tightly knit immigrant community. Turn-of-the-century lower Manhattan, teeming with street peddlers and budding alliances, is shot in soft earth tones. Here is where Vito's family is born and its close ties sealed. But by the end of the modern-day section, the family has left New York for its compound in Nevada. Family solidarity has been splintered by business, jealousy, and violence. An innocent and proud war veteran at the beginning of *The Godfather*, by the end of *Part II* Michael Corleone, having killed his own brother, and with his power consolidated, sits atop his throne a lonely man. He is a long way from Little Italy.

The Cowboy in New York

Just one year before *Midnight Cowboy*, Don Siegel had explored some of the same terrain in *Coogan's Bluff*, sending a Western lawman to the big city. But Siegel's film only glanced at what Schlesinger's film directly confronted. Drawing upon Clint Eastwood's Western persona, the film tells the story of Arizona Deputy Sheriff Walt Coogan sent to New York to bring John Ringerman, hippie thug, back west for trial. In New York, Coogan is subjected to taunts, a pool-hall beating, and the city's criminal justice bureaucracy. But whereas the city would transform Joe Buck, it merely amuses and frustrates Coogan. His cowboy apparel gets mocked throughout, making him the object of desire for two gay men standing in the 23rd precinct. "Look at all that … in two inch heels," one muses as the two ogle Coogan. Later, a fellow hotel guest calls him a "Texas faggot." But these encounters say little about Coogan's sexuality and much about the revision of sexual iconography by contemporary New York. The cowboy's hetero-magnetism is confirmed by his pursuit and eventual seduction of probation officer Julie Roth.

While Coogan's sexual aims and traditional chivalry are immune to urban corruption, his old-West individualism cannot be so freely asserted. Coogan's trip to New York serves as a civics lesson on the difference between city and desert Southwest. "This isn't the OK Corral around here," Lieutenant McElroy lectures Coogan, "this is the city of New York. We've got a system, not much, but we're fond of it. We don't like it when some two-for-a-nickel cowboy thinks he can bend it out of shape." Unwilling to wait for a state judge to order Ringerman's release, and the doctors at Bellevue to authorize it, Coogan bluffs his way into the hospital, takes the prisoner into custody and then proceeds to lose him. Coogan's search for Ringerman takes him through an almost comic underworld of violent beatniks in which the man of the West ultimately captures his prisoner. Indeed, Siegel remains far too indebted to the genre for his hero to be undone by New York. Rather, he uses the Westerner to argue that the city has corrupted everything from justice to gender roles, America's youth to nature itself. Coogan's tracking skills, first introduced in the film's opening scene in which he locates an Indian in the desert, succeed where urban police methods do not, culminating in a motorcycle chase scene around the grounds of The Cloisters. Coogan's disdain for the dense structural pattern of the city gets articulated when Julie asks him what he is thinking as he looks out over the cityscape: "Trying to picture it the way it was. Just the trees and the river before people came along and fouled it all up."

Siegel makes it clear that Coogan has not totally conquered the city. Coogan's Bluff is not just one man's gambit to end run the rules, it is also a section of upper Manhattan overlooking what was once the Polo Grounds, and it is where the Westerner, prisoner recaptured, learns he must still wait out the city's bureaucratic procedures. Still, by this point, those procedures function as something like comic relief, the product of eastern liberals, Julie Roth among them, who have created a system that leaves no room for men like Coogan. Whereas Joe Buck is redefined by New York, Coogan is merely delayed. The clash of mise-en-scène figures the difference between these films. Joe is devoured by the city, a point made consistently by Jon Voigt's immersion in the real streets of New York. Siegel sets Clint Eastwood on location at various points but relies considerably on studio exteriors that awkwardly situate Coogan in a space resembling a much smaller town.

Coogan's Bluff rests at a point of transition, still invested in the romance of the cowboy lawman, but aware, perhaps nervously so, of his shifting status for urban America. Coogan heads back to the desert, his generic identity dented but still intact. For Joe Buck, there would also be a future but it would have to come without the cowboy getup and far away from the punishing streets of New York. But for Rico Rizzo, the child of immigrants, there would be no retirement to Florida. What would come true for one generation of Jews and Italians, reared in New York, prosperous enough to spend their senior years under the sun, did not come true for everyone. Rico's immobility, both economic and geographical, a condition figured by his one bad leg, stands in for another wave of New Yorkers, African-Americans and Puerto Ricans for whom New York would be a far less hospitable place. For this population, many of whom arrived in the post-World War II period, the New York of the 1960s and 1970s would be characterized by white flight to the suburbs, a diminishing tax base, and shrinking municipal services. Although Rico makes it out of New York, he does not make it out alive. Unlike Joe, but like so many minority New Yorkers at this time, Rico remains bound to the streets, trapped in an abandoned building and a deteriorating city.

The Crisis and Black New York

This is not to suggest of course that the New York cycle simply displaced representations of African-Americans onto ethnic minorities. While the representation of black city-dwellers in these films is complex, we can identify at least two important tendencies. The less pronounced identifies blacks as local residents and bystanders often depicted as caught up in the urban tumult or resisting as a chaotic mass. They populate the madhouse that is the precinct station in *Across 110th Street*, or they are on the streets picketing in *The Hospital*. As such, they are the victims, an angry yet largely powerless crowd and a sign of widespread discontent at the heart of the ungovernable city. Hal Ashby's *The Landlord*, while functioning for the most part as a white integrationist fantasy, was one of the few mainstream films to represent black city-dwellers as something beyond bystanders and other than action figures. In the Brooklyn apartment building that Elgar Enders (Beau Bridges) purchases as his first official adult act, the black residents consistently defy the expectations of their white landlord, exposing the naiveté of the privileged outsider.

The second tendency serves to compensate for the first, asserting the fantasy of power for a black population struggling to survive the city in crisis. This is perhaps less the case in *Across 110th Street*, where Lieutenant Pope's ascent to power eclipses the role of Mattelli, the old-school Italian detective whose methods combine violence, racism, and bribery. In this film, the black icons of the day – Malcolm X, Angela Davis, Muhammad Ali – function as interior decoration, as powerless as the struggling and sympathetic black thieves caught between the police and the mob. In this New York, black power is split between Doc Johnson's underworld control of Harlem and the new NYPD embodied by Pope. *Across 110th Street* refers, of course, to a piece of geography, the point at which a predominantly white neighborhood changes over to African-American. But *Shaft* refers to an individual, the private detective who embodies independence, both professional and sexual. He is not tied down to one woman and he is not indebted to either the black underworld run by Bumpy Jonas or the white police establishment. It is John Shaft who most thoroughly compensates for a population victimized by urban decline. In contrast to the era's prevailing image of a ghetto community increasingly dependent on overtaxed social services, Shaft embodies personal agency. In John Shaft, the revolutionary Ben Buford, and the gangster Bumpy Jonas, the film articulates three paths toward very different forms of empowerment. We might suspect that Shaft's alliance is with Ben, but ultimately the film celebrates his independence. He is neither intimidated by the mob nor a pigeon for the cops, but is respected by both. It is no accident that Shaft lives in Greenwich Village, a sure sign of his independence from the uptown scene. At film's end,

Figure 7.2 Cops and the criminal underworld collide in Barry Shear's racially charged *Across 110th Street* (1972, producers Fouad Said and Ralph Serpe).

he will neither accompany Bumpy's daughter Marcy back to Harlem, nor join Ben and the revolutionary cause. Rather, after a taunting phone call to the cops, of whom he has been one step ahead, he walks off into the night by himself, back to the Village.

But the city was less kind to those in its employ. Although the films of the New York cycle endowed its cop heroes with a rogue individualism and a toughness commensurate with their beat, it just as frequently concluded that the troubled city had now grown beyond their capacity to police. For one thing, the chronic illness spreading throughout the city had now infected the force itself. Cops on the take are a central issue in *Serpico*, *Across 110th Street*, *The Detective* (1968), and *Madigan*. As a result, the protagonists in these films find themselves pitted against two enemies – comrades on the inside and criminals on the outside. To underscore how the city had changed and how an earlier generation of representational values could no longer contain it, *Madigan* (Richard Widmark as Madigan), *The Detective* (Frank Sinatra as Joe Leland), and *Across 110th Street* (Anthony Quinn as Mattelli) cast aging Hollywood stars as cops at the end of the line. Madigan gets his man at the end but is killed in the process. *Across 110th Street* functions to a great extent as a eulogy for Captain Mattelli, gesturing, at points, with admiration in his direction, but ultimately suggesting he belongs to an age gone by. His emotionalism and bareknuckle tactics now seem immature compared to Lieutenant Pope's rationality. The last indignity comes when it is revealed that Mattelli has been on a mobster's payroll. Now fully compromised, his once considerable power undermined, Mattelli, like Madigan, is killed at film's end. In *The Detective*, third generation cop Joe Leland, convinced the NYPD does little more than apologize for, if not enforce the city's mistreatment of its ghetto citizens, hands over his badge. When his commanding officer asks why, Leland's anti-establishment response is simple: "Because there are things to fight for and I can't fight for them while I'm here." In each film, the charismatic lawman with roots in a pre-1960s New

York, and played by a star from the studio era, falls victim to the unmanageable city. Even Popeye Doyle in *The French Connection*, a new generation cop whose rule-bending would make Madigan blush, meets failure in the end. He may act as though he owns the streets, but ultimately he loses the French drug smuggler Charnier, accidentally kills FBI agent Mulderig, and gets removed from the narcotics division.

The Urban Road Film

Midnight Cowboy begins and ends with a road trip, defining flight as a possible and often necessary tactic of survival. The road films of this period – *Easy Rider* (1969), *Two Lane Blacktop* (1971), *Scarecrow* (1973), *Bonnie and Clyde* – punctuated a postwar fascination with cross-country travel, a restlessness that rejected domestic stability. This fascination with the scenes and structures of the highway got articulated in the 1950s by Beat writers and captured in the photographs of Edward Ruscha and Robert Frank. Mobility in and of itself was endorsed as the antidote to the stasis of bourgeois life, the nuclear family, and suburban tranquility. "Movement is always preferred to inaction," Norman Mailer wrote in his essay "The White Negro"; it was the existential response to the horrors of World War II and the ever-present threat of atomic destruction (Mailer 1959, 350). Even the political action of the late 1960s echoed with the tropes of mobility – Freedom Rides, antiwar marching, it was the era of movements.

But in *The French Connection* and *The Seven Ups* (1973), *The Taking of Pelham One Two Three* and *Taxi Driver*, New York bent the open road into a winding circuitry of avenues, cross-streets and tunnels. White-lined pavement running to the horizon, a metaphor for limitless possibilities and an escape to new beginnings, gets replaced in the New York cycle by a crowded and dangerous street life. More than half of William Friedkin's policier takes place outdoors as Detectives Russo and Doyle and Charnier and his American partner, Sal Boca, perform an intricate ballet on foot, in cars, and on the subway across the streets of Manhattan and Brooklyn. What emerges from *The French Connection* is an understanding that the city is home to parallel worlds, one crowded by busy New Yorkers, the other an interplay, largely invisible, of crime and pursuit. In this New York, surfaces can be deceiving. We first meet Popeye Doyle dressed as Santa Claus and Russo as a street vendor; we later see Russo dressed as a postman. On any given street there might be a stake-out in progress; the man walking up the block might be tailing a suspect, the car parked at the curb might be part of an international drug deal.

Beyond anything else, the film is a record of mobility. Yet the movement is circular not linear, it is tightly focused and bounded by the sharp edges of buildings and the constraints of traffic, all of it accruing a tension that will be only temporarily released by the celebrated chase scene in which Doyle commandeers a car and pursues the French killer, Frog 2, trying to flee on an elevated Brooklyn train. Here is the urban (in)version of the cross-country road trip. Whereas the open highway could produce a meditative journey, part ethnographic and part self-discovery, the urban chase is obsessively single-minded. Its pleasure derives largely from its liberation from the rules of the road in a place where the rules are a matter of life and death. As Doyle drives in the wrong lane, ignores red lights, and crashes freely into everything that might impede his progress, the chase becomes the ultimate expression of the need to break the law in order to enforce it. A *tour de force* sequence in Friedkin's film, the New York City car chase also punctuated *The Seven-Ups*, an echo of *The French Connection* with its undercover cops and similar cast. Here, two cars race north through the Upper West Side along Central Park West and Riverside Drive. As if trying to escape the dangerous network of city streets, the lead car, driven by stunt chase coordinator and actor Bill Hickman, heads for the George Washington Bridge and the (relatively) open road of the Palisades Parkway in New Jersey. Now beyond his city jurisdiction, Buddy (Roy Scheider), in pursuit of the criminals, crashes his car into the back of a truck stalled on an exit ramp, his body intact, his car destroyed.

In fact, what New York did to cars certified its status as the American dream in reverse. There is little doubt that for many Americans, owning a new model car was the sign of middle-class achievement, its maintenance a weekend pastime. In *Two Lane Blacktop*, the era's quintessential road film, the 1955 Chevy driven by the two protagonists is the centerpiece of their lives, a hand-built, finely tuned reason for being. In *American Graffiti*, perhaps the most popular city road film of the era, the car is a prized and deeply personal extension of one's self and a central force in the film's nostalgic appeal. But in New York, the car is a target for theft and abuse. In its cover story of April 1, 1969, *Look* magazine asked if the dream city had now turned into a nightmare, and reported that in 1968, 1,500 cars were stolen every week in the city (Astor 1969, 62). Popeye Doyle even steals one in the line of duty. In the New York cycle, cars are not emblems of identity so much as pawns in a larger game, always vulnerable to accident or crime, either frustrated by traffic or a tire-screeching threat to pedestrian life. In *The Seven-Ups*, Buddy's car is incrementally destroyed during the chase, losing hubcaps, having its windshield shot through, getting its sides smashed and having the front hood blown off, leading up to the final crash in which its top gets sheared away. In *The French Connection*, Friedkin's camera relishes the dismantling of the smuggler's Lincoln in the NYPD body shop as Doyle and Russo hunt for the heroin. The city as dangerous encounter between car and pedestrian is summed up in what has become one of *Midnight Cowboy*'s signature moments, the scene in which Rico and Joe are almost hit by a taxi. "I'm walkin' here," Rico yells as he slams his hand down on the front hood. The authenticity of this scene, testifying to the film's realism, is only enhanced by the story that this was an unscripted moment and that Dustin Hoffman brilliantly stayed in character despite almost being run over.

In the New York cycle of this period, the road does not point toward boundless horizons. Rather, it marks a threshold in the verticality of the city, a plane beneath which despair, confusion, and loss circulate. Joe Buck's fall from optimistic grace is registered precisely in such spatial terms. From his first hotel room overlooking mid-town and the penthouse where Cass lives, the course of Joe's descending fortunes travels downward to where he walks the empty subway tunnels at night, the cop on the beat and a crazed woman looking for Grand Central his only company. Subterranean New York is also central to the nightmare montage that mixes black-and-white with color as Joe pursues Rico through empty subway train cars. The haunting nether world of underground Manhattan becomes intertwined with Joe's memories of sexual assault in Texas, something of an archaeological path through repressed images.

When it came to imagining humanity's worst nightmare, Hollywood rested it precisely on top of a buried New York. At the end of *Planet of the Apes* (1968), George Taylor comes to realize he has traveled not through space but through time, his journey winding up at New York Harbor and a half-buried Statue of Liberty. In *Beneath the Planet of the Apes* (1970), astronaut Brent finds Taylor after venturing below ground and finding the ruins of his old home. His journey takes him to what is left of St Patrick's Cathedral where he finds a mutant strain of humanity praying to its last remaining atomic bomb. New York as the graveyard on which the post-apocalyptic future would be built might have made sense to those who already saw the city as signaling the end of civilization. For those who preferred the metaphor of city as jungle, Taylor and Brent had found that as well, a planet now ruled by an empire of violent apes.

For Brent, his nightmare is fully realized when he stumbles upon the ruins of the Queensboro Plaza subway station. As David Pike has persuasively suggested, "the deterioration of the subway came to stand in for the deterioration of the social fabric as a whole" (1998, 11). Unreliable service, crime, and graffiti all came to characterize the transit system and the city's neglect of its citizens. In *The Taking of Pelham One Two Three*, gunmen commandeer a crowded subway car and demand a million dollars ransom. But this is New York in 1974, a city that in the previous decade had witnessed teachers, transit, and sanitation workers walk off the job, where the annual murder rate the previous two years had topped 2,000, and where the economy was now on the brink of bankruptcy. As a result, those in charge of municipal operations have grown so weary it is hard for them to tell a crisis from a nuisance. Bedridden with the flu, the city's cowardly mayor responds to the ransom demands by saying the city does not have a million dollars. Annoyed that the hijacking has thrown off the train schedule, Frank Correll, the head of operations, yells, "Screw the god-damned passengers. What do they expect for their lousy thirty-five cents? To live forever?" Trapped below, the straphangers have a vastly different perspective. Filmed on location in New York and steeped in realistic details about the mass transit system, *The Taking of Pelham One Two Three* suggested that city dwellers in 1970s America were all potential, if not fully realized, hostages.

The mise-en-scène of urban crisis had little room for the abstract beauty of the cityscape. The early American avant-garde had found in the architecture of Manhattan a bold, modernist aesthetic. In Paul

Strand and Charles Sheeler's *Manhatta* and Robert Florey's *Twenty-Four Dollar Island* (1924), the city is arranged as a series of geometric compositions with its spanning bridges and triumphant verticality. In Jay Leyda's *A Bronx Morning*, the city comes to life with a pronounced lyricism, the camera swirling to follow birds in flight or catching sunlight falling on the linear arrangement of fire escapes. Woody Allen would restore some of this interest in *Manhattan* (1979) and *Hannah and Her Sisters* (1986). But the films of the realist cycle featured rubble-strewn lots and garbage-filled alleys. Chain-linked fences cordoned off deserted swaths of property. Toward the beginning of *The French Connection*, Doyle and Russo chase a suspect from residential blocks into a no-man's land of abandonment, an apt spatial metaphor for their methods that go beyond traditional boundaries. The film ends in another abandoned structure, this time a rusted-out and mud-filled public facility on Ward's Island, a site not to be found on any tourist's itinerary. But even a film set within one of New York's most elegant residences suggested that sinister elements lurked within. Roman Polanski's *Rosemary's Baby* begins with an aerial pan of the city before it comes to rest on a high angle long shot of the Dakota Apartment house. After hovering over its intricate roof of gables and dormers, the camera, along with Rosemary and Guy Woodhouse, moves inside where the newly married couple will ultimately fall prey to a coven of Satan worshippers. Presciently inaugurating a decade of films that will argue New York is some form of modern-day hell, Polanski's film literalized the idea, as the devil impregnates Rosemary, a pretty white woman from Omaha who has moved to the big city.

Conclusion

In 1976, Martin Scorsese's *Taxi Driver* brought the New York cycle to its violent culmination. Eight years after *Rosemary's Baby*, it, too, imagined a young white girl victimized by terror city. But whereas Polanski's nightmare was nestled within the eccentric confines of luxury living, an upscale New York haunted house, Scorsese punctuated almost a decade of films set in the streets. Indeed, one can understand *Taxi Driver* as the last urban road film of the era, presenting the pavement as a menacing parade of hookers and pimps, of gun violence and seedy pleasures. The car chases of *The French Connection* and *The Seven-Ups* – and one could perhaps add here the one in *Bullitt* (1968), set in San Francisco – can be understood as highly charged assertions of agency, interruptions of a sort in which the clash between individual action and urban obstacles gets distilled into a single frenetic passage. But as a taxi driver, Travis Bickle has sacrificed all personal agency to be in the service of others, taking them "anywhere, anytime." Popeye Doyle stops for no one; the doors to Travis's cab are open to anyone. Travis is on the road but traveling in circles and the meditations produced by his mobility, rendered largely through his journals, build toward an alienation for which the only remedy will be a violent catharsis.

In *Taxi Driver* the documentary impulse that had fueled many films in the cycle gets routed through Travis, be it through point-of-view shots or reflections in his rear-view mirror, and is ultimately replaced by a more expressionist mise-en-scène. Interiors such as the cold, pasty white colors of Travis's apartment or the office-bland tones of the Pallantine campaign headquarters stand in stark contrast to the psychologized exteriors of New York at night. Underground steam, water-splayed colors, and faces bathed in neon orange and red combine to project a near hallucinogenic space. Seen now in highly personal terms, saving the city can only be understood in personal terms as well. As a result, Travis embraces, as perhaps the film does also, the old-West convention of lone justice. What can be saved in *Taxi Driver* is not the city but the myth of the gunfighter. According to this logic, the city is beyond renewal and the Pallantine campaign ("we are the people") signals the empty rhetoric of contemporary politics. Travis has the power, not to transform his environment, but to temporarily satisfy his own violent desire, to temporarily overcome his feelings of alienation and romantic failure with Betsy. This is certified by her appearance at the end and her look of semi-admiration for him from the back seat. All along, the film has defined the city as sinful in sexual as much as economic terms. Still, the conclusion of *Taxi Driver* is mired in ambiguity. While it takes pleasure in the violent retribution handed out to Sport, it also refuses to fully embrace what Travis has done. Indeed, after his taxi pulls off into the night in the film's final shot, and the credits roll, Bernard Herrmann's score hits the same three notes found in his score for Hitchcock's Norman Bates. Travis may be more psycho than savior.

At the end of *Taxi Driver*, Iris, the young prostitute rescued by Travis, flees the city and returns home to her working-class parents. In doing so, she joined an exodus begun years earlier by Joe Buck and Rico Rizzo, one followed by Bree Daniels (*Klute*), Frank Serpico (*Serpico*), and Paul Kersey (*Death Wish*). In fact, taking flight did not just end many of the New York films, but was a primary feature of the New Hollywood, bringing an uncertain narrative closure to *Five Easy Pieces*, *The Graduate*, *One Flew over the Cuckoo's Nest* (1975), and *Catch-22* (1970).

But it is in *The Hospital*, Paddy Chayefsky's salute to middle-class responsibility, that the impulse to escape gets explicitly stated and then rejected. Dr Herman Bok (George C. Scott) is invited to flee the city and follow the young and alluring Barbara (Diana Rigg) to New Mexico. Besieged by a hospital gone mad, incompetent doctors, a killer loose among the patients, as well as his own alcoholism and decline, Bok refuses to walk away from the crisis. "Someone has to be responsible," he tells Barbara at film's end. "Everybody's hitting the road, running away, running to the hills. Someone has got to be responsible." The Bronx-born Chayefsky, who had come of age at mid-century, had cut his artistic teeth writing for early television and the New York stage and had created sympathetic portraits of working- and middle-class New Yorkers with *Marty* (1955) and *The Catered Affair* (1956). It made sense, then, that as the city fell into crisis, Chayefsky would offer, in Herman Bok, a flawed hero who refused to walk away from New York.

But in the eight years between *The Hospital* and his screenplay for *Network* (1976), a period roughly parallel with the New Hollywood and the cycle of urban crisis films, even Chayefsky's faith appears to have diminished. Perhaps even more than *Taxi Driver*, it is *Network* that punctuates the cycle. Here, the protesting citizenry, as unorganized and undisciplined as it might be in *The Hospital*, has been transformed into an impotent if outraged television audience, their collective passion registered only as ratings points. In the film's *tour de force* sequence, New Yorkers blindly follow the instructions of crazed newsman-prophet Howard Beale, throw open their windows and scream "I'm mad as hell and I'm not going to take this any longer." Over the course of 15 shots, director Sidney Lumet cuts from medium long shots to long shots to one final extreme long shot of the entire wall of a huge apartment building as its tenants release their pent-up anger and frustration. And during this scene, *Network* briefly strays from realist satire into horror film as lightning and thunder explode and echo across the frame. Removed from the streets, the people have been atomized, imprisoned in their separate apartments, their only recourse an empty, TV-prompted complaint shouted at the top of their lungs. It is horror city in the televisual age.

As its economic crisis passed and the New Hollywood gave way to an era of more robust box office figures, New York on screen was no longer defined as horror city. Traces of the cycle recur, most notably perhaps in John Carpenter's *Escape from New York* (1981) in which Manhattan is now the site of a maximum-security prison. But as a coherent cluster of films, the urban crisis cycle had run its course. It is difficult to imagine Woody Allen's *Manhattan* being made in 1969. A decade later, however, the New York auteur could present his favorite town in polished black-and-white set to a George Gershwin score. Its opening montage, cutting from Greenwich Village to Yankee Stadium, Broadway to Park Avenue could end with fireworks over the skyline, the city once again a cause for celebration.

References

Astor, Gerald. (1969). "New York Dream or Nightmare?" *Look*, 33.7, April 1, 61–64.

Bremer, Sidney. (1992). *Urban Intersections: Meetings of Life and Literature in United States Cities*. Urbana: University of Illinois Press.

Canby, Vincent. (1974). "New York's Woes Are Good Box Office." *New York Times*, November 10, 14, 19.

Cook, David. (2000). *Lost Illusions: American Cinema in the Shadow of Watergate and Vietnam 1970–1979*. Berkeley: University of California Press.

Elsaesser, Thomas. (1975). "The Pathos of Failure: Notes on the Unmotivated Hero – American Films of the 1970s." *Monogram*, 6, 13–19.

Floyd, Kevin. (2001). "Closing the (Heterosexual) Frontier: *Midnight Cowboy* as National Allegory." *Science & Society*, 65.1, Spring, 99–130.

Kael, Pauline. (1973). *Deeper into Movies.* Boston: Little, Brown.

Mailer, Norman. (1959). "The White Negro: Superficial Reflections on the Hipster." In *Advertisements for Myself* (pp. 337–358). New York: Putnam.

Pike, David. (1998). "Urban Nightmares and Future Visions: Life beneath New York, *Wide Angle*, 20.4, October, 9–50.

Sanders, James. (2001). *Celluloid Skyline: New York and the Movies.* New York: Knopf.

Schatz, Thomas. (1993). "The New Hollywood." In Jim Collins, Hilary Radner, & Ava Preacher Collins (eds), *Film Theory Goes to the Movies* (pp. 8–37). New York: Routledge.

Teaford, Jon C. (1990). *The Rough Road to Renaissance: Urban Revitalization in America, 1940–1985.* Baltimore: Johns Hopkins University Press.

Weiler, A. H. (1969). "*New York Is Scene of 45 Movies This Year.*" *New York Times*, December 9, 66.

8

Nashville: Putting on the Show
Or, Paradoxes of the "Instant" and the "Moment"

Thomas Elsaesser
Professor Emeritus, University of Amsterdam, The Netherlands

Thomas Elsaesser discusses **Robert Altman**'s ***Nashville*** (1975) – released at the end of the **New Hollywood** era – as a film of multi-layered **paradoxes** that shape its compelling "**constructive instability**." The film comments ironically on a media-saturated culture in which personal emotions and political action exist only as **public performance**, dissolving boundaries between reality and image, story and spectacle, actor/character and audience. Altman's use of setting, complex camera work, sound design, and editing patterns, as well as his revisionist blending of the **backstage musical** and **family melodrama**, work to thematize "**spectacle as compulsive ritual**" in a film deeply **reflexive** of its own construction. In his exceptional model of close formal analysis, Elsaesser also contextualizes *Nashville* in its cultural/historical moment, when "a transfer of ideological tasks ... was underway from 'Hollywood' and popular movies, to 'Nashville' and popular music (with television both mediating and presiding over the transfer)." Elsaesser's essay shares ground with Derek Nystrom on the New Hollywood and Charles Warren on direct cinema documentary in this volume.

Additional terms, names, and concepts: ensemble film, overlapping dialogue, multi-track (unmixed) sound, zoom lens, improvisation, spectator-displacement, "architecture of the look," "architecture of make-believe"

> *Nashville*, that's the new Hollywood, where people are hooked on instant stars, instant music, instant politicians.
>
> Robert Altman

The Loser as Winner

Robert Altman's career can stand as the epitome of the direction the American cinema in the 1970s might have taken – but did not. After an especially "long march" from industrial filmmaking in Kansas City to *Bonanza-type* television work, a break on *Alfred Hitchcock Presents* and a worthy but unappreciated attempt

American Film History: Selected Readings, 1960 to the Present, First Edition. Edited by Cynthia Lucia, Roy Grundmann, and Art Simon.

at making an "outside the box" Hollywood film (*That Cold Day in the Park*, 1969), the enormous success of *M*A*S*H* (1970) promised Altman a degree of control that until then was barely thinkable within the American film industry. It seemed to predestine him to play a leading role in transforming the moribund studio system into a leaner, more dynamic and more responsive "New Hollywood" for the post-Vietnam era and generation.

Why it did not quite work out that way, either for him or for others of his talent, stamina, and temperament, is a question that has kept film scholars preoccupied for the last two decades. There is a general consensus that the years between 1967 and 1975 were one of the more crucial periods in the history of the American cinema, and that – for reasons as diverse and inconclusive as the influence of European New Waves, revisions in the Motion Picture rating system, the loss of the family audience to television, changes in exhibition practice, the Zeitgeist of the anti-Vietnam War protests and the rise of popular music – Hollywood produced a string of remarkably unconventional films and gave a number of remarkably gifted filmmakers breakthrough opportunities. There is less consensus whether this shift of gears and of generations was merely an interim phase in the otherwise consistent historical development of a conservative, risk averse, but adaptable industry, or whether the interlude, however brief and serendipitous, altered the character of American cinema forever. The filmmakers sensed the desire for change and captured the mood of a disillusioned, perhaps more realistic America, but only some of them were able to turn their iconoclasm into the new mainstream. Consequently, there is little agreement about names and labels: New American Cinema, New Hollywood, the cinema of the "movie brats" and "mavericks," just as there is no clear definition of the resulting style: postmodern, postclassical, or merely a minor modification of classical narrative and the canonical storytelling formats. Altman, so much is certain, was a key player in all these games and battles, even if, in retrospect, it is still not clear whether he belonged to the "winners" or "losers," or, indeed, whom time will declare the winners. During his lifetime, it often seemed as if Altman was among the losers, judged by the commercial failure of so many of his projects, and by the fact that his way of making movies did not become the template of Hollywood in the 1980s and 1990s. Yet, given that he was able to make 33 films in 38 years, right up to the time of his death, of which some eight or ten have become classics, his record is impressive and his stature as one of the American cinema's great directors is assured.[1]

Putting on the Show

In light of these ambivalences, it is worth taking another look at *Nashville* (1975), pivotal in that it is Altman's most ambitious film and certainly his best remembered, but also because it premiered the same year as Steven Spielberg's *Jaws*, the director and the film that – by common consensus – did transform Hollywood, reinvented the classical style, by capturing a different cultural moment and representing another America.[2] Altman tried to reinvent Hollywood by perfecting his own (television) techniques, and certainly discovered a daringly original way of making large-cast ensemble films, of the kind excelled in by Hollywood in the musicals of the 1930s and the spectacular epics of the 1950s. But he did this in the idiom of the 1970s, and in a manner that redefined the core Hollywood virtue: the dynamic relation and creative tension between realism and artifice, "life" and "show." Nathaniel Rich, in a retrospective essay, pays tribute to Altman's "acrobatic" style in *Nashville* and his knack for action-as-perpetual-motion, praising what one might call the film's *constructive instability*, as it "always feels poised on the brink of chaos, and it balances there until the final minutes, when an assassin's bullet sends it over the edge" (Rich 2010).

Since it first screened 35 years ago, *Nashville* has remained one of the most written about films in the canon of New Hollywood cinema. Articles too numerous to count, chapters in the many monographs devoted to Altman's works, Joan Tewksbury's screenplay with the writer's commentary, a blow-by-blow account of its making (*The Nashville Chronicles*), as well as extensive, in-depth interviews have left few questions unanswered and even fewer interpretive avenues unexplored.[3] What then, by common consent, makes for the originality of Altman's masterpiece? Overlapping dialogue, and the innovative use of multitrack sound (un)mixing are among the techniques most often mentioned,[4] as is Altman's eye for telling incidental detail, made possible by a camera-style that manages to "cover" several actions at once, while combining the unobtrusiveness of the fly-on-the-wall documentary with the authorial intentionality of the zoom. Beyond these technical and stylistic traits (which, of course, make for an ethic and a worldview in themselves), *Nashville* is seen as Altman's most perfect expression of his perplexingly paradoxical genius. A film quintessentially of its time[5] and uncannily prescient;[6] brilliantly relying on improvisation (see Wexman 1980), and tightly organized in its narrative deep-structure;[7] a heartless satire of the shallow world of Country & Western and a deeply humane vision of an America at the crossroads; a film about the cancerous invasion of show business into politics and a film that merely uses politics and popular music to "get at" the petty tribalism of Hollywood. Altman's uneven box office record made him the Hollywood insider's outsider, and he never quite resolved his own ambivalences concerning the movie colony. Hesitating between Malibu and New York for the best part of his life, Altman, with *Nashville*, did not just enter the art versus popular culture debate, but also reopened an older cultural divide, now not between Hollywood and Broadway, but between *Variety* and the *New Yorker*.[8]

In the early days of the film's impact and fame, I was myself among those who could not get enough of *Nashville*. Having made Altman the hero of a previous essay (1975), I wrote an article for the French journal *Positif* (1977), whose editors were also great admirers of Altman. Although proposing some of the same antinomies and paradoxes that subsequently became the cliché of Altman criticism, I was more interested in another aspect, which had already caught my attention in the earlier attempt to define the New Hollywood: the way Altman, along with other directors, flamboyantly broke conventions of classical storytelling while simultaneously reaffirming or reinstating so many others. This seemed especially true of his approach to genre, where, by reviving the musical, *Nashville* became something like an ode or elegy to the "society of the spectacle."[9]

Nashville as the Stage for a Family Melodrama

Nashville, which fits several possible genre designations,[10] is most robustly "Hollywood" when approached in the tradition of those backstage musicals whose action revolves around the trials and tribulations of "putting on a show." The stage being the eponymous city of Nashville, in the days preceding the Tennessee presidential primary; the show being John Triplette's (Michael Murphy) attempt to mount a preelection rally in order to promote Hal Philip Walker, presidential hopeful and quite possibly sole registered member of the Replacement Party. The conjuncture of show business, sex, and politics is as evident as in the Warner musicals, but there is little of the foot-stomping verve and aspirational brio of the 1930s "New Deal" musicals. Instead of a concerted focus on the final performance, in *Nashville* the energies are "distributive": pointing downward and outward, and dissipating into shabby political deal-making, marital infidelities, and lackluster performances in front of ill-assorted audiences. Whereas in *Footlight Parade* or *42nd Street*, the different individuals and their ambitions were blended and melded together by a ringmaster turned drill sergeant, to culminate in a firework of choreographed energy and a military singleness of purpose, the point about Triplette's show in *Nashville*'s Centennial Park is how reluctantly the participants have assembled there, energized only by Haven Hamilton (Henry Gibson), after he has been shot and the star act has been carried off-stage. Until then, they have been cajoled, persuaded, even bribed into performing on a political platform, not because they support this "New Deal" of taxing the property of churches and bringing politics into the family budget ("when your automobile costs more than what it cost Columbus to discover this continent, that's politics"), but because everyone has a personal motive that Triplette – helped by Del Reese (Ned Beatty), his local organizer – succeeds in synchronizing with his own plans and appears to further with his casually proffered promises. If Haven Hamilton is intimated a state governorship (which recalls both the unsuccessful Roy Acuff and the successful Ronald Reagan) and Barbara Jean (Ronee Blakley) attends because her husband feels the need to restore a tarnished image with her fans, Sueleen Gay (Gwen Welles) and Albuquerque (Barbara Harris) have long been waiting for a chance to perform, while Tom, Bill, and Mary (Keith Carradine, Allan Nicholls, and Cristina Raines) are persuaded to stay, not least prompted by their internal jealousies and rivalries as a trio. In each case, their indifference to politics, whether those of H. P. Walker (a "small government" conservative in a liberal's "tax the rich" clothing) or of the local Southern Democrats, is heavily underscored by Altman, who intimates that the show as promotional tool for special interests – as hidden as the presidential candidate remain faceless – never connects with the personal motivations of the performers that eventually bring the rally into being.

These personal motivations, on the other hand, are not private, in the sense of preserving a sphere of intimacy, protected from the public realm. The characters use show business to test their self-worth and to become celebrities, but even more they need spectacle as a language, a context, and a setting that give the personal the flavor of the intimate, by the very fact that it is performed in public, where it is always on the verge of tipping into indiscretion or banality, shame or embarrassment. This flirting with failure – neatly captured in Barbara Jean's collapse in the middle of her triumphant homecoming and her lapse into incoherence when wandering off-message – is part of the promise and challenge of Nashville itself.

Having to live up to its reputation as unofficial capital of White America's "soul," the home of Country & Western music, Nashville blends the pomposity of its replica Parthenon with the heartfelt hospitality of a plantation mansion barbecue. The image which Nashville connotes and *Nashville* promotes may be corny to the core, but it is one that Altman celebrates as much as he satirizes it: The South as a warm, friendly place where everyone belongs, where one has roots to return to and memories to cling to. It epitomizes a community bonded by patriotism, religion, conjugal love, and above all, by once more declaring the patriarchal family as sacred, while deprecating party politics. But the show sold every night at the Grand Old Opry and packaged by day in the city's recording studios is political in precisely the way Hal Philip Walker understands it: First highlighting the discrepancy between reality and the image, it then offers the image as remedy.[11]

Altman's *Nashville* is of its time and about its historical moment. It documents how a transfer of ideological tasks across the mainstream media was under way, from "Hollywood" and popular movies, to "Nashville" and popular music (with television both mediating and presiding over the transfer).[12] The director rightly sensed that within the culture at large, music by the early 1970s had taken over from the movies as the *lingua franca* of American society's most volatile energies as well as its most traditional values: in the case of Motown and Soul, to assert a "crossover" appeal that wanted to blur racial divides and blend sexual identities, and in the case of Nashville and "country," to reaffirm – after Vietnam and Watergate, and on the far side of civil rights, student protests, or the women's movement – the family as the focal point in the national mythology of primary-instinct emotions and primary-color loyalties. However, songs like "My Idaho Home" or "For the Sake of the Children," no less than "I'm Easy" or "I Never Get Enough," are penned and performed by characters who seem to be in the music business – almost without exception – in order to escape from ties and obligations, broken hearts and bad relationships, traumatizing memories and unhappy longings negatively centered on the family. Hence the seriously ambiguous status of the songs in the film, confirmed by Keith Carradine and Ronee Blakley, key songwriter-performers in *Nashville* (Ciment 1975). Both have commented on the fact that Altman makes ironic-satirical use of songs written "straight," heart-on-my-sleeve, without any tongue-in-cheek. Ronee Blakley pinpoints the crucial dichotomy when she says that in "My Idaho Home" she was able to express in public and through the character of Barbara Jean something she could not tell her own parents in private. Subdued by a bullying husband whose role it is to keep her in an enforced childhood of dependence, fragility, and infirmity ("I've been running your life for quite a while now, and I've been doing pretty well"), the secret of Barbara Jean's appeal is not only that she is everybody's doll and Nashville's sweetheart, but that so powerful a presence (on stage) can combine with so fragile a personality (also on stage). Choreographed around the need to perform "presence" in public, in order to exorcise a dysfunctional marriage in the present and disturbing memories of a past that must have been as traumatic as she claims it was bucolic – her stage acts punctuate the film and provide the subterranean motivation for the violent denouement, not least because the vulnerability and hurt she displays so defiantly are a real threat to the patriarchal order on which Nashville depends. Haven Hamilton offers a further conspicuous example of how the family has to be celebrated in song or on stage, because its reality is so precarious. He is the most patriarchal figure in the film, obsessively paying back-handed compliments to his son in public, while Tom, the most "macho" of the younger generation, is manifestly incapable of a meaningful relationship in private, wooing his women in public with an intensely private love-song: In each case, it is as if the private sphere could be validated only when presented to an audience – in the confessional mode.

Indeed, *Nashville*'s mosaic of mini-narratives proliferates around the disintegration of the family as a viable emotional unit. Its resurrection as projected fantasy or "phantom limb" memory turns the "togetherness" of the family into the "altogether now"-ness of the spectacle. As a substitute or surrogate, "Nashville" offers the synthetic family of performer and audience, where domestic scenes of emotional indifference (Del Reese's home life), cruelty (Tom Frank's bed), and violence (Bill and Mary's marital spats) are exchanged for a song of heartfelt regret ("Since You've Gone"), a hymn to defiance ("We Must Be Doing Something Right") and a gospel of acquiescence ("... It Don't Worry Me").

In other words, *Nashville*'s Country music numbers and stage acts serve to live out in public, as ritual, so many variations on the family melodrama, which Hollywood, 20 years earlier, played straight and in the tragic mode, rather than as musical and satire.[13] The women in particular – no feminist among them – rebel against preordained gender roles; they escape from being wife, lover, mistress, daughter, niece: Albuquerque in perpetual flight from her husband; Sueleen Gay estranges her loyal boyfriend in order to sing on stage "Let Me Be the One" to an indifferent and hostile audience; Haven Hamilton's mistress Lady Pearl (Barbara Baxley) resists by insisting on her outsider-Catholicism, and L.A. Joan (Shelley Duvall), anxious not to be the niece of Mr Green and his dying wife, escapes into the role of a supergroupie with one-night stands.

Once Altman establishes on every level of the action and in every relationship a similar double-bind that motivates the spectacle as compulsive ritual, he plays through the shifting configuration of constituent terms: performers, places, spectators. In order for the sense of togetherness to sustain itself, it has to be endorsed by an audience for only its participation renders the illusion real and efficacious. *Nashville* progresses by assigning to its players particular roles, fixing degrees of distance and participation, at once replacing hierarchies and reorganizing them. Jeff Goldblum's Tricycle Man embodies the flattening effect of the film's decentered circularity, as well as being the minimalist among the army of performers: A silent, mischievous Ariel figure on an Easy Rider chopper, he is both central and marginal, linking places and people, while staying on the sidelines and performing party-magic only for the minutely attentive. While the message of the spectacle is thus couched in the language of the nuclear family, the social "order" that corresponds to this disavowal of deterritorialized randomness presents itself as a fine gradation of poses and postures – from detached observer, mute spectator, faithful fan, and groupie to frustrated would-be performer, star, and superstar – flanked by the paraphernalia of supporting parts necessitated thanks to the logistics and technology of performance: attendants, bodyguards, sessions musicians, sound technicians, photographers, journalists, impresarios, chauffeurs, and hustlers. Given the possible vantage points from which the phenomenal revival of Country & Western music as the successor-rival to Rock and Soul could be viewed, it is remarkable how Altman balances his insight into the politics of this music and the extent of its commercialization with such close attention to the effects spectacle has on the sense of self, and on the distributive positions of audience and performer in social life. When power relations shift from real inequality to the asymmetries and double reflections of the show, putting it on is not enough: "the show must go on," as the film's ending suggests, if both performers and audience are not to be pushed "over the edge."

Altman's Mise-en-Scène

To suggest that *Nashville* belongs to the genre of the musical whose plot is motivated by the different logics of the show is to foreground an aspect that viewers might regard as quite minor, considering the urgency and forward drive typical of the genre is here so singularly lacking. *Nashville*'s characteristic is the meandering plot and the serendipitous narrative, familiar from 1960s European cinema, following Michelangelo Antonioni's *L'Avventura* (1960), Alain Resnais's *Last Year at Marienbad* (1961), and several films of French *nouvelle vague*. This and other examples of "plotless" filmmaking in the 1970s briefly became the hallmark of the "liberal" wing among New American cinema directors, associated with the names of Bob Rafelson, Dennis Hopper, Jerry Schatzberg, and Monte Hellman. But Altman's seemingly laid-back acceptance of contingency and chance in *Nashville* and several of his previous films also manages to lay bare a contrast of attitudes with wider cultural resonance: between those who consider life as a project, to be designed and planned, whose progress has to be monitored and self-assessed, and those who treat life as an adventure, as the opportunity for encounters, possibly or preferably those that will radically change both the direction and meaning one gives to existence. Consequently, a more or less fatal tension develops between protagonists whose behavior is goal-oriented – "pure" idealists like Brewster (*Brewster McCloud*, 1970) and Bill (in *California Split*, 1974), or "anachronistic" idealists like McCabe (of *McCabe & Mrs. Miller*, 1971) and Marlowe (in *The Long Goodbye*, 1973) – and those who relate to the world across quite another level of motivation, communicating with people on impulse or whim (often, the heroes' partners or antagonists, and above all, the women in their lives). Their behavior might seem random, but could also be called "entropic" and likened to the laws of particle physics. Although *Nashville* is a carefully plotted film, with all the narrative pieces eventually fitting together and both mood and tenor subtly modulated to prepare the denouement, one's first perception is that of randomness and accident, both literal and metaphoric, yet – proving the point about plotting – one does not feel either confused or overloaded.

Of the cast of 24 principal protagonists each is etched indelibly with the first encounter, and while their commerce with each other could be described as "molecular" (in the Deleuze–Guattari sense of implying "intensive potential"), their nomadic souls are also in "Brownian motion" (Marks 2006, 81). Like particles in an enclosed space they bounce off each other and ricochet; their contact, fleeting though it is, increases their disjunctive velocity. It is as if we sense the patterns, but our perceptual or even cognitive capacities fall short of grasping or naming them. Haven Hamilton's son Bud, for instance, seems to come into contact with L.A. Joan and Opal solely to launch these ladies in diametrically opposite directions. Like in no other of his films, the gambler's passion and aleatory instincts of Altman here find ample expression without needing to be enacted literally, as in *California Split*, and yet the pathos that can emerge from such chance encounters, as that of Sergeant Kelly and L.A. Joan in the hospital, carries the poignant irony of "bad timing" usually found only in full-blown melodrama.

For some, the risks of involvement, improvisation, and interaction are such that remaining outside the flux of particles that energize themselves through mutual collision feels worse than to accept the synthetic community of "instant stars, instant music, and instant politicians." The character of Opal is a case in point: She is incapable of losing herself or "going with the flow." Her self-conscious perspective on America and on events prevents her from entering into the reciprocating tension of performer and audience. Confined in another kind of sensibility (or insensibility), Opal scans the visual field for depth of meaning of a rather more old-fashioned kind. She is – the satirical treatment of her shallowness notwithstanding – another of Altman's idée fixe idealists. Her pathetic ramblings in the school bus compound or in the car with Linnea during the freeway pile-up are in truth frantic and desperate attempts to extract from the surface of things, from their collage-collision, something like a valid metaphoric language: "vertical" custodian of meaning that to the literary mind ("from the BBC") is meant to survive the evaporation of truth in the performance.

Altman's roving camera movements, his probing zooms and shifting perspectives, along with the overlapping sound from multichannel recordings, undoubtedly help to open up the narrative along the horizontal: The interplay of several media inputs activates different sensory bands and triggers chains of association which create the illusion of richly varied visual and densely textured aural surfaces.[14] But this should not be mistaken for a wholesale abandonment of the more linear, cause-and-effect sequence of actions and events of classical narrative. While the artfully loose string of incidents, typical of the musical with its "numbers," liberates potentialities in the protagonists that emphasize a readiness for taking risks in some, and revealing dangerous idées fixes in others – apart from Opal, mainly those who take no part in the world of the spectacle, like Mr Green, Star (Albuquerque's husband), Lady Pearl who is obsessed with the Kennedys, and of course, Kenny, the loner with the guitar case – the inner logic of Altman's mise-en-scène in *Nashville* nonetheless flows from the

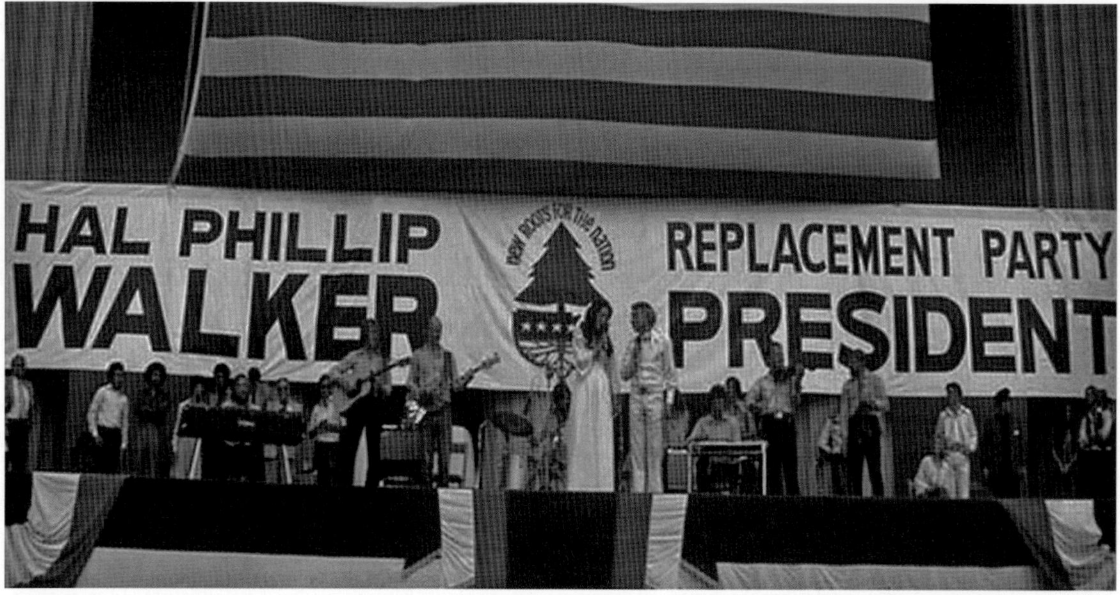

Figure 8.1 Barbara Jean and Haven Hamilton: Nashville gods in front of their own Parthenon, in *Nashville* (1975, director and producer Robert Altman).

exigencies of the central paradox that his film explores so persistently: The spectacle is a festival of the body and the senses, but as a reification of time and space, it freezes social relations, paralyzes political action, and suspends the individual in the permanent "now."

It is this two-sidedness that fascinates the director – the show as the celebration and realization of a new type of community: "instant," spontaneous, unstable, molecular, open toward possibility and chance, and yet also projecting a dysfunctional, neurotic, fragmentary mode of existence, one that pulverizes the very category of "experience" into isolated stimuli and ephemeral sensory shocks. Nashville, the place, is nothing but a succession of stages and ministages: permanent, like the Grand Old Opry; transitional, like the bars with their aspiring nightly acts; improvised, like the airport reception; or "accidental," like the mass pile-up on the freeway. Each time, as soon as movement comes to a halt, the scenes divide up and split into audience and protagonists; the show develops, blossoms, consumes time and space and transforms the world into a communal fairground, which is also a commercial enterprise and a social vacuum. In this, the film recalls Billy Wilder's *Ace in the Hole* (1951), in a humorous key, when ice cream vendors or popsicle stalls appear as if out of nowhere, right in the middle of the freeway. The dynamic of incidents opening out into spectacle renews itself incessantly, and is nourished by the fortuitous presence of any two out of the triad: spectator, place, performer. Not only can every place become a stage if there is a public, but if there is an audience there will be performers willing to fill the hiatus of waiting: the drum-majorettes at the airport from the Tennessee twirling academy, or Albuquerque mounting a platform rig and singing inaudibly against the roar of engines on the race track. Speed, mobility, and spectacle appear as the only modalities that afford the experience of feeling oneself "real."

In interviews, Altman was careful to both promote and sidestep the impression that his films are "improvised" (Rosenbaum 1975, 91). Rightly so, because improvisation as inspired impulse or formal variation of a given theme were certainly his *topics*, but they were part of his *method* only insofar as they helped him get closer to something that to him was "real."[15] When, much to screenwriter Joan Tewksbury's chagrin, he allegedly told the actors to "toss away the script,"[16] it was because he made sure they had internalized their part, that is, they knew their place and function in the unfolding Altman landscape, extended before director's inner eye. This is perhaps why Michael Henry called the director of *Nashville* an action-painter, treating the actors as so many colors or daubs on his "palette" (Henry 1975b). But one wonders whether Altman, rather than the Jackson Pollock of the New Hollywood, is not also second cousin to Jean Tinguely, master of the sculpted happening-machine, elaborately setting up conceits of mechanical parts that take on a life and a dynamics of their own: "In *Nashville* more than any other film, what we did was sort of set up events and then just press the button and photograph them, pretty much like you would a documentary" (Altman quoted in Byrne & Lopez 1975–1976, 15). Through the logic of the happening, that category of the auto-generated, non-purposive event in which otherwise hidden energies are allowed to emerge, Altman becomes the ethnographer of spectacle in the very idiom of spectacle, letting a world transfixed by the treacherous substantiality of the image "document" its slippages between performance, person, and personality, and thus enact its own "professional deformation." In other words, this paradox or dilemma is the "script," and the command to "toss it away" is Altman's ironic comment on the very impossibility to do so.[17]

A History of the Present: One-Dimensionality, Flatness, and the Spaces in Between

The documentary or ethnographic method in *Nashville* does not contradict Altman's dramaturgical concern with the clashes of different points of view, his love of oblique or impossible angles, the fragmentation and *mise-en-abime* of his images: They all serve to establish how worlds function that consist mainly of mutually reflecting fantasies, at the intersection of people's imaginary projections. It is a theme abundantly evident in his films before and after *Nashville*, from *McCabe & Mrs. Miller* (1971) and *Images* (1972), to *Buffalo Bill and the Indians* (1976), *Health* (1980), and *Come Back to the Five-and-Dime, Jimmy Dean, Jimmy Dean* (1982), which helps inscribe a continuity in his work, but also gives consistency to Robert Benayoun's claim of Altman as an "American moralist."[18] It places his films in an American literary tradition, as well as in a cinema pedigree we think of as both "classical" and "European." His self-confessed "obsession with reflections, images"[19] puts him in a line of descent from Hitchcock, Ophuls, Preminger, via Cukor, Minnelli, Sirk, to Billy Wilder, Frank Tashlin, and Blake Edwards, all of whom are directors whose works have provided a running commentary on the United States as a country and a people living by the self-fashioning as well as self-deceiving iconography of its media. Altman's box office problem – his seeming lack of popular appeal at the time each film premiered (if one excepts *M∗A∗S∗H* from the early period and *The Player* (1993), *Short Cuts* (1993), and *Gosford Park* (2001) from the final decade) – stems in part from the fact that his films can rarely be summed up in a sentence,[20] but also that they addressed, through wit and satire, an audience that had internalized celebrity and show business so completely that any version of reality inherently not in the mode of the show, or critical of the performance of self, lacks plausibility and conviction. Altman's satire is so deadpan or slippery because it has to operate without a position shared with the audience, from which it could direct its jabs. As a result, it appears sour and misanthropic, leaving spectators at a loss how to take the tone.[21] The same applies to the protagonists: Parallel to Carradine and Blakley's discomfort at seeing their songs used ironically, the Country & Western community at first distrusted the film, regarding it as mean-spirited and elitist.[22] With time, Nashville has come round to embracing *Nashville*: nostalgia, narcissism, and cult status no doubt helping.[23]

Yet, in a wider sense, too, time has been on Altman's side. Reified to the point where it is the touchstone of the real, the spectacle is in the sphere of perception and self-perception what money is in the sphere of economics and the market: a great leveler, a force subjecting all other values to its own laws. It is in this sense that (feminist) film theory regarded narrative and spectacle as hostile to each other. Narrative is an affirmation of progress and development, of energies inflected toward meaning and purpose, with an implicit acknowledgment of history as propelled by a telos or purpose; while spectacle in this respect is not only a form of looking and being looked at, of dividing the world into performers and spectators, but an arbitrary, contiguous distribution of energies, the suspension of goal and direction, the sacrifice of history in favor of the eternal recurrence of ritual, defined by a spatial configuration, where the horizon of aims and means collapses as they get caught up in the mirroring gazes of mutual self-confirmation. Altman, after giving America in *Nashville* the history of the present (his present for the Bicentennial, as it were), set out in search of past American history with *Buffalo Bill and the Indians* (his film immediately after *Nashville*), to discover already back in 1885 only prearranged tableaux, staged scenes, and fake images. His Buffalo Bill is the very type of hero unable to assume a role as performer without being constantly tempted into becoming the narcissistic spectator of his own mise-en-scène. Even the myth of the Conquest of the West, containing too much narrative (and a telos that by 1977 much of Hollywood felt obliged to discredit and repudiate), shrinks to the "one-dimensionality" of the Wild West show.

But if action is reduced to the suspended animation of spectacle, this spectacle in itself need not be one-dimensional; layered by the multiple points of view that sustain its reality-effects, Altman in *Nashville* provides critical leverage without becoming distant. Hence the fruitful ambiguity in his mise-en-scène: capable of suggesting a mental space – the abstract form of all these events, the inner theater of a collective mind, so to speak – he also depicts these events with the pure externality of a "mural tapestry" (Henry 1975a). In line perhaps with the reigning avant-garde orthodoxy of the period, *flatness* is Altman's aesthetic credo even more than one-dimensionality is his critical theory.[24] Enacting a kind of zero-degree of perspectival vision through the use of the zoom, he implies the possibility that film technology has intervened, if not in the mutations of human perception, then in the fine arts aesthetics. It suggests a hidden dialectic between high culture and popular media that once more marks the historical moment: the technical advance in sound recording, the increased mobility of video, contrasted with the stasis or stagnation in the apparatus of cinema. For the dialectic also extends to the relation between movies and music mentioned earlier: The more the movie's aural soundscape provides depth, layeredness and "perspective," the more the imageplane can content itself with pure surface and explore the spatiality of human interaction.

The abstract or cerebral aspects of Altman's mise-en-scène make *Nashville*, in more than the sense indicated by the quotation heading this essay, a film about the cinema, but not necessarily in the usual mode of self-reflexivity. What is striking – perhaps even more so in retrospect – is that the cinema finds itself reworked in the idiom of music, insofar as it needs a cinematic imagination in order to appreciate and comprehend the pattern of participation, performance, and presence which sustains the spectacle.[25] The opening scene in the recording studio, the gala night at the Grand Old Opry, Tom Frank singing at the Exit Inn, and the final rally in Centennial Park are almost textbook exercises of how to dramatize space through the rhythm of seeing, looking, being seen. In each location, camera angles and editing punctuate and structure the event in order to "place" the viewer inside the show, involve him (Altman leaves no doubt about "the male gaze") by privileging his vision, only then to relegate him to the casual and peripheral witness that he also is. When Connie White (Karen Black) performs at the King of the Road, she says to the audience: "that's what I like about this place – I can't see you and you can't see me." She makes explicit what the film recalls at crucial moments: the hazards of being a spectator, and not just its pleasures. Sueleen Gay's striptease at Trout's Club is given neither soft-porn velvet glamor, nor the suggestion of hardcore brutishness: Altman, who shows the assembled male audience's deterioration into ogling and leering drunks without explicit didacticism, enforces the point of our discomfiture by placing his camera at the crucial moment in a most disadvantageous position, with the young woman's frail nudity blotted out by the bandstand.

The cinemagoer, as voyeur or uninvited guest, has to make do with a particularly poor seat at the show, because to flatter the spectator at this point would be to render invisible a key critical dimension of the film, which is the most palpable sign of Altman's authorial presence.

The sequence where Tom Frank sings "I'm Easy," the number that won Carradine an Oscar and a Golden Globe, is outstanding for its complex handling of emotional tensions as well as its architecture of looks. Composed of shots that take a physical space and make it erotic by the indeterminate gaze of Tom, as it intersects with the longing or radiant look of the four women to whom he seems to be individually addressing himself, the scene has such a lingering impact because of a further dimension, which inscribes a presence that is visually absent. For the point of intersection is the spectator rather than either Tom or the individual women. All characters involved look directly into the camera: The

Figure 8.2 Linnea Reese (Lily Tomlin) and Tom Frank (Keith Carradine) in *Nashville* (1975, director and producer Robert Altman).

conventional sense of a real space "out there," in relation to which we are mere observers, does not materialize; the type of shot one most expects at such a dramatic moment, such as a reverse-field shot – returning the look, say, between Tom and Linnea (Lily Tomlin), to confirm the visual axis and generate the impression of three-dimensional space – is suppressed in favor of a visual openness that draws in the spectator and makes him the stand-in for the fictional character, rather than vice versa, as is the rule. Altman's multiple cameras insinuate themselves within a visual field that cannot be comprehended within a top-down, or male–female hierarchy: The scene demands a spectator-displacement in some ways as radical as in a play by Brecht, while being orchestrated by means of a mise-en- scène that is as classical (in its momentary transgression of the rules) as that of any of the Hollywood directors mentioned above.

If withholding the master-shot, the close-up, or shot-counter-shot at the expected places creates a critical gap that involves the spectator emotionally via "perception and its dislocation," the show at the Grand Old Opry becomes a claustrophobic nightmare by the sheer surfeit and redundancy of spectatorial presences, layer upon layer. The promiscuity of audiences on-stage, offstage, and in the auditorium is already stifling, before the performers themselves begin to play at being spectators. Haven Hamilton is looking at the audience while the camera looks at his back, thus assuming the point of view of his entourage, sitting as audience on stage while in full view of the auditorium. Photographers are below-stage and up-stage, as emcees introduce the performers and then lead the applause; each new star brings on stage his or her own family or associates, while the camera picks out the faces of those who are to be the main protagonists in the final act of the drama. As a dizzy uncertainty about who is watching whom envelops the scene, a further Pirandellian twist is introduced with a cut to the hospital room, where the show has its irritated listeners in Barbara Jean and her husband Barnett (Allen Garfield), already engaged in a bad marital fight, with Barbara Jean badmouthing her replacement Carol White, while having to endure Haven Hamilton's sentimental appeal to her fans not to forget that "she cried real tears" about not being able to perform at the show.

By contrast, at the final rally in Centennial Park, these various architectures of the look and of spectatorial displacement make way for a different architecture of make-believe. First, it is the camera, distant, hovering, or zooming in, but each time flattening out all sense of depth, that gives the event no more than surface texture. Second, such flatness befits a place whose landmark is a plaster-of-Paris replica of the Parthenon, a mere piece of stage scenery, originally built for another show, and which the citizens of Nashville had rebuilt in concrete and stone to commemorate their own presumption. This piece of self-conscious history of American image-making with borrowed plumes Altman ingeniously appropriates for his film's final grand design, muffling its monumentality in a sea of faces and the mediocrity of the songs. Despite Haven Hamilton's protestations ("This isn't Dallas, this is Nashville") destined to become the scene of another national cliché – the "lone-nut" assassination – the Parthenon is also a sign that the spectacle in *Nashville* was indeed a political category all along, not only because Triplette had managed to co-opt Nashville stars to collude in a political propaganda show, but because in Nashville the very signs of history signal the "end of history," in the sense of Jean Baudrillard's (1983) simulacrum, where the copy's hyperreality destroys the original by making it obsolete. Casting a wary eye at what was implied by "postmodernism" before the term had gained currency, Altman found a uniquely emblematic as well as enigmatic shot to encapsulate this message. When Hal Philip Walker is finally about to appear in a motorcade of black limousines, the camera zooms in on his arrival, but our view is conspicuously blocked by the very pillars of Nashville's monument to artifice. With the oversized symbol of the city's pretension of being "the Athens of the South" as an obstructing backdrop, this black Cadillac, possibly not even containing a presidential candidate of doubtful credentials, is an appropriate update of the Emperor's New Clothes, now in the automotive idiom that resembles a funeral.

Nashville and Vanitas: Country Music's Funereal Baroque

As virtually every vista of transparent perception (the classic cinema's way of establishing the realism of its representations) is partially obscured by obstacles, by spectators' backs, or a deliberately skewed and awkward camera angle, one realizes why Altman, in so many ways the most classical director among the New Hollywood generation, is also a harbinger of the post-classical, in a mode that makes him a bridging figure of transition, comparable in this respect perhaps only to Stanley Kubrick's equally pivotal role. Rather than a postmodern cynic or relativist, Altman shows himself in *Nashville* possessed of that same Baroque sensibility of vanitas and melancholia, of mirror mazes and trompe l'oeil effects that had served Kubrick from *Lolita* (1962) and *2001 – A Space Odyssey* (1968) to *Barry Lyndon* (1975) and *The Shining* (1980) to give his skeptical realism an unsettling edge of cosmic doubt. Despite the seeming openness and loosely joined narrative of *Nashville*, Altman's final tableau is one of claustrophobia and menace, into which the shot from Kenny's gun bursts as if to break the spell that the spectacle of so much make-believe had cast over the people and the place. But this fatal shot, despite the brief shock it causes among performers and audience, and despite the grieving cortege that takes Barbara Jean's prostrate body offstage, fails to deliver finality or closure, because it leads, in true Baroque spirit, merely to another spectacle. As a terrified Albuquerque grabs the microphone and with it her chance to become a star, present fear and past trauma reveal themselves as the true reasons why "the show must go on," on this stage, as well as on the one of national politics. As the song's refrain "it don't worry me" is quickly taken up by the crowd, the performer most in need of the spectacle is the audience itself, defiantly in denial. With a slow backward track, Altman extends an invitation of participation to those in the cinema seats, and an eerie feeling of something peeling off the screen overcomes the spectator when the heads in front of the movie spectator imperceptibly begin to merge with the backs of the chanting crowds in Centennial Park, prompting not the famous question, posed in Jean Renoir's *The Golden Coach*: "where does the spectacle end and life begin?" but rather: Where does the show end and our collective death-in-life begin?

Such intimations of a Baroque *memento mori* beneath the rhinestone-and-taffeta glamour of Country music, of Nashville and what it stands for, clearly appeal to one side of Altman's saturnine imagination, but the director himself has also suggested a less apocalyptic and more equivocal reading:

> That song [at the end] is double-edged. I think it's both a negative and a positive comment. In one way you can say Jesus, those people are sitting there singing right after this terrible thing happened; that shows their insensitivity. … You ever watch an automobile accident? People will sit there and gawk, then get back in their car, turn

the radio on and finish their Pepsi-Cola ... So what you really have to wonder about is the reason for it or the lack of reason for it. We sit and demand such great answers in our drama but in our lives we'll accept anything. (Altman quoted in Byrne & Lopez 1975–1976, 25)

In *Nashville*, we accept the paradoxes of the "instant" and the "moment" that is the cinema: most vividly "present" when "putting on the show," most thrillingly alive when poised precipitously close to death.

Notes

Chapter epigraph from Paul Gardner, "Altman Surveys *Nashville* and Sees Instant America," *New York Times*, June 13, 1976, II, 26.

1. "Has there ever been another director who failed at the box office so often, and so regularly? Most Hollywood directors don't survive one flop, let alone twenty-five. But Altman the gambler, the schemer, kept finding ways to make films" (Rich 2010).
2. For a symptomatic reading of these two films, as the recto and verso of the US Zeitgeist and its ideology at this point in time, see Hoberman 2004.
3. See Wexman & Bisplinghoff 1984, and the listing of articles (only up to 1999) at http://www.filmreference.com/Films-My-No/Nashville.html (accessed April 2011). The twenty-fifth anniversary in 2000 produced another slew of books and articles, including a survey by Ray Sawhill (2000) in *Salon.com*.
4. "[W]e used an 8-track system and it's really unmixing rather than mixing sound. We'd just put microphones on all the principals ... [and] they all go down on different tracks, pretty much the way music is done today. And in our musical sequences we had an additional 16 tracks" (Altman quoted in Byrne & Lopez 1975–1976, 15).
5. "Nashville is one of the great examples of why 'dated' is sometimes impotent criticism to level at a movie. This one was made to be dated, and as such it is a brilliant satire of America immediately prior to the Bicentennial. It is a movie about the moment, but the moment lives on." At http://www.brightlightsfilm.com/32/nashville.php (accessed April 22, 2011).
6. Altman has been credited of having predicted – and accused of having inspired – the assassination of John Lennon, five years later. See the director's response in an interview included in the 2000 DVD release of *Nashville*, also cited verbatim on the film's Wikipedia page, http://en.wikipedia.org/wiki/Nashville_%28film%29 (accessed August 10, 2010).
7. "Altman's storytelling is so clear in his own mind, his mastery of this complex wealth of material is so complete, that we're never for a moment confused or even curious. We feel secure in his hands, and apart from anything else, 'Nashville' is a virtuoso display of narrative mastery" (Ebert 1975).
8. Almost as famous as the film is Pauline Kael's gushingly enthusiastic, but perceptive prerelease review in the *New Yorker*, which apparently irritated many industry professionals on the West Coast, unless it merely made them envious (Kael 1975).
9. The term had made its entry a few years earlier, with Guy Debord's manifesto *La Société du spectacle*, first published in 1967 and translated into English in 1970 and 1977 (Debord 1977).
10. "It is a musical ... It is a docudrama about the Nashville scene. It is a political parable, written and directed in the immediate aftermath of Watergate ... It tells interlocking stories of love and sex, of hearts broken and mended. And it is a wicked satire of American smarminess" (Ebert 2000).
11. "Country music, like much of our popular culture, feeds on contradictions – extremes of long-suffering and self-indulgence, mildness and brutality, piety and hedonism, discipline and misrule" (Clark 1976).
12. "[*Nashville*] is, in one significant respect, a popular film *about* popular film and about popular culture in general, though, paradoxically, it implies that popular film is less popular, less central to popular culture, than such media as television, radio, and records. However, as a film, *Nashville* also bridges the gap between popular and 'elite' culture by being at once an entertainment and a formidably artistic metaphor for nothing less than the United States of America in the latter quarter of the twentieth century" (Rollin 1977, 41).
13. For family melodramas in the tragic mode during the 1970s, the central reference is Francis Coppola's *Godfather II* (1974), which, in the genre of the gangster film, details the corrosive effects of capitalism – as well as show business – on the family and on gender roles.
14. At the airport arrival scene, Altman prominently features the presence of the local TV news, to which his own camera provides the counterpoint. While the TV camera pans left to anticipate some action, Altman's camera leisurely sweeps to the right, in a movement that commands attention as it takes control, putting the rival in the junior place.
15. For a detailed discussion of Altman, *Nashville*, and improvisation, see Wexman 1980.
16. Geraldine Chaplin, who plays Opal, remembers the first day on the set: "Altman said, 'Have you brought your

scripts?' We said yes. He said, 'Well, throw them away. You don't need them'" (quoted in Rich 2010, from Zuckoff 2010).

17. As Buck Henry observed: "An Altman set was different because everyone felt they were collaborating – of course they weren't." Quoting this line, Nathaniel Rich (2010) concludes: "The deepest contradiction with Altman lies in this disparity between the spontaneous, anarchic feel of his films and the rigorous planning that produced them."
18. Robert Benayoun (1975) has compared Altman with Kurt Vonnegut, Jr. Vonnegut in turn has called *Nashville* "a spiritual inventory of America, frank and honest" (1975, 103).
19. See Michel Ciment's interview with Carradine and Blakley (1975), from which the remarks here attributed to them are taken.
20. "Commercially the biggest problem with the film is that it doesn't have a shark. So nobody really knows except by word of mouth ... And you say What's it about? And, well, you can't answer that. So that's the problem every time you do a film that doesn't have an absolute, one focal point" (Altman quoted in Byrne & Lopez 1975–1976, 13).
21. "To a considerable extent, Altman resists [the] temptation [of satire], electing to strive for something that is far more difficult, more ambitious, and in the end more humane – a depiction of our national character that is as comprehensive as one movie will allow, employing a variety of points of view ranging from the satiric to the sympathetic" (Rollin 1977, 42).
22. "The *Nashville Banner* ran a big front-page headline saying 'Altman's *Nashville* Down on Nashville.' – [W]e had a screening before we opened in New York for the people in Nashville who contributed to the film. They had a lot of press down there, but it didn't amount to very much. The musicians like it. Some people thought it was too long. Some people thought that the music was not authentic, and some thought it was. It was kind of a bore" (Altman quoted in Byrne & Lopez 1975–1976, 16). For more on *Nashville* in Nashville, see Stuart 2004.
23. There is still some uncertainty as to whether *Nashville* was considered by the industry a success or not. Altman claims that it was the first of his films since *M**A*S**H* to make him any money, but Hollywood producers seem to have thought otherwise: "Originally I came out here with a script with a lot of scenes in it and a lot of characters. A former head of Columbia, who was the producer I was talking to at the time, said, 'Oh, that's very Nashvilleian.' And I said, 'Oh, great!' I took it as a positive, not knowing he meant it as a negative" (MacDonald 2003, 7).
24. The reference here is to Herbert Marcuse's then widely read *One-Dimensional Man: Studies in the Ideology of Advanced Industrial Society* (1964), which argued that the supposed freedoms of liberal democracy disguised the coercion to consume and entailed the unfreedom of neurotic needs. The final song in *Nashville*, with its refrain "some might say that I ain't free, but it don't worry me" could be taken as an ironic response to Marcuse.
25. "I don't think we've found a format for movies yet. I don't believe the film should be limited to the photographing people talking or walking from a car into a building, that kind of stuff we do. It can be more abstract, impressionistic, less linear" (Altman quoted in Holdenfield 1975, 31).

References

Baudrillard, Jean. (1983). *Simulations*. New York: Semiotext[e].

Benayoun, Robert. (1975). "Altman, USA." *Positif*, 176, December, 32.

Byrne, Connie, & Lopez, William O. (1975–1976). "*Nashville*." *Film Quarterly*, 29.2, Winter, 13–25.

Ciment, Michel. (1975). "Jouer avec Altman: Rencontres avec Ronee Blakley et Keith Carradine." *Positif*, 176, December, 45–49.

Clark, Roy P. (1976). "Unbuckling the Bible Belt." *New York Times* (national edn), July 6, sec. E.

Debord, Guy. (1977). *Society of the Spectacle*, trans. Fredy Perlman. London: Compendium. (Originally published as *La Société du spectacle*, 1967.)

Ebert, Roger. (1975). "*Nashville*." Review, January 1. *Roger Ebert.com*, at http://rogerebert. suntimes.com/apps/pbcs.dll/article?AID=/19750101/REVIEWS/501010346/1023 (accessed April 2011).

Ebert, Roger. (2000). "*Nashville*." Review of DVD re-release, August 6. *Roger Ebert.com*, at http://rogerebert.suntimes.com/apps/pbcs.dll/article?AID = /20000806/REVIEWS08/8060301/1023 (accessed August 10, 2010).

Elsaesser, Thomas. (1975). "Pathos of Failure: Notes on the Unmotivated Hero." *Monogram*, 6, October, 13–19.

Elsaesser, Thomas. (1977). "Ou finit le spectacle?" *Positif*, 197, September, 23–27.

Gardner, Paul. (1976). "Altman Surveys *Nashville* and Sees Instant America." *New York Times* (national edn), June 13, sec. 2.

Henry, Michael. (1975a). "Altmanscope (sur le plateau de *Nashville*)." *Positif*, 166, February, 19.

Henry, Michael. (1975b). "La Palette de l'action painter." *Positif*, 166, February, 3–7.

Hoberman, J. (2004). "'*Nashville* Contra Jaws': Or 'The Imagination of Disaster' Revisited." In Thomas Elsaesser, Alexander Horwath, & Noel King (eds), *The Last Great American Picture Show: New Hollywood Cinema in the 1970s* (pp. 195–222). Amsterdam: Amsterdam University Press.

Holdenfield, Chris. (1975). "Zoom Lens Voyeur." *Rolling Stone*, July 17.

Kael, Pauline. (1975). "The Current Cinema." Preview of *Nashville*. *New Yorker*, March 3.

MacDonald, Scott. (2003). "Hollywood Insider–Outsider: An Interview with Chuck Workman." *Film Quarterly*, 57.1, Autumn, 2–10.

Marcuse, Herbert. (1964). *One-Dimensional Man: Studies in the Ideology of Advanced Industrial Society*. Boston: Beacon Press.

Marks, John. (2006). "Molecular Biology in the Work of Deleuze and Guattari." *Paragraph*, 29.2, July, 81.

Rich, Nathaniel. (2010). "The Gambler." *New York Review of Books*, 57.4, March 11, at http://www.nybooks.com/articles/archives/2010/mar/11/the-gambler-3/?page=2 (accessed October 25, 2010).

Rollin, Roger B. (1977). "Robert Altman's *Nashville*: Popular Film and the American Character." *South Atlantic Bulletin*, 42.4, November, 41–50.

Rosenbaum, Jonathan. (1975). "Improvisations and Interactions in Altmanville." *Sight & Sound*, 44.2, Spring, 90–95.

Sawhill, Ray. (2000). "A Movie Called '*Nashville*.'" *Salon.com*, June 27, at http://www.salon.com/entertainment/movies/feature/2000/06/27/*nashville*/index.html (accessed April 2011).

Stuart, Jan. (2004). *Nashville Chronicles: The Making of Robert Altman's Masterpiece*. New York: Limelight.

Vonnegut, Kurt. (1975). "*Nashville*." *Vogue*, June.

Wexman, Virginia Wright. (1980). "The Rhetoric of Cinematic Improvisation." *Cinema Journal*, 20.1, Autumn (special issue on film acting), 29–41.

Wexman, Virginia Wright, & Bisplinghoff, Gretchen. (1984). *Robert Altman: A Guide to References and Resources*. Boston: G. K. Hall.

Zuckoff, Mitchell. (2010). *Robert Altman: The Oral Biography*. New York: Knopf.

9

Cinema and the Age of Television, 1946–1975

Michele Hilmes
Professor, University of Wisconsin–Madison, United States

Although the advent of television posed box office challenges to the film industry, the artistic relationship between the two was initially collaborative, as Michele Hilmes points out. Later court rulings, springing from the **1948 Paramount decision**, however, enforced a seemingly adversarial structure that soon would be overcome. Tracing affiliations between the broadcast and film industries (including **radio**), Hilmes illustrates the shared creative efforts among producers, directors, and talent working in all three mediums. As in early cinema, women played a crucial role in early television production companies and programming – with such key figures as **Lucille Ball**, **Joan Davis**, and **Loretta Young**. **Hannah Weinstein's Sapphire Productions**, with the help of **British television**, employed many of **Hollywood's blacklisted writers**, whose pseudonyms signaled high-quality programming, while also indirectly subverting the ideology that had ousted them. Hilmes traces the evolving film–television relationship from the 1950s through the 1970s, when the concept of **synergy** took hold. Her essay shares ground with Derek Nystrom on the New Hollywood and Barbara Klinger on Hollywood and cable television in this volume.

Additional terms, names, and concepts: voiceover narration, newsreel, theater television, subscription TV, FCC, UHF, Fin-Syn rules, situation comedy, three-camera live, Desilu Studios, serialization, Four Star Productions, anthology drama program, package productions, MCA, Monogram formula, pan and scan, miniseries, prime-time soaps

Hollywood's relationship with broadcasting goes deep, back to the days of the 1920s, before radio networks had yet established themselves. Far-sighted entrepreneurs like Harry Warner of Warner Bros. set up radio stations as publicity vehicles for films and film stars, and advertisers turned to the glamour of Hollywood to promote their products on air. Indeed, American broadcasting could not have developed as it did without the influence of the movie industry, nor would Hollywood be what it is today without

American Film History: Selected Readings, 1960 to the Present, First Edition. Edited by Cynthia Lucia, Roy Grundmann, and Art Simon.

its considerable connection to broadcasting. Unlike Britain, where film producers regarded the public monopoly British Broadcasting Corporation (BBC) as purely a competitor, likely to use up film properties and celebrities without adequate compensation, Hollywood studios and stars eagerly teamed up with radio in the early 1930s in the mutual pursuit of profit, not only as a medium of publicity but in the development of sound technology and practices and as a vibrant venue of mutual creative interaction. This continued and intensified as television debuted in the late 1940s, bringing visual aesthetics and techniques of film production to the serial forms of broadcasting. By the late 1970s, it had become impossible to speak of the film and television industries as separate entities: television networks both produced and aired movies; film studios originated the vast majority of prime-time programs on the networks; and cable television had begun to transform both industries as a new site of hybrid creativity.

This chapter picks up the story of cinema's engagement with broadcasting as television emerged in the mid-1940s, and traces a few of the more important lines of mutual interaction, both in the industry and in the films and television programs that this productive relationship engendered. With glances backwards at the important establishing period of radio, it demonstrates that there has never been a firm boundary between film and broadcasting; in fact, in terms of sites of production, the trajectory of creative personnel, the development of genres, texts, and styles, and the audiences who viewed them, film and television differ mainly in their method of distribution – airwaves versus theaters – and not always even that, as theatrical films began to figure significantly on television in the mid-1960s. The theatrical feature film – "cinema" as we know it – represents the highly visible tip of the motion picture iceberg, supported and sustained by a vast number of nontheatrical forms with television foremost among them.

Transitions

By the late 1930s, Hollywood was the center of radio as well as film production, prompted by the movies' conversion to sound, the development of the transcontinental landline business, and the rise of sponsor-funded national networks. Both NBC and CBS, along with most of the largest advertising agencies, built studios in Los Angeles. The networks drew increasingly on Hollywood's glamour and talent, and the studios relied increasingly on radio not only for publicity but for a constant flow of new stars and new ideas. Their growing synergy took place on variety shows and celebrity gossip programs as well as in high-profile drama and film adaptation venues like the *Lux Radio Theatre* and in guest spots on series programs (Hilmes 1990). Conversely, radio stars like Rudy Vallee, Bob Hope, Bing Crosby, Jack Benny, and George Burns and Gracie Allen (as well as a host of less-known radio acts, like *Lum and Abner*, the *Hoosier Hotshots*, and a glut of singing cowboys, to give only a few examples) became staples of popular film, particularly the "B" films that filled out the bottom half of a double bill (Murray 2005). Certain genres, like the Hollywood "women's film" and the thriller drama, built on conventions established in daytime and prime-time radio series; and certain stylistic elements common to radio – such as voiceover narration and dramatic uses of music – influenced cinema aesthetics (Kozloff 1988; Altman 1994). A growing number of creative artists primarily associated with cinema either got started in radio – such as director Orson Welles and composer Bernard Herrmann – or moved productively between them, such as Welles himself, director Alfred Hitchcock, and actor Peter Lorre, to name only a few (Heyer 2005; Thomas 2008).

By 1945, both the motion picture industry and network broadcasting had reached a pinnacle of popularity and social centrality. Boosted by their significance during the war years as morale-lifting entertainment as well as sources of news and propaganda, both film and radio unwittingly stood upon the precipice of significant change. For cinema, that change stemmed from industry reorganization resulting from the Paramount decision of 1948, which forced studios to divest themselves of their theater holdings, as well as from the privatizing leisure habits of the suburban baby-bearing audience. In broadcasting, the introduction of television by the very companies that owned the radio networks, and the rapid transfer of talent, properties, and advertising to the new medium that resulted, left radio bereft of its former cultural role even as it evolved another: promoting popular music for an expanding recording industry. Television didn't kill the movies, as many predicted at the time, but it did sound the death knell for some film genres such as the newsreel and short documentary as theatrical attractions; these shifted over to television almost immediately. Not until the late 1950s would the major Hollywood studios move into production for television, but cinema and television intersected in ways that were important to both during the transitional period.

Contrary to depictions current at the time of Hollywood studios as "ostriches with their heads in the sand," several studios saw clearly that the future of the film business would be linked with television and made efforts to get in on the ground level. In 1938, Paramount purchased a 50 percent interest in Allen B. DuMont Laboratories, a company involved in the development of television technology, which eventually received licenses and built stations in three cities: WABD New York, WTTG in Washington, DC, and WDTV in Pittsburgh (Weinstein 2004). Paramount also applied for a total of six other stations, through various subsidiary companies, and by 1948, operated two stations, KTLA-Los Angeles and WBKB in Chicago (Hess 1979, 89). Paramount proved the most successful in obtaining licenses, though other studios applied as well, with Fox and Loew's-MGM the most active. However, the taint of the 1948 Paramount antitrust suit blackened the reputation of the movie industry with federal regulators, resulting in rejection of most license applications in the reordering that took place between 1948 and 1952. By then, other television-related technologies beckoned, such as theater television (the broadcast distribution of films to theaters for exhibition) and subscription TV. The rejection by the Federal Communications Commission (FCC) of the idea of an ultra-high-frequency (UHF) "movie band" for distribution of movies to theater television, and its subsequent quashing of subscription television in the face of broadcasting industry objections, effectively ended Hollywood studio attempts to enter the broadcasting industry from the distribution and exhibition angles (Hilmes 1990). Production for television's hungry schedules, on the other hand, would eventually lead to Hollywood domination of the television business, culminating in the corporate merger of studio and network interests in the 1980s and 1990s.

During the period of transition between radio and television, as Hollywood studios tried a variety of approaches to the new medium, a few areas of mutual influence and interaction stand out. One is Hollywood's role in the development of the domestic situation comedy, long a television staple. It first emerged on radio in the late 1940s, as a handful of Hollywood's supporting comediennes, including Lucille Ball, Joan Davis, Ann Sothern, Eve Arden, and Marie Wilson, became leading ladies in prime-time radio and from there moved to television. They were aided by changes in the tax laws that encouraged stars to detach themselves from studios and sponsors and incorporate themselves as independent producers. CBS's new initiative to produce its own programming in resistance to the power of the sponsor abetted such plans, along with the attraction of the regular work of a radio series combined with a greater degree of control over their careers. These women built programs around their comic personas, established first in the movies, with far-reaching effect on both the television industry and the film business (Hilmes 2005).

The best-known innovator is Lucille Ball, who played the madcap wife or girlfriend in a string of films under RKO contract, as well as in a few musical features at MGM, from 1935 to 1947. In July of 1948, she debuted on prime-time radio in *My Favorite Husband* with costar Richard Denning. The radio series ran until 1951, by which time Ball and husband Desi Arnaz had incorporated their own independent production company, Desilu. *I Love Lucy* became television's first hit series shot on film, using the "three-camera film" system innovated by Desilu which adapted television studio techniques ("three-camera live") to filmed production (Schatz 1990). This enabled the series not only to take advantage of multiple takes and postproduction editing but to thrive in syndication for evermore – somewhere, a television channel is playing an *I Love Lucy* rerun even as you read this today. It also enabled the show to become the first international blockbuster as it was sold to television systems worldwide.

Not only *I Love Lucy* but a parade of hit television programs emanated from the Desilu Studios, among them Eve Arden's comedic series *Our Miss Brooks*. Arden filled supporting roles in more than 25 motion pictures between 1937 and 1945, most notably *Stage Door* (1937) and *Mildred Pierce* (1945). Playing a sharp-tongued but kindhearted high school teacher in a small Midwestern town, Arden debuted as Miss Brooks on radio in 1948, then joined Desilu when she adapted her role for television in 1952; it ran on CBS for five years to highly favorable reviews. Another B actress, Joan Davis, known for her comic

Figure 9.1 Joan Davis in trouble again in *I Married Joan* (1952–1955, NBC, producers Joan Davis, James Bank, P.J. Wolfson, and Richard Mack). (Wisconsin Center for Film and Theater Research).

roles in such forgettable programmers as *Love and Hisses* (1937), *Hold That Co-Ed* (1938), and a series of geography-based titles including *Two Latins from Manhattan* (1941), *Two Senoritas from Chicago* (1943), and *Kansas City Kitty* (1944), became one of the first high-profile female radio program hosts when she replaced Rudy Vallee on his variety show in 1943, then gained her own program, *The Joan Davis Show*, in 1945. CBS created a package series around her in 1948, titled *Leave It to Joan*. Under the title *I Married Joan* it moved to CBS television in 1950, then went to NBC in 1952 under Davis's own production and ownership, where it ran until 1961 (Hilmes 2005).

As radio comedy began to move away from its earlier vaudeville-based variety format into more serial, "recurring sketch" forms, such stars molded the series comedy into its 1950s domestic manifestation, shaped by Hollywood's B traditions. This process of "serialization," mandated by the unique "streaming" properties of the broadcast medium, became one of television's most striking and fundamental narrative characteristics. Though the serial form has deep cultural roots that have found expression in virtually every medium (Stedman 1977), serialized dramatic narratives evolved as the very backbone of radio programming, well suited to its technology, social function, institutional practices, and economics. Yet radio series, produced live, were limited by their aural-only nature to relatively small casts, reduced situational complexity, and short episodic duration. It is when broadcasting's seriality met the possibilities inherent in film's visuality and permanence that television programs as we know them today began to take shape. Conversely, television's episodic schedule gave filmed narratives the chance to develop over time and across narrative variations in a way rarely possible in theatrical cinema. Filmed serials for television also opened up a lucrative new market, giving broadcast programs a fixed and highly saleable form relatively new to the medium (though see Russo 2004 on the history of radio transcriptions). Film extended broadcast programs' lifespan in syndicated sales far beyond the original network broadcast, not to mention a new transportability through space that would begin to build television beyond live radio's national scope toward a new international field of distribution, such as film had long enjoyed.

Innovative independent production companies like Desilu were the first to perceive this emerging opportunity. They were quickly joined by the first wave of filmed television producers, such as Jerry Fairbanks Productions, Hal Roach Studios, Ziv Television, Jack Webb's Mark VII Ltd., and many more, along with a few of the more prescient studios like RKO and Columbia's Screen Gems division (Marc 1990). One of the most successful was Four Star Productions, founded by three major Hollywood stars – Dick Powell, Charles Boyer, and David Niven – who produced and often appeared in an early filmed anthology drama, *Four Star Playhouse* (ABC 1952–1956), that brought major studio talent to the airwaves in shows produced by this talented trio. The company later diversified not only into a fourth star – adding Ida Lupino as a partner in 1956 – but into somewhat less prestigious but more popular productions like *Dick Powell's Zane Grey Theater* (CBS 1956–1962) and the sitcom *Hey Jeannie!* (CBS 1956–1957) (Becker 2008, 56–58).

This early period of productive innovation influenced not only American television, but television around the world. The story of Hannah Weinstein's Sapphire Productions illustrates the transnationality of early filmed television, and also reveals how the politics of the era shaped the film/television relationship. During the peak of the Cold War, as the House Un-American Activities Committee and publications like *Red Channels* hounded many established Hollywood writers, directors, and actors out of the business, "runaway" productions overseas provided a productive refuge. By 1952, a group of astute blacklisted Hollywood artists were living in Paris. Among them was a young political activist named Hannah Weinstein, who had little experience in the film industry but had been active in left-wing Hollywood organizations; by 1947, she had become executive secretary of the Hollywood branch of the Independent Citizens Committee of the Arts, Sciences, and Professions (HICCASP), a group that would soon be denounced as a "communist front organization" by the House Un-American Activities Committee. After producing a short film on the French resistance that she sold to American television, as she later recalled, "I began to look for other material and came up with some offbeat English mysteries which we went to London to make because it was cheap at that time" (Gross 1977). In 1952, she produced a three-part series, *Colonel March of Scotland Yard*, in partnership with Boris Karloff (who also starred in the program), based on the novels of John Dickson Carr. It was later released as a feature film, *Colonel March Investigates* (1953); 22 more episodes were produced in 1954 and released in the US in syndication by Official Films; later they would also be broadcast in Britain (Neale 2003).

What makes this series memorable today is not so much the content of the programs themselves, but their production credits. Many were written by "Leslie Slote" – actually the "nom de blacklist" (among others) of two well-known Hollywood writers, Walter Bernstein and Abraham Polonsky, who had turned to writing for television when film work dried up. However, it was British television that turned this one-off production unit into a small transnational television empire. Britain had initiated television service well before the United States, in 1937, but until 1955 the BBC provided a noncommercial monopoly in television as it did in radio and showed little interest in popular entertainments. Only in 1955 did commercial television make its debut, after a long and contested political struggle. One of the new commercial franchisees was Lew Grade, owner of a British talent agency, who formed his Incorporated Television Company (ITC) in conjunction with Associated TeleVision (ATV) to make a bid for the Midlands service. It was successful, and Grade's ITC would become well known for its internationally circulating television serials (*The Saint*, 1962; *The Prisoner*, 1967) as Grade himself emerged as a popular culture impresario. However, the television market in Britain was not yet large enough to support expensive filmed production, and import quotas prevented the broadcast of more than a small proportion of US-produced series and films.

Grade purchased the *Colonel March* series and aired it with favorable ratings in 1955. Based on that success, he invested in Hannah Weinstein's new production company, Sapphire Films, with the objective of producing adventure series in Britain for ATV that could also be syndicated in the United States. Sapphire's big advantage was that it could draw on blacklisted talent of a far higher quality than television production could count on normally, making its shows stand out on both sides of the Atlantic. Sapphire's first hit was the series *The Adventures of Robin Hood*, which did well not only in the US and Britain but around the world, including Canada, Australia, Japan, Norway, Italy, Mexico, and Argentina. Its pilot was the work of Oscar-winning screenwriter Ring Lardner, Jr (*Woman of the Year*, 1942; *Laura*, 1944), who with Ian McLellan Hunter (A *Woman of Distinction*, 1950) wrote most of the series's episodes under a variety of pseudonyms such as Lawrence McClellan, Oliver Skene, Robert B. West, Eric Heath, Ian Larkin, and many more. Other exiled writers for this and other series included Waldo Salt, Robert Lees, Bernard Gordon, Norma and Ben Barzman, and Donald Ogden Stewart, to name only a few (Neale 2003, 247–248).[1]

Sapphire produced several subsequent series, including *The Adventures of Sir Lancelot* (1956–1957), *The Buccaneers* (1956–1957), *Sword of Freedom* (1958–1960), and *Four Just Men* (1959–1960). Besides giving work to blacklisted Hollywood talent, the advantage of filming these series in England included getting around broadcast import quotas and taking advantage of British tax incentives designed to encourage indigenous production. They were produced at Nettlefold Studios in Walton-on-Thames but found their largest audiences in the United States and internationally. Such series were true cultural hybrids, drawing on distinctively British historical legends and fictional characters to tell stories that often seemed to relate strongly to the American politics that so concerned their writers. As Ring Lardner, Jr was later to note,

> *The Adventures of Robin Hood* gave us plenty of opportunities for oblique social comment on the issues and institutions of Eisenhower-era America ... perhaps, in some small way, setting the stage for the 1960s by subverting a whole new generation of young Americans. (Lardner 2000, 141)

Here the filmed seriality of television intersected with politics and policy to create a program written by Cold War exiles from Hollywood, produced in Britain with British talent, for a company funded by both US and British investors. Though unique in many ways, the story of Sapphire Films marks the arrival of the filmed dramatic series as television's dominant narrative form, both domestically and internationally, that would serve as the reliable base of film studio economics for decades to come. Hollywood studios may have been prevented from entering the broadcasting network business in its earliest decades, but soon they would take it over from the inside.

However, early television is more prominently remembered as the era of live studio production, most notably the live anthology drama. This sphere of production also drew on, and more significantly produced, writers and directors who would go on to do their primary work in film. Television's initial emphasis on live production stemmed from its legacy in radio, where the networks had always insisted on the superiority of live over recorded radio programs. In part this was derived from FCC regulations, which considered recorded programming less desirable in station license renewals and frequency assignments. And, up until the postwar years when magnetic tape made its appearance, recording technologies, mostly on disc, did not allow for easy editing or reproduction. Yet by the end of the war the ban on "transcriptions," as they were called, had been largely lifted (Russo 2004); early television's preference for live programming must be understood as an attempt by the networks to hold off the threat of film industry domination as much as a positive aesthetic choice. And, too, live studio production had developed into a sophisticated art by the late 1940s which the networks logically wished to draw on as they made their initial forays into television, as well as to preserve the association of television with the higher status of the theater rather than the suspect film industry (Boddy 1990).

The list of filmic talent honed in live television is an impressive one, and would include, at a minimum, directors John Frankenheimer, Franklin J. Shaffner, Sidney Lumet, Arthur Penn, George Roy Hill, Delbert Mann, and Robert Mulligan. Frankenheimer's career is typical. Starting out as a director and floor producer at CBS, Frankenheimer directed programs as diverse as soap operas and Edward R. Murrow's interview program *You Are There* before moving into

Figure 9.2 Ed Wynn, Jack Palance, and Keenan Wynn in Rod Serling's *Requiem for a Heavyweight* (1956, producers CBS and Playhouse 90). (Wisconsin Center for Film and Theater Research.)

the live anthology drama in which he made his reputation. In series including *Playhouse 90*, *Climax!*, *Danger*, and *Studio One*, Frankenheimer worked with writers such as Rod Serling, Leslie Stephens, Abby Mann, and Reginald Rose, in adaptations of famous novels and plays and in works written originally for television. He moved into film directing as the live era came to an end, becoming known for taut political thrillers like *The Manchurian Candidate* (1962) and *Seven Days in May* (1964), up to one of his most recent films, HBO's *Path to War* (2002). Numerous leading actors, too, garnered their initial acclaim in live anthology drama; a list of a few of the most prominent would include Paul Newman, James Dean, Joanne Woodward, Hope Lange, Rod Steiger, Colleen Dewhurst, Anne Francis, Anthony Perkins, and George C. Scott.

Hollywood stars also frequently served as hosts of anthology series, both during the early live period and during the late 1950s as anthologies shifted to filmed production. The filmed anthology, like the sitcom, provided many actors and actresses with the opportunity to bypass both sponsor control and network schedules by distributing their shows in syndication to local television stations. By 1956, six top-rated syndicated anthology series were filmed in Hollywood and touted their star connections even in their titles: *Crown Theater with Gloria Swanson* (1953), *Ethel Barrymore Theater* (1953), *Edward Arnold Theater* (1954), *Ida Lupino Theater* (1956), and *Douglas Fairbanks, Jr. Presents* (1953–1957) (Becker 2008, 107). Two of the most successful and longest running network anthologies featured stars whose personas linked closely with their programs: Loretta Young and Ronald Reagan. As Christine Becker notes, Young went the route of her sitcom sisters by incorporating her own production company around her anthology series, at first titled *Letter to Loretta* but later changed to *The Loretta Young Show*. Introducing each episode with the device of a letter from a fan requesting guidance through a knotty problem, Young also starred in a number of the episodes. With an address directed squarely toward the female audience, and an emphasis on stories that tended toward the melodramatic, Young's show was as disdainfully dismissed by critics as it was embraced by audiences; it anchored NBC's Sunday night schedule from 1953 until 1961 (Becker 2008, 112–115). Ronald Reagan, on the other hand, used his association with his sponsor as host of the *General Electric Theater* not so much to revive a sagging acting career but to build up his public presence as a spokesman for American industry, a role he would later carry to the Governor's mansion in California before heading for the White House (Becker 2008, 120).

More than a few feature films grew out of live anthology productions. These include *Requiem for a Heavyweight*, *The Helen Morgan Story*, *Days of Wine and Roses*, *Judgment at Nuremberg*, and *Twelve Angry Men*. The anthology drama program, in both its live and filmed versions, represents a high point in original, stand-alone drama for television, killed off as much by the talent-devouring demands of television's weekly schedule as by audience preference for the familiar continuities of serial drama. Yet its voracious appetite for talent provided an entrée into film and television production for many young artists, and a new public persona for not-so-young ones, that neither cinema nor serials could rival.

A Maturing Relationship

By the mid-1950s, most of the major studios had at least dipped their toes into prime-time television production, led by Disney Studios' long-running *Disneyland* in 1954 and joined the next year by Warner Bros. (*Warner Brothers Presents*), Twentieth Century-Fox (*20th Century-Fox Hour*), and MGM (The *MGM Parade*). It is no coincidence that three out of four of these debuted on the ABC network; itself the former NBC Blue network that had split from its parent after federal investigations, it had merged with United Paramount Theaters, the divested theater subsidiary of the Paramount Corporation, in 1953, and under president Leonard Goldenson offered a welcoming venue for the Hollywood majors. The next decade saw the major film studios develop into the veritable cornerstone of the network television business, a profitable enterprise that helped the film industry through its post-studio system doldrums but that benefited the television networks far more. As Christopher Anderson persuasively argues, "The rise of telefilm production in Hollywood represented the consolidation of a particular type of text that has dominated prime-time television ever since … the history of American TV is the history of Hollywood TV" (1994, 12). From their earlier model of live anthology, variety, and game shows in prime time and live serials and talk shows during the day, the networks by the early 1960s had shifted into the filmed series programming that would mark the "classic network system" still emblematic of American television and influential even today.

One of the most successful of the new Hollywood film/television hybrids was MCA, the company led by Lew Wasserman that by the 1960s dominated the television production industry and had moved into film production with its acquisition of Universal Pictures in 1962. Starting out as a music booking agency in Chicago under the direction of Jules Stein, it grew into one of the most successful talent agencies in Hollywood. Wasserman, hired by Stein in 1939, is credited by many with first realizing the tax advantages of "package productions," which brought star, writer, director, and property together in a one-time corporation produced by the talent agency (Gomery 2007). Also seeing the enormous potential in television for this sort of package, Wasserman formed MCA subsidiary Revue Productions (after a timely intercession by client and Screen Actors Guild president Ronald Reagan to obtain a waiver of SAG stipulations against this sort of agent-led production), one of the largest and most successful television production companies in Hollywood by the mid-1960s. Its biggest hit was *Wagon Train* (1957–1965), but its properties included a long list of other solidly popular series: *The Adventures of Ozzie and Harriet* (1952–1966), *Alfred Hitchcock Presents* (1955–1965), *McHale's Navy* (1962–1966), *The Danny Thomas Show/Make Room for Daddy* (1953–1964), *The Andy Griffith Show* (1960–1968), and many others.

In 1960, with its purchase of Paramount's pre-1948 film library, MCA also aggressively pursued the increasingly important practice of distributing theatrical films to television. Though no one doubted that theatrical films would hold great appeal for television audiences, despite the networks' "pro-live" rhetoric, circumstances in both the film and television industries had militated against it through the early 1950s. First of all, early television screens were very small, had poor resolution, and of course remained black-and-white only, making the small screen an unfavorable venue for Hollywood's current releases. In fact, television stations at first would have preferred to screen older movies in the 16mm format that studios used for release to the military, schools, and nonprofit groups. Hollywood's unanimous refusal to sell 16mm films to television prompted a Justice Department suit in 1952 against all the major studios, accusing them of a conspiracy to restrain trade. Backed up by the vociferous objections of theater owners to the idea of 16mm films on TV, the studios resisted by suing the Justice Department and received a favorable verdict in US District Court in 1955.[2]

However, even for those stations or networks willing to purchase 35mm films, the situation was complicated. The powerful Hollywood talent guilds and unions, having won a battle for residual payments for recorded music in 1941, insisted that a similar system of residual rights should apply to the release of films to television as well. Until sufficient economic incentive existed for the studios to come to such an agreement, television briefly became a showcase for the British film industry. Over the next five years, more British films reached American audiences via television than had ever been seen in theaters. Leading the foreign invasion were not the networks, who were holding firm to a "no film" stance, but some of the nation's more powerful independent stations, which saw theatrical films as a way to rival their network-affiliated competitors. WPIX-New York purchased a package of 24 films from British film producer Alexander Korda in 1948, bringing such major stars as Vivien Leigh, Laurence Olivier, and Charles Laughton to television for the first time. Universal began to distribute features made by J. Arthur Rank Studios in 1949, and smaller studios like Monogram, Republic, and Eagle-Lion also ventured into the trade, mostly with packages of the "B" pictures for which they were known. When Monogram attempted in 1950 to release a package of 144 features made before 1946, the American Federation of Musicians called a strike, refusing to work for Monogram until all 144 films could be rescored using the same number of musicians as in the original production, plus a payment of 5 percent of the distribution fee. The Screen Actors Guild also objected, leading to Monogram's agreement to pay each actor 12.5 percent of his or her original salary for each film released for under $20,000 and 15 percent for those sold for more. The Screen Writers Guild bargained for a similar deal, which became known as the "Monogram formula."[3]

Even by 1951, however, it seemed clear that theatrical film distribution to television might become more than a strategy for struggling independent stations. CBS purchased a package from Monogram for its *Film Theater of the Air* series in 1951. At this point the major studios became more interested, negotiating a contract with the Screen Actors Guild that relinquished television distribution royalties for films made before 1948 in return for an agreement to negotiate a "TV new deal" for post-1948 product; both the Screen Directors Guild and the Writers Guild of America signed off on this as well. While they were negotiating, a few smaller producers forged ahead. David O. Selznick broke the "A" picture barrier by selling 12 of his films in 1951 for a price of more than $2 million, which several large stations were willing to pay. The DuMont Network purchased a package of older but still "A" quality features from distributor Quality Films in 1951 as well.

Another important milestone occurred in 1954, when the studios won a court decision confirming that their pretelevision agreements with talent and craft labor unions gave them an "implied right" to distribute those films to the new medium (Lafferty 1990, 236). However, until the watershed year of 1955, it was neither sufficiently financially rewarding for major studios to release their films to television in large numbers, since their compensation for each individual screening simply came nowhere near what they could earn in theatrical distribution, nor was theatrical film programming sufficiently attractive to networks given their investment in live television. Independent stations, however, as well as network affiliates in larger cities who saw a way of filling in nonnetwork parts of their schedules, were willing to negotiate with the smaller studios, in particular, for the packages of recognizable cinema hits. As William Lafferty notes, by 1953, "CBS's New York flagship station used 30 hours of feature films a week," mostly in "fringe" times and during the summer (1990, 238).

Not until 1960, though, did the studios finally reach an agreement with the craft and labor unions for residual payments for post-1948 films released to television. And not until 1961 did the major networks finally feel secure enough in their profit structure to begin to incorporate regular screenings of relatively recent Hollywood theatrical feature films into their schedules. NBC's *Saturday Night at the Movies* debuted on September 23, 1961, with a prime-time screening of *How to Marry a Millionaire* (1953) as the first of a package of 32 Twentieth Century-Fox feature films intended to fill up its first season on the air. In April 1962, ABC followed with its Sunday evening *Hollywood Special*, later renamed the *ABC Sunday Night Movie*. NBC added *Monday Night at the Movies* in 1963, while CBS only capitulated to the regularly scheduled feature film series in 1965, with its *Thursday Night Movies*. Studios by this time could command substantial prices for single films and for packages. In 1966, ABC paid Twentieth Century-Fox more than $20 million for a package of 17 films, while MGM received $52.8 million for 45 films from CBS. Blockbusters could bring considerably more: Warner Bros received $1 million for two showings of *The Music Man* from CBS in 1967, followed by Columbia's $2 million deal with ABC for two broadcasts of *The Bridge over the River Kwai*. By the end of 1968, network schedules featured seven movie slots per week in prime time, one for every night of the week – this in spite of the fact that the cinema's increasing emphasis on wide-screen production meant that features had to be "panned and scanned" to fit television's 4:3 aspect radio – cutting off up to 50 percent of the picture in the process.

However, it would soon become apparent to the networks that relying on Hollywood feature films as central prime-time programming components had its drawbacks. First of all, the market for high-quality features rapidly became tight; television's voracious demand quickly exceeded supply and prices rose sharply into the mid-1960s. Second, as Lafferty explains, the feature film was going through some fundamental transformations. With the gradual phasing out of the Production Code, influence from European cinema, and a changing theatergoing demographic, many mid- to late 1960s feature films proved too controversial or racy for the domestic environment of the small screen (1990, 248). The mid-1960s, therefore, see the entry of the networks themselves into feature film production – not only the "made-for-TV movie" so generally critically reviled but films intended for theatrical release as well. NBC had, in 1962, teamed with Universal TV – the consolidated company formed by MCA's Revue Productions' purchase of Universal Pictures – on a nearly feature-length, 90-minute weekly, high-prestige Western series, *The Virginian*. It was only a short conceptual step to an NBC/Universal partnership in stand-alone "mini-movies," as they were called. Their first joint effort, as Gary Edgerton relates, was an adaptation of an Ernest Hemingway story, "The Killers," which Don Siegel directed in 1963 with a cast including John Cassavetes, Lee Marvin, Angie Dickinson, and Ronald Reagan. Deemed "too spicy, expensive, and violent" for TV, it was in fact released as a theatrical feature, bypassing television exhibition. Their next effort would be more successful; *See How They Run* premiered on October 17, 1964, setting off the made-for-TV movie phenomenon in earnest (Edgerton 1991, 114). By 1967, both ABC, with its ABC Pictures, and CBS with its CBS Cinema Center, had taken the trend to its next logical step, setting up wholly owned subsidiaries to specialize in the production of theatrical feature films that would eventually be screened on their respective networks – and often subsequently released as features overseas. This network foray into the studio business ultimately failed – all three network subsidiaries folded by 1972 – but by that time other players had entered the "telefeature" field. According to Gary Edgerton, six studios dominated the field by 1973: Universal TV, Aaron Spelling Productions, Paramount TV, Twentieth Century-Fox TV, Columbia's Screen Gems, and Metromedia, a station group owner based on the old DuMont Network combined with David A. Wolper Productions. They would go on in the 1970s to bring the made-for-TV movie to new prominence made possible by special prime-time slots created by all three networks: NBC's *World Premiere Movies*, CBS's *New Friday Night Movie*, and ABC's *Movie of the Week*. With the Peabody Award-winning *Brian's Song*, produced by Columbia Screen Gems for ABC and premiering November 30, 1971, the made-for-TV movie rose to a peak of respectability outshone perhaps only in 1983 by ABC's *The Day After*, which attracted 62 percent of American TV viewers to its all-star version of nuclear holocaust in the homeland (Edgerton 1991). The telefeature would eventually fade from major network schedules as it became the backbone of cable TV production in the 1980s and 1990s.

The telefeature's near cousin is the miniseries, arising slightly later than its stand-alone counterpart but finding strong critical resonance with pay-cable channels a few decades later. This particular form, a cornerstone of the BBC schedule for decades, had arrived on American shores in the form of British historical sagas and literary adaptations aired on National Educational Television (NET), soon to become enshrined on the schedule of NET's successor, PBS. A miniseries combines elements of the serial form and the standalone feature by stringing anywhere from two to more than 20 episodes of a single serialized property over several evenings, weeks, or even months, airing one to two hours at a time. The NET's BBC-produced hit *The Forsyte Saga* ran over 26 weeks in the fall of 1969 and the spring of 1970, bringing John Galsworthy's lengthy series of novels to enthralled American audiences. ABC and Universal TV took a more modest, and also a more lowbrow, approach in 1976 with their adaptation of Sidney Sheldon's bestselling novel *Rich Man, Poor Man* in six two-hour segments over six weeks, but it remained for the national impact of *Roots* – an eight-part series based on Alex Haley's novel produced by David L. Wolper Productions for ABC in 1977 – to bring the form to mainstream network legitimacy.

Struggles for Control

By the mid-1960s, the network television business had stabilized into a highly lucrative three-network oligopoly, with a solid advertising base, a network affiliate station in virtually every US city, and a standardized schedule of filmed series programs that drew in large national audiences at a relatively low cost per episode. With the regulatory turmoil of the 1950s and early 1960s largely resolved in their favor, the networks had little to fear from competition with independent stations in most markets. This fact led to a "buyer's market" in television programs, putting the networks in the driver's seat in negotiations with studios large and small. With the three major networks the only game in town for television series sales, they were able to take an ownership position in most of the programs on their prime-time schedules. This meant that studios saw little benefit when a successful show went into syndication after its network run; that stream of revenues went back to the networks. All three networks had created subsidiary companies to handle their syndicated distribution, both domestic and international, with CBS Enterprises (later to become known as Viacom) the largest and most successful. By 1965, over 90 percent of the programs aired in prime time were owned by the network themselves, either whole or in part.

In Hollywood, production for television had become a steady, profitable component of the film business. Once past their initial urge to use the medium as a means of film promotion, studios settled into turning out the filmed series that the networks demanded, often acting as distributors for smaller independent production companies as well (Alvey 1997). Production for television helped the studios ride out the rough spots in the new "blockbuster" era that had emerged in the 1960s, as competition for a small number of "hit" films replaced the reliable "A" and "B" system of former decades. Still focused primarily on the Technicolor, Cinemascope, all-star-cast theatrical features that brought in the big bucks in the 1960s, most major studios deliberately kept television production budgets to a minimum, adopting streamlined "factory" production methods to turn out the maximum number of episodes at the smallest possible cost, aware that they could be readily undercut by smaller, leaner production companies. Thus, the period of American television from 1965 to 1975 is marked by the highest level of standardization, centralization, and homogenization in its history. The studios and their associated independents turned out low-budget, formulaic programs, most of them series rather than true serials (with standalone episodes rather than continuing storylines) for ease of syndication: They could be aired in virtually any order, and viewed without concern for sequence. Half-hour situation comedies, with frequent spin-offs, and assorted hour-long crime, medical, and adventure dramas alternated with feature films on prime-time schedules.

Virtually no one but the networks, however, was happy with this situation. Advertisers reached large audiences but paid high prices to do so in a tightly controlled market, and when their target demographic conflicted with a network's brand image, they were out of luck – as happened with the sponsors of CBS's rural comedies in the early 1970s, booted off to make way for more hip, youth-friendly programs. Film studios chafed at their lack of ability to innovate beyond successful formulae, or perhaps more accurately at the limited profits on the sale of programs to the big three oligopoly that would have encouraged them to innovate. In particular, the idea that ownership rights to a program belonged to the network that aired it, and not to the company that produced it, went against deep Hollywood traditions – it was as though theater owners and distributors had teamed to keep studios in thrall to the exhibition business, an unthinkable abrogation of Hollywood business strategy.

Furthermore, US policy makers were no happier. In 1965, an FCC study had noted the degree of monopsony control held over the television program market by the three national networks, and in 1970, proposed and passed a set of rules designed to redress the balance-of-power issues their studies had uncovered. One axis involved network control over their affiliates' schedules; the Prime Time Access Rule aimed to free the first hour of prime-time Monday through Saturday (7–8 p.m. EST; 6–7 p.m. CST) from network programming and require that local stations develop their own programs in that time slot. Stations responded by moving their local news broadcasting into the first half-hour and filled the second with highly profitable syndicated series, either off-network or first-run shows. This did provide a boost for independent production of game and quiz shows, in particular, and made the business of off-network rerun sales even more lucrative. However, it was with the Financial Interest and Syndication Rules that the FCC's actions most directly affected the film industry. These rules not only mandated that syndication rights return to programs' original producers after one or two airings on the network, but that networks must in the future limit themselves to owning or taking a financial interest in only a small percentage of their prime-time shows – 15 percent, excluding news and sports. All three networks appealed the implementation of these rules in 1970, though CBS was first to see the writing on the wall. It announced plans to spin off its syndication arm, CBS Enterprises, in 1971, forming Viacom, a company that would go on to become a larger media conglomerate than its parent. The Fin-Syn rules were upheld in federal court in 1972, and NBC and ABC followed CBS's lead by divesting distribution in 1973 (Kompare 2005, 87), though they continued to appeal other aspects of the new regulations into the early 1980s.

The Prime Time Access and Fin-Syn rules, combined with the increase in numbers of independent stations in the UHF band and the slow advent of cable television channels, opened up the market for both first-run and off-network syndication throughout the industry, and quickly reshaped the studio/network relationship, giving the studios an advantage they had long sought. Both major studios and independent producers were quick to respond, innovating new programs and beginning to explore film/television tie-ins again, such as Paramount's *Entertainment Tonight*, a news program covering the entertainment business, which would debut in 1981. By the end of the 1970s, television had begun to break out of the classic network system mold. Not only miniseries like *Roots* but also prime-time soaps like *Dallas* (Lorimar/CBS, 1978) and *Dynasty* (Spelling/ABC, 1981), and "quality" series with a more heavily serialized narrative structures such as *Cagney & Lacey* (Orion/CBS, 1982) and *Hill Street Blues* (MTM/NBC, 1981) began to lead the ratings and fill the schedules. Films were adapted into television series, as with *M*A*S*H* (Twentieth Century-Fox/CBS, 1972), and occasionally television series spun off movies, as with the ongoing *Star Trek* franchise (Paramount/NBC, 1967; Paramount Pictures, 1979).

And Hollywood itself adopted some of the tricks of the television trade as it attempted to stabilize the new blockbuster market with an increased emphasis on film sequels and serials. As Tino Balio explains, a sequel picks up the situation and action where a previous film left off, resulting in a "premarketed" property that allows audiences to anticipate what the film will be about. "Film titles with Arabic numbers, Roman numerals, or such phrases as 'Return of,' 'Beyond the,' and 'Beneath the'" (1990, 261) began to appear in about 10 percent of Hollywood releases in the 1970s. Series films use the same characters from previous pictures but place them in a different situation. Series films (including many based on broadcasting stars and programs) had made up a part of Hollywood's "B" strategies for many decades but now such properties became "A" business, with the James Bond, Dirty Harry, and – for a different kind of television-based example – the *Muppet* series of films.

Eventually, too, the "Hollywoodization" of television, along with the new kinds of channels made available by satellite distribution's expanded universe, would result in the international spread of American television. Hollywood programs began to dominate the world's small screens the way its films had long filled the theaters. Though initially confined to the "cheap and cheerful" fringe slots on international schedules – pulling in audiences at low purchase costs so that scarce public funds could be used for "quality" productions – by the 1990s American television began to be recognized as much for its own frequently excellent cinematic quality as for its pervasiveness. This was particularly true for the films, miniseries, and documentaries produced for pay-cable channels like HBO and Showtime, insulated from advertising support, but mainstream network programs like *Friends*, *E.R.*, *The Simpsons*, *Law and Order*, and the various *CSI* manifestations gained not only dollars but critical respect – in contrast to the horrified reaction to the "Dallasification" of an earlier era. It is no coincidence that complex serial narratives now outnumber the once prevalent episodic series, as the recombined production, distribution, and exhibition corporations seek to make the most of their long-lived properties.

Finally, of course, by the mid 1990s, the television and motion picture industries would simply merge their now no longer differentiated activities in the multimedia conglomerates so dominant today. Prompted by the immanent repeal of the Fin-Syn rules (which were set to expire in the early 1990s), major production companies perceived that there was an acute advantage to owning their own channels of distribution, as they had attempted to do back in the 1940s and 1950s. Rupert Murdoch's Twentieth Century-Fox Corporation broke through the old studio/network divide by starting up the Fox network in 1988; Warner Bros. and Paramount followed in 1995 with The WB and UPN, respectively; while NBC and its parent GE merged with Universal, ABC became a part of the Disney empire, and CBS, in a typical twist of fate, was acquired by its former subsidiary, the Viacom Corporation. In 2006, CBS/Viacom, which by this time also owned Paramount Pictures and the UPN network, swallowed up rival WB to form the CW network.

Conclusion

In the end, the major distinction between television and the cinema as media rests not on their inherent textual qualities nor on production practices, ownership, or appeal, but on the difference between live and recorded distribution: between cinema's stand-alone textual closure and television's streaming seriality. Early regulators established a strong incentive for broadcasting to remain a live medium, so little motivation existed for developing sound-only recording technologies that would have allowed the flexible editing and postproduction of film, until the late 1930s. By then, however, both television and the war loomed on the horizon. Though captured German magnetic tape technology and other related developments would finally bring sound recording into a new era, the attention of the industry had turned to television. A host of circumstances preserved live production and distribution for television's first 10 years, but by the mid-1960s most of television was shot and distributed on film. Hollywood interests were held at bay, kept to a fairly rigid and standardized production regime, for another decade or two before further government regulation stimulated the merger of the two industries that we are witnessing today. In this era of DVD distribution, on-demand services delivered through cable, satellites, and the internet, and the high-definition home theater, not to mention the increasingly digital distribution of theatrical feature films, it is only the ghosts of lingering differences that remain.

Notes

1. Other production companies took advantage of this situation as well, such as Danziger Brothers Productions and Douglas Fairbanks Ltd. See Mann 2008.
2. *Variety*, April 27, 1955, 5; July 27, 1955, 1.
3. *Variety*, July 6, 1949, 2; May 4, 1949, 26.

References

Altman, Rick. (1994). "Deep-Focus Sound: *Citizen Kane* and the Radio Aesthetic." *Quarterly Review of Film and Video*, 15.3, 1–33.

Alvey, Mark. (1997). "The Independents: Rethinking the Television Studio System." In Lynn Spigel & Michael Curtin (eds), *The Revolution Wasn't Televised: Sixties Television and Social Conflict* (pp. 139–160). New York: Routledge.

Anderson, Christopher. (1994). *Hollywood TV: The Studio System in the 1950s*. Austin: University of Texas Press.

Balio, Tino (ed.). (1990). *Hollywood in the Age of Television*. Boston: Unwin Hyman.

Becker, Christine. (2008). *It's the Pictures That Got Small: Hollywood Film Stars on 1950s Television*. Middletown, CT: Wesleyan University Press.

Boddy, William. (1990). *Fifties Television*. Urbana: University of Illinois Press.

Edgerton, Gary. (1991). "High Concept, Small Screen: Reperceiving the Industrial and Stylistic Origins of the American Made-for-TV Movie." *Journal of Popular Film and Television*, 19, 114–127.

Gomery, Douglas. (2007). "Talent Raids and Package Deals: NBC Loses Its Leadership in the 1950s." In Michele Hilmes (ed.), *NBC: America's Network* (pp. 153–170). Berkeley: University of California Press.

Gross, Linda. (1977). "She Battles for Minorities." *Los Angeles Times*, July 28, 14.

Hess, Gary H. (1979). *An Historical Study of the DuMont Television Network*. New York: Arno Press. (Originally a PhD dissertation, Northwestern University, 1960.)

Heyer, Paul. (2005). *The Medium and the Magician: Orson Welles, the Radio Years, 1934–1952*. New York: Rowman & Littlefield.

Hilmes, Michele. (1990). *Hollywood and Broadcasting: From Radio to Cable*. Urbana: University of Illinois Press.

Hilmes, Michele. (2005). "Femmes Boff Program Toppers: Women Break into Prime Time, 1943–1948." In S. Brinson & J. E. Winn (eds), *Transmitting the Past: Historical and Cultural Perspectives on Broadcasting* (pp. 137–160). Tuscaloosa: University of Alabama Press.

Kompare, Derek. (2005). *Rerun Nation: How Repeats Invented American Television*. New York: Routledge.

Kozloff, Sarah. (1988). *Invisible Storytellers: Voiceover Narration in American Fiction Film*. Berkeley: University of California Press.

Lafferty, William. (1990). "Feature Films on Prime-Time Television." In T. Balio (ed.), *Hollywood in the Age of Television* (pp. 235–256). Boston: Unwin Hyman.

Lardner, Ring, Jr. (2000). *I'd Hate Myself in the Morning: A Memoir*. New York: Thunder's Mouth Press.

Mann, Dave. (2008). "From Obscurity to Authority? The Changing Status of the Screenwriter during the Transition from 'B' Features to TV/Film Series (1946–64)." *Journal of British Cinema and Television*, 5.2, 280–299.

Marc, David. (1990). "The Screen Gems Division of Columbia Pictures: Twenty-Five Years of Prime Time Storytelling." In Robert J. Thompson & Gary Burns (eds), *Making Television: Authorship and the Production Process* (pp. 137–144). New York: Praeger.

Murray, Susan. (2005). *Hitch Your Antenna to the Stars: Early Television and Broadcast Stardom*. New York: Routledge.

Neale, Steve. (2003). "Pseudonyms, Sapphire, and Salt: 'Un-American' Contributions to Television Costume Adventure Series in the 1950s." *Historical Journal of Film, Radio and Television*, 23.3, 245–257.

Russo, Alexander. (2004). "Roots of Radio's Rebirth: Audiences, Aesthetics, Economics, and Technologies of American Broadcasting, 1926–1951." PhD disssertation, Brown University.

Schatz, Thomas. (1990). "Desilu, *I Love Lucy*, and the Rise of Network TV." In R. J. Thompson & G. Burns (eds), *Making Television: Authorship and the Production Process* (pp. 117–135). New York: Praeger.

Stedman, Raymond W. (1977). *The Serials: Suspense and Drama by Installment*. Norman: University of Oklahoma Press.

Thomas, Sarah. (2008). "A 'Star' of the Airwaves: Peter Lorre – 'Master of the Macabre' and American Radio Programming." *Radio Journal: International Studies in Broadcast and Audio Media*, 5.2–3, 43–156.

Weinstein, David. (2004). *The Forgotten Network: DuMont and the Birth of American Television*. Philadelphia: Temple University Press.

Part II

1976–1990

10

Setting the Stage
American Film History, 1976–1990

In the summer of 1975, a great white shark appeared on the horizon of the American movie industry. Steven Spielberg's *Jaws* took moviegoers out of the crumbling cities to the beach where they encountered a new yet familiar sense of horror. It was familiar insofar as there had been a long tradition of screen heroes fighting to subdue a monster – of some alien force – be it earthly or interplanetary, invading American life and threatening its families. But given its arrival in 1975, it offered something different in its menace. Over the previous decade, moviegoers had been battered by representations of what, by the mid-1970s, seemed like intractable problems – ungovernable cities, inadequate public institutions, corrupt police. Beyond the movie screen, the nation wrestled with the reality of these problems plus the aftermath of a divisive war, the resignation of a criminal president, and an energy crisis that threatened the economy. But *Jaws* posed a problem that was not chronic, a frightening disturbance, to be sure, but one that could be isolated and vanquished. The menace of Spielberg's shark exposed a callous mayor worried about summertime profits, but it celebrated a local police chief and father, Roy Scheider's Martin Brody, who overcame fears and restored his place at the helm of public safety.

Indeed, on numerous fronts, *Jaws* became emblematic of what we can call contemporary Hollywood. As scholars Thomas Schatz and Justin Wyatt have pointed out, *Jaws* helped the industry set a new course in distribution and marketing (Schatz 1993, 19; Wyatt 1994, 113). It was an exemplary high-concept project, that is, one in which the story could be summarized in a couple of sentences and conveyed for advertising through a single iconic image. As an uncomplicated idea, it could then be used as the centerpiece for a wide marketing scheme that included the manufacture and sale of related products. This search for a synergy between film and a range of ancillary markets would dominate the industry for the next three decades. *Jaws* also signaled the potential of saturation booking – the simultaneous release of a single film across the country in hundreds of theaters (later it would be thousands), accompanied by a simultaneous television advertising blitz in order to maximize attendance for a film's opening weekend. As David Cook has pointed out, the saturation release strategy had for many years been reserved for films anticipated as flops and therefore used as a way to earn some profits before bad reviews or word of mouth could spread (2000, 42). But in the case of *Jaws* it proved successful for an accomplished action film,

American Film History: Selected Readings, 1960 to the Present, First Edition. Edited by Cynthia Lucia, Roy Grundmann, and Art Simon.

one that would continue on a record-breaking run all year.

Industry and Economics

Despite its economic crisis and high-profile flops in the late 1960s and early 1970s, which temporarily resulted in a relative openness to taking risks and experimenting with topics and filmmakers more in tune with the counterculture, the industry had, in fact, never abandoned high-budget filmmaking. During the 1969–1970 release season, the action drama *Airport* outgrossed most competitors at the box office, promptly triggering multiple sequels and the birth of a whole cycle of disaster films, including *The Poseidon Adventure* (1972), *The Towering Inferno* (1974), *Earthquake* (1974), *Rollercoaster* (1977), and *The Swarm* (1978). Quaint by today's standards and invariably much heavier on talk than action, these films nonetheless were clear indications that Hollywood's faith in commercial formula filmmaking was unwavering. But it was the enormous success of *The Godfather* (1972) that made an offer the industry could not refuse. This wisdom was confirmed by the success of *The Exorcist* (1973) and *Jaws* and then, toward the end of the 1970s, by the even greater profits *Star Wars* (1977) generated. These latter films helped signal the end of the New Hollywood or, as some scholars have suggested, the arrival of yet another.

Horror, disaster, and science fiction would come to dominate the box office, moving away from the realism that had defined films like *The French Connection* (1971) and *Midnight Cowboy* (1969). It was perhaps the work of auteur-entrepreneur George Lucas that most thoroughly embodied a cinema fleeing from recession realism, either through the nostalgia of *American Graffiti* (1973) or the outer space fantasies of his *Star Wars* franchise. Made for $11.5 million, *Star Wars* earned over $260 million after its rerelease run ended in 1979 (Cook 2000, 50). As important as its technical wizardry was its role in a lucrative merchandizing campaign. Toys, T-shirts, beach towels, and lunch boxes carried the *Star Wars* brand, certifying, in a whole new dimension, the place of movies within a larger system of commoditization. Ideologically, Lucas's film looked ahead to the 1980s Reagan era. Its optimistic catchphrase, "May the Force be with You," stood in stark contrast to the fatalism of "Come on Jake, it's Chinatown."

While the incredible success of *Jaws* took to new heights the blockbuster strategy initiated by *The Godfather* and *The Exorcist*, it did so without the narrative complexities of Coppola's gangster film or the R-rated perversities of Friedkin's horror classic. Its PG-13 pitch toward a younger, predominantly male audience would be a model for the blockbuster successes to follow – Lucas's *Star Wars*, *The Empire Strikes Back* (1980), *Return of the Jedi* (1983), and Spielberg's own *Raiders of the Lost Ark* (1981), *E.T. the Extra Terrestrial* (1982), and *Indiana Jones and the Temple of Doom* (1984). In the high-stakes blockbuster game, films that were too adult-oriented and lacked ancillary marketing schemes traveled a rough road, as true of Paramount's high-profile remake of *The Great Gatsby* (1974). While *Gatsby* was relatively successful, other films such as *The Hindenburg* (1975), *Sorcerer* (1977; a remake of the French classic *The Wages of Fear*, 1955), and *The Wiz* (1978; a black cast adaptation of the Broadway musical based on *The Wizard of Oz*, 1939, featuring superstar Diana Ross and young Michael Jackson) were out-and-out failures. None, however, was as big a bust as Michael Cimino's auteurist prestige Western, *Heaven's Gate* (1978), which, like *Cleopatra* 15 years before, almost brought a studio to its knees.

These flops notwithstanding, the Spielberg–Lucas approach seemed to insure a new box office record every year. Yet as Stephen Prince has pointed out, the startling grosses recorded during this time were largely a function of higher ticket prices. The number of ticket buyers remained essentially the same as during the previous 20 years (2000, 19). With the number of moviegoers holding steady, the purveyors of film had to look for revenues from beyond the big screen. Product tie-ins, as noted, were one angle, but thanks to two other emerging formats – the sale of movies on video and exhibition on cable television networks – the industry was able to generate profits through a strategy of repackaging aimed at home viewing. In 1976, JVC launched its Video Home System (VHS), a half-inch videotape cassette that could record and play back images. In 1976, Paramount agreed to the sale of its film library on videocassette and, a year later, Twentieth Century-Fox did the same. In 1977, the first video store opened in Los Angeles and the delivery of the movies was forever changed. The movies had been made smaller decades earlier when the studios had sold their libraries for broadcast on television. But now the movie fan was no longer at the mercy of TV station programmers and began tape-recording his or her favorite movies broadcast on television. In its 1984 decision in *Sony versus Universal* (the Betamax case), the Supreme Court declared that the copying of television shows at home did not constitute copyright infringement and, furthermore, that Sony, as manufacturer of the home recording machine, also could not be held liable. Films-on-video would remain the industry standard for home use – despite the introduction of the Video Laser Disk by Philips in 1978 – until the Digital Video Disk (DVD) was developed by several companies in 1995. It is difficult to overstate the economic windfall generated for the studios by the migration of films into the home. By 1989, sales and rentals for home video were twice that of the domestic box office and, as we shall see, played a crucial role in the continued spread of Hollywood product around the globe (Balio 1998, 58).

The emergence of cable networks and the role they have played in film production and exhibition are much more complicated than the rather straightforward advantages presented by film-on-video sales. As Barbara Klinger discusses in this volume, Home Box Office (HBO) became, by the early 1980s, the dominant force in pay cable television and an important player in the financing of films for theatrical release. Its majority share position within the cable market enabled it to obtain very friendly terms for cable casting rights to films made by the studios. HBO, along with its primary premium channel competitor, Showtime, and outlets such as The Movie Channel further expanded the exhibition sites for theatrical films. Unlike the broadcast networks, many cable channels could present Hollywood movies uncut or without traditional commercial interruption. Moreover, by the end of the 1980s and throughout the 1990s, many films by-passed theatrical exhibition entirely and moved directly to video or exhibition on cable TV.

As the cost of film production increased, home video and cable television became crucial ways for a movie to recoup costs or turn a profit. At the beginning of the 1980s, the average negative cost for a film – the cost of obtaining a property, hiring talent, building sets, and actually shooting the movie – was $9 million. By decade's end, that figure had risen to $23 million (Prince 2000, 20). And by 1995, the average production cost for a film was close to $39 million (Maltby 1998, 37). The average ticket price also rose steadily, although not quite at the same pace as the cost of film production. In 1980, the average ticket price was $2.69, but by 2009, that figure stood at $7.50. To be sure, moviegoers in urban centers like New York and Los Angeles paid more for a ticket and might have marveled at the matinee prices still in effect in many smaller cities throughout the country. Admissions rose consistently after 1982, contributing to a healthy industry that also witnessed an increase in the number of indoor theaters. In 1990, there were 22,904 movie screens in the United States. By 2009, there were more than 38,000 and that did not count the just over 600 drive-in theaters still in business.[1]

The numbers, however, do not tell the complete story. Even before much of American film-watching moved home on video and later DVD, it moved from urban centers to the suburbs, from the once grand movie palaces to the multiplex that was often in close proximity to the indoor shopping malls that dated back to the opening of the Southdale Center in Edina, Minnesota, in 1956. The American flight to the suburbs relocated moviegoers to theaters that now discarded the ornamental designs of an earlier era. During the 1960s and 1970s, downtown movie palaces turned to exhibiting pornography, got converted to mega-churches, or were abandoned all together. Now much of the nation saw its movies in smaller, box-like theaters with diminished screens. The suburban theater dominated movie-going after 1980, and while the Cineplex-Odeon chain tried to offer a more luxurious experience through its well-appointed theaters, for many viewers, going to the movies remained a minimalist experience, often at a theater attached to a strip or enclosed mall.

The Return of Vertical Integration

Among the most dramatic events of this period was the industry's return to vertical integration – the ownership of production-distribution-exhibition by a single company that had been declared monopolistic by the Paramount decree in 1948. Taking advantage of the original consent decrees it had signed that ruled out trade practices such as blind and block booking but that had not strictly forbidden its ownership of theaters, Paramount, which in 1966 had become a subsidiary of Gulf+Western, turned to the acquisition of theaters in 1986. So, too, did Universal (owned by MCA) and Columbia, the two never having been part of the 1948 High Court decision since, at the time, they had not owned theaters. The Justice Department, under the far less regulatory administration of President Ronald Reagan, would eventually permit Warner Communications to enter the exhibition market as well. By 1986, these companies were once again vertically integrated with control of over 3,500 screens out of a total of 22,000 nationwide, a percentage, as Richard Maltby has demonstrated, equivalent to the holdings of the affiliated majors in 1938 (1998, 38).

The return to vertical integration was both preceded and accompanied by a renewed round of movie industry mergers and acquisitions, this time to a degree far in excess of that which had characterized the 1960s. During the 1980s and 1990s, almost all the well-known studios, themselves already part of larger conglomerates, either merged with other media companies or were acquired by even larger entities. By 2010, six conglomerates controlled the movie business – Time-Warner, Sony, News Corporation, Viacom, NBC/Universal, and the Walt Disney Company. The Disney Company, which had been in the animation business since 1923, had emerged in the late 1980s and 1990s as one of the most successful and powerful forces in entertainment. Under the leadership of Michael Eisner and Jeffrey Katzenberg, it underwent a renewal of its animation division, with hits like *Who Framed Roger Rabbit* (1988) and *The Little Mermaid* (1989), acquired Miramax Films in 1993, and took over the ABC and ESPN television networks. Although Eisner and Katzenberg would be gone by 2005 – in 1994, Katzenberg helped found Dreamworks with Spielberg and David Geffen – Disney's business would stay strong, fueled in great measure by its purchase of the Pixar Animation Studios in 2006.

Thus, between 1980 and 2010, the movie business was at the center of a general trend toward media mergers and consolidation, attached to companies whose holdings included internet services; television production and station ownership; radio broadcasting; satellite ownership; book, magazine, and music publishing; and theme parks. Unlike the conglomerate ownership of the 1960s, these companies were more dedicated to a unified strategy of manufacturing entertainment products or providing leisure services, although, of course, they remained thoroughly involved in the licensing of their brands for sale in ancillary markets. The merger musical chairs reminds us that while audiences know these company names – to the extent they know them at all – as producers of entertainment, for shareholders and acquisitive boardrooms they are pieces in a larger business strategy aimed at the synergistic exploitation of media and leisure on a global scale (Elsaesser 2004, 55).

In 1983, the US produced approximately 350 films. Just five years later that number would approach 600 (Balio 1998, 58). With the major studios meeting less than a quarter of this demand, companies such as Orion, Carolco, New Line, and Cannon could enter the market and find ready consumers. But the demand for more films was not limited to the domestic arena. After 1980, the globalization of Hollywood accelerated at a remarkable pace, in terms of both US films exported overseas and the influx of foreign-born filmmakers working in the US. As Richard Maltby and Tino Balio have pointed out, film-on-video permitted American films to further saturate global markets. By the end of the 1980s, the most important source of Hollywood revenue coming from overseas was video (Maltby 2003, 215). As the number of commercial television stations in Europe grew, along with cable and satellite operations, new and voracious venues opened up for American films. Furthermore, theaters throughout Europe and Asia – and Japan in particular – underwent a long overdue restoration during this period with hundreds of new screens opening on both continents. "By 1994," Tino Balio writes, "the overseas market surpassed the domestic in film rentals for the first time" (1998, 60).

Genre Cinema and Its Audiences – Trends and Cycles

In 1993, Bill Murray starred in *Groundhog Day*, a mildly amusing comedy in which he plays Phil Connors, a weatherman sent to cover the eponymous event only to get trapped inside it, waking up every morning to relive the same day. After 1980, the American moviegoer could be forgiven for identifying with Phil, for each year of new releases brought first a startling and then quite predictable sense of déjà vu. Indeed, perhaps the most distinguishing aspect of film production during this period was its reliance on the sequel. Not surprisingly, perhaps, it was a strategy applied largely to horror, science fiction, and action cinema, although there were three installments of *The Godfather*. Horror films, especially the slasher subgenre, led the way. Between 1978 and 2009, there were 10 *Halloween* films, 12 in the *Friday the 13th* franchise, and nine installments of *A Nightmare on Elm Street*. Given the low and then modest budgets for these films, they were incredibly profitable vehicles as each franchise grossed in excess of $200 million over the years.[2] These franchises represented single concept filmmaking reduced to its essence, a repetition, with slight variation, that required virtually no introduction of characters and modest development of their motives. And while such franchises did rely on viewer familiarity, anyone who had fallen behind could get a quick tutorial on home video.

But slasher films barely scratched the surface. The action-adventure–sci-fi genres produced four installments of *Rambo* (1982–2008), four of *Lethal Weapon* (1987–1998), and four *Raiders/Indiana Jones* (1981–2008) titles. There were three *Robocop* films (1987–1992), six rounds of *Rocky* (1976–2006), three resurrections of the original *Alien* (1979–1997), and four aptly titled *Die Hard* installments (1988–2007). The *Star Trek* franchise, discussed by Ina Rae Hark in the hardcover/online edition, produced 10 films (1979–2002) – and the mission continues. Superheroes such as Superman, Batman, and Spider-Man, as well as those first drawn for Marvel Comics, have had a remarkable reincarnation on the big screen with no end in sight, as Bart Beaty illustrates in this volume. Comedy – particularly its lowbrow version – was not exempt, with National Lampoon's vacation series (four between 1983–1997), *Police Academy* (six between 1984 and 1989), and *Scary Movie* (four between 2000 and 2006). Sequels proved to be a low-risk/high-return formula, popular with the all-important youth market and attractive, not to mention enormously profitable, for the stars on whom the series depended.

A Cinema of Spectacle

The three genres most closely associated with sequel franchises were also those most thoroughly bound up with the new cinema of spectacle, that is, films that relied to a significant extent on special effects, animated or computer-generated images, and innovations in sound technology such as Dolby and THX. David Cook applies the term "cinema of attractions" – which Tom Gunning has used to characterize the early years of American film when visual presentation trumped narrative – to describe a similar tendency in blockbusters of the 1970s. Cook explains this return to an earlier mode on the basis of the industry's return to a pre-vertically integrated industrial structure (2000, 44). Invoking the cinema of attractions is a useful approach, as is Cook's reminder that with genres such as the musical and horror film (and we might add the Western), classical Hollywood never fully abandoned this impulse. The new cinema of spectacle continued to expand well into the era of renewed vertical integration. Its emergence in this period can certainly be tied to developments in image and sound technology and their capacity to make the impossible or unreal appear plausible or authentic. As Michael Allen has argued, the goal of technological experiments in color, sound, and image is aimed toward "reducing the spectators' sense of their 'real world,' and replacing it with a fully believable artificial one" (1998, 127). This believable artificial world is the foundation for films that imagine an otherworldly future time (the *Star Wars* and *Star Trek* films) or an earthly future time (*Robocop* or the *Terminator* series), or that integrate the known world with fantasy science and action (the *Spider-Man* films). A similar impulse fuels films that are wholly animated (the *Toy Story* series) or rely on CGI to give scale and depth to an imagined past (*Gladiator*).

The contemporary cinema of spectacle rather neatly matches the high-concept approach to film production. While some films like *Terminator 2: Judgment Day* (1991), present a complicated story, many films pivot around simple stories in which complexities receive little explanation, with deployment of special effects rather than representation of social or psychological problems of primary importance. It is not only image morphing, digital compositing, or 3D that characterizes this new mode, but also editing, which is used as much for percussive effect as for narrative exposition. Indeed, even in films located entirely in the "real world," cutting for sense stimulation – to match actions such as explosions or to synchronize movement with music – often works to construct a believable yet radically fragmented phenomenal world, as Kristen Whissel and Bart Beaty point out in this volume. Although the cinema has always been invested in spectacle – from *Ben-Hur* in 1925 to the 1959 remake and *Cleopatra* (1963) – with editing a key rhythmic device to stimulate the senses and build suspense, after 1980, spectacle was the main "attraction" in many instances. Rather than conceal the signs of spectacle as part of an integrated mise-en-scène in support of narrative, the contemporary mode tends to revel in these signs, declaring that spectacle *is* the story.

In the 1980s, the cinema responded to two other image-based forms – music television and video gaming. The MTV network was launched in 1981 and its combination of music with fast cutting created an aesthetic for a key movie demographic – 15- to 25-year-olds – that would inform the editing styles of many films. Video gaming for domestic use began in 1972 and would have little impact on film in its primitive early stages. But as the gaming industry developed more sophisticated imaging technology, its penetration into the American market was registered across age and gender groups. In the 1980s and 1990s, Disney, Spielberg's DreamWorks, and LucasArts all invested in video game development. As gaming could be applied to three different venues – consoles (such as television), computers, and mobile devices – its versatility extended its potential competition with film and broadcast television. According to one industry estimate, revenues generated by video gaming in 2008 were close to $12 billion.[3] These were figures the movie industry could not ignore, and high-profile filmmakers continued to look at the artistic and financial possibilities of creating video games. Moreover, the special effects of big screen movies had begun to reflect the explosive visual dynamics of video gaming and a reciprocal aesthetic, not to mention market, was firmly established.

Films that featured special effects were hardly incompatible with a serious, socially aware cinema. Ridley Scott's *Blade Runner* (1982), adapted from a novel by Philip K. Dick, was among the first dystopian visions of a future world, one in which humanity must confront the artificial life of its own creation. Unlike, say, the *Terminator* films, *Blade Runner* creates a future world that harkens back to the urban maze of film noir but is now a fully globalized city and, as in earlier German Expressionist films like *Metropolis* (1927), a city divided between the wealthy living above the fray in high-tech, high-rise structures and the poor and working classes living on the steamy, rainy street level (in *Metropolis* the workers also inhabit subterranean factories). *Blade Runner*'s opening shots introduce a skyline of fiery explosions over a dark city of monumental structures, the antithesis of an America that had long identified itself with frontiers of open land. *The Matrix* (1999), by contrast, explores and gives visual dimension to the conflict and interpenetration of reality and simulation, imagining a world that, for many, is both a product of and uniquely described by the cinema and its special effects.

Changes in film technology went far beyond its impact on the movie-going experience and reshaped film production in profound ways. In the late 1970s and 1980s, filmmakers began to use video monitors during shooting in order to gain instant access to their work rather than waiting to look at dailies. Additionally, transferring film to video for editing purposes provided cost and efficiency benefits. By the mid-1980s, developments in technology permitted the transfer of footage to digital storage so that editing could be done on computers. Shots could now be edited together and whole sequences assembled without any celluloid film actually being cut. By the mid-1990s, software had been developed that permitted digitized images to play at the 24-frames-per-second film standard, rather than the 30-frames-per-second video standard.

If the post-1980 period witnessed something of a revolution in editing equipment, an equivalent change took place with the invention of the Steadicam. Developed by cinematographer/inventor Garrett Brown, and first used commercially in 1976, the Steadicam was a device that stabilized the hand-held camera image. A combination movie camera, video monitor, and waist-shoulder harness, the Steadicam permitted the camera operator to move where cranes and dollies could not go and to follow action without having an eye fixed to a viewfinder. Hand-held shots could now be as smooth as traditional tracking shots but with an intimacy and dexterity not available to bulkier equipment. In its first generation of use, the Steadicam found its most prestigious employer in Stanley Kubrick who shot virtually all of *The Shining* (1980), and especially its signature hallway traveling shots, with the new apparatus.

The contemporary cinema of spectacle also helped create an important new adjunct to the industry – the special effects house. The most important of these has been Industrial Light and Magic (ILM), founded by George Lucas in 1975 to create the visual effects for *Star Wars*. For the next 35 years, ILM would pioneer advances in computer-generated technologies, contributing to hundreds of films, including *Jurassic Park* (1993), *Forrest Gump* (1994), *Titanic* (1997), and the *Harry Potter* series (2001–2010). With Skywalker Sound, Lucas also oversaw the creation of the most advanced technology for recording, editing, and mixing sound. With ILM and Skywalker, Lucas, more than any other individual, moved the cinema toward the digital age, providing tools that fueled the new cinema of spectacle.

Oedipus in a Time Machine

Hollywood during the 1980s became an index of the Reagan years and the conservatism that swept the former mid-level studio-era actor into the White House. The return to vertical integration was made possible by Reagan's sweeping deregulation of business at the core of his economic philosophy. The aesthetic makeover that fueled the Reagan revolution – insisting that America see itself as ever victorious rather than defeated and defeatist – was reflected in the new visual pyrotechnics and genre friendly productions of the age. The high-concept approach to film production – its narrative simplicity and technical bravado – both directly and indirectly expressed the tightly scripted, well-choreographed sound-bite politics of Reagan's two terms. Even the name given to his proposed strategic missile defense system – Star Wars – adopted and echoed the fantasies emanating from Hollywood, as Susan Jeffords details in this volume.

From Shirley Temple and Andy Hardy to the Dead End Kids and Beach Party teenagers, Hollywood by no means ignored the appeal of child and teenage protagonists, building stars and cycles around their characters and concerns. The post-1980 period was no exception. But films of this era represented the loss of innocence in terms of ideological paradoxes central to Reagan's presidency: Preparing for the future meant returning to America's allegedly simpler past, and real-life political challenges became just another Hollywood movie plot to be solved. Jeffords finds much of the sci-fi, fantasy, and horror/comedy fare of the period driven by plots that strap Oedipus into a time machine, a move underscored by the desire either to secure the son's future through the past (*Star Wars*) or to restore the father's "rightful" place in the present (*Back to the Future* and its sequels). If innocence ultimately could not be regained, redemption became a formulaic second choice – a logic prominently reflected in the smug pragmatism of many of the period's protagonists.

The recalibration of youth rebellion into an entitled sense of disaffected boredom in the 1980s produced its own group of filmmakers. As Thomas Doherty points out in the hardcover/online edition, writer-director-producer John Hughes specialized in ensemble teen-oriented films (with the so-called Brat Pack) that combined light comedy with coming-of-age angst. Two films starring Matthew Broderick imagined radically different outcomes for his clever, rule-breaking high school persona. *Ferris Bueller's Day Off* (1986) features its eponymous hero as the master of hooky, fooling his parents and outsmarting the high school dean of students, as he takes his two best friends on a joy ride through Chicago. The power of the mildly subversive teenager is represented by Bueller's ability to break the fourth wall at points and narrate his life directly to the audience. In John Badham's *War Games* (1983), Broderick plays a high school teen whose computer hacking mischief almost leads to global nuclear war. Here, breaking the rules affords a much more terrifying education, but still one that is ultimately life affirming.

The direct camera address of Hughes's films and the MTV-style aesthetics of fragmented screens and flash-edits that characterize many of the decade's movies did not exactly constitute a radicalization of style. Staging narratives of ideological recuperation, 1980s films placed style over substance. As such, they were part and parcel of an era that, perhaps for the first time in history, sought conservative renewal via the superficial incorporation of older, more progressive, or even apparently radical tropes. Just as Reagan's urging to return to old-fashioned values on the surface seemed to mimic the left's argument that, in order to deal responsibly with the present, one has to understand the past, what looked like the entertainment industry's charting of new creative paths amounted to little more than a plundering of past styles or icons – often those of the counterculture – which, in the process, became eviscerated of substance and ideologically retooled.

In *An Officer and a Gentlemen* (1982), one of the first big commercial and critical triumphs of Reaganite entertainment, Richard Gere's post-Vietnam protagonist seeks a career in the armed forces. While his motorcycle vaguely echoes the 1960s counterculture and its expression of freedom and individualism, the film disavows the anti-establishment politics present in such films as *Easy Rider* (1969) – a strategy copied in subsequent pro-military films like *Top Gun* (1986). The film preaches self-reliance, moral conservatism, and traditional gender values. But Hollywood liberals, too, skewed more conservative, offering up carefully wrought narratives of restoration. Robert Redford made his much acclaimed directorial debut with the family drama *Ordinary People* (1981), whose story about a psychologist's treatment of a dysfunctional teenager shrewdly displaced politically charged problems of the Vietnam era. Intergenerational strife and survivor guilt are defined in terms of personal trauma, which therapy is able to resolve. Through the formation of a male triad – father, son, therapist – and the expulsion of the mother, the film indirectly seeks to reconcile generational rifts created a decade earlier during the anti-war movement.

Stars

The Reagan-era 1980s and early 1990s witnessed a revival of the star system, and, because stars tend to be associated with archetypal roles, the era saw a renaissance of certain genres and subgenres. Second-wave feminist desires to see women in substantial roles arguably helped bring about the renewal of the woman's film and the retooling of traditional male-centered genres, like the Western (*The Ballad of Little Jo*, 1993; *Bad Girls*, 1994; *Buffalo Girls*, 1995) and the courtroom drama (*Jagged Edge*, 1985; *Suspect*, 1987; *The Accused*, 1988; *Music Box*, 1989) to position women as figures in leading roles. The latter group – with no fewer than 21 films produced featuring female lawyers between 1985 and 1999 – did nevertheless betray the industry's unease with such shifting formulas;. While women are positioned as protagonists, initially, narrative trajectories often see male leads eclipse the women or undermine their power through various contingencies marking the female lawyer as unworthy or unqualified (Lucia 2005). During this period came the rise of such new names as Kathleen Turner (*Body Heat*, 1981; *Peggy Sue Got Married*, 1986), Debra Winger (*An Officer and a Gentleman*, 1982; *Terms of Endearment*, 1983), Glenn Close (*Fatal Attraction*, 1987; *Reversal of Fortune,* 1991), Jessica Lange (*Tootsie*, 1982; *Sweet Dreams*, 1985), and Cher who already was a popular singer and television star (*Silkwood*, 1983; *Moonstruck*, 1987).

First and foremost among this group was Meryl Streep, one of the few female actors of this period whose fame and popularity endured significantly far beyond the decade. From an academic acting background that led to gradually more prominent roles in the late 1970s (*Julia*, 1977; *The Deer Hunter*, 1978; *Kramer vs. Kramer*, 1979), Streep brought her Method-inflected approach to the woman's picture, which she almost single-handedly redefined in a string of high-profile prestige films – *The French Lieutenant's Woman* (1981), *Sophie's Choice* (1982), *Silkwood*, *Out of Africa* (1985), *Ironweed* (1987), and *The Bridges of Madison County* (1995). Celebrated as the best female actor in Hollywood, if occasionally lampooned for her catalogue of mannerisms and accents, Streep's success well into the new millennium has been an exceptional case that signaled the 1980s industry resolve to recapture a tradition of stardom in which a single player could convey the nexus of great acting, prestige entertainment, and star glamour – a tradition that largely had been lost, at least for female stars, since the 1960s and remains elusive for many performers of both sexes in an industry that markets performers as *either* actors *or* stars. No female performer came close to Streep in terms of longevity, critical recognition, or consistent success. Julia Roberts and Sandra Bullock, of a younger generation and sold as stars primarily, have earned industry awards in part as recognition of their box office power. For short periods Sally Field, in the 1980s, Susan Sarandon, in the 1980s and 1990s, and Jodie Foster (who has gone on to direct films) were considered among the best at their craft. But with few exceptions, the industry was not kind to its female stars as the emphasis on youthful good looks came down consistently harder on women than it did on men.

The most accomplished male actors of the earlier period – Dustin Hoffman, Al Pacino, Robert De Niro – delivered the occasionally acclaimed performance (*Rain Man*, 1988; *The Insider*, 1999; *Cape*

Fear, 1991, respectively) but spent much of their time in less than inspiring films. Jack Nicholson, on the other hand, became almost a cult figure whose enduring popularity matched his consistent critical praise for films such as *The Shining* (1979), *Terms of Endearment* (1983), *Prizzi's Honor* (1985), *A Few Good Men* (1992), *As Good As It Gets* (1997), and *The Departed* (2006). Among the new generation of stars, Eddie Murphy and Tom Hanks came from television. Murphy successfully transitioned from late night comedy to films that were action-comedy hybrids (*48 Hours*, 1982; *Trading Places*, 1983; *Beverly Hills Cop*, 1984). Hanks also started out in comedy (*Splash*, 1984; *Big*, 1988) before moving into the top echelon of industry players with his much-praised performances in *Philadelphia* (1993), *Forrest Gump* (1994), and *Saving Private Ryan* (1998).

The biggest career launched during the 1980s was that of Tom Cruise, who parlayed his youthful good looks into stardom in *Risky Business* (1983) and *All the Right Moves* (1984) and rose to superstardom with *Top Gun*. But he showed he had more serious ambition in *Rain Man* (1988), *Born on the Fourth of July* (1989), *Eyes Wide Shut* (1999), and *War of the Worlds* (2005). Cruise is arguably the quintessential 1980s star, having tailored his persona around characters that are cynical, if charming, materialists with a capacity to reform (*Rain Man*; *A Few Good Men*; *Jerry Maguire*, 1996). The decade's obsession with father–son and other intergenerational male relationships found expression through the mutually beneficial casting of prestigious older stars such as Dustin Hoffman (*Rain Man*) and Paul Newman (*The Color of Money*, 1986) alongside the much younger Cruise.

Perhaps the most acclaimed actors of the post-1980 period were Sean Penn and Denzel Washington. Each displayed a remarkable range and an explosive intensity – Penn in *The Falcon and the Snowman* (1985), *Casualties of War* (1989), *The Thin Red Line* (1998), *Mystic River* (2003), *Milk* (2008), and Washington in *Cry Freedom* (1987), *Glory* (1989), *Malcolm X* (1992), *Training Day* (2001), in particular. In a career spanning more than four decades, Jeff Bridges moved comfortably between drama and comedy in films that included *The Last Picture Show* (1971), *Jagged Edge* (1985), *The Fabulous Baker Boys* (1989), and *The Big Lebowski* (1998). Perceived as a sexy star early in his career, his acting talent earned him industry respect and considerable praise for his flawed, middle-aged heroes in *Crazy Heart* (2009) and *True Grit* (2010).

A Socially Engaged Cinema

However much American film after 1980 appears dominated by spectacles and sequels, it would be wrong to characterize the era as engineered strictly for the family or teen audience. Indeed, while one historiographic narrative might posit a transition from the New Hollywood of *Midnight Cowboy* and *The French Connection* to a New New Hollywood (or New Hollywood II, as Derek Nystrom refers to it in this volume) of *Jaws* and *Star Wars*, it would be wrong to see here a complete break in the trajectory of American film. The industry and the culture had changed, but important tendencies of the earlier period remained and scores of new films invigorated the post-1980 era. Genres like the biopic and the literary adaptation, that had been staples of studio era production, also continue as important forces in contemporary film. So, too, has the war and returning veteran picture.

For the long years of the Vietnam War, the Hollywood cinema remained largely silent on the subject. One can certainly read war films like *The Dirty Dozen* (1967) and *M*A*S*H* (1970) or a Western such as *Little Big Man* (1970) as addressing some aspect of America's involvement in Vietnam, but as a subject for explicit representation there was little beyond a pro-victory, pro-war *The Green Berets* (1968) and Peter Davis's independent anti-war documentary *Hearts and Minds* (1974). This changed dramatically within a few years after the fall of Saigon in 1975. Over the next 15 years, dozens of films, and some of the era's most provocative, produced vivid depictions of jungle combat and the psychological damage wrought by the war. A short list of the most important films in this genre includes *Coming Home* (1978), *Who'll Stop the Rain* (1978), *The Deer Hunter* (1978), *Apocalypse Now* (1979), *First Blood* (1982), *The Killing Fields* (1984), *Platoon* (1986), *Good Morning, Vietnam* (1987), *Gardens of Stone* (1987), *Hamburger Hill* (1987), *Full Metal Jacket* (1987), *Born on the Fourth of July* (1989) and *In Country* (1989). Many of these films avoided the war narrative cliché in which combat turns a boy into a man, preferring instead to represent the profound physical and psychological

Figure 10.1 Young soldier Chris (Charlie Sheen) witnesses the brutal and senseless murder of innocent Vietnam villagers in Oliver Stone's *Platoon* (1986, producer Arnold Kopelson).

devastation done by wartime service. But few of these films turned their anger directly upon the policymakers of the Vietnam era or placed the conflict in a wider critique of Cold War ideology. Still, the luster that had accrued to the US military from the representations of World War II glory was certainly worn off by many of these films, as soldiers returned as victims not heroes, decorated with scars not medals. Indeed, *Coming Home*, *The Deer Hunter*, and *Full Metal Jacket* all registered a deeply self-destructive if not suicidal impulse that, for many, characterized the nation's involvement in Southeast Asia.

While it was in Oliver Stone's *Platoon* (1986) and *Born on the Fourth of July* that American cinema spoke with the greatest clarity and insisted that the nation confront the casualties of a tragic foreign policy, Stone was not the only director to offer a larger perspective on questions of historical responsibility. Between the late 1970s and early 1990s, several artistic approaches to this complex subject emerged, each signaling a profoundly different worldview. Like Coppola's *Apocalypse Now*, *Platoon* acquired landmark status for its frank and visceral depiction of the horrors US troops experienced and the horrors they caused by obliterating whole villages. While in loosely adapting Joseph Conrad's *Heart of Darkness*, Coppola was more interested in reading America's involvement in Vietnam as an extension of colonialism and western hubris, Stone replaced the language of art cinema with the genre conventions of the combat film. Stone's own frontline experiences in Vietnam lent *Platoon* historical authenticity. At the same time, to make the trauma of war crimes palatable to American audiences and to help them confront issues of national guilt and historical responsibility, Stone felt compelled to frame his story in Oedipal terms, with a young soldier caught between an ethical and an unethical, if not downright evil, father figure. We encounter Vietnam primarily as a moral dilemma, seen through the eyes of an innocent protagonist, rookie soldier Chris Taylor (Charlie Sheen), who stands between the immoral and ruthlessly pragmatic Staff Sergeant

Barnes (Tom Berenger) and the principled but self-effacing Sergeant Elias (Willem Dafoe). This dramaturgy proposes that the ethical quagmire of war and the ineluctability of historical guilt can be confronted and rationalized through clear-cut choices, suggesting that no war is too dark to disable our capacity for moral integrity, which, so the film suggests, will help bring about at least a symbolic resolution.

By contrast, Kubrick's *Full Metal Jacket* proposes a modernist vision of warfare that portrays military training and frontline combat as utterly consistent in sharing a homicidal and dehumanizing vision, which no individual can escape. Co-written by former war correspondent Michael Herr and set during the Tet Offensive, the film follows James T. "Joker" Davis (Matthew Modine) from bootcamp to Vietnam, where he works as a combat correspondent. Joker naively believes that his education and critical awareness of the US role in Vietnam will place him above the fray. By film's end, he has performed the mercy killing of a female Vietcong sniper, and his smug belief that he is at a critical remove from the war has been replaced by the hollow gaze of a soldier who has been exposed to the inferno of combat, which has turned him into a killer. In Kubrick's film, moral integrity is a fanciful fiction that becomes quickly eroded by the reality of psychic deformation under combat conditions and the naked will to survive.

In addition to this cycle of Vietnam War/returning veteran films, the serious Hollywood cinema turned to representing contemporary history in films like *Missing* (1982), *The Right Stuff* (1983), *Silkwood, Salvador* (1986), *Mississippi Burning* (1988), and *JFK* (1991) – a tradition continued by such films as *Quiz Show* (1994), *Apollo 13* (1995), *The Insider*, and *Good Night, and Good Luck* (2005). Each of these films anchors its critique in real events, exposing corporate and government crimes in the 1950s, 1960s, and 1970s. And among this group of filmmakers, no other mainstream director would be more associated with a post-1960s liberal project than *Platoon*'s Oliver Stone. As Robert Rosentone discusses in the hardcover/online edition, perhaps more than any other director of the period, Stone consciously attempts to write the history of the 1960s and 1970s, from Jim Morrison (*The Doors*, 1991) to Richard Nixon (*Nixon*, 1995). In *JFK* (1991), Stone wove together a dense collage of images – archival and reenactment in color and black-and-white – in order to summarize nearly three decades of conspiracy theory. Stone's film introduced the assassination controversy to a new generation while it also raised questions about the relationship between film and the project of authoring history (see Simon 1996).

The biopic reemerged during this period as well, in films as diverse as *Bound for Glory* (1976), *The Elephant Man* (1980), *Coal Miner's Daughter* (1980), *Mommie Dearest* (1981), *Reds* (1981), *Frances* (1982), *Amadeus* (1984), and *Sweet Dreams* (1985) – an interest that extended into the next decade and the new millennium with films such as *Hoffa* (1992), *Boys Don't Cry* (1999), *Erin Brockovich* (2000), *American Splendor* (2003), *Capote* (2005), and *Lincoln* (2012). *Gandhi*, a 1982 British production, gained considerable critical and popular success in the US. Not since the Warner Bros. biopics of the 1930s did the movie industry make such a deep investment in telling the stories of real people. The genre attracted some of the era's most acclaimed auteurs, who sought to infuse the biopic with political significance – indeed, whose very choice of topics was already intended as a political statement. Before specializing in satires on American gangsterism (*Bugsy*, 1992) and politics (*Bullworth*, 1994), Hollywood liberal Warren Beatty co-wrote, produced, and directed the ambitious epic *Reds* (1981), the story of American writer John Reed, who witnessed the Soviet revolution and wrote about it in *Ten Days that Shook the World*. Spike Lee decided to leave his Brooklyn habitat and venture into the Hollywood lion's den to make *Malcolm X* (1994) as a mainstream film that would receive wide distribution.

But it is *Raging Bull* (1980), Martin Scorsese's tale of Italian-American middle-weight champion Jake LaMotta, that stands out as the most distinguished biopic, and certainly one of the most distinguished films of the era. While the classical sports biopic, like *The Pride of the Yankees* (1942) and *Knute Rockne All American* (1940), had been vehicles for building American heroes, the boxing film had always been something of an antidote. In *Raging Bull* Scorsese continued that legacy with black-and-white cinematography that recalled *Body and Soul* (1947) and *The Set-Up* (1949). Here, the pride of the Bronx is exposed as a brutal man, consumed by sexual jealousy. The golden era of New York sports culture is demythologized, as is the immigrant story of upward mobility – from the Bronx to Madison Square Garden – by a portrait in which masculinity

Figure 10.2 On his first "date" with his future wife Vickie (Cathy Moriarty) in Martin Scorsese's *Raging Bull* (1980, producers Robert Chartoff and Irwin Winkler), the already married boxer, Jake La Motta (Robert DeNiro), takes her to his mother's apartment, where they admire a photo of Jake and his brother (Joe Pesci) adorned with rosary beads.

rests at the intersection of domestic violence, masochism, and blood sport. Whereas earlier films in the genre had functioned as social critique in their depiction of the fighter as victim exploited by a corrupt system, Scorsese's treatment looked inward, assigning LaMotta's fall to his own personal demons.

Writer-Directors and Other Auteurs

By 2010, Scorsese had consolidated his status as one of the era's recognized auteurs, the product of critical reception to be sure, but also the result of his longevity and ability to collaborate with actors of his own generation – Robert De Niro in particular – and those of the next as well, most notably Leonardo DiCaprio. But his career is characterized less by a unified oeuvre than by his alternation between genre pictures – largely gangster films – and more idiosyncratic projects like *The King of Comedy* (1982), *After Hours* (1985), *The Last Temptation of Christ* (1988), *Kundun* (1997), *The Aviator* (2004), and *Hugo* (2011). His work, moreover, has pivoted around two passions seemingly at odds with each other. The first is his signature imprint on the gangster film. Scorsese's fascination with the criminal world is less invested in its law-breaking than in its rigid codes of behavior – the hierarchies of power, the semiotics of dress, the slippery ethos of loyalty, the macho posturing, and the commitment to gun violence. In these pictures, the nuclear family has been eclipsed by the family of men, despite the rebellious voice given to Karen Hill (Lorraine Bracco) in *GoodFellas* (1990). These worlds revolve around patriarchal relationships of mentoring, paranoia, and betrayal. Scorsese's second passion is music – a world that is light years away from the destructive order of gangland. In *The Last Waltz* (1978), *No Direction Home: Bob Dylan* (2005) and *Shine a Light* (2008), Scorsese documents the creative energy and performance of The Band, Bob Dylan, and the Rolling Stones, respectively.

Viewed in this way, Scorsese appears very much an artist torn between two ancestries – the child of immigrants and also the child of the 1960s, a combination figured by the presence of The Who, Cream, and Derek and the Dominoes on the soundtrack of *GoodFellas*. By the time he won his first Oscar for directing *The Departed* (2006), Scorsese had assumed the mantle of industry elder statesmen, an oral historian of American film and a leading force behind its preservation.

Whereas Scorsese directed his first feature (*Who's That Knocking at My Door*, 1967) at age 25, Clint Eastwood would not get behind the camera until he was 41 and well established as a movie star. Although he directed his first film in 1971, it would not be until the late 1980s that his critical reputation would begin to take shape. Perhaps he needed to grow out of his onscreen personas such as high plains drifter and rogue cop, before he could be regarded seriously as a mature filmmaker. The first glimmer of this new understanding of Eastwood surfaced in 1988 with *Bird*, his biopic about Charlie Parker, and culminated four years later with *Unforgiven* (1992), his Oscar-winning Western. A eulogy for and a perpetuation of the gunfighter, *Unforgiven* features Eastwood as William Muny, an aging Westerner driven to strap on his holster one last time. Having retired to raise pigs and two children on his farm, he still could unleash the deadly force necessary to avenge the murder of a friend and kill a sadistic local sheriff. The gunfighter returns in *Unforgiven*, not in the name of the law but in the name of justice. This was territory Eastwood knew well, not only as an actor, but also as the disciple of filmmakers Don Siegel and Sergio Leone. As a filmmaker himself, however, this was not territory he would settle in. He followed *Unforgiven* with the remarkably sensitive *A Perfect World* (1993), in which Eastwood's Texas Ranger must wrestle with the humanity of the escaped killer he has tracked down. His closing remark and the film's last lines, "I don't know nothing. Not one damn thing," resonates with Eastwood films to come. Indeed, he would go on to direct himself in *Million Dollar Baby* (2004) and *Gran Torino* (2008), two films centered on the re-education of the iconic tough loner. In neither film can Eastwood fully relinquish this persona and to a great extent that is what these films are about – both a recognition and a refusal of aging, and the unexpected commitments and loss of certainty that come with it.

Since the 1980s, no one has moved between the roles of director and producer more prolifically and successfully than Steven Spielberg. During this period he served as producer on an array of films, from *Poltergeist* (1982) to *Back to the Future* (1985), from *Men In Black* (1997) to *Flags of Our Fathers* (2006). Indeed, perhaps no filmmaker is so thoroughly identified with the American cinema during this era. After *Jaws*, Spielberg established his career with action-adventure pictures that, with the exception of *1941* (1979), were box office successes. *Raiders of the Lost Ark* (1981), *E.T. the Extra-Terrestrial* (1982), and *Jurassic Park* (1993) fueled his authority within the industry. While two artistically ambitious projects of the 1980s, *The Color Purple* (1985) and *Empire of the Sun* (1987), failed to gain Spielberg the kind of critical respect he had hoped to achieve, he finally demonstrated that he was more than a director of family fare with his adaptation of *Schindler's List* (1993). The American cinema had always trod lightly in representing the Holocaust – Sidney Lumet's *The Pawnbroker* (1964), for example, explored the psychological wounds of survival more than the history of extermination. Spielberg presented stark images of Jews being rounded up and suffering in the death camp as it told the based-in-fact story of industrialist Oskar Schindler and his saving of close to 1,200 Jews in his employ. Greeted with near unanimous acclaim, it disturbed some that Spielberg had centered his Holocaust epic on the heroic efforts of a German Christian and that Jewish agency was largely obscured. But the film's success would fuel the Shoah Foundation, Spielberg's enormous project to preserve the voices and images of survivors and witnesses of Hitler's final solution. After *Schindler's List*, Spielberg would alternate between adult-oriented drama (*Catch Me If You Can*, 1992; *Munich*, 2005) and action films (*War of the Worlds*, 2005), but he would nevertheless remain closely tied to the representation of World War II through his *Saving Private Ryan* (1998) and his work as producer on Clint Eastwood's *Flags of Our Fathers* and *Letters from Iwo Jima* (2006).

The reconsolidation of the industry in the 1980s was not kind to everyone, and the era's most significant casualty may have been Francis Ford Coppola. Perhaps it was too much to ask any director to continue along a path begun with the first two *Godfather* films, in 1972 and 1974, *The Conversation* (1974), and *Apocalypse Now* (1979). In 1969, he created his own studio, American Zoetrope, which he founded as an alternative to established studios in order to spearhead independent filmmaking on the periphery of Hollywood. American Zoetrope produced such films as *The Conversation, Apocalypse Now,* and Carroll Ballard's *The Black Stallion* (1979).[4] But the studio would not become the successful, alternative production model Coppola had envisioned. *One From the Heart* (1982) and *The Cotton Club* (1984), while expressions of the director's innovative visual style, were box office failures, saddling Coppola with debts he would spend the decade paying off – or trying to. Had he not pursued the dream of Zoetrope with such hubris, perhaps Coppola could have remained an artistic force within the industry. But it could be that his darker sensibilities were simply out of touch with the Reagan 1980s, a period that saw the rise of Spielberg and Lucas and the decline of such figures as Robert Altman and Arthur Penn.

As the new era of entertainment conglomeration witnessed media giants extending their reach throughout foreign markets, a new wave of foreign filmmakers broke through to success in Hollywood. They were a diverse set of directors, already with auteurist reputations in their home countries, whose work spread across multiple genres. Paul Verhoeven came from the Netherlands and scored major hits in the sci-fi action genre with *Robocop* (1987) and *Total Recall* (1990) before directing the glossy murder mystery *Basic Instinct* (1992), controversial within the gay and lesbian community for its depiction of a murderous lesbian (Sharon Stone), and then the equally controversial *Showgirls* (1995), the first high-budgeted ($40–45 million) studio film released with the NC-17 rating. German-born director Wolfgang Petersen used the critical praise for his World War II drama *Das Boot* (1982) to gain an entrée to Hollywood and the production of the high-budget action films, such as *In the Line of Fire* (1993), *Air Force One* (1997), and *The Perfect Storm* (2000).

Contributing to the artistry of many films and, indeed, to the authorship of many filmmakers is the musical composer. Chief among them is John Williams, a Juilliard alumnus who, after playing piano in New York jazz clubs and recording studios, went on to become perhaps the most successful film score composer of the post-1960 period, with accomplishments extending well into the new millennium. Over his decades-long career, Williams has composed or adapted the music for a remarkable number of films across multiple genres, gaining his greatest recognition through his association with Steven Spielberg, for whom he scored the music to virtually all of the director's work. His music has provided the aural foundation for Spielberg's *Jaws, Schindler's List, Raider's of the Lost Ark* (1981) (and the entire *Indiana Jones* series to follow), as well as for such diverse film as *The Poseidon Adventure* (1972), *The Towering Inferno* (1974), and *JFK,* to name just a few. He supplied the music for the *Star Wars* franchise and for the first three installments of the *Harry Potter* series. Williams has been particularly adept at creating the grand sounds required for the cinema of spectacle. Jerry Goldsmith would have a four-decade career scoring films beginning in 1962. After success in television and radio, he went on to work in the movies as the New Hollywood was emerging and wrote scores for *The Planet of the Apes* (1968), *Patton* (1970), and *Chinatown,* among many others. In *Chinatown,* in particular, he creates a lush atmosphere imbued with a haunting mixture of nostalgia, longing, and inscrutable mystery.

Women in Hollywood

While women had played important roles as screenwriters and directors during the silent era, their access to jobs behind the camera had been limited throughout the classical studio years. Directors Dorothy Arzner and Ida Lupino had been exceptions to the rules that only began to be rewritten in the 1970s, most notably with Elaine May, whose off-beat comedies *A New Leaf* (1971) and *The Heartbreak Kid* (1972) put her on the map, before her directing career experienced a setback with *Mickey and Nicky* (1976). May, however, did continue to find success as a screenwriter with *Heaven Can Wait* (1978), before making another notoriously ill-fated return to directing with *Ishtar* (1987). But it was not until the post-1980 period that a diverse set of women directors gained access to mainstream production and a (solitary) woman assumed the position of studio chief. In 1980, after a brief acting career and various jobs at MGM and Columbia, Sherry Lansing became the first woman president of a major studio – Twentieth Century-Fox. Twelve years later she took the reins at Paramount and oversaw a successful run at that studio before stepping down in 2004. While many attributed her success to her "disowning" a feminist sensibility – with productions like *Fatal Attraction* (1987) and *Indecent Proposal* (1993) – she did nevertheless produce *The Accused* (1988), which ostensibly, at least, supported the victim of a gang rape (Jodie Foster, in an Academy Award winning performance.)

Throughout the 1970s and 1980s, there was probably no more important woman artist in Hollywood than Barbra Streisand. Like Bing Crosby and Frank Sinatra before her, she achieved enormous success across three popular arts – as recording artist, cabaret singer, and box office movie star. But unlike her male predecessors, she would achieve success behind the camera as well. After founding Barwood, her own production company, she wrote, directed, and starred in *Yentl* (1983), the story of a shtetl girl who impersonates a boy so as to study in a yeshiva. She would produce and direct herself again in *The Prince of Tides* (1991) and *The Mirror Has Two Faces* (1996).

As for the new class of women directors who did not get their start in front of the camera, their films reflected a diverse set of interests and resist simple labeling under the term "woman's picture." Among that group are Amy Heckerling (*Fast Times at Ridgemont High*, 1982), Amy Jones (screenplay for *Mystic Pizza*, 1988), Callie Khouri (screenplay for *Thelma & Louise*, 1991), and Penelope Spheeris (*Wayne's World*, 1992). Nancy Meyers, Penny Marshall, and Kathryn Bigelow had the most consistent success. Meyers started out as a writer of such women-centered comedies as *Private Benjamin* (1980), *Baby Boom* (1987), and *Father of the Bride* (1991), and then took on directing her own screenplays in *Something's Gotta Give* (2003) and *It's Complicated* (2009). Marshall strung three hits together with *Big* (1988), *Awakenings* (1990), and *A League of Their Own* (1992), the latter centering on an all-female baseball team during World War II. Bigelow consistently worked within the action genre typically dominated by men. Her deep understanding of the structural dynamics of genre cinema (showcased in intelligent form in the teen vampire story *Near Dark*, 1986), as well as her dynamic sense of editing and gift for pacing and suspense, informed the cop films *Blue Steel* (1989) and *Point Break* (1991). Her direction of *The Hurt Locker* (2008), about an army unit in Iraq charged with disarming improvised explosive devices, earned her the first-ever Oscar awarded to a female director.

Gay and Lesbian Representation and Queer Cinema

Just as it had taken Hollywood more than a decade to turn attention to the Vietnam War, so, too, it would not be until the mid-1980s, roughly 15 years after the Stonewall uprising in New York City, that Hollywood would engage openly, and in a culturally nuanced manner, with homosexuality. John Sayles's *Lianna* (1983), an independent and modestly budgeted film, told the story of its title character, the wife of a college professor whose affair with her own female teacher leads to the end of her marriage and her pursuit of a new sexual identity. *Personal Best* (1982) and *Desert Hearts* (1985) also attempted sensitive portrayals of lesbian romance – a far cry from William Friedkin's *Cruising* (1980) and its lurid misrepresentation of a homicidal Greenwich Village gay community. Skittish and conservative as it is, the industry was slow to represent the AIDS crisis. The first films dealing with the disease were Bill Sherwood's independent film *Parting Glances* (1985) and the PBS-financed *Longtime Companion* (1990), which received a theatrical release, as Michael Bronski discusses in this volume.

In the late 1980s and early 1990s, however, independent cinema responded to Hollywood's avoidance of AIDS and its exploitation mentality with a series of alternative and indigenously authored portrayals of gay men, most notably Tom Kalin's *Swoon* (1992), a reworking of the Leopold and Loeb story, Greg Araki's *The Living End* (1992), a New Wave-influenced drama about AIDS and young male rebels on the lam, Todd Haynes's avant-gardist episodic film, *Poison* (1991), and Gus Van Sant's *My Own Private Idaho* (1993), set among queer juvenile delinquents and male prostitutes in the Pacific Northwest. The same region is also the setting for the director's overlooked early masterpiece, *Mala Noche* (1986), about the erotic attraction shared by two men who speak different languages but do, nevertheless, manage to communicate their desire. Key proponents of what came to be called the New Queer Cinema, these filmmakers created work that flew in the face of mainstream attitudes about homosexuality, as each crafted honest portrayals about the dignity of gay desire without ideological alibis, embellishments, or censorship. Such attitudes were furnished by Jonathan Demme's prestigious AIDS drama, *Philadelphia*, however, which invited mainstream approval of the topic through the traditional homophobic formula of isolating its gay characters from politics, from one another, and eventually, from life itself. A mainstream box office success that garnered several Academy Awards, *Philadelphia* was regarded as a concession, of sorts, to the gay community's vociferous protest against the polemically charged portrait of a mentally disturbed, sexually perverse serial killer in Demme's previous film, the spectacularly successful thriller, *The Silence of the Lambs* (1991). Its star, Jodie Foster, was outed by the gay community in the course of its protests. As Michael Bronski explains, independent queer cinema, too, gradually changed in the course of the 1990s through the influence of mainstream culture, turning gradually more assimilationist and, thus, losing its radical edge over the entertainment industry, which soon "discovered" white middle-class gays as a valuable demographic.

Independent Film

As much as the post-1975 period can be framed in terms of the spectacle blockbuster, it can also be defined by the expansion of independent production. As Geoff King points out in this volume, independence in film is a rather unstable concept or at least one that has a wide spectrum of applications – with one category of independent production so closely tied to the studio mainstream that its independence is only of degree not kind. And some of the companies that found initial success with modestly budgeted first-time projects made a very smooth transition to larger productions featuring bigger stars. Perhaps the most important of these was Miramax, a production-distribution company founded by Bob and Harvey Weinstein in 1979. Miramax functioned as an independent producer both separate from and under the ownership of one of the Big Six, in this case Disney, which purchased Miramax in 1993 and sold it in 2010. Miramax was responsible for dozens of films at the heart of independent cinema over the past 30 years, producing or distributing *sex, lies and videotape* (1989), *Reservoir Dogs* (1992), and *Pulp Fiction* (1994). Perhaps the other most successful independent production company of this period was Orion. Founded in 1978, Orion had consistent success during the 1980s with a string of Oscar winners – *Amadeus*, *Platoon*, *Dances with Wolves* (1990) and *The Silence of the Lambs*. It also produced a cluster of critically praised films by Woody Allen – *Zelig* (1983), *Hannah and Her Sisters* (1986) and *Crimes and Misdemeanors* (1989).

But there was also a segment of independent production operating at a greater distance from the studios. Jim Jarmusch and John Sayles spearheaded this movement in the 1980s. Jarmusch's *Stranger Than Paradise* (1984) was a breakthrough for low-budget, personal filmmaking aimed at a niche audience open to a deliberative, non-glossy form and minimal narrative. Its detached treatment of three quirky characters who travel from New York to Cleveland to Florida hinges on long takes, claustrophobic interiors, and slow camera movement. Its austere, black-and-white cinematography perfectly captures the spirit of late punk lower Manhattan – a spirit its main characters take with them on the road. The film's modest box office success on a budget of approximately $100,000 signaled to other filmmakers that there just might be opportunities for them, as well, outside of mainstream studio production. Sayles would prove to be one of the more prolific filmmakers of the 1980s, and in *Lianna*, *The Brother From Another Planet* (1984), and *Matewan* (1987) his creative independence was devoted to politically charged subjects. On the West Coast, the independent scene produced *Chan is Missing* (1982), directed by Wayne Wang in collaboration with a community of Asian and Asian-American film artists, many of whom had studied at San Francisco State University. The film uses a stolen money mystery as a means of representing life within the Chinese-American community. With its intimate, black-and-white images, many devoted to the alleys and streets of San Francisco's Chinatown, it offered a much-needed perspective on a minority culture whose cinematic identity had long been defined by studio-era products like Charlie Chan and martial arts imports. A half-generation later, the independence represented by Jarmusch and Wang would fuel the early work of Richard Linklater (*Slacker*, 1991; *Dazed and Confused*, 1993) and Kevin Smith (*Clerks*, 1994).

Female directors who preceded Kathryn Bigelow and Nancy Meyers operated with modest success on the independent margins at least a decade earlier, as well. In 1978, Claudia Weill made the female relationship film *Girlfriends* and, after winning critical acclaim, was able to obtain studio distribution, which helped her follow up with a Hollywood production, *It's My Turn* (1980), featuring rising star Jill Clayburgh. One of the most prolific women directors of the 1970s and 1980s was Joan Micklin Silver; whose independent film *Hester Street* (1975) is set in the late 1880s Jewish immigrant community in New York's Lower East Side. In 1977, she made *Between the Lines*, a film about the alternative newspaper publishing scene. Her most accessible feature is the 1988 independent comedy *Crossing Delancey*, set among present-day Jewish immigrants on the Lower East Side. Following the strategy of many other women filmmakers, Micklin Silver also directed for television.

Other notable independent women directors of the 1980s include Susan Seidelmann and Allison Anders. Like Micklin Silver's work, Seidelman's early films, *Smithereens* (1982) and *Desperately Seeking Susan* (1985), affectionately focus on New York City in the early 1980s. The former, with its alternative music track, often is classified as a punk musical, and the latter film features performers who would soon become famous, particularly Madonna, which helped make the film a hit and launched Seidelman's Hollywood career. Anders, too, has roots in the alternative music scene. In 1987, she co-directed *Border Radio*, a story about three rock musicians who flee to Mexico. Her critically acclaimed 1992 feature *Gas, Food, Lodging* is an intimate family drama about a waitress and her daughters living in a small Western town.

Since the mid-1970s, independent film has been a crucial venue for black filmmakers wishing to represent black history and culture through stories that do not depend on white liberal Hollywood and its marginalizing tendencies. Three decades after Oscar Micheaux, black independent film saw the beginnings of a renaissance, as several black film students at UCLA made films that sharply contrasted with white liberal fantasies of black nobility and with racially charged stereotypes of black hyper-masculinity. As Janet Cutler discusses in this volume, the films of Charles Burnett, Billy Woodberry, Haile Gerima, Julie Dash, and other members of the UCLA group, often called the L.A. Rebellion, were informed by the insights of postcolonialism and third world politics. While most of their projects began as student films and had marginal distribution, films such as *Bush Mama* (1975, released 1979), *Killer of Sheep* (1979, not released theatrically in the US until 2000), *Bless Their Little Hearts* (1984), and *Illusions* (1983) are now ranked among the most important and valuable of the period, by virtue of both their thematic and artistic treatment of the struggles of working-class and lower middle-class African-Americans.

The East Coast also saw the rise of major black independent auteurs. Like his white peer Jim Jarmusch, Spike Lee had been a filmmaking student at NYU and, inspired by *Stranger Than Paradise*, directed his first independent feature, *She's Gotta Have It*, in 1986. Lee would go on to a distinguished career founded initially on stylish urban fiction and, later, on documentary as well. Perhaps more than any other film of the era, Lee's *Do the Right Thing* (1989) exposed the still raw nerve of racial conflict in America at the end of the twentieth century and has continued to resonate powerfully in the new millennium. In this film, set on a single block in Brooklyn on a scorching hot day, pent-up frustrations and scars of historical injury ignite when a young black man from the neighborhood is killed by an NYPD officer. Mookie, the central character played by Lee, retaliates by throwing a garbage can through the window of Sal's Pizzeria, where the conflict began, sparking a riot and the burning of the pizzeria – and challenging its audience to make sense of the title's declaration to "do the right thing." For Lee, the question of tactics was as vital in 1989 as it had been to an earlier generation. How does black America balance Martin Luther King's pacifist civil disobedience with Malcolm X's admonition to bring about freedom "by any means necessary"? Lee chose an aesthetic at odds with the urban realism of the early 1970s and the cool black-and-white look of Jarmusch. In *Do the Right Thing*, emotional excess and racial tumult are rendered through the use of vivid color and stylized shot compositions, with canted low angles that declare the director's authorial presence. Lee's film expresses political content through a distinctively personal style – an approach eschewed by the big studios but very much the métier of independent production. This combination of idiosyncratic style and content related to black history and culture are impressively on display also in Lee's *Mo' Better Blues* (1990), starring Denzel Washington as a jazz trumpeter, *Jungle Fever* (1991), an interracial love story starring Wesley Snipes and Annabelle Sciorra, and *Clockers* (1995), an adaptation of a Richard Price novel about a young drug dealer in the 'hood.

Throughout this period, Lee remained the leading figure within a groundswell of independent as well as Hollywood-based black filmmaking that included the work of John Singleton (*Boyz n the Hood*, 1991), Mario Van Peebles (*New Jack City*, 1991), and Bill Duke (*Deep Cover*, 1992), which, as Keith Harris explains in the hardcover/online edition, either directly deployed or implicitly benefited from crossover dynamics. An exciting period for black narrative feature films, the early 1990s witnessed the return of some members of the L.A. Rebellion – Charles Burnett staged a widely noted return with his family drama *To Sleep With Anger* (1991), while Julie Dash released her highly acclaimed *Daughters of the Dust* (1992), a family portrait of Gullah women on the island of St Helena in the early years of the twentieth century. A ravishingly beautiful film, *Daughters of the Dust* became an art house hit, despite the sometimes difficult-to-understand dialect spoken by its protagonists. Dash notwithstanding, women, too, were a minority in the black filmmaking scene. Notably, however, Leslie Harris made the low-budget feature *Just Another Girl on the IRT* (1992) about the painful maturation of a young black woman in New York. Black independent film also intersected with queer cinema in the work of Cheryl Dunye, whose *Watermelon Woman* (1994) is a fictional biopic that presents a revisionist black lesbian historiography.

During this period, working primarily with independent producers Rollins-Joffe and Orion Pictures, Woody Allen continued to co-write and direct a film every year – a pattern that has continued into the new millennium. In much of his work from 1976 to 1999, Allen contemplates the nature of status – how it is gained, lost, and internalized with consequences that cut to the very core of identity and self-esteem. Arguably, this has been a central theme in almost every one of his films since the Oscar winning *Annie Hall* in 1977, which many regard as a turning-point in Allen's career, leading away from the broader comedy of his earlier films to those comedies infused with melancholy and to melodramas centered on female characters – both of which explore personal, romantic relationships and their characters' tenuous sense of self within a larger social sphere. Allen's characters continually negotiate their perceived positions in relationship to others as they formulate dreams, desires, and aspirations. Whether in the maternal melodramas *Interiors* (1978) and *September* (1987), the clever mock documentary *Zelig* (1983), whose title character exhibits a chameleon-like personality; the story of a comically unlucky bottom-rung talent agent in *Broadway Danny Rose* (1984), the reflexive serio-comic fantasy centered on the romance of the movies in *Purple Rose of Cairo* (1985), or on a bygone era in *Radio Days* (1987), or in serio-comedies centered on marriage and family relationships in *Hannah and Her Sisters* (1986), *Another Woman* (1988), and *Alice* (1990), Allen invites viewers to ask whether emotional sincerity is possible in a world driven by collective desires for material acquisition, acceptance, and approbation. Allen continually asks whether love and desire can function apart from perceptions of status.

He most explicitly addresses this question and its ethical implications in *Manhattan* (1979) – featuring black-and-white cinematography that is both lush and somber – in which characters feel compelled to "trade up" in their relationships. Although the teenage Tracy (Mariel Hemingway) appears exempt from such motives in her relationship with Allen's Isaac Davis, some 30 years her senior, her final words are pivotal: "Not everybody gets corrupted – you need to have a little faith in people." The sustained look of uncertainty, longing, and ironic resignation these words evoke in Isaac encapsulates much of what Allen explores and expresses in his films to follow – so many of which are dedicated to testing out Tracy's thesis. And as its title makes clear, this film also is as much about a place as it is about the people who inhabit it. In so many of his films of the period, New York City functions as a character in its own right – providing nostalgically comic glimpses of working-class life in 1940s Brooklyn or idealized, iconic backdrops of upper middle-class privilege in Manhattan, where artists of all sorts find inspiration and endless opportunities for romance that, at the same time, easily undermine commitment. Allen's typical use of existing jazz recordings on his soundtracks heightens the romance, the nostalgia, and the playful commentary on characters and situations, at turns.

Crimes and Misdemeanors (1989) is perhaps Allen's darkest film, with ironic twists that tap into themes of fate, chance, expediency, and morality. Judah Rosenthal, a highly successful opthamologist (Martin Landau), literally gets away with murder, disposing of his mistress (Anjelica Huston) who has become too demanding, threatening to topple his insular world of privilege in which his marriage and family are defining anchors. Viewers are immersed in Judah's hushed, well-appointed world in which material comfort hides the incomprehensible moral chaos beneath, involving both serious crimes, such as Judah's, and the misdemeanors of others – so conveniently swept under the carpet yet part of the same ethical continuum. Judah is not without feelings of guilt, however, and when he relives a Passover Seder of his boyhood, watching as family members debate issues of ethics, morality, and religion, the claustrophobic framing and mise-en-scène evoke an anxiety he now has internalized. As in *Manhattan* and so many of his films, Allen here contemplates a world in which crime so often goes unpunished and individual morality offers dubiously fragile hope. Allen's own Jewish heritage deeply informs such concerns in almost all of his work, but most explicitly in this Seder scene. In many of his films, his Jewish identity also is a source of hilarity, as in *Annie Hall*, in which Allen's paranoid Alvy Singer sees anti-Semitism everywhere – even when a colleague asks, "Did you [eat lunch]?" Alvy only can hear, "Jew, Jew eat lunch?"[5]

More broadly and consistently comic than Allen, Mel Brooks also foregrounds his Jewish heritage and relies on many traditional tropes of Jewish humor. Although not nearly as prolific a filmmaker as Allen, Brooks, like Allen, wrote, directed, and acted in many of his movies of the period, produced independently by Crossbow Productions. His work almost exclusively centers on clever, self-reflexive parody – of film genres (*Blazing Saddles*, 1974; *Spaceballs*, 1987), film series (*Young Frankenstein*, 1974), periods in film history (*Silent Movie*, 1976), and the work of film directors (*High Anxiety*, 1977). *High Anxiety* is a broadly humorous yet carefully executed parody of Hitchcock's films, not only imitating, elaborating upon, and ultimately transforming iconic scenes from the auteur's work, like *Psycho*'s shower scene and attacks in *The Birds*, but also foregrounding and sending up Hitchcock's signature forward tracking camera, his use of diegetic and nondiegetic sound, and his themes so often centered on the self-reflexive examination of voyeurism as central to film viewing pleasure. *The Producers* (1967) – about two shyster stage producers who mount a musical about Hitler and the rise of the Nazis – is, perhaps, the most recognizable of Brooks' work, given its afterlife as a highly successful and critically acclaimed Broadway musical.

Avant-garde Cinema

By 1980, there was a clearly established canon for the American avant-garde. The films of Maya Deren, Kenneth Anger, Bruce Conner, Bruce Baillie, Ken Jacobs, Paul Sharits, and Ernie Gehr had been subjected to scholarly treatment and were essential viewing for film students. Others, such as Andy Warhol, were being rediscovered in the 1980s and yet others, such as Stan Brakhage and Michael Snow, continued to produce new work. In the 1970s, many experimental filmmakers had professionalized their practices by moving from the artisanal support networks of independent co-ops to association with museums and universities, where their work continued to thrive long after the countercultural tumult had receded. Others became key figures in the newly developing video art scene, which formed around two poles – the institution of alternative television, spearheaded by WGBH Boston, and the urban gallery scene that, in the 1970s, became receptive to video art exhibition. The avant-garde also retained its interest in working with found footage or fragments of early cinema – a practice, as Scott MacDonald discusses in this volume, pursued methodically or even obsessively by Ken Jacobs. Among the new generation of experimental filmmakers, Lewis Klahr's cutout animation also borrowed ready-made images but in his films these tended to come from magazine advertisements of the post-World War II era. Klahr gave motion and personality to these already highly coded emblems of consumer society, recreating intimacies and atmospheres that echoed both suburban life and the world of film noir. Other notable new filmmakers included Pat O'Neill and Nathaniel Dorsky, both working on the West Coast. A master of the optical printer, O'Neill combined cutout animation with live action footage and stills. His film *Water and Power* (1987) is a grandly conceived alternative mythology about the Los Angeles region through several centuries – a response of sorts to Bruce Baillie's 1966 classic *Mass for the Dakota Sioux*. Dorsky over his long career gained recognition for his meticulously conceived lyrical films that he himself has described as devotional cinema.

Since the 1970s, American avant-garde cinema also has produced a venerable group of women filmmakers whose work is both influenced by and, in turn, has provided new impulses within feminism. Yvonne Rainer is a key figure in this group. Having begun as a dancer in the 1960s, Rainer went into filmmaking in the 1970s. Her feature-length films explore various dimensions of female identity and oppression in a patriarchal world. Highly influenced by psychoanalysis and 1970s theories about the social construction of identity, works such as *Film about a Woman Who…* (1974), in a radically self-reflexive way, explore the impact of language on women's perceptions of themselves. Rainer's reflexivity responds to the self-limiting logic of those feminists who, in accordance with the psychoanalytic theories of Jacques Lacan, posit female sexuality as lacking in cultural power. This system implies not only that women have no option beyond patriarchal language through which to analyze their situations and politicize themselves, but also that any such gestures at female agency ultimately are compromised and deferred, as they exist only in relation to, and as a lesser variant of, a larger phallocentric system. While some filmmakers responded to this ideology with an exorcizing austerity in their art, others, particularly from the 1980s forward, reintroduced sensuality into their films as both a libidinal vector and an epistemological tool for feminism. One such filmmaker is Su Friedrich, whose highly cinephilic work, much of which includes found footage, expresses a concern with the specifically cinematic qualities of the image. Other filmmakers in this category include Lizzie Borden, Abigail Child, and Peggy Ahwesh, who in the 1980s and 1990s developed bodies of work on a variety of subjects that placed them at the forefront of American avant-garde cinema.

Starting in the 1970s with Barbara Hammer (*Superdyke*, 1975; *Multiple Orgasm*, 1977), and Michael Wallin (*The Place Between Our Bodies*, 1975) and continuing with Greg Bordowitz and others in the 1980s and 1990s, gay and lesbian avant-garde cinema continued to be an important venue for self-expression, first in the era of gay liberation and then during the AIDS crisis. One of the most important artists of this period is Marlon Riggs, whose 1987 video essay *Ethnic Notions* explored the long history of racial stereotyping in American culture. In 1989, Riggs's landmark video *Tongues Untied*, which used autobiography to explore the life of black gay men besieged by racism, homophobia, and AIDS, became the subject of controversy. It was singled out by Republican Senator Jesse Helms as an argument against federal taxpayer funding of the arts through the National Endowment for the Arts (NEA).

The avant-garde has traditionally blurred the boundary between fiction and documentary forms, producing a range of hybrids that have, by now, developed their own traditions. One such tradition is that of the experimental ethnographic film, with one of its key contributors in Trinh T. Minh-ha, whose work combines two related concerns, feminism and postcolonialism. Such films as *Reassemblage* (1982), *Naked Spaces – Living Is Round* (1985), and *Surname Viêt Given Name Nam* (1989) analyze the oppression of women in relation to the oppression of non-white races and non-Euro-American ethnicities and peoples. Her work reflects the increasing influence of postcolonial theory on the academy since the 1980s, as well as a growing awareness of America's problematic involvement in the oppression of Third World countries. Minh's work also anticipated the growing interpenetration of American and global avant-garde cinema and media since the 1990s, made possible through a growing international network of avant-garde festivals and showcases.

Certainly not all experimental filmmakers followed such a studied or theoretical plan, choosing to embrace instead a more chaotic aesthetic, one at considerable distance from the rigor of Jacobs or Rainer. Jon Moritsugu's work, for example, reflects the rough-edged and raucous impulses of punk rock. "Postmodernism? Who cares!" screams the narrator of *Der Elvis* (1987), Moritsugu's tribute to the king of rock 'n' roll. Funny and angry, aggressively committed to celebrating the overweight, drug-soaked Elvis over his smooth, younger self, the film continues in the tradition staked out by an earlier generation of underground artists. In *Sleazy Rider* (1988), Moritsugu parodies the hippie classic with the story of two young women hitting the road on motorcycles. In the 1990s and beyond, Moritsugu brought his violent punk energy to such aptly titled features as *Mod Fuck Explosion* (1994), *Fame Whore* (1997), and *Scumrock* (2003).

In the United States, the most important venues for avant-garde work since the 1970s have been the experimental film section of the New York Film Festival, "Views from the Avant-garde," and the annual Flaherty Seminar. But with the widespread shift to digital video in the 1990s, the avant-garde has become increasingly dispersed over a range of media outlets and is an essential component of film communities from the San Francisco Bay Area to Midwestern cities and Anthology Film Archives still operating in New York City's East Village.

Documentary

To an unprecedented degree during this period, the American film landscape made room on many of its first-run screens for non-fiction cinema. Venues expanded largely because the subject matter of documentary filmmakers was richly diverse as were approaches to filming those subjects. Not only did 1960s direct cinema and cinéma vérité pioneers like D.A. Pennebaker, the Maysles brothers, and Richard Leacock exert influence through their work, but many actively mentored the younger generation of filmmakers – some formally through their teaching at such universities as MIT, which helped establish Boston as a mecca for aspiring documentarians. Although direct cinema and cinéma vérité approaches are evident in the films of this younger generation, including Ross McElwee, Errol Morris, and Michael Moore, their work more often reflects a mixture of modes, including the interweaving of observational and archival footage, the centrality of lyrical or satirical voiceover narration, the use of stylized reenactments, and the presence of penetrating interviews, either in the casual context of talking with subjects going about their daily routines or the more formal "talking heads" mode. Personal concerns and heavy doses of subjectivity – the filmmakers themselves sometimes are their own most compelling protagonists – often are central to the films, whether as ends in themselves or as a means of addressing larger cultural or political themes. Most importantly, however, subjectivity here becomes a form of resistance and commentary on the illusion of objectivity implied by the "fly-on-the-wall" direct cinema approach. McElwee and Moore, in particular, as well as Morris in his earlier films, tend to seek out eccentric individuals whose presence on camera is debatable as either gratuitously entertaining and even potentially exploitative or as central to the core themes and overarching social critiques the films offer.

Ross McElwee's first feature documentary, *Space Coast* (1979), co-directed with Michel Negroponte, is set in Cape Canaveral, Florida, and examines the culturally and economically impoverished lives of those who live near the NASA/Kennedy Space Center, creating a tapestry of quirky character studies echoed later in *Something to Do with the Wall* (1991), co-directed with McElwee's wife Marilyn Levine. Both, however, are placed in a larger cultural/historical context – whether the country's myopic and extraordinarily costly space race or the presence, then destruction, of the Berlin Wall. Originally filmed in 1986 against the backdrop of the 25th anniversary of the Wall, *Something to Do with the Wall* takes an unanticipated turn when protests erupt and the Wall is demolished, forcing the filmmakers to readjust the focus of their project.

Citing Ed Pincus's *Diaries* (1982) as a key influence, McElwee produced, in effect, personal essays in his most noted films of the period, chief among them *Sherman's March: A Meditation on the Possibility of Romantic Love in the South during an Era of Nuclear Weapons Proliferation* (1985). A transplanted Southerner living in Boston, McElwee retraces the steps of the Civil War general who laid waste to the South. But, mostly, McElwee visits his old girlfriends and takes up with new ones along the way. Camera on shoulder wherever he travels – even into the homes of old friends – McElwee contemplates his own state as a filmmaker who lives life through the viewfinder of a camera, which becomes both a fortress and a weapon. McElwee's funny yet poignant narration clarifies, comments upon, and complicates the visual track, pondering the complexities of gender, Southern culture today, and the ever-present possibility of nuclear annihilation. In *Time Indefinite* (1993) McElwee documents his engagement to documentary filmmaker Marilyn Levine, the birth of their son Adrian, and the death of his father, again with reflective, beautifully crafted narration that deftly captures and balances comic, joyful, and melancholy moments (see Lucia 1993). *Time Indefinite* follows a pattern in 1980s and 1990s documentary popularized by Ira Wohl in his Oscar-winning *Best Boy* (1979), in which the personal involvements of the filmmaker form the subject of the film. Wohl documented the difficulties his elderly aunt and uncle faced in moving their middle-aged, mentally handicapped son Philly into a group home, after his having lived with them all of his life. In keeping more closely to the cinéma vérité tradition, however, Wohl became a catalyst, urging his reluctant relatives to acknowledge their own advanced age and poor health in order to arrange for Philly's future care and aid in his transition while they still were able.

Michael Moore, beyond all others, however, is the figure most responsible for the widespread, mainstream appeal of documentary during this period. Highly influenced by McElwee, Moore weaves together personal narrative and political/economic analysis, home movies and observational footage, interviews and quirky character studies, along with humorous, satirically incisive narration.[6] In *Roger & Me* (1989), Moore exposes the role played by General Motors, and its chairman, Roger Smith, in the economic decline of his hometown of Flint, Michigan. Film crew in tow, Moore repeatedly attempts to gain access to Smith and is continually denied – a trope replayed throughout the film that indicts corporate privilege, insularity, and callous disregard for the lives of workers. In 1992, Moore followed up with a short television documentary, *Pets or Meat: The Return to Flint*, revisiting some of the more memorable characters in *Roger & Me* and continuing to bear witness to a city irreparably damaged.

Unlike McElwee and Moore, Errol Morris relies not on voiceover narration but on probing interviews, often mixed with archival images and stylized reenactments, exploring subjects as diverse as capitalist greed motivating pet cemetery owners in *Gates of Heaven* (1978) and, much later, the criminal abuses of Abu Ghraib in *Standard Operating Procedure* (2008), a film discussed by Patricia Aufderheide in this volume. *Gates of Heaven*, along with *Vernon, Florida* (1981), share with McElwee an interest in eccentric, off-beat characters as a means of capturing a slice of American culture and its ideological underpinnings. It is with *The Thin Blue Line* (1988), however, that Morris gained significant critical and popular acclaim. In this story of a Dallas death-row inmate, whose conviction Morris questions, stylized, fragmented reenactments shot in slow motion represent eyewitness and police department versions of the roadside shooting of a police officer. Through these obviously staged and conflicting reenactments, Morris interrogates the justice system's heavy (and perhaps conveniently self-serving) reliance on eyewitness testimony, drawing reflexive attention to the very act of seeing. The inmate, Randall Adams, later was freed as a result of Morris's compelling evidence and the outrage of activist viewers. Morris's stylized approach to reenactment in this film came to influence many reality television crime shows in the decades to follow. To facilitate his interviews, Morris later invented a device he calls the "Interrotron," which, through a series of mirrors and lenses, enables his subjects to make direct eye-contact with the camera and hence (somewhat eerily) with the viewer, as they look at Morris, who always remains off-camera – in marked contrast to McElwee and Moore who are very much present in their own films (see Grundmann & Rockwell 2000).

In *American Dream* (1990), Barbara Kopple, who had broken through in 1976 with her award-winning *Harlan County U.S.A.*, employs the vérité style to document a six-month strike at a Hormel meatpacking plant in Austin, Minnesota. In contrast to Kopple's approach, filmmakers Jayne Loader, Kevin Rafferty, and Pierce Rafferty, in *The Atomic Café* (1982), create a collage of archival government-funded instructional film footage to present a damning historical portrait of America's nuclear arms testing and Cold War paranoia that resonates powerfully during the ramped-up aggression of the Reagan era. Several notable oral history films of the period, including *The Life and Times of Rosie the Riveter* (Connie Field, 1980) and *The Good Fight: The Abraham Lincoln Brigade in the Spanish Civil War* (Noel Buckner, Mary Dore, and Sam Sills, 1984), interweave archival government propaganda footage and photos with present-day interviews to draw a portrait of government manipulation and hypocrisy. In *Rosie* this strategy centered on luring women into the workforce during World War II, only to force them out at war's end and, in *Good Fight*, on prohibiting Americans from engaging in Spain's battle against fascism. As "character films" these documentaries present intimate portraits of a mere handful of individuals – everyday folks who reflectively look back on what they experienced and how they rebelled – lending a highly personal, emotional dimension to these moments in history.

Frederick Wiseman continued with remarkable energy to bring his observational style to the documenting of American institutions. Turning to

American military and political operations overseas in the mid- and late 1970s, his *Canal Zone* examines the workings of the Panama Canal and the lives of military and government workers, as well as private citizens living in the "zone"; in *Sinai Field Mission* (1978) Wiseman examines the US/UN military-run buffer zone between Israel and Egypt, established in 1976; and in *Manouevre* (1979) he observes war games staged by NATO in Western Europe, following a US tank company as they participate. In *Missile* (1987), Wiseman takes his camera to Vandenberg Air Force Base, following the officers who oversee the intercontinental ballistic missiles for the Strategic Air Command. In the early 1980s, Wiseman turned his attention to American consumerism in *Model* (1980), following female models, their agencies, the process of getting work, and rigorous photo shoots. In *The Store* (1983) he examines the workings of the Neiman Marcus store and corporate headquarters in Dallas. During the mid-1980s Wiseman's work concentrated, again, on education, but now visiting institutions devoted to the education of disabled children and adults: *Multi-Handicapped* (1986) observes classroom and counseling sessions at the Helen Keller School; *Deaf* (1986) visits the School for the Deaf at the Alabama Institute; *Adjustment and Work* (1986) explores the work done at Alabama's E. H. Gentry Technical Facility; and *Blind* (1987) visits kindergarten through high school classrooms at the Alabama School for the Blind. In *Near Death* (1989), Wiseman invites his viewers into a six-hour record of life inside the ICU of Boston's Beth Israel Hospital. Wiseman's unique relationship with Public Broadcasting promises him an audience, and he presents them with alternating images of bureaucratic excess, human cruelty, and apathy on the one hand, along with kindness, caring, and humor on the other. The structure of his work is as subtle and as complex as the institutions he examines. Although Wiseman's editing and framing choices shape our experience of each institution – and his aesthetic invites experiencing rather than simply observing – many of his films during this period skillfully withhold judgment.

Wiseman's work, along with that of other documentarians, avant-garde, independent, and mainstream filmmakers, attests to the remarkably varied, rich, and constantly changing cinematic landscape of the period.

Notes

1. These figures are drawn from the National Association of Theater Owners website: www.natoonline.org (accessed March 4, 2015).
2. These figures can be found at boxofficemojo.com (accessed March 4, 2015).
3. Cited in https://depts.washington.edu/critgame/wordpress/2010/04/fyi-video-game-statistics-by-the-entertainment-software-association/ (accessed March 4, 2015).
4. See Lewis 1995.
5. Parts of this discussion are drawn from Lucia 2008.
6. When interviewing McElwee in 1993, Cynthia Lucia recalls his telling her that, although he did not know Moore personally, Moore sent him a rough cut of *Roger & Me* hoping for feedback.

References

Allen, Michael. (1998). "From Bwana Devil to Batman Forever: Technology in Contemporary Hollywood Cinema." In Steve Neal & Murray Smith (eds.), *Contemporary Hollywood Cinema* (pp. 109–129). London and New York: Routledge.

Balio, Tino. (1998). "'A Major Presence in All of the World's Important Markets': The Globalization of Hollywood in the 1990s." In Steve Neal & Murray Smith (eds.), *Contemporary Hollywood Cinema* (pp. 58–73). London and New York: Routledge.

Cook, David A. (2000). *Lost Illusions: American Cinema in the Shadow of Watergate and Vietnam 1970–1979*. Berkeley: University of California Press.

Elsaesser, Thomas. (2004). "American Auteur Cinema: The Last – or First – Great Picture Show." In Thomas Elsaesser, Alexander Horwath, & Noel King (eds.), *The Last Great American Picture Show: New Hollywood Cinema in the 1970s* (pp. 37–69). Amsterdam: Amsterdam University Press.

Grundmann, Roy, & Cynthia Rockwell. (2000). "Truth Is Not Subjective: An Interview with Errol Morris." *Cineaste* 25.3 (Fall), 4–9.

Lewis, Jon. (1995). *Whom God Wishes to Destroy ... Francis Ford Coppola and the New Hollywood*. Durham, NC: Duke University Press.

Lucia, Cynthia. (1993). "When the Personal Becomes Political: An Interview with Ross McElwee." *Cineaste*, 20.2, 32–37.

Lucia, Cynthia. (2005). *Framing Female Lawyers: Women on Trial in Film*. Austin: University of Texas Press.

Lucia, Cynthia. (2008). "Status and Morality in *Cassandra's Dream*: An Interview with Woody Allen." *Cineaste*, 33.2, 40–43.

Maltby, Richard. (1998). "'Nobody Knows Everything': Post-Classical Historiographies and Consolidated Entertainment." In Steve Neal & Murray Smith (eds.), *Contemporary Hollywood Cinema* (pp. 21–44). London and New York: Routledge.

Maltby, Richard. (2003). *Hollywood Cinema*. 2nd edn. Malden, MA and Oxford: Blackwell.

Prince, Stephen. (2000). *A New Pot of Gold: Hollywood under the Electronic Rainbow 1980–1989*. Berkeley: University of California Press.

Schatz, Thomas. (1993). "The New Hollywood." In Jim Collins, Hilary Radner, & Ava Preacher Collins (eds.), *Film Theory Goes to the Movies* (pp. 8–36). New York and London: Routledge.

Simon, Art. (1996). *Dangerous Knowledge: The JFK Assassination in Art and Film*. Philadelphia: Temple University Press.

Wyatt, Justin. (1994). *High Concept Movies and Marketing in Hollywood*. Austin: University of Texas Press.

11

Seismic Shifts in the American Film Industry

Thomas Schatz
Professor, University of Texas at Austin, United States

Thomas Schatz surveys major changes in American cinema since the mid-1970s, with an emphasis on industry analysis. He distinguishes three key phases – **recovery (1976–1988)**, **resurgence (1989–1998)**, **reintegration and retrenchment (1999–present)** – during which Hollywood restructured itself in successive waves of **mergers** and **acquisitions** closely bound up with reconceptualizing big budget filmmaking (the **blockbuster phenomenon**) and with the advent of new technologies, enabling film exhibition on **cable television**, **home video**, **DVD**, and the **internet**. Schatz claims that, in the new millennium, the industry was a well-calibrated system in which established studios collaborated with **boutique production** houses owned by shared **parent companies**, while also coexisting with bona fide **independents**. Schatz's historical account resumes with Jon Lewis on "The End of Cinema as We Know It" in the online edition. His essay also shares ground with Geoff King on independent film since the 1980s, J. D. Connor on independent blockbusters, Barbara Klinger on Hollywood and cable television, Bart Beaty on the superhero genre, Paul Wells on computer animation, and Kristen Whissel on CGI in this volume.

Additional terms, names, and concepts: convergence, globalization, deregulation, digital revolution, ancillary markets, Sony decision, Paramount decree, FCC, Fin-Syn rules, high definition 3-D

The commonplace assumption that the American film industry entered a new era in the mid-1970s, a period generally referred to as the New Hollywood, has given way more recently to the view that the industry entered yet another phase in the 1990s and 2000s – variously termed Conglomerate Hollywood, Convergent Hollywood, and Global Hollywood, epithets that well indicate the dominant forces at work in contemporary cinema. These views are quite compatible and in fact are crucially interrelated, in that the trends toward conglomeration, convergence, and globalization – and other key trends as well – took

American Film History: Selected Readings, 1960 to the Present, First Edition. Edited by Cynthia Lucia, Roy Grundmann, and Art Simon.

root in the burgeoning New Hollywood, as the industry reversed three decades of deep decline and entered a period of sustained growth, economic resurgence, and structural transformation that continues to this day. This recovery has involved an array of social, economic, technological, and aesthetic forces that have evolved and interacted in different ways over time, resulting in three distinct phases of industry development since the late 1970s – phases that are implicit in the organization of this volume, with separate sections focusing on the late 1970s and 1980s, the 1990s, and the 2000s.

To cite a few salient examples: Consider the explosive growth of home video, which came out of nowhere in the late 1970s with the introduction of the VCR (videocassette recorder) and by the late 1980s surpassed the box office as a revenue source for the film industry, then surged to far greater heights with the introduction of the DVD (digital video disc) in the late 1990s. Consider the impact of the Reagan-era media deregulation campaign and free-market economic policies of the 1980s, which led to a series of media merger-and-acquisition waves, beginning with the Time–Warner and Sony–Columbia mergers of 1989, that reconfigured the industry. Consider the plight of the major Hollywood studios, which foundered through the early recovery of the late 1970s and 1980s, regained their bearings in the 1990s as conglomeration took hold, and in the 2000s reclaimed virtually complete control of the American film industry – albeit as subsidiaries of a half-dozen global media giants. Consider the digital revolution, which swept through the United States in the 1980s with the introduction of the PC (personal computer) but did not significantly impact the film industry until the 1990s, when it rapidly transformed the production and delivery of movies, giving rise to a distinctly "digital cinema" during the 2000s – as was emphatically underscored with the release of *Avatar* in late 2009.

And consider the movies themselves, particularly the new breed of blockbusters that emerged in the late 1970s with films like *Jaws* (1975), *Rocky* (1976), and *Star Wars* (1977), which sparked Hollywood's economic recovery and have dominated and defined its filmmaking trajectory ever since. The blockbuster syndrome went into another register in the burgeoning conglomerate era with films like *Batman* (1989), *Beauty and the Beast* (1991), and *Jurassic Park* (1993), megahits geared to both the expanding movie marketplace and the far-flung media and entertainment operations of the studio's parent company. The blockbuster ethos intensified even further in the new millennium, as a spate of fantasy and superhero franchises – the *Matrix*, *Harry Potter*, *Lord of the Rings*, *Spider-Man*, *Shrek*, *Batman*, and *Iron Man* series, et al. – became the coin of the global entertainment realm. Countering this blockbuster syndrome, however, has been a trend toward low-budget independent, art-cinema, and specialty films – a distinctly "off-Hollywood" trend in the 1980s that steadily went mainstream in the wake of breakthrough 1989 hits like *sex, lies, and videotape*, *Roger & Me*, and *Do the Right Thing*. As the independent sector flourished and an indie-film movement coalesced in the 1990s, the conglomerates inevitably stepped in, launching their own indie-film divisions and buying up successful independents. That seemed to signal a new golden age in American film, as the studios, the indie-film divisions, and the genuine independents flourished. But in the course of the 2000s, as conglomerate control intensified and the studios' blockbuster franchises generated record revenues year after year, even in the face of a global economic crisis, the indie-film movement waned and the independent sector all but collapsed.

As even this brief rehearsal suggests, the American film industry has undergone profound and fundamental changes since the late 1970s, a reversal of fortunes as acute and significant as its sudden collapse in the late 1940s. Not since that earlier collapse, in fact, has such a range of social, political, economic, and technological forces assailed the industry, and not since the postwar collapse of the studio system has Hollywood seen such a wholesale transformation. The aim of this essay is to chart those forces and to gauge their impact on the industry – and on Hollywood films and filmmaking – through the successive phases of Hollywood's long and quite remarkable resurgence.

Recovery (1976–1988)

The late 1970s saw three developments that fundamentally transformed the American film industry in the ensuing decade. The first was a new breed of blockbuster that signaled key changes in the aesthetics, the marketing and distribution, and the sheer commercial impact of top box office hits. The second was the introduction of the VCR, which sparked the steady if highly conflicted emergence of "home video" as a new delivery system and an increasingly important revenue source for Hollywood. The third was cable television, whose explosive growth through the late 1970s and 1980s created a huge demand for filmed entertainment – not only movies but Hollywood-produced television series as well.

Of these three developments, the new breed of blockbusters had the most immediate and significant impact on the struggling movie industry. Several films in the early 1970s like *The Godfather* (1972) and *The Exorcist* (1973) anticipated this trend, but the real game-changer came in 1975 with *Jaws*, a genuine breakthrough on multiple fronts. In terms of story and style, *Jaws* was a high-speed, high-concept, male action-adventure film that melded elements of the disaster, horror, and buddy-comedy genres into a hyper-efficient entertainment machine. It was propelled by a nationwide "saturation" release campaign, opening in a then-record 400-plus theaters and supported by an unprecedented TV network ad blitz. An "event" film and prototype summer blockbuster, *Jaws* redefined the profit potential of a major movie hit and spawned a multimedia franchise via sequels, reissues, licensed merchandise, theme-park rides, and myriad other tie-ins.

This blockbuster trend continued with megahits including *Rocky* (1976), *Star Wars* (1977), *Close Encounters of the Third Kind* (1977), *Saturday Night Fever* (1977), *Animal House* (1978), *Grease* (1978), *Superman* (1978), *Star* Trek (1979), and *Raiders of the Lost Ark* (1980). The most important of these was *Star Wars*, which like *Jaws* was a high-speed, genre-blending, male-action film but proved to be even more popular with audiences and more strategically open to reiteration, licensing, and serialization. An early template for what Henry Jenkins has termed "transmedia storytelling," *Star Wars* was quickly and strategically expanded through blockbuster sequels (*The Empire Strikes Back*, 1980, *The Return of the Jedi*, 1983) and a far wider array of media iterations than *Jaws* that steadily expanded and exploited the narrative world conjured up in the original film (Jenkins 2006). Steven Spielberg and George Lucas, who directed *Jaws* and *Star Wars*, respectively, quickly emerged as the chief architects of what Variety's A. D. Murphy called "the modern era of the super-blockbuster films" (1989, 26). Not only were they the dominant filmmakers of the era (including their collaboration on *Raiders of the Lost Ark* and the ensuing Indiana Jones series, which Lucas produced and Spielberg directed), but also production executives and emergent moguls with highly successful companies: Lucasfilm Limited and its industry leading special effects counterpart, ILM (Industrial Light and Magic); and Spielberg's Amblin Entertainment, which produced scores of films and television shows in the 1980s, including top movie hits like *Back to the Future* (1985) and *Who Framed Roger Rabbit* (1988).

Lucas and Spielberg were charter members of the "movie brat" generation of the early 1970s – a group of maverick filmmakers that included Francis Ford Coppola, Dennis Hopper, Hal Ashby, William Friedkin, Peter Bogdanovich, Martin Scorsese, Brian De Palma, and Paul Schrader. But the American New Wave generated by these headstrong auteurs had ebbed by the late 1970s, swamped by the blockbusters of Lucas, Spielberg, et al., and undercut by their own self-indulgence and overreaching. The last gasp came with films like Coppola's *Apocalypse Now* (1979), Bob Fosse's *All That Jazz* (1979), Scorsese's *Raging Bull* (1980), and Michael Cimino's *Heaven's Gate* (1980). While Lucas and Spielberg charged to the top of the industry in the 1980s, the other movie brats found it increasingly difficult to find work, and the art-cinema ethos they had shaped all but disappeared from mainstream Hollywood.

That alternative art-cinema impulse did survive, although primarily "off-Hollywood" in an independent film movement centered in New York during the 1980s and spearheaded by a new generation of writer-directors out of the NYU (New York University) film school including Jim Jarmusch (*Stranger Than Paradise*, 1984), Joel and Ethan Coen (*Blood Simple*, 1984), Oliver Stone (*El Salvador*, 1986), and Spike Lee (*She's Gotta Have It*, 1986). Also on the margins were exploitation filmmakers working in a tradition that extended back for decades but enjoyed a significant surge in the late 1970s and the 1980s, thanks largely to the success of writer-director John Carpenter's *Halloween* (1978), which spurred a significant trend in low-budget teen horror and "slasher" films (*Nightmare on Elm Street* and *Friday the 13th* series, et al.) during the 1980s.

Another crucial factor in Hollywood's economic recovery involved radical changes in moviegoing and film consumption, which quickly transformed both the theatrical and "ancillary" markets. The traditional exhibition sector underwent a sea-change in the late 1970s and 1980s with the proliferation of mall-based multiplex theaters, a development geared both to changing social conditions (suburban migration, shopping centers, and so on) and also to the studios' escalating wide-release strategies in marketing blockbuster films. During the 1980s, the number of indoor movie screens in the US and Canada increased from 14,000 to 22,000 as the multiplex became the predominant theatrical venue (MPAA 1990). Meanwhile the ancillary (secondary or subsequent) markets of home video and cable television simply exploded. Ironically enough, the early VCR systems – Betamax (introduced by Sony in late 1975) and VHS (introduced in 1977 by JVC, et al.) – caught on with American consumers as a means to record and "time shift" television programs. Meanwhile, the Hollywood studios, several of which were developing video-disc systems of their own, tried to keep the VCR out of the US. In 1978, Universal and Disney filed a copyright infringement suit against Sony that went all the way to the US Supreme Court. Sony ultimately prevailed after a six-year legal battle, although by then Hollywood welcomed the outcome, since the VCR had become a standard home appliance and the home video industry had become a crucial revenue source for the studio-distributors. Home viewing of movies on broadcast and cable television also grew at unprecedented rates, with the TV networks paying record fees for Hollywood films, especially blockbuster hits, while the cable market developed a voracious appetite for filmed entertainment. Another key innovation during that era was the pay-cable "movie channel," which was pioneered by HBO in 1975 and in the course of the 1980s became a vital revenue source with the emergence of new cable networks like Showtime, Cinemax, and The Movie Channel.

Another new technology and nascent media industry in the 1980s was the personal computer industry, propelled primarily by the introduction of the IBM PC in 1981 and the Apple Macintosh in 1984. The potential import of the PC industry – and of digital technology generally – to the film industry was not readily evident. Warner's ill-fated decision to buy Atari during the first rush of videogame fever in the early 1980s signaled the movie industry's interest in digital technology but also its uncertainty about how to utilize or exploit it. LucasFilm also developed a computer-based "nonlinear" editing system in the 1980s that would revolutionize postproduction over the next decade. But LucasFilm's uncertainties about digital media also were evident in its decision to unload an internal startup, Pixar, which was experimenting with computer animation. (More on this below.) On another front, the impact on the music industry of the CD (compact disc) – a technology that actually spun off the video laserdisc in the late 1970s – convinced many in Hollywood that digital video would be the "next generation" of home movie viewing.

The intensifying blockbuster syndrome and emerging video markets resulted in record movie revenues in the 1980s, as the industry entered a full-blown recovery mode after three decades of deep economic decline. The domestic box office steadily climbed from \$2.75 billion in 1980 to a record \$5 billion in 1989, driven not only by inflation but also the first real uptick in movie attendance since the mid-1940s (MPAA 1990). The ancillary markets had a massive – and steadily increasing – effect on the studios' bottom line as well, and home video's impact was simply staggering. During the 1980s, a revenue source that was nonexistent a decade earlier became the studio-distributors' single largest revenue source, surpassing the surging theatrical market. Hollywood's overseas revenues also began to climb in the late 1980s, with foreign income beginning to eclipse the domestic box office on a number of top hits. Moreover, Hollywood's intensifying blockbuster syndrome was further provoked by the fact that the home video, television, and foreign markets all proved to be as blockbuster-driven as the theatrical market. When all of these revenue streams were taken into account, the full extent of Hollywood's recovery was starkly evident. According to a Goldman Sachs study, the studios' movie-related income from all sources climbed from \$2.9 billion in 1981 to \$10.25 billion in 1989 (Goldman Sachs 1995).

Despite this economic recovery, however, the major Hollywood studios were in relative disarray in the 1980s, and their control over the production process was uneven at best. The "big three" talent agencies – Creative Artists (CAA), William Morris, and International Creative Management (ICM) – wielded enormous authority over project development, especially the high-stakes, talent-heavy blockbusters that were generating huge paydays for top stars and filmmakers, along with hefty commissions for their agents. In fact, the agencies' packaging of movie projects – particularly the key elements of star, director, and script – gave them more power over the development of many of the top films than the studios that financed and released them. Meanwhile, "instant majors" like Orion, TriStar, Cannon, and Vestron continually sprang up, fragmenting the market and further undercutting the major studios' once hegemonic control. Thus, the studios remained remarkably undervalued and ripe for acquisition even as the industry recovery took hold. In 1981, Kirk Kerkorian snatched up United Artists for $380 million and merged it with MGM. A year later Coca-Cola bought the relatively healthy Columbia Pictures for $750 million. And in a two-stage deal in 1984–1985, Rupert Murdoch's Australian company News Corp bought Twentieth Century Fox for $575 million (Prince 2000; Schatz 2008).

The News Corp deal was engineered by Barry Diller, the Fox studio head who already had run the ABC network and Paramount Pictures. Diller convinced Murdoch not only to buy Fox but also to launch a fourth US television network, Fox Broadcasting – a huge risk but also an indication that the US broadcast television system itself was in disarray due to the onslaught of cable and home video. In fact, all three of the traditional TV networks – ABC, CBS, and NBC – changed hands in the mid-1980s, and like the movie studios were picked up at bargain basement prices (Auletta 1991). None of those network TV deals involved an alliance with a movie studio, since the Federal Communications Commission prohibited joint ownership of a broadcast network and a movie studio. The Fox television venture both skirted and directly challenged these FCC regulations, and Murdoch and Diller were willing to risk federal interference or a Justice Department lawsuit because their efforts were very much in line with the Reagan administration's deregulation campaign – and particularly the rollback in media constraints under FCC chairman (and Reagan appointee) Mark Fowler (Holt 2001–2002).

Since its emergence in the 1910s and 1920s, the Hollywood film industry had undergone alternating waves of merger-and-acquisition on the one hand, and government efforts to restrict ownership and control (usually in the form of antitrust prosecution) on the other. The most significant government intervention was, of course, the Supreme Court's historic Paramount decree of 1948, which forced the studios to sell their theater chains and to discontinue the unfair trade practices that had given them a lock on the American movie marketplace. In the wake of that ruling, the FCC restricted the film studios' participation in the emerging television industry, relegating them in effect to subcontractor status as the networks took command. But network power over the booming TV industry became so intense (and monopolistic) during the 1960s that the FCC, in an effort to curb that control, restricted network ownership and distribution of primetime programming via the so-called Fin-Syn ("Financial Interest and Syndication) Rules. This was actually a boon to the movie studios, which produced most of the networks' prime-time fictional series, since it ensured the studios' exclusive ownership of their series and control of the lucrative syndication markets. But now the Reagan-era media deregulation campaign, which would continue under Presidents George H. W. Bush and Bill Clinton, was gradually rolling back these restrictions. In the process, the federal government fostered a new mode – and a new age – of media integration wherein film studios, TV broadcast networks, cable networks, and other media entities (publishing, music, and so on) could coexist within the same corporation.

This radical shift in media regulation was tied to the Reagan administration's free-market economic policies, which allowed major industries to self-regulate in response to market forces and to compete more openly in the increasingly competitive international marketplace. This coincided with another crucial Reagan-era policy strategy, the escalation of the Cold War throughout the 1980s, which was conducted on both a military front (via an arms buildup) and an economic front (via pressure on the Soviet Union and Chinese bloc countries to move toward a competitive, capitalist system). By 1989, as Bush took office, it was clear that this strategy was succeeding as the Soviet Union was in a state of collapse and as economic reforms were enacted by communist countries throughout Europe and Asia, including China. It was not yet clear how extensively these developments would impact the movie industry, although in light of the already improving foreign markets, the studio powers had reason to be optimistic about the expanding global marketplace.

Resurgence (1989–1998)

The year 1989 was a watershed in American film history. It was the year of *Batman* and *sex, lies, and videotape* – the first modern blockbuster and seminal indie film, respectively, that established a dual filmmaking agenda that still prevails. It was also the year of the Time–Warner and Sony–Columbia alliances, which set off a merger-and-acquisition frenzy that quickly transformed the industry. *Variety* dubbed 1989 "the year of the Bat," due to *Batman's* runaway hit status in both the theatrical and home video markets, where it trounced the high-profile sequels to the *Indiana Jones*, *Ghostbusters*, *Back to the Future*, *James Bond*, *Star Trek*, and *Lethal Weapon* series (Putzer 1990). Director Tim Burton's offbeat style, production designer Anton Furst's nightmare vision, Jack Nicholson's wacked-out villain, and Warner Bros.' savvy marketing campaign all distinguished *Batman* from the competition – and from earlier blockbusters as well. Equally distinctive were Warner Bros.' ownership and control of the *Batman* property and Time Warner's capacity to parlay the film's success into a global marketing bonanza, as the licensing and merchandising revenues quickly surpassed the box office returns (Pendleton 1992).

While *Batman* marked a significant advance in blockbuster filmmaking, for independent film impresario John Pierson, 1989 was "the year it all changed" due to the momentous impact of *sex, lies, and videotape* (Pierson 1995).[1] An edgy, erotic, highly personal debut film from writer-director Steven Soderbergh, shot in his home town of Baton Rouge for just over $1 million (versus *Batman*'s $51 million budget), *sex, lies, and videotape* made its mark on the festival circuit – initially at the US Film Festival (later renamed Sundance) and then at Cannes, where it won the Palme d'Or – prior to its summer release. It grossed just under $25 million, only one-tenth of *Batman's* industry-leading box office take but an unprecedented achievement for an "art film" and also a huge leap for its then obscure distributor, Miramax Films. *Sex, lies,*

Figure 11.1 James Spader and Andie MacDowell in *sex, lies, and videotape* (1989, director, writer, and editor Steven Soderbergh and producers Robert F. Newmyer and John Hardy), which sparked the indie film movement of the 1990s.

and videotape gave Miramax a foothold in the industry, which was further secured in late 1989 with the release of *My Left Foot* and *Cinema Paradiso*, both of which were solid hits as well. Thus, while Peter Biskind in his chronicle of Miramax and Sundance in the 1990s aptly describes *sex, lies, and videotape* as "the big bang of the modern indie film movement" (2004, 26), it was scarcely an isolated phenomenon in the independent realm. In fact, the studios in 1989 were moving into the independent sector as well via "negative pickup" deals – Warner Bros.' release of Michael Moore's first feature, *Roger & Me*, for instance, and Universal's decision to finance and distribute Spike Lee's breakout film (and third feature), *Do the Right Thing*.

While *Batman* and *sex, lies, and videotape* signaled a sharp division on the filmmaking front, the Time–Warner and Sony–Columbia mergers marked an epochal rift in the structure and operations of the film industry. Hollywood from its very beginnings had been shaped by merger-and-acquisition waves, but this one was different from any in industry history in that it involved a cadre of global media giants moving aggressively into Hollywood – and into other US media industries as well. A key antecedent here was the News Corp–Fox alliance and the launch of Fox Broadcasting, which augured a new species of media conglomerate. The gradual evolution and eventual success of that venture, along with the explosive growth of cable and home video, the government's media deregulation campaign, and Hollywood's steady economic recovery, combined to induce other media giants to go after major film studios. The first to take the plunge was Time, Inc., which announced in early 1989 that it was merging with Warner Communications to create the world's largest media corporation (valued at about $15 billion), combining not only film and publishing interests but also Time's considerable "video" assets that included HBO and a massive cable system. Shortly after that announcement, Paramount's parent company, Gulf+Western, changed its name to Paramount Communications (having sold off its nonmedia assets) and launched a hostile takeover bid of Time, Inc. (Saporito 1989). As Time successfully fended off that assault in the courts in July, the Japanese electronics giant Sony announced that it was acquiring Columbia Pictures and its sister studio, TriStar, for $4.8 billion. These deals dwarfed the News Corp–Fox deal of just five years earlier, clearly indicating how much the stakes had risen in the resurgent movie industry. In fact Sony closed out that turbulent year by hiring producers Peter Guber and Jon Peters, whose recent hits included *Rain Man* (1988) and *Batman*, to run Columbia, with the Guber–Peter deal alone costing Sony as much as Murdoch had paid for the entire Twentieth Century Fox Studio in 1984–1985 (Griffin & Masters 1996).

The Time–Warner and Sony–Columbia deals initiated a merger-and-acquisition wave that crested in 1994–1995, with several major transactions: the acquisition of Paramount Pictures and the Blockbuster home video by global syndication giant Viacom; the acquisition of Universal Pictures by Seagram; Time Warner's purchase of Turner Broadcasting (TBS), a major media conglomerate in its own right; and Disney's purchase (for $18.3 billion) of the ABC television network, its parent company Cap Cities, and various cable holdings including ESPN. These deals coincided with the FCC's final phase-out of the Fin-Syn restrictions in 1995 and Congressional passage of the US Telecommunications Act of 1996, culminating the media deregulation crusade begun by Reagan and officially sanctioning the integration of once-distinct media industries into a vast entertainment empire ruled by a cadre of media conglomerates (Schatz 2008).

Disney's acquisition of Cap Cities/ABC was perhaps the most crucial of these deals for several reasons. By 1995, Disney was the only Hollywood-based company still in control of its own destiny, and one that avoided being swallowed up by another media conglomerate by becoming one. Moreover, Disney's rise from perennial "mini-major" to major studio status in the late 1980s and then to conglomerate status in the 1990s speaks volumes about the seismic shifts in the film industry over the previous decade. Disney in the early 1980s was a foundering studio with a minuscule market share when founder Walt Disney's nephew Roy seized control of the company in an internal power struggle and brought in new management – Michael Eisner as CEO, Frank Wells as president, and Jeffrey Katzenberg as head of production. The studio soon rose to the top of the movie industry via two very different strategies. One was the systematic reissue of its animated classics (*Snow White and the Seven Dwarfs*, *Peter Pan*, et al.) in theaters and then as sell-through VHS cassettes, an innovative and enormously profitable enterprise. The other was the production of modestly budgeted, slightly risqué, live-action comedies and comedy-dramas like *Ruthless People* and *Down and Out in Beverly Hills* in 1986; *Three Men and a Baby* and *Good Morning Vietnam* in 1987; *Cocktail* and *Beaches* in 1988; *Dead Poets Society* and *Turner & Hooch* in 1989 – all under its Touchstone label (as was the PG-rated *Who Framed Roger Rabbit* in 1988) to avoid sullying the Disney brand. Meanwhile Eisner oversaw the upgrading and expansion (on a global scale) of Disney's theme park and resort operations, while Katzenberg focused on the studio's once vital but now moribund animation division, which had not produced a hit since the early 1960s (Stewart 2005).

The first animated feature created under Katzenberg was *The Little Mermaid*, which was Disney's third-biggest hit in 1989 (after *Dead Poets Society* and *Honey, I Shrunk the Kids*) but without question its most important film in decades – and, along with *Batman*, a defining hit of the burgeoning conglomerate era. *The Little Mermaid* reasserted the venerable Disney brand and spurred an animation renaissance that included *Beauty and the Beast* (1991), *Aladdin* (1992), and *The Lion King* (1994), which took the company's five-year resurgence to another level. *The Little Mermaid* set the tone, style, and the narrative thrust of Disney's new run of animated films, which wed its traditional fairy-tale impulse to something quite new: a full-blown Broadway musical treatment. It also created a new template for Disney's global entertainment franchises. *The Little Mermaid* soundtrack sold three million copies (on Disney's label) while the film itself was a massive sell-through hit on VHS. Disney followed it with both prequels and sequels that went straight to VHS and to its cable channel, and the company also produced a Broadway musical version – the first of several stage hits that helped rehabilitate New York's theater district in the 1990s. Disney also had started a chain of retail stores in 1987, where *The Little Mermaid* became a merchandising bonanza. The film was further reworked for Disney's theme parks, resorts, and hotels, which under Eisner focused more heavily on the family market. This latter point was crucial to Disney's enormous success in the contemporary era. In that watershed year of 1989, despite the number of top hits with a strong family focus (including *Honey, I Shrunk the Kids*, *Look Who's Talking*, and *Parenthood*), *The Little Mermaid* was the *only* G-rated film (general audiences, suitable for all ages) among the top 40 box office releases. Somehow Hollywood had lost contact with the core family audience, and Disney reversed that trend with a steady output of franchise-spawning animated hits. Other companies followed suit, as the G-rated family film once again became an industry staple.

Disney's expansion also included the acquisition of Miramax Films in 1993 – one of several key moves by Hollywood's major powers into the independent film realm as the indie film movement quickly coalesced. In late 1991, Sony became the first conglomerate to launch an indie film division, Sony Pictures Classics, which enjoyed immediate success with *Howard's End* (1992); News Corp followed suit with Fox Searchlight in 1995, and eventually all of the majors launched divisions geared to the independent sector. The conglomerates also began buying up successful independents, usually allowing them to operate autonomously from the major studio – as was the case with Miramax, whose founders Harvey and Bob Weinstein continued to control the company after the Disney buyout. Miramax was riding high at the time, thanks to 1993 hits like *The Crying Game* and *The Piano*, and among its first releases after the buyout was *Pulp Fiction* (1994). Another key acquisition at the time involved New Line, which with Miramax was the top independent in the early 1990s. Founded in the late 1960s by Robert (Bob) Shaye, New Line rose to prominence in the 1980s via low-end genre films, most notably its *Nightmare on Elm Street* teen horror series and offbeat comedies like John Waters's *Polyester* (1981) and *Hairspray* (1988). New Line's *Teenage Mutant Ninja Turtles* grossed over $125 million in the US in 1990 to become the most successful independent release ever. In a move to counter Miramax in 1991, New Line created an art-film division, Fine Line Features, which enjoyed immediate success with *The Player*. Miramax in turn created Dimension, a genre film subsidiary to counter New Line, which cranked out horror, action, and teen fare à la its *Hellraiser* and *Halloween* series. New Line was purchased by TBS in 1993, which in turn was bought by Time Warner, bringing New Line and Fine Line into the conglomerate's filmed entertainment division, with the fiercely independent Bob Shaye maintaining control of both subsidiaries and operating in complete autonomy from Warner Bros. (Connolly 1998; Mehler 1992; Stevenson 1992; Wyatt 1998).

Thus, by the mid-1990s, a new class of Hollywood studio had emerged, the conglomerate-owned indie-film division, signaling one of the most significant developments in recent industry history. Indie divisions like Sony Classics, Fox Searchlight, Miramax, and New Line occupied an aesthetic and commercial space that was fundamentally distinct from both the major studios and the scores of true independents, whose numbers and output steadily increased as well. These indie subsidiaries had a huge advantage over true independents due to the resources of their parent companies, particularly in terms of production and marketing budgets and assured access to distribution in both the theatrical and crucial ancillary markets. This new "Indiewood" sector, as it came to be termed, blurred the distinctions between studio and independent filmmaking, particularly as Miramax and New Line began producing more expensive and blatantly "commercial" fare designed to compete with the major studio releases. Miramax, in particular, steadily raised the bar after its acquisition by Disney with "indie blockbuster" hits like *The English Patient* (1996), *Good Will Hunting* (1997), and *Shakespeare in Love* (1998) (Perren 2001–2002). Another clear indication of the indie film boom was the 1995 launch of DreamWorks SKG, a purportedly independent studio created by consummate Hollywood insiders Steven Spielberg, Jeffrey Katzenberg (who left Disney after the death of Frank Wells and a falling out with Eisner), and media mogul David Geffen. By 1997, DreamWorks was turning out its own brand of high-end indie films, and the 1998 Oscar race was dominated by a much publicized "battle of the indies" that centered on Miramax's *Shakespeare in Love* and DreamWorks's *Saving Private Ryan* for best picture (which went to Miramax) (LaPorte 2010).

DreamWorks's 1998 slate also included *Antz*, an initial foray into animation in a plan to compete with Disney and another indication of a major shift in 1990s filmmaking. *Antz* was Hollywood's second computer-animated feature, employing the same new imaging technology as *Toy Story*, the 1995 hit produced by the upstart Pixar, a company owned by Steve Jobs, whose films were financed and distributed by Disney. Although Katzenberg had been dismissive of computer animation before *Toy Story*, he was now convinced it would revolutionize animated filmmaking. Eisner was dubious as well, but Disney continued to support Pixar's efforts as it developed several new computer-generated features, including *A Bug's Life* – a film whose similarities to *Antz* was no coincidence, according to personnel at Pixar who accused Katzenberg of stealing the idea which was in development when he left Disney. Pixar also was developing *Toy Story 2*, which began as a direct-to-video project but was upgraded and successfully released theatrically in 1999 (Price 2008).

These computer-animated films were early harbingers of digital cinema as films fully created with digital technology. Cinema was still a film-based medium, of course, in that the vast majority of feature films were still being shot and released (and thus projected) on celluloid. But Hollywood filmmaking had already entered the digital age in several key areas, particularly the use of computer-generated (CG) special effects, computer-based postproduction (digital editing), and digital sound. CG effects were vital to Hollywood's blockbuster ethos, of course, whether to create photo-realistic imagery in films like *Jurassic Park* (1993) and *Titanic* (1997), or blatantly outrageous spectacle in films like *Independence Day* (1996), *Men in Black* (1997), and *Armageddon* (1998). Online delivery of filmed content was widely anticipated in light of the explosive growth of the internet and the world wide web in the 1990s, as was the convergence of the PC, video game, and movie industries. While these developments remained tantalizing prospects just out of reach, one new digital delivery technology did arrive in 1997 that wielded an enormous impact on the film industry. This was DVD, a new home-video format that enjoyed the most rapid "diffusion of innovation" of any technology in history due to the unprecedented cooperation of the film, PC, and consumer electronics industries in its development and rollout, and due also to new technology's clear superiority over VHS in terms of quality, cost, and convenience. Hollywood also used the DVD rollout as the opportunity to shift from a rental to a sell-through strategy, which returned a larger portion of home-video revenues to the distributor (Taylor 2006; Sebok 2007).

The impact of DVD on the home-video market was complemented by the phenomenal growth of Hollywood's foreign markets in the late 1990s, as the market reach of the global media conglomerates paid dividends, literally and figuratively – especially for the studios' high-stakes blockbusters, which performed extremely well in the international marketplace.

Titanic, to take the most obvious and striking example, became the most successful film to date after its December 1997 release, generating $600 million in its domestic theatrical release, $1.25 billion in foreign theatrical, $55 million in US television rights, and steadily ascending home-video returns through a succession of reissues. *Titanic* was the first film to generate over one million DVD units (in its initial home-video release), and a decade later one reliable source put its worldwide home video revenues at well over $1 billion.[2]

Reintegration and Retrenchment (1999–)

The new millennium brought a number of key changes to the film industry, most notably the consolidation of conglomerate control, the tremendous acceleration of both the home video and international markets, the rapid rise of a new class of blockbuster film franchises, and the gradual, seemingly inevitable collapse of both the indie film and independent sectors while the major studios enjoyed record revenues. The era began with another merger-and-acquisition wave and a brief period of intense upheaval, due largely to the collapse of the "digital economy." In 1999, Viacom acquired CBS (its former parent company) for $35.6 billion, twice what it had paid five years earlier for Paramount and Blockbuster combined. This old media (film and television) deal was soon overshadowed by two massive new media deals spurred by the astounding growth of the internet and the web – and by the assumption that online moviegoing was finally at hand. In early 2000, the internet giant AOL (formerly America Online) announced that it was acquiring Time Warner in a stock deal for over $150 billion – roughly 10 times the value of the Time–Warner merger a decade earlier and a clear indication of both the extravagance and the unbridled optimism of media corporations at the height of the dot-com boom. Months later the French water-and-power giant Vivendi, which had been moving aggressively into telecommunications and media, announced that it was buying an 80 percent stake in Universal Pictures from Seagram for $34 billion. By the time these two deals were finalized in 2001, however, the dot-com bubble had burst, the digital economy was in free fall, and both mergers were doomed. In 2003, AOL-Time Warner reverted to Time Warner, with AOL as a mere subsidiary (which Time Warner eventually sold). In 2004, Vivendi sold its stake in Universal to General Electric, owner of NBC, which promptly launched "NBC Universal" (Schatz 2009).

With those three deals the Big Six media conglomerates consolidated their control of the film and television industries in the United States, by far the world's richest media market, as well as their collective domination of the global movie marketplace. Their Hollywood studios were the conglomerates' crown jewels, even though movie revenues comprise a relatively modest portion of the conglomerates' media-related income – generally less than 20 percent. Those revenues are substantial, however, and are continually rising as the global media-and-entertainment industry steadily expands, driven largely by the home video and foreign markets. While domestic box office grosses remained fairly steady in the $9–10 billion range from 2002 to 2009, foreign box office surged from $9 billion to over $19 billion – with no end in sight, given the growth of overseas markets, the studios' coordination of domestic and foreign release campaigns, and the worldwide appetite for Hollywood blockbusters. The studios' home video revenues surged as well, thanks to the massive impact of DVD technology. In 2002, home video revenues reached a record $20.3 billion (versus worldwide theatrical revenues of $19.8 billion), with DVD surpassing VHS for the first time and sell-through surpassing rental (Hettrick 2003). Home video hit $24 billion in 2004 and then began to level off, with the studios capturing the lion's share of the market and relying on DVD returns for nearly one-half of their movie-related income. This includes revenues not only from current releases but their film and television libraries as well, marking another key distinction between the VHS and DVD eras. And as in the VHS era, Disney far surpassed its competitors in the triangulation of its theatrical, television, and home video operations and in the transmedia franchising of its products – spinning off DVD and cable sequels to its animated classics, for instance, or parlaying *High School Musical* (which began as a 2006 Disney Channel movie) into a worldwide theatrical film, television, home video, concert, stage, and recording industry phenomenon.

One key to conglomerate control over the US market has been ownership of multiple delivery "pipelines," particularly television networks and cable channels. Having been announced in 2009, Comcast's acquisition of NBC Universal from GE was completed in 2013 after a lengthy and complicated process due mainly to regulatory issues. As of 2015, four of the Big Six own the four US broadcast TV networks, and together with a fifth conglomerate they dominate and effectively control the US cable network system as well. The only media conglomerate without significant television holdings, Sony, has focused instead on hardware–software synergy, relying on its filmed entertainment division to help move its consumer electronics hardware. This includes Sony's Blu-Ray system, the HD (high definition) DVD home video format that Sony owns and controls, as well as its HD and 3-D televisions and videogame systems. Sony is the only conglomerate with both a "computer entertainment" and a consumer electronics division, which puts it in a class by itself among the Big Six. Moreover, the Sony PlayStation game console has the capacity to play and stream high-definition movies, thus creating both a delivery pipeline and a potential site of convergence between movies and gaming.

Sony's dearth of traditional television pipelines curbed its investment in TV series production, where the other conglomerates remain very productive. In its feature filmmaking operations, however, Sony has been quite consistent with the rest of the Big Six. By the 2000s, all of the conglomerates had developed a dual approach, with their major studios focusing on high-end films for worldwide release, while their indie divisions turn out low- to mid-range films for more specialized audiences. In the early 2000s, Miramax and New Line continued to dominate the indie-division ranks and push into the high-stakes realm of the major studios, most notably with New Line's decision to finance and distribute the *Lord of the Rings* trilogy (2001–2003), a blockbuster franchise developed alongside – and in direct competition with – another Time Warner franchise, Warner Bros.' *Harry Potter* series. Meanwhile the growing ranks of genuine independents consistently secured about 15 percent of the domestic movie market, turning out successful niche market films as well as occasional breakout hits like *The Blair Witch Project* (Artisan, 1999), *Traffic* (USA Films, 2000), *Memento* (Newmarket, 2001), *My Big Fat Greek Wedding* (IFC Films, 2002), *The Passion of the Christ* (Newmarket, 2004), and *Fahrenheit 9/11* (Lionsgate, 2004). In fact, the independent market was sufficiently robust that the conglomerates continued to expand their indie-film divisions and to acquire successful independents – as when Universal absorbed USA and Good Machine into its newly launched Focus Features subsidiary in 2003.

Thus, the film industry had reached an equilibrium of sorts in the early 2000s, with the three-tiered system of major Hollywood studios, conglomerate-owned indie subsidiaries, and genuine independents operating in relative harmony. But this balance began to shift rather severely in 2006 in two significant ways. First, the major studios were doing so well financially that it became difficult for the conglomerates to rationalize the costs and relatively higher risks of their indie subsidiaries. As recently as 2005, these subsidiaries comprised 13 of the top 25 distributors in the US and enjoyed a market share of over 15 percent. But in 2007, due to pressure from Wall Street and stockholders, as well as the box office performance of their top studio releases, the conglomerates began selling off or shutting down their indie subsidiaries, or folding them into their major studios. By 2009 only three indie divisions – Sony Classics, Focus, and Searchlight – were still operating on anywhere near the same level they had been a few years earlier, as the output of indie division films fell sharply along with their market share.[3]

A second aspect of this shifting balance has been the collapse of the independent sector. With the notable exception of just two companies, Lionsgate Films and Summit Entertainment, the hundred-plus independent producer-distributors found it difficult if not impossible to turn a profit after 2006. Those two successful independents relied on genre franchises to keep them afloat – Summit with *Twilight* (2008) and the series it spawned, and Lionsgate with its torture-horror *Saw* and *Hostel* series, its *Transporter* action franchise, and the remarkable run of the *Tyler Perry* "urban" (African-American) comedies. In 2009, Summit and Lionsgate earned more than all of the conglomerate-owned indie divisions combined, and more than all of the genuine independents combined as well.[4] In a sense, Lionsgate and Summit had become the Miramax and New Line of the new millennium, but without succumbing to conglomerate acquisition and without the overreaching and executive hubris that doomed both Miramax and New Line. The independent landscape underwent a significant change, however, when Lionsgate acquired

Summit in 2012 while still remaining independent of the Big Six conglomerates. Commercial and structural forces have induced other successful independents (and quasi-independents like DreamWorks and Pixar) to submit to conglomerate acquisition, however, and it may only be a matter of time until Lionsgate and Summit join them.

It is important to note that neither Lionsgate nor Summit specializes in "art films," which remain the domain of the surviving indie subsidiaries where the Coen brothers, Wes Anderson, Ang Lee, Danny Boyle, Alexander Payne, et al., continue to find safe haven. But the ranks of indie auteurs have steadily dwindled, due not only to the diminishing number of indie division releases (and indie subsidiaries) but also the studios' penchant for recruiting name-brand indie filmmakers to direct franchise blockbusters – a trend anticipated by Tim Burton on *Batman* that coalesced in the new millennium as filmmakers with independent credentials like Peter Jackson, Bryan Singer, Sam Raimi, Christopher Nolan, Jon Favreau, David Yates, Guy Ritchie, Marc Forster, Michel Gondry, and Kenneth Branagh signed on to direct studio franchise films. These assignments have a certain artistic cachet, thanks especially to Jackson's work on the *Lord of the Rings* trilogy and Nolan's on the rebooted *Batman* franchise. But the primary impulse clearly is professional and commercial more than anything else; franchise blockbusters are increasingly the only game in town for top filmmaking talent and thus represent the proverbial offer that simply cannot be refused.

Which is to say that the fate of top filmmaking talent in the new millennium, like that of the independent sector and the indie film movement generally, has been shaped by (and at the mercy of) the studios' growing preoccupation with franchise filmmaking. Hollywood's blockbuster mentality intensified in 1999 with *The Matrix*, *The Phantom Menace* (the first *Star Wars* film after a 16-year hiatus), and *Toy Story 2*, and then went into another register altogether with a veritable onslaught of new blockbuster franchises: *Harry Potter*, *Lord of the Rings*, and *Shrek* in 2001; *Spider-Man* and *Ice Age* in 2002; *Pirates of the Caribbean* in 2003; and Pixar's remarkable run of single-film franchises (*Monster's Inc.*, 2001; *Finding Nemo*, 2003; et al.). As these high-stakes, high-profile series blitzed the global movie marketplace and were parlayed by the conglomerates into global entertainment brands and veritable subindustries unto themselves, the franchise became Hollywood's prime objective and its consummate renewable resource – a product line that could increase its yield over time, not despite but precisely because of its predictable and formulaic nature and thus its capacity for systematic reformulation. And as the franchise mentality coalesced, so did a range of formal, stylistic, and aesthetic protocols.

The Matrix, as Henry Jenkins notes, was a breakthrough in "transmedia storytelling" (2006, 93–130), a narrative designed to expand through multiple iterations on an array of media platforms. The expansion of both the narrative world and the story itself speaks to the serial (versus series) nature of these franchises, as well as their strategic migration into other media formats. Digital technology is a key factor here, particularly in terms of the computer-generated effects and spectacular fantasy worlds created in the films and in their other media incarnations. Indeed, something of a seismic shift aesthetically in these new blockbuster franchises has been the prevalence of fantasy – by no means a strong tradition in Hollywood filmmaking, but a governing narrative paradigm in the new millennium. A number of other rules are worth mentioning as well: the reliance on a presold story property, the male protagonist and frequent coming-of-age motif, the Manichean moral universe of absolute good versus evil, the hero's alternating struggles with external foes and his own internal darker side, the chaste love story, the stylized violence and PG-13 rating (parents strongly cautioned for children under 13), the mythic quest and inevitable happy ending (tentatively in the individual installments, and then decisively when and if the serial story is concluded).

The revived *Star Wars* series was a breakthrough in digital cinema as well, with Lucas touting *Episode I: The Phantom Menace* in 1999 as Hollywood's first completely digital motion picture. The Pixar films shared this distinction, and along with DreamWorks' *Shrek* franchise proved to be far more influential in the animated realm than the *Star Wars* films in the live-action arena, as one studio after another entered the computer-animation fray during the 2000s. In terms of live-action production, in fact, digital filmmaking was far more pronounced outside the studio blockbuster realm, ranging from low-budget DV (digital video) projects like *The Blair Witch Project* and *Frozen River* (2008), to mid-range features involving top directors who veered into digital cinema as the high-end, high-quality HD technology rapidly evolved. These included Robert Rodriguez, an early adopter whose *Sin City* (2005), which he shot, edited, and codirected with Frank Miller, was a technical and stylistic *tour de force*, particularly in its blending of live action and animation and its onscreen realization of a graphic novel. Another was Michael Mann who, in films like *Collateral* (2004), *Miami Vice* (2006), and *Public Enemies* (2009), gave traditional Hollywood styles and genres a new "look" with a distinctively video quality. Danny Boyle in *28 Days Later* (2002) and *Slumdog Millionaire* (2008) mixed documentary-style, run-and-gun video techniques with remarkably slick, sophisticated digital effects and editing. Sci-fi/horror proved to be especially amenable to digital filmmaking, with several major hits like *Cloverfield* (2008) and *District 9* (2009) following Boyle's lead in freely mixing documentary-style DV cinematography with state-of-the-art CG effects.

The development of digital cinema took an enormous leap with the December 2009 release of *Avatar*, whose writer-director-producer-editor James Cameron had been redefining the limits and capabilities of digital filmmaking as both a filmmaker and a technological innovator for the previous two decades – dating back to *The Abyss* (1989), *Terminator 2: Judgment Day* (1992), and of course *Titanic* (1997). *Avatar* proved to be a breakthrough in two distinct ways. In terms of filmmaking, it marked key advances in the amalgamation of animation and live action, in its use of 3-D motion-capture technology (much of it developed by Cameron), and in its creation of a digital fantasy realm. In terms of exhibition, *Avatar*'s high-definition digital 3-D technology had a sudden and decisive effect on film projection and theatrical moviegoing – constituting what Charles Acland (2010) termed a "technological tentpole" by fueling the conversion of theaters worldwide to digital 3-D and enhancing the appeal and commercial prospects of the 3-D films that inevitably followed. Simply stated, *Avatar* raised the bar for digital filmmaking and redefined the immersive viewing experience, and it rewrote the box office record books in the process, grossing $2.75 billion worldwide in its initial release.

Whether digital 3-D represents a seismic shift in filmmaking and exhibition remains to be seen. At the very least, it is another important step in digital innovation not only for the movie industry but also for the conglomerates and adjacent media industries as well. Disney launched the ESPN 3D cable channel in June 2010, for instance, and that same month Sony announced 3-D upgrades for its PlayStation game system and its Bravia HD televisions. The notion that *Avatar* and other 3-D movies will fuel 3-D development in other media undercuts the frequent comparisons between the current trend and the short-lived, ill-fated 3-D "craze" in the early 1950s. Whereas that earlier 3-D rollout was motivated by Hollywood's struggle to compete with the television, the current rollout is yet another effort to integrate film, television, home video, and various other modes of media consumption. That said, it also remains important for the movie industry to differentiate the theatrical 3-D experience, and to convince moviegoers that it is more immersive, more spectacular, more thrilling than other 3-D media experiences.

As the 3-D trend accelerated, several industry leaders including Joe Roth of Revolution Studios (and former head of Fox and Disney) and media mogul Mark Cuban (Magnolia Pictures, Landmark Theaters, HDTV, et al.) encouraged the studios' return to theater ownership (Garret 2010; Pond 2010). They argued that the studios were not likely to face antitrust challenges in the era of deregulation and media diversification, and that reverting to vertical integration made sense for several very good reasons: Hollywood's deepening commitment to wide-release blockbusters; the compatibility of these spectacular, CG-driven films with digital 3-D projection; and the fact that the conversion to digital projection would be accompanied, inevitably, by a conversion to digital distribution, which would eliminate the enormous costs of striking and shipping 35mm film prints. Studio ownership of theater chains, they noted, would give them far more efficiency and flexibility in the handling of wide releases, and thus greater profitability once the costs of conversion to digital delivery and projection were absorbed.

The prospect of the major studios reverting to theater ownership conjures up visions of the vertically integrated studio system of old – a biting irony, to be sure, and another indication of the industry's resurgence and the studios' reassertion of power. Indeed, Hollywood in recent years has seen a veritable rebirth of the studio system, with the Big Five integrated major studios of the classical era replaced by the Big Six conglomerate-owned majors of the contemporary era. But the studios are not likely to rush back into theater ownership, given the enormous success of their distribution operations on the one hand, and the pitfalls and uncertainties of theatrical exhibition on the other. Blockbusters again are a key factor, in that the studios command a huge portion of the box office gross (often as high as 70–80 percent) on high-end films during the first few weeks of release, when blockbusters do the lion's share of their business. The studios then take a sizable distribution fee (usually 25–35 percent) of these box office revenues "off the top," before settling with investors, coproducers, participating talent, and so on. Thus, the studios are quite content to stand pat on the current arrangements, waiting to see if and when the exhibition market heats up enough to warrant a gamble on theater acquisition. The other "pipelines" owned by their parent conglomerates already provide viable outlets for their films, while the steadily expanding foreign markets enable the studios to hedge their bets against fluctuations in the US theatrical market. And even though theatrical release remains the most vital stage in the launch and ultimate commercial performance of a hit movie, it comprises an ever decreasing portion of a film's total revenues (currently about 20 percent). Digital 3-D may increase a major hit's theatrical take, particularly in light of the increased ticket prices in 3-D venues, but it is unlikely to change the distribution–exhibition protocols of the modern blockbuster era.

What's far more likely to change the current system – and what's likely to precipitate the next seismic shift in the American film industry – is the simultaneous "day and date" release of movies in theaters, online, on cable television, and on DVD. This prospect now appears to be all but inevitable, given the prevailing economic, technological, and social conditions – not to mention the configuration of the media conglomerates, all of which would stand to benefit from such a change. In fact the recent acquisition of NBC Universal from GE by the cable giant Comcast increases this likelihood (Arango 2009; Kang 2011). The current system is generating record revenues for the major studio-distributors year after year, however, so this kind of massive change is more likely to originate elsewhere and to develop more incrementally, either through the conglomerate-owned indie divisions or, more likely, in the genuine independent sector. Indeed, with the soaring costs of theatrical release and the daunting odds against success in that high-stakes market, bypassing the theatrical venue altogether may be the only way that true independents – and the alternative filmmaking ethos they foster – can hope to survive.

Notes

1. This quotation is actually a chapter title in Pierson's professional memoir: "1989: The Year It All Changed" (Pierson 1995).
2. Nash Information Services, Titanic: "Total U.S. Gross"; "Worldwide Gross"; "Worldwide Video and DVD Sales and Rentals"; at http://the-numbers.com.
3. According to the MPAA (Motion Picture Association of America), the conglomerate-owned indie divisions released an average of 80 films per year from 2000 to 2007; their output fell to 60 in 2008 and 47 in 2009, when their market share dropped below 6 percent. Interestingly enough, the major studios' output did not increase as they absorbed these indie divisions; in fact it declined from an average of 190 per year between 2000 and 2007 to 168 in 2008 and 158 in 2009.
4. According to Nash Information Services, the combined market share of Lionsgate and Summit in 2009 was 8.3 percent, while the combined share of the conglomerates' indie division was under 6 percent, as was the combined share of the hundred-plus independents: at http://the-numbers.com.

References

Acland, Charles R. (2010). "*Avatar* as Technological Tentpole." *Flow*, January 22, at http://flowtv.org (accessed February 2011).

Arango, Tom. (2009). "G.E. Makes It Official: NBC Will Go to Comcast." *New York Times*, December 3.

Auletta, Ken. (1991). *Three Blind Mice: How the Networks Lost Their Way*. New York: Random House.

Biskind, Peter. (2004). *Down and Dirty Pictures: Miramax, Sundance, and the Rise of Independent Film*. New York: Simon & Schuster.

Connolly, John. (1998). "Flirting with Disaster." *Premiere*, July, 84f.

Garrett, Diane. (2010). "Biz Told to Alter Its DNA at Summit." *Variety*, May 4.

Goldman Sachs. (1995). *Movie Industry Update*.

Griffin, Nancy, & Masters, Kim. (1996). *Hit and Run: How Jon Peters and Peter Guber Took Sony for a Ride in Hollywood*. New York: Touchstone.

Hettrick, Scott. (2003). "Home Video Business Bounds Past $20 Billion Mark." *Video Business*, January 10, at http://www.videobusiness.com.

Holt, Jennifer. (2001–2002). "In Deregulation We Trust: The Synergy of Politics and Industry in Reagan-Era Hollywood." *Film Quarterly*, 55.2, Winter, 22–29.

Jenkins, Henry. (2006). *Convergence Culture: Where Old Media and New Media Collide*. New York: New York University Press.

Kang, Cecilia. (2011). "Update: FCC, Justice Approve Comcast and NBC Joint Venture." *Washington Post*, January 18.

LaPorte, Nicole. (2010). *The Men Who Would Be King*. New York: Houghton Mifflin Harcourt.

Mehler, Mark. (1992). "Shaye: Steady Hand on the Fast Track." *Variety*, August 10, 35.

MPAA (Motion Picture Association of America). (1990). *U.S. Economic Review*. Los Angeles: MPAA.

Murphy, A. D. (1989). "20 Years of Weekly Film Ticket Sales in U.S. Theaters." *Variety*, March 15–21.

Pendleton, Jennifer. (1992). "Manic Bat-marketing Underway." *Variety*, April 20, 3.

Perren Alisa. (2001–2002). "Sex, Lies and Marketing: Miramax and the Development of the 'Quality Indie' Blockbuster." *Film Quarterly*, 55.2, Winter, 30–39.

Pierson, John. (1995). "1989: The Year It All Changed." In John Pierson, *Spike, Mike, Slackers and Dykes: A Guided Tour across a Decade of American Independent Cinema* (pp. 126–132). New York: Hyperion.

Pond, Steve. (2010). "Mark Cuban to Studios: Buy Theater Chains." *The Wrap*, June 6, at http://www.thewrap.com (accessed February 2011).

Price, David A. (2008). *The Pixar Touch: The Making of a Company*. New York: Knopf.

Prince, Stephen. (2000). "2. Merger Mania." In Stephen Prince, *A New Pot of Gold: Hollywood under the Electronic Rainbow* (pp. 40–89). New York: Scribner's.

Putzer, Gerald. (1990). "Box Office Blasts Off in the Year of the Bat." *Variety*, January 3, 1.

Saporito, Bill. (1989). "The Inside Story of Time Warner." *Fortune*, November 20, 164–210.

Schatz, Thomas. (2008). "The Studio System and Conglomerate Hollywood." In Paul McDonald and Janet Wasko (eds), *The Contemporary Hollywood Film Industry* (pp. 13–42). Malden, MA: Blackwell.

Schatz, Thomas. (2009). "New Hollywood, New Millennium." In Warren Buckland (ed.), *Film Theory and Contemporary Hollywood Movies* (pp. 19–46). New York: Routledge.

Sebok, Bryan. (2007). "Convergent Hollywood, DVD, and the Transformation of the Home Entertainment Industries." PhD diss., University of Texas, Austin.

Stevenson, William. (1992). "Fine Line Finesses Art-House Mainstays." *Variety*, August 10, 40.

Stewart, James B. (2005). *DisneyWar*. New York: Simon & Schuster.

Taylor, Jim. (2006). *DVD Demystified*. 3rd edn. New York: McGraw-Hill.

Wyatt, Justin. (1998). "The Formation of the 'Major Independent': Miramax, New Line and the New Hollywood." In Steve Neale and Murray Smith (eds), *Contemporary Hollywood Cinema* (pp. 74–89). London: Routledge.

12

Independent Film

1980s to the Present

Geoff King

Professor, Brunel University London, United Kingdom

Independent filmmaking since the 1980s has taken on multi-faceted definitions shaped by individual **artistic vision**, **industrial factors**, and **cultural/ideological implications**. Geoff King explores the impact on film content and style of **new technologies**, such as lightweight film and digital cameras, and a changing **distribution infrastructure**. The altering independent landscape has had dual, sometimes contradictory effects. Artistic originality has been both severely threatened and surprisingly invigorated; **crossover potential** has increased exponentially; and new **indie** phenomena, such as "**mumblecore**," have emerged. The past 30 years have witnessed the rise of uncompromising visionaries like **Jim Jarmusch**, **Todd Haynes**, **Todd Solondz,** and **Kevin Smith**, but it also has seen the commercialization of the **Sundance Film Festival** and **Miramax**'s industrial branding of independent film – all part of a larger historical narrative about the vicissitudes and triumphs of filmmaking outside the major studios. King's essay shares ground with Eric Schaefer on low budget exploitation, Alex Lykidis on black representation in earlier independent films, Janet Cutler on "L.A. Rebellion" filmmakers, and Michael Bronski on queer cinema of the 1990s in this volume.

Additional terms, names, and concepts: Indiewood, Independent Feature Project, New Queer Cinema

They were often grainy, sometimes monochrome; they tended to be talky rather than full of movement or action, and they frequently betrayed their low-budget origins. But they were also marked as "new," fresh, and inspiring to others. There had always been independent features, of one kind or another, as long as there had been a Hollywood or any other establishment against which such distinctions could be made. During the 1980s and into the early 1990s, however, the notion of American independent cinema gained a new currency. Rather than being a catchall term, taken more or less literally to describe a range of very different types of nonstudio filmmaking, ranging from the avant-garde to exploitation-oriented

American Film History: Selected Readings, 1960 to the Present, First Edition. Edited by Cynthia Lucia, Roy Grundmann, and Art Simon.

genre cinema (including, at one extreme, pornography), "independent" came primarily to signify a particular type of lower-budget feature production. This was something akin to an American "art" cinema in certain respects: Although blended in many cases with more popular generic components, often characterized as "quirky" or "off-beat," it became widely celebrated as an accessible alternative to the Hollywood mainstream. It also gained a new label of its own: "indie," not just "independent," which suggested something of the particular territory that was involved (a term that brought resonances from some similar developments in the same period in the field of popular music), as opposed to wider and less specific connotations of independence. Work of this type had its own earlier history in American cinema, not least in the films of John Cassavetes in the preceding two decades. What marked the period from the 1980s onward as different and gave it a more established identity was a gathering momentum. Rather than being perceived as occasional one-off occurrences, or the persistent work of isolated individuals such as Cassavetes, independent films began to gain a sustained presence that had the appearance of a distinct movement in both the cinematic and the wider cultural discourses of the time.

What, exactly, this variety of "independence" has constituted, and how it should be judged, has never ceased to be a topic of debate, both within the independent community and among academic and other commentators. The term "independent" is a heavily loaded one, in which a range of investments are held. For some, it is a concept the boundaries of which seemed to be in need of tight policing, a concern that came especially to the fore as the indie sector became increasingly institutionalized during the 1990s and the distinction between independent and Hollywood film became less clear-cut in some instances. The notion of independence is one that has almost constantly been considered to be in "crisis" in some way, partly as a result of its own success, a phenomenon that persists today. Part of the problem is the vague nature of the term and the different ways in which it can be and has been defined. It is best understood, I suggest, as a relative concept rather than an absolute, something that exists in a range of degrees rather than as a binary independent/not-independent alternative. And the quality of independence is one that can be defined, in these relative degrees, at a number of levels. In this essay, as elsewhere (King 2005; 2008), I adopt three principal dimensions in which to examine degrees of independence: the industrial-economic (budget level, sources of finance, type of distributor, manner of distribution, box-office/home-viewing revenues/expectations), the formal-aesthetic (stylistic dimensions such as narrative structure, camerawork/photography, editing or use of sound) and the social, cultural, or political/ideological implications that might be drawn, more or less explicitly, from the material presented by the work in question.

At each level, a range of possibilities exists, from the radically alternative to something much closer to the qualities associated with the Hollywood mainstream, as does a variety of combinations of different degrees in each dimension. In some cases, indie status may be clearly apparent at all three levels, but what can result is a complex and nuanced balance of qualities: a complexity seen by some as a muddying of the waters, but one that I would argue only adds to the richness of this part of the cinematic landscape as an object of study. The term "indie" is useful, I suggest, in signifying a particular region of the cinematic landscape, the product of a specific historical context, that gets its definition from a mixture of qualities identifiable at all three levels. This can be opposed to more literal definitions of independence that tend to be restricted to the industrial-economic and, as a result, become so wide-ranging as to lose anything other than a negative specificity; that is to say, to encompass films of any kind that are neither funded and produced nor distributed by the major studios or their offshoots, a definition that can be taken, depending on how exactly it is conceived, to include everything from the smallest-scale experimental cinema to big-budget unambiguously mainstream films such as *Terminator 2: Judgment Day* (1991) or *Star Wars: Episode One: The Phantom Menace* (1999) (see Tzioumakis 2006, 4–5).

To make even the more restricted topic of indie cinema manageable in the confines of this essay, I focus on three broad phases in the period from the 1980s until the time of writing. The first is the early period in which the variety of independent cinema sketched briefly above came to fruition, from the 1980s until the early 1990s. The second runs from the mid-1990s to the early 2000s, a period in which the increasingly institutionalized status of parts of the independent sector led to significant blurring of some key distinctions between it and the realm of the

Hollywood studios. This included the creation of a zone of overlap that became known as "Indiewood," a development viewed by some as a threat to the status of any distinct notion of independent feature production and distribution. The final part of the essay challenges the latter perspective, however, by examining the scope that still exists in the early years of the twenty-first century for the production of independent features that can clearly be distinguished in kind from the output of either the major studio divisions or the Indiewood territory in between the two. In each of these sections, broader background is combined with closer examination of representative individual case-study examples.

Breakthrough and Consolidation: The Development of the "Indie" Recipe

The breakthrough achieved by independent film by the end of the 1980s began slowly, with the modest box office success of a quite small group of features in the early years of the decade, including *Return of the Secaucus Seven* (John Sayles, 1980), *My Dinner with Andre* (Louis Malle, 1981), *Chan Is Missing* (Wayne Wang, 1982), *Smithereens* (Susan Seidelman, 1982), and *El Norte* (Gregory Nava, 1983). Nothing very specific linked these films, beyond their low budgets and a general sense that their material was not that of the typical Hollywood studio production. On their own, their presence might not have signified anything more than a passing trend, but many more were to follow, generating increased momentum and increasingly wider recognition. A key landmark, by general consensus (see Pierson 1995), was the appearance in 1984 of Jim Jarmusch's first commercially distributed feature, *Stranger Than Paradise*, a film that seemed to crystallize some of the key features of the new independent movement. Others that followed, and have since gained the status of indie "classics," included *Blood Simple* (Joel and Ethan Coen, 1986), *She's Gotta Have It* (Spike Lee, 1986), *sex, lies, and videotape* (Steven Soderbergh, 1989), *Slacker* (Richard Linklater, 1991), *Reservoir Dogs* (Quentin Tarantino, 1992), and *Clerks* (Kevin Smith, 1994). The appearance of such films, and many more, was attributed in many cases to the emergence of a new generation of filmmaking talent, although the origins of those involved were highly variable (from New York University film school graduates such as Joel Coen and Spike Lee to the self-taught). What really marked this period as distinctive, however, and created the potential for something like a sustained movement rather than the occasional isolated breakthrough, was the development of a supporting infrastructure, beyond the work of individuals or even groups of filmmakers.

A number of key institutions came either into existence or into fruition during the 1980s, building in some cases on roots established in the previous two decades. These included independent film distributors, film festivals, and bodies such as the Independent Feature Project (IFP), a membership-based support organization. Of these, distributors were the most important, establishing a specialized channel for the release of both American independent features and overseas imports. The two biggest players in the 1980s and especially into the 1990s were Miramax and New Line Cinema, both of which came from small beginnings in the preceding decades (Miramax founded in 1979, New Line dating back to 1967). They were joined in the late 1970s and early 1980s by others, including Samuel Goldwyn, Island/Alive, Cinecom, and First Run Features. Some of the Hollywood studios also dipped a toe briefly in the independent water at this time. United Artists, Twentieth Century-Fox, and Universal created their own "classics" divisions to handle domestic and overseas "art" films. The growth of a network of independent distributors gave the sector a sustained presence, beyond the impact of any individual title, and led to the development of strategies tailored to the specific requirements of smaller films that needed careful nurturing if they were to fulfill their potential. The latter typically involved a small-scale "platform" release accompanied by low-cost forms of marketing, usually based around favorable reviews or the winning of festival prizes, and/or "grass-roots" campaigns focused on the very particular constituencies that might be attracted by particular films (see Rosen 1990). The development of the festival circuit was another important ingredient, providing sources of early reviews and positive word-of-mouth, as well as a release circuit in its own right for films that failed to achieve further distribution. By the early 1990s the Sundance Film Festival (formerly the US Film Festival, originally created in

1978) had established its status as the most high-profile event/institution in the independent landscape, followed by the IFP's Independent Feature Film Market in New York. The Sundance festival in particular, in its association with successes such as *sex, lies, and videotape*, played an important role in increasing the prominence of indie cinema in the wider culture of the period.

If these kinds of institutions played a crucial role in the development of what was, by the early 1990s, to become a booming independent feature sector, a number of broader underlying factors provided the economic basis for expansion. The most important was the rapid expansion during the 1980s of home video as a viewing medium, which created a large new market for film product (along with the simultaneous growth of cable television and an increase in the numbers of cinema screens in the United States). The video boom coincided with a period in which production by the Hollywood studios had been reduced as part of a strategy in which the studios concentrated their resources primarily around relatively small numbers of potential blockbuster hits and star vehicles. This left a big gap in demand that made financing for independent productions much easier to obtain, from sources that included video distributors and television companies overseas as well as in the United States. The financial territory at home was made even more hospitable by the debt-based financial system adopted under the Reagan administration during the 1980s, although this came to a halt with the stock market crash of 1987. Public funding also played an important part in the support of some independent features in this period, from national and local sources and from the Public Broadcasting Service (PBS), although these faced substantial cuts by the early 1990s. The involvement of public funds was a significant contributor to the perception that this variety of independent film included an orientation toward the expression of alternative perspectives, as Yannis Tzioumakis suggests, at a time when the Hollywood mainstream became associated with a broadly conservative backlash against the radical currents included in some of its products in the decade from the late 1960s until the late 1970s.

Low budget, distributed largely outside the major studio system, and handled in a manner distinctly different from the wide releases typical of Hollywood product, the indie films of the 1980s and early 1990s were quite clearly marked as independent at the industrial level. What exactly "low budget" meant was somewhat variable, but still well beneath the radar of what would usually be contemplated by the studios. For some of the films cited above, inexpensive meant hundreds of thousands of dollars, compared with the millions or tens of millions characteristic of Hollywood production. By the early 1990s an even lower budget tendency came to the fore, partly as a result of the financial squeeze that followed the 1987 crash. This tendency was exemplified by *El Mariachi* (Robert Rodriguez, 1992, \$7,000), *Laws of Gravity* (Nick Gomez, 1992, \$38,000), and *The Living End* (Gregg Araki, 1992, \$22,700). The key to production at such minimal cost was the structuring of projects around resources already available to the filmmaker, the use of borrowed equipment and the availability of casts and crew prepared to work without any initial payment. The highlighting of extreme low budget became a significant source of publicity for the indie sector, promoting a romantic notion of the pursuit of filmmaking dreams on credit card debt or other innovative means of finance. The reality was that much higher costs were involved in the process of actually getting the films in front of viewers (blowing up 16mm footage to the exhibition standard of 35mm, rerecording poor quality sound, and the distribution expenses of marketing and striking prints – costs that could dwarf those of the initial production).

Low or very low budget production also played a strong part in shaping the aesthetics of the indie cinema of this period. Grainy footage was a frequent hallmark, whether monochrome or color. Camerawork was often fixed and static – or the opposite, hand-held and unsteady – the two options easiest to achieve with limited resources (*Stranger Than Paradise* is a striking example of the former, shot in long static takes, *Laws of Gravity* of the latter, employing a verité-style mobility that gives the impression of catching the reality of life on the streets). The results ranged from a formalist distance to the creation of impressions of documentary like authenticity, each distinguishable from the predominant norms of mainstream Hollywood. In other cases, a variety of formal markers of distinction were created on the cheap through such means as innovative and inexpensive camera motion (developed by Sam Raimi for *The Evil Dead*, 1981, and *The Evil Dead 2*, 1987, and by the Coen brothers for *Blood Simple* and *Raising Arizona*, 1987) to create overtly stylized effects appropriate to the genre territories in which these filmmakers worked (in these cases, horror/horror spoof, noir, and screwball comedy). The employment of these different formal strategies, and the resonances that resulted, provides a useful indication of the kind of territories crossed by the indie cinema of the time, ranging from (and sometimes combining) elements of the "arty," the "worthy," and the kind of work that sought to bring "quirky," "offbeat" qualities to more popular generic ground.

Narrative is another formal ground on which many of these films were marked as clearly different from the Hollywood norm, with a leaning at the lower-budget end of the scale toward attenuated or downplayed narrative forms, deliberately eschewing the conventional plot points and character arcs usually associated with studio production. This was, as with the aspects of visual style considered above, the result of a mixture of factors. Practical necessity played a role, films in which little happens or the canvas is small and intimate generally being much easier to produce on limited resources. However, there was also a more positive commitment to the presentation of something closer to the exigencies of real life, a strain that can be traced from the films of Cassavetes through a range of indie features including the early works of Jarmusch and other noted indie features including *Laws of Gravity*, *Working Girls* (Lizzie Borden, 1986), *Clerks*, and *Gummo* (Harmony Korine, 1997). If downplayed narrative forms made claims to authenticity and realism similar to those of hand-held camerawork (the two sometimes, but far from always, combined), the narrative equivalent of more formalist or stylized visuals constituted countertendencies in some work to complicate or draw more overt attention to narrative structure. Some productions demonstrated multi-stranded narratives, two of the most striking examples being *Slacker*, a grainy, low-budget compilation of a series of fragmentary meetings and conversations, and *Poison* (Todd Haynes, 1991), in which the viewer is invited to make connections between three entirely separate stories. Multiple strands often required greater resources, however, especially when woven more smoothly into wider fabrics, a characteristic of a group of higher budgeted later 1990s features including *Short Cuts* (Robert Altman, 1993), *Happiness* (Todd Solondz, 1998), and *Magnolia* (Paul Thomas Anderson, 1999). The earlier period also witnessed a number of more formally experimental narrative structures, including the revisiting of events from different perspectives, notable examples being Jarmusch's *Mystery Train* (1989) and *Night on Earth* (1991), and *Flirt* (Hal Hartley, 1995) (for more on these, see King 2005).

Many indie films of this period and afterwards are more conventional in narrative or other formal qualities, however, or mix various degrees of difference at different levels. Independent features tend, generally, to abide by "classical" Hollywood conventions such as the use of continuity editing regimes in the assemblage of shots. And even if some departures are found in the realm of narrative, many of the ingredients familiar from Hollywood and other mainstream/commercial cinemas are retained, including the logic of cause-and-effect in the organization of plot material (even if in an attenuated and throw-away manner in some examples) and a central focus in most cases on a small number of major characters (even if they do not always perform the kinds of actions or have the kinds of characteristics usually found in studio productions). The "difference" by which indie features were and have continued to be marked tends to be relative rather than absolute, closer to Hollywood in most respects than to the more radical avant-garde or experimental ends of the cinematic spectrum. The same can be said of the sociocultural or political content of these films and its implications. Difference from Hollywood in these terms is sometimes implicit rather than explicit. Downplayed narrative forms that deny major arcs of character action or development or that refuse the familiar Hollywood affirmative ending have significant sociopolitical implications, but these are far from always drawn to attention. The most frequent sources of more overt or radical intervention in sociopolitical territory have tended to focus on areas such as race and particularly gender.

The emergence of a number of black filmmakers was one key ingredient of the period from the mid-1980s to the early 1990s. Most notable is the work of Spike Lee, the success of whose *She's Gotta Have It* demonstrated the existence of a viable audience for black indie features that opened up a space for others to follow. Lee remained the dominant presence, however, taking on issues of racial politics more directly in the films that followed, especially *Do the Right Thing* (1989), a feature that was distinctly indie in quality (and over which Lee maintained full control, including final cut), despite being a studio-funded production. Lee's approach in such films was a characteristic mixture of serious content and sassy "in-your-face" style, a recipe that proved commercially appealing and marked a clear difference between the dominant trend in black indie cinema (and, arguably, indie cinema more generally) and the more seriously political orientation of an earlier black independent film movement, the L.A. School of the 1970s (for more on this, see King 2005, 203–209).

Gender politics also loomed large in some of the most notable indie features of the period, including the polemical feminism of Lizzie Borden's near-future science fictional *Born in Flames* (1983) and the more conventional day-in-the-life treatment given to prostitution in *Working Girls*. A number of other women filmmakers emerged as part of the indie movement, including Allison Anders (best known for *Gas Food Lodging*, 1992), although the sector remained almost as male-dominated in some respects as its Hollywood equivalent, with women filmmakers generally finding it much harder than their male counterparts to make the crucial move from achieving the release of one feature to obtaining funding for others to follow (black women filmmakers had it hardest of all in this respect, as evidenced by the inability of Julie Dash to produce a theatrical release to follow her critically acclaimed period piece *Daughters of the Dust*, 1991). The most eye-catching dimension of the gender politics of the indie scene in this period was what became known as New Queer Cinema, constituted by an assertively homocentric group of films that were distinctly independent in both form and content. The appearance of New Queer Cinema marked a rejection of a more conventional strand of gay-oriented independent film exemplified by titles such as *Desert Hearts* (Donna Deitch, 1985), *Parting Glances* (Bill Sherwood, 1986), and *Longtime Companion* (Norman René, 1990) that quietly made the case that gay or lesbian existence could be treated as entirely "normal," itself a move some distance from the stereotypical caricatures usually found in Hollywood. The label New Queer Cinema was given to a group of features that appeared far more uncompromising in their approach, products of a context that witnessed an aggressive campaigning fight-back against early AIDS-era homophobia, including *Poison*, *The Living End*, and *Swoon* (Tom Kalin, 1992), films that were far from being designed to make portrayals of homosexuality comfortable for the wider audience.

By the early years of the 1990s, the combinations of these different strains – the more "arty" or formalist; the more "gritty" or seemingly authentic, the avowedly stylish, "quirky" or "offbeat," the more sociopolitically oriented, all of which were subject to a variety of blends – was sufficient to suggest the existence of a particular territory that was distinctive in its relationship with the rest of the cinematic spectrum without being anything like a monolith. It also gained a high level of visibility in the broader culture of the time, establishing the terms "indie" or "independent" as signifiers of a brand of cinema of greater cultural worth than that associated with the Hollywood mainstream (Tzioumakis 2006). The successes of numerous indie films produced on very low budgets provided inspiration to others to follow in their tracks, as evidenced in the anecdotes produced by many filmmakers of the time (*Slacker* is cited by Kevin Smith, for example, as having demonstrated to him that making a film of that kind was something of which he would be capable; Smith's *Clerks* played the same role, in turn, for others). The result was an ever increasing volume of production, although by no means was every film able to achieve theatrical distribution. A recurring problem in the latter half of the 1990s and into the following century was the oversupply of films in competition with each other for a limited amount of space. This was just one of several respects in which the success of the sector was to become widely viewed as one of its own worst enemies.

Case Study: *Clerks* (Kevin Smith, 1994)

Clerks is a by-now classic example of low-budget production that makes the most of available resources, almost entirely shot (on a budget of $27,000, much of it raised on credit cards) in the New Jersey convenience store at which writer-director Kevin Smith was employed at the time. From its opening seconds, *Clerks* is instantly recognizable as indie fare, its heavily textured black-and-white footage – in which the grain clearly dances and fizzles, especially against pale backgrounds – announcing its inexpensive origins and marking the film as very distant from the Hollywood mainstream. The camera is mostly static, often in long takes dominated by conversation. Most of the performers were nonprofessionals at the time, although the lead, Brian O'Halloran, who plays the reluctant and heavily put-upon clerk Dante Hicks, called in to

Figure 12.1 Dante (Brian O'Halloran) and Randal (Jeff Anderson) in Kevin Smith's *Clerks* (1994, producers Scott Mosier and Kevin Smith, who was also the writer), distracted by a debate about the finer points of *Return of the Jedi*.

work on what should be his day off, had previous part-time experience on the stage. The film adopts a day-in-the-life narrative structure, built primarily around a succession of comic scenes and dialogue riffs involving the strange array of customers who visit the store, along with Dante's relationship with nearby slacker video-store clerk Randal (Jeff Anderson). The nearest *Clerks* comes to featuring conventional plot material is in its portrayal of Dante's love life, including visits from his current girlfriend Veronica (Marilyn Ghigliotti) and the background presence of his ex, Caitlin (Lisa Spoonaur), but any developments along these lines are mostly subordinate to the impression of evoking a particular and somewhat warped slice of life, punctuated by chapter headings (the original more dramatic and downbeat ending, in which Dante is shot dead by a robber, was cut after the film's first screening, at the Independent Feature Market).

Clerks is also typical of the breakthrough period of indie cinema in the early 1990s in what was disguised by the headline budget figure. That was the cost of the original shooting on 16mm but not of the version that made it into theaters after the film was picked up for distribution by Miramax. "Completion costs," including a remix of the original sound and blow-up to the theatrical standard 35mm, were an additional $200,000, on top of which could be added more than $1.7 million spent by the distributor on advertising in print and electronic media (Pierson 1995, 231). From a sociocultural perspective, the film's marker of difference from the mainstream is the sexually explicit nature of parts of the dialogue, much of which would be inconceivable within a more mainstream feature, including a list of outlandish porno titles ordered by Randal. *Clerks* was originally given an NC-17 rating (no one under 17 admitted) that would have restricted it to very marginal distribution, although this was changed to "R" (under-17s to be accompanied by parent or adult guardian) on appeal.

Crossing over (and Selling out?): Expansion, Incorporation, and the Blurring of Lines

Some of the greatest commercial triumphs of the indie sector have been viewed, in retrospect, as having created some of its biggest problems for the future. In the course of the 1990s, expectations began to change. In the early period, during the 1980s, an independent feature was considered to have been a financial success if its US box office gross was in the region of $1–2 million dollars, or even less in some cases. It was a modest business with modest expectations (even if the costs of production remained well beyond the individual means of most of those involved) and, as a result, there was relatively low pressure to surrender artistic ends to more immediately commercial ends. Many films enjoyed healthy cost-to-profit ratios without a requirement for spectacular performance at the box office. This was changed, however, by a series of "breakout" successes that altered all understanding of the kind of financial ceiling that might be expected. The first was Soderbergh's *sex, lies, and videotape*, a hit at the Sundance festival that won the prestigious Palme d'Or at Cannes and grossed a then unprecedented $25 million in the US on a budget of $1.2 million, an event that marked a milestone in the development of the indie sector. It was followed by others, most prominently Quentin Tarantino's *Pulp Fiction* (1994), which upped the ante even further, topping the $100 million barrier that had not so many years previously been the exclusive preserve of the successful Hollywood blockbuster, and *The Blair Witch Project* (Daniel Myrick and Eduardo Sánchez, 1999), which grossed $140 million.

The result was not that all films were expected to achieve such box office heights, but a broad shift was detected by many industry commentators in how the nature of the indie business came to be perceived. Films such as *sex, lies, and videotape*, *Pulp Fiction*, and *The Blair Witch Project* gained their success by crossing over into a broader audience than usually associated with the independent sector. This was achieved through the use of wider release strategies and more aggressive (and expensive) marketing campaigns, approaches that increased the overall cost of distribution and generally raised the stakes involved. Such strategies did not suit all indie features alike, most of them not having the potential to reach larger audiences, but they became increasingly prevalent as the 1990s developed. This, combined with heightened competition among escalating numbers of indie features, put an increased emphasis on the need for films to earn rapidly or lose their place in theaters. Less space was generally available for films to build slowly, according to the traditional art or indie recipe, while spending on advertising became increasingly important to enable any individual work to gain attention. The fear expressed by many was that more commercial-seeming independent features were likely to succeed in this environment at the expense of those with less immediately obvious appeal beyond a smaller niche audience – fears that were only increased by a new wave of Hollywood studio involvement in the indie sector.

The success of films such as *sex, lies, and videotape* and *Pulp Fiction*, and plenty of more modest examples since the latter 1980s, did not go unnoticed in Hollywood, prompting a more concerted investment in the indie sector during the 1990s. By the early 2000s, all of the major studios had created their own indie-related offshoots, known in the trade as "specialty" divisions, through either the creation of new subsidiaries from scratch or the incorporation of existing producers and/or distributors. The two most prominent moves came in 1993, when Miramax was bought by the Walt Disney Company and New Line was sold to Ted Turner, subsequently becoming part of the Time-Warner conglomerate. Sony Pictures Classics was created in 1992, followed by Fox Searchlight in 1994 and Paramount Classics in 1998. Universal went through a number of maneuvers before settling on the creation of Focus Features in 2002, an entity that included the takeover of Good Machine, a leading presence in the New York indie scene. Warner Independent Pictures was created in 2003 (although its closure was subsequently announced as part of a rationalization in 2008). The specialty divisions retained significant degrees of autonomy from their studio parents, although these varied in scope from one to another. The result of studio ownership was to give renewed industrial clout to a former independent such as Miramax, a company that had suffered from periodic instability and insufficient capitalization, enabling it to drive many of the more mainstream-oriented trends outlined above. Flush with Disney cash and able to draw on the studio's numerous existing deals for video and television sales, Miramax was able to expand its number of indie film acquisitions in the latter part of the 1990s, forcing up prices all around and obliging others to follow its more aggressive buying and marketing strategies if they were to compete (Biskind 2004, 193). It was Miramax, in particular, distributor of both *sex, lies, and videotape* and *Pulp Fiction*, that drove the push for wider releases and bigger box office returns and that was the chief architect of the blurring of lines between the indie and studio sectors that gained momentum during the decade.

Miramax was also at the forefront of a move increasingly into production as well as distribution from the latter part of the 1990s. The indie business of the 1980s and early 1990s was founded on a process in which US distribution rights were usually bought after completion of a film (overseas theatrical and video/television rights were often sold in advance in separate packages, as suggested in the previous section, to raise production finance). The typical procedure would be for distributors to view films at or around festivals such as Sundance and for bidding wars to occur for what appeared to be the most attractive features. The announcement of the results of the bigger deals became one of the most prominent sources of media coverage for the indie sector, especially in cases in which the agreed fees appeared to be excessive. The heightened competition of the late 1990s drove distributors to invest increasingly in production, to gain an early stake in and privileged access to desirable projects. This increased the risks involved in the business, however, and was viewed as another potential source of conservatism in the nature of the productions most likely to be supported (Biskind 2004, 159–160).

The outcome of these developments was the creation of a hybrid zone that became known as Indiewood, a term usually used as one of abuse by critics who saw its creation as a threat to the existence of a more distinctive independent sector. Indiewood is defined most clearly at the institutional level, in the shape of the specialty divisions, although it can also be used to characterize individual films, or groups of films, that themselves seem to embody a blend of indie and more mainstream-oriented qualities (King 2008). The distinction between indie and Indiewood at the textual rather than the institutional level is far from clear cut, the indie sector itself representing a hybrid territory that has drawn upon a variable blend of the traditions of Hollywood, art, and exploitation cinemas. It is not simply a question of textual qualities specific to films produced or distributed by the studio divisions, the slates of which also include overseas imports and some American films that appear quite clearly to remain within the norms of indie production (small scale, low-budget, "offbeat," and generally not star-led). Examples of the latter from the mid-2000s include *Napoleon Dynamite* and *Garden State* (both 2004) distributed by Fox Searchlight, *The United States of Leland* and *Northfork* (both 2003) from Paramount Classics, *The Station Agent* (2003) from Miramax, and *Brick* (2006) distributed by Focus Features. For some commentators, the problem with such films was that, by the end of the 1990s and into the 2000s, they appeared precisely to be following a recipe that had become conventionalized in some of its ingredients, including a willful "quirkiness" that seemed to be too carefully designed as such to fit a particular bill rather than being simply the outcome of unchanneled creative vision (although the latter notion is perhaps somewhat naive, as if any forms of cultural production existed in a vacuum).

At the same time, the Indiewood divisions were also involved in the production and/or distribution of larger, more ambitious features that appeared to be designed more consciously with crossover potential in mind. It is this sense of more actively seeking access to broader audiences, rather than gratefully accepting such success as an occasional bonus, that is one of the markers of a distinctly Indiewood tendency at the textual level. A number of different strains of such production can be identified, including literary-oriented films, sometimes marked as "epic" in their qualities. Examples include *The English Patient* (Miramax, 1996), *Cold Mountain* (Miramax, 2003), and *Brokeback Mountain* (Focus, 2005), along with combinations of literary and "heritage" signifiers in the likes of *Shakespeare in Love* (Miramax, 1998), *Possession* (Focus, 2002), and *Pride and Prejudice* (Focus, 2005). At its more formally innovative, Indiewood has tended to combine its markers of distinction from the mainstream with the presence of substantial stars and/or more conventional underlying genre frameworks, as is the case with the Focus releases *Eternal Sunshine of the Spotless Mind* (2004, with Jim Carrey, Kate Winslet, and romantic comedy as mainstream ingredients underpinning elements of nonlinear narrative and surreal visual effects) and *21 Grams* (2003, Sean Penn, Naomi Watts, with emotional melodrama underlying a highly fragmented narrative form) (King 2004; 2008). Another aspect of this crossover was a tendency for the major Hollywood studios themselves, not just their specialty divisions, to fund or distribute indie-type films. One prominent example of the late 1990s was *American Beauty* (1999, produced and distributed by DreamWorks). In some cases studio backing was more of a necessity for films with some indie dimensions but larger budgetary requirements than would usually be associated even with the products of the Indiewood sector, as was the case with two striking contributions released in 1999, *Fight Club* (David Fincher, Twentieth Century Fox) and *Three Kings* (David O. Russell, Warner Bros.). Some individual filmmakers whose work manifests a distinctly indie approach have worked consistently with the majors, including Wes Anderson, whose first feature, the offbeat comedy *Bottle Rocket* (1996), was produced and distributed by Columbia Pictures (part of the Sony empire) and whose subsequent films *Rushmore* (1998), *The Royal Tenenbaums* (2001), and *The Life Aquatic with Steve Zissou* (2004) were products of mainstream divisions of the Walt Disney brand, Touchstone Pictures (*The Darjeeling Limited*, 2007, was distributed by Fox Searchlight).

Increased studio involvement in the indie sector can be explained in a number of ways. The most obvious attraction was the desire to share some of the extreme windfalls that accompanied the most successful breakout indie features – like *Pulp Fiction* and *The Blair Witch Project* – but also the substantial if less spectacular revenues generated by solid but more modest performers. The tendency of the specialty divisions in their role as distributors has been effectively to cherry-pick the relatively small numbers of indie products that appear most likely to achieve success at either of these levels. A degree of involvement in the indie sector has also been viewed as a useful way to establish relationships with promising new filmmakers, at least some of whom would be happy subsequently to be recruited to handle more mainstream studio productions. The same goes for the building or maintenance of relationships with stars, some having made clear their desire in the late 1990s to work with the younger generation of indie-oriented talents such as Wes Anderson or David O. Russell (Waxman 2005, xviii). The other principal motivation for the studios was the prestige that could be gained through either the release of independently produced features or their own involvement in such work from the start. Prestige does appear to have a value in its own right to the Hollywood studios, as parts of corporations whose role in dominating large swathes of audiovisual culture is a frequent target for attack on various grounds. Fortunately, from the studio perspective, it is also often readily translatable into economic gain, especially via major award-giving processes such as the Academy Awards, the most high-profile event in the annual film calendar. The 1990s was a period in which indie or indie-related films often dominated the Oscars, usually receiving significant boosts at the box office as a result.

Case Study: *Sideways*

Sideways (Alexander Payne, 2004) is not a particularly ambitious-seeming film that would have been expected to achieve enormous crossover success; nor is it star-led or accompanied by other ingredients that would make it one of the most obvious candidates for breakout box office returns. In a number of other somewhat more modest ways, however, it offers a good example of what might be interpreted as a "softening" of the edges of indie-style cinema, as performed from within the auspices of a studio specialty division. It was both produced and distributed by Fox Searchlight on the relatively low budget of $16 million (large by traditional indie standards) and grossed a very healthy $71 million at the US box office (it is important also to note that the film was distributed on DVD by Twentieth Century Fox Home Entertainment, the main home-viewing outlet of the studio). *Sideways* is a mostly low-key, character-centered piece, one of its more indie-seeming features being the cranky nature of the main protagonist, Miles (Paul Giamatti), a depressive unpublished middle-aged writer who embarks on a "road trip" through California wine country with craggy small-time television actor Jack (Thomas Haden Church), the latter seeking a last sexual fling before his upcoming marriage. Miles is a difficult, bitter, and in some ways unattractive character (he steals money from his elderly mother before sneaking out without saying goodbye on her birthday after an overnight visit), qualities that mark departures from the norms of the mainstream. But the film also includes a number of somewhat unlikely and movie-conventional dimensions, primarily the relationship he establishes with the attractive Maya (Virginia Madsen), even if this is subject to some awkwardness and qualification. *Sideways* concludes with an open ending, in the romantic dimension, that offers a balance characteristic of many Indiewood features. Where a happy ending would be de rigueur in Hollywood and a downbeat conclusion might typify a more "honest" strain of indie production, less prone to such consoling fantasies, *Sideways*

Figure 12.2 A matter of taste distinction, on and off screen, as Miles (Paul Giamatti), the wine connoisseur in Alexander Payne's *Sideways* (2004, producers Michael London and George Parra), is observed by the skeptical Jack (Thomas Haden Church).

closes with Miles knocking on Maya's door, seeking to reestablish their connection after the apparent end of the relationship. The possibility of a positive resolution is left intact, and the impression created is that it remains a reasonable likelihood, but the film seems to want to have its cake and eat it, too; to offer something akin to an upbeat ending but also to avoid the cliché of its actual enactment on screen. It seems no accident, in the context of the way the film seeks to position itself, that its subject matter is also partly about acts of cultural distinction through taste, as manifested through the role of Miles as a wine connoisseur, distinguished from the "crass" tastes represented by Jack. If the film presents a clash between the two, it also seems in some aspects of its own fabric to offer a combination of the qualities they might be taken to represent, including a blend of poignant character-based drama, gentle humor, and occasional excursions into broader and more knockabout comic routine.

Still Indie after All These Years: "Mumblecore" and Other Lower-Budget Productions

It would be wrong to assume that the story of indie cinema from the mid-1990s onwards is just one of incorporation, deradicalization, and loss of any alternative "edge." That has become one of the dominant narratives surrounding the sector in recent years, but it is a partial account. The same could be said of some of the more romantic accounts of the earlier breakthrough period. It is easy to exaggerate exactly how radical or "different" commercially distributed indie cinema was in the heyday of the late 1980s and early 1990s, a tendency likely to increase the extent to which the following years are seen as a period of decline or "betrayal." Plenty of indie production in the earlier period was solidly conventional in many respects. And plenty of distinctly indie production has been sustained in the face of the encroachments of Indiewood, from the later 1990s and into the new century.

While some of the developments outlined in the previous section have created pressure to increase reliance on more conventional material, and to give increased power to the larger players, others have offered some countervailing forces in favor of smaller-scale and potentially more innovative production. The most significant is the new potential created by the advent of digital video (DV) as a viable means of production and distribution. Digital video cameras and editing software have, for the first time, made ownership of the means of production an affordable prospect for those with limited means, without sacrificing all potential for subsequent theatrical distribution. Light and portable DV cameras are also well suited to a fast and mobile "guerrilla" style of production, with small crews and low impact that can escape the need for the expensive shooting permits required in many locations. The fact that filmmakers can afford to have their own camera and edit on a home computer makes it much easier for films to be shot and edited over extended periods of time, a necessity often for those who still have to rely on day jobs. A favorable climate for experimentation is also created by the reusable nature of the recording medium, whether digital tape or hard drive, as opposed to the expensive and one-time-only use of celluloid. In some of these respects, the use of digital video has increased the accessibility of modes of filmmaking traditionally associated with the low-budget indie sector, but some are more ground-breaking, as is the potential created by digital forms of distribution.

Distribution, as always, remains the key to the business end of independent cinema. If the use of ultra-low-budget digital video has opened up new potential for production, it is distribution that remains the sticking point. The strength of the larger players, especially the studio divisions, is such that they continue to dominate access to conventional theatrical distribution. The studios have also begun to make moves into distribution via the internet and digital download, but this is an arena that offers a number of particular advantages to low-budget independents. At one end is self-distribution by the filmmaker directly onto a website, or the use of a website as window for direct sales onto DVD. This is a low-cost approach that entirely avoids the bottlenecks, costs, and studio domination of traditional forms of distribution. Films sold directly online provide an immediate large share of revenue to the producers, free from the potential influence of traditional distributors on content. The biggest remaining problem is finding ways of gaining any attention for a production released in this manner: One of the most important dimensions of conventional theatrical distribution, and one of the sources of dominance by the big players, is the cost of marketing (hence the particular importance of the festival circuit, as a source of attention, to the lower-budget end of the indie spectrum).

A range of low-cost online forms of promotion have also been explored, although this is also a crowded and competitive territory. One of the most notable success stories in this domain to date is Susan Buice and Arin Crumley's *Four Eyed Monsters* (2005), which built an audience through a combination of strategies. These included eye-catching web-posted video podcasts focused on the emotional dimensions of the making and early screenings of the film, information gathered about viewers who took up an invitation to respond to the podcasts, a selective theatrical release that followed from the interest generated by the latter, direct sales on DVD, and the screening of the entire film on YouTube, the latter leading to a deal for retail release. New outlets for download or video streaming were appearing at regular intervals at the time of writing, although only beginning to offer the prospect of substantial revenues. These ranged from competing more directly with the mainstream in established channels such as the Apple iTunes store to agreements available for DVD distribution or downloads via Amazon's Create-Space platform (the biggest player in this arena at the time of writing was New York based New Video Digital, which claimed in 2008 to have acquired the rights to more than 5,000 hours of independent film and television content (Kohn 2008)). Other forms of digital exhibition have also been attempted or proposed, including low-cost installations in nontraditional venues or new small-scale theatres.

Digital video has made its own, sometimes distinctive, contributions to the aesthetics of indie cinema. It can produce far longer single takes than are possible on film, a capacity exploited to original effect in the simultaneous four-strand 93-minute takes of *Timecode* (Mike Figgis, 2000). At its lower grades or in low levels of light, or when manipulated for deliberate effect, the image plane can become an impressionistic pixellated surface, as used to potent effect in Harmony Korine's *Julien Donkey-Boy* (1999). Alternatively, in other usages, DV can produce a harsh unflattering quality of the image that heightens the impression of authenticity sought by some indie filmmakers. The latter is very much to the fore in a group of films that appeared around the mid-2000s and acquired the label "mumblecore" on the basis of a shared low-key naturalism that included mostly hand-held DV footage along with low-fi sound quality and the vocal hesitancies of nonprofessional performers, among them a number of the filmmakers themselves. How far mumblecore can be said to constitute a "movement" in any real sense, rather than a marketing ploy – the latter associated particularly with the South by Southwest Film Festival in Austin, Texas, at which the notion appeared to crystallize in 2005 – remains subject to debate (see Taubin 2007). The films and filmmakers with which it is associated can reasonably be said to represent a distinctive version of some more familiar indie formats, however, the most characteristic features being ultra-cheap DV aesthetics and a quite narrow focus on the everyday relationship foibles of a "twenty-something" MySpace/YouTube-oriented generation.

Among the most critically lauded filmmakers to whom the label has been attached is Andrew Bujalski, an unrepresentative figure in one respect, given that his work, starting with *Funny Ha Ha* (2002) and *Mutual Appreciation* (2005), has been shot on film rather than DV and has received somewhat wider (although still marginal) theatrical release. As a rule, "mumblecore" features have been restricted to festival screenings, web-based distribution, or very small-scale and short-lived commercial openings. The most prolific of these filmmakers to date has been Joe Swanberg, whose third feature, *Hannah Takes the Stairs* (2007), demonstrated the limited theatrical potential of most such productions: opening on just one screen, with a first weekend gross of $5,901, reaching a maximum of two screens and a total US gross of $21,152 (figures from the Internet Movie Database, imdb.com). *Hannah Takes the Stairs* is typical of the qualities associated with Swanberg's work, and with mumblecore more widely, with its handheld camerawork (sometimes relatively steady, sometimes involving awkward pans and occasional loss of focus), its flat unflattering lighting, and its tendency to use long takes in its more sustained sequences. The aesthetic is partly a reflection of practical exigencies, but also seems well suited to the material. The nonprofessional performers often seem uncomfortable on camera, an impression that fits the discomfort experienced by the characters they play. Narrative development is minimal, tracing a series of awkward relationships experienced by Hannah (Greta Gerwig) but with no sense of any real progression, the emphasis of the film being on sequences in which the protagonists "hang out" together, sitting or lying around talking hesitantly about themselves and the uncertain states of their relationships. Swanberg's style, more so than those of his contemporaries, is heavily reliant upon improvised performance and dialogue, his name in the writing credits being accompanied by those of several other members of the cast (which includes fellow filmmakers Bujalski and Mark Duplass in two of the central male roles, a reflection of various personal connections and overlappings that exist within the mumblecore-related community).

A rather different aesthetic is found in the films of Aaron Katz, *Dance Party, USA* (2006) and *Quiet City* (2007), which include more lyrical and carefully designed audiovisual qualities while charting similarly minimal character engagements at the level of narrative. *Quiet City* begins with striking images, featuring carefully composed orange-toned skyscapes, and its account of the time spent together by a couple who meet by chance, which shows little conventional evidence of developing into anything romantic (she visiting New York and unable to make contact with the friend with whom she is meant to stay), is punctuated throughout by cutaway interludes that include shots of trees and semi-abstracted parts of the urban landscape. These, along with the use of silences and slow piano pieces on the soundtrack, give a quiet, contemplative quality to the film, adding an extra dimension to more familiar mumblecore ingredients such as long takes, hand-held camerawork, and hesitant, largely improvised conversational material (and earning comparison by some critics with the work of the Japanese director Yasujiro Ozu). *Dance Party, USA* and *Quiet City* also make use of backlighting and generally warmer tones that stand in contrast to the flatter, more unvarnished visuals typical of mumblecore and many other low-fi indie productions.

Recurring implicit themes in mumblecore include difficulties of communication within relationships, with the particular twist of being mediated via ubiquitous channels such as cellphones, text messaging, email, and the internet. The films grouped together under this banner can be understood as a distinctly contemporary take on material familiar in this respect from the history of art/indie cinema, although they have also been criticized for a narrowness of scope. The world of mumblecore is an overwhelmingly straight, white, middle-class domain, vaguely leaning in many cases toward a not-quite established artistic milieu (many of the characters are aspiring musicians, writers, and the like). While women often feature as central characters, the filmmakers are primarily male and some have faced accusations of male-oriented voyeurism (especially Swanberg's first feature, the sexually explicit *Kissing on the Mouth* (2005), which includes footage of the director masturbating onscreen). One notable exception is So Yong Kim's first feature *In Between Days* (2006), a low-key DV portrait of the life of an adolescent Korean girl recently relocated to the US, the visual qualities of which include numerous striking compositions and a use of light akin to that of Katz. It is also far less reliant on dialogue than the typical mumblecore feature and as a result considerably more affecting than most, which might be one reason – along with its different milieu – for its less frequent inclusion in the group of films associated with the term. The concerns expressed by all of these filmmakers are exclusively personal in focus, which is in keeping with a great deal of indie and art cinema but is a quality for which they have been singled out for criticism from some quarters.

More politically oriented strains have generally been less prominent in low-budget indie features of the early twenty-first century than was the case in the early 1990s, although with some exceptions. Some of the newer generation media forms that constitute part of the background fabric of mumblecore are even more central to *Redacted* (2007), a much higher budget production ($5 million) by the established Hollywood director Brian De Palma. Based on real events, including the rape and murder of civilians by American marines during the occupation of Iraq in 2006, *Redacted* is comprised of a mixture of audiovisual forms built around the video diary kept by one soldier, other components including scenes presented as coming from a French documentary film, Arabic and other television news reports, security cameras, and sequences of computer-window video footage from sources including radical Islamic groups and antiwar protesters. The somewhat more mainstream roots of the project are betrayed by the rather too neat way in which all of these come together to develop a single narrative thread, but it remains a clearly independent entity at the industrial level, produced by the high-definition television channel HDNet and given theatrical distribution by Magnolia Films.

Other independent filmmakers have also continued to produce work of a provocative nature, too uncomfortable to find distribution at the more mainstream or Indiewood end of the spectrum, even if it has often struggled to gain more than marginal distribution. Notable figures include Todd Solondz, whose *Palindromes* (2004) offers an unremittingly uncomfortable take on the deeply divisive subject of abortion rights via a story in which the central character is played successively by eight performers of different ages, races, and genders. Feature filmmakers with more "maverick" reputations, continuing after many years to operate largely or entirely outside the major established indie institutions, include Jon Jost (whose work tends to blend feature-length with more avant-garde and less narrative-centered qualities) and Rob Nilsson (often identified as an heir to the tradition established by John Cassavetes), whose recent work includes the nine-volume "9@Night" films (2000–2007), a series of improvisation-based collaborative features focused on a world of street-level outsiders. There also remain plenty of new filmmakers constantly refreshing the indie pool, whether their work is distributed through the traditional theatrical route or new channels including the internet. Others have chosen the time-consuming option of self-distribution, taking their films around the country themselves in search of a wider range of viewers and a better financial return, as in the case of Lance Hammer's striking debut feature, *Ballast* (2008).

Case Study: *Primer*

Winner of the Grand Jury Prize at the Sundance Film Festival in 2004, *Primer* (Shane Carruth, 2004) is a good example of how low-budget indies can continue to revisit and refresh otherwise familiar genre material. In this case the format is a variety of science fiction, given a distinctively indie twist that combines a timetravel scenario with characters and aesthetics closer to the "everyday" world of mumblecore. The narrative concerns two young white-collar engineers, Abe (David Sullivan) and Aaron (Shane Carruth), whose out-of-hours garage business experiments result in the inadvertent creation of a device that permits short-term steps backwards in time. The extraordinary/fantastical dimensions of the latter are blended with the quotidian texture of a world of suburban kitchens, dull motel rooms, and the anonymous chamber of a storage facility from which the time-travel experiments are conducted. The early stages of the film are filled with a thick texture of unexplained scientific-technical jargon, part of a low-key naturalistic aesthetic that includes the flat, grainy Super 16mm footage, blown up to 35mm for release. Much is shot close, sometimes hand-held, while a number of jump-cut sequences contribute to the overall impression of dislocation that increases as the film progresses. The narrative becomes gradually more complex and remains in many respects opaque, as the viewer becomes aware of strange temporal overlaps and previously unknown acts of time-shifting, not to mention the unexplained consequences of the fact that a double of the character is created each time such an event occurs. Distrust and uncertainty multiply, following the initial intentions of the protagonists to exploit the device in order to make their fortune through the use of advance knowledge of the movements of stocks. The usual conventions of time-travel movies are largely avoided, or handled in a low-key and oblique manner that offers a highly effective renewal of the generic territory. *Primer* was produced for an initial $7,000, which puts it in the ultra-low-budget category, with the self-taught first-time writer-director Shane Carruth, formerly an engineer, also editing, writing the music, and playing one of the lead roles. The device at the center of the narrative is assembled on the cheap, key components being obtained through the cannibalization of assorted domestic products, including the catalytic converter from a car, in a manner that reflects the "available resources" production ethic that largely governs work of this kind. After its success at Sundance, the film gained theatrical distribution by the non-studio affiliated THINKFilm, earning a total gross of $424,760 at the US box office, along with widespread critical praise.

Films such as *Primer* and the works that have been grouped together under the mumblecore label return us in many ways to the kinds of qualities with which this piece opened: grainy image quality, an emphasis on character and talk rather than the kinds of action or narrative development more typically associated with the commercial mainstream. During the period in between the 1980s and the late 2000s, much changed in the American independent landscape. It became a far more crowded, contested, and institutionalized terrain, with indie features having to fight among themselves to gain recognition and/or the theatrical distribution that is still generally considered to be the clearest marker of success, both commercially and artistically. The concept of "indie" or "independence" also became increasingly contested in itself, and is likely to remain so in the future. The late 2000s witnessed a number of particular difficulties, including a renewed squeeze on indie finance and distribution during the deep recession that started toward the end of the decade, and problems of their own for the specialty divisions (the closure of Warner Independent was followed by the effective shutdown of its equivalent at Paramount and the radical downsizing and then sale of Miramax by Disney). Whatever else recent history has shown, however, it has demonstrated that there will continue to be feature filmmakers, either struggling or relatively more established, whose work or ambition does not fit into the confines of the more commercial mainstream, either that of Hollywood or that represented by the studio specialty divisions. Some forms of indie cinema might seem somewhat formulaic in their own ways, as is perhaps inevitable in any such form of production once it becomes an established part of the wider cultural landscape, but examples such as *Primer* and *Palindromes* demonstrate a continued ability for the sector to produce work that is fresh, surprising, and challenging, even if the bounds of difference remain limited when compared with the realm of the more radically alternative or avant-garde.

References

Biskind, Peter. (2004). *Down and Dirty Pictures: Miramax, Sundance and the Rise of Independent Film*. New York: Simon & Schuster.

King, Geoff. (2004). "Weighing Up the Qualities of Independence: 21 Grams in Focus." *Film Studies: An International Review*, 5, November, 80–91.

King, Geoff. (2005). *American Independent Cinema*. London: I. B. Tauris.

King, Geoff. (2008). *Indiewood, USA: Where Hollywood Meets Independent Cinema*. London: I. B. Tauris.

Kohn, Eric (2008). "New Video Digital Aiming 1,600 Films at Itunes, Other Platforms." August 15, at www.indiewire.com/biz/2008/08/new_video_digit.html.

Pierson, John. (1995). *Mike, Spike, Slackers and Dykes*. London: Faber & Faber.

Rosen, David. (1990). *Off-Hollywood: The Making and Marketing of Independent Films*. New York: Grove Weidenfeld.

Taubin, Amy. (2007). "All Talk." *Film Comment*. November/December, at www.filmlinc.com/fcm/nd07/mumblecore.htm.

Tzioumakis, Yannis. (2006). *American Independent Cinema: An Introduction*. Edinburgh: Edinburgh University Press.

Waxman, Sharon. (2005). *Rebels on the Backlot: Six Maverick Directors and How They Conquered the Studio System*. New York: Harper.

13

Reclaiming the Black Family
Charles Burnett, Julie Dash, and the "L.A. Rebellion"

Janet K. Cutler
Professor, Montclair State University, United States

Janet Cutler examines the work of black filmmakers who studied at UCLA in the mid-1970s and became known as the "**L.A. Rebellion**" or "**L.A. School**." She concentrates on **Charles Burnett's *Killer of Sheep*** (1977) and **Julie Dash's *Daughters of the Dust*** (1991) as films that, in very different ways, inscribe the nuanced intersections of race, gender, heritage, and family to represent "the rich diversity of black life." She historicizes this group of filmmakers and their funding and exhibition struggles, claiming that, through rejecting boundaries separating style and content and commercial cinema's "misconceptions and distortions," they pioneered a cinema that addresses the intertwining components of oppression and survival central to the **black diaspora**. Cutler's in-depth formal analysis captures the films' emotional power and authentically indigenous status, at the same time illustrating their narrative, stylistic, and cultural hybridization of African and American influences. Cutler's essay shares ground with Alex Lykidis on earlier white-authored representations of African-Americans, Scott MacDonald on the contemporary avant-garde, Geoff King on independent film, and Michael Bronski on queer cinema in this volume, and with Ed Guerrero on Blaxploitation and Keith Harris on black crossover cinema in the hardcover/online edition.

Additional terms, names, and concepts: Third World Film Club, neorealism, Gullah tradition, "speculative history," collective memory

In the mid-1970s, a loosely knit group of black graduate students at the University of California at Los Angeles (UCLA) produced a body of films designed to challenge Hollywood cinema thematically and stylistically. Working individually and collectively, members of what Clyde Taylor labels the "L.A. Rebellion"[1] and some others call the "L.A. School" crafted an alternative cinema in the shadows of nearby Hollywood studios, often focusing on working-class and poor blacks in the inner city.[2] Despite their differing concerns and approaches, these filmmakers shared an urgent desire to counter mainstream cinema's misconceptions and distortions and to adopt modes of expression uniquely suited to representing the rich diversity

American Film History: Selected Readings, 1960 to the Present, First Edition. Edited by Cynthia Lucia, Roy Grundmann, and Art Simon.

of black life. Chief among these student filmmakers were Charles Burnett (*Killer of Sheep*, 1977), Larry Clark (*Passing Through*, 1977), Ben Caldwell (*I and I: An African Allegory*, 1977), Haile Gerima (*Bush Mama*, 1979), and later Alile Sharon Larkin (A *Different Image*, 1982), Julie Dash (*Illusions*, 1983)[3] and Billy Woodberry (*Bless Their Little Hearts*, 1984). In the decades that followed, many continued to produce provocative works, including Burnett's *To Sleep with Anger* (1990), Dash's *Daughters of the Dust* (1991), and Gerima's *Sankofa* (1993).

Charles Burnett, one of the principal members of the first wave of the "L.A. Rebellion," explains the group's resistance to Hollywood, especially the industry's then-popular "Blaxploitation" crime melodramas that sensationalized ghetto violence and celebrated larger-than-life macho action heroes like Superfly and Shaft:[4]

> The commercial film is largely responsible for … how one views the world. It reduced the world to one dimension, rendering taboos to superstition, concentrated on the ugly, creating a passion for violence and reflecting racial stereotypes, instilling self-hate, creating confusion rather than offering clarity: To sum up, it was demoralizing. (1989, 224)

If not an outright rebellion,[5] what emerged in the crucible of UCLA was a selfconsciously anti-Hollywood film movement committed to offering counternarratives of black experience. Participant Ntongela Masilela emphasizes that the "intellectual and cultural coordinates of this Black independent film movement are inseparable from the political and social struggles and convulsions of the 1960s" (1993, 107), citing the civil rights, antiwar, and women's movements, along with the battles for national liberation in Africa, Asia, and Latin America:

> The arrival of Charles Burnett at UCLA in 1967, two years after the assassination of Malcolm X and the Watts Rebellion and … of Haile Gerima in 1968, the year of the assassination of Martin Luther King … were generative events in the formation of the Black independent movement in Los Angeles. (1993, 107)

At the time that Charles Burnett entered UCLA, there were few black students or professors, and Third World cinema was not yet a part of the curriculum (Reynaud 1991, 327). As David James points out, the conditions that nurtured the "L.A. Rebellion" developed when demands for educational reforms sparked aggressive minority recruitment and new academic programs; as a result of these initiatives, black students at UCLA had the opportunity to study and to collaborate, gaining access to professional quality production and postproduction equipment.[6] Ironically, UCLA and the University of Southern California (USC) served at the time as training and feeder facilities for the film industry, whose products were anathema to "L.A. Rebellion" students (Bambara 1993, 119). In fact, it was not UCLA's "official" film school but rather the Ethno-Communications Program of its Anthropology Department, founded by Elyseo Taylor, which taught minority students about alternative cinema, urged them to make films about their communities, and enthusiastically supported their fledgling efforts.[7]

In addition to working on each other's films,[8] black students at UCLA engaged in intense debates in classrooms, film societies, and study groups.[9] Film scholar Teshome Gabriel, with Burnett, Masilela, Gerima, Caldwell, Clark, and others, launched UCLA's Third World Film Club that between 1974 and 1976 held campus screenings of films emerging from Cuba, Brazil, and Africa. Defying the US State Department, the Film Club's founders helped to break the embargo against bringing Cuban films to America (Masilela 1993, 110). These screenings provoked lively exchanges regarding appropriate models to adopt in creating a new black cinema.

Female students contributed to the "L.A. Rebellion's" second wave, producing innovative films that privileged black women's experience and culture. Valerie Smith includes UCLA's Julie Dash and Alile Sharon Larkin among "the emergent black women independent filmmakers and video artists of the late seventies and eighties … [who] search for the enduring political implications of private, domestic relationships that the mainstream has trivialized or ignored" (1987). In addition, many of the women filmmakers were deeply engaged by Afrocentrism, using cinema to explore the "cultural and political identification with Africa" (Masilela 1998, 23).[10] According to Toni Cade Bambara, their works served to clarify the "L.A. Rebellion's" central themes: "family, women, history, folklore" (1993, 120).

This essay focuses on two exemplars of the "L.A. Rebellion's" goals and achievements: Charles Burnett's *Killer of Sheep*, arguably the masterwork of the 1970s black independent cinema, and Julie Dash's *Daughters of the Dust*, a 1990s culmination of the "L.A. Rebellion's" aspirations. Burnett and Dash succeeded in bringing nuanced depictions of black experience to the screen as students, went on to produce major feature films, and continue to struggle to secure funding and distribution for their work, while maintaining and deepening their artistic vision.

What is oppositional about these two films is both their formal innovation – each employs a distinct, unconventional narrative structure – and their celebration, in a decidedly nondidactic way, of the complexity and integrity of black communities, and especially of black families. Burnett stresses the fundamental decency and resilience of families beset by attacks from outside and within. In Burnett's view, "There has always been the attempt to destroy our consciousness of who we were, to deny the past, and to destroy the family structure" (1989, 225). Dash focuses on the capacity of black women to keep families together and to draw on generations of women's knowledge, especially of African traditions. As she explains, "I wanted to show black families, particularly black women, as we have never seen them before" (1992, 32). Both filmmakers bring new modes of black masculinity and femininity to the screen.

This essay argues further that, in very different films, Burnett and Dash endorse the elusive yet essential connections between the past and the present, warning of the dangers of the denial or loss of that continuity. Their works explore the conflicts and rewards inherent in embracing the past – its traumas and sustaining values – especially for characters who are profoundly torn between tradition and modernity.

While family and community are central to both films, each posits a different present moment and historical past. Burnett's 1970s characters recently migrated to California from the South and, while intent on assimilation, carry in their hearts "precious memories"[11] of life in rural America as a source of comfort in the urban North. For Dash's turn-of-the-century family, isolated on the idyllic Sea Islands, the past is more complicated. For older figures, it encompasses the history of slavery, but also of African communities underpinned by rich cultural traditions. Younger characters enjoy the kinship that links their extended family, for the most part accepting and practicing the Gullah version of African life; yet they stand ready to migrate North, even if it means scattering and dissipating their unique community and the culture that sustains it. As Dash explains, "I feel that one of the major gaps in our narrative as black people is that no one talks about the psychic loss that black people experienced when we left the agrarian South to move to the industrialized North" (1992, 42). A third group of "modern" characters denounce Afrocentric ways in favor of progress, technology, and Christianity. Both filmmakers present deeply conflicted individuals who consciously suppress their collective past ("country" in Burnett's work and "hoodoo" in Dash's film), yet long for its regenerative power.

In contrast to mainstream films that play a role in the erasure of a black historical continuum, Burnett and Dash create continuity and connection through their work. Believing that there are ways of life that deserve visibility and preservation, they use film to document black communities and provide a bridge between generations and their disparate cultures. Their films record memories of an otherwise unseen past: they contribute to the retrieval and rewriting of black history.

Killer of Sheep: Redeeming the Everyday

A close analysis of *Killer of Sheep* seems timely, given the film's much delayed theatrical release over three decades after its completion. Beautifully wrought, it features a number of striking images, unforgettable incidents, and a compelling musical soundtrack. In certain ways, *Killer of Sheep*'s distribution history is emblematic of the obstacles faced by nonmainstream films. Completed in 1973, it was released and sporadically shown in 1977 and was ignored or dismissed by the press. In her review for the *New York Times*, Janet Maslin dismissed the film as "amateurish and boring" (Hozic 1994, 471).

Nonetheless, *Killer of Sheep* won an ardent following: In the years between its completion and its long-awaited, wide distribution, the film was enthusiastically received by the relatively small audiences of museums, colleges, libraries, and festivals. It received positive reviews in France and was awarded the coveted Critics Prize at the 1981 Berlin International Film Festival. A decade later, it was among the 100 films selected by the Library of Congress's National Film Registry as "culturally, historically, or aesthetically significant." In 2000, it was preserved and transferred from 16mm to 35mm by UCLA Film and Television Archives, and in 2002, it was named by the National Society of Film Critics as one of the "essential films of all time" (Hedges 2007, 4). Burnett lacked the finances to purchase the rights to the songs he compiled to accompany and comment on incidents in *Killer of Sheep* until 2007, and this constituted a major stumbling block to the film's general circulation.[12] When it finally enjoyed full theatrical and DVD distribution in 2007, *Killer of Sheep* garnered glowing reviews and articles. Until then, however, it was virtually unknown to the general public.

From the outset, Burnett's talent and perseverance overcame the meager resources at his disposal. *Killer of Sheep* was his UCLA thesis film, shot in black and white for $10,000, with Burnett serving as writer, producer, director, and cameraman. It was set in Burnett's home community[13] – South Central Los Angeles's devastated Watts ghetto – and drew its actors almost exclusively from among Burnett's friends and neighbors (Reynaud 1991, 328).[14]

Scholarly writing on *Killer of Sheep* frequently emphasizes the film's debt to the Italian neorealist film movement of the 1940s and 1950s, citing their shared affinity for nonprofessional actors,[15] location shooting, and plots centering on the daily lives of ordinary people. In his program notes for Whitney Museum of American Art screenings of *Killer of Sheep*, Clyde Taylor writes, "Obviously influenced by neorealism, Burnett's narrative is striking for its perceptions of the unpretty, tragicomic poetry of everyday life among the oppressed" (1986). And Chris Norton writes of *Killer of Sheep*, "The neo-realist period obviously influenced Burnett deeply" (1997, 2). However, Burnett makes clear that he had not seen Italian neorealist films prior to completing *Killer of Sheep* in 1973, and he specifically dismisses the idea that neorealism inspired that film.[16] Rather, he states that its chief influences were documentaries: Pare Lorentz's *The Plow That Broke the Plains* (1936) and *The River* (1938),[17] and other works shown in Basil Wright's UCLA documentary cinema class.

Wright had been the first to join the celebrated film unit of John Grierson, leader of the 1930s British documentary film movement, and he remained Grierson's lifelong colleague. Wright directed some of the British documentary's most heartfelt works about dispossessed people: his *Song of Ceylon* (1934), a poetic meditation on a chilling topic – the disenfranchisement of the Ceylonese by British colonial powers – is a clear antecedent of Burnett's work.[18] As Burnett's teacher and mentor, Wright was the person who encouraged him to become a filmmaker (Masilela 1993, 112). Burnett was especially moved by the humane way in which the documentaries Wright showed treated their subjects:

> Basil Wright's class started a lot of things for me. In the films he discussed, every shot contained a human element and touch. The subjects in front of the camera were treated like people not just props and objects and things to be manipulated ... reverence was visible throughout the work. (Reynaud 1991, 328)

Indeed, Burnett asserts that "*Killer of Sheep* is supposed to look like a documentary" (Wali 1988, 20). Anyone expecting *Killer of Sheep* to employ the sort of straight-ahead narrative or melodramatic strategies that inform Italian neorealism will be surprised by the film's highly episodic, fragmented structure and unsentimental tone. Its intricately orchestrated incidents resist linear time and continuous space. Taken together, they convey the texture and rhythm of the protagonist's life in a dead-end environment – a world of vacant lots and abandoned buildings where survival with dignity is itself a heroic achievement.

It would be futile to attempt to trace the "narrative arc" of *Killer of Sheep*, since Burnett eschews the conventional plot structure demanded by commercial film audiences; there is no introduction of characters, presentation of an overriding conflict, or resolution of a story. As Paula Massood points out, Burnett opts instead for a form that interweaves three distinct bodies of material, each shot in its own style and set in its own location (1999, 28). When juxtaposed, they detail an incident-filled yet essentially static situation, one lacking real opportunities for personal or collective growth. In this world, the protagonist must summon up great internal resources (at considerable cost) simply to shrug off disappointments and carry on as a wage-earner, husband, and father.

Burnett's first feature film alternates between several kinds of footage. There are hand-held, fluid shots of the interior of the slaughterhouse where Stan, Burnett's protagonist, and his fellow workers – often viewed as body parts in close-up drifting in and out of the frame – perform a dance of death with their victims: shape-shifting sheep who suddenly appear as huge clouds of swirling white wool, or as lean, skinned corpses whose skeletal faces jostle upside down from meat hooks, or as chopping block subjects of a skull-splitting, brain-scooping worker. The slaughterhouse sequences contain no dialogue, but rather are accompanied by classical, jazz, and blues recordings, and at times by the ambient sounds of sheep bleating and metal meat hooks scraping on overhead tracks. Burnett shot this extraordinary footage – a leitmotif throughout the film – in a single weekend.[19]

In addition, there is elegant and strikingly composed footage of unsupervised children (including Stan's son and daughter) at play in brightly sunlit vacant lots, alleys, and rooftops. Sync sound is used to capture their shouts of joy and pain during violent fighting, wrestling, and "war games," as well as ambient sounds of the neighborhood. Sometimes their play spills out into the streets (riders abandon their bicycle to oncoming traffic when attacked by snarling dogs) and front porches (two boys perform lengthy handstands, timed by a third). At times, sync sound gives way to recorded music, often to ironic effect, as when Paul Robeson sings the utopian "The House I Live In" ("The children in the playground, the faces that I see / All races, all religions, that's American to me") as children play in squalor, then sit on a wall throwing stones. While most of the shots involving the children are static or involve slight reframing, occasional sweeping camera movements stand out as lyrical. The long shot taken from inside a moving train of boys running alongside and the tightly framed shot taken from a moving car of boys laughing as they run around a residential corner in slow motion momentarily liberate the subjects from the confines of their impoverished lives.

Finally, the film includes primarily static, often claustrophobically framed sync sound footage shot in interiors of Stan's and his neighbors' homes and local businesses like the liquor store. In these scenes, Stan and the other characters often appear trapped, surrounded by a hostile environment – offscreen dogs growl, sirens wail – just outside the frame. The music in these sequences is diegetic, as when Stan's daughter, Angela, bounces her doll and sings along to a recording she plays of Earth, Wind and Fire's "Reasons" ("Now, I'm craving your body / Is this real / Temperatures rising / I don't want to feel / I'm in the wrong place to be real"). This material makes up the bulk of the film, and Burnett uses formal variety – especially in his camera placement and compositions – to make his shots visually arresting.

Stan is an unfamiliar film protagonist. The antithesis of an "action hero," he is a member of the working poor and a family man whose dead-end life is nevertheless treated as layered and complex.[20] First seen as a bare torso laboring under a kitchen sink, Stan is revealed to be a slaughterhouse worker and an exhausted insomniac. Reminded by his friend Bracy that he seldom sleeps and must be "counting sheep," Stan does not smile (in fact, his wife says, "you never smile any more").[21] Neither does he return his wife's caresses. "I have worked myself into my own hell ... no peace of mind," he tells another friend, Oscar, obliquely. Oscar flippantly responds, "Why don't you kill yourself?" Yet Stan is more concerned about his growing rage: "No, no, I won't kill myself but I got the feeling that I might have to do somebody else some harm." The reasons for Stan's state of mind are more complex and ambiguous than the film's title suggests.[22] Although it provides brief glimpses of Stan's dehumanizing work, the film focuses more intensely on his devastated community and strained domestic life – his relationship with immediate family and close friends, his attempts to repair his house, and his struggles to obtain a functioning car.

Living adjacent to LA's bustling freeway system, many of Burnett's characters cannot afford to purchase reliable automobiles. One running joke in the film involves the dilapidated, noisy cars Stan and his friends drive, contrasted to the criminals' flashy new model that silently glides through the frame. At one point, a man in the front seat of his clunker reaches for a beer on the hood, revealing that the car has no windshield. When Stan's family and friends try to drive to the racetrack, Gene's car has a flat, but there is no spare tire. They return home, one of many indications that Stan and his friends are unable to escape life in South Central. In a bravura sequence, Stan and Gene buy a used car motor and immediately break it. Tightly framed, hand-held camera movements follow the two men as they carry the bulky engine down a seemingly endless flight of narrow wooden stairs and finally hoist it onto the bed of a pickup truck. The sequence has some of the tragicomic detail of Laurel and Hardy trying to move a piano up a flight of stairs in *The Music Box* (1932).[23] As the truck starts moving, the motor falls to the street, bounces threateningly toward the camera, and is destroyed. An extended camera movement from the truck as it pulls away from the abandoned motor reinforces the men's fading hopes. This moment, which underlines the futility of the characters' efforts, receives deadpan treatment, signaling that such setbacks are common occurrences.

Surrounded by poverty and urban decay, unable to secure a car or a new job, Stan nonetheless maintains his dignity and values: He rejects offers of lucrative criminal activity from petty gangsters, Smoke and Scooter, who pressure him to be the third man in a murder, then sits passively while his wife angrily shoos them away, arguing with their claim that violence signals manhood. Despite Smoke's comment that "he don't even have a decent pair of pants," Stan refuses to be defined as poor: He tells Bracy that his family can make donations to the Salvation Army, something the poor cannot do. He happily takes cash to Gene and offers to share his can of peaches with Gene's wife. Stan's ability to maintain his sense of morality is not explained in the film: It is simply a fact, like his desensitizing job and lack of sexual desire.

Stan is a family man, but his relationships with his wife and children suffer as a result of his malaise.[24] His wife's failed attempts at intimacy are particularly poignant. She studies her reflection in a pan's lid, then applies makeup. Holding Stan's hand, she invites him to go to bed, but he chooses instead to remain at the kitchen table with daughter Angela on his lap, stroking his face. Angela glances back and forth from her mother to her father, while the wife looks on, devastated by this tableau of affection. In one of the film's most evocative and longest takes, Stan and his wife dance to Dinah Washington's "This Bitter Earth," framed and silhouetted by a large background window. The lyrics of the song – "What good is love that no one shares" – underscore their misery; the static shot continues beyond the point the record stops, as the wife tries to parlay their dancers' embrace to one of lovers. Stan extricates himself and walks out of the frame, but the camera lingers on his wife, standing alone. This unexpected set piece stands out vividly as a culminating moment of pain and despair.

Figure 13.1 Stan and his wife dance to "This Bitter Earth" in Charles Burnett's *Killer of Sheep* (1977, producer Charles Burnett).

Stan's daughter Angela is introduced in the film wearing what looks like a sad-eyed Droopy Dog mask, "perhaps in imitation of her father" (Hoberman 2007, 63). The easygoing relationship Stan and Angela share is contrasted with Stan's alienation from his son, Stan Jr. In their few interactions, Stan is gruff, angrily telling his son not to call his mother "mot dear" because it defines him as "country." Stan's desire to assimilate makes him encourage his children to shed their Southern roots, but Stan Jr is already an initiate into urban criminality and violence. He ignores his father's attempts to make him stop pulling at his sister's mask, leaves the front door unlocked, and climbs onto the roof to hide when his mother calls him. Over a bowl of cereal, he urgently tells his sister, "I need some money!" Away from his family, he helps two robbers stealing a television to avoid the police, warning them that a man who witnessed the crime is reporting it.

The relatively tense episodes involving Stan at home are punctuated by scenes of anarchic children at play – bullying and wounded, joyful and pensive, sweet and cruel – often acting out mini-wars in which groups of them throw rocks at each other and at passing trains. The kinetic energy of the children stands in sharp contrast to the stasis of the adults, especially the benumbed Stan. Children constitute an ongoing presence in the film, playing, fighting, or intently witnessing adult behavior unless explicitly told to leave (Angela especially observes her mother's failed flirtations, tension between her parents, and adult inability to acquire a motor or get to the racetrack). Throughout the film, children can be seen deep in the background or entering and exiting the frame. Some of the most striking moments in the film involve images of children; the low angle shots of them leaping from roof to roof and the long shot of the four boys sitting on a wall throwing stones reinforce the relationship of danger and play. In no way does Burnett romanticize childhood or find charm in poverty, but his images insist that children act as witnesses to and mirrors of the adult world.

The privileged position of children is established in the film's opening. Over a black screen a mother and child sing a lullaby. A close-up of a boy's face, described in the screenplay as "almost paralyzed with fear," listens to an angry lecture: "You let anyone jump on your brother and you just stand and watch, I'll beat you to death." The camera pulls back and reveals the father, who says that no matter who started the fight, his sons ultimately have only each other. When the film cuts to the mother, who has been comforting the boy's brother, she walks over and slaps the boy's face. The scene fades to black, and Paul Robeson's voice takes up the lullaby, singing "O, my baby, my curly headed baby." This vignette establishes the generational imperative for boys to embrace violence as an essential part of manhood. Immediately, Burnett identifies family as the determining factor – right and wrong are linked to family loyalty, rather than abstract values.

Burnett also embeds child–adult parallels in the film (sometimes as purely formal echoes), unobtrusively demonstrating how quickly and thoroughly children observe, then adopt, adult behavior. These scattered couplets begin in the film's opening scene as the father insists that violence and manhood are linked: "Look, you're not a child anymore; you'll soon be a god damn man. So start learning what life is about now, son." This resonates when the petty gangsters try to shame Stan into joining them by saying, "You can be a man if you can, Stan." In the film's second scene, a child is viewed in close-up peeking out from his plywood "shield" at what is revealed to be an opposing band of similarly shielded rock throwers. Later, a man in a military uniform peeks out in close-up from behind a wall that shields him from what turns out to be an angry, gun-toting woman. A rock-throwing child sustains a head wound, as does a bandaged man, James, who lies on the floor next to the used car engine Stan and Gene buy. Gene hurts his hand carrying the car engine, and in the following scene a boy injures his hand at play. Burnett films workers hanging sheep upside down in the slaughterhouse, then boys perform lengthy handstands on their porch. Stan's daughter and a grown woman are at different points in the film chastised for coming outside barefoot, behavior deemed more appropriate to the rural South. A young girl tries with some effort to hang her wet laundry, but is disappointed when a group of boys run by tossing dirt, just as adults finally succeed in acquiring a car engine only to be defeated when they accidentally destroy it. As the children grow older, Burnett implies, their pains and pleasures will continue, but will become less playful and more severe.

Burnett's visual style is as daring and varied as his subject matter, his episodic structure, and his unsentimental tone. This is especially true of his approach to framing.[25] Often, his camera is unusually close to characters or objects. Knees, legs, and arms fill the frame. Sometimes Burnett begins a scene by withholding the context for an image, disorienting the viewer before revealing the surrounding space. As noted earlier, the brief scene that begins the film initially shows a frightened boy in a dark room, then the camera pulls back to reveal the offscreen father who threatens him. However, *Killer of Sheep* never makes clear who these characters are.[26] The next scene begins even more mysteriously; the left half of the frame is in darkness while in the brightly lit right side a boy's face in close-up bobs in and out of the frame for split seconds, peering toward the camera. It is only when the boy rushes forward that Burnett cuts to a wide shot revealing a war game between boys in an empty lot, each group shielded by a sheet of plywood from behind which they peek and throw rocks at their opponents.

One of Burnett's pictorial strategies involves darkening the frame with objects on the set, dividing the image horizontally or vertically, as in the shot discussed above, half-masked by the plywood board. Rather than cutting, Burnett simply blocks part of the frame, creating a kind of imbalance: The wife is lit as she puts on makeup, but the other side of the frame is cast in shadows; the wife sits in darkness in the bedroom, while Stan and Angela are illuminated on the other side of the frame. At other times, Burnett uses light and shadow to create frames around characters, as when Angela dresses near a bathtub in a shaft of light, flanked on either side by the doorway we peer through. Burnett's elegant, disorienting use of interior framing to isolate his characters in space is complemented by an opposite strategy – his use of compositions in which action occurs in all parts of the frame simultaneously, inviting viewers to scan many sorts of visual information at once. Burnett often dynamizes the entire frame, presenting shots with widely scattered groups of characters (children struggle with a bicycle at the top of a flight of stairs while others play in the yard below). Another unconventional strategy employed by Burnett involves having characters emerge from surprising parts of the frame. Most radically, they enter or exit from behind the camera, sometimes pausing for seconds at a time so near the lens that their clothing completely blocks the deep space in which action is taking place.

Burnett's compositional strategies also reinforce the idea that *Killer of Sheep* occurs in the real world, a setting that continues beyond the frame. This is conveyed by abundant sound effects that activate off-screen space (sometimes acknowledged by glances of characters): recurring music from an ice cream truck, the barking of dogs, the sounds of children playing. Sound effects are also part of Burnett's strategy to capture the texture of the world: the pinging of the rocks against the plywood shields, the rhythmic creak of the chain link fence as Angela seductively leans against it, the harsh scraping of meat hooks sliding across metal tracks, and the clanging of kitchen cooking utensils as Stan's wife prepares dinner.

The musical soundtrack, thoughtfully selected by Burnett, plays an especially varied and complex role. In the slaughterhouse, music ranges from Paul Robeson's rendition of "Going Home" (over the sheep being led to slaughter) to William Grant Still's "Afro-American Symphony" to Little Walter's "Mean Old World." Cecil Gant's "I Wonder" begins as the camera pulls away from the men with the stolen television; a mournful Scott Joplin rag, "Solace," plays as Stan and Gene abandon their broken car engine; Louis Armstrong's "West End Blues" accompanies the failure of the film's principals to drive to the racetrack. Burnett's soundtrack provides an additional layer to the experience; music makes the images more beautiful or more surprising, often commenting ironically on what is seen onscreen. In addition, as David James suggests,

> in the soundtrack [Burnett] loosened the realism and used music to access other times and spaces, and so introduce a historical dimension and a sense of continuity, whose destruction he regarded as primarily responsible for the degradation of the black community. (1998, 40)

Burnett's choice of widely diverse African-American music from different genres and time periods links his characters to the collective experiences of African-Americans in America.[27]

Throughout, Burnett's filmmaking strategies constitute striking alternatives to conventional Hollywood narrative. By presenting unfamiliar subject matter in an unexpected style, he presents a unique representation of black urban life in poetic, documentary-like film language. Burnett even withholds a happy ending or conventional resolution, though the film ends with signs of intimacy: Stan drops his opposition to all things "country," employing a folk saying to tell Angela that rain is just the "devil beating his wife," then smiles slyly and strokes his wife's legs. Another glimmer of optimism follows: a crippled young woman informs her friends of her pregnancy, but this precedes the final scene in which Stan herds the sheep onto the killing floor. The film is far more interested in meditating on the heroism of Stan's struggle than in positing a hopeful future. For Burnett, that is enough:

> The only thing you can ask someone to do is to stay alive, to continue moving. It's hard, but as long as you keep your values in perspective, that's all you can ask of anybody. And that was what *Killer of Sheep* was showing, his values. (hooks 1996, 154)

Burnett faithfully depicts a family man who survives because he must. Stan lives in a demonstratively imperfect, deteriorating world.[28] As Burnett explains,

> my community ... does not have an elder statesman, and more important, does not have roots ... Life is going to work, coming home, making sure every entrance is firmly locked to keep thugs out, thinking on how to move up in the world or being a member of a street gang ... (1989, 225)

This environment damages Stan and those he cares about. As Paul Arthur concludes, the film conveys

> the sense of decent people going nowhere, turning inward on themselves and those they love to do the damage they want to do to the system. Burnett's real talent is for the rhythms and mini-dramas of domestic life, [countering] blaxploitation without sanitizing the grim realities of S. Central LA. (1999, 10)

In a film that denies Stan point-of-view shots, it is clear that his situation stands for the dilemmas of his community – the dehumanization of workers and the devastation of poverty. Paula Massood suggests that the film's strategies extend

> what first appears as a sole focus on a singular hero and suggest that Stan's existential dilemma is undeniably linked to a larger community crisis. With this connection Burnett shifts the conventional narrative identification from the individual to the community, thus adapting the film's narrative for an African American collectivity. (1999, 36–37)

The most provocative feature of Burnett's uncompromising vision of the endemic difficulties of life in Watts is its celebration of people who persevere in the face of misery and pervasive despair. Exhausted by his stultifying job, dispirited by day-to-day hardship, and surrounded by urban decay, Stan nevertheless maintains his decency and integrity. One of Stan's defining traits is his unswerving commitment to living an ethical life in the midst of chaos and doing his best to hold his family together. To this end, he endures deadening employment, rejects the promise of quick money through criminal behavior, and demurs when offered a job predicated on sexually servicing his employer.

Thus, *Killer of Sheep* fulfills Burnett's central goal for filmmaking:

> A major concern of story-telling should be restoring values ... The issue is that we are a moral people ... and it should be continuously presented in some aspect of a story, as [it was] for example in the negro folklore which ... was a source of symbolic knowledge that allowed one to comprehend life. (1989, 224–225)

For Burnett, film is a tool to counteract the dislocation and dissolution of families; it helps restore the sense of continuity and cultural values that are crucial to sustaining black communities.

In his depiction of a community in peril, Burnett examines the connection of present-generation families in urban South Central to their roots in the rural South. [29] Stan wants to distance himself and his family from their past (the last time he was in church was "back home"), but his happiest family moment comes when he cites folk wisdom to explain the rain to his daughter. Stan's wife is sustained by memories of the South when she feels most rejected by him. After their dance, she picks up baby shoes and says in startlingly poetic voiceover:

> Memories that don't seem mine, like half eaten cake and rabbit skins stretched on the back yard fences. My grandmother, mother dear, mot dear, dragging her shadow across the porch. Standing bare headed under the sun, cleaning red catfish with white rum.

Racial memory is complex: it encompasses both rich folklore and devastating nightmares. As Nathan Grant points out,

> "back home" ... is paradoxically the site of both the values that have a potential to sustain in the unforgiving, fragmenting, disillusioning city, and the elements of a clandestine, insidious evil that can forever mark us by turning our deepest fears and anger further inward. (1997, 149–150)

These problems are internalized in the family: Their attempt to find a better life away from the segregated South yields disappointment in the "promised land" of the North. According to Hozic, "Most of the characters in Burnett's films are, much like Burnett himself, first or second generation transplants from the South. Uprooted yet again, they are continuously torn between remembering and forgetting" (1994, 472). This tension between the past and the present played out by family members propels both Burnett's and Dash's films.

Daughters of the Dust: Imagining History

Julie Dash's work celebrates black women of widely varying ages and experiences.[30] Indeed what is important in films like *Daughters of the Dust* is the centrality of black women's voices, the connections between them, and the role they play in passing on tradition. Women are guardians of the past, valuable sources of a history that might otherwise be forgotten. Like Burnett, Dash is concerned with the way that African-Americans have lost a sense of continuity with their families and their culture; however, she values what she calls "speculative history" – her films show "what could have been, what might have been, and now what *is* on record" (Mellencamp 1994, 93). Respecting the subjective ways that the past is recalled through storytelling, Dash uses her films to reclaim and revise the history of black experience.

The structure of *Daughters of the Dust* is specifically designed to emulate the unique qualities of African oral history. As Dash tells Houston Baker,

> I decided I was not going to stay with the usual approach of Western narrative. Instead, my narrative structure is based upon the way an African griot would recount ... a family's history over a period of days ... and how the stories would expand outward and then come back inward ... (Baker 1992, 151)[31]

In this way, *Daughters of the Dust*, like *Killer of Sheep*, is nonlinear and multilayered, actively avoiding the codes of conventional narrative. It too presents striking, poetic images and stresses the importance of preserving family and community values. The film presents a world – the Gullah or "Geechee" community on the Sea Islands off the coast of South Carolina and Georgia – virtually unknown to film audiences, yet part of Dash's own history (her father was a descendant of Gullahs). But if Burnett's subject is the everyday struggle, Dash's subject is the extraordinary moment (in this case, the day a community migrates to the mainland). Unlike his devastated South Central, her lush, fertile Sea Islands (and especially the beauty of its women) make inconsequential the lack of material wealth. Furthermore, the look of the film, shot in glowing color, is the antithesis of Burnett's documentary-like realism: its lovely, magical images linger in the mind like memories.

In *The Cinematic Jazz of Julie Dash* (1992), a biographical documentary directed by Yvonne Welbon, Dash articulates her desire to commit black cultural tradition to film, to keep it from being forgotten or destroyed, and to prevent it from being superseded by conventional forms employed by the mainstream film industry.[32] She mourns the absence of family photos and notes that black women would instead treasure a button from a grandfather's shirt, keeping it safe for years before handing it down to the next generation. Dash sees her filmmaking as the equivalent of this process: her works visually collect and pass on remembrances, reconstruct cultural history, and validate experiences, primarily transmitted by black women across generations.

Like Burnett's *Killer of Sheep*, *Daughters of the Dust* was an especially difficult project to bring to fruition. Using her 1981 Guggenheim fellowship, Dash spent 10 years researching the African-based Gullah tradition at libraries of UCLA, the Smithsonian, and the Schomburg Collection. Seven years into this work, she scripted and shot a trailer to raise funds, but it was almost two years later, when PBS's American Playhouse agreed to finance the film in 1989, that production could begin. Even then, additional funding was needed to complete the film.[33] Although cinematographer A. J. (Arthur Jafa) Fiedler won first prize for Best Cinematography in a Dramatic Film for *Daughters of the Dust* at the 1991 Sundance Film Festival, it was rejected by Cannes and other major film festivals, Toronto being a significant exception. The resistance to *Daughters of the Dust* was, in Dash's view, due to the film's focus on black women, especially the absence of characters who conform to racial stereotypes or a plot dealing with racial conflict.[34] Dash describes her experience with one distributor unwilling to take on the film:

> [He] said *Daughters of the Dust* wasn't an authentic African American film. It wasn't ... from the hood, which is interesting to me having grown up in the hood. Ironically, those filmmakers who make the "hood" films haven't necessarily grown up in the hood. It's exotica to them. (Martin 2007, 7)[35]

However, as Amy Taubin reports, "While distributors continued to tell Dash that there was no audience for the film, *Daughters* drew 1,500 people at the Black Filmmakers Hall of Fame screening in Oakland and even more at the Black Light Film Festival in Chicago" (1991, 66).

Eventually *Daughters of the Dust* was picked up by Kino International, a distributor known primarily for championing archival and foreign films. In 1992, it became the first feature film by an African-American woman director to be released nationwide. And, despite its "unfamiliarity," it enjoyed great success. The film attracted an art house following, and more importantly, its publicity campaign built an audience in the black community by targeting black radio stations, churches, and newspapers. Downtown, the theater manager at Film Forum observed: "It's been a big surprise. It's primarily a middle-class black female audience. We sell out weekend performances, and during the week, we get busloads of church groups, high schools, and senior-citizen groups coming in for matinees" (Brouwer 1995, 13).

The story takes place in 1902 when most members of the Peazant family are set to migrate from the island to the mainland. The Peazants are descendants of African slaves who worked on indigo, rice, and cotton plantations. The decision of many to emigrate signals the breakup of the large, extended family, and the scattering of the Gullah traditions that have remained intact in this isolated community, as the opening titles of the film explain:

> At the turn of the century, Sea Island Gullahs, descendants of African Captives, remained isolated from the mainland of South Carolina and Georgia. As a result of their isolation, the Gullah created and maintained a distinct, imaginative, and original African American Culture. Gullah communities recalled, remembered, and recollected much of what their ancestors brought with them from Africa.

On one level the film concerns the events of a single day – that of the planned migration – when members of the family meet at Ibo Landing, welcome a boatload of relatives from the mainland, picnic on the beach, and then either depart or stay. The film's primary conflict – the debate over whether to go or remain behind – reveals other tensions in the community.

Dash's central characters represent a broad range of Gullah women – from those with firsthand knowledge of slavery to yet-to-be-born children. Nana Peazant, the 88-year-old grandmother, struggles to keep the family intact while preserving African rituals. She is the keeper of memories and a source of folk wisdom, who wants to give her children the sense of dignity and identity that comes from history and tradition: "I'm trying to teach you how to track your own spirit. I'm trying to give you something to take North besides big dreams."

As one of the film's narrators, Nana makes clear the roots of her devotion to safeguarding family history:

> They didn't keep good record of our birth, our death, and the selling of the slave back then. A male child might get took from a mother and sold at birth. Then, year later, this same person might have to mate with his own mother or sister, if they were brought back together again ... So it was important for the slave theyself to keep the family tales just like the African griot who would hold his record in his head. The old souls in each family could recollect all the birth, death, marriage, and sale. Those 18th century Africans they watch us, they keep us, the ancestors.

The film's other narrator, the Unborn Child of Eli and Eula, has been summoned by the "old souls" to help solve her parents' dilemma: "My story begins before I was born. Nana saw the family coming apart. Flowers to bloom in distant places. And then there was my ma and daddy's problem." Their marriage is in turmoil because Eli is infuriated by the thought that Eula may be carrying the child of the white landowner who raped her. To keep Eli from taking revenge, Eula refuses to tell him the identity of the rapist. Yellow Mary, one of the women who returns to Sea Island for the reunion, concurs with Eula's decision: "There's enough uncertainty in life to wonder what tree your husband's hanging from." Yellow Mary knows the perils of the mainland, having first served as both a domestic worker and wet nurse, then as a prostitute. The island community treats her like an outcast who "went off and got ruint." Despite the general hostility toward Yellow Mary, Eula fiercely insists on the connections the women share:

> As far as this place is concerned, we never enjoyed our womanhood ... Deep inside we believed that they ruined our mothers, and their mothers before them ... Even though you are going up North, you all think about being ruined too. You think you can cross over to the mainland and run away from it?

These characters eventually choose to remain on the island, but not Haagar, one of Nana's daughters-in-law; she disdains African traditions and hopes her children will have better lives in the North: "I'm an educated person ... and I'm tired of Nana's old stories ... This is a new world we're moving into and I want my daughters to grow up to be decent 'somebodies.'" Eula argues a different position: "Do you understand who we are? We are the daughters of those old dusty things Nana carries around in a tin can!" However, Viola, a visitor from the mainland, strongly supports Haagar's views. Having become a devout Christian, she suppresses her African roots and embraces her new faith; a fervent missionary, she immediately organizes Bible lessons for the island's children.

Figure 13.2 Trula and Yellow Mary on a boat in Julie Dash's *Daughters of the Dust* (1991, producers Julie Dash, Arthur Jafa, and Steven Jones). (Courtesy of Julie Dash.)

Through the depiction of Yellow Mary and her lesbian lover, Trula, Dash addresses the complex meanings of color within the black community. It is in part because of Yellow Mary's lighter skin that she is regarded as morally inferior and excluded from activities like the preparation of the feast on the beach. In addition, Caroline Streeter adds context to the women's feelings toward Yellow Mary and Tula, which arise from a "constellation of traumatic associations ... including rape, incest, miscegenation, racial passing, homosexuality and prostitution" (2004, 772). However, Yellow Mary departs from the "tragic mulatta" stereotype of mainstream films. She is not a victim, but rather a "new kind of woman" – strong, independent, and modern. Arriving with a tin of cookies from a mainland store, she explains, "You know I don't like messing around in no kitchen."

Setting *Daughters of the Dust* in a single time and place, Dash weaves together many stories that, over the course of the film, incorporate disparate time periods and locations. Thus, the film embodies the characteristics of ancestral storytelling as it layers indelible images, collages multiple voices, and proceeds at a contemplative pace. By conflating time (past, present, future) and conjoining spaces (Africa, the Sea Islands, and the mainland), Dash gives the film a narrative that deepens as it moves forward. The film's structure reflects Dash's conviction that stories deserve to be told and viewed in more than one way. For example, the tale of the Africans coming to the Sea Islands in chains, rejecting the future they see ahead of them, and turning back as one is told twice in the film. In Eula's version, the Africans walk on water all the way home to Africa. The same story told by Muslim Bilal is not miraculous: it records mass suicide. In addition, scenes are viewed from an unusually wide range of distances and angles. The film includes long takes, allowing the audience to spend intimate time with the characters and settings, but also offers many perspectives on each space, as in the varied setups used to cover the extended scene in which Trula and Yellow Mary recline in a tree and debate their beliefs with Eula. In sum, Dash explains, "I wanted a very visual film, memories recalled from the past, floating in a time continuum" (Thomas & Saalfield 1991, 26).

Not an ethnographic documentary (nor meant to look like one), *Daughters of the Dust* has a decidedly imaginative quality: Houston Baker calls it "a magically historical world midway between revelation and cultural memory. Occupying both real and mythical Sea Island territories off the coast of South Carolina and Georgia ... it refigures Gulla history" (1992, 150). Dash employs varied techniques to foreground the film's lyrical embrace of the past and the spirit world. "In *Daughters*' slow fades, moments of dreamy slow motion, asynchronous flashbacks, and scenes of spiritual possession, Dash gestures to the continuing ghostly presence of that history, as sedimented in and animated by displaced spirits and ancestors, or 'old souls'" (Kaplan 2007, 515).

Dash's film quite literally brings memories to life: there are flashbacks to Eula and Eli as young lovers at the beach and to Nana as a young slave on the plantation. It also pictures the spirit world: Pixelated images of the Unborn Child as a young girl romping across the screen capture the future while simultaneously recalling the past, the ancestors who have sent her to restore her father's confidence in the "old ways." Spirits are made concrete, as when the Unborn Child invades her mother's body or when Eli experiences a trance-like interaction with his ancestral spirits. Dash's visual imagery is often meant to be poetic, rather than factual: "the story unravels through an evocative, dreamlike series of tableaux" that underscores the ideas of memory (Hurd 2007, 68). A sculptural object that floats in the brackish water is the figurehead of a slave ship, "symbolic of the African Warrior in the New World" (Baker 1992, 165). Though not historically accurate, Nana's hands are stained blue to remind viewers that during slavery she and other women hand-dyed fabric with indigo in huge stone crocks.[36] Thus, Dash imaginatively links different time periods; she allows vivid, concrete signs from the past to appear in the film's present, creating a continuity that does not separate what was from what is.[37]

At the heart of the film is a sense of the importance of preserving spiritual connections to the past, including maintaining ritual observances and protecting ancient objects. In *Killer of Sheep*, the wife is comforted by remembered images from her Southern childhood – rabbit skins, red catfish, white rum. In *Daughters of the Dust*, connections to the past are more palpable: frizzled chickens, bottle trees, coins, roots, and flowers; a sense of security comes from things in Nana's pocket or in the tin can she carries. In order to speed her family on its journey, Nana makes an amulet out of some of the objects she cherishes: her mother's hair (cut "before they sold her away from me") and Yellow Mary's St Christopher medal, bound around a Bible with twine. All the characters except Haagar eventually kiss the amulet, promising to remember their family traditions while facing their new life. However, this ritual underlines that memories and objects are indeed ephemeral and fragmentary: One of the grandmothers teaches children the few African words she remembers; and there are only vestiges of Africa in the crafts, hairstyles, and hand gestures of community residents.[38]

In *Killer of Sheep* the characters have assimilated to Los Angeles and are ambivalent about their roots in the rural South; characters in *Daughters of the Dust* are on the verge of that transition.[39] As Jacquie Jones points out,

> The great Black migrations ... [distanced] African Americans from family and roots. Away from the elaborate support systems of extended family and community an uprooted Southerner had only the artificial constructs of neighborhoods and government and the more insular nuclear family to rely upon for guidance and practical education. (1993, 23)

Daughters of the Dust explicitly addresses the role film can play in preserving traditions. Mr Snead, the photographer, comes from the mainland at Viola's request to document this important family event, recording a culture that will soon disappear from view. The assignment forces him to confront his own African past. In fact, he alone can see the Unborn Child through the viewfinder of his camera, though her image disappears when he looks away. Thus, the camera allows Snead (and Dash's audience by extension) to see the ordinarily hidden world of spirits and memories. The kaleidoscope Mr Snead brings as a gift also provides new ways of seeing, as does the stereopticon with which he shows the children pictures of the mainland. Unlike *Killer of Sheep*, *Daughters of the Dust* includes extended debates over the relative merits of the past and present. In Dash's film the modern is represented by the camera: Through the character of Mr Snead, questions are raised about the relationship between film and the subjects being photographed, as well as the possible contributions film can make to cultural history.

If, as Burnett and Dash suggest, the loss of continuity between the ancient and the contemporary is a significant threat to already fragmented black communities, then mainstream film is complicit in this process of erasure. These two filmmakers fulfill the anti-Hollywood aspirations of the "L.A. Rebellion" by using film to instate memories and recover the past. As Burnett asserts, "I think that it is the artist's job to establish links with the past, to give some self-respect to the people, to create the sense of a center. I think that erosion of memory is the design of the establishment" (Hozic 1994, 475). Dash explains, "the images I wanted to show, the story I wanted to tell ... had to take them back, take them inside their family memories, inside our collective memories" (1992, 5). For Burnett and Dash, family and tradition are sustaining. As Yellow Mary says, "I need to know I can come back and hold on to where I come from." The fact that their films do not conform to mass audience expectations allows them to provoke intense reactions and spark discussions. In Burnett's view, "The idea is not that something is going to change but that you should create some form of debate and open up the problems" (Hozic 1994, 476). But thc humanistic, socially conscious films of Burnett and Dash accomplish much more: They are the new "scraps of memories,"[40] evidence that deepens an appreciation of individual integrity, strong families and rich, complex black communities.

Notes

My thanks to Sam McElfresh and Hiram Perez for their useful comments on this essay.

1. Clyde Taylor – a scholar who writes extensively about this generation of filmmakers – consistently characterizes the "L.A. Rebellion" as a coherent, radical movement. He distinguishes it from several other periods of filmmaking featuring African-Americans, including pre– and post–World War I Hollywood cinema, pre–World War II films by black independent producers, and 1960s–1970s "blacksploitation" films. Taylor notes that "What separates the new black cinema from these other episodes is its freedom from the mental colonization that Hollywood tries to impose on all its audiences, black and white" (1983, 47).
2. Black filmmakers on the East Coast most often turned to documentary, seizing on its rhetorical stance as "truthful" and "authentic" to provide alternate images of black experience. That was especially true of the trailblazing PBS television series *Black Journal*: In the late 1960s, under the supervision of Williams Greaves, it became a training ground for documentarians like St. Clair Bourne, Stan Lathan, and Madeleine Anderson. The East Coast also had its share of independent black narrative filmmakers, including Kathleen Collins (*Losing Ground*, 1982) and Charles Lane (*Sidewalk Stories*, 1989).
3. Julie Dash initially came to Los Angeles in 1975, spending two years as a Fellow at the American Film Institute's Center for Advanced Film Studies; she then went on to earn an MFA in film and television production at UCLA.
4. The success of Melvin Van Peebles's *Sweet Sweetback's Baadasssss Song* (1971), along with Gordon Parks's *Shaft* in the same year, paved the way for a series of black exploitation films, especially popular with urban black audiences. These films featured glamorized images of empowered black pimps, gangsters, and prostitutes. However, they were decried by members of the L.A. independent film community. Still, because of its experimental style, *Sweetback* was a complicated case: as Toni Cade Bambara writes, "Some of *Sweetback*'s techniques and procedures were acceptable to the insurgents but its politics were not" (1993, 119).
5. Charles Burnett has often claimed that, at the time, the movement was not understood as a "rebellion" by its participants: "I began making films wanting to tell a story about all the people I knew and worked with, the problems that they're facing, and how they were going on ... It's not that I set out purposely to create an alternative cinema" (hooks 1996, 152).
6. In *Allegories of Cinema*, David James disputes Clyde Taylor's claim that a "new black cinema was born out of the black arts movement," contending instead that it "developed from the educational reforms projected by the Black movement rather than from the movement itself ... Not until the increased Black enrollment in higher education in the seventies did an ongoing independent Black cinema emerge in university and semi-academic milieus" (1989, 178). For an understanding of the way UCLA and other schools played a pivotal role in independent black filmmaking of the 1970s, see James 1998, 32, 36, 37, n18. James points out the importance of UCLA's Ethno-Communications program which was "founded in 1968 in the wake of the 1965 Watts rebellion and the civil rights movements and in immediate response to student complaints about the racial exclusivity of the film school itself" (n20).
7. Burnett was a teaching assistant in this program that encouraged students to find their own stories and their own aesthetic (Kim 2003, 2). Burnett and his

contemporaries stayed at UCLA as long as possible in order to take advantage of the resources of the university, especially the filmmaking equipment (MoMA notes for the What's Happening series, Museum of Modern Art, New York, 1980).

8. For example, Charles Burnett scripted and shot Billy Woodberry's *Bless Their Little Hearts*; he also photographed Alile Sharon Larkin's *Your Children Come Back to You* and Julie Dash's *Illusions*. He is listed as one of two cinematographers on Haile Gerima's *Bush Mama* and as camera operator on Larry Clark's *Passing Through*.
9. Toni Cade Bambara describes an off-campus screening and study group that included "cadres from two periods – Charles Burnett, Haile Gerima, Ben Caldwell, Alile Sharon Larkin, and Julie Dash – engaged in interrogating conventions of dominant cinema ... discussing ways to alter previous significations as they relate to Black people ... [and] developing a film language to respectfully express cultural particularity and Black thought" (1993, 119–120).
10. Alile Sharon Larkin's *A Different Image*, for example, concerns a young black woman's attempts to define herself in contrast to the destructive images perpetuated by the dominant culture (on billboards, magazines, etc.), as well as to the sexist attitudes of her male contemporaries. In the film, the protagonist Alana develops her own African-based identity.
11. "Precious Memories," sung by Sister Rosetta Tharpe, accompanies the opening of Burnett's *To Sleep with Anger* in which the central character, dressed in his Sunday finest, has a nightmare of burning in hell before the dissolve to an image of his bare feet, a signal (as Nathan Grant suggests) of a return to "down home" ways (1997, 149).
12. Even so, the song that ends the film was not Burnett's original choice: Unable to secure the rights to Dinah Washington's "Unforgettable," Burnett replayed her rendition of "This Bitter Earth," also used in an earlier scene (Burnett's commentary on the Milestone DVD).
13. Burnett himself was from Mississippi and moved to South Central Los Angeles with his family at the age of three (Grant 1997, 137).
14. Burnett describes his childhood in Watts as an impetus to his filmmaking. "You grew up seeing ... your friends getting into trouble ... maybe because I have a serious speech impediment I always felt like ... an observer. I really liked ... the kids ... [and] felt an obligation to write something about them, to explain what went wrong with them. I think that's the reason I started to makes these movies" (Reynaud 1991, 326). Like Martin Scorsese's asthma, which often kept him housebound and watching from his window, Burnett's early speech impediment made him a spectator rather than a participant in his peers' activities, granting him observational skills that became invaluable in his work. Through filmmaking, he found an alternative means of personal expression.
15. According to Burnett, "The cast was originally non-actors. Henry Sanders who has been in other films was a last-minute replacement after my main character failed to get his parole in time. Charles Bracy got involved with acting and has since had jobs acting. Kaycee Moore has turned to acting as well." From a written statement for MoMA, 1980.
16. In a phone interview with Phyllis Klotman (March 26, 1992), Burnett emphasizes that he had not seen Italian neorealist films until after making *Killer of Sheep*. He also denies the influence of neorealism on *Killer of Sheep* in an interview with Nelson Kim, conducted in 2001 and revised in 2003 for *Senses of Cinema* (Kim 2003, 6). In an email exchange, Burnett states, "neorealist films were not important to me until later ... I think documentary films had the most impact on the style of *Killer of Sheep* ... In fact it was Basil Wright who helped me to work out my notion of what filmmaking is for ... *Bicycle Thieves* and other Italian films reaffirmed my style of filmmaking" (Burnett email to the author, October 2010). Indeed, I would argue that the differences in structure, tone, and style may be even more significant. As Armond White says, "Burnett's astringent view of poverty ... is the opposite of DeSica's plangent sentiment" (DVD notes, 2007). Burnett's discovery of Third Cinema, which opened his eyes to new ways of thinking about film, also came after he completed *Killer of Sheep* (Reynaud 1991, 328).
17. From Burnett's email to the author.
18. Prior to *Song of Ceylon*, Wright's most celebrated film was *O'er Hill and Dale* (1932). Employing a nonjudgmental, observational style, and shot by Wright without a crew, it focuses "on a day in the life of a shepherd ... alone in a bleak [Scottish] landscape ... during the lambing season ... Wright considered it his best camerawork and his most personal film to date." It was one of the "Imperial Six," a handful of Grierson unit films that enjoyed theatrical release (Jon Hoare in BFI Screenonline, at www.screenonline.org.uk/film/id/530356/, accessed February 2011).
19. From Burnett's commentary on the Milestone DVD.
20. *Killer of Sheep* makes clear Burnett's objection to both the "positive" images of social problem films and the "negative" images of Blaxploitation: "The middle class blacks wanted to emphasize the positive and the inner city wanted 'Superfy'; neither had any substance, however, both were detrimental" (1989, 224).

21. Dorothy, the heroine of Haile Gerima's *Bush Mama*, is also something of a somnambulist, but in that explicitly political work, Dorothy becomes a militant.
22. Although many published interpretations focus on Stan's job, rather than the other aspects of his life, the title of the film is open to various readings. On one level, Stan is both the killer of sheep and like them – helpless and unable to escape his fate. The crushing conditions of urban America life threaten Stan and his community, although neither capitalism nor racism is an explicit topic. What the film shows is that in Watts, people like Stan work for insufficient wages, live in poverty and try to take care of their families at the end of exhausting days.
23. Charles Burnett has said: "I know the world's a struggle – like the guy in *Killer of Sheep*, the only thing he can do is try and continue to try. That's the metaphor of Sisyphus, pushing the rock up the hill. You can't turn round and swim back now. You're too far gone" (Wali 1988, 22).
24. Burnett has pointed out: "I think that most problems exist within the family. It is the base of civilization, and its erosion and breakdown, the destruction of the extended family, are a constant theme for me" (Reynaud 1991, 326).
25. Inez Hedges sees Burnett's framing as a form of "signifyin'" because Burnett reverses the expectations of Hollywood films, "decentering the spectator." She explains, "in black culture the 'signifyin'' speaker tries to establish his superiority by displaying verbal cleverness, most often in the form of putting down the addressee" (2007, 141).
26. Burnett has said that this is one of Stan's childhood memories (Kim 2003, 4).
27. Music is an important source of continuity in Larry Clark's *Passing Through*: A jazz musician released from prison struggles in the film industry and searches for his grandfather, an older musician who provides the inspiration he needs to face the future.
28. By 1984, the sense of futility and hopelessness is even greater. As Ed Guerrero writes of *Bless Their Little Hearts*, the film "is set in an historical moment occurring only an instant before the genocidal explosion of drugs and gang violence in black communities across the nation" (1993, 321–322).
29. This is the central issue in Burnett's *To Sleep with Anger*, in which Harry, a wily trickster from "back home," arrives in South Central to visit the middle-class Gideon and his family who have lost touch with their roots in the South. Harry's presence triggers conflicts that have been simmering below the surface, forcing characters to question their values and confront their demons. The family emerges stronger – problems revealed and repaired – as a result of its confrontation with this character from folklore.
30. Julie Dash has said that she had "always wanted to make films about African American women. To tell stories that had not been told. To show images … that had not been seen" (1992, 4).
31. Dash cites the written work of Toni Cade Bambara as an important influence on the structure of the film (Baker 1992, 150, 153). She considers her film aesthetic most like that of Euzhan Palcy (*Sugar Cane Alley*) (Martin 2007, 7).
32. In *Illusions*, Dash takes on Hollywood in an explicit way, calling attention to the commercial cinema's systematic erasure of black people, concealing their contributions to history (including film history); she subverts Hollywood conventions by making a film that features black female protagonists working inside the system, using their presence to comment on sexism and racism.
33. Dash deliberately chose actors from the independent film movement who had previously worked for little or no pay, including Barbara O (*Bush Mama* and *Child of Resistance*), Adisa Anderson (*A Different Image*), Kaycee Moore (*Killer of Sheep* and *Bless Their Little Hearts*), and Cora Lee Day (*Bush Mama*) (Dash 1992, 113–114).
34. According to Dash, "Hollywood studios … could not process that a black woman filmmaker wanted to make a film … with characters who weren't killing each other and burning things down" (1992, 8).
35. Valerie Smith discusses the realist aesthetic, a feature of many black fiction films, in reference to Spike Lee's *Do the Right Thing* (1989), Mario Van Peebles's *New Jack City* (1991), John Singleton's *Boyz n the Hood* (1991), and Matty Rich's *Straight Outta Brooklyn* (1991) which "contain referents or markers that gesture toward an externally verifiable 'real life'" (1992, 58). Smith's concern is primarily with the black documentaries that have been overlooked in favor of these works which have been assigned a kind of authority over black experience almost as part of their marketing strategies.
36. Dash wanted a new poetic image of slavery to replace whip marks and chains (1992, 31).
37. For more on the importance of the color blue and the way it provides a link to Nana's dress, Eula's skirt, and the ribbon in the Unborn Child's hair, see Gourdine 2004.
38. For more on the connection to African culture see Ogunleye 2007.
39. Comparing *Daughters of the Dust* to Burnett's *To Sleep with Anger*, Jacquie Jones identifies the tension between "reconciling collective memory and the legacy of slavery with upward mobility and the American Dream," saying that, for the directors, "the two are not mutually

exclusive, provided there is a continuum of tradition and family" (1993, 20).

40. Dash uses E. Franklin Frazier's term to describe "where we hold and store things ... our secrets ... our private things" (Dash 1992, 43).

References

Arthur, Paul. (1999). "*Killer of Sheep*." Unpublished personal journal entry, volume 21, March 1999–September 1999, 10.

Baker, Houston. (1992). "Not without My Daughters: A Conversation with Julie Dash." *Transition*, 57, 150–166.

Bambara, Toni Cade. (1993). "Reading the Signs, Empowering the Eye: *Daughters of the Dust* and the Black Independent Cinema Movement." In Manthia Diawara (ed.), *Black American Cinema* (pp. 118–144). Bloomington: Indiana University Press.

Brouwer, Joel R. (1995). "Repositioning: Center and Margin in Julie Dash's *Daughters of the Dust*." *African American Review*, 29.1, 5–16.

Burnett, Charles. (1989). "Inner City Blues." In Jim Pines and Paul Willemen (eds), *Questions of Third Cinema* (pp. 223–226). London: British Film Institute.

Dash, Julie. (1992). *Daughters of the Dust: The Making of an African American Woman's Film* [with Toni Cade Bambara and bell hooks]. New York: New Press.

Gourdine, Angeletta K. M. (2004). "Fashioning the Body [as] Politic in Julie Dash's *Daughters of the Dust*." *African American Review*, 38.3, 499–511.

Grant, Nathan. (1997). "Innocence and Ambiguity in the Films of Charles Burnett." In Valerie Smith (ed.), *Representing Blackness: Issues in Film and Video* (pp. 135–155). New Brunswick, NJ: Rutgers University Press.

Guerrero, Ed. (1993). *Framing Blackness: The African American Image in Film*. Philadelphia: Temple University Press.

Hedges, Inez. (2007). "Signifyin' and Intertextuality in Black Independent Films." *Socialism and Democracy*, 44, 21.2, 133–143.

Hoberman, J. (2007). "L.A. Story." *Village Voice*, March 20, 63.

hooks, bell. (1996). "A Guiding Light: An Interview with Charles Burnett." In bell hooks, *Reel to Real: Race, Sex, and Class at the Movies* (pp. 152–169). New York: Routledge.

Hozic, Aida A. (1994). "The House I Live In: An Interview with Charles Burnett." *Callaloo*, 17.2, 471–491.

Hurd, Mary G. (2007). *Women Directors and Their Films*. Westport, CT: Praeger.

James, David E. (1989). *Allegories of Cinema*. Princeton: Princeton University Press.

James, David E. (1998). "Toward a Geo-Cinematic Hermeneutics: Representations of Los Angeles in Non-Industrial Cinema – *Killer of Sheep* and *Water and Power*." *Wide Angle*, 23–53.

Jones, Jacquie. (1993). "The Black South in Contemporary Film." *African American Review*, 27.1, Spring, 19–24.

Kaplan, Sara. (2007). "Souls at the Crossroads, Africans on the Water: The Politics of Diasporic Melancholia." *Callaloo*, 30.2, 511–526.

Kim, Nelson. (2003). "Charles Burnett." *Senses of Cinema*, March, at http://archive.sensesofcinema.com/contents/directors/03/burnett.html (accessed February 2011).

Klotman, Phyllis. (1991). *Screenplays of the Black Experience*. Bloomington: Indiana University Press.

Martin, Michael. (2007). "Making Movies That Matter: A Conversation with Julie Dash." *Black Camera*, 22.1, 4–11.

Masilela, Ntongela. (1993). "The Los Angeles School of Black Filmmakers." In Manthia Diawara (ed.), *Black American Cinema* (pp. 107–117). Bloomington: Indiana University Press.

Masilela, Ntongela. (1998). "Women Directors of the Los Angeles School." In Jacqueline Bobo (ed.), *Black Women Film and Video Artists* (pp. 21–41). New York: Routledge.

Massood, Paula. (1999). 'An Aesthetic Appropriate to Conditions: *Killer of Sheep*, (Neo) Realism, and the Documentary Impulse." *Wide Angle*, 21.4, 20–41.

Mellencamp, Patricia. (1994). "Making History: Julie Dash." *Frontiers*, 15, 76–101.

Norton, Chris. (1997). "Black Independent Cinema and the Influence of Neo Realism: Futility, Struggle and Hope in the Face of Reality." *Images Journal: A Journal of Film and Popular Culture*, 5, at www.imagesjournal.com (accessed February 2011).

Ogunleye, Foluke. (2007). "Transcending the '*Dust*': African American Filmmakers Preserving the Glimpse of the Eternal." *College Literature*, 34.1, 156–173.

Reynaud, Bérénice. (1991). "An Interview with Charles Burnett." *Black American Literature Forum*, 25.2, 323–334.

Smith, Valerie. (1987). "The Black Woman Independent: Representing Race and Gender." New American Filmmakers Series, Exhibitions of Independent Film and Video, 34. New York: Whitney Museum of American Art.

Smith, Valerie. (1992). "The Documentary Impulse in Contemporary African American Film." In Gina Dent (ed.), *Black Popular Culture, a Project by Michele Wallace* (pp. 56–64). Seattle: Bay Press.

Streeter, Caroline A. (2004). "Was Your Mama Mulatto? Notes toward a Theory of Racialized Sexuality in Gayl Jones's *Corregidora* and Julie Dash's *Daughters of the Dust*." *Callaloo*, 27.3, 768–789.

Taubin, Amy. (1991). "Art and Industry." *Village Voice*, November 26, 66.

Taylor, Clyde. (1983). "New U.S. Black Cinema." *Jump Cut*, 28, April, 46–48.

Taylor, Clyde. (1986). "The L.A. Rebellion: A Turning Point in Black Cinema." New American Filmmakers Series, Exhibitions of Independent Film and Video, 26. New York: Whitney Museum of American Art.

Thomas, Deborah & Saalfield, Catherine. (1991). "Geechee Girl Goes Home." *Independent*, July, 25–27.

Wali, Monona. (1988). "Life Drawings: Charles Burnett's Realism." *Independent*, 11.8, October, 16–22.

White, Armond. (2007). "*Killer of Sheep*: More Than a Masterpiece." Essay with the Milestone DVD.

14

Feminism, Cinema, and Film Criticism

Lucy Fischer
Distinguished Professor, University of Pittsburgh, United States

It was not until the advent of the 1970s **Women's Liberation** movement that radical political promises of the 1960s were largely but not completely realized, including significant and sweeping demands for **equal rights** in the home and the workplace. In this context Lucy Fischer discusses the rise of **feminist film criticism** and **feminist film theory**, citing key essays and books by feminist film scholars and their intersection with **women's filmmaking practices** on both sides of the camera – inside and outside of the commercial domain. From **feminist documentaries** and **feminist experimental films**, to **female-directed narrative features** of the 1970s and 1980s, Fischer examines the complex challenges and dilemmas women have faced in response to mainstream culture's superficial assimilation of and, at times, reactionary opposition to feminist concerns. Her essay shares ground with Shelley Stamp on women in early cinema, Veronica Pravadelli on cinema and the modern woman, and Cynthia Lucia on Natalie Wood in Volume I; with Janet Cutler on Julie Dash and Scott MacDonald on the feminist avant-garde in this volume, and with Jane Gaines on women in early film in the hardcover/online edition.

Additional terms, names, and concepts: first wave feminism, second wave feminism, NOW, the woman's film, film noir

Second Wave Feminism: The Context

Before it is possible to discuss American feminist film criticism and film practice between 1976 and 1988, it is necessary briefly to trace the social/historical context in which such activities took place – "second wave" feminism in the United States. The "first wave," of course, refers to events that transpired in the nineteenth and early twentieth centuries that were focused largely on women's property rights, opposition to chattel marriage, and the quest for suffrage. The "second wave," on the other hand, marks occurrences that took place from the 1960s to the

American Film History: Selected Readings, 1960 to the Present, First Edition. Edited by Cynthia Lucia, Roy Grundmann, and Art Simon.

1980s, drawing upon the gains of the prior women's movement.

As we know, the 1960s in the US were associated with a variety of social protests: against the war in Vietnam, traditional college education, established sexual mores, conformity, and consumer culture. While women were engaged with these movements and the sexual revolution challenged conventional norms of female erotic behavior, 1960s culture remained largely sexist (despite the founding of the National Organization for Women (NOW) in 1966). The joke in political circles was that, while the men planned demonstrations and authored manifestos, women often served coffee and ran the mimeograph machines. In the early 1970s, however, women began to question whether the youth revolt in which they participated might not also include a revolution in sexual politics and a rebellion against patriarchy. It was with those thoughts and hopes that second wave American feminism truly began – under the banner of the Women's Liberation Movement (or Women's Lib, as it was sometimes called). But what were some of its signal events?

The year 1970 saw the publication of *Sisterhood Is Powerful, An Anthology of Writings from the Women's Liberation Movement* (edited by Robin Morgan), as well as that of *Our Bodies, Ourselves* (which educated women about female physiognomy, sexual receptivity, and reproductive health). Speaking for feminists of color, Tony Cade published *The Black Woman*; the North American Indian Women's Association was founded, as was the Comisión Femenil Mexicana. Finally, addressing the concerns of aging women, Maggie Kuhn organized the Gray Panthers.

In 1971, Bella Abzug (elected to Congress the previous year) along with Shirley Chisholm, Betty Friedan, and Gloria Steinem organized the National Women's Political Caucus. *Ms.* magazine (edited by Gloria Steinem) released its premier issue in January of 1972. Puerto Rican women held their first conference and Shirley Chisholm (an African-American) ran for the Democratic Party's presidential nomination. Finally, Congress passed Title IX, an Act that forced educational institutions to support women's sports.

In 1973, Congress allowed the first female page to work in the House of Representatives. The national Black Feminist Organization was formed and Naiad Press (a lesbian book publisher) was founded. The year 1974 saw the Equal Credit Opportunity Act passed which prevented discrimination against women in financial matters (thus allowing them to gain more independence). In Washington, Helen Thomas (who had covered the city for 30 years) was finally named a White House reporter. Moreover, homosexuality (male and female) was removed from the American Psychiatric Association's list of mental disorders, ameliorating the prejudice felt by lesbians.

In 1975, the United Nations sponsored its First International Conference on Women in Mexico City. And, in the same year, Susan Brownmiller published *Against Our Will* (a highly influential book about the ubiquity of rape). Finally, NOW sponsored "Alice Doesn't Day," asking women to strike. In 1976, ERAmerica was launched to promote the ratification of the Equal Rights Amendment (an effort dating back to the 1920s). Unfortunately, the Amendment ratification process eventually expired in 1982, effectively killing the measure. Also in 1976, the Organization of Pan Asian American Women was formed, and Barbara Jordan became the first African-American female to give the keynote speech at the Democratic National Convention. In 1977, the National Association of Cuban-American Women was organized, as was the National Coalition Against Domestic Violence – highlighting a longstanding problem conventionally minimized or ignored. Finally, the Air Force graduated its first female pilots.

In 1984, Geraldine Ferraro became the first woman to run for vice-president (on the Democratic ticket with Walter Mondale). In 1986, the *New York Times* agreed to use the term "Ms" instead of "Miss" or "Mrs" for its formal mention of females and, in the same year, Maryland's Barbara Mikulski became the first Democratic woman to be elected to the Senate without having succeeded her husband. With her appointment, the number of women in the Senate doubled (from one to two). Finally, in 1987, Congress declared March "Women's History Month" – an event that is celebrated to this day.

Feminist Film Criticism and History: Images of Women

As Marjorie Rosen pointed out in one of the early books of feminist film criticism,

> [while] abundant material is available about film techniques and editing, about directors and Western heroes, about Hollywood myths, the star system, the studio system, about blacks in film, Indians in film, sex in film, even animals in film … about women, there is virtually nothing … In all the pedestal pushing and crumbling, nobody has a thought to study woman's role in cinema. (1973, 9)

Second wave feminism helped scholars become aware of this gap, and they concluded that (1) male onscreen roles and genres had been emphasized in studies of cinema (as in Robert Warshow's work on "The Westerner" and "The Gangster"), and (2) female movie roles had, historically, been stereotypical and problematic. This led to a plethora of writing on "images" of women in which critics focused on the narrative level of cinematic construction and how female characters were portrayed within the drama. Often their representation was subjected to "positive" or "negative" evaluations, depending on whether the figure in question was deemed "progressive" or "regressive" in terms of women's issues (sexpots having a negative valence and career women a positive one). Furthermore, screen portrayals were often judged for how closely they conformed to the "real" situation of women in a particular time, place, or segment of the population.

Several pioneering works of this kind were published within a few years of each other. Both Marjorie Rosen's *Popcorn Venus* (1973) and Molly Haskell's *From Reverence to Rape* (1974) adopted a historical approach to American cinema, examining screen roles for women on a decade-by-decade basis. Thus, Rosen has a chapter on "Mary's Curls, Griffith's Girls" in which she discusses the Victorian, goody-two-shoes roles played by actresses like Mary Pickford or Lillian Gish in the teens. She then moves on to such iconic representations as the "flapper" in the 1920s (often played by Coleen Moore, Clara Bow, or Joan Crawford) and to the later era of "Mammary Madness" in the 1950s (dominated by the likes of Marilyn Monroe, Jayne Mansfield, and Mamie van Doren). While, in a similar mode, Haskell critiques such figures as Janet Gaynor for embodying passive "virgin-heroines" in *Seventh Heaven* (1937) and *Street Angel* (1928) (though "sublimely"), she also champions performers like Katharine Hepburn and Rosalind Russell for portraying strong, independent females. As she observes about the former,

> Hepburn was one of the few, if not the only, actresses allowed to sacrifice love for career, rather than the other way around. The explanation usually offered is that her arrogance and eccentricity exempted her: She was neither a "regular guy" … nor a representative of the American woman. (1974, 181)

While both Haskell and Rosen produced diachronic surveys of American film, Joan Mellen concentrated mostly on the contemporary era in *Women and Their Sexuality in New Film* (1974). Thus (in her writing on American cinema), she examined the "bourgeois woman" in *Diary of a Mad Housewife* (1970), the sexual female in *Carnal Knowledge* (1971), the lesbian in *Rachel, Rachel* (1968), and the feminist-era housewife in *Up the Sandbox* (1972). Her first chapter is clear, however:

> One searches in vain the contemporary cinema for a new perception of women which assumes their capacities and value. An international … women's movement has induced the cinema to be only slightly more self-conscious about its patronizing and hostile portrayal of women as flawed creatures. (1974, 15)

In addition to monographs on the issue of female representation in cinema, a magazine on the topic premiered in 1972: *Women and Film* (which was published until 1975). In 1977, a more academically oriented journal emerged (with ties to the now-defunct earlier publication): *Camera Obscura*, edited by a "collective" including Janet Bergstrom, Sandy Flitterman, Elisabeth Hart Lyon, and Constance Penley. The first few issues offered articles on such diverse filmmakers as Yvonne Rainer, Alfred Hitchcock, Chantal Akerman, Dorothy Arzner, Maya Deren, and Sally Potter and published theoretical pieces by the likes of Jean-Louis Baudry, Raymond Bellour, Bertrand Augst, and Thierry Kuntzel (the French influence very clear).

While the books by Rosen, Haskell, and Mellen were sold to the general public, additional scholarly texts in this vein soon appeared. Sumiko Higashi's *Virgins, Vamps and Flappers* (1978) concentrated exclusively on silent cinema, a far more esoteric field, and examined such figures as Lillian Gish as Victorian heroine, Mary Pickford as American Sweetheart, Theda Bara as Vampire, and Joan Crawford as New Woman. At the same time, E. Ann Kaplan's edited volume *Women in Film Noir* (1978) took on a particular genre of the 1940s that fascinated feminist critics for its troubling but captivating vision of the femme fatale. Thus, Pam Cook wrote on "duplicity" in *Mildred Pierce* (1945), Kaplan wrote on the "place of women" in *The Blue Gardenia* (1953), and Richard Dyer wrote on "resistance and charisma" in *Gilda* (1946). As Janey Place notes in her essay, though film noir "is a male fantasy" in which woman "is defined by her sexuality," it nonetheless "gives us one of the few periods of film in which women are active, not static symbols, are intelligent and powerful, if destructively so, and derive power, not weakness, from their sexuality" (1978, 35).

In a volume that focused (like Higashi's) on a particular film historical period (though one of the sound era), Brandon French, in *On the Verge of Revolt* (1978), investigated the image of women in American movies of the 1950s, writing on such works as the Gothic *Sunset Boulevard* (1950), the romantic *Picnic* (1956), and the comic *Some Like it Hot* (1959). As she comments:

> On the surface, fifties films promoted women's domesticity and inequality and sought easy, optimistic conclusions to any problems their fictions treated. But a significant number of movies simultaneously reflected, unconsciously or otherwise, the malaise of domesticity and the untenably narrow boundaries of the female role. (1978, xxi)

Taking on a far narrower topic, Karen M. Stoddard in *Saints and Shrews* (1983) considered the vision of aging women in American film. Proceeding decade by decade from the 1930s, she examined such roles as the older mother (*The Grapes of Wrath*, 1940), the over-the-hill stage actress (*All About Eve*, 1950), and the widowed wife (*All That Heaven Allows*, 1955). While many of these female images are retrograde, Stoddard concludes that "the media cannot totally be condemned for the images they project of older women; it can be argued that [these] images … are more indicative of social attitudes and myths held by the audience toward older women" (19783, 6). In one of the first anthologies to be published on the topic of women and film (*Women and the Cinema*, Kay & Peary 1977), Janet Maslin questioned whether contemporary heroines (in films like *Alice Doesn't Live Here Anymore*, 1974, or *A Woman under the Influence*, 1974) are really different from earlier iterations. On the one hand, both are portrayed as "victims," but, on the other, each is depicted with great "compassion" (Kay & Peary 1977, 44).

Questions of race began to be broached at this time. Though not a book written from a feminist perspective, Donald Bogle's *Toms, Coons, Mulattoes, Mammies & Bucks* (1973) took on the stereotype of the black maternal female so prominent in American films like *Gone with the Wind* (1939) and television shows like *Beulah* (1950–1953). As he notes, the mammy figure is similar to a "comic coon" but distinguished by "her sex and her fierce independence. She is usually big, fat, and cantankerous." One of her offshoots is the "Aunt Jemima" who is "blessed with religion" as well as being "sweet, jolly, and good-tempered" (Bogle 2001, 9).

Investigations by American critics of female representation in non-Hollywood film also were launched. In *Kino and the Woman Question* (1989), Judith Mayne examined the image of females in such Soviet works as *Strike* (1925), *Bed and Sofa* (1927), *Mother* (1926), *Fragment of an Empire* (1929), and *Man with a Movie Camera* (1929). She demonstrates that the way in which

> the woman question is posed in films of the 1920s offers a critical vantage point from which to comprehend the narrative strategies central to the development of Soviet cinema; and … that these narrative strategies are central to an understanding of the representation of women in relation to cultural and political change. (1989, 15)

Feminist Film Criticism and History: Female Film Practitioners

As Claire Johnston pointed out in 1975, "The last few years have witnessed a radical re-assessment of the role women have played in the cinema" (1975, 1).While examining portrayals of women onscreen was one aspect of this investigation, documenting the history of women filmmakers was another. This shift was signaled by a major arts event: the First International Women's Film Festival, held in New York City, June 5–21, 1972, at the Fifth Avenue Cinema. It comprised 13 features, four documentaries, and 13 programs of short subjects and sought both to revive interest in "lost" filmmakers of the past and to celebrate those of the present. Among the feature films shown were Mai Zetterling's *The Girls* (1967), Dorothy Arzner's *The Wild Party* (1929), Ida Lupino's *The Bigamist* (1953), Agnès Varda's *Cleo from 5 to 7* (1962), and Barbara Loden's *Wanda* (1970). Among the documentaries screened were Perry Miller Adato's *Gertrude Stein, When This You See, Remember Me* (1970) and Kate Millett's *Three Lives* (1971). As George Gent wrote in the *New York Times*, the festival was "an outgrowth of the new female self-consciousness fostered by the women's liberation movement" (1972, 46). The year 1974 saw Chicago's Films by Women Festival and 1976 saw the Second International Women's Film Festival in New York. Similar festivals followed in Canada and Great Britain.

Within short order, a focus on female cineastes surfaced in the critical literature as well. Thus, in the Kay/Peary anthology, Ruth McCormick and Ellen Willis wrote on Lina Wertmuller's *Swept Away* (1974); Gerald Peary wrote on Alice Guy-Blaché; Richard Koszarski wrote on Lois Weber; William Van Wert wrote on Germaine Dulac; Dannis Peary wrote on Stephanie Rothman; Debra Weiner interviewed Ida Lupino; and Molly Haskell posed the question: "Are Women Directors Different?" referencing Elaine May, Liliana Cavani, and Nelly Kaplan. Aside from essays on directors, the volume also included pieces on or interviews with actresses: Jane Fonda, Liv Ullmann, Mae West, Brigitte Bardot, and Marlene Dietrich, along with articles *by* performers Louise Brooks and Greta Garbo. Finally, it paid homage to film editor Dede Allen and screenwriter Leigh Brackett.

This interest in women workers in the American film industry continued throughout the 1970s and 1980s. In 1975, British critic Claire Johnston published *The Work of Dorothy Arzner* – a book that investigated the oeuvre of one of the pioneer female directors of the American studio system who made such films as *Christopher Strong* (1933), *Craig's Wife* (1936), and *Dance Girl Dance* (1940). As Johnston remarks, her volume did not seek to portray Arzner as "some cult figure in a pantheon of Hollywood directors" (1975, 1), but rather to "understand the real achievement of her work" and to "locate it within the constraints imposed by the … studio system" (1975, 2). Other more encyclopedic volumes about female cineastes followed. *Women Directors* (1988) by Barbara Koenig Quart gave attention to such historic American artists as Blaché, Weber, Arzner, and Lupino, while also examining the work of contemporary artists like Elaine May, Joan Micklin Silver, Claudia Weill, Susan Seidelman, Joyce Chopra, Martha Coolidge, Donna Deitch, Barbra Streisand, and Goldie Hawn (along with numerous European figures) and remarking that "women directors, almost invisible just fifteen years ago, have from the late 1970s on, and especially in the 1980s, been entering feature filmmaking in unprecedented numbers" (1988, 1). Quart found in their work "a subtly different kind of vision … directed at everything from kitchen work, to nuances of sexual experience, to the dark areas of pornography and violence" (1988, 5). In addition to directors, the legacy of women scenarists began to be considered, given the large number working during the silent era. *What Women Wrote* (1987) is a microfilm collection of screenplays by such authors as Frances Marion (*The Wind*, 1928), Anita Loos (*A Cure for Suffragettes*, 1913), Alice Guy-Blaché (*The Monster and the Girl*, 1914), Josephine Lovette (*Our Modern Maidens*, 1929), and Jeanie MacPherson (*The Ten Commandments*, 1923).

Some critical works of the era discussed women filmmakers within a more theoretical context. E. Ann Kaplan (in *Women and Film: Both Sides of the Camera*, 1983) wrote about French author/director Marguerite Duras's *Nathalie Granger* (1972), noting that "European women filmmakers began producing independent feature films long before women in the USA" (1983, 91). She also penned a chapter on German cineaste Margarethe von Trotta's *Marianne and Julianne* (1981), focusing on how, while the director "refuses to provide idealized images for the female spectator," she also depicts "female characters [who] are seen as actively engaged in a struggle to define their lives, their identities, and their feminist politics" (1983, 104–105). In my own book *Shot/Countershot: Film Tradition and Women's Cinema* (1989), I contextualized the work of numerous female directors in relation to the male tradition, establishing an intertextual framework. Thus, I compared Ingmar Bergman's *Persona* (1966) (about an actress) to Mai Zetterling's *The Girls* (1968) (also about female performers), or George Cukor's *Rich and Famous* (1981) (about female friendship) to Claudia Weill's *Girlfriends* (1978) (also about the same topic). I quoted Yvonne Rainer, who noted that "films are a way through which [artists] can re-imagine" canonical works (Fischer 1989, 1).

While most of the feminist critics cited above concentrated on fiction/feature film directors in the US or Europe, some examined the work of avant-garde artists. A group called The Legend of Maya Deren Project formed to highlight and circulate the artist's work and to publish her notebooks and theoretical writings. In *Women and Film*, Kaplan wrote about two works by Rainer: *Lives of Performers* (1972) and *Film about a Woman Who...* (1974). Speaking of the former she notes that Rainer attempts to "deconstruc[t] the soap-opera like 'script' through foregrounding its 'performance'" as well as by "introducing unexpected elements into the 'script'" (1983, 118). In *Shot/Countershot*, I examined another Rainer film, *The Man Who Envied Women* (1985), which I see as a highly dialogic text that makes use of clips from male-authored films (e.g. *Un Chien Andalou*, 1929, *Dangerous*, 1935, *Double Indemnity*, 1944), in order to "talk back" to traditional cinema. In *The Hand That Holds the Camera* (1988) Lynn Friedman Miller conducted interviews with seven female avant-garde filmmakers: Doris Chase, Michelle Citron, Kavery Dutta, Tami Gold, Amalie Rothschild, Meg Switzgable, and Linda Yellen. The best known of these were Chase (for film and video dance pieces), Amalie Rothschild (for documentaries like *Conversations with Willard Van Dyke*, 1981), and Michelle Citron (for the faux-home movie *Daughter Rite*, 1980). Not surprisingly, in her introduction to the volume, Miller notes that "generally, women film directors have had more success with experimental and independently produced feminist documentary films than with Hollywood commercial films" (1988, vii). Furthermore, she inquires: "How does the work of an independent woman filmmaker or video artist help women rethink themselves and the society?" (1988, viii).

The work of female documentary filmmakers was also a subject of discussion. In a 1988 article on the "emergent black woman director," Valerie Smith stated that it is only recently that "black women emerge[d] as filmmakers in ... significant numbers" (1988, 711) and noted that "most black women independents tend to explore the formal possibilities of realism instead of experimenting with daring modes" in part for accessibility and in part for financial reasons (1988, 711). Writing as an artist herself, Alile Sharon Larkin noted how black women filmmakers "make films about [such real life subjects as] incest, male–female relationships, and other subjects considered women's issues ... [They] strive to present the total picture in an effort to heal and unite our community" (Pribram 1988, 168).

While, given the foregrounding of identity politics at the time, much writing on women's cinema looked for a sign of a female aesthetic or feminist point of view, critics were also wary of this assumption. As Molly Haskell wrote: "Polarities do exist, but they don't necessarily correspond to gender. All we can do is hope that women filmmakers become, like their counterparts in the other arts, merely *filmmakers*" (quoted in Kay & Peary 1977, 435).

Feminist Film Criticism and History: Feminist Film Theory

While many of the critics already mentioned examined either onscreen representations of women or the work of women directors, others in this period forged an innovative brand of criticism that concentrated more on gender in relation to cinematic ontology and form. As Diane Waldman noted: "Meaning is to be located in the interaction between reader and image and not in the images themselves" (1990, 18). In part, this move came from dissatisfaction with the realist thrust implied in foregrounding onscreen images – an approach now seen as too "sociological," as lacking complexity, and as ignoring the specifics of the medium. In this regard, an important interplay arose between writing in Great Britain and the US. In particular, American scholars were much influenced by Laura Mulvey's seminal essay, "Visual Pleasure and Narrative Cinema," first published in 1975 then reproduced in the Kay/Peary anthology (as well as in a later one edited by Constance Penley in this era).

Mulvey's Freudian-based investigation of such psychological drives as scopophilia and fetishism led to an interest in issues of cinematic voyeurism, which positioned the prototypical spectator as masculine and the object of sight as feminine. Hence, in *Women and Film*, Kaplan inquired: "Is the Gaze Male?" and challenged the notion of the female spectator as barred entirely from the cinematic scene. Of course, Mulvey herself would modify her position in a companion essay: "Afterthoughts on Visual Pleasure and

Narrative Cinema" (1981). There, she asserted that the female viewer was not simply locked into the hopeless and masochistic position of identifying with the passive heroine. Rather, Mulvey now saw the woman viewer in a more nuanced manner, as shifting among a multiplicity of identifications. In fact, she asserted that such a viewer "may find herself secretly, unconsciously almost, enjoying the freedom of action and control over the diegetic world that identification with a hero provides" (quoted in Penley 1988, 70). Arguing against Mulvey's assumption that men in film are generally powerful "ego ideals" who confront ineffectual females, Gaylyn Studlar (1992) highlighted the opposite dynamic in the work of Josef von Sternberg in which the "hero" (e.g. Dr Rath in *The Blue Angel*, 1930) often stands in masochistic and infantile relation to the awesome "maternal" heroine (e.g. Lola Lola in the same film).

This focus on the politics and psychology of film viewing was continued in *Female Spectators*, edited by Deidre Pribram (1988), which considered not only movies but television. Pribram called for a more rigorous analysis of female spectatorship that would proceed along three avenues: "the individual female spectator, shaped by the psychic and social processes of subject formation; female spectators as historically and socially constituted groups; and female audiences, participants in film's (and television's) broad popular base" (1988, 5). Contributors like Linda Williams and Jeanne Allen provided readings of such works as *Mildred Pierce* (1945) and *Rear Window* (1954); Christine Gledhill took on the question of pleasure and cinema; Jacqueline Bobo focused on the black female viewer; and Jacqueline Byars returned to Freudian discourse to expand on theories of gendered film and television viewing.

Beyond issues of spectatorship, feminist film criticism also tackled questions of dramatic structure and the potential gender bias contained in classical form. In a chapter of *Alice Doesn't* (1984) entitled "Desire in Narrative," for instance, Teresa de Lauretis returned to ancient myth for a paradigm found in contemporary film – that of the active hero who encounters various "obstacles" in the course of his journey to manhood. De Lauretis saw these impediments as gendered female (as are Circe and the Sphinx that Odysseus meets). Clearly, these dangerous figures must be ruthlessly destroyed; moreover, whatever their fate, they remain characters "in someone else's story, not their own" (1984, 109). In my own work, I related de Lauretis's theory to Orson Welles's *The Lady from Shanghai* (1947) – where a naive sailor (Welles) meets and falls in love with the evil Elsa Bannister (Rita Hayworth), yet must ultimately abandon and transcend her in order to continue on his masculine life journey unscathed (Fischer 1989, 32–49).

While the aforementioned critics focused on the female film spectator as constructed by and through the text, Kathy Peiss in *Cheap Amusements* (1986) concentrated on real, turn-of-the-century New York working-class moviegoers. Thus, she found that "movies altered women's participation in the world of public, commercial amusements," with their attendance soaring when film moved from the arcade to the nickelodeon. As she notes: "Wives with their husbands and mothers with children crowded into the movie houses, breaking down the segregated and noncommercial orientation of married women's leisure" (1986, 148).

In her influential 1975 essay, Mulvey had argued that the satisfaction enjoyed by most mainstream cinema viewers was one steeped in rampant sexism, and she called for a more advanced form of filmmaking that would harness the "destruction of pleasure" as a "radical weapon" (1975, 712). On a related note, Claire Johnston's essay "Women's Cinema as Counter-Cinema" (1973; reproduced in another American anthology, Erens 1979) was also highly influential, giving critics a way to envision the work of women artists as productively opposed to the standard male-authored fare. Hence, following that lead, in *Shot/Countershot* I placed works like Busby Berkeley and Ray Enright's *Dames* (1934) and Arzner's *Dance Girl Dance* (1940) in a "diptych" frame, highlighting how they present divergent visions of the showgirl, how the latter "rewrites" the former. The notion of feminist reformulation is also central to *Re-vision* (1984), an anthology edited by Mary Ann Doane, Patricia Mellencamp, and Linda Williams. In their introduction the editors note how, after nearly a decade of feminist film theory, the critic is faced by a double-bind:

> she can continue to analyze and interpret various instances of the repression of woman, of her radical absence in the discourses of men … or she can attempt to delineate a feminine specificity, always risking a recapitulation of patriarchal constructions and a naturalization of "woman." (1984, 9)

The essays (written by not only the editors but writers like Judith Mayne, B. Ruby Rich, and Christine Gledhill) included attempts to confront this "dilemma" as they examine such films as Leontine Sagan's *Mädchen in Uniform* (1931) or Nicolas Roeg's *Bad Timing* (1980).

While, as noted, in the first few decades of academic film study, the genres that received the most attention were traditionally "masculine" ones (Westerns, crime films, action movies, thrillers) – directed by such cineastes as John Ford, Howard Hawks, and Alfred Hitchcock – as feminist film theory took hold, attention shifted to melodrama and, specifically, to the "woman's picture," especially popular with female audiences in the 1930s and 1940s and, traditionally, denigrated by male critics. While many journal articles engaged this topic, the major treatise on the subject was *The Desire to Desire* (1987) by Mary Ann Doane, which examines several subcategories of the form – including the romance (e.g. *Humoresque*, 1946), the maternal narrative (e.g. *Stella Dallas*, 1937), the Gothic (e.g. *Rebecca*, 1940), and the medical drama (e.g. *Dark Victory*, 1939). Her title signals that heroines in these works (unlike traditional heroes) have trouble actively desiring, a fact related to their positioning as women in a constraining patriarchal culture. Beyond that, Doane sees a certain de-eroticization of the gaze in these films, as well as a substitution of "masochistic fantasy" for sexuality (1987, 79).

Other feminist critics took on the broader genre of melodrama. Writing in Christine Gledhill's anthology *Home Is Where the Heart Is* (1987), Lea Jacobs examined censorship in the "fallen woman cycle," Janet Walker wrote about Freud and the vision of women in post–World War II American cinema, and Julia Lesage investigated anti-Asian racism and rape in *Broken Blossoms* (1919). At this time, not only film but also television melodrama began to receive considerable attention for its address to a female audience. Annette Kuhn examined this topic in the Gledhill anthology but, even earlier, Tania Modleski published *Loving with a Vengeance* (1982) in which she took a look at both soap operas and Harlequin romance books. Here, she attempted to validate female fantasy by resisting the attitudes she found prevalent in women's criticism of popular feminine narratives: "dismissiveness; hostility … [and] a flippant kind of mockery." Rather, she asserted that these kinds of stories "speak to very real problems and tensions in women's lives" (1982, 14). As part of discussions of cinematic "weepies" and novelized romances, the point was made that popular culture often was coded as female in general. Applying this notion to TV studies, Patrice Petro wrote in 1986 of the "attribution of 'feminized' values" to that medium, calling for the scrutiny of "our critical vocabularies which assign hierarchal and gender-specific value to difference" (1986, 6, 7).

Theorizations of cinema, gender, and race also began to be formulated in this era (as evidenced by the Lesage essay mentioned above). In "White Privilege and Looking Relations" (1986), Jane Gaines questioned the whitewashing of feminist film criticism, noting that "just as the Marxist model based on class has obscured gender, the feminist mode based on the male/female division under patriarchy has obscured the function of race" (Gaines 1999, 294). She analyzes the film *Mahogany* (1975), a work which actually frustrates and repudiates the male gaze, but only for the black man (1999, 299). Also confronting cinema and race, Michelle Wallace commented upon the image of black women in works by both white and African-American filmmakers. Writing on *The Color Purple* (1985), she found that Steven Spielberg "juggles film clichés and racial stereotypes fast and loose, until all signs of a black feminist agenda are banished, or ridiculed beyond repair" (1990, 972). She is equally skeptical of Spike Lee's *She's Gotta Have It* (1986), "the showpiece of the new black aesthetic … about a black woman who couldn't get enough of the old phallus, and who therefore had to be raped" (1990, 101). Taking an alternate position, Darcy De Marco asserted that the Lee film "breaks new ground for black women by liberating their sexuality from traditional Hollywood constraints" (1986, 26).

While the cinematic image had received the greatest amount of attention in writing on women and film, the issue of sound also began to be addressed. In *The Acoustic Mirror* (1988), Kaja Silverman concentrated specifically on the rarely used female voice-over in cinema – a technique most associated with the feminist avant-garde (e.g. Betty Gordon's *Empty Suitcases*, 1980) rather than with the mainstream cinema (which often used the male voice-off in genres like film noir). On a theoretical level, she tied the voice-off to the body of woman in another way by foregrounding how, for the baby *in utero*, the mother's voice is the original disembodied vocalization. Furthermore, the work of European feminist film critics (beyond the British) began to be translated into English, as in Giuliana Bruno and Maria Nadotti's *Off Screen: Women and Film in Italy* (1988).

In the same year, yet another anthology of feminist criticism appeared – *Feminism and Film Theory*, edited by Constance Penley, a work whose title proclaims the shift in discourse away from the earlier "images of women" approach. In this volume, not only films are examined (those by Arzner, Walsh, Lol Stein), but also the writing of other female critics is reviewed, as in Bergstrom's article "Rereading the Work of Claire Johnston" (1979). This piece not only attests to the centrality and sophistication that feminist film theory had assumed but also to the continuing interchange on this subject between Great Britain and the United States.

The Film Scene

As always, most American films of this period proffered images of women (how could they not?), whether in works of fiction, documentary, or experimental cinema. But the simple appearance of females onscreen did not make a work of especial interest to the question of women and film – in that era or any other. On the one hand, films by female directors gained prominence, often just for the fact of being woman-authored. On the other, so did certain films made by men that either sympathetically took on women's issues or hostilely rejected them – both moves that gained critical notice. That films were often categorized in this period by the gender of their creators is clear from Patricia Erens's 1979 anthology *Sexual Stratagems* which is divided into two sections: "The Male-Directed Cinema" (which includes my own essay on *Dames*, 1934, and Birgitta Steene's essay on Ingmar Bergman) and "Women's Cinema" (which includes B. Ruby Rich's piece on Leni Riefenstahl and Marsha Kinder's essay on *Jeanne Dielman*, 1975).

Feminist Documentaries

Part of the dynamics of the second-wave feminist movement involved the practice of "consciousness-raising," attempting to educate women concerning the restrictions of their existence in patriarchal society (whose ideology had become "natural" to them), as well as the means for transcending those limitations. This practice took the form of discussion groups (where women's issues could be raised in a collegial setting), political groups (where activism was discussed and engaged), and even physiology groups (where women learned about their bodies, health, and sexuality in a sometimes literal and graphic manner). Female-authored films (often documentaries) functioned to augment, illustrate, and engage many of the issues considered in these groups – most shown in noncommercial venues, such as homes, schools, libraries, community centers, health clinics, and museums. Occasionally, such works would be screened at festivals and/or gain commercial release (always difficult for nonfiction films and even more challenging for those with a feminist orientation). As Julia Lesage has pointed out, most of these films "used a simple format" with information "told directly by the protagonists to the camera" (1978, 222).

One of the earliest works of this type was *Growing up Female* (1971) made by Julia Reichert and Jim Klein, which took on issues concerning the socialization of women in America by featuring six women and girls. Also in 1971, Kate Millett (known for her book *Sexual Politics*, 1970) had a theatrical release for *Three Lives*, which told the stories of several women: Millett's sister, a chemist, and a bohemian free spirit. While, in general, the 1970s women's movement was criticized as being "lily white," some documentaries confronted issues of race. Madeline Anderson's *I Am Somebody* (1970) chronicled a strike by black female hospital workers in South Carolina. Likewise, *Fannie's Film* by Fronza Woods (1979) was a study of a 65-year-old cleaning woman that challenged stereotypical conceptions of domestic workers and women of color.

In a similar vein, Barbara Kopple raised issues of class in *Harlan County, U.S.A.* (1976), in which she recorded a miner's strike in Kentucky, focusing a great deal on the role of women in organizing and sustaining the strike. The film was given a major theatrical release and won the Oscar for Best Documentary. The Western bias of the women's movement was challenged by Claudia Weill and Shirley MacLaine in *The Other Half of the Sky: A China Memoir* (1975), a film that explored the situation of downtrodden Chinese women. Clearly, because of MacLaine's celebrity, the film had greater visibility than most and was nominated for an Academy Award. In the area of women's medical care, *Taking Our Bodies Back* (Margaret Lazarus and Renner Wunderlick, 1974) explored ten areas important to women's health. On another note, Donna Deitch's *Woman to Woman* (1974) gave an overview of the concerns of diverse American women by interviewing a mural painter, housewives, a psychiatrist/lesbian, a telephone operator, girls, children, activists, and prostitutes.

Some feminist work in this era was highly autobiographical. In 1972, Joyce Chopra made *Joyce at 34*, a film that examined the effect of her own pregnancy on her filmmaking career. In 1976, Martha Coolidge made *Not a Pretty Picture*, a docudrama that reenacted her high school trauma of date rape. In *Nana, Mom and Me* (1975) Amalie Rothschild presented a triptych portrait of three generations of women in her family: herself, her parent, and her grandparent. Similarly, in *David On and Off* (1972) Coolidge filmed her brother; and in *Old-Fashioned Woman* (1974) she explored the life of her New England grandmother.

Most interesting of all was a work that merged the documentary with the fictional: Michelle Citron's *Daughter Rite* (1980), which used family home movies (though not those of the filmmaker) accompanied by a voice-over narration (other than her own) that spoke from the daughter's perspective of contradictory feelings toward the mother. Citron's own remarks reveal the complex, liminal status of the work:

> Over the years, I've steadfastly maintained that *Daughter Rite* is not autobiographical. After all, I told myself … I had interviewed many daughters prior to writing the film and later hired actors to speak the text. The film was about mothers and daughters in general, not my mother and her daughters specifically … Of course, the reality of the film's verisimilitude is more complex. (Citron quoted in Waldman & Walker 1999, 276)

Feminist Experimental Cinema

The mention of *Daughter Rite* leads us to a consideration of the feminist experimental cinema (of which it is also a part). Eschewing a dramatic/fiction format, this brand of film attempted to do several things: oppose the male-authored canon, forge a feminist aesthetic, and surface some of the problematic aspects of women's position in masculine culture. Hence, Kaplan calls this genre the "theory film" (1983, 142), largely because of its abstraction and didactic function. In truth, some of the most discussed and lauded films of this kind were not American, but British. Hence, Laura Mulvey and Peter Wollen's *The Riddles of the Sphinx* (1977) took on the question of motherhood in Western society, and Sally Potter's *Thriller* (1979) examined the victimhood of woman within art and culture.

Some films of this type, however, were made in the US. *Sigmund Freud's Dora: A Case of Mistaken Identity* (1979) directed by Anthony McCall, Claire Pajaczkowska, Andrew Tyndall, and Jane Weinstock is both a reenactment and critique of Freud's analysis of a patient chronicled in one of his famous case studies. In the film, rather than help Dora, Freud bullies her by putting words in her mouth and denying the validity of the sexual assault she experienced and reported.

Perhaps the most accomplished female director of experimental films in this period was Yvonne Rainer – though she famously refused to label her films as "feminist" early on (Camera Obscura Collective, 1976). Her first feature, *Lives of Performers* (1972), is about a man caught between two women, ruining the lives of both. It draws on Rainer's prior work as a dancer and choreographer. *A Film about a Woman Who…* (1974) uses conventions of soap opera to fashion a narrative about female sexuality. *Kristina Talking Pictures* (1976) tells the unlikely story of a Hungarian female lion tamer who travels to New York to become a choreographer. *Journeys from Berlin/1971* (1980) conjoins the subjects of political terrorism and psychoanalysis in its focus on a woman undergoing therapy. Finally, *The Man Who Envied Women* (1985) is one of Rainer's most complex works, with its composition based on quotation from the classical and experimental cinema – incorporating film clips from *Un Chien Andalou* (1929), *Dangerous* (1935), *Double Indemnity* (1944), and *Wavelength* (1967), to name but a few. In taking this approach, Rainer expands the notion of women's cinema as "remaking" the canon – not only alluding to male-authored films but recycling them for her own aesthetic/ideological purpose.

The film's title, for example, directly alludes to two movies by male auteurs (François Truffaut and Blake Edwards), each called *The Man Who Loved Women* (1977 and 1983 respectively), about characters who

Figure 14.1 In *The Ties That Bind* (1984) Su Friedrich creates a portrait of her mother. (Courtesy of MoMA film stills archive.)

are inveterate womanizers. The clip from *Double Indemnity* (a film with a script by Raymond Chandler) has particular meaning in Rainer's work, since that author's name is mentioned in the dialogue.

Su Friedrich was another highly productive filmmaker during in this period. *Cool Hands, Warm Heart* (1979) examines women's quotidian beauty routines: shaving legs, fixing hair, etc. As B. Ruby Rich has noted, "Building on proverbs, metaphor, and the principles of a radical feminist imagination, Su Friedrich creates a world in which women's private rituals become public spectacles" (Friedrich website). In *Gently Down the Stream* (1981) Friedrich confronts the oneiric realm, with the film constructed from 14 dreams. As Bruce Jenkins writes: "Friedrich's film becomes a public exorcism, one that continually exposes and infects the viewer with the psychic consequences of religious constraints, familial binds and sexual conflicts" (1986–1987, 196). A similar dream theme characterizes *But No One* (1982), which, like the earlier work, uses a poetic word text etched into the film's emulsion. As Friedrich herself notes: "The blunt, vernacular images, which were shot on the streets of the Lower East Side, are set in contrast to the strange images conjured by the text" (Friedrich website). Her best-known work of the era is *The Ties That Bind* (1984), a portrait of her mother who immigrated to the US after World War II with Friedrich's father, an American soldier. In particular, Friedrich struggles here with her mother's status as a German citizen during the Nazi period, attempting to learn how she positioned herself vis-à-vis the Third Reich. Again, Friedrich uses the technique of words etched on the screen to represent her own interrogative voice. Finally, in *Damned If You Don't* (1987), Friedrich relates a tale of lesbian love involving the seduction of a nun.

Barbara Hammer is another experimental filmmaker of this era whose work addressed questions of homosexuality. *Dyketactics* (1974) celebrates lesbian sensuality; *Double Strength* (1978) is a poetic study of a lesbian relationship; *Women I Love* (1979) is a collective portrait of several of Hammer's paramours; and *Sync Touch* (1981) juxtaposes images of lesbians with clichés about them. Finally, *The Female Closet* (1998) investigates the lost histories of lesbians, bisexuals, and gays in Western culture.

Kathy Rose's experimental films (like those of Rainer) drew on the art of dance. In *Primitive Movers* (1983) she performs live in real time against a background of animated and abstract "chorus girls" who move with her – harking back to the musicals of Busby Berkeley. Similarly in *Strange Ditties* (1983) she dances against a projected background; but this time it is often white, and she uses her body to purposefully block the projector's beam, casting mobile and graceful shadows on the screen.

While not really an experimental film, Julie Dash's *Illusions* (1982) is a short dramatic work that would have no exhibition possibilities outside the domain of schools, museums, universities. Made and set in 1942 Hollywood, it concerns the paradoxes facing African-American women in the film industry. One of the main characters is a black, light-skinned, female studio executive who is "passing" and the other is a black woman who provides the singing voice for a white star.

Women's Independent and Commercial Cinema

The audience for experimental film (whether female- or male-authored) was, of course, small at this time (as it is now), and many artists sought to enter the broader realm of theatrical exhibition. One of the earliest to break into this market was Barbara Loden, whose film *Wanda* (1970) employed a cinema vérité style to tell the tale of a working-class woman (played by Loden) living in the rust belt and caught in a web of abusive relationships. Loden was married to director Elia Kazan (which helped the film get made) and had appeared in such mainstream films as Kazan's *Splendor in the Grass* (1961). Writing in the *New York Times*, Roger Greenspun opined: "I suppose it is significantly a woman's film in that it never sensationalizes or patronizes its heroine and yet finds her interesting" (1971).

Another early success in the feature market was Joan Micklin-Silver's *Hester Street* (1975), a work in black-and-white set in the early twentieth century that concerns the immigration of an Eastern European Jewish couple to the US. As in many cases, the husband Jake (Steven Keats) comes to the country before his wife does, but in her absence becomes Americanized. When his wife, Gitl, arrives (with her old-fashioned clothes and traditional wig), he is ashamed of her and rejects her in favor of more modern women. As played by Carol Kane, Gitl is the focus of our sympathy, especially as she rebels against her oppressive treatment. Writing in the *New York Times*, Roger Eder spoke of Micklin-Silver's "fine balance between realism and fable" and calls the film "an unconditionally happy achievement" (1975).

Claudia Weill's *Girlfriends* (1978) was also groundbreaking in a variety of ways. First of all, it was shot in 16mm, but ultimately received a theatrical release. Second, it took on the subject of female friendship (between two artists), not a prevalent topic in the annals of Hollywood. As Judy Klemesrud wrote in the *New York Times*: "The stereotype [of friendship] was of women at each other's throats as they competed for men. Now that stereotype has been dealt a blow" (1978). The film starred Melanie Mayron as Susan Weinblatt, a Jewish New Yorker (adding an ethnic twist to the subject). Unlike most screen actresses, Mayron is not a beauty (with her glasses, kinky hair, and full face), but she is nonetheless treated as attractive and is sought after by men. Again in a manner that counters clichés of screen romance, her lover in this case is an aging, married rabbi (Eli Wallach) – hardly the usual leading man. Additionally, Susan befriends another woman, Ceil (Amy Wright), a lesbian, who is treated very sympathetically.

In the next decade, Weill goes on to make a big-budget second film with Hollywood stars: *It's My Turn* (1980). In the narrative Jill Clayburgh plays Kate, a female academic who is focused on her career and lives with Homer, an architect (Charles Grodin). At a wedding, she meets former baseball player Ben (Michael Douglas) who wins her affection and passion – though difficult choices about her job and living location remain to be solved when the film ends. Roger Ebert (1980) found the film too dogmatic: "The people in this movie don't seem to be having conversations; they seem to be marching through current feminist issues." Writing in the *New York Times*, Carey Winfrey, on the other hand, asserted that Weill was on her way to becoming "a successful female practitioner of a craft long dominated by men." She did wonder, however, if the narrative's

Figure 14.2 Susan (Melanie Mayron) and Rabbi Gold (Eli Wallach) in *Girlfriends* (1978, director and producer Claudia Weill).

second-guessing the choices of an overachieving woman asks: "Has feminism gone too far?" (1980).

Susan Seidelman also has an interesting career during this era. Her first feature was *Smithereens* (1982), which she wrote, produced, directed, and edited. A youth film, it concerns a young New Jersey woman (a free spirit type) who comes to New York to make it in the underground Punk scene – only to have hopes dashed at the end. Janet Maslin of the *New York Times* asserted that Seidelman presented her character "with wit, style, and even more nerve than the heroine's own" (1982b). The director's next film was a more commercial venture featuring known players: *Desperately Seeking Susan* (1985). Here Madonna takes the role of Susan, a down-and-out con woman on the run, who corresponds with her boyfriend through a series of personal ads in a local New York City newspaper. These ads are read by a bored, wealthy, suburban housewife, Roberta (Rosanna Arquette), who follows Susan around the East Village. Through a stroke of fate, an act of mistaken identity, and a case of amnesia, Roberta "becomes" Susan and meets one of her friends, Dez (Aidan Quinn) – falling in love with him and deciding to leave her spa salesman husband. The film humorously critiques the bourgeois life of women and paints a curious but moving portrait of the bond between two extremely different females. Roger Ebert was impressed with "the complexities of this movie" as well as its "dizzying plot" and "interesting characters" (1985). Seidelman's final film in this era, *Making Mr. Right* (1987), was far less successful. It is about a shy and retiring scientist (John Malkovich) who builds a robot double for a long-term space mission. He hires a PR woman (Ann Magnuson) to teach the robot about human emotions and the latter, surprisingly, falls in love with her. Rita Kempley of the *Washington Post* joked that "we can only conclude that women have decided that machinery is less trouble than men" (1987).

A few of the documentarists of this period also moved into the realm of fiction/dramatic cinema. Joyce Chopra, who had earlier made a movie about her pregnancy, directed *Smooth Talk* (1985) starring Laura Dern. Based on a story by Joyce Carol Oates, it concerns a teenage girl's sexual awakening and experimentation. It won the Grand Jury Prize at Sundance in 1986 and the respect of critics like Roger Ebert, who noted: "The movie is almost uncanny in its self-assurance, in the way it knows that the first hour, where 'nothing' happens, is necessary if the payoff is to be tragic, instead of merely sensational" (1986b). Similarly, Donna Deitch (who had earlier made a documentary about diverse American women) directed *Desert Hearts* (1985), which, like John Sayles's *Lianna* (1983), was one of the few movies at this time to broach the subject of lesbianism. Unlike the latter, however, *Desert Hearts* is set, not in the contemporary period, but in the 1950s, and concerns a female university professor who goes to Nevada for a divorce and unexpectedly falls in love with a ranch owner's daughter. Ebert praised Deitch's handling of the love scene, writing: "Instead of turning it into some kind of erotic music video – in which the real subject is not sex but the director's cleverness – she lets the scene build according to its own rhythms. The result is one of the few genuinely powerful erotic passages in recent movies" (1986a). Mirra Bank (who had been an editor on *Harlan County*) along with Ellen Hovde (who had codirected the documentary *Grey Gardens*, 1975, with the Maysles brothers) made another moving dramatic film in the 1980s, *Enormous Changes at the Last Minute* (1983), an adaptation of stories by Grace Paley. It comprises three unrelated (but thematically tied) segments about women caught in trying situations: abandonment by a husband, dealings with an aged father, and pregnancy after an affair. It also boasts a cast of soon-to-be-famous actors: Ellen Barkin, Kevin Bacon, and David Strathairn. Janet Maslin of the *New York Times*, however, complained that the film "seems [too] determined to lionize the rueful, independent women who are [its subjects]" (1985).

Some women directors got their start in the teenpic – a low prestige genre often assigned to females. However, in *Fast Times at Ridgemont High* (1982), New York University and American Film Institute graduate Amy Heckerling transcended the limitations of the form and made a truly biting and sardonic satire of American youth culture. Focusing on California high school students, the film mocks their education, sexual exploits, leisure antics, and consumer habits, and garners wonderful performances from Jennifer Jason Leigh, Sean Penn, Phoebe Cates, and Judge Reinhold. In 1983, it received a Writers Guild award and in 2005 it was added to the National Film Registry. At the time of its release, *New York Times* critic Janet Maslin was qualified in her response to it, finding it "both worthwhile and disappointing simultaneously. There's a lot to make [the] film likable, but not much to hold it together" (1982a).

The female director most identified with the teenpic in this period is Martha Coolidge, formerly a documentarist – though her films have not won the respect that greeted *Fast Times*. *Valley Girl* (1983) tells the tale of a suburban girl who breaks ups with her boyfriend and meets a city boy from Hollywood and must decide whether to start a relationship with him despite the disapproval of her friends. As Maslin remarked: "On the West Coast, where they know about such things, *Valley Girl* may conceivably strike a funnier and a more familiar chord than it does in New York, but I doubt it. Too much of the film is too aimless" (1983). One champion, however, was Ebert, who found it "a little treasure, a funny, sexy, appealing story" (1983). Coolidge's *Joy of Sex* (1984) focuses on a teenage girl who, believing she will soon die, embarks on a quest to lose her virginity. Then in *City Girl* (1984), Coolidge considers the world of a more adult woman – a photographer who explores a cult in a local club, living out her sexual fantasies in the process. *Real Genius* (1985) returns to youth culture, this time focusing on two boys who work together on a school science project that they learn, to their dismay, their teacher will turn over to the government to use as a weapon. Finally in *Plain Clothes* (1988), an undercover policeman disguises himself as a high school student in order to prove the innocence of his teenage brother who has been accused of murdering a teacher. In the *New York Times*, Maslin opined that "Martha Coolidge has directed *Plain Clothes* in an adequate but mostly lifeless style" (1988). Thus, none of Coolidge's films gained the kind of critical kudos or respect that marked the work of directors like Heckerling, Chopra, or Seidelman.

While this period saw advances in the place of women in the film industry, the situation was still discouraging. Producer Henry Jaglom (who started a division within his company to enable women to direct) told film scholar Annette Insdorf: "Women are still the most disenfranchised group in Hollywood; in order to succeed, they have to tailor their humanity to male distortions. They have to try to think what will succeed among male studio executives" (Insdorf 1988).

Women's Cinema: Trickle-Down Feminism

A third area of interest in the film scene of this period is the male-authored cinema that began to take on feminist issues (perhaps in order to be politically correct or *au courant*) – some more successfully than others. The beginning of the era was signaled by the release of two comic works: *Diary of a Mad Housewife* in 1970 and *Up the Sandbox* in 1972. Both concerned the trials and tribulations of contemporary wives and mothers, surrounded by absent or insensitive men. While, on the surface, the plots of these works and others contained "positive images" of women, or exposed constraints in patriarchal society, few would (or did) stand up to analyses by feminist critics, who looked beyond their surface narratives toward less progressive underlying themes and stylistic tropes.

As noted, John Sayles's *Lianna* (1983) is a work that sensitively portrays the growing love and erotic attraction between two women, one happily married and the other her professor. *The Turning Point* (1977) directed by Herbert Ross, on the other hand, tells the story of Deedee (Shirley MacLaine), a former dancer – now a fulltime wife and mother – who must confront her lost career when her daughter joins a dance company and they both encounter Deedee's college friend Emma (played by Anne Bancroft) who pursued her art and became a star. Another film that explored female friendship was George Cukor's *Rich and Famous* (1981) about two college pals (both would-be writers), one who remains single and becomes a serious novelist (Jacqueline Bisset), and the other (Candice Bergen) who marries and authors trash fiction. In Fred Zinnemann's *Julia* (1977) – based on the memoir of Lillian Hellman – two women take on the heroic tasks of espionage in World War II. Thus, Hellman (Jane Fonda), at the behest of her friend Julia (Vanessa Redgrave), smuggles money through Germany in order to help the antifascist cause.

During the 1970s, many feminist critics had bemoaned the lack of complex and prominent roles for women in film and had pointed to foreign directors like Ingmar Bergman, who had featured female players in such works as *Persona* (1966), *The Passion of Anna* (1969), and *Cries and Whispers* (1972). On some level, Robert Altman's *Three Women* (1977) was seen to address this issue with its tale of Pinky (Sissy Spacek), a sanitarium worker who becomes involved with a coworker, Millie (Shelley Duvall). In a move that seems to parallel *Persona* (as does the setting of the Altman film), the two women seem inexplicably to swap identities. A third woman (Janice Rule), a local artist, also enters into the narrative universe. Perhaps the most celebrated of the male-authored films was *An Unmarried Woman* (1978), directed by Paul Mazursky, which concerns Erica (Jill Clayburgh) an upper middle-class New York wife whose husband leaves her for a young salesgirl he has met while shopping. Erica must come to terms not only with psychological rejection but with her career and romantic hopes for the future. While she soon meets and begins a relationship with a highly attractive artist (Alan Bates), the film won praise for the fact that she does not immediately drop her gallery job to move away with him when he so requests. Clearly, people saw the film as a modern revision of the classic Hollywood love story.

Curiously, two films starring Dustin Hoffman also drew a great deal of critical attention and, in some cases, ire. *Kramer vs. Kramer* (1979) directed by Robert Benton, pitted Hoffman (as Ted Kramer) against his wife, Joanna (Meryl Streep), in a bitter divorce and child custody dispute. Joanna had become enraged at Ted's careerism and refusal to take responsibility for his child, so she deserts the family and Ted must learn how to be a loving and dependable father. When Joanna resurfaces and wants to take charge of her son once more, Ted resists, having learned the joys of parenting. Feminist critics condemned the film on two scores: its portrayal of Joanna as a heartless mother, and its sentimental depiction of Ted as a superior nurturer. On some level, their complaints about the film were encapsulated in a statement made by *New York Times* critic Vincent Canby:

> [The film is] about fathers and sons, husbands and wives, and most particularly, perhaps, about the failed expectations of a certain breed of woman in this day and

> age … Joanna is not an easily appealing character, especially when she returns after eighteen months of therapy in California and seeks legal custody of the child she walked out on. (1979)

Then in *Tootsie* (1982), directed by Sydney Pollack, Hoffman plays Michael, an unemployed actor, who, in order to get work, pretends to be a woman so as to secure a female role in a daytime soap opera. For most of the film, Hoffman plays the part of the matronly Dorothy in drag, as she wins popularity (within the narrative) with female viewers and fellow performers, encouraging them to break free from the control of men – individuals precisely like the real Michael. Again, many reviewers harshly criticized the film for demonstrating that men make the best feminists.

Drawing on the same theme as *Kramer vs. Kramer* but transposing it to comic form, two films envisioned men as replacing the role of women in the family. *Mr. Mom* (1983) starred Michael Keaton as a married husband and father who loses his job and becomes the stay-at-home parent, wreaking temporary havoc upon the household but ultimately triumphing. In *3 Men and a Baby* (1987) a group of bachelors become the unwitting parents to a child that one of them allegedly has fathered (whose mother has left it on their doorstep). After a series of humorous fits and starts, they, of course, succeed as loving dads. As I noted in my book *Cinematernity* (1996, 111–130), a hostile stance toward the mother has always been part and parcel of comic discourse, but coming in the late 1980s – on the heels of two decades of feminist activism – this reiteration of the motif seems to have an especially malevolent thrust. As Susan Faludi would note in her 1991 book *Backlash*:

> the last decade has seen a powerful counter-assault on women's rights, a backlash, an attempt to retract the handful of small and hard-won victories that the feminist movement did manage to win for women. This counterassault … stands the truth boldly on its head and proclaims that the very steps that have elevated women's position have actually led to their downfall … [and] that women's "liberation" [i]s the true contemporary American scourge. (1991, xviii)

Thus, ironically, Faludi suggested that, as the 1990s dawned, we were entering an era of stark reaction against the women's movement, now seen as an even greater threat than at its outset due to its enormous gains, cinematic and otherwise.

References

Bergstrom, Janet. (1979). "Rereading the Work of Claire Johnston." *Camera Obscura*, 1–2, 21–31.

Bogle, Donald. (2001). *Toms, Coons, Mulattoes, Mammies & Bucks*. New York: Continuum.

Bruno, Giuliana, & Nadotti, Maria (1988). *Off Screen: Women and Film in Italy*. London: Routledge.

Camera Obscura Collective. (1976). "Yvonne Rainer: Interview." *Camera Obscura*, 1, Fall, 76–96.

Canby, Vincent. (1979). Review: *Kramer vs. Kramer*. *New York Times*, December 19, C23.

de Lauretis, Teresa. (1984). *Alice Doesn't: Feminism, Semiotics, Cinema*. Bloomington: Indiana University Press.

De Marco, Darcy. (1986). "Liberating Black Female Stereotypes." *Black Film Review*, 2.26, 7, 34.

Doane, Mary Anne. (1987). *The Desire to Desire: The Woman's Film of the 1940's*. Bloomington: Indiana University Press.

Doane, Mary Anne, Mellencamp, Patricia, & Williams, Linda (eds). (1984). *Re-vision: Essays in Feminist Film Theory Criticism*. Frederick, MA: University Publications of America.

Ebert, Roger. (1980). Review: *It's My Turn*. *Chicago Sun-Times*, at http://rogerebert.-suntimes.com/apps/pbcs.dll/article?AID=/19801028/REVIEWS/10280301/1023 (accessed February 2011).

Ebert, Roger. (1983). Review: *Valley Girl*. *Chicago Sun-Times*, at http://rogerebert.suntimes.com/apps/pbcs.dll/article?AID=/19830429/REVIEWS/304290302/1023 (accessed February 2011).

Ebert, Roger. (1985). Review: *Desperately Seeking Susan*. *Chicago Sun-Times*, at http://rogerebert.suntimes.com/apps/pbcs.dll/article?AID=/19850329/REVIEWS/503290301/1023 (accessed February 2011).

Ebert, Roger. (1986a). Review: *Desert Hearts*. *Chicago Sun-Times*, at http://rogerebert.suntimes.com/apps/pbcs.dll/article?AID=/19860606/REVIEWS/606060301/1023 (accessed February 2011).

Ebert, Roger. (1986b). Review: *Smooth Talk*. *Chicago Sun-Times*, at http://rogerebert.suntimes.com/apps/pbcs.dll/article?AID=/19860509/REVIEWS/605090305/1023 (accessed February 2011).

Eder, Richard. (1975). "Pathos and Wit Light Up Hester St." *New York Times*, October 20, 44.

Erens, Patricia (ed.). (1979). *Sexual Strategems: The World of Women in Film*. New York: Horizon Press.

Faludi, Susan. (1992). *Backlash: The Undeclared War against American Women*. New York: Anchor.

Fischer, Lucy. (1989). *Shot/Countershot: Film Tradition and Women's Cinema*. Princeton: Princeton University Press.

Fischer, Lucy. (1996). *Cinematernity: Film, Motherhood, Genre*. Princeton: Princeton University Press.

French, Brandon. (1978). *On the Verge of Revolt: Women in American Films of the Fifties*. New York: Ungar.

Friedrich, Su. (website). http://www.sufriedrich.com/content.php?sec=films&sub=film_1979_chwh (accessed February 2011).

Gaines, Jane. (1999). "White Privilege and Looking Relations: Race and Gender in Feminist Film Criticism" (1988). In Sue Thornham (ed.), *Feminist Film Theory: A Reader* (pp. 293–307). New York: New York University Press.

Gent, George. (1972). "Women Filmmakers: Doors Opening." *New York Times*, June 15, 46.

Gledhill, Christine (ed.). (1987). *Home Is Where the Heart Is: Studies in Melodrama and the Woman's Film*. London: British Film Institute.

Greenspun, Roger. (1971). "Young Wife Fulfills Herself as a Robber: Barbara Loden's Film Opens at Cinema II. *Wanda* Improves with Its Turn to Action." *New York Times*, March 1, 22.

Haskell, Molly. (1974). *From Reverence to Rape: The Treatment of Women in the Movies*. Chicago: University of Chicago Press.

Higashi, Sumiko. (1978). *Virgins, Vamps and Flappers: The American Silent Movie Heroine*. New York: Eden Press.

Insdorf, Annette. (1988). "Women Film Directors Make a Strong Comeback." *New York Times*, April 24, A19.

Jenkins, Bruce. (1986–1987). "Gently Down the Stream." *Millennium Film Journal*, Fall/Winter, 195–198.

Johnston, Claire. (1975). *The Work of Dorothy Arzner: Towards a Feminist Cinema*. London: British Film Institute.

Johnston, Claire. (1979). "Women's Cinema as Counter-Cinema" (1973). In Patricia Erens (ed.), *Sexual Strategems: The World of Women in Film* (pp. 133–143). New York: Horizon Press.

Kaplan, E. Ann. (1983). *Women and Film: Both Sides of the Camera*. London: Routledge.

Kay, Karyn, & Peary, Gerald (eds). (1977). *Women and the Cinema: A Critical Anthology*. New York: Dutton.

Kempley, Rita. (1987). "Making Mr. Right." *Washington Post*, C7.

Klemesrud, Judy. (1978). "'Girlfriends' Director on Female Friendship: Changing Attitudes 'Like a Kinship.'" *New York Times*, August 4, A12.

Lesage, Julia. (1978). "The Political Aesthetics of the Feminist Documentary Film." In Patricia Erens (ed.), *Issues in Feminist Film Criticism* (pp. 222–237). Bloomington: Indiana University Press.

Maslin, Janet. (1982a). The Screen: "*Ridgemont High*." *New York Times*, September 13, C6.

Maslin, Janet. (1982b). The Screen: "*Smithereens*." *New York Times*, November 19, C10.

Maslin, Janet. (1983). "*Valley Girl*: A Coast Comedy." *New York Times*, April 29, C10.

Maslin, Janet. (1985). Film: "3 Paley Stories." *New York Times*, April 11, C25.

Maslin, Janet. (1988). "An Undercover Return to High School." *New York Times*, April 16, 18.

Mayne, Judith. (1989). *Kino and the Woman Question: Feminism and Soviet Silent Film*. Columbus: Ohio State University Press.

Mellen, Joan. (1974). *Women and Their Sexuality in New Film*. New York: Horizon Press.

Miller, Lynn Friedman. (1988). *The Hand That Holds the Camera*. New York: Garland.

Modleski, Tania. (1982). *Loving with a Vengeance: Mass Produced Fantasies for Women*. London: Routledge.

Mulvey, Laura. (1975). "Visual Pleasure and Narrative Cinema." *Screen*, 16.3, 6–18.

Mulvey, Laura. (1981). "Afterthoughts on 'Visual Pleasure and Narrative Cinema': Inspired by *Duel in the Sun*." *Framework*, 15/16/17, Summer, 12–15.

Peiss, Kathy. (1986). *Cheap Amusements: Working Women and Leisure in Turn-of-the-Century New York*. Philadelphia: Temple University Press.

Penley, Constance (ed.). (1988). *Feminism and Film Theory*. New York: Routledge.

Petro, Patrice. (1986). "Mass Culture and the Feminine: The 'Place' of Television in Film Studies." *Cinema Journal*, 25.3, 5–21.

Place, Janey. (1978). "Women in Film Noir." In E. Ann Kaplan (ed.), *Women in Film Noir* (pp. 35–67). London: British Film Institute.

Pribram, Deidre (ed.). (1988). *Female Spectators: Looking at Film and Television*. London: Verso.

Quart, Barbara Koenig. (1989). *Women Directors: The Emergence of a New Cinema*. New York: Praeger.

Rosen, Marjorie. (1973). *Popcorn Venus: Women, Movies, and the American Dream*. New York: Avon.

Silverman, Kaja. (1988). *The Acoustic Mirror: The Female Voice in Psychoanalysis and Cinema*. Bloomington: Indiana University Press.

Smith, Valerie. (1988). "Reconstituting the Image: The Emergent Black Woman Director." *Callaloo*, 11, 709–719.

Stoddard, Karen M. (1983). *Saints and Shrews: Women and Aging in American Popular Film*. Westport, CT: Greenwood Press.

Studlar, Gaylyn (1992). *In the Realm of Pleasure: Von Sternberg, Dietrich and the Masochistic Aesthetic.* New York: Columbia University Press.

Waldman, Diane. (1990). "There's More to a Positive Image than Meets the Eye." In Patricia Erens (ed.), *Issues in Feminist Film Criticism* (pp. 13–18). Bloomington: Indiana University Press.

Waldman, Diane, & Walker, Janet (eds). (1999). *Feminism and Documentary.* Minneapolis: University of Minnesota Press.

Wallace, Michelle. (1990). *Invisibility Blues: From Pop to Theory.* London: Verso.

Winfrey, Carey. (1980). "Claudia Weill: It's Her Turn Now." *New York Times*, December 7, D1.

15

American Avant-Garde Cinema from 1970 to the Present

Scott MacDonald
Professor, Hamilton College, United States

During the 1970s, the American avant-garde underwent unprecedented diversification into smaller movements and trends defined by race, ethnicity, gender, cultural and ideological position, academic institutionalization, and modes of production. Scott MacDonald identifies six areas of experimentation that exemplify many larger avant-garde developments during the past 40 years: **new feminist filmmaking**, **ethnic cinemas**, **personal/autobiographical filmmaking**, **found footage filmmaking**, **"home-made" cinema** (or **microcinema**), and the rejuvenation of older and broader **avant-garde traditions** devoted to re-educating the eyes and mind through **formal experiments**. Because most experimental film is contingent on the creative vision of an individual artist or small collective, MacDonald's approach is necessarily **auteurist**, but not without acknowledging that most avant-garde film and media is keenly sensitive to its environment and to broader socio-political, cultural and/or ecological concerns. MacDonald's essay shares ground with Janet Cutler on "L.A. Rebellion" filmmakers and Lucy Fisher on feminist film in this volume and with Jan-Christopher Horak on the American avant-garde before World War II and Jared Rapfogel on American underground film in Volume I.

Additional terms, names, and concepts: expanded cinema, structural film, Anthology Film Archives, "essential cinema," The Film Farm, "devotional cinema"

Much of what has happened during the past three decades of American avant-garde film history is a result of the explosion of creativity that characterized the 1960s and early 1970s.[1] Not only did a remarkable number of interesting filmmakers emerge during this moment, but filmmakers who had been productive during the 1950s and 1960s found a new audience. The American film society movement, energized by Amos Vogel's Cinema 16 in New York and Frank Stauffacher's Art in Cinema in San Francisco and Berkeley, spread across the nation during the late 1940s and the 1950s, and began a transformation

American Film History: Selected Readings, 1960 to the Present, First Edition. Edited by Cynthia Lucia, Roy Grundmann, and Art Simon.

in American film awareness that culminated during the next decade, producing a very wide range of interesting avant-garde films, plus an abundance of what Gene Youngblood (1970) called "expanded cinema" (that is, multimedia presentations and happenings that expanded the use of motion pictures beyond the movie theater), as well as the beginnings of what came to be called "video art." Much of the creative energy of this moment was devoted to rebelling against conventional American society and in particular against the social standards that had come to seem "normal" during the 1950s and early 1960s. This rebellion took two general forms, evoking the traditional distinction between the Apollonian and the Dionysian in Greek art.

The approach that for many came to seem the quintessential contribution of the late 1960s and early 1970s was what P. Adams Sitney (1974) called "structural film." While Sitney's use of the term reflected his belief that what was unusual about the films he called "structural" was a rigorously formal organization that called attention to itself *as* structure, a somewhat less problematic way of defining these films is to see them as attempts by the filmmakers to transform explorations of the apparatus of cinema into works of art. Structural film was largely a result of the filmmakers' attempts to be taken seriously as visual artists, often working in modes that echoed what seemed to be the most productive modern directions in painting, sculpture, literature, and experimental music, as well as a function of the new importance of film studies in academe: for those beginning to teach film history and film production, an exploration of the cinematic apparatus seemed fundamental. The most notable films identified with structural film – Tony Conrad's *The Flicker* (1966), Michael Snow's *Wavelength* (1967), Ken Jacobs's *Tom, Tom, the Piper's Son* (1969, revised 1971), Hollis Frampton's *Zorns Lemma* (1970), Ernie Gehr's *Serene Velocity* (1971), Anthony McCall's *Line Describing a Cone* (1973), J. J. Murphy's *Print Generation* (1974) – demonstrated a passionate intellectual engagement with cinema. This intellectual engagement included an extension of duration that demanded a new form of cinematic attention (a cinematic analogy, perhaps, to the expansive canvases of new American painting of the era following the arrival of abstract expressionism), along with serious attention to aspects of the film experience that had usually been taken for granted, even by earlier avant-garde filmmakers: the way the zoom lens shapes space, the details of film grain, the degree to which a print of a film subtracts from the visual quality of the original, and so forth.

While structural film was a particularly important new direction during the period, it quickly found as many enemies as friends. In addition to the primary audience for popular cinema, which had little interest in avant-garde experiments, most serious cineastes – those fascinated with the auteur dimensions of American cinema and/or with the new "art cinema" coming from Europe, Japan, India – looked askance at structural film's demands on audiences and its seeming lack of traditional filmic craft. Further, the intellectual, implicitly academic dimensions of structural film aggravated a good many avant-garde filmmakers who saw structural film as a betrayal of the rebellion against repression that had energized avantgarde filmmakers in the 1960s. The "Dionysian" strain of American avant-garde filmmaking – evident early on in the work of Kenneth Anger (*Fireworks*, 1947; *Inauguration of the Pleasure Dome*, 1954; *Scorpio Rising*, 1963), Jack Smith (*Flaming Creatures*, 1964), and Bruce Conner (*Cosmic Ray*, 1962) – found additional adherents in Robert Nelson (*Oh Dem Watermelons*, 1965), George and Mike Kuchar (their early 8mm films), Paul Morrissey (*Trash*, 1970), and John Waters (*Multiple Maniacs*, 1970; *Pink Flamingos*, 1972; *Female Trouble*, 1974), and by the end of the 1970s, in the work of such "punk" or "no wave" filmmakers as Beth B and Scott B (*Black Box*, 1978; *Letters to Dad*, 1979; *The Offenders*, 1979; *The Trap Door*, 1980), Vivienne Dick (*She Had Her Gun All Ready*, 1978), and Manuel DeLanda (*Incontinence*, 1978; *Raw Nerves*, 1980). These filmmakers were defiantly nonintellectual, or at least resolutely nonacademic; indeed, traditional academe was seen as part of the repression these filmmakers were bent on defying.

The conclusion of this period was defined by the appearance, during the early 1970s, of a series of books that charted the trajectory of avant-garde cinema up until the beginning of that decade: David Curtis's *Experimental Cinema: A Fifty-Year Evolution* (1971), Jonas Mekas's *Movie Journal: The Rise of a New American Cinema, 1959–1971* (1972), Sitney's *Visionary Film: The American Avant-Garde* (1974), Amos Vogel's *Film as a Subversive Art* (1974), Sitney's *The Essential Cinema: Essays on the Films in the Collection of Anthology Film Archives* (1975), and Malcolm Le Grice's *Abstract*

Film and Beyond (1977). These books, along with the opening of Anthology Film Archives in December 1970 (and its repertory of "essential cinema" – "the essential works of the art of cinema" – chosen by a committee of five: James Broughton, Ken Kelman, Peter Kubelka, Jonas Mekas, and P. Adams Sitney), seemed to suggest not only that avant-garde film had a distinguished history, but also that this history had now culminated in forms of self-reflexive cinema (structural film) that represented a deeper awareness of the evolution of the cinematic apparatus.

While the "essential cinema" is most sensibly read as an attempt by its selection committee to propose a new, rather more broad-ranging sense of film as an art form than had been evident during earlier decades – the eclectic list included Brakhage, Buster Keaton, Yasujiro Ozu, Jean Renoir, the Kuchar brothers, Charles Chaplin, Robert Breer, Luis Buñuel, Andy Warhol, Maya Deren, Robert Flaherty, F. W. Murnau, Harry Smith, Leni Riefenstahl, and Roberto Rossellini – many of those in avant-garde circles, and especially the generation of filmmakers coming of age in the late 1970s, found "the essential cinema" precisely the opposite of "broad-ranging"; indeed, the "essential" in "the essential cinema" came to be seen by many as less a progressive intervention within conventional senses of film history, than as a cinematic version of what came to be called "essentialism." The establishment of the Collective for Living Cinema in New York City in 1973 was in some measure a reaction to the perceived elitism of Anthology Film Archives.

These days, the most obvious failure of the "essential cinema" canon would seem to be its refusal to admit the achievements of major auteurs of industrial narrative cinema: Can the Anthology Selection Committee really have thought that Douglas Crockwell, Ian Hugo, and Frank Stauffacher were more important to the evolution of cinema as an art form than John Ford, Alfred Hitchcock, and Douglas Sirk? But during the decades that followed the establishment of Anthology Film Archives, a wide range of other forms of rebellion against both commercial moviemaking and the exclusivity of Anthology and of those chronicling avant-garde history developed. Indeed, the cinematic accomplishments of the final 25 years of the twentieth century and the first decade of the twenty-first are so numerous and diverse that the best one can do in a short history is to enumerate and track a number of these accomplishments. Further, it is useful to see this history as a series of often overlapping tendencies within which individual filmmakers have worked in a variety of ways and with a variety of goals.

Before these tendencies are described, however, it is important to recognize that while some of the major contributions to the creative explosion of the 1960s were confined to that decade (Warhol's remarkable productivity as a filmmaker lasted only a few years, from 1963 to 1968; the same is true of Jack Smith, though Smith continued to perform, and at times to appear in films by others), some filmmakers who established themselves during the 1950s and 1960s continued to make important contributions throughout the rest of the century and into the new millennium. The most obvious instance of this, of course, is Stan Brakhage whose remarkably prolific career lasted until the final moments of his life (Brakhage died on March 8, 2003); indeed, it is difficult either to simplify or to define any creative falling off in this long career that in later decades continued an ongoing exploration of the filmmaker's domestic environment, including the *Sincerity* series (five sections, 1973–1980) and *The Loom* (1986); and that produced dozens of subtle and beautiful explorations of light, including *The Text of Light* (1974), *The Roman Numeral Series* (1979–1980), *Commingled Containers* (1997), and many films made by painting and etching on the filmstrip, including *The Dante Quartet* (1987), *Preludes, 1–24* (1996), and *Chinese Series* (2003), made in the final days of Brakhage's life as he scratched into film emulsion with his fingernails.

Other filmmakers whose longevity has been impressive include Larry Jordan, George Kuchar, and Andrew Noren. Jordan, who went to high school in Denver with Brakhage and helped to found San Francisco's Canyon Cinema, is best known as an experimental animator/collagist (he's made other kinds of films as well) who established his reputation in the 1950s. Major works of more recent decades include *The Rime of the Ancient Mariner* (1977) and the feature-length *Sophie's Place* (1986). Like Brakhage, Kuchar is relentlessly productive. For two decades he produced and directed several trash melodramas a year, some for himself, others as collaborations with his classes at the San Francisco Art Institute; and when he switched to video during the 1980s, he became so productive that for a time his video distributor, the Video

Data Bank in Chicago, published a separate catalogue listing his works. Keeping up with Kuchar is nearly impossible, but particularly impressive is the series of "Weather Diaries" he made in Oklahoma's "tornado alley" beginning in 1986. Noren established himself in the 1960s, only to lose nearly all his early films in a fire, then began what became the ongoing project, *The Adventures of the Exquisite Corpse*, a diary of light as it reveals his personal world, in 1968. So far, *Adventures* has produced *Huge Pupils* (1969), *False Pretenses* (1974), *The Phantom Enthusiast* (1975), *Charmed Particles* (1979), *The Lighted Field* (1987), *Imaginary Light* (1995), *Time Being* (2001), *Free to Go (Interlude)* (2003), and *Aberration of Starlight* (2008), the last three made with a digital camera.

The remainder of this chapter describes six tendencies that have characterized American avant-garde cinema since the 1970s: three of them, ideological tendencies (with, of course, formal implications) primarily evident in the 1970s and 1980s; and three of them, formal tendencies (with, of course, ideological implications) somewhat more evident in recent decades. The 1970s and 1980s revealed considerable interest in using cinema as an adjunct to feminist political action and as a means of coming to grips with the problematic depiction of women in nearly a century of commercial cinema. African-Americans, Asian-Americans, and Latinos, too, found means of exploring territories, ethnic territories in particular, distorted or made invisible by the commercial media industry. And new forms of personal cinema, more fully engaged with the political realities of the moment, were developing. Recent decades have seen the emergence of "found-footage film" or "recycled cinema," as William C. Wees (1996) has called it, as a major arena for exploration; an increasing fascination with hand-crafted cinema; and new forms of film dedicated to retraining perception – in particular, perception of place.

My brief survey of these tendencies is presented with an important caveat: While the focus of this essay is the recent history of *American* avant-garde cinema, this does not mean that we should understand this history as a national enterprise. The arts and artists have always functioned internationally and transnationally, and this is particularly true of avant-garde film. In the 1960s few film artists had more impact on American avant-garde filmmaking than Michael Snow, a Canadian living in New York; or than Peter Kubelka, whose trip to the United States in 1966 to show *Unsere Afrikareise* ("Our Trip to Africa," 1966) was personally transformative for Kubelka ("[in America] I encountered a completely different approach to my work and to myself. I gained a new life" (MacDonald 2005, 178)) and influential on the American filmmakers who saw Kubelka's masterpiece (the completion of *Unsere Afrikareise* was financed by American Jerome Hill). Similarly, the visits to Europe and elsewhere by P. Adams Sitney and others who presented American work to new audiences instigated new developments in independent filmmaking wherever the American filmmakers' work was seen. Taka Iimura, who spent time in the United States in the late 1960s, made film portraits of Brakhage, Jonas Mekas, Jack Smith, Stan Vanderbeek, Warhol, and himself – and subsequently became an important contributor to structural film, with *Models* (1972) and *1 to 60 Seconds* (1973). This interplay between the United States, Canada, Europe, Japan, and other nations has continued in more recent decades. One of the fictions of a history such as this one is that we can separate artistic approaches or movements along lines of national history and identity. The (relatively few) mentions of non-American filmmakers in the following pages must be understood as clues to what is, in fact, a far more complex set of historical/geographical relationships.

New Feminisms

What came to be understood as a new kind of feminist cinema during the 1970s not only resisted the depictions of women that had become common in commercial cinema during the 1960s – depictions in which women were increasingly exposed and their sensuality and sexuality exploited – but refused those 1960s avant-garde feminist strategies that seemed to echo commercial exploitation. During the 1960s cinematic feminism had rebelled against the sexual repression so characteristic of middle- and upper middle-class American society during the 1950s and early 1960s.

In Bruce Conner's *Breakaway* (1966), for example, Antonia Christina Basilotta (Tony Basil) dances erotically to her song "Breakaway" – breaking away from the idea that women's sensuality need be controlled; and Carolee Schneemann's openly erotic *Fuses* (1967) bravely exposed her lovemaking with partner James Tenney. During the early 1970s, some women filmmakers were providing feminist critiques of this kind of erotic self-exposure – and of course, the sexual exposure of women increasingly evident within the burgeoning hard-core porn industry. Gunvor Nelson's *Take Off* (1972), during which a stripper not only removes her clothing but also her hair, arms, legs, and breasts, provides a *reductio ad absurdum* of the striptease (and of all forms of female "striptease" in commercial cinema), as does Anne Severson's *Near the Big Chakra* (1972): Severson presents a series of silent close-up images of the vulvas of women of various ages, as if to say, "Is this what you desire to see? – take a good look!" Some of the earlier spirit of liberating female sexuality remained evident, however, in Chick Strand's *Soft Fiction* (1978).

The feminist cinema that made the greatest impact on the 1970s and 1980s, however, especially within American academe, took an entirely different approach. By the late 1970s, representing women as erotic objects of what Laura Mulvey had defined in 1975 as "the male gaze" in "Visual Pleasure and Narrative Cinema," the most widely reprinted and influential theoretical essay of the era (Mulvey 1989), had come to seem out of bounds for progressive cinema, including progressive avant-garde cinema. Mulvey's own film, *Riddles of the Sphinx* (1977), co-created with Peter Wollen, provided a remarkable (and, by the twenty-first century, remarkably underappreciated) demonstration of the ideas in her canonical essay: In *Riddles* women are represented as workers, as intellectuals, as people coming to grips with the realities of class, and absolutely not as erotic objects. *Riddles of the Sphinx* was a British film, but it found a considerable American audience, especially in colleges and universities, and had an impact on many filmmakers, both women and men.

The most important woman filmmaker to emerge from the 1970s, however, was American dancer/choreographer-turned-filmmaker, Yvonne Rainer. Her austere, feature-length melodramas (*Lives of Performers*, 1972; *Film about a Woman Who*..., 1974; *Kristina Talking Pictures*, 1976; *Journeys from Berlin/1971*, 1980) avoided virtually all conventional forms of erotic sensuality, and especially sensuality that could be seen to denigrate women. While both Mulvey and Rainer can be understood as rebelling against male-dominated cinema in all its aspects, including the male-dominated formalism of structural film, both rebelled in part by incorporating dimensions of structural film within an entirely new gender-political context. The organization of *Riddles of the Sphinx* is as rigorously formal as the organization of any structural film; and both Mulvey and Rainer demand just the kind of patience on the part of audiences that the canonical structural films demand: Here too, audiences are asked to focus for extended durations on dimensions of the cinematic apparatus, but in this case, not on the chemistry or mechanics of the apparatus, but on the ways in which the apparatus tends to reflect the larger society's assumptions about women.

Some feminists rebelled not only against the erotic exploitation of women, but against all forms of sensual self-indulgence and self-expression that had characterized so much of the avant-garde cinema of the 1950s and 1960s, including the pursuit of beautiful imagery of any kind and the fetishizing of craft. This rigorously non-sensual attitude was increasingly evident in Rainer's films (especially once Babette Mangolte ceased to be her cinematographer after *Film about a Woman Who*...), and in films by others struggling with sexual politics: for example, in the widely discussed, gender-collaborative *Sigmund Freud's Dora* (1979), made by McCall and Tyndall, with Claire Pajaczkowska and Jane Weinstock. Even James Benning, who had become identified with structural film, contributed to this new sensibility: his *American Dreams* (1984) reveals parallels between Hank Aaron's quest to surpass Babe Ruth's home run record, Arthur Bremer's quest to assassinate a president, and Benning's own obsession with rigorous structure – confirming the filmmaker's awareness of the problematic ways in which men function in contemporary society. The increasing elimination of traditional forms of cinematic sensuality in favor of an engagement with political ideology resulted in what Mulvey was to call "scorched earth" cinema (MacDonald 1992, 334), and by the early 1980s in a new kind of rebellion, led by two disparate figures: Su Friedrich and Trinh T. Minh-ha.

For Friedrich, whose feminist credentials were developed in part through her work on the feminist art journal *Heresies*, the idea that feminist cinema must rigorously avoid sensuality came to seem fundamentally counterproductive: it unwittingly reconfirmed the idea that women were defined by lack. Having made short "scorched earth" films in the late 1970s, Friedrich began to change her direction with *Gently Down the Stream* (1982), a short psychodrama made up of a set of troubling dream narratives (mostly having to do with the struggle between her Roman Catholic upbringing and her lesbianism) presented as visual texts in which Friedrich paid particular attention to the sensual dimensions of the presentation: chiaroscuro, texture, and the poetic timing of the texts. Five years later, in *Damned If You Don't* (1987), Friedrich declared her independence from puritan film feminism: If the choice was between a sensual cinema that sometimes pleased men and an utterly non-sensual cinema – if one was "damned" either way – a feminist filmmaker must choose the former. Friedrich's exquisite handling of black-and-white cinematography, her painstaking editing, and a finale during which a woman undresses the nun she has been pursuing romantically and the two make love provided her answer to scorched earth feminist cinema, and offered any number of younger feminist filmmakers a new alternative. In *Sink or Swim* (1992) Friedrich's focus was her troubled relationship with her father – before, during, and after his divorce from her mother. It is clear in the film that Friedrich's development as a filmmaker, and in particular her abilities as a cinematographer and an editor, have been her means of coming to terms with her father's absence and with the ways in which, present and absent, he has undermined her self-esteem.

Trinh T. Minh-ha brought a multicultural perspective to cine-feminism. A Vietnamese immigrant, Trinh declared her independence from the male-dominated tradition of ethnographic documentary in particular and male-dominated cinema in general, first in *Reassemblage* (1982), and subsequently in the series of films that followed, including *Naked Spaces – Living Is Round* (1985) and *Surname Viêt Given Name Nam* (1989). *Reassemblage* is a 40-minute sound-image montage on the theme of Senegal, focusing particularly on the everyday activities of women. The film pretends to no particular expertise, draws no totalizing conclusions, and while its imagery of Senegal is sensuous and engaging, the film uses a variety of tactics that undermine a conventional, male, exoticizing gaze. Trinh's use of a hand-held camera, for example, can be read as a response to the gestural, self-expressive camerawork so characteristic of early Stan Brakhage: She seems at pains to avoid drawing attention either to her personal feelings about what she sees or to her "understanding" of the culture she is visiting.

Other responses to "scorched earth" feminist cinema included Lizzie Borden's *Born in Flames* (1983), which provided a politicized, intellectualized action-adventure entertainment (reminiscent of Jean-Luc Godard) in which an America in the throes of revolution saw radical feminists crossing racial lines to join other rebels; and *Working Girls* (1986), a narrative focusing on several call girls for whom prostitution is necessary labor, which was sensual without being conventionally exploitive (the male tricks are as fully exposed in *Working Girls* as the women who service them). Abigail Child's *Mutiny* (1983) and *Mayhem* (1987), and Peggy Ahwesh's *The Deadman* (1990, co-made with Keith Sanborn) were also instances of a new, more sensual feminist cinema.

In more recent years this return to a progressive, feminist sensuality has been confirmed by a younger generation of filmmakers, including Jennifer Todd Reeves and Shirin Neshat, who was studying in the United States at the time of the Islamic revolution in Iran and has remained here. Reeves's *Chronic* (1996) reveals the effects of a gang-rape at a fraternity party on its young protagonist and the slow healing that results in the carefully crafted film we see. Neshat's frustration with the repression of women in her native land, as well as her personal isolation in America, are expressed in her photographs and in her films and installations, including *Turbulent* (1998), *Rapture* (1999), *Fervor* (2000), *Soliloquy* (1999), and *Passage* (2001). Gina Kim, a Korean national who studied at CalArts and now lives in the United States, finished *Gina Kim's Video Diary* in 2002; the long, intimate video charts the filmmaker's gradual coming to terms with her body and its desires.

Ethnic Cinemas

The 1970s and 1980s saw a developing interest in, on one hand, cinema that was produced by filmmakers from particular, underserved ethnic communities, often rebelling against conventional representations of these communities; and on the other hand, new forms of cinema produced by filmmakers interested in working across conventional ethnic (linguistic, cultural, and political) boundaries toward a global consciousness that was respectful of difference. While on one level, the films that represent these two tendencies can seem quite different, they are best understood as two aspects of a single quest.

As cinema studies became ensconced in American academe, a set of particular approaches to film history became conventional, in large measure as a means of organizing college courses. In some instances, the practical need to delimit subjects of study caused rifts between otherwise closely related cultural projects. For example, avant-garde film and African-American film have usually been understood as distinct histories, despite their commonalities: Both avant-garde filmmakers and African-American independents have seen commercial cinema and television as at best mixed blessings that have consistently distorted and obscured social reality in the name of the status quo, have generally reduced human beings to mindless consumers, and have stifled many forms of resistance and creativity. Both cultural projects have evolved as counter-cinemas to these tendencies and both have explored a range of alternatives to the mass media with generally limited means. Nevertheless, the histories of African-American cinema have generally ignored avant-garde work, assuming that avant-garde filmmakers are committed to art for art's sake, and chroniclers of avant-garde film have often ignored even those films produced by African-Americans that are obviously relevant for avant-garde history.

This still widespread tendency became increasingly problematic during the 1990s once scholars began to realize that the "race filmmaker" Oscar Micheaux (who produced a considerable body of independent films from the 1920s through the 1940s) might be considered experimental in ways that relate to filmmakers identified with the avant-garde; and once William Greaves's *Symbiopsychotaxiplasm: Take One* was rediscovered. Greaves's feature, shot in 1968 and finished in a first version in 1972, is increasingly understood as a major contribution to the American avant-garde; it can even be classified as a structural film, in the sense that it explores the fundamentally collaborative dimension of filmmaking in a manner analogous to the way in which other structural films explore other dimensions of the cinematic apparatus.

The late 1970s and early 1980s were a heyday for the production of independently produced, often experimental forms of narrative focusing on African-Americans. In the wake of Melvin Van Peebles's influential *Sweet Sweetback's Baadasssss Song* (1971), the University of California at Los Angeles (UCLA) became home to the "L.A. Rebellion," a group of young, independent filmmakers working with very limited financial resources, who used neorealist tactics to reveal dimensions of contemporary black life in Los Angeles. Landmark films include Haile Gerima's *Bush Mama* (1975), Charles Burnett's *Killer of Sheep* (1977), Billy Woodberry's *Bless Their Little Hearts* (1984), and Julie Dash's *Illusions* (1982; Dash's best-known film, *Daughters of the Dust*, 1991, is an experimental narrative feature about black life on the Sea Islands off the Atlantic coast at the turn of the last century). From a later vantage point, it seems clear that many of these films could have been understood under the rubric of what an influential special issue of *October* (no. 17; Summer, 1981) called "The New Talkies" – the issue focused on Michael Snow, Yvonne Rainer, Hollis Frampton, and video artist Martha Rosler, avant-garde makers who were incorporating sound into new forms of narrative – that is, as rebellions against more than one form of "silence."

Figure 15.1 Director and producer William Greaves in *Symbiopsychotaxiplasm: Take One* (1972). (Courtesy William Greaves.)

During recent decades, African-Americans working independently have contributed a variety of films and videos to the American avant-garde. Marlon Riggs's *Tongues Untied* (1989) has much in common with Su Friedrich's *Damned If You Don't* in its confrontation of the repression of gay experience and identity (in this instance, black male gay experience and identity) within American culture and American cinema; and in its use of a composite form that mixes narrative, document, and performance to confront the homogeneity of commercial genres. Zeinabu irene Davis's *Cycles* (1989) is closely related to the psychodrama: It explores the rituals a young woman performs in honoring her monthly cycles. Cauleen Smith's *Chronicles of a Lying Spirit (by Kelly Gabron)* (1992) is a brief personal chronicle that explores the mediation of history by film, television, and the print media. During the 2000s, Tony Cokes, who established himself with *Fade to Black* (1990), an experimental documentary on the depiction of African-Americans in American cinema, has produced a considerable body of what he calls "Evil" videos: short, highly formal pieces that use visual text to engage various dimensions of contemporary social and political reality; and Kevin Jerome Everson has produced a series of lovely portraits of everyday people and activities, including *Undefeated* (2008) and *Ninety-Three* (2008).

The histories of Asian-American cinema and what Chon Noriega has called "Chicano Cinema" (Noriega & Lopé 1996) were developing alongside African-American cinema during the 1980s and 1990s and bear much the same relation to the American avant-garde. The UCLA Ethno-Communications program, which was instrumental in instigating the "L.A. Rebellion," provided impetus to new Asian-American cinema as well. Several veterans of the Ethno-Communications program established Visual Communications in 1970, with the goal of supporting filmmaking that was more respectful of Asian-American history and culture, and had a hand in producing a wide range of films. Wayne Wang's neorealist experimental narrative *Chan Is Missing* (1982) was a breakthrough for West Coast Asian-American cinema. Widely seen, it gave notice that Asian-Americans were also rebelling against conventional cinema and its often laughable depictions of Asian-Americans ("Chan," of course, refers to Charlie Chan).

During the 1980s Christine Choy, who got her start working with Third World Newsreel during the 1970s, was involved in a series of experimental documentaries, including *Mississippi Triangle* (1984), made as an interethnic collaboration with Allan Siegel and Worth Long, focusing on the intersections of multiple ethnicities in the Louisiana Delta; and *Who Killed Vincent Chin?* (1988, co-made with Renee Tajima), an exploration of the murder of a Chinese-American by several Detroit men who assumed he was Japanese and thus part of the Japanese auto industry. Also of note are *Yellow Tale Blues* (1990), co-made with Tajima, a personal documentary about Choy's immigrant Chinese/Korean-American family and Tajima's native Japanese-American family, and Choy's experimental evocation of artist Barbara Takanga, *Five Chapters* (1992). Tajima (now Tajima-Peña) has continued to make films, including more recently *Calavera Highway* (2008), an engaging road movie chronicling the journey taken by her Chicano husband and his brother into their past along the Texas-Mexico border and into the complexities of ethnicity.

A topic of particular interest to Japanese-American filmmakers during the 1990s was the internment of Japanese-Americans during World War II. In 1991, Rea Tajiri finished her experimental documentary *History and Memory*, which focuses on four generations of her family and the ways in which the internment of her grandmother and her mother (her father was in the American military!) has affected both older and younger generations. In 1994, Robert A. Nakamura, a veteran of Visual Communications, finished *Something Strong Within*, a film about Japanese-Americans in American internment camps during World War II, constructed entirely from home movies made by the prisoners in those camps.

The 1970s and 1980s also saw a variety of experimental films and videos produced by Mexican-Americans and Puerto Rican-Americans. Significant figures include four teenagers from East LA – Harry Gamboa Jr, Gronk, Willie Herrón, and Patssi Valdez – who called themselves Asco (Spanish for "nausea") and in 1973 initiated *No-Movies*, a series of performance pieces and other public art actions that functioned as Dada responses to the exclusion of Chicanos from mainstream filmmaking and even from established avant-garde film venues. On the East Coast, Puerto Rican-Americans were also making contributions, including video artist Edin Vélez (*Meta Mayan II*, 1981), Diego Echeverria (*Los Sures*, 1984), and Raphael Montañez Ortiz, a New Yorker of mixed heritage who has worked in a variety of ways since the late 1950s. During the 1980s and 1990s Ortiz produced a considerable body of what he called "digital/laser/videos," in which he deconstructed and reconstructed moments from commercial cinema that he felt embodied societal repression and oppression (more detail on the digital/laser/videos later).

The interest in transnational cinema that was developing during this same period was a macrocosmic version of the same quest that was energizing the development of the ethnic cinemas: the production of cinematic alternatives to contemporary definitions of community that serve the interests of parochial nationalism and unbridled capitalism. During the 1970s and 1980s a number of filmmakers worked at creating transnational cinematic forms, films in which a single cut might move viewers not simply from one action to the next, but across national, ethnic, and linguistic boundaries. While the ethnic cinemas focused primarily on narrative, on telling a different set of stories in inventive ways, the transnational films focused primarily on montage, attempting to model a global consciousness within films that, to borrow the title of an Alan Berliner film, take us "everywhere at once."

Filmmakers who made a commitment to a more global sense of cinema include Warren Sonbert, in *The Carriage Trade* (1973) and the series of montage films that followed; Yvonne Rainer, in *Journeys from Berlin/1971* (1979); Trinh T. Minh-ha, in *Naked Spaces – Living Is Round* (1985) and *Surname Viêt Given Name Nam* (1989); Godfrey Reggio, in *Powaqqatsi* (1988); and Ron Fricke, in *Baraka* (1992). The most ambitious of these transnational films was Peter Watkins's *The Journey* (1987), a $14^1/_2$-hour critique of media representation, shot in 11 nations with community groups from each location, using funding raised by those groups. The ways in which ethnicity functions politically was a major theme in *The Journey*, especially in the American episodes shot in central New York State (*The Journey* was shot in three American locations), where the Mohawk Valley support group for the film psychodramatized some of the implications of race for civil defense planning.

New Engagements with the Personal

A third avant-garde tendency with a political edge that became important during the 1970s involved a redirection of the idea of personal cinema. Of course, the 1940s psychodramas were often personally revelatory in ways that had political implications (Kenneth Anger's *Fireworks*, 1947, can serve as a case in point); and Carolee Schneemann's focus on her sex life in *Fuses* (1967) and on her quotidian life with Anthony McCall in *Kitch's Last Meal* (in various two-screen versions, 1973–1978) certainly had political dimensions. But by the early 1970s new kinds of politically inflected personal films were being produced. In his *Reminiscences of a Journey to Lithuania* (1972) and *Lost Lost Lost* (1976) Jonas Mekas reworked footage shot during earlier decades into explorations of the ways in which his life was transformed first by the Nazis, then after World War II by the Soviet takeover of Lithuania, and how Mekas found a new, aesthetic community of artists and played an increasing role in the political and art-political realities of American life during the 1960s and 1970s. Robert Huot, who had established himself as a painter while becoming increasingly frustrated with the hypercommercial, apolitical aspects of the New York art world, dropped out after "disappearing" more and more fully as a minimalist and conceptualist painter, moving to central New York State where he produced a series of diary paintings and diary films – *One Year (1970)* (1971), *Rolls: 1971* (1972), *Third One-Year Movie – 1972* (1973), *Diary 1974–75* (1975), *Super-8 Diary 1979* (1980) – that revealed the filmmaker's attempt to reconstruct a personal and social life during a time of political turmoil.

By the 1980s several younger filmmakers were exploring new approaches to the personal. In *The Ties that Bind* (1984), Su Friedrich confronted her mother about her experiences growing up in Germany during the rise of Nazism and, after World War II, marrying an American and moving to the United States. Friedrich reveals the ties that bind her mother's experiences with the filmmaker's own attempts to play an active role in resisting the arms buildup of the Cold War. In both *The Ties That Bind* and in its companion piece, *Sink or Swim*, Friedrich's intricate and subtle editing of sound and image provides order within the chaos of international and familial politics. Alan Berliner confirmed Friedrich's exploration of family history within the political and gender-political realities that inform it, in a pair of films that, like Friedrich's, focus on his maternal family history (*Intimate Stranger*, 1991) and on his relationship with his father (*Nobody's Business*, 1996). In Berliner's films, as in Friedrich's, exquisite craftsmanship functions as an emblem of the filmmaker's attempt to maintain coherence and equilibrium within the complex changes wrought within individual families by both personal and sociopolitical developments.

The use of personal history as a means of reflecting and engaging current political and social issues was also a focus in Jill Godmilow's *Far from Poland* (1984), which was inspired by the filmmaker's inability to get permission to travel to Poland to document the workers' revolution and resulted in an exploration of the interplay between her personal relationships and her political sensibilities. And *Privilege* (1990), Yvonne Rainer's deflected autobiographical film about her years as a young dancer/choreographer in New York, reveals and explores Rainer's early struggles with issues of race, gender, and class within the context of her more recent struggles with aging and the onslaught of menopause. In *Privilege* filmmaking becomes a kind of utopia, a way of modeling progressive politics.

That Godmilow's films and Berliner's are usually categorized as documentaries reveals what has become an interesting convergence of two histories traditionally thought to be distinct. As is true of the canonical 1920s "city symphonies," which are claimed by both avant-garde and documentary history, the personal avant-garde films by Mekas, Huot, Friedrich, Berliner, and Gina Kim seem quite close in spirit, and sometimes in formal ways, to that branch of documentary history known as the "personal documentary": the autobiographical films of Ed Pincus (*Diaries*, 1980), Alfred Guzzetti (*Family Portrait Sittings*, 1975), Camille Billops and James Hatch (*Finding Christa*, 1991), Ross McElwee (*Backyard*, 1984; *Sherman's March…*, 1986; *Time Indefinite*, 1993), Robb Moss (*The Same River Twice*, 2004), and Nina Davenport (*Operation Filmmaker*, 2007).

This intersection of avant-garde film and documentary is also evident in Todd Haynes's *Superstar: The Karen Carpenter Story* (1987) and Jonathan Caouette's *Tarnation* (2003). *Superstar* is a documentary of Karen Carpenter's life as a singer and her succumbing to the anorexia and bulimia that led to her death. It uses Barbie dolls as characters, mixing a range of approaches similar to *Damned If You Don't* and *Tongues Untied*; and it is structured in a manner reminiscent of Bruce Conner's films and of Anger's *Scorpio Rising* (1964) – that is, popular songs become the ground against which Haynes figures the activities of Carpenter and her family. Refused exhibition by the standard avant-garde sites during the 1980s (and under threat of suit from the music and toy industries), it found a home in clubs, especially gay clubs, and within the underground circulation of videotapes. *Tarnation* is the horror film of personal documentary (Caouette grew up within a dysfunctional environment – his mother received many shock treatments and suffered extended institutionalization, and he himself was abused in foster homes), but reveals the considerable influence of low-budget horror films, trash cinema (John Waters in particular), and avant-garde forms of editing. Like *Superstar*, it uses popular songs, in the Conner manner, to structure particular periods of Caouette's early life. Both Haynes and Caouette were influenced by avant-garde cinema from an early age, and both *Superstar* and *Tarnation* are sexually political in the sense that they implicitly/explicitly reveal the ways in which gay identity is suppressed and released by various forms of family trauma and social pressure. In the films that followed *Superstar*, Haynes often evoked the avant-garde filmmakers who were crucial in his own development – Conner, Jean Genet, Jack Smith, Kenneth Anger, Leslie Thornton – and his commercial feature *I'm Not There* (2007) uses avant-garde strategies to question the nature of identity itself.

Recycled Cinema

By the final quarter of the twentieth century, working with found footage had developed a long tradition. Esfir Shub had pioneered the reuse and recontextualization of previously shot footage in *The Fall of the Romanov Dynasty* (1929); in 1936 Joseph Cornell reedited a Hollywood feature into *Rose Hobart*; and Bruce Conner and Raphael Montañez Ortiz were experimenting with new ways of working with found materials during the late 1950s (Conner in *A Movie*, 1958; Ortiz, in *Cowboy and "Indian" Film* and *Newsreel*, both 1958). But as film history continued to accumulate and access to it developed, an interest not simply in avoiding commercial approaches to cinema, but in literally confronting these approaches and their material manifestations became increasingly common. During the 1970s and 1980s, Conner continued to refine his approach of reediting found materials into inventive montages that could speak in quite complex ways. *Take the 5:10 to Dreamland* (1976), *Valse Triste* (1977), *Mongoloid* (1978), *America Is Waiting* (1981), and *Mea Culpa* (1981) number among Conner's finest works.

In 1969, while teaching at Binghamton University (then Harpur College and subsequently the State University of New York at Binghamton), Ken Jacobs used re-photography to develop an epic investigation of the textures, the chiaroscuro, the tiny gestures evident in the original *Tom, Tom, the Piper's Son,* produced by Biograph in 1906, and transformed the results into his own *Tom, Tom, the Piper's Son.* During the following decades, Jacobs invented a variety of new ways of recycling artifacts from earlier eras of cinema in his many "Nervous System" pieces: performances produced with projection devices Jacobs designed. These devices made possible a variety of effects, including in some cases, a kind of pulsating 3-D. Among the most memorable of the Nervous System works are *XCXHXEXRXRXIXEXSX* ("Cherries," in various versions since 1980), which recycles a bit of French pornography; *TWO WRENCHING DEPARTURES* (in various versions since 1989), which commemorates the deaths of two early Jacobs collaborators: Jack Smith and Bob Fleischner; and *THE MARRIAGE OF HEAVEN AND HELL (A FLICKER OF LIFE)* (various versions since 1995). Jacobs's switch to digital image-making in the 2000s unleashed a remarkable creative effusion that lasted through the first decade of the millennium, producing a range of works employing recycled material, including *Celestial Subway Lines/Salvaging Noise* (2005, a collaboration with John Zorn), *New York Ghetto Fish Market 1903* (2006), *Razzle Dazzle (The Lost World)* (2007), *Nymph* (2007), and *Capitalism: Slavery* (2007) – these last two, short digital works that recycle nineteenth-century stereopticon photographs.

The influence of Jacobs and *Tom, Tom, the Piper's Son* was evident during the late 1970s and early 1980s in the work of students who had studied with him at Binghamton University in the early 1970s. Alan Berliner produced a series of short found-footage films, including *City Edition* (1980) and *Everywhere at Once* (1985), and then a feature, *The Family Album* (1986), which recycles 16mm home movies made by Americans during the previous generation into a vision of American family life that reveals both the idealization of the family (in the visuals) and the sad realities that underlay this idealization (in family members' comments on the soundtrack). Berliner has continued to use recycling as a central filmmaking tactic. Phil Solomon's films have involved a reworking of recycled materials using the optical printer. His *The Secret Garden* (1988), *The Exquisite Hour* (Super-8mm version, 1989; 16mm version, 1994), *Remains to Be Seen* (Super-8mm version, 1989; 16mm version, 1994), *Clepsydra* (1992), and the series of "Twilight Psalms," including *Walking Distance* (1999), *Night of the Meek* (2002), and *The Lateness of the Hour* (2003), are mysterious and beautiful evocations of loss and the fear of mortality – both human mortality and the mortality of cinema itself.

Two very different approaches to recycling are evident in the work of Morgan Fisher and Abigail Child. In *Standard Gauge* (1984) Fisher presents a series of 35mm artifacts he collected during his years of working in and around the Hollywood industry, in a continuous, 35-minute 16mm shot (his subtle way of using an avant-garde film gauge to critique the industry and the limitations of 35mm "standard gauge"). Fisher describes the experiences that resulted in his acquiring these particular artifacts with dry humor, revealing the aesthetic and political implications of the filmstrips and of the usually invisible markings on the filmstrips that reveal contributions to commercial cinema that are normally repressed. In his *( )* (2003) Fisher transforms inserts from Hollywood films (images that are necessary to clarify narrative storytelling, but have no other function) into the central focus of a film: "I wanted to make a film out of nothing but inserts … to release them from their self-effacing performance of drudge-work, to free them from their servitude to story" (Fisher's program notes). In her *Prefaces* (1981) and in *Covert Action* (1984), which uses home movie material from one of the collections that Berliner used in *The Family Album* and *Mercy* (1989), and in parts 3, 4, and 7 respectively of her seven-part exploration of cinematic sound-image relationships, *Is This What You Were Born For?*, as well as in such recent films as *Surface Noise* (2000), Child creates intricate, complex, high-speed, sound-image montages that subtly and obliquely express her engagement with current sociopolitical realities, while providing challenges to the viewer's perceptual and conceptual abilities.

The 1980s also saw several attempts to rework and explore the implications of quintessential moments from Hollywood films. Some of the first of these to come to the attention of American avant-garde audiences came from Europe: most obviously, the Austrian Martin Arnold's *pièce touchée* (1989) and *passage à l'acte* (1993), both of which deconstructed and reconstructed typical Hollywood moments – a husband coming home to his waiting wife, a family around the dinner table – in ways that were witty and insightful. But other filmmakers had preceded Arnold in this kind of work. In 1985, Raphael Montañez Ortiz began his extensive series of "digital/laser/videos." Using an Apple computer, along with a Deltalab Effectron II sound effects generator, Ortiz would choose a moment from a commercial film that he felt encapsulated a societal problem (racism, sexism, the subtle brutalities of class) and then, having carefully studied this moment, he would "shred" and refashion it in an attempt to exorcize the problematic elements. For 10 years Ortiz worked with this method in a variety of ways, producing dozens of videos, including *The Kiss* (1985), *My Father's Dead* (1991), *The Briefcase* (1992), *The Drowning* (1992), *The Critic* (1996), and *The Conversation* (1996). Far less aggressive than either Arnold or Ortiz, Chuck Workman, who studied film history with Amos Vogel in New York before moving to Los Angeles, has become widely known for recycling moments from Hollywood films in *Precious Images* (produced for the Directors Guild of America in 1986) and *Pieces of Silver* (produced for Eastman Kodak in 1989), and in the many montages he has created for the annual Academy Awards shows.

A very different approach to found-footage film represents another crossover between documentary history and avant-garde history: the recycling of earlier film artifacts, particularly artifacts made as American government propaganda or for other government purposes, into critiques of the government and its policies. Erik Barnouw's recycling of suppressed government footage of the aftermath of the bombings of Hiroshima and Nagasaki, in *Hiroshima-Nagasaki August 1945* (1970) is an important early instance, as is Bruce Conner's *Crossroads* (1976), which recycles American government documentation of the Crossroads nuclear testing at Bikini Atoll in the summer of 1946. In their landmark compilation documentary, *The Atomic Café* (1982), Kevin Rafferty, Jayne Loader, and Pierce Rafferty use government propaganda and "educational" films from the 1940s and 1950s to reveal the construction of American paranoia during the Cold War; and, more recently, San Franciscan Craig Baldwin has found a variety of ways to rework many forms of found materials in surreal satires and burlesques of American historical and political realities, in such films as *Tribulation 99: Alien Anomalies under America* (1991), *¡Oh No, Coronado!* (1992), and *Spectres of the Spectrum* (2000).

A variety of other approaches to cinematic recycling have been evident in recent decades. Some filmmakers have been fascinated not simply with the filmic past, but with the process of decay that often transforms the original cinematic artifacts. The pioneers in working with filmic decay include the Italians Yervant Gianikian and Angela Ricci Lucchi (*From the Pole to the Equator*, 1987) and the Dutch filmmaker Peter Delpeut (*Lyrical Nitrate*, 1991). But several Americans have made contributions to this approach, including Peggy Ahwesh in *The Color of Love* (1994) and Bill Morrison, most notably in *Decasia* (2002). Pornographic film artifacts have also been explored, not only by Jacobs in *XCXHXEXRXRXIXEXSX*, but by Scott Stark and Naomi Uman. Stark's *NOEMA* (1998) recycles only those moments from a modern porn film during which the sexual partners are changing positions; the result is both surreal and poignant. Naomi Uman used nail polish and bleach to remove the women's bodies from a passage of 1970s European porn, in *Removed* (1999).

Finally, during recent decades some filmmakers have recycled their own earlier material into new work. A notable instance is the late Warren Sonbert's *Friendly Witness* (1989) for which the filmmaker, who had foresworn sound for two decades, returned to sound (pop songs and Gluck's overture to *Iphigénie en Aulide*) and to his own personal film archives to fashion a remarkable montage celebrating the panoply of life he saw around him as he traveled the world. In 1996, Bruce Conner returned to his 1960s film, *Looking for Mushrooms*, refashioning it into a new, longer form. And in 2004, Ken Jacobs released a new (DVD) version of his epic, *Star Spangled to Death*, shown in various versions from 1956 until 1960; the new version includes a wide variety of cinematic artifacts, from the complete Nixon "Checkers speech" to the spectacular and spectacularly racist "Going to Heaven on a Mule" number from Busby Berkeley's *Wonder Bar* (1934) and passages from Oscar Micheaux's *Ten Minutes to Live* (1932). *Tom, Tom, the Piper's Son* has recently been reworked digitally and released on DVD, as have a number of the Nervous System works.

Home-Made Cinema and the Microcinema Movement

In an influential essay published in the winter, 1989–1990 issue of the short-lived *Motion Picture*, Tom Gunning suggested that the generation of filmmakers coming of age in the 1980s represented "a minor cinema," adapting the term "minor literature" from Gilles Deleuze and Félix Guattari's *Kafka: Towards a Minor Literature* ("There is nothing that is major or revolutionary except the minor. To hate all languages of masters"). For Gunning, the films of Nina Fonoroff, Peter Herwitz, Peggy Ahwesh, Mark Lapore, Louis Klahr, and Phil Solomon asserted "no vision of conquest, make no claims to hegemony"; these filmmakers "proudly wear the badge of the ghetto," in the sense that they "recognize their marginal position outside the major cinematic languages" (1989–1990, 2). This essay was the most articulate response to what was seen by some as the pretentiousness of the International Experimental Film Congress that had been held in Toronto in the late spring of 1989, and its focus on older masters of avant-garde film. Gunning's insight was prescient of the generation of filmmakers that came of age at the end of the century, and can be seen as representing another tendency that has become pervasive.

While the filmmakers Gunning listed in his essay may have agreed with Solomon in feeling "alienated from the whole avant-garde filmmaker rock-star road show," which seemed a new version of "the whole tradition of the Cedar Bar macho artist" (Solomon 2005, 203), it was a still younger set of filmmakers who would most fully exemplify Gunning's minor cinema, making a commitment to work, insofar as possible, not only outside of the commercial industry, but away from the world of art museums and established avant-garde film venues. Many of these filmmakers returned to the idea of a hand-crafted cinema, often working directly on the filmstrip, learning to hand-process their own footage and to welcome the accidental inscription of their home-made processes into their work.

Important influences on this new tendency included filmmaker Saul Levine, working out of the Massachusetts College of Art, and the Canadian Phil Hoffman's "Film Farm," a week-long summer workshop for independent filmmakers established in 1994. Levine's engaged, informal teaching, his commitment to handcrafted cinema, and his own films inspired a number of filmmakers, including the obsessive diarist Anne Charlotte Robertson, whose Super-8mm films, and especially her on-going *Diary*, became a way of dealing with sexism, issues of the body, and her own struggles with bipolar syndrome. In 1988, *Diary*, then 40 hours long, was presented at the Museum of the Moving Image in New York, not only with Robertson in attendance providing in-person narration, but within a set that recreated Robertson's bedroom at her home in Framingham, Massachusetts. David Gatten has described his experience of Hoffman's Film Farm:

> I was expecting a film studio and was really surprised to arrive at a farmhouse and a barn, where there were ten Bolexes, ten tripods, ten light meters, some chickens, some cows …
>
> We learned to process the film ourselves and this was certainly not the pristine lab environment that I had been taught to expect, where your film is processed very carefully, transferred to video, and sent back to you as a videotape – so that you never touch the film, because if you touch the film, you could damage it: you always needed to have an untouched back-up negative at the lab. What we were doing at the farm was shooting the six rolls and processing them ourselves in buckets and spraying the film with a garden hose. In the process the film might fall on the rough floor and you might step on it; the dog might come over and chew on it. And we projected the original. (2009, 203–204)

The Film Farm nurtured young filmmakers committed to working on and with celluloid, and the resulting films were exhibited by a developing network of "microcinemas," small, intimate screening venues spread across North America.

This younger generation of filmmakers includes Jennifer Todd Reeves, who has done psychodramatic narratives (*Chronic*, for example, and *The Time We Killed*, 2004); a series of impressive hand-painted films, including *The Girl's Nervy* (1995) and *Fear of Blushing* (2001); and more recently live performances mixed with projected film (*When It Was Blue*, for example, performed since 2008). David Gatten established himself with *Hardwood Process* (1996) and *What the Water Said, 1–3* (1998), both made by working directly on the filmstrip, and has devoted himself to his *Secret Life of the Dividing Line* project, a projected nine-film suite, often using hand-crafted processes of his own invention. As of 2010 the *Secret Life* project included *Moxon's Mechanick Exercises, or the Doctrine of Handy-works Applied to the Art of Printing* (1999); *The Enjoyment of Reading, Lost and Found* (2001); the title film, *Secret History of the Dividing Line* (2002); and *The Great Art of Knowing* (2004). All four films relate in a variety of direct and oblique ways to the life of William Byrd II of colonial Virginia, who founded the city of Richmond, led the surveying party that drew the original boundary (the "dividing line") between Virginia and North Carolina, wrote *History of the Dividing Line* – one of the first detailed descriptions of American nature – and assembled one of the two largest libraries in colonial North America. Gatten's *Secret History* project asks viewers to engage with his ongoing research into the history of the Byrd family and its implications for the present, and with his various ways of "researching" the material bases of cinema.

Another accomplished filmmaker identified with this hand-crafted tendency is Lawrence Brose. In *De Profundis* (1997) Brose uses formal manipulations of both photographed and recycled gay porn imagery as a means to an overtly sexually political end: a new sense of gay rights that does not involve the suppression of "queerness." For Brose, the direct manipulation of the filmstrip formally *materializes* the widespread fascination with drag. And there is Luther Price, who has produced a considerable body of work, often working directly on the filmstrip and combining cinema and performance; and Greta Snider – for *Flight* (1996) she used hand-processing and a rayogram technique to evoke her relationship with her deceased father; and the legendary Bay Area collaborative SILT (Jeff Warrin, Christian Farrell, Keith Evans), which became well known after 1990 for a variety of ingenious film processes and performances; and Jeanne Liotta – she calls her *Loretta* (2003) "a photogram opera"; and the performance artists Sandra Gibson and Luis Recoder who use 16mm loops, spray bottles, colored gels, unfocused lenses and hand-shadows to create, as Ed Halter (2008) has suggested, "slowly mutating light sculptures: morphing color fields, angel-white auras, fusing penumbrae, pulsing vertical lines ... ethereal experiences." Michelle Smith has produced a series of epic hand-crafted films (*Regarding Penelope's Wake*, 2002, for example) using what she describes as "frame-by-frame collage/montage/hand-painted/ripped/cut/etched found footage" (program notes).

Closely allied in spirit to the filmmakers committed to hand-crafting are informal documentary filmmakers like Matt McCormick, whose *The Subconscious Art of Graffiti Removal* (2001) reveals the unconscious "art form" created when another, conscious art form (graffiti) is erased; Naomi Uman, whose *Leche* (1998) and *Mala Leche* (1998) document the lives of a rural Mexican family with scratched, dyed, hand-processed imagery; and Bill Brown, whose *Roswell* (1994) and *The Other Side* (2006) depict American place in a personal, quirky manner reminiscent of George Kuchar's video work (indeed, Kuchar's Weather Diary series and his many video postcards represent one canonical filmmaker's psychic alliance with, and influence on, younger filmmakers who represent this sense of cinema). In 1996, McCormick was the founder of Peripheral Produce, which has become a distributor (on DVD) of the films of Bill Brown, Naomi Uman, Bryan Frye, and the late Helen Hill.

The history of the microcinema movement remains to be written, though some of its originators are clear. Using Bruce Baillie's community-oriented Canyon Cinema, established during the early 1960s, as inspiration, San Franciscans Rebecca Barton and David Sherman created Total Mobile Home, where the couple hosted filmmakers in their home, once a week from 1994 until 1997. Total Mobile Home, in turn, inspired other venues that ministered to small audiences of devoted cineastes, many of them located in private homes, some of them with a more public visibility. By the 1990s, these venues formed a nationwide network that included The Other Cinema, founded in 1987 by Craig Baldwin in the Mission District of San Francisco; Ocularis established by Dónal Ó Céilleachair in 1996 as a rooftop screening series in Williamsburg, Brooklyn (it offered programs until 2006); the Robert Beck Memorial Cinema in New York City (named for an American soldier in World War I who was struck deaf and dumb by shellshock and cured by seeing a film), founded by Bryan Frye on the Lower East Side of Manhattan in 1998 (the Robert Beck presented events regularly until 2002); the Aurora Picture Show, founded in 1998 in Houston, Texas, by Andrea Grover; and the Cinema Project in Portland, Oregon, established in 2003 by Autumn Campbell and Jeremy Rossen.

Perceptual Retraining

One final tendency that has been pervasive during the past 20 years has involved the use of the film experience to retrain and reinvigorate viewer perception of cinematic space and time, and in particular, the representation of place. While the filmmakers committed to hand-crafting and hand-processing constituted a rebellion against the commercial domination of film *production*, Peter Hutton, James Benning, Ernie Gehr, Nathaniel Dorsky, Warren Sonbert, Alfred Guzzetti, Sharon Lockhart, and the other filmmakers and videomakers who can be identified with this tendency have seen their work as a confrontation of conventional *reception*, a confrontation that has tended to take one of two rather different forms: a serialist/ minimalist direction epitomized by the films of Hutton, Benning, and Gehr; and a new approach to montage evident in the films of Sonbert, Dorsky, and Guzzetti.

Beginning in the early 1970s, Gehr, in *Still* (1971), Larry Gottheim, in his *Fog Line* (1971) and other single-shot films, in *Barn Rushes* (1971) and in *Horizons* (1973), Robert Huot, in *One Year (1970)* (1971), Peter Hutton, in *New York Near Sleep for Saskia* (1972), *Images of Asian Music (A Diary from Life)* (1974), and *Florence* (1975), and James Benning, in $8^1/_2 \times 11$ (1974), 11×14 (1976), and *One Way Boogie Woogie* (1977), reenergized the contemplative/meditative way of experiencing the cinematic representation of place pioneered by Austrian émigré Henwar Rodakiewicz in *Portrait of a Young Man* (1931), and by Rudy Burckhardt in a long series of films beginning in the 1940s. Using extended, continuous, often silent shots, filmed from a stationary or near-stationary camera, these filmmakers asked that viewers slow down and explore each image, not for clues to a narrative direction, but as extended moments-in-time that offered the possibility of renewed perceptual engagement and awareness.

The late 1970s and the 1980s saw several significant contributions to this tendency. Peter Hutton remained consistent in his approach to both landscape and cityscape in a series of short, black-and-white studies of New York City – *New York Portrait, Part 1* (1977); *Part 2* (1980); and *Part 3* (1990) – and, once he had moved into the Hudson Valley to teach at Bard College, in a series of landscape studies of his new environs, beginning with *Landscape (for Manon)* (1987), a homage to Hudson River School painter Thomas Cole. Rudy Burckhardt completed *Around the World in Thirty Years* in 1982; and Nathaniel Dorsky finished *Hours for Jerome, Parts 1 and 2* in 1982 (it had been shot during the 1960s) – along with Larry Gottheim's *Horizons*,

Hours for Jerome is American cinema's foremost celebration of the seasonal cycle. Michael Rudnick contributed *Panorama* (1982), a time-lapse 360-degree panorama of San Francisco; and in 1983, Babette Mangolte, who had become the premiere avant-garde cinematographer of the 1970s and 1980s (providing the camerawork for Yvonne Rainer's *Lives of Performers* and *Film about a Woman Who*..., for Chantal Akerman's early features, and for *Sigmund Freud's Dora*), finished *The Sky on Location*, a stunning, thoughtful excursion through the geography and history of the American West. Dominic Angerame began what was to become a series of San Francisco films with *Continuum* (1987) and *Deconstruction Sight* (1990).

During the 1990s the interest in place began to find the audience it had lacked during earlier decades. Ernie Gehr's *Side/Walk/Shuttle* (1991), arguably his most remarkable and engaging film, is a 41-minute panorama of San Francisco, made up of long, continuous shots filmed, often clandestinely, from an elevator on the outside of the Fairmont Hotel, near the spot where Eadweard Muybridge photographed his photo-panorama of the city. Each shot provides the time to experience this urban space and the myriad ways in which Gehr's camera angles reframe and transform it. *This Side of Paradise*, Gehr's study of a Polish flea market in West Berlin, was finished the following year; and his digital video *Glider* made at "The Giant Camera," a camera obscura in San Francisco, followed in 2001. Hutton continued his studies of the Hudson Valley in *In Titan's Goblet* (1991), *Study of a River* (1996), and *Time and Tide* (2000), his first foray into color since 1970. And Jem Cohen finished *Lost Book Found* (1996) and *Amber City* (1999), impressive evocations of New York and an unnamed Italian city (actually Pisa), respectively.

James Benning's move to California in 1988 to teach at the California Institute of the Arts inaugurated what was to become the most accomplished period of his career, beginning with *North on Evers* (1991), a record of two cross-country motorcycle journeys – one presented in a rolling text, the other

Figure 15.2 Moosehead Lake, Maine, in *13 Lakes* (2004, director and producer James Benning). (Courtesy James Benning.)

in imagery and sound – from his home north of Los Angeles to New York City through the Southwest and the South, and back through the Midwest. *North on Evers* doesn't fit the paradigm of contemplative cinema, but it can be seen as a survey of the territory that Benning would explore during the following decades, in *Deseret* (1995), his depiction of the geography and history of Utah; *Four Corners* (1997), about the region where Arizona, New Mexico, Colorado, and Utah meet; *Utopia* (1998), about the border territory between California and Mexico; and in his California Trilogy (three films, each made up of 35 two-and-a-half-minute shots): *El Valley Centro* (1999), *Los* (2000), and *Sogobi* (2001). Two of Benning's most rigorous films – *13 Lakes* (2004) and *Ten Skies* (2004) – followed: Each asks audiences to engage a series of minimally organized, 10-minute shots. This particularly demanding approach was inspired by Sharon Lockhart's use of 10-minute shots in her *Goshogaoka* (1997), a depiction of a young female Japanese basketball team; and Benning's use of the 10-minute shot may in turn have inspired Lockhart's *Pine Flat* (2006), rigorously composed, 10-minute shots of young people in a tiny town in the mountains north of Los Angeles.

The two films Lockhart had completed before *Pine Flat* are also impressive engagements with place: her *Teatro Amazonas* (1999) is a 35-minute, 35mm shot of the opera house in Manaus, Brazil, made famous by Werner Herzog's *Fitzcarraldo* (1982); the opera house is crowded with citizens from Manaus who listen to a choral piece during which, one by one, the singers drop out, until at the conclusion of the film, the audience in Manaus and we in the theater seem to be sharing the same space. Lockhart's *NŌ* (2003) creates the illusion of a single, 30-minute shot (there is one nearly invisible cut) of two Japanese farmers spreading hay on a field; at first, the film seems a simple documentary, but slowly we realize that the farmers are only spreading the hay on that portion of the field revealed by the camera – and the farmers are implicitly transformed into art-workers doing a Yvonne Rainer-esque choreographic piece. Recent films by Hutton (*Skagafjörður*, 2004; *At Sea*, 2007), Benning (*RR*, 2007; *casting a glance*, 2008), Naomi Uman (*Kalendar*, 2008), and Ben Russell (*Let Each One Go Where He May*, 2009) have reconfirmed the vitality of this approach, as have Lucien Castaing-Taylor and Ilisa Barbash in their videos on sheepherders in Montana, *Sweetgrass* (2009) and *Hell Roaring Creek* (2007). The switch to digital image-making by Gehr, in *Waterfront Follies* (2008), by Benning, in *Ruhr* (2009), and by Lockhart, in *Lunch Break* (2008) and *Double Tide* (2009), has provided a new tool for exploring this tendency.

Other major contributors to the depiction of place include Pat O'Neill, who established himself as a master of the optical printer in the 1970s in such films as *Sidewinder's Delta* (1976), and whose surreal depiction of Los Angeles in *Water and Power* (1989) is one of this nation's finest city symphonies. Anthropologist and seminal ethnographic filmmaker Robert Gardner finished *Forest of Bliss*, his city symphony of Banares, India, in 1986. And J. Leighton Pierce has produced evocations of American domestic space that transform the ordinary into the remarkable. While Hutton and Benning tend to work in long shot, Pierce tends to work in close-up, sometimes in miniature, expanding viewer awareness of the particular. Like Benning and Lockhart, Pierce has always been much involved with sound, and his early videos – *Principles of Harmonic Motion* (1991) and *Thursday* (1991), for example – and such 1990s films as *Red Shovel* (1992) and the domestic epic *50 Feet of String* (1995) create distinctive, lovely, and mysterious (and mysteriously familiar) sound-image worlds. Pierce's switch to digital video in the 2000s resulted in a series of lovely, painterly personal films, and this was followed by an increasing commitment to installation work.

Like the serialist/minimalist approach, the montage approach to place represented by Sonbert, Dorsky, and Guzzetti also demands of viewers a greater attention to the particularities and nuances of individual images than conventional cinema normally asks, but within a different formal context. In Benning's and Hutton's films, the regularized editing structure tends to create a ground against which the details of successive images can be figured. The montage films of Warren Sonbert and Nathaniel Dorsky rely on what Dorsky has called "polyvalent editing." In contradistinction both to Eisenstein's dialectical editing, where successive shots "collide" with one another, and to the conventional additive montages used at transitional moments in Hollywood films, each shot in a polyvalent montage simultaneously collides with and adds to the shots that immediately precede and follow it, and each shot contributes to a variety of visual and conceptual motifs and themes that emerge from the montage as a whole. Sonbert's *The Carriage Trade* (1971) was an early demonstration of the approach. *The Carriage Trade* was followed by *Rude Awakening* (1976), *A Woman's Touch* (1983), *The Cup and the Lip* (1986), *Honor and Obey* (1988), *Friendly Witness* (1989), and *Short Fuse* (1992). More generally appreciated in Europe than in the United States, Sonbert's montage films allowed him to see personal and political issues within a global context. Nowhere is this more evident than in his final two films where his struggles with HIV and AIDS reconfirm his passion for engaging the sensual and aesthetic fascinations of the world.

While the density of Sonbert's individual shots and their brevity make his films a bit overwhelming, Nathaniel Dorsky's films ask viewers to slow down; indeed, Dorsky's films are designed to be shown at what he calls "sacred speed" (that is, at silent speed, rather than at 24 frames per second) because this slower velocity helps him achieve what, in an influential pamphlet (2003), he has called "devotional cinema." Dorsky's imagery is subtle, suggestive, often mysterious, and consistently beautiful; the films ask that viewers engage the many subtleties of each image and the myriad formal and metaphoric interrelationships between both successive and nonsuccessive shots. Dorsky's increasing confidence in his approach to polyvalence made the late 1990s and the 2000s his most productive period: *Four Cinematic Songs – Triste* (1996), *Variations* (1998), *Arbor Vitae* (2000), *Love's Refrain* (2001) – was followed by *Two Devotional Songs: The Visitation* (2002) and *Threnody* (2004), and more recently, by *Winter* (2008), *Sarabande* (2008), *Compline* (2009), *Pastourelle* (2010), and *Aubade* (2010).

Alfred Guzzetti's film *Air* (1971) and his recent videos are in some senses quite different from Sonbert's and Dorsky's films, but their montage structures ask and reward a similar engagement on the part of viewers. Unlike Sonbert and Dorsky, Guzzetti uses image and sound as equal partners: Both tracks are comparably subtle and dense and create complex image and sound interplay; and in his videos – including *The Stricken Areas* (1996), *What Actually Happened* (1996), *Under the Rain* (1997), *A Tropical Story* (1998), *The Tower of Industrial Life* (2000), and *History of the Sea* (2004) – Guzzetti also works inventively with visual text, mostly dream texts. Guzzetti has a background in music, and his videos feel much like musical compositions that reveal his attempts to navigate the Scylla of violence and chaos in the world at large and the Charybdis of our personal mortality by acknowledging the wonder and mystery of his experience and demonstrating the artist's ability to transform angst into song.

Note

1. I am using "avant-garde" here in the most general sense: that is, to designate a body of cinema, or really several bodies of cinema, that have generally been called "avant-garde" during recent decades. Some of these films can be defined as politically progressive, others as formally inventive, some as both. Some of the filmmakers I am designating as "avant-garde" would surely resist the term, preferring "experimental," "underground," or another designation.

References

Curtis, David. (1971). *Experimental Cinema: A Fifty-Year Evolution*. New York: Dell.

Dorsky, Nathaniel. (2003). *Devotional Cinema*. Berkeley: Tuumba Press.

Gatten, David. (2009). "Interview with Scott MacDonald." In Scott MacDonald, *Adventures of Perception: Cinema as Exploration* (pp. 296–329). University of California Press.

Gunning, Tom. (1989–1990). "Towards a Minor Cinema: Fonoroff, Herwitz, Ahwesh, Lapore, Klahr and Solomon." *Motion Picture*, 3.1–2, 2–5.

Halter, Ed. (2008). "Live Cinema: A Contemporary Reader." MS.

LeGrice, Malcolm. (1977). *Abstract Film and Beyond*. Cambridge, MA: MIT Press.

MacDonald, Scott. (1992). *A Critical Cinema 2*. Berkeley: University of California Press.

MacDonald, Scott. (2005). *A Critical Cinema 4*. Berkeley: University of California Press.

MacDonald, Scott. (2009). *Adventures of Perception: Cinema as Exploration*. Berkeley: University of California Press.

Mekas, Jonas. (1972). *Movie Journal: The Rise of a New American Cinema, 1959–1971*. New York: Collier.

Mulvey, Laura. (1989). "Visual Pleasure and Narrative Cinema" (1975). In Laura Mulvey, *Visual and Other Pleasures* (pp. 14–30). Bloomington: Indiana University Press.

Noriega, Chon A., & Lópe, Ana M. (eds). (1996). *The Ethnic Eye: Latino Media Arts*. Minneapolis: University of Minnesota Press.

Sitney, P. Adams. (1974). *Visionary Film: The American Avant Garde*. New York: Oxford University Press.

Sitney, P. Adams (ed.). (1975). *The Essential Cinema: Essays on the Films in the Collection of Anthology Film Archives*. New York: New York University/Anthology Film Archives.

Solomon, Phil. (2005). "Interview with Scott MacDonald." In Scott MacDonald, *A Critical Cinema 5* (pp. 199–227). Berkeley: University of California Press.

Vogel, Amos. (1974). *Film as a Subversive Art*. New York: Random House.

Wees, William C. (1993). *Recycled Images*. New York: Anthology Film Archives.

Youngblood, Gene. (1970). *Expanded Cinema*. New York: Dutton.

16

A Reintroduction to the American Horror Film

Adam Lowenstein
Associate Professor, University of Pittsburgh, United States

Acknowledging that ***The Texas Chain Saw Massacre***, ***The Omen***, and ***Halloween*** are modern horror classics, Adam Lowenstein insists that they – and larger trends in 1970s and 1980s horror film production – merit renewed scholarly attention. Validating many of the pioneering insights of earlier horror scholars, he simultaneously seeks to reframe and reevaluate their critical approaches – a project implicitly informed by Lowenstein's place among a younger generation of horror fans whose rapport with the films expresses appeals and attractions previous scholars have overlooked. He argues that **Robin Wood**'s comparative study of *Texas Chain Saw Massacre* and *The Omen*, for instance, suffers from a false binary linking aesthetically sophisticated art to **politically progressive themes**, and that **Carol Clover**'s largely ahistorical approach to the **slasher sub-genre** too heavily relies on theories of **identification** at the expense of the affective impact of **spectacle**. Lowenstein's essay reframes questions of **spectatorship** within debates on **high and low art** and in relation to contemporaneous historical/cultural phenomena. Lowenstein's essay shares ground with Michael Sicinski on the biopic as a genre and Susan Jeffords on Hollywood and Reagan's America in this volume and with Thomas Doherty on the teenpic in the hardcover/online edition.

Additional terms, names, and concepts: repression, oppression, the Other, reactionary politics, subjective/I-camera, final girl

One of the most important innovations affecting the American horror film during the years 1976–1988 belongs not to any one particular film, but to a film festival. In 1979, the critic Robin Wood (collaborating with Richard Lippe) organized The American Nightmare, a special retrospective at the Toronto International Film Festival (then the Festival of Festivals) highlighting what he saw as evidence that "the true subject of the horror genre is the struggle for recognition of all that our civilization represses or oppresses" (Wood 1979, 10). By arranging screenings of films by, and discussions with, directors such

American Film History: Selected Readings, 1960 to the Present, First Edition. Edited by Cynthia Lucia, Roy Grundmann, and Art Simon.

as Wes Craven, Brian De Palma, George A. Romero, Stephanie Rothman, and David Cronenberg (the lone Canadian), Wood set out to locate the contemporary American horror film at the center of American culture. The American Nightmare bravely sought to move beyond the conventional associations attached to the horror genre: heartless exploitation, slipshod filmmaking, gratuitous violence, unrelieved misogyny, and an inherent silliness that precludes any substantial aesthetic or political ambitions. Against all odds, Wood wanted to take the horror film seriously. In fact, he titled his wide-ranging essay that opens the program notes "An Introduction to the American Horror Film," with its unmistakable connotations of wiping the slate clean, of showing us anew something we thought we understood perfectly well (or never deigned to understand at all).

By almost any measure, Wood's mission was remarkably successful. "An Introduction to the American Horror Film" quickly became the single most influential critical essay on the horror film ever published; it is frequently cited and reprinted even today. Before Wood, it was relatively rare for critics and scholars to ascribe much psychological or cultural significance to the horror film. After Wood, studies of the horror film emerged that argued the genre could teach us valuable things about female sexuality, homosexuality, racial difference, family dynamics, philosophy, critical theory, historical trauma, cultural history, and the nature of cinematic spectatorship. Nearly all of these studies, whether explicitly or implicitly, owed much to Wood's trailblazing convictions about why the horror film deserves serious critical consideration.

Today, more than 30 years after The American Nightmare, we need a reintroduction to the American horror film. Not because Wood's claims are necessarily incorrect or outdated, but because they have been so foundational to critical discussion of the horror film that a number of their premises have gone largely unchallenged. By surveying the American horror film from 1976 to 1988, we return to the historical moment of Wood's essay and discover an opportunity to review his findings alongside the films that shaped them. As my own essay title suggests, returning to Wood constitutes both a tribute to his work and a desire to reframe it. My attempt to reintroduce the American horror film seeks not to leave Wood behind, but to see his arguments in a new light that recasts the genre's history.

"An Introduction to the American Horror Film"

When Wood argues that "the true subject of the horror genre is the struggle for recognition of all that our civilization represses or oppresses," what exactly does he mean? For Wood, outlining the similarities and differences between repression and oppression forms a primary critical task. Repression, following the political economist Gad Horowitz, comes in two varieties: basic repression, which "makes possible our development from an uncoordinated animal capable of little beyond screaming and convulsions into a human being," and surplus repression, which makes us into "monogamous, heterosexual, bourgeois, patriarchal capitalists" (Wood 1979, 7–8). Wood focuses on surplus repression, which he subdivides into psychological and cultural components. He refers to the psychological aspects of surplus repression as simply "repression," defined along Freudian lines as an internal, unconscious process of disavowing all that threatens the individual from within. The cultural aspects of surplus repression become "oppression," defined along Marxist lines of social alienation, where the threat emanates from social sources outside the individual. For Wood, oppression is socially expressed repression. For example, "our social structure demands the *re*pression of the bisexuality that psychoanalysis shows to be the natural heritage of every human individual, and the oppression of homosexuals." Wood concludes that "the two phenomena are not identical" but "closely connected": "what escapes *re*pression has to be dealt with by *op*pression" (1979, 8). So when the horror film seeks to recognize what we have repressed psychologically and oppressed socially, it confronts us with a combination of internal and external otherness.

The concept of "the Other" occupies the center of Wood's argument. The Other is "what bourgeois ideology cannot recognize or accept but must deal with" through rejection, annihilation, or assimilation. Examples include women, the proletariat, foreign cultures, racial or ethnic minorities, homosexuals, alternative political ideologies, and children (Wood 1979, 9–10). For Wood, these Others enter the American horror film as monsters that threaten American society's investments in monogamous, heterosexual, bourgeois, patriarchal capitalism ("bourgeois ideology" or "normality" for short). Here Wood arrives at his influential "basic formula" for the horror film: "normality is threatened by the Monster" (1979, 14). The flexibility and utility of this formula offsets its obviousness and simplicity, according to Wood. The formula's three variables (normality, monstrosity, and the relationship between them) offer the means to categorize horror films as politically "progressive" or "reactionary" (1979, 23). Progressive horror films challenge conventional distinctions between normality and monstrosity by generating ambivalence between the two – through a sympathetic monster, for instance, or a doubling between the forces of normality and monstrosity. Reactionary horror films consolidate the status quo divisions between normality and monstrosity by squelching any possible ambivalence – most often through aligning the monster with such complete negativity that normality's oppressions are rationalized and reinforced. The two films Wood compares and contrasts in his initial presentation of the horror film's progressive and reactionary tendencies are *The Texas Chain Saw Massacre* (Tobe Hooper, 1974) and *The Omen* (Richard Donner, 1976). Examining how Wood draws distinctions between the progressive *Massacre* and the reactionary *Omen* will allow me to conclude my summary of "An Introduction to the American Horror Film" and begin the work of reintroduction.

The Texas Chain Saw Massacre and *The Omen*

The Texas Chain Saw Massacre depicts the encounter between a group of young friends traveling in rural Texas and the terrifying, murderous family they meet there. The friends set out in a van to visit the empty house that belongs to relatives of Sally and her brother Franklin, who is confined to a wheelchair. Accompanying Sally and Franklin are Sally's boyfriend Jerry and the couple Kirk and Pam. The family of unemployed slaughterhouse workers who live nearby now survive through a meager service station business that sells barbecue made from the unlucky human victims who cross their path. This family includes the brothers Hitchhiker and Leatherface (named for his habit of wearing masks made of human skin), their father the cook, and their ancient grandfather. The slaughterhouse family kills the young people one by one, until only Sally remains. After a harrowing, protracted series of captures and escapes, Sally, now nearly unrecognizable through the blood stains that soak her and apparently driven mad, manages to ride off with a passing driver. The Hitchhiker is crushed on the highway while pursuing her and a wounded Leatherface swings his chainsaw wildly in the air in the film's final shot.

In *The Omen*, the prominent American diplomat Robert Thorn and his wife Katherine, stationed in Rome, exchange their stillborn child for an infant born at the same time. This child, Damien, will grow up surrounded by a series of violent "accidents" that result in the spectacular deaths of those who get too close to him. These "accidents" point more and more definitively to his concealed identity as the prophesied Antichrist, the spawn of Satan who will lay waste to the world. Robert slowly comes to realize that he must destroy his son, but he ultimately fails and dies himself in the attempt. The film ends with the revelation that Damien has now been adopted by the president and first lady of the United States, making his rise to power all the more inevitable.

Wood begins his comparison of the two films with a "chart of oppositions." These oppositions include the status of *The Omen* as "bourgeois entertainment" versus the "nonbourgeois 'exploitation'" of *Massacre*, as well as the sense that in *The Omen* "traditional values" are "reaffirmed" while in *Massacre* they are "negated" (1979, 19). Another major difference Wood observes between the two films does not appear on the chart but crystallizes its organization: *The Omen* does not qualify as a "work of art" while *Massacre* "achieves the force of authentic art" (1979, 19, 22). These key contrasts illustrate how Wood distinguishes between progressive and reactionary horror films, but I will argue that they also indicate how such distinctions are ultimately insupportable.

In many ways, Wood's sense of the basic differences between *The Omen* and *Massacre* rings true. *The Omen*'s lavish production values and use of major stars such as Gregory Peck and Lee Remick diverge sharply from *Massacre*'s obviously low budget and unknown cast. But Wood's decision to label this difference as one between bourgeois entertainment and nonbourgeois exploitation equates mode of production with ideological stance in problematic ways. *The Omen*, a major Hollywood studio film produced by Twentieth Century-Fox, therefore becomes aligned with "good taste" and the reaffirmation of traditional social values, while the independently produced *Massacre* is filed under "bad taste" and the negation of traditional social values (Wood 1979, 19). *Massacre*'s distance from Hollywood and proximity to bad taste helps to prove its progressiveness, just as *The Omen*'s studio mode of production points toward its reactionary tendencies. Wood's desire to rescue *Massacre* from the category of "exploitation," a label he sees as the enemy of serious critical consideration, forces a hasty and simplistic equation of the independent mode of production with the progressive (nonbourgeois) and the studio mode of production with the reactionary (bourgeois). But can mode of production really provide such a clear-cut guide to a film's political meaning? Are the connections between Hollywood and bourgeois good taste, alongside those of independent film and nonbourgeois bad taste, really as distinct as Wood's chart of oppositions seems to indicate?

Despite their titles that may suggest otherwise, graphic gore – a time-honored hallmark of bad taste and exploitive gratuitousness – anchors *The Omen* at least as powerfully as *Massacre*. In fact, *The Omen* depends upon a visual logic of escalating graphic violence for its dramatic impact in a way that *Massacre* does not. The "accidents" of *The Omen* must convey an increasingly vivid sense of Damien's evil essence, since the appearance and actions of the child himself over the course of the film change only in very limited ways. So the accidents progress accordingly. First, a nanny's suicidal hanging captured mostly in extreme long shot, with very little warning granted beforehand. Second, the impaling of a priest in much more detail, complete with an extended buildup where he is chased by wind and lightning and stares screaming at the falling rod that kills him. Third, the shocking fall of Katherine caused physically by Damien, which includes a slow-motion descent as well as a close-up of Katherine once she hits the floor with blood trickling from her mouth. Fourth, the attack on Robert and the photographer Jennings by a pack of dogs in which no one dies but where the visual ante is upped through a more graphic presentation of imagery present in the previous two accidents: Robert's arm is impaled on the cemetery gates while he tries to escape, the blood now more plentiful than Katherine's after her fall. Fifth, Katherine's death, which is relatively brief but functions visually in a manner similar to the dog attack, embellishing previous imagery in more spectacular detail: she falls again, only this time breaking through an upper-story window and crashing through the roof of an ambulance below. The sequence ends by zooming in to a close-up of Katherine's face, but this time blood streams from her nose *and* mouth. The final accident is the most spectacular of all: Jennings decapitated by a sheet of glass, filmed in slow motion and complemented by two graphic aftermath shots displaying the severed head.

In contrast, *Massacre* resists graphic escalation as its dominant visual logic. The film begins with some of its most explicit and disturbing images: a series of close-ups of decaying body parts. But the presentation of these close-ups foreshadows the unconventional approach to graphic spectacle characteristic of the film as a whole. The close-ups are shot in the brilliant but instantly fading light of Polaroid flash photography at night, resulting in images often more puzzling than identifiable. The sounds of digging alert us to the possibility that the images may represent unearthed corpses, but not until the flash photographs are replaced with a sunlit close-up of a corpse's decomposing face do we gain confidence about that assessment. This close-up, without a cut, becomes a slow tracking shot away from the corpse that reveals the full extent of the labor caught only in fragments by the flash photographs: the corpse's entire body has been attached to the top of a tall gravestone, with the phallic monument protruding obscenely from the corpse's groin. The corpse's hands cradle the severed head of a second corpse above its groin, suggesting a bizarre simulation of fellatio or intercourse. A radio broadcast voiceover accompanies this tableau, explaining that grave-robbing incidents have been reported in rural Texas. The announcer's voice describes the construction made by the grave robbers, which we now realize we are viewing, as "a grisly work of art."

And so it is. A work of art in bad taste, perhaps, at least in terms of its repellent use of corpses for material and crude sexual metaphor for meaning. But in terms of cinematic presentation, this is good taste epitomized. The complex interplay between sound and image, the alternation of showing and telling, the balance between a static and moving camera, the transition from briefly glimpsed, nearly abstract images at night to a long take that unveils those images in the illuminating detail of daylight – all of these techniques pertain to good taste in cinematic form, not bad taste.

Figure 16.1 The opening "work of art" in Tobe Hooper's *The Texas Chain Saw Massacre* (1974, producers Tobe Hooper and Kim Henkel).

Indeed, *Massacre* in its entirety functions along lines indicated by this opening sequence: "good taste" in cinematic form collides with "bad taste" in content.

One major way in which good taste ultimately overshadows bad taste in *Massacre*, contrary to Wood's assertions, is its avoidance of precisely the kind of one-dimensional visual logic of graphic escalation characteristic of *The Omen*. The film's opening corpse tableau is followed by scenes of violence that emphasize not mechanical increases in graphic spectacle, but the process of revealing more and more about who the slaughterhouse family is and how they live. This process climaxes with Sally's captive participation in a macabre family dinner at the home of the slaughterhouse clan, where she sees the entire family in more detail than ever before. The dinner concludes with Grandpa's attempt to kill Sally, but he is so feeble that Sally escapes with a minor head wound. This wound barely registers as graphic spectacle when compared with the corpse tableau that begins the film, and the family's refusal to acknowledge Sally's sexual offer in exchange for her life during the dinner ("I'll do anything you want," she whimpers) eliminates the possibility of enacting the sort of sexually explicit spectacle suggested by the obscene arrangement of dead bodies in the opening sequence. So the promises of bad taste intimated by the film's beginning go unfulfilled at the film's end, while what transpires in between varies widely between graphic display and implicit suggestion. Even the film's most nightmarish conceit, that the family robs graves and kills people in order to support a barbecue business, is established more by connotation than denotation.

Although Wood acknowledges that *Massacre's* "*mise-en-scène* is, without question, everywhere more intelligent, more inventive, more cinematically educated and sophisticated than that of *The Omen*," he still aligns *Massacre* with bad taste and *The Omen* with good taste based on mode of production. For Wood, *Massacre* is "raw" and "unpolished" in terms of "the overall effect of the film, as it seems to be generally experienced" – only after multiple viewings, as one "gets over the initial traumatizing impact" (bad taste), can one "respect the pervasive felicities of camera placement and movement" (good taste) (1979, 19). What Wood misses here is how the *coexistence* of good and bad taste in *both* films cannot be resolved through differences in mode of production. *Massacre*'s good taste in cinematic form and tasteless mode of production (where "unpolished" and "traumatizing" become linked), as opposed to *The Omen*'s bad taste in cinematic form and tasteful mode of production, cannot be reduced to the dichotomy between *Massacre*'s bad taste and *The Omen*'s good taste that Wood insists upon. Isn't *Massacre*'s commitment to tasteful cinematic form, even art (no matter how grisly), just as "bourgeois" as *The Omen*'s investment in Hollywood studio production values? Isn't *The Omen* challenging conventional bourgeois taste when it wallows in an "unrespectable" visual economy of graphic escalation?

Wood's inability to address such questions stems from the equivalences he draws between *Massacre*'s progressive politics and its status as an authentic work of art, on the one hand, and *The Omen*'s reactionary politics and its failure to be a work of art, on the other. Wood claims *Massacre* for art by describing the film as "profoundly disturbing, intensely personal, yet at the same time far more than personal … as a 'collective nightmare' it brings to focus a spirit of negativity, an undifferentiated lust for destruction that seems to lie not far below the surface of the modern collective consciousness" (1979, 22). *The Omen*, meanwhile, falls beneath the requirements for art: "the most one could say is that it achieves a sufficient level of impersonal professional efficiency to ensure that the 'kicks' inherent in its scenario are not dulled" (1979, 19).

Aligning *Massacre* with personal art and *The Omen* with impersonal professionalism highlights how much Wood's argument depends on the critical paradigm of auteurism. Shaped by a complicated exchange of currents in film criticism between France, Britain, and the United States from the 1950s through the 1970s, auteurism argued for the recognition of directors as the true "authors" of their films, with an important index to the artistic value of a director's film or body of films based on the amount of personal expression stamped on it. Auteurism provided an essential critical apparatus for lionizing the European art cinema of the day, but it also legitimated the past and present efforts of such mainstream Hollywood directors as John Ford and Alfred Hitchcock. Indeed, Wood's own pioneering auteurist study of Hitchcock, *Hitchcock's Films* (1965), begins by resolving to take Hitchcock as "seriously" as we take Ingmar Bergman or Michelangelo Antonioni (Wood 2002, 57). So Wood's willingness to elevate *Massacre*, but not *The Omen*, to the level of art cannot be interpreted as an inherent preference for independent film over Hollywood film. In fact, "An Introduction to the American Horror Film" tends to equate "Hollywood cinema" with American cinema in general, therefore understanding a film like *Massacre* as produced in a low-budget, "exploitation" mode, but within "Hollywood" rather than outside it – it is still an American film (Wood 1979, 19). I will return to Wood's inaccurate, blanket use of "American" later, but for now, the issue of art demands further attention.

If *Massacre* achieves the status of art for Wood, it is not solely by means of recognizing director Tobe Hooper as an auteur. It is also through the film's definition as a "collective nightmare." This critical move toward social and psychological concerns rather than pure auteurism reflects the seismic changes in film studies that began during the mid-1970s and collected around the British academic film journal *Screen*. Innovations in film theory at *Screen* included applying particular strands of Marxist and psychoanalytic thought to analyses of cinema as an ideological instrument. The politicizing of film studies at *Screen* involved the belief that criticism could and should unmask the ideological messages embedded in cinema, particularly the dominant, mainstream style of narrative film associated with Hollywood. "An Introduction to the American Horror Film" participates in this politicization, but with a difference. Wood mentions *Screen* by name as a reference point in his essay, but he qualifies his debt to the journal by wondering whether its "new academicism" may prove "more sterile than the old … driving its students into monastic cells rather than the streets" (1979, 7). As a result, Wood distances himself from the preferred theorists of *Screen*, Louis Althusser on Marxism and Jacques Lacan on psychoanalysis, by turning to Gad Horowitz's synthesis of Freud, Wilhelm Reich, and Herbert Marcuse. Wood's distrust of academic approaches to film criticism dovetails with his sense that those who study film should be working toward a particular form of social revolution, one he summarizes as "the overthrow of patriarchal capitalist ideology and the structures and institutions that sustain it and are sustained by it" (1979, 7). Wood's convictions that such a revolution is the only way to imagine desirable social change, that it must come from action rather than thought, and that its realization may be imminent undergird all of the claims in "An Introduction to the American Horror Film," including the distinctions between *Massacre* as nonbourgeois, progressive, authentic art and *The Omen* as bourgeois, reactionary, inauthentic entertainment.

But when it comes to film, can critical judgments lodged in auteurism (art versus entertainment) map themselves so neatly onto political judgments (progressive versus reactionary)? I think not, as I hope my account of Wood on *Massacre* and *The Omen* has begun to demonstrate, but even Wood himself appears to strain under the weight of this method. He tempers his dismissal of *The Omen* as reactionary by maintaining that "the film remains of great interest" because "'normality' [bourgeois patriarchal capitalism] is not merely threatened by the monster, but totally annihilated: the state, the church, the family" (1979, 19). Here Wood gestures toward a problem that eventually undermines his critical apparatus: If a typical progressive horror film introduces ambivalence into the relationship between the "normality" of bourgeois patriarchal capitalism and the "monstrosity" of those elements that threaten it, then what could be more progressive than a film that attacks, in explicit, systematic fashion, the state, the church, and the family? *The Omen* depicts a state so blind that it happily embraces forces of evil bent on destroying it (the president adopts the Antichrist), a church infiltrated by priests who have sold their souls to the devil (representatives of the church scheme and murder to make Damien's birth and adoption possible), and a family so dishonest with each other that they seal their own doom (Robert never tells his wife what he knows from the beginning, that Damien is not their biological child).

Massacre, by comparison, remains relatively silent on church and state. Even its assault on "normal" conceptions of family seems less obvious than in *The Omen*. Wood claims that *Massacre* presents its slaughterhouse family as sympathetic, despite their monstrousness: "We cannot cleanly dissociate ourselves from them ... *they* are victims, too – of the slaughterhouse environment, of capitalism – *our* victims, in fact" (1979, 21). But is sympathy of this kind very likely in relation to a family so clearly intended, first and foremost, to terrify and disgust with their acts of murder, torture, grave robbing, and cannibalism? Wood is right that *Massacre* channels much more creative energy toward the monstrous family than the young friends whom they kill, but does the film's management of creative energy translate into sympathy for its monsters from viewers?

For Wood, the slaughterhouse family "does not lack that characteristically human quality, an aesthetic sense, however perverted its form," due to the fact that some "artworks among which the family live ... achieve a kind of hideous aesthetic beauty" (1979, 21–22). The "artworks" Wood refers to appear most prominently when Pam enters the house of the slaughterhouse family. She stumbles into a room furnished with an array of decorations, including a couch whose arms are supplemented by the arms of a human skeleton and a human skull hanging upside down with an animal horn through its gaping mouth. Without doubt, these decorations are constructed and shot in such a manner that viewers are invited to admire the skillful craft of the filmmakers in imagining them, right down to the witty play with the notion of "arms." But admiration for cinematic craft outside the film is not the same as sympathy for the slaughterhouse family within it. Indeed, Hooper frames these decorations as an extended series of point-of-view shots from Pam's perspective, whose wariness about the house transforms into terror and disgust as she soaks in the surroundings of the room. Through Pam's distressed perspective, the effect of the sequence is not appreciation for the slaughterhouse family's taste in interior design, but an alarming sense of danger, death, and disorder.

This sequence's soundtrack combines eerie, nondiegetic washes of metallic echoes (emphasizing Pam's subjective response) with the diegetic clucking of a chicken, trapped in a cage hanging from the ceiling. The sound and image of the chicken, coupled with the floor strewn with feathers and the many scattered bones that toss together human and animal remains indiscriminately, point not to the presence of Wood's proclaimed sense of "characteristically human" qualities for the slaughterhouse family, but their absence. This family does not comprehend the boundaries between human and animal, a far more basic human trait than an aesthetic sense.

When Pam retches and flees the room, her disgust solidifies, rather than challenges, the viewer's sense of the slaughterhouse family as closer to animals than humans. Viewers, unlike the unknowing Pam, add to this impression by incorporating the recent horrifying images of Kirk's death. Leatherface slaughters Kirk just like an animal, with sledgehammer blows to the skull accompanied by the spastic convulsions of Kirk's dying body. Leatherface's guttural squeals, closer to the grunts of a pig than the voice of a human being, only enhance the overall atmosphere of animality within the house, a place where meaningful distinctions between the human and the animal have disintegrated.

Again, Hooper establishes this atmosphere of animality with masterful cinematic skill, but the evidence for a sophisticated aesthetic sensibility on the film's part should not be equated with a sympathetic, "human" aesthetic sensibility displayed by the slaughterhouse family themselves. *Massacre*'s art primarily involves conveying the animality of the family, not generating sympathy for its humanity. By the same token, admiration for *Massacre*'s art need not lead necessarily to admiration of its "progressive" politics, nor should distaste for *The Omen*'s art lead necessarily to disapproval of its "reactionary" politics. Wood's critical methodology radically simplifies the relations between art and politics, leaving little room for those polyvalent negotiations that might result in artful reactionary films, artless progressive films, or films that careen between such categories or resist integration into the categories at all. For example, a horror film where sympathy for the monster is beside the point need not automatically condemn that film to reactionary oblivion the way Wood often suggests. *The Omen* does not devote much effort to making Damien sympathetic, but that does not detract from (and may even enhance) its power to mount an institutional critique of bourgeois patriarchal capitalism.

Wood attempts to resolve the contradictions that arise when trying to demarcate between progressive and reactionary horror films by distinguishing between politically productive, "apocalyptic" negativity and politically counterproductive, "*total* negation" (1979, 24). The latter phrase emerges when Wood attacks David Cronenberg's *Shivers* (aka *They Came from Within* and *The Parasite Murders*, 1975), *Rabid* (1977), and *The Brood* (1979) as reactionary. I have explained elsewhere how this distinction between apocalyptic negativity and total negation fails to account for the aesthetic and political complexity of Cronenberg's films, so I will not rehearse that here (see Lowenstein 2005, 154–164). However, I do want to pause to note how Wood's desire to assimilate Cronenberg, a Canadian director, into the catch-all category of the "American" horror film betrays his antipathy for reckoning meaningfully with questions of national identity or even the differences between studio and independent versions of American cinema (as I mentioned earlier). Another film that Wood champions in "An Introduction to the American Horror Film" is *Raw Meat* (aka *Death Line*, 1972), a British horror film that Wood describes as "American-derived" and not truly British because its director, Gary Sherman, is American (1979, 16). The problem here is obvious: Important contexts for understanding a film disappear as "horror film" and "American horror film" become synonymous.

A related problem surfaces in Wood's analysis of *The Omen*, when he remarks that one of the film's most "obvious" reactionary traits involves how "'horror' is disowned by having the devil-child a product of the Old World, unwittingly *adopted* into the American family" (1979, 19). Actually, *The Omen*'s detailed attention to multiple national locales (moving between action in Italy, Britain, Israel, and the United States) constitutes more than just a touristic display of glossy production values – it simultaneously embeds the film's events in a wide geopolitical context that hardly resembles a simple "Old World versus New World" dichotomy. There are even glimmers of recognition in *The Omen* that imagining radical evil historically in the old-fashioned terms of Old World and New World no longer works after Auschwitz: Robert first mistakes the sign of the devil on a priest's body for a concentration camp tattoo, intimating that the sins of the fathers have historical as well as supernatural implications. This important suggestion, however tentative and fleeting in the film itself, goes unnoticed in Wood's schema where horror "owned" is American and horror "disowned" is non-American.

Wood concludes his essay by lamenting that the genre's most recent commercial successes, most notably *Alien* (1979) and *Halloween* (1978), fail to realize the progressive potential of late 1960s and 1970s horror films such as *The Texas Chain Saw Massacre*, *Night of the Living Dead* (1968), *Sisters* (1973), and *God Told Me To* (aka *Demon*,1976). Wood perceptively observes how *Alien*, at least "at first glance," appears to be "little more than Halloween-in-outer-space" (1979, 26). What he could not have known then was just how influential the barebones narrative structure of *Halloween* would prove over time: the story of a masked male killer hunting down and butchering a series of mostly young, mostly sexually active women (along with their male partners) only to be defeated in the end by a resourceful young female who converts her virginal sexual state into effective combat and survival tactics. This is the narrative blueprint for the slasher film, a subgenre birthed by *Halloween*'s phenomenal success that would dominate the American horror film during the 1980s and then reformulate itself in the 1990s and beyond as the ambitious serial killer film (*The Silence of the Lambs*, 1991; *Zodiac*, 2007) and the self-knowing slasher film (Wes *Craven's New Nightmare*, 1994; *Scream*, 1996). Not that *Halloween* invented the slasher film single-handedly, as its debts to *Psycho* (1960), *The Texas Chain Saw Massacre*, and the Canadian film *Black Christmas* (1974) (among others) are considerable, but it certainly ushered in a flood of imitators in a way that made the slasher film visible as never before. Studying the slasher film means picking up where Wood leaves off.

The Slasher Film

If Wood gave critical shape to the American horror film before the rise of the slasher film, then Carol J. Clover did so afterwards. Clover's essay "Her Body, Himself: Gender in the Slasher Film" (1987) and her subsequent book *Men, Women, and Chain Saws: Gender in the Modern Horror Film* (1992) have been just as important as Wood's essay for defining the genre in groundbreaking ways. Clover, a scholar of Scandinavian and comparative literature, draws on Wood's work but approaches the horror film quite differently. Where Wood emphasizes questions of art and politics, Clover turns to matters of cinematic spectatorship.

For Wood, the ultimate goal is to classify individual horror films as progressive or reactionary. For Clover, the horror film's primary interest lies not with any one particular film, but with the cumulative effect of so many similar films telling versions of the same story over and over again. Wood wishes to raise *The Texas Chain Saw Massacre* to the level of art by virtue of the politics expressed within the film itself; Clover is drawn to films like *Massacre* and its slasher imitators for their artlessness, for their "crudity and compulsive repetitiveness," because these qualities convey "a clearer picture of current sexual attitudes, at least among the segment of the population that forms its erstwhile audience, than do the legitimate products of the better studios" (1992, 22–23).

In the transition between Wood and Clover, then, we can detect a shift from film to spectator as the center of critical gravity. Clover avoids the conflation of art and politics that hobbles Wood's model by turning to the audience for meaning in a way that Wood resists. Not surprisingly, Clover embraces precisely the sort of film theory Wood rejects: psychoanalytic constructions of spectatorship as pioneered in *Screen*. By placing her research in conversation with this rich, ambitious body of scholarship, Clover can theorize how these films are seen, not just what the films show. Not least among Clover's many impressive achievements in this regard is her ability to integrate the horror film into a discussion within film theory where it was not hitherto central, changing the nature of that discussion in the process. In fact, Clover's engagement with the single most influential document of the *Screen* moment in film theory, Laura Mulvey's "Visual Pleasure and Narrative Cinema" (1975), makes it difficult to read Mulvey in the same way afterwards.

Mulvey's essay is a compellingly formulated, still-forceful feminist manifesto on cinematic spectatorship. She argues that classical Hollywood film delivers pleasure to the spectator by presenting male characters onscreen as active agents of looking while female characters occupy the passive role of "to-be-looked-at-ness" (Mulvey 1986, 203). By implication, then, all film spectators are positioned as "male" and "heterosexual" by the films themselves, with the spectacle of women drained of their potentially threatening psychoanalytic substance (castration anxiety) through the visual and narrative strategies of voyeurism (the sadistic investigation and punishment of the female) and fetishistic scopophilia (the masochistic overvaluation and fragmentation of the female) (Mulvey 1986, 205). In the years since Mulvey published "Visual Pleasure and Narrative Cinema," many scholars (including Mulvey herself) have come to question a number of the essay's assumptions, including its lack of room for spectators who may not identify as male and heterosexual, or whose race, class, national, or other identities may shape their experiences as viewers. Clover intervenes not so much to posit a specific, concrete spectator in place of Mulvey's hypothetical, universalized spectator – Clover's determination of "the younger male" as the primary audience for the horror films she studies is, by her own admission, largely anecdotal and hardly exhaustive (1992, 7) – but to challenge Mulvey's division of spectator experience into sadistic voyeurism and masochistic fetishism.

Clover describes the possibilities of sadomasochistic spectatorship, where the younger male spectator of a slasher film can switch "back and forth with ease" between a sadistic position of terrorizer and a masochistic position of terrorized (1992, 62). To call the former position "male" and the latter position "female" is not really accurate, since Clover demonstrates how the killer in a slasher film tends to be an anatomical male in "gender distress" and the hero an anatomical female, a "Final Girl," who becomes masculinized in her climactic victory over the killer (1992, 27, 35). In short, the slasher film's sadomasochistic spectatorship, where viewer identifications shift between killer, victim, and victim/killer (the Final Girl), illustrates how "gender is less a wall than a permeable membrane" (Clover 1992, 46). Clover's most striking departure from Mulvey is her suggestion that it is the masochistic side of spectatorship that functions most powerfully for audiences of the horror film, so that Mulvey's sadistic male spectator is replaced by Clover's masochistic male spectator – even within a subgenre like the slasher film where most critics would assume Mulvey's sadistic male gaze would be overwhelmingly dominant.

For all the differences between Wood and Clover, they resemble each other when they encounter certain seemingly puzzling aspects of horror film spectatorship. Wood reports his "terrifying experience" while watching *The Texas Chain Saw Massacre* "with a large, half-stoned youth audience who cheered and applauded every one of Leatherface's outrages against their representatives on the screen." He cannot really fathom this reaction, except as a sign of "a civilization condemning itself, through its popular culture, to ultimate disintegration, and ambivalently … celebrating the fact" (Wood 1979, 22). Similarly, Clover comes up short when she observes that slasher film audiences respond to the extremely graphic gore routinely offered up by these films through "uproarious disgust" as well as "fear," suggesting a "rapid alternation between registers – between something like 'real' horror on one hand and a camp, self-parodying horror on the other." Like Wood, Clover appears stumped by the audience's behavior: "Just what this self-ironizing relation to taboo signifies, beyond a remarkably competent audience, is unclear" (Clover 1992, 41). These moments of puzzlement in both Wood and Clover point toward certain uncharted aspects of spectatorship in their models. In my own discussion that follows, I will use the period's most influential slasher film, *Halloween*, to map some of this uncharted territory in terms of what I will call "spectacle horror": the staging of spectacularly explicit gore for purposes of audience admiration and giddy delight as much as shock or terror, but without necessarily breaking ties with narrative development or historical allegory.

Halloween and Spectacle Horror

Halloween tracks the murderous deeds of Michael Myers, an unstoppable masked killer who commits his first crime as a young child on Halloween night: After spying on his older sister, Judith, before and after she has sex with a boyfriend, he dons a mask and stabs her to death. After spending the next 15 years in a mental institution under the supervision of the psychiatrist Dr Sam Loomis, he escapes and returns to his hometown of Haddonfield, Illinois, on Halloween to murder others who seem to remind him of his sister – young, attractive, sexually active women (and their boyfriends, if they happen to get in the way). But Michael expresses a special fascination with Laurie Strode, a virginal, bookish student who spends more time on her homework and babysitting than on dates with boys. In the climax of *Halloween*, Michael turns from killing Laurie's friends Annie and Lynda to stalking Laurie herself. Laurie fights back tenaciously, first outrunning and then wounding Michael. By the time Loomis finally arrives on the scene to shoot Michael repeatedly, Laurie seems to anticipate what Loomis then witnesses: the disappearance of Michael's corpse. Laurie may have won her safety, for now, but the relentless Michael will not die.

In many ways, *Halloween* lacks the sort of explicit carnage characteristic of spectacle horror. I have argued elsewhere that the common perception of Alfred Hitchcock as the master of cinematic suggestion, of horror implied rather than horror shown, is more reductive fantasy than consistent reality (Lowenstein 2004). But director John Carpenter, clearly under Hitchcock's spell while making *Halloween* (Laurie is played by Jamie Lee Curtis, the daughter of *Psycho*'s star Janet Leigh; Dr Loomis is named after a character in *Psycho*), often strives to mimic the fantasy of Hitchcockian restraint. This quality in *Halloween* becomes apparent when comparing it to the gorier horror films that preceded it, such as *Night of the Living Dead* or *Last House on the Left* (1972), and those that followed it, such as *Friday the 13th* (1980). But the staging of over-the-top set pieces as occasions for audience admiration of cinematic technique and the sheer enjoyment of outrageous explicitness can still be found in *Halloween*.

The film's opening sequence unfolds as a thrilling exercise in fluid camera movement. In long takes composed to evoke a single, restless tracking shot, a roving subjective camera travels outside and inside a middle-class suburban home, capturing the point of view of an unidentified "character." From outside the house, this subjective camera as "character" spies Judith Myers making out with her boyfriend on a downstairs couch, then the couple heading upstairs together. The "character" enters the house and acquires a large knife from a kitchen drawer. While heading toward the staircase, the "character" pauses to remain unseen, allowing the boyfriend, still putting his shirt back on, to descend the stairs and leave the house. Then the "character" climbs the stairs and, upon reaching the landing, picks up a clown's mask discarded by the boyfriend. Now the point of view of the "character" is filtered through the eyes of the mask. The masked "character" moves to the bedroom, where a topless Judith brushes her hair while seated at a mirror. She does not notice that she is being watched until the camera/character is nearly upon her. "Michael!" she calls out, identifying the bearer of the subjective camera's visual perspective. Staying within the mask's line of sight, Michael stabs Judith multiple times in the chest as she screams, then leaves her bloody corpse crumpled on the floor. He exits the room quickly, heads down the stairs and out the front door. At just that moment, a car pulls up in front of the house and a middle-aged couple steps out. "Michael?" the man asks, removing the mask. With the mask off and the source of the subjective camera's agency now finally revealed, we see that Michael is a young boy in a clown suit, still holding the bloodied knife. As the sequence ends, Michael's parents stare at him with uneasy disbelief.

Halloween's opening articulates the structure of spectacle horror without providing the full dose of explicit spectacle. The presentation of Judith's nudity, the plunging of the knife into her body, and the image of her bloody corpse are certainly graphic, but they are tempered through the subjective viewpoint of the mask, which necessarily obscures portions of the frame. Many of *Halloween*'s slasher successors will dispense with this kind of restraint, but they will retain the formula for graphic spectacle as a pairing of explicit female nudity with explicit violence. A number of them will also imitate the subjective or I-camera technique, providing the illusion of putting the viewer behind the eyes of the killer. Although this technique may seem to literalize the sadistic male gaze, I believe Clover is closer to the mark when she refers to it as a "visual identity game," one in which the spectator can "view the action in the first person long before revealing who or what the first person is" (1992, 56). Clover also notes that such subjective/I-camera sequences in the slasher film are "usually few and brief" compared to the extended climaxes where the point of view shifts to the Final Girl (1992, 45). *Halloween*, at least at first glance, appears to offer no exception in this regard.

The I-camera sequence that begins *Halloween* has its complement near the end of the film, when Laurie battles Michael. Laurie's subjectivity motivates most of the action in the last part of the film, after her friends, Annie and Lynda, have died at Michael's hands. Indeed, the film's final section commences when Laurie temporarily leaves the house where she is babysitting to enter the house across the street where Annie has been babysitting and where Lynda and her boyfriend Bob have come to have sex. Carpenter films the spatial transition between the two houses, one of safety and sleeping children, the other (as Laurie will discover but as the audience already knows) of danger and dead bodies, in a manner that recalls *Halloween*'s opening. Laurie's point of view generates tracking shots that take us closer and closer to the house of death, just as Michael's subjective point of view inspired similar camera movements toward the similar-looking Myers house (right down to a nearly identically placed jack o' lantern on the front porch) when the film began. The difference now is that we know who Laurie is (in contrast with Michael's mysterious subjectivity) and that Carpenter inserts reaction shots of Laurie's responses as he returns to her face, following eyeline matches that show the house from her point of view.

But the resemblance between the two sequences in terms of mise-en-scène and camera movement highlights a motif that runs throughout *Halloween*, one that ultimately challenges Clover's treatment of Michael's subjective/I-camera perspective as a relatively isolated exception: the mirrored relations between Michael and Laurie (note that the jack o' lantern occupies the right side of the porch at the Myers house, while it sits on the left side at the house Laurie approaches – mirror images). Both characters motivate tracking shots that take us toward houses of nondescript normalcy on the outside, but of sexual transgression and death on the inside. Clover points out how the somewhat feminized male killer (proficient in murder, but not regular sexual functioning) and the somewhat masculinized female Final Girl (physically active once the killer attacks, but sexually inactive beforehand) ease the sadomasochistic, back-and-forth movement of spectator positions in the slasher film, with its reliance on "cross-gender identification" (1992, 46). But for Clover, who is rightly dedicated to interrogating "the astonishingly insistent claim that horror's satisfactions begin and end with sadism," the analytic weight rests with how the young male audience of the slasher film must identify across gender boundaries with the Final Girl (1992, 19).

Although I agree with Clover that the interstitial gender status of the Final Girl and young male viewers searching for a stable sexual identity helps enable cross-gender identification, I want to suggest also that this exchange involves a more intimate incorporation of the killer's point of view – not as a "sadistic" identification in opposition to a "masochistic" identification with the Final Girl, but as a mirroring of the subjectivities of killer and Final Girl, resisting concepts of "identification" altogether. If identification does not tell the whole story, or even the primary story, of spectatorship in the slasher film, then neither do the attendant assumptions of sadism, masochism, and the exclusivity of a young male audience. Let me explore these claims by returning to *Halloween*.

When Laurie's subjectivity rushes to the forefront most flamboyantly, we seem to have a perfect visual complement to *Halloween*'s opening sequence – we see through her eyes as she squirms inside a locked closet, following her gaze upward in low-angle shots from the closet floor as Michael attempts to break in. But just as identification with Michael's gaze in the opening sequence is complicated by the absence of a reaction shot – the fact that we do not yet know to whom this gaze belongs – our identification with Laurie's gaze here is complicated by our knowing too much about the context within which this gaze is situated. Identifying solely with Laurie as the determined Final Girl scrambling to survive collides with a fascination linked to the growing relationship between Laurie and Michael. Perhaps theirs is no ordinary romantic relationship, but it does unfold visually as a sort of dance – by the time Laurie hides in the closet, she and Michael have already engaged in so many choreographed moves together (surprise, flight, pursuit, confrontation, wounding, resurrection) that this feels like an inversion of the prom date Laurie never managed to secure. And "choreographed" is the key term here, for the spectator's identification with Laurie's point of view must compete not only with the mirroring established with Michael that has become a shared relationship by this time, but also with the mechanics of spectacle horror.

Spectacle horror does not rely primarily on spectator identification with characters. Instead, spectacle horror more closely resembles the mode of viewer address film historian Tom Gunning describes when characterizing early cinema (1895–1906) as a "cinema of attractions." Gunning describes the cinema of attractions as "directly soliciting] spectator attention, inciting visual curiosity, and supplying pleasure through an exciting spectacle." He goes on to say that "an attraction is offered [directly] to the spectator by a cinema showman" such that "theatrical display dominates over narrative absorption, emphasizing the direct stimulation of shock or surprise at the expense of unfolding a story." He points out that character psychology is not of central concern, but instead the "energy [that] moves outward towards an acknowledged spectator rather than inward towards the character-based situations essential to classical narrative" (1990, 58–59).

In *Halloween*, one striking moment of "attraction" occurs while Laurie searches the house of death. Viewers know that Laurie's calls for Annie, Lynda, and Bob will go unanswered, since we have seen them brutally murdered by Michael. Therefore, when

Laurie enters an upstairs bedroom to find Annie's dead body on the bed beneath Judith Myers's relocated gravestone, we do not share fully in her level of knowledge. We know Annie is dead. We know Michael has stolen Judith's gravestone. With narrative concerns stripped away, we focus instead on the shock and pleasure of display, on the attraction itself. The sense of a "cinema showman" addressing us directly – "look at this!" – is heightened by a musical sting (a synthesizer screech) that coincides with the presentation of the attraction, paired with a slow tracking shot that moves in to magnify the details of the spectacle. The presence of a "cinema showman" becomes even more palpable as the sequence continues. Laurie, horrified by the sight of Annie, backs away from the bed only to have Bob's swinging, upside-down corpse almost knock her over when it emerges without warning from a nearby closet. Again Laurie backs away, but this time the cabinet she stands next to opens of its own accord to reveal Lynda's strangled body. Carpenter's direct address to the audience comes through loud and clear – he is quite literally pulling the strings on this series of attractions, right down to opening cabinet doors, without any evident onscreen agency.

Common audience responses to this sequence that I have observed fit squarely within Clover's and Wood's puzzled accounts of horror viewer behavior: squeals of surprise or fright followed by giddy laughter and appreciative hoots and hollers. Such behavior is more easily explained as a response to an aesthetic of attractions, rather than a response to the forms of narrative-based identification Clover and Wood favor. The mixed viewer affect of fear, excitement, humor, and admiration must be understood, then, as a response to the direct address of the "cinema showman," not as viewer identification with onscreen characters or situations. When it comes to spectator engagement with attractions, sadistic identification with the killer or masochistic identification with the Final Girl is beside the point. In fact, "identification" itself, at least in the conventional, psychologized sense, does not apply. Attractions do not require an audience, whatever their gender may be, to identify with any particular male or female character, or to respond to ways in which these characters embody relative degrees of masculinity or femininity. Viewer involvement occurs elsewhere, no longer chained to forms of identification.

So is *Halloween* really a textbook case of spectacle horror as simply equivalent to attractions? It's important to remember that it is not just Carpenter outside the film but Michael within the film who orchestrates these attractions. In this way, the spectacle represented by these three corpses does indeed function as an attraction, but it also develops the film's narrative and thematic content. The choreographed corpses are yet another maneuver in Michael's "dance" with Laurie, another bid to "impress" her in his own twisted way. And Laurie's discovery of the corpses emphasizes once again her mirroring of Michael – she retraces the steps he walked himself in *Halloween*'s opening sequence, first outside the house, then through the ground floor, then up the stairs to the bedroom. The line between Michael's "making" the corpses and Laurie's discovering them grows more blurry as the film proceeds to its conclusion, with Laurie herself twice "creating" a fallen body (at least temporarily) as she wounds Michael with a knitting needle, a hanger, and finally his own knife.

When Laurie takes possession of Michael's knife and uses it against him, their mirrored relations have all but converged to establish one shared being. This is why Laurie's subsequent unmasking of Michael – a brief, quickly corrected event – carries no dramatic charge whatsoever. What is the point of unmasking the killer when the Final Girl and the killer are no longer dueling entities, but two halves of a whole? At this juncture in *Halloween*, we sense that seeing Michael means not removing his mask, but observing Laurie's interactions with him.

Clover's emphasis, then, on identification between the spectator and the Final Girl minimizes the viewer's investment in the killer's point of view, which I have argued is part of a constitutive mirroring of the Final Girl's point of view, not its opposite. Clover's account of spectator identification, even shifting, sadomasochistic, cross-gender identification, misses the thrill of the attraction and its resistance to psychologized processes such as identification. Gunning's attraction, at least when imported to the context of the slasher film, misses the ways in which attractions simultaneously lend themselves to certain forms of narrative and thematic knowing, such as the mirrored relations between Michael and Laurie. Therefore, my own theorization of spectacle horror aims to combine cinematic narrative and cinematic attractions, along with the possibility of historical allegory. I have described elsewhere how the horror film's interface with historical trauma might be imagined, in particular cases, as a series of "allegorical moments" that testify to "a shocking collision of film, spectator, and history where registers of bodily space and historical time are disrupted, confronted, and intertwined" (Lowenstein 2005, 2). Spectacle horror may or may not generate allegorical moments in which horror illuminates historical trauma, for such moments depend on the specificities of the film, spectator, and history. What of *Halloween* in this regard?

For all of her illuminating work on spectatorship, Clover remains relatively silent on questions of history. In a rare moment of historical hypothesizing on the slasher film, she writes, "The fact that the typical patrons of these films are the sons of marriages contracted in the sixties or even early seventies leads me to speculate that the dire claims of that era ... were not entirely wrong." For Clover, these claims revolve around the notion that "the women's movement, the entry of women into the workplace, and the rise of divorce and woman-headed families would yield massive gender confusion in the next generation" (1992, 62). I agree with Clover when she attributes the historical crises addressed by the slasher film to social developments connected to feminism, but I disagree with her presenting these crises as a list of unspecified and presumably equivalent phenomena that fall under the exceedingly general umbrella of "massive gender confusion." In concluding my discussion of *Halloween*, I will argue that it is one of these social factors in particular that preoccupies the slasher film and forms the basis for its historical allegories: an explosive increase in the divorce rate.

Between 1960 and 1980, the divorce rate in America "jumped ninety percent," meaning that during those years, "the number of divorced men and women rose by almost two hundred percent" (D'Emilio & Freedman 1988, 331). These staggering statistics begin to inform Clover's work, at least implicitly, when she suggests that social gender confusion manifests itself in the slasher film via the feminine male killer standing in for a "parent" and the masculine female Final Girl standing in for "everyteen" (1992, 63). What this account obscures is precisely what I have posited as central to my own analysis of *Halloween*: the mirroring between killer and Final Girl that makes them intimates, not opposites; the failure of "identification" to explain adequately the interaction between spectator and film.

To describe Michael as a parental figure, for example, erases significant aspects of how the film visualizes him. Not just his introduction as a young boy, but "childish" traits expressed later on such as his curious, seemingly uncomprehending stare at Bob's lifeless body and his subsequent masquerade (complete with bed sheet and glasses) as Bob's "ghost." In these ways, Michael more closely resembles the children Laurie babysits than an adult. So the violence Michael wreaks need not be interpreted necessarily as "parental" punishment meted out to a misbehaving teen, but rather the fantasies of domination and revenge directed toward parents by the child of divorce. Indeed, the teens Michael murders before stalking Laurie may be eager for sex and beer in ways that match conventional images of their age group, but their place within the mise-en-scène aligns them with parents more than anything else. Annie substitutes for absent parents as a babysitter, spending most of her time in the domestic spaces of the kitchen and laundry room, while Lynda and Bob occupy the parents' bedroom.

Annie, Lynda, and Bob, like Judith Myers and her boyfriend at the beginning of the film, fill spaces left vacant by their proper residents: parents. Absent or impotent parents in the slasher film are nearly as ubiquitous as masks, knives, and screams. The image of Michael's parents in *Halloween*'s opening sequence crystallizes the typical parental presence in the slasher film: oblivious, away when they're needed, returning too late, saying nothing, paralyzed. Annie's father, Sheriff Brackett, is kind and well intentioned, but ultimately incapable of protecting his town or his daughter. Loomis, as Michael's "guardian," proves similarly ineffective in providing all but the most belated intervention to Michael's crimes. We only glimpse Laurie's father briefly (her mother is entirely absent) when he reminds her to deliver a key to the Myers house so some prospective buyers can get in. There is no warmth at all in Mr Strode's hailing of Laurie, whom we are seeing for the first time. In fact, it's all business – Strode is a realtor attempting to sell the Myers place. The distance between Laurie and her father is underlined visually when they are prevented from sharing the same frame. Carpenter cuts between medium shots of Mr Strode and long shots of Laurie, who continues to walk away from her father when he speaks, even as she promises to do the work he's asked of her.

By comparison, Laurie's encounter with Tommy, the young boy she babysits, is a model of warm parental interaction – smiles, jokes, physical playfulness, patience, reassurance. Laurie runs across Tommy right after leaving her father, so the contrast between the two episodes is pronounced. In short, our first impression of Laurie codes her as an idealized parent, yet also a child somewhat removed from her own parents. Our first impression of Michael codes him as a demonized child, yet one capable of exacting the sort of recognition and revenge often craved emotionally by the child of divorce. Again, Michael as demonized child and Laurie as idealized parent are not finally opposing roles but mirror images. They are *both* children of absent parents; they are *both* capable of improvising forms of parental power, whether that takes the shape of brute strength or kind understanding; they are *both* suspended between child and adult roles by their lack of romantic partners.

What draws Michael and Laurie together as a "couple," then, are their commonalities and their shared needs – they not only see themselves in each other, but they also see the opportunity to fill the void left in their lives by their absent parents. The spectator, in turn, as a hypothetical teenage child of divorce, sees in Laurie and Michael's "union" the trauma of divorce (violence, danger, aggression) as well as a sort of fantastic resolution to that trauma – two parents who keep coming back together again, who seem destined for each other (if only to continue fighting as a result); and/or two children overcoming their divorce-induced fear of romantic relationships by reaching out to each other, however treacherous the odds (a "dance," a "prom date"). After all, Laurie delivers the "key" (literal and figurative) to Michael's house. Not surprisingly, Carpenter follows up the distant parent–child interaction between Laurie and her father and the intimate parent–child interaction between Laurie and Tommy in two ways: first, with a "scare" (Michael suddenly appears behind the door as Laurie drops off the key) and then with a "romantic" moment between Laurie and Michael. As Laurie walks away from the Myers house, Michael's left shoulder enters the frame – he stands behind her, unseen. Michael breathes heavily in the frame's foreground, while Laurie sings dreamily in the background: "I wish I had you all alone / Just the two of us …"

In these four linked moments, *Halloween* conveys the divorce-related parent–child fantasies that govern the entire film: Laurie/Michael as traumatized "children" of absent parents *and* as potential "parents" with the power to take revenge for or even overcome the trauma of that absence together. Such fantasies do not depend upon the spectator identifying with Laurie as "everyteen" or with Michael as a "parent" – instead, the mirrored relations between Laurie and Michael allow for viewer investments that transcend character identification in favor of situations that evoke not only spectacle horror, but also allegorical moments connected to the trauma of divorce. *Halloween* ends with a montage depicting the domestic spaces – a stairway, a living room, a front porch – where Laurie and Michael have "danced" together. These spaces are now empty, animated only by Michael's breathing and our memories of what took place there. The final shot presents the Myers house, where it all began – not just the spectacular murder that opens the film, but the first encounter between Laurie and Michael, the first time they share the frame. The Myers house *is* a haunted house, then. It is haunted by the audience's relief that the horror that began there is now over, as well as by the audience's regret that the domestic spaces like it, once so full of thrilling cinematic spectacle and rich affective fantasy, are now empty. In this sense, Michael's breathing is not so much a threat as a reassurance – somehow, someday, these empty spaces will be filled again.

Conclusion

Of course, the many sequels to and imitators of *Halloween* proved that spectators desired to revisit the threat and reassurance offered by the slasher film again and again. So the story of the slasher film's popularity in the wake of *Halloween*, from *Friday the 13th* to *A Nightmare on Elm Street* (1984) and everything in between, is in many ways the dominant story of the horror genre between 1978 and 1986. My analysis of *Halloween* speaks to this phenomenon, particularly in terms of how Carol J. Clover's important scholarship illuminates certain aspects of it while passing over others that do not fit easily under the rubric of psychologized identification.

But the slasher story is not the whole story. Horror films that participated in what I have described as spectacle horror were not limited to the slasher film during this period. Other noteworthy trends within spectacle horror included the zombie/cannibal apocalypse (*The Hills Have Eyes*, 1977; *Dawn of the Dead*, 1979; *The Evil Dead*, 1981; *Day of the Dead*, 1985; *The Texas Chainsaw Massacre 2*, 1986), the return of classic horror and science fiction in newly graphic guises (*Martin*, 1978; *Invasion of the Body Snatchers*, 1978; *Alien*; *An American Werewolf in London*, 1981; *The Howling*, 1981; *The Thing*, 1982; *Cat People*, 1982; *Q* (aka *The Winged Serpent*), 1982; *Re-Animator*, 1985; *The Fly*, 1986), and the supernatural thriller (*Carrie*, 1976; *The Amityville Horror*, 1979; *Phantasm*, 1979; *The Fog*, 1980; *The Shining*, 1980; *Ghost Story*, 1981; *The Entity*, 1981; *Poltergeist*, 1982). These films, often directed by "name" horror auteurs like John Carpenter, Larry Cohen, Wes Craven, David Cronenberg, Brian De Palma, Tobe Hooper, and George A. Romero, tend to fall within the critical terrain so influentially explored by Robin Wood. In my analyses of *The Texas Chain Saw Massacre* and *The Omen*, I have argued that Wood's categories of "progressive" and "reactionary," with their troublesome ties to the designation of "authentic art," cannot produce adequate political or aesthetic evaluations of these kinds of horror films, let alone the apparently "apolitical" and "artless" slasher films that surround them.

In a more recent essay Wood reflects on developments in the horror genre since The American Nightmare, asking, "Aside from *Day of the Dead*, is there *any* American horror movie made since 1980 that could be championed as any sort of radical statement about our impossible (so-called) civilization?" For Wood, the answer is a resounding no, and he places the blame squarely on the slasher film. This subgenre, according to Wood, functions "on a very low level of artistic or thematic interest," where it is barely possible to draw "certain distinctions": "The original *Halloween* ... was a well-made and effective film; the entire *Friday the 13th* series fully deserves to go, with Jason, to hell; the *Nightmare on Elm Street* films have ... a certain flair in invention and design. What more can one say?" (2004, xviii).

As I hope my reintroduction to the American horror film has suggested, there is much more to say, then and now, about the history of this film genre.

Note

This essay is dedicated to the memory of Robin Wood, 1931–2009.

References

Clover, Carol J. (1987). "Her Body, Himself: Gender in the Slasher Film." *Representations*, 20, 187–228.

Clover, Carol J. (1992). *Men, Women, and Chain Saws: Gender in the Modern Horror Film*. Princeton: Princeton University Press.

D'Emilio, John, & Freedman, Estelle B. (1988). *Intimate Matters: A History of Sexuality in America*. New York: Harper & Row.

Gunning, Tom. (1990). "The Cinema of Attractions: Early Film, Its Spectator and the Avant-Garde" (1986). In Thomas Elsaesser and Adam Barker (eds), *Early Cinema: Space-Frame-Narrative* (pp. 56–62). London: British Film Institute.

Lowenstein, Adam. (2004). "The Master, the Maniac, and *Frenzy*: Hitchcock's Legacy of Horror." In Richard Allen and Sam Ishii-Gonzáles (eds), *Hitchcock: Past and Future* (pp. 179–192). London: Routledge.

Lowenstein, Adam. (2005). *Shocking Representation: Historical Trauma, National Cinema, and the Modern Horror Film*. New York: Columbia University Press.

Mulvey, Laura. (1986). "Visual Pleasure and Narrative Cinema" (1975). In Philip Rosen (ed.), *Narrative, Apparatus, Ideology: A Film Theory Reader* (pp. 198–209). New York: Columbia University Press.

Wood, Robin. (1979). "An Introduction to the American Horror Film." In Robin Wood & Richard Lippe (eds), *The American Nightmare: Essays on the Horror Film* (pp. 7–28). Toronto: Festival of Festivals.

Wood, Robin. (2002). *Hitchcock's Films Revisited*. Rev. edn. New York: Columbia University Press.

Wood, Robin. (2004). "Foreword: 'What Lies Beneath?'" In Steven Jay Schneider (ed.), *Horror Film and Psychoanalysis: Freud's Worst Nightmare* (pp. xiii–xviii). Cambridge: Cambridge University Press.

17

Back to the Future
Hollywood and Reagan's America

Susan Jeffords

Professor and Vice Chancellor, University of Washington Bothell, United States

It is no coincidence, as Susan Jeffords argues, that during **Ronald Reagan**'s presidency – touted as a "**revolution**" by the New Right – numerous box office hits centered on simplistic **good versus evil** and **father–son themes**, suitable to evolving **special effects technology**. As a former movie star, Reagan seamlessly meshed policy rhetoric with Hollywood tropes and catchphrases. He borrowed "**the evil empire**" from ***Star Wars*** to describe the Soviet Union, unearthing **Cold War** animosity and denouncing détente, while also appropriating the series title for his **anti-missile defense plan** that negated earlier nuclear arms reduction efforts. Reagan's mission to **"change"** the country back to its imagined glory before **Vietnam defeat**, is given allegorical expression in ***Back to the Future*** movies that restore the father (and country) to positions of patriarchal privilege. The ***Rambo*** films dutifully rewrite history in concert with Reagan's mission to reassert US dominance and erase the shadow of military defeat, as Jefffords's analysis of these films and their ideological underpinnings conveys. Her essay shares ground with Kristen Whissel on CGI in this volume and with Ina Rae Hark on the *Star Trek* films and Thomas Doherty on teen films in the hardcover/online edition

Additional terms, names, and concepts: "Reaganomics," Iran–Contra, paternalism

The 1980s marked the beginning of what came to be called "The Reagan Revolution." The lynchpin of the Reagan Revolution was "Reaganomics," a supply-side economic theory that argued for government deregulation, tax cuts, and limiting growth of social spending. On the international front, the Reagan Revolution adopted a confrontational stance toward communism and the Soviet Union, labeling it "the evil empire." This political philosophy included an end to détente, a ramping up of the US military, and the development of what came to be known as "Star Wars," the Strategic Defense Initiative focused on an effort to create a "shield" in space that would protect the United States against missile attacks.

American Film History: Selected Readings, 1960 to the Present, First Edition. Edited by Cynthia Lucia, Roy Grundmann, and Art Simon.

As the very naming of this time period suggests, the Reagan "revolution" of the 1980s adopted a common theme centered on "change." One of the defining paradoxes of the period, however, is that a president who himself was an icon of an earlier era articulated this message of change. Ronald Reagan, 70 years old at the time of his inauguration, not only represented the 1980s "revolution" that adopted his name, but he also represented the 1930s and 1940s, the period when he achieved Hollywood fame. Harkening back to a simpler time before nuclear conflict, before the Cold War, before the Vietnam War, and the Civil Rights and feminist movements, Reagan represented for many Americans a return to older values and more traditional ways of life. Popular culture in the 1980s reflected this tension by creating stories about change and stability, about continuity and discontinuity. Many of the decade's most popular films take up these themes, among them some of the biggest box office draws of the era: *Star Wars* (1977), *The Empire Strikes Back* (1980), and *Return of the Jedi* (1983); *Raiders of the Lost Ark* (1981), *Indiana Jones and the Temple of Doom* (1984), and *Indiana Jones and the Last Crusade* (1989); *First Blood* (1982), *Rambo: First Blood, Part II* (1985), and *Rambo III* (1988); Robert Zemeckis's *Back to the Future* (1985), *Back to the Future, Part II* (1989), and *Back to the Future, Part III* (1991). It is no accident, given these themes, that the films themselves became sources of seemingly endless continuity through sequels that carried their stories forward. Relying heavily on special effects – presented by the film industry as a technology of the future, much in the same vein as Reagan touted his "Star Wars" technology – it is also no accident that these films were marketed and appealed to a youthful, largely teenage audience.

Strongly expressing these themes of change and stability, continuity and discontinuity, George Lucas's *Star Wars* fundamentally changed American filmmaking by setting new expectations for special effects and imagery, altering not only the kinds of films that were made but the resources required to make them. Lucas formed his own visual effects company – Industrial Light and Magic – as a way of achieving the effects he wanted in *Star Wars* and introducing effects to filmmaking that have since become staples of the Hollywood action film. Through the remainder of the 1970s and into the 1980s, Hollywood became enthralled with the special effects blockbuster. Beyond the films already mentioned, some of Hollywood's top-grossing films appeared between 1977 and 1989: *Superman* (1978), *Rocky II* (1979), *Superman II* (1981), *E.T.* (1982), *Blade Runner* (1982), *Ghostbusters* (1984), *Top Gun* (1986), *Batman* (1989). The special effects trend worked to further support and compellingly express the themes of the "Reagan Revolution," particularly for a younger audience drawn to these effects extravaganzas.

Such films also represented Hollywood's response to the expansion of cable television offerings, which, more than ever before, provided a wider variety of programming, more viewing options, and – with the founding of HBO in 1972 – new opportunities for watching films directly on home television sets. Hollywood responded, first and foremost, not only by appealing to teenagers – the demographic least likely to want to stay at home – but also by increasing its production of film experiences that could not be duplicated on the television set at home. While watching an intense character drama might be just as appealing – or maybe even more so – in an intimate home setting, the special effects extravaganza required the large screen and sophisticated sound system to be fully appreciated. What makes the period of 1977–1988 special in this regard, then, is that it marks the arrival of the special effects blockbuster and a teen-focused marketing strategy that has since dominated the Hollywood industry.

Reagan Era Hollywood and the Battle of Good versus Evil

While a common characteristic of Reagan-era Hollywood is the shift to special effects blockbusters catering to a teen audience, common narrative themes emerge in these films as well, clearly reflecting the political and social times in which they were produced. Although technical features reveal the effort to appeal to a largely teenage audience, the content of the films is not determined only by the technology available to filmmakers. For that, we must turn to the events of the time in order to understand why this content explores issues of such strong appeal to target the audience.

The top-selling films of the period are largely allegories of *good versus evil*. The *Star Wars* series is the

Figure 17.1 Obi-Wan Kenobi fights Darth Vader in the spectacular battle of good against evil in George Lucas's *Star Wars* (1977, producer Gary Kurtz).

most obvious example, with the entire sequence of films narrating the battle waged for domination of the universe by the "dark side" and the "Force," that which, according to Obi-Wan Kenobi, "binds the galaxy together." The same can be said of the *Indiana Jones* series, along with the *Rocky*, *Rambo*, and *Superman* series. Although the contest between "good" and "evil" has been one of the main themes of storytelling for thousands of years, its emergence in films of the mid-1970s can be partially explained by the role of special effects. With the special-effects emphasis on spectacular imagery, complex plots give way to spectacle as a means of capturing audience interest and encouraging them to leave their homes (and televisions) and pay for a movie ticket.

The straightforward conflict between "good" and "evil" formed a ready scaffold for the spectacular film sequences characterizing the most popular films of this period. And the simplified good-versus-evil political rhetoric of the era was neatly reinforced for audiences accustomed to hearing it in the broader culture with Reagan's election in 1980. Film critic Peter Biskind captures this sense of simplicity in his study of Hollywood films of this period, concluding that "when all was said and done, Lucas and Spielberg returned the 1970s audience, grown sophisticated on a diet of European and New Hollywood films, to the simplicities of the pre-1960s Golden Age of movies ... They marched backward through the looking-glass" (1998, 343).

Star Wars: Securing the Son's Future through the Past

Along with good versus evil, *change*, as previously noted, was also a prominent theme of the era, one most notably addressed in films that centered on the relationships between fathers and sons. Relationships between fathers and sons carried an obvious emotional overlay for audiences, particularly for teenage sons navigating relationships with their own fathers. The dynamic was simple as was the narrative question it posed: How do fathers and sons get along? Stories about fathers and sons did not require much in the way of plot explanation or background; they were stories already familiar to all and could therefore easily accommodate the hallmark spectacles of these films. Moreover, because these stories by definition traced the passage of time, films about fathers and sons engaged with questions of change that permeated the culture of the time: How, for example, do things change from one generation to the next? How does a younger generation define itself against the mistakes of the past? How can a new generation be freed from the way things were done in the past, while simultaneously establishing a sense of continuity with the past? These questions became metaphors for larger political, social, and cultural debates that defined the era.

The first *Star Wars* films clearly reflect the Cold War culture out of which they emerged, with the battle between an "evil empire" that wants to dominate the universe, and a small group of rebels who stand true to "the Force," an alternative political and social system that stands for freedom across the universe. As we first meet Luke Skywalker, that older system of "the Force" seems antiquated and only the stuff of fantastic tales, while the Empire is gaining power and stability. The debate that energizes all of the films is whether this antiquated world that belonged to an older generation can be revitalized by a new generation willing to join and defend "the Force." The relationship between Luke and Darth Vader – between father and son – becomes the central defining narrative for the universe, as Luke Skywalker's personal quest to learn about his father intertwines with his rebellion against the dictatorial rule of the Emperor who sets out to destroy not only the democracy that the rebels wish to advance but also the potential bond between fathers and sons, as he knowingly orders Darth Vader to kill his own son. It is finally only the reconciliation of Skywalker with his estranged father that enables the rebellion to succeed, as Vader chooses to kill the Emperor rather than sacrifice his son. And though Vader had gone over to "the dark side," his blood is what guarantees Skywalker will become the Jedi knight with the potential to lead a revolution throughout the universe. Perfectly displaying the paradox between stability and revolution, *Star Wars* shows that, without this genetic continuity of father to son, there can be no rebellion; yet, without the rebellion, there could have been no chance for Skywalker to learn about and come into his own genetic heritage.

And, of course, father and son narratives neatly reflect the predominantly male focus of Hollywood films, especially Hollywood action films. The demographics of Hollywood's audiences and film stars indicate an increasing attention to male audiences and male actors during this period, resulting, in part, from the coming of age of the Baby Boom generation. The teen date-movie ritual at the time yielded a greater emphasis on male movie interests than on female interests, with *Variety* magazine opining, in 1972, that women's movie attendance was "dominated by their male companion's choice of screen fare" (Maltby et al. 2007, 22). Along with this came a tilting toward the male preference for action and special effects and for the stars most frequently cast in this genre. Film historian Richard Maltby summarizes this shift by pointing out that "in Classical Hollywood a roughly equal number of male and female stars appeared in exhibitors' polls of leading box-office attractions. Since the late 1960s, however, these lists have become increasingly dominated by men to a proportion, by the late 1980s, of nine to one" (Maltby et al. 2007, 22).

Consequently, films aimed at this younger male audience came to redefine Hollywood filmmaking not only in terms of special effects and genre, but also in terms of gender emphases and the kinds of stories that went with them. In this way, the father-and-son story became more than a convenient plot frame for spectacular filmmaking. It became the framing worldview of Hollywood's most successful films of the period and, therefore, indelibly influenced the film industry's direction for decades to come.

Back to the Future: Restoring the Father's "Rightful" Place in the Present

One of the best examples of this shaping influence and way in which the dominant themes of the era played out is the *Back to the Future* series. Starting in 1985 and continuing with sequels in 1989 and 1990, *Back to the Future* was the top-grossing film of 1985, out-earning *Rambo* and *Rocky IV*. The three *Back to the Future* films configure anxieties about the continuity between past and present explicitly in terms of a father-and-son relationship, as the teenager Marty McFly travels to the past to meet his own father, to the future to meet his son, and to the Old West to meet his great-grandfather. The films use Marty's personal excursions into the past and the future to symbolize large-scale social and economic changes that took place between the generations: his father's, his own, and that of his future children. What makes these films more than humorous stories about an individual's family history are the plot lines that tie Marty's life to the character of the entire community in which he lives – on his successes or failures rest the fate of all who live in Hill Valley. Underscoring the themes of continuity, Marty's actions and their consequences take place in relation to his father/great-grandfather/son. Underscoring the theme of revolution, the *Back to the Future* films insist that, indeed, one man *can* change the world.

And change is precisely the subject of these films, as Marty works to change some events, while preventing others from changing. In keeping with this dual purpose, the narratives pose change as a source of both profit and fear. "Doc" Brown, the inventor of a time-travel machine, is always reminding Marty that any action he takes in the past could have drastic effects on the future (their present). Not only can he potentially change the present world he returns to, but should he or Doc meet "himself" in the past or in the future, this could tear apart "the fabric of the universe" and destroy all life. Marty's actions in the past threaten his very life: As his presence in the past diminishes the possibilities for his parents' union, Marty finds that his family photograph begins to fade, suggesting that he, his brother, and his sister are being eliminated altogether, losing all chance of being born. (This is the most extreme anti-abortion message of the decade: If your mother believed in abortion, you couldn't return to the past to rescue her.) At the same time, Marty profits from some changes in the past, as his own poor and dysfunctional family becomes, through his intervention, the perfect, wealthy family of his dreams. Both messages converge in determining how, during the Reagan era, change was to take place. By insisting that not *all* change is good, these plots delineate not only what changes were to occur but, and perhaps most important, for whose benefit and at whose direction they were to take place.

When Marty McFly returns accidentally to the year 1955 in *Back to the Future*, he risks his own future existence, ironically, by trying to save his father from an oncoming car. In doing so, Marty takes his father's place in the affections of Lorraine (his future mother), who takes him in to nurse him back to health after his accident. The remainder of the film follows Marty's efforts to reunite his father George and his mother and make them fall in love. Successful as a matchmaker, Marty also alters their relationship by enabling George to rescue Lorraine (rather than the other way around) as she is attacked by the brutish Biff Tannen. Consequently, the George McFly who was to become a doormat for Biff, a failure at his job, and a weak role model for his children, now – in the alternate future Marty has created – is cast as Biff's superior, a best-selling author and community leader, a loving husband, and a well-rounded father. The film's opening presents us with a McFly family in which the father is a wimp who delights in *Three Stooges* comedies, the mother is an alcoholic, the uncle is in jail, the brother works at a fast food restaurant, the sister cannot get a date, and the house is a cramped collection of junk and trash. After Marty's intervention in the past, however, he returns home to find an immaculate and well-furnished home, his parents returning from a morning tennis game, his brother dressed in a suit and tie and heading for his office, his sister unable to keep track of the many boys who call her, and himself with the truck he had coveted parked in the garage.

In contrast, the destructive nature of change is shown in the plot of *Back to the Future, Part II*, when the McFly family nemeses – the Tannens – acquire a copy of a sports history almanac that Marty had purchased in the future, a magazine that details all of the sports scores of the twentieth century. Returning from 2015 to 1955 to give the magazine to "himself," Biff Tannen manages to change the entire course of time by becoming, through the assistance of the magazine, "America's greatest living folk hero," according to the "Biff Tannen Museum" erected in Hill Valley in his honor. The world that Biff has created is governed by gambling, overrun by criminals, and violent beyond repair. Schools have been burned down, housing developments have been allowed to deteriorate, and even Marty's mother, now Biff Tannen's wife, has been forced to succumb to Biff's fetishistic wishes by having her breasts surgically enlarged to distorted proportions. But perhaps the most telling sign of how bad the future world has become is when we learn that Marty's father, George, was killed in 1973. Only by returning again to 1955 and retrieving the magazine does Marty manage to return the "present," not to its original form in the beginning of *Back to the Future*, but to its altered and happier form that Marty brought about through his first return to 1955. Change in these films is, consequently, both good and bad, depending on the direction it takes and whom it benefits. Although Doc is concerned that any change in time may put the universe itself at risk and Biff's acquisition of the magazine, indeed, produces a future full of terror and abuse, Marty's minute actions in the past have improved not only his own life but that of his entire family.

What is the difference between the changes that brought about these dystopian and utopian worlds? Biff Tannen's desire for personal profit and the power that he accrues because of it produce a world that is violent, racist, ignorant, and depraved, in which

Figure 17.2 Marty McFly plays matchmaker to reunite his parents and change his own future in Robert Zemeckis's *Back to the Future* (1985, producer Steven Spielberg).

the personal desires of one man have taken precedence over the interests of the community. In contrast, Marty's efforts to reunite his parents are not self-serving in material terms – his only desire is to ensure his own future birth – but altruistic: He works throughout the film to help his father develop a stronger character. In spite of the fact that he does profit from his efforts, he has no idea at the time that he will; he is as surprised as anyone when he wakes up to a changed world. The film's message is clearly that change for personal gain is bad, but change for the improvement of the family – especially the father – is good. At the opening of the first film in the series, Marty is confronted by Mr Strickland, the school disciplinarian, with his fate as his father's son: "You remind me of your father. He was a slacker too … You're too much like your father. You don't have a chance. No McFly ever amounted to anything in the history of Hill Valley." Marty's reply – at the time an empty retort – anticipates the film's narrative trajectory: "Yeah; well, history is gonna change." The plot of *Back to the Future* turns around Strickland's edict so that not only is Marty a success but his reconstructed father is as well. Now, in the altered world of the future, Strickland's insult – "You're too much like your father" – is transformed as an epithet of praise.

This strategy of reversal was central to Reagan's America – to rewrite the recent past so that the charge "You're too much like your father" is turned from an insult – "America in the 1980s is too much like America of the 1970s and doesn't have a chance" – to a compliment. To accomplish this reversal, heroes must return to the time before things went wrong; they must return to the 1950s, before the Democratic vision of the Great Society took over the government, and they must reinvent the characters who will shape the future. Just as Marty coaches his father from being a wimp to becoming a hero, Reagan, it is implied, is coaching America from acting the part of the "wimp" as the doormat for communism and fundamentalist Islamic revolutions during the "weak" Carter years, to becoming the economically and socially successful international father-figure of the Reagan years. From the man/country who gave his children/citizens only shame, George McFly, along with the America he figures, is transformed into a father who can give his children just what they want and need – a well-rounded family marked by material success.

Another key year figured in the films is that of George McFly's murder at the hands of Biff Tannen in *Back to the Future, Part II*. George is killed in 1973, the year of final US withdrawal from Vietnam. That is the year, this film seems to be saying, in which the nation lost its direction and was given over to a period of destructive liberal values – in other words, the year in which the nation lost its father. As a result of George's death, Uncle Joe is back in jail, Marty's sister is in debt, and Marty himself has been sent to boarding school in Switzerland. Biff and Lorraine live in a penthouse at the top of his gambling casino, where Biff entertains women in his hot tub. Lorraine, physically and verbally abused by Biff, has resorted again to drinking. She has been turned from a nurturer to a sex object; her children have been abandoned; their home has been turned into a business venture. All of this results when the family is cut off from its rightful father. As goes the McFly family, so, the dates of this film would suggest, goes the nation. With the "father" gone, American children/citizens have been abandoned to lead lives of self-indulgence, addiction, and crime, all because they have been severed from their "family" by a leader who cares nothing for "family values." The home has been taken over by a "false" father who was never intended to have a family at all. All of this began in the devastating year of 1973, when an otherwise happy and thriving family/nation was cut off from its source of guidance and leadership by an untimely death. That George McFly was murdered by Biff suggests, as well, that the nation's troubles were brought about by an unjust assault on the father. It is, according to *Back to the Future, Part II*, the job of faithful and dutiful sons to retrieve not only their fathers' memory but their very bodies from the grave, and in so doing, to save the community from a future full of misery. In this context, and because the future can be altered for the worse as well as for the better, Doc's edict never to disrupt history takes on a qualified meaning. Biff Tannen has falsified history, and it is up to Marty and Doc to do everything they can to return history to its rightful path, the path in which Hill Valley is still a pleasant and peaceful community, one that honors writers like George McFly and not criminals like Biff Tannen.

But the "history" to which Doc and Marty want Hill Valley to return is in fact itself an altered history, the one in which George McFly is a hero rather than a wimp. Consequently, these narratives suggest, changing history – and risking the fabric of the universe – is worthwhile, not for personal profit, but only for the good of the father, because, as Marty's story makes clear, what is good for the father is good for the family and the community as a whole. Only Biff Tannen profits from the information in the sports magazine of the future, but everyone profits from George McFly's success. This is "trickle-down" historiography with a vengeance. Like these films, Reaganism would argue that the changes it effected – in the tax structure, in corporate regulations, in government support of social service programs, and in the size of the federal deficit – were meant to benefit not just the wealthy few – not, in other words, to create a Biff Tannen future – but to benefit the many, the family, and community as a whole, as everyone would profit from this restructuring of the role of the father to produce a heroic future.

In order to create these benefits not only the present but the past itself would have to be changed. This was to be one of the key insights of the Reagan ideologues: they could sell their vision for the present if they could invent a version of the past that validated it. For a president apparently incapable of distinguishing Hollywood from history, this proved to be a snap. From commemorating a tomb for an Unknown Soldier from the Vietnam War to put an "end" to that troubling part of the nation's past, and refiguring the mercenary Nicaraguan Contras as "freedom fighters," to vilifying the actions of the Carter presidency, Reagan reworked history in order to produce, like Marty McFly, the happy "present" he desired. And, like Marty McFly, he hoped that a present full of poverty, failure, and social dysfunction could be mended, not by offering social programs to assist those bearing these burdens, but by waving the magic wand of "history" over such scenes and thereby manufacturing a rosy image of those same lives. When Marty and Doc first discover, on their return to 1985, the disastrous world that Biff has created, Marty wants simply to return to the future to put back the sports magazine that would lead to Biff's wealth. But Doc warns that the future, from which they had just returned, is now closed off to them, since it was the future of another time line that now has been realigned through Biff's intervention. With urgency in his voice, he explains to Marty,

> Our only chance to repair the present is in the past, at the point where the time line skewed into this tangent. In order to put the universe back as we remember it and get back to our reality, we have to find out the exact date and the specific circumstances of how and where young Biff got his hands on that sports almanac.

By articulating this Reagan strategy of rewriting history, Doc acknowledges that there are alternate possibilities, not only for the future but also for the past, and that it is the job of faithful sons and ethical technologists to make sure the "right" time line is adhered to.

Without consulting any of Hill Valley's citizens, Doc and Marty "know" which time line is "right," which future will be the best for the entire community, and they take it on themselves to secure that future for everyone. This paternalistic attitude, in which "national security" was offered as a screen of trust behind which presidential actions and decisions determining the futures of entire countries were to be made without consultation with US citizens or their Congressional representatives, proved to be the hallmark of the Reagan administration. As in the case of Iran–Contra, the President simply *knew*, regardless of Congressional restraints, how to "correct" the flaws of history (such as a successful Marxist revolution) and get back to the world as we remember it.

Back to the Future, Part II even figures Reagan in its future scenarios. To follow changes in history, Marty and Doc frequently have recourse to newspapers and historical records. It is in fact a newspaper headline that prompts Doc to take Marty to the future, where he is to save his son from a jail sentence. As evidence of the bad future that Biff Tannen has created, Doc shows Marty a copy of the *Hill Valley Telegraph* with a headline that reads, "Emmett Brown Committed," above a story about how Doc has been declared insane under Biff's direction, presumably in order to prevent him from revealing the source of Biff's wealth. As part of this negative future, beneath this headline is a story with the lead, "Nixon to Seek Fifth Term, Vows End to Vietnam War by 1985." After Marty retrieves the magazine from the 1955 Biff, thereby restoring the "true" history of the film, these headlines change. The feature story now shows Doc Brown being honored for his inventions, but what is more interesting is how the Nixon headline has been altered: "Reagan to Seek Second Term, No Republican Challengers Expected." The negative and destructive future is associated with a continued Nixon presidency and an endless war in Vietnam; the positive future puts Ronald Reagan back in the White House, unopposed.

But over which "future" is Reagan presiding? The one in which George McFly is a wimp? Or the one in which he is a celebrated author and successful businessman? When Doc triumphantly declares, "The future is back," to which future is he referring? Because Marty returns home again to the altered McFly residence, audiences can only conclude that it is the second, heroic "future" that will elect Reagan president and over which his unchallenged image will reign. The prosperity of the American future is associated with a continued Reagan presence, one that will make it possible for him to seek a second term as president, unopposed, because he, like the new future he represents, was the author of the nation's "true" history all along.

Whereas time seemed a potential enemy for the Reagan Revolution in its early years – with the memories of the Vietnam War still not put firmly to rest, with Reagan's own age a possible deterrent to the continuation of the revolution, and with the United States–Soviet conflict at its potentially worst state in decades – by the end of the 1980s, time seemed to have embraced the Reagan version of history with open arms, sanctioning its rewritten narrative of American prowess and progress with the defeat of communism, the founding of a Republican dynasty, the increased political influence of the religious right, the defeat of the Sandinistas in Nicaraguan elections, and the final placement of the United States as the lone superpower in the world. Having seen his version of history triumph in progressively larger circles of time – from 1985 to 1955 to 2015 to 1885 – Doc Brown, like Reagan, is now able to see time as his ally, not his enemy. "The future is," he intones, "whatever you make of it," indicating that time, which had once controlled him and Marty, is now in their hands. This may have been, in the long run, one of the chief accomplishments of the Reagan Revolution – to have made history a tool of social control, to have pressed the past into service to one of "history's" newest sagas, "The Reagan Revolution." For who is Doc Brown other than Ronald Reagan himself? He has allied himself with technology in the name of progress; survived an assassination attempt (at the hands of one of Reagan's chief targets, Libyan terrorists!); acted as a surrogate father; turned to science fiction tales for his inspiration (Doc's childhood reading led him to want to build a time machine; Reagan's viewing of *The Day the Earth Stood Still* prompted him to envision his own "Star Wars" program); fought a future filled with crime, drugs, and idleness; enabled a dysfunctional lower-class family to improve its wealth and social status; returned an American family to its values of nurturance and success; and found his own personal history not in the hothouse parlors of the East but in the open spaces of the Wild West. Ranging over history, apparently in control of time, Ronald Reagan and Doc Brown come to stand as surrogate fathers, supplying symbolic leadership to a generation of youth whose futures seemed to have been opened up by their visions of technological wizardry and moral instruction. Both, by the end of the decade, seem to have gone beyond time itself, to have left the limitations of history and entered into the realm of fantasy, glory, and dreams.

Know Thy Father, Find Thyself, and Save the World

The *Star Wars* films provide the first of these scenarios in which the fate of the entire universe depends upon the successful reunion of a father and son. *Star Wars* suggests that knowledge of the father is such an important part of an individual's identity that, without that knowledge, the individual cannot realize his true skills and abilities. Until Luke Skywalker learns that his father was a Jedi knight, he remains a frustrated farmer. And because it is Luke, using the powers that he has inherited from his father, who finally saves the universe from the evil Emperor, the plot suggests that if Luke had stayed a farmer and if he had remained unaware of his parentage, the universe would have been doomed to misery. (There is no suggestion that he could have inherited these skills from his mother.)

One of the key features of this and other father–son stories in the 1980s is the gradual transformation of that relationship. Rambo, once trained by Colonel Trautman to be a "killing machine," rescues him from the Soviets in the final film of that sequence. Similarly, Marty McFly, initially awed by Doc Brown's knowledge and at the mercy of Doc's inventions, finally rescues Doc from his own death in 1885, enabling him to go on to become a father to his own time-traveling family. In the *Star Wars* series, Luke is initially tormented by and divided from his then unknown father. But by the final movie, Luke has rescued his father from the "dark side" and has returned him to the heavenly world of the "Force." Even the final *Indiana Jones* film reunites Indiana Jones with his long-estranged father, whom he must rescue from his Nazi jailers. This list comprises a substantial selection of Hollywood's blockbuster film series of the period.

What does it mean when a group of films so diverse in plot content – from fighting intergalactic wars to rescuing Vietnam prisoners of war to traveling through time to recovering ancient artifacts – should be so similar in structure and in narrative sequence? While it is not possible to assert that the Reagan Revolution *caused* such stories to be written or to be so popularly viewed, it is possible, however, to suggest that both the Reagan Revolution and these films captured in some sense the concerns of the American electorate/audiences and offered a resolution to their anxieties through the restoration of a happy father–son relationship to the benefit of the community/nation/universe. It is not hard to conjecture about such concerns. It is a commonplace in discussions of the Vietnam War that it brought the United States its first military defeat (the Korean War is seen in such analyses as a standoff). Coming a few years after the final, ignominious withdrawal of American forces from Vietnam was the hostage crisis in Tehran. During this same period, the United States experienced several recessions (the most significant of which was during the Carter presidency) at the same time that increased international competition became a source of concern for US manufacturing industries. With all of this, it is not hard to imagine how narratives of continuity could well capture the attention of large sectors of the American public, concerned as they were with the central question of whether US power, ascendant after World War II, would be able to continue that ascendancy in the future. And, in the face of signs that US power was diminishing, what kind of "revolution" would be called for to restore that power? Invoking the days before that power waned, Ronald Reagan, Colonel Trautman, Doc Brown, Dr Jones, and Obi-Wan Kenobi all stand as emblems of a personal and national identity that could be recaptured. But because those men seemed themselves too old or too weak to restore that time, it became important to put forward younger men who could, through rescuing these elderly mentors, rescue the nation that needed them as well. For a while, Reagan was himself that "younger man," with his image of vitality, health, and agelessness. But, throughout the Reagan presidency, George Bush stood waiting to take on the role he would adopt in 1988, as the son who would receive his inheritance from his acknowledged father.

Time and the Triumph over Evil

The plots of the Reagan-era special effects blockbusters present a successful father–son relationship as essential to the defeat of evil and the triumph of good. In *Raiders of the Lost Ark*, that evil is one of the most readily acknowledged demons of twentieth-century Western history – Nazism. In *Star Wars*, the evil emanates from a similarly despotic ruler who is attempting to crush all freedoms from the universe. In *Rambo*, the evil is the overtly communist enemy who has made Americans hostage to their own freedoms. And in *Back to the Future*, the evil of the small-minded and greedy Tannens represents not just a bad family but a crime-ridden and lawless future world. In each case, the interlocking themes of "good versus evil" and of "fathers and sons" stand out. Such terms may seem simplistic, but they are exactly the terms whereby Reagan carried out his own narrative of American history. Externally, the Soviet Union was an "evil empire," and Marxist revolutionaries in Latin America were merely surrogates of that evil. Internally, non-normative families and peoples were bringing about the decline of the nation as a whole.

The theme of "time" shows up as well, in that these films all take on the span of time as their subject, with Indiana Jones an archaeologist who explores artifacts from early biblical to ancient Indian religions, with Luke Skywalker the last in a long line of Jedi knights, with Rambo fighting the wars of America's recent past, and with Marty McFly traveling through time itself. Consequently, one key to the success of these films is not only their resolution of the father–son relationship but also their appropriation of time. In each case, a "happy" ending depends upon the ability of the hero to overcome the limitations of time, to rewrite history, to restructure the future, or to rescue the father from the burdens of time itself. Indiana Jones literally holds time in his hands, or rather carries it in his knapsack in the form of the artifacts of lost civilizations. Luke Skywalker's success as a Jedi depends on his ability to see what no one else can – the ghosts of his past: Obi-Wan Kenobi, Yoda, and, finally his own father, Darth Vader, as they join the afterlife of the "Force." Rambo transforms the first American military defeat into a victory with his resounding defeat of the Vietnamese and Soviet armies. And, while Marty McFly turns his own dismal life into one of prosperity, Doc Brown moves beyond his own lifetime to become a master of time itself.

If, as the Reagan Revolution suggested, stories of American decline and loss are to be rewritten and the emblems of previous times are to be retrieved, then history must come under the control of the present. All of these films, in keeping with this idea, rewrite the pasts they have inherited. In successive battles Rambo rejects the narrow middle-class economy, bureaucratic government leadership, and a self-serving multinational corporate mentality. Marty McFly rejects the unmotivated and self-defeating image of his economically incompetent father and his own middle-management future to become the author of his own open life. Luke Skywalker rejects his uncle's limited agrarian goals as well as Darth Vader's service in the authoritarian empire of evil to align himself with the forces of rebellion. All of these films insist on the value of the father to the health of the community, but they also caution that restoring the father will not be enough, that the habits of the father will not ensure a successful future. Instead, in each case, the son must develop his own individual qualities, under the mentorship of the father, to produce a set of abilities appropriate for his future. Continuity must be combined with revolution to produce a happy ending.

But this combination of continuity and change indicates an important qualification of the Reagan ideology. Many criticized Reagan for wanting to return to the past, for retrieving the images, characters, and values of an earlier time; but Reagan's strategy was much more complex. He did indeed invoke those earlier times to advance much of his agenda – whether centered on the strengthening of the heterosexual, domestic family unit, on the positioning of the United States as triumphant international police officer, or on insisting upon a single, heteronormative sexual model – but he also combined those nostalgic images with an up-to-date technology and a "new" economic theory. And, perhaps more than anything, Reagan himself stood paradoxically for continuity and change, extending into the present images and narratives of earlier decades at the same time as lobbying for immediate change in a departure away from

Democratic leadership and its social service agenda. The film narratives centered on father–son relations, consequently, help both to show how change is possible (the son replaces the father) and to caution against change taking too radical a form (the son models himself after the father). They serve largely to justify a conservative agenda that can be adjusted to accommodate different economic and political policies while maintaining the general framework of a narrative of continuity. "Family values" thus comes to mean a great deal more in the Reagan era than simply which parent works and whether teenagers abstain from sex until marriage; it provides the ideational paradigm for the very structure of mainstream social narratives in the 1980s, as fathers and sons pass on the stories of national identities, agendas, and futures.

By the late 1980s and early 1990s, the moviegoing public's fascination with the father–son plot seemed to have dwindled, with the appearance of many popular brother and buddy films eclipsing father–son narratives. Ivan Reitman's *Twins* (1988) and Barry Levinson's *Rain Man* (1988) are the most explicit examples, while interracial buddy films like *Lethal Weapon 2* (1989), *Flight of the Intruder* (1991), *Diggstown II* (1992), *White Men Can't Jump* (1992), and *Die Hard with a Vengeance* (1995) were among the most popular of these narratives. Perhaps the growing recession, increasing joblessness, and decreasing US economic standing led some viewers to feel less concern about continuity than about the need for a "revolution" in their own economic positions, a tendency that the presidential campaign of Bill Clinton successfully recognized and capitalized upon as a political strategy.

References

Biskind, Peter. (1998). *Easy Riders, Raging Bulls: How the Sex-Drugs-and-Rock 'n' Roll Generation Saved Hollywood*. New York: Simon & Schuster.

Maltby, Richard, Stokes, Melvyn, & Allen, Robert C. (eds). (2007). *Going to the Movies: Hollywood and the Social Experience of Cinema*. Exeter: Exeter University Press.

18

"Stayin' Alive"
The Post-Studio Hollywood Musical

Karen Backstein
Independent scholar

The American film musical thrived during Hollywood's studio era – with all of the technology and people in place to stage lavish production numbers inside narratives of **utopian promise**, if occasionally peppered with darker moments. Karen Backstein takes a look at what happened to the musical in the **post-studio**, **postmodern** era when ready resources no longer existed and hard-edged **realism** became the dominant narrative mode onscreen. ***West Side Story*** (1961) – with its urban setting, location shooting, and narrative centered on ethnic gang warfare – set the stage for later **show musicals** like ***Cabaret*** and ***Chicago***, infused with darkness and discontent, and **dance films** like ***Saturday Night Fever*** and Disney's ongoing ***Step Up* franchise**, that thematize real-world issues. Grounded in representations of stage or street performances, these films manage to maintain a level of realism appealing to contemporary audiences. Through the lens of **residual**, **dominant**, and **emergent styles** that theorist Raymond Williams provides, Backstein also discusses the heightened **reflexivity**, that is simultaneously authentic and artificial, nostalgic and seriously **revisionist**, in films like Martin Scorsese's ***New York, New York*** and Francis Ford Coppola's ***One from the Heart***. Backstein's essay shares ground with Desirée Garcia on the folk musical in Volume I.

Additional terms, names, and concepts: balleticization, Brechtian distancing, film genre, musical, postmodern musical

Overture: The Studio System Fades

Perhaps more than any other genre, the musical – at least in its classic Hollywood model – benefited from the studio system and its mode of organization and working. Often featuring a plethora of dancers, a full-size orchestra, and costly production numbers requiring hours of rehearsal, musicals placed huge demands on time and budgets. Inevitably, as the system, with its underlying ideology, began to crumble, the musical suffered a crisis. Without a solid institutional structure to provide support, the production of

American Film History: Selected Readings, 1960 to the Present, First Edition. Edited by Cynthia Lucia, Roy Grundmann, and Art Simon.

wholly original film musicals dwindled as the 1960s came to a close and the 1970s arrived. The savvy professionals who had labored under set-in-stone contracts – like those that bound talents such as choreographer Jack Cole and his dance troupe to Columbia Pictures – were no longer on call. Teams like Arthur Freed's fabled unit at MGM faded into oblivion. The personnel who replaced them were less dedicated to and less practiced in the genre and the specific demands it placed on filmmaking technique and style. Many new productions took a conservative approach, depending on the built-in buzz of a previous Broadway hit. Those directors who did try to innovate during the 1970s often met with critical and financial failure, although time has often proven kinder to their work. And as commercial cinema's reliance on fairy tales gave way to grittier dramas, it was easy to forget the many moments of darkness, even in the traditional musical (as in most fairy tales), and to regard them as old-fashioned and out of step with the times.

The truth is, in a medium as conventionally associated with the "real" as cinema, there is a certain discomfort when characters spontaneously burst into song and dance. Filmmakers – the term is used here to include not only the director but also the many artists who bring a movie to life – always realized this difficulty and employed a wide variety of cues to create seamless transitions from everyday sequences to lavish production numbers. These strategies have been well analyzed from different points of view by such theorists as Peter Wollen, Rick Altman, Richard Dyer, and Jane Feuer.[1] Simple walks gradually build into choreography. Whistling and humming transform into a tune. Backstage and performance spaces make theatricality "natural." A character's bubbling emotions grow more and more agitated until they boil over – and need an outlet for release. Even a film like *An American in Paris* (1951) – with its lengthy and highly formal final ballet – anchored its choreography in the protagonist's reverie, providing both psychological motivations (Kelly's misery at losing his girl) and cinematic signals (extreme close-ups) to cue the viewers' expectations. But the increasing balleticization of the musical from the late 1940s to the early 1960s shifted the parameters, taking dance (and with it the music) further and further away from the popular, social forms like tap, jazz, and ballroom that had permeated the genre early in its development.[2]

In Bob Fosse's words when he was preparing to make *Cabaret* (1972),

> all the Gene Kelly, Fred Astaire musicals – they're classics. But they represent another era. Today I get very antsy watching musicals in which people are singing as they walk down the street or hang out the laundry. In fact, I think it looks a little silly. (Tropiano 2011, 51)

Underlying Fosse's concern is a belief in film's innate tendency to capture reality. A musical like *Cabaret* caters to this inherent surplus realism through its backstage setting, which indirectly also references the tradition of the music hall with its modest spaces, small-scale acts, tin-pan orchestras, and lower-class audiences. Severing such a connection to the real would require an altogether new text that steps entirely outside of its boundaries, thoroughly refashioning the real. Such is the appeal of *Rocky Horror Picture Show* (1975), in which that white-bread couple Janet and Brad enter a mock-horror world that completely upends their suburban expectations and their identities. That cult audiences attending *Rocky Horror* eventually chose to fully break the wall between the theater and the screen by actively participating indicates how successful a full departure from naturalism could be for the musical – something Disney has since discovered in linking the musical with animation, a form entirely divorced from the real.

The final notes for the type of musical Fosse refers to really began to sound in 1961 with *West Side Story*, an elaborate choreo-opera (to use the term coined by codirector and choreographer Jerome Robbins) that took the genre to its furthest point and also exploded it. In some respects, *West Side Story* was the culmination of Gene Kelly's push toward ballet and toward longer and longer pure dance numbers in his later films; one can even point to *It's Always Fair Weather* (1955) as a harbinger of the contemporary musical's turn to darkness and discontent.[3] (Notably that film itself was Kelly's "sequel" to his adaptation of Robbins's own *On the Town* (1949), in what was a clear give-and-take between the two most popular American brands in ballet and filmdance.) Admittedly, the choice of *West Side Story* is to some degree arbitrary. Some very old-style musicals became wildly popular even after its release, and when exploring the canon, it is always possible to find individual cases that fly in the face of more general trends. In this respect

Figure 18.1 Shot on location, Robert Wise and Jerome Robbins's *West Side Story* (1961, producers Walter Mirisch, Robert Wise and Saul Chaplin) places formalist balletic dance moves on gritty New York City streets.

Raymond Williams's (1977) concept of residual, dominant, and emergent styles proves especially useful in examining the rich body of musical texts: At any one time, these three modes coexist, with some films serving as throwbacks to earlier styles while others, ahead of their time, seem to flash-forward. Residual musicals during the 1970s and 1980s aimed to resemble the classical Hollywood product (*Fiddler on the Roof*, 1971; *Man of La Mancha*, 1972; *Funny Lady*, 1975; *Annie*, 1982), while the emergent texts often found their impetus in non-American filmmaking – especially the European new waves – that veered from commercial fare (*At Long Last Love*, 1975; *Pennies from Heaven*, 1981). *West Side Story* pushed the envelope both in its choreography and its cinematic choices. While the film looks back to the previous decade, its commercial and artistic success sent ripples into the future more than other later blockbuster musicals like *The Sound of Music* (1965). *West Side Story* raises the central question of how a "realistic" story can be told through music and dance. The issues confronted during its production – particularly how to achieve the proper balance of realism and theatricality – continued to attract directors who later grappled with the genre once studio rules had disappeared.

Taking its complex jazz-ballet and symphonic styling from the studio into the street, *West Side Story* mixed the most artificial of forms with a gritty, contemporary story of ethnic gang warfare. The combination of extreme formalism and on-location realism had gone about as far as it could go, as balletic hoodlums crossed an actual rubble-strewn New York City landscape while executing pirouettes, *jetés*, and *battements*. It owed as much to the ballet stage – where, ironically, many of the dance numbers have finally settled – as to Broadway, and many critics perceived an irresolvable stylistic clash between the subject matter and the presentation. In this, Gene Kelly's statement comes to mind: "There was no character … that couldn't be interpreted through dancing if one found the correct choreographic language. What you can't have is a truck driver coming on stage and doing an *entrechat*" (Wollen 2012, 22). But *West Side Story* came close to doing just that. Although the film proved hugely popular at the box office and won 10 Academy Awards, the pendulum had begun to swing, and no one since has tried to duplicate *West Side Story*'s achievement. But its stylistic choices have reverberated through the decades, whether through rejection or postmodern imitation.[4] These thorny issues of realism versus stylization have influenced the creation of such films as Julien Temple's *Absolute Beginners* (1986) and music videos like *Beat It* and *Bad* (1987). Such issues obsessed Bob Fosse as he worked on *Cabaret*, and in a different way, they formed the framework on which Martin Scorsese and Francis Ford Coppola would build their own postmodern musical texts, *New York, New York* and *One from the Heart*, respectively. More recently, these concerns became a central dilemma for Rob Marshall as he transformed Fosse's *Chicago* (2002) from a "vaudeville" revue into a movie.

The parameters of the classical Hollywood musical and its downward trajectory, in terms of popularity and number of films released, mirror the decline of the studio system. Of course, as with many other Hollywood genres, the musical underwent change, particularly in the 1960s and 1970s. Whereas the gangster film and the Western remained rooted in aggression, power, and paranoia, however, the musical could never quite abandon and, therefore was forced to grapple with, its utopian vision. The musical did not so much disappear as undergo a sea change. Unlike the two other genres whose innate violence and pessimism lent itself to historical revisionism, however, the musical's revisionist variations seemed intent on wrestling with both its Brechtian distancing devices and its much-lauded (by such critics as Richard Dyer) utopian tendencies. Even in revisionist rejection of what the musical was, there remains a kind of nostalgia for the genre's potential to express joy, community, and a more egalitarian social system.

At the same time, the problem producers had to confront as the 1960s ended and the 1970s arrived, was American cinema's penchant for harder-edged filmmaking, with darkness magnified. How would the musical, redolent of fantasy, fit into this new American cinema, forged by directors like Robert Altman (*McCabe & Mrs. Miller*, 1971), Martin Scorsese (*Mean Streets*, 1973; *Taxi Driver*, 1976), and Sam Peckinpah (*The Wild Bunch*, 1969)? American filmmakers like Peter Bogdanovich, Scorsese, and Coppola were savvy cinephiles and therefore aware of the work of such European directors as Jacques Demy and Jean-Luc Godard, many of whom had turned a deconstructive eye on the musical form with films like *Les Parapluies de Cherbourg* (1964) and *Une femme est une femme* (1961). At the same time, in America, the studios were not entirely dead, and there was still a hope that they might repeat the successes of the past – like the money-making, multi-award-winning *The Sound of Music* or *Funny Girl* (1968). Nothing completely died out, but more varied approaches lived on, both competing with and influencing each other.

Yet a more fundamental question began to arise during this time: What actually constitutes a musical after the genre's deconstruction? Considering that many critics rejected the musical label for *Cabaret*, now universally acknowledged as such, instead preferring to call it "a drama with music" (Tropiano 2011, 92), it is clear that the parameters of the genre have shifted. Does *Dirty Dancing* (1987) qualify, given the importance of dance both to the narrative and audience pleasure? What about the original *Footloose* (1984), with its soundtrack songs and "duped in" dancing? Or *The Adventures of Priscilla, Queen of the Desert* (1994)? How would one characterize *Saturday Night Fever* (1977), a seriously dramatic film with a brilliantly successful soundtrack, featuring songs, again not sung by onscreen performers, and with highly choreographed social dance that mirrored what was occurring at clubs and discos night after night? In short, what happens to a genre when actual amateurs take over the singing and dancing once performed by professionals who strove to impart the "joys of being an amateur"? (Feuer 1982, 13).

None initially becoming dominant, numerous approaches to the genre emerged, including: adaptations of stage musicals; postmodern musicals that deliberately deconstruct the ideology beneath the genre, such as *Pennies from Heaven* (1981), based on the British TV series; and musicals that channel the fresh burst of energy MTV created as a force to be reckoned with – one built on musical and choreographic bricolage, liberally plucking images and tropes from the past.

All these permutations – from backstage to Brechtian to "music video" style – will be examined in relation to the issues that film theorists have debated in discussing the classical musical: professionalism; the idea of work as play; the formation (or fragmentation) of community; utopianism. Given the large body of musicals and the limited parameters of this essay, "samples" or "examples," are chosen, of necessity, to illustrate and raise various theoretical and cultural points. Obviously, many other works (and many other categories) can alternatively be explored.

Although this essay aims to raise some central issues, it cannot possibly answer all the potential questions.

From Stage to Screen: The Show Musical

From *The Gay Divorcee* and *On the Town* to contemporary theatrical hits like *Les Misérables*, Broadway has always served as a "feeder" for Hollywood, providing musicals that already had proven their popularity and garnered critical acclaim. While we tend to think of the golden age of musicals through the eyes of film innovators like Busby Berkeley, Fred Astaire, and Gene Kelly, the studios never stopped looking to the stage for product. As the musical genre diminished in the post-studio era, this built-in recognition factor assumed more importance: Musicals were hard to sell, but it might be easier if an established fan base already existed. The move from the theatricality of a stage to the "reality" of the screen, however, usually required extensive revisions – especially when the studio back lot, with its curious mix of imitation and artificiality, had disappeared. A few throwbacks, like Gene Kelly's commercially unsuccessful 1969 adaptation of *Hello, Dolly!*, might have suggested that hewing to an older style could not work with contemporary audiences. But others, including *Fiddler on the Roof* (1971), fit the "residual" mode as they came to the screen, finding their audience without radically departing from earlier cinematic styles or greatly modifying the original text. In its way, *Fiddler* fits into the long line of traditional translations from an earlier era, like *Oklahoma!* (1955), *Carousel* (1956), or *The King and I* (1956). While its shtetl setting eliminates the utopian dimension Dyer has pointed to, it also firmly places the story in the past, with a "folk" feeling that links the singing and dancing in both culture and ritual – most especially in the celebrated wedding scene. Though the narrative deals with actual historical prejudice and violence, the physical space on the screen suggests an "otherwhere," long ago and far away.

Complicating matters is the fact that during this same time the theater also underwent its own period of innovation: reconceiving narrative (*A Chorus Line*, *Chicago*, *Dancin'*, *Contact*), becoming more operatic in form with almost fully sung texts (*Phantom of the Opera*, *Les Misérables*), and later, like cinema, moving toward predigested product with a high recognition factor (jukebox musicals like *Mamma Mia!* and *Jersey Boys*). In the case of some of Broadway's biggest hits, decades elapsed before they came to the screen, with the cultural ground shifting beneath them in the meantime. And when the transformation to celluloid happened, the cinematic magic often didn't. *A Chorus Line*, with its unique and deeply personal "audition" structure, based on the actual struggles of its original cast, was not a singular sensation on the screen. The show premiered in 1975; the film, directed by Richard Attenborough, opened a decade later. No truly cinematic means had been found to replace what the theater provided: the impassively godlike offstage voice of a never-seen director, controlling the fates of the auditioners; the intimacy of the actors delivering their heartfelt monologues, one by one, in what felt like a direct address to individual audience members; and the reflexive collapsing of the onstage "narrative" space with the spectatorial space of the auditorium.

Attenborough struggled against the minimalism of the original, with its one set (the stage itself) and its self-conscious theatricality. But the conventional "opening up" of the story – which included shots outside the theater and flashbacks – only diminished the play's emotional rawness and emphasized the narrative's lack of forward impetus. Even the choreography, the star of the play, could not be suitably reworked for the two-dimensional medium. (It did not help that its creator, the innovative Michael Bennett, was a victim of AIDS and no longer living.) Whereas on stage the movement often began small and then grew in power and complexity, in harmony with the dancers' heightened emotions and revelations, that kinetic energy simply did not come across consistently in Attenborough's filming. Nor did Attenborough find a substitute for the dynamics among the auditioners; on stage, when one dancer performs a solo, the audience is always aware of the others watching, judging, often approving, and always wondering if this person performing will get the job they all really need. Cutting to reaction shots – a favorite strategy in pre-Astaire musicals that Attenborough uses here to inscribe the perspectives of Zach, the auditioning director, and his assistant – destroys the integrity of the choreography. Moreover, in conveying Zach's impressions, the film reveals information that remains (necessarily) inaccessible to the theater audience. But to stay with the choreography would limit the film to the stage as a single setting and potentially diminish access to the emotions and thought processes of the group. In an effort to add cinematic power, during the first large audition, well before the director has weeded down to the last few hopefuls, the camera hovers over the packed stage, before swooping in through the dancers. But in focusing on individuals as the camera tracks forward, the film contradicts the story's very ideology. Despite the characters' memorable individuality that shines through during the director's inquisition, they ultimately aim to shed their individuality and prove their capacity for blending in – something the camera undermines by signaling viewer attention to this or that character. In another instance, cutting patterns – including a flashback – deny viewers the chance to grow ever more amazed as the show-offy "I Can Do That" progresses, piling on increasingly difficult tricks. Nor can the movie resist the impulse to overemphasize the faded love story between Zach (Michael Douglas) and his former star dancer, Cassie (Alyson Reed) – a romance that played only the smallest part in the original.

Similarly, it took over 20 years for the film adaptation of Andrew Lloyd Webber's *The Phantom of the Opera*, premiering onstage in 1986, to appear onscreen. Famed for its crashing chandelier that gave the audience a frisson of near-fear as it almost fell right into the orchestra seats, this film, too, found no visual equivalent to a highly theatrical experience. *Phantom*'s practically operatic and lushly orchestrated score, with minimal spoken text, influenced later Broadway productions, but was a rarity in contemporary cinema. And with cinematic translations of humongous theatrical hits, the potential wrath of millions of fans always is possible: The casting of Gerard Butler, with the "rock 'n' roll sensibility" supposedly required to bring in young audiences backfired, for this inferior singer ironically was hidden behind makeup that destroyed any chance of real star sex appeal. While the 1998 film earned roughly $155 million worldwide, given its $70 million budget, it could hardly be called a brilliant success and certainly did not achieve the stature of its Broadway equivalent as the longest-running musical.

The film adaptation of *Les Misérables* (2012), another operatic spectacle, was more conventionally successful, winning several Oscars. Despite the breadth and grandeur of its revolutionary story with its potential for multiple locations and expansive battle scenes – a scenario well suited to escaping the confines of the stage – the film chose instead to go smaller, with intensely tight close-ups in which faces loom large, with the camera practically peering down the actors' throats as they sing. (Interestingly, this strategy might work far better on television than on the large screen.)

This raises the question of what makes an effective transition when a film director has to jettison the theatricality, the personal presence of a star, and even the participatory role that the audience plays when humans on and off stage exchange energy. *Mamma Mia!*, the play, not only had superb singers, but also benefited from theatergoers who joyfully rose from their seats and began dancing and singing along with catchy ABBA tunes they already knew. This didn't happen with the screen version (2008), which, with a few exceptions, featured a roster of well-known actors who were also painfully poor singers. As a result, performances in the film adaptation failed to endear themselves to audiences as they had onstage or as such amateurish singing had in film musicals like Woody Allen's *Everyone Says I Love You* (1996). Obviously, viewers are sometimes simply eager to see the show, as in *Fiddler on the Roof*, even without cinematic redefintion. But several landmark films did turn a fresh eye on the process of adaptation, including Miloš Forman's *Hair* (1979). The play, which premiered in 1967, emerged from the bourgeoning counterculture of hippies and anti-war protesters. By the time the adaptation opened, the country had lived through the shock of Watergate and Nixon's resignation. Forman used the musical to look back at a faded period of hopeful revolution, but also to a time of lively street life when young people joined sit-ins and love-ins, and played their guitars in Central Park. That contemporary youth would sing and dance in the open, turning the world into a stage, was a given. He opened the story up, using the park itself and chose as a choreographer Twyla Tharp, who started out working in alternative, non-proscenium spaces. Her uniquely loose, quirky movement, often full of humor, matched the relaxed, often marijuana-fueled, hippie style. Forman also understood that the songs could work on a double level: to describe the protagonists' emotions, but also to allude to the larger political turmoil enveloping the country. *Hair* managed to gaze backward at its theatrical origins while at the same time seeming completely contemporary – and never trapped within the confines of the theater.

Cabaret and *Chicago*: Fosse redefining and redefined

On all levels – cinematically, critically, and financially – *Cabaret* (1972) proved both successful and significantly influential on films to follow. Like *West Side Story*, *Cabaret* examined a serious subject: the twilight of Germany's Weimar era and the coming of "a tomorrow" that belonged to the National Socialist Party. But Fosse went in the opposite direction of Wise and Robbins. With one crucial exception ("Tomorrow Belongs to Me," the chilling Nazi anthem sung in a beer garden), the music and choreography take place entirely in the Kit Kat Klub, the site of the eponymous nightclub revue. No more bursting into song and dance anytime, anywhere: Now the singers and dancers conform to conventional notions of reality, performing only in the expected locales. This approach is something that producer Cy Feuer, and director Bob Fosse (after his abject failure of *Sweet Charity* in 1969) immediately agreed upon. As Feuer proclaimed: "There can be no unjustified singing on the screen" (Tropiano 2011, 50). *Cabaret* is thus a film divided. A dramatic, non-musical half chronicles the ill-fated romance of the lowbrow singer Sally Bowles (Liza Minnelli) with the writer and sometime English teacher Brian Roberts (Michael York), along with another romantic subplot concerning the Jewish heiress Natalia Landauer (Marisa Berenson) with Fritz Wendell (Fritz Wepper), Brian's student and a closet Jew himself. On the other hand, the film showcases the spectacles of the Kit Kat Klub, the seedy cabaret where Sally performs, hosted by an unnamed and somewhat menacing Emcee (Joel Grey). The former has forward narrative propulsion; the latter provides both pleasure and commentary on the offstage action.

A well-respected dancer and choreographer of stage and screen, Fosse remains a crucial link between the big-name creators of the past, like Gene Kelly and Jerome Robbins, and future director/choreographers like Susan Strohman and Rob Marshall. Additionally, Fosse's then-wife Gwen Verdon had danced for renowned screen choreographer Jack Cole at Columbia, and she was, by all accounts, deeply involved in every aspect of his work, thus conveying her own experience and knowledge and providing another link to the past (see Tropiano 2011 and Wasson 2013). When he began working in film, Fosse, like Busby Berkeley, developed a method of shooting in harmony with his movement choices – one based on editing that highlighted the already-fragmented gestures, the jazzy isolations of the body that he tended to choreograph. Tropiano speaks of how the traditional musical captures the whole body in space and respects the time over which a dance evolves. *Cabaret* goes in a different direction, he points out, because the editing "fills a thematic function" that goes beyond questions of simply viewing the dance. "In an effort to keep it authentic, Fosse avoided some of the common cinematic tricks used in movie musicals," Tropiano explains. "He staged the musical numbers within the confines of the small stage, rather than making the space larger to accommodate the choreography" (Tropiano 2011, 71).

Fosse extended this method of presenting musical numbers in later works, including his autobiographical *All That Jazz* (1979), in which these very same signature fragmented moves were used in the opening, specifically, because they reflexively evoked the director/choreographer. One glimpse and audience members recognize the creator, which is precisely the point. While Fosse may literally have kept within the confines of his small stage in *Cabaret*, editing became another way of expanding that space. Perhaps with the exception of "If You Could See Her Through My Eyes," there is little effort in *Cabaret*'s musical numbers to maintain the integrity of space in the Kit Kat Klub throughout any one number. Film space can be infinite, as opposed to the dramatic space of the storytelling, where we are crucially aware of the tightness of rooms and of people walking in and intruding. In the Kit Kat Klub, everything is flexible, even though Fosse generally shoots each musical scene with a relatively full view of the stage – at least when it begins. But when Liza's Sally Bowles sings "Maybe This Time," bright lights bathe her, the camera moves slightly around her, and her momentary hopefulness seems unbounded by the walls of a mere building. Similarly, "Mein Herr," becomes a tangle of faces, legs, and chairs, with quick cuts among the dancers. It's a carved-out film space that contrasts radically with the non-musical scenes.

Despite the "realism" of the musical setting, Fosse did draw a line in the sand. As some critics carped – including Christopher Isherwood, who wrote the stories on which the show is based – the Kit Kat Klub is supposed to be second rate and Sally Bowles a starry-eyed hopeful with dreams bigger than her minimal talent. On stage, the women who have portrayed her – even to this day – are regarded as pure actresses rather than as accomplished singers and dancers. Obviously, Minnelli departs from the typical casting, and the film musical's added songs ("Mein Lieber Herr," "Maybe This Time," and "Money Makes the World Go Round") all serve to showcase her considerable talent. *Cabaret* helped turn Minnelli into the type of star Bowles longed to be. At least in 1972, it was inconceivable that the star of a musical would not sing and dance well – even if s/he had to be dubbed, as many were in *West Side Story*. It was, in fact, integral to the film's pleasure: Producer Feuer hired director Fosse precisely because he knew that the musical numbers had to work in order for the film to succeed (Tropiano 2011, 51–52). The setting had to be realistic, the dancing and singing carried out in a logical arena, but the actual performances didn't have to match the characters' reputed talents, or lack thereof.

An interesting contrast with *Cabaret* is the 2002 film adaptation of Fosse's own *Chicago* – first on stage in 1975 and appearing onscreen almost three decades later, directed by Rob Marshall rather than Fosse, despite Fosse's best efforts in the intervening years.[5] Fosse had subtitled the original show "A Musical Vaudeville." Based on a play from 1926, and with a loose narrative structure, *Chicago* centers on Roxie Hart's murder of a faithless lover, her quest for exoneration at trial, and her even more dogged pursuit of fame – particularly the fame possessed by another showgirl/murderess, Velma Kelly, locked up in the same prison. Originally starring two of Broadway's best-known and most highly skilled dancers, Gwen Verdon and Chita Rivera, the music and dance evoked the Roaring Twenties by intimating, rather than directly imitating, dance styles of the period. (According to Sam Wasson, Fosse was insistent that his assistants "keep [him] away from the Charleston!" (2013, 382).) In more crucial ways, *Chicago* looked ahead to what would become our present-day obsession with celebrity and the media's complicity. Although the show received several Tony nominations upon its original release, *Chicago* was not largely well received: Cold, cynical, and deliberately Brechtian, it challenged the audience, offering no characters with whom to easily identify. When a new, revised production opened in 1997, however, its themes resonated and audiences had grown more receptive. In 2002, choreographer Marshall directed the adaptation, and made it clear in interviews that his first order of business involved finding a structure for the musical pieces: "They've been trying to make this film for the past 20 years. People toyed with ideas of how it could be done and there were a lot of scripts and a few directors along the way … It really was a problem: how do you get into this movie? How do people start singing? How is that natural?" (BBC 2002). Marshall also did, as so many directors before him, bring up the troubling question of how to integrate the music and dance: "It really was a problem: how do you get into this movie? How do people start singing? How is that natural?" (Marshall 2011). Marshall's solution was to turn all of the musical numbers into external manifestations of the characters' internal thoughts – particularly those of Roxie Hart. Thus, rather than the songs providing independent, Brechtian commentary on such social issues as the judiciary and journalism, they turned into the stuff of individual hopes and dreams. This strategy didn't entirely negate the story's critique, especially as specific characters embody and act out particular ideas of fame and entitlement prevalent in our culture. But Marshall's question – "how is that natural?" – presupposes that "naturalness" is an innate virtue. Perhaps, commercially, it is a virtue but cinematically, not necessarily. Clearly, given the big budget from an "independent" but still large producer, creating a Godardian text was still outside the realm of possibility.

Chicago as a stage show had the flashiness that fit the high-end vaudeville productions the show's subtitle alluded to. While "flashiness" describes the film to some degree, not all flash is quite the same. Some critics, including Elvis Mitchell in his *New York Times* review, pointed to the influence of Baz Luhrmann's *Moulin Rouge* (2001), with its high-speed kinetics and over-the-top fantasy (2002).

Love it or hate it, Luhrmann created a visual feast – richly colorful, with elaborate sets and blissfully daring anachronisms. *Moulin Rouge* had fun playing with clichés about turn-of-the-century Paris, including a courtesan ill with consumption living in the artists' quartier of Montmartre. (Note that Lurhmann had also directed a stage version of *La Bohème* on the same topic.) While its lead actors, Nicole Kidman and Ewan McGregor, were not necessarily the strongest singers, they were puzzle pieces in a hugely elaborate jigsaw that didn't depend too heavily on the quality of their voices. Questions of "the natural" that so consumed Marshall did not even enter into the equation. Mitchell, in his review, similarly referenced Dennis Potter's TV musical mini-series, *Pennies from Heaven* (1978) and *The Singing Detective* (1986), which flagrantly flout reality with songs that are obviously lip-synched.[6] But Potter's work is deliberately Brechtian, with artificiality now presented as a virtue. This approach differs radically (in every sense of the word) from Marshall's *Chicago*.

Marshall's reworking of Fosse's choreography retains its signature gestures, calling up memories for anyone who has seen Fosse's dances. His cutting mimics Fosse's own chopped, percussive editing. But these are surface imitations with no depth of meaning underneath. The harmony of Fosse's camera/choreography combination does not exist here. Partly, it has to do with the leads: Fosse always worked with specially chosen dancers whom he trained to perfection. Even a swiftly passing gesture in a Fosse shot resonates with a physical clarity the dancer delivers. But *Chicago*'s Renée Zellweger and the passably decent Catherine Zeta-Jones are not on that level, and Richard Gere even less so in his lengthy tap-dance sequence. Here, the editing serves to obscure movement rather than to highlight a crisply executed jazz isolation or the beauty of a dance-built body. While there is a professional dance corps – the women in the jail – they get far less to do, and again, editing does not spotlight their skills. In this respect it is illuminating to consider the differences in casting between *Cabaret* and *Chicago*. In the decades between the two, a shift had occurred in the preference for professional dancers and singers in cinema. It is almost as if their very skill contributes to the "unnatural" effect directors seemed desperate to avoid. Additionally, without a Fosse, whose own name carried weight, it is hard to imagine a musical director who could sell his film without a "star." Hugh Jackman, a genuine musical theater performer, remains unique in that respect. When *Les Misérables* was released in 2012, publicity trumpeted the fact that the actors were singing "live" as they were filmed – as if the ability to do so were something rare among musical performers in film.[7]

But "amateur" performances can also be used for a different reason – to depart from, and comment on, the classic musical and its ideology. These more modern texts call attention to the fact that the actors lack extensive professional training as musical artists. The audience is always aware that they're not watching an Astaire and Rogers blissfully dancing cheek-to-cheek or hearing a Judy Garland break our hearts with her voice. Someone less than perfect can remind us either that the world of the past has vanished, or that there can be sweet emotion in the ordinary.

Musicals in the Age of Postmodernism

The same lack of naturalism that some filmmakers saw as a problem to be solved became for others an opportunity for exploration. The 1970s was a period of transformation in American cinema, when a new breed of independently minded directors came to the fore, savvy cinephiles who knew both European trends and American film history, and they too turned their attention to established genres with an eye to revise. If such creators as Robbins and Fosse came out of theater and dance, Scorsese, Coppola, and many (but not all) of their cohorts were pure products of cinema/cinephilia, anchored in movie lore and technique. It's possible to trace the influence of their musical efforts to, and place them in the context of, contemporary European cinema, especially the *nouvelle vague*, which had already recast the musical in Brechtian terms in such works as Godard's *Une femme est une femme* (1961), as well as later efforts like Ken Russell's brilliant Berkeleyesque spoof *The Boyfriend* (1971). But if Godard was Brechtian in his desire simultaneously to explore and dissect the pleasures of the genre, Coppola and Scorsese approached the musical with different eyes. They wanted to recreate the musical for a new age, working on a large scale. Godard had begun, by the early and mid-1960s, to grow disillusioned with the classic cinema. Scorsese and Coppola were still, in their own ways, in love with it. But because both Scorsese's *New York, New York* (1977) and Coppola's *One from the Heart* (1982) came at a great financial cost and failed critically at the time of release – and although they have since benefited from critical reassessment – they became not models to follow, but lessons to learn from. While Woody Allen, who works with a minimal budget and has a small but devoted fan base, released his musical

Everyone Says I Love You (1996) with nary a blip, the experience proved difficult, even disastrous, for others who waded into the musical waters.

If Richard Dyer focused on the classical musical's sense of utopia ("not how it would be organized, but how it would make you feel"), with its creation of community, its depiction of work as play, its insistence on the existence of love (1981, 177–178), it became clear in the post-1960s that people found this idea hard to believe in anymore – at least as this cinematic utopia had once been depicted. But the musical's juxtaposition of narrative and spectacle, its alleged Brechtian qualities, became the locus of the New Hollywood musical. Fosse's *All that Jazz* wedded his customary razzle-dazzle choreography to a story of drug abuse, illness, and death, turning the old idea of "let's put on a show" into a nightmare scenario. Dennis Potter's TV series *Pennies from Heaven* foregrounded the musical's artificiality by having the actors burst into obviously lip-synched production numbers that ironically commented on their discontented lives: In that TV mini-series, the focus was as small and tight as its medium, the tiny dreams fed by the cheery old tunes in the sheet music the protagonist sold. Three years later, it became a film musical using the same conceit, but changing the inspiration to suit both cinema and the United States: Now the silver screen fueled the fantasies, the production numbers grew in size, and everything had the expansiveness of America and the American dream, despite its Depression-era setting, much in keeping with the musicals produced during that historical period.

Revisionist and postmodernist meta-musicals like *New York, New York* and *One from the Heart*, in extremely different ways, look back to the heyday of the genre with a knowing eye. Both have a fascination with the genre's allure, but specifically with its deliberately false surface. At issue here is a nostalgic longing for what the characters and audience understand no longer can be – in some respects echoing Godard, whose former love for Hollywood is tempered by a steely-eyed clarity about the uses of entertainment.

Scorsese spoke about shooting *New York, New York* in LA, "like the old films I used to see as a kid." He went on to say that he "tried to fuse a fantasy – the movies I grew up with as a kid – with the reality that I experience myself" (Brunette 1999, 72).[8] Bright and colorful and brassy – perhaps a bit abrasive as the city it's named for – *New York, New York* marries the city and Hollywood in more ways than its physical, studio production. To a large degree, Scorsese's essay on the past, and the incompatibility of NY and LA, are literally embodied by its two stars. Robert De Niro, by then, was a symbol of in-your-face New York attitude in both *Mean Streets* and *Taxi Driver*, and his entrance as saxophonist Jimmy Doyle is loud, brazen, pushy, almost unpleasant in his dogged pursuit of a resistant Francine Evans (Liza Minnelli). Minnelli, on the other hand, carried old Hollywood in her very genes, via her mother (Judy Garland) and father (Vincente Minnelli). Her character's doomed romance with Jimmy, moreover, poignantly recalls both her mother's unhappy off-screen love affairs and several of her mother's onscreen roles as well – in *A Star Is Born* most powerfully. That Minnelli is frequently called upon to sing torch songs, including some that recall her mother performing "The Man that Got Away," heightens the film's allusive resonance. Not surprisingly, in the film's schema, Jimmy remains associated with music, seedy clubs, and black culture, while Francine moves on a path toward film stardom – with a top-tier nightclub gig thrown in, further echoing Garland.

Scorsese flirts with many of the iconic images and tropes from the classic musical, and then twists them around. The opening sequence, a loud, crowded, rambunctious celebration on V-J Day, follows Jimmy as he wanders through the hall where sailors and their girls jitterbug and twirl. A big band plays, liquor gushes, people seem mad with joy, and Scorsese's camera, flowing through the packed space and capturing the eddying stream of movement on the dance floor, is gloriously choreographic in and of itself. And Jimmy could almost be, for a moment, Gene Kelly on the town – but the more hardened, bitter Kelly of *It's Always Fair Weather*. When Jimmy settles on Francine, he hangs on like a pit bull despite her firm refusal; Thomas Sotinel describes his persistent attentions as "clumsy and brutal" (2010, 38). But the brutality is only slightly different from that in many a musical, in which stubbornly persistent heroes win out – only, in those other cases, with more surface charm. As the divergent career paths of Francine and Jimmy split them apart, the narrative echoes those of many other musicals, most especially, once again, *A Star Is Born*. Through the backstage element, Scorsese weaves the music in smoothly, from Jimmy's first audition when Francine steps in to rescue him, to performances on tour, and finally to the triumphant club show in which Francine sings the song that she and Jimmy had composed together. But just as in the initial party scene, Scorsese infuses the film with a harsh, scorching reality. Jimmy remains violent and selfish, devoted to his music and willing to sacrifice love and friendship in hopes of becoming the artist he dreams of being. There is no softening of his treatment of Francine, nor of Francine's situation in the wake of the relationship's dissolution. If spectacle in the traditional musical is a thing of pleasure, here, despite the actual beauty of the music and singing, it is always darkened by complicated emotional underpinnings and dramatic reversals, with never a release.

In spite of the urge to the utopian that Dyer posits, early 1930s musicals often did have a dark edge. The Busby Berkeley-choreographed *Gold Diggers* films, for instance, were colored by the Depression: think of "My Forgotten Man," with its breadlines and lines of soldiers; or the "Broadway Melody" number, which ends with a suicide. Gene Kelly's later movies also hinted at failed dreams. The desire for joyful resolution, and the impossibility of that desire, are themes not only of *New York, New York*, but of the production number that makes up its film-within-a-film (literally called "Happy Endings"). Given a look which includes montage sequences straight from 1930s Busby Berkeley musicals, it features Francine playing a movie usherette dreaming of love. In true Hollywood fashion, she accidentally meets a "Prince Charming" in the theater who sweeps her up, leading to romance, wealth, and happiness as a chorus dances around her. Only, it turns out to be a daydream ... until it all begins again, leaving her staring wide-eyed at the camera. It is a dizzying achievement – one that promises the finale we presumably want, snatches it away, and then teasingly holds it out again, all while perfectly evoking a long-gone cinematic style. Scorsese's narrative depicts an endless cycle of disillusion. Yet the joy of his bravura filmmaking makes it clear that he looks back with love, even if the utopian universe portrayed in those glorious Hollywood musicals is a hard sell in an age of cynicism insistent on realistic representations. He acknowledges our hunger for the satisfying conclusion without feeding it, either in the film-within-a-film or in *New York, New York* itself, which perhaps may account for the movie's lack of success.[9] What happy ending is possible? How can the audience desire the reconstitution of a couple who have met in a manner most women would consider harassment in real life and whose relationship is redolent of anger, infidelity, and betrayal?

One from the Heart: It's Only a Paper Moon

An absolute financial and critical failure upon its release, Francis Ford Coppola's *One from the Heart* (1982), with an estimated budget of $27,000,000 and a US box office gross of $900,000, stands as the film that sunk a studio – notably Coppola's own American Zoetrope, mortgaged to the hilt in order to finance this production.[10] It is no surprise that Philip French, in *The Guardian*, declared that, in spite of Coppola's former *Godfather* glory, "he actually achieved disaster with *One From the Heart*, a grand folly comparable with Spielberg's *1941* and Scorsese's *New York New York*" (2012). Along with *New York, New York*, *One from the Heart* is a plaintive reminder of why large-scale musicals became so hard to produce after the studio system had vanished. Everything Coppola and Scorsese had to create from scratch previously existed (seemingly) permanently on MGM's back lot. It also is hard to imagine a commercially made movie more fully devoted to the idea of artificiality, fakery, and simulacra than Coppola's musical is. Vera Dika, in *Recycled Culture*, calls it a "self-conscious comment on the changed status of the real (that is, a real now dominated by simulation) in contemporary society" (2003, 171).

Reviewers saw no heart beneath the visually startling surfaces or in the tale of a couple who argue, separate, spend a night with new lovers, and ultimately return to each other. Not only did Coppola set his love story in Las Vegas, a city that's already an artificial construct and tourist playground, he then piled simulacra upon simulacra by building and filming on an elaborate stage set. Like Scorsese, he was clearly attracted to the concept of a studio back lot and its historical evocations. There is dazzling beauty in the resulting mix of saturated colors, neon, and fabricated streets filled with showgirls, buskers, and circus performers. It is an environment where anyone can break into song and dance without notice. Sets crumble to the touch and ceilings rip like paper, all intentionally insubstantial. Adding to the holiday atmosphere, the entire story takes place on the Fourth of July. Once the two protagonists, Hank (Frederic Forrest) and Frannie (Teri Garr) leave the very ordinary house they share – a place of home-cooked dinners, beer, and fights about family finances – they step into a fantasy world devoid of nature, save for the come-hither images in Frannie's travel agency window that promise paradise with every blinking palm tree. But even the desire to travel is less a desire to visit a real place than a longing to enter the sets Frannie has designed to entice customers.

Unlike Scorsese, and more on the line of what Baz Lurhmann would later do, Coppola mostly cast actors with limited musical backgrounds (although, for *New York, New York*, De Niro learned how to play saxophone in order to look more authentic, while the actual sax performances were dubbed). Raul Julia as Ray, Frannie's love interest, had starred in numerous Broadway musicals, and was the notable exception, although Garr had some brief experience as a dancer. In keeping with the film's title, music and dance were meant to be expressions of the heart, not demonstrations of skill. But the amateur quality is the point, along with the fact that many of the songs capturing the characters' emotions are on the soundtrack and not sung by the protagonists themselves as they gallivant through Vegas. As both Jane Feuer and Heather Laing have noted, in musicals the spoken tends to become sung, and language is transfigured (Feuer 1982; Laing 2000). In this sense, sung dialogue signals the characters' desire to reconcile with their own alienated selves and with the world. But the disconnect between the characters' dialogue and the music in *One from the Heart* implies that protagonists lack the potential to achieve this longed-for reconciliation. Coppola's strategy suggests not only the stifling of emotion, but also the need for characters (and the audience) to find those missing emotions outside of themselves in earlier, more "genuine" texts. He slips in allusions to the past, as Frannie hip hops on and off the curb like Gene Kelly in his "Singin' in the Rain," number and as she and Ray sway to the same "Copacabana" that got Astaire and Rogers moving in *Flying Down to Rio* (1933). But more than traditional dance and song, *One from the Heart* conjures up the musical through a generalized sense of performance, of the entire universe choreographed to a soundtrack. Nastassja Kinski's Leila, a contortionist for the Circus Max, serves as a human signifier of the film's visual and thematic concerns. She's a constructed persona, a painted goddess who is, upon request, willing to disappear. Coppola at one point superimposes her face over the street, her eyes gazing watchfully as Hank searches for her.

In some respects, *One from the Heart* might be called a mock-carnivalesque musical. Bakhtin's (1984) concept of carnival involves a time when rules are suspended, when power is overturned, and when gender roles become fluid. It's a brief moment of liberation that provides a taste of what life could be like. Coppola plays with this idea, but Hank and Frannie's carnival does not offer true freedom. Despite their smiling faces when they first venture out, newly costumed, for their adventure, the two seem as trapped in their world as the characters in Sartre's *No Exit*. When they greet each other back home, with relief and a hug, the question remains open as to whether it is love or a sense of futility has brought them there. When it is only a paper moon, is it worth trying to fly there?

Gotta Dance: The Dance Film (or: You Should be Dancing, Yeah)

"Dance" films – ones that center directly on characters who label themselves as dancers, professional or not, and have production numbers showcasing dance – diverge from musicals of the past in that they divorce movement from singing and most often work to a prefabricated soundtrack that may mix and remix newly written and already popular songs. By their nature, almost all of these films focus on youth, often rebellious, but most frequently without strong political beliefs or an interest in genuine social change. In that sense, they differ from 1970s and 1980s rock 'n' roll musicals like *Tommy* (1975), *Quadrophenia* (1979), or *Pink Floyd The Wall* (1982), which access genuine rage that comes straight from the sensibilities of the adult, often working-class British bands that created them. Rather than "a teenage wasteland," these narratives instead portray teenage discontent, or at the most, an incoherent anger at the workings of a system little understood.

The American dance film upended traditions – eschewing stage dance for street dance, the classical for the popular, and, in moving from the 1970s into the 1990s, abandoning long shots that capture the whole figure in movement for dazzlingly, vertiginous shotgun-fast short takes of the body in fragments. MTV was launched in 1981, and its music videos pointed the way forward with an increasing predominance of recorded soundtracks. With only minimal narratives, MTV videos never pretended to realism; performance was the point, and that shift bled into film. Technology altered the voice; singing characters, expressing their deepest emotions in lyrics, vanished in films such as *Saturday Night Fever*, which instead substituted a wall of prerecorded tunes that functioned almost as a Greek chorus. Intensive cutting fractured the body, making it easy to substitute dance doubles (as in *Flashdance*, 1983, or *Footloose*) or simply to create choreography from a catalogue of images rather than depending on the dancer to master steps and space. This set the stage for such films as Disney's *Step Up* series, which also focused on popular music and vernacular dance, as well as a cinematic style predicated on editing. But this series also ushered in the return of the backstage musical – with the meaning of "backstage" more loosely defined.

It is possible to identify the dance film in two waves – the first, in the 1970s and 1980s, represented by *Saturday Night Fever*, *Dirty Dancing*, and *Footloose*, among others,[11] and the second, in the new millennium, represented primarily by the *Step Up* franchise. These films, about nonprofessionals, posit dance as a form of bodily liberation and personal freedom from an oppressive social ideology. As in *West Side Story*, movement offers release from closed-off possibilities and uncertain futures, from unfair rules and rigid class structures, and in short, in the more recent films, provides access to pleasures demonized by a grownup world. And, of course, dance signifies sex. It is the utopia in a dystopian narrative world, with dance numbers providing as much joyful release for viewers as for the protagonists onscreen. Upon the film's release, and for a long time after, the Bee Gees

Figure 18.2 John Travolta as Tony Manero dominates the film frame in John Badham's *Saturday Night Fever* (1977, producer Robert Stigwood).

blockbuster soundtrack and John Travolta's exhilarating hip-jutting, finger-pointing movement became iconic sounds and images of the disco era. This was all set, however, within a blue-collar world filled with frustration, desperate aspirations, violence, and death. Dance here is also amateur and placed, with a few exceptions, within the delineated space of the disco or rehearsal hall, where such performances would recognizably occur in real life. The first group of dance films fall most uneasily into the musical category, precisely because they place such heavy emphasis on narrative, on soundtrack scores, and on the mostly social, everyday nature of the dance. Yet the popularity of the films hinges completely on the music and choreography, and on performance as a defining factor in characterization.

Tony Manero (John Travolta) in *Saturday Night Fever* is defined by his body, whether he's strutting down the street, telling you how he feels by the way he uses his walk, leading a group of disco dancers across the floor, or romantically partnering with the many women eager to dance at his side. The camera incessantly focuses on him, whether fetishizing individual body parts, watching the full figure dominate the space, or moving in and around him to capture the dizzying, romantic spinning of his competition performance with Stephanie (Karen Lynn Gorney). The camera's freedom and flexibility in these sequences, along with the dancers' dynamism, speak to the fundamentally utopian nature of these dancing moments for Tony. The cinematography and editing when Tony is at the disco or on the streets seem directed by his movement. They rarely imprison his body in space, except in those scenes set in his uninspiring hardware store job or in his home crowded with parents and siblings.

Interestingly, despite the presence of women in these films – Gorney, Jennifer Grey in *Dirty Dancing*, and Lori Singer in *Footlose* – the male stars (or in *Footloose* Kevin Bacon's stand-in) are the true dancers and are positioned as objects of the gaze.[12] Aside from the joyful finale in *Footloose*, in which teens end the town's ban on dancing, the most memorable moment centers on an angry Ren McCormack (Bacon) who releases his fury in an athletic, acrobatic dance, based on running, that moves laterally across space, breaking out of the film frame over and over again. As in the classical musical, it is a moment when words cannot suffice, when the welling-up of emotion proves so powerful that it has to explode in motion. Interestingly, given the fact that dance is "naturalized" in *Footloose* as something social and ordinary, this number occurs completely in public space, yet neither viewers nor critics perceived it as breaking with reality – attributable, perhaps, to the music video it resembles (and which it later came to be). A way of listening and viewing had, by then, been normalized through MTV, allowing cinema to incorporate the style wholesale. In fact, many non-musical narrative films of the MTV era incorporated an obligatory musical montage, later replayed on or sometimes retooled for MTV as a marketing tool to encourage record/CD, box office ticket, and video/DVD sales. It is worth adding, as well, that with the rise of hip hop street culture and skateboarding, the use of public space for acrobatic and ballet-like dance performances became more commonplace – no longer just the stuff of movie fantasies.

Films like *Dirty Dancing* also initiated their own small explosion of ballroom-based movies, many of which turned to Latin-inflected dances – including a direct sequel set in Havana during the Cuban revolution. A series of lambada films arrived when that craze hit, all of which happily played with stereotypes of Brazilian eroticism. (*The Forbidden Dance* (1990) ridiculously attributed the form to Brazilian Indians, and imbued it with ancient spiritual power.) *Dance with Me* (1998), starring Vanessa Williams, is set in a dance studio and uses the romantic tension between a ballroom-trained teacher and a "real Latin" to explore the idea of authenticity in dance. This scenario itself dances around the question of which is better: the stylized, studied, and skilled version performed by the teacher or the "street" version performed by a sexy Latin man. (The answer: It is best, professionally and personally, when the two come together, when training meets passion.) But this choreographic clash is part of a much larger pattern of mapping onto gender roles other archetypal binaries – centered on race, class, geography, education, and skills. Most often these films set up a tension between white femininity and dark masculinity, uptown/upper-class women vs. downtown/lower-class men, a ballet-school-trained female vs. a street or hip hop, self-trained male. These binaries become fodder for romance, giving each partner the opportunity to embrace new worlds and meet in the middle, not unlike the dynamics of the 1930s fairy-tale musical as Rick Altman defines them, although now unfolding in very different settings and with differing narrative circumstances (Altman 1989). Each partner learns to appreciate the value of what the other has to offer.

The second wave of dance films can, interestingly, be traced to a non-musical: *Save the Last Dance* (2001), the story of a white would-be ballerina (Julia Stiles) who jettisons her dreams after a failed audition. Moving from New York to Chicago, she becomes involved with a much poorer young black man involved in hip hop culture (Sean Patrick Thomas). The juxtaposition of classical dance with black vernacular club dance, and the healing power of characters who embody each form, enable them to "save each other," a trope that would later dominate the popular *Step Up* series. But *Save the Last Dance* also "saved up" the dancing, which did not play as strong a role in the film as the drama did – perhaps because the brief ballet sequences reveal Stiles's limited dance skills.

The *Step Up* franchise – which began in 2006, extending to the time of this printing and likely beyond – embraces and shares with musicals of the past the view of dance as freedom, success, community, and even social engagement. The series, to greater or lesser degrees, consists of backstage stories with at least one character aspiring to a professional career. The first, eponymous film unfolded in the insular world of a performing arts school, to which a youth (Channing Tatum) must perform community service after he vandalizes the building. He and Nora (Jenna Dewan, now Jenna Dewan-Tatum), one of the school's most promising dancers, come together romantically and professionally to the benefit of both. The concept of the *Step Up* films can be almost summed up in the words famously applied to Astaire and Rogers: He gave her class and she gave him sex. But in the *Step Up* films, the genders are reversed.

The "revolution" in *Step Up: Revolution* (2012) is of two types: A street collective pushes its political goals with flash-mob tactics that displease the powerful elite but delight spectators, and a rich white girl embarks on a personal journey to become a professional dancer against her father's wishes. When she falls in love with a member of the secretive collective, they reluctantly allow her to join in their struggle to stop her father, a developer, from razing the homes and small businesses in a poor black and Latino community. The stylish musical sequences staged by the collective reflect the changes in popular performance, particularly those wrought by the reality TV competition show, *So You Think You Can Dance*. (In the film, the role of rich girl Emily is played by one of that show's dancers, Kathryn McCormick.) *So You Think You Can Dance* sets ballerinas against B-boys, and puts lockers and poppers and hip hoppers alongside Broadway, ballroom, and jazz dancers. For the most part, they all must attempt to dance in each other's styles, as well as in those generally unfamiliar to all, like Bollywood. Their performances are usually full production numbers, and the influence of that choreography permeates *Step Up: Revolution*. Because the guerrilla entertainers want to remain anonymous, they set up carefully and quietly, hiding their equipment and always wearing elaborate masks and costumes when they make their sudden appearance. When Emily joins them, she brings a different type of training to the mix, enriching their choreography.

The street, of course, is the natural stage both for this type of dance and this type of political agitation. It also creates a large and free dance space. Before viewers know who anyone is or what is happening, the opening number explodes onto the Miami landscape. The camera peers into a car where two young men nod at each other. It cuts to the other side of the car to look in the opposite direction, as the driver honks, setting the dance in motion and also, if you will, igniting the music. In a series of quick shots, a young woman blasts hip hop from the machine she has hidden in what looks like an ice truck; the camera tracks forward through lines of automobiles, and bodies begin to somersault and fly in the air from every direction. A crowd gathers, cellphones get pulled out, and traffic snarls. What the film has already communicated is the new world order – one in which street dance is equivalent to stage dance (as clearly professional as it is the purview of amateurs) and one in which social media can transform entertainment into activism. It is a literal political "movement" in which protests can be both pleasurable and effective. Occupy!

The *Step Up* films combine bits of the traditional Hollywood fairy-tale narrative of rising to success with grittier, more modern stories usually linked to poverty and race. The negotiation of ballet and vernacular dance has long been an issue of the musical, and these films are the latest iteration. It bears adding, however, that, despite their dazzling dance numbers, the *Step Up* series' engagement with social conflict is superficial and the proposal of solutions to these conflicts patently false – a trademark of Disney's opportunistic construction of skin-deep social pluralism that shrewdly steers clear of hot-button issues.

Conclusion

Musicals, of course, continue to be planned and produced. Rob Marshall, director of *Chicago* and *Nine* (2009), has adapted another Broadway musical to the screen – Stephen Sondheim's very adult fairy tale *Into the Woods*, to the screen. Produced by Disney, the film, even before appearing, stirred a storm of controversy when Sondheim – very supportively – confirmed news of "family-friendly cuts" and "major plot changes" (Khatchatourian, 2014). Clint Eastwood, whose only prior association with the genre was over 40 years ago when he acted in *Paint Your Wagon* (1969), has adapted the Tony Award winning jukebox musical *Jersey Boys* (2014), about the rise to fame of the Four Seasons pop group. Interestingly, Eastwood cast mostly actors from the original stage production, rather than big-name stars, to play Four Seasons singers. *Annie*, filmed twice earlier (for the movie theater in 1982 and for television in 1999), has gotten a modern-day reboot, this time with an African-American cast. *Step Up All In* (2014) has brought the successful franchise to Las Vegas for a dance crew battle. Lin-Manuel Miranda's stage musical *On the Heights*, about uptown New York's Latino community, seems likely to reach the big screen also.[13] And of course, a steady stream of animated musicals – like *Frozen* (2013) or *Rio 2* (2014) – is likely to continue flowing, given huge successes.

What seem to be off the agenda, at least in the United States, are live-action musicals that experiment with, comment on, and play with the conventions of the genre. The type of original and playfully postmodern work, created by Peter Bogdanovich, Martin Scorsese, Francis Ford Coppola, and Herbert Ross in the 1970s and early 1980s, is nowhere to be found among mainstream filmmakers. The form has congealed, apparently, into either stage adaptations or soundtrack dance musicals with a backstage bent. Few of the actors can both sing and dance, and, outside of the animated movies, it is rare for a film to showcase an entirely new score. (One interesting exception is Joss Whedon's *Dr. Horrible's Sing-Along Blog* (2008), but that initially was made only for online viewing.)

At the same time, partial restagings of classic musicals, like *Carousel* (2014), regularly air on PBS. NBC also enjoyed such a huge success with its production of *The Sound of Music* (2014) that the network has planned a remake of *Peter Pan*, featuring Christopher Walken as a tap-dancing Captain Hook. Popular TV shows like *Glee* and *Smash* pay homage to Broadway, while reality television competitions, like *So You Think You Can Dance* and *Dancing with the Stars*, have introduced a new generation to ballroom and a host of other styles – sometimes quite self-consciously referencing and imitating the choreography of Astaire, Kelly, and Fosse. Celebrities from these shows, along with stars like Neil Patrick Harris and Hugh Jackman, possess both audience appeal and the requisite musical skills. But the genre remains constricted by an essentialist belief in cinema's connection to the real and the financial failure of postmodern musicals from decades past. The only recent exception that comes to mind is Julie Taymor's *Across the Universe* (2007), which benefited from the beloved Beatles' songbook as well as from nostalgia for the 1960s. Firmly embracing the idea that her characters would sing their feelings, Taymor also realized (as was the case in Forman's *Hair*) that the songs could paint a social portrait of an era that many view fondly. A strong visual stylist and revered puppet-maker, Taymor allowed her film to dip liberally into fantasy (as with the song "Lucy in the Sky with Diamonds," for example), giving *Across the Universe* a magical feel even as it dealt with social revolution. But save for that unusual musical, the persistent questions of why anyone would sing and dance, and how to make it appear natural, haunt the genre – or, at least, the big-budget, big distributor manifestation of the musical. It continues to stay alive, but is perhaps not living life to its fullest.

Notes

1. Peter Wollen (2012) provides a particularly excellent analysis of how cues work in his close reading of Gene Kelly's "Singin' in the Rain" number. See also Altman 1989; Dyer 1981; Feuer 1982.
2. John Mueller (1985, 12–13) argues that the classical musical began falling apart in the mid-1950s as a result of decreased revenues and increased cost. This analysis makes *West Side Story* a perfect interim text. The Astaire/Kelly model is gone, but still has some

influence, and the newer postmodern musicals had not yet come into existence.

3. Of course, classic musicals like *Oklahoma!* (1955) and *Carousel* (1956) also have a large measure of darkness, including beatings, threats of rape, and death. Their overall setting in the past, however, and their folksiness differ from later works like *West Side Story* or *One from the Heart* that are grounded in contemporary reality.
4. For a detailed production history of *West Side Story*, see Acevedo-Muñoz 2003.
5. Apparently, after seeing Baz Luhrmann's *Strictly Ballroom* (1992), Miramax producer Harvey Weinstein wanted to do *Chicago* with Luhrmann, but the director said, "I wouldn't dare touch the work of Bob Fosse" (Priggé 2004, 42). Lurhmann's statement reveals that he fully understood the differences between the type of musical he produced – almost entirely based on cinematic and other visual strategies – and musicals that depended on actual choreography and singing. (In *Strictly Ballroom*, Paul Mercurio could easily handle his own choreography, which most dancers in that genre do.)
6. Dennis Potter also chose to call the TV version of his *Pennies from Heaven* a "drama with music, rather than a musical" (Biesen 2014, 157).
7. Not surprisingly, this publicity prompted a bemused reaction from Broadway stars like Michael Cerveris, who, in a mocking tweet, pointed out that stage singers manage to do that every night.
8. For Scorsese's own perspective on *New York, New York*, and the influence on traditional Hollywood musicals, see his interviews in Christie and Thompson (2003, 69–74).
9. Although the film eventually was given an alternate ending, that was not part of the original release, which is my primary concern.
10. *One from the Heart* was not the only musical that bankrupted a studio. Biesen also points to the film version of *Pennies from Heaven* as costing $20 million and only earning $7 million, "a record-breaking loss that accelerated [MGM's] postclassical demise" (2014, 157).
11. Lesley Vize argues that dance films like *Saturday Night Fever* and *Dirty Dancing* "constitute a separate genre" (2003, 24). Notably, she refers to synesthesia to describe the way one sensory experience transfers into another (e.g., listening to the Bee Gees brings images of John Travolta dancing to mind). She does not use the word kinesthesia, however, to describe the phenomenon by which our own bodies begin to move, or want to move, while watching the dance.
12. For more about male dancers in the musical and their feminization, see Cohan 1993.
13. For Miranda's views on the upcoming film adaptation, see *Broadway World* 2014.

References

Acevedo-Muñoz, Ernesto R. (2003). *West Side Story as Cinema: The Making and Impact of an American Masterpiece.* Lawrence: University of Kansas Press.

Altman, Rick. (1989). *The American Film Musical.* Bloomington: Indiana University Press.

Bakhtin, Mikhail. (1984). *Rabelais and His World*, trans. Hélène Iswolsky. Bloomington: Indiana University Press.

BBC. (2002). "Rob Marshall: From Broadway to Hollywood." December 11. At http://news.bbc.co.uk/2/hi/entertainment/2714325.stm (accessed March 17, 2015).

Biesen, Sherri Chinen. (2014). *Music in the Shadows: Noir Musical Films.* Baltimore: Johns Hopkins University Press.

Broadway World. (2014). "Lin-Manuel Miranda Talks *In the Heights* Movie Adaptation: Wants to Make It as Good as Possible." March 5. At http://www.broadwayworld.com/article/LinManuelMiranda-Talks-IN-THE-HEIGHTS-Movie-Adaptation-Wants-to-Make-It As-Good-as Possible-20140305#.U9CcmbEwITA (accessed July 24, 2014).

Brunette, Peter. (1999). *Martin Scorsese: Interviews.* Jackson: University Press of Mississippi.

Christie, Ian, & David Thompson. (eds). (2003). *Scorsese on Scorsese.* Revised edition. London: Faber & Faber.

Cohan, Steven. (1993). "Feminizing the Male: Fred Astaire and the Spectacle of Masculinity in the Hollywood Film Musical." In Steven Cohan & Ina Rae Hark (eds), *Screening the Male: Exploring Masculinities in the Hollywood Cinema* (pp. 46–69). London: Taylor & Francis.

Dika, Vera. (2003). *Recycled Culture in Contemporary Art and Film: The Uses of Nostalgia.* Cambridge, UK: Cambridge University Press.

Dyer, Richard. (1981). "Entertainment and Utopia." In Rick Altman (ed.), *Genre: The Musical* (pp. 175–189). London: Routledge & Kegan Paul.

Feuer, Jane. (1982). *The Hollywood Musical.* Bloomington: Indiana University Press.

French, Philip. (2012). "*One from the Heart*" DVD review. *The Guardian*, January 14. At http://www.theguardian.com/film/2012/jan/15/one-from-heart-coppola-dvd (accessed March 17, 2015).

Khatchatourian, Maane. (2014). "*Into the Woods* to Get Family-Friendly Disney Plot Changes." *Variety*, June 18. At http://variety.com/2014/film/news/into-the-woods-plot-changes1201223496/ (accessed July 26, 2014).

Laing, Heather, (2000). "Emotion by Numbers: Music, Song and the Musical." In Bill Marshall and Robynn Stilwell (eds), *Musicals: Hollywood and Beyond* (pp. 5–13). Exeter, UK: Intellect.

Mueller, John E. K. (1985). *Astaire Dancing: The Musical Films*. New York: Knopf Doubleday.

Mitchell, Elvis. (2002). "'*Chicago*,' Bare Legs and All, Makes It to Film." *New York Times*, December 27. At: http://nytimes.com/2002/12/27/movies/film-reviewchicago-bare-legsand-all makesittofilm.html?module=Search&mabReward=relbias%3Ar%2C[%22RI%3A7%22%2C%22RI%3A12%22 (accessed July 26, 2014).

Priggé, Steven. (2004). "Martin Richards" in *Movie Moguls Speak: Interviews with Top Film Producers* (pp. 34–49). Jefferson, NC: McFarland & Co.

Sotinel, Thomas. (2010). *Master of Cinema: Martin Scorsese*. Paris: Cahiers du cinéma.

Tropiano, Stephen. (2011). *Cabaret: Music on Film*. Milwaukee: Limelight Editions.

Vize, Lesley. (2003). "Music and the Body in Dance Film." In Ian Inglus (ed.), *Popular Music and Film* (pp. 22–38). New York: Wallflower Press.

Wasson, Sam. (2013). *Fosse*. Boston: Houghton Mifflin Harcourt.

Wollen, Peter. (2012). *Singin' in the Rain*. 2nd edition. London: Palgrave Macmillan

Williams, Raymond (1977). "Dominant, Residual, and Emergent." In Raymond Williams and Steven Lukes (eds.), *Marxism and Literature* (pp. 121–127). Oxford: Oxford University Press.

Part III

1991 to the Present

19

Setting the Stage
American Film History, 1991 to the Present

On Pearl Harbor Day, 2001, less than three months after the attacks on the World Trade Center in New York City and on the Pentagon in Washington, DC, Warner Bros. released *Ocean's Eleven*, a glossy, star-studded caper about a Las Vegas casino heist. Embraced by critics and audiences alike, the film's success proved that Hollywood was still capable of fulfilling its old mission of entertaining a broad swath of the adult moviegoing public, particularly at a time when Americans were trying to recover from such traumatic events. *Ocean's Eleven* scarcely holds the significance in film history that September 11 has assumed for the course of American politics and the shaping of America's image at home and abroad. But its elegant update of a classic genre provides a sardonic commentary about a society on the cusp of a new millennium, a nation in between two presidencies, and a movie studio in the wake of a fateful merger. Looking at *Ocean's Eleven* in slightly more detail is instructive for understanding American cinema from 1991 to the present.

In remaking the 1960 film of the same title, which featured members of the Rat Pack as World War II veterans deploying their respective areas of expertise to rob five casinos on the famous Las Vegas "Strip" in one night, director Steven Soderbergh did not aim to recreate period-specific detail or wax nostalgic about American Cold War bravado. Like other remakes of 1950s and 1960s heist films released after *Ocean's Eleven* box office success – *Welcome to Collinwood* (2002), *The Good Thief* (2002), *The Italian Job* (2003), and *The Ladykillers* (2004) – *Ocean's Eleven* recasts the past as style by projecting a certain attitude centered on male-coded professionalism, camaraderie, and gentlemanliness (Gallagher 2013, 159). In an era that saw studios wooing young audiences with gross-out comedies featuring twenty-something slackers defiantly wallowing in their own immaturity, *Ocean's Eleven* celebrated the suave antics of Rat Pack masculinity but without the misogyny of the Cold War era. As the heist plot hinges on subterfuge and role-playing before surveillance cameras as a ploy to breach casino security, the film's display of male performance, as Mark Gallagher puts it, "acknowledges the perils of visibility, but transforms them into benefits" (2013, 161).

If *Ocean's Eleven* suggests, tongue-in-cheek, what is at stake for male performance in the twenty-first century, the film's 2001 release date also made it resonate as a statement about the perils of public office – specifically, the trials and tribulations of two successive presidents, Bill Clinton and George W. Bush, in their respective attempts to maneuver an unsparing, volatile media. Both presidents operated under

American Film History: Selected Readings, 1960 to the Present, First Edition. Edited by Cynthia Lucia, Roy Grundmann, and Art Simon.

Figure 19.1 Danny Ocean (George Clooney), as heist "director" in Steven Soderbergh's *Ocean's Eleven* (2001, producer Jerry Weintraub), supervises a costume fitting for one of his "players," Saul Bloom (Carl Reiner), as "producer" Reuben Tishkoff (Elliott Gould) looks on.

watchful media eyes, yet criticism of the recently elected Bush for a delayed response to the World Trade Center and Pentagon attacks paled in comparison to the more intensive and focused coverage Clinton had received for lying about his sexual relations with White House intern Monica Lewinsky. Liberal Hollywood, however, made it clear for whom it rooted. The beguiling charm of *Ocean Eleven*'s leads, Danny Ocean (George Clooney) and his partner in crime, Rusty Ryan (Brad Pitt), is stoked by their unmistakably Clintonesque flair. Privileging personal charisma and a vaguely populist anti-authoritarianism over any need to play by the rules, their comportment elegantly abstracts Clinton's adulterous predisposition into the carefree homosocial world of heist professionalism. It thus falls to the antagonist, casino owner Terry Benedict (Andy Garcia), whose surveillance-heavy operation stands for "big business, class condescension, and affectlessness" (Gallagher 2013, 161), to allude to Bush.

Ocean's Eleven and its sequels added big budget movie-making to Soderbergh's artistic portfolio, which also includes independent film (his 1989 Palme D'Or-winning feature debut, *sex, lies, and videotape*), art cinema (*King of the Hill*, 1993), revisionist genre films (*The Underneath*, 1995; *Magic Mike*, 2012), biopics with niche appeal (*Che*, 2008; *Beyond the Candelabra*, 2013), social message dramas (*Traffic*, 2000; *The Informant!*, 2009), television (*The Knick*, 2014), experimental video (*Bubble*, 2005), and documentary shorts (*An Amazing Time: A Conversation about End of the Road*, 2012). This diversity makes Soderbergh, Gus Van Sant, the Coen Brothers, and several of their peers part of a new generation of cinephile directors. Their self-sufficiency enables them to pursue small, personal films, while their knowledge of cinema helps them create big studio productions that are more sophisticated, infusing them with reflexivity and intertextuality.

The narrative and visual style of *Ocean's Eleven* indicates that Soderbergh has modified some of the hallmarks of classical cinema – such as linear, unobtrusive editing, psychological transparency, and compositional unity – with idioms of New Hollywood and global art cinema, giving his remake greater formal elasticity, while still adhering, however self-consciously, to basic narrative conventions. In fact, the film's plot arguably functions as a double Hollywood allegory: first, it allegorizes the modern Hollywood movie-making process, with "director" Danny recruiting his pals as "stock crew" for a package deal underwritten by "movie producer" Reuben

(Elliott Gould), Danny's rich friend. The resulting "movie" is the video of the faked raid on the casino vault (a movie set replica of the real vault) that distracts Benedict from the actual raid and, in fact, turns him into an unwitting accomplice, similar to the ways in which the cinema, according to some theorists, seduces spectators with its illusionism. Second, the make-believe antics with which Danny and Rusty seduce Reuben into joining their caper resemble nothing so much as the corporate flights of fancy that drove the historic merger of Warner Bros.'s parent company, Time Warner, with the internet provider AOL – a deal that was brokered in 1999 and announced in January 2000 (Arango 2010), before *Ocean's Eleven* went into production, but that instantly soured when the dot-com bubble burst later that year, making the whole deal look like a heist gone bad.

Reflexivity and intertextuality are features Soderbergh shares with many classic auteurs – and, as *Ocean's Eleven* shows, they remain key to defining the contemporary auteur as a creator of sophisticated, multi-layered popular art. But before the advent of the New Hollywood in the 1970s, it was usually critics and scholars who bestowed the auteur status on a director in a process aimed at unifying his (and, in rare cases, her) body of work. This approach seems as vital as ever, given the new auteurs' academically fueled eclecticism (some would call it inconsistency or erraticism) in choosing genres and themes. But one thing notably distinguishes Soderbergh and his peers from previous waves of serious-minded filmmakers. As Thomas Elsaesser has recently pointed out, the new auteur is required to develop a public persona that becomes an important and integral part of the discursive frameworks within which a movie is marketed, presented to the public, and received by viewers and the press (Elsaesser 2012, 282). The auteur is now used by studios as a promotional device, as stars once had been. As part of an intensified strategy in the new millennium that was initiated during the New Hollywood, the auteur has become the movie industry's spokesperson and what might be termed a media intellectual.

But why should Hollywood care about auteurs? To answer this question, it is necessary to revisit the industry's recent past, for the new auteurism has been shaped as much by industry and business factors as by personal vision, and these must be traced back to the late 1980s. During this period, American film developed a double-tiered structure, on the one hand, growing its traditional capital- and labor-intensive productions and, on the other, generating and cultivating a new independent film scene. In contrast to earlier decades, however, independent film was no longer considered subordinate to big studio filmmaking. As the 1980s turned into the 1990s, indie film became increasingly intertwined with big budget filmmaking and big studio financing and, ultimately, became fully integrated into what we continue to call Hollywood, as Geoff King powerfully argues in this volume.

Independents in a Changing Industry

Hollywood's reconsolidation during the Reagan years and the emergence of new media markets through pay TV and home video created a voracious demand for feature films, as Barbara Klinger points out in this volume. The industry responded by multiplying and diversifying its production units (Balio 2013, 115). While some of these were short-lived, and the entertainment business as a whole was folded into large conglomerates and multinational corporations, the industry did become more permeable to outsiders and newcomers in the late 1980s and 1990s, due mainly to three factors: the rise of specialty distributors-turned-studios, premium cable channels' boosting of feature film production through pre-sales agreements, and the major studios' founding of boutique divisions that specialized in small, off-beat films and mid-size character-driven dramas (Balio 2013, 115).

Among specialty distributors that rose to prominence during the period, Miramax stands out. Its rise exemplifies how portions of the industry found economically viable ways of tapping into the taste of specialty audiences and, in the process, cannibalized artistic talent from the fringes. That Miramax's first three hit releases – Jim Sheridan's *My Left Foot* (1989), Guiseppe Tornatore's *Cinema Paradiso* (1990), and Soderbergh's *sex, lies, and videotape* (1989) also won prestigious awards illustrates the company's knack for branding unconventional films as quality fare. In the process, it launched the careers of such filmmakers as Quentin Tarantino, who developed a cult reputation with the 1992 *Reservoir Dogs*, a grungy homage to European new wave gangster flicks, before gaining fame and multiple awards with his 1994 global box office hit *Pulp Fiction*. A three-hour multi-story film about small-time gangsters that features graphic language and imagery (including an extended anal rape scene), *Pulp Fiction* stunned the film establishment, its success suggesting that Hollywood was now open territory for geeks whose main credentials consisted of having spent years working behind the counter of a video store. The film's *tour-de-force* pastiche implicitly confirms home video's role in educating and shaping the work of cinephilic directors like Tarantino, as well as its pervasive impact on the larger culture. Tarantino's efforts as director, writer, and producer would continue to display his eclectic love of Hollywood history, art cinema, martial arts, grindhouse, and Blaxploitation movies. His persona, a palimpsest of successive generations of auteurs and movie brats brought up-to-date by postmodern geek spirit, became central to promoting his films.

That Miramax executives Bob and Harvey Weinstein would allow Tarantino to indulge in his favorite revenge theme at such length (in feverish fantasies of Kung Fu justice in *Kill Bill, Vol. I*, 2003, and *Kill Bill, Vol. II*, 2004; Nazi terror in *Inglourious Basterds*, 2009; and black slave rebellion in *Django Unchained*, 2012), indicates that their notion of counter-programming went beyond the middle-brow costume genre exemplified by *Shakespeare in Love* (1998). In turning their company into one of global cinema's major gateways to the American market, the Weinsteins shrewdly renewed the promise European art cinema had made to American audiences in the 1960s – that prurience could be redemptive, provided it was linked with social awareness and cultural reflection. This logic shaped many Miramax releases, including *Kids* (1995), a low-budget film directed by Larry Clark, written by Harmony Korine, and co-produced by Gus Van Sant, about at-risk teens, and *The Crying Game* (1992), an IRA drama with a shrewdly marketed transsexual subplot. Miramax's star rose in 1993, when Disney bought the company. But in 2005, Disney also bought out the Weinsteins in response to their bloated production budgets and payrolls and their backing of projects not in line with Disney's politics, such as Michael Moore's rabble-rousing antiwar documentary *Fahrenheit 9/11* (2004). Thereafter, high-profile releases would be few and far between for Miramax, leading to its sale in 2010 (Balio 2013, 137). Between 1996 and 2007, however, Miramax produced or distributed four films awarded the best picture Oscar – *The English Patient* (1996), *Shakespeare in Love*, *Chicago* (2002), and *No Country for Old Men* (2007).

By contrast, New Line Cinema outlived many of its competitors. Best known for *A Nightmare on Elm Street* (1984) and its sequels, the company gradually expanded to off-beat comedies and dramas, such as Paul Thomas Anderson's feature debut, *Boogie Nights* (1997), a nostalgic satire about the golden age of 1970s hard-core pornography, before becoming a major player with its production of the *Lord of the Rings* trilogy.

During the same period, the major studios created their own art house divisions, enabling them to develop and exploit off-beat material in a risk-free way. Working in conjunction with independent writer-directors, art house "shingles" operated with a close eye on the Academy Awards season and the festival scene that boomed in the 1990s, signaled by the rise of the Sundance Film Festival. In 1991, Sony created Sony Pictures Classics, which became an important foreign art cinema distributor and also co-produced its own films. Notable examples are *The Celluloid Closet* (1995), a documentary based on Vito Russo's book concerning queer representations in Hollywood cinema; *Waiting for Guffman* (1996), an off-beat Christopher Guest ensemble comedy about a small-town amateur theater group convinced they will make it big; *Crouching Tiger, Hidden Dragon* (2000), the Oscar-winning Ang Lee swordplay action-drama; *Capote* (2005), a biopic that probes the complex relationship between author Truman Capote and the subjects of his famous book, *In Cold Blood*; and *Kill Your Darlings* (2012), about the young poet Allen Ginsberg's sexual and artistic growing pains before achieving Beat fame.

Fox's art house division, Fox Searchlight, specialized in low- and medium-budget films, such as *The Ice Storm* (1997), Ang Lee's drama about upper middle-class sexual ennui and disaffection in suburban Connecticut; *Boys Don't Cry* (1999), Kimberly Pierce's drama-biopic about the murder of transgender teenager, Brandon Teena; the biopic *Kinsey* (2004), about American sex researcher Alfred Kinsey; and Alexander Payne's sleeper hit *Sideways* (2004), an indie bromance involving two 40-ish men on a road trip and the women they meet on the way. Two Fox Searchlight films became big box office hits – the off-beat family road trip comedy *Little Miss Sunshine* (2006) and Danny Boyle and Loveleen

Tandaan's international blockbuster *Slumdog Millionaire* (2008). The company's $10–$20 million budget range, still modest by industry standards, has given independent directors such as Payne (*The Descendants*, 2011), Darren Aronofsky (*Black Swan*, 2010), Wes Anderson (*The Grand Budapest Hotel,* 2014), and Steve McQueen (*Shame*, 2011; *Twelve Years a Slave*, 2013) an opportunity to work with stars and court a larger audience, in addition to competing for awards. This strategy also generated *The Tree of Life* (2011), Terrence Malick's poetic meditation on the significance of family, the function of memory, and the meaning of life, which grossed over $50 million.

Although art house division slates of domestic and foreign releases tend to be eclectic, some divisions have built a portfolio around specific topics, such as minority issues. A case in point is Focus Features, a company that, over the years, has released several films with gay, lesbian, or transgender themes that enjoyed considerable critical and box office success. The first was Todd Haynes's *Far From Heaven* (2002), a 1950s period film and queer-themed remake of *All That Heaven Allows* (1955), Douglas Sirk's socially critical melodrama about the forbidden love between a middle-class New England widow and her gardener. Unconstrained by movie censorship, Haynes adds two 1950s social taboos, race and homosexuality, to Sirk's indictment of WASP hypocrisy. He gives the housewife (Julianne Moore) a closeted husband (Dennis Quaid) and makes the gardener an African-American man (Dennis Haysbert). The film's style shows that Haynes is content to pay homage to Sirk's mise-en-scène without rehearsing its trademark Brechtian irony.

In 2005, Focus Features released *Brokeback Mountain,* Ang Lee's adaptation of Annie Proulx's story about the secret love between two Montana sheepherders, which became a global box office hit, garnered several Oscars and Golden Globe awards, and turned into a cause célèbre for liberal America. *Far from Heaven* and *Brokeback Mountain* poignantly depict the social and political isolation of their respective protagonists. Yet, the fact that Lee's film ignores gay liberation – even though its setting is historically concurrent with the movement – has been read as Hollywood's depoliticizing of minority topics. And while the homosexually active male protagonists in both films have wives, in *Brokeback Mountain* the use of bisexual story elements functioned to shield movie heroes from being called gay. But these shortcomings are offset by the film's abiding emotional power and the fact that it confronts mainstream viewers with widescreen images of rugged Westerners engaged in anal intercourse – aspects that made *Brokeback Mountain* one of the most widely discussed American films of the 2000s.

The members of the Academy of Motion Picture Arts and Sciences could not yet bring themselves to award Heath Ledger and Jake Gyllenhaal Oscars for their performances in *Brokeback Mountain.* Two years later, however, they awarded one to Sean Penn for *Milk* (2008), Focus Feature's biopic about San Francisco city supervisor and gay activist Harvey Milk. Hollywood has an infamous record of falsifying images of gays and lesbians, but Focus Feature's 2010 queer family dramedy, *The Kids Are All Right* – a story about two female lovers' efforts at running a queer family – signaled the extent to which gays and lesbians could now be imagined as middle-class citizens rather than as liminal figures. The mainstreaming of these characters is tied closely to consumerist white privilege, however, and comes at the expense of the subtly racist treatment of at least one non-white character – a Hispanic gardener. In 2013, the company released *Dallas Buyers Club*, a drama about a straight man who, when diagnosed with AIDS in the mid-1980s, antagonizes the Food and Drug Administration by setting up a commercial exchange for the distribution of unapproved medication. This film, too, garnered a Best Actor Oscar, but has been widely criticized for spinning actual events into a story that glorifies individualism and the capitalist marketplace, while demonizing state-sponsored healthcare and marginalizing the historical significance of AIDS activist collectives.

A New Auteur Cinema

As a consequence of the diversification of the production scene in the late 1980s and early 1990s, an increasing number of emerging directors, only a few of whom can be discussed here, began to take their place alongside seasoned filmmakers like Martin Scorsese. Differing widely in themes, styles, and budgets, their films overtly concern themselves with American society, either in testing the viability of the American Dream, or through investigating questions of family, social responsibility, and the relation between individuals and the community. A concern with these classic themes places directors like Gus Van Sant, the Coen Brothers, and Paul Thomas Anderson in a tradition of socially interested cinema that includes the work of Frank Capra, Orson Welles, William Wyler, John Huston, Elia Kazan, John Frankenheimer, Robert Altman, and most filmmakers of the first New Hollywood.

Gus Van Sant began his career with the micro-budget *Mala Noche* (1986), a gay-themed triangle romance, shot on black-and-white 16mm, involving a white gay store assistant and two Mexican teens that – like his subsequent films *Drug Store Cowboy* (1989), *My Own Private Idaho* (1991), and *Even Cowgirls Get the Blues* (1993) – exemplifies independent cinema through a loosely constructed, regionally specific story (in his case, the Pacific Northwest). Following his breakthrough success in the black comedy *To Die For* (1995), Van Sant brought his interest in social outsiders to mainstream audiences. *Good Will Hunting* (1997), a male friendship tale between a Harvard student and his hyper-intelligent, psychologically challenged janitor friend (played by co-writers Ben Affleck and Matt Damon respectively), explores psychotherapy as a tool for social readjustment. In contrast to Robert Redford's 1980 drama *Ordinary People*, however, Van Sant's film questions the very notion of social readjustment. After *Psycho* (1998), a formally close remake of Hitchcock's classic that riled critics with its seemingly gratuitous depictions of sexual outsider Norman Bates's desires, Van Sant returned to making low-budget films (with the exception of the studio-backed biopic *Milk*). Like his early work, most of these later films are set among alienated young adults and interrogate violent, senseless death that, in some cases, is depicted as a nihilistic rebellion against assimilation. *Gerry* (2002) is a partially improvised, non-linear two-person drama involving two desert hikers that ends with one killing the other; *Elephant* (2003) is a fictionalized treatment of the 1999 Columbine High School massacre, which – like Soderbergh's Liberace biopic, *Beyond the Candelabra* (2013), and Van Sant's next film, *Last Days* (2005) – was financed by HBO and premiered at Cannes. *Last Days*, which depicts a rock musician's final days before his suicide, is inspired by the story of Nirvana front man Kurt Cobain.

Their sexual or racial alterity and their status as young malcontents define Van Sant's protagonists as outsiders from the start. By contrast, many of Joel and Ethan Coen's protagonists are more firmly embedded in society before getting pushed to the margins, either because their luck evaporates in a series of ill-fated turns or because their hubris and short-sightedness do them in. Through unusual plot twists the Coens infuse their films with a unique blend of comedy, drama, suspense, and horror – all resulting in self-reflexive uses of genre that arise from unpredictable, uneven apportioning of these elements, as William Luhr discusses in the hardcover/online edition. From their 1986 cinematic debut with the noirish thriller *Blood Simple*, throughout the 1990s, the Coens' love of pastiche, as in the dark comedy *Raising Arizona* (1987), and their synthetic take on screwball tradition, as in *The Hudsucker Proxy* (1994), have helped shape their reputation as cult jesters for a generation raised on MTV and late night reruns of Hollywood classics. This sensibility peaked with another addition to the cult canon, *The Big Lebowski* (1998), a paean to the abiding virtue of hippie values in a self-indulgent, materialist world. What gives these films substance beyond the sheen of postmodern irony is their smartly written, offbeat dialogue that forms the connecting tissue between seemingly disparate layers of low-key drama, dead-pan humor, and similarly dead-pan violence.

The critical and commercial success of *Fargo* (1996), a cross between suspenseful policier and absurdist farce, gave the Coens greater leverage in realizing their projects. Characteristic of other independent directors who experience mainstream success, the Coens have since oscillated between larger studio-backed productions (which, in the case of the 2004 *Ladykillers* and the 2010 *True Grit*, are remakes of classics) and smaller films, such as *A Serious Man* (2009) and *Inside Llewyn Davis* (2013). A melancholic look at the early 1960s folk music scene, *Llewyn Davis* has thrown into relief the Coens' core concerns – their investigation of the corrosive impact of the profit motive on American society and their deep empathy with grassroots culture and the notion of "folk," which is already present in *The Big Lebowski* and is made more explicit in the Depression-era musical *O Brother, Where Art Thou?* (2000).

Llewyn Davis's modest budget and box office performance are appropriate to the film's subject, a story about a morose musician whose uncompromising vision of his art and ambivalence toward success define him as a self-defeating slacker in the eyes of some

Figure 19.2 Bowling partners – the Dude (Jeff Bridges), Walter (John Goodman), and Donnie (Steve Buscemi) in *The Big Lebowski* (1998, directors, producers, and writers Joel Coen and Ethan Coen) – are sympathetic slackers who serve as antidotes to capitalist, achievement-driven values.

friends and family members and lead him through a series of uncomfortable mishaps. An astoundingly original defense of the moral integrity of underperforming (in every sense of the word), the film becomes a radical reminder of what is most viable about the American Dream – qualities that, so the Coens suggest, can only be pursued tentatively, as they require us to remain skeptical of materialism and on our guard against hubris. Whether played in a low-key register as in *Llewyn Davis*, through generic high jinks, as in the satirical comedy of errors, *Burn After Reading* (2008), or as Gothic neo-Western in *No Country for Old Men* (2007), one of their biggest critical and commercial hits to date, the Coens' unique mixture of pragmatism, skepticism, and absurdism has created one of the most remarkable bodies of films in recent American cinema. In *No Country for Old Men* the single-minded, indeed pathological, search for cash embodied by Anton Chigurh (Javier Bardem), wreaks havoc across a population of criminals and innocents, driving the ageing sheriff, Ed Tom Bell (Tommy Lee Jones), to recognize that this is no country for old men. In this contemporary gangster-Western, the violence that resonates throughout much of their work comes to dominate a simple but deeply troubling chase story. As it had in so many Westerns of the past, the desert landscape comes to stand for the realm of limitless brutality, its sublime beauty littered with the victims of human greed.

The drive for success is a central theme for Paul Thomas Anderson, who set his early films in a suburban world, where familial dysfunction lurks beneath the sheen of a prosperous, commerce-driven, media-saturated culture. Whether to escape or conquer this world, Anderson's protagonists compulsively commoditize themselves, falling prey to what Jason Sperb has characterized as the trifecta of "excess, egomania, and greed" (Sperb 2013, 3). *Boogie Nights* tracks the rise and fall of a gullible hunk who finds fame during the 1970s porn film boom, before drugs, crime, and the advent of video jeopardize his career. Most characters in the ensemble cast of *Magnolia* (1999) engage in some form of exploitation or self-exploitation, driven by the petty opportunism that determines their meandering paths. As Sperb argues, however, Anderson's films "often end on a cautious note of reconciliation that implies patriarchal capitalism is the solution to the same problems it created" (2013, 3). *There Will Be Blood* (2007) and *The Master* (2010) are stern warnings against the gospel of materialism. Each film casts its respective tycoon tale – of a monstrous, post–gilded-age oil baron in the former and a Cold War religious demagogue and quack in the latter – as a dark parable of the consequences of the success myth.

Film music is an often overlooked but nevertheless crucial element in the success of many films and the auteur status accorded many filmmakers. During this period, John Williams continued to compose film scores for the *Star Wars* and *Indiana Jones* franchises and for Steven Spielberg films, including *Saving Private Ryan* (1998), *Minority Report* (2002), *Munich* (2005), and *Lincoln* (2012), among others. Arguably the most prolific film composer in cinema history, Williams, in some given years, has up to four feature film scores to his credit. Danny Elfman also has contributed contemporary film scores of note through collaborations with directors Tim Burton, Gus Van Sant, and Sam Raimi, to name just a few. Elfman successfully creates the grand sounds necessary for science fiction and superhero films, such as *Batman Returns* (1992) and *Spider-Man* (2002), as well as the subtler, often dramatically tense compositions for films such as *Good Will Hunting* (1992), *To Die For* (1995), and *Milk* (2008). Also during this period, critically acclaimed singer-songwriter Randy Newman, with a following loyal to his smart lyrics and pop melodies, went on to become an honored film composer whose work is perhaps best associated with Pixar Animation and the scores for the *Toy Story* series (1995–2010), *Monsters, Inc.* (2001), and *Cars* (2006).

International directors made the successful move to Hollywood during the studio and post-studio eras, a migration that continues into the new millennium. Taiwanese native Ang Lee, while not obtaining the cult status of mainland China's John Woo, achieved considerable recognition within the industry. Arriving in the US in 1979, Lee studied at New York University (where he worked with Spike Lee) and devoted his first feature filmmaking efforts to a trilogy – *Pushing Hands* (1992), *The Wedding Banquet* (1993), *Eat Drink Man Woman* (1994) – about generational clashes within Taiwanese-American culture. He would break through to popular and critical acclaim with a string of successes that included *Sense and Sensibility* (1995), *Crouching Tiger, Hidden Dragon, Brokeback Mountain*, and *Life of Pi* (2012). The best-direction Oscar awarded him for *Brokeback Mountain* cemented his role as a leading filmmaker in the US. Indeed, between 1992 and 2012, Lee released, on average, a film every two years. Lasse Hallström came from Sweden, where he made *My Life as a Dog* (1985), a film that would gain international attention and praise. Among his prominent US films are *What's Eating Gilbert Grape* (1993), featuring Leonardo DiCaprio as a mentally challenged adolescent in one of the most prominent of his early screen roles; *Chocolat* (2000), a US–UK co-production, and adaptations of John Irving's novel, *The Cider House Rules* (1999), and Annie Proulx's novel, *The Shipping News* (2001).

In the new millennium three Mexican filmmakers established themselves as players within the industry, working with major stars and big budget projects. In *21 Grams* (2003) and *Babel* (2006), Alejandro González Iñárritu, in collaboration with screenwriter Guillermo Arriaga, experimented with complex narrative construction, weaving together the lives of multiple characters, frequently through a non-linear sequencing of events. Guillermo del Toro found a niche with films such as *Hellboy* (2004), *Hellboy II* (2008), and *Pan's Labyrinth* (2006). Similarly, Alfonso Cuarón broke through with the immensely popular *Harry Potter and the Prisoner of Azkaban* (2004) and followed that with the sci-fi drama *Children of Men* (2006). Iñárritu and Cuarón established themselves within the industry through their treatment of the fantasy-adventure film, the kind of fare that has been central to American cinema in the post-1980 period.

Female Directors in Hollywood

Since the 1990s, women directors have become more visible in American cinema. While some operate without studio backing, others successfully maneuver between small indie productions and mid-size films released by larger distributors, while also working for television and in the advertising and music video industries. Sofia Coppola arguably has a special status, as her projects have traditionally been backed by her father's American Zoetrope studio. After an early acting career that included roles in the *Godfather* films, she quickly became a notable writer-director, garnering a Best Screenplay Oscar for her second feature, *Lost in Translation* (2003). The film is about a developing friendship between a successful, middle-aged actor (Bill Murray) and a young college graduate (Scarlett Johansson) who, while staying at the same Tokyo hotel, bond over loneliness, spousal neglect, and a lack of purpose in life. Johansson's Charlotte resonated with generation-X audiences all over the world. She exemplifies Coppola's penchant for creating characters who, their youth and social privilege notwithstanding, reflect the paradoxical status and contradictory expectations society has created for women – whether in the suburban setting of *The Virgin Suicides* (1999), in the French court of *Marie Antoinette* (2006), or in the elite circles of Beverly Hills in *The Bling Ring* (2013).

Stories about women, gender, and sexuality are also of interest to Kimberly Peirce and Patty Jenkins, whose films explore the deformation of the individual and the family as a consequence of economic inequality and sexual and gender oppression. Peirce achieved global acclaim with *Boys Don't Cry* (1999) with its dramatic treatment of the transgender teenager Brandon Teena, who was raped and murdered in Nebraska when his biological femaleness was discovered by his girlfriend's clique. Jenkins wrote and directed *Monster* (2003), a film about real-life serial killer Aileen Wuornos, who turned to prostitution while growing up in a broken home and later killed seven men. Each film returned its investment multiple times over, and each also garnered numerous awards, including Best Actress Oscars for their respective leads, Hilary Swank and Charlize Theron.

Kathryn Bigelow has traditionally placed her heroines in a male-centered world, although several of her recent films have also shown the dehumanizing impact of that world on men. This is particularly true of *K-19: The Widowmaker* (2002), which is based on the real-life near-fatal accident of a nuclear-powered Soviet submarine during the Cold War; *The Hurt Locker* (2008), which depicts the nerve-wrecking work of a US military bomb disposal unit during the Iraq War; and *Zero Dark Thirty* (2012), which dramatizes the US military and intelligence hunt for Osama Bin Laden. Through these military settings Bigelow explores what happens when masculinism becomes synonymous with, and is fueled by, officially sanctioned values like patriotism and male hero worship. While *K-19* and *Hurt Locker* hauntingly depict the alternately terrifying and exhilarating dynamics of male homosocial worlds, *Zero Dark Thirty* places a female protagonist, CIA officer Maya Lambert (Jessica Chastain), at the center of the narrative. Although *Hurt Locker* garnered Bigelow a Best Director Oscar (the first for a female feature film director), *Zero Dark Thirty* is especially of interest in terms of female representation in the context of its controversial, if implicit, endorsement of government-sanctioned torture, euphemistically referred to as enhanced interrogation. Though the film implicates male and female agents in the violence of these interrogation techniques, by assigning its female protagonist a key role in the tactics leading to the capture of Bin Laden, it clearly complicates and recontextualizes the question of torture. The film individualizes – and thereby deflects from – government agency and responsibility by focusing on a female protagonist and several secondary male figures. The implication that women who exercise power in today's world must share in responsibility for the effects of that power is an inarguable premise, consistent with Bigelow's early genre films that revolve around women attempting, with varying degrees of success, to insert themselves into male systems of power and masculinist value systems. Although loosely based on actual individuals and events, and while mildly acknowledging that the female investigator (played by Jessica Chastain) is but a small cog within a vast male-dominated security apparatus, the film's portrayal of female exceptionalism ultimately functions to distract from interrogating key officials in the Bush administration and the President himself, who were largely responsible for the inhumane treatment of prisoners – some of whom were wrongly accused.

Black Filmmakers in Hollywood

Historically, African-Americans remained barred even longer than women from becoming writers, directors, and producers in Hollywood. It was not until the late 1980s and 1990s that a significant wave of studio-backed black-authored films emerged, most of them written and/or directed by film-school educated directors like Spike Lee and John Singleton, as well as self-taught directors like Robert and Allen Hughes. When the 'hood film genre began to wane in the mid-1990s, however, it once again became more difficult to identify larger trends and shared concerns in black filmmaking. But in the late 1990s and early 2000s, three notable new black directors emerged – Kasi Lemmons, Lee Daniels, and Tyler Perry – all of whom share an ability and willingness to work in multiple artistic capacities, including acting, writing, producing, and directing. While African-Americans have always been part of the entertainment industry, contemporary black filmmakers have had somewhat greater success in obtaining positions of creative control.

Lemmons initially sought an acting career, which led to employment in television and substantial supporting roles in feature films, including Spike Lee's *School Days* (1988) and Bernard Rose's *Candyman* (1992). She made her debut as a writer-director with *Eve's Bayou* (1997), a critically acclaimed, commercially successful family drama set in upper middle-class black circles. After her next feature, *The Caveman's Valentine* (2001), Lemmons directed *Talk to Me* (2007), a biopic about legendary black radio DJ Ralph "Petey" Greene (played by Don Cheadle) who, with the help of a radio promoter (Chiwetel Ejiofor), became a media personality in the 1960s and 1970s. The film invites comparison with Lee's *Malcolm X* (1992) through its use of the Sam Cooke song "A Change Is Gonna Come," considered a Civil Rights anthem. Lee uses the song as a prelude to Malcolm X's assassination, folding it into a larger dialectic of racism and black liberation "by any means necessary." Lemmons, by contrast, uses it as a eulogy for Martin Luther King Jr., when played on the air by Greene after King's assassination in order to redirect black anger away from looting and rioting. Yet, far from being accommodationist, Lemmons's story of Greene's rise and fall pinpoints the DJ's subsequent fame as a different form of black containment.

Lee Daniels came to directing after success as a talent manager and producer of socially conscious dramas. His directorial projects are equally grounded in social commentary, whether in edgy genre films like *Shadowboxer* (2006) and *The Paperboy* (2012), or in social message movies like *Precious: Based on the Novel "Push" by Sapphire* (2009). *Precious* is about an obese, illiterate Harlem teenager who, during her second pregnancy (she already has one child with Down Syndrome), learns she is HIV-positive and tries to transcend the circumstances of her broken home, while coming to term in her preganancy. Shown at Sundance and Cannes, the film earned rave reviews and became a cause célèbre for blacks in the entertainment industry. Co-produced by Daniels, Oprah Winfrey, and Tyler Perry, among others, it garnered several Oscars and became a major box office hit. Daniels scored a similar success with *Lee Daniels' The Butler* (2013), a historical drama based on the life of Eugene Allen, a black man who worked as a butler in the White House for several decades. Textbook examples of liberal mainstream cinema, Daniels's films deal with complex socio-historical issues through a single protagonist. *Precious* showcases its heroine as a spectacle of disenfranchisement, while *The Butler* editorializes history. It hopscotches across symbolically crucial moments of black struggle, mildly satirizing Nancy Reagan's social hypocrisy, while ignoring Reaganomics' systematic, longer-term disenfranchising of African-Americans.

Beyond *Precious*, which she executive-produced, Oprah Winfrey produced and acted in *Selma* (2014), notably and surprisingly the first American theatrically released biopic about Martin Luther King, Jr. *Selma* avoids many of the "great man" narrative biopic clichés, instead providing a nuanced portrait of the man in the context of his complicated political and personal relationships. That said, the script sometimes delivers heavy-handed speechifying dialogue, even at the most intimate of moments. The film also incited controversy at the time of its release for the representation of President Lyndon Baines Johnson (LBJ) as a resistant figure in advancing voting rights and other causes central to the Civil Rights Movement. At the same time, *Selma* admirably exposes the inner workings of the movement and conflicts between King's Southern Christian Leadership Conference (SCLC) and the grassroots Student Nonviolent Coordinating Committee (SNCC). *Selma* director Ava DuVernay had won various awards for her earlier films (*Middle of Nowhere*, 2012, about a black female medical student, and *I Will Follow*, 2010, about a black female artist). In the context of *Selma*'s subject, its cinematic treatment, and DuVernay's directing credentials, it is difficult to explain the Academy of Motion Pictures Arts and Sciences generally dismissive treatment of the film, nominated only in two Oscar categories – Best Motion Picture of the Year, which it did not win, and Best Original Song, which it did win for "Glory," written by John Stephens and Lonnie Lynn. The Academy fell silent on admirable performances by David Oyelowo as Martin Luther King, Jr., Carmen Ejogo as Coretta Scott King, and Tom Wilkinson as LBJ. And, while Oscar awards and nominations are not necessarily indicative of film quality, this absence of recognition did strike some critics and others in the film community as disturbing, particularly in light of Golden Globe nominations for DuVeray as Best Director and Oyelowo as best actor, the American Film Institute (AFI) naming *Selma* "Movie of the Year," the African-American Film Critics Association (AAFCA) awarding it best actor, best music director, and best picture awards, and the Alliance of Women Journalists conferring Best Director and Female Icon of the Year awards to DuVernay.

Tyler Perry's prolific efforts as playwright, screenwriter, actor, producer, and director make him one of the highest paid artists in the entertainment industry. The themes and style of his films, which are shaped by his religious and artistic background, give Perry's work a paradoxical quality. His first film, *Diary of a Mad Black Woman* (2005), is based on his own play for which he created and performed in drag the character of Madea, an overwrought, elderly woman who is combative but good-hearted. The film became a success and formed the beginning of the Madea franchise, which has since added seven more films, and in which the character fights all manner of bias, but also solves feuds and mentors family and friends. The contradictions in Perry's work – it is rowdily burlesque low art informed by Christian values – have earned him similarly contradictory accusations of perpetuating black minstrelsy while advocating outdated middle-class ideologies of black uplift. Yet, Perry's popularity is hardly puzzling, if one considers that his films strongly resonate with non-urban and church-going audiences, a demographic that often is ignored or dismissed by influential urban critics.

Hollywood in the New Millennium

On Wednesday, June 11, 2013, Steven Spielberg and George Lucas publicly predicted that the American film industry was headed for what Spielberg termed an inevitable "implosion" (Bond 2014). Speaking to students and faculty at the University of Southern California (USC), Spielberg lamented that character- and content-driven films – including biopics and historical dramas such as his own 2012 *Lincoln* – are of little interest to a spectacle-driven industry seeking to recoup its skyrocketing production and marketing budgets through increased ticket prices. Spielberg's warning that the industry would self-destruct if only a handful of mega-budget movies were to fail perhaps indirectly referenced Disney's dramatic flop with the fantasy extravaganza *John Carter* (2012), which earned $73 million domestically on a budget of $250 million (marketing not included). Even its foreign box office of $211 million could not salvage a film that would have needed to make $600 million to break even (*National Post* 2012). Another Disney (Buena Vista) release, *The Lone Ranger* (2013), a special effects-driven action Western based on the TV series, estimated to have cost $375 million to produce and market, would have needed to earn $800 million worldwide just to break even (Barnes 2013). The film grossed less than $90 million at the American box office for a worldwide total of $260 million.[1] Universal Pictures' supernatural buddy cop movie, *R.I.P.D.* (2013), based on a comic book, cost $130 million to make (marketing not included) and grossed a total of $78 million (with less than half coming from the US box office).[2] Another Universal release, the martial arts film *47 Ronin* (2013), grossed $38 million domestically (and only $112 million internationally) for a $175 million production budget (marketing not included).[3]

Despite the huge success of *The Hunger Games* and superhero franchises based on Marvel and DC Comics characters, Hollywood's business model seemed to have gone awry. Yet, somehow, Spielberg's prediction did not come true. By the end of the 2013 summer season, a few heads may have rolled in Hollywood, but one year later the industry appeared very much intact, about to embark on another round of movie apocalypses – such as *Transcendence* (2014), a sci-fi film that cost $100 million (before marketing) and ended up earning $23 million in North America and a mere $80 million internationally.[4] By comparison, it is interesting to consider how the few traditional, content-driven productions released in 2013 and 2014 fared. By the end of 2013, *Lee Daniels' The Butler* had earned $176 million on a budget of $30 million,[5] while the Jackie Robinson biopic *42* had made nearly $100 million on a budget of

$40 million.[6] By spring 2014, Steve McQueen's *12 Years a Slave* had returned $188 million on its $20 million budget;[7] the US/UK produced maternal melodrama *Philomena*, directed by Stephen Frears, grossed $100 million worldwide on a budget of $12 million;[8] and the AIDS drama *Dallas Buyers Club*, directed by Jean-Marc Vallée, grossed $55 million on a budget of $5 million.[9] By mid-summer 2014, *The Fault in Our Stars*, a love story about two terminally ill teenagers, had returned over $250 million worldwide on a $12 million budget.[10]

Such figures might prompt studios to rethink their production palettes. Yet, with the exception of comedies and horror films, Hollywood has shown little interest in moderately budgeted productions and outright disdain for low-budget ones, even when such films show big returns. By the early to mid-2000s, many studios had once again shuttered their specialty divisions, acting mainly as distributors of small, content-driven films that were now being produced by business-savvy independents. Compelled by their parent companies to turn movies into serialized tie-in devices and advertisements for a global toy market, Hollywood studios in the new millennium had become tent-pole mills, producing films expected to support both the production company itself and the ancillary products spinning off from the movie. Spielberg's complaint, understandable as it may be, feels slightly disingenuous, if one recalls that it was his and Lucas's concept of movie entertainment that paved the way for the serialization or "sequelitis" that sealed the industry's resurgence in the 1980s. Now both moguls seem to fear eviction from the house they built.

As the 2013 and 2014 release seasons indicate, films are no longer designed as films. They are small particles in comprehensive franchises, churned out by a sprawling industry with huge overhead, a high-cost infrastructure (including armies of post-production and computer-generated effects [CGE] specialists), and tax-related incentives that can sustain itself only by releasing big movies all the time. While even many small productions now rely on CGE, films like *Philomena* or *Dallas Buyers Club* do not keep an industry alive – not because they do not make enough money, but because they do not cost enough. Asking Hollywood to focus on such films would be like asking General Motors to manufacture bicycles.

The tent-pole business model emerged fully only after the industry had completed its 1990s wave of mergers and acquisitions. By the 2000s, studios were streamlining their product into three overarching categories – comic book franchises, family films, and 3-D showcases. These were defined less by themes, plots, and iconography than by their intellectual property (IP) profile (based on successful novels, plays, television shows), their main target demographic, and the technologies that determined their consumption (Balio 2013, 25). Sequels based on characters created by Marvel and DC Comics benefited as much from the 3-D boom as animated films for the whole family, such as *Up* (2009) or *Ice Age: Continental Drift* (2012), which succeeded with a large audience by addressing children and grown-ups on separate levels. The industry reaped tremendous box office success with films like *Toy Story* and its two sequels (1995–2010), *Shrek* and its three sequels (2001–2010), *WALL•E* (2008) and *Monsters, Inc.* (2001). Synergistic ties with youth-oriented television, like the Nickelodeon cable network, further fueled production cycles aimed at a pre-teen or early teen demographic. But the lukewarm box office performance of *Cars 2* (2011) signaled that animated film could no longer afford to rely solely on 3-D to attract audiences, as families became less willing to pay increased ticket prices to see 3-D releases.

While Hollywood movies remain rooted in genre cinema, classic genres lost some of their significance as a means of communication between studios and audiences. They were eclipsed by franchises and by the studios themselves, which once again became publicly recognizable brands in their own right. Warner Bros. was the largest, most profitable, and most stable studio in the first decade of the new millennium (Balio 2013, 40). It launched the *Harry Potter* franchise and the *Dark Knight* trilogy, but also benefited from its subsidiary, New Line Cinema, which developed the *Lord of the Rings* films. The studio also struck lucrative distribution deals with several production firms, including Village Road Show Pictures, for which it released both the *Matrix* and the *Ocean's* franchises. Disney turned one of its classic theme park rides into the profitable *Pirates of the Caribbean* franchise. Paramount rebooted the *Star Trek* series and co-produced two *Transformers* movies. As Bart Beaty points out in this volume, Marvel Comics founded its own studio to make films based on its comic book characters, although *Spider-Man* remained in the hands of Sony, which also adapted Dan Brown's bestseller *The Da Vinci Code* (2006). Fox was in charge of George Lucas's new installment of the *Star Wars* trilogy, but the company also developed the *X-Men* franchise and co-produced James Cameron's *Titanic* (1997) and *Avatar* (2009) together with Paramount.

The Meaning of Movies: Universalizing Content for the Global Market

By the 2010s, the foreign revenue of Hollywood films out-grossed American box office by three to one. Yet, given the escalating budgets for big studio movies, a tent-pole's global earnings are now essential to pushing it into the black – which, for example, was the case with *Pacific Rim* (2013), an auteurist monster movie directed by Guillermo del Toro that earned back only half of its $180 million budget domestically and might have become another box office disaster, had it not performed well in Asia (Mendelson 2013). Keenly aware of their significance, the industry now makes concessions to foreign markets on several levels. Big-budget films have recently boasted ethnically and nationally diverse casts. Marketing considerations also motivate studios' strategic adjusting to foreign censorship codes, as was the case with *Django Unchained* (2013) and *Iron Man 3* (2013), both of which were reedited for the Chinese market that, in 2012, had grown 36 percent (Thompson 2014, x).

Recent studio strategizing aside, Hollywood has long sought to make its high-budget productions culturally legible to as many audiences as possible. Yet, rarely does a blockbuster's appeal rest on a lowest common denominator approach, with *Avatar* (2009) as case in point. As Thomas Elsaesser has very effectively argued, the film achieved global success not because it is all things to all people but because it succeeds in being very different things to different people (2012, 289). Environmentalists embraced the film with the same enthusiasm as the Na'vi – the story's extra-terrestrial aborigines – embraced their sacred tree. By contrast, urban columnists panned the film for its "white messiah" fable that constructs earthlings as saviors of the natives, who are portrayed as noble savages about to be colonized (Elsaesser 2012, 292). Elsaesser references political theorist Slavoj Žižek, who contributed to the *Avatar* debate, claiming that the film manipulates audiences into sympathizing with the noble tribe without endorsing its political cause. *Avatar*'s story, as Žižek adds, eerily echoes the fate of actual citizens of India who recently fought companies trying to mine their land. But, countering Žižek's Marxist view of these citizens as victims, Elsaesser takes into account the ways in which they mobilized the media to their own advantage. Upon learning that their struggle was becoming global news, these Indian citizens likened their children to *Avatar*'s protagonists in a YouTube campaign, and lobbied director Cameron to support their cause – a move that, in turn, inspired oppressed groups around the world and became further proof of Hollywood's abiding power as the lingua franca of a globalized world (2012, 294).

That *Avatar* can be read both as self-congratulatory enactment of colonialism and as skeptical fable about capitalism is indicative of how Hollywood today, not entirely unlike Hollywood of yesteryear, shapes its films in order to give multiple audiences stratified access to one and the same text.

Something similar can be said of superhero movies, which are allegorically overwrought from the outset. In the case of *The Dark Knight*, the second installment of Christopher Nolan's post-millennial *Batman* trilogy, which premiered in 2008 in an America divided over controversial practices used by the Bush government in combating terrorism, it was the figure of the Joker (Heath Ledger) that sparked opposite interpretations. Conservative columnists read the Joker as an open homage to what they perceived as Bush's moral courage (Klavan 2008), while opponents of the war read the same character as a dramatic device demonstrating that a democratic nation, even when fighting terror, must never abandon its principles (Landesman 2008). Its double allegory helped make *The Dark Knight* one of the most successful and most widely discussed films of all time. Yet, the exact interpretation of such allegories is not preordained.

Meaning emerges through a complex dialectic between a given studio's corporate culture, the decisions of the film's creative team (writers, director, and producers), and, last, but not least, the vast community of vocal fans of a franchise, who sometimes are more familiar with it than even the franchise owners or the movie studio producing the films. Hollywood has, of course, always been keenly aware of fan communities, and the management of fandom has long been among the main tasks of PR departments. It was not until the late 1990s, however, with the emergence of online platforms and the rising significance of fan conventions like Comic-Con International, that marketing experts began to engage fans in a closely interactive manner (Balio 2013, 76). A primer was New Line Cinema's launch of the official *Lord of the Rings* website in May 1999, six months before shooting started. When a plethora of alternative fan-run sites sprang up to compete with the official site, the studio decided to engage rather than suppress or ignore the franchise's unruly fan base (Balio 2013, 84).

Certain films inevitably come to bear the stamp of the corporation that bring them to life – particularly if the film in question is a high-profile blockbuster, whose financing and design require contentious boardroom meetings fueled by competing philosophies and whose performance will determine the fates of hundreds or thousands of people involved in its production. Film scholars J. D. Connor and Jerome Christensen have read high-budget films as internal corporate texts in which studios dialogue with their managers and staff about risks, goals, and strategies. Christensen has discussed Tim Burton's *Batman* (1989), released during the 1989 merger negotiations between Warner and Time Inc., as a veiled message to corporate insiders (Christensen 2012, 281). (As demonstrated earlier, a similar kind of reading can be performed for *Ocean's Eleven* and the AOL–Time Warner merger.) Connor, who focuses on Hollywood's allegorical expressions of its own restructuring efforts, argues in this volume that high-budget productions like *Hulk* (2003) narrativize their paradoxical status as industrially authored "independent" films.

Competing Screens and (not so) New Ways of Seeing

Although *Hulk* underperformed at the box office, the success of blockbusters like *Avatar* and *The Dark Knight* enabled the industry to maintain control over a fickle market threatened by declining DVD sales, the fragmentation of audiences, and the hard-to-gauge impact of the internet and social media on consumer preferences and Hollywood marketing practices (Balio 2013, 65). The irony of this period rests with the juxtaposition, indeed, the contradiction of image and exhibition. While the accent is placed on spectacle, on visual abundance that gains maximum effect on the biggest of screens, movies have begun to be exhibited on ever smaller screens – televisions, computers, and hand-held devices. One could argue that the post-1980 spectacles, like CinemaScope in an earlier era, were yet another effort to counter the ubiquity of domestic small screens with an overwhelming visual display. But the fact remains that movie exhibition venues continue to diversify, as personal computers, tablets, and cell phones have become popular sites of image consumption. Still, these small screens are transient – carried to work and viewed while commuting, shared with friends outside the home – and a growing number of Americans have balanced the hand-held frame with the installation of ever larger screens and sound systems at home, seeking to import the theater experience into the living room. In the process, the movies defended their place alongside other media in a dramatically expanding screen-based society.

One of the notable developments in this new society has been the transformation of television into a medium of serious, ambitious storytelling. The trend began in the late 1990s, when HBO, to beef up its slate of original productions, launched *The Sopranos* (1999), a scripted series about the trials and tribulations of the leader of a mob clan. The series' tremendous popularity created a new concept – scripted programming – with such series as *Six Feet Under* (2001), a black comedy about a family who owns a funeral home, *Deadwood* (2004), a Western series about a seedy frontier town, *Breaking Bad* (2008), a series about a high school teacher turned crystal meth producer, and, perhaps most significantly, *The Wire* (2002), a multi-faceted, deeply vernacular portrait of the Baltimore underworld through the eyes of drug dealers and the police. While *The Wire* was less popular than other series, its combination of intelligent storytelling with local color and incisive social critique instantly placed it as comparable to a long line of socially conscious movies, ranging from pre-blacklist films like Jules Dassin's *The Naked City* (1948) to the New Hollywood of Jerry Schatzberg's *Panic in Needle Park* (1971) and Sidney Lumet's *Dog Day Afternoon* (1975) and *Prince of the City* (1981).

Television, as *The Wire* proved, was not merely the new place for artistically ambitious and socially responsible entertainment – it now also presented itself as the better place, as it claimed to bring higher-quality stories made for less money to more people, and this was true not only for scripted series but also feature films.[11] Small surprise, then, that projects for cable TV soon attracted top industry talent, such as David Fincher, known for edgy Hollywood films such as *Fight Club* (1999), *The Curious Case of Benjamin Button* (2008), and *The Social Network* (2010), who in 2013 began directing the hit series *House of Cards*, as well as Martin Scorsese, who executive produced *Boardwalk Empire* (2010) and directed its 2010 series premiere. Steven Soderbergh decided to make his Liberace biopic, *Behind the Candelabra* (2013) not as a theatrical feature, but for HBO, which reduced the budget from $70 million to $23 million (Thompson 2014, xi). The film earned an Emmy, not an Oscar, but still premiered at Cannes to much fanfare and favorable reviews.

In his USC address Spielberg also expressed horror at the prospect of moving a large-scale biopic like *Lincoln* – or, for that matter, Lucas's co-produced and co-directed World War II Tuskegee Airmen drama, *Red Tails* (2012) – to the small screen, a concern that rings a bit false. His concern seems less about cable TV's viability as a home for epic movies than about the director's self-image as auteur, who embraces television only for certain projects, and then usually (though not always) as a producer. Like Spielberg, *Avatar*'s James Cameron is one of the most artistically and business-savvy filmmakers in the business, yet he seems more willing to move between large and small screens, high- and low-tech formats, and solitary lab work and large-scale industrial delivery. Cameron has made these disparate aspects part of his public image. As Hollywood enters a period of technological transformation – establishing new synergies with TV, digitizing production and exhibition, and creating movies and software for mobile consumer platforms – what distinguishes Cameron is that, like the industry itself, he openly embodies the art/business and art/science oppositions.

Seismic shifts in the industry can rarely be attributed to just a few individuals, but it should be noted that Cameron and Lucas have been forces in Hollywood's large-scale efforts to move toward digitization. Since the 1990s, both directors have been lobbying for the retirement of 35mm film as a production and exhibition medium (Lucas's *Star Wars: Episode One* became a test case for digital projection in multiplexes). When, by the end of 2012, digital projection had de facto eclipsed 35mm projection as the standard format for theatrically exhibiting films in the US (Thompson 2014, xiv), the plunge into the digital age was irreversible. Whether or not the reintroduction of 3-D constitutes a similar sea change remains to be seen. The danger of moviegoers rejecting 3-D on aesthetic or narrative grounds (a topic long debated by film theorists and critics) may now be a moot point. But as the recent peaking of ticket sales for 3-D films seems to indicate, audiences may balk at bankrolling the industry's promotion of 3-D.

What may ultimately be at stake, however, is making 3-D user friendly for mobile devices like laptops, tablets, and smartphones – in other words, turning it from a theatrical attraction foisted on the public by a spectacle-driven industry into a mundane, semi-private mode of consumption that would trigger a paradigm shift not merely in imaging technologies but in the very notion of "seeing" (Elsaesser 2012, 303). The availability of 3-D for home consumption, so Elsaesser speculates, may be what ultimately motivates Cameron. Heavily invested as artist *and* entrepreneur in developing 3-D technologies and holding several patents in processes that convert 2-D to 3-D, Cameron seems to conceive of *Avatar* – and also of *Titanic* (1997), which underwent a costly conversion to 3-D for its 2012 rerelease – not as movies, but as software advertisements for new technologies of mass image consumption, whose scale, once unfolded, would render a movie's theatrical revenue largely irrelevant (Elsaesser 2012, 301).

Hollywood's reintroduction of 3-D in the first decade of the new millennium was commercially motivated. This does not mean, however, that the 3-D aesthetic is limited to animation or fantasy films. Martin Scorsese's *Hugo* (2011), a historical drama about a boy who grows up in the Gare Montparnasse railway station in Paris, uses 3-D to underscore the film's homage to early cinema – a period that also witnessed numerous experiments with projecting stereoscopic slides (Elsaesser 2013, 221). Baz Luhrmann's 2013 adaptation of F. Scott Fitzgerald's classic jazz age novel, *The Great Gatsby*, uses 3-D to give spatial expression to the distance separating the story's main characters from their dreams and ideals – and also from each other. 3-D enables Luhrmann to build a mise-en-scène that foregrounds both the elusiveness and the synthetic nature of the American Dream by pulling apart its disparate material and imaginary components and setting them in dialogue with each other. This tension, in which diverse elements supplement and feed off each other without fully harmonizing, makes Luhrmann an intriguing, though hardly obvious, conceptual heir to Orson Welles, who also depicted American culture by mobilizing and orchestrating disparate literary, visual, and tonal registers in one and the same film. Artistic efforts such as those of Scorsese and Luhrmann are proof that 3-D has garnered the attention of artistically ambitious filmmakers.

Independent Film

Historically, American independent film has benefited from lightweight cameras and accessible equipment. Beginning in the late 1980s, the introduction of industrially viable camcorders (and, later, digital video cameras) reinforced this trend and created a boon for filmmakers seeking to develop their projects outside established industry structures. The same period also saw a greater permeability between dominant and marginal modes of filmmaking. Festivals like the Sundance Film Festival, acting as a clearinghouse for indie projects, made it more likely that a low-budget or micro-budget indie film could pique the interest of a mainstream distributor.

This famously became the case with *The Blair Witch Project* (1999), a micro-budget horror movie that ended up grossing $250 million. Its creators, Eduardo Sánchez and Daniel Myrick, financed the project by promoting their only asset, a short, homemade tape purportedly about the mysterious disappearance of three filmmaking students in the woods. Embellished with fake news coverage – an element that would remain central to the subsequent marketing campaign – the tape attracted investors who financed its development into a feature film. It eventually premiered at the 1999 Sundance Film Festival and was picked up by Artisan Entertainment, an erstwhile video distributor, that bought it for $1 million but spent $25 million on an innovative internet marketing campaign that suggested the film was about real events. While harking back to the early horror films of Roger Corman rather than to John Cassavetes and John Sayles, Sánchez and Myrick's film proved that a low-budget indie approach, particularly if it favors improvised acting, is suitable for genre films (the film's sequel, *Book of Shadows: Blair Witch 2,* 2000) by contrast, was a glossy but stale studio product that was widely panned).

Other independent films of the period also pursued the micro-budget route. Most members of the "mumblecore movement," which was at its peak from 2002 to 2010, crafted their ultra-low-budget films from loosely scripted or improvised scenarios and used amateur actors. Defined by Geoff King, in this volume, as films of "low-key naturalism" shot with a handheld camera, and with low-fi sound and "the vocal hesitancies of nonprofessional performers," mumblecore gained visibility when several of its films, including Andrew Bujalski's *Mutual Appreciation* (2005), Joe Swanberg's *Kissing on the Mouth* (2005), and Mark and Jay Duplass's *The Puffy Chair* (2005), screened at the 2005 South by Southwest Film Festival, which would become a champion of mumblecore. More recent examples include *Tiny Furniture* (2010), written and directed by its main actress, Lena Dunham, and *Frances Ha* (2012), whose main actress, Greta Gerwig, appeared in several mumblecore films and emerged as the movement's only star. While their minimal plots and low-key dramas fly in the face of dominant cinema, mumblecore films are relatively homogenous in their focus on young white heterosexual college graduates in crisis or limbo.

Micro-budgets, hand-held equipment, and improvised stories and performances are also the mark of Greg Araki's films. The graphic sex, meandering plots, and minimalist treatments of *Totally Fucked Up* (1993), *The Doom Generation* (1995), and *Nowhere* (1997) defy mainstream conventions even more than do mumblecore films. Araki's casts – alienated queer youth on the fringes of society – can be compared to the characters of Gus Van Sant's independent films. But the 2004 *Mysterious Skin* marked a departure for Araki. Formally more polished, it won acclaim for its imaginative and sensitive adaptation of Scott Heim's novel about children's strategies of dealing with sexual abuse. Children and young adolescents are also at the center of David Gordon Green's *George Washington* (2000), which follows a group of small town kids in the South, who cover up a fatal accident the title character inadvertently initiated. Its quietly powerful depiction of children is reminiscent of Charles Burnett's indie classic *Killer of Sheep* (1977). Green has since also directed comedies for larger studios, while intermittently realizing independent projects, such as the 2013 drama *Joe*, that illustrate his abiding interest in the challenges of growing up in a world of absent or neglectful parents.

Richard Linklater's budgets have ranged from $20,000 (for his 1991 debut, the near-plotless bohemian comedy *Slacker*) to $30 million for mainstream comedies like *The Newton Boys* (1998), *Bad News Bears* (2005), and the highly popular *School of Rock* (2003). This range identifies Linklater as a beneficiary of the interpenetration of independent and mainstream film. His films made for under $3 million, such as the cult comedy *Dazed and Confused* and the off-beat romance *Before Sunrise* (1995), as well as its two sequels, *Before Sunset* (2004) and *Before Midnight* (2013), tracing the evolving romance between an American man (Ethan Hawke) and a French woman (Julie Delpy), also define Linklater's work and have made him into something of a dean of American independent film. His status has been confirmed with *Boyhood* (2014), a nearly three-hour-long drama that tracks the maturation of the film's protagonist, Mason (Ellar Coltrane), from boy to man. Like Linklater's romantic trilogy, which spans nearly two decades, *Boyhood* depicts its characters at different stages in their lives. Filmed intermittently over 12 years, with the same cast, the characters take on an organic authenticity unique in the realm of fiction film and conceptually comparable only to Michael Apted's biographical non-fiction project *7 Up* and its sequels. Linklater's innovative zeal also is evident in *Waking Life* (2001), an animated drama rendered through computerization of live action footage.

Anna Boden and Ryan Fleck's early films are carefully scripted, highly complex character studies about men's conflicted relations to their own careers and ideals. *Half Nelson* (2006) is the story of a junior high school teacher whose drug addiction gradually compromises his commitment to his job. Free of moralizing clichés, the film builds its drama quietly through the exploration of the main character and the bond he forms with a student. Boden and Fleck's second film, *Sugar* (2008), depicts a Dominican baseball player's struggles to adjust to life in the US after having been recruited by the minor leagues. Independent film is said to generate fresh impulses for Hollywood, but a comparison between Boden and Fleck's first and second films serves as a caveat to this notion. *Half Nelson* became a breakout hit, mainly as a result of Ryan Gosling's portrayal of Dan, the troubled history teacher, which earned the former Disney teen-star-turned-indie-actor comparisons with Marlon Brando, an Oscar nomination, and a career in melodramas with "indie flair," such as *Blue Valentine* (2010) and *The Place Beyond the Pines* (2013). Every bit as engaging as *Half Nelson*, *Sugar*, by contrast, struggled to find an audience. Its story, set among Caribbean immigrants in New York, and its realist, non-melodramatic style, notably diverged from Hollywood's formulaic, sentimental treatment of baseball. The film remains the sole credit of its male lead, Algenis Perez Soto, an amateur actor from the Dominican Republic, who learned English for the film.

A similar contrast characterizes two female-centered films directed by women. Debra Granik's *Winter's Bone* (2010) is about the struggle of an Ozark teenager, who takes care of her mentally unresponsive mother and two younger siblings, and who desperately searches for her drug-dealing father to avoid her family's eviction from their home. Courtney Hunt's *Frozen River* (2008) follows a white store assistant and a Native American bingo parlor employee, who try to earn money by smuggling illegal immigrants from Canada into the US across a frozen river. Like Boden and Fleck's *Half Nelson*, Granik's film benefitted from a breakthrough performance by Jennifer Lawrence, whose rising star and Oscar nomination helped the film earn $13 million at the box office. *Frozen River*, while also profitable, had a much lower profile, though it, too, furthered the careers of its leads, Melissa Leo, who already was an established actress before *Frozen River*, and Misty Upham, who went on to obtain supporting roles in other films and on TV before her untimely death.

Sugar and *Frozen River* confirm that American independent film has been the traditional home for stories featuring non-white Americans or immigrants – as has also been the case with Chicano-themed films like *El Norte* (1985), *Stand and Deliver* (1988), *American Me* (1992), and *Mi Vida Loca* (1994). Stories about border-crossers also recently have become the focus of international co-productions. *Sin Nombre* (2009), a US–Mexican film, produced by Mexican star Gael García Bernal, tells the story of Sayra (Paulina Gaitán), a Honduran girl who tries to immigrate to the US. *Maria Full of Grace* (2004), a US–Colombian co-production about a Colombian girl (Catalina Sandino Moreno) hired as a drug smuggler, earned an astounding $13 million at the box office.

No account of American independent film in the new millennium can ignore the achievements of Kelly Reichardt, who, since her 1994 debut feature, *River of Grass*, has made road movies about unconventional relationships explored in long takes, capturing quiet conversations, and a minimalist but poetically evocative mise-en-scène. *Old Joy* (2006) is the story of two former college friends who, during a weekend reunion, experience a dimension of male intimacy that transcends traditional categories. *Wendy and Lucy* (2008) follows a woman and her dog on a trip to Alaska that tests the woman's commitment to keeping the dog. *Meek's Cutoff* (2010) is a frontier tale about the unusual bond between a settler woman and a Native American that develops during an ill-fated wagon trail. Reichardt's films illustrate that American independent film has retained its interest in genre without rescinding its commitment to unconventional, uncompromising storytelling. The same might be said for non-fiction and avant-garde production, on which diversified technologies of production and consumption have also had an impact.

Non-fiction and the Avant-garde

Errol Morris and Michael Moore have continued to produce documentaries of note from 1991 to the present, as has long-time filmmaker Frederick Wiseman. While digital video technology has ushered in a new golden age for nature documentaries, it also has been crucial in the production of 9/11, Iraq War, and economic crisis documentaries – the new millennium's cataclysmic political and economic crises having triggered numerous films with incisive commentary, many of which have received theatrical distribution.

Michael Moore has continued to make his mark in the new millennium, most notably with his incendiary *Fahrenheit 9/11* (2004), in which he assails the foreign policy of President George W. Bush and his response to the World Trade Center and Pentagon attacks of September 11, 2001. For Moore, the nation was then guided by a fear stoked at the highest levels of government that masked the economic ties of ruling elites among the US and its allies. In *Sicko* (2007), Moore takes on the healthcare industry, attacking the for-profit American system while marveling at international models of state-run care. Moore's films are first-person narrated inquiries that pit his indignant, populist persona against corporate and governmental power. As the most financially successful documentarian in the history of American film (four of his films are among the top 10 grossing documentaries of all time), Michael Moore has benefited from a production/distribution relationship with Miramax/the Weinstein Company that, at least before its 2010 takeover by Disney, had assured the reach of his films deep into the mainstream marketplace. Moore's success had convinced the exhibition sector that there is a substantial audience for non-fiction cinema, especially for films that take an advocacy stance, as those interrogating the Iraq War most certainly do.

In documenting the Iraq War, as Susan Carruthers discusses in this volume, two filmmakers emerge as centrally important figures: Charles Ferguson and Alexander Gibney. Ferguson's 2007 film *No End in Sight* examines multiple perspectives on the war, including those of Iraqi citizens – most notably a young boy – in order to illustrate US responsibility for the morass of suffering, brutality, misunderstanding, and ineptitude that characterized the war and US occupation of the country. In the same year, Gibney directed *Taxi to the Dark Side*, a scathing indictment of US interrogation methods that resulted in the brutal torture and death of an innocent Iraqi taxi driver. Ferguson went on to make *Inside Job* (2010), interrogating government and corporate collusion that resulted in the 2008 financial crash, with actor Matt Damon as narrator. In 2005, Gibney directed *Enron: The Smartest Guys in the Room*, a caustic exposé of corporate corruption and the middle- and working-class victims who lost everything as a result. Although a deeply committed political documentarian, Gibney has a range of interests, including counterculture literature and funk music, which he explores, respectively, in *Gonzo: The Life and Work of Dr. Hunter S. Thompson* (2008), and *Mr. Dynamite: The Rise of James Brown* (2014).

Errol Morris's *Standard Operating Procedure* (2008) shares ground with Gibney's *Taxi to the Dark Side*, although his interest and emphasis differ. Morris creates visual tropes and reflexive stylistic devices aptly suited to his themes that contemplate the nature of truth, reality, and the mind's easy susceptibility toward self-deception. The many levels and layers of self-deception form thematic strands running through almost all of Morris's work, from *The Thin Blue Line* (1988) to *Mr. Death: The Rise and Fall of Fred A. Leuchter, Jr.* (1999) – the portrait of a self-proclaimed execution expert who eventually comes to deny the Holocaust on the basis of his "empirical" evidence. This theme also is present in *The Fog of War: Eleven Lessons from the Life of Robert S. McNamara* (2003) and *The Unknown Known* (2013), both portraits of US Secretaries of Defense – the former in the Kennedy and Johnson administrations during the Vietnam War; the latter, Donald Rumsfeld in the George W. Bush administration during the Iraq War. In *Standard Operating Procedure* archival footage of Rumsfeld's press conferences supports the film's premise that the responsibility for appalling, and often fatal, abuse of inmates in Iraq's Abu Ghraib prison cannot necessarily be blamed on "a few bad apples" – the words Rumsfeld used to describe the young, low-ranking US military men and women assigned to the prison. As Patricia Aufderheide explains in this volume, Morris's intensive interviews with some of the military involved, including the publicly reviled Lynndie England, not only suggest a larger top-down dynamic at work but also reflexively invite careful interrogation of the photographic images placed in evidence – returning once again to Morris's decades-long concern with vision and images, themselves, as questionable means of accessing truth.

Morris's bent toward philosophy perhaps finds its most direct expression in *A Brief History of Time* (1991), a portrait and extended interview with conceptual physicist Stephen Hawking, whose paralysis that confines him to a wheelchair and renders him without speech stands in poignant contrast to his cosmological research and theories concerning time and the universe. In Hawking's work, physics undeniably meets philosophy – and some might even say spirituality – a point made palpable through Morris's haunting use of chiaroscuro lighting, slowly circling camera movements, and eerily ethereal low camera angles (see Grundmann & Rockwell 2000).

Along with Moore and Morris's work, the Oscar-winning film, *An Inconvenient Truth* (2006), certifies the prestige potential of theatrically released documentaries, positioning certain films over and above the current-events function of television news operations. Distributed by Paramount Classics and directed by Davis Guggenheim, the film amplifies former Vice President Al Gore's global warming lecture tour to the level of national dialogue. The film inspired and is among the most recognized in a long line of eco-documentaries to follow, including *Chasing Ice* (2012), in which time-lapse photography captures the effects of global warming on glaciers and which also features a soundtrack song performed by actress Scarlett Johansson. In Jessica Yu's *Last Call at the Oasis* (2011), Erin Brockovich-Ellis, among others, discusses a global water crisis not yet felt by Western nations. And *Gasland* (2010) investigates the controversial fracking process of extracting gas, that enriches corporations while contaminating water supplies and laying waste to the land.

Not in the least because of its urgent ecological messages and because nature has continued to be a source of fascination for documentary audiences, the wildlife genre also has enjoyed soaring popularity. *March of the Penguins* (2005), a French production, opened in just two theaters in the United States, but would go on to play in over 2,500 more and gross over $77 million, second only on the all-time list behind *Fahrenheit 9/11*. *Earth* (2009), a 90-minute condensation of an 11-hour television documentary, was released by Disney in 1,800 theaters and would go on to gross in excess of $32 million. Though less widely released than *March*, two earlier films, also from France, were well received in the US: *Microcosmos* (1996), which fascinated American audiences with its close-up look at insect life, infused with gentle humor through its cleverly composed musical track, and *Winged Migration* (2001), which follows the migratory patterns of birds over several years and seven continents. Producers discovered that 3-D technology is especially well suited to this genre, seemingly able to transport viewers directly into the animal habitats onscreen. Multiple 3-D wildlife documentaries found distribution, most notable among them, *To the Arctic 3D* (2012), featuring actress Meryl Streep.

In a very different mode, the lives of urban youth gain attention in Steve James's immensely popular *Hoop Dreams* (1994), about two African-American high school kids in Chicago with ambitions to play in the NBA. The film follows the boys and their economically strapped parents as they attempt to navigate the waters of establishment institutions, a subject Martin Bell also explored a decade earlier in *Streetwise* (1984) – a film about homeless teens living on the streets of Seattle – and much earlier with a different emphasis in Frederick Wiseman's *High School* (1968). Appealing to younger audiences, the relationship between music and documentary that had been nurtured a generation earlier in *Monterey Pop* (1968), *Woodstock* (1970), and *The Last Waltz* (1978) was sustained by *Madonna: Truth or Dare* (1991), the era's most popular celebrity documentary. In its juxtaposition of behind-the-scenes black-and-white footage with performances of Madonna on stage in color, it packaged the pop star as an entertainer without secrets, blurring the lines between performance and personality.

Wiseman, in *High School II* (1994), celebrates the work being done at Central Park East Secondary School in New York, a stark contrast with the environment he critiqued over two decades earlier in *High School.* Wiseman again returned, almost two decades later, to the subject of education in *At Berkeley* (2013), his 244-minute look at university life and decision-making at one of California's most prestigious academic and research institutions. His *Public Housing* (1997) examines the Ida B. Wells housing project in Chicago's South Side and resonates, in many ways, with his earlier *Welfare* (1975), in which both workers and recipients in the New York City welfare system are shown as victims of an overwhelming, nearly incomprehensible bureaucracy. In *Domestic Violence* (2001) and *Domestic Violence II* (2002), Wiseman observes the operations of a shelter for abused women and children in Tampa, Florida, and their struggles with the court system. In his characteristic observational mode, which eschews voiceover narration, written titles, or formal interviews, Wiseman represents the emotional and psychological complexities and trauma as women meet individually with counselors and with each other during group sessions.

In the new millennium, Wiseman also has ventured outside the US to make *La danse* (2009), focusing on the production process of the Paris Opera Ballet, as he had in 1996 with *La Comédie-Française ou L'amour joué.* And in *Crazy Horse* (2011) he observes the eponymous club in Paris, famous for its dashing nude dancing. His 2014 *National Gallery* observes the meticulous work of those who restore paintings at London's National Gallery – their painstaking attention to detail in many ways a metaphor for the entire body of Wiseman's work, in which attention to the details of working and living fascinate the filmmaker and mesmerize those viewers similarly inclined. One of Wiseman's crowning achievements, *Belfast, Maine* (1999), captures the multifaceted workings of this town, from its fish-canning factory and dry-cleaning shops to its town council meetings and community theater rehearsals. Wiseman poignantly captures both the beauty and the evanescence of human activity in this and, by extension, any other American town. His fascination with observing people as they negotiate with each other, with institutional power, and with the very nature of necessity defines this filmmaker as undeniably masterful – as an American treasure whose work offers an unparalleled view, and often an incisive critique, of American culture, institutions, and ideology over the incredible range of six decades.

Two recent additions to the group of notable American documentary filmmakers are Joshua Oppenheimer and Lucien Castaing Taylor. While not strictly an American film but a Danish-British-Norwegian coproduction, Oppenheimer's 2012 debut feature, *The Act of Killing,* received global attention and an Academy Award nomination for Best Feature Documentary for its experimental portrayal of a group of Indonesians who, during the 1960s, had served as a death squad in the genocide of tens of thousands of Indonesians deemed communists. After spending extensive time with his subjects, Oppenheimer sensationally succeeded in coaxing them to reenact their killings in front of the camera, soliciting disturbing and complex reactions, ranging from prideful commemoration to convulsive expressions of grief and sorrow. The film triggered a global debate about the ethical implications of its own refusal to judge its subjects. Lucien Castaing-Taylor also displays a notable skill in getting close to his subjects. These, however, are Americans working in formerly essential occupations now relegated to the margins. The 2009 film *Sweetgrass,* co-directed with Ilisa Barbash, is an intimate, at times moving, portrait of a family of Montana sheepherders whose livelihood is increasingly shaped by the demands of modern commerce and technology. His 2012 film *Leviathan,* co-directed with Vèrèna Paravel, portrays the grueling work of fishermen on a trawler. Both films copiously draw on extensive long take close-ups of minute details, as well as the surrounding seascape in *Leviathan* and wind-swept grasslands of Montana in *Sweetgrass*. A member of Harvard's Sensory Ethnography Lab, Castaing-Taylor seeks to redefine ethnographic cinema along the lines of increased sensory perception, viscerally subjecting spectators to the impact of cinematic aesthetics.

Avant-garde cinema also has expanded its range. Occupying one end of the spectrum are such high-budget productions as video artist Bill Viola's large-screen video installations, *An Ocean without a Shore* (2007) and *Observance* (2002), which dissect facial and bodily expressions with the aid of videographic effects. Also a high-budget project is multi-media artist Matthew Barney's *Cremaster* cycle (1994–2002), a series of five films that, in strikingly poetic manner, explore different aspects of creation. Named after a muscle linked to male sexual organs, the *Cremaster* films' imagery includes individuals in revealing costumes, full-body makeup, and special effects, blending different planes of human knowledge with explorations of mythic themes and landscapes. While Viola's video walls were exhibited at international art fairs and biennials and also became box office attractions for newly created branches of large urban museums such as the Guggenheim, Barney's *Cremaster* cycle was among the first of avant-garde films to receive theatrical release in the US since Warhol's *The Chelsea Girls* (1966). And not unlike Hollywood films, whose release is accompanied by extensive promotional materials, Barney's films were part of a larger group of art works issued by the author, which included sculptures, photographs, and drawings.

Occupying the low-budget end of the spectrum are small-scale films, such as Jonathan Caouette's autobiographical avant-garde psychodrama *Tarnation* (2003), which also received theatrical distribution and mainstream critical attention. Other examples in this category include the films of David Gatten, which represent various forms of found text on the screen and explore the possibilities of transforming the written word into moving image. Gatten relies on an optical printer to scan and scroll along extensive portions of written texts, exploring one whole library, in the case of William Byrd II (1674–1744).

Among the boldest of contemporary avant-garde works is Christian Marclay's *The Clock* (2010). As a 24-hour montage, Marclay's film combines the extreme duration of a Warhol film and the collage aesthetics of Bruce Conner. In *The Clock*, Marclay references the entire history of cinema, using shots from thousands of films that refer to or include in the frame virtually every minute of a 24-hour cycle. In some excerpts time is a central component, either of dialogue or the mise-en-scène, while in others a clock might be positioned in the corner of the frame or in the background. Screenings of Marclay's film are synchronized, moreover, with the time of spectatorship so that a viewer entering the theater at, say, 4 p.m. will begin watching just as it is 4 p.m. onscreen. Borrowing from seemingly every national cinema and genre, including some television, as well as the silent and sound periods, *The Clock* functions as something of a history of the medium. But this history is fragmented in the service of a larger claim – that all movies, no matter the story they tell, are at the mercy of time's passage. Time becomes the story, so to speak, as tension builds not from narrative action but from the unstoppable march of the hands around the faces of watches and clocks. The spectator comes to anticipate time rather than event, but in order to keep the past from being assigned entirely to oblivion, Marclay occasionally cuts back to clips the viewer has seen before. The result is a monumental meditation on the cinema – one that marks the intersection of its past and its ontology, the countless films that have been made, and the defining power of temporal duration. Marclay's work is part of a broader trend among avant-garde artists such as Martin Arnold and Stan Douglas who use and reshape classical Hollywood cinema for their gallery exhibitions.

American Film in the Twenty-first Century

American film in the twenty-first century is characterized by paradoxes. The established film industry still goes by the name of Hollywood, but because it differs both from the old Hollywood of the classical studio era and the New Hollywood that superseded it, it has been called the New New Hollywood or the New Hollywood II, as Derek Nystrom refers to it in this volume. But the New New Hollywood bears surprisingly close resemblance to the old Hollywood from which it is twice removed. After decades of dismantling its structures and contending with declining business, the industry reconsolidated during the laissez-faire boom years of the 1980s. It entered the new millennium with its main tiers once again vertically integrated, many of its top companies still bearing the illustrious names of the golden age. These banners, however, are now integrated into much larger global corporations that regard movies as delivery devices for merchandise in addition to distinct pieces of entertainment, art, or social commentary.

The industry not only has reconsolidated, but it also has, paradoxically, become more segmented, with numerous independent companies calling Hollywood their home. At once enabled and jeopardized by the volatile marketplace, movies are financed in novel ways and "packaged" through ever shifting ventures. What Eduardo Sánchez and Daniel Myrick, the creators of *The Blair Witch Project*, have in common with Danny Ocean of *Ocean's Eleven* and the merger-happy CEO of that film's Warner Bros. studio, is that, no matter the nature and scale of the project, fundraising tactics tend to become even more make-believe than the projects themselves. With movies as far afield as *Blair Witch* and *Ocean's Eleven*, American film has entered a period of considerable diversification. But the variety of films is less discernible at the multiplex than in the richly stratified media landscape that includes cable television, streaming services, and video on demand (VOD).

The colliding of new media with old media, termed "convergence culture" (Jenkins 2008), along with the industry's synergized exploitation of every aspect of a movie, has dramatically redefined filmmakers' roles, causing them not only to reinvent their films and their craft, but also to revinvent themselves. Baz Luhrmann gets major studios to back his remakes of old classics of American film and literature because he films them in 3-D and/or furnishes them with pop and hip-hop soundtracks, and edits them for online consumption. James Cameron regards himself as an experimental filmmaker and high-tech tinkerer, although he never operates outside the bounds of the established industry. Mark Webb and Darren Aronofsky debut with micro-budget independent films and, within a few years, get pegged to direct blockbusters. Steven Soderbergh charts the reverse course – or, more accurately, oscillates between blockbuster projects and independent films. Greater access to the means of production has enabled the number of American films to skyrocket – with the result that literally thousands of films fail to obtain distribution and go directly to DVD and/or online exhibition.

Did the industry change with its audiences or vice versa? For several decades, Hollywood anxiously targeted what it perceived to be its main demographic, young adolescent males, while neglecting other segments. Given the rising number of action films and fairy tales with female protagonists (mostly notably, perhaps, Disney's highly successful animated feature *Frozen*, 2013, and its 2014 reworking of the Sleeping Beauty story in *Maleficent*), however, it appears that the industry is expanding the potential of "niche" markets. New technologies, online platforms, and social media have changed viewing habits and expanded consumer demographics. As electronic media now deliver the bulk of movie revenue, theatrical exhibition, although still the main rationale for launching the production of movies, now functions more as a tool for promotion than as the primary source of profit. That said, however, the movie theater remains an appealing venue for entertainment – sometimes because it offers artistic enrichment and sometimes because it offers the "first look" at highly publicized blockbusters.

Just as in the early days of the Nickelodeon, the unmistakable allure of watching movies as part of a community of viewers in a shared public space is an enlargement of the experience, in visual terms, of course – as in the early days of the cinema of attractions – but also in the intangible realms of heightened perceptual, intellectual, and social engagement. In choosing to adapt F. Scott Fitzgerald's *The Great Gatsby* in high-tech form, Baz Luhrmann might be said to have captured the desires of American film viewers whose sustained attraction to the projected image parallels that of Fitzgerald's title character, who "believed in the green light, the orgastic future that year by year recedes before us" (Fitzgerald 2004 [1925], 180). The cinema joins its audience in a dual desire: It forges ahead into new technologies, yet uses them to produce and reimagine enduring myths. The final line of Fitzgerald's novel speaks directly to the historian's project, as well – as the discipline moves forward, it is compelled to reexamine the past. Elusive as it may be, this dynamic unites many of us – filmmakers, viewers, students, and scholars – as we "beat on, boats against the current, born back ceaselessly into the past" (p. 180).

Notes

1. http://www.boxofficemojo.com/movies/?id=loneranger.htm (accessed July 20, 2014).
2. http://www.boxofficemojo.com/movies/?id=ripd.htm (accessed July 29, 2014).
3. http://www.boxofficemojo.com/movies/?id=47ronin.htm (accessed July 29, 2014).
4. http://www.boxofficemojo.com/movies/?id=transcendence.htm (accessed July 29, 2014).
5. http://www.boxofficemojo.com/movies/?id=butler.htm (accessed July 29, 2014).
6. http://www.boxofficemojo.com/movies/?id=42.htm (accessed July 29, 2014).
7. http://www.boxofficemojo.com/movies/?id=twelveyearsaslave.htm (accessed July 29, 2014).
8. http://www.boxofficemojo.com/movies/?id=philomena.htm (accessed July 29, 2014).
9. http://www.boxofficemojo.com/movies/?id=dallasbuyersclub.htm (accessed July 29, 2014).
10. http://www.boxofficemojo.com/movies/?id=faultinourstars.htm (accessed July 29, 2014).
11. See Jaramillo 2002.

References

Arango, Tim. (2010). "How the AOL–Time Warner Merger Went So Wrong," *New York Times*, January 10, at http://www.nytimes.com/2010/01/11/business/media/11merger.html?pagewanted=all&_r=0 (accessed July 29, 2014).

Balio, Tino. (2013). *Hollywood in the New Millennium*. London: BFI Publishing.

Barnes, Brooks. (2013). "Masked Lawman Stumbles at the Gate." *New York Times*, July 7, at http://www.nytimes.com/2013/07/08/movies/masked-lawman-stumbles-at-the-gate.html?_r=0 (accessed July 20, 2014).

Bond, Paul. (2014). "Steven Spielberg Predicts 'Implosion' of Film Industry." *Hollywood Reporter*, June 12, at http://www.hollywoodreporter.com/news/steven-spielberg-predicts-implosion-film-567604. (accessed July 20, 2014).

Christensen, Jerome. (2012). *America's Corporate Art: The Studio Authorship of Hollywood Motion Pictures*. Stanford, CA: Stanford University Press.

Elsaesser, Thomas. (2012). *The Persistence of Hollywood*. New York: Routledge.

Elsaesser, Thomas. (2013). "The 'Return' of 3-D: On Some of the Logics and Geneaologies of the Image in the Twenty-First Century." *Critical Inquiry*, 39, 217–246.

Fitzgerald, F. Scott. (2004 [1925]). *The Great Gatsby*. New York: Scribner.

Gallagher, Mark. (2013). *Another Steven Soderbergh Experience: Authorship and Contemporary Hollywood*. Austin: University of Texas Press.

Grundmann, Roy, & Cynthia Rockwell. (2000). "Truth Is Not Subjective: An Interview with Errol Morris." *Cineaste* 25. 3. Fall, 4–9.

Jaramillo, Deborah L. (2002). "The Family Racket: AOL Time Warner, HBO, The Sopranos, and the Construction of a Quality Brand." *Journal of Communication Inquiry* 26, 59–75.

Jenkins, Henry. (2008). *Convergence Culture: Where Old and New Media Collide*. New York: NYU Press.

Klavan, Andrew (2008). "What Bush and Batman Have in Common. *The Wall Street Journal* July 25. At http://online.wsj.com/news/articles/SB121694247343482821 (accessed July 29, 2014).

Landesman, Cosmo. (2008). "*The Dark Knight* – The Sunday Times Review." *Sunday Times* (London), July 27, at http://entertainment.timesonline.co.uk/tol/arts_and_entertainment/film/film_reviews/article4386375.ece (accessed July 29, 2014)

Mendelson, Scott. (2013). "*Pacific Rim* and More Domestic 'Flops' that Became Global Hits." *Forbes*, September 2, at http://www.forbes.com/sites/scottmendelson/2013/09/02/pacific-rim-and-more-domestic-flops-that-became-global-hits/ (accessed July 29, 2014).

National Post. (2012)."*John Carter* May Set Guiness Record for Biggest Box Office Flop of All Time." *National Post*, March 21, at http://arts.nationalpost.com/2012/03/21/john-carter-may-set-guinness-record-for-biggest-box-office-flop-of-all-time/?__federated=1 (accessed July 20, 2014).

Sperb, Jason. (2013). *Blossoms and Blood: Postmodern Media Culture and the Films of Paul Thomas Anderson*. Austin: University of Texas Press.

Thompson, Anne. (2014). *The $11 Billion Year: From Sundance to the Oscars, an Inside Look at the Changing Hollywood System*. New York: HarperCollins.

20

The Queer 1990s
The Challenge and Failure of Radical Change

Michael Bronski
Professor, Harvard University, United States

The **New Queer Cinema**, first identified as such by **B. Ruby Rich**, takes on multi-dimensional and sometimes contradictory forms throughout the 1990s and beyond. Michael Bronski identifies three historical **LGBT film production cycles**: **resistance (late 1980s–early 1990s)**, **reaffirmation (mid-1990s)**, and **regulation (late 1990s)**, arguing for a queer reading of ***Mrs. Doubtfire*** as a mildly implicit resistance film and for ***Longtime Companion***, produced at the height of the **HIV-AIDS crisis**, as a strongly explicit resistance film. With the health crisis relatively controlled, came mid-1990s reaffirmation films like ***The Adventures of Priscilla, Queen of the Desert*** and ***The Birdcage***, in which LGBT characters, while asserting their own identity and desires, ultimately serve to support and confirm the heterosexual status quo. The sexuality of their late 1990s successors is displaced in films like ***The Next Best Thing***, and thereby "regulated," in part, by a focus on more generalized "gender," often turning LGBT characters into "best friends" of straight protagonists. Bronski's essay shares ground with Geoff King on independent film in this volume and with David Lugowski on queer images in 1930s films and Jared Rapfogel on underground film in Volume I.

Additional terms, names, and concepts: Stonewall Riot, Gay Liberation Movement, Gay Rights Movement, the woman's film, GLAAD, "repressive tolerance," gay best friend cycle

The 1990s are unique in the history of lesbian-gay-bisexual-transgender (LGBT) cinema in that they saw the release of an unusually large number of LGBT-themed films – more than 75, including Hollywood productions, independent productions, and British and European films released in the United States. This output spans a wide range of themes, genres, and artistic and narrative approaches and, as will be argued below, it reflects a spectrum of political perspectives. This cinematic embarrassment of riches makes perfect sense when viewed against the background of the decade's extraordinarily vibrant political and social

American Film History: Selected Readings, 1960 to the Present, First Edition. Edited by Cynthia Lucia, Roy Grundmann, and Art Simon.

developments. In retrospect, the 1990s were clearly a pivotal period for LGBT politics and artistic endeavor.

With the advent of the Stonewall Riots and the birth of the Gay Liberation Movement in 1969, discussion within the LGBT community about representation became far more public than it ever had been. Gone was the tacit acceptance of past mainstream images of gay people in which the existence of homosexuality was always repressed, and the "homosexual" often died or turned out to be straight. The new focus was on "authentic" images created outside of commercial constraints and from within the community. Through this notion of authenticity gay liberationists sought to publicize images of homosexuals that were as complex and varied (good, bad, beautiful, and ugly) as those of heterosexuals.[1]

This same time frame also saw the rise of the Gay Rights Movement, a new LGBT movement that, in various ways, constituted both a counterforce and a supplement to the Gay Liberation Movement.[2] While the Gay Liberation Movement promoted a grassroots direct action approach to politics that was predicated on the idea that political action was a direct outcome of personal experience – summarized by the phrase "the personal is the political" – the Gay Rights Movement was more concerned with the institutional process of attaining specific political and legal rights within the existing system. In order to accomplish this, the focus was placed on promoting wholly "positive" portrayals of LGBT people in the mainstream news and entertainment media. It was in this context that Vito Russo, who was a member of New York's Gay Activists Alliance (nationally one of the first gay rights groups), wrote his groundbreaking 1981 *The Celluloid Closet: Homosexuality in the Movies*. His methodological focus on representations of LGBT people in film was limited to an analysis of film content. While *The Celluloid Closet* broadly popularized the discipline of LGBT film studies, it also simply celebrated "positive" representations of LGBT people and denounced "negative" ones.

Within two years of the publication of Russo's book, the political context would radically shift with the advent of the AIDS crisis and the onslaught of grassroots AIDS activism.[3] The simultaneous advent of queer theory – and particularly queer film/media theory – opened new approaches to analyzing film and media representations of homosexuality. Rather than focusing on the concept of homosexuality *in* film, this more sophisticated critical and political apparatus allowed for consideration of the historical and political context of LGBT representation as well – that is, homosexuality *and* film.[4] Reflecting in one way or another the see-saw political movements of the 1970s and 1980s, LGBT films of the 1990s can be located at the intersection of mainstream ("straight") and independent ("queer") cinema. They reflect the full spectrum of political strategies ranging from radical/separatist to assimilationist. The, at times, contradictory tone adopted by these strategies makes it difficult to obtain an historical perspective on LGBT cinema during this period.

While it is impossible to build a historiographic and theoretical framework that will encompass all of the films of a period, it is helpful to understand how, during the 1990s, LGBT films moved through several overlapping, though relatively clearly defined stages. The stage of "resistance" began in the late 1980s and produced some of the most transgressive films of the period, which completely transformed the very nature of LGBT cinema. This continued for three years and was followed by a period of "reaffirmation" during which these new transgressive images were gradually acknowledged by a wider, mainstream audience and, while often remaining controversial, became part of a national, commercial media consciousness. In the final stage, the once transgressive representations were now being appropriated by the mainstream and used as a form of cultural "regulation," which kept LGBT images visible but did not allow them to change, to become more radical, or to transgress established social norms. This phenomenon reflected what political theorist and philosopher Herbert Marcuse called "repressive tolerance," a process that seemingly promotes tolerance and acceptance, but only so as to secure the political and social status quo (2007, 32–59).

Resistance

If several exciting LGBT-themed films emerged in the late 1980s, it was their reception by critics that made them into "queer cinema." The key role in this regard falls to queer critic B. Ruby Rich's foundational article, "New Queer Cinema." Essentially a report from a series of film festivals, Rich's essay noted a drastic sea-change in the then current representations of LGBT characters and themes. The main films that Rich placed in this category of "New Queer Cinema" were Laurie Lynd's *R.S.V.P* (1991), Christopher Munch's *The Hours and the Times* (1991), Tom Kalin's *Swoon* (1991), Todd Haynes's *Poison* (1991), Isaac Julian's *Young Soul Rebels* (1991), and Gregg Araki's *The Living End* (1992). Rich argued that these films covered a wide range of topics, themes, and aesthetic visions (2004, 53–60). Aside from the message that emerged from festivals where these films were shown that "queer is hot," the films themselves were unapologetic in their depictions of queer life. In addition, their embracing of pop culture and its myths constituted a decisive break from the mainstream conventions that had hampered previous efforts at providing "authentic" representations.

New Queer Cinema rejected the idea of "positive" images as being a useful political tool for seeking equality or social and political acceptance for LGBT people and, instead, tackled what is left out by or disavowed and repressed in the production of "positive" images. Tom Kalin's *Swoon* is a meditation on the 1920s homosexual murderers Nathan Leopold and Richard Loeb that explores how their homosexuality was integral both to their lives and their legal prosecution. Other films of this wave were about particularly racialized or marginalized subgroups within the LGBT community, such as drag queens and hustlers. Jennie Livingston's *Paris Is Burning* (1990) chronicles the lives of men involved in New York's African-American "ball culture," and Gus Van Sant's *My Own Private Idaho* (1991) is about the complex personal relationships between male prostitutes. Several films of this wave explore historical subject matter and offer profoundly revisionist interpretations of accepted historical data. Derek Jarman's *Edward II* (1991) recasts the doomed monarch as a victim of homophobia and Christopher Munch's *The Hours and the Times* boldly, and not without some evidence, imagines a love affair between John Lennon and the Beatles manager Brian Epstein. There was also a rejection of cinematic conventions in these films, especially in queering the dramatic, romantic moment. Gregg Araki's *The Living End* posits HIV-infected lovers as the new, still ultimately doomed, Romeo and Juliet. As Monica Pearl (2004) points out, particularly in dealing with HIV-AIDS, the films of "New Queer Cinema" defy the conventions of how films have represented death and dying – either in an attempt to humanize people battling with HIV-AIDS in the face of massive mainstream disdain (as is the topic of Laurie Lynd's elegiac *R.S.V.P.*) or to reimagine the conventions of representing death as a different genre altogether. Todd Haynes included a "1950s science fiction parody" section in *Poison*, and John Greyson used a variety of musical comedy conventions in *Zero Patience* (1993) to undercut mainstream thinking about HIV-AIDS; he also rewrote history as he reanimated the life of homosexual Victorian explorer and sexologist Sir Richard Burton to "explain" racist and erotophobic theories about HIV-AIDS.

While Rich's article was directly on target about this new zeitgeist in queer filmmaking, what had begun as a piece of casual reporting eventually came to stand as a manifesto for a certain school of LGBT filmmakers. In fact, what Rich termed "New Queer Cinema" is but a slice of the overall output of LGBT cinema in the early 1990s and is best understood in a larger context. American New Queer Cinema was also influenced by a tradition of non-American films of the 1970s and 1980s, most significantly films such as the extensive body of work by Derek Jarman in England and Rosa von Praunheim in Germany, both of whom were heavily influenced by the radicalism of Gay Liberation in the early years of the 1970s.[5]

To show the impact of films made in this phase of New Queer Cinema's "resistance," it may be useful to examine two films that were made outside its canon and, thus, usually ignored: *Longtime Companion* (1989) and *Mrs. Doubtfire* (1993). Both films were granted substantial theatrical releases. The latter was a high-end Hollywood production with bankable stars and a major director; and the former was financed by PBS and featured rising stars. Both relied on traditional narrative structures, and, on the face of it, reinforced fairly traditional views of the world. Yet, in their own respective ways, each of these films contains transgressive elements that place them more in line with New Queer Cinema than with more conventional representations.

Longtime Companion, written by award-winning playwright Craig Lucas and directed by his frequent stage collaborator Norman René, was one of the first theatrical releases – in May of 1990 – of a fiction film or a documentary dealing with HIV-AIDS (Rose von Praunheim's compilation of shorts, *Die Aids-Trilogie*, played festivals later in the 1990s).[6] Structurally, *Longtime Companion* follows a fairly traditional form as it narrates, beginning in 1981, the lives of a group of (mostly) gay male friends in New York City as they deal with illness and death. Lucas's screenplay uses short scenes and vignettes to move the action across ten years and increasingly dire circumstances, as the original group of nine friends are gradually reduced to only four. To a large degree the power of *Longtime Companion* resides in its straightforward recounting of the physical horrors of HIV infection. René never hesitates in allowing us to grasp the profound physical devastation of HIV on the human body. This was a bold move in 1990 when people with AIDS were routinely blamed for their illnesses or their physical condition. Death like this was simply not commonly seen by mainstream audiences.

But the brilliance of Lucas's script, and *Longtime Companion*'s primary connection to the transgressiveness of early 1990s LGBT film, is that it takes a traditional melodramatic narrative and – in the manner of Douglas Sirk's films of the mid to late 1950s – forces us to reevaluate the basic conventions of the soap opera and the "woman's film." It is not simply that Lucas introduces the topic of HIV-AIDS into what amounts to a series of distinct, but overlapping, domestic dramas, but rather that he completely reimagines them in the context of a growing epidemic that is disproportionately affecting gay men in a very specific urban culture.

This connection to the traditional "tragedy" as conveyed in the conventional Hollywood woman's films is clearly evident in a comparison of Marguerite's death scene at the end of George Cukor's *Camille*, for instance, to Sean's death scene just past the midpoint of *Longtime Companion*. Cukor's film – which sets a standard for the lavishly produced woman's film of the 1930s – presents us with a languishing, yet beautiful Greta Garbo propped up on lush bedding, who succumbs gracefully to both tuberculosis and unfulfilled love. Just before her death, her maid Nanine (Jessie Ralph) and her lover Armand (Robert Taylor) surround her. A few moments later Armand holds her in his arms, urging her to get well and live, as Camille

Figure 20.1 Robert Taylor (Armand) and Greta Garbo (Marguerite) in the death scene from George Cukor's *Camille* (1936, producers Bernard H. Hyman and Irving Thalberg).

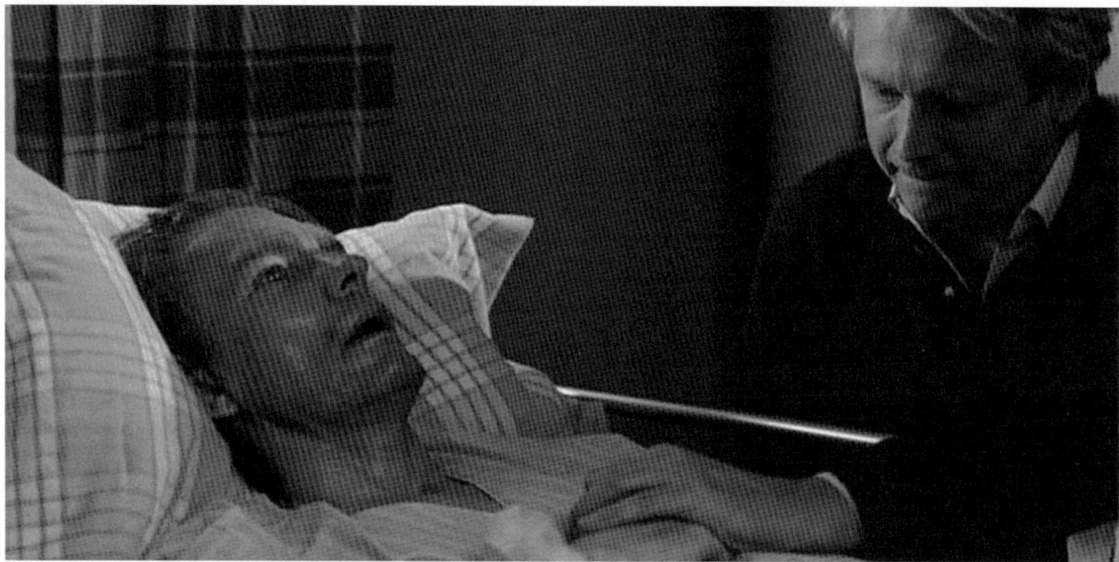

Figure 20.2 Mark Lamos (Sean) and Bruce Davison (David) in the death scene from Norman René's *Longtime Companion* (1989, producer Stan Wlodkowski).

swoons off to the afterlife looking both peaceful and beatific.

An almost identical scene in *Longtime Companion* presents us with a far different reality. Here Sean (Mark Lamos), who writes television soap operas, is in the last stages of AIDS, unable to speak more than repetitive, guttural sounds and strapped to a stark hospital bed in his well-appointed apartment. Just before his death, he, too, is surrounded by his lover David (Bruce Davison) and a home health aide, Henry (Pi Douglass), who, in this case, have to change his diapers and clean his soiled bed sheets. As the scene continues, David sends Henry out on errands and then sits quietly next to Sean, who continues to make inarticulate sounds, and gently urges him to "let go" and die. Both the similarities and the differences to the *Camille* scene are vivid and expose how Lucas has both interrogated and upended the original conventions.

Lucas's rewriting of the traditional woman's melodrama narrative does not end there, however. If the woman's film genre is essentially one of the domestic drama – and even when Sirk moves outside of the home as he does in the theater scenes in *Imitation of Life*, it is only to heighten the at-home drama – Lucas clearly breaks from this convention by having his surviving characters join community-based political groups as a way of confronting the "domestic" crisis. In doing so he radically suggests that what looked like, at first, a conventional "domestic drama" was in reality a far more extensive, and very public, political drama.[7] While the influence of ACT UP is clearly present in von Praunheim's documentaries – he interviews and films activists at meetings discussing their work – and while the group's anger is viscerally present in *The Living End*, it is Lucas's *Longtime Companion* that boldly, and for the first time on film, breaks the fourth wall and introduces the world of queer political community building as a counterweight, as well as solution, to the idea of the domestic problem drama.

A similar synergy between art and politics, although perhaps not as direct, can be seen in Chris Columbus's 1993 *Mrs. Doubtfire*. By most measures, *Mrs. Doubtfire* is a highly commercial, very mainstream and, thus, ultimately apolitical genderswitch comedy about a divorced father who disguises himself as a female Scottish nanny in order to be able to see his own children. While drag has always been integral to exploring gender binaries in theater and film – international stage and screen versions of Brandon Thomas's 1892 West End play *Charley's Aunt* have been popular for over a century – since the advent of the second wave of feminism in the late 1960s and the growth of the Gay Liberation and then Gay Rights movements in the 1970s and 1980s, the social explorations of drag have taken on a very specific political character. Ironically, many of the films that had garnered a solidly queer audience during this time – Edouard Molinaro's *La Cage aux Folles* (1978), Sidney Pollack's *Tootsie* (1982), Blake Edwards's *Victor Victoria* (1984) and *Switch* (1991) – were ultimately far more invested in reaffirming gender binaries than in expanding or breaking them. And while it would be disingenuous to say that the pro-family message of *Mrs. Doubtfire* was as transgressive as New Queer Cinema, there is a sense in which *Mrs. Doubtfire*, as mainstream as it is, was a decisive break from these earlier gender-bending comedies.

While Jennie Livingston's *Paris Is Burning* documented the playful aspect of gender performance in Harlem's famed "ball culture" and Rosa von Praunheim's *I Am My Own Woman* (1992) focused on gender as lived performance, *Mrs. Doubtfire*, quite distinctly, focused on gender performance within the biological, heterosexual family. This reflected radical feminist themes that had been articulated by such diverse writers as Shulamith Firestone in *The Dialectic of Sex* (1970) and Dorothy Dinnerstein in *The Mermaid and the Minotaur: Sexual Arrangements and Human Malaise* (1976). Both essential feminist texts were concerned with the gendered relationships between the sexes in relationship to the family and child rearing.

Mrs. Doubtfire's narrative centers on Daniel Hillard (Robin Williams), a too-easygoing father who drives his wife Miranda (Sally Fields) to seek a divorce because of his own childish antics with their children. Given only limited visitation rights to his children, Daniel – with the help of his gay, cosmetician brother Frank (Harvey Fierstein) – invents a strict, no-nonsense nanny named Mrs Doubtfire who whips the kids into shape, makes the house run smoothly, and makes life easier for the beleaguered Miranda. The plot of *Mrs. Doubtfire* is clearly inspired by Mrs Henry (Ellen) Wood's enormously popular 1861 sensation novel *East Lynne* – which had a remarkably vital, decades-long life as a stage melodrama and has been filmed 16 times since 1902 – in which a wife and mother, ignored by her emotionally withholding husband, has an affair, is deserted, and later returns to her home as a governess to raise her own children. Contemporary critics view Wood's novel as a critique of bourgeois masculinity, rather than as a panegyric to Victorian motherhood. The enormous popularity of *Mrs. Doubtfire* was no doubt in part due to the exaggerated, and by now predictable, antics of star Robin Williams – his parody of Tom Cruise's air-guitar dance in *Risky Business*, his constant reiteration of cute cartoon voices, his lighting his false bosoms on fire while cooking. But one of the reasons why the film struck a chord with early 1990s audiences was that its basic premise held that both traditional masculinity – as embodied by Stuart Dunmeyer (Pierce Brosnan), Miranda's new love interest – and the abandonment of "masculine" and, thus, fatherly responsibility were both detrimental to children.

What "queers" this story, to a large degree – and what constitutes it as a precursor to the popular 2003 reality television show *Queer Eye for the Straight Guy*, in which five gay men "makeover" various heterosexual men in the service of "normal" heterosexual and gender relationships – is that, before refocusing attention on gender roles within the family, the film details Daniel's transformation as facilitated by his gay brother Frank.[8] In its own middle-of-the-commercial-road way, *Mrs. Doubtfire* insists on the queer presence not only to correct the dangerous inconsistency of gender behavior and performance, but also to repair and heal the family itself. While *Tootsie* and *Switch* suggest that men would become "better" at performing their own gender by experiencing what it would be like to be a woman – an evaluation clearly connected to more mainstream feminist thought – *Mrs. Doubtfire's* critique is more in line with radical feminism. Ultimately, however, *Mrs. Doubtfire* turns sentimental and refuses to make good on its own premise – that all gender roles need to be critiqued and that children are at the mercy of these roles within the biological family – but compared to other gender-bending films in the years before and after its release, the politics of *Mrs. Doubtfire* nevertheless comes far closer to a transgressive sensibility.

Two very distinct cultural impulses emerged and collided during this period. The frisson of New Queer Cinema created a public space that allowed a wider dissemination of LGBT images, but by mid-decade the potential for radical "resistance" these images offered had largely evaporated in their more mainstream manifestations. At the same time, however, the explicit representations of queer sexuality and antisocial themes that could be found in Haynes's Genet-like sexual humiliations in *Poison* or Araki's revengeful AIDS-infected killers in *The Living End* engendered a backlash against the foundational transgressive nature of this new, and short-lived, cinema movement. As Rich notes, New Queer Cinema arose at the same moment that such Hollywood productions as *The Silence of the Lambs* (1991) (in which the murderer could be read as either homosexual or transsexual) and *Basic Instinct* (1992) (in which the main character was a murderous bisexual woman) were being protested by direct action groups such as Queer Nation for alleged "negative images" of LGBT people – adding another layer of context. The irony here is that the political visibility, predicated on headline-grabbing transgressive political actions promoted by these groups, is what also gave mainstream producers permission to create "negative" depictions of LGBT people in the first place.[9] These contradictory urges within both camps continued to find some resolution in the cultural mandate to discuss issues that had long been of concern to feminism – in particular gender, but also the idea of alternative family domesticity – without the burden of an explicitly feminist marker.

Reaffirmation

Part of a larger move away from gay male related HIV-AIDS narratives in mainstream film took place with the emergence of a new approach that replaced discussions of sexuality and sexual activity with discussions of gender. After advances in medical treatment of HIV-AIDS in the mid-1990s, AIDS activist groups were far less in the forefront of either creating or being subjects of news reports.[10]

Overwhelmingly, the new discussion of gender was focused only on cross-dressing and situated in a culture and tradition of gay male camp. While the films produced often ostensibly promoted the idea of nonbiological gay-male families, they always did so at the expense of locating sexual relationships in these domestic groupings. This domestication of gay male culture and life was perhaps a reaction to the more explicitly promiscuous, and often public, sexuality in the films of New Queer Cinema, such as Jarman's *Edward II* and Gus Van Sant's *My Own Private Idaho*. With the exception of independent American films – such as Greg Bordowitz's personal 1994 documentary dealing with HIV-AIDS and his family, *Fast Trip, Long Drop*; Rose Troche's 1994 lesbian love drama, *Go Fish*; and Cheryl Dunye's 1996 fictional investigation of black American lesbian history, *The Watermelon Woman* – the reality and the cultural excitement of New Queer Cinema was over.[11] This de-sexualization also allowed mainstream films to discuss issues of gender, as opposed to sexuality. This shift was culturally reinforced by many younger second-wave feminists who were resisting what they saw as the preoccupations of older feminists about the "correct" way for a woman to behave and who rejected the label of "feminist." In the broader cultural context of the mid-1990s, in which a backlash to second-wave feminism was manifest in the popularity of books such as Katie Roiphe's *The Morning After: Fear, Sex, and Feminism* (1993) and the advent of Camille Paglia's monthly, and frequently antifeminist, columns in Salon.com, this makes perfect sense.

This coalition of cultural concerns and imperatives produced three very popular films about gay men in drag – *The Adventures of Priscilla, Queen of the Desert* (1994), *To Wong Foo, Thanks for Everything! Julie Newmar* (1995), and *The Birdcage* (1996) – and also produced two mainstream films about women, sex, and gender: the 1995 road adventure *Boys on the Side* and the 1996 faux-noir thriller *Bound*. Notwithstanding *Boys on the Side* and *Bound*, it is important to point out that lesbianism held a very liminal – or, perhaps more accurately, marginalized – place in New Queer Cinema. Almost all of the films usually discussed in relationship to the movement are by and about men. Rich does mention some videos by Sadie Benning, as well as films by Cecilia Dougherty and Cecilia Barriga, but these works, important as they were, have been completely overlooked in most articles on New Queer Cinema. In her essay "New Queer Cinema and Lesbian Films," Anita Pick makes the point, quoting Amy Taubin, that New Queer Cinema "is figured in terms of sexual desire and the desire it constructs is exclusively male." Pick notes that the "gender neutral queer fails to adequately acknowledge a lesbian presence" and adds that the same might also, historically, be said of the broader terms "woman" and "feminism" (2004, 103–118).

When lesbianism did come to New Queer Cinema it was toward the end of its lifespan, with Rose Troche's *Go Fish* and Cheryl Dunye's *Watermelon Woman*. Both films are very important not only in mapping out a cinematic rhetoric of lesbian desire but also in setting the stage for a public discussion of lesbian community and family. While each in its own way was an important link to past lesbian and feminist filmmaking – specifically the European directors Chantal Akerman and Ulrike Ottinger, as well as the American filmmakers Yvonne Rainer and Su

Friedrich – neither film, as compared with some of the male films of New Queer Cinema, had much, if any effect on mainstream sensibilities or spectatorship. This was, to a large degree, because outside of a very narrowly defined heterosexual, and sexual, male gaze, lesbianism has never had a clearly defined place in mainstream cinema. It would be difficult, then, for independent, lesbian-feminist films – which were paid even less attention than their gay male counterparts – to make a substantial impact on this cinema.

But the problem may also have been the approach of the directors to their material. Troche's *Go Fish* is a detailed examination of a series of friendships and relationships among a small circle of lesbian friends including "Max" (Guinevere Turner), Ely (V. S. Brodie), Kia (T. Wendy McMillan), Daria (Anastasia Sharp), and Evy (Migdalia Melendez). Troche had been deeply interested in the political fragmentation within the lesbian community – particularly over the issue of lesbians having sex with men. While the film is also the story of a young woman looking for a girlfriend, this emotional and romantic drama is overshadowed by the more overtly political content dealing with the foundational question: "What makes a lesbian?" Cheryl Dunye also foregrounded overt political content in *Watermelon Woman*. Dunye plays a young, black, lesbian filmmaker, and using her own name, researches cinema history to uncover the women-centered erotic and emotional life of Fae Richards, a fictional black female performer of "mammy" roles who was best known as "the watermelon woman" in films such as *Plantation Days*. Dunye discovers not only Richards's possible involvement with the butch, white director but also her probable long-term relationship with a black woman. The fictional investigation into lesbian and film history is the metanarrative for the central, contemporary story of the filmmaker's involvement with a white woman which, in part, parallels Richards's own life. Dunye is deeply interested not only in the process of uncovering a lesbian past and a clear history of sexual and racial representation but also in uncovering the roles that race and butch and femme play in lesbian lives. The film is methodical in its discussion of these topics.

While these lesbian feminist films did not have the same influence on more mainstream filmmaking, they emerged at the very moment Hollywood was making films about lesbians that dealt with nearly the same themes. Both were responding to the larger political moment in their own way. Pairing *Go Fish* and *The Watermelon Woman* with *Boys on the Side* and *Bound* presents us with complementary, if very different, visions and demonstrates how lesbian themes were easily accommodated into mainstream spectatorship.

Boys on the Side, directed by Herbert Ross from a script by Don Roos, charts similar community-of-women territory as Troche does in *Go Fish* and specifically addresses the question of "what makes a lesbian." While Troche's film was located entirely in one, clearly defined geographic locale, *Boys on the Side* uses a female road film narrative crossed with a series of domestic dramas that involve a murder trial and a profound betrayal of friendship. The film centers around the friendships of Jane (Whoopi Goldberg), a lesbian rock singer who has a tendency to fall in love with heterosexual women, Holly (Drew Barrymore), a pregnant free spirit who chooses the wrong men and accidentally kills her abusive boyfriend, and Robin (Mary-Louise Parker), a middle-class real estate agent with simple romantic dreams who is living with HIV-AIDS contracted from a casual liaison with a bartender. Screenwriter Roos peppered *Boys on the Side* with the staples of the traditional "woman's film" – female friendships, romance, mother–daughter conflicts, a fatal illness, and a final, joyful, if tearful, reconciliation. On a basic level, the film performs a blending of Vincent Sherman's *Old Acquaintance* (1943), King Vidor's *Stella Dallas* (1937), Edmund Goulding's *Dark Victory* (1939), and Douglas Sirk's *Written on the Wind* (1956) and *Imitation of Life* (1959). What makes it completely contemporary, however, is not simply that Roos has introduced HIV-AIDS into the plot – the new, more socially conscious version of Bette Davis's brain tumor in *Dark Victory* – but rather that he has re-imagined the female-friendship networks of all of these films into what Adrienne Rich, in her foundational 1980 essay, "Compulsory Heterosexuality and Lesbian Existence," calls the lesbian continuum – that is, a deep bond between women that makes them, with or without same-sex sexual experience, the most important people in one another's lives. This is a clear extension of 1970s lesbian-feminist rhetoric of the "woman identified woman" (Rich 1985, 24–75). It is made explicitly clear toward the end of the film when Robin, in the witness box, explains her connection to her friends in language that echoes, not quite word for word but close, Rich's arguments. This clear articulation of a lived lesbian continuum is also clearly an echo of a scene in *Go Fish*, in which Kia explains to her women's studies class that lesbian lives have rarely been visible to historians. The difference between the two scenes is that *Boys on the Side* presents it through dramatic action and not, literally, through a lecture.

What Roos and Ross had done in *Boys on the Side* – the very title indicates that women can be with women exclusive of men – was to place lesbian-feminist rhetoric into a fully realized, dramatically convincing narrative that posits an idealized world of female-bonding networks across lines of class, color, and sexual orientation. While *Go Fish* was a substantial move forward for women and independent queer cinema – it was made for 15,000 dollars and was considered commercial enough for Samuel Goldwyn to pick up for distribution – its basic themes were disseminated far more widely in *Boys on the Side*, which relied on the basic conventions of the women's film to present a fairly radical feminist message.

A similar case can be made for Larry and Andy Wachowski's *Bound* (1996), a film that uses the basic structures and prototypes of the noir crime drama to explore a lesbian relationship deeply predicated on butch and femme roles. *Bound* – which takes its cues both from Billy Wilder's 1944 double-crossing relationship thriller *Double Indemnity*, and such split-second crime capers as Stanley Kubrick's *The Killing* (1956) – is clearly intended to be nothing more than a mainstream thriller. Its central relationship, however, of a butch–femme lesbian couple stealing two million dollars of laundered money from the Mafia lover of one of the women (whom she eventually murders) refigures many of the themes in independent LGBT cinema in a completely mainstream format. The narrative and sexual tension of *Bound* revolves around the relationship of Violet (Jennifer Tilly), the femme, flirtatious moll who comes on to Corky (Gina Gershon), a very butch, recently released convicted-felon-now-construction-worker whom she enlists as partner in both sex and crime. The intricate, hair-trigger plot to heist the two million dollars from Violet's minor-Mafia-player lover Caesar (Joe Pantoliano) is in constant juxtaposition with the possibilities of Violet or Corky betraying either one another or the clearly articulated gender roles they assume. (It is not accidental that the Wachowskis hired cultural sex expert and critic Susie Bright as an advisor for the lesbian scenes in the film as they clearly understood that it was this central narrative that had to carry the weight of the movie.)

In contrast to lesbian filmmaker Dunye, who was clearly interested in uncovering a cinematic and an actual, lesbian past in *The Watermelon Woman*, the Wachowski brothers were interested in mining classic noir plots and female stereotypes to see what they would yield. What is remarkable about the film is that under its rather crude, if complicated heist plot is a fairly well-developed meditation on female gender roles in noir films. According to the openly lesbian text of *Bound*, the very familiar gender roles open to women in the classic noir narrative are essentially, to take Adrienne Rich's paradigm slightly out of context, part of a lesbian continuum of women who are perfectly capable of acting independently of men and in their own interests. The butch affect of actors such as Barbara Stanwyck is obvious, but *Bound* brings to mind the fluctuating butch–femme gender roles of performers such as Marie Windsor, Audrey Totter, Ann Savage, Gloria Graham, and Colleen Grey. Clearly, *Bound* hit a nerve with LGBT audiences since it won an Honorable Mention for the Grand Jury Award at LA Outfest in 1996, and a Gay and Lesbian Alliance against Defamation (GLAAD) Media Award for Outstanding Film in 1997.

The GLAAD Award is notable because it was the highly publicized nationwide protests against the "negative" images of *Basic Instinct* (1994) that put the organization squarely in the forefront of the mainstream media and allowed it to grow exponentially into a multimillion dollar per year nonprofit organization with stable ties to the entertainment industry in a variety of roles including advisor to productions featuring LGBT themes or characters. GLAAD's award to *Bound* is, in a notable way, a turning point in 1990s representation of LGBT images in film because, in essence, *Bound* is not all that different in theme, plot, or even tone from *Basic Instinct* – the film that GLAAD wholeheartedly condemned three years earlier as not only a negative portrayal of bisexual and lesbian women, but as a potential cause of harm for LGBT people. So what made the difference here? Why was the murderous bisexual lesbian in *Basic Instinct* a "negative" image and the murderous bisexual lesbian in *Bound* an award winner? Clearly, New Queer Cinema's rejection of the "negative" image concept in the early 1990s had a tremendous effect on queer filmmakers as well as on the mainstream. In the early years of the 1990s, however, cultural license for these images was granted to openly LGBT artists such as Kalin, Haynes, and Araki, while self-avowed heterosexual filmmakers such as Jonathan Demme (*The Silence of the Lambs*) and Paul Verhoeven (*Basic Instinct*) were vilified for similar work. While this is understandable as an intracommunity move to claim control over the production of images, what is surprising is that this cultural change could happen so quickly four years later. In this "reaffirmation" stage, mainstream films made by heterosexual men would be praised for what were once considered transgressive images of lesbians. It is this turning point that, to a large degree, also marks the transition from reaffirming a period that saw the effect of these new images of LGBT people to a new period that saw their regulation within a mainstream system of cultural production.

This transition from affirming to regulating is most evident in the appearance, and considerable popularity, of three films in a two-year period of time. Stephan Elliott's *The Adventures of Priscilla, Queen of the Desert* (1994) is a drag road movie in which two gay men, Tick aka Mitzi (Hugo Weaving) and Adam aka Felicia (Guy Pearce), and a trans woman, Bernadette (Terence Stamp), travel on a bus, the eponymous Priscilla, across the Australian outback to do a show at a small resort run by Tick's estranged wife. Beeban Kidron's 1995 film *To Wong Foo, Thanks For Everything! Julie Newmar* charts the road trip of two professional drag queens, Noxeema (Wesley Snipes) and Vida (Patrick Swayze), and a novice, Chi-Chi (John Leguizamo), as they journey from New York to Los Angeles to enter a drag pageant. On the road their car breaks down in a small heartland town where they, passing as women, become involved in the lives of the locals and help solve many of their relationship problems. Mike Nichols's *The Birdcage* (1996) is a remake, set in Miami, of the highly successful 1978 French farce, *La Cage aux Folles*. Businessman Armand Goldman (Robin Williams) and his lover Albert Goldman (Nathan Lane), who performs in drag under the name Starina, run *The Birdcage*, a classy drag club. Val (Dan Futterman), Armand's son from a former marriage, is about to marry Barbara Keeley (Calista Flockhart), the daughter of a prominent right-wing religious politician, and has misrepresented his parents to his intended in-laws. When the Keeleys insist on visiting their prospective in-laws, the Goldmans must pretend to be heterosexual, respectable, and Christian, and they have to act the parts of a government-employed cultural attaché and his housewife – as Val has invented them to his future in-laws.

The popularity of these three films was enormous. *The Birdcage*, earning 185.3 million, was the top-grossing LGBT themed film in US history at that point, and while *Priscilla* and *To Wong Foo* were not blockbusters, both achieved critical and popular support. They were all indicative of a new, transitional moment in LGBT representation. These films continued the public discussion of gender roles that had begun with second-wave feminism and was enacted in films like *The Crying Game* and *Mrs. Doubtfire*, but they were also very much a backlash to the experimentation and sexual explicitness of much of New Queer Cinema. Each of these films gloried in, and capitalized upon, gay male drag culture. While cross-dressing had always been a part of both mainstream stage and screen entertainment, this was the first time that it was fully acknowledged as integral to gay male culture. The radical aspect of *The Adventures of Priscilla*, *To Wong Foo*, and *The Birdcage* was that each presented the audience with openly gay men who identified as a part of a cohesive – and public – gay male culture. This arguably progressive aspect of the films was overshadowed, at the same time, by the films' major theme: the reinforcement and solidification of the biological nuclear family and traditional social norms. At the end of *The Adventures of Priscilla*, Tick is reunited with his eight-year-old son (who has been living with his estranged wife), and they form a new family. In *To Wong Foo*, Noxeema, Vida, and Chi-Chi perform a series of "makeovers" that help the townswomen become more attractive to their spouses (following *Mrs. Doubtfire* as a precursor to *Queer Eye for the Straight Guy*), put a stop to a brutal case of domestic abuse, and reinvigorate the annual celebration of small-town life – the Strawberry Social. In *The Birdcage*, Armand and Albert are willing to humiliate themselves to ensure the success of their son's heterosexual relationship, and the film, predictably, ends with his marriage.

The Birdcage presents Armand and Albert as an old married couple who are asexual, while *The Adventures of Priscilla* and *To Wong Foo* incidentally flirt with the idea that these men are sexual before quickly avoiding the reality of that idea. If the films had allowed their drag queens and older men to have full sexual lives, or even to discuss their sexual desires, they would have been unable to fulfill their primary goals of reinforcing mainstream, heterosexual values. Just as importantly, they also – simply by hinting at gay male sexual activity – would have raised the specter of HIV-AIDS in the minds of most viewers. The AIDS epidemic was now fully in its second decade, and while it was no longer considered only a "gay male disease" – Ryan White, an HIV-infected boy who had gained enormous media attention, died in 1990, and a year later, avowedly heterosexual basketball star "Magic" Johnson announced that he had tested positive for HIV – its cultural linkage to gay male sexuality was unavoidable.

By mid-decade LGBT characters and themes found a secure place in mainstream Hollywood films. To a large degree this was a response to the cultural changes that had been wrought by both the mainstream LGBT gay rights organizations as well as groups such as ACT UP and Queer Nation. It was also a sign that the political, cultural, and social changes that had been evolving with the emergence of national, and well-publicized, Gay Liberation and Gay Rights movements since 1969 had incited backlash. It was these multiple convergences that defined the "reaffirmation" stage as having a profound and lasting impact on the ability of mainstream audiences to watch, comprehend, and enjoy a variety of LGBT representations on screen, while simultaneously leading both mainstream and independent LGBT cinema toward greater compromises.

Regulation

In the last years of the decade, LGBT representation moved into a third stage, which is, in essence, an attempt to contain and control the deluge of LGBT images that had begun to appear in Hollywood and even in independent film. Some films in this period still pushed boundaries. Todd Haynes's *The Velvet Goldmine* (1998), for example, was a complicated dissection of sexual mores and sexual identities of the British glam rock craze of the early 1970s in which Haynes took many of his cinematic stylizations from New Queer Cinema and applied them to a more mainstream palette. Bill Condon's *Gods and Monsters* (1998), based on Christopher Bram's novel *Father of Frankenstein* (1995), was an imagined examination of the last months in the life of noted 1930s director James Whale, while also a complicated meditation on history, art, and the AIDS epidemic. Kimberly Peirce's *Boys Don't Cry* (1999), also an interpretative biography, was a hard-hitting account of the 1993 rape and murder of Brandon Teena, a young transgender man. Aside from these and a few other examples, the majority of LGBT films in the last third of the decade were comedies or comedy-dramas that featured substantial, sometimes even substantive, LGBT characters but that also assiduously avoided controversial subject matter or challenging narrative forms. Even when the films were independent productions with considerable LGBT artistic input and relatively wide distribution – in and of itself a breakthrough for LGBT-themed films – they were very safe films that bore little relationship to the New Queer Cinema of the early years of the decade. Films such as Tony Vitale's 1997 ethnic comedy of mistaken sexual identity, *Kiss Me Guido*, David Moreton's sweet coming-out story *Edge of Seventeen* (1998), Simon Shore's comedic, but realistic coming-out comedy *Get Real* (1998), Tommy O'Haver's innocuous comedy *Billy's Hollywood Screen Kiss* (1998), and, in 1999, Jamie Babbitt's mediocre *But I'm a Cheerleader*, all took advantage of the cultural and social space that New Queer Cinema opened for LGBT artists but pursued none of the exciting intellectual and artistic risks they also pioneered.

While there were certainly more LGBT characters in mainstream and independently produced films, and on more screens by 2000, their position had drastically shifted (in most cases) from outsiders to insiders, from critics of society to accepted players. This was, to a large degree, a product of the political climate. If the Gay Liberation and Lesbian Feminist Movements of the early 1970s insisted that LGBT people had the ability to radically challenge the status quo and, with a progressive political and social vision, change the world, the later Gay Rights Movement set as its goal the inclusion of LGBT people within the existing social and political frameworks. This political ideology is clearly mirrored in the more mainstream Hollywood productions during the same years. It is very telling that a majority of Hollywood films of the period featured a narrative trope of the "gay best friend to the female heterosexual lead." The films ranged from serious comedies, like James L. Brooks's *As Good as It Gets* (1997), and romantic heterosexual relationship comedies, like P. J. Hogan's *My Best Friend's Wedding* (1997), Nicholas Hytner's *The Object of My Affection* (1998), and Dan Roos's *The Opposite of Sex* (1998), to serious domestic drama, like John Schlesinger's *The Next Best Thing* (2000). This narrative device reached its apex in the television comedy series *Will and Grace* (1998–2006). The rise of the "gay best friend" genre is, in a sense, the logical conclusion of the trends of the decade and is, by and large, a conservative rhetorical move that places gay male characters in major roles while, at the same time, sidelining them within a heterosexual narrative context. They, or their lives, are rarely – in any obvious way – the center of these films. This is certainly the case with *As Good as It Gets* and *The Object of My Affection* in which the gay male characters – played by Greg Kinnear and Paul Rudd, respectively, and with an acceptable but unmistakable level of stereotyping – are completely incidental to the heterosexual narrative.

These films are clear examples of, as noted above, Herbert Marcuse's concept of "repressive tolerance" – the illusion, not the reality, of full acceptance. This illusion flourished for a number of reasons, the primary of which was that the cultural spaces opened by New Queer Cinema, and then vacated by its demise, made commercial productions the most visible representations of LGBT characters and themes. Concomitantly, a certain political reality was crystallizing: the agenda of the Gay Rights Movement, harkening back to the ideas of Vito Russo, embraced many of these representations as "positive images." Thus, the now very visible LGBT community – that has its roots in the early publications and cultural collectives of the Gay Liberation Movement including groups such as GLAAD – now gave a queer imprimatur to many of these films.

Ironically, this queer imprimatur for certain films was granted not only officially by GLAAD, but also, just as importantly, through extensive affirmative press coverage in national gay publications such as *The Advocate* and *OUT*, as well as in many local LGBT newspapers. Not surprisingly this press coverage was often published in conjunction with full-page, expensive advertisements for the films that appeared in the same issue. This synergy between positive press coverage and the film distributors' ability to buy advertising space – certainly not unique to LGBT-themed films – was a direct result of the industry's growing understanding of a large, increasingly lucrative market for LGBT films. Given this mutually supportive economic context, it is not surprising that one of the main impulses of mainstream Hollywood and independent film at the end of the decade was to present safe, socially and politically acceptable images of LGBT people for the largest possible audience. While there were certainly films earlier in the decade intended for both heterosexual and LGBT audiences they, to a large degree, placed LGBT people or themes in subordinate roles through a number of rhetorical maneuvers in both the script and the advertising. In *Philadelphia* (1993), for example, the dying Andrew Beckett is less the focus of the film's dramatic arc than Joe Miller, the homophobic lawyer who overcomes his prejudice. The tagline for the film – "No one would take on his case ... until one man was willing to take on the system" – was an indication that, while the plot centered on a gay man with AIDS, the real hero was the courageous lawyer. By the end of the decade, the film industry began to produce some films in which the gay protagonist and the LGBT theme were central to the narrative, and this was not understood by the creative and marketing teams to be a hindrance in securing a wide, mostly heterosexual audience. This attempt at creating a LGBT crossover movie epitomized the process of "regulation" that tolerated and even promoted certain, already established, queer images but at the same time made sure that they did not transgress accepted norms or moralities.

A prime example of this evolution from reaffirmation to regulation is Frank Oz's *In & Out* (1997). Written by openly gay playwright Paul Rudnick, the film tells the comic coming-out story of Howard Brackett (Kevin Kline), a small-town, Midwestern high school drama teacher who does not realize he is gay, even though he evidences every trope of gay male life and gay affect, ranging from being incredibly fussy about his clothing to knowing the details of Barbra Streisand's recording career. His first inkling that he is gay occurs when former student, now Oscar-winning actor, Cameron Drake (Matt Dillon) outs him at the Academy Awards for inspiring him to play an openly gay character in a film. The accidental – and, to Brackett, surprising – outing is a parody of Tom Hanks's thanking his own high school drama teacher, Rawley Farnsworth, who was gay, when he accepted his Oscar for *Philadelphia*. The outing becomes a national news story, and as Brackett, who is engaged to fellow teacher Emily Montgomery (Joan Cusack), strives to convince everyone in town that he is heterosexual, he gradually comes to the realization that he is, indeed, gay. Paul Rudnick's script, really a series of *bons mots* and astute observations on contemporary culture, charts Brackett's coming out with forthrightness but never presents him in sexual situations – the exception being a single, surprising yet comic kiss by openly gay news reporter Peter Malloy (Tom Selleck) who is covering his story – thus taking away any sexual threat he may present. By relying on the cultural ephemera of gay male culture – Broadway musicals, disco, female movie stars – as signifiers for homosexuals, Rudd created a highly lovable character who is so unaware of his own sexual desires that he is completely acceptable to mainstream audiences. (This forms an interesting comparison to Andrew Beckett in *Philadelphia* who is presented in the film as partnered, but highly sexual in his frequenting of porno movie theaters, although he must suffer for this by contacting HIV-AIDS.)

To complete this process of regulating gay male (sexual) identity, Rudnick relied on two narrative ploys, both of which are allusions to previous films. In the first, Brackett's queer identity is clearly understood not in terms of sexual identity but in terms of gender. In an attempt to bolster his masculinity Brackett orders a set of cassette tapes that will instruct him on the art of being more manly. The tapes are a disconcerting mixture of bullying, sarcasm, and preternatural knowledge of Brackett's spontaneous responses. The more the tough male voice on the tape insists on Brackett's acting in a "butch" manner, the more he fails and then rebels against the demands of socially constructed traditional masculinity. The entire scene is a nearly word-for-word reinscription of a pivotal scene in *Strike Me Pink* (1936) in which milquetoast, small college town, Jewish tailor Eddie Pink (Eddie Cantor) attempts to learn how to be a real man.[12] While the conflation of effeminacy with homosexual identity and practice is quite common (including the deviation from traditionally defined gender roles) – in the 1930s, Cantor referred to his blackface character as a "cultured, colored pansy" – Rudnick's use of the imagery here works quite well in distracting the viewer from questions of sexuality or sexual activity.

While this conflation of gender with sexual orientation to define homosexual orientation is constantly reinforced by the use of gay male cultural artifacts rather than sexual behavior, Rudnick ends the film with a rousing spectacle of tolerance and acceptance. As his homosexuality becomes nationally known and he finally acknowledges that he is gay, Brackett is fired from his job. In a show of support, his fellow faculty and students, along with his neighbors, announce at a town meeting that they are also gay. In a parody of the climactic scene in Stanley Kubrick's *Spartacus* (1960), in which hundreds of Roman slaves claim his identity (and face death) in order to save the leader of a slave revolt, Brackett is not only saved but becomes a hero.[13] Rudnick's ending is funny, and in some sense progressive since it places Brackett's personal life within a clearly defined community, but it also has the – consciously intended – effect of further desexualizing him, thus making the film acceptable to a wide audience. And while gratifying as a communal political action, this energetic show of support has the unintended effect of erasing even a specific homosexual identity from the film. If everyone is gay here (and no one but Brackett is) then in essence, no one is actually gay.

If late 1990s regulation was in full force in *In & Out*, it took a more nuanced form in the new century in John Schlesinger's *The Next Best Thing* (2000), a serious spin, with comic moments, on the gay best friend theme that had become so prevalent. While the gay best friend narrative was essentially used as comic rhetoric, Schlesinger attempted to move it into the realm of the socially meaningful domestic drama. This was not a surprise, for Schlesinger had pioneered serious, important portrayals of gay men and gay sensibility since the mid-1960s. *Billy Liar* (1963) is a prime example of how a clearly defined gay male sensibility can define a film about heterosexual characters, and *Darling* (1965) (along with Tony Richardson's 1961 *A Taste of Honey*) featured one of the first central, openly gay characters. *Midnight Cowboy* (1969) and *Sunday, Bloody, Sunday* (1971) essentially defined how the contemporary cinema could deal with adult themes of fluid sexuality (including overt homosexuality) and relationships. The television adaptations of Alan Bennett's short plays *An Englishman Abroad* (1983) and *A Question of Attribution* (1991) also brought a level of emotional and political sophistication to the usually homophobic narrative of the homosexual spy. The premise of Tom Ropelewski's screenplay for *The Next Best Thing* showed promise.

Abbie Reynolds (Madonna) is a heterosexual woman who is ready to settle down and raise a child. She has no luck finding a heterosexual male lover who will also be a partner, but after a drunken one-night fling with Robert Whittaker (Rupert Everett), her gay best friend, she finds herself pregnant. She decides to keep the child, whom they name Sam (Malcolm Stumpf), and they raise him together. Five years later, Abbie meets heterosexual Ben Cooper (Benjamin Bratt), falls in love, and the two decide that they want to raise Sam without Robert's involvement. When Robert resists their plan, Abbie and Ben raise the political and emotional stakes with homophobic arguments for Robert's exclusion from the child's life, eventually taking the case to family court.

At heart, *The Next Best Thing* is a film at war with itself. Ropelewski's screenplay and Schlesinger's direction indicate that they intended the film to be a serious retelling, from a gay male perspective, of the traditional Hollywood woman's story. The film clearly draws on examples like *Stella Dallas* (stage production, 1924; filmed in 1925, 1937, and 1990, and on a popular radio show from 1937 to 1955) and *Madame X* (stage production 1910, filmed internationally at least 15 times since 1910, and a Brazilian television series in 1966) that depict a loving mother estranged from her child as a result of social and sexual indiscretion, while further drawing upon Douglas Sirk's domestic/paternity drama *Written on the Wind* (1956). *The Next Best Thing* places a gay man denied access to his child in the role of the alienated mother and brings up questions of whether it is appropriate or even feasible for gay men to father children. At the political and emotional center of the film is the question of whether or not parenting (in all of its incarnations from conception to the raising of children) constitutes a heterosexual prerogative and whether or not homosexuals are fully equal under the law. With such hot-button issues as children and homosexuality – Abbie and Ben raise questions of Sam's safety with Robert – *The Next Best Thing* comes close to grappling with complicated topics such as the limits of heterosexual tolerance for gay identity, as well as the broader question of the structuring of public policy on the, usually, unquestioned prejudice of prioritizing institutionalized heterosexuality over any form of homosexuality. What *The Next Best Thing* does well, by borrowing from these earlier women's genres, is predicating its narrative on the idea that the emotional and political tensions that exist between normative heterosexuality and tolerated homosexuality can be resolved by "friendship."

As with *Mrs. Doubtfire*, and its borrowing the plot and motifs of *East Lynne*, the rhetorical move of replacing the socially unacceptable, excluded mother with the socially stigmatized gay man was both thematically daring and politically savvy. Such a move might have skillfully foregrounded questions of sexuality, gender arrangements, social stigma, and the equal application of US family law. Unfortunately, as a result of its misguided script, sluggish direction, and miscasting – with Everett and Madonna in the leads, suggesting a cross between the sentimentality of *My Best Friend's Wedding* and the manic comedy of *Desperately Seeking Susan* – *The Next Best Thing* never realized its potential or benefits from Schlesinger's usual artistry as a director. One of the film's tag-lines at the time was "Best friends make the best mistakes," indicating that friendship, even one that involved a sexual encounter, might be the neutral ground between these often antagonistic positions.[14] The other tag-line used in the film's promotion was "He was smart, handsome and single. When her biological clock was running out, he was … the next best thing," which may have been meant ironically, but in the regulatory systems of the later 1990s was understood literally. The film opened well and was second in that weekend's box office, but soon failed with critics and audiences. The film was tantalizing enough, however, in Schlesinger's dealing with the tensions between the political resistance of the early years of the decade and the social regulation that ended it. Whatever the considerable problems with *The Next Best Thing* were, the reality is that by the late 1990s, mainstream and independent cinema were presenting images that often showcased lesbian and gay characters but did so in such a way that securely and firmly placed them into safe and unthreatening categories. This was, to a large degree, in clear, if noncausal, concert with the activities of the Lesbian and Gay Rights Movement during that time.

While HIV-AIDS had not been eradicated, more effective drugs had made it a manageable illness. The urgency of the HIV-AIDS epidemic, which had engendered so much of New Queer Cinema in the late 1980s and early 1990s, had now ended and the main preoccupation of the movement was refocused on antidiscrimination battles. The Employment

Non-Discrimination Act (ENDA) was introduced in Congress in 1994 and has continued to be a major focus of the movement since then. Along with ENDA, enormous financial, social, and political attention has also been paid on another antidiscrimination measure: the securing of the right of same-sex marriage in all of the 50 states. From 1991 on, when the first state-based same-sex marriage case, *Baehr v. Lewin*, was filed in Hawaii, up until early 2015, when 37 states and the District of Columbia allow same-sex couples to legally wed and 13 states have passed constitutional amendments against it, same-sex marriage has become the most visible of gay rights causes. This turn to reformist politics from a more radical critique of political and social culture is clearly the immediate cause, as well as the background, charting how the LGBT films of the decade moved from resistance to regulation. Viewed in this context, the radical impulses of *The Next Best Thing* were doomed to fail as the very idea of a heterosexual woman and a gay man raising a child – and thus breaking down certain established, entrenched binary cultural ideas about sexuality and gender – were seen as nowhere nearly as important as replicating a heterosexual marriage ideal with a same-sex version.

The 1990s saw a drastic upswing in the number of LGBT-related themes and characters in Hollywood and independent films, and this exciting cinematic moment was, viewed in retrospect, a time of enormous radical change; even if it would eventually become eclipsed by a deep desire to maintain the culture's basic status, it did so while allowing lesbian and gay lives simply to become more visible – as long as they did not threaten the accepted social and political paradigms.

Notes

1. The move from discussing, or simply accepting, mainstream representation to valuing specifically LGBT-produced representation was facilitated enormously by the rise of a widespread and very active national and local lesbian and gay press in which such publications as *Fag Rag*, *Amazon Quarterly*, *Gay Sunshine*, *The Gay Liberator*, and *Dykes and Gorgons* demanded that LGBT people take seriously the mandate of self-representation. This mandate was materially enacted, as well, by political collectives of artists dedicated to producing posters, dramatic productions, painting, graphics, and film. It was in this political climate that filmmakers such as Jan Oxenberg (*A Comedy in Six Unnatural Acts*, 1975), Mickie Dickoff (*Monday Morning Pronouns*, 1975), and Tom Joslin (*Black Star: Autobiography of a Close Friend*, 1977) got their start. This was the rise of independent LGBT cinema which would eventually morph, with some political and cultural transformations, into the New Queer Cinema of the 1990s.
2. The Gay Rights Movement continued the goal of the early homophile groups of the 1950s.
3. When the political approach of the Gay Rights Movement proved inadequate for dealing with the HIV-AIDS epidemic, new political groups, such as ACT UP and Queer Nation, reverted back to the direct action models of the Gay Liberation Front. The HIV-AIDS direct action group ACT UP was founded in New York in 1987 and the grassroots, community-based visibility group Queer Nation followed in 1990. These groups were vital in the formation of a new "queer identity."
4. The political ramifications of "and" versus "in" are significant. This is particularly true for Hollywood and some international films in the 1990s. The "and" analysis has a firm historical grounding in a variety of sources, particularly B. Ruby Rich's essay "New Queer Cinema," as well as the psychoanalytically inflected film theories of Teresa de Lauretis and other postmodern thinkers. Michele Aaron's anthology *New Queer Cinema: A Critical Reader* (2004), has examined in detail the content, significance, and ramifications of LGBT cinema of the early 1990s, but little extensive work has been done on the decade.
5. The themes and even the content of New Queer Cinema can certainly be traced in Jarman's work back to *Sebastiane*, his 1976 homoerotic re-creation of the martyrdom of St Sebastian. Von Praunheim's 1990 three-part film *Die Aids-Trilogie* documented both AIDS activism as well as artistic responses to the epidemic, but his filmmaking career began before the Stonewall Riots. His 1971 *It Is Not the Homosexual Who Is Perverse, but the Society in Which He Lives* laid the groundwork, in many ways, for the film.
6. Although *Longtime Companion* came after John Erman's 1985 made-for-television movie *An Early Frost*, starring Aidan Quinn and Gena Rowlands, and after Bill Sherwood used HIV-AIDS as a backdrop to look at three generations of gay men in *Parting Glances* (1986), it preceded Gregg Araki's *The Living End* and John Greyson's *Zero Patience*, which would be heralded as the beginning of a cinematic response to the epidemic that was already nearly a decade old.

7. Contrast this with the idea of "domestic drama" in *Philadelphia*, the award-winning Jonathan Demme film that was released three years later. While lauded by critics and both straight and gay audiences, the film – although it does chart the physical ravages of HIV-AIDS on Andrew Beckett (Tom Hanks), its central character – is not only removed from gay political action groups (ACT UP had now been active for nearly seven years) but severed from a gay community. Except for a fairly brief part in which we meet Andrew and his lover's friends, there is no sense in *Philadelphia* that HIV-AIDS actually affects a community or that there is a well-organized, sustained, and relatively effective community response to it. The intense privatization of AIDS in *Philadelphia* – and its insistence that Andrew's private "domestic drama" is in fact his heterosexual biological family's drama as they are the most supportive of him – is an indication of how the mainstreaming of LGBT representation would become, by the end of the decade, a form of strict, and conscious regulation of queer images, which would become culturally prevalent, but extraordinarily nonthreatening.
8. It is instructive to think about this "queering" – which is both incidental yet vitally important to the plot – in comparison to Neil Jordan's critically acclaimed and extraordinarily popular *The Crying Game* that was released exactly, almost to the date, the year before and had garnered six Academy Award nominations and one win for best screenplay written directly for the screen. While *The Crying Game* is a better made, more complex film, and Jordan's political intentions, especially the connections here between sexuality and nationalism, are far more evolved than anything in *Mrs. Doubtfire*, the gendered "secret" at the heart of the film – which, in true 1950s movie publicity-stunt fashion, audiences were urged not to tell their friends – essentially cheapens the queerness of the film, turning it into a plot device with an exotic allure, as at a Victorian stage melodrama entire audiences would gasp at the shocking "revelation." Mainstream audiences flocked to *The Crying Game* because it allowed them to be, indeed insisted upon them being, shocked by the "otherness" of gender discord. This was a purely American response. In Great Britain, where the film did not fare well because of its sympathetic view of the IRA, the issue of gender was far less pertinent.
9. Rich notes that the fact that Tom Kalin, whose *Swoon* flirted with the same transgressive material, supported the protests against *Basic Instinct* only adds to the irony, and reality, that by the early 1990s the intersections between LGBT politics and the production of LGBT images had already taken a number of unexpected turns. This responsive trend of replicating the binary of negative/positive stereotypes has continued to Trey Parker's animated *South Park: Bigger, Longer and Uncut* (1999), in which Satan is sexually and romantically involved with Saddam Hussein, and the 2001 *L.I.E.*, which is a sympathetic examination of a middle-aged man's relationship with several teenage boys. In their denouncement of these films, both radical and assimilationist strands of the LGBT movement were deeply influenced by the simplistic interventionist logic of a Gay Rights analysis of mainstream media. This influence continues today through the work of organizations such as Gay and Lesbian Alliance against Defamation (GLAAD).
10. While there is not a direct year-by-year correlation here, the winding down of New Queer Cinema – even as its enormous aesthetic and political effects were still reverberating among audiences and more mainstream filmmakers – coincided with a shift in grassroots political activity as well. While ACT UP, Queer Nation, and Lesbian Avengers were still active and vocal in many parts of the country, the advances in medical treatment of HIV-AIDS that were enormously helpful to people living with HIV-AIDS must at least indirectly be attributed to the impact of eight years of concerted AIDS activism; at the same time, these advances also helped muffle the urgency of those calls for change that went beyond issues of treatment and addressed larger political problems relating to the oppression of LGBT people. It must be noted, however, that while the AIDS epidemic that affected gay men was less in the news and on the screen, the epidemic among women of color, as well as other groups, was just getting media attention – but almost no visibility on the screen. This was, among other reasons, because the many lesbians and gay men had education and social status that allowed them access to funding that other, differently marginalized groups did not have.
11. There was some continued work from a few directors – Gregg Araki's 1994 *All Fucked Up* and his 1995 *The Doom Generation* (that was promoted with the tagline "A Heterosexual Film by Gregg Araki") continued themes he explored in *The Living End* – but many of the directors who emerged earlier in the decade such as Tom Kalin and Jennie Livingston dropped out of view, or, like Todd Haynes, emerged later in the decade with new work. The reasons for this are unclear. Both Kalin and Livingston received a great deal of attention, and while her film was far more commercially successful than his, she never released another commercial film. Kalin did some work as a producer of independent films such as *Go Fish* in the 1990s. His next full work was the 2007 *Savage Grace*. Haynes made an easier transition to mainstream cinema with the 1995 *Safe* and then the

1998 *Velvet Goldmine*, perhaps because his subject matter became more conventional and his visual aesthetic more accessible to a mass audience.

12. The narrative here – by Walter DeLeon, Francis Martin, and Frank Butler – is a loose plot about gangsters, mixed with a series of vaudeville jokes, and is obsessively concerned with the comedy produced by the ineffectual Jewish man in a gentile world. *Strike Me Pink*, and most of the other Eddie Cantor movies of the 1930s, relies on a clearly defined history of the effeminization of the Jewish male that was a staple of Jewish comics in vaudeville. The most notable example of this is Bert Lahr, born Irving Lahrheim, with his character Cowardly Lion in Victor Fleming's *Wizard of Oz* (1939). This trope of the effeminized Jewish man at war with the world was carried on to the 1950s and early 1960s in almost all of the films of Jerry Lewis and Danny Kaye.
13. This denouement of community and collegial support also appears in Denis Dugan's *I Now Pronounce You Chuck and Larry* (2007) in which two New York City firefighters pretend to be a male couple in order to get domestic partner benefits.
14. This idea of queering relational dichotomies through the concept of "friendship" has great currency in writing by such theorists as Alan Bray, who explored it in his last work, *The Friend* (2002), as well as some of the ideas in Sharon Marcus's *Between Women: Friendship, Desire and Marriage in Victorian England* (2007).

References

Aaron, Michele (ed.). (2004). *New Queer Cinema: A Critical Reader.* Edinburgh: University of Edinburgh Press.

Bram, Christopher. (1995). *Father of Frankenstein.* New York: Dutton.

Bray, Alan. (2007). *The Friend.* Chicago: University of Chicago Press.

Dinnerstein, Dorothy. (1976). *The Mermaid and the Minotaur: Sexual Arrangements and Human Malaise.* New York: Harper & Row.

Firestone, Shulamith. (1970). *The Dialectic of Sex.* New York: Farrar, Straus, Giroux.

Marcus, Sharon. (2007). *Between Women: Friendship, Desire, and Marriage in Victorian England.* Princeton: Princeton University Press.

Marcuse, Herbert. (2007). *The Essential Marcuse: Selected Writings of Philosopher and Social Critic Herbert Marcuse*, ed. Andrew Feenberg & William Leiss. Boston: Beacon.

Pearl, Monica. (2004). "AIDS and New Queer Cinema." In Michele Aaron (ed.), *New Queer Cinema: A Critical Reader* (pp. 23–35). Edinburgh: University of Edinburgh Press.

Pick, Anit. (2004). "New Queer Cinema and Lesbian Films." In Michele Aaron (ed.), *New Queer Cinema: A Critical Reader* (pp. 103–118). Edinburgh: University of Edinburgh Press.

Rich, Adrienne. (1985). *Blood, Bread and Poetry: Selected Prose 1979–1985.* New York: Norton.

Rich, B. Ruby. (2004). "New Queer Cinema" (1992). In Harry Benshoff & Sean Griffin (eds), *Queer Cinema, the Film Reader* (pp. 53–61). New York: Routledge.

Roiphe, Katie. (1993). *The Morning After: Sex, Fear, and Feminism on Campus.* Boston: Little, Brown.

Russo, Vito. (1981). *The Celluloid Closet: Homosexuality in the Movies.* New York: Harper & Row.

Wood, Ellen. (2005). *East Lynne*, ed. Elizabeth Jay. New York: Oxford University Press.

21

24/7

Cable Television, Hollywood, and the Narrative Feature Film

Barbara Klinger

Provost Professor, Indiana University, United States

A mutually enhancing affiliation between Hollywood studios and popular media dates back to the silent era. With **cable television** and **subscriber pay services**, the rapport grew markedly, revising "the concepts of film's specificity as an industry, an aesthetic, a narrative form and a viewing experience," as Barbara Klinger explains. Cable TV supplies Hollywood with an essential **aftermarket** – providing a virtual 24-hour film archive for the exhibition of canonical and independent films, thus situating film as "a social presence that extends well beyond the theater." Klinger discusses the legal, technological, and business-oriented changes that assisted the growth of cable TV and permitted its role in creating original content and mounting its own studio productions. While acknowledging small screen limitations on the aesthetics of film exhibition, Klinger insists that this cannot be a ground for dismissal. Rather, as a discipline, film studies must take account of the vast changes cable television has brought about to the reception and, indeed, the very meaning of cinema. Klinger's essay shares ground with Michele Hilmes on cinema and television from 1945 to 1975, Thomas Schatz on seismic film industry changes, and Patricia Aufderheide on post-1999 documentary in this volume.

Additional terms, names, and concepts: network television, satellite distribution, TBS, fiber optic cable, HBO, conglomerates, cross-fertilization

An integral part of American film history resides in Hollywood's extensive relationships to new media and technologies, especially as they have acted as vital forums for movie production, distribution, and exhibition. In the second half of cinema's existence, a particularly strong configuration of intimate business associations has materialized between film studios and a number of new media and technology concerns, from broadcast and cable television to DVD and the internet. Adjudicated by complex forces, these developments have clearly affected the film studios' organization and economic profile. Such advances have also had a significant impact on the very meaning of cinema as a medium and an experience, deeply

American Film History: Selected Readings, 1960 to the Present, First Edition. Edited by Cynthia Lucia, Roy Grundmann, and Art Simon.

influencing the aesthetics, public reputation, and modes of consumption of films, as well as their sheer presence in everyday life.

This chapter focuses on the affiliations between Hollywood and one of these influential advancements: cable television. Although cable TV has existed since the 1940s (when it was named CATV, or Community Antenna Television, and served to retransmit broadcast signals to rural areas), its place in US television gained more serious national traction in the late 1970s. With this in mind, my account will focus on cable's impact on the narrative feature film, beginning in the 1980s. During this decade, basic cable, as an aftermarket for Hollywood features, overtook the theatrical box office in revenues for the first time; in the early 1990s, it earned more than double the amount of theaters, while pay cable proceeds rivaled those of theaters (Wasko 1995, 3). As cable, along with VHS, became indispensable to home film exhibition, the major broadcast TV networks at the time (ABC, NBC, and CBS) began to lose the position they had long claimed as central purveyors of features for this market. On a different front, cable networks' expanding fortunes from the 1980s onward led them to become more than recycling centers for Hollywood fare; with pay channel HBO in the lead, cable created and distributed original programming, including motion pictures.

As showcase, generator, and supplier of feature films, cable television has been a potent force in the cinemascape. As such, it provides insight into the fundamental inter-media conditions of cinema's material existence and circulation. In considering aspects of the alliance between cable TV and cinema since the 1980s, I will also be concerned, then, with the larger question of what this chronicle means to film history and to film study more generally. Since films have been shown on TV for more than 60 years, what role does cinema's televisual history – its exhibition on TV monitors in the home and other contexts from the early post–World War II broadcast days to the DVD era – play in illuminating cinema's story as a major mass entertainment form? How has cinema's delivery through television shaped its identity and circulation? Granting that there are differences, how do the continuities between these two media affect concepts of film's specificity as an industry, an aesthetic, a narrative form, and a viewing experience?

Cable TV, of course, represents only a part of cinema's televisual history. However, with cable's prodigious appetite for film content, roots in broadcast network TV practices before it, and central place in contemporary media conglomerates, it offers a strategic and representative site for studying films as they thrive in off-theater locales – locales that have been instrumental in giving movies an intimate place in audience's lives. Given the complex amalgam of economic, regulatory, and technological factors that define the evolution of the relationship between cinema and cable, my chronicle of the latter's function as exhibitor, distributor, and producer of films from the 1980s to the early 2000s will necessarily be selective, focusing on a number of developments that have helped to make it into a capacious and powerful venue for narrative features.

Cable Television as Aftermarket

Until the mid-1980s, movie theaters remained Hollywood's primary source of exhibition revenue. This state of affairs changed dramatically as cable TV and VHS became enormously profitable as aftermarkets for feature films. In fact, with the combined force of ancillary exhibition and theatrical box office, the major studios at the time (Paramount Pictures, Universal Pictures, Warner Bros., Twentieth Century Fox, Columbia Pictures, and MGM/UA) earned more money from their films in 1987 than in any previous year (Gomery 1988, 83). The film industry flourished, then, not despite competition from rival media, but because of the income they generated for the studios. Moreover, while ABC, NBC, and CBS had already made feature films available in great numbers to viewers long after their first runs, cable and VHS escalated the pervasiveness of Hollywood cinema in the home. As Douglas Gomery states, by the late 1980s, "The North American public [enjoyed] the greatest access to feature films in the medium's history" (1988, 83).

As this bustling business indicates, despite turf battles between the cable and film industries (see Hilmes 1990, 171–181), the former has been vital to studio interests and to its products' visibility. Similarly, Hollywood films have been central to cable's development and popularity. Like that of the broadcast networks before it, the evolution of cable programming relied heavily on Hollywood fare. While premium movie channels such as HBO and superstations such as TBS have occupied a prominent place in cable's history as an aftermarket, many nonsports cable networks, from A&E (Arts and Entertainment) and AMC (American Movie Classics) to TCM (Turner Classic Movies) and USA have prominently featured recycled films and TV series in their lineups.

Part of the reason for this dependence resided in commercial cinema's appeal to subscribers and cable networks alike. In the 1970s, basic cable subscribers numbered below 15 million. In the 1980s, that figure rose substantially to nearly 50 million and hovered around 65 million in the 1990s and early 2000s (NCTA 2011). Although having a lower subscription rate, pay cable's fortunes similarly improved from tens of thousands of households in 1974 to over 30 million in the 1980s and building to 53 million by 2007 (NCTA 2008). According to early preference studies across diverse audiences, the strongest incentive for signing up was to gain greater access to old and new movies (Heeter & Greenberg 1988, 256). Further, a 1986 survey found that, while 25 percent of basic cable programming consisted of movies and TV series already shown in theaters and/or on broadcast networks, subscribers spent nearly half of their viewing time watching it. Such recycled fare constituted 91 percent of premium cable offerings and captured 85 percent of premium subscribers' viewing time (Waterman & Grant 1991, 180). Many customers, weary of watching censored films with commercial interruptions, wanted to see movies uncut and uninterrupted – a desire that helped HBO (which commenced operations in 1972) and later premium movie channels build subscriber bases.

For cable networks hungry for content and not yet breaking even on start-up costs, Hollywood films constituted ready-made and, often, relatively inexpensive programming. From the 1980s to the early 1990s, sports and rerun movies and TV series dominated cable programming. Besides attracting viewers, theatrical films and broadcast TV series had (and continue to have) significant functions for cable. Among other roles, they helped to define a cable network's brand by embodying programming types that could secure its identity, thereby attracting its targeted audiences (Mullen 2003, 134, 138). For example, the Sci-Fi Channel, launched in 1992 (and now called the Syfy channel), has focused on science fiction, horror, and fantasy content. In its early history, its fare included Flash Gordon space adventure movie serials (1936–1940), *Dracula* (1931), and TV vampire soap opera *Dark Shadows* (1966–1971) (Carter 1992). The *Star Trek* movies and TV series and spin-offs have also been important branding properties. As specialty channels and cablecast original programming (e.g., made-for-cable movies, miniseries, and TV series) have grown exponentially, reruns have retained their branding function, while providing a "promotional bed," a block of time leading up to and providing space for advertising original content (Segrave 1999, 169).

Of course, cinema's multifaceted importance to cable owed to the fact that recycled Hollywood fare had already proven popular in broadcast network distribution. At the same time, during its history, cable's perceived advantages over the major broadcast networks have included improved signal reception, a larger number of channels, narrowcasting (specialized programming for diverse and fragmented groups that more efficiently delivers specific audiences to advertisers), less censorship on some channels in terms of sex, violence, and language (as HBO's *The Sopranos* (1999–2007) attests), competitive quality original programming, and expansion into new media, including broadband internet service. From the early 1980s to the early 1990s, cable grew from 10 to 26 percent of TV viewership. By 2003, it claimed more than 50 percent of this viewership (Stelter 2008a; NCTA 2008, 6; Edgerton 2008, 5). Today, cable has clearly superseded ABC, NBC, CBS, and Fox as a movie destination: While one can easily navigate the "Big Four" without encountering a feature film, channel surfing in a cable household without such an encounter would be almost impossible.

A combination of regulatory, programming, and technological factors in the 1970s and beyond substantially enhanced cable's ability to show Hollywood films. In 1977, for example, HBO challenged the Federal Communications Commission (FCC) to loosen its restrictions on cable programming. Previously, the government body, in an attempt to protect "free" traditional broadcasting, limited the kinds of movies pay cable could offer.[1] While the government's attempts to regulate cable continued, HBO's successful challenge resulted in a period of increasing deregulation that allowed cable companies to compete relatively unrestrained with the main broadcast networks. With fewer restrictions, cable TV could program more theatrical films and more cable channels entered the market (Segrave 1999, 163–165). By 1980, besides HBO, several other premium cable movie channels appeared, including HBO's sister channel Cinemax, and competitors Showtime and the Movie Channel. During the 1980s, these four pay channels together showed thousands of different films annually, repeating titles several times during the course of a month to capitalize on their investments. In 1981/82, these channels were also the first to go to a 24/7 (24 hours a day, 7 days a week) programming schedule. As other pay movie channels (such as Starz, introduced in 1994) and basic cable channels followed this schedule, feature films, among other kinds of programming, were increasingly deployed to fill new hours. As Kerry Segrave writes of this turn of events, "Nobody benefited more than the Hollywood majors" (1999, 165).

From a different angle, technological developments, such as satellite distribution, fiber optics, and digital transmission and compression technologies, have also supported a growth in channel options and reach that have affected movie exhibition on TV. The ability to uplink cable stations to satellite dramatically facilitated both pay and basic cable's penetration of US and international markets.[2] HBO, for example, was the first to go to satellite distribution in 1975. With the help of satellite uplink, HBO viewers rose from a total of 57,000 US households in 1974 to 6 million five years later. In 1976, Ted Turner uplinked the signal from his Atlanta-based independent station TBS (Turner Broadcasting Systems), creating the first "superstation," an independent channel (unaffiliated with any network) with broad national presence on cable. As in HBO's case, satellite distribution resulted in TBS's substantial growth; by the late 1980s, TBS reached more than 40 million US homes, becoming the single most watched cable station (Gomery 1988, 86). Other cable networks quickly followed, including superstation WGN (originating in Chicago) and pay cable channels, such as Showtime (Segrave 1999, 160–162; Gomery 1992, 264). As Patrick Parsons and Robert Frieden comment, "With the availability of satellite-delivered programming, cable television quickly migrated from a localized, self-contained, and somewhat sleepy distribution service to a nationally and globally connected infrastructure rich in diverse content" (1998, 5). Satellite distribution thus meant that stations once dependent on locally originated sources of programming could access content from the much broader area provided by the satellite's "footprint;" through satellite hookup, a particular station's signal could be distributed nationally and internationally.[3]

Numerous other technological developments have affected cable TV. For example, fiber optic cable (as it replaced coaxial cable) carries more information, meaning increased channel capacity. In addition, new compression technologies enable more information to be "squeezed" into cable wires, allowing broadcasters to transmit several program services over one channel and to offer digital cable subscribers hundreds of new channels options, including HD channels. Such developments led to the multiplexing of cable channels, an idea launched by HBO in 1991 and later adopted by other channels (Granger 1993). In addressing the consequences of multiplexing for programming, a commentator succinctly wrote that it would mean "movies, movies, and more movies" (Greenstein 1991). It would also mean more narrowcasting, with movies and other kinds of programming used to target specific audiences. Thus, as one instance of this phenomenon, in 1998, HBO created "HBO the Work," a collection of channels oriented toward different viewers that includes HBO Signature (for women), HBO Family, and HBO Latino. As a consequence of a host of technological developments, then, a channel like HBO has uplinked to satellite, expanding its service in the United States and in more than 150 countries abroad (Time Warner 2010), and multiplexed. It has also offered pay-per-view and video-on-demand services, become available (in 1994) on DBS (direct broadcast satellite), and gained a presence on other digital platforms. As a representative of industry advancements, HBO's example demonstrates how movies have become a strong currency within proliferating windows of access.

Business arrangements that characterize the relationship between cable and film industries have resulted in a relatively stable supply of product. During the course of this relationship's history, studios have tried altogether to circumvent the pay movie cable channels by establishing their own.[4] However, a practice already used by the broadcast networks – the exclusive distribution agreement – has been more the norm. In such agreements, a studio offers a package of its films, for a licensing fee, to a certain movie channel, giving the channel sole access for a designated period of time (a year or more). Thus, for example, between the 1980s and 1990s, HBO had long-term affiliations with Paramount, Twentieth Century Fox, Warner Bros., and Columbia Pictures (Hilmes 1990, 181). In 1994, Starz signed such agreements with Disney and MCA Inc., parent company then of Universal Pictures (Ginsberg 1994). In such agreements, the cable channel pays the studio a fee for each of its titles (in the early 1980s, approximately \$6 to \$8 million a film, although blockbusters could command higher prices), plus a share of per household subscriptions. At this time, by some estimates, the film industry was bringing in \$600 million annually from pay cable rerelease of its films (Sherman 1984, 208). Of course, basic cable channels also routinely enter into exclusive distribution arrangements, as in the case of separate package deals USA Network made with Paramount, Universal, and Twentieth Century Fox in 1989–1990. USA paid approximately \$2 million apiece for the roughly 20 films it purchased from each of these studios (Segrave 1999, 174). Today, such agreements continue to hold lucrative potential for dealmakers (Goldstein & Nordyke 2008).

Extensive in-house film libraries provide another means of securing reliable sources of programming. In a famous example, in 1986, Ted Turner bought the MGM/UA Entertainment Co. for more than a billion dollars. Due to financial distress, he sold MGM back to former owner Kirk Kerkorian at a loss, but kept the library of thousands of films from MGM, Warner Bros. and RKO. Valuable properties in the Turner library included *Gone with the Wind* (1939), *The Wizard of Oz* (1939), *Citizen Kane* (1941), *Casablanca* (1942), and the musicals of Fred Astaire and Ginger Rogers. This acquisition supplied Turner with an arsenal of movies to stock TBS (where films comprised almost half of the station's daily offerings) and, later, TNT (Turner Network Television, launched in 1988) and TCM (Turner Classic Movies, launched in 1994), while keeping programming costs low (Fryman & Hudson 1993, 190–196). In the mid-1990s, to continue stocking his stations, he spent \$25 million for exclusive distribution rights lasting 10 years for approximately a hundred of Paramount's classic and contemporary titles (Segrave 1999, 175). In 1995, Time Warner became the home of Turner's cable empire and film library. Other cable networks too gained access to libraries as a result of corporate takeovers – this was the case, for example, with superstation WOR after it was purchased in 1987 by MCA with its Universal Pictures' catalog (Gomery 1992, 270–271). Still others were launched by studios as outlets for their archives. As a joint venture between Paramount Pictures (bought by Viacom in 1994) and MCA/ Universal, the Sci-Fi channel, as I have mentioned, screened Paramount's *Star Trek* franchise and Universal horror such as *Dracula* (Carter 1992).

As these last examples suggest, the centralization of media ownership during the last 30 years in which large media corporations, such as Time Warner, Viacom, and the Walt Disney Company, purchased cable and other media concerns (such as film studios, music companies, and book publishers), felicitously affected the cable programming of Hollywood features. As Megan Mullen writes, media giants "supplied the cable networks they controlled with major movie and television syndication libraries, contributing significantly to cable's existing reliance on recycled programming materials." Cable, in turn, "offered syndicated program suppliers one more distribution/exhibition window for their products, creating an incentive to build even larger libraries" (Mullen 2003, 133). The move toward mergers and conglomeration produced a vital reciprocity, then, between parts where recycled Hollywood fare vividly emerged as central to the growth and operations of cable and film businesses alike. Whether movie libraries were accessed through exclusive distribution agreements, outright purchase, corporate takeovers, or joint ventures into channel creation, this rerun fare was critical not only to industry economics, but to the experience of films for cable subscribers given access to thousands of movies, old and new.

Given the multiple factors that have entered into the feature film's pervasive presence on cable TV, key questions arise: How does cable present these movies to customers? What issues do its modes of presentation raise about film aesthetics, the film experience, and film history more generally?

When theatrical movies were broadcast on network TV, they were edited for length or content, interrupted by advertisements, and, in the case of widescreen films, panned and scanned to fit TV screens. Such transformations resulted in sometimes dramatically altered showings of the original, with scenes deleted, characters left out of the frame, and new "camera movements" inserted. These practices remained largely unchanged on most basic cable channels, including TBS, TNT, and USA. In addition, in the 1980s, some black-and-white films were colorized for cablecast, with Ted Turner as a proponent of this computerized transfiguration. Turner's decision to colorize certain films in his library (including classics like *Casablanca*) to make older titles attractive to contemporary audiences elicited an outcry amongst many who saw colorization as another act of aesthetic sabotage directed at theatrical cinema by those involved in the aftermarket. Premium movie channels changed some of the conditions typically governing the televised theatrical, when they presented films without commercial interruption or editing. With some exceptions, though, these venues tended to show widescreen films panned and scanned, rather than in letter-box formats. The channel dedicated to the uninterrupted airing of movies can still come up short in this regard, even today.

Many in the field of Film Studies thus regard cable as a despoiler of theatrical films, a status that has often relegated it to the back burner of serious inquiry. Yet, even drastic alterations do not provide sufficient grounds for dismissing the phenomenon of the ancillary text *tout court*. Such metamorphoses are an intimate part of a film's history and social story and thus merit examination outside the register of aesthetic alarm that often defines scholarly response to televised theatricals. Since cable TV is a central forum for film circulation, like other ancillary venues, its participation in a film's history has material effects worth considering. In fact, movies in the aftermarket raise more interesting questions than reservations about aesthetics and reception, once cinema is understood as a medium with a social presence that extends well beyond the theater.

In terms of explicit historical functions, cable, like the broadcast networks before it, has acted as a vast film library, film archive, and revival house – facts easy to overlook today as DVD, with its reputation for high-quality renditions of films, has aggressively assumed these roles. However, a reviewer in the late 1980s wrote that TNT, a beneficiary of Turner's 1986 film library purchase, provided enthusiasts with "reel after reel of rare movies ... most of which had not been seen on television or in the dwindling revival houses for years, if ever. Some of the films ... had not left the vault since their first release decades ago" (Alexander, 1989). Films such as *Baby Face* (1933) and a double bill of *Trader Horn* (both 1931 and 1973 versions) were shown, many appearing in "mint condition" through remastered transfers from original prints (Alexander 1989). Channels such as AMC (launched in 1984 as a classics channel, but later revamped to feature more contemporary films) and TCM have similarly served as revival houses, screening numerous films from yesteryear that might otherwise have remained in obscurity. Moreover, TCM (like AMC before it) is connected to film preservationists and the preservation movement, enhancing its status not only as a quasi-archival site, but as a place for serious movie fans. Meanwhile, channels such as IFC (the Independent Film Channel, launched in 1994) and Bravo (launched in 1995) present foreign and independent features and shorts that, outside of urban areas and without a Netflix membership, are difficult to find. With narrowcasting and cable's expansion of channels, specialized movie channels have continued to grow, providing not just reruns of *Top Gun* (1986), but of almost every sort of film. Hence, like an official film archive or museum, cable TV re-presents the past and thus attains a historical function with regard to "old" films and TV shows. Cable is one of the ways in which the US film heritage is put on display and reencountered by interested viewers (see, e.g., Klinger 2006, 91–134). Further, the rhetoric it uses to characterize this past affects how and what films mean to audiences.

To wit, cable programming has often organized films into festivals and marathons and/or showcases for certain stars, directors, genres, and themes.[5] To name a few instances, AMC has aired festivals of Marx Brothers' comedies, John Wayne's films, and Oscar Micheaux's oeuvre. TNT, TBS, and Spike TV have each featured marathons of James Bond films. Cable has also packaged programming via special shows: USA's *Up All Night* (1986–1998), hosted by comedians such as Gilbert Gottfried, featured low-budget films like Troma Entertainment's *Toxic Avenger* (1985); TNT's *Monstervision* (1993–2000), hosted by Joe Bob Briggs for most of its history, screened mainly B movies and held festivals, for example, of Hammer Films; and, perhaps the most familiar of such forums, *Mystery Science Theater 3000* (1988–1999), cablecast on a number of channels, including Comedy Central and Sci-Fi, also aired mainly low-budget films.

Given its pervasiveness and longevity, justice cannot be done to the impact cable recycling has had on film presentation and reception. If we widen the circle, we can see too that its programming strategies are not unique; they have characterized other forms of ancillary exhibition, including theatrical reissue, network broadcast, VHS, and DVD. Older movies are constantly being "refreshed" for contemporary audiences by strategies that reorganize them into catchy, thematically coherent frameworks. Cable TV reframes films via programming themes and, when relevant, host commentaries – devices that might redefine any aspect of a film, from its genre to its director's reputation. Indeed, *Mystery Science Theater 3000* is famous for the mocking commentaries offered by its character hosts (a man and his robot friends) on films, turning them into camp or cult fare. From the robots to the gray-haired, well-groomed, and earnest Bob Dorian on the early AMC, "redneck" Briggs on TNT, and scathing, shrieking Gottfried on USA, the "host-effect" also helps to situate films for audiences. Moreover, the fact that festivals and marathons are often timed for the holidays and other special occasions (e.g., James Bond films for Christmas and Fourth of July, and *Friday the 13th* marathons for Halloween), indicate that cable and other ancillary venues position movies as part of national, family, and fan rituals, thereby weaving films further into everyday life. Even without such fanfare, cable characterizes movies by placing them into legible programming mixes (e.g., Lifetime airs romances and other women's films interspersed with commercials aimed at female audiences) and by branding them with the network's identity. As I have mentioned and as the Lifetime example demonstrates, the logic of narrowcasting demands that each channel signal its unique identity in the multichannel universe in part through the kinds of recycled movies it shows. Here, movies provide a way of promoting the channel's brand by demonstrating its difference from competing cable stations.

Through multiple means, then, the aftermarket's recycling of films has considerable effects on film identity and consumption. As Derek Kompare argues, rerun movies or TV series are involved not in a passive process, but in a "vital economic and semiotic" enterprise: "In presenting familiar programming, cable networks do not merely run it; they strip it, promote it, repackage it, and recombine it." Even when a cable channel develops original programming, "a popular, familiar rerun" remains its "lifeblood," forming the "core" of its appeal to advertisers and audiences alike (Kompare 2005, 171–172). The imperative of recycling always involves a meaning-generating process that muscularly affects how a film or a TV series appears to the public, as well as the nature of their allure.

A film's canonical fortunes can also be deeply affected by televisual recycling. Recycling, as it inevitably resuscitates the past, literally makes that past memorable, while attracting old and new audiences. In terms of social fortunes, for example, the place Frank Capra's *It's a Wonderful Life* (1946) occupies in the US consciousness would be impossible to gauge without taking stock of TV's role in its destiny. How would this longtime perennial holiday favorite have fared in cultural memory and, for that matter, in the canon, without the incessant replay it enjoyed on network and cable TV and in other forms of ancillary circulation? A film's reputation and place in popular as well as academic canons can be greatly influenced by replay. In addition, by being given a "second chance" in the aftermarket, a film can clearly become cult – the case with, more recently, such titles as *Scarface* (1983), *The Princess Bride* (1987), and *The Big Lebowski* (1998). Further, an entire generation may associate a film with television – for example, cable replay of *The Breakfast Club* (1985) and other John Hughes films – helping to fuel nostalgia for the 1980s for these viewers (Klinger 2006, 174–181). In no uncertain terms, cable replay, among other venues, thus influences film legacy, the creation of diverse canons and fandoms, and affect itself.[6]

No matter whether movie cablecasts represent aesthetic advantages or disadvantages (as in the rerelease, respectively, of rare prints in good condition or edited prints that damage the original), cinema's recirculation on cable constitutes a major aspect of the medium's history. Even the mangled print is part of a film's material history, part of its family tree, and should be considered as such, enlarging our sense of the many forms that movies assume in their social circulation (Klinger 2007, 289). Moreover, as we have seen, an intimate symbiosis exists between cable TV and the film rerun that has effects worth considering, from the material semiotics of meaning construction for the text to canon formation and beyond. Since so many films have for so long been exhibited after their theatrical premieres, ancillary circulation becomes more than an economic fact; it provides keys to a more robust understanding of film history in all of its intermedia intricacies.

Despite its prominent place in film history, the cable aftermarket for Hollywood features does not exhaust the former's involvement in the life of the latter. Although recycled theatrical fare and TV series remain important commodities, the cable networks' expansion into original programming, beginning in the 1980s and mushrooming in the 1990s and into the 2000s, provides further insight into the vital relationship between these two enterprises.

Production/Distribution

While their function as purveyors of the cinematic past is perhaps the most visible aspect of their relationship to film, cable networks have not simply been in the business of exhibiting theatrical features. Like the broadcast networks before them, they have produced and distributed feature films as part of programming strategies that include signature original content from comedy specials to TV series. HBO, for example, a channel that initially made its reputation for showing uncut, uninterrupted feature films, is now known as much, if not more, for original TV series (e.g., *Sex and the City*, 1998–2004, and *The Sopranos*, 1999–2007), miniseries (e.g., *Band of Brothers*, 2001), and documentary films (e.g., *Capturing the Friedmans*, 2003) as it is for rerunning theatrical releases. Other cable networks too are deeply invested in producing content; in the realm of TV series alone, original programming is found in shows from AMC's *Mad Men* (2007–2015) to USA's *Burn Notice* (2007–2013).

Trade journalists and scholars depict cable's shift toward original programming as owing to multiple factors. As Mullen explains, when HBO assumed its position with what was then Time Inc. (now Time Warner) in 1989, it acquired access to Warner Bros. films and distribution networks, but it also gained the financial foundation necessary for developing original content. While other cable networks recovered their start-up costs sufficiently to produce original content by the mid-1990s, HBO's situation gave it a head start (Mullen 2003, 2, 146). Other developments making original content both more financially viable and attractive include the growth of the aftermarket (e.g., syndication and video rentals and sales) for cable shows (Santo 2008, 21–24, 36) and the continued importance of branding. Original programming enabled cable networks to individuate themselves strategically to compete for advertisers and viewers in a media marketplace defined by scores of channels and an ever-expanding aftermarket replete with DVD box sets of classic TV shows and movies (Stelter 2008b). In terms of use value, then, original shows could perform both as signature elements of an innovative and distinctive brand and as material destined to be recycled. New programming has also helped cable channels avoid substantial churn rates (wherein subscribers drop channels) generated by the glut of reruns necessitated by 24/7 scheduling (Segrave 1999, 166).

Part of cable networks' embrace of original content has involved the production, coproduction, and distribution of first-run theatrical pictures, made-for-pay-cable movies, and "orphaned theatricals" – films abandoned by studios and picked up by cable. When original series and miniseries, as long-form storytelling modes, are added to this mix – a point to which I shall return – then cable's contribution to narrative film grows exponentially. In any case, particularly against the backdrop of the heady synergisms characteristic of horizontally integrated media conglomerates, these different types of involvement with cinema raise intriguing questions about the place of cinematic specificity in the contemporary mediascape.

Granting that the practice of creating and airing original movies has been legion historically on broadcast and other cable networks, HBO offers an especially pointed example of cable's interrelation with feature film production. The oldest and most successful of the pay-cable channels and widely considered to be the foremost innovator of original content among cable networks, HBO was the first to produce a made-for-pay-cable movie (*The Terry Fox Story*, 1983), as well as cable miniseries (*All the Rivers Run*, 1984), and cable series (*Not Necessarily the News*, 1983–1990) (Edgerton 2008, 6). *The Terry Fox Story*, a biopic about a Canadian cancer patient/amputee who ran across the country to raise money for cancer victims, was shown on HBO and then distributed as a first-run picture in Canadian theaters. The film went on to win Best Picture and five other Genies, Canada's main national film award. From such roots, HBO would eventually earn a reputation as "quality TV," producing programs with high production values and adult (i.e., topical or controversial) content that drew top honors at awards ceremonies (e.g., Emmies for made-for-cable movie *And the Band Played On*, 1993, based on Randy Shilts's best-selling book about the early years of the AIDS epidemic, and *The Sopranos*). In any case, between 1996 and 2001, HBO's original programming rose from comprising 25 to 40 percent of its schedule; meanwhile, from 1995 to 2007, its subscriber base jumped more than 50 percent. The company's move into original programming and its interests in the broadcasting, motion picture, home video, and digital industries have been part of its diversification, a diversification "crucial to its success" (Edgerton & Jones 2008, 315, 7).

Much earlier, in 1977, as a projected cost-saving gambit, HBO began buying cable rights to theatrical films before they were made. Instead of paying the studios for rights after they had released a film (when its true market potential could be assessed), HBO opted for a "pre-buy" arrangement: It paid a sum toward a film's production costs, while gaining exclusive cable rights and a profit share. Thus, HBO helped to finance such films as *On Golden Pond* (1981), *Sophie's Choice* (1982), *Tootsie* (1982), and *King of Comedy* (1983) (Hilmes 1990, 180; Wasko 1995, 77). Since *On Golden Pond* was a huge box office hit, it represented a particularly gratifying windfall for the pay cable company. By moving aggressively into financing films and "forging partnerships with dozens of filmmakers and producers," HBO not only found the "key to ... success," it became "a force" with which studios and other media concerns had to reckon (Balio 1990, 265).

In the 1980s, HBO invested more heavily in multiple ventures in theatrical film production and distribution, continuing to expand its operations, while maintaining the practices of cost sharing and securing features for exclusive cable runs. In 1983 and 1984, respectively, HBO helped to form Tri-Star Pictures and Silver Screen Partners. Tri-Star (later TriStar), the first new film studio in roughly four decades, was created from HBO's partnership with Columbia Pictures and CBS. Among Tri-Star's earliest releases were 1984's *The Natural*, a baseball movie starring Robert Redford, *The Muppets Take Manhattan*, and *Places in the Heart*, featuring Sally Field's Oscar-winning turn, and the 1985 teen comedy *Real Genius*. Tri-Star distributed other titles theatrically, including blockbuster *Rambo: First Blood II* (1985). HBO produced seven films with financing from Silver Screen Pictures, including the Patsy Cline biopic *Sweet Dreams* (1985), the Tom Hanks comedy *Volunteers* (1985), and horror thriller *The Hitcher* (1986). With some exceptions, HBO/SSP's films were comedies and adventures targeting the 18–24 age demographic, a younger viewership than the middle-aged audiences typically drawn to HBO's more overtly serious fare (Silver Screen Partners 1997; Smith 1984).

HBO's relationship with both ventures was short-lived – by 1986 both CBS and Time Inc. had sold HBO's shares in Tri-Star to Columbia, while SSP became affiliated with the Disney Company. Yet such arrangements provided evidence of the synergies possible between pay cable and multiple-media concerns: Columbia produced films for Tri-Star that were later cablecast exclusively on HBO and then shown on CBS (Hilmes 1990, 192); in the case of SSP, Tri-Star distributed its films theatrically with HBO covering the cable and home video markets (Silver Screen Partners 1997). These alliances also clearly represented strategic moments in HBO's growing commitment to feature film production.

In the 1980s HBO developed a number of divisions to produce original programming (for itself and for broadcast and other cable networks), from comedy specials and sports shows to made-for-cable movies and theatrical features. These divisions included HBO Pictures, HBO Independent Productions, HBO Showcase, HBO NYC Productions, and HBO Films. HBO as a studio not only introduced its feature films and documentaries at major film festivals, such as Cannes and Sundance, it had in-house production and theatrical and non-theatrical distribution deals with other media concerns, locking film product in from inception. By making films and controlling distribution, HBO not only gained exclusive rights to show films it produced or coproduced, but profited from the aftermarket, earning revenue from sales to broadcast and cable TV and other venues (Smith 1984).

Beginning operations in 1983, HBO Pictures produced such made-for-cable films as supermodel biopic *Gia* (1998), starring Angelina Jolie. Showcase, also mainly a banner that produced television content, operated between 1986 and 1995, producing Emmy-winning made-for-TV movie *Age Old Friends* (1989) and more than 25 other telefilms, many based on actual events (e.g., *Tailspin: Behind the Korean Airliner*

Tragedy, 1989) ("Colin Callender" 2008). Showcase was replaced by NYC Productions in 1996, a banner designed to focus on "edgier" made-for-TV fare such as an anthology drama on abortion, *If These Walls Could Talk* (1996), with segments directed by Nancy Savoca and Cher.

Independent Productions has made both TV and theatrical features, including the teen comedy *Don't Tell Mom the Babysitter's Dead* (1991), the surprise blockbuster *My Big Fat Greek Wedding* (2002), and *American Splendor* (2003), a biopic about comic book artist Harvey Pekar. Since 1999, HBO Films (a reorganization of HBO Pictures and NYC Productions) has continued producing made-for-cable movies and miniseries, as well as low-budget independent and "A" theatrical features. It coproduced and distributed across first-run and ancillary media Gus Van Sant's Columbine-inspired *Elephant* (2003), which won the Palme d'Or and Best Director prizes at Cannes. HBO Films also made *Maria, Full of Grace* (2004), a drama about the Colombian drug trade, along with numerous award-winning documentaries, and John Frankenheimer's last feature-length film, the made-for-cable *Path to War* (2002).

In 2005, HBO joined with New Line Cinema (a Time Warner subsidiary since 1996, it was absorbed into Warner Bros. studio in 2008) to launch Picturehouse Entertainment, mainly an acquisitions and distribution arm. Among other titles, HBO Films coproduced and Picturehouse released director Mary Harron's biopic *The Notorious Bettie Page* (2005); meanwhile, Picturehouse distributed Robert Altman's *A Prairie Home Companion* (2006) and acquired North American distribution rights to Guillermo del Toro's *Pan's Labyrinth*. In 2008, however, HBO considered moving away from full immersion in the theatrical business. Along with Warner Independent Pictures, Picturehouse closed in 2008, with its last release a big-screen remake of the 1930s classic, *The Women* (Picturehouse 2008).

This follows an industry-wide trend of shuttering independent film divisions, despite the fact that their films often perform well during awards season. How long this trend will last and how it will affect cable companies' relationship to theatrical cinema is as yet unknown.

If developments since the 1980s imply the complexity of determining what "counts" as a film, the "orphaned" theatrical expressly raises the issue. For

Figure 21.1 Linda Fiorentino as the irresistible Bridget Gregory with Peter Berg (Mike) in John Dahl's *The Last Seduction* (1994, producer Jonathan Shestak).

example, when Columbia Pictures rejected film producer Ray Stark's proposal to adapt the best-selling book, *Barbarians at the Gate*, for theatrical release, HBO made the adaptation for $7 million. Released in 1993, *Barbarians* won not only its time slot, but an Emmy for Best Made-for-TV Movie (Fabrikant 1993). Another case involving Columbia found the studio prepared to shelve one of its productions, director John Dahl's *Red Rock West* (1992), which starred Nicholas Cage. The movie went straight to HBO, where it was shown repeatedly in 1993. It then had a limited theatrical release, where it gained critical acclaim for its inventive blend of neo-noir and Western elements. Similarly, John Dahl's *The Last Seduction* (1994) aired on HBO before its theatrical release. Since the rules of the Academy of Motion Pictures Arts and Sciences (AMPAS) oblige theatrical first-runs for films under consideration for an Academy Award, star Linda Fiorentino's standout turn as a femme fatale was not eligible for nomination (Pinsker 1994). The role such circumstances play in determining where a film first appears also works in reverse. In earlier broadcast history, Don Siegel's *The Killers* (1964) was produced to be the first made-for-TV movie; however, after being deemed too violent for television, it gained theatrical release (Brooks & Marsh 1999, 687).

Such turns-of-fate are not unusual; nor are they without consequence for Film Studies. They invite reflection on what constitutes a film – what comprises cinematic specificity – with respect not only to film form, but to details of production, distribution, and exhibition. They also, as we shall soon see, encourage consideration of the place of made-fors and long-form TV narratives (such as cable series) in cinema history. In fact, HBO's multifaceted involvement in film production and distribution, from pre-buys and made-for-pay-cable movies to its theatrical divisions and adoption of orphaned theatricals, indicates that making distinctions about what is and is not a film is a productively tangled affair.

If first-run theatrical exhibition is the bottom line in determining the division between telefilms and theatrical pictures, as it is for AMPAS, HBO films premiering in theaters would clearly qualify as cinema. Films produced and then orphaned by a major studio that have their first and subsequent runs, respectively, on cable and in theaters would fall short. However, such distinctions are unstable, once we consider the issue of circulation more broadly. Orphaned theatricals and certain kinds of made-for-cable films introduced on US cable or video are often exported to global markets as first-run theatrical features and experienced by their audiences as such (Gale 2001; O'Connor 1995). Add to this films with origins on TV abroad, such as Stephen Frears's *My Beautiful Laundrette* (1985), which was shown on British television and was then released theatrically in the United States, and the circle seems complete. Such cases help to qualify any easy assumptions about origins.

The circuitousness of a film's identity as film in terms of distribution and exhibition also applies to its production. Made-for-cable movies and series are not always as easily recognized, as they once were, by low production values, sensationalistic issues, and absence of A-list stars. Even if they were, similar elements range across numerous films that have had first-run theatrical distribution (e.g., *The Blair Witch Project*, 1999), suggesting the unreliability of such benchmarks. In any case, as embodiments of "quality television," HBO's made-fors and series have distanced themselves from old standards, sometimes touting their adoption of cinematic values. In one of many such instances, Alan Ball, creator of the series *Six Feet Under* (2001–2005), searched for a cinematographer who would bring a "cinematic sensibility" to the show (Magid 2002, 71–72). Certainly with its calling card, "It's not TV ... it's HBO," the company tries to distinguish itself from other networks and from the low expectations often associated with television. However, the intermixing of television and cinema aesthetics is part of a much larger picture. As John Caldwell argues (1995), the mingling of aesthetics, along with narrative modes, techniques, and personnel, took extensive root in the 1980s and has been pervasive ever since.

Beyond prompting reflection on production and exhibition as distinctive foundations for cinema, this intimate relationship raises issues about authorship and genre. Personnel identified with Hollywood filmmaking regularly "cross over" into work on cable programs. In fact, each industry has exchanged and capitalized upon the talent of executives, directors, writers, performers, and others who fluidly move between corporations and media. As just one example of this, John Frankenheimer (who began his career helming dramas for CBS's *Playhouse 90*) directed films such as *The Birdman of Alcatraz* (1962), *The Manchurian Candidate* (1962), *Ronin* (1998), and *Reindeer Games* (2000). He also directed "made-fors" for HBO (including *Against the Wall* (1994), *The Burning Season* (1994), and *Path to War* (2002)) and for TNT (*Andersonville* (1996) and *George Wallace* (1997)). Further, he produced a short for a BMW-sponsored internet omnibus production (*The Hire* (2001–2002)), thus working in broadcast television, film, cable, and the internet during his career. Such crossings do not erase all distinctions among media industries; rather, they continue to indicate a pervasive reciprocity among them. In this light, authorship emerges as an inclusive and capacious category, where analyzing a director's work in all media is essential. Multiple media animate the development of a director's themes and style, indicating, from a different angle, the significance of continuities among film, cable, and other industries for the study of directors regarded as film authors.

The example of John Dahl suggests, as well, that cable films have implications for genre criticism. *Red Rock West* and *The Last Seduction* offer inventive nuances to the noir formula, setting the action in a small town rather than an urban milieu, a change with which others, like the Coen Brothers, have also experimented. In such cases, the decay and despair characterizing the genre's slick urban streets find their way into America's heartland, demonstrating that the corrosive effects of ennui and corruption know no regional bounds. Moreover, *The Last Seduction* is hailed as a film by "modern film noir expert Dahl" that boasts a femme fatale who makes Barbara

Stanwyck in *Double Indemnity* (1944) "look like Snow White" (Maltin 2008, 772). In Dahl's capable hands, then, the film lends new ruthless and hypersexual dimensions to the genre.

Since Dahl's films were given theatrical exhibition, their cable origins become a moot point and they tacitly find a place in the genre's history and canon. However, cable movies without US theatrical distribution – including long-form narratives, such as series and miniseries – are also clearly a part of these histories. For instance, created by David Milch, HBO's Western series *Deadwood* (2004–2006), with its cramped, muddy town and depiction of progress as defined by successive waves of increasingly corrupt and brutal forms of capitalism, deconstructs both the genre's classic visual tropes of magnificent vistas and its themes of progress via enlightened capitalist enterprise. Taking to excess the Western's typical focus on drinking and bloodletting, the series also emphasizes the grotesque Rabelaisian body, with its primary functions and afflictions on full display. By virtue of its critical position on the genre's mythology, the cable series occupies an important place in its history. Like *The Sopranos*, *Deadwood* also demonstrates how thoroughly defined texts are, whether they originate on television or in theaters, by generic intertexts drawn from multiple sources – from pulp fiction and TV to theatrical pictures (see, e.g., Heller 2008, 42–51). Cable Westerns, gangster shows, family melodramas, and other genres belong not only to TV genre history, but to a history that recognizes and studies cross-media manifestations as integral to scholarship and teaching. In this mediaverse of revolving doors, the Milchs and Chases of cable have already emerged as auteurs within these genres (see, e.g., McCabe & Akass 2008, 86–89), making distinctions between film and television genres additionally difficult to sustain.

Informing and underlying this cross-fertilization and concomitant reconsideration of media specificity is, of course, the media industries' increasing conglomeration and diversification since the 1970s. Recognizing that conflicts of interest between different media concerns still occur, Michele Hilmes comments: "The 1980s atmosphere of across-the-board deregulation combined with a sudden burst in technological development of distribution channels removed the artificially maintained barriers to previous integration of the various arms of the entertainment business" (1990, 195). HBO is both part and beneficiary of the vertical and horizontal integration of media conglomerates. Its parent company, Time Warner, is involved in the publishing, film, broadcast, cable, and satellite TV, music, print, and theme park businesses, exemplifying the kind of horizontal integration and diversification characteristic of major media conglomerates. Along with its fellow conglomerates, Time Warner demonstrates vertical integration as well. It has, for instance, used its subsidiaries (such as Lorimar Telepictures Corporation and film studio Warner Bros.) to create programming for its cable stations, while these stations in turn have distributed films produced by Time Warner companies.

HBO's adaptation of Candace Bushnell's *Sex and the City* represents a vivid recent example of horizontal and vertical synergy. Grand Central Publishing, a licensee of HBO, originally printed the novel, which HBO then made into a TV series of the same name. In 2008, four years after the series ended its run, HBO coproduced with fellow Time Warner subsidiary New Line Cinema, the first movie version, followed by another in 2010. The TV series *Sex and the City* has been syndicated on TBS and WGN, both owned by Time Warner; the theatrically released films were distributed, via Warner's home video division, on HBO and other networks. From the ground up, multiple media are vitally linked to one another in a shifting series of relationships, endorsing a dizzying circularity among parts.

The growth of media conglomerates and the aftermarket has distinct implications for the feature film narrative. In these contexts, film is necessarily renarrativized and repositioned for consumption. Scholars writing about the media convergence that has resulted from horizontal integration discuss "transmedia storytelling" as an overarching principle that defines the contemporary repurposing and circulation of narrative across media platforms. In transmedia storytelling, a text's fictional world is spun off into different media, including video games, animated movies, novels, action figures, and so on (see, e.g., Jenkins 2006, 20–21, on *The Matrix*, 1999).

As in the case of *Sex and the City* – its existence as novel, TV series, film franchise, and merchandising epicenter – narrative is potentially indefinitely prolonged, told and retold, through a successive and selective foregrounding of its various elements for redeployment in new media or forms. As we have seen, the reissue – another form of repurposing – results in renarrativizing and prolongation as well, albeit in a different way. Recut, censored, digitally remastered, repackaged into film festivals or marathons, defined as an exemplar of a network's brand, and shaped by host commentary into classic, camp, and/or nostalgia piece, the same film undergoes transformation. As it circulates, the proliferation of reissues on cable and in other media converts the film into a never-ending and continually refined story. In the process, it may appear to be omnipresent, becoming especially memorable to viewers, subject to reassessment, or relegated to the status of video wallpaper – a backdrop to household activities.

As Dana Heller argues, conglomerates and the aftermarket make the "lines separating systems of production and channels of distribution" especially permeable, while demonstrating the "ongoing merger between the film and television industries." As film has become a medium intimately associated with the home, the "difference between movies made for television and movies made for theatrical distribution" becomes all but irrelevant (Heller 2008, 44). As we have seen, movies enter into patterns of production, distribution, and exhibition that clearly unite the film and cable industries and their artifacts. With constant recycling in the aftermarket, a film's origin – in a film studio or cable network, for example – matters less with regard to its specificity as a medium than the principle of its continued circulation – its lifeblood. In fact, as almost every commercial narrative is released in ancillary formats, narrative origins may become obscured or ultimately inconsequential. Although some outlets may categorize their holdings and thus maintain distinctions (e.g., in video stores TV series on DVD often are displayed separately from films), from a consumer's point of view films and broadcast and cable series each provide consumable narrative worlds that can be distinguished by length, if by no other means. While theaters and home spaces offer different kinds of viewing experiences, the realms of exhibition and consumption suggest possibilities of blurring between these experiences. That is, feature films can become part of a series or become serialized – as in, respectively, the TV marathon or the case of the home viewer who watches a film in installments – just as a cable series can attain the flowing, uninterrupted status of a coherent feature experience via boxed sets of series or viewer marathons that transcend the parameters of a single episode. Since most feature narrative forms in the US end up in the home market, achieve their most prolonged life and exposure in this venue, and are subject to these and other varied modes of consumption, sites such as cable achieve lasting importance aesthetically and experientially as places of cinema. While this impact is often associated with the rise of digital technology, cable has long tested the boundaries of what is ordinarily conceived of as film in the midst of a complicated mediascape.

Conclusion

Despite the onslaught of competitive forms such as VHS and DVD, cable TV has continued to represent a significant exhibition venue for films and, hence, a major means of accessing movies for audiences. In its capacity as producer, distributor, and exhibitor of feature films, cable has, since the late 1970s, represented an extraordinarily important purveyor of Hollywood cinema. As a bountiful recycler of features, cable represents an archive or "treasure trove" of films old and new, an influential means of branding and reframing film identities through programming strategies, a site that affects the creation of classic and cult movies, and an instigator of nostalgia. Further, the study of cable as producer and distributor of films can productively complicate notions of theatrical cinema, promote a more inclusive sense of authorship and genre history, interrogate the specificity of cinema as a medium in an era of media convergence, and raise questions about what happens to notions of specificity and narrative in the distribution and reception of feature-length and long-form storytelling.

Cinema's televisual history and cable TV's role in that history prompt examination of cinema's social life, its migration and mutation across time and space by virtue of its relationship to television, digital media, and other windows of access waiting in the wings. This is an issue that pertains not only to film history, but to an understanding of the medium itself. Cable, like other Hollywood connections, produces and presents movies in ways that inalterably affect them, in the process raising aesthetic, critical, and historical issues, as well as enlarging our sense of the many forms that motion pictures assume in their ambient lives. By recognizing cinema's indelible inter-media associations, film studies can more fully engage the de facto complication of film as an object of inquiry – not to flatten all distinctions between media, but to examine and weigh the complex relationships between narrative forms that have characterized film's long ties to television and other industries and media involved in its production and circulation.

Notes

1. A 1975 FCC decision restricted pay cable to films that were either more than ten or less than two years old. At the time, a quality Hollywood film would go through several runs on the big screen over a two-year period. Through the FCC's provision, pay cable could only show films that were either old or, if more recent, of inferior quality. Thus, the decision allowed Hollywood to maintain hold, for a time, over its most valuable properties for theatrical reissue and for the broadcast syndication market.
2. Satellite distribution, itself, was affected by President Richard Nixon's "Open Skies" policy and a 1972 compliant FCC ruling that allowed big business, among other interests, to enter freely the satellite industry (see, e.g., Mullen 2003, 90–91).
3. Although we might think of cable and satellite TV as distinctly different, insofar as direct satellite delivery of programming to homes operates without the cable company as middleman, cable TV, as we now know it, would not exist without the satellite assist.
4. See Segrave 1999, 170–172, and Arango 2008 on the attempts to create, respectively, the Premiere Channel in 1980 and the Epix channel in 2008–2009 (the latter of which is still in business).
5. See Mullen on cable's multiple methods of reframing rerun material (2003, 163–172).
6. Since the aftermarket allows viewers intimate contact with films in their private surroundings, it also has a direct impact on film viewing. With the assistance of various technologies, viewers can copy and manipulate the films they watch at home, while also being able to amass their own libraries, stoking the activity of collecting and the personalization of film libraries.

References

Alexander, Ron. (1989). "Movie Buffs Find a Trove on Cable." *New York Times*, January 12, at http://www.nytimes.com/1989/01/12/arts/movie-buffs-find-a-trove-on-cable.html (accessed December 2010).

Arango, Tim. (2008). "Paramount Ready to End Movie Sales to Showtime." *New York Times*, April 21, C1, C6.

Balio, Tino (ed.). (1990). *Hollywood in the Age of Television*. Boston: Unwin Hyman.

Brooks, Tim, & Marsh, Earle (1999). *The Complete Directory to Prime Time Network and Cable TV Shows, 1946–Present*. New York: Ballantine.

Caldwell, John. (1995). *Televisuality: Style, Crisis, and Authority in American Television*. New Brunswick, NJ: Rutgers University Press.

"Colin Callender." (2008). Hollywood.com. At http://www.hollywood.com/celebrity/Colin_Callender/192194 (accessed December 2010).

Carter, Bill. (1992). "Television Notes." *New York Times*, March 31, at http://query.nytimes.com/gst/fullpage.html?res=9E0CE7D6113DF932A05750C0A964958260&sec=&spon=&pagewanted=2 (accessed December 2010).

Edgerton, Gary. (2008). "Introduction." In Gary. R. Edgerton & Jeffrey. P. Jones (eds), *The Essential HBO Reader* (pp. 1–20). Lexington: University Press of Kentucky.

Edgerton, Gary, & Jones, Jeffrey. (2008). "HBO's Ongoing Legacy." In Gary. R. Edgerton & Jeffrey. P. Jones (eds), *The Essential HBO Reader* (pp. 315–330). Lexington: University Press of Kentucky.

Fabrikant, Geraldine. (1993). "The Media Business: Making 'Barbarians' Had Its Perils for HBO." *New York Times*, March 29, at http://www.nytimes.com/1993/03/29/business/the-media-business-making-barbarians-had-its-perils-for-hbo.html (accessed December 2010).

Fryman, John E., & Hudson, Jerry. (1993). "Turner Network Television (TNT)." In Robert G. Picard (ed.), *The Cable Networks Handbook* (pp. 190–196). Riverside, CA: Carpelan.

Gale, Thomson. (2001). "Three Tiers of Made-for-TV Movies." *Video Age International*, 21.2 (February), 1.

Ginsberg, Steve. (1994). "Media Moguls Launch New Cable TV Movie Channel." *Los Angeles Business Journal*, February 7, at http://www.allbusiness.com/north-america/united-states-california-metro-areas/429129–1.html (accessed December 2010).

Goldstein, Gregg, & Nordyke, Kimberly. (2008). "Showtime Signs Movie Deal with Weinstein Co." *Hollywood Reporter*, July 15, at http://uk.reuters.com/article/industryNews/idUKBNG12597320080716 (accessed December 2010).

Gomery, Douglas. (1988). "Hollywood's Hold on the New Television Technologies." *Screen*, 29.2, 82–89.

Gomery, Douglas. (1992). *Shared Pleasures: A History of Movie Presentation in the United States*. Madison: University of Wisconsin Press.

Granger, Rod. (1993). "After a Quick Start, Plexing Finds Niche." *Multichannel News*, March 15, at http://www.highbeam.com/doc/1G1–13885660.html (accessed December 2010).

Greenstein, Jane. (1991). "HBO Begins to Plex Muscles." *Multichannel News*, August 5. at http://www.highbeam.com/doc/1G1–11151140.html (accessed December 2010).

Heeter, Carrie, & Greenberg, Bradley S. (1988). *Cable Viewing*. Norwood, NJ: Ablex.

Heller, Dana. (2008). "Films." In Gary. R. Edgerton & Jeffrey. P. Jones (eds), *The Essential HBO Reader* (pp. 42–51). Lexington: University Press of Kentucky.

Hilmes, Michele. (1990). *Hollywood and Broadcasting: From Radio to Cable*. Urbana: University of Illinois Press.

Jenkins, Henry. (2006). *Convergence Culture: Where Old and New Media Collide*. New York: New York University Press.

Klinger, Barbara. (2006). *Beyond the Multiplex: Cinema, New Technologies, and the Home*. Berkeley: University of California Press.

Klinger, Barbara. (2007). "Cinema's Shadow: Reconsidering Non-Theatrical Exhibition." In Richard Maltby, Melvyn Stokes, & Robert C. Allen (eds), *Going to the Movies: Hollywood and the Social Experience of Cinema* (pp. 273–290). Exeter, UK: University of Exeter Press.

Kompare, Derek. (2005). *Rerun Nation: How Repeats Invented American Television*. London: Routledge.

McCabe, Janet, & Akass, Kim. (2008). "It's Not TV, It's HBO's Original Programming." In Marc Leverette, Brian L. Ott, & Cara Louise Buckley (eds.), *It's Not TV: Watching HBO in the Post-Television Era* (pp. 83–93). New York: Routledge.

Magid, Ron. (2002). "Family Plots." *American Cinematographer*, 83.11, 71–72.

Maltin, Leonard. (2008). *2008 Movie Guide*. New York: Signet Books.

Mullen, Megan. (2003). *The Rise of Cable Programming in the United States*. Austin: University of Texas Press.

NCTA (National Cable & Telecommunications Association). (2008). "2008 Industry Overview," pp. 1–19, at http://i.ncta.com/ncta_com/PDFs/NCTA_Annual_Report_05.16.08.pdf (accessed December 2010).

NCTA (2011). "Basic Video Customers, 1975–2010," at http://www.ncta.com/Stats/BasicCableSubscribers.aspx (accessed July 2011).

O'Connor, John J. (1995). "Critic's Notebook; Those Hybrid Made-for-TV Movies." *New York Times*, April 20, at http://www.nytimes.com/1995/04/20/arts/critic-s-notebook-those-hybrid-made-for-tv-movies.html (accessed December 2010).

Parsons, Patrick R., & Frieden, Robert M. (1998). *The Cable and Satellite Television Industries*. Needham Heights, MA: Allyn & Bacon.

Picturehouse. (2008). "Picturehouse and Warner Independent Pictures to Cease Operations." *Picturehouse*, May 8, at http://www.picturehouse.com/press/20080508_picturehouse.php (accessed December 2010).

Pinsker, Beth. (1994). "Pop Culture News: John Dahl." EW.com. December 30, at http://www.ew.com/ew/article/0,,305089,00.html (accessed December 2010).

Santo, Avi. (2008). "Para-television and Discourses of Distinction: The Culture of Production at HBO." In Marc Leverette, Brian L. Ott, & Cara Louise Buckley (eds.), *It's Not TV: Watching HBO in the Post-Television Era* (pp. 19–45). New York: Routledge.

Segrave, Kerry. (1999). *Movies at Home: How Hollywood Came to Television*. Jefferson, NC: McFarland.

Sherman, Stratford P. (1984). "Coming Soon: Hollywood's Epic Shakeout." *Fortune*, April 30, p. 208.

Silver Screen Partners. (1997)."Silver Screen Partners LP Annual Report." US Securities and Exchange Commission, at http://www.secinfo.com/dUK18.77.htm#1stPage, pp. 2–3 (accessed December 2010).

Smith, Sally B. (1984). "HBO Starts Producing Movies for Theaters." *New York Times*, February 13, C18.

Stelter, Brian. (2008a). "Cable Networks Trying to Build on Their Gains in Ratings." *New York Times*, May 26, C5.

Stelter, Brian. (2008b). "No Longer Young, Nick at Nite Plans to Show It Can Be Nimble." *New York Times*, July 29, C8.

TimeWarner. (2010). "HBO."At http://www.timewarner.com/corp/businesses/detail/hbo/index.html (accessed December 2010).

Wasko, Janet. (1995). *Hollywood in the Information Age: Beyond the Silver Screen*. Austin: University of Texas Press.

Waterman, David, & Grant, August. (1991). "Cable Television as an Aftermarket." *Journal of Broadcasting and Electronic Media*, 35.2, 179–188.

22

Plasmatics and Prisons

The Morph and the Spectacular Emergence of CGI

Kristen Whissel

Professor, University of California at Berkeley, United States

In the age of **computer-generated images (CGI)** and **digital visual effects**, a question arises as to whether such technological advances are simply crowd-pleasing gimmicks or central tropes in advancing the larger aesthetic design and thematic/ideological concerns of the films that incorporate them – as most films now do, to greater or lesser degrees. Kristen Whissel, in compellingly close readings of ***Terminator 2: Judgment Day***, ***Dark City***, ***The Matrix***, and ***X-Men***, argues that the **digital morph** is a technique central to the ideological project of each film. Rooted in the **protean possibilities** first explored in early **film animation** that "collapses distinctions and violates systems of classification," the morph becomes thematically crucial in narratives counterposing incarceral conditions of enslavement with the desire for liberation, thus enabling characters magically to transcend restrictive boundaries. In films more grounded in everyday life, like *The Mask* and *The Nutty Professor*, Whissle argues that the morph "allows 'repressed' elements of the protagonists' psyches … to find expression through the new selves they embody." Her essay shares ground with Bart Beaty on the blockbuster superhero and J. D. Connor on independent blockbusters in this volume and with Kirsten Thompson on cel animation in Volume I.

Additional terms, names, and concepts: time-lapse photography, plasmaticness

In the final decade of the twentieth century, the use of computer-generated images (CGI) and digital visual effects became a hallmark of popular, live-action American blockbusters. Accomplished mostly in postproduction, such practices ranged from color adjustment at the level of the pixel to spectacular visual effects designed to astonish audiences. One of the first such recognizable spectacular effects was the digital morph, which created smooth transformations of a "source" image into a "target" image using software programs to cross-dissolve and warp images. In Ron Howard's *Willow* (1988) and James Cameron's

American Film History: Selected Readings, 1960 to the Present, First Edition. Edited by Cynthia Lucia, Roy Grundmann, and Art Simon.

The Abyss (1989), characters and creatures shape-shift their surface appearance in single scenes organized around the display of this astonishing effect; in later films, particularly in Cameron's *Terminator 2: Judgment Day* (1991), the Wachowski Brothers' *The Matrix* (1999), and Bryan Singer's *X-Men* (2000), the ability to morph defines characters who exercise this (spectacular) power with thrilling dramatic effects. In addition to giving bodies seemingly unfettered capacity for instantaneous change, the morph also allowed landscapes and cityscapes to transform themselves with fluid ease in films like Peter Jackson's *Heavenly Creatures* (1994) and Alex Proyas's *Dark City* (1998), while in films like Chuck Russell's *The Mask* (1994) and Tom Shadyac's *The Nutty Professor* (1996) morphing gave the human body comic plasticity that allowed it to stretch, bulge, and bend in often comic and cartoonish fashion.

The morph's cultural and aesthetic precursors are numerous, yet within the history of the cinema, its chief forerunner is the overlapping dissolve, which originated in nineteenth-century magic lantern shows, was a staple of early trick films, and was an important optical effect in creating monstrous metamorphoses in classical films such as Rouben Mamoulian's *Dr. Jekyll and Mr. Hyde* (1932). Scott Bukatman has argued that the rapidity of the morph's transformations and its exaggeration and acceleration of everyday perceptions of continuity and discontinuity place its origins, in part, in time-lapse photography (2003, 134–136). Perhaps the most important precursor, though, is the digital morph's relation to film animation. Unbound by the laws of physics, animated bodies and objects have transcended the fixed categories and oppositions that define our experience of the world and have given otherwise discrete, solid forms the ability to stretch, expand, shrink, flatten, merge, and transform. Lev Manovich has argued that digital practices such as the morph, which make it possible to "cut, bend, stretch and stitch digitized film images into something with perfect photographic credibility," represent a return to the proto-cinematic practices of the previous century, whereby images were painted and animated by hand:

> At the turn of the twentieth century, cinema delegated these manual techniques to animation and defined itself as a recording medium. As cinema enters the digital age, these techniques are again becoming commonplace in the filmmaking process. Consequently, cinema can no longer be clearly distinguished from animation. (2001, 295)

Manovich's arguments about the return of cinema to its origins in animation are apt for thinking about the relationship of the photo-realistic digital morph to the pliant, fluid, graphic transformations that have always been the province of animation. As scholars have argued, the digital morph exploits the liberation of the computer-generated image from indexicality and the laws of physics to which the photographic film image is subject. This freedom – which is the freedom of animation – was the focus of Sergei Eisenstein's critical writings on Disney (first published in 1941), which provide an important conceptual framework for thinking about how cinematic metamorphosis has historically functioned in the films in which it appears. Eisenstein begins his analysis of Disney's animated shape-shifting creatures by describing the sheer joy he experiences watching the figural transformations undergone by sea creatures in *Merbabies* (1938). He cites as "an unforgettable symbol" of Disney's "whole creative work" the image of "a family of octopuses on four legs, with a fifth serving as a tail, and a sixth – a trunk" and exclaims, "How much (imaginary) divine omnipotence there is in this!" (1986, 5). Eisenstein argues that such images display a sustained "mockery of form" that exploits "the appeal of the myth of Proteus" – that is, the ability physically to assume any form without restriction or restraint. He gives this protean power the name "plasmaticness" and explains:

> for here we have a being represented in drawing, a being of definite form, a being which has attained a definite appearance, and which behaves like the primal protoplasm, not yet possessing a "stable" form, but capable of assuming any form and which, skipping along the rungs of the evolutionary ladder, attaches itself to any and all forms of animal existence. (Eisenstein 1986, 21)

Plasmatic images provoke delight not simply because of their inventive playfulness or potential as a "flashy trick" (indeed, Eisenstein rejects the latter); rather, for Eisenstein the plasmatic image fascinates precisely because it violates standardized forms of classification. Hence, he continues:

> In *Merbabies*, a striped fish in a cage is transformed into a tiger and roars with the voice of a lion or panther. Octopuses turn into elephants. A fish – into a donkey. A departure from one's self. From once and forever prescribed norms of nomenclature, form and behavior. (Eisenstein 1986, 5)

Plasmaticness mobilizes the fantasy of transcending any type of categorization or boundary – zoological, behavioral, social, spatial, and temporal. Hence it is not simply the physical boundaries of the body that plasmaticness transcends, but all of the attending categories or forms of classification that attach themselves to any being. In the process, plasmaticness makes possible the temporal dream of "skipping along the evolutionary ladder," making a leap forward as possible and as pleasurable as a regression back to a more "primal" state of being – that of "originary plasma" itself. Hence plasmaticness brings to life a delightful, upended world that collapses distinctions and violates systems of classification and laws that prescribe, delimit, hierarchize and confine. Indeed, Eisenstein arrives at the conclusion that "a single, common prerequisite of attractiveness shows through in all these examples: a rejection of once-and-forever allotted form, freedom from ossification, the ability dynamically to assume any form" (1986, 6).

Just as Bukatman links the digital morph to cultural fantasies surrounding its "promise of endless transformation and the opportunity to freely make, unmake, and remake oneself" (2003, 134), Eisenstein argued that delightful images of plasmaticness were particularly valuable and appealing in the context of modernity's regimentation and regulation of every aspect of life. In this regard, Eisenstein explains, "Metamorphosis is a direct protest against the standardly immutable" and enacts a "triumph[s] over *all* fetters, over *everything* that binds" (1986, 43, 4). Standardization, hyperrationalization, fetters that bind – these are the defining features of modern life that call forth both Disney's playfully metamorphic characters and his audiences' gleeful response to them. Indeed, Eisenstein claimed that

> [in] a country and social order with such a mercilessly standardized and mechanically measured existence, which is difficult to call life, the sight of such "omnipotence" (that is, the ability to become "whatever you wish"), cannot but hold a sharp degree of attractiveness. (1986, 21)

Hence, the plasmatic merbabies provide audiences with "a momentary, imaginary, comical liberation from the timelock mechanism of American life" (1986, 22).

The following will consider the way in which the digital morph takes up – and even mediates – this dialectic between the "omnipotence of plasma" and "everything that binds" in the fictional cinematic worlds in which it appears. It is precisely the struggle between an ossified, standardized existence that imprisons and enslaves and the dynamic shape-shifting of metamorphosis that is at stake in a number of films made at the end of the twentieth century that feature the digital morph, particularly *Terminator 2: Judgment Day*, *Dark City*, *The Matrix*, and *X-Men*. In these films, the morph embodies and enacts this narrative struggle even as it functions as an astonishing, spectacular effect. This dual function should be no surprise, for, as Eisenstein argues of animated films featuring plasmatic metamorphosis,

> It's natural to expect that such a strong tendency of the transformation of stable forms into forms of mobility could not be confined solely to means of form: this tendency exceeds the boundaries of form and extends to subject and theme. (1986, 22)

Prison Worlds and Liquid Metal

James Cameron's groundbreaking film *Terminator 2: Judgment Day* is set in a world divided between two potential states: one defined by radically closed, carceral settings in which human identity and history are predetermined, and another in which identity and time can be made and unmade by human agency set upon an "open road" toward an unknown future. The film's narrative follows an arc that begins in the first extreme and by the end, reaches for the second. At the beginning of *Terminator 2*, the fate of humanity seems predetermined: Sarah Connor's voiceover narration confirms that Judgment Day has come and gone, the war against the machines is well underway, and that SkyNet has sent a second terminator to the past to eliminate her son, John Connor, the leader of the human resistance against the machines. Following the title sequence, which displays a violent battle in the war taking place in the year 2029, the film takes us back in time as the first terminator, the T-101, arrives in Los Angeles when John is just a boy and Sarah is incarcerated for crimes committed in her attempt to prevent the rise of SkyNet and the arrival of Judgment Day. Her prior attempts to escape the asylum have failed, leaving her to dream repeatedly of the impending moment when nuclear bombs will kill three billion people on earth. Given the film's flashback structure and the content of Sarah's voiceover narration, the arrival of Judgment Day seems inevitable – an historical *fait accompli.*

Given such a context, in which history functions like a "time-lock mechanism" that moves inexorably toward annihilation, it is not surprising that identity has become ossified and that space is defined by radically closed settings surrounded by prison gates, chain-link fences, armed guards, and high-tech surveillance. In *Terminator 2*, neither Sarah nor John has an identity beyond the respective roles they both will play in relation to the impending war with the machines: John is humanity's savior and Sarah is his mother and protector. There is no mystery to the process of becoming for either: Even before he was born, John Connor was already and inescapably his future self – the "great military leader" who sends a comrade back in time to make sure he is conceived; in turn, Sarah's identity is a matter of her success or failure to fulfill her predestined role as John's mother and guardian. If she succeeds humanity will endure; if she fails, humanity is doomed. To protect John, Sarah must escape from the maximum-security wing of an asylum and destroy the hand and chip of the T-1000, which is protected behind layers of high-tech security at the Cyberdyne headquarters. Moreover, in *Terminator 2*, space is locked down and hierarchized, such that the protagonists cannot simply pass through it; rather, they must break through formidable barriers that segment, restrict, and confine. Even the spaces through which the protagonists flee throughout much of the film – the hallways of the asylum, LA's aqueducts and freeways, the corridors running behind stores in a mall, and the steel plant where the film ends – are like mazes through which the T-1000 (and the dreaded future he represents) relentlessly pursues them. Even in Sarah's dreams, all escape routes lead directly to the spatiotemporal dead end of Judgment Day. Hence, after she is beaten by hospital orderlies, Sarah dreams of Kyle, who leads her out of the asylum through doors that open onto the perimeter of a fenced-in playground moments before the blinding flash from the nuclear strike awakens her from her too-real nightmare. Throughout *Terminator 2*, the chain-link fence – which Sarah rattles while screaming unheard warnings to parents and children on the other side – materializes the historical impasse Judgment Day imposes before future human history.

Two scenes linked by cross-cutting are particularly important to the connection the film makes between Sarah's incarceration and inevitable arrival of Judgment Day. The camera cuts from Sarah as she awakens from her nightmare to the room where she undergoes her review. A close-up of a monitor shows a video recording of Sarah narrating the same nightmare from which we have just seen her awaken. The shot dollies out from the monitor to reveal windows caged by chain-link fencing and later, a steadicam shot pulls back even further into an observation room behind a large pane of one-way glass where medical students videotape and analyze the current interview. As the multiple framed layers of security and surveillance suggest, this review will not lead to the new freedom Sarah desires (transfer to minimum security and a better chance for escape), without which her fate – along with humanity's – is sealed. To emphasize this idea, halfway through the interview the camera cuts to Miles Dyson at Cyberdyne headquarters as he moves through layers of security to retrieve the T-1000's CPU and arm – the very technology that will enable him to invent SkyNet. Hence all the elements that keep history moving toward nuclear Armageddon – Sarah, the chip, and the cybernetic arm – are locked away in high-security spaces. Though Sarah initially disavows the nightmare she has just watched herself narrate onscreen, the present-day interview ultimately ends in the same manner as the previous one: Sarah hysterically warns Dr Silberman about Judgment Day and is violently restrained, sedated, and confined to her cell. The repeated motif of the nightmare – dreamed, recounted, disavowed, then reaffirmed – defines the present purely in relation to Judgment Day: As she says to Dr Silberman in the video, "God, you think you're safe and alive? You're already dead! Him, you, everybody – you're dead already! … Cause I know it happens! It happens!" The asylum itself is meant to be terminal: It is a locked-down, deadly space in which Sarah, and with her, future human history, might come to an end.

It is no surprise that a fictional world in which space, time, and identity are so starkly overdetermined and so thoroughly closed should call forth a figure of radical plasmaticness that possesses the power to transcend space (it can pass through any barrier), time (it travels to the past in order to change the future), and identity (it can mimic the superficial appearance of anyone) that the protagonists lack. In contrast to Sarah's imprisonment and powerlessness to thwart the arrival of Judgment Day, the T-1000 moves back in time to change the course of history and demonstrates, even before he appears onscreen, his ability to transcend the material barriers that confine Sarah: The film signals his arrival by a large circle burned through the same kind of chain-link fence that defines the mise-en-scène of the asylum and Sarah's nightmare. The T-1000's transcendental plasticity is most spectacularly demonstrated, of course, by his ability to morph, a power that gives dramatic and even terrifying elaboration to the violent conflict the film stages between the protagonists' desire for freedom and the machines' drive for complete control. Hence, the T-1000's most spectacular morphs take place in scenes in which the protagonists struggle to escape locked-down spaces and in the process, their predetermined futures.

In keeping with this idea, the T-1000's efforts to break into the maximum-security ward parallel Sarah's efforts to break out. To penetrate the asylum's security system, the T-1000 mimics the facility's architecture and personnel: first, it "becomes" the hall floor to evade notice, then morphs its surface appearance from the checkerboard floor to the security guard, Louis, to gain entry into the maximum-security wing. By mimicking the security system he must bypass, the T-1000 demonstrates the purpose of its own digital morph: It is the perfect technology for overcoming such systems. In the process, the T-1000's morph foregrounds what the film has already made clear at the level of story and character: By incarcerating Sarah and leaving John unprotected, the law unwittingly colludes with the machines to make Judgment Day, and a machine-made future without John Connor, into reality. There is, therefore, an inverse relationship between the T-1000's figural plasmaticness and its programmed function: Its ability to transform itself and its potential to change the future are in the service of ending humanity's ability to transform itself through time and to make and unmake its own fate. The T-1000 is a terminal figure of transcendental freedom that works on behalf of humanity's "end."

The T-1000's spectacular morphs allow the broader dialectic of radical freedom and confinement that structures the film to find dramatic expression when the T-1000 arrives at the asylum just after Sarah has seen surveillance images of the T-101 (which she assumes has been sent to terminate John) and her desire to escape becomes most acute. Indeed, Sarah's efforts to break out of the asylum parallel the T-1000's efforts to break in. Both initially evade hospital personnel passively (the T-1000 mimics the surface of the floor; Sarah feigns catatonia and lies motionless on her cot) only to assault and steal the weapons of the security personnel each tricks. Even Sarah's use of "Liquid Rooter" (which she threatens to inject into her hostage, Dr Silberman, if the guards and orderlies don't obey her commands to unlock gates and doors) is a low-tech version of the digital plasmaticness that allows the T-1000 to ooze through the prison bars that stand in his way. In this protracted sequence, Sarah and the T-1000 embody opposing relations to history: While her struggle for freedom serves the idea that "the future is not set: there is no fate but what we make for ourselves," the T-1000's plasmatic brutality and spatial transcendence work to foreclose upon humanity's future and ensure that much of humanity is, as Sarah warns, "dead already."

The spectacular morphs that take place in these scenes elaborate and charge with visual pleasure this conflict between freedom and "fetters," possibility and fate. The most astonishing transformation – the floor-to-guard morph – takes place immediately after the T-1000 enters the asylum. After asking a receptionist for Sarah's location, the T-1000 disappears when Silberman and a group of detectives and security guards walk toward the reception area. After Louis, the security guard, locks the door behind the police, a close-up shows his shoe strike the linoleum floor as he walks back toward reception, and the T-1000 begins to rise slowly out of the floor. The camera cuts to Louis at the coffee machine as the T-1000 continues to rise up and morph behind him, still covered with the checkerboard pattern of the linoleum floor. The sound of coffee filling (and taking the shape of) the cup provides an apt sound effect for the liquid metal man as it "pours" itself into the form of the

Figure 22.1 T-1000 morphs from checkerboard floor to security guard in *Terminator 2: Judgment Day* (1991, director and producer James Cameron).

guard. As he morphs into a perfect mimicry of Louis, the latter announces to the receptionist that the vending machine has dispensed him a coffee cup (printed with playing cards representing a hand of poker) with a full house; this seems like an inside joke between the two machines, for the two pairs of jacks visible on the side of his cup match the "two of a kind" (of decidedly different suits) now standing in the hallway. As Louis examines the cup, the surface of the T-1000 changes from the checkerboard pattern, to liquid metal to a perfect copy of Louis. When Louis turns around, he stands face to face with his double. The T-1000 points his index finger between Louis's eyes; the finger morphs into a metal lance that instantly pierces through Louis's head and kills him. The T-1000 drags the guard into a closet and walks calmly to the reception area and is buzzed into the maximum-security wing where Sarah is confined. Hence the morph allows T-1000 to embody an extreme and deadly version of everything Sarah desires for herself and humanity: freedom of mobility through space and time and the radical freedom to become, to make and remake one's self and one's fate. Just as the T-1000's morph enacts the violent appropriation of identity that implies the death of the target, the machine's possession of such qualities is itself an appropriation, a violent theft of internal, human desire (rather than simply outward, superficial appearance) that implies the termination of the "target" – humanity itself.

As Vivian Sobchack has noted, the radical freedom of form displayed by the T-1000's morphs – including the Janelle-T-1000 morph, or the T-1000-amorphous blob morphs that enable it to ooze through small openings – imply a transcendental relation to the major binaries used to differentiate and classify phenomena (human versus machine, male versus female, animate versus inanimate, subject versus object, liquid versus solid) (2000, 139). Yet, at the same time that it enjoys such freedom, it is important to note that the T-1000 is bound by codes and rules, a paradox suggested by the default persona the T-1000 assumes upon its arrival: that of a clean-cut white cop in the LAPD. On one hand, as the scenes detailing the T-1000's arrival at the asylum demonstrate, the terminator's cop persona, combined with his ability to morph, gives it the potential to be anybody, anywhere without raising suspicion (which contrasts sharply with the T-101, whose appearance alarms most who see him). In short, it gives him extraordinary freedom of mobility, and functions as an outward sign of the cyborg's masterful transcendence of the laws (of physics, of the state, etc.) that govern human existence. On the other, the cop persona is also an outward sign of the T-1000's subjection to another set of rules and laws – those that govern machine rather than human existence. By alluding to the law, the cop persona simultaneously implies the freedom *and* the limitations to which it is subject, for the T-1000's consistent return to this surface appearance contextualizes its radical plasmaticness to remind us that it is a machine programmed to complete a single mission – to kill John Connor. Built into the spectacle of his floor-to-guard transformation is the idea that the T-1000's morphs are controlled by a program and that the cyborg does not – and cannot – act independently. As Patrick Crogan notes, the black and white checkerboard pattern that covers the surface of the T-1000 as it morphs references the "standard surface rendering option in 3D computer imaging software packages" used to create morphs before *Terminator 2*, and thereby functions as a moment of computer-generated self-reflexivity (2000, 5). Moreover, Crogan argues that the checkerboard pattern "schematizes the computer screen's field of pixels and, more fundamentally still, the simple alternatives of the binary code – 'off' or 'on,' '0' or '1' – that are the building blocks of digital circuitry in computer chips" (2000, 5).

The foregrounding of software programs and code as the sources of the T-1000's figural freedom points to the idea that the T-1000 cannot deviate from his program, question it, change it, or rest until it is complete. Indeed, as the T-101 explains to John, anytime a Terminator is sent to the past, SkyNet sets its CPU to "read only." Hence all of the T-1000's actions – including his spectacular morphs – are harnessed to a single, inescapable goal. We can say then, that at the level of character, concept, and spectacular visual effects, the T-1000 embodies the dialectic between radical freedom and control, boundaries and their transcendence, that structures the entire film: The radical plasticity and (digital) figural freedom elaborated by the morph are the effect of a rule-based program that has been designed to help SkyNet eliminate John Connor, the last threat to machine sovereignty over humans and the only hope for future human sovereignty over machines.

Hence *Terminator 2*'s plasticity terrifies by virtue of its potential mechanization of historical time such that the course of human history is to be entirely made and unmade by machines and shaped toward a single end – the destruction of humanity – by liquid metal. In the process, history becomes radically plasmatic as well. The future can be known in advance, thanks to machines. The past can be altered from the future, so that a different future – the subordination of all time, space, and matter to machine life – shall come to pass. Hence the narrative of *Terminator 2* sways between radically opposed relationships to historical time that can be summed up by two phrases: "You're already dead!!!" and "The future is not set. There is no fate but what we make for ourselves." While the locked-down spaces of the first half of the film work in the service of the fatalist model, the open road becomes the spatial figuration of the second model. Indeed, as Sarah, John, Dyson, and the T-101 drive to Cyberdyne Headquarters to destroy the technological remains of the T-1000, Sarah's voiceover remarks, "The future, always so clear to me, had become like a black highway at night. We were in unchartered territory now, making up history as we went along." The open road becomes a structuring metaphor for the possibility of changing humanity's fate only after Sarah and John change the T-101's CPU from "read only," in the process changing humanity's future from "read only" as well.

"They're guarding all the doors and holding all the keys"

Like *Terminator 2*, *Dark City* and *The Matrix* feature spectacular morphs that are elaborated within prison-worlds populated by characters that have no control over their own fate. The eponymous Dark City, for example, is populated by a group of citizens stolen from earth by a race of aliens who experiment on them in order to find the "secrets" of the individual human soul. The Dark City that serves as the laboratory for these experiments is a discrete, isolated cityscape enclosed by a brick wall that, when pierced, opens on to the void of outer space. Here, the architectural body of the cityscape is plasmatic rather than the body of a character: Each midnight, the city's skyline morphs so that buildings expand in size or shrink, tenements turn into stately mansions, staircases stretch upwards or contract, doorways appear and disappear, and skyscrapers sprout from the ground and twist upwards toward the night sky. Hence, the Dark City is simultaneously a radically closed and radically variable setting – a prison with plasmatic walls – from which the protagonists cannot escape. Eddie, a cop who has come to realize he is the subject of a cruel experiment, wails as he observes the protagonist, John Murdoch, trying to find the express train that will take him out of the city to Shell Beach: "There's no way out you know! There's no way out of the city – believe me, I've tried!" The spiral Eddie draws obsessively in his notebooks and the maze in which another character, Dr Schreber, sets loose his lab rats invoke the topography and function of the city as a whole. Though the film waits until the end to disclose the true nature of its setting as a prison-laboratory floating in space, it hints at the truth of its inhabitants' enslavement throughout.

The plasmatics of the urban landscape in *Dark City* correspond to the plasmatics of individual human identity and history: Each midnight as the cityscape morphs, the aliens force their human captives to sleep so they can inject them with new memories and new identities. This process of transformation – called "tuning" by the aliens – robs the humans of their individual pasts (none of their memories are their own; rather, they are in possession of an amalgamation of memories that have been removed from the prisoners and mixed together by the aliens "like so much paint") and take away any ability to become and to exert a measure of agency over their own individual and collective futures. Put differently, the prisoners of the Dark City live in a perpetual present tense that is a collocation of variable pasts formed and reformed into different combinations. Only after John Murdoch awakens during a tuning does he understand the radically ahistorical, immaterial context in which he and his fellow "citizens" exist as he watches the city transform around him. Freedom for the protagonists of *Dark City* is the freedom to become (physically, psychologically) over time. Murdoch defeats the Strangers and before he destroys their technology, he "tunes" the city to restore human, earthly temporality to everyday life: He exposes the cityscape to a sun and surrounds it with water, creating tides and daytime that will alternate with night and thereby create the sense of a future and a past and, with both, the experience of duration.

Like *Terminator 2* and *Dark City*, *The Matrix* sets much of its action in prison-worlds: Both the digital world of the Matrix and the real world function as carceral spaces that keep humanity effectively enslaved by machines. When Morpheus first meets Neo, he defines the Matrix in a now familiar exchange:

> MORPHEUS: The Matrix is everywhere. It is all around us. Even now, in this very room. You can see it when you look out your window or when you turn on your television. You can feel it when you go to work, when you go to church, when you pay your taxes. It is the world that has been pulled over your eyes to blind you from the truth.
>
> NEO: What truth?
>
> MORPHEUS: That you are a slave Neo. That like everyone else, you were born into bondage, born into a prison that you cannot smell or taste or touch. A prison for your mind. Unfortunately, no one can be told what the Matrix is. You have to see it for yourself. This is your last chance. After this, there is no turning back. If you take the blue pill, the story ends and you wake up in your bed believing what you want to believe. You take the red pill you stay in Wonderland and I show you how deep the rabbit hole goes.

In *The Matrix*, the real-world-as-prison is veiled over by a machine-made, digital illusion that enables humans to experience enslavement as freedom. It is not incidental that Morpheus alludes to *Alice in Wonderland* as he explains to Neo the (pharmaceutical) options at hand, for in doing so he refers not simply to the protagonists' adventures in an alternate world that subtends the real one, but also to the plasticity of bodily form that both Alice and Neo experience in those alternate worlds. The strong relation between plasmatics and prisons (here, the former seems a response to or the outcome of the brute fact of the latter) is made clear when Neo, preparing to have his consciousness returned to his real body and the tiny plastic cell where it passively resides, touches the reflective surface of a cracked mirror only to have it ripple like a pool of liquid metal that slowly begins to engulf him as it provides a conduit to the real world. Once in the real world, such liquidity refers not to the "omnipotence of plasma" or the "myth of Proteus," but instead to the final form taken by each prisoner, who, upon death is liquefied and fed to the living. And while the carceral existence of humanity is invisible inside the Matrix, wide shots of the battery towers offer a terrifying glimpse of the real-world-as-prison: Tens of thousands of inert bodies occupy transparent, coffin-sized cells arranged on a series of massive towers that recede into deep space, giving credence to Morpheus's later assertion that, "As long as the Matrix exists, the human race will never be free."

In *The Matrix*, as in *Terminator 2*, the morph is the outcome of a dialectic that brings the narrative desire for radical freedom into violent conflict with settings starkly defined by incarceration and enslavement. Indeed the origins of the Matrix are associated with the human exploitation of digital plasmatics as a means for liberating humanity from bondage. Morpheus tells Neo, "when the Matrix was first built, there was a man born inside who had the ability to change whatever he wanted, to remake the Matrix as he saw fit. It was he who freed the first of us, taught us the truth." In the brief history narrated by Morpheus, the digital prison gives birth to the morph.

With this in mind, it is not surprising that the characters most strongly linked to the ability to morph – the Agents – exercise this power within the digital prison of the Matrix. Throughout the film, we see the Agents morph out of the bodies of a range of minor characters – a helicopter pilot, several military policemen, and a homeless man asleep on a subway platform. As Morpheus explains of the Agents, "They can move into and out of any software still hard-wired to their system. That means anyone we haven't unplugged is potentially an agent. Inside the Matrix, they are everyone and they are no one." This ability to morph into and out of any digital body gives the Agents an alarming ubiquity that allows them not just to be anyone, but also to be just about anywhere. Morpheus continues, "We survived inside by hiding from them and running from them. But they are the gatekeepers. They're guarding all the doors and holding all the keys." Here, Morpheus links the Agents' power to morph to their broader function within the Matrix: They police the thresholds that separate the real and digital worlds, the material prison and the machine-made illusion that keep humanity enslaved. Once again, the figure of the digital morph provides a subject and a theme for the film in which it appears, for it emblematizes and even mediates the violent narrative conflict between freedom and imprisonment.

Given this strong link between the figure of the morph and the film's concern with the protagonists' drive for freedom, it is not surprising that the greatest display of digital plasmaticness occurs during violent struggles organized around scenarios of confinement and escape inside the Matrix. The agents often morph into a scene at the moment when the protagonists are about to exit the Matrix, transforming each departure into a flight for life and freedom. For example, no sooner does a cop locate the crew of the Nebuchadnezzar climbing through the wall of the digitally sealed Heart O' the City Hotel than Smith morphs into his body to prevent Morpheus's escape from the Matrix. Later, as Neo and Trinity rescue Morpheus from Smith, an Agent morphs into the digital "body" of a helicopter pilot on the scene; when Smith is shot during the extended fight sequence, he morphs out of and abandons the digital body of the dying policeman he had taken over and morphs into the body of another uninjured cop in a different room. Later, as Trinity, Neo, and Morpheus try to exit the Matrix through a payphone in a subway station, Smith morphs through the body of a homeless man lying on the platform and he shoots the phone's receiver, thereby destroying Neo's means for escape. Inside the Matrix, then, the morph is a weapon used to keep humanity imprisoned, mind and body, in both the Matrix and in the real world. It is an effect designed to intensify emotionally scenarios of potential confinement and escape by endowing the "gatekeepers" with a degree of mobility and power that exacerbates and emphasizes the protagonists' ongoing status as cornered quarry.

The omnipotence and omnipresence Smith seems to enjoy thanks to digital plasmatics are not, however, a sign of the Agents' *own* freedom and power but that of the machines that control *them*. Like the T-1000's morph, the Agents' morph is a sign of their own rule-bound, subordinate existence, for they are nothing more than sentient programs that must carry out a mission. Indeed, at the level of characterization, the morph simultaneously provides evidence of Smith's relative power within the Matrix *and* his control by machines as it gives spectacular expression to his own violent pursuit of freedom from confinement. This becomes clear in the scene in which Smith tries to break into Morpheus's mind to obtain the codes for the mainframe in Zion, the last real-world city where free humans reside. As he tortures the shackled Morpheus (an image that links humanity's enslavement in the real world with the transatlantic slave trade), he explains,

> I hate this place – this zoo, this prison, this reality – whatever you want to call it. I can't stand it any longer. I must

> get out of here … I must get free. And in this mind is the key. My key. Once Zion is destroyed there is no need for me to be here.

Whereas earlier Morpheus defined the Agents as gatekeepers to humanity's prison, here Smith defines Morpheus as the gatekeeper to his own prison. Through Smith, the morph becomes a visual-effects emblem for the (unfulfilled) desire for freedom from constraint that drives the narrative forward. Hence, rather than indicate their liberation from the laws of physics, the digital liquidity that gives the Agents their freedom of form, radical mobility, and speed is the perfect expression of their subjection and control. As Morpheus explains to Neo,

> I've seen an agent punch through a concrete wall. Men have emptied entire clips at them and hit nothing but air. Yet their strength and their speed are still based on a world built on rules. Because of that they will never be as strong or as fast as you can be.

Each time the agents morph, they simply confirm that the entire world of the Matrix – and hence their own power – is defined and delimited by a program. This idea is reinforced by the green binary code that becomes momentarily visible as one figure morphs into the other.

In contrast to the agents' programmed and rule-bound morph, Neo's increasingly powerful plasmaticness inside the Matrix derives from a compulsion to bend and break rules evident from the beginning of the film. After Neo arrives late to work, his boss chides, "You have a problem with authority, Mr. Anderson. You believe that you are special, that the rules do not apply to you. Obviously you are wrong." When first taken into custody at the beginning of the film, Smith confronts Neo with the fact that he is "guilty of virtually every computer crime we have a law for." These crimes are committed in the process of searching for Morpheus and the truth about the Matrix – one that will eventually reveal the true conditions of humanity's existence. The narrative arc of the film traces the transformation of this drive from petty criminality and minor acts of insubordination against authority to violent resistance against a regime of mass enslavement. This arc simultaneously follows Neo's transformation into a digital being able to bend and even exploit the rules of the Matrix as the "One" able to fight the machines and lead the human resistance. It is not surprising then that the first morph in the film takes place inside a police station when Agent Smith interrogates Tom Anderson/Neo for information on Morpheus's location. When Neo refuses to cooperate and, citing his rights, asks for his phone call, Smith morphs Neo's face so that his mouth seals itself shut. The other agents then hold Neo down as Smith dangles in the air an electronic bugging device that morphs from inanimate object into a wriggling, crawling electronic insect that burrows into Neo's body through his navel.

In this scene, the morph provides a high-tech, spectacular demonstration of the fact that Neo's body is not his own, and that, like any other slave, he is not a subject but an object to be controlled and exploited. Importantly, the morph that seals Neo's mouth stifles his demand for his phone call (as Agent Smith asks, "What good is a phone call if you have no mouth?") and thereby hints at the true conditions of his existence: He has no rights and the self and free will he experiences in the Matrix are merely computer-generated fabrications. *The Matrix* uses the morph's figural freedom to give terrifying expression to Neo's state of bondage: Both the mouth and bug morphs reveal that Neo's body has no physical integrity and that the boundaries that normally separate inside and out (skin, orifices) to distinguish the self from the rest of the world are illusions drawn from a human past that no longer exists. Hence, while Smith digitally seals Neo's mouth in the Matrix, in the real world the machines have imposed new openings into the bodies of their captives to harvest their energy. Moreover, the quick cut from the interview room to Neo's bedroom (which leads Neo to believe the incident was only a dream) hints at the truth that will later be revealed: There is no "outside" of the prison just as there is no outside of the dream/illusion. It is precisely Neo's desire to awaken from his dream (and in the process to be freed from the prisons that confine his mind and body) that drives his criminal activities. In the end, he temporarily defeats Smith in a manner that echoes and exceeds Smith's use of the morph to occupy the digital bodies of "hard wired" humans in the Matrix: He leaps directly into Smith's body to take possession of it, and makes it stretch and contort until it finally explodes into bits of code, leaving Neo's digital image standing triumphantly in Smith's place. Itself an emblem of programmed freedom, the digital morph mediates the violent struggle for freedom from confinement waged between the Agents and the rebels as they fight each other in an effort to free themselves from the control of the Matrix. Neo's ability to master the morph within the Matrix signals his appropriation of the digital power to transcend the barriers and controls used by the machines to enslave humanity, an idea clearly expressed in the voiceover addressed to the machines that ends the film:

> I know you're out there. I can feel you now. I know that you're afraid. You're afraid of us. You're afraid of change. I don't know the future. I didn't come here to tell you how this is going to end. I came here to tell you how it's going to begin. I'll hang up this phone and then I'm going to show these people what you don't want them to see. I'm going to show them a world without you. A world without rules and controls, without borders and boundaries. A world where anything is possible. Where we go from there is a choice I leave to you.

Mutation and Morphological Becoming

Just as *The Matrix* alludes to the transatlantic slave trade to frame its representation of humanity's enslavement, *X-Men* places its narrative origins in the Holocaust to provide an historical framework for imagining the future persecution of mutants. *X-Men* opens in 1944 as German soldiers imprison the teenaged Eric Lensherr (Magneto) and his family in a concentration camp. As the Lensherrs are herded with other Jews into the camp, point-of-view shots reveal Eric's focus on the tattooed forearms of emaciated concentration camp victims to establish the dominant anxiety of the film: the classification, imprisonment, and destruction of an overpowered minority by a dominant majority. As in *Terminator 2*, *Dark City*, and *The Matrix*, digital plasmaticness in *X-Men* mediates the clash between two violently opposed forces – one associated with the violent denial of liberty, the other with an unyielding desire for freedom. As guards drag Eric away from his screaming parents, he reaches toward the closed gates that separate them and they begin to pull apart, creaking and groaning as they bend toward Eric's outstretched arms. Only by knocking Eric/Magneto unconscious are the guards able to stop his newly emergent powers. In this way, the internal process of genetic mutation finds external expression through – and becomes defined as – the potential power to break down structures (ideological and physiological as well as material) that separate, hierarchize, and confine.

The *X-Men* prologue establishes the theme used to represent digital plasmaticness in the film, for, in the "not too distant future," Magneto continues to use his power to control metal and magnetic fields as a means for resisting new attempts to classify and imprison a newly despised minority – genetic mutants. In *X-Men* the concept of mutation gives expression to the genetic rejection of "once and forever prescribed norms of [human] nomenclature, form and behavior." Indeed, some mutants embody the categorical breakdown – in *Merbabies* fashion – between previously distinct human and animal species, such as Sabretooth, Wolverine, and Toad. Other mutants embody a synthesis between the human body and the elements, again breaking down categories that separate different phenomena: While Magneto controls magnetic fields, Storm can control the weather. Other mutants have the ability to transcend the physiological barriers that separate different bodies and "contain" individual consciousness: Charles can access and control anyone's mind, while Rogue can absorb the vital energy or powers of those she touches – a variation on the concept of the "omnipotence of plasma" represented by a morph that raises the veins on her skin and her victim's while draining the latter of color. In turn, mutation's inherent plasmaticness – its tendency to collapse difference – is sometimes doubled by bodily plasticity: Toad's tongue can stretch to great lengths to be used as a weapon, while Wolverine's regenerative flesh heals instantaneously (much in the manner of the T-1000) as wounds morph back to smooth skin in seconds. At the same time, the characterization of various mutants idealizes the unique, for no mutant seems to duplicate the plasmatic traits or powers of any other. Articulated through the body, the concept of mutation and the visual effect of the morph work together to give expression to the protagonists' drive for freedom from classification, control, and confinement and the right to self-determination.

It is no surprise, then, that "registration" – the act of identifying, categorizing, and (potentially) imprisoning mutants – functions as the conceptual counterforce to the transcendence of boundaries and barriers that mutation implies and morphing enacts. Hence, in the opening sequences of the film, which take place in the "not too distant future," we understand that the world stands on the brink of another holocaust as the Mutant Registration Act is being debated in Congress. In response to Dr Jean Grey's argument against registration, the film's chief antagonist, Senator Kelly, argues,

> I have here a list of names of identified mutants living right here in the United States. Now here's a girl in Illinois who can walk through walls. Now what's to stop her from walking into a bank vault, or into the White House, or their houses [points to audience in the gallery]? And there are even rumors of mutants so powerful they can enter our minds and control our thoughts, taking away our God-given free will. Now I think the American people deserve the right to decide if they want their children to be in school with mutants, to be taught by mutants. Ladies and Gentlemen, the truth is that mutants are very real and they are among us. We must know who they are and above all we must know what they can do.

Senator Kelly broadly defines the mutant "threat" as the imminent breakdown of formerly impenetrable barriers (walls, gates, the cranium) that separate "inside" and "outside." For Kelly, to be a mutant is to enjoy radical freedom from any barrier – a freedom that he makes inseparable from the *loss* of free will for nonmutants. The solution to the problem of mutant plasmaticness is the creation of new systems of identification and classification in the service of discrimination, segregation, and even imprisonment (Magneto warns Xavier, "Let them pass that law and they'll have you in chains with a number burned onto your forehead!"). Registration will have the effect of identifying mutants principally as such in order to convert "mutant" into a reductive, limiting identity category able to counter the "protean possibilities" of mutation's plasmaticness. Moreover, the determination of what mutants can do, one senses, would be in service either of harnessing mutant power for nefarious purposes (Wolverine's adamantium skeleton is the result of military experiments on mutants) or eliminating the omnipotence of plasma altogether by transforming "mutation" back into a "standardly (im)mutable" form of the human species (indeed, the third film of the franchise, *X-Men: The Last Stand* (2006), sees the emergence of a medical "cure" for mutation).

Mise-en-scène joins the morph in giving visual expression to the conflict between constraint and freedom when Magneto discusses the Mutant Registration Act with Xavier against the backdrop of a dome made of crossed beams that materializes the dialectic between imprisonment and liberty that structures the film and its use of the morph. On one hand, the crossed beams recall the wires of the concentration camp gates seen in the prologue (a pattern that appears again when the film introduces Wolverine, who is first seen cage-fighting behind chain-link fencing), suggesting impending incarceration. On the other, the dome's design also forms a pattern of Xs and Ys that evokes chromosomes and their potential for plasmatic mutation and, perhaps, the ultimate triumph of mutant freedom over human control. The means for accomplishing such freedom is itself a matter of violent conflict: For while the X pattern symbolizes the X-Men's method for promoting tolerance, the XY pattern foreshadows, perhaps, Magneto's plan to achieve freedom by transforming the world's leaders into genetic mutants. If the freedom emblematized by mutant plasmaticness exists in a dialectical relationship with the threat of imprisonment, it is not surprising that Magneto is aided by his sidekick, Mystique, who is the only mutant meta-morph able to transform her body into a replica of any other. Together, Magneto and Mystique embody the fantasy of a mutant existence in which the human body and the material world are utterly malleable and subordinate to individual will.

X-Men thoroughly narrativizes the dialectic of imprisonment and freedom emblematized by mutation and the morph in the scene when Toad and Mystique kidnap Senator Kelly for Magneto. The kidnapping begins with a shot of Kelly sitting in his helicopter with his Congressional aide. After trying to convince another legislator to vote for the registration act on his cell phone, Kelly remarks to his aide, "You know this situation, these mutants, people like this Jean Grey, if it were up to me, I'd lock them all away. It's a war. It's the reason people like me exist." Moments after expressing in clearest terms the threat he truly poses to mutant freedom, we see Kelly's aide morph (back) into Mystique – an image of digital plasmaticness that has a broadly transformative effect that extends beyond the figural change of Mystique's surface appearance. As the morph ripples across Mystique's body, the associations of power and freedom initially connoted by setting, mise-en-scène, and dialogue as the Senator peddles influence in his helicopter are immediately converted into their opposite.

No longer an image of privileged hypermobility, the helicopter is suddenly a trap – a claustrophobic space of confinement that strips him of his power and makes him vulnerable, even helpless, while the "private" expression of his political will serves to provoke (and perhaps justify) his enemy's aggression. Kicking the Senator into unconsciousness, Mystique retorts, "It's people like you who made me afraid to go to school as a child." Consistent with the link between the mutant drive for freedom and the threat of imprisonment, the morph that shape-shifts the figure of a nonmutant into that of a mutant even provides visual shorthand for Kelly's fate: Magneto kidnaps the Senator in order to transform him into a mutant, thereby forcing him to embody the genetic/bodily plasmaticness that he opposes ideologically.

Once his mutation is complete, Kelly's body becomes quite literally plasmatic: The digital morph allows his rubbery form to stretch with comic elasticity (and so, when Magneto visits Kelly in his cell he asks, "How are we feeling, Senator? Relaxed, I hope"), thereby linking computer code to genetic code in this struggle over identity, power, and difference. At precisely the moment Magneto endows the Senator with bodily plasmaticness, he burdens him with a new self, threatened with the loss of liberty that "mutant registration" entails, once again making mutation and the morph inseparable from a play between freedom and control. Hence, it is not surprising that Kelly's new mutant body becomes the means by which he escapes his cell: First, he oozes his rubbery head through the bars on his window and then eludes Sabretooth's attempt to pull him back into the cell as his arm stretches and slips from his grasp. After swimming from Magneto's island hideout to shore, Kelly emerges from the ocean and walks along the beach as his body morphs from a gelatinous, indistinct mass back into recognizable human form after he passes by a young boy who, as he pokes a jellyfish with a stick, is urged by his sister: "Let it go, Tommy, let it go!" This child's play recapitulates the captivity and torture that will be the fate of all mutants, including Kelly, should the Mutant Registration Act pass. Yet Kelly's future will not entail enduring all that "registration" implies in the film; rather, he will embody the most extreme form of plasmaticness possible. In the end, his body morphs once again from distinct, human form, to a formless blob as he takes the shape of Eisenstein's "originary plasma" stripped entirely of its omnipotence.

It is worth remembering that Senator Kelly's transformation is simply a test case for Magneto's larger plot to transform world leaders into mutants so that, as he explains, when they return home from a United Nations summit in New York "our [mutant] cause will be theirs." That he carries out his plan from the top of the Statue of Liberty is no coincidence. Historically, of course, the iconic statue emblematizes the idea of freedom and declares the United States as a place where self-determination, unrestricted becoming, and escape from imposed limitations are possible; however, the form this icon takes – an "ossified" and unchanging copper figure – conflicts with the notion of bodily plasmaticness that *X-Men* links so strongly to (the desire for) freedom. Indeed, the use of the statue for the final fight sequence provides the ideal setting for the final violent conflict between the X-Men and Magneto. On one hand, the fight sequence features the greatest display of the protean power of human mutation as the X-Men battle Magneto and his henchmen. The Statue of Liberty thus becomes the setting for the extraordinary exercise and display of plasmaticness, thereby reaffirming the site's association with freedom and the transcendence of barriers and boundaries. On the other, Magneto changes the meaning of the statue by temporarily transforming it into an instrument for confining and exploiting other mutants: He uses copper beams to shackle the X-Men to the inside of the statue and handcuffs Rogue to his mutation machine on top of its crown so he can use her in his place to mutate the members of the United Nations summit. Magneto argues that this transformation, which requires the sacrifice of Rogue's life, is necessary because the statue itself has become a hollow, empty promise of freedom cast in metal. The world's leaders must be changed into mutants precisely because, he explains, "there is no land of freedom, no tolerance – not here or anywhere else." Indeed, by attempting this mass mutation from the top of the statue, he effectively seeks to change and update the meaning of the statue for a new era poised on the threshold between mutant freedom and registration. His drive to update and refashion the symbolic resonance of the statue is best represented when a replica of the Statue of Liberty in the gift shop is ultimately revealed to be Mystique, who has morphed her form into a simulation of this seemingly immutable symbol of freedom.

The play between the ossified and the plasmatic that organizes the film's narrative continues through the film's conclusion, for in the end, Magneto's fate is as fitting as Senator Kelly's. Just as Kelly's staunch opposition to mutant plasmaticness resulted in his own unstoppable metamorphosis into a plasmatic state, Magneto's attempt to create a new brotherhood of mutants by transforming the world's leaders results in his imprisonment in a hard, transparent, plastic cell. While his new prison makes it impossible for Magneto to create magnetic fields or subject metal to his will, it also represents the "ossification" of that which was formerly pliant and plasmatic. And just as Kelly's short prison sentence resulted in an evolutionary leap forward (after he is transformed, Magneto says to him, "Welcome to the future, brother"), the plastic prison effectively transforms Magneto into an earlier life form – a mere human unable to control magnetic fields. And despite the fact that – or precisely because – Senator Kelly has been returned to the primal state of liquidity, his place in the Senate can be taken up by the mutant who embodies the very omnipotence of plasma he sought to contain: The film ends with the revelation that Mystique now masquerades as the Senator, who now opposes the Registration Act in favor of mutant rights. The morph mediates the struggle between freedom and control, joining the two in a digital effect that thematizes and spectacularizes their inseparable nature.

Conclusion

As the above analyses of the morph *Terminator 2*, *Dark City*, *The Matrix*, and *X-Men* suggest, the films in which new digital visual effects appeared in the last decade of the twentieth century often display a masterful use of new digital techniques while simultaneously expressing a deep ambivalence about their place in popular narrative cinema. While one might attribute this to the ambivalence with which technology is often treated in science fiction films, we can see this same dynamic at work in comedies that feature the digital morph, such as *The Mask* and *The Nutty Professor*. In both films, the digital morph allows "repressed" elements of the protagonists' psyches – especially sexual/romantic desire and (comic) violent aggression – to find expression through the new selves they embody thanks to their acquired ability to morph their own bodies. In these films, consciousness and repression turn the everyday self into a sort of prison that traps and smothers aspects of the unconscious longing to be free. Needless to say, the new personas that emerge along with the protagonists' transformed bodies and personalities are not entirely appealing and, as Bukatman notes, amount to the unrestrained "Id" (2003, 152). With respect to the ambivalence it generates, the digital morph is similar to other computer-generated images of the 1990s, such as the digital dinosaurs in Steven Spielberg's *Jurassic Park* (1993) and *The Lost World* (1997), which simultaneously produce astonishment and anxiety, awe and fear in the fictional worlds in which they appear and in the spectators who flocked to cinemas to see them in record numbers. Given that computer-generated images have effected a transformation in cinema parallel to the shift to synchronized sound at the end of the 1920s, such ambivalence is unsurprising. For, much like the morph itself, computer-generated images make possible a new type of filmmaking that liberates the photorealistic image from the limitations of indexicality and the laws of physics, while displacing many production practices from the studio or the location to the confines of the computer.

References

Bukatman, Scott. (2003). *Matters of Gravity: Special Effects and Supermen in the 20th Century*. Durham, NC: Duke University Press.

Crogan, Patrick. (2000). "Things Analog and Digital." *Senses of Cinema*, April, 1–13.

Eisenstein, Sergei. (1986). *Eisenstein on Disney*, ed. J. Leyda. Calcutta: Seagull Press.

Manovich, Lev. (2001). *The Language of New Media*. Cambridge, MA: MIT Press.

Sobchack, Vivian. (2000). "'At the Still Point of the Turning World': Meta-Morphing and Meta-Stasis." In Vivian Sobchack (ed.), *Meta-Morphing: Visual Transformation and the Culture of Quick Change* (pp. 131–158). Minneapolis: University of Minnesota Press.

23

Mainstream Documentary since 1999

Patricia Aufderheide
Professor, American University, United States

The term "**documentary**" elicits mixed, usually negative reactions from the general public, as Patricia Aufderheide notes, briefly surveying international documentary film history to unearth the roots of such misguided perceptions. Examining new-millennium documentaries, as her primary subject, Aufderheide acknowledges the important role of **public television** in supporting the ongoing work of **Bill Moyers** and of **cable television** in funding and exhibiting works that range from corporate-driven formulaic drivel to incisive exposés. She provides informative close readings of **Werner Herzog**'s ***Grizzly Man***, **Errol Morris**'s ***Standard Operating Procedure***, **Judith Helfand** and **Dan Gold**'s ***Blue Vinyl***, **Alex Gibney**'s ***Enron: The Smartest Guys in the Room***, and **Michael Moore**'s ***Sicko***, among others, to illustrate the multiple modes, production contexts, and ideological arguments that have captured larger audiences through the mid-2000s. Although the fervor for movie-theater documentary has since dampened, Aufderheide notes the self-distribution potential of **YouTube** and other online sources. Her essay shares ground with Charles Warren on direct cinema documentary, Barbara Klinger on cable television and Hollywood since the 1990s, and Susan Carruthers on Iraq War films in this volume.

Additional terms, names, and concepts: cinéma vérité, for-profit television documentaries, "factual television," personal essay films, HBO, Kartemquin Films, reenactment, Interrotron camera, self-reflexivity, Michael Moore persona, "gotcha interview"

From the 1930s to the 1990s, documentary was a rather dowdy cinematic category; to many, it even represented a subordinate cinematic form. "Is it a movie or a documentary?" was an entirely expectable question. That all changed by the end of the 1990s. The first decade of the twenty-first century was one of unprecedented burgeoning of documentary production and consumption that entailed a great increase in output and some qualitative advances. While televisual documentary came to be associated with

American Film History: Selected Readings, 1960 to the Present, First Edition. Edited by Cynthia Lucia, Roy Grundmann, and Art Simon.

certain factory values that reflected the TV industry's vast need for programming, theatrical documentary came in this period to be seen as a much more individually crafted, courageous, human-scale response against social injustice and the abuse of power. Hence, the era also raised questions about the social role of documentary, including the responsibility of filmmakers to serve the public's informational needs and to honor traditional journalistic goals, such as accuracy.

Documentary, a term that the dour Scottish documentary entrepreneur John Grierson crafted, has at its core a promise to say something about real life truthfully. There was the Griersonian legacy, for one. If cinema were food, for Grierson documentary was the spinach. He recommended it as a tool of education and persuasion for governments and businesses alike; documentary was supposed to do the business of managing the social peace (Aitken 1990). What followed were decades of educational films, a business born in the wake of governments' use of 16mm film in World War II. After that war, businesses and filmmakers found ready clients in schools that expected and would receive fare that was laced with paternalism. Then there was television, which, before the advent of the cable era, tended to favor a radio-influenced, portentous format of "white paper" style public affairs documentary – important stuff but rarely, well, fun (Barnouw 1993). Through the combined impact of these factors, documentary became associated with the grim authority of teachers, bureaucrats, and portentous journalists. All too often, documentaries were first deployed in disciplinary scenarios – in schools, workplaces, and religious institutions. Viewers probably encountered the least aesthetically adventurous work first, films hewing to conventions such as the voice-of-God narrator, the authoritative expert host, and mutually reinforcing words and images. When a documentary actually succeeded in both stimulating and pleasing viewers, a common response was, "It was a good film, not like a regular documentary." However, viewers did not merely carry away a sense that documentaries were boring. They also implicitly expected documentaries to be uncontroversial in accuracy and authoritative about their subject matter.

This widespread impression of documentary, of course, contradicted a rich aesthetic and social history. Documentarians, as historian Erik Barnouw noted, have seen themselves as poets, buglers for causes, chroniclers, and reporters, among other roles. Documentary had begun, with Robert Flaherty, in films that poetically imposed a man-versus-nature drama on reality; *Nanook of the North* (1922) for instance, employed masterfully suspenseful storytelling in both image and editing. Documentary had challenged the viewer to reexamine his or her own notions of truth, as Luis Buñuel's *Las Hurdes* (1933) did. It even aspired to induce synesthesia, as Joris Ivens's filmic poem *Rain* did in combining the representation of natural events with musical composition. But most viewers at the end of the twentieth century had likely never seen these films. It took the advent of home video, the emergence of satellite-fed cable channels, the development of minimajors among distributors, and the expansion of theaters into multiplexes to create the conditions to make documentary into a consumer-friendly kind of cinema. The lowered cost of digital production and distribution affected all aspects of the supply chain. It made documentary a cheap source of programming on proliferating channels and screens that demanded, 24 hours a day, to be fed with new material. It also made possible the development of theaters specifically designated for documentaries and other niche audience fare within cineplexes, a tactic pioneered by the Landmark Theaters in the early twenty-first century.

By that time, there had already been generations of independent US filmmakers armed with video cameras (the Sony PortaPak was introduced in 1967). Documentary had become an important feature of the Civil Rights Movement and of antinuclear and peace activism since the late 1960s. Such documentarians, whether they worked as advocates or as chroniclers, often resisted or directly opposed the voice-of-authority image of documentary, rather styling themselves dissidents, activists, and truth-tellers against the grain of reigning ideologies. They cultivated a range of styles that were as unlike televisual conventions of the time as possible: cinéma vérité (*Salesman*, 1968, Maysles brothers; *Harlan County, USA*, 1976, Barbara Kopple), oral histories (*With Babies and Banners*, 1979, Lorraine Gray; *The Good Fight*, 1984, Noel Buckner and Mary Dore), unnarrated compilation films (*Atomic Café*, 1982, Jayne Loader and Kevin Rafferty), reflexive essays (*The Thin Blue Line*, 1988, Errol Morris) (Aufderheide 2007). Many of these filmmakers were nurtured – sometimes with forbearance, sometimes reluctantly – by public service television. Indeed, they mobilized in the late 1970s to force public television to provide more space to social documentary, an effort that succeeded by 1988, when the Independent Television Service was created as a production arm for "underrepresented" voices and viewers, as part of public broadcasting (Aufderheide 2000, 99–120).

Documentary was finally positioned for popularity. Cable TV channels that were devoted to documentary multiplied and went global in the 1990s. Box office success, however, had to wait for the twenty-first century. In 2008, the widely used website box office calculator, Box Office Mojo, listed 25 of the 30 top-grossing theatrical documentaries of all time in the US (excluding performance films, reality TV and IMAX) as having been produced since 2002. The business trend may well be short lived. By 2006, theatrical box office was already declining. However, the transformation of the image of documentary from being earnest and education-oriented to constituting entertainment with a purpose was definitive. The vast proliferation of screens in people's lives, ranging from home-based HD to iPods on the go, has been met with a vast expansion of nonfiction production, much of it in television. The evolution of documentary form in this period hailed from two different sources: corporate and individual. Corporate cable documentaries, driven by bottom-line values and typified by formulas that promised both dependability and novelty, contrasted with documentaries made out of an individual creator's passion. These two strands interacted creatively, both to feed high-quality talent into the corporate sector and to introduce market opportunities into the non-market-driven field.

Already in the 1990s, a business emerged in for-profit television documentaries. Documentaries produced for the new cable and satellite channels took on a factory look (for instance, a Discovery Health Channel's *Birth Day*, the BBC's *Big Cats*, the National Geographic series *Seconds from Disaster*). In these series, personality was methodically expunged in favor of brand identity. Indeed, Discovery channels pioneered the notion that all credits for the film – the recognition of individual authorship – should be relegated to websites in order to maximize brand identity and minimize the time span in which viewers might decide to switch channels. (The move was stopped by vigorous protest from filmmakers' organizations, especially the International Documentary Association.) Sentiment and the drama around violence and reproduction typically propelled story. Cinematography and editing styles were drawn both from fiction and from news television. Designed for the small screen, they were graphics heavy and typically featured headline-style narration. They provided unsubtle musical and special-effects cueing for emotional response. Lighting clichés developed, such as fog, mist, and haze over reenactments and shocking blasts of light for transitions. Documentaries borrowed narrative drama from reality television, leading to "factual television" hybrids such as Discovery's *Junkyard Wars* series and Spike TV's *Manswers*.

Formulaic, commercial documentary technique in this period was designed to capture and keep viewer attention, with techniques ranging from shock to titillation to innuendo. The formulaic choices also effectively allayed questions about the accuracy, ideology, or significance of the real-life material being portrayed. Omniscient and authoritative narrators, portentous music, and tautly constructed narratives left little room for ambiguity, reflection, or participation. These formulaic documentaries reinforced viewers' stereotypes about documentary's relationship with truth and accuracy. They buried questions of representation behind layers of convention and the thrills of suspense and adventure. At the same time, they studiously avoided questions of social implications of the phenomena they described.

Theatrical venues also showcased for-profit documentaries, which usually depended on some novelty or shock effect. The large-screen, high-tech, museum-friendly IMAX film was a high-end profit center, featuring subjects with a big wow factor (celebrity, novelty, mega-fauna) and skirting social or political frameworks. According to trade journal *Variety*, in 2008, *Space Station 3D* (2001), after seven solid years on the circuit, was still drawing revenues and adding to its $76 million lifetime gross receipts; *Nascar 3D* (2004) consistently picked up a steady $7–8 million a year. Performance films, such as concerts and the 2003 standup comedy hit *Blue Collar Comedy Tour* were dependable ticket-sellers. *The Aristocrats* (2005), a slightly more complex film showcasing a variety of comedians' approaches to the same hoary joke, also did well in theaters. So did *Metallica: Some Kind of Madness* (2004), a close-up look at a midlife crisis in the history of the eponymous heavy metal group. The 1991 concert tour film *Madonna: Truth or Dare* is one of Box Office Mojo's top 10 grossing documentaries of all time. Sports documentaries, especially extreme sports – for instance Dana Brown's 2003 *Step into Liquid*, Brian Sisselman's 1998 *Freeriders*, and Stacy Peralta's 2004 *Riding Giants*, all about extreme surfing – were another dependable for-profit documentary genre. From France the 2005 *March of the Penguins* was a spectacularly successful commercial wildlife film, one of the all-time best-selling documentaries with nearly $128 million worldwide gross by 2009. (For comparison, the 2008 James Bond film *Quantum of Solace* took in $544 million worldwide in a year.) It cheerfully anthropomorphized penguins, misrepresented their habits and patterns (for instance, implying that they mate for longer than a season), and overlaid narration and a musical score marked by patronizing sentimentality (although less so in English than in the original French).

At the same time, for-conscience documentaries also flourished and built relationships in the cracks of the for-profit system. They benefited from the proliferation of movie screens and the internet-fueled ability to promote a film to targeted passionate audiences. They depended on a combination of public service television, film festivals, donors, and foundations to make films that often had short theatrical runs (sometimes purely for the purpose of making them eligible for the Academy Awards). They demonstrated a broad range of aesthetic choices, all of them challenging the expectations generated by commercial cable documentary formulas. They also positioned documentary as a teller of truths being withheld by those in power, or untold because of societal bias. The filmmakers who made these films with journalistic and artistic ambition, and who sometimes spoke from conscience, were not household names, but their audience-friendly formats were also fostered by the new golden age – or at least golden moment – for documentary. There were competition films, preferably with a socially marginalized group or disadvantaged kids or both: the trend-setting Jeffrey Blitz's *Spellbound* (2002), about the national spelling bee; Marilyn Agrelo's *Mad Hot Ballroom* (2005), about urban kids in a ballroom-dancing competition; Scott Hamilton Kennedy's *O.T.: Our Town* (2002), about kids in a desperately poor Los Angeles neighborhood putting on a play; Patrick Creadon's *Wordplay* (2006), about crossword puzzles; Henry Alex Rubin and Dana Adam Shapiro's *Murderball* (2005), about wheelchair-bound rugby players. There were crime dramas (preferably with a maudlin or stomach-turning psychological twist), such as Vikram Jayanti's *James Ellroy's Feast of Death* (2001), Andrew Jarecki's *Capturing the Friedmans* (2003), and Kurt Kuenne's *Dear Zachary: A Letter to a Son about His Father* (2008). Ken Burns, working exclusively in television, had long since developed a genre of archival storytelling unto himself, featuring creative filming of archival photographs. His first work in the new century included *Jazz* (2001), *The War* (2007), and *The National Parks: America's Best Idea* (2009).

The personal essay continued to be a common format in the work of Alan Berliner, Doug Block, Ross McElwee, Robb Moss, and Susan Smiley, among others. Some environmentally conscious nature films focused on climate change, such as Jacques Perrin's international coproduction *Winged Migration* (2001) and Davis Guggenheim's *An Inconvenient Truth* (2006). In part thanks to the high visibility of former vice-president Al Gore and the publicity investment of Participant Productions, the latter became one of the best-selling documentaries of all time, and has been credited with a shift in public awareness toward the urgency of the climate change issue. The ebullient business environment for documentaries also favored established production houses that had long nurtured and sustained independent and critical voices. Such houses included Arts Engine, Firelight Media, Lumiere Productions, and Skylight Pictures. (Another good example, the legendary Blackside Productions, which had produced *Eyes on the Prize*, 1987, and other hallmark historical documentary series for television, collapsed after the 1998 death of founder Henry Hampton.) The production at the beginning of the twenty-first century from these houses showed continuity with documentary's history of political engagement and reflected a sophisticated understanding of the needs of the documentary niche in the entertainment marketplace. For instance, the nonfiction work of prolific African-American film director Spike Lee was supported at the beginning of the twenty-first century by contracts with the premium cable channel HBO. HBO expected prestige and awards from its relationship with Lee, whose films are strongly inflected with outrage about the effects of racism in the US. They got what they wanted. With his longtime coproducer and editor Sam Pollard, Lee made *When the Levees Broke*

(2006) about the disaster of Hurricane Katrina in New Orleans. *When the Levees Broke* chronicles the testimony of people who experienced the horror of the hurricane and its aftermath. Their treatment is vivid testimony to both long-term and immediate neglect of people deemed not worth paying attention to by authorities and the powerful. The unnarrated work lets survivors' and rescue workers' testimony speak for itself, with powerfully affecting music providing the emotional cueing. By the time viewers watch Barbara Bush, the US President's mother, blandly opine that survivors had better conditions in their refugee camps than they had been living in, they need no prompting to sense their own outrage.

Kartemquin Films in Chicago also demonstrated the role of production houses in maintaining the vitality of the independent voice in documentary. It had been founded in the 1960s with a social issue, social change mandate. It exclusively produced documentaries, often about or with working-class subjects in Chicago. Its work was supported at times by a collective structure, sometimes with foundation grants, regularly with subsidy from commercial work and equipment rental, and by modest sales. The Kartemquin style is marked by a belief that viewers can, with the help of filmmakers, enter into the lived experiences – the challenges, the pain, the achievements – of people they might otherwise never encounter or even think about. Kartemquin founder Gordon Quinn understands this approach as a political act, one that can invest viewers in a wider understanding of the society they live in and encourage greater engagement with their challenges as members of it.

Kartemquin had broken into mainstream consciousness with *Hoop Dreams* (1994), made by director Steve James and other members of the second generation of filmmakers in a tradition carefully cultivated by Quinn, the film's executive producer. *Hoop Dreams* tracks over five years the lives of two inner-city Chicago, African-American boys given basketball scholarships in a cinéma vérité style (an umbrella term for the non-narrated film style that presented viewers with the impression that they were watching unconstructed, unedited experience). Like the earlier cinéma vérité documentary *Salesman* (1968), it reveals not only individual drama but an investment in an American dream of success that is regularly betrayed.

Kartemquin went on in the first decade of the twenty-first century to produce an explosion of work, some like Steve James's *Stevie* (2003), about James's guilt-ridden relationship with a troubled young man for whom he had been in a Big Brother program, debuting in theaters. Other works, like the seven-hour series *The New Americans* (2004), showed primarily on television. *The New Americans* tracked immigrants to the US from their homes through their first year of acculturation. It was made at a time of great public controversy about immigration and its effects on American culture. It follows five stories of US immigrants – Kenyan, Mexican, Indian, Palestinian, and Dominican. In each case, the stories begin in the immigrants' home country, in order to place them within their home context before the viewer encounters them stripped of it.

The cinéma vérité approach of the series allows viewers to come to their own conclusions about the decisions they watch unfolding; indeed, the distinctive Kartemquin editing, marked by measured pacing and surefooted construction of emotional drama, requires viewers to decide for themselves. The immigrants are not treated as emblematic or representative, but as people with family ties, fearful challenges, and a set of assets they use to confront their new world. There are no bad guys, though there is no shortage of problems. The Mexican family abandons what seems like a relatively good situation, because of unbearable homesickness for family. A Dominican baseball player does not make the cut, and must go home. The Kenyan political refugees find their family riven by cross-generational conflict, as the young people absorb American values that the elders resist. Viewers also watch the ways in which immigrants manage the complex process of maintaining ties with their worlds of origin while building new networks in the US; what might otherwise seem small achievements – a certification as a nurse's aide for instance – become milestones that can trigger catharsis.

The New Americans has had several lives, as is typical of Kartemquin work (and of much work produced by such social documentary production houses). For instance, modules focusing on particular issues, such as cross-generational conflict, were created for social workers and medical personnel who deal with immigrants. The film and these modules have both been widely used in education of service workers and volunteers working with immigrants. They have even changed policies of those organizations, which were able to adapt their procedures better to immigrants' needs based on what they had learned.

Figure 23.1 Kartemquin films, one of the documentary production houses that flourished in the documentary boom, had theatrical success with Steve James's *Stevie* (2003, producers Steve James, Adam D. Singer, and Gordon Quinn); here, Stevie (left) with Steve James.

The abundance of work in this period made possible a stable transfer of knowledge to later generations of Kartemquin producers, who maintained the group's historic interest in class, diversity, injustice, and democracy. For instance, David Simpson's *Milking the Rhino* (2008), shown on US public television and internationally, explored the challenges of economic innovation in Africa. Their work was increasingly supported directly by the documentary marketplace, by public television coproducers, cable television, theatrical contracts, and DVD sales of both old and new work. Production values and storytelling were consistently high, making festival and theatrical screenings a routine feature of their releases.

The burgeoning commercial opportunities also favored seasoned documentary auteurs, the literary lions of the documentary world. The auteurs had developed during the flourishing of film culture in the 1970s and early 1980s, when directors were heralded as artistic heroes of their culture who had an independent voice. Ironically, in film culture they had often been second-class citizens, people admired more for their subject matter than for their art. Many of them had grown up in the first flush of cinéma vérité, in which David and Albert Maysles, Robert Drew, Richard Leacock, D. A. Pennebaker (later working with Chris Hegedus), Fred Wiseman, Allan King, and Jean Rouch were pioneers (Mamber 1974; Benson & Anderson 1989; Feldman 2002; Rouch & Feld 2003). The cinéma vérité styles that these artists variously explored and established had become, by the twenty-first century, a default cinematic language for auteurist documentary, with some of these legends continuing to work into the new century.

Examples of such documentary auteurs who flourished at the turn of the twenty-first century include Werner Herzog (a German artist and longtime resident of the California Bay Area), Barbara Kopple, and Errol Morris. Each of these auteurs over decades has honed a powerful storytelling craft and communicated to viewers an intense experience of their subjects. They also have developed distinctive styles, which approached the challenge of negotiating the promise of truth-telling with different tools and tone. Their recent work showcases the range of expression revealed during the early twenty-first century flourishing of authorial, for-conscience documentary. This aesthetic and strategic range, featured on theatrical screens, on premium cable channels, and in public service television series, was an important counterpoint to the formulaic nature of commercial television series.

Each of these artists wrestles with the challenge of saying something truthful about reality and the challenge, too, of saying it differently. All see themselves as artists, using the documentary form as a nontransparent means of expression, and all in one way or another are making an intervention in public discourse. However, both the objectives and the means are wrapped around the powerful stamp of the individual's vision. Kopple employs a fly-on-the-wall approach to representation of reality, carefully crafting narratives that draw viewers into situations that require moral decision and action. Herzog and Morris explore fundamental issues of meaning and purpose in life as philosophers of the image. All of them craft stories around compelling, often troubling characters.

In Kopple's work one sees the legacy of the observational cinema style made memorable by the Maysles brothers, with whom Kopple studied (Wintonick 1999). This style is used to reveal the ways in which people assert their own humanity and courageously resist injustice and the cruelly unfair hand of fate. Kopple's career choices were shaped in the highly politicized atmosphere of the late 1960s and 1970s, as much by anti-imperialist organizing as by feminism (Aufderheide & Zimmerman 2004), and she has long produced socially critical documentaries on topics that deal with the underdiscussed issue of class in America (*Harlan County, USA*; *American Dream*, 1990). She has also, as her career has progressed, directed television and made documentaries that wander from the cutting edge of politics, such as *Wild Man Blues* (1997). Her films consistently approach the challenge of truth-telling by establishing an intimate relationship with her subjects and then minimizing her own presence in the scene. The illusion thus created is that the viewer is an invisible part of the action, a friendly observer. This relationship generates trust, loyalty, affection, and commitment toward the people whose experiences Kopple captures and shares with viewers.

Her 2006 film *Shut Up and Sing* (codirected with old friend Cecilia Peck) boldly continues the tradition of fly-on-the-wall filmmaking. In it, she and Peck follow the Dixie Chicks, a popular southern country-music girl band, on a tour that takes a disastrous turn. On the eve of the Iraq invasion, the band's leader, Natalie Maines, blurts out to an adoring audience of British fans that the band is ashamed that George Bush is from Texas. This crowd-pleasing comment then reverberates back home, and country music stations refuse to play the Dixie Chicks' new album. The film tracks the evolution of Maines's and the band's political and aesthetic change and growth. Maines moves from a position of chagrin to political awareness of the importance of defending free speech rights; the band moves out of its country-music niche onto the radar of the general audience and into the limelight of the Grammy awards. The story is told at eye-level with the band members, as they sit on hotel-room beds and fret over developments, practice in each other's houses, and chat with each other about babies and death threats. Kopple, with Peck, brings viewers into the room with an immediacy that is shockingly intimate in retrospect but sleepover-comfortable at the time. The viewer has the illusion of participating in the intensely feminine interplay of the women in the group.

The film is, however, far from an iterative recording of events. It is carefully shaped, with a powerful moral lesson. The film's editing is complex. The story is not told chronologically, but rather in alternating moments, between the events of March 2003 that precipitated the group's crisis of identity, and the release of their crossover album in early 2007. The earlier scenes act as extended flashbacks that explain the present. They also guide the viewer's attention, so that scenes whose significance might otherwise be obscure are made instead revelatory, thus taking a real-life crisis and giving it a tight dramatic arc. The characters of each of the women are revealed in multiple ways. They respond to interview questions; we watch them on stage and backstage; we see them at home, with their children (by the end of the film the three women have seven children); and we watch them working through the hard questions together. The film thus convinces the viewer that he or she is watching the complexity of real lives under crisis, rather than an essay about it or explanation of it. The fluidity of the cinéma vérité sequences goes far to erase the viewer's awareness of the constructedness of the presentation. At the same time, the presentation of each character is far more a collage than a portrait.

The question driving the film is: How will the women manage this career crisis? Initial panic and dismay over the commercial crisis cedes to reflecting upon and recasting the problem as a political one of free speech, which in turn becomes about creative triumph when the group writes new songs and develops a sound that reaches beyond the original country demographic. The film provides economic and political context for the group's moral decisions. It includes interviews with country music station directors and radio executives, who explain the economics of country music, and also features a Congressional hearing on media concentration. The Dixie Chicks' manager, Simon Renshaw, testifies that two large companies control access to most of the country music stations.

This story thus acts, as Kopple's work often does, as an instructive and engrossing tale about how people behave when their rights are threatened. The women involved, while talented, need to blunder and ponder their way through to formulating a feasible response to the crisis, just as the rest of us do. They are never confused about their loyalty to each other or their need to defend their right to speak. But every deliberation implies contingency, as there are many decisions that could possibly be made; the consequences are always (to them at least) unknown. The fact that the viewer knows the band's future is secured – even though in a way different from how the members had planned – allows the viewer to focus on the way they face their difficult decisions. Further, the film with its contextualizing information illuminates for the viewer why the band members face the obstacles they do. This information helps viewers understand the band's dilemma as one created by large forces, not merely bad individuals.

Interrogating Reality

Both Herzog and Morris position themselves as philosophic critics, analyzing perception as much as fact. Werner Herzog, who was part of the 1970s New German Cinema movement – a cinema associated with socially critical and formally experimental work – from early on in his career has positioned himself as a nonconformist railing against complacency (Herzog & Cronin 2002; Prager 2007). Like some experimental filmmakers such as Stan Brakhage, Herzog uses images of reality to peel back layers of expectation and habit in order to shock viewers into seeing anew. Herzog is notoriously contrarian, resisting received critical judgment. Although most of his dozens of films are considered documentaries, he rejects the label. "The boundary between fiction and 'documentary' simply does not exist; they are all just films," he has told an interviewer. He claims to despise mere "fact," feeling free to invent elements in his films such as an imaginary quote attributed to Pascal. He particularly sneers at cinéma vérité, provocatively calling it "the cinema of accountants." At the same time, he claims a reverence for extreme landscape and situations, which seem to defy interpretation and confront him (and his viewers) with the non-negotiable nature of reality at base.

Notwithstanding Herzog's own skepticism toward the fact/fiction binary, many of his films do, in fact, fall into the broader category of documentary. They usually feature a character whose personality or situation in its extremity forces a confrontation with fundamental questions about the purpose and nature of being. For instance, in 1977 in *La Soufrière*, he went to an island on the verge of volcanic eruption and interviewed the lone holdout; in 1984, in *The Dark Glow of the Mountains*, he explored the motivations of daredevil mountain climbers; in 1997 he made *Little Dieter Learns to Fly*, about a German-born US Navy pilot who was captured in Laos during the Vietnam War and escaped; his 2004 *The White Diamond* was about an engineer who flies a blimp over Guyana in a high-risk situation, where his cinematographer has died; the 2007 *Encounters at the End of the World* is concerned with the dreams of the scientists and workers who run the McMurdo Research Station in Antarctica.

His 2005 work *Grizzly Man* was, unlike most of his documentaries, a major theatrical release. The project was funded by Discovery Docs, a division of the global media company that produces documentary programming for cable and satellite. That division was designed to win prestige for the company. (It was shortlived and was eliminated in 2008 when the company changed strategy.) Discovery producers arranged for British singer-songwriter Richard Thompson to write the score, and closely supervised the filmmaking process. Nonetheless, the product was recognizably Herzogian. The "grizzly man" is Timothy Treadwell, a naturalist and sometime videographer in Alaskan bear country. Herzog worked with video left from the last summer that Treadwell spent in bear country, during which he and his girlfriend were killed and partially eaten by bears. The video left behind, pored over meditatively by Herzog, who also narrates the film, reveals a sadly obsessive, angry, sentimental, and unstable man who regularly behaves in ways that court disaster. Herzog freely uses this material, along with his own videography of the starkly beautiful region, to ask his hallmark questions about the meaning of life and even the meaning of asking unanswerable questions about the meaning of life. He narrates a close reading of Treadwell's footage, which he showcases not the least for its unintended revelations. For instance, he calls attention to the camera's capturing of landscape before Treadwell enters a shot, attributing to it a "strange, secret beauty." He turns the video self-reflexive by running in sequence several successive takes that Treadwell botched before getting an entrance right. In a hallmark moment, Herzog takes the viewer on a dizzying overview of the stark landscape, and in voiceover scathingly describes the difference between Treadwell's sentimental vision of the world and his nihilistic one. For himself, he says, nature is violence and chaos. The film holds viewers in part by the tension between two kinds of obsessive individuals – Treadwell and Herzog.

Perhaps the film's most notable way of forcing viewers to consider the meaning of representation and the non-negotiable nature of reality, as D. T. Johnson has noted (Johnson 2008), is its treatment of the audio record of the couple's deaths. The tape does not appear until the end of the first hour, after which viewers, knowing Treadwell to be dead, have seen him manically alive at great length. Herzog visits one of Treadwell's friends, who has the tape and lets him listen to it. Solemnly listening, he then equally solemnly pronounces that she must never listen to it, a pronouncement that also implicitly includes the viewers. Herzog in one moment demonstrates his power over viewers, his concern for the relationship between representation and reality, and his horror and fascination with the rupture of the extreme in daily life. *Grizzly Man*'s quest for truth is not about the circumstances of Treadwell's death, although viewers beginning the film might be forgiven this assumption. Rather it is a quest to discover more interior truths about perception and purpose. Herzog uses the tools of personal narrative, reflexive video, and perspective (for instance the contrast between the vastness of the land and the backpackers in it) to do this. Herzog benefited from a favorable theatrical climate for documentaries to repeat a philosophical exploration that he had done many times before. His film was favorably reviewed and widely seen in theaters before screening on cable TV, although it irritated some naturalists, who felt that he slighted Treadwell's record of high-quality nature photography.

Errol Morris has long made films that ask viewers to reconsider what it is that they think they know by seeing, as Linda Williams has discussed (1998). He has also produced television commercials, which have produced a steady stream of income for him. Born in the first wave of the baby boom, he was shaped as well in a highly politicized era. He has combined a deep interest in philosophical questions of epistemology with a background that includes work as a criminal investigator. Like Herzog, Morris has (in his columns in the *New York Times* among other places) loudly rejected the claims of cinéma vérité to any superior kind of truth; he argues that the philosophical problems of interpreting reality, "the Cartesian riddle" – the question of what the world is like, what is true – remain (Leitner 1998; Cunningham 2005). His films all root this question in the study of particular practice. His approach, as Jonathan Kahana has noted (2008), features the cultivation of doubt in the viewer, forcing viewers to reconsider received wisdom. His techniques include reenactment and a starkly confrontational visual technique in interviewing, using his trademarked Interrotron camera to enable interviewees to "see" him in the lens of the camera and thus have direct eye contact with it.

Morris's early film *Thin Blue Line* (1988) reconstructs visually the testimony of a variety of witnesses to a crime for which a man had been sentenced to death, and was profoundly influential on subsequent documentaries as well as on crime television. His film eventually was entered as evidence to reopen the case, at the conclusion of which the man was released. His 2008 film *Standard Operating Procedure*, an exploration of the meaning of photographs taken by soldiers at Abu Ghraib prison, continues Morris's lifelong fascination with the interpretation of reality. He challenges received wisdom that the soldiers' photographs simply provide evidence of "bad apples" in the armed forces who willfully flouted military procedure and tortured

Figure 23.2 Still images presented as objects of study, problems to solve in Errol Morris's *Standard Operating Procedure* (2008, producers Julie Ahlberg and Errol Morris).

prisoners. The film was widely seen and played a role in vigorous public discussion about torture, amplified by his columns in the *New York Times*.

Morris argues in the film that, in fact, what civilians would call torture is routine military practice, and that the photographs can be read differently. He does this with interviews of the soldiers and experts, by repeated and meditative examination of the photographs, and by enactments that illustrate the version of reality that interviewees provide. The viewer re-sees photographs that have become part of public memory, such as one of a hooded prisoner in a Christ-like pose. The viewer is eventually pushed to reconsider some of the soldier interviewees as being other victims of the military's "standard operating procedure" in Iraq. Like Morris's other films, *Standard Operating Procedure* is elaborately and even ostentatiously crafted at every point. Representation is systematically denaturalized. Interviews are almost clinical in their close-up framings. Reenactments are deliberately stylized. Photographs are openly presented, not as evidence but as problems to solve. The doubt Morris instills does not, however, go unresolved. His conclusion is damning – that government and media alike chose to shift responsibility for atrocity and to condemn the least powerful by misreading the data.

Herzog and Morris both use self-reflexive techniques that, in their distinctiveness, comment implicitly on documentary public affairs conventions and on fictional or fictionalizing elements. They use these elements in order to address the nature of representation and to ask how we know what we think we know about reality. Herzog's visceral resistance to intellectual synthesis stands in stark contrast to Morris's approach, however. Morris believes and argues to the viewer that it is possible both to acknowledge confusion, distortion, self-deception, and ideological framing and also to use their analysis to come to some shared conclusion about reality – for instance, that the wrong man was given the death penalty – or to ask the right questions, such as whether the right people were charged with the right crimes in Abu Ghraib.

As documentary auteurs who developed their expectations for the craft and art of documentary film at the height of 1960s and 1970s film culture, Kopple, Herzog, and Morris produce works of art aimed at a theatergoing, Netflix-subscribing viewership. Shaped differently from one another by the furious and polarized politics of the period, they each select stories that correspond with their own inquiries about the possibilities and consequences of individual choice in difficult circumstances.

Moral Investigations

Another strand of conscience-driven documentary work is executed by people who primarily understand themselves as interlocutors with the public – that is, viewers in their role as democratic citizens and active members of their own society. These films address a broad American public, composed of people who work and vote. They assume that democracy can work, is worth caring about and fighting for. They speak to people who are paying taxes, believe in the democratic process, and expect accountability. They associate knowledge with the act of getting involved with political change and monitoring corruption.

Often these makers have thought of themselves less as filmmakers than as journalists, reporters, or even activists. Frequently, their works have come close to being audiovisual equivalents of well-researched, issue-based feature articles in national magazines such as the *New Yorker*, *Harper's*, *Vanity Fair*, and *The Atlantic*. Here, documentary is sought out as an effective form of nonfiction communication with a general audience. Typically these works were designed not only to introduce information but to reframe an issue so that viewers might take action as they see fit. At their best, these works are marked by high journalistic standards, compelling storytelling, and strategies designed to cross ideological and cultural barriers. They use a broad range of strategies to achieve their communication goals, addressing themselves to people who might use them to reimagine both a problem and the viewer's own capacity to act on it. Three very different examples of such work in early twenty-first-century US documentary can be found in the films of Bill Moyers, Judith Helfand, Eugene Jarecki, and Alex Gibney.

Bill Moyers entered the twenty-first century as a seasoned veteran of public-service documentary. He was a legendary figure in public broadcasting, having as a young man been instrumental in creating it. (He had worked in the Lyndon Johnson White House on the 1967 legislation creating public broadcasting.) Raised in Texas, trained as a journalist, and ordained as a Baptist minister, he spent a decade in public service before turning to news and commentary production for public broadcasting with *The Bill Moyers Journal* in the 1970s (he revived it in 2007). He later worked for CBS before returning after 1986, with his wife, to documentary production. His distinctive style of exhaustively researched, thematic documentary on environmental, political, and cultural topics – typically addressing directly the question of how to define the public good – has created cultural markers. His series of interviews with philosopher Joseph Campbell, *The Power of Myth*, made a profound cultural impact. Moyers infused the classic public affairs documentary style with moral inquiry and civic passion. Developed in the heyday of network television and notoriously pricey, this documentary style has remained a powerful format even in a multi-screen, digital era. But few outside of Moyers and a handful of others could command the resources from private foundations to execute the sober long-form journalistic works that had once been the TV networks' fulfillment of their public-interest obligation.

The 2001 *Trade Secrets*, made with his longtime producer Sherry Jones, demonstrates the classic public affairs documentary style. The film aims to inform an active (prime-time public broadcasting) audience who, beyond taking individual action, would presumably take this information into decisions about supporting particular legislation or candidates, although these types of actions were not guided by a film-related campaign. *Trade Secrets* addresses, in the tradition of legendary broadcast journalist Edward R. Murrow, a general prime-time public broadcasting viewing audience (the so-called "intelligent layman"). It methodically exposes dangerous chemical industry practices that affect everyone's daily life, made possible by a lack of regulation. It features, in particular, the dangers of polyvinyl chloride production. The two historically dominant frames of reference for the chemical industry – the social progress emphasis of "better living through chemistry" and the event-driven focus on the Thalidomide scandal – were replaced by Moyers's emphasis on public accountability of industry and government's obligation to protect the public.

Moyers, the narrator and host, acts both as fair-minded journalist and upholder of moral standards in the exalted tradition of Edward R. Murrow. Interviews are key to the documentary's argument. Moyers attentively interviews victims of chemical industry malfeasance (as well as their loved ones), scientists, doctors, lawyers, historians, and political functionaries. Eschewing, as always, a "gotcha" approach in the *60 Minutes* style, he respectfully explores with his interview subjects not what happened but how it happened, how it was allowed to happen, and what the human consequences are. The other major element of the film is revelation of journalistic research, which uncovered industry documents revealing knowledge of poisonous and carcinogenic effects of chemical production processes. This is revealed textually, with the camera scrolling down actual documents.

This film was powerfully controversial, not least because the Chemical Society protested it. It also constituted rigorously researched and documented journalism, with the imprimatur of public television and Moyers's own journalistic reputation. The documentary's website was rich in additional information substantiating claims of the film. The website also offered recommendations as to how individuals can become personally involved in the issue by informing themselves, by reducing chemical use in the home, and by discussing the issue with friends and coworkers.

Contrasting sharply with this traditional and sober approach is Judith Helfand and Dan Gold's treatment of the same general topic, the carcinogenic effects of polyvinyl chloride, in *Blue Vinyl* (2002). The style of the film, which won numerous awards and was shown on the prestige cable channel HBO, is highly personal and even idiosyncratic, following on Helfand's earlier personal essay film *A Healthy Baby Girl* (1997). In that film, Helfland chronicled in video-diary form her family's coming to terms with her uterine cancer as a result of her mother being prescribed DES, an antimiscarriage drug that the pharmaceutical company knew could be deadly. *A Healthy Baby Girl* is artfully artless, seemingly a girlish video diary, but of a hideously premature, near-death experience. The chronicle of personal recovery evolves into expression of grief and then awareness of systemic corporate irresponsibility. The victims of a health crisis reimagine themselves as civic activists. The film, which won a Peabody Award for Excellence in Journalism and Public Education, was both an exposé of the social devastation caused by chemical company negligence and also a mother–daughter relationship story.

Blue Vinyl (codirected with Dan Gold) takes Helfand on a search for the environmental implications of vinyl, which her parents have chosen as the new exterior of their home. She finds that polyvinyl chloride creates cancer-causing dioxin at the beginning and end of its life cycle. By this time, Helfand's artfully artless persona was well honed. That persona takes a walk around the world in the film, with a piece of her parents' new vinyl siding under her arm. She visits victims (some the same as in *Trade Secrets*), factory workers, neighborhood residents in highly polluted areas, and a spokesperson for the Vinyl Institute. Viewers watch her nervous, flustered preparations to interview this industry representative; his slick, suited performance contrasts markedly with her disheveled and disarming questions, reinforcing viewers' allegiance to her perspective and also their awareness of the knowledge and power imbalance. She becomes the personification of the little guy in a big corporate world, but one who simply refuses to be a victim.

Where Moyers is the Murrow-esque, steady guide through a thicket of information, Helfand carefully models herself as the clueless consumer, demonstrating the obstacles to discovering the implications and consequences of consumer choices. Her sometimes comical efforts to find answers to what should be simple questions and to find an alternative to vinyl siding for her parents' home function to reframe the public issues from consumer choice to a wider consideration of public health and public will. She not only exposes chemical industry malfeasance, but also addresses directly why consumers find it difficult to take action. She shares with viewers her own, her family's, and Louisiana shop clerks' desire not to have to deal with this at all. She also builds the case, interview by interview, vinyl siding under the arm the whole time, that none of us can afford to avoid it.

Both films address issues of public concern, deploying different styles and generating different expectations for the role of documentary. *Trade Secrets* maintains a distinct journalistic role, with Moyers as an expert trusted guide. Even the film's website has only consumer-action information. The citizen, now armed with alarming information, will presumably demand better regulation from his or her legislative representatives. *Blue Vinyl*, by contrast, was designed as a tool for activism. The film itself encourages people to become active citizens and informed consumers, not least by Helfand's indomitable example. The film also became the anchor of a campaign. Helfand and Robert West, through their separate outreach organization Working Films, have supported organizations that resist incinerators which put dioxin into the air. They have also worked with businesses to limit use of vinyl packaging. The action campaigns that have emerged through the film have done so because individuals across communities have discovered shared problems for which the film has helped provide a vocabulary to articulate those common interests and concerns.

Between these extremes there exist journalistic and op-ed style documentaries, also motivated by a commitment to engage viewers as members of the public and often produced for a cable environment that demands brisk pacing, bold cueing, and provocative framing. Two filmmakers working in this mode are Eugene Jarecki and Alex Gibney, who collaborated on *Trials of Henry Kissinger* (2002), a film that sparked international furor with its portrayal, following Christopher Hitchens's book, of the eponymous statesman as a war criminal. Although it had a solid theatrical run and was shown in 30 countries, including on the BBC, it was only shown in the US on the small Sundance Channel.

Jarecki, armed with an elite education and blessed with family money, wanted to use documentary to promote a more liberal geopolitical agenda in a conservative era. He was chastened by the experience of his Henry Kissinger film – dismayed, as he told the BBC, that people easily targeted Kissinger the man as the villain: "I wanted to have a much more holistic approach that really took on the whole system." His 2005 film *Why We Fight* attempts to change the framework within which people understand US geopolitical choices and actions – what Jarecki understands as US imperialist policies. The film was widely praised but little seen. Like the Kissinger film, *Why We Fight* had a successful theatrical presence but, perhaps because of its explicitly political critique, only a small televisual window in the US (although it showed on television in many other countries).

Why We Fight is a sober, hard-hitting indictment of fecklessness in military, legislative, industry, and even media sectors, leading to a betrayal of democratic values. It builds its explanation for US imperialist policies on the warning that President Eisenhower issued in his farewell address, to beware the military-industrial-legislative complex (as it was in the first draft of his speech). Jarecki traces that warning in Bush-era geopolitics, which his essay film represents as being driven by parochial and counterproductive pressures from the "complex." The film mixes presentational modes of network public affairs documentaries – B-roll, tight-shot interviews, archival footage – with the op-ed style of argument from prestige newspapers. It attempts to act as a public alarum, much as Murrow did – for instance, as in the end to *Harvest of Shame*, when Murrow spoke directly to the American people as citizens about their need to demand that their legislators take action against migrant labor injustices. In this case, however, Jarecki, without the journalistic stature of Murrow (or Moyers), acts as a ventriloquist, letting his viewpoint emerge from carefully chosen leading characters – middle-class, middle-of-the-road conservatives, such as President Eisenhower, longtime establishment military critic Chalmers Johnson, an anti–Iraq War New York cop whose son died in 9/11, and a harshly critical retired Air Force officer. All are models of independent thinkers who believe that their actions count; his choosing these characters illustrates Jarecki's concern with reaching middle-class, middle-of-the-road viewers as citizens.

In the last few minutes of *Why We Fight*, the retired Air Force lieutenant colonel, Karen Kwiatkowski, has the last word. Seen at home in an exurban setting where she raises horses, she says, "Why we fight? I think we fight 'cause too many people are not standing up, saying 'I'm not doing this anymore.'" She issues a frank, direct, non-ironic appeal to voters – people who have always assumed they have agency, people who think that at some point earlier democracy did work, people who can be upset that they are betrayed.

With the same expectations for using documentary journalism to affect public life, Alex Gibney reflects a more careful balance between the entertainment needs of today's cable audiences and the values and concerns of someone who came of age in the 1970s. Gibney comes from a family tradition of social responsibility and of journalism, and has produced and directed a wide range of solidly reputable, crisply executed, strategically timed documentaries.

Enron: The Smartest Guys in the Room (2005), which was nominated for an Academy Award, chronicles the greatest financial scandal of its time (later dwarfed by ensuing economic disasters). Drawing upon a bestseller by Bethany McLean and Peter Elkind, Gibney reframes the story as an epic drama rather than a "financial story." Voices overlap in the first few minutes of the film: "It's not about numbers, it's a story about people"; "It's a tragedy." As if unspooling a detective story, Gibney sketches the characters of several key actors in the Enron company and follows their astonishing trajectory of greed and overweening, testosterone-fueled hubris. He shows the complicity of the financial sector, financial journalism, and even regulators in believing the unbelievable. The rise of heroes, including two women (one whistleblower inside the company, one journalist), mirrors the catastrophic downfall of Enron.

The film ratchets up the classic public affairs documentary style to fit cable standards. It is quicker, louder, and brassier, but not fundamentally different in form from the style that Jarecki and Moyers draw on. Murrow is still in the wings, but the film's narrative tone is more like that of liberal TV commentator Keith Olbermann (although the narrator is Peter Coyote). Popular songs typically cue events through their lyrics. We hear the jazz song lyrics, "I'm going ... right to the top ..." as Enron's fortunes soar. Singer-songwriter Tom Waits is frequently heard, his raspy, cynical voice underlining the narrator's judgmental stance. (Gibney himself, in an interview, called the music "a toe-tapping Greek chorus.") Deliberately stagey reenactments and arch use of Hollywood films such as *It's a Wonderful Life* sharpen the ironies that feed outrage. The film showcases the audiotapes (revealed in the legal process) of brutal salesmen knowingly destroying the California electrical supply infrastructure as they jack up prices. This revelation comes after tracking the building, by the executive class known as the "guys with spikes," of the corporate culture that did not merely permit but mandated such brutality. The film intends to trigger disgust and indignation, not just about corporate greed – one expects that – but about the failure of government to protect citizens from its wider consequences, challenging viewers to demand more transparency from industry and better government.

Perhaps the most notable documentarian of this period, Michael Moore, was also the most distinctive. Moore combined in one large celebrity package the authorial role of the artist, the crusading role of the independent journalist, and the entertainer role that cable television had chosen for documentarians. Moore permanently destabilized the Griersonian set of expectations for documentary – that it be dowdy, paternalistic, anonymous, earnest. He also challenged the popular expectation, born of decades of mediocre educational fare and public affairs television, that documentary be balanced or neutral. Three of the top 10 grossing documentaries of all time are Moore documentaries. People who know nothing else of documentary film know his name. Many of them think that Michael Moore does not make "real documentaries" because of his obvious persuasive purpose. This is in part a reflection of the fact that Moore works very hard to position himself as the anti-Grierson, the anti-Murrow, the anti-Moyers. He is selfconsciously uncouth, slovenly, seemingly uninformed, impetuous, even reckless (Sharrett & Luhr 2005).

Moore did not emerge from the film community, but rather from his experience as a left-wing print journalist. His film work, from the start, has been high profile and audience grabbing. Its conventions resemble those of reality television, such as the staged adventure, and draw from those of investigative public affairs programming like *60 Minutes*, such as the gotcha interview. *Fahrenheit 9/11* (2004), which had taken in $222 million worldwide by 2009, plays a unique role in documentary history. The film broke through what had been, in the US, a suffocating barrier of silence about the growing public sentiment against the war in Iraq, and, by gaining the top award at the Cannes Film Festival, registered international antiwar protest. Moore's film boldly, even rudely, accuses the Bush administration of lying about the reasons to go to war, coddling its Saudi allies, and recklessly conducting the war. The film's overwhelming success was much more a political statement by viewers than it was an aesthetic or entertainment one. Its success made possible the release of many more documentaries on Iraq by distributors that had been diffident in the earlier climate of fear.

Moore's style is personality centered and designed to be at least contentious if not controversial; his documentaries are structured as quests and all are extended personal performances, with Moore's persona dominating every scene. As the representative of the average person – someone who has no inside knowledge but an abundance of common sense won through harsh experience with injustice – he takes upon himself the job of telling truths to power. His weapon of choice is faux naiveté.

In Moore's films, the average person is sometimes working class and sometimes a member of the middle and professional classes that tend to watch documentaries. The audience he actually addresses is the middle-class documentary film-going audience. What is common among the actual, implied, and putative audiences for the films is that they have been betrayed by those in power and are voiceless and even helpless. The charging polarity is between the victims and the powerful. Moore's signature gesture is ridiculing and humiliating the powerful, as he did in an interview with Hollywood celebrity Charlton Heston and an attempted interview with TV personality Dick Clark in his *Bowling for Columbine* – a film that addresses but does not recommend policy on guns and gun control. His ability to use ridicule and contempt for savage entertainment is also evident in his setups, which are designed to demonstrate power relations. For instance, his attempt to interview the CEO of General Motors in *Roger and Me*, other CEOs in *The Big One*, and his attempt to get medical treatment at Guantanamo military base for 9/11 rescue workers suffering from chronic illness in *Sicko* are all acts of faux naiveté.

As the representative of the victims, Moore thus brazenly employs tactics that would be off-limits to a journalist. He uses the weapons of the weak – laughter, ridicule, shame – to point fingers at the powerful. Techniques that may seem unfair – a gotcha interview, a setup designed to embarrass or humiliate the interviewee, editing that unfairly suggests a cause-and-effect relationship or even a relationship (for instance, an official laughing at a comment made in a different context, voiceover mocking the people shown in the video) are implicitly justified because of the inequity that Moore assumes and describes to viewers between his speaking position and those in authority. This is a different project from invoking agency – celebrating and calling on people to assume the power they have, as is typical in the work, for instance, of Kopple, Moyers, Helfand, Jarecki, and Gibney. It is also extremely entertaining, for anyone who perceives their interests poorly served by those in power and perceives themselves disempowered to do more than sneer. At the same time, Moore's insouciant stance also models a disruptive disrespect, which can be a prompt to action (as it was in 2004).

Moore sometimes does make a direct call to action, typically addressed to his core audience of middle-class, educated Americans. For instance, at the end of *Fahrenheit 9/11*, he and his crew pound the streets around the Capitol building in Washington, DC, buttonholing Congressional representatives. Moore uses his trusty technique of shaming by asking Congressmen if they have a child fighting in Iraq and if they will urge their colleagues to send their children – a snicker-inducing scene. Immediately Moore cuts to scenes of appalling urban and rural poverty and anomie; in voiceover, he says that the poorest of the poor are the ones who fight America's war, and "all they ask of us is that we not send them into harm's way" without a good reason. With these references to "they" and "we," Moore has repositioned the viewer away from complicity as a victim into a social actor on behalf of victims. "Will they ever trust us again?" he asks boldly. Suddenly, the viewer is no longer the victim, but the victim's caretaker. Immediately, however, he shifts to a collage of images of totalizing power, and describes war as a familiar tool to maintain power by intimidation and fear. These images then thrust the viewer back into the powerless role of victim. He then models a response – his familiar one of impudence, the victim who retaliates, by "talking back" in voiceover to President George W. Bush. By using the weapon of the weak – the cheap jibe – he ends by restoring the viewer to victimhood.

Sicko, his 2007 documentary (one of the top three highest grossing documentaries of all time), goes a step beyond ridicule and contempt. He argues in this film for nationally subsidized and regulated health care. He uses the full repertoire of unabashed unfair reportorial techniques. He deploys hidden cameras and lies to officials about his motives. He poses as more naive than he assuredly is in asking questions. He holds official error – for instance then-President Bush's common malapropisms – up for viewer scorn. He uses edits to ridicule officials, such as one in which Congressmen are seen laughing after Moore describes the abysmal world rating of the US in health care. He conducts stunts, such as bringing chronically ill people who worked in the cleanup in New York after 9/11 to Cuba. He brays into a bullhorn off Guantanamo Bay to a nearby US military patrol: "I have three 9/11 rescue workers; I just want some medical attention, the same kind the evildoers are getting." He roams a British hospital, wide-eyed, asking how much everything costs, while people keep telling him they pay nothing. The film delivers, nonstop, entertainingly vengeful victories for the little guy. In the end, the case is clear: There are plausible, viable, even successful health-care alternatives, and all that is stopping the US government from exploring them is health-care industry lobbying and venal politics.

The outraged faux-naif role has, in the wake of Moore's success, become a trope, used profitably by other documentarians. In that role, the documentarian takes on the character of a naive, uninformed everyman who intrepidly reveals scandal, bad behavior, even immorality. The documentarian plays this role comically, exaggerating the character's common-man cluelessness in order to dramatize revelations. The audience can both empathize with the lead character's common-man position and also savor the way he or she turns the knowledge tables on the insiders. Morgan Spurlock played the role of faux-naif in his well-received *Super Size Me* (2004), in which he made his own body an experiment in the perils of fast food. Ben Stein assumes an aggrieved, outraged attitude – shocked at his apparent discovery that freedom of expression has been muffled – with the 2008 *Expelled: No Intelligence Allowed*, which asserts that scientists espousing intelligent design (anti-Darwinism) are persecuted. Bill Maher, equally faux-naif, is astounded at the idiocy of people who believe in God in *Religulous* (2008).

These films were issued in the geopolitically fraught period of the Bush presidency and were marked by an attitude of resistance to official authority. The Obama administration, however, created the conditions of greater optimism for social equality, while the economic crisis created an acute awareness of the instability of privilege. The era of affluence that had floated documentary into public view, into a spot on the entertainment docket of millions, and into a revitalized role in public life seemed to have come to an abrupt end.

At the same time, a new generation of creators was swarming onto the scene, with the advent of YouTube in 2005. The video-sharing site created a new venue for documentaries, a new way to critique and comment upon the work of others, and a chance to discover relationships between works. YouTube even made it possible for individuals to create their own video channels. Followed soon by open-source video platform Miro, the service motivated many new creators to see themselves as video storytellers, documentarians, and public witnesses. Much of the first-generation material on YouTube was banal, trite, and vulgar. Some of it made bold political criticism, such as a video made during the Iraq War that recut political speeches by political allies George Bush and Tony Blair, making them appear to lip-sync to the song "Endless Love."

The online video environment opened up a new distribution channel, for new voices and uses. The human rights organization WITNESS used it to post both human rights-related documentation and human rights documentaries. Entire long-form documentaries appeared there. The BBC journalist Adam Curtis's *The Power of Nightmares*, positing a connection between the rise of US neoconservatives and the Muslim Brotherhood, was posted online by enthusiasts frustrated by its lack of US distribution. The innovative video advocacy organization Brave New Films, led by veteran Hollywood insider Robert Greenwald, moved away from making long-form films such as *Outfoxed* (2004) and *Wal-Mart: The High Price of Low Cost* (2005) and focused on making short films for use in activist campaigns, using email and social media to prompt people to watch, recommend, and spread them. Michael Moore posted his *Slacker Uprising* (2008), a get-out-the-vote film, online. By the end of 2008, in the US alone, some 13 billion videos were being viewed monthly, with figures constantly escalating.

In the first decade of the twenty-first century, documentary rose to unprecedented significance in American media, succeeding not only in establishing a commercially viable niche in the filmic landscape but also having discernible impacts on public opinion, public actions, and even public policy. Viewer experience with a wide range of styles challenged long-established stereotypes about the form and raised new questions about the ethical responsibilities of the documentarian (Aufderheide et al. 2009). Documentarians acted as entertainers, journalists, and artists or performers; Michael Moore attempted a trifecta, and has the box office to prove his success.

Documentary ended the decade with new crises, as traditional mass media distribution business models continued to crumble. The rise of online video and, in particular, of the mashup created the conditions for people formerly known as viewers to become close readers, analysts, and makers of popular culture as never before. The question of how to represent the real, a question addressed with great thought by leading documentarians of the time, had overnight evolved into a question faced by millions. As the most popular and critically well-received documentaries of the decade demonstrated, they had a wide range of options in saying something true about something real.

References

Aitken, Ian. (1990). *Film and Reform: John Grierson and the Documentary Film Movement*. London: Routledge.

Aufderheide, Patricia. (2000). *The Daily Planet: A Critic on the Capitalist Culture Beat*. Minneapolis: University of Minnesota Press.

Aufderheide, Patricia. (2007). *Documentary Film: A Very Short Introduction*. New York: Oxford University Press.

Aufderheide, Patricia, & Zimmerman, Debbie. (2004). "From A to Z: A Conversation on Women's Filmmaking." *Signs*, 30.1, 1455–1473.

Aufderheide, Patricia, Jaszi, Peter, & Chandra, Mridu. (2009). *Honest Truths: Documentary Filmmakers on Ethical Challenges in Their Work*. Washington, DC: Center for Social Media, American University.

Barnouw, Erik. (1993). *Documentary: A History of the Non-fiction Film*. New York: Oxford University Press.

Benson, Thomas, & Anderson, Carolyn. (1989). *Reality Fictions: The Films of Frederick Wiseman*. Carbondale: Southern Illinois University Press.

Chanan, Michael. (2007). *The Politics of Documentary*. London: British Film Institute.

Cunningham, Megan. (2005). *The Art of the Documentary*. Berkeley: New Riders.

Feldman, Seth. (2002). *Allan King: Filmmaker*. Toronto: Toronto International Film Festival.

Herzog, Werner, & Cronin, Paul. (2002). *Herzog on Herzog*. London: Faber & Faber.

Johnson, David. (2008)."'You Must Never Listen to This': Lessons on Sound, Cinema, and Mortality from Herzog's 'Grizzly Man' (Werner Herzog)." *Film Criticism*, 32.3, 68–82.

Kahana, Jonathan. (2008). *Intelligence Work: The Politics of American Documentary*. New York: Columbia University Press.

King, John. (2000). *Magical Reels: A History of Cinema in Latin America*. London: Verso.

Leitner, David (1998). "Director: Errol Morris." *Millimeter*, October 1, at http://digitalcontent-producer.com/mag/video_director_errol_morris/ (accessed March 4, 2008).

Mamber, Stephen. (1974). *Cinéma Vérité in America: Studies in Uncontrolled Documentary*. Cambridge, MA: MIT Press.

Prager, Brad. (2007). *The Cinema of Werner Herzog: Aesthetic Ecstasy and Truth*. London: Wallflower Press.

Rouch, Jean, & Feld, Steven. (2003). *Ciné-ethnography*. Minneapolis: University of Minnesota Press.

Williams, Linda. (1998). "Mirrors without Memories: Truth, History and *The Thin Blue Line*." In B. K. Grant and J. Sloniowski (eds), *Documenting the Documentary: Close Readings of Documentary Film and Video* (pp. 379–396). Detroit: Wayne State University Press.

Sharrett, Christopher & Luhr, William (2005). "*Bowling for Columbine*: A Review." In A. Rosenthal & J. Corner (eds), *New Challenges for Documentary* (pp. 253–265). Manchester: Manchester University Press.

Wintonick, Peter. (1999). *Cinéma Vérité: Defining the Moment*. Montreal: National Film Board of Canada.

24

Truthiness Is Stranger than Fictition
The "New Biopic"

Michael Sicinski
Independent scholar

The **biography picture** or **biopic** has undergone a remarkable resurgence since 1999, with star-centered **prestige films** an important component of Hollywood's production line. Michael Sicinski situates this phenomenon within an international history of the genre, concluding that the contemporary American biopic is aesthetically and ideologically impoverished in serving up "**truthiness**," or plausible simulation of biographical fact, as a means of reinforcing dominant beliefs – ironically at a time when the **public sphere** is "governed by falsehood and fabrication." Adopting studio-era conventions, the contemporary biopic assumes that individual psychology is accessible through a collection of facts and that history is a neat, linear progression in which unique individuals shape their times. Sicinski argues the superiority of the **critical biopic** – as exemplified by ***Ali*** and ***I'm Not There*** – that pivots not on the accuracy of facts but on close readings of textuality. In these films cinematography and editing de-center the individual, who is now embedded within history rather than an exceptional sculptor of it. Sicinski's essay shares ground with Susan Jeffords on Hollywood and Reagan's America in this volume and with Robert Rosenstone on Oliver Stone as historian in the hardcover/online edition.

Additional terms, names, and concepts: New Biopic, "Old" Biopic, impersonation vs. interpretation of character

The "New Biopic" as Cultural Symptom

Before turning to a consideration of the odd prevalence of "biopics" (or biographical films about well-known historical or cultural figures) among recent Hollywood and Indiewood prestige pictures, it may be useful to consider some aspects of the larger cultural landscape into which they insert themselves. Filmmaker Michael Moore, who in many ways has revitalized the documentary form precisely by adopting the stylistic mannerisms of sketch comedy and

American Film History: Selected Readings, 1960 to the Present, First Edition. Edited by Cynthia Lucia, Roy Grundmann, and Art Simon.

specious reasoning by montage one finds in every bit of propaganda from Eisenstein to Fox News, took the podium at the 2002 Academy Awards to loudly declare that "we are living in fictitious times." In some sense this contention is fairly obvious, although whether the period from 1999 to the present represents some unique nadir of deceit is highly debatable. Still, from Bill Clinton's minor obstructions of justice through the fraudulent 2000 election and the seemingly limitless, deadly prevarications of the Bush forty-third presidency, one can easily say that the public sphere is one governed by falsehood and fabrication (or, as Moore misspoke that night, "fictition").

In an ironic twist that only an army of critical-theory armed scholars could parse, this moment of high theater within the realm of the political sphere has been accompanied by an increasing demand within American culture that our art be truthful. Rather than treasuring the imagination as a means by which to explore new options for the creation of better worlds, or more humane paths for living, there has been an increased demand for lockstep verisimilitude, "art" that must reflect the world as we think we know it to be.

Bertolt Brecht warned us that in reactionary times we would cling to distorted forms of "realism," that copied the surface of things but deliberately failed to comprehend the deeper social structures that produced the world we inhabit. The New Biopic can best be understood, I believe, in the context of the present decade's popular desire for a form of hybrid art which provides an illusion of transparency, an overcoming of "artiness" in favor of what fake TV journalist Stephen Colbert cannily refers to as "truthiness." "Truthiness" reflects the vague sense of an idea seeming plausible or accurate by operating comfortably within the vein of other widely held, dominant truths. What Colbert has done, of course, is rename the concept of ideology for our allegedly postideological age.

Certainly our era is filled with copious examples of the drive toward greater reflection of the surface affectations of reality and its concomitant ideologies. Perhaps the insistence that contemporary forms hew to a recognizable "real" provides consolation in our "fictitious times." But outside of the realm of cinema, the clearest example of this is within the publishing industry. While it has long been true within the industry that nonfiction outsells fiction, the current decade witnessed an unprecedented boom in memoir sales. For writers, the message has been loud and clear: If it didn't really happen (preferably to *you*), we aren't interested. Of course, this insistence was bound to result in a backlash. The perpetrator of the great memoir hoax of the decade, or the victim of the anti-art publishing zeitgeist, depending on your point of view, is obviously James Frey. In spring of 2003, Doubleday published his memoir of drug addiction and recovery, *A Million Little Pieces*. Soon, the veracity of specific details of the memoir came under scrutiny by internet investigators, and Frey was subjected to a rather brutal interrogation on the Oprah Winfrey Show for deceiving the host and her book club audience. In his own defense, Frey maintained that he spent years shopping *A Million Little Pieces* around as a novel, but no publishers (including Doubleday) were interested. He also claimed that his publishers advised him to retool the book into a memoir for sales purposes.

What the whole Frey issue occludes, of course, is textuality itself. Regardless of how accurate "the facts" of any given memoir or biopic may be, there is still, one hopes, a style or a form that gives them a texture over and above mere denotative meaning. But more and more, this question of textuality – the physical *stuff* of the work of art – seems to be what the popular arts are striving to overcome. Granted, this is impossible. But the work of the text, its shape and organization, its locutionary force and mode of address, can be more and more adroitly disguised through adherence to agreed upon terms of vulgar mimesis. This urge to copy, and the pleasure of appreciating the copy *as* such, strikes me as one of the defining characteristics of the New Biopic.

In the most basic terms, a biopic is a realist film centered on the life and achievements of a single woman or man, her or his biography (or a substantial segment of it) providing the dramatic shape for the work. I also want to make a second distinction between proper biopics, which treat the single individual as a central figure in history, and those biographical films based on real-life stories whose interest value lies more in the subject's "typicality" or their representation of a larger issue or class of citizens. I would argue that *Boys Don't Cry* (Kimberly Peirce, 1999), *Erin Brockovich* (Steven Soderbergh, 2000), *A Beautiful Mind* (Ron Howard, 2001), and a pair of films directed by painter Julian Schnabel, *Before Night Falls* (2000) and *The Diving Bell and the Butterfly* (2007), fall into this category. These films are not arguing for the world-historical stature of their subjects. Rather, they argue on behalf of the fascinating, even heroic qualities of the ordinary lives so profiled, and their value as representative of a larger identity group or political issue (e.g., transgender people, political muckrakers, stroke patients).

But if we consider the vast majority of biopics made, in Hollywood and around the world, overwhelmingly they adhere to certain genre tropes, and these must be part of our definition as well. Biopics, almost by their nature, assume that the human subject is fundamentally knowable, that he or she has a psychology that can be explained through a progression of biographical facts, and that the assembly of such facts will, in the end, produce a rather coherent portrait of some "self." What's more, that subject or self is understood by the traditional biopic to be an active shaper of history. But too often, the conventional biopic, for the sake of dramatic license of three-act closure, fails to address certain fundamental questions that any good biographer ought to face.

These include how history functions in fits and starts rather than as a linear progression; how the individual is shaped by his or her times as much as he or she shapes them; how interior psychology is but one mode of understanding the individual onscreen, and not necessarily the most useful for gaining a fuller understanding of the individual as a sociological creature; and finally, that cinematic style and form, in the form of obvious work upon the sound and image of a film, can serve to disrupt easy identification with the individual profiled, or complete suspension of disbelief in the "pastness" of the diegetic world, instead asking us as viewers to think critically about how the subject of the biopic and his or her history might have resonances for our own time.

Rather than examining how individuals are shaped and constrained by the social and material circumstances in which they find themselves, traditional biopics chart the series of accomplishments of some exceptional personage who is an active shaper of the larger world. In short, the biopic proffers a bourgeois conception of the human subject and of history, not as dialectical processes, but as sculptor and clay, respectively.

The Biopic as Prestige Object, and Other Alternatives

It seems fair to say that the New Biopic serves several functions. These functions are cultural, industrial, as well as creative within certain parameters. Just as the truth of the story is the chief guarantor of merit for the memoir, the New Biopic derives its cultural authority from bringing presumably important true-life stories to the big screen. The fact that big-budget biopics have, in the present decade, been overwhelmingly released from mid-October on – that is, the Oscar season – demonstrates that the industry has a high degree of faith in these pictures' perception and overall worth as prestige items. During the period from 1999 through the end of 2008, 46 US-produced biopics were released to Manhattan theaters. Of these films, slightly over two-thirds of them opened between October and December.[1]

Those that predated the Academy Awards sweet spot generally fall into three categories. Several are studio releases that were being dumped onto the market, reputed to be either bad films or the result of troubled productions. These include *Isn't She Great* (Andrew Bergman, 2000), which starred Bette Midler as *Valley of the Dolls* author Jacqueline Susann; *Miss Potter* (Chris Noonan, 2006), the Beatrix Potter biopic featuring Renée Zellweger as the children's author; and *De-Lovely*, Irwin Winkler's 2004 Cole Porter biopic featuring Kevin Kline and Ashley Judd. While *De-Lovely* opened in the United Kingdom during the usual October awards season, it was rushed into release in July in the US, following a critically lambasted world premiere at the Cannes Film Festival in May.

A few fall into a smaller, second category of films whose target audience is more likely to exist within some small niche that is not, strictly speaking, defined by an interest in cinema per se. These include "artsploitation" pictures, films which freely combine elements of the arthouse with those of the grindhouse, such as *Freeway* auteur Matthew Bright's *Ted Bundy* (2002) (a film, like most of Bright's work, that is of significant interest even if it is never wholly successful), and David Jacobson's complex, somewhat Fassbinder-inflected *Dahmer* starring Jeremy Renner. Also falling under the nonprestige, niche-market umbrella are religious-themed (or "Godsploitation") films such as 2003's *Luther* and the most successful independently released film of all time, Mel Gibson's *The Passion of the Christ*.

Of course, when certain other biopics have forgone the typical prestige packaging – October to December rollout, with key actors on the talk show circuit and major studio campaigning inside the industry for Academy Award nominations – there have been other material exigencies, not necessarily related to the film's quality, or its perceived prestige value. In many cases, these are independent and/or auteurist biopics, and although many of them hew to the same basic structure and formula as their better-funded Hollywood cousins, some have adopted complex approaches to the form, stretching and even undermining the biopic's very gold standard – its perceived truth value. Often these film foreground cinematic signification, the very work that an artist or group of artists *performs* on the basic set of biographical facts. These "anti-biopics," or "critical biopics," all of which were commercially released well before the October awards-season prestige berth, include *American Splendor*, a self-reflexive film about the life of cartoonist Harvey Pekar; *Baadasssss!*, in which director Mario Van Peebles draws on his own childhood memories in order to portray his father Melvin in the process of creating his landmark 1971 film *Sweet Sweetback's Baadassss Song*; *The Notorious Bettie Page*, a revisionist consideration of the life and work of the late BDSM pinup, played with astonishing intelligence by Gretchen Mol; and Sofia Coppola's *Marie Antoinette*, a frankly anachronistic period piece likening the court at Versailles to the British postpunk era.

The only other film of the period to significantly break with the traditional biopic form, Todd Haynes's Bob Dylan film *I'm Not There*, is the sole exception to the pre-October rule, having been released in November. It would appear, however, that this had less to do with its studio's overall hopes for prestige positioning and commercial potential and more to do with a desire to capitalize on Oscar buzz surrounding Cate Blanchett's strange distaff riff on mid-period Bob Dylan. (She scored the coveted Best Supporting Actress nomination.) We will discuss this film in more detail below.

These films are working against the set of anti-art assumptions that govern the New Biopic's popularity. They are also drawing on earlier modes of counter-cinematic address, some of which have engaged with the biopic form before. We will discuss this in time. But first, it will be necessary to establish some basic parameters for what a biopic is, how its older forms have evolved historically, and what's so new about the New Biopic, circa 1999 to the present.

The "Old" Biopic in the US: A Brief History

The earliest film works were in fact documentaries of ordinary people, although the films served to emphasize their ordinariness, not their uniqueness. But alongside the traditional *actualités*, filmmakers also used the device to restage events in the lives of famous personages, particularly executions, such as those of President McKinley's assassin, Leon Czolgosz (in a 1901 Edison short), and Mary, Queen of Scots (Alfred Clark, 1895). Since, strictly speaking, the biopic depends on a substantial narrative thrust, it cannot be said to exist until the advent of longform narrative cinema. Nevertheless, the major works of the silent era tended toward grander scales of inquiry, examining epochal world events or employing the new-found power of montage to combine different, even distant lives together, rather than to zero in on the details of a single individual. A grand exception of this period is Abel Gance's *Napoleon* (France, 1927), a gargantuan, decade-spanning achievement wherein the director follows the life of Napoleon Bonaparte from his grade school days through the French Revolution, finishing off with the General's invasion of Italy. Running well over five hours, Gance's film is only one part of a planned multipart biopic that never came to fruition, although the expansive power of that fraction of *Napoleon* he was able to realize in no way feels lacking. In addition to being the first film to fully operate within the form that we now understand as the modern biopic, *Napoleon* also anticipated Cinemascope with an unprecedented triple-projection technique.

The biopic has been a staple of Hollywood production since the earliest days of the sound era. D. W. Griffith's first sound film, in fact, was a biopic, 1930's *Abraham Lincoln*. The early incarnations of the Academy Awards were consistently filled with nominations for industry biopics which are largely overlooked today, films such as *Disraeli* (1929) and *The Story of Louis Pasteur* (1935). Well into the era of the studio system, biopics continued to function as prestige productions, many making a big splash at the time. Some, such as *The Pride of the Yankees* (1942, about Lou Gehrig), remain sentimental favorites. Others, such as *Madame Curie* (1943) or *Wilson* (1944, about President Woodrow Wilson), are rather obscure today, turning up now and then on Turner Classic Movies for the curious cinephile.

Still others, such as *The Life of Emile Zola* (1937), have accumulated greater currency over the years, less due to interest in their ostensible subject than in the material surrounding him, in Zola's case, the Dreyfus Affair. And there are those films that maintain our interest primarily because of their formal elegance as works of cinema, or due to the overall excellence of the careers of those who made them. Examples of these might include *Gentleman Jim* (Raoul Walsh, 1942, about boxer Jim Corbett), *The Glenn Miller Story* (Anthony Mann, 1954), or for that matter, *Citizen Kane* (Orson Welles, 1941), understood as being, among so many other things, a crypto-biopic of newspaper magnate William Randolph Hearst.

The period from the 1950s to the end of the 1960s saw a turn away from large-scale biopics by and large, although a few certainly made their mark, such as *Funny Girl* (1968, about Fanny Brice). From the 1970s onward, the biopic continued to be a staple of Hollywood prestige programming, with profiles of military leaders (*Patton*, 1970), rock stars (*The Buddy Holly Story*, 1978), comedians (*Lenny*, Bob Fosse, 1974, about Lenny Bruce), and eventually even biopic directors (*All That Jazz*, Bob Fosse, 1979, about Bob Fosse) getting the full treatment.

This is to say nothing of developments within the New American Cinema, that branch of off-Hollywood filmmaking that revitalized the industry from the late 1960s to just before the age of the blockbuster. Directors like Arthur Penn created brash new spins on the genre such as *Bonnie and Clyde* (1967), a hyperviolent crime romance which maintains the biopic essentials but disrupts the generic trappings by centering on an infamous duo. Members of this New American Cinema group, partly influenced by developments in the American avant-garde such as the diary films of Jonas Mekas and the first-person camera of Stan Brakhage, would take the biopic into bold new directions in the 1980s. The most notable film of this period is *Raging Bull* (1980), Martin Scorsese's densely layered portrait of boxer Jake LaMotta. Using complex montage structures and centering on a transformative performance by Robert De Niro, *Raging Bull* set a new standard for psychological and formal complexity within the biopic which few films since have matched. Another triumph of the 1980s came from Robert Altman. His highly unconventional *Secret Honor* (1984) adopted the stage-bound, one-act play format to allow his actor, Phillip Baker Hall, to portray Richard Nixon in "conversation" with his Oval Office tape recorder, going over various events in his life in the halting, fragmented order of tormented human thought. All the events one would expect from a Nixon biopic are present in *Secret Honor*, but Altman eschews the usual mimetic pleasures of re-creation, instead zeroing in on his subject's mental anguish.

Although by the 1970s and 1980s we can begin to see American filmmakers stretching the biopic form, the vast majority of Hollywood biopics are holding fast to the basic structure that defined the genre from the outset: Follow the trajectory of a single individual's life in an essentially realist filmic mode, using the chronology of significant events in the subject's life to provide the overall shape of the film. If one were to select a film that typifies this approach, *Gandhi* (1982) would be as good as any. Virtually devoid of any purely cinematic interest, the film trades solely on the inherent importance of its subject matter. In fact, one could argue that it is a film that should not have been a biopic at all, since its subject, by his own reckoning, was a representative of a movement rather than its sole historical standard-bearer. Rarely viewed today, *Gandhi* exists as "a good film" in the abstract, an edifying idea of cinema that few are actually interested in undertaking as a viewing experience. Even the continued evolution of its star, Ben Kingsley, as one of his generation's finest actors has done little to stoke continued interest in *Gandhi*.

By the same token, an equally successful biopic of the period, *Amadeus* (1984), has retained only a slightly higher degree of aesthetic longevity, primarily due to its brisk, comedic pace and Tom Hulce's whimsical take on the character of Wolfgang A. Mozart. However, *Amadeus* effectively killed the career of its Oscar-winning lead actor, F. Murray Abraham, who has since been trapped in an endless run of direct-to-video schlock films. These films were released to great acclaim, hit their marks, and sank into the deep pool of cable programming that belies their prestige status within the industry.

The "Old" Biopic as a Critical Form: International Influences

Running counter to this bland trend, and much more in sympathy with the line of innovation that runs through *Citizen Kane*, *Bonnie and Clyde*, and *Raging Bull*, are the developments in international auteur cinema, and frequently the biopic came into the crosshairs of the film artists involved. However, in most cases, the filmmakers pushed the boundaries of the genre, questioning what it means to bring a human life before others on the screen. Attempts at a transparent realism were eschewed in favor of obvious stylization, a deliberate and unmistakable work upon the sounds and images contained within the film. Furthermore, many of world cinema's masters engaged with the biopic precisely to challenge or undermine its fundamental assumption, which is so seemingly self-evident that it usually goes unspoken – that history is shaped by great and powerful individuals. Instead, many filmmakers chose to explore how social and political forces also applied pressure upon their subjects in a dialectical give-and-take.

During the heyday of the Soviet Union, for example, the tenets of official Socialist Realism often favored biographical films, mostly of great historical figures whose efforts glorified or otherwise shored up the communist state. At the same time, these great men were understood to be "typical," in the sense that they were "of the people," members of the Bolshevik class and not elitist intellectuals or other ostensible enemies of the working class. Against this wholly mechanical Stalinist model, the great film artist (and noncommunist) Andrei Tarkovsky used the biopic form to reconsider the social and spiritual place of the artist in society. His masterwork, *Andrei Rublev* (1966), flouts Soviet orthodoxy by profiling the life of a renowned fifteenth-century icon painter as he observes a century marred by ethnic fighting and sectarian strife. Unlike the "great man" model of history favored by the biopic, *Andrei Rublev* mostly depicts its subject as a receiver and interpreter of events rather than a prime mover.

In a similar vein, Alexander Sokurov, a contemporary Russian filmmaker highly influenced by the Tarkovskian mode – patient, observational, spiritual, rarely overtly political – has created a series of biopics profiling infamous despots of the twentieth century. In most of the films, the men are seen less as shapers of history than as deranged accidents of their times, both perverting and perverted by objective social forces. In the finest of these films, *The Sun* (2005), Sokurov depicts Japan's Emperor Hirohito as a childlike, sheltered man burdened with world-historical duties for which his sequestered existence could scarcely prepare him. A penetrating and even sympathetic portrait, *The Sun* garners significant power from Sokurov's deliberate, uninflected pacing and a remarkably inward lead performance by Issei Ogata. By refusing to play along with the biopic's presumption of psychological interiority, artists like Tarkovsky and Sokurov return objective social and historical conditions to their rightful place.

To a large extent, the European New Wave cinemas of the 1960s and 1970s steered clear of biopics, chiefly for the reason implied above. That is, filmmakers of the French New Wave, the Italian Neorealist movement, the New German Cinema, the "angry young men" of British cinema, and post-Franco Spanish cinema were much more interested in broader social questions that could not be so easily explored through biography. What's more, the general assumption of linearity in the biopic – that is, a structure that will follow the basic trajectory of an individual life – was at odds with the radical collage experiments of Godard, the surrealist gamesmanship of Buñuel, or the charge that Italians and especially the Germans so acutely felt, to employ cinema as a tool for exploring the damaged psychology and traumatic memories associated with World War II. Radical form and broadly based sociological subject matter, rather than great-man hagiography, seemed the way to forge a new cinema for a new age.

There were major exceptions to this "rule," of course, and if any one thing unites these disparate films and filmmakers, it is the fact that they chose to adopt the biopic form in order to subvert its basic premises. To recall, in this period these were more than stylistic questions; they were openly political ones as well. The focus on the singular individual as the primary unit of historical analysis, which the biopic in its usual form implies, was seen not only as faulty but as retrograde, a bourgeois affectation. A more radical cinema would of necessity "decenter" the individual in favor of an open, legible analysis of social forces, within which the single person, no matter how great his or her achievement may have been, could be properly understood to be merely one "node."

Among the Italians, Roberto Rossellini and Pier Paolo Pasolini were the major contributors to the critical biopic model. Although most of Pasolini's major works were either adaptations of classical literature or original works of social commentary, he created what has become one of the most faithful and yet most formally radical of all adaptations of the life of Christ, *The Gospel According to St. Matthew* (1964). Rather than focusing on Christ as a holy being or miracle worker, or as the Christian martyr, Pasolini presents him first and foremost as a political rhetorician, demonstrating the radical power of Christian teaching when isolated from the institutions that have formed in its wake. Similarly, although in a very different tone, Rossellini's late "didactic" films made for Italian television, such as *Socrates* (1971), *Blaise Pascal* (1972), and *Descartes* (1974), adopted a patient, discursive style that favored the elaboration of ideas over traditional notions of dramaturgy. Rossellini's technique favored long takes and extended passages of dialogue, often delivered with a tamped-down, expository performance style. In these films, the true subjects are the social contests between differing views of the world, not the men themselves.

Among the practitioners of what came to be known as the New German Cinema, few filmmakers were as stern and austere in their unadorned modernism as the duo of Jean-Marie Straub and the late Danièle Huillet. Like Pasolini, Straub and Huillet were Marxist filmmakers dedicated primarily to exploring the dialectical materialist potential within already existing works of art. However few directors in the history of the medium have taken the concept of cinematic adaptation in such stark, transformative directions. In their groundbreaking anti-biopic *The Chronicle of Anna Magdalena Bach* (1968), Straub and Huillet tell the story of Johann Sebastian Bach through a strict dialectical process. In lengthy unbroken takes using direct sound, *The Chronicle* shows virtuoso musician Gustav Leonhardt playing Bach and performing his compositions in their entirety. Against this material we hear a female voiceover reading letters written by Bach's wife Anna Magdalena, detailing her husband's struggles as well as the family's material hardships. In short, Straub and Huillet debunk the myth of transcendent genius by revealing the daily economic underpinnings that permitted Bach to create, or in some cases prevented him from working. Whereas most biopics isolate the individual, treating career and family as opposing forces operating upon him, *The Chronicle of Anna Magdalena Bach* demonstrates their coextensive reality.

Among British filmmakers, the key figure to have adopted the biopic form and made it his own is undoubtedly Peter Watkins. A maverick in every sense of the word, Watkins has worked in documentary, feature filmmaking, and eventually as a wholly independent producer of long-form political films bearing his trademark style, a combination of news and documentary technique (including interview and direct questioning) within a fictional diegetic format. His long-form video film about the life of playwright August Strindberg, *The Freethinker* (1994), combines elements of the subject's childhood, marriage, and work life to demonstrate a multi-tiered individual drawing creative energy from all facets of life, including his engagement with the social sphere. But Watkins's masterpiece, and probably the greatest of all critical biopics, is *Edvard Munch* (1974). This three-and-a-half-hour opus traces ten years in the life of the Expressionist painter as he struggles to create his work and gain acceptance within the taste-making circles of Europe. However, Watkins's purview takes in examinations of nineteenth-century gender relations, child labor, burgeoning class-consciousness, and the overall place of art within society. In fact, there are frequent passages of the film in which Munch is not present at all, receding into the larger background of social relations. Furthermore, Watkins has his character, and his actors, speak directly to the camera to articulate their impressions of what's happening around them, and to give their own ideologies the best possible hearing. A critical biopic in any meaningful sense of the term, *Edvard Munch* takes as its fundamental charge the demonstration that the individual is both an actor within history and a product of his times.

Although the critical biopic mode has certainly been an undercurrent, it has nevertheless made its impact felt on more mainstream projects. In the intervening years, some American films have successfully incorporated elements of the critical mode into projects whose overall thrust was a more traditional great-man narrative. A prime example of this approach would be *Malcolm X* (1992), wherein writer-director Spike Lee adheres to the linear trajectory of Malcolm X's autobiography. The film also positions Malcolm X as a prime mover, a singular force, and in this regard follows the standard great-men view of history proffered by the traditional biopic. However, following Malcolm X's assassination, which would be the logical conclusion of such a narrative, Lee surprises with a diegetically disruptive coda, featuring contemporary schoolchildren of many races and genders standing up to declare, "I'm Malcolm X." The film concludes with then-recently-freed South African leader Nelson Mandela speaking X's line, "by any means necessary." Lee's phatic gesture is clear: This biopic, this life, cannot be safely consigned to the past. The struggle continues. (In a darkly ironic twist, Matthew Bright's aforementioned Ted Bundy biopic appropriates Lee's intervention wholesale, following Bundy's execution scene with a series of average kids, one holding up a dead cat, declaring, "I'm Ted Bundy.")

To sum up this necessarily quick-and-dirty survey of the vicissitudes and shifting fortunes of the biopic, we can see that the social purpose of the form has varied significantly over time and in different cultural contexts. Although early Hollywood biopics, particularly under the studio system, were considered prestige efforts much as they are today, the prestige seems to have derived from a sense of the subject matter's inherent importance. Whether because of America's understandable sentimental attachment to Lou Gehrig or a class-based duty-bound desire to edify oneself about the particulars of the Dreyfus Affair, the story's connection to the real world provided much of the luster of films like these in the face of competing product. But even when Hollywood begins producing successful biopics without presumed importance as their hook, they share one element in common with their forebears. Absolute verisimilitude is secondary to some form of interpretation of the material, an allowance that actors will create characters out of real life personages. When we view *Gentleman Jim* or *The Glenn Miller Story* today we are not bowled over by Errol Flynn's or James Stewart's uncanny impersonation of the subject, nor is that the point. As we have seen with a project such as *Gandhi*, however, that old commitment to importance and "uplift," when combined with a drive toward ever greater replication of the surfaces of people and things, can result in films of little lasting value. Moving along the other, less traveled track, those makers of critical biopics have, in various ways, provided contemporary filmmakers with a set of tools for attaining a deeper understanding of biography and its relationship to history. What's more, they have pointed the way toward a careful consideration of the act of cinematic inscription, and the ways in which filmic style and organization encourage certain interpretations over others. As many have noted in the years since the 1970s and 1980s heyday of "countercinema," it's possible for all of these approaches to become a "style" in themselves, a rote laundry-list of techniques no more critical than any other. Nevertheless, when applied with purpose and acuity, for reasons organic to the film-text's creation, they can be useful methods for disrupting conventional habits of perceiving the past.

The "New Biopic" as Recuperative Form: 1999–2008

Although for the sake of ease and organization I have made a division between Hollywood and non-Hollywood production, these modes are certainly not mutually exclusive. In fact, both have much to provide the contemporary filmmaker, since the biopic, at its best, will engage serious questions of social history and collective memory, as well as the problems of filmic enunciation and historiography. That is to say, rank replication of "the world" as it appears to be is a shallow option indeed when compared with early Hollywood's (perhaps misplaced) attempts as uplift and countercinema's (not always successful) methodology of discontinuity and social mapping. There have been numerous biopics made in the intervening years, some of which have drawn on the potentials found in the biopic's lineage.

But most have not. Instead, in recent years many in the industry have been content to take a movie star, coach him or her in a convincing impression, and build a film around it. If there is a New Biopic, it is characterized by a disappointing popular retreat into historical exceptionalism, a conception of history as the work of uniquely endowed individuals who stand head and shoulders above their brothers and sisters. But even more than this resurgence of a quaint notion of history (which squares quite nicely with a renegade president's projected image to the world as the lone justice in a mad world), the New Biopic tends to remove the guesswork for aesthetic evaluation. How can the craft of acting be judged? Do we have to rely on fuzzy concepts like the Stanislavsky method or some medium-specific rules for moving the process between the theater and the movie set? No. Contemporary biopics demand of us one question: Does Cate Blanchett look, talk, and move like Katherine Hepburn? Did Jamie Foxx manage to fully assimilate Ray Charles's vocal mannerism and unique physical tics, providing a perfect simulacrum without lapsing into offensive caricature? How well do Marion Cotillard and her makeup artists manage to capture the outsized flamboyance of Edith Piaf, and when we watch clips of *La Vie en Rose* side by side with actual archival footage, are we floored by the uncanny likeness? Too many recent films biopics have offered very little aside from the satisfaction of mimicry, a fetishistic concern with the surfaces and postures of the recent past.

Will the New Biopics have a lasting impact? Films such as *Walk the Line* (2005), *Ray* (2004), and *Monster* (2003) have few if any aesthetic properties aside from their ability to create a neutral space for their lead actors' Method mimicry. They come and go; they are the *Gandhi*s of our decade. But those are just the populist and artsploitation titles. For the new prestige set, we are offered insight into presumptively fascinating literary or artistic figures, whose life stories serve (cf. the memoir) to ratify the artists' creations in the jury of public opinion. Ed Harris's take on *Pollock* (2000) flies in the face of Modernism by narrativizing the painter's canvases, emphasizing the drips as the gestures of frustrated macho bravado. Once-abstract art now tells a story. Meanwhile, *Frida* (2002) takes Kahlo's autobiographical artwork and de-allegorizes it, following Frida (Salma Hayek) through a point-by-point chronology which blends the diegetic world with the imagery of her art. Instead of gaining an understanding of how Kahlo transformed her life into images, *Frida* gives us a portrait of a damaged visionary who simply saw the world in different, magical terms. The labor of her art is largely effaced.

But perhaps the most critically lauded straight-ahead biopic of the present decade is *Capote* (Bennett Miller, 2005), a film whose mode of address is that its makers have high prestige in their sights, and will attain it at all costs. Like *Frost/Nixon* (2008) but in a far more self-serious key, *Capote* invests minor celebrity and pop cultural ephemera with an almost ladled-on gravitas. Hardly a terrible film but certainly unremarkable, *Capote*'s biggest flaw is the self-importance permeating every frame. It works extra hard to stake its claim on significance, particularly with Miller's somewhat static, contemplative views on prairie vistas, his too-neat dialectic between urban *bon vivant* decadence and the square-jawed fortitude of the men of Kansas, and above all Philip Seymour Hoffman's fey, lacquered impersonation, conjuring Truman Capote with a helium lisp and slicked-back hair which, together with his immaculate black suit and tie, recall 1990s robotic TV character/Coca-Cola pitchman Max Headroom. Hoffman's is a performance devoid of discovery or spontaneity, as it is so intent on duplicating the Capote seen chatting up talk-show hosts Johnny Carson or Dick Cavett. Like so many other stately prestige films, *Capote* flattens moral complexity, serving up a predigested version of it. Here, it is an oscillation between A and B poles: Capote's compassionate identification with the killer he is interviewing for his book *In Cold Blood*, versus the self-serving dissimulation of appearing to provide the criminal legal assistance and a truly sympathetic ear. One holds sway, then the other, and back again, until the "ambivalent" ending when B is saturated with a listless anger at itself for not being capacious enough to accommodate more A. *Capote* is somewhat unusual in that it centers on a rather recessive, even depressed gay protagonist, one whose place in history is rather of the footnote variety even in literary circles. But like *Ray* and *Walk the Line*, although with somewhat more highbrow stakes, *Capote* is for the most part a drab vacuum of a film that is filled with Hoffman's "perfect likeness." The relative exoticism of Truman Capote does not cancel the pleasure in watching him replicated, Hoffman doing an *objectively* good job. And this, above all, provides the New Biopic's deepest satisfactions in an anti-art age.

Like the memoir craze, these New Biopics have achieved ascendancy because they trade in a safe, cozy, and false one-to-one correspondence model of artistic creation. But in two films discussed below, I hope to show this retrograde process breaking down to varying degrees, allowing for more radical potentials. These films offer significant alternatives to the Cult of Truthiness. They do not completely avoid surface realism, but neither do they make it into a totalizing fetish object. They both focus on a single exceptional individual to some degree, but they also, again to varying degrees, adopt a more nuanced view of the human subject as a historical work-in-progress, a discontinuous being shaped by the material and discursive potentials of his or her era. Amidst the junkpile of rote mimicry and received ideas that for the most part constitutes the New Biopic, I believe these films demonstrate some of the potential critical avenues that remain open to further exploration.

Shards of History: *Ali*

My first example comes from the film *Ali*, Michael Mann's 2001 biopic chronicling 10 pivotal years in the life of Muhammad Ali. The film's subject, of course, is one of the most colorful individuals ever to have graced the sporting world, but whereas typical biopics would zero in on his singularity, this film aggressively demonstrates Ali's historical "typicality," the social formation of his identity and public persona. Earlier in this chapter I described how Spike Lee's *Malcolm X* adopted the dominant biopic mode only to depart from it at its conclusion, opening the text outward rather than closing it down. In a highly similar gesture – unsurprising, considering the dovetailing subject matter – Mann's film starring Will Smith as Ali opens with a complex, almost dreamlike montage, presenting not only the film but Ali himself as a multilayered, contradictory text.

The dominant image of the montage consists of close-ups of Smith as Ali, working out in the gym at a punching bag, offering a semidiegetic framework for the other images we see. We could, presumably, be witnessing the fleeting thoughts of Ali as he punches, the nonlinear work of memory. However, the sequence uses the punching as pure visual and auditory rhythm, and Mann's contrapuntal deployment of a live performance by R&B legend Sam Cooke (David Elliott) complicates our ability to clearly locate the sequence's point of enunciation.

Let us take a closer look. Over the opening studio logos and the black screen featuring the film's initial titles and credits, we hear the noise of the crowd just before Cooke takes the stage, followed by his introduction. In the first proper shot of the film, we see Ali (still Cassius Clay) in close-up, running down the street just before dawn, in a left-to-right tracking shot. A gray hoodie obscures his face. The shot contains the date stamp, "February 24, 1964." Shot 2: We see Cooke at the microphone from behind, asking the crowd, "you doing okay?" He is in silhouette, shown from the waist up, and is bathed in a transcendent blue-white spotlight. Shot 3: Ali running in L-to-R tracking shot, this time in long shot, down a sidewalk against closed shops. The street and sidewalk are at a 30-degree angle. Shot 4: Continuation of Ali's run, same location, but in medium shot, and at a 45-degree angle, creating a deeply recessed space against a black, cloud-strewn sky. Streetlights are hazy and haloed. Shot 5: Cooke begins to sing, the camera pivoting around his left side, still bathed in light. Shot 6: A low-angle shot of the street where Ali is running, right down the central axis. The shot is static, and Ali runs through the shot from the extreme distance on the right, through to the foreground, crossing in front of the camera to the left. By the end of the shot, his brown pants are a blur which dominates the frame. Shots 7 and 8: Cooke again, playing to an increasingly frenzied, all-black crowd, dominated in the foreground by elegant women enthusiastically desiring Cooke. By this point, the purpose of the Cooke material is clear both intuitively and rhetorically. Mann is showing us African-American male performance at the apex of its power, beauty, and seductiveness. Cooke and those around him are luminous, almost heavenly bodies, lifted out of the mundane world into a realm of radiant possibility.

Shot 9: Ali runs along a low white fence, as clouds gather in a turbulent, deep purple sky. The moon shines through the clouds. Mann's use of high-definition video results in a swirling, pixellated grain in the sky. This extended shot tracks left to right at an upward, 30-degree angle past several streetlights that provide a starburst halo effect. Shot 10: Cooke from behind, a silhouetted guitar neck anchoring the right side of the frame. For the first time, the audience is seen before Cooke in the distance. Shot 11: Close-up on Ali's face, bobbing through the frame straight on as he runs down the street. The street, trees, and streetlights behind him are a blur of light and motion. Shot 12: A police car with two white cops comes down the street behind Ali, bisecting the frame, its lights piercing the visual field. The officer driving the squad car leans out and asks Ali, "What you running from, son?" Shot 13: Ali from the waist up, center frame, the cop car minimized in the lower left. The camera tracks backward. Shot 14: The squad car, same framing as shot 12, only the camera halts as the car exits

Figure 24.1 The hand of Sam Cooke anoints the faithful in Michael Mann's *Ali* (2001, producers Michael Mann and A. Kitman Ho).

the frame on the left hand side. Shot 15: Ali from the abdomen up, slightly to the right of frame, as the street at night unfolds behind him in deep Renaissance perspective, at 30 degrees to the right. He jogs on toward the camera, which continues to track back with him. Shot 16: The same setup, only a tighter framing of Ali's head and shoulders. Shot 17: Cooke holds the microphone and waves his arm on the left of the frame as the women in the center of the audience as illuminated by a central shaft of light. Shot 18: A close-up of Cooke's suit-clad midriff with the camera following the gesture of his pointing arm, left to right. His spotlit arm and finger recall the Sistine Chapel. He pulls his arm back as women's waving arms enter the frame from the right.

What the first part of *Ali*'s opening montage suggests is that the African-American male body is, for better or worse, a spectacle. It does not enjoy the privileges of presumed "invisibility" afforded to the white male body. What young Cassius Clay is in the process of learning is how, when, and where to take control of the spectacle that is his own body. How can he harness its strength? How will he articulate a style of being which combines selfhood with a degree of performativity? Within the bounded space of the concert hall, an African-American public sphere, Sam Cooke uses performance – not only his voice but his body as well – to transform himself into something luminous. By the time Mann shows us Cooke's divine finger anointing the swoony devout, it is clear that the singer has achieved a kind of secular transfiguration.

By contrast, Ali, in these opening moments, is conditioning his body in public, a hostile public arena dominated by racist white authority. Mann and Smith show us Ali's run through the nighttime streets, illuminated by the diffuse lamplight and cloud-obscured moon, as a display of African-American male beauty and luminosity equal to Cooke's. However, Ali's bodily transformation is inward, private, and subject to racist interference, which arrives in the form of the police (who, truth be told, utter a remark to Ali and drive on).

The remainder of the opening montage, which lasts nearly 10 minutes, becomes even more complex after this. After another pair of shots of Ali on the road and Cooke performing, Ali is seen working out on the speed bag at daybreak. His face a blurred silhouette, his fists a whirlwind in center frame. The next shot shows Ali straight on, in perfect focus, slightly to the left of center frame. The next shot is somewhat pivotal: A medium shot of Ali in the same position as reflected in a mirror on the opposite wall, which Mann then suddenly brings closer to us via a rapid zoom. In the new framing, Ali pounds the bag in close-up. The next shot ambiguously pans around the back of Ali's shoulders, left to right, with his head, gloved fists, and rattling bag all whipping so quickly through the frame, and photographed from such close range, that this icy blue composition devolves into an almost Futurist abstraction of pure motion, color, and light. At the end of this shot, Mann introduces slow motion, so that we can see the still-hazy fists of Ali pummeling the bag, with an inevitability that is almost holy writ.

At this point, we begin seeing flash-frame inserts of concrete historical events as well as moments from Ali's past. The first is a first-person shot of Sonny Liston (Michael Bentt) in the ring taking a punch at his opponent/the camera. Next shot: back to a close-up of Ali's face. There is an extended montage of the Liston fight as the heavyweight champion decimates his opponent. Mann shows the event from all angles, continually cutting back to Ali at the punching bag, its rhythm and back-and-forth pendular swing turning the film into a kind of phenakistoscope. From this point Mann begins to provide glimpses of Ali's psychological makeup, the events that helped shape him and, in essence, all the things he's fighting when he enters the ring. We witness young Cassius looking quizzically on as his father paints a church mural of an exaggeratedly Caucasian Jesus Christ, clearly experiencing a cognitive dissonance in his spiritual life. We see the boy and his father as they move to the back of a bus. We see the young man skim a newspaper headline about the murder of Emmett Till – Till, a 14-year-old boy from Chicago, became an early cause célèbre for the Civil Rights Movement when he was brutally murdered while visiting relatives in Mississippi, for allegedly flirting with a white woman. We are shown an extended passage of Ali standing in the back of a hall as Malcolm X (Mario Van Peebles) addresses his assembly about the teachings of Elijah Muhammad and the right of African-Americans to defend themselves against tyranny. During and after the workout we are introduced to Ali's principal trainers, Angelo (Ron Silver) and Bundini (Jamie Foxx). During the sequence, Ali utters only two, barely audible words. He and his team march down the corridor to their weigh-in for the Liston bout. And all the while, Sam Cooke sings on, achieving an ecstatic crescendo. He is in complete control of the performance space, and this is what Ali has to achieve as well.

At the end of this meticulous montage sequence, whose construction of meaning is almost exclusively visual and suggestive rather than directly expository, Ali busts into the weigh-in and begins talking shit about Liston to the reporters. He has the verbal swagger that was Muhammad Ali's trademark. The remainder of *Ali* follows a much more conventional, linear path through the next 10 years of the man's life, from capturing the heavyweight title, through his conversion to Islam, his conscientious objection to service in Vietnam, his ban from US boxing, and his struggle to overcome that setback. This plays out in relatively straightforward ways, and at times Smith's performance in the title role lapses into mere mimicry. But there are moments when instead of impersonating the surface affectations, the look or the voice of Ali, he captures the frustration and distance inherent in being a famous, well-connected outsider, a man whose personal choices ostensibly spat in the eye of the nation that embraced him. In addition to smart choices on Smith's part, Mann is to be commended, as usual, for his expressive, medium-specific use of digital video. *Ali* favors shallow compositions for interiors, rack focus and a slightly smeared, impressionistic use of light that lends the film a painterly texture, particularly inside the boxing ring.

Make no mistake. The remainder of *Ali* in no way delivers on the radical promise of its first 10 minutes. While the rest of *Ali* is an above-average biopic for the reasons described above, it cannot truly be called a critical film. Nevertheless, what makes *Ali* a far more complex biopic than usual, one that, I would argue, has at least partially absorbed the lessons of the critical biopics of the past, is that Mann boldly presents many of the film's key themes in microcosm before "the movie" proper has even begun. We understand Ali's life and career as being shaped by an acute consciousness of America as a racist nation. But more significantly, Mann's opening montage complicates Ali as an individual, locating him as a multifaceted subject who is formed and informed by history. Rather than spending the first 10 minutes of the film establishing Muhammad Ali as an active protagonist, *Ali* displays him as a somewhat passive observer and listener, someone taking in information and processing it both intellectually and through his pugilistic art. Even though the remainder of the film is far more conventional, *Ali* gives us this thickly layered historical prism at the start, one with which to interpret everything that follows. But perhaps most significantly of all, *Ali* disrupts the notion that Muhammad Ali, or by extension any person, has an essential self that a biographical project can simply reveal. Instead, the running, boxing, and thinking, juxtaposed with Sam Cooke's electrifying stage presence, give us a picture of the black male body codified as spectacle in racist society. In the opening running scenes, this is a threat for Ali, but for Cooke, this is a scene of great power. The question, then, is how one takes charge of that spectacle, how one develops a performative style of being. So, when Mann concludes this highly introspective montage of Ali's bodily existence and his interior life with "Muhammad Ali," the loudmouth boxer who "floats like a butterfly, stings like a bee," he is showing us that this persona is a cultural and historical product, and not some essence waiting to be discovered. *Ali* operates on the assumption that the outsized bravado that was "Muhammad Ali" was, among other things, political theater. Given that Ali remains, to this day, the most famous and beloved American Muslim in history, this seems a safe assumption, and a productive one on which to base a progressive contemporary biopic.

Shards of Identity: *I'm Not There*

Earlier in this chapter, I made some stipulations about how we could define the biopic for the purposes of this argument. The primary definition was as follows: A realist film centered on the life and achievements of a single woman or man, her or his biography (or a substantial segment of it) providing the dramatic shape for the work. Over the course of this chapter, naturally we have encountered examples of films which have expanded, toyed with, or subverted some aspects of this basic definition, as well as some which have followed it to the letter. The final film I wish to consider in depth is one that breaks what is probably the most basic rule of the biopic. It is not really about its subject. As its title suggests, Todd Haynes's *I'm Not There* (2007) is a film about a structuring absence, and its ostensible subject Bob Dylan – appears only in the final minutes of the film in a single archival performance clip, and the name "Bob Dylan" is never uttered once. The main body of the film has many characters and events, most of which allude to some specific details of Dylan's life and legend. But they serve to highlight the inability of the film to offer "Bob Dylan" to the hungry eye of the viewer. And so, *I'm Not There* is a biopic constructed almost entirely from negative space.

The first spoken words of narration in *I'm Not There* seem to indicate right off the bat that the film's project will not be playing by the standard rules of the biopic. Instead of providing context or a personal introduction to the film's subject, the voice offers fragments of doleful reverie: "There he lies. God rest his soul, and his rudeness. A devouring public can now share the remains of his sickness and his phone numbers." Following an opening tracking shot in black and white, which is filmed from the point of view of a musician backstage getting ready to go on, Haynes gives us a whiteout. Next we see a close-up of a booted foot revving a motorcycle. The next shot is one of a low, flat desert landscape, which the microscopic figure traverses laterally across the very bottom of the screen. The title appears, blinking: I / he / I'm / her / not her / not here. / I'm not there. As the figure on the bike exits frame right, we hear a thump, followed by a shot of the dead Jude Quinn (Cate Blanchett) on the slab. A male voiceover intones the words at the start of the paragraph as a coroner makes the first incision. Then, in rapid succession, we are shown The Dylans: poet Arthur Rimbaud (Ben Whishaw); folksinger Jack Rollins (Christian Bale); outlaw Billy the Kid (Richard Gere); Woody Guthrie (Marcus Carl Franklin), a young runaway riding the rails; Robbie (Heath Ledger), a movie star playing Jack Rollins in a film; and of course Jude (Blanchett), the most Dylan-like Dylan, dealing with his post-electric rock star fame. As the dead body is shown once again, the voiceover informs us, "Even the ghost was more than one person."

Built into the very structure of Haynes's film is a total theoretical engagement with what it means to attempt to depict a historical personage as mythic as Bob Dylan, from so great a historical remove. Rather than collapse the contradictions that Dylan the man contains and inevitably displayed through his public career and private life, *I'm Not There* openly displays the impossibility of a singular, coherent self, static and unchanging across time. What's more, Haynes complicates the notion of identity as sticking to particular bodies and body times, casting "Dylan" as older men, younger men, an African-American boy, and a woman. If nobody can truly be summed up through the reassuring fictions of the linear biography, then Dylan, whose work was an all-pervasive force throughout the culture, could just as reasonably be embodied by Franklin or Blanchett as by Bale,

Figure 24.2 Jack Rollins (Christian Bale) is a Dylanesque figure defined by isolation and negative space in Todd Haynes's *I'm Not There* (2007, producer Christine Vachon).

Whishaw, Ledger, or Gere. Haynes is showing us that there is not only Bob Dylan but, more importantly, the Dylan Effect, and that is uncontainable. Spike Lee had schoolchildren stand up and declare, "I am Malcolm X," in order to demonstrate a similar force, one that far exceeds the boundaries of a single human life. Haynes has taken Lee's principle and made it his dominant structuring principle.

Haynes also employs different film styles to accelerate the sense of textual discontinuity. Each "Dylan" has its own accompanying film style (e.g., Godardian/Felliniesque for Jude Quinn, Southern pastoral for Woody Guthrie, standard "Behind the Music" documentary for Jack Rollins, etc.), and at first *I'm Not There* tends to move somewhat sequentially through the Dylans. But by about the middle of the film there is considerable interweaving between the personae and the styles, resulting in startling juxtapositions and formal pastiche. Just as Haynes is telling us that the traditional biopic cannot proffer a singular identity that is "Bob Dylan," his method of cinematic construction demonstrates his belief that the traditional biopic's linear realist mode of narration, coupled with its tendency toward stylistic neutrality, sacrifices engagement with the multifaceted complexities of history and subjectivity in favor of quaint, prepackaged, "truthy" stories about the doings of Great Men.

Against the "Fictition" of "Truthiness"

Although Haynes cannot avoid the pitfalls of the biopic entirely – the final 15 minutes of *I'm Not There* tends to smooth out ambiguities and force linkages between the segments and personae which had been left in productive suspension, and we then end on the real Dylan's image – *I'm Not There* is a clear demonstration of the critical potential that exists for filmmakers who choose to explore the intellectual options still possible within the New Biopic.

Luckily, Haynes is not alone. As before, the quest to revitalize the biopic is an international one. Recently, British installation artist Steve McQueen made his debut feature film, *Hunger* (2008, UK), a highly unconventional biopic about Irish Republican hunger striker Bobby Sands. By spending the first third of the film showing fragments of the world around Sands – his cohort, the prison environment, the daily life of a guard – before turning to the specific arguments for and against the hunger strike for recognition as political prisoners, McQueen places Sands into the larger framework of the movement he led, and the system he challenged. Using close-ups whose meaning only becomes apparent later in the film, McQueen constructs *Hunger* as a series of synecdoches, a fitting approach to a biopic about a man who committed his life to the representation of something greater than himself.

Another promising new direction can be glimpsed in the work of Canadian filmmaker Clive Holden. His biographical film installation *Ken Dryden* draws strategies from both avant-garde portraiture and the biopic traditions. The piece is a poetic consideration of the image and careers of Dryden, a legendary National Hockey League goalie currently enjoying a second life as a Liberal MP in Canadian Parliament. In the work, multiple images of Dryden are projected in a mobile grid – shots from the hockey days, images from Parliament, and other abstract images that relate to Dryden only obliquely. Against the image sequence, and operating as a semi-independent loop, is an audio recording of Dryden on a radio program discussing a gang rape case involving a varsity hockey team, and the culture of machismo in professional sports. Holden's unconventional bio-installation complexifies the idea of how one man's different life phases relate to one another, physically marking out that disphasure as a sculptural fact.[2]

Rank mimicry and the slavish presentation of a simplified view of both history and the individual will always be comforting fictions. Ideology is not going anywhere. Nevertheless, filmmakers have the choice, even within the relatively conservative form of the biopic, to break with convention, buck the trends of our fictitious times, and provide images of human life that cast "truthiness" aside, instead attempting to move us closer and closer to actual truth.

Notes

1. See Mike D'Angelo's yearly list of New York releases, from 1999 through 2015, at his website, http://www.panix.com/~dangelo.
2. Holden's film, part of his larger *Utopia Suite* project, can be explored in more depth at http://www.utopiasuite.com.

25

"Asia" as Global Hollywood Commodity

Kenneth Chan
Associate Professor, University of Northern Colorado, United States

The so-called "**Asian Invasion**" refers to the heightened presence and influence of Asian films in the US, beginning in the mid-1990s – whether in theatrical exhibition, Hollywood's importing of filmmakers and actors, its remaking of prominent Asian films, or its international co-productions of films set in Asian locations. Kenneth Chan traces Hollywood's historical record, interrogating contemporary **continuities** and **discontinuities** with earlier **Orientalist** or more aggressively racist representations. Chan argues that, while certainly moderated, similar attitudes continue to inform contemporary Hollywood's packaging of **"Asia"** as a "cinematic smorgasbord" of "choices," thus reinforcing **capitalist ideology** by selling "Asia" as a series of consumerist commodities that include the **kung fu** and ***wuxia*** **genres**, **Asian crime films**, **Asian horror**, **Bollywood spectacles**, dramatization of **cultural politics**, and representations of **global diversity as American multiculturalism**. Through close readings of ***Slumdog Millionaire*** and ***The Karate Kid***, Chan concludes that, while Hollywood has progressed, it "still has a long way to go in transcending reductive modes of ethnic typology." His essay shares ground with J. D. Connor on independent blockbusters in this volume and with Diane Negra on immigrant stardom in the hardcover/online series.

Additional terms, names, and concepts: "Global China," Fifth Generation filmmakers, global Hollywood, J-Horror

Introduction

Beginning in the mid-1990s and gathering particular force in the first decade of the new millennium, an "Asian Invasion" – as some critics have described it – emerged in Hollywood.[1] The fact that this history of American cinema devotes an entire chapter to the subject of Hollywood's relationship to Asia specifically within the context of American film's contemporary history (1999 to the present) testifies to the significance of this cross-cultural phenomenon. But this temporal historicist bracketing of Hollywood and Asia as a recent cultural occurrence offers a convenient disjunctive moment to reflect on the discursive

American Film History: Selected Readings, 1960 to the Present, First Edition. Edited by Cynthia Lucia, Roy Grundmann, and Art Simon.

and material continuities *and* discontinuities that have characterized this fraught relationship. I speak of continuity in a sense that, materially, American film has always had an intimate connection to Asia in terms of both film production and market distribution since the very beginning of cinema's technological emergence,[2] a point that reinforces the notion of film as a transnational capitalist commodity, with global Hollywood as a prime instance (Miller et al. 2001). The developed film industries of China, India, Japan, and Hong Kong, for instance, have often confronted Hollywood competition reactively, thereby inflecting the aesthetic and technological development of these national cinemas, while innovations emerging from Asia, in turn, have helped reconfigure and challenge cinematic culture in Hollywood.[3] Or, as Bliss Cua Lim more effectively puts it, "Hollywood ... pillages from its rivals, a conspicuous instance of national–regional counterflows, in which the centre imitates its cinematic elsewheres, lest we forget that film is truly global" (2007, 124). On the discursive front, Hollywood has also deployed, throughout its history, "Asia" as a representational category of cultural otherness invoking, for example, fears of the "yellow peril" which, according to Gina Marchetti, "combines racist terror of alien cultures, sexual anxieties, and the belief that the West will be overpowered and enveloped by the irresistible, dark, occult forces of the East" (1993, 2). Historically, these fears were visually embodied in the Orientalist stereotypes of the evil Fu Manchu, Flash Gordon's arch nemesis Ming the Merciless, and the voluptuous prostitute Suzie Wong. While these figurations have now deservedly been relegated to Hollywood's overtly racist historical past (and a relatively recent past at that), their discursive underpinnings persist today, often in a liberal multiculturalist guise. In briefly registering these continuities, I am not only making the obvious but necessary contextual point that the contemporary Asian invasion, as we are witnessing it so far, does not occur in a historical and discursive vacuum, but also bringing in the notion that these continuities suffer elision – a convenient historical amnesia – in Hollywood's current politically correct propensity to embrace exotic ethnic cultures, now in the spirit of liberal multiculturalism, in order to sustain its global hegemony.

Conversely, to mark the "newness" of Hollywood's contemporary focus on Asia – hence, its discontinuity from Hollywood's previous encounters with the "Orient" – is a project grounded in the realities of Pacific Rim international relations of the 1990s. The rise of the People's Republic of China (PRC) as a super economic powerhouse, after Deng Xiaoping's reconceptualization of "socialist nationalism ... through a reengagement with global capitalism" in terms of a new "model of Asian capitalism" (Ong 1999, 37–38), has become a geopolitical concern that the United States must now confront. Mainland China's economic ascendancy cannot be delinked from the cultural pull it maintains on ethnic Chinese across the globe, a transnational network that Michael Curtin labels as "Global China" (2007, 295). Curtin contends that

> this vast and increasingly wealthy Global China market will serve as a foundation for emerging media conglomerates that could shake the very foundations of Hollywood's century-long hegemony ... Hollywood has dominated for so long that many of its executives have difficulty envisioning the transformations now on the horizon. (2007, 3–4)

While Curtin may be correct to play up Hollywood's slow uptake concerning Global China's impact, it is an error for us to dismiss Hollywood's capitalist tenacity and dexterity, considering its complex corporate ties to global conglomerates and the continued cultural cachet that Hollywood commodities still retain worldwide.

Hollywood's response to the migration of the Hong Kong film industry's stars, directors, and industry stalwarts to the United States – especially after the Tiananmen Square massacre of 1989, and right up to and after Hong Kong's transfer from British colonial hands to the People's Republic of China in July 1997 – demonstrates, in part, this tenacity and dexterity. Corporate Hollywood clearly saw the cultural and economic advantages of incorporating this established talent into its labor pool, which includes major stars like Jackie Chan, Jet Li, Michelle Yeoh, and Chow Yun-fat; auteur directors such as John Woo, Tsui Hark, and Wong Kar-wai; and martial arts choreographers like Yuen Woo-ping (who also happens to be a talented director). Prior to this cinematic migration, Asian cinemas occupied a minor place in American film consumption patterns, with enthusiastic cinephiles, followers of Asian cult films, kung fu cinema fans, international film festival attendees, and minority Asian communities constituting the bulk of the audience. Mainstream American audiences rarely had the chance, or the inclination, to watch Asian films, except for the occasional flash of kung fu action cinema interest (Bruce Lee being the classic example). The Hong Kong migration in the 1990s, therefore, provided a historically opportune moment to catalyze interest in Asia and Asian cinemas, which Hollywood has seized upon rather successfully. In locating it as part of Hollywood's "history of foreigners and émigrés," Kwai-Cheung Lo conceptualizes this "influx of Hong Kong filmmakers and stars … as part of the continuous self-rejuvenating process of Hollywood industry" (2005, 132–133).

The introduction of Chinese directors, actors, characters, and/or narrative elements in the 1990s began this trend, in films like *Hard Target* (1993), *The Wedding Banquet* (1993), *Rumble in the Bronx* (1995), *Broken Arrow* (1996), *Chinese Box* (1997), *Face/Off* (1997), *Lethal Weapon 4* (1998), *Rush Hour* (1998), and *Anna and the King* (1999). Ang Lee's *Crouching Tiger, Hidden Dragon* (2000) is a watershed title in that, by generating fascination with the *wuxia pian* (Chinese sword-fighting film) and kung fu cinema, it also directed critical and mainstream attention to Chinese and Asian cinemas in general. What is fascinating about the film's place in this phenomenon is that Ang Lee hails from Taiwan and received his film education from New York University, thus suggesting that the Hong Kong migratory effect has drawn into its wake other ethnic Chinese cinematic streams such as the PRC, Taiwan, and the Chinese diaspora, including Chinese-American cinema. Riding a parallel wave that eventually merged into this Chinese-in-Hollywood tidal wave, for instance, is the cinema of the Fifth Generation filmmakers from mainland China, bringing us directors like Chen Kaige and Zhang Yimou, and stars like Gong Li and Zhang Ziyi, who now populate Hollywood's firmament. But this wave has widened and deepened its sweep even more, transcending the ethnic Chinese, to include representatives from Japan, India, and South Korea, to name a few, constituting a diverse ethnic visuality that is Hollywood "Asia."

What is the ideological nature of this visual collage called "Asia" within Hollywood's representational discourse today? What are some of the key trends defining this Hollywood-meets-Asia phenomenon that relies on the politics of this ethnic categorization? In attempting to address these questions, this chapter charts the contradictory reformulations of "Asia" from racist alterity to a liberal multiculturalism, as part of Hollywood's capitalist commoditization of ethnicity for both local US consumption and global export. The chapter will then deploy this conceptual framework in reading the trends emerging out of the Hollywood–Asia connection, before tackling two recent high-profile films as significant examples of Hollywood ethnic commodities: Danny Boyle's *Slumdog Millionaire* (2008) and Jackie Chan's latest star vehicle, *The Karate Kid* (2010).

"Asia" as Ethnicity

To begin the project of inscribing the emerging history of Hollywood's engagement with Asia in the past decade, I first need to theorize what constitutes this category called "Asia" beyond its obvious geographical and cultural denotations. In locating the term within quotation marks, I am suggesting that "Asia," while being rooted materially and visually in a geopolitical reality, has also been discursively deterritorialized and reformulated into a category of otherness that resonates as "ethnicity" within the context of American racial politics. In her insightful book *The Protestant Ethnic and the Spirit of Capitalism*, Rey Chow argues that "ethnicity exists in modernity as a boundary – a line of exclusion – that nonetheless pretends to be a nonboundary" – the notion that everyone is ethnic, which she goes on to say acts as "a framework of inclusion, only then to reveal its full persecutory and discriminatory force whenever political, economic, or ideological gains are at stake" (2002, 30). She concludes:

> ethnicity, rather than being a condition equal to all, has often been a source of oppression – indeed, a liability – to those who are branded "ethnics" [and] articulations of ethnicity in contemporary Western society are thoroughly conditioned by asymmetries of power between whites and nonwhites. (2002, 31)

By exposing the contradictory structure of ethnicity's inclusionary/exclusionary logic as a liberal ideological blind spot, Chow implicates multiculturalism's (unwitting) role in "reconstituting and reinvesting racism in a different guise," despite its "well-intentioned disaffiliations from overt racist practices" (2002, 17). Chow goes on to point out that "this liberalist cultural logic … democratizes these [exclusionary] boundaries rhetorically with honorable terms such as 'multiculturalism' and 'diversity' and practically by way of the proliferation of enclaves and ghettos" (2002, 29).

Hollywood's contemporary deployment and representations of "Asia" feed into this multiculturalist discourse of racial and cultural diversity and tolerance, reflecting the notion that Hollywood "has become more multicultural and politically correct as a result of catering to the increasingly diversified tastes of the world market" (Lo 2005, 133). According to Minh-Ha T. Pham, "Hollywood is not threatened by the increased presence of Asian and Asian American actors and filmmakers" per se, but this presence "enhances Hollywood's image as a racially inclusive, equal opportunity, global industry" (2004, 122). Of course, I am in no way suggesting here that Hollywood has completely abandoned Orientalist and racist stereotypes, which continue to provide studios with a convenient representational default mode in pandering, either strategically or lazily, to mainstream America's reductive conceptions of ethnic minorities. Though the unpacking of these "negative" representations is a project deserving attention, this chapter also takes to heart, in its critical agenda, Robert Stam and Louise Spence's suggestion that "the insistence on 'positive images' … obscures the fact that 'nice' images might at times be as pernicious as overtly degrading ones, providing a bourgeois façade for paternalism, a more pervasive racism" (1983, 3). While Stam and Spence are deconstructing colonialist cinematic imagery's Manichean articulation of the good versus bad "native," their advice rings true in reading the patina of ideological correctness that Hollywood's multicultural portrayal of "Asia" offers.

Beyond problematizing "Asia" as a part of Hollywood's ethnic plenitude, I want to follow Rey Chow a step further in her exploration of ethnicity as capitalist commodity, in order to extend this theoretical narrative to its logical end. In discussing what she terms "the ethnicization of labor," whereby ethnicity is conditioned and defined by late capitalist logic, Chow cites the work of Immanuel Wallerstein (1991) to argue that "ethnicization must thus be linked to the racism specific to the operations of modern capitalism with its twin objectives of maximizing profits and minimizing production costs" (Chow 2002, 34). "Asia" as global Hollywood ethnicity, therefore, accrues cultural value within a "capitalist ethos of objectification and reification, whereby what is proclaimed to be human must also increasingly take on the significance of a commodity, a commodified spectacle" (Chow 2002, 48).[4] The Hollywood visuality of "Asia" lends itself perfectly to this commoditization of ethnic spectacle, whereby supposedly sensitive and positive cultural portrayals of Asian otherness as multicultural difference are not only conceived of as being worthy of cinema (as spectacle) but also this "positivity" ameliorates the guilt of objectifying the spectacular. Another way of looking at this commoditized spectacle is to see it the way Kwai-Cheung Lo does, that "the larger the share Hollywood can get of the Asian Pacific market, the more yellow and brown faces will probably be seen in the mainstream American cinema and television" (2005, 173).

"Asia" as Cinematic Smorgasbord

Part of the pleasure of capitalist consumption is the reified notion of choice. Implicit in this choice are the apparent freedom and agency consumers treasure, that inevitably mask the lines of ideological control shaping taste and opinion. The multiplicity presented as Hollywood "Asia" functions in this fashion. We envisage in this Asian smorgasbord cultural, racial, national, and even genre offerings that simulate the heterogeneity of choice – a cornucopia of filmic trends evincing global cultural chic and cosmopolitan savvy. In delineating some of these choices or trends emerging out of the Hollywood–Asia engagement, my goal is to both highlight and, in some cases, begin the process of critically unpacking these trends in order to demonstrate not only how this cinematic smorgasbord of diverse Asia, as a whole, is itself emblematic of the commoditized ethnic spectacle but also how each individual trend is, in very specific ways, implicated in the politics of multicultural correctness. The list that follows is, of course, meant to be illustrative and is far from comprehensive, and from a hermeneutical standpoint it is intended to be descriptive rather than prescriptive.

1. *Kung fu and* wuxia *genres and elements. Crouching Tiger, Hidden Dragon* is a contemporary version of the *wuxia pian* (the Chinese sword-fighting

film).[5] The fact that Ang Lee's film has helped intensify the American audience's appetite for Asia through martial arts is indicative of the ease with which kung fu spectacle, as it intersects with the mainstream proclivity for action genres, transforms into Hollywood's ethnic commodity par excellence. As a transnational coproduction involving companies such as China Film Co-Production Corporation, Columbia Pictures Film Production Asia, and Sony Pictures Classics, *Crouching Tiger, Hidden Dragon* both ignited a global interest in the genre and set the coproduction standard for future *wuxia* and kung fu films to follow, including titles like *Hero* (2002), *House of Flying Daggers* (2004), *Kung Fu Hustle* (2004), *Jet Li's Fearless* (2006), *The Warlords* (2007), and *Red Cliff* (2008). While it may not have been directly involved (in a traditional sense) with the production of the majority of these films, Hollywood did ultimately benefit from both distribution rights and, in a number of cases, transnational coproduction efforts.[6] The fact that these films helped sustain audience interest through the decade allowed later Hollywood-produced films – like DreamWorks's animated *Kung Fu Panda* (2008) and the Jet Li–Jackie Chan matchup in *The Forbidden Kingdom* (2008) – to join the action. Columbia Pictures' 2010 remake of *The Karate Kid* is the latest addition to this series of kung fu-related cinema, to be discussed later in the chapter. But, for now, I would like to speculate on two possible reasons why martial arts films, including the *wuxia pian*, find easy accommodation in Hollywood's ethnic multiculturalism: First, the historical persistence of the kung fu stereotype in the mainstream American imagination of Chinese and certain East Asian groups solidifies the cultural and historical gravitas accorded to martial arts cinema, making it the obvious candidate for culturally signifying ethnic Asia. (I have very liberal and well-meaning Anglo-American friends whose fetishism of kung fu and kung fu cinema is marked by utmost respect and stoic seriousness.) Second, martial arts as a culturally flexible spectacle can easily be reconfigured and emplaced within Hollywood's action genres, where cultural specificities and historical temporalities matter little. For example, *The Touch* (2002), *Bulletproof Monk* (2003), *Dragonball: Evolution* (2009), and *The Last Airbender* (2010) invoke "Asian" cultures and characters of vague or nonspecific national or cultural origins. Gordon Liu's Pai Mei character in *Kill Bill: Vol. 2* (2004) is historically out of place, thus functioning perfectly in Tarantino's cinematic pastiche. Even the *Star Wars* prequels and *The Matrix* trilogy[7] incorporate fighting sequences reminiscent of kung fu techniques in Hong Kong cinema (see Hunt 2003, 31 and 179–181).

2. *Asian crime films*. The fact that most Asian crime films are often hybrid martial arts films makes Asian criminality a similarly popular ethnic commodity in Hollywood. Particularly in films with contemporary settings, gangland criminality frequently involves the spectacularly violent and cruel Chinese triads and Japanese Yakuza in their rapacious exploitation of their own minority communities and in their occasional forays into the American mainstream to terrify white suburbia. *Lethal Weapon 4*, the three *Rush Hour* films, *The Replacement Killers* (1998), *The Corruptor* (1999), and *Kill Bill* are important instances. So taken was Martin Scorsese by Andrew Lau and Alan Mak's *Infernal Affair* (2002) that he remade the Hong Kong triad crime flick into the Leonardo DiCaprio star vehicle *The Departed* (2006). A fascinating subcategory of this genre draws out minority interracial connectivity and/or violence, specifically representations of African-American and Asian/Asian-American conflagrations and/or alliances: *Rumble in the Bronx*, the *Rush Hour* series, *Romeo Must Die* (2000), *Cradle 2 the Grave* (2003), and, of course, the remake of *The Karate Kid*.[8] The construction of ethnic alterity in the guise of a criminal other finds its historical antecedent in the yellow peril stereotypes. While one could argue that the containment of gangland turf wars and violence within the confines of ghettoized spaces (such as Chinatowns) in these recent films has helped spotlight the realities of urban social problems in minority

communities, the persistence and evolution of binary figurations – the bad Asian (triad criminal) versus good Asian (Chinese victim) – allow the stereotype of Asian submissiveness to temper and contain Asian criminality, making the latter politically safe for mainstream American consumption. The Asian criminal other can thus securely take its place among Hollywood's multiculturally correct offerings.

3. *Asian horror.* The spectacle of horror cinema parallels that of action cinema in its appeal to young audiences who constitute a major sector of Hollywood's target consumers both in the United States and across the globe. Believing that Asian horror, especially in the Japanese tradition, is too culturally alien for American audiences, studios have resorted to less effective Hollywood remakes of contemporary Asian horror classics by, for instance, Americanizing the setting or replacing the main Asian protagonist with a generally Anglo-American one – what Bliss Cua Lim calls the "deracinating acts of cultural appropriation" (2007, 115). *Dark Water* (2005), *The Grudge* (2004), *The Grudge 2* (2006), *The Ring* (2002), and *The Ring Two* (2005) are Hollywood-ized versions of what film scholars have termed "J-Horror," Japanese horror cinema. *The Eye* (2008) is a remake of a similarly titled contemporary Hong Kong horror film, made in 2002 by the Pang brothers. Reflecting on the popularity in the United States of such "extreme" films from Asia, Jinhee Choi and Mitsuyo Wada-Marciano theorize that "'Asia' just becomes a spatial fix or an empty signifier for being cool, rather than providing an entry point for the [young] viewer to be exposed [*sic*] and learn about the originating countries" (2009, 6). Furthermore, as with Asian criminality, Hollywood's appropriation of Asian horror displaces cultural difference into representations of the monstrous – as Robin Wood points out, "the true subject of the horror genre is the struggle for recognition of all that our civilisation *re*presses or *op*presses" (1985, 201). The nightmare scenario that is Asian horror allows for audiences to grapple with cultural difference in an acceptable fashion – the cinematic figures are supernatural ones anyway – without needing to directly confront Asian difference in all its troubling humanity.

4. *Bollywood spectacles.* While one could argue that the Chinese cinematic wave has helped pique and intensify Hollywood interest in Asian cinemas in general, Bollywood films included, Indian cinema in Hollywood historically has ridden separate tidal streams, focusing mostly on diasporic Indian experiences. Key North American directors include Mira Nair, director of films such as *Mississippi Masala* (1991), *Kama Sutra: A Tale of Love* (1996), *Monsoon Wedding* (2001), *Vanity Fair* (2004), and *The Namesake* (2006), based on the eponymous novel by Pulitzer prize winner Jhumpa Lahiri, and Deepa Mehta, a Canadian director whose oeuvre boasts award-winning films like her trilogy *Fire* (1996), *Earth* (1998), and *Water* (2005). From aesthetic and political standpoints, both Nair and Mehta have raised the bar very high, never shying away from difficult issues, while unabashedly embracing the ludic possibilities of Bollywood camp. Much as there is to celebrate in the political interventions of their work, the risk these filmmakers take, especially Mehta in her trilogy, is that political critique – of India as a flawed postcolonial experiment of democracy mired in fundamentalist religious fanaticism and conservative traditionalism – can turn itself into a commoditized spectacle for American audiences. Furthermore, Bollywood as cinematic spectacle can work on a carnivalesque register that would then proffer a Bahktinian mode of subversion in films like *Vanity Fair*, *The Guru* (2002), and Baz Luhrmann's *Moulin Rouge!* (2001), or it can be reduced to sheer (multicultural) spectacle for its own sake, as in *Slumdog Millionaire* and *The Love Guru* (2008).

5. *Dramatizing cultural politics.* As in the case of *Slumdog Millionaire*, Hollywood has recently taken on certain political causes by embedding its critique in historical and political dramas: American criticism of China's human rights abuses becomes the narrative premise of *Red Corner* (1997) starring Richard Gere, whose activism against Chinese oppression is legendary. This criticism has translated into American celebrity support for Tibet, spawning films like *Seven Years in Tibet* (1997) and *Kundun*

(1997), with its release coinciding perfectly with the 1997 British transfer of Hong Kong to Chinese rule. Clint Eastwood's double-feature critiques of American militarism, released in the post-9/11 era – *Flags of Our Fathers* (2006) and *Letters from Iwo Jima* (2006) – are politically complicated films that eschew the reductive us-versus-them politics of George W. Bush. The latter film is an attempt at offering a genuine and very human Japanese perspective on World War II. Director Rob Marshall's campy adaptation of Arthur Golden's *Memoirs of a Geisha* (2005) examines the plight of girls abusively shaped into geishas. And Tom Cruise's star-turn as *The Last Samurai* (2003) demonstrates how understanding the traditionalism of Japanese Bushido practices can help generate cross-cultural sensitivity and respect. While these representational moments of political critique and/or cultural sensitivity, as framed within US multiculturalism, are laudable goals, what is problematic about this trend is that "Asia" becomes a space of cultural and political "primitivism." As Rey Chow explains, China "is 'primitive' in the pejorative sense of being 'backward' … when compared to the West, it is also 'primitive' in the meliorative sense of being an ancient culture (it was there first, before many Western nations)" (1995, 23). "Asia" is thus reduced to an instrumental role in furthering the American political logic of multiculturalism, while remaining locked in a static, museum-ized conception of traditional Asian culture and history.

6. *Global diversity as American multiculturalism.* In Roland Emmerich's summer blockbuster *2012* (2009), a series of apocalyptic disasters descending upon the world are foretold by Indian scientist Dr Satnam Tsurutani (Jimi Mistry). While the prescient scientist does not survive a tsunami crashing into the Himalaya mountain range, many characters – including various Asian characters hailing from China and Tibet – do eventually make it to modern-day arks to survive another day. Films like this one that feature global scenarios (including the NBC television series *Heroes*) populate their cast with Asian actors to signify global diversity. This diversity is shorthand for American multiculturalism because these filmic narratives are really about America's hegemony in international politics. With Asians in Hollywood as the ethnic flavor of this past decade, casting directors' token inclusion of an Asian face is a quick way to signal cultural diversity. *Pirates of the Caribbean: At World's End* (2007), *The Mummy: Tomb of the Dragon Emperor* (2008), *Around the World in 80 Days* (2004), *Shanghai Knights* (2003), and the action-star reunion bash *The Expendables* (2010) appear like Benetton ads with the token casting of Asian actors or stars. Hollywood also realizes that including Asian stars can extend the overseas box office reach of films in Asian markets, where the fan base of such stars readily constitutes an established audience group for studios and distributors, while at the same time giving their films a chic ethnic gloss. Take, for example, Gong Li's minor roles in *Miami Vice* (2006) and *Hannibal Rising* (2007); Ken Watanabe's appearances in *Batman Begins* (2005) and *Inception* (2010); Michelle Yeoh's inclusion in *Tomorrow Never Dies* (1997), *Sunshine* (2007), and *Babylon A.D.* (2008); and mega pop star Jay Chou's American debut as Kato in the remake of *The Green Hornet* (2011).

Slumdog Millionaire: Bollywood Bombast Meets Political Paternalism

When in a class I first verbalized my critical frustration with Danny Boyle's *Slumdog Millionaire* (after it swept eight wins out of ten nominations on Oscar night, including Best Picture), an eager film student, who also happened to be a devoted fan of the director and the film in particular, confronted me, as genially as he could, with a measure of righteous political indignation at my apparent lack of appreciation – not only of what the film had achieved for Bollywood in the United States but also of how it had shone global attention on the destitute social conditions of poverty and exploitation in India. My student clearly had his political heart in the right place, and I applauded him for that. What I want to do here, however, is to situate the sentiment he expressed squarely within the rhetorical logic of a Western paternalism that confronts "Third World" poverty, exploitation, crime, and human rights abuses in a way that nominally satisfies liberal multiculturalism's conceptions of political sensitivity to ethnic and cultural differences. My choice of this British production as one of two exemplary instances of Hollywood's Asia is premised not only on its appeal to American audiences, but also on how, as a film distributed by Twentieth Century Fox and Warner Bros. Pictures, it typifies the global Hollywood production and distribution network strategies I mentioned earlier.

With a track record of excellent films to his credit, including *Shallow Grave* (1994), *Trainspotting* (1996), *The Beach* (2000), *Millions* (2004), and *Sunshine* (2007), Danny Boyle turned to Simon Beaufoy's screenplay adaptation of Vikas Swarup's novel *Q&A* to tell the story of how an 18-year-old teenager has survived the slums of Mumbai to take part in the globally syndicated television game show *Who Wants To Be a Millionaire?* in order to find Latika, the girl he loves. The narrative success of the film lies in Boyle and Beaufoy choosing not to tell Jamal's tale in a strictly chronological fashion; the plot instead begins *in medias res* with Jamal's interrogation and torture at the hands of the Mumbai police in their attempt to ascertain how an uneducated "slumdog"[9] can possibly have been successful in getting this far in the competition. Or, as the police inspector bluntly puts it, "Professors, doctors, lawyers, general knowledge wallahs never get beyond 16,000 rupees. He's on 10 million. What the hell can a slumdog possibly know?" The film ingeniously cuts between three different narrative threads involving Jamal, with parallel editing that moves between different time periods in his life. The narrative present involving the police interrogation allows Jamal to describe and explain his motivations for getting on the show and how the questions he answered are miraculously tied to his life experiences – all with the diegetic help of a video of his participation in the show screened on the station television. Challenging verisimilitude, the questions perfectly align with the chronological narration of his youthful experience, illuminating for the audience Jamal's ability to answer the questions and the motivations that drive him as an individual.

A significant consequence of this plot structure is the stark contrast the film offers between the destitution and chronic violence the underclass suffers and the glossy, brightly lit television dream world that *Who Wants To Be a Millionaire?* presents as a media fantasy narrative of escape. When Jamal finds Latika trapped in the gangster Javed Khan's house watching the program, he asks her, "Why does everyone love this program?" She replies, "It's a chance to escape, isn't it? Walk into another life." Screening this program to millions of India's poor is like cruelly dangling an entire Thanksgiving meal in front of the hungry homeless without the intention of ever feeding them. Javed Khan's casual mockery of the show, asking why Latika bothers to "watch this shit TV" since he is already "a millionaire," exposes the ideological interpellation in which reality TV traffics: It deludes the masses into buying fantastical narratives of wealth attainment as real and reachable life goals, when the ultra-rich like Javed Khan effortlessly blur the boundaries between criminality and legal capitalist enterprises in order to amass wealth for themselves and the few, thus widening an already cavernous divide between the rich and the poor. The complicity of programs like *Who Wants To Be a Millionaire?* the film acknowledges; however, ironically, it appears less conscious of its own role in such neoliberal capitalist discourses. The film's ending with Jamal correctly answering the final question and thus winning the 20 million rupees, while getting the girl at the same time, raises the troubling question: In what sense does *Slumdog Millionaire* parallel the ideological structure of *Who Wants To Be a Millionaire?*, especially when Jamal diegetically (and the film as fantasy text) functions as a vicarious figure of capitalist hope and possibility – a poor old woman presses up against the car ferrying Jamal to the studio and utters, "Go son, go with my blessing and win it all. We love you Jamal." This final triumph is capped with the requisite concluding dance sequence in a train station during the final credits – a song-and-dance mise-en-scène that is characteristic of many Bollywood flicks – to mark, rather spectacularly, Jamal and Latika's third and presumably final reunion. Both Hollywood and Bollywood, hence, are guilty of the happy ending that dissolves the ideological contradictions that their narratives sometimes expose and that neutralize critique necessarily initiated by a film like *Slumdog Millionaire*. Bollywood as ethnic spectacle ends the film, leaving American audiences emotionally satisfied that our couple will walk away into bourgeois comfort and conventionality (20 million rupees is worth only about US $500,000) and the horrors of slum life are but a distant and ugly memory.

Figure 25.1 The Bollywood-style dance finale of Danny Boyle and Loveleen Tandan's *Slumdog Millionaire* (2008, producer Christian Colson).

Controversies over the film, especially after its Oscar win, took on an extratextual form, something to be expected when the filmmakers take on a subject of this nature. Accusations soon surfaced that the producers did not sufficiently pay the child actors, a number of whom were actually plucked from the slums. According to various news outlets,

> Rubina Ali (the youngest Latika) and Azharuddin Mohammed Ismail (the youngest Salim) were both poorly compensated for their original, monthlong [*sic*] acting work and have not shared in the film's financial windfall ... Fox Searchlight, Boyle and Colson [the producer] have declined to say what their actual compensation was. (Horn 2009)

The filmmakers' statement denied such exploitation, with the distribution companies also stating that "the welfare of Azhar and Rubina has always been a top priority for everyone involved in 'Slumdog Millionaire.'" The official statement goes on to say that "for 30 days' work, the children were paid three times the average local adult salary" and then to boast that "we are extremely proud of this film, and proud of the way our child actors have been treated" (Horn 2009). The filmmakers even bought the child actors apartments when their families "lost their homes ... after civic authorities demolished parts of the slum where they lived" (Kinetz 2009). Evident here are the ethical and moral consequences of cinema attempting to double as commodity spectacle and political intervention. The filmmakers likely took insufficient account of the anthropological dilemma that film as social presence creates when it seeks to intercede (as social text) on behalf of and exploit (as capitalist commodity) its object simultaneously. Boyle reflects on what he calls "a difficult moral question": "Do you exclude kids from the slums? If you exclude them, then it feels morally wrong. But if you include them, it raises another set of moral questions – how do you care for them after the movie is finished?" Regarding the children's desire to attend the Oscars ceremony, Boyle muses, rather appallingly I might add, that "you have to worry about exposing them – even if it's just a flash – to this world" (Horn 2009). He adopts (unwittingly, one would hope) a neo-imperialist discursive posture in assuming the moral right to intrude, if only to make a film, into an exotic world that he can objectify, while assuming that boundaries ought to be maintained to contain that very world from encroaching into his – and all for the supposed benefit of that world.[10]

Criticisms of the filmic representational discourse run the gambit, particularly those coming from Indian viewers. A *Los Angeles Times* article, eliciting cultural "insider" responses, presents a range of views. A Mumbai film professor points out that the film is "a white man's imagined India ... It's not quite snake charmers, but it's close. It's a poverty tour." Adding to this notion that the film offers a stereotypical image of what India is like in the Western imagination, the same professor argues that "there is still a fascination [among Indian audiences] with seeing how we are perceived by white Westerners ... It's a kind of voyeurism." Some note how *Slumdog Millionaire* joins "other foreign depictions over the years that they consider inaccurate, distorted or obsessed with poverty and squalor," raising objections from other critics who see the potential critique in the film's "focus on issues some in India would rather downplay." One response explains that "the world's second-most populous country after China has seen enormous benefits from globalization. But 'Slumdog' raises questions about the price paid by those left behind and the cost in eroding morality." A University of Chicago film scholar argues in tandem that "we're too quick to celebrate 'Incredible India' ... But there is an underbelly. To say we don't have problems is absurd" (Magnier 2009).

While it is possible to agree, to varying degrees, with these various critical positions, and to find the dialectic emerging from intersections productive, it is interesting to see how they generally fall into and depend on positive/negative categorization of ethnic representations. To offer a slightly different nuance to the critical logic here, I will suggest that the film mobilizes a political critique of Indian society (the "negative" representations) in a way that self-consciously and purposefully inverts its gaze on its own complicity, even if only momentarily (with the happy ending and Bollywood dance sequence significantly and necessarily excluded, of course), as a means of articulating a liberal politics (a "positive" political mode) crucial to its contribution to Hollywood's ethnic multiculturalism. Two sequences in the film come to mind. The police inspector's spurning the West's attempts to expose human rights abuses in Asia – "Now we'll have Amnesty International here next, peeing in their pants about human rights" – immediately after he has subjected a battered Jamal to electric shocks highlights the ease with which such inhumane abuses go unreported and how systemic these abuses are. This reference to human rights also brings into focus the lightly interconnecting network lines of transnational capitalism that morally implicate corporate responsibility, while paradoxically permitting ethical disavowal and legal protection at the same time. For instance, the producer of *Who Wants to Be a Millionaire?* inquires about but then turns a blind eye to a kidnapped Jamal as he is bundled into a police vehicle. It is too difficult to resist noting that *Slumdog Millionaire* is caught in its own web of political cleverness when the film itself is a player in what Rey Chow (in a discussion about human rights and China) identifies as "an ongoing series of biopolitical transactions in global late capitalism, transactions whereby human rights ... are the commodity par excellence" (2002, 20).

The second equally spectacular example is present in the Taj Mahal segment. In realizing that petty theft of tourist shoes can only get them so far, Jamal and his brother Salim move on to more creative entrepreneurial tactics of survival by trading on touristic ignorance. In a serendipitous fashion, Jamal discovers that he can whimsically indulge in fabulation, imaginatively reconstructing history to enthrall tourists with his tales. Are the exploitative modes of self-exoticism and self-orientalism he trades in any worse than the West's exploitation of the Taj Mahal as the romanticized backdrop for the operatic performance of Christoph Willibald Gluck's *Orphée et Eurydice*? The best moment comes when Jamal brings well-meaning American tourists, who wish to see the "real" India, to visit a river community. When juvenile thieves strip the tourist couple's rented car of its tires, the Indian driver blames Jamal for the crime and assaults him. The American couple come to his defense, as Jamal plays the tourist sympathy card: "You wanted to see a bit of real India, here it is." The tourists' response, "Well, here is a bit of the real America, son," is materially backed by a monetary gift. The film delights in its ability to shift between ideological positions by questioning both Jamal's "native" craftiness and the American tourists' presumptive deployment of the all-powerful greenback as the definitive capitalist resolution. Once again, one can only hope that the filmmakers are cognizant of the ironic parallel between this fictive moment and their own attempt to resolve the controversies surrounding the use of the child actors by agreeing to pay for the children's new apartments in Mumbai.

Finally worth noting is a humanistic strain that undergirds the narrative structure of the film, exemplifying Rey Chow's notion that American ethnicity "pretends to be a nonboundary" when it is politically advantageous to the majority (2002, 30). The very desire that drives the narrative is one of love as a universal value: Jamal confesses to the inspector, after the latter lets him go, that he "went on the show because ... [he] thought she'd be watching." It is not money that motivates Jamal but his love for Latika. Though heterosexual romantic love is a common narrative strategy in cinema, what is worth examining is its universal valuation as a human trait, so to speak, transcending cultural, national, and ethnic specificities. Love over money brings Jamal to Latika, while rewarding him with 20 million rupees at the same time; love for his brother redeems Salim when he kills Javed Khan and dies as a consequence; and love for the truth convinces the police inspector of Jamal's innocence. Ethnic specificities must turn instrumental in conveying universal values in order to serve multiculturalist politics. The nasty and messy issues of destitution, poverty, and violence witnessed in the slums cannot eclipse what Danny Boyle senses to be "a dynamism" there: "It is not a static thing, a slum ... It is actually a thriving, bustling mini-metropolis ... with a communicating and supplying, and cheating each other, and helping each other, just like in all communities."[11] Or, as an Indian commentator points out, "These ideas, that there are still moments of joy in the slum, appeal to Western critics" (Magnier 2009). The "universal" lessons drawn from *Slumdog Millionaire* mask the need for further engagement with the oppressed ethnic other, as demanded by liberal imperatives, for the film, through its representational and narrative discourses, eventually contains that other in a humanistic fantasy of hope and triumph over adversity.

The Karate Kid: Cross-Cultural Transmission

The Karate Kid series has come a long way from its comic book roots. After Pat Morita had cinematically immortalized the role of Kesuke Miyagi, the Japanese karate master, in the first installment in 1984, Hollywood had him reprise the role three more times: *The Karate Kid, Part II* (1986), *The Karate Kid, Part III* (1989), and *The Next Karate Kid* (1994), with the then unknown Hilary Swank replacing Ralph Macchio in the final film of the series. Given the recent Hollywood fascination with Asia, it would only be a matter of time before Hollywood executives would go dusting through old scripts looking for a potential remake. The result was *The Karate Kid* (2010) starring Jackie Chan and Jaden Smith (Will Smith and Jada Pinkett Smith's son). The plot closely follows that of the first film but changes the location from California to the People's Republic of China (a fascinating setting update to reflect globalization's impact on making the world a smaller place, California no longer constructed as inhabiting the very border of American ethnic otherness), and the remake has an African-American actor play the Karate Kid. After the death of Dre Parker's father, his mother Sherry (Taraji P. Henson) is transferred by her employers to China to assume a position, with Dre (Jaden Smith) reluctantly in tow. Before they can even unpack and settle in, Dre gets into a fight over a Chinese girl, Mei Ying (Han Wenwen), and is targeted by the group of bullies for harassment. Mr Han (Jackie Chan), the Parker's maintenance man, comes to Dre's rescue in one particularly bad situation and agrees to teach him kung fu in order that Dre will be able to challenge the bullies honorably at a national martial arts competition. After the requisite training from Mr Han, Dre acquits himself by rising to the challenge, despite a severe injury. His victory not only earns him the respect of the bullies, but it also restores the respectability of Mr Han as the martial arts teacher de jure.

The film works through the standard kid-friendly conventions of the underdog story but with the added element of kung fu and the China setting to give it its ethnic gloss. The lessons it teaches include the all-American never-say-die motif, musically accentuated by Justin Bieber's pop ditty "Never Say Never" during the final credit sequence. But this key lesson is achieved through cross-cultural transmission, building in additional pedagogical moments for its teenage target audience to convey the notion of cultural respect as part of US multiculturalism. A brief reading of the film through two formulations of this notion of cultural respect can be revealing: one involving the film's touristic gaze of China and the other involving the figure of the kung fu master and his relationship to his American pupil.

Cinema as touristic gaze is problematic for Asian and Asian-American viewers given the historical precedence this gaze has established from the emergence of cinema. In her illuminating study of actuality films by Thomas Edison and the American Mutoscope and Biograph companies, which include titles like *Dancing Chinamen – Marionettes* (1898) and *Chinese Rubbernecks* (1903), Sabine Haenni contends

Figure 25.2 A training sequence atop the Great Wall of China in Harald Zwart's *The Karate Kid* (2010, producers Ken Stovitz, James Lassiter, Jada Pinkett Smith, Jerry Weintraub, and Will Smith).

that the depiction of Chinatown and its inhabitants in these films helped "to invent [white] subjects that could pleasurably experience the newly racialized metropolis by simultaneously consolidating a new kind of 'white' hegemony, and by assigning the Chinese to a limited and constrained space" (2002, 25). Hollywood cinema has the ability to generate vicarious anthropological experiences as audiences intrude into cultural spaces without bearing the risk of real or imagined dangers, or assuming the ethical responsibility involved in cross-cultural contact, as *Slumdog Millionaire* demonstrates. *The Karate Kid* is likewise implicated through its tour-through-the-major-sights-of-China perspective: As in a tourist promotion board video, audiences are treated to a panoramic vista of the Forbidden City and a requisite kung fu training montage atop the Great Wall of China, imagery consonant with Jackie Chan's public role as the promoter of Hong Kong and Chinese tourism.[12]

On the other hand, the film seems deeply conscious of the cultural politics this commoditized gaze invokes, and it works particularly hard in the beginning segments of the film to circumvent it. On multiple occasions, the narrative establishes a stereotypical vision of China in order to debunk it immediately as an object lesson for both the characters and the audience. Dre's mother, for example, forces him to learn Mandarin in preparation for what she imagines to be "a quest to start a new life in a magical new land." In the typically embarrassing manner of parents subjecting their children to instruction, Sherry commands Dre, on their flight to China, to ask, in Mandarin, a Chinese-looking passenger across the aisle what his name is. Dre's stumbling attempts are met with the humorous American-accented response, "Dude, I'm from Detroit," a response that disrupts the place of racial typology in the construction of contemporary American national identities. In fact, to have African-American characters make this racial mistake – forgetting that Asian-Americans are Americans too – is to mitigate what would be otherwise a more egregious cultural faux pas if committed by an Anglo-American character. The film brings the message home when Harry, Dre's new blonde American neighbor, in welcoming the Parkers to their new apartment home in Beijing, advises Dre to learn Chinese: "This is China. Might not be a bad idea." Respect for China and its place in the global economy is the new cultural literacy for the transnational corporate elite. Another instance of this pedagogical structuring is again found in the film's expositional moments: Dre complains to his mother on the plane that "in China, everything is old. There's old houses, old parks, old people" and holds up a magazine photo of a bearded geriatric figure to make his point. As they are driven from the airport to their new apartment in the city, the newcomers catch glimpses of both old and new Beijing, including point-of-view shots of the National Stadium (affectionately known as the Bird's Nest Building) and the Central China

Television Headquarters (a Rem Koolhaas creation), cool architectural additions to Beijing's rapidly shifting landscape. Mother Parker seizes this teachable moment to point out to Dre (and the film's young audience) that "there's nothing old in China, huh?" The articulation of Chinese modernity functions as a corrective to the Orientalist tendencies in traditionalist media representations of China. It is also crucial to observe that the film shuttles between images of the old and the new, from a Chinese puppet theater scene to one of Mei Ying on a dance machine gyrating to Lady Gaga's "Poker Face." This cultural shuttling between the old and the new is especially worth noting in the master/student relation.

The kung fu master and student relationship is a narrative standard in the history of Chinese martial arts cinema. This convention is brought into Hollywoodized versions of the kung fu film and granted an East–West cultural configuration, with the Asian master transmitting his skills and philosophical values to his Western student: Chow Yun-fat's Monk with No Name takes on Seann William Scott's Kar and Jaime King's Jade as twin students in *Bulletproof Monk*; Jet Li and Jackie Chan team up to mentor Michael Angarano's Jason Tripitikas in *The Forbidden Kingdom*; and Quentin Tarantino enlists Hong Kong kung fu icon Gordon Liu to play the cruel master of Beatrix Kiddo (Uma Thurman) in *Kill Bill: Vol. 2*. The Hollywood East–West, master–student dynamic may be viewed, probably prematurely, as a symbolic passing of the kung fu cinematic torch.[13] But what are more interesting about this cultural transmission between master and student are the primitivist terms in which it is couched, as Rey Chow has delineated. The Asian master represents "primitivism," firstly, "in the meliorative sense of being [part of] an ancient culture" and therefore should be respected for his historical value to the Western student – the student can learn the ancient art of kung fu and its positive philosophies to apply to his present situation – and, secondly, the master is also primitivist in a "pejorative sense of being 'backward' … when compared to the West" (1995, 23), thereby requiring his erasure, reconstitution, or containment after he has successfully transmitted all that is valuable to the student. "Asia" has once more played a role of utility, even in the culturally respectful climate of Hollywood multiculturalism.

In fitting into this character profile, Master Han is not only acquainted with the art of "ancient Chinese healing," but he is also armed with fortune cookie quips like "You think only with your eyes, so you are easy to fool"; "When fighting angry, blind men, best to just stay out of the way"; and "Kung fu is for knowledge, defense. Not to make war, but create peace," all of which function as code for ancient Chinese wisdom. His attempts to transmit this "wisdom" to Dre require cultural translation, which his student provides in the form of American pop cultural language: "Chi" is compared to "The Force in *Star Wars*." Master Han is transfigured into "Yoda" in all his alien otherness, while Dre proudly dons the Jedi title. There is also a clear hint that the ancient philosophical wisdom being transmitted plays a mythological role in catalyzing an American sense of self-worth and fortitude within Dre. On the train trip the two take, Mr Han brings Dre to the Dragon Well to tell him a story that his father had told him: "I stood here with my father when I was your age. He told me it's magic kung fu water. You drink, and nothing can defeat you." Mr. Han bestows on his surrogate son Dre this mythic tale handed down from his father that serves to shore up Dre's self-confidence, a lesson he learns well, as he demonstrates in his conversation with Mr Han before Dre's final duel with his arch nemesis:

MR HAN: You don't need to fight anymore. You have proven everything you need to prove.

DRE: What, that I can get beat up easy and then quit? That's not balance. That's not real kung fu. You said that when life knocks you down, you could choose whether or not to get back up. Well, I'm trying to get back up, and why don't you help me? …

MR HAN: Just tell me, *Xiao* Dre, why? Why you need to go back out there so badly?

DRE: Because I'm still scared. No matter what happens, tonight, when I leave, I don't want to be scared anymore.

Dre has learned this final lesson of self-confidence and integrity on his own. Master Han has served his function in Dre's life and will fade into the background as the kung fu teacher of Chinese students he has acquired, thanks to Dre's impressive performance and display of character at the competition (until, of course, Hollywood reenlists Han for a potential sequel to the film). The kung fu master as the teacher of respect for ancient Chinese culture, and as the facilitator of transmuted "American" values has fulfilled his ideological task.

Conclusion

My attempts to think through this concept of "Asia" as global Hollywood commodity have been tinged with a certain political anxiety and ambivalence. Hollywood has come a long way in terms of ethnic representations of racial minorities, progress that one wants to champion and encourage. While I hope the United States as a nation also will take a politically progressive direction, with Hollywood either representing society or leading the way, box office and bottom-line constraints suggest that Hollywood still has a long way to go in transcending reductive modes of ethnic typology to allow for more nuanced depictions of cultural complexity and interaction, beyond simply paying lip service to multicultural correctness. By mapping the trends and confronting the newer entries to Hollywood Asia, I am expressing, through the most critical of language no doubt, my hope for better things to come from this intersection between Hollywood and Asian cinematic cultures.

Notes

1. Pham conceives this notion of an "Asian invasion" as "an American construct." Her argument that "the Asian invasion of Hollywood is framed by an increasingly popular discourse of multiculturalism" (2004, 122) parallels my point in this chapter.
2. I deal with this issue in the introduction of my book (Chan 2009, 12–19).
3. There is also the complex question of Asian-American cinema and its relationship to Hollywood's Asia that deserves an essay of its own. For more on this matter, see Feng 2002a and 2002b, and Hamamoto & Liu 2000.
4. Chow is discussing this commoditization in relation to China and human rights, but the principle still applies to our understanding of Hollywood's Asia.
5. For a more detailed definition and rigorous study of the genre in both its historical and contemporary guises, see Teo 2009. See also Hunt's *Kung Fu Cult Masters* for "the transcultural impact of 'kung fu'" (2003, 2).
6. Corporate entities such as Columbia Pictures Film Production Asia and Warner China Film HG Corporation signal an important trend in which Hollywood studios, as part of larger conglomerates, engage in strategies of globalization to partake of coproduction models that depend much more on localized talent. According to Time Warner's Asia Pacific Profile 2006, "in 2004, Warner Bros. partnered with China Film Group and Hengdian Group to form Warner China Film HG Corporation, the first filmed-entertainment joint venture with a foreign company in the history of China, making Warner Bros. the first non-Chinese company empowered to market and distribute Chinese films (both acquired and produced) in China": at www.timewarner.com/corp/aboutus/fact_sheet.page/TW_AsiaProfile2006_all.pdf (accessed October 26, 2010). Warner China Film HG Corporation coproduced Peter Chan's *The Warlords*.
7. See Feng 2009 for a racialized reading of *The Matrix*. Yuen Woo-ping is instrumental in the fight scenes in the trilogy.
8. Studies on this complex cross-cultural interaction include Jayamanne 2005; Kim 2004; Lo 2005, 153–157; Marchetti 2001; Pham 2004.
9. According to Danny Boyle, "Simon [Beaufoy] invented this word 'slumdog' which I thought was a kind of a regular word, but nobody's heard of this word ... It's a word for a slum kid, a kid from the slums." Beaufoy's clever neologism is unfortunate, particularly in terms of the loftier political goals of the film. Boyle's statement is from "Slumdog Dreams: Danny Boyle & the Making of Slumdog Millionaire," a special featurette available in the 2009 Twentieth Century Fox DVD release of the film.
10. I cautiously and tentatively marshal this critique of Boyle's public statement with the understanding that one can only read such citations in news articles at face value when one is not privy to the entire interview and its context.
11. "Slumdog Dreams: Danny Boyle & the Making of Slumdog Millionaire."
12. From 1995, Chan officially assumed the position of "Hong Kong Tourism Ambassador." "His 'performance' on and off screen has been considered by others and himself as having a direct impact on Hong Kong tourism, including tourist perceptions of the territory" (Pang 2007, 206).
13. The buzz that recent Hollywood martial arts cinema generated globally has seemingly reinvigorated Hong Kong and Chinese productions of the genre, particularly as regional or international coproductions. Exemplary titles include *Seven Swords* (2005), *The Promise* (2005), *The Myth* (2005), *The Banquet* (2006), *An Empress and the Warriors* (2008), *Three Kingdoms: Resurrection of the Dragon* (2008), *Mulan* (2009), *Storm Warriors* (2009), *14 Blades* (2010), *True Legend* (2010), and *Little Big Soldier* (2010).

References

Chan, Kenneth. (2009). *Remade in Hollywood: The Global Chinese Presence in Transnational Cinemas.* Hong Kong: Hong Kong University Press.

Choi, Jinhee, & Wada-Marciano, Mitsuyo. (2009). Introduction. In Jinhee Choi & Mitsuyo Wada-Marciano (eds), *Horror to the Extreme: Changing Boundaries in Asian Cinema* (pp. 1–12). Hong Kong: Hong Kong University Press.

Chow, Rey (1995). *Primitive Passions: Visuality, Sexuality, Ethnography, and Contemporary Chinese Cinema.* New York: Columbia University Press.

Chow, Rey (2002). *The Protestant Ethnic and the Spirit of Capitalism.* New York: Columbia University Press.

Curtin, Michael (2007). *Playing to the World's Biggest Audience: The Globalization of Chinese Film and TV.* Berkeley: University of California Press.

Feng, Peter X. (2002a). *Identities in Motion: Asian American Film and Video.* Durham, NC: Duke University Press.

Feng, Peter X. (ed). (2002b). *Screening Asian Americans.* New Brunswick, NJ: Rutgers University Press.

Feng, Peter X. (2009). "False Consciousness and Double Consciousness: Race, Virtual Reality, and the Assimilation of Hong Kong Action Cinema in *The Matrix.*" In Tan See-Kam, Peter X. Feng, & Gina Marchetti (eds), *Chinese Connections: Critical Perspectives on Film, Identity, and Diaspora* (pp. 9–21). Philadelphia: Temple University Press.

Haenni, Sabine. (2002). "Filming 'Chinatown': Fake Visions, Bodily Transformations." In Peter X. Feng (ed.), *Screening Asian Americans* (pp. 21–52). New Brunswick, NJ: Rutgers University Press.

Hamamoto, Darrell Y., & Liu, Sandra (eds). (2000). *Countervisions: Asian American Film Criticism.* Philadelphia: Temple University Press.

Horn, John. (2009). "'Slumdog Millionaire' Makers Respond to Criticism over Pay to Two Young Actors." *Los Angeles Times*, January 30, at http://articles.latimes.com/2009/jan/30/entertainment/et-slumdog30 (accessed October 30, 2010).

Hunt, Leon. (2003). *Kung Fu Cult Masters: From Bruce Lee to Crouching Tiger.* London: Wallflower Press.

Jayamanne, Laleen. (2005). "Let's Miscegenate: Jackie Chan and His African-American Connection." In Meaghan Morris, Siu Leung Li, & Stephen Chan Ching-kiu (eds), *Hong Kong Connections: Transnational Imagination in Action Cinema* (pp. 151–162). Durham, NC: Duke University Press.

Kim, James. (2004). "The Legend of the White-and-Yellow Black Man: Global Containment and Triangulated Racial Desire in *Romeo Must Die.*" *Camera Obscura*, 55, 19.1, 151–179.

Kinetz, Erika. (2009). "Slumdog Child Star Finally Gets New Home." *Huffington Post*, July 5, at http://www.huffingtonpost.com/2009/07/04/slumdog-child-star-moves-_n_225672. html (accessed October 30, 2010).

Lim, Bliss Cua. (2007). "Generic Ghosts: Remaking the New 'Asian Horror Film.'" In Gina Marchetti & Tan See Kam (eds), *Hong Kong Film, Hollywood and the New Global Cinema: No film Is an Island* (pp. 109–125). London: Routledge.

Lo, Kwai-Cheung. (2005). *Chinese Face/Off: The Transnational Popular Culture of Hong Kong.* Urbana: University of Illinois Press.

Magnier, Mark. (2009). "Indians Don't Feel Good about 'Slumdog Millionaire.'" *Los Angeles Times*, January 24, at http://articles.latimes.com/2009/jan/24/world/fg-india-slumdog24 (accessed October 30, 2010).

Marchetti, Gina. (1993). *Romance and the "Yellow Peril": Race, Sex, and Discursive Strategies in Hollywood Fiction.* Berkeley: University of California Press.

Marchetti, Gina. (2001). "Jackie Chan and the Black Connection." In Matthew Tinkcom & Amy Villarejo (eds), *Keyframes: Popular Cinema and Cultural Studies* (pp. 137–158). London: Routledge.

Miller, Toby, Govil, Nitin, McMurria, John, & Maxwell, Richard. (2001). *Global Hollywood.* London: British Film Institute.

Ong, Aihwa. (1999). *Flexible Citizenship: The Cultural Logics of Transnationality.* Durham, NC: Duke University Press.

Pang, Laikwan. (2007). "Jackie Chan, Tourism, and the Performing Agency." In Gina Marchetti & Tan See Kam (eds), *Hong Kong Film, Hollywood and the New Global Cinema: No film Is an Island* (pp. 206–218). London: Routledge.

Pham, Minh-Ha T. (2004). "The Asian Invasion (of Multiculturalism) in Hollywood." *Journal of Popular Film and Television*, 32.3, 121–131.

Stam, Robert, & Spence, Louise. (1983). "Colonialism, Racism and Representation: An Introduction." *Screen*, 24.2, 2–20.

Teo, Stephen. (2009). *Chinese Martial Arts Cinema: The Wuxia Tradition.* Edinburgh: Edinburgh University Press.

Wallerstein, Immanuel. (1991). "The Ideological Tensions of Capitalism: Universalism versus Racism and Sexism." In Étienne Balibar & Immanuel Wallerstein, *Race, Nation, Class: Ambiguous Identities* (pp. 29–36). New York: Verso.

Wood, Robin. (1985). "An Introduction to the American Horror Film." In Bill Nichols (ed.), *Movies and Methods: Volume II: An Anthology* (pp. 195–220). Berkeley: University of California Press.

26

The Blockbuster Superhero

Bart Beaty
Professor, University of Calgary, Canada

From **Superman** and **Batman** to **Spider-Man**, **Iron Man,** and **X-Men**, Bart Beaty provides a comprehensive look at superheroes – their comic book origins and the many film franchises they have inspired. He argues that, "it is not the pedigree of the superhero that determines a film's success, nor the absolute fidelity of the adaptation to the source material, but the ability of a filmmaker to capture the tone of the contemporary comic book onscreen." Locating the birth of the superhero in 1938, with the appearance of Superman in *Action Comics* #1, Beaty traces the history and growth of such key publishers as **DC Comics** and **Marvel Comics** as they expanded into film production. He uses the ***Batman* franchise**, spanning six decades, as a case study of evolving **synergy** among the print, broadcast, and film industries; the impact of advancing **film technology**; and shifting inscriptions of **ideology**, as mediated by story, characterization, casting, production design, and tone. Beyond ***Batman***, Beaty examines other superhero films through issues of authorship and occasionally divergent critical and box office reception. Beaty's essay shares ground with J. D. Connor on independent blockbusters and with Kristen Whissel on CGI in this volume.

Additional terms, names, and concepts: "summer event," second wave superhero, reboot, retcon

In a post-credit scene included at the end of *Iron Man* (Jon Favreau, 2008), the titular hero (Robert Downey, Jr) returns to the home of his alter ego and is confronted by an intruder, S.H.I.E.L.D. director Nick Fury (Samuel L. Jackson). Fury asks him: "You think you're the only superhero in the world? Mr Stark you've become part of a bigger universe. You just don't know it yet." While Tony Stark lacks a sense of the bigger picture, the same can hardly be said of the filmgoers who came to this film armed with a background in the superhero comics produced by Marvel Comics. The audience of knowledgeable comic book fans anticipates key relationships, character developments, and actions that cannot possibly be encompassed by a feature-length film. These spectators are alert to such things as the foreshadowing

American Film History: Selected Readings, 1960 to the Present, First Edition. Edited by Cynthia Lucia, Roy Grundmann, and Art Simon.

of the emergence of War Machine, the rival to Iron Man that will be taken on by his friend James Rhodes (Terrence Howard, replaced for the sequels by Don Cheadle), or the background shots of Captain America's partially assembled shield on Stark's workbench, an allusion to Iron Man's partner and sometime rival in Marvel's *Avengers* comic book series. Thus, when Fury, with the last line of the film, informs Stark that he would like to speak to him "about the Avenger Initiative," it not only serves to anticipate Fury's role in the *Iron Man* sequel scheduled to be released two years later, but also begins the process of advertising the *Avengers* film scheduled for release for the first weekend in May 2012. In the world of Marvel Comics, The Avengers is the superhero team that originally featured Iron Man, Captain America, Thor, the Hulk, Ant-Man and the Wasp. In the world of Marvel Studios, *Iron Man* was the second Avengers-related film, following *Hulk* (Ang Lee, 2003) and preceding, by one month, *The Incredible Hulk* (Louis Leterrier, 2008); it was followed by *Thor* (Kenneth Branagh, 2011) and *Captain America: The First Avenger* (Joe Johnston, 2011), with the casts of those four franchises combining for the mega-event film *The Avengers* (Joss Whedon, 2012). Significantly, Fury's specific use of the term "universe" directly alludes to the lexicon already in place in the comics world referring to the fictional worlds inhabited by characters across different titles and series. This quick scene informs the audience that Iron Man exists in the same world as the heroes of previous films based on Marvel characters, including Spider-Man, the Hulk, the Fantastic Four, and the X-Men, and it also anticipates future films.

The short post-credits scene in *Iron Man* brings to cinema a narrative sensibility developed in the American comic book industry in the 1980s, uniting a chain of seemingly stand-alone blockbuster films into a rich and varied matrix. In other words, *Iron Man* is not simply a film based on a popular character from another medium. Rather, it is the cinematic version of a particular narrative tradition that seeks to transform the superhero film from its origins in serial fiction and stories for young children into the kind of contemporary blockbuster that can attain both critical and box office success. The rise to prominence of the superhero as the dominant generic basis for summer blockbuster films in the 1990s and 2000s is the result of a diverse array of causes and influences ranging from developments in computer generated special effects and the synergistic business opportunities stemming from the conglomeration of media industries. Yet, at the same time, the wave of superhero films that was initiated by the record-shattering $115 million opening weekend of *Spider-Man* (Raimi, 2002)[1] has been organized with attention to the particularities of what I have elsewhere called the "comics world," a unique cultural field that has evolved since the rise of the Silver Age of Comics (1954–1970) and the later Underground movement (1968–1976). The socioeconomic components that subtended the emergence of this world included the establishment of organized comic book fandom in the United States with its major conventions and cultural events, such as the annual Comic-Con International in San Diego. But it also brought about formal advances such as heightened levels of psychological realism, intensified narrative syntheses (termed "crossovers"), and the integration of disparate characters into a single diegetic world. From this perspective, the storytelling style adopted by Marvel Studios in the 2000s sought to replicate the editorial vision introduced into Marvel Comics in the 1960s, focusing on the creation of a realistic and shared "Marvel Universe" inhabited by characters of all types who could selectively interact depending on storytelling needs. By adopting this strategy, Marvel Studios, in partnership with young filmmakers like Jon Favreau and Sam Raimi who grew up during the Marvel Comics era, sought to transform the superhero genre into a potent creative and economic force. Thus, Marvel Studios is currently creating nothing less than a new storytelling and business model aimed at leveraging the history of almost 50 years of Marvel Comics production for a new cinematic audience constructed in the image of comics fandom.

The contribution of the Marvel style to the history of American comic books is generally attributed to Stan Lee, editor of Marvel's superhero titles and the primary writer associated with the Marvel line during the 1960s.[2] Along with artists Jack Kirby, Steve Ditko, and others, Lee helped create many of the best-known characters of the second wave of superhero comic books in that decade. The costumed comic book superhero had its origins with the first appearance of Superman in *Action Comics* #1 (1938), published by what is now DC Comics, Marvel's chief rival. This debut was cemented into a genre by a wave of copy-cat heroes seeking to capitalize on DC's sudden success. Nonetheless, while the superhero comic book was the force that initially crystallized and stabilized the nascent American comic book industry, enthusiasm for the genre was burned out by the end of World War II and many superhero comic book series were cancelled due to poor sales. Only comics featuring Superman, Batman, and Wonder Woman, all properties of DC Comics, continued long past the end of the war.[3]

The superhero wouldn't reemerge as the dominant force in the American comic book industry until the early 1960s. In the mid-1950s the industry was challenged by a number of setbacks, including the rise of television, a distribution crisis, and a public backlash against the industry that linked comic books to juvenile delinquency (see Beaty 2005; Hajdu 2008; Nyberg 1998). To combat these assertions, in 1954 the industry adopted a self-regulating code that was akin to the Hayes Code, thereby all but eliminating the production of the horror and crime comic books that were among the best-selling magazines of the period. The resulting Code strictures, with their emphasis on wholesome values and child-friendly entertainment, laid the foundation for the return of the superhero. In the early 1960s, Lee challenged the staid output of DC Comics by introducing a new line of superhero characters featuring The Fantastic Four (1961), Spider-Man (1962), the Hulk (1962), Thor (1962), Iron Man (1963), and the X-Men (1963). Lee thereby reinvigorated the genre, attracting a new generation of young readers as well as an older generation nostalgic for the kinds of heroic adventures that they themselves had read as children who were attracted to the more sophisticated Marvel style. While DC's superheroes had long occupied a shared universe and appeared in each other's stories and titles, Marvel took the universe concept much more seriously and made guest appearances of popular characters a commonplace in their publications, carefully maintaining narrative and character continuity so that events in one character's title would have effects in the titles of other characters in the shared universe. DC's superhero comics focused on stand-alone stories that could be logically deciphered by any first-time reader to the extent that any new appearance of the villainous Joker in a Batman comic book bore little or no relationship to previous appearances by the same character. By contrast, Marvel adopted the storytelling conventions of the televised soap opera, with its vast open-ended continuity, allowing its characters to gradually age and develop as personalities. Significantly, upon reintroducing a villain in a Marvel superhero comic book, the company would directly refer to the previous encounters, even going so far as to footnote the issues and dates of the earlier stories for readers.[4]

Thus, while the comic book industry's two leading publishers of superhero stories, DC and Marvel, targeted similar audiences within the same genre, their products had notably distinctive narrative styles. Marvel tended to knit stories together into one coherent universe, but DC maintained a fuller separation between series and even issues from the same series. Over time, the popularity of the Marvel model caused DC to emulate their strategies, and, by the 1970s, both companies had begun to lay out extremely elaborate models of internal continuity. This tendency was heightened by the emergence of a new generation of artists and writers who had grown up reading earlier superhero comics and who now sought to find ways to reconcile heretofore contradictory plot points in an effort to bring complete coherence to the fictional worlds. By the 1980s, each company was engaged in the creation of universe-wide mega-events known as crossovers that would have ramifications for all or most of the company's titles. By having events in one character's title directly impact those in another, the concept of the integrated diegetic world was reinforced and, importantly, readers were obliged to purchase comics they might not have otherwise in order to read the whole story.

The success of Marvel's *Marvel Super Heroes Secret Wars* (1984) and DC's *Crisis on Infinite Earths* (1985) introduced a "summer event" sensibility into the comics industry that was directly imported from Hollywood blockbuster filmmaking of the same era. Moreover, each new blockbuster offered the opportunity to reset the fictional universe in new ways, thereby overcoming some of the burden of continuity that had, over the course of time, become overly convoluted and contradictory as successive writers sought to reconcile one plot point against another. *Crisis on Infinite Earths* was marketed as an attempt to clarify DC's extraordinarily complicated diegetic history by consolidating material into a canon. This attempt is one of the most significant examples of the retroactive continuity change (retcon), a deliberate narrative strategy in the field of superhero comic books that would later be adopted in such films as *Superman Returns* (Bryan Singer, 2006). The 1990s saw the acceleration of universe-wide event comics, and the 2000s even more so. For example, DC's *Crisis on Infinite Earths* spawned a sequel, *Zero Hour: Crisis in Time* (1994) that was intended to address the continuity problems that had been created by the first correction. A decade later, DC would launch six additional company-wide crossover events in successive years: *Identity Crisis* (2004), *Countdown to Infinite Crisis* (2005), *Infinite Crisis* (2005–2006), *52* (2006–2007), *Countdown to Final Crisis* (2007–2008) and *Final Crisis* (2008), suggesting that adjustments to company-wide continuity had become a permanent concern for creators.

The Evolution of Batman from the 1940s to the 2000s

As Batman has been the subject of films in four distinct historical periods, the franchise provides an excellent opportunity to assess the historical development of storytelling in the superhero film genre. Batman debuted as one of a dozen feature stories in the twenty-seventh issue of the anthology title *Detective Comics* (May 1939).[5] Following the successful launch of the Superman character in 1938, DC Comics, and many of its competitors, quickly flooded the comic book market with new superhero concepts. Batman, whose creation is credited to artist Bob Kane and writer Bill Finger, was one of the most successful superhero characters to have been launched in the early period of the first superhero comic book boom. Batman was so popular that, by the spring of 1940, he was the star of his own comic book, as well as the primary feature in *Detective Comics*. In 1943, a Batman comic strip by Kane and collaborators began appearing in American newspapers, running until 1946. While the character was never featured in his own radio series, he did appear occasionally in *The Adventures of Superman* starting in 1945, where he was voiced by actors including Matt Crowley, Stacy Harris, and Gary Merrill.

On 16 July, 1943, a 15-part Columbia Pictures serial debuted The Batman as a cinematic character. Starring Lewis Wilson and featuring Douglas Croft as his sidekick, Robin, the serial followed Batman's attempts to thwart the villainous plots hatched by Prince Daka (J. Carrol Naish), a Japanese spy who turned his adversaries into pseudo-zombies. More than Universal or Republic, Columbia was interested in capitalizing on the success of newspaper comic strips in serial form, adapting no fewer than 14, including fellow superheroes Superman and The Phantom. The Batman serial was the most lavish of Columbia's productions up to that point in time, and was marketed like a stand-alone feature (Cline 1997, 25). While the serial introduced the concept of the Bat's Cave to the Batman mythology (changed to Batcave in the comics), it tended to ignore the obligations of the comic book genre. Notably, no attempt was made to present a Batmobile, and Batman and Robin were simply chauffeured about town by their butler, Alfred, in a black Cadillac. Similarly, very little was made of the idea that the character was a "super" hero. In the film, Bruce Wayne is a government agent battling fifth columnists during World War II, and the fact that he dresses in a superhero costume is barely addressed. In this way, the character had much more in common with traditional detective and secret agent characters than with someone like Superman, and the trappings of the superhero genre fit uneasily in the serial. In *The New Adventures of Batman and Robin*, a second serial released in 1949, the characters again battled a traditional serial villain in the form of a mad scientist (Leonard Penn) bent on world domination, rather than a villain from the comic book. In this film Robert Lowery and Johnny Duncan played the respective lead roles. The two Batman serials produced in the 1940s evinced very little connection with the comic books that were being presented during the same era, and there was little connection between the individual films.

With the decline of serial filmmaking in the 1950s, Batman remained dormant on the screen until the debut of ABC's *Batman* television show in January 1966 (see Spigel & Jenkins 1991). The show ran on two consecutive nights in primetime. On Wednesdays, the episode would end with Batman (Adam West) and Robin (Burt Ward) in a dire predicament that would be resolved at the opening of Thursday's program. The show featured various well-known character actors as supervillains, including Burgess Meredith (the Penguin), Cesar Romero (the Joker), Frank Gorshin and John Astin (the Riddler), Vincent Price (Egghead), and Julie Newmar and Eartha Kitt (Catwoman). The show was initially a hit, with both nights' airings ranking among the top 10 programs of the 1965–1966 season, but it quickly burned out and saw a precipitous decline in interest in 1967, and was cancelled in 1968. The producer, William Dozier, also brought the property to the cinema for a feature-length film between the first and second season. In *Batman: The Movie* (Leslie Martinson, 1966), four supervillains (Penguin, the Joker, the Riddler, and Catwoman (this time played by Lee Meriwether)) combine forces to challenge Batman and Robin, seeking world domination by dehydrating world leaders at the United World Security Council. Like the television series that spawned it, *Batman: The Movie* was knowingly and joyfully campy. The rising interest in the Pop Art of painters Roy Lichtenstein and Andy Warhol in the early 1960s served as the visual inspiration for the television series and film, which featured explosive, brightly colored "Pow," "Bang," and "Thud" effects during fight sequences. Robin's constant punning ("Holy heart failure, Batman!"), and the ridiculousness of the plots, sets, and acting in the film and series contributed to the idea that the 1960s version of Batman was children's fare, with the serial-derived plot elements and comic book background highlighting the lack of seriousness with which the character was presented. The idea of a serious superhero film would have to wait until the children raised on Bat-camp grew up.

In many ways, the Tim Burton-directed *Batman* feature in 1989 opened the door for the current superhero movie boom. While Richard Donner's *Superman* (1978) initiated the trend toward superheroes on the silver screen, its three sequels (1980, 1983, 1987) had reduced the luster of that particular franchise, and, particularly by the third and fourth installment in the series, reiterated the campy-comical approach to the genre. Burton's film was notable for the dramatic shift in tone that aligned the character more closely with its contemporary comic book counterpart than with his cinematic predecessors. In the mid-1980s, two milestone comics dramatically transformed the Batman character. Frank Miller's *The Dark Knight Returns* (1986) depicted Batman as an aging crime-fighter emerging from retirement to renew his war on crime, and Alan Moore and Brian Bolland's *The Killing Joke* (1988) added a layer of psychological complexity to the Batman/Joker relationship. Each of these works, which featured grimly adult psychosexual themes rarely found in the superhero comic books up to that period in time, contributed to a remasculinization of the Batman mythos in the wake of the feminizing effects of the 1960s camp version. In short, each of these works reconceptualized Batman within a tough-guy pulp/noir tradition that was then taken up by Burton in the film version.

Batman tells the story of the crime-fighter's (Michael Keaton) war with the psychotic mass killer known as the Joker (Jack Nicholson). Shot at Pinewood Studios in England, the film is largely defined by Anton Furst and Peter Young's Academy Award-winning set designs, which employed a postmodern Gothic sensibility emphasizing darkness, shadows, and the verticality of Gotham City's decaying skyline. This dark vision of *Batman* was an overwhelming success with filmgoers in a way that the two previous incarnations of Batman on film had not been. The film opened in 2,194 theatres on June 23, 1989, establishing a new record for largest initial weekend box office gross at $43.6 million. The film would eventually gross $411 million worldwide in 1989, and spawned a "Batglut" of merchandise totaling more than $750 million worth of T-shirts, toys, soundtrack albums, and assorted tie-ins. Importantly, *Batman* was the first superhero franchise film to generate significant synergies horizontally across a single media empire, as the film was released by Warner Brothers, based on a comic book series from DC Comics – which had been part of Time Warner since 1971 – with a soundtrack on Warner Bros. Records featuring the work of contract recording artist Prince, and so on (Meehan 1991). From this standpoint, it, and its sequels, solidified the superhero template previously established by the *Superman* franchise but with a far more serious tone and a more comprehensive marketing approach.

Keaton and Burton returned to Batman for a sequel in 1992: *Batman Returns*. This film featured Batman combating a trio of villains: the Penguin (Danny DeVito), Catwoman (Michelle Pfeiffer) and politician Max Shreck (Christopher Walken). The film opened strongly on the weekend of June 19, earning $45.7 million, but was ultimately less successful than its predecessor, grossing only $266 million worldwide. The film's reduced financial performance was largely attributed to a conservative backlash against the film's darkness, violence, and sexual situations that led to McDonald's discontinuing their Happy Meal cross-promotion with the movie. While the film was

Figure 26.1 Heath Ledger's Academy Award-winning performance as the Joker in *The Dark Knight* (2008, director and producer Christopher Nolan).

better critically appreciated than *Batman*, Warner Brothers opted to move in a more family-friendly direction with the next installment in the series. *Batman Forever* (1995) was directed by Joel Schumacher and introduced Val Kilmer in the role of Batman when Keaton turned down the part. In this film, the caped crusader takes on the twinned villains of the Riddler (Jim Carrey) and Two-Face (Tommy Lee Jones), and Robin (Chris O'Donnell) is introduced into the series for the first time as Batman's sidekick. The lighter touch found success at the box office, as the film had the highest grossing opening weekend of 1995, and outperformed *Batman Returns*, but not Burton's first film. Schumacher returned for a fourth Batman film, *Batman & Robin*, in 1997 with George Clooney taking on the lead role. In the final installment of the third Batman cycle, the hero confronted two major new villains (Mr Freeze (Arnold Schwarzenegger) and Poison Ivy (Uma Thurman)) and was joined by a second sidekick, Batgirl (Alicia Silverstone). Schumacher's second film broke markedly from the tone established by Burton, returning to the camp sensibility of 1966's *Batman: The Movie* in an effort to appeal to families and generate toy sales. The strategy turned out to be a mistake. *Batman & Robin* grossed only $238 million worldwide, making it the least successful film in its cycle, and was criticized for its bloated style. While Schumacher, Clooney, and O'Donnell had been expecting to make a fifth Batman film, *Batman Triumphant*, for release in 1999, Warners discontinued the film cycle and began exploring the possibility of a live-action version of the futuristic *Batman Beyond* animated television series, as well as a film based on the highly acclaimed 1987 Frank Miller/David Mazzucchelli origin comic book series, *Batman: Year One*, neither of which came to fruition.

After an eight-year hiatus, and the explosion of interest in the superhero genre that the Batman franchise largely spawned, Batman returned to the screen in 2005 in *Batman Begins*, the character's fourth cinematic iteration. Directed by Christopher Nolan, and starring Christian Bale, two stalwarts of the independent cinema movement of the 1990s, *Batman Begins* bears no relationship to any of its predecessors. Nolan's vision of the *Batman* franchise was largely influenced by, although not straightforwardly adapted from, the Miller/Mazzucchelli story *Batman: Year One*, and by the Batman comics that Jeph Loeb and Tim Sale produced in the late 1990s. This Batman was the most realistic within the limitations of the genre, and the vision of Gotham City was of a modern metropolis. Significantly, this was the first Batman film to make extensive use of computer-generated special effects. While the opening weekend grosses of *Batman Begins* were below expectations, its final tally of $372 million worldwide meant that it surpassed the performance of every other Batman film except for Burton's original 1989 *Batman*, thus ensuring a sequel.

The Dark Knight in 2008, also directed by Nolan and retaining much of the same cast from *Batman Begins*, is, in many ways, the high-water mark for the superhero film genre, in terms of both global audience appeal and critical esteem. The film, which is the third-highest grossing movie of all time (behind James Cameron's 1997 *Titanic* and 2009 *Avatar*), at more than $1 billion in receipts, was nominated for eight Academy Awards, and won two: a technical award for Best Sound Editing (Richard King) and the first acting award ever given to a superhero film, Best Supporting Actor (Heath Ledger). In returning to the story of the Batman/Joker relationship established in the first of Burton's films, Nolan highlighted certain post-9/11 cultural themes, including the war on terror and the deployment of extralegal strategies in combating irrational violence, earning it comparisons with the foreign policy of the Bush administration (Klavan 2008). At the very least, *The Dark Knight* sought to bring moral complexity into a film franchise that had previously abjured it, with the result being a summer blockbuster with broad yet very adult appeal. The idea that a superhero film could attract a mature audience with no prior investment in the genre or characters now firmly had its grip on Hollywood.

The road that the Batman character traveled from the subject of low-budget serial films in the 1940s to critical and box office success was far from a direct one, and it raises a number of important issues about the history and the development of the genre. What best explains the phenomenal success of *The Dark Knight* and the rise to prominence of the superhero film genre? Certainly, striking advances in the area of special effects were a major factor. The Batman films of the 1940s and 1966 lacked elaborate special effects, and featured heroes in mundane action sequences while dressed in ridiculous costumes. The centrality of visual spectacle in recent decades, and the transition from optical to digital processes, have made it possible for the superhero to be represented cinematically in as spectacular a fashion as on the printed comic book page, while still maintaining a certain realist aesthetic. There is no doubt that, for movie studios, superhero films are attractive franchises: They arrive with built-in audiences, they have a large number of potential characters and storylines, and they can be used to generate significant corporate synergies across horizontally integrated media companies. Nonetheless, the appeal of the franchise concept does very little to explain the attraction of (some) superhero films to the public, nor does it explain why some superhero films that hew closely to the formula fail.

It is certainly possible to read, as many have, the success of a film like *The Dark Knight* as resulting from an ideological alignment of the individual vigilante hero acting outside society with contemporary norms and beliefs. However, suggestions that the success of *The Dark Knight* stems from its ideological correspondence with the Bush administration seem inadequate insofar as the film's success was essentially coterminous with the resounding repudiation of the Bush presidency by the American electorate. Moreover, while comic book superheroes had once constituted a short-lived fad for the public in the infancy of the genre (1938–1945), a significant level of sustained interest in the genre has existed in North America since at least the early 1960s with little abatement. Further, the interest in superhero movies generally has done very little to drive interest in superhero comic books, whose overall sales have remained relatively flat since the superhero movie boom began in the 2000s.[6]

Another argument for the success of these films is the presence of A-list stars and critically acclaimed directors attached to the project. Following the lead of Marlon Brando in *Superman* (1978) and Jack Nicholson in *Batman* (1989), the most popular of contemporary superhero films are awash with well-regarded actors. *The Dark Knight*, for example, cast two Academy Award winners, Michael Caine and Morgan Freeman, in supporting roles. It also marked Heath Ledger's first appearance in a major studio release after his Oscar-nominated performance as a gay cowboy in the critically acclaimed *Brokeback Mountain*. Similarly, 2008's other superhero blockbuster, *Iron Man*, included three Oscar nominees, Robert Downey, Jr, Jeff Bridges, and Terrence Howard, and one winner, Gwyneth Paltrow, as its lead characters. Moreover, the films themselves are increasingly overseen by directors with a great deal of artistic credibility particularly in independent and film festivals circles. When Tim Burton was hired to direct *Batman* (1989) he had only two features (*Pee Wee's Big Adventure*, 1985, and *Beetlejuice*, 1988) to his name. It was the success of his version of *Batman* that cemented his reputation as an idiosyncratic A-list director and demonstrated to filmmakers how the genre could be successfully used to generate cultural capital within Hollywood. Similarly, Sam Raimi had cultivated a dedicated following for both his horror films, the *Evil Dead* series (1981, 1987, 1992), and smaller dramatic films such as *A Simple Plan* (1998) before taking on *Spider-Man* in 2002. In recent years, even higher profile young filmmakers with an indie-auteur reputation have been entrusted with major superhero franchises. Thus Bryan Singer (*X-Men*, 2000; *Superman Returns*, 2006) moved to superheroes from high-end thrillers such as *The Usual Suspects* (1995) and *Apt Pupil* (1998). Jon Favreau took on *Iron Man* after finding success as a writer and actor and sometimes director in a series of independent films, most notably *Swingers* (Doug Liman, 1996). Christopher Nolan came to the Batman series after his Oscar-nominated small budget crime films *Memento* (2000) and *Insomnia* (2002). The trend toward A-list participants says something about the shifting hierarchies of genre, as superhero films are no longer considered merely lucrative but also prestigious.

Narrative, Seriality, and Superhero Auteurism

The transition from superhero narratives of the 1980s and 1990s, such as *Batman* and *Superman*, which are loosely connected by the lead figure but which stand alone narratively, to the principle of serial continuity can be seen clearly in the respective differences between the first and second *Spider-Man* films (Sam Raimi, 2002 and 2004), and the first and second *X-Men* films (Bryan Singer, 2000 and 2003). Despite the fact that both of these franchises took great liberties with the storylines presented by their source comic books, significantly altering the established superhero canon, they were nonetheless well received by comic book fans for their respectful treatment of the characters and ability to strike the proper tone. Among the significant changes made to Spider-Man in the first film are his web-slinging powers, which, in the film, are biological while they are mechanical in the comic book, and his relationship with Mary Jane Watson (Kirsten Dunst), a character who was not introduced until the forty-second issue of the Spider-Man comic book (November 1966) and did not go to high school with Peter Parker (played by Toby Maguire in the film).

X-Men makes an even greater number of changes from comic book to film. Stories featuring the X-Men, more than any other comic book superhero team, have been structured in a manner reminiscent of televised soap operas. At various times, literally dozens of Marvel mutant characters have been members of the team led by Professor X (Patrick Stewart), although the founding members from the 1963 version of the series were Cyclops, Marvel Girl, Iceman, Beast, and Angel. Of these, only Cyclops (James Marsden), Marvel Girl (Famke Janssen, who does not use the name Marvel Girl in the film), and Iceman (Shawn Ashmore) appear in the first film. In 1975, Marvel Comics relaunched the X-Men series with both a new creative team (Len Wein and Dave Cockrum) and a new cast of mutant superheroes. Initially, only Cyclops remained from the original team, and he was joined by Colossus, Nightcrawler, Storm, Thunderbird, Banshee, Sunfire, and, the most popular new character, Wolverine. The X-Men film opts for a mixture of these two teams, composed of Professor X, Cyclops, Jean Grey/Marvel Girl, Storm (Halle Berry), and Wolverine (Hugh Jackman) as the primary team, and Iceman and Rogue (Anna Paquin), a character introduced to the Marvel universe in 1981, as newly recruited students. Other important X-Men characters, including Kitty Pryde (Sumela Kay), Jubilee (Katrina Florece) and Pyro (Alex Burton), are included in what are essentially cameo roles as students at Professor Xavier's School for Gifted Youngsters.

Unlike their sequels, both *X-Men* and *Spider-Man* are largely self-contained films. Although each was intended to be the basis of an ongoing franchise when it was created, the films build to conclusions that would be satisfactory had no sequels been forthcoming. While *X-Men* concludes with the vanquished Magneto (Ian McKellen) vowing to continue his fight, which suggests the possibility of a sequel, the ending is strikingly different from the conclusion of *X2*, which signals the rebirth of Jean Grey as the Phoenix, one of the pivotal characters in the X-Men mythology. The birth of the Phoenix at the end of *X2* virtually necessitates a third film in the series, much as, for example, the capture of Han Solo in *The Empire Strikes Back* (Irvin Kershner, 1980) served as prelude to a third film in that series. Similarly, *Spider-Man* ends in a fashion that is largely self-contained, though also unsatisfactory. Peter Parker's decision to spare Mary Jane the knowledge that he is Spider-Man means that the film ends on a somber note of disappointment. While this ending stresses the probability of a sequel to resolve the romantic tension aroused by the first film, that is hardly enough to satisfy continuity-hungry superhero fans. At the end of *Spider-Man 2*, however, the film returns to the story of the first film. Harry Osborne (James Franco), whose role was diminished for the sequel, is haunted by visions of his dead father, the Green Goblin (Willem Dafoe), who was the vanquished villain from the first film but had no role in the second. Then, after the denouement of Spider-Man's showdown with the second film's villain, Doctor Octopus (Alfred Molina), and an apparent narrative closure of the film, Harry unwittingly discovers his father's weapons cache. The stage is set for a confrontation that will open the third film in the sequel. The transition, therefore, represented by these films results from developing a situation that lends itself to forming the base of a sequel to one that virtually commands one, as continuity increasingly takes central stage in the world of the filmic superhero.

While continuity-based cross-referencing is fast becoming a hallmark of a "good" superhero film, it can also be troubling for the genre on a number of levels. Continuity problems arose in American superhero comic books for several reasons. Among these is the fact that, in the mid-century period in particular, comic books were widely denigrated as mass cultural children's fare. One result of this was that comics were one of the least prestigious parts of the culture industry, and often attracted creators who could not be bothered to adhere to anything resembling a character bible, but were simply churning out material to meet a monthly deadline. Related to this, a high degree of creator turnover was a natural function of the business cycle because superhero characters were owned by their publishers and not by the people who initially created them. As new writers and artists came to a title, they often had decidedly different visions of the characters than their predecessors and would shift the direction of the title, emphasizing only those aspects of the continuity that particularly suited their needs. The resulting contradictions often generated heated debates within the superhero comic book fandom over what constituted the canon of the superhero universe. *Superman Returns* brought this issue squarely to the world of the superhero film. Warner and director Bryan Singer sought to position the film as a continuation of the previous *Superman* films that had starred Christopher Reeve. However, Singer, along with many fans of the character, felt that only the first two of those four films were canonical, and so opted to situate *Superman Returns* after the events of *Superman II* (1980), proceeding, therefore, as if the events of *Superman III* (Richard Lester, 1983) and *Superman IV: The Quest for Peace* (Sidney J. Furie, 1987) had never taken place. This is a quintessential retcon, or a change to established character continuity made after the fact, and is generally accepted among superhero comic fans when it is perceived that the change makes for a better story. At the same time, Singer's film jettisoned key elements and characters from the first two canonical *Superman* films, including the characters of Lex Luthor's sidekick Otis (Ned Beatty) and companion Eve Teschmacher (Valerie Perrine). This selective use of past works, while typical of strategies employed within the field of comic books, created an awkward chronology for the character completely divorced from the comic book version of Superman, and at odds with significant portions of the film series.

A similarly awkward relationship exists between the two movies featuring the Hulk. Ang Lee's 2003 *Hulk* opened to a strong box office total of more than \$62 million, but it was the first movie in history to open with more than \$20 million in its first weekend, only to decline by at least 65 percent the following week. Its cumulative worldwide gross of \$245 million was considered a disappointment, and it has the dubious distinction of being the best opening film not to gross at least \$150 million in the domestic box office. Nonetheless, Marvel had invested heavily in the concept and the character, not just as a standalone franchise but as the buildup to a larger integrated media strategy, and the film had succeeded in boosting merchandising sales, so a sequel was ordered with a new director (Louis Leterrier) and an entirely new cast. Eric Bana was replaced by Edward Norton as Bruce Banner/The Hulk, while Liv Tyler replaced Jennifer Connelly as his ex-girlfriend, Betty Ross. While the recasting of lead roles in superhero films is not novel or even extraordinary (consider the range of actors who have portrayed Batman, or, in another genre, James Bond), *The Incredible Hulk* (2008) went much further, acting essentially to negate everything established in *Hulk*. Alongside the completely overhauled cast was the decision to act as if the first film, released only five years earlier, had never happened. Thus, *The Incredible Hulk* is not a sequel to *Hulk*, but an entirely new venture, complete with a different origin story, new villains, and a much different tone and visual style. Importantly, the film also contained a cameo appearance by Robert Downey, Jr as Tony Stark immediately before the credits in which he indicates to General Ross (William Hurt) that "we are putting a team together." This second nod to the forthcoming *Avengers* film, coming, as it did, in a film that opened only a week after *Iron Man*, helped to cement the concept of the shared superhero universe, even for viewers who might have missed the implications of the more subtle Nick Fury appearance after the credits in *Iron Man*. With *The Incredible Hulk*, which only barely outgrossed the Lee version, Marvel Studios adopted a strategy lifted directly from the Marvel Comics: rebooting a character in order to bring it more closely into line with what is perceived as a more elaborate and canonically significant undertaking (see J. D. Connor's essay in this volume). Importantly, however, neither the reboot nor the retcon can guarantee audience success even among curiosity-driven superhero fans.

The reboot and the retcon are important strategies by which a superhero franchise can be maintained, and they have been used with great frequency since the 1990s in the American comic book industry, where, for instance, a character such as Captain America has been the subject of nearly continuous reconceptualization by changing creative teams. Interestingly, while Batman has been successfully rebooted on several occasions, both *The Incredible Hulk* and *Superman Returns* were failures in this regard. Plans for a sequel to *The Incredible Hulk* were put on hold by Marvel Studios until after the release of *The Avengers*, and Warner has decided to reboot *Superman*, thereby retconning the *Superman Returns* retcon for any films in the series moving forward. Both of these decisions foreground the issue of failed superhero films. From the standpoint of the movie studio, a failure in the superhero genre is not only costly, given the tremendous expenses that are associated with special-effects driven action films, but potentially damaging over the long term insofar as superhero films are envisioned as the basis for long-running franchises that will multiply audiences. The question of why some superhero films fail helps to assert the primacy of certain tendencies in the contemporary superhero genre. Failed properties tend to share specific characteristics: an overreliance or unwarranted faith in the lead actor's drawing power at the box office, the selection of a lesser known superhero as the basis for a film, and the adoption of the action-adventure blockbuster formula with little attention to quality writing and direction.

The Fallen Superhero

There can be several stumbling blocks for the superhero film at the box office, including the wrong director, the wrong cast, the wrong character, or the wrong take on the character. In many ways, the reasons for the failure of a superhero film are self-evident in that it does not present a vision that resonates with an audience. It is worth noting, however, that underperforming films based on less well-known superheroes, like *Daredevil* (Mark Steven Johnson, 2003), *Elektra* (Rob Bowman, 2005), and *Ghost Rider* (Mark Steven Johnson, 2007), all involved A-list stars (Ben Affleck, Jennifer Garner, and Nicolas Cage respectively) working with little-known or inexperienced directors. By way of contrast, the *Hellboy* films directed by Guillermo del Toro (2004, 2008) feature an Oscar-nominated filmmaker working with a cast of virtually unknown or character actors. Based on a relatively little-known superhero, the films haven't enjoyed blockbuster status but are well regarded critically and financially and enjoy a certain cult following more akin to a sleeper indie hit. The superhero film that is synonymous with failure, however, is *Catwoman* (Pitof, 2004), which fared poorly at the box office despite its Batman-derived pedigree and Academy Award-winning star (Halle Berry). The failure of *Catwoman* is attributable to a number of factors, including an inexperienced director, a star with no real track record of box office success outside the ensemble *X-Men* films and the James Bond franchise, and a take on the character that was largely at odds with the characterization from the comic books. *Catwoman*, which won the Golden Raspberry awards for Worst Film, Worst Actress, Worst Director, and Worst Screenplay in advance of the Oscars, demonstrated better than most films that it is not the superhero genre itself that generates strong results, but individual works within it. Specifically, it is those works that take seriously the visual and narrative complexity of the genre and develop a formula more in keeping with the production of independent filmmaking than with star-driven vanity projects. Determining the right formula is a risky proposition but one with enormous long-term benefits to studios and their parent media conglomerates.

While actors may not be the primary drivers of superhero success, the characters themselves do seem to bring a certain cachet. In this sense, superhero films diverge from other forms of genre filmmaking such as the Western or science fiction. As the mixed success of many superhero films has demonstrated, one problem inherent in the genre is the relatively small number of well-known superheroes in American culture. While a genre like the Western might be endlessly open to new characters and narrative possibilities, the superhero film is limited by the range of characters that have dominated the field in their original comics form; names like Superman, Batman, and Wonder Woman from DC Comics, and Spider-Man, the X-Men, Captain America, and the Hulk from Marvel remain the gold standard within the field. While a few non-Marvel and non-DC superheroes have served as the basis for successful series (*Teenage Mutant Ninja Turtles*, 1990, 1991, 1993, 2007) and unsuccessful films (*Spawn*, Mark Dippé, 1997; *Barb Wire*, David Hogan, 1996), the quest to turn second-tier heroes into top-tier franchises has proved challenging. While *Iron Man* made a tremendous success of a character that was only marginally popular in comic book form, the examples of *Daredevil* and *Ghost Rider* indicate the challenge that is involved with relying predominantly on the ability of a lead actor to bring audiences to little-known superhero properties.

Increasingly, the successful superhero franchise is not merely a career-making vehicle for movie stars, but a credibility-building forum for aspiring auteurs. As the superhero film becomes legitimated as an important outlet for serious filmmaking, and not just fodder for popcorn sales, it has become an attractive venue for directors who might not otherwise have been conceived as the makers of special-effects driven action movies. The decision by Marvel Studios to hire four-time Academy Award nominee Kenneth Branagh, best known for his Shakespearean work, to direct *Thor* (2011) highlights the way that commercial and critical interests have intersected to elevate filmmaking within the genre. Significantly, by 2009, the narrow range of A-list superhero characters available to Hollywood had some directors frustrated about being shut out of the boom, as Brett Ratner, director of *X-Men: The Last Stand* (2006), publicly bemoaned the fact that he did not have a superhero franchise to call his own (Seijas 2009).

One outcome of the limited pool of superhero resources has been Hollywood's effort to create new superhero stories from scratch. For example, Pixar's animated superhero film *The Incredibles* (Brad Bird, 2004) offered an elaboration of many of the melodramatic themes found in the Lee/Kirby *Fantastic Four* comic books, and, significantly, featured a cast of four characters whose powers were analogous to those found in that comic book, presenting superheroism as a form of social exceptionalism privileged over the mundane qualities of everyday life. The film was both a critical and commercial smash, the fifth-highest grossing film of 2004 and the winner of two Academy Awards (Best Animated Feature, and Best Achievement in Sound Editing), and it ushered in a tidal wave of tie-in merchandising. One of the important attributes of *The Incredibles* was the creation of a fully fleshed out superhero universe, including subsidiary heroes like Frozone (Samuel L. Jackson) that allowed the family of heroes to function within an entire superhero universe. The opposite tack was taken by the makers of the film *Hancock* (Peter Berg, 2008), starring Hollywood mega-star Will Smith, who challenged his image as the likeable leading man of summer blockbusters by playing a despised alcoholic superhero in contemporary Los Angeles.

Only two superpowered beings exist in *Hancock*, the titular character and his ex-wife Angel (Charlize Theron), one of the smallest conceivable superhero universes. Nonetheless, this proved to be of little consequence for moviegoers, as the film was the fourth-highest grossing film in 2008 (behind *The Dark Knight*, *Iron Man* and the fourth Indiana Jones film), and made

Figure 26.2 Will Smith's Hancock rescues an injured police officer in Peter Berg's *Hancock* (2008, producers Michael Mann, Akiva Goldsman, James Lassiter, and Will Smith).

more than $624 million at the worldwide box office. The success of *The Incredibles* and *Hancock* is suggestive of the way that superhero films have the possibility of becoming divorced from their comic book origins, if they remain true to the spirit of superhero canonicity: fully fleshed out characters inhabiting a complex moral universe, with innovatively rendered worlds and realist narratives, well-crafted dialogue and character development. A-list stars and eye-popping special effects are no longer sufficient for the discerning, and increasingly sophisticated, superhero audience.

Conclusion: From Market Synergies to Aesthetic Synergies

The ability of the contemporary superhero film to capitalize on the core elements of the superhero comic book has been dependent upon the ability of filmmakers to create the superhero film as a genre distinct from, albeit related to, the traditional science fiction or action blockbuster. In turn, this directorial freedom is intimately related to the changing business models in the production of superhero movies, particularly at Marvel Studios. For many years, even while the Superman and Batman franchises were generating significant revenue for DC Comics, Warner Brothers and parent company Time Warner, the rights to popular Marvel Comics characters were tied up in a complicated contractual situation with independent producers, including Carolco and the Cannon Group, who were unable to raise the capital to finance blockbuster films.[7] In 1986, Marvel was sold to New World Entertainment, and then, in 1989, to junk bond trader Ronald Perelman's MacAndrews & Forbes Holdings. Perelman took the company public in 1991 and also founded Marvel Studios in 1993 as a subsidiary company to license characters for films. A series of poor business decisions led to the bankruptcy of Marvel Entertainment in 1996. Control of the company eventually landed with the owner of Toy Biz, Isaac Perlmutter, and Avi Arad, the head of Marvel

Studios. Following the bankruptcies of Marvel, Cannon, and Carolco, Marvel was able to reacquire the rights to their most popular characters, and licensed them to various studios, including Twentieth Century Fox (X-Men) and Columbia Pictures/Sony (Spider-Man). In 2004, following the success of the initial films coproduced by Marvel Studios, the company opted to move into production directly and raised $525 million to produce 10 films for which they would then outsource the distribution. *Iron Man* and *The Incredible Hulk* in 2008 were the first of the films produced by Marvel Studios, and, not surprisingly, are the ones that most clearly reproduce the storytelling styles of Marvel Comics.

It may be argued that superhero films may not have risen to such prominence in Hollywood were it not for the rapid conglomeration of media companies and new corporate models of synergy. Yet, the success of the genre is not only tied to these corporate developments but is intricately bound to the evolution of the cultural status of the American comic book. In 1986, just a few years before the explosion of interest in superhero-based films was launched by Burton's *Batman*, three comic books were widely heralded in the press as exemplifying the new seriousness of the comic book form. These were Art Spiegelman's Holocaust memoir *Maus*, Frank Miller's dystopic futuristic Batman series *The Dark Knight Returns*, and Alan Moore and Dave Gibbons's intricately plotted critique of fascist tendencies within the superhero genre, *Watchmen*. Significantly, the latter two books are firmly rooted in, if critical of, the superhero genre that has dominated the American comic book industry, and the history of the superhero film would be deeply structured by the creators of these works.

Frank Miller is a well-regarded comic book writer and artist who first came to fame in the early 1980s as the creative force on Marvel's *Daredevil* (both the films *Daredevil* and *Elektra* are based on his particular plots and his vision of those characters). By 1986, he was a star in the comic book field, and DC entrusted him to radically overhaul one of their most popular characters. The resulting hyperviolent vision of Batman contributed to Burton's vision of the character and made Miller a sought-after talent. Miller broke with DC Comics at the end of the 1980s in a dispute over a proposed ratings system for comics and began working with smaller, independent comic book companies where he would maintain an ownership stake in characters and work that he created. Miller also worked briefly in Hollywood, penning the sequels *Robocop 2* (Irvin Kershner, 1990) and *Robocop 3* (Fred Dekker, 1993), an experience he found extremely unfulfilling.[8] At the same time, he began publishing the black-and-white neo-noir comics set in the fictional town of Sin City for Dark Horse Comics, and, in 1998, serialized *300*, about the Battle of Thermopylae, for the same publisher. In the 2000s he returned to work at DC, creating a *Dark Knight* sequel, *The Dark Knight Strikes Again*, and a new Batman series with artist Jim Lee. In 2005, Miller returned to the film industry, working with director Robert Rodriguez on a filmic adaptation of *Sin City* and, in 2008, he wrote and directed his first film, *The Spirit*, an adaptation of Will Eisner's celebrated newspaper superhero comic strip.

Including *Daredevil* and *Elektra*, four of Miller's comics have been directly adapted for the screen, his treatments of Batman have influenced both Burton and Nolan, and he himself has made a film based on the comics work of another creator. Neither *Daredevil* nor *Elektra* were well received by comic book fans, although each film fared reasonably well at the box office. *Sin City* and *300* (Zack Snyder, 2006), on the other hand, while not strictly superhero films, are notable for their slavish fidelity to their source material. Each of the films was produced on a digital backlot with computer-generated sets and effects. Moreover, each film pays close attention to the original source material, replicating individual panels from the comics on the screen as moving images and adhering closely to Miller's dialogue. Each of the films fared well at the box office. *Sin City* grossed more than $158 million worldwide and received generally positive reviews, while *300*, which received mostly poor reviews and was widely attacked as racist, imperialist, and homophobic, grossed more than $456 million worldwide. Both films are anticipated to produce theatrical sequels but, in the meantime, have spawned their own TV series. Nonetheless, Miller's success in the film industry was diminished somewhat at the end of 2008 when he released his version of *The Spirit*, one of the worst reviewed of all superhero films and also one of the biggest money losers with a worldwide gross of only $38 million. The film was roundly condemned within comics fandom for taking unnecessary liberties with Eisner's creation, altering its tone in order to bring it more in line with Miller's own right-wing political leanings. Interestingly, of all the film projects based on comics that Miller has been involved with, the most successful, by far, are those that maintain the greatest level of fidelity to the original comics, the digital backlot films that enable filmmakers like Rodriguez and Snyder to replicate the visual elements of the comics with near exactitude, while the works that take the greatest liberties, *Elektra* and *The Spirit*, have fared the worst with critics and the public. Thus, it seems that it is not Frank Miller himself who inspires cinema-going audiences but the attraction of his particular comic book style. This logic flies in the face of Hollywood's tendency to rely on well-known names rather than well-established styles to sell an intended blockbuster. Arguably, a Miller-created version of the iconic Eisner property *The Spirit* should have been a recipe for a smash hit, despite the fact that the character was not widely known outside comic book fandom. Yet, by failing to adhere to the canonical narrative and tone of the original comic, Miller faced a hostile backlash from fans aghast by his hubris, and his work found very little traction.

In contrast to Miller's embrace of Hollywood, Alan Moore remains an idiosyncratic outsider. For that he has earned a devoted following within comics but is little known or valued beyond this subculture. The British writer entered the comic book industry through the music press in the 1970s, eventually coming to work for the British comics magazines *2000 A.D.* and *Warrior*, where he initially launched *V for Vendetta* as a critique of Thatcherism in the 1980s. He entered the American comic book industry working for DC on the low-selling monster title *Swamp Thing*, which he reenvisioned as a more serious and adult work filled with commentaries on environmental issues. It was in the pages of *Swamp Thing* that he made his name as a serious and experimental writer in the comic book form and where he introduced the character of John Constantine. In 1986 and 1987, he wrote the 12-part miniseries *Watchmen* (with art by Dave Gibbons), a dark and dense novelistic treatment about the political and philosophical ramifications of superheroes in American culture that is widely credited with beginning a trend toward the deconstruction of superheroes in the American comic book industry. Like Miller, Moore had a falling out with DC Comics at the end of the 1980s over issues including royalty payments and the proposed ratings system, and stopped working with the company. At the time he turned his attention away from superhero comics, launching *Big Numbers* (with Bill Sienkiewicz), a comic book series about fractal mathematics, *From Hell* (with Eddie Campbell), about Jack the Ripper, and *Lost Girls* (with Melinda Gebbie), a pornographic comic with literary overtones. In the 1990s, he returned to superhero comics, working with Image comics on a number of titles, and launching his own line of comics, America's Best Comics, which included his *League of Extraordinary Gentlemen* with artist Kevin O'Neill.

Alan Moore's comics have been adapted for the screen with even greater frequency than have Miller's, including *From Hell* (Albert and Allen Hughes, 2001), *The League of Extraordinary Gentlemen* (Stephen Norrington, 2003), *Constantine* (Francis Lawrence, 2005), *V for Vendetta* (Andy and Larry Wachowski, 2005), and *Watchmen* (Zack Snyder, 2009). Unlike Miller, however, Moore has openly shunned Hollywood. He was involved with the sale of his rights for the films *From Hell* and *League of Extraordinary Gentlemen*, but was so unhappy with the resulting works that he turned his back on the film industry, vowing never to watch a film based on one of his comic books. On subsequent films, including *V for Vendetta* and *Watchmen*, he has asked that his name be removed from the credits, and has sought to distance his own work from the films that are based upon it. In this way, Miller and Moore, the two most influential superhero comic book creators of the 1980s, have come to occupy opposite positions within the field. Miller is the quintessential comics industry celebrity who has been embraced by Hollywood and who has, in turn, embraced it, while Moore retains a reputation as a controversial outsider untainted by the film industry. Interestingly, and despite their renown within comics fandom, Hollywood has had trouble selling films based on their contributions alone, as, for instance, both *V for Vendetta* and *Watchmen* have been high-profile box office disappointments despite the fact that they are adaptations of works frequently held to represent the aesthetic pinnacle of the superhero comic book genre. Ultimately, it seems that it is not the pedigree of the superhero that determines a film's success, nor the absolute fidelity of the adaptation to the source material, but the ability of a filmmaker to capture the tone of the contemporary superhero comic book on screen. The comics work of Miller, Moore, and dozens of other comic book creators since the mid-1980s has been oriented toward elevating the superhero story by encumbering it with greater narrative and moral complexity so as to strip it of its pulpish roots. So, too, with superhero movies, which increasingly look to superhero comics as an important forerunner of the turn away from simple-minded action movie tropes and toward more realist-inspired character development, art direction, and special effects in the superhero blockbuster. Just as superhero comic book creators in the 1980s were inspired by the psychological complexity of underground and independent comic books to raise the level of their genre, so too in the world of film have superhero filmmakers borrowed from the lessons of independent filmmaking to transform the adventure blockbuster into a respectable cinematic genre.

Notes

1. Unless otherwise indicated, all data on box office receipts are taken from BoxOfficeMojo.com.
2. For a history of Stan Lee and the Marvel style, see Raphael and Spurgeon 2003.
3. For an overview of the development of the American comic book industry see Gabilliet 2009.
4. For example, when a line of dialogue on the second page of *Fantastic Four #6* (September 1962) indicates that "the [Human] Torch has been scouting for signs of Doctor Doom," a footnote directs readers back to *Fantastic Four #5* (July 1962) for the reasons why. Further, the events of *Fantastic Four #6* are footnoted when Dr Doom returns in *Fantastic Four #10* (January 1963).
5. For detailed readings of the history and significance of Batman, see Brooker 2001 and Pearson & Uricchio 1991.
6. A notable exception would be sales of Alan Moore and Dave Gibbons's *Watchmen*, whose sales surged tremendously in 2008 in advance of the 2009 film release.
7. For a history of Marvel Entertainment see Raviv 2002.
8. Miller delivered a scathingly anti-Hollywood speech at the 2000 Harvey Awards presentation.

References

Beaty, Bart. (2005). *Fredric Wertham and the Critique of Mass Culture*. Jackson: University Press of Mississippi.

Beaty, Bart. (2011). *Comics vs. Art: Comics in the Art World*. Toronto: University of Toronto Press.

Brooker, Will. (2001). *Batman Unmasked: Analyzing a Cultural Icon*. New York: Continuum.

Cline, William C. (1997). *In the Nick of Time: Motion Picture Sound Serials*. New York: McFarland.

Gabilliet, Jean-Paul. (2009). *Of Comics and Men: A Cultural History of American Comic Books*, trans. Bart Beaty and Nick Nguyen. Jackson: University Press of Mississippi.

Hajdu, David. (2008). *The Ten-Cent Plague: The Great Comic-Book Scare and How It Changed America*. New York: Picador.

Klavan, Andrew. (2008). "What Bush and Batman Have in Common." *Wall Street Journal*, July 25.

Meehan, Eileen. (1991). "'Holy Commodity Fetish, Batman!' The Political Economy of a Political Intertext." In Roberta E. Pearson & William Uricchio (eds), *The Many Lives of the Batman* (pp. 47–65). New York: Routledge.

Nyberg, Amy Kiste. (1998). *Seal of Approval: The History of the Comics Code*. Jackson: University Press of Mississippi.

Pearson, Roberta E., & Uricchio, William. (1991). *The Many Lives of the Batman: Critical Approaches to a Superhero and His Media*. New York: Routledge.

Raphael, Jordan, & Spurgeon, Tom. (2003). *Stan Lee and the Rise and Fall of the American Comic* Book. Chicago: Chicago Review Press.

Raviv, Dan. (2002). *Comic Wars: How Two Tycoons Battled over the Marvel Comics Empire – And Both Lost*. New York: Diane.

Seijas, Casey. (2009). "X-Men 3 Director Brett Ratner Says 'There's Nothing Left' in Comics for Him to Adapt." *MTV News Splash Page*, March 19.

Spigel, Lynn, & Jenkins, Henry. (1991). "Same Bat Channel, Different Bat Times: Mass Culture and Popular Memory." In Roberta E. Pearson and William Uricchio, *The Many Lives of the Batman* (pp. 117–148). New York: Routledge.

27

Limited Engagement
The Iraq War on Film

Susan L. Carruthers
Professor, Rutgers University–Newark, United States

The post-9/11 Iraq War and protracted fighting that followed President George W. Bush's declaration of "**mission accomplished**" was haunted by a **"meta-contradictory" paradox**, as are many of the documentary and narrative films representing it: "How do we understand – and what do we call – a war that was long since declared over, in which the enemy remains largely invisible yet remains ubiquitous?" Susan L. Carruthers provides close readings of **the first wave of documentaries** in 2005–2006, including ***The War Tapes*** and ***Gunner Palace***, the former of which casts soldiers as cinematographers recording their own experiences, and the **second wave** in 2007–2008, including ***Taxi to the Dark Side*** and ***Standard Operating Procedure***, which cast soldiers as both perpetrators and victims in the contexts of Abu Ghraib and other atrocities. During this same period narrative films, many of which center on soldiers' homecoming, attracted little audience interest or critical attention, a response with political and ideological implications that Carruthers probes, ***The Hurt Locker***'s success notwithstanding. Her essay shares ground with Pat Aufderheide on the contemporary documentary in this volume and with Stephen Prince on post-9/11 film in the hardcover/online edition.

Additional terms, names, and concepts: war film, combat film, embedded journalists

Imagine a landscape of desolate streets strewn with vast mounds of garbage and burnt out vehicles. Buildings – an indistinguishable jumble of shops and homes, punctuated by golden-domed mosques and filigreed minarets – are pock-marked by artillery rounds where they haven't been pulverized into rubble. Everything chokes with dust. And everyone is armed – armed with a camera if not also with more lethal weapons. Cellphones serve both to detonate improvised explosive devices and to document the carnage. While "jihadis" film beheadings and suicide bombers record their last messages before martyrdom, American troops engage in their own obsessive digital self-documentation. Flurrying shutters click to produce a gruesome montage of grins, grimaces, tears, blood, corpses, and severed body parts.

American Film History: Selected Readings, 1960 to the Present, First Edition. Edited by Cynthia Lucia, Roy Grundmann, and Art Simon.

Or so it would seem as a distant conflict comes into blurry focus from the welter of photographs, videoclips, and feature-length films that collectively constitute "Iraq" as American viewers apprehend it. Indeed, it has become something of a truism that never before in history has a conflict-in-progress been subject to such relentless imagistic documentation. In whatever other ways Iraq's intractability may or may not resemble the quagmire of Vietnam, cultural critics have pointed to one striking discrepancy. Vietnam – the first "television war" – was avoided by the film industry until it was over, Hollywood studio executives reluctant to tackle a war that was both too divisive and too visible. Iraq, by contrast, having been largely abandoned by network news after the first flush of "mission accomplished" euphoria, has attracted an unprecedented number of filmmakers eager to fill the void.

This dichotomy may be a little too schematic. It is easy to forget that *The Green Berets* (1968), John Wayne's hyperpatriotic tribute to the Special Forces, was not the only film to be made about the war in Vietnam while it was in progress. Several documentaries, some broadcast on television, some released theatrically, aired in the United States before American troops pulled out in 1973.[1] But historical record-straightening aside, the profusion of documentary films made about Iraq nevertheless remains striking. To date, at least 40 have appeared, together with a smaller number of narrative films distributed by major studios.

Here, I will chart the key thematic preoccupations of American filmmakers as they have engaged the war's origins, course, and consequences. How far have their political concerns, emotional investments, and aesthetic strategies shifted over time? To what end has Iraq been the most heavily "documentaried" war to date? If everyone is making pictures, who has actually been looking, and what have they seen?

The Soldier as Cinematographer

Given the daunting number of war-related films, I propose to begin by taking a close look at one that condenses many key features of Iraq war cinema more broadly. After its premier at the 2006 Tribeca Film Festival, Deborah Scranton's *The War Tapes* garnered widespread critical acclaim and an Oscar nomination for best documentary film (lost to Al Gore's *An Inconvenient Truth*). Like other films that preceded it such as Michael Tucker and Petra Epperlein's *Gunner Palace* (2005) and Garrett Scott and Ian Old's *Occupation: Dreamland* (2005), *The War Tapes* sets out to document a year-long tour of duty in Iraq, in this case by members of C Company of the New Hampshire National Guard. Unlike those earlier productions, however, the "war tapes" in Scranton's film are supplied by men on active duty, providing this documentary with a distinctive promotional hook: the first war film to be shot by soldiers themselves. Having declined an offer to embed with the National Guard, Scranton instead sought permission to give cameras to the guardsmen themselves. Ten volunteers received a one-chip Sony MiniDV camera, tripod, microphones, an array of lenses, and a stack of blank tape.[2] Some sent Scranton only raw footage, while others maintained regular contact via email and instant messaging. Edited into final form, *The War Tapes* foregrounds the camerawork and reflections of three men in particular. Specialist Mike Moriarty, Sergeant Steve Pink, and Sergeant Zack Bazzi offer a compelling study in contrasts: Moriarty, a "substantially patriotic" father of two, laid off from his forklift-driving job and struggling to shore up his imperiled masculinity; Pink, a cynical 24-year-old carpenter with writerly inclinations, hoping to eliminate debts accrued as a college English major; and the laconic, *Nation*-reading, Arabic-speaking Bazzi, the apple of his Lebanese mother's teary eyes.

This biographical mise-en-scène, introducing Moriarty's wife, Pink's girlfriend, and Bazzi's mother, occupies *The War Tapes*' first 15 minutes. From the outset, then, it is clear that the relationship between "over here" and "over there" – between domesticity and military service, between men and women, family and country – is central to Scranton's mission of establishing "the possibility of empathy in the middle of war." A film about the first-hand experience of soldiers, *The War Tapes* also reflects the experience of the women who wait and worry at home: a portrait of relationships strained by prolonged absence, and under threat of fatal termination, that can't be readily resumed "as normal" by men who return home altered, angry, and estranged. This looming alienation is foreshadowed at the outset when, on the eve of his deployment, Moriarty films his four-year-old son running across a parking lot to greet him. Seen through night-vision lenses, he is an eerily luminescent little figure – tinged in green, not quite of this world – who interrupts filming by jumping up for a hug.

Then, with little orientation (it is November 2004 in the turbulent city of Fallujah), *The War Tapes* plunges viewers into the maelstrom. Since no single narrator lends overall coherence to the video collage, we are left to make our own sense of the disorienting experience of soldiering in Iraq. Chaos reigns. Firefights erupt from nowhere and end just as suddenly: a blizzard of bullets; a din of expletives, commands, and yells; a confusion of injuries; vehicles on fire; blood on the road; the camera upended. If it is impossible to tell who is firing at whom, it is also hard not to question the wisdom of soldiers doing double duty as cinematographers, when their sights might more appropriately be trained elsewhere.

Throughout *The War Tapes*, Iraq is mainly viewed through the windscreen or turret of an armored personnel carrier: a blasted wasteland of arid countryside and cratered streetscapes moved through at speed. At rest, the soldiers of C Company face daily mortar and rocket attacks on their flimsy encampment near Bilal. But while they are in constant danger, they also present a lethal menace to the civilian population of Iraq. Barreling down single-gauge highways at 50 miles per hour, the armored convoys stop for no one. Iraqi drivers who move too slowly are bulldozed aside, their cars furiously bumped off the road like fairground dodgems. Heedless pedestrians face a more lethal fate. In one of *The War Tapes*' most disturbing sequences, also rendered in night-vision's ominous green, Moriarty's vehicle plows into a young Iraqi woman who had dashed out to cross the road. By the time they lurch to a halt, her body lies in pieces, dimly captured on video as several guards struggle to drag her remains off the road before more trucks hurtle past. Troubled by the indignity of her death, one soldier remarks on the crumbled remains of cookies she'd been carrying – a badge of her innocence and their culpability. "The Iraqi people are who we're here to help, and we just killed one of them," a guardsman notes. Revolted by the sight of "pieces of her head," which he urges another soldier not to look at, he is instantly aware that such a scene is never forgotten. And it isn't. On return to New Hampshire, this vision of wasted life haunts Moriarty in post-traumatic flashback.

Pink adopts a more defiant attitude toward death – avowedly eager to "kill insurgents at a rate fast enough that [he] can see them fall to the ground and die." His ambition is realized. In one scene, Pink recounts his role in killing several insurgents, whose disfigured corpses are shown in a series of still close-ups. With studied disdain, he tells a story of how he had been upbraided for continuing to film when a dog came sniffing at the bodies and started to eat the flesh. "I didn't see a problem with that," Pink announces. "Good for him. I hope he fills his belly." But Pink's commanding officer apparently took a different view, upbraiding him for having shot the dog with a video camera rather than with his rifle – a contingency not in the rule book, Pink fumes in self-defense.

Pink's attitude to the US mission in Iraq demonstrates a similarly hard-nosed realism. He drips scorn over those naive dopes who think the military should be patching up a broken country, building bridges to win hearts and minds. ("We're not the Peace Corps.") And for those who think the war is all about oil, he has an equally belligerent riposte: "This had *better* be about oil. This had *better* be about money. And we'd better *get* that money and that oil ... Somebody other than Dick Cheney better be getting their hands on it pretty soon." Pink's point of view is echoed, albeit with less vehemence, by Moriarty. He too regards America's thirst for oil as a mandate to do whatever it takes to secure supplies. His gripe, a familiar post-Vietnam complaint, is rather that those in command refuse to apply sufficient force to prevail. The answer? "Shit or get off the pot."

Together the protagonists of *The War Tapes* provide candid insights into the operation of untrammeled greed in what one of them dubs the "war for cheese." They are well placed to do so, for the primary mission of C Company is providing armed protection for convoys of trucks operated by Kellogg, Brown and Root (KBR, a Halliburton subsidiary) as they deliver supplies to military bases across Iraq. As Pink explains, desperate TNRs (third country nationals) receive a pittance to drive unroadworthy vehicles through hostile territory while hapless "rear echelon motherfuckers," who had never expected to see combat, ride in the most vulnerable position – poised to fire at insurgents who might ambush them en route. KBR, meanwhile, profits handsomely: empowered to do so by a monopolistic deal that lets it run everything from laundries, to canteens, to PXs and barbershops, egregiously bilking the Pentagon for services the military hitherto undertook itself. Even those soldiers who robustly champion America's right to profit through the exploitation of others draw the line at KBR's inequitable divvying of the spoils. That the US Vice President also happened to serve as CEO of the war's biggest beneficiary hardly passes them unnoticed.

The War Tapes thus provides raw material for a trenchant critique of US purposes and practices in Iraq. But unlike some polemical works that both preceded and followed it – a vein tapped by Robert Greenwald in *Uncovered, Outfoxed*, and *Iraq for Sale* – Scranton's film avoids direct authorial argument.[3] Implying rather than asserting, it adopts an approach more typical of Iraq war documentaries: an approach that privileges identification with men in uniform. The parameters of criticism are thus established by *their* appreciation of the war's dangers, possibilities, stupidities, and injustices. In this case, viewers might suspect that Scranton harbors more sympathy for Sgt Bazzi's position that Bush's "war of choice" is not a fight he personally would pick than for the gung-ho patriotism and unabashed materialism of Pink and Moriarty. But since the director remains voiceless throughout, authorial hints are dropped more obliquely by the editing. While Bazzi quips that "one day Iraqi will bloom" – thanks to the liquid sewage that US troops, under C Company escort, spray over the Iraqi countryside – she cuts to footage of President Bush, declaiming the nobility of America's democracy-bearing mission: a gesture of pungent debunking.

Critics applauded *The War Tapes*, in part precisely because of its ideological understatement. According to film scholar Charles Musser, the strident populism of Michael Moore's loved-and-loathed *Fahrenheit 9/11* (2004) had left audiences (or at least critics) fatigued by such full frontal polemicism (2007, 12–13). Reviewers duly commended Scranton's film as a nonpartisan offering that would elicit viewers' sympathy irrespective of their attitudes toward the war – views that had become thoroughly polarized by the time of its release in mid-2006. If critics of the war detected a kindred spirit in Scranton, supporters could hardly charge her with being disrespectful of "the troops" since soldiers had shot and narrated much of the film themselves. *The War Tapes*, in other words, was sufficiently open a text that it could be read as supportive of various incompatible viewpoints. What looked like an exposé of corporate war profiteering to some struck Michael Atkinson of the *Village Voice* as "a worthless ration of war propaganda – ethnocentric, redneck, and enabling" (2006).

This kind of indeterminacy typifies numerous films about the Iraq War. While few espouse an enthusiastically supportive stance, many filmmakers have also avoided an explicit antiwar politics, preferring a skepticism – or more direct hostility – aimed primarily at Bush rather the particularities of the war itself. In *The War Tapes*, as in several other documentaries, footage of the administration's optimistic assertions about the "mission accomplished" forms a recurrent counterpoint to images of Iraq's chaos. One guardsman flawlessly replicates the official line about the United States bringing democracy and peace to the Middle East before sardonically appending, "and then we'll buy everyone in the world a puppy." But if the commander-in-chief is an object of suspicion, ire, or ridicule, so too are the "mainstream media" – one of Pink's bunkmates refusing to answer his questions on camera because Charlie Company has been warned not to speak to the media.

Mutual antipathy between journalists and men in uniform has a long history on screen and in war zones alike. Reporters regularly serve in fictional war movies as hate figures, whether of the right (as in John Wayne's *The Green Berets*) or the left (as in David O. Russell's *Three Kings*, 1999). It is no surprise, then, that the only US-made narrative film to be set entirely in Iraq takes a journalist as its central protagonist – although in Philip Haas's *The Situation* (2006) Connie Nielson functions as an object of desire rather than detestation. More novel to Iraq War cinema is the recurrent trope of soldier as filmmaker or photographer first established by Scranton, later reprised by Brian De Palma in *Redacted* (2007), Kimberley Peirce in *Stop-Loss* (2008) and elsewhere. This collapsing of identities not only blurs the boundary between "media" and military (as Pink reminds his truculent bunkmate) but also sharpens soldiers' awareness of who is, or is not, paying attention to the pictures they take. For some, notably the photographer/torturers of Abu Ghraib, attention is entirely unwelcome. For others, like *The War Tapes*' Moriarty, civilians' inattentiveness even to photographs that they may have expressly *asked* to see – as his workmates do – emblematizes the home front's infuriating indifference to the war.

Figure 27.1 Sgt Steve Pink films his fellow National Guardsmen as their convoy comes to a halt in Iraq in Deborah Scranton's *The War Tapes* (2006, producers Steve James and Robert May).

Devoting its final 20 minutes to C Company's New Hampshire homecoming, *The War Tapes* anticipates a series of films – fictional narratives like *Home of the Brave* (2006), *The Valley of Elah* (2007), and *Stop-Loss*, and documentaries such as *The Ground Truth* (2006), *Lioness* (2008), and *Body of War* (2007) – devoted to the tribulations of soldiers returning to a tuned-out America. As this focus on service personnel suggests, the overriding preoccupation of US filmmakers has been with the war as an *American* experience: an experience all too vivid for those who serve and all too invisible to those who choose to avert their gaze. Very few filmmakers have situated themselves among Iraqis to observe the occupation and its consequences as a wrenching chapter of Iraqi history. In this regard, *The War Tapes* is also typical. Iraqis, always male, appear infrequently and fleetingly – generally as comic relief, from the young boys hawking ornamental swords and enquiring of Bazzi whether he owns a donkey back in Amerikah to the trainee Iraqi police whose inept marksmanship elicits derision from the guardsmen.

Opening Shots: American Cinema's First Cycle of Violence

For many, the terms "war film" and "combat movie" surely appear synonymous. (What else would a war film be about than men – more specifically, *our* men – in battle?) Predictably, then, the first theatrically exhibited documentary to deal with the war in Iraq made American soldiers its subject. Released in March 2005, two years after the launch of Operation Iraqi Freedom and 22 months after Bush had declared a victorious end to "major combat operations," *Gunner Palace* enjoyed the widest release of any nonfiction Iraq War film to date. Critics enthusiastically greeted its portrayal of the 2/3 Field Artillery as they go about the daily business of pacifying Baghdad, headquartered in a bombed-out palace formerly inhabited by Uday Hussein.

Pitched squarely at the MTV generation and its YouTube siblings, *Gunner Palace* deploys a familiar cultural motif: the surrealism of war. Of the various contradictions it exposes, none glares more garishly than the palace itself. Crammed with oversize chandeliers, swags of satin, and circular beds, and plastered in gold leaf, it symbolizes the corruption, bombast, and megalomania of the deposed regime – a monument to kleptocratic excess. Yet the palace is hardly a five-star residence. Partially demolished, it is in a precarious condition, as is its plumbing. It is, then, an unlikely place for soldiers to call home. The toilets don't flush, but the swimming pool seems to work just fine, and when the unpleasant work of raiding Iraqi homes is done, poolside partying is the order of the day.

The meta-contradiction, however, is the war itself. This paradox persistently marks films on Iraq: How do we understand – and what do we call – a war that was long since declared over, in which the enemy remains largely invisible yet seemingly ubiquitous? For the makers of *Gunner Palace* and their protagonists the answer seems to be a mess. Asked by the unseen director what they make of their mission, the gunners' responses darken over time, as frustration and rage deepen that the Iraqis are so wretchedly ungrateful for being "helped," and that the hajjis won't fight fair. Pissed off about being tasked with the impossible, their anger runs on both adrenalin and vengeance, so while war may be hell, retribution has its rewards.

Like Scranton, Tucker and Epperlein treat the administration's claims about the sanctity and success of Operation Iraqi Freedom with utter skepticism. But their own position on the war is unclear – willfully muddied by ironic devices that place distance between them, their soldier subjects, and the least edifying elements of occupation soldiering (Grajeda 2007). Thus a segment of the film documenting the gunners as they conduct house-to-house searches is entitled "Scaring the Natives," while another sequence detailing the nighttime raid on a suspect insurgent's home ("The Majid Raid") unspools to the accompaniment of Wagner's "Ride of Valkyries." This heavy-handed aural allusion to *Apocalypse Now* reinforces the soldiers' claims that they are "living in a movie" but does little to clarify how the filmmakers would have us understand this particular production. Sheik Majid, it turns out, is not at home. Nor, it is later acknowledged, is he one of the bad guys. Nevertheless his house, like those of many other "natives," is burst into after an APC (armored personnel carrier) plows into the door. Heavily armed soldiers then abruptly shove terrified women and children aside, while they rifle through possessions, disparaging the crude condition of Iraqi homes and subjecting male residents to more invasive scrutiny. When men protest at being forced onto their knees at gunpoint and told to "shut the fuck up," the gunners escalate their response, "zipping up" the indignant householders in flexicuffs, hooding them, and bundling them off in trucks. If Tucker finds any of this objectionable, he certainly does not let on. And since he and his camera participate in the violation of domestic space, the viewer also becomes an accessory to Iraqis' degradation. The natives are scared, at least in part, for *our* edification.

With its ambiguous anti-Bush, pro-military sensibility, *Gunner Palace* set the tone for much of what would follow, positioning soldiers as the sole objects of viewers' attention and empathy – fundamentally decent guys assigned a lousy mission by a mendacious president abetted by a sycophantic press. In so doing, the filmmakers accord epistemological primacy to "being there": the embedded cameraman a superior source of knowledge about Iraq in comparison to the mainstream media. Tellingly, *Gunner Palace*'s promotional tagline, "Some war stories will never make the nightly news," promised to make good the deficit with its unexpurgated footage and language.[4] No mere fly-on-the-wall observer, Tucker casts himself as the gunners' buddy, confidante, and champion. He shares their privations. But he uses a mordant authorial voiceover to enunciate the privilege he enjoys and they do not – namely, the ability to quit at any time.

At no point, though, does he dwell on those other stories more thoroughly absent from the nightly news than the gunners' tribulations. As in *The War Tapes*, Iraqis are peripheral presences. They are the shadowy figures whose houses are broken into, or they are the Americans' mocked and mistrusted translators. Nicknamed "Basil" and "Elvis," these Iraqis function as court jesters at the palace. As the interpreters' powers of mimicry grow, however, they also come under increasing suspicion as traitors at the gate, spying for the resistance. One is later arrested and taken to prison. His story isn't told.[5]

A handful of American documentaries belonging to this first wave (2005–2006) did place Iraqis at the center of the frame, however. James Longley's *Iraq in Fragments*, Laura Poitras's *My Country, My Country* (both Oscar nominees in January 2007), and Andrew Berends' *The Blood of My Brother* (2006) all eschew the use of authorial voiceover in favor of a more quietly observational style, though their tone and mood differ considerably.

A triptych of vignettes, *Iraq in Fragments* strives to capture the texture of Iraqi life under occupation. Its three cameos focus in turn on a fatherless 11-year-old in Baghdad, radicalized Shiites in Najaf, and a Kurdish boy and his father: a structure suggestive of the country's disintegration along ethno-religious fault-lines. While the protagonists' emotions waver between nostalgia, despair, fury, and fatalism, the film's mood is woozily dreamlike. Longley presents a succession of arrestingly juxtaposed images: a red London double-decker reflects passers-by in its convex windows; a luminous tropical fish swims by in a tank; donkey carts share city roads with tanks; a mosque's gilded dome shimmers into focus; gauzy drapes, stirred by a breeze, afford glimpses into Iraqi homes. Only fleetingly do US soldiers or tanks heave into view. Their absence – an uncanny inversion of most filmmakers' marginalization of Iraqis – led some critics to wonder whether this apparent oversight wasn't also an evasion of responsibility, implying that Americans really had very little to do with Iraq's fragmentation.

Where Longley shows little inclination to indict, Poitras suggests a more skeptical viewpoint in *My Country, My Country*, the narrative arc supplied by the six-month buildup to Iraq's January 2005 national elections. The multiple contradictions of importing electoral procedure into a country too lawless for candidates to campaign publicly without fear of assassination, where insurgents threaten to behead all those who vote, and the US military devolves the work of policing the polling to foreign mercenaries – lest the whole business look too much like the orchestrated sham it undoubtedly is – are brought into plain view.

Figure 27.2 Dr Riyadh visits Abu Ghraib prison in Laura Poitras's *My Country, My Country* (2006, producers Laura Poitras and Jocelyn Glatzer). (Photo Paul Cobaugh.)

So too are the dilemmas and dangers of political campaigning in wartime Baghdad, with Poitras's close-up lens trained on Dr Riyadh: physician, patriarch, patriot, and candidate for the Iraqi Islamic Party.

In Dr Riyadh, Poitras locates virtually the sole "good Iraqi" to appear in any film about the war. A softly spoken, round-shouldered man possessed of a robustly opinionated wife and houseful of spirited daughters, he is a man of faith, science, and humanity beset by irresolvable, escalating predicaments. As a doctor, he attempts to treat a surfeit of patients suffering from dried-up incomes, scars of conflict, and the typical maladies that afflict devastated cities without reliable sanitation, water, or electricity. As a city councilor, he intercedes with US officers to protest the detention of young children in Abu Ghraib and the humanitarian catastrophe of Fallujah after its November 2004 bombardment. And as a family man, he beseeches his family to venture out on election day – to the accompaniment of not-so-distant explosions and gunfire – to vote for him, even though his party has already announced that its candidates will not participate in the new puppet government if elected. Underscored by Kadhum al Sahir's plaintive refrain ("Oh my country, may you have a happy morning/Reunite everyone; heal your wounds"), *My Country, My Country* sounds a prolonged note of despair. The filmmaker observes the Riyadh household in intimate detail, charting the disintegration of middle-class domesticity as basic services falter and Adhamiya (also home to the gunners' palace) becomes too dangerous for the women to venture out. Poitras is in their living room when a relative arrives with news that his teenage son has just been kidnapped, recording his stricken face after a bungled attempt to arrange a ransom payment. When he insists that the country is "going to hell," and they are all going with it, it's hard to disagree. Where others have conjured Iraq as a country bereft of women, teeming with fanatical men, Poitras "normalizes" Iraqis while documenting the violent abnormality of life in Baghdad – a feat that clearly relied on a deep bond of trust between filmmaker and family.

As Iraq's insecurity deepened in 2005, trust joined the lengthening list of commodities in exceedingly short supply. Logistical difficulties and life-threatening danger surely played their part in ensuring that no other US filmmaker would attempt to replicate Poitras's achievement. But by the time *My Country, My Country* premiered in mid-2006, it was already clear that viewers attracted to Iraq warfare were also a rare commodity.

A few months earlier, critics had hailed the gritty immediacy of *Gunner Palace*, which claimed the novelty of being the first Iraq war film to reach US movie theaters. Yet despite high-profile advertising and favorable notices, it didn't linger. When *Occupation: Dreamland* – a more traditional vérité style treatment of the experiences of the 82nd Airborne's Alpha Company 1/501 – opened in September 2006, it struggled considerably harder to find an audience. The pattern was set, with filmmakers battling first to secure distributors and second to fill theaters. Like Moriarty's coworkers in *The War Tapes*, American civilians appeared singularly uninterested in looking at pictures of Iraq. Fox Television pulled its Iraq War series *Over There* after just one season. And when Hollywood released its first Iraq-related feature, Irwin Winkler's *Home of the Brave* in December 2006, it lasted just one week in New York City before sinking ignominiously under the weight of hostile reviews and audience indifference – this despite the lure of big name stars like Samuel L. Jackson, Jessica Biel and, in his first acting role, Curtis Jackson (better known as rapper 50 Cent).

As the war progressed, the "occupation documentary" became ever less visible, though not altogether extinct. Whether deterred by rising casualty rates in Iraq or escalating civilian displeasure with the war in America, professional documentary filmmakers largely surrendered this terrain to soldier amateurs, who continued to produce video records of their tours that continued to fare badly at home.[6]

The Soldier as Perpetrator – and Victim

If few civilians appeared interested in pictures of counterinsurgency soldiering, and even fewer in portraits of Iraqi life, there were nevertheless some pictures that every media-sentient American had seen – whether or not he or she cared to scrutinize what these images depicted. These were the infamous pictures of naked Iraqi prisoners stacked in human pyramids; men forced to masturbate for their camera-wielding American guards; inmates chained in crucifixion postures with women's panties over their heads; a hooded figure with arms outstretched and wires dangling from his fingers; a female MP (military police) ghoulishly posing by a corpse, grinning and giving the thumbs-up. In short, Abu Ghraib.

By the time HBO broadcast Rory Kennedy's prize-winning documentary *Ghosts of Abu Ghraib* in February 2007, the furor that first erupted in April 2004 had long since dimmed. President Bush had apologized, or at least attempted to explain to outraged foreigners that Americans did not *do* torture, and that when wayward soldiers did misbehave, democratic states ordered transparent investigations. Numerous investigations, of varying degrees of opacity, were duly conducted. As a result, Brigadier General Janis Karpinski was dishonorably discharged, and a "few bad apples," as Donald Rumsfeld memorably termed the miscreant MPs in the notorious photographs, were sent to prison. Seemingly defused, at least on the home front, the crisis had passed. One American poll conducted in 2006 found that a majority of those questioned could not identify "Abu Ghraib." The touchy subject of torture soon became safe enough for scatological gross-out humor in the form of *Harold and Kumar Escape from Guantanamo Bay* (2008). To paraphrase Marx, this was history returning – the second time as farts.

Kennedy's was the first of a series of films dedicated to disinterring the "ghosts of Abu Ghraib." It was soon followed by Alex Gibney's *Taxi to the Dark Side* (2007), Michael Tucker and Petra Epperlein's *The Prisoner, Or How I Tried to Kill Tony Blair* (2007) and Errol Morris's *Standard Operating Procedure* (2008), all of which contributed to a larger Anglo-American cycle of films tackling atrocities in Iraq and the "war on terror" more broadly: Michael Winterbottom's *The Road to Guantánamo* (2006), Nick Broomfield's

The Battle of Haditha (2008), in addition to *The Situation* and *Redacted*.

Of these investigations, Gibney's applies the widest angle lens to the commission of atrocities, tracing the evolution and circulation of what came to be "standard operating procedures" from Guantánamo bay to Bagram air base in Afghanistan and thence to Abu Ghraib: way-stations along the "war on terror's" *via dolorosa*. He and Kennedy share an interest in tracing the chain of culpability up from the lowest echelons of the military, where the top brass deposited it, back to Secretary of Defense Rumsfeld, Attorney General Gonzalez, and others who furnished legal arguments in support of the constitutionality of "harsh interrogation" techniques or of Guantánamo's extraterritorial exemption from US law. Along the way, the Justice Department, with Rumsfeld's blessing, came to redefine torture so narrowly as to permit almost any form of prisoner abuse short of "organ failure, impairment of bodily function or ... death": a formulation supplied by John Yoo, who appears in the film. As Gibney vividly demonstrates, when death alone forms the outer limit of permissible force, it is easy for guards and interrogators (torturers by any other name) to misrecognize the moment at which to desist from further "softening up" – or not to be too scrupulous about respecting the final, lethal frontier in such permissive circumstances.

Illustrating the point, Gibney frames his legal enquiry with the story of Dilawar, an unfortunate young Afghan taxi-driver, turned over to the Northern Alliance by a pecuniary bounty-hunter and subsequently imprisoned at Bagram. There he was shackled to the wire mesh ceiling of his cage, his leg "pulpified" by American guards irritated by his imprecations for Allah's mercy. A military-issued death certificate (written in English and plainly stating blunt force injuries as the cause of death) was later given to his uncomprehending family. Later still, this document was tracked down by *New York Times* reporter Carlotta Gall, one of many talking-heads to appear in Gibney's reconstruction of Dilawar's death and the larger context that rendered torture a quotidian feature of the "war on terror" – a policy by design, not the organic outgrowth of an atrocity-producing situation.

Kennedy's film reaches a similar conclusion, though it does more to establish Abu Ghraib as a site of horror for guards and prisoners alike. Its fetid corridors still adorned with lurid Baathist-realist murals of Saddam, and seemingly still echoing with the screams of thousands of inmates executed there during his dictatorship, Iraq's largest prison is hardly a secure environment, coming under regular mortar and sniper attack. Not surprisingly, the former MPs, soldiers, and civilian interrogators interviewed in *Ghosts of Abu Ghraib* make much of these mitigating circumstances. The heat, the stench, the fear, and the *ghosts* – not merely the "undead" victims of Saddam's executioners but the term applied to prisoners brought in undocumented with a view to their possible disappearance.

Kennedy's guiding question might be distilled as *who authorized this?* What "this" is, the filmmaker takes more or less for granted, the Justice Department's Jesuitical approach to the definition of torture notwithstanding: an abomination, a moral calamity, a national disgrace. Using a similar set of interviewees – Karpinski, Lynndie England, Sabrina Harman, Roman Krol, Javal Davis, and others – Errol Morris adopts a different tack in *Standard Operating Procedure*. The acclaimed director of *The Thin Blue Line* (1988), *Mr. Death: The Rise and Fall of Fred A. Leuchter, Jr.* (1999) and *The Fog of War* (2003) appears largely unconcerned with the legal and ethical questions that preoccupy Kennedy and Gibney. Instead, Morris adopts Abu Ghraib as an opportunity to ponder epistemological questions about the nature of photographic evidence, and the hazy ontological status of events "known" only because photographed.

Promotional material for *Standard Operating Procedure* deployed an ironic tagline, "The War on Terror Will Be Photographed." The War on Terror was not, after all, *meant* to be photographed or televised, at least not those aspects that might disturb viewers and corrode support for the enterprise of delivering freedom to Iraq: hence the administration's injunction against pictures of US casualties and coffins, bodies and body bags. And hence too a prohibition against photography inside Abu Ghraib – an ordinance observed, it would seem, entirely in the breach. Where Kennedy's documentary takes the photographs as more or less transparent illustrative material, Morris probes both the content of the images and the practice of picture-taking by snap-happy guards. What were they doing? And what were they *thinking?* Would there even have been "an Abu Ghraib" without the pictures, Morris enquires, following the lead of Javal Davis, who poses this variant of the philosopher's tree question in both *Ghosts of Abu Ghraib* and *Standard Operating Procedure*.

Clearly, the photographs were constitutive of the scandal. Without them there would indeed have been "no Abu Ghraib": no international outcry; no investigative reports; no US soldiers imprisoned. But does that mean that without the pictures there would accordingly have been no torture? Surely not. Yet here Morris embarks on a more contrarian line of argument signaled by his documentary's second provocative tagline: "The scandal was a cover-up." The *real* crime of Abu Ghraib, he proposes, was not abuse of prisoners but the scapegoating of guards, who were effectively punished for the crime of taking pictures or of being caught in the frame – but not necessarily in the act. Those who *really* hurt, or even killed, prisoners at Abu Ghraib were never punished. Thus a second line of defense, repeatedly plied by his interviewees, is that the photographs mystify the character of the acts they apparently depict. When Morris has them contextualize several of the most notorious images, England duly explains that she was not dragging the prisoner on the leash ("you can see the slack," she protests), and that Charles Graner was merely *posing* in the act of assaulting a naked prisoner. Similarly, there was no live electricity attached to the wires dangling from the fingertips of "Gus," the prisoner on the wooden box depicted with arms outstretched in black burlap hood and sack, like an inverted Klansman uniform.

What exactly is the problem, then, these disgraced former soldiers seem to be saying? Perhaps their picture-taking was unwise: a reflex they ought to have checked. But Sabrina Harman also repeatedly makes the case that her photography was in fact *heroic*: the work of a putative whistle-blower keen to gather evidence of atrocities that no one would believe had happened without visual corroboration. Her letters home, read aloud and spotlighted as though by torchlight, suggest that the picture-taking was done on behalf of a projected future prosecution – neither in a spirit of sadistic fun nor as a grisly memento (like cutting ears from dead Japanese soldiers), and certainly not as a unique form of degradation, compounding other acts of humiliation, abuse, and torture.

Morris gently burnishes the "bad apples" to a soft sheen. England, Harman, and Ambuhl appear made-up and made-over, guileless victims of a mendacious administration determined to pass the buck ever downward. While his voice is heard four or five times posing supplementary questions, rarely does he interrogate his witnesses' special pleading. (When exactly did Harman plan to blow the whistle? So what if there was slack in the leash and no live electricity running through those wires?) Despite voicing chagrin that no one had ever thought to talk to the people in the pictures, Morris exhibits precisely no interest in the *other* people in the pictures: the prisoners. He encourages us to see, and invites his interviewees to scrutinize, solely the American figures in the photographs – as though the Iraqi inmates' nakedness had somehow rendered them invisible. (Without the clothes, there is no person? Inverting the story of the emperor's new clothes, nakedness here does not stimulate the bestowal of imaginary raiment but effaces the unclad subject altogether.) If Morris wanted to ascertain what was going on in these pictures by asking those who appear in the frame, then clearly his curiosity only extended so far. Not, we might suppose, because he feared compounding the harm already done or from any sense that torture defies articulacy – that it serves to render those in pain mute while claiming to compel speech – but because Iraqis' subjectivity just is not interesting to him. Like other filmmakers, he is drawn to Iraq only insofar as it is an *American* story, with American villains and heroes. In this case, his larger purpose is to redeem those falsely accused, demonstrating that the ostensible perpetrators of atrocity were themselves victims of circumstance, calumny, and calculation.

The politics of this move, however, troubled most reviewers less than Morris's payment of interviewees for their services and his preferred aesthetic strategies: elliptical "reconstructions" artfully suggestive of abuse, and insistent background music that establishes a mood of brooding disquiet. Some critics duly complained that Morris confused what really occurred at Abu Ghraib with what he had imaginatively staged. It does not, however, take a skillfully trained eye to distinguish between "found" and "made" footage in *Standard Operating Procedure*. What's more problematic is whether the aestheticization itself obscures the brute fact of physical and psychological violence: suffering that Morris's film discursively minimizes in multiple ways.

Operation Homecoming: The Veteran as Cipher

The returning warrior is a favored figure of classical literature and classical Hollywood alike. Not for nothing is the amputee protagonist of William Wyler's

The Best Years of Our Lives (1946) named Homer. But while homecoming lends itself to sentimentality, narratives of return have commonly assumed darker shadings. Since war is neither easily left behind by soldiers nor readily comprehended by civilians, friction ensues: the brief bliss or reunion giving way to protracted struggles to readjust, recuperate, and achieve equilibrium if not the status quo ante. As Wyler showed, and as others like John Huston and Fred Zinnemann documented more unflinchingly in films like *Let There Be Light* (1946) and *The Men* (1950), the "good war" did bad things to those who fought it. And if this was true of World War II, the less popular wars that followed it produced increasingly conflicted on-screen characterizations of the veteran. After the Korean War, the combat veteran seemed to fall from cinematic fashion altogether, supplanted by the former prisoner-of-war – a hapless or more malign victim of communist "brainwashing" like Laurence Harvey in *The Manchurian Candidate* (1962). As for Hollywood's Vietnam veteran, he was as apt to be plagued by what he had done to Vietnamese civilians as by what the VC had done to him.

Given American cinema's extensive repertoire of veteran types – from garlanded hero to pent-up psycho, paraplegic demon-lover to brainwashed assassin – can we discern novel patterns in the filmic representation of soldiers returning from Iraq? Two striking phenomena immediately stand out. First, we might note the extraordinary number of films (documentary and narrative features alike) that foreground the veteran, and second, at how early a date this concentration became evident. Almost as soon as there were films about the war in Iraq, there were films about soldiers returning home, bearing the physical and psychological scars of service. If *The War Tapes* blazed this particular trail, it did not take others long to follow Scranton's lead. The veteran is thus no longer an artifact of postwar – as we might have hitherto imagined – but rather a disruptive reminder of what many civilians appear apt to forget: that the war in Iraq is still going on. How, after all, would one know?

A unifying motif of homecoming films is thus the immovable indifference of civilian America to an ongoing war that's over neither in reality nor in the consciousness of those who fought it. That the war constitutes unfinished business is underscored by the fact that many veterans remain on active duty, whether by personal choice or military fiat, thanks to the policy of "stop loss" that gives Kimberley Peirce's film its name. Remobilization looms. This theme, first explored in Irwin Winkler's *Home of the Brave*, which ends with one of the distressed returnees reenlisting, unable to slide back into the oblivion of civilian life, would resurface in Kathryn Bigelow's *The Hurt Locker* (2008), whose protagonist is similarly incapable of swapping the adrenalin highs of bomb disposal for the steady thrum of domesticity.

A distinct subgenre, these films raise a variety of issues: the rehabilitation of gravely wounded men and women (*Home Front*, 2005; *Fighting for Life*, 2008); grief and mourning (*Jerabek*, 2007; *Operation Homecoming*, 2007; *Grace is Gone*, 2007); the pernicious effects of post-traumatic stress disorder (PTSD) (*Home of the Brave*; *The Ground Truth*, 2006; and, to varying degrees, almost all these films); the veteran as antiwar activist (*Body of War*); conscientious objection (*Stop-Loss*; *Breaking Ranks*, 2007); the novel phenomenon of women in combat, and the particular problems of readjustment faced by female soldiers when their front-line service is obfuscated by a military that does not formally permit such a thing (*Lioness*).

Where front-line documentaries tended to fly-on-the-wall understatement, many of these films adopt a more strident mode of address. If their purpose is illustrative, the visceral confrontation of viewers with uncomfortable evidence of damage also serves to rebuke. Emotional in their appeal to viewers' sympathies, these filmmakers press insistent claims on behalf of soldiers suffering a deficit of military care and civilian attention. The traumatized veteran thus provides a powerful vehicle for oppositional critique – an emblem of the war's wastefulness suggestive of the larger blows "Iraq" has dealt the American body politic. Where Vietnam era documentaries such as *Winter Soldier* (1972) and *Hearts and Minds* (1974) enlisted the veteran to attest US war crimes perpetrated against the Vietnamese, the Iraq War veteran serves more as testament to self-inflicted injury. This time, the wounded soldier isn't the war criminal but evidence of a war crime, victimized by a reprehensible war of choice. Nowhere is this message more forcefully driven home than in Phil Donahue and Ellen Spiro's *Body of War*, which centers on paraplegic veteran and antiwar activist Tomas Young, whose severely incapacitated body, paralyzed from the chest down, is presented as an unanswerable interrogative: The war was worth *this?*

But however generative of outrage the maimed soldier may be, this figure need not, and does not, enunciate one message alone. The architects of war commonly press soldiers' suffering into service as its own justification for war. When other rationalizations fail to rally support, and crudely material motives remain unutterable (by political leaders if not by grunts themselves), casualties become a reason to continue fighting – the tinder to reignite popular conviction. If victory alone vindicates loss, then the original sacrifice can only be avenged and redeemed through further pain. And so the war continues.

Americans encountered this (il)logic in Korea and Vietnam, and it has not been absent from the Iraq War either. Some filmmakers have turned to the wounded veteran for purposes of martial rededication. In its depiction of a young marine's body being repatriated from Iraq, accompanied back by Lt Col. Michael Strobl to Dubois, Wyoming, for burial, *Operation Homecoming* offers an unusually clear illustration of how military ceremonial strives to emboss death with patriotic value. Similarly, documentaries like *Baghdad ER* (2006) and *Fighting for Life* endow military medics and wounded soldiers – emblems of heroic endurance both – with a much more affirmative meaning. With their emphasis on the virtues of unquestioning service, these films ostensibly bracket the war's politics, thereby offering an implicit endorsement.

Finally, we might note that Hollywood has been far more attentive to the home front than to Iraq in its few war-related features to date. With the exception of Brian De Palma's Mahmoudiya atrocity reconstruction, *Redacted*, other studio releases – *Home of the Brave*, *The Valley of Elah*, and *Stop-Loss* – are homecoming dramas that cast the traumatized veteran as a source of murderous danger to himself and others, or the dead soldier as a source of unspeakable grief (as in James C. Strouse's *Grace is Gone*).

Of these, *The Valley of Elah* merits particular attention. The work of Oscar-winning director Paul Haggis, it occasioned more excited anticipation than most Iraq-related films on release in September 2007. Tommy Lee Jones soon claimed an Oscar nomination for his performance as a bereaved father who attempts to fathom his returned soldier-son's murder by tracing clues in corrupted digital images retrieved from the boy's cellphone. But while these markers of critical esteem distinguish Haggis's film, *The Valley of Elah* is also a perfect distillation of Hollywood's prevailing mood: one that has taken the war primarily as an occasion for patriotic lamentation. Where conservative critics interpreted the offerings of Haggis, Winkler, and Peirce as the predictably jaundiced output of a liberal institution, it would be truer to say that these directors are not so much *anti*war as war-*averse*. Iraq itself occupies little if any space in their work. The opening sequences of *Home of the Brave* and *Stop-Loss* are both set in Iraq, detailing the ambushes that explain their protagonists' physical and psychological wounds.

Neither scene lasts more than 15 minutes, and neither was filmed there. In *The Valley of Elah*, Iraq is rendered solely in the form of indecipherable pictures and footage: images that prove impossible to read without contextual clarification. The problem confronting Tommy Lee Jones's character – how to make sense of entirely murky events – stands as an overburdened metaphor for the filmmakers' own predicament: How to render intelligible a war that so thoroughly resists representation?

Most have turned away from this daunting task, seemingly less interested in the war per se than in what this debacle might reveal of a country in grave trouble. If the military (or its upper echelons) appear in an unflattering light, civilian America looks even worse – bloated, complaisant, distracted. In both documentary and narrative film, America emerges as a wilderness of flat landscapes and flattened aspirations: an endless succession of shabby strip-malls and tawdry strip clubs, unappetizing diners and anodyne motels, where meth and easy credit dull the pangs of protracted postindustrial depression. The civilian counterpart to PTSD, this malaise is also the recruiting sergeant's most effective ally.

In the hands of Haggis, Winkler, and Peirce, "Iraq" is less shorthand for a ruinous war than a marker of precipitous national decline. Their jeremiads strain with yearning for America to be "good again" – as patriotic in their own way as more conventional, flag-waving war movies. Indeed, Haggis's moral in *Elah* is underscored by the prominence it attaches to the flag. When we first see the stars and stripes, it is fluttering upside down outside a school in New Mexico, where Tommy Lee Jones's character has gone to investigate his son's disappearance from Fort Rudd. Appalled, he stops to tell the El Salvadoran janitor responsible for this lapse that the flag must *never* fly upside down: that the inverted flag is an international distress signal, denoting the need for assistance in dire peril. In the final scene, he returns to the school to hoist aloft the flag his son has left behind. This time, he inverts the flag himself. If the janitor's initial action was inadvertent, it turns out not in fact to have been a mistake. Disturbed by his son's death and the military's attempt to cover up fellow soldiers' responsibility, the father has lost faith in war's nobility, in martial justice, in national virtue. America requires rescue.

An Audience of One

By common critical consent, the war in Iraq has produced few great films – arguably none at all. By unanimous accord, it has produced a glut of mediocre treatments and several execrable failures, particularly among Hollywood's offerings such as De Palma's *Redacted* and Strouse's "grief porn," *Grace is Gone*, about a man so far gone in denial when his wife dies in Iraq that he cannot break the news to his two daughters, taking them instead on a road trip to a Florida amusement park. It is also clear that American audiences have populated theatrical screenings of these films in inverse proportion to the latter's profusion. In other words, the Iraq War has proven to be a very poor box office draw indeed. This disinclination to watch has encouraged some directors like the prolific polemicist Robert Greenwald to avoid commercial distribution networks altogether in favor of "guerrilla screenings" in activists' living rooms, church halls, or wherever the already persuaded congregate.[7]

The patterns are clear enough: many films produced with a limited repertoire of themes that few Americans are watching. But how do we account for the peculiarities of Iraq War cinema and its critical and popular rejection? Most of the standard answers do not withstand closer scrutiny. Some cultural commentators propose that it is simply *too soon* for this war to have been transmuted into cinematic art, pointing out that many of the most enduring films of World War II appeared in the 1950s, just as Hollywood's definitive treatments of Vietnam appeared at the tail end of the 1970s and in the 1980s. Others contend that there are simply *too many* films, leaving audiences fatigued by the surfeit of war-related offerings. Or alternatively, that it is precisely because most Iraq-related films are not great cinematic art that they have failed to lure audiences, the up-close immediacy of several early Iraq documentaries having made it hard for Hollywood's narrative features to convince viewers of their own verisimilitude. Why pay to see B-list actors – with trainer-honed physiques and radiant dentition – playing soldiers from unglamorous red states where teenage recruits most assuredly do not resemble these perfect-skinned imposters? Despite their claims to facticity (and *Redacted*, *Stop-Loss*, and *Elah* all loudly touted their real-life referents), these films did not seem as "authentic" as those made by people who had visited, or indeed served in, Iraq. An imploded country is no place to make a movie, "Iraq" being played by Morocco in *Home of the Brave* and *The Situation*, and by Jordan in *Redacted* and *The Hurt Locker*.

But these propositions do not add up to a coherent explanation. Great films *do* emerge from the midst of war, generally from the very thick of it. (Think, for example, of John Huston's *Battle of San Pietro*, 1945, or Gillo Pontecorvo's *Battle of Algiers*, 1966.) Similarly, three of the most acclaimed recent films – Oscar-nominated documentaries *The War Tapes*, *Iraq in Fragments*, and *My Country, My Country* – are vérité style treatments made about and in Iraq at war. Yet they did not achieve strikingly greater box office success than several later productions that were panned, and this at a conjuncture when popular/populist documentary filmmaking had become a resurgent commercial force in US cinema.[8] Audience indifference to these lauded documentaries also makes it hard to credit the suggestion that Hollywood's narrative offerings fared poorly because audiences were unwilling to suspend disbelief that Morocco was really Iraq, and actors were soldiers. Viewers could only have become mistrustful of claims to realism – or fatigued by overload – had they already reached documentary saturation point. Since early releases fared just as poorly as later ones, we can reasonably assume they had not.

Alternative explanations are thus required, and we might begin by inverting one of the familiar hypotheses. Perhaps Americans' resistance to war-related material is not a function of the proximity of these events but rather of their own distance? In other words, potential viewers have shied away from films about the war less because these productions are insufficiently compelling or excessively numerous but rather because most Americans were already detached and disinclined to view. The real task, then, is to fathom how and why "Iraq" is at once broadly yet shallowly unpopular in the United States – for the same forces productive of public aversion to certain forms of inquiry also structure filmmakers' limited engagement with the war.

To say that Americans are, by and large, tuned out from the war in Iraq is hardly to venture a controversial assertion. Yellow ribbon decals aside, there's little discernible evidence in broad swathes of the country that US troops are fighting in both Afghanistan and Iraq. This is not wartime as normal. Yet if there is no surge of patriotic fervor among a population increasingly attenuated from a downsized and outsourced military, nor is there much sign of widespread disaffection either: few protests, few placards, no broad-based social movement rallying opposition. Unlike its predecessor in Vietnam, this unpopular war has given rise to no "war at home." Antiwar sentiment, if we can call it that, exhibits far greater national self-absorption than transnational solidarity.

As evidenced by the films surveyed here, the affective response aroused by the war ranges from vague skepticism to splenetic apoplexy. Very few filmmakers have proffered outright support. But if most have no trouble in saying – or at least insinuating – that the war is wrong, *why* it is wrong has generated much confusion, and no consensus.[9]

Choked with inchoate rage, filmmakers have frequently struggled to articulate their precise animus against the war – other than that it is *Bush's war* and as such, the apotheosis of everything stupid, misguided, and mendacious about his presidency. Viewed through the prism of liberal nationalism, the war is thus wrong because it has squandered America's patrimony and prestige; because it has generated profits only for its corporate beneficiaries and architects; because consent was fraudulently mustered; because it has turned ordinary decent Americans into torturers and war criminals; because the victory proclaimed prematurely has proven so elusive; because the war was badly planned or simply because Iraq is a huge confounded mess, and there's "no end in sight."

This catalog of discontent encompasses contending interpretations. For some, like Charles Ferguson, the problem is framed as "good intentions gone bad" – thanks largely to internecine bureaucratic infighting, which led the occupation's more thoughtful planners to be sidelined in favor of the true believers who imagined that Iraq's de-Baathification would be a "cakewalk." For others, Iraq holds greater appeal as an allegory than as a policy puzzle. Thus Errol Morris, introducing a rough cut of *Standard Operating Procedure* at Brandeis University, announced that what had drawn him to the subject of Abu Ghraib was its richness as a metaphor for the moral anomie of the Bush administration – a directorial vision of jaded purposelessness that seems hard to square with the self-evident calculation behind Iraq's invasion, and the precise calibration of acceptable forms of "harsh interrogation."

But what remains most telling about these films, a handful of notable exceptions aside, is their treatment of – or rather their refusal to inspect – Iraq itself: a charge also applicable to Bigelow's multiple Oscar-winning *The Hurt Locker*, which generates suspense from improvised explosive devices (IEDs) without exploring the politics of those planting the bombs, an inquiry deferred by the urgency of disposal. The reasons for this are complex, and my interpretation is necessarily speculative. In part, however, this aversion would seem to spring from a profound ambiguity about America's purposes in Iraq. It is worth recalling that many liberals (filmmakers included) were initially supportive of Operation Iraqi Freedom. Far from seeing it as an egregious violation of international law, a violent rending of Iraqi sovereignty, they endorsed "preemption" as a way to depose a noxious dictator. That the war did not *go* wrong but *was* wrong is a viewpoint that finds only muted expression in the whole roster of films concerned with Iraq. For many liberal critics, a central objection is that the Bush administration failed to instantiate democracy, one of its core stated objectives, and that the other aims – ridding Iraq of weapons of mass destruction and severing the alleged nexus between al-Qaeda and Baghdad – proved bogus: the products of faulty intelligence, if one accepted the official line, or outright fabrications if one did not.

Dissecting these operational failures and uncovering administration falsehoods have not been difficult, and several filmmakers have duly documented lapses and lies that were hardly well hidden.[10] Much harder, however, is the task of explaining Iraq's unraveling and doing so with some empathy – for Iraqis rather than simply for the US military. Other than Steve Connors and Molly Bingham's *Meeting Resistance* (2007), the war's filmic record offers remarkably little guidance as to precisely who contested the occupation and, more broadly, who is fighting whom in Iraq and why. Do filmmakers believe that US audiences simply aren't interested in, or capable of grasping, such complexity? Or are they themselves too uninterested, too impatient, or too irked by Iraqi intransigence to chart the contours of Iraq's crisscrossing vectors of conflict?

Near the end of Philip Haas's Sunni triangle-set love triangle, *The Situation* (2006), the journalist (played by Connie Neilson) turns to her CIA officer boyfriend for assistance in charting Iraq's sectarian landscape. His answer, though less than helpful, speaks volumes: "It's just the situation, Anna. It's just *Iraq*." If Sunni and Shia have been killing each other since, like, forever, what's really to be explained? And what else is to be expected except an endless cycle of bloodletting? At only slight risk of exaggeration, one might propose that a similar compound of intellectual laziness tinged with anti-Muslim disdain saturates much American filmmaking about the war in Iraq and explains why so few films have examined Iraq: as though hands have been collectively thrown up in the face of confounding, sometimes infuriating, complexity – and *ingratitude*. For filmmakers are surely not all immune from antipathy toward people who, dammit, ought to have been more thankful for their liberation, stepping up boldly to freedom's gilded plate. Yet the Iraqis failed to do so. Instead, they turned on their liberators before turning on one another. So, if their wretched country is now fouled up beyond all recognition, is that not essentially their own fault?

This point is made somewhat allegorically in Nina Davenport's *Operation Filmmaker* (2007) about a middle-class Iraqi film student plucked from Baghdad to intern on Liev Schreiber's *Everything is Illuminated*. As the Iraqi ingrate becomes ever more recalcitrant and demanding, his benefactress begins to wonder what she had expected would happen in this ill-conceived rescue venture. More than that, she is desperate to locate an "exit strategy" from this unwinnable war of nerves. Similarly, much US antiwar opinion stems from a desire to shake off a bothersome burden, letting Iraqis get on with the business of slaughtering one another alone. And there we find the nub of what distinguishes Iraq's unpopularity from Vietnam's. While antiwar sentiment over Vietnam undoubtedly had many determinants and variegations, a thoroughgoing critique of imperialism and an emancipatory impetus nevertheless drove a good deal of the movement. Forty years later, with the radical left near extinction in the United States, such sentiments are embraced by only a peripheral coterie, and though "imperialism" may have been much discussed during the Bush years, it was not always with distaste for imperial ventures. In the aftermath of the World Trade Center attacks, many (including liberal public intellectuals like Michael Ignatieff) urged Americans to assume the "burden" of world-ordering: to plant the flag in lawless trouble-spots, and stay put.

If contemporary antiwar sentiment is striking in its singular lack of emotional affiliation with suffering Iraqis, this may seem entirely predictable. Necessarily at least a two-sided business, war is often rendered one-dimensional by commercial media that sequester sympathy for "our side" alone. When Randall Wallace's *We Were Soldiers* appeared in 2002, critics were quick to remark that it was the first American production to render a North Vietnamese officer sympathetically – 30 years after America's withdrawal. But in pointing this out, such commentators often replicated the same oversight at work in claims that *The Green Berets* was the only Vietnam War film made before it ended. Equating film with narrative features alone, they neglected the documentaries that emerged during the war. One distinctive facet of the latter was their willingness to engage the war from multiple perspectives, including those of Vietnamese peasants and guerrillas. Like other radical antiwar activists, avant-garde filmmakers embraced Che Guevara's injunction "two, three, many Vietnams," insisting on the indivisibility of liberation struggles: in Vietnam, on the Mall, in the ghetto.

Iraq, by contrast, has neither inspired cinematic experimentation of the kind essayed by Emile de Antonio in *The Year of the Pig* (1969) and Nick Macdonald in *The Liberal War* (1972), nor stirred solidarist sentiment more broadly. Third worldism is no longer in fashion. More than that, though, it's considerably harder for today's antiwar activists to find common cause with the Badr brigades, the Mahdi Army, al-Qaeda in Mesopotamia, or myriad other groups fighting against the US occupation – and/or against fellow Iraqis – than it was for New Leftists in the 1970s to proclaim solidarity with the Vietnamese liberation struggle. Other than wanting out, what is an American activist to want in Iraq?

It remains to be seen when and how this war will end, how it will be inscribed in US popular memory, and what role film will play in shaping that consciousness. It also remains to be seen how future scholars and critics will make sense of the films discussed in this essay. If Barack Obama, having repudiated Iraq as not *his* war, succeeds in affirming Americans' desire to feel virtuous once again, it is possible that these works will be conceived less as "Iraq War films" than as cinema of the late Bush era – when good Americans were bamboozled into a bad war by their least popular president. After all, they offer a far more comprehensive index of American dissatisfactions than of Iraq's destruction. Just as Salon.com's Andrew O'Hehir observed of *Taxi to the Dark Side* that it was "not about America at war in Iraq or in Afghanistan but America at war with itself" (quoted in Filasteen 2007), so the same might be said of a whole series of films that have domesticized the war without ever bringing it home.

Notes

This essay draws on three contributions the author made to *Cineaste*: "Say Cheese! Operation Iraqi Freedom on Film," 22.1 (Winter 2006), 30–36; "Question Time: The Iraq War Revisited," 22.4 (Fall 2007), 12–17; "Bodies of Evidence: New Documentaries on Iraq War Veterans," 34.1 (Winter 2008), 26–31.

1. For a detailed chronology of war-related documentary and narrative films released from 1954 onwards on the subject of Vietnam, see Dittmar & Michaud 1990.
2. See http://www.thewartapes.com/2006/03/living_journalism.shtml (accessed March 2011).
3. This essay does not discuss a number of films concerned with the deceptions behind Washington's launch of "Operation Iraqi Freedom," most notably the series of documentaries made by Robert Greenwald. On these, see Musser 2007; Gaines 2007; Aufderheide 2007.
4. Equally tellingly, the biggest ruckus caused by *Gunner Palace* was over the award of a PG-13 certificate to a film that used the most taboo four-letter word no fewer than 30 times in 87 minutes.
5. It should be noted, however, that Tucker and Epperlein later returned to the scene of the Majid Raid, telling the story of one of the young men "zipped up" and taken to Abu Ghraib in their 2006 documentary *The Prisoner, Or How I Tried to Kill Tony Blair.*
6. See, for example, John Laurence's *I Am an American Soldier* (2007) and Jeremy Zerechak's *Land of Confusion* (2008). Meanwhile, the war in Afghanistan – for long far less visible than that in Iraq – received its first full-scale documentary treatment with Sebastian Junger and Tim Hetherington's *Restrepo* in 2010.
7. Other films dealing with the "war on terror" in its Afghan location, or elsewhere, such as Robert Redford's *Lions for Lambs* (2007) and Gavin Hood's *Rendition* (2007) fared just as badly.
8. It is also instructive to note that *The Hurt Locker*, which would subsequently garner six Oscars in 2010, grossed just $145,352 during its opening weekend in US theaters in June 2009.
9. Explicitly pro-administration films are few and far between, but would include the supposedly nonpartisan film made "by the Iraqi people" (with US government money), *Voices of Iraq* (2004).
10. The administration's rationalizations are treated with outright disbelief in Greenwald's films, as also in Eugene Jarecki's *Why We Fight* (2005), Danny Schechter's *WMD: Weapons of Mass Deception* (2004), and David Wald's *Buried in the Sand: The Deception of America* (2004).

References

Atkinson, Michael. (2006). "Casualties of War." *Village Voice*, May 23, at http://www.villagevoice.com/2006–05–23/film/casualties-of-war/ (accessed March 2011).

Aufderheide, Patricia. (2007). "Your Country, My Country: How Films about the Iraq War Construct Publics." *Framework*, 48.2, 56–65.

Dittmar, Linda, & Michaud, Gene. (eds) (1990). *From Hanoi to Hollywood: The Vietnam War in American Film*. New Brunswick, NJ: Rutgers University Press.

Filasteen. (2007). "*Taxi to the Dark Side*." December 2, at http://filasteen.wordpress.com/2007/12/02/taxi-to-the-dark-side/ (accessed March 2011).

Gaines, Jane M. (2007). "The Production of Outrage: The Iraq War and the Radical Documentary Tradition." *Framework*, 48.2, 36–55.

Grajeda, Tony. (2007). "The Winning and Losing of Hearts and Minds: Vietnam, Iraq, and the Claims of War Documentary." *Jump Cut*, Spring, 49, at http://www.ejumpcut.org/archive/jc49.2007/Grajeda/index.html (accessed March 2011).

Musser, Charles. (2007). "War, Documentary and Iraq Dossier: Film Truth in the Age of George Bush." *Framework*, 48.2, 9–35.

The Biggest Independent Pictures Ever Made
Industrial Reflexivity Today

J. D. Connor
Assistant Professor, Yale University, United States

"**Film reflexivity**" is a frequently used term with multiple meanings contingent upon historical, industrial, generic, authorial, and theoretical contexts, especially so in connection with **modernism** and **postmodernism** – concepts that are sometimes equally amorphous. J. D. Connor teases out the many implications of reflexivity present in these contexts and in another increasingly ambiguous one: **independent film production**. Connor surveys three strands of scholarly thought on reflexivity by **Stanley Cavell**, **David Bordwell and Noël Carroll**, and **John Caldwell**. He complicates their arguments through analysis of **"independent" blockbusters**, including ***Raiders of the Lost Ark***, ***Hulk***, and ***WALL•E*** – all products of studio-owned independent production houses, raising the question of what "indie" really means. Connor identifies the **"library"** as a trope, implicitly or explicitly present in these films, and allegorically expressive of the industry's archiving of content, images, and characters in order to build a storehouse of "reflexive" references available for profit-driven **sequels** and **reboots**. Connor's essay shares ground with Geoff King on independent film, Thomas Schatz on contemporary shifts in the film industry, and Bart Beaty on the blockbuster superhero in this volume, and with Jon Lewis on the end/future of cinema in the hardcover/online edition.

Additional terms, names, and concepts: Ang Lee, James Schamus, Focus Features, Independent Feature Project (IFP), "intensified continuity," Pixar, bibliotechnologies

Last of the Independents

Upon receiving his Lifetime Achievement Award from the Independent Feature Project (IFP) in September 2002, Ang Lee was looking forward to his next picture, *Hulk*, which was due to open the following summer: "I guarantee you it's the biggest independent film ever made" (Traister 2003). He had reason to be nervous. His longtime partner, the producer and writer of *Hulk*, James Schamus, had just

American Film History: Selected Readings, 1960 to the Present, First Edition. Edited by Cynthia Lucia, Roy Grundmann, and Art Simon.

sold his own company, Good Machine, to Universal and had agreed to head the studio's new independent arm, Focus Features. Anthony Kaufman of the *Village Voice* was apocalyptic: "The death of American independent film has been prophesied more than once over the last few years, but finally we have a date on which to pin our grief" (Kaufman 2002). If Lee also seemed slightly embarrassed, some of that feeling was a hangover from Schamus's rather infamous IFP keynote address in 2000. Schamus had argued, somewhat tongue-in-cheek, that the IFP should be shut down and started anew. It should be shut because, simply, the indies had won. "The IFP has already, and fabulously, achieved its goals" (Schamus 2000). The indie market had grown exponentially alongside the expansion of the media conglomerates, while at the same time those major players were making more and more films with an "'independent' feel." "The successful integration of the independent film movement into the structures of global media and finance has wrought untold benefits to American filmmakers." He was, many felt, far more gracious than necessary when he argued that

> There is no logical reason why the towering artistic achievements of films like *Boys Don't Cry* and *Election*, brought to us by the News Corporations and Viacoms of this world, should not be celebrated, and we ought to be genuinely grateful that caring and savvy people who work for those corporations have cleared a path in the marketplace for these kinds of films. (Schamus 2000)

In place of the de rigueur defense of independent film, Schamus contended that the IFP should defend independent expression more generally – fighting the extension of the conglomerates, supporting local distribution networks around the world, working to repeal parts of the Telecommunications Act of 1996. If this speech was the theory, the integration of Good Machine into Universal and the launching of *Hulk* were the practice.

Six years after Lee's guarantee and eight years after Schamus's rant, Mark Gill, speaking at the Los Angeles Film Festival, announced that "Yes, the sky really is falling" (2008). Surveying the landscape of studio-based indie labels and real indies, he noted the implosion of various production companies (Warner Independent and Picturehouse, New Line and ThinkFilm), the evaporation of Wall Street financing (this even before the credit panics later that summer), skyrocketing production and marketing costs, and the generally bleak competition for leisure time and dollars. It was clear from his title that an epoch had passed, and in what followed he offered ways to navigate through what would remain of the indie sector.

Paradoxically, the notion of independence was more prominent than ever. Gill noted that "for the first time in the roughly 20 years I've been looking at this data, more than 10% of the audience now is telling pollsters they prefer independent films" (2008). What he did not specify (because the poll did not ask it) was whether those "independent films" came from a studio or a true indie. (Indeed, the response to "Would you prefer to see a film from Fox Searchlight or ThinkFilm?" is most likely "Wha?") And yet the survival of the term and the notion of the independent film among producers who produce nothing of the kind suggests that the invocation of independence does not in these cases refer to a mode of production or distribution but rather to a relationship of responsibility and of authorship and an aspiration to quality of a particular kind. Independence is nearly identical with an ideology of art; it is, after all, a spirit.

Director Andrew Stanton described *WALL•E* in just these terms:

> I almost feel like it's an obligation to not further the status quo if you become somebody with influence and exposure. I don't want to paint the same painting again. I don't want to make the same sculpture again. Why shouldn't a big movie studio be able to make those small independent kinds of pictures? Why not change it up? (Onstad 2008)

The notion of *WALL•E* as a "small" picture is ludicrous, of course. It cost $180 million and it opened in nearly 4,000 theaters in the US. It earned $224 million domestically and $283 million abroad, making it the eighth highest grossing film of 2008.[1] But is Stanton's recourse to a discourse of "independence" any less ludicrous? How does it play out in *WALL•E*? And what alternatives to this self-contradictory aesthetic are available today? To put it more pointedly: If studios are "changing it up" when they make their "indie" films, what are they doing when they practice what we might call "normal" studio filmmaking?[2]

Before answering these questions, though, we might account for their origins slightly differently.

The speeches by the producers Schamus and Gill bookend a particular economic period in the history of indie filmmaking, but they are also highly staged instances of industrial reflexivity. These are public addresses; the speakers have been chosen for their ability to narrate compellingly. Structurally, these are self-conscious performances by producers who are simultaneously part of the system (Schamus at Good Machine/Focus, Gill at The Film Department) and called upon to render an opinion about the system as a whole. Even more, these controversial speeches required elaboration and response, comment and questions, rebuttals and denunciations, contextualization and renarrativization.[3] They are nodes in the discourse of industrial reflection, a place where wisdom (conventional or not) finds explicit formulation and around which collective energy might gather. That is, in part, why it makes sense to point to them as landmarks and to build a story around them: from hubris to realism in the indie film community. Something similar is true of the remarks by Lee and Stanton, although in their cases the reflection tends *away* from the industrial no matter how cannily the directors understand the system. Instead, their professions of independence are compared with their actual situations. Because they are Hollywood directors, we more readily ask how (or, in the suspicious mode, whether) their films reflect their beliefs.

Questions about independence, then, appear within a broader context of reflexivity. That reflection is natural to cinematic creativity, necessary to professional identity-formation, endemic to professions of criticism, and assimilable to the qualifiedly public discourse of marketing, education, and appreciation that surrounds mass arts. In what follows, I want to bring more specificity to the current configuration of reflexivity so that we might see how its various aspects are brought to bear within and just outside particular films. Beyond the particular examples, we may begin to answer the larger question of how industrial reflexivity has changed within what we might think of as Hollywood's "order of composition."[4]

Realms of Reflexivity

Three ways of thinking about reflexivity bracket this discussion of the ideology of independence. The first, derived from Stanley Cavell's *The World Viewed* (1979), is more philosophical and considers the relations between films that reflect on their own nature and our general capacity for reflection within and outside art. The second, developed in the work of David Bordwell and Noël Carroll, is more immanent. In place of a general reflexivity, they concentrate on the proliferation of cinematic allusions. From this they conclude that contemporary Hollywood storytelling struggles against an overarching "belatedness." Late to the party, today's filmmakers must grapple with their precursors, one way or another. The third avenue for reflection, which follows from John Caldwell's *Production Culture*, is more immanent still. Caldwell examines the myriad ways in which film production workers understand their positions within their crafts, the industry, and the culture at large. Where Cavell excavates "the thought of movies," and Bordwell and Carroll the rise of "iconographic coding," Caldwell takes up the "deep texts" of the film/television industry – brochures, demo reels, trade shows, producers' script notes – in his effort to detail the anxiety-fueled current production culture (Cavell 1984; Bordwell 2006, 7; Carroll 1982; Caldwell 2008).

In what follows, I hope to show how contemporary Hollywood films have served as communicating channels – imperfect, to be sure – between the deep textual situations of workers and the marketing efforts of the executive corps; between the discourses of authorship and the ideals of viewership. More than a collection of instances, or a story of the filmmaking process, these readings provide an account of the degree of coherence of the system as a whole. In short, I read feature films as nodes in the ongoing process of industrial reflection. Yet these reflections have been under new pressures of late. To understand the ways those pressures have affected and been affected by filmmaking, to understand why we live in the era of the biggest independent pictures ever made, we need to read Cavell, Bordwell and Carroll, and Caldwell historically.

Writing at the dawn of the New Hollywood, but looking back to films like *Contempt* (1963), Stanley Cavell turned naturally enough to problems of reflexivity and what he called "the camera's implication" (1979). While in some of its historical lineaments Cavell's argument seems to accord with widely available notions of postmodernism, the conceptual consequences of each step he takes run counter to narratives in which postmodern referentiality comes between viewers and their "natural" appreciation of the cinema. On his account, in the classical era, implications of the camera and breaches in the fourth wall functioned as inside jokes. And these jokes "confirm[ed] for the insiders a strong sophistication in moviegoing, a proof that their increasing consciousness of moviemaking routines [would] not jeopardize the film's strength for us" (1979, 124). Now, circa 1970, baring the device no longer lightens or enlightens. "The world's presence to me is no longer assured by my mechanical absence from it, for the screen no longer naturally holds a coherent world *from* which I am absent" (1979, 130). And this "loss of conviction in the film's capacity to carry the world's presence" has made it necessary to insist on the camera's existence. Reflexivity amounts to candor. Hence "the shakings and turnings and zoomings and reinings and unkind cuts to which [the camera] has lately been impelled" (1979, 128).

Until this contemporary moment, then, the distance between the world viewed by the camera and the world we inhabit had been automatic. The camera needed only to document the division between the world and the audience. But where once the world exhibited itself, now film has "tak[en] over the task of exhibition" (1979, 132). This last idea, that film "exhibits" itself, explains a final complication in Cavell's account, namely, that he does not call this new aesthetic "postmodernism." Rather, he regards the reflexive, exhibitionist, "theatrical" turn as the delayed arrival of modernism in the cinema.[5] Modernism, in this definition, appears when an art first discovers its freedom ("now anything can be exhibited and so tried as art") and subsequently recognizes the problem that entails, "that perhaps *all* you can do with your work and works is to exhibit them" (1979, 120). The autonomy of the artwork occasions a search for connection. Reflexivity is a solution to the problem of freedom; it asserts a connection where connection has been lost. "The object itself must account for the viewer's presenting of himself to it and for the artist's authorization of his right to such attendance" (1979, 121). Put another way, reflexivity is the tribute art pays to marketing (Caldwell 2008, 275, 309).

A decade later Noël Carroll drew attention to the increasing allusiveness of Hollywood cinema (1982). What had been inside jokes were now extended beyond the comic into other registers where they might serve as shorthand invocations of thematic or historical density. These allusions could, at the same time, ground the authority of post-studio directors who wished to (or needed to) assert what Cavell called their right to our attendance. Yet, after a period in which reflexive irruptions seemed to be everywhere (whether they were, in Cavell's terms, "serious" or not), Hollywood filmmaking settled down into an era of what David Bordwell calls "intensified continuity" (2006). Flashing forward to the 1990s, viewers continued to encounter all those attention-grabbing devices and more, yet these moments hardly functioned as instances of reflexivity at all; indeed, they barely register as technical flourishes. (Think here of digital lens flare and its banality.) Instead, other features seem to dominate the style. Shot lengths shorten; the depth of field contracts; close-ups get bigger. This is the era of Bordwell's "mannerist" or "referential" or perhaps "belated" classicism; what I and others have called neoclassicism (Bordwell 2006, 188–189, 23–24; Connor 2000; Smith 1998, 10). What are the stakes of this difference in terminology?

"Intensified continuity" carries with it a critique of histories that regard Hollywood cinema as fundamentally postclassical. On these accounts, to put it briefly, the fragmentation of the production process attendant upon the breakup of the studios is reflected in the fragmentation of the narrative and spatial worlds of the film. But for Bordwell, the general homology between industrial form and narrative form is beyond dubious. Yet Bordwell and Carroll recognize that something general has changed. Within their argument, then, the ideas of belatedness and allusionism amount to a *de minimis* version of postmodernism, one so small that it might still be subsumed by a nearly timeless classicism.[6]

We might, though, reframe the argument about the relationship between art and industry in a way that would avoid any necessary reflection or homology between the product and the process. Intensified continuity editing, multiple plotlines, and the general referential substrate are the (potential) reflection and (necessary) demand made of (not made *by*) the production process. Contemporary filmmaking solicits its reflection; there is no reason why that reflection might not make itself apparent in the films themselves. After all, if Cavell is right, film as an institution routinely reinterprets its own automaticity and its own requirements.

Here Caldwell's ethnographic work among everyone from below-the-line workers up through the executive ranks helps explain how this aestheticized homology works, how allegory wends its way through the industry. "Film and television companies, in particular, acknowledge image making as their primary business, and they use reflexive images (images about images) to cultivate valuable forms of public awareness and employee recognition inside and outside of the organization" (2008, 110). In the ever more fragmented and flexible film and television industry of the last two decades, industrial reflection has become increasingly fraught:

> Within the nomadic labor and serial employment system now in place, any area that wishes to remain vital – in the face of endless new technologies, increased competition, and changes in production – must constantly work, through symbolic means, to underscore the distinctiveness and importance of their artistic specialization. (Caldwell 2008, 116)

The "deep texts" are routinely reflexive; they are "native theories" of practitioner groups at various levels of the hierarchy. The system is manic and anxious. Unable to achieve balance in the work-lives of its practitioners ("If you want work–life balance, go get a government job," said Gill), it sought that balance in various ways on screen. Whether those films might exert any sort of control over the system as a whole is a question, but it is a question that should remain open.[7]

Bibliotechnologies

If the modernism of the New Hollywood lined up all too well with postmodernism, the subsequent decades found the studios reascendant, in what looked like a kind of corporate recidivism. In 1971, Cavell could contend: "Self-reference is no more an assurance of candor in movies than in any other human undertaking. It is merely a stronger and more dangerous claim, a further opportunity for the exhibiting of self" (1979, 124). Yet what does it mean when, for the sake of argument, the modernist moment in the development of a particular aesthetic institution coincides with the postmodern moment in the culture (and the economy)? We have a much better sense of this combined and uneven development 30 years on. Within Hollywood, that precarious moment was followed by a reinstitutionalization, a neoclassicism.

For industrial reflexivity to exist, there has to be an industry to reflect, but those reflections are distributed across innumerable levels, from the lowliest term-contracted computer compositor to the CEO, from union work-rule campaigns to Motion Picture Association lobbying efforts. In a context of potentially overwhelming anxiety, symbolic forms of coherence replaced durable arrangements of labor and capital. In that period, coherence was provided, I have argued, by the idea of the classical Hollywood studio itself. Central to that idea was a very particular understanding of the office of the motion picture. In 2001, Howard Stringer, then chairman and CEO of Sony Corporation of America, told PBS's *Frontline*:

> You could make the case that the movie is the most fundamentally symbolic piece of content that any media company develops. It drives all your content. It's the most visible. It's the most conspicuous. It's the most dangerous. It's the most exciting … And it lives forever. (*Frontline* 2001)

In the modern media conglomerate, then, the motion picture may have been displaced from the center of the company's finances but it remained, somehow, the center of its corporate identity: "the most fundamentally symbolic piece of content." The movie was the home of collective reflection, where competing visions of the current industrial configuration could play out.

Stringer, though, is describing the system as it consolidated in the 1980s and flourished in the 1990s. Early in the new century, however, several of the imperial medialiths had begun to sense the limits of their expansion. Where before the trends in corporate behavior and corporate representation were uniform and mutually reinforcing, recent conglomerate and studio activity has been diffuse and inconsistent. Three have been in retreat. Time Warner has sought to unwind its merger with AOL and to spin off its cable arm; Viacom cleaved in twain, leaving the slow-growth television networks on one side and the potentially higher growth media properties, as well as the studio, on the other; and Vivendi simply imploded. In the last instance, the instant French media conglomerate coughed up Universal, which

GE merged with NBC, thereby recreating a 1970s-style interindustrial conglomerate. In contrast to the unwinding conglomerates, Sony has been content with Columbia, although it did become embroiled in the latest incarnation of MGM/UA to no great success. News Corp. has retained some of the go-go atmosphere of a decade ago, while Disney has made two crucial acquisitions, Pixar and Marvel.

Have things changed sufficiently to regard today's Hollywood as different in kind from that of merely half a dozen years ago? How would we mark the change? Does Time Warner CEO Jeff Bewkes's June 2006 declaration that synergy is "bullshit" (Karnitschnig 2006) constitute an epochal event in the history of Hollywood? Does the flattening of DVD revenues (LaPorte 2009) mark the transition? What of the disruption of long-term labor relations – made notorious by the 2007–2008 writers' strike but epitomized in the drastic changes in the workflow and hierarchies of production designers, cinematographers, and editors? Or the foreseeable completion of the digitalization of the industry – not simply digital production, but distribution and exhibition as well? Of course it will be difficult to assess the depth of such transformations at such close range, yet we might suspect that the convergence of radical changes in corporate aims, rates of market growth, and the division of labor suggests that some breakpoint is at hand.

What might be replacing the neoclassical order? One compelling reading of this new era would contend that the principal locus of corporate reflection has simply shifted to television. Time Warner's landmark HBO series such as *The Wire* (2002–2008), News Corp's *American Idol* (2002–), Disney's *High School Musical* (2006), and NBC Universal's *30 Rock* (2006–) are, in their different ways, emblems as central to their corporations as *Batman* (1989), *Die Hard* (1988), *The Lion King* (1994), and *Waterworld* (1995) were, respectively, in the high neoclassical period. Indeed, the emergence of a broad, auteurist strand of show-running, and its concomitant popular and critical endorsement may amount to what we would call "The New Television" after "The New Hollywood" of the 1970s.

Yet, in the precession of corporate reflexivity, the residual film studios offer an interesting contrast to this new world of authored television. One nonclassical feature of the current order of composition has been the lurch toward radically immersive forms, in this case explicitly three-dimensional forms, at all phases – production, distribution, and exhibition. A second feature, and the one I will concentrate on here, is the pervasive adoption of the discourse of independence as the next step in the rationalization of Hollywood's industrial reflection. While there are incisive and thorough histories of American independent cinema from critics as different as Peter Biskind (2004), Geoff King (2005), and John Berra (2008), there has been little attempt to understand independence through its reflections within studio filmmaking. The notion of studio independence is self-contradictory, to be sure, but not necessarily more self-contradictory than any other ideology of authorship within a highly capitalized, collaborative industry of mass entertainment.

The anaclitic relationship between studio and independent is breaking down. In the neoclassical era, the formal division of labor between the studios and the independents was fairly stable. The studios made deniable allegories of the motion picture process – development (*Notting Hill*, 1999), production (*Jurassic Park*, 1993), distribution (*Outbreak*, 1995), exhibition (*Speed*, 1994) – and the indies made undeniable critiques of that process (*Sleep with Me*, 1994; *Swimming with Sharks*, 1994; *State and Main*, 2000).[8] As studios identify themselves as indies, though, their reflexive allegories are leaking out all over. In the *New York Times*, Katrina Onstad asked Stanton directly,

> Is the ubiquitous, all-powerful Buy n Large a sly dig at Disney, Pixar's new corporate bedfellow? With a fervent head shake no, Mr. Stanton turns company man. "Part of the contract was: 'You can't touch us, you can't change what we do,' and that's actually gained them such a level of respect and trust they wouldn't have gotten if they'd tried to be Draconian." (Onstad 2008)

Allegory is still deniable, but only barely so. Despite his protestations that *WALL•E* is an "indie" film, Stanton "turns company man": defending his own independence amounts to defending Disney against the allegorical stories his independence makes possible, which is to say that defending Pixar's independence amounts to defending Disney's corporate culture. Pixar, in 2008, had become as overbranded as Disney itself.

We can see that in the initial teaser trailer. Stanton, on-screen, harkened back to an initial pitch meeting, years ago. "In the summer of 1994, there was a lunch." The sentence is banal, but the cinema is portentous. As saccharine music plays we dissolve into an empty, almost abandoned-looking Hidden City Café. "So at that lunch we knocked around a bunch of ideas that eventually became *A Bug's Life*; *Monsters, Incorporated*; *Finding Nemo*, and the last one we talked about that day was the story of a robot, named WALL•E." Setting aside the skeptical interpretation – that 14 years on Pixar had finally run out of better options and decided to make the robot romance – the implication was that, as an audience, our associations with Pixar would be strong enough to motivate our desire to see anything the company produces. But even more precisely, the implicit appeal of that first trailer was to our nostalgia for the founding moments of Pixar as a production company, and for its independence. Alongside that nostalgia there was also a sense that the films pitched that day belonged together, that they constituted a unified sensibility, a library waiting to be born. The trailer fosters that continuity linking one filmscape to another: the *Bug's Life* grass island, *Monsters, Inc.*'s vault of doors, and *Nemo*'s jellyfish. All of Pixar is available to us, the viewers, and all at once.[9]

Indeed, while *WALL•E* has been taken as a fable of ecological destruction and overconsumption, of politics left and right, one thing that has gone suspiciously unremarked is its interest in filing and retrieval. "Filing and retrieval" hardly seem like fodder for the marketing machine, whatever their appeals to juvenile discoveries of order, but they are the necessary backdrop for the film's invocations of individuality and independence. WALL•E's occupation is ostensibly trash compacting – he makes cubes and places them in grand architectural structures. But his romance lies not in the Watts Towers aesthetic of his trash cubes – they are simply a stunning byproduct of his day job – but in his retrievals – the bits and pieces of the world that he collects. (Eve's "directive" is retrieval, too; she is supposed to collect any sign of "ongoing photosynthesis" and return it to the Axiom.)

The film opposes active retrieval to passive consumption. In the dystopia, Buy n Large is a vast warehouse retailer that has taken over the entire world, an already shopworn joke from its appearance in *Idiocracy* (Judge, 2006) (where the ultrastore is an actual Costco)[10] and a 2003 *Saturday Night Live* skit about Walmart ("Bathrobes with patriotic ducks is in aisle 6,000 and, here, you're gonna need this poncho because I think it's rainy season in that part of Walmart"). In contrast, WALL•E is a DIY recycler. His home entertainment system consists of an old VCR wired to an iPod and viewed through a CRT screen as a magnifier. His walls are lined with racks for other WALL•E units, but they have all been mined for spare parts. Their places are now filled with the detritus that has struck his emerging subjectivity as worth preserving. (Hidden among the shelves, naturally enough, are characters from earlier Pixar movies.)

On the mother ship (we won't call it Disney), the captain need do nothing but let the autopilot (we won't call it the brand) run everything. Eventually, he discovers just how vast the computer's stores of knowledge are, and surfs its databanks from one entry to another. The troika of WALL•E, Eve, and the captain share more than a commitment to the transformative power of recall; they share Pixar's corporate pedigree. WALL•E's startup sound is the Apple C-major chord, Eve's design was vetted by Apple's chief designer Jonathan Ive, and, slightly more speculatively, the captain is empowered by his computer to throw off the shackles of his autopilot.[11]

Pixar had been owned by Apple CEO Steve Jobs until 2006, when Disney paid $7.4 billion for the company, a move that installed Jobs on Disney's board and Pixar chief John Lasseter as Chief Creative Officer of both Pixar and Disney (Holson 2006; Solomon 2006). This is why the *New York Times* reporter asked Stanton if the criticism of Buy n Large was a "dig" at Disney. In the film's version of the change in corporate control, the acquisition of Pixar saves Disney from its own infantilizing complacency. Pixar's own well-tended corporate culture drives that subversive reinvention: The arrival of the Pixar robots leads the captain to unlock the knowledge dormant in the vault. The robots are the keys to the library, and the library is the key to the rediscovery of human purpose.

Libraries may do many things on film. They frequently serve as locations of hidden, total knowledge, as in *Toute la mémoire du monde* (1956) or *All the President's Men* (1976) or *The Time Machine* (2002) or *National Treasure 2* (2007). In *Jumper* (2008), the library is a refuge. When David Rice first discovers his ability to teleport, he arrives (twice) in the Ann Arbor public library. ("Escape to your library" reads the helpful poster.) In *Alexander* (2004), Anthony

Hopkins as Ptolemy narrates the story from the library of Alexandria, vouching for its historical reality. In *Se7en* (1995), the library is the locus of obsession; in *A.I.* (2001), the "room where they make you read" is the place where David lashes out against his own double, against his own identity as a product. The library as such has no single meaning.

Just offscreen, though, we see that libraries have become the anchors of corporate identity. Legacy libraries feed individual productions. The RKO library is being opened up for remakes (Ice Cube's *Are We There Yet?* (2005) remakes *Mr. Blandings Builds His Dream House* (1948), for example). Libraries also drive mergers and acquisitions. The MGM/UA library was the most enticing element for the private equity investors in the most recent sale of the studio, while the DreamWorks library was monetized in order to make the Paramount/DreamWorks deal possible. Libraries reliably spin off cash that can be plowed into production, as at Lionsgate or Luc Besson's EuropaCorp. In short, library rights are the legal order that makes a culture of "the long tail" possible.

Postmodernism is often understood as a recycling of certain modernist moments in collage form – as pastiche, bricolage, remix, and so on. But within the ordered narrative worlds of contemporary Hollywood, postmodernism (or Cavellian modernism) works through cataloguing and recall, and both of those depend on an underlying structure of reliable availability. The satisfactions of knowing the inside joke align viewers with the property regime of the authoring institution. Theories of the postmodern, like theories of creativity, may emphasize notions of disorder or spontaneous order – the rhizomatic, the playful, the autopoetic, the networked. But the imperatives that organize intellectual property and revenue streams in Hollywood foster a much broader organization of entertainment. That organization has its enforcement side in various Digital Rights Management technologies and the festering legal campaign against individual BitTorrent downloaders. The pseudocreative flipside is a personalized bibliotechnology that entices users to more intently manage the entertainment they already have the rights to; iTunes Genius playlists, Netflix queues, and TiVo protocols are not simply ways of cataloging what one owns, but are ways of shaping future consumption along the lines of present desires.

The industrial commitment to maximum exploitation of intellectual property and the consumer's commitment to a maximum availability of popular culture offer an explanation for the reappearance within contemporary Hollywood of a version of the "jukebox musical" (*Magnolia*, 1999; *Across the Universe*, 2007; and, most prominently, *Mamma Mia!*, 2008). The fan of a particular artist enjoys the double pleasure of the music for its own sake, on the one hand, and the anticipation of the deployment of particular songs from the oeuvre, on the other, while the production companies benefit from a unified rights situation and the chance to capitalize on the stored value of the song catalog. As Robert Kraft, director of Fox Music, explained, the difficulties in producing a soundtrack like *Juno* (2007) or *Moulin Rouge!* (2001) make *Mamma Mia!* "a dream" (author interview, January 24, 2008).

Some features of Hollywood's "bibliothecarian imagination" are almost constant, such as the oppositions between reserve/prolepsis, stasis/circulation, artifact/idea.[12] In what follows, I will look at two additional ways in which the potential of the library as technology or social form or concept is realized. In the first, typified by Marvel Studios' aggressive self-understanding, the library functions as a reserve of characters and stories through which producers and audiences renegotiate the terms of franchise identity. The Marvel example shows how Hollywood balances innovation and consistency today. The second example, *Indiana Jones and the Kingdom of the Crystal Skull*, turns even further inward, toward the histories of its creators. Yet *Crystal Skull* casts the disordered archive of its own history (of film) as an analogue for both its own practice and its reception. The differences between these three deployments (including *WALL•E*) suggest the contours of a broad swath of contemporary reflection. Through them we approach not the meaning of the library, but the possibilities of meaning and creative work defined through the library. Which is to say that we begin to answer the question of Hollywood's order of composition.

From Library to Reboot

Returning to the biggest independent film ever made, *Hulk* (2003), famously, was a disappointment – an odd disappointment, given that it grossed $245 million worldwide. But it was only a disappointment, not a flop. By the following summer, it had become possible to imagine a sequel – at least outside Universal. In July, *The Onion* published a column by the Hulk himself headlined "Why no one want make *Hulk* 2?" (*The Onion* 2004). In a world where franchises exist, in Caldwell's phrase, to be strip-mined, the notion of a character in search of a sequel was only slightly implausible. The *Onion* piece turns the Hulk into a wheedling self-promoter with his characteristic fractured English intact. He drops articles and prepositions, ignores verb tenses, and remains trapped in the third person. Still, he has a keen sense of craft of the sequel: "Hulk work out treatment for next movie Hulkself. It have everything in *Hulk*, only more intense." Hulk is working on the pitch, which will tie up some of the loose ends in the sequel-porous initial installment and capitalize on the array of characters already available in the comic: "Many unanswered questions from last *Hulk* movie. What happen to puny human Banner in rainforest? Is there cure for Hulk? … Is there future with Betty Ross? Where villains that make comic so great?" But he is also thinking up merchandising possibilities ("If Hulk Hands big hit, Hulk Feet even bigger hit!") and marketing campaigns ("This time it personal").

If much of Hulk's column seems persuasive – why not make *Hulk 2* indeed? – the tagline gives the game away in its allusion to the campaign for *Jaws: The Revenge* (1987), a film widely regarded as the worst sequel ever made. The industrial logic of sequels ("everything in *Hulk*, only more intense") is inexorable but risks franchise-killing, clichéd badness. Hulk recognizes this possibility, too. "First studio exec to suggest Joel Schumacher get smashed!" In place of the *Batman Forever* director, he pins his hopes on the indie credentials of Schamus ("Him really get what Hulk all about") and Lee.

> Why no one appreciate daring vision of Ang Lee? Aaargh! Ang Lee genius! Maybe panels on screen gimmicky, but him try something new. When last time you try something new?! Ang Lee willing to work in unfamiliar genres. Him brave like Hulk. Hulk wish for him to work on *Hulk 2*, if he willing, but Hulk understand if he not want to. Ang Lee like Hulk: He not stay in one place for too long. Him working on gay western right now. That prove Hulk's point.

In the paramarketing world of insider-styled coverage of Hollywood, what Justin Wyatt calls the "enfotainment" complex, every interpretation is also a defense of certain choices, of certain ideologies (Wyatt and Vlesmas 1998). Alongside interpretation, then, there is also plenty of room for accusation: "When last time you try something new?!" Even if that accusation would be utter bad faith (this is a sequel pitch; it is trying something *again*), it stings, and it stings whether it is directed at the "puny humans" in the general public who want the same thing, only more of it, or the gutless producers who have not greenlit the sequel. Finally, within this defensive castigation of the audience, Hulk offers an auteurist allegory, though it is unfocused. Lee's genre-bending is evidence of both his Hulk-like bravery and, somehow, his Hulk-like persecution ("Sometimes Hulk so sad and alone").

In this last respect, *Hulk*'s claim to be the biggest independent film ever made was Marvel and Universal's attempt to duplicate the strategy that had worked for Fox on *X-Men* and, before that, for Warner Bros. with *Batman*. If one could put a franchise in the hands of an indie director, there could be something fresh and enticing to audiences; it would not seem rote.[13] At the same time, though, the franchise had to deliver on the promises of the underlying property ("Where villains that make comic so great?").

The original *Hulk* marketing campaign already embodied this two-sidedness; it suggested deep reserves of independent authorship beneath its "popcorn" facade. For Ang Lee, the indie-auteur model

Figure 28.1 Director Ang Lee dons the motion capture suit in order to generate the data that will become The Hulk in *Hulk* (2003, producer James Schamus). The roll of carpet stands in for Jennifer Connelly.

succeeded. The *New Yorker* ran a long profile of him with particular attention to his role not simply as a director but as a performer (Lahr 2003). Lee had begun as an actor at Indiana University and had put that talent to work in *Hulk* by donning the motion capture suit and providing the initial data points for the computer rendering of the monster. (The DVD release included plenty of behind-the-scenes footage of him hulking out.) The protagonist was not simply a plausible allegory of the director but was actually – that is, kinetically – him. In an era when digital effects are contracted out, potentially leaching the director's control over the process, Lee's performance background became the means of bringing effects back under his signature.

For Schamus, though, the model failed. He wrote a piece in the *Times* touting the Hulk as "a perfect embodiment of American repression, a curiously asexual rampaging id" and *Hulk* as an exploration of the nearly timeless notion of the hero:

> Spectacles hold little fascination without the heroic figures who are inscribed within them. It is the constant testing, reconfiguring and evolution of such heroes that make these movies so compelling, and the Hulk provides the opportunity to explore a particularly complex member of the heroic tribe. (Schamus 2003)

The backlash against the piece suggests the dangers of indie insistence. The sense of a structural interpretive imbalance captures some of what made it possible for *Hulk* to seem "disappointing" regardless of the numbers.[14]

The problem with *Hulk*'s marketing was not the simple fact that there were two registers of meaning directed at two audiences ranked in a hermeneutic hierarchy. As Richard Maltby has argued, that split audience was a foundational principle of classical Hollywood (1996). Instead, the problem with *Hulk*'s split marketing was that it had violated the implicit division of labor between the neoclassical studios and the independents. In indie fashion, *Hulk* made its reserves of authorship *explicit*, thus insistently forcing the "popcorn" audience to contend with a denigration of the "mere entertainment" that it sought, while, at the same time, *Hulk* short-circuited the "deep" interpretive work of the audience for whom that work constitutes entertainment. For any classical aesthetic, this loss of balance is fatal.

The Onion's Hulk was two years too early in his sequel pitch. If, that is, *The Incredible Hulk* (2008) is actually a sequel to *Hulk*. It would be hard to know even apart from the lack of a numeral. The characters remain, but all the actors are new. And despite Hulk's plea, Ang Lee and James Schamus were not part of the film; Louis Leterrier directed while *X-Men* writer Zak Penn did the screenplay. The origin story is rehearsed behind the opening credits, as is typical in a sequel, but this version is aligned not with the universe of *Hulk* but with that of the 1970s television show. All these things make *The Incredible Hulk* less a sequel than what today is called a "reboot."

The reboot has taken the place of the sequel in the way that the reimagination has taken the place of the remake. Each new term has been inserted into the rhetoric of the intermittent franchise narrative and its attendant, pulsed revenue streams in order to capitalize on the discontinuities inherent in the lags between installments. These terms do this work in four ways. First, where the sequel and the remake suggest a smooth continuity and a machinic replication, the reboot and the reimagination locate creativity in delay. Second, at the same time that they vouch for the creativity in the system, the terms also promise to purge older stories of whatever might have become problematic in them – whether those are problems of politics, narrative balance, pacing, or, most generally, style. Third, rebooting and reimagining also more directly solicit the audience's reflection on the differences and connections between the incarnations. That reflection is aided by the release of new, more feature-laden DVDs that promise to take the audience not simply behind the scenes but behind the decision-making that led to the now-outmoded version. Ultimately, though, the efforts to intensify certain viewers' attention to difference and connection are not in the service of a radical problematization of the text, for the studios' aims stop short of such a complete deconstruction of identity. Instead, the reboot and the reimagination posit a real property that can be the hermenaut's true object of desire. There is value in the library. The studios know this, they defend that intellectual property extraordinarily vigorously, and in the reboot and the reimagination, they inculcate that belief in the audience.

The reboot may veer away from fundamental critique, but at the heart of *The Incredible Hulk* lie potentially radical worries about identity and replication.

Figure 28.2 "This is all you": Bruce Banner (Edward Norton) discovers the library made from his blood in the reboot, Louis Leterrier's *The Incredible Hulk* (2008, producer Kevin Feige, Gale Anne Hurd, and Avi Arad).

When Banner intentionally draws his blood to send it back to a willing researcher (Mr Blue) he unwittingly gives rise to a library. He arrives in New York to test out a possible cure and discovers that Blue has generated a vast collection from that initial sample. "You didn't send me much to work with so I had to concentrate it and make more," says Mr Blue. Here, Blue gives voice to the film's hybrid identity as reboot-sequel. The franchise must be rebooted (because "you didn't send me much to work with") while it fulfills the demands of a sequel ("concentrate it and make more"). It is, for the researcher, a utopian scene of production and reproduction: "This is potentially Olympian ... We will unlock hundreds of cures." Characters are libraries or bibles, filled with data and stories. "Bruce, this is all you," says Blue, gesturing to the library. At the same time libraries are populated by the exploits and potentials of the characters they catalog. This vacillant equivalence lies at the heart of the latest wave of industrial reflexivity. What has become more explicit is the stored value that can be unleashed, Hulk-like, when necessary. "It has to be me, you have to take me back there," Banner says, before dropping out of a helicopter and into the fray against Abomination.

But if the *Hulks* were intended to be summer tentpoles and were, therefore, important occasions for a studio and its employees to ponder their own fates, then they might for the same reason be isolated occasions. If, however, the *Hulks* are part of a strategic pivot in which the assertion of a reflexivity corpus now occupies a crucial space in Hollywood, then we should find similar reflection even in down-market properties. And in the case of *The Punisher*, that is exactly what we find.

When Lionsgate released *The Punisher* in 2004, Marvel (under Avi Arad) had become a zealous developer of its intellectual property, and its studio brand had begun to vie with its distributors' for prominence.[15] *The Punisher* is odd and unique: Its broody hero vies with subtropical sun (Tampa, Florida), the aesthetic is neon moderne in a too-crisp, video-edged way reminiscent of *CSI: Miami*, and the tone veers from broad, absurdist violence, to domestic comedy, to (supposed) melodrama. Itself a relaunch from a Dolph Lundgren vehicle from 1989, the version starring Thomas Jane reads as low budget as its hero.

The 2008 reboot *Punisher: War Zone* puts the Punisher back in New York City, and while it is a cold, wet New York, overly familiar from the *Batman* films and *Grand Theft Auto IV*, the setting better explains the baleful, retributive moralizing of the film than even Frank Castle's own tragic backstory. Five years have elapsed since Castle's family was gunned down. In the meantime he has been busy meting out justice. Friends on the police force look the other way, feeding him inside information, until Castle accidentally kills an undercover FBI agent. When the dead man's partner, Agent Butiansky, joins the "Punisher

Task Force" (staff of one), he is directed to a basement library. The endless rows of metal shelves and archival boxes are the materialization of the department's bad faith. The locale makes it all too clear that the police have no interest in arresting Frank. Still, Butiansky intends to persevere. When he asks for the Punisher case files, he is told they are right here. "Which drawer?" "All of them." As with Mr Blue's "Olympian" fantasies, this represents the producers' dream. The Punisher library provides a narrative equivalent of the hardware racks on which Frank stores his armory. And just as each weapon promises a different way to die, so each drawer promises a different death. These libraries are extensions of a character, but they are also, in the Marvel universe, the equivalent of characters. The film's final battle at the Brad Street Hotel takes this cataloging to the next level by literalizing the characters involved. The city's ethnic gangs have been invited to take their best shot at Frank, their shared nemesis, and each gang occupies a different space in the hotel, filed neatly away in rooms ready to launch into the fight and the story.

If *The Punisher* was part of Marvel's attempt to exploit its lesser properties – to see, in effect, how the new "Marvel Knights" label would match up with the zeitgeist – *War Zone* was also part of a more conscious attempt to bring all of Marvel together. A frozen Captain America would have made a cameo appearance at the beginning of *The Incredible Hulk*, but it was later cut. However, Robert Downey Jr's Tony Stark did appear at the end, visiting from Marvel's Fox release, *Iron Man*. Across studios and seasons the pieces are being assembled, cataloged, and held in readiness. "We're putting a team together," says Downey. The plan to bring Hulk, Iron Man, Captain America, Thor, and the Ant-Man together came to fruition in 2012 with Joss Whedon's *The Avengers*. With the Spider-Man series ensconced at Sony and the Fantastic Four/Silver Surfer cross at Universal, Mr Blue speaks as the genius of the (Marvel) system: "With a little more trial and error there's no end to what we can do."

Indy and the Indie

Hulk may have been the biggest independent picture ever made, but at the box office the biggest Indy is Indiana Jones. The first installment, *Raiders of the Lost Ark* (1981), was a triumph of deal-making: Lucas and Spielberg received nearly half of the gross; they participated in the music and merchandising; they had control over the poster and trailers; and Paramount reduced its distribution fee (Dick 2001, 187). Culturally, the film drove home the nostalgia at the heart of the Lucas–Spielberg axis of postmodernism by cloaking its 1930s setting in something like the form of an old serial. It looked like narrative "slumming," and it was quickly diagnosed by Fredric Jameson as part of the Reaganite populism of the era (Jameson 1998). But it also advanced a serious aesthetic claim, namely, that the attempt to comprehensively recapture a period's authentic look and feel ought to be marked by that period's demotic narrative forms even as it elevates those forms to the center of film art. This winking historicism mixes the pleasures of childhood with a recognition that something separates this film from the serials it evokes. That "something" is quality, a recognition that, despite its narrative and formal debts, *Raiders* is good by our standards and not those of the past. In its famous concluding joke, *Raiders* tucks the Ark of the Covenant in some vast warehouse where it is in principle cataloged but in actuality lost. The political lesson is simple enough: The fate of independence and adventure is bureaucratization, the loss of control to "top men."

The fourth installment released in 2008, *Kingdom of the Crystal Skull*, begins at that warehouse, which we come to learn is Hangar 51, putative resting place of the aliens who crashed at Roswell, NM. Like the "book of secrets" in *National Treasure 2* (2007), this warehouse-cum-soundstage is the place "where you and your government have hidden all of your secrets," and the new adventure is triggered by the arrival of the ultimate bureaucrats, the Soviets and their top woman. Where the Americans hid things away for the good of the citizenry, the communists desire total knowledge. The glimpse we get of the Ark as they leave the warehouse makes the irony of their fate clear from the outset.

The merger of 1930s tale and 1930s telling from *Raiders* gives way to a 1950s version of the same. As Lucas put it, "It was the idea of taking the genre from the 1930s serials, action-adventure serials, to the B science fiction movies of the 50s … I wanted to rest it on a cinematic antecedent, like we did with the other one." The entire Lucas–Spielberg team still operates within a classicist/nostalgist aesthetic. These are the basic terms of their art. Screenwriter David Koepp describes it as needing to adhere to "the rules" of the series while somehow being "fresh." Sound designer Ben Burtt will say, "When I think of the Indy films, I always think I want to give things a classic sound." But if these are "classic" sounds they are also new: "There's been a conscious choice to create the supernatural sounds as if maybe they were created for movies back in the 1950s. I've tried to derive a style from those movies, to make new sounds in that old style." Composer John Williams will describe the Crystal Skull's musical motif as a product of this same effort:

> The crystal skull, certainly for its various appearances in the film, needed to have some musical identification, and what I tried to do was to try to get some kind of homage if you like to the science fiction films of the 50s that would bring an aspect of nostalgia into this piece.[16]

The filmmakers may be trying to merely update their 1980s neoclassicism, but *Crystal Skull* is decisively inflected by a reading of its period in a way that *Raiders* was not. Spielberg, describing Lucas's pitch to him, drifted in and out of quotation, but even when it is unclear who is speaking, it is absolutely clear that the shared terms of the discussion are interpretive:

> But George insisted, and he said, "This will be like a B movie. It'll be like those 1950s B movies, *Earth vs. the Flying Saucers*, and all those exploitation movies that were really about government paranoia, Cold War fears and things like that, and Hollywood turned them into *Invaders from Mars*."[17]

It is a truism of film history that the alien invaders of the 1950s movies represent the marching forces of communism, or conformity, or both. On this understanding of Cold War culture, social and political anxieties would occasionally find more literal expression in social problem or exploitation films – juvenile delinquency in *Rebel without a Cause* or nuclear anxiety in *On the Beach*. *Crystal Skull* stages both aspects of this reading via confrontations between the actual period threats and their allegorical period stand-ins: The (actual) Russians want to know everything the (allegorical) aliens know. If communists came to 1950s cinema dressed as aliens, *Indy*'s communists now want to *be* aliens. (Indeed, Cate Blanchett's black bob, drawn cheeks, and bulging eyes make her an alien manqué.) Meanwhile, the film offers us the ultimate conformists in the form of TV-watching mannequins who populate a Potemkin Eisenhower suburb. They will soon perish in a nuclear test strike. If the social discipline of suburban conformity was the complement of the anxieties of the nuclear age, *Crystal Skull* takes that functionalism a step further: Its suburbs exist only in order to be destroyed by the bomb.

What to make of the film's reliance on such a reading? Is *Crystal Skull* a critique of 1950s paranoia or an endorsement of it? In truth, the film is neither. The McCarthyite thugs who badger Indy about his loyalties are off-track not because there are no communist subversives on campus, but because there are actual Soviet spies all over the country, stealing its secrets. The populuxe design of the fake suburb and the intended glee that greets its destruction imply that the film endorses the critique of suburban homogenization, and yet it brings that critique to ground when it nukes the place. The further implication seems to be that if you think that the suburbs are full of consumerist mannequins who "deserve it," you are no different than the bombers. Whether this conclusion amounts to a critique of the critique, whether it reverts to an "endorsement" of suburbanism or not, is unclear. Regardless, the whirl of interpretation verges on the ludicrous. Indy rides out the bomb in a lead-lined refrigerator; fans and critics everywhere object. "Nuke the fridge" replaces "jump the shark" in the critical lexicon.

In Spielberg's work, the collapse of the oppositions between cultural resistance and approval, on the one hand, and between allegory and literalism, on the other, had actually occurred by the time he made *War of the Worlds* (2005). Where *Jurassic Park* (1993) had maintained a studied ambivalence about the relationship between showman and exploiter, *War of the Worlds* couldn't keep its allegory straight. Spielberg explained that the humans fighting off the aliens were like 9/11 victims fleeing Manhattan, while Koepp told *USA Weekend*, "You can read our movie several ways ... It could be straight 9/11 paranoia. Or it could be about how U.S. military interventionism abroad is doomed by insurgency, just the way an alien invasion might be" (Barboza 2005). To Koepp, it did not matter which account was right. All that mattered was that there be some story, *any* story to link the summer sci-fi blockbuster to terrorism and war. Those plucky Americans fighting off the aliens might be the plucky Americans they appeared to be, or they might be members of al-Qaeda in Iraq. Regardless, the horizons of interpretation had been opened for the audience. The mission in *Crystal Skull* was very much the same.

Crystal Skull begins by excavating hidden secrets; it ends with a nightmare of total recall. At the climax of *Raiders*, Indy's nemesis Belloc looks at the angels rushing around the Ark and proclaims, "It's beautiful!" – just before he becomes a column of fire. In *Crystal Skull*, the problem is not too much beauty but too much knowledge. "I want to know everything. I'm ready," Cate Blanchett's Spalko tells the alien. She is not. Bombarded with too much knowledge, Spalko attempts to turn away from the alien's eyes, but it refuses to let her go. Reanimated, the creature from another dimension reveals itself to be a postmodern connoisseur of irony. Fountains of knowledge will come streaming out of her eyes and mouth like so much ectoplasm. Spalko vaporizes because her skull lacks the capacity of the scaphocephalic aliens. Indy, though, will survive because he doesn't want to know everything the aliens do; he simply wants to be able to access it. She wants to be the library; he wants to be the librarian.

But we can be even more explicit: *Crystal Skull* tells the story of the digitalization of library access. *Raiders*' concluding joke was analog. As Michael Rubin, Lucasfilm veteran and author of *Droidmaker: George Lucas and the Digital Revolution*, put it,

> If you want to know what editing was like before George came along, visualize that warehouse at the end of *Raiders of the Lost Ark* … If you shot a movie like *Star Wars*, you had 300,000 feet of film and sound rolls that had to be code numbered and matched by hand. If you wanted to cut the scene where Luke was doing this and Han Solo was doing that, some poor schmuck had to find those pieces so you could fit them together with tape. It was like the Library of Congress with no librarian. (Silberman 2005, 141–142)

When *Crystal Skull* revisits that warehouse, Indy becomes that librarian, tossing handfuls of gunpowder in the air and allowing the strong magnetic field of the alien sarcophagus to lead the way to the alien's crate. In this new magneto-digital world, the randomness of the library's arrangement becomes irrelevant: your data knows you want it.

At this point, it becomes difficult to sort through the multilayered grid of historical references behind *Crystal Skull*. Sloshing around in the film we find the 1950s of its setting, the 1930s of its origins, the 1980s of the series' origins, a healthy dose of Lucas's late 1960s libertarian paranoia (the politics of *THX–1138*), and, of course, the contemporary. In characteristic fashion, the film stages this pastiche as self-reflection. Standing in the antechamber to the crystal aliens' chamber, among the bric-a-brac of thousands of years of civilization gathered from across the globe, Indy recognizes his own profession: "They were collectors … Archeologists." The room may be as haphazardly arranged as the boiler room in *Citizen Kane*, but the aliens know what they have. As their saucer rises through the shell of the temple, it looks for all the world like a spinning hard drive.

When IBM debuted the hard disk drive in 1956 (in plenty of time for the events of *Crystal Skull* the next year), they announced it this way:

> [The] 305 RAMAC and 650 RAMAC [are] two electronic data processing machines using IBM's random access memory, a stack of disks that stores millions of facts and figures less than a second from management's reach. Because transactions are processed as they occur, the fresh facts held in a random access memory show business as it is right now, not as it was hours or weeks ago. (IBM 1956)

The total library, stocked with "fresh facts" and instantly available: this has been a remarkably durable commercial utopia. The digital library promises to make sense of the convergent flux of filmmaking practices, corporate mythologies, and audience involvements; it promises *to show business as it is right now*. That is what Schamus and Gill were promising as well, when they played their parts in one of dozens of self-reflexive Hollywood rituals.

In this new era, when it is impossible to distinguish between the indie blockbuster and the blockbuster as such, both "the biggest independent pictures ever made" and their less-indie complements are drawn from a standing reserve, a library of stories and storytelling. Yet the library is not simply a theme or a motif, the way that the absent father (in Spielberg) or the recognition of impending climate change (at Fox, home of the *Ice Age* series) are. While themes and motifs bring order or coherence to a film or group of films, the library offers the possibility of imagining order as such – an order that is not merely narrative, but always potentially so; an order that is not necessarily "logical," but nested within the social and aesthetic practices of Hollywood. Libraries look most thematically insistent when they suggest the parameters of self-understanding in general. Today's Hollywood films are themselves industrial reflections even as they serve as communicating channels between the layers of reflexivity that compound into the evanescent industrial self-consciousness. Whether we attribute that reflection to the studio, the indie director, the author of the source text, the community of fans, or the assembly of artists and artisans is a matter to be decided in each case. Yet the order of reflexive composition in contemporary Hollywood makes our decision one the film has already imagined – imagined, and filed away.

Notes

1. All figures here and later from boxofficemojo.com.
2. The idea of the "normal" film derives from Thomas Kuhn's account of normal science. But filmmaking does not progress in the ways that science does, and it may be that what is "normal" is both always undergoing transformation and yet, at the same time, only defined in contrast to something else ("indie kinds of filmmaking"). What would it mean then to speak of "normal" filmmaking? It might mean something like the "average" film of the sort analyzed in Bordwell, Staiger, and Thompson's *Classical Hollywood Cinema* (1985), where random sampling is supplemented by a selection of other landmark films to provide a portrait of a broad range of Hollywood filmmaking. But I am less interested in the average or baseline film than in a competing positive notion of what studio filmmaking might entail. To look ahead: If independence is associated with the endlessly renewed surprise of creativity, normal filmmaking will be aligned with the inherently sustainable, with films that look like models.
3. For responses to Mark Gill's speech, see Thompson 2008, Goldstein 2008, Poland 2008, and Macaulay 2008, who begins: "I'm blogging from Paris where, the other night, I had dinner with two Palme d'Or-winning French producer friends. 'What did you think of the Mark Gill article?' one wanted to know. Yes, Gill's speech is dinner conversation across the Atlantic. In fact, the producer had printed it out and circulated it among her staff." He goes on: "I've commented before on the Gill piece, which I mostly agree with. Now we're seeing a second wave of responses to the article, and one must-read for indies is by writer/director John August, who blogs about the release of his Sundance film The Nines and relates it to the speech."
4. This notion is derived from T. J. Clark's *The Painting of Modern Life: Paris in the Art of Manet and His Followers*. The crucial sentence appears in a note: "It matters what the materials of a pictorial order are, even if the order is something different from the materials, and in the end more important than they are" (Clark 1985, 78). Cinema has more than a pictorial order (there is, at the very least, a sonic order), but the principle holds. In what follows, I address a comparatively special case in which the materials and the order have converged; one of the questions I want to answer is how materials matter.
5. His use of "theatrical," here, is heavily indebted to Michael Fried's development of the same term.
6. This is a characteristic move. After a decade of denying that "high concept" constituted anything at all, in *The Way Hollywood Tells It* Bordwell contends that Justin Wyatt's notion of high concept "skillfully captures a distinct trend in early 1980s cinema, but the films' fashion-layout gloss remains a fairly isolated phenomenon" (2006, 7).
7. Caldwell puts it this way: "Ultimately I will suggest that material and conceptual uses of space do impact the sense of space and narrative that viewers experience when watching the screen at home or in the theater. But this connection between the space of making and the space of watching is more circumstantial than direct" (2008, 69).
8. Within the system, movie-movies from the studios would seem to offer a more candid reflection of the industry, but they are almost invariably played for laughs. In this comedic form they preneutralize their critique of the system – as in Bowfinger (1991), or in the mirthless spoofs that stretch endlessly from *Not Another Teen Movie* (2001) to *Epic Movie* (2007) and *Disaster Movie* (2008), and, doubtless, beyond.
9. Of course the story was mythical, and even Stanton could not remain committed to it. When Steve Weintraub asked him, "Was this kind of the end maybe of the first generation of Pixar?" Stanton answered: "I mean, that lunch got a little mythologized once we got the fully-formed ideas, like it was the only lunch we ever had. But it is funny that, out of that lunch, came *A Bug's Life* and *WALL•E*, but there were many other lunches

and meetings that, eventually, those seeds turned into *Monsters, Inc.* and *Finding Nemo*" (Weintraub 2008).

10. Although *Idiocracy* was given a token release in 2007 it had languished on Fox's shelf for a year following disastrous test screenings.
11. For the history of the Mac startup sound, see Whitwell 2005. For Ive's visit to Pixar see Weintraub 2008: "I had two things. One, I had the making-fun-of-the-iPod joke, I was having the Apple sound joke and I also had decided that if I was going to make the prettiest robot in the world, for a machine, what would that be and we all agreed that, currently, Apple products are the most gorgeous looking machines in the world. They could be art objects without adding a function. We didn't want to literally make her be Apple, but we wanted her to feel that same design sensibility, where the functions are hidden. It's a mystery and you're not exactly sure how it all works, but it seems almost magical and everything is almost perfectly molded into one another. It became obvious to us, but I wanted Steve to be comfortable with it and he said we should have Johnny Ive come over and see what he thinks, because he designs everything for Apple. He came over and pretty much fell in love with immediately and it was the biggest shot in the arm. He didn't have anything to approve on, he just said, 'I love her.' It was a great afternoon with him that was pretty much the stamp of approval."
12. There seems to be no common adjective meaning library-like in English.
13. Caldwell points to another possibility, that such a film might be made more efficiently because its indie-based creative team would not be beholden to union work-rules and divisions of labor. In the case of summer tentpoles, though, that advantage tends to fade. The sheer bulk of effects work puts the responsibility for squeezing efficiencies out of a budget in the hands of the ultra-competitive effects shops themselves.
14. Regardless of the numbers: This is a crucial point. Whether the estimation of Hollywood films by Hollywood can escape the tyranny of the numbers is an open question. When it looks like it does, this suggests that certain discourses (or ideologies) have sufficient sway that they might, at times, overpower the economic.
15. See Donahue 2002. This history is encapsulated in the leaders running before the three installments of the *X-Men* series. I discuss that series in the opening chapter of *The Studios after the Studios* (2015).
16. "Adventures in Post Production," transcript from DVD feature, *Indiana Jones and the Kingdom of the Crystal Skull*, Blu-Ray 2-Disc Special Edition, Lucasfilm, 2008.
17. "The Return of a Legend," transcript in ibid.

References

Barboza, Craigh. (2005). "Imagination Is Infinite." *USA Weekend*, July 15, at http://www.usaweekend.com/05_issues/050619/050619spielberg.html (accessed March 24, 2009).

Berra, John. (2008). *Declarations of Independence: American Cinema and the Partiality of Independent Production*. Bristol: Intellect.

Biskind, Peter. (2004). *Down and Dirty Pictures: Miramax, Sundance, and the Rise of Independent Film*. New York: Simon & Schuster.

Bordwell, David. (2006). *The Way Hollywood Tells It*. Berkeley: University of California Press.

Bordwell, David, & Carroll, Noël (eds). (1996). *Post-Theory: Reconstructing Film Studies*. Madison: University of Wisconsin Press.

Bordwell, David, Staiger, Janet, & Thompson, Kristin. (1985). *The Classical Hollywood Cinema: Film Style and Mode of Production to 1960*. New York: Columbia University Press.

Caldwell, John Thornton. (2008). *Production Culture: Industrial Reflexivity and Critical Practice in Film and Television*. Durham, NC: Duke University Press.

Carroll, Noël. (1982). "The Future of Allusion: Hollywood in the Seventies (and Beyond)." *October*, 20 (Spring). Reprinted in Noël Carroll, *Interpreting the Moving Image* (pp. 240–264), Cambridge: Cambridge University Press, 1998.

Cavell, Stanley. (1979). *The World Viewed*. Enlarged edn. Cambridge, MA: Harvard University Press.

Cavell, Stanley. (1984). "The Thought of Movies." In Stanley Cavell, *Themes out of School: Effects and Causes* (pp. 3–26). Chicago: University of Chicago Press.

Clark, T. J. (1985). *The Painting of Modern Life: Paris in the Art of Manet and His Followers*. Princeton: Princeton University Press.

Connor, J. D. (2000). "The Projections: Allegories of Industrial Crisis in Neoclassical Hollywood." *Representations*, 71 (Summer), 48–76.

Connor, J.D. (2015). *The Studios after the Studios: Neoclassical Hollywood (1970–2010)*. Stanford: Stanford University Press.

Dick, Bernard F. (2001). *Engulfed: The Death of Paramount Pictures and the Birth of Corporate Hollywood*. Lexington: University of Kentucky Press.

Donahue, Ann. (2002). "Above the Line: Avi Arad: Turnabout? It's Marvel-ous." *Variety*, May 19, at http://www.variety.com/article/VR1117867142.html (accessed March 24, 2009).

Frontline. (2001). "The Monster That Ate Hollywood." At http://www.pbs.org/wgbh/pages/frontline/shows/hollywood/etc/script.html (accessed March 24, 2009).

Gill, Mark. (2008). "Yes, the Sky Really Is Falling." *Indiewire*, June 22, at http://www.indiewire.com/article/first_person_film_departments_mark_gill_yes_the_sky_really_is_falling/ (accessed March 24, 2009).

Goldstein, Patrick. (2008). "The Sky Is Falling on Indie Film." *L.A. Times* blog, June 23, at http://latimesblogs.latimes.com/the_big_picture/2008/06/the-sky-is-fall.html (accessed March 24, 2009).

Holson, Laura M. (2006). "Disney Agrees to Acquire Pixar in a $7.4 Billion Deal." *New York Times*, January 25, at http://www.nytimes.com/2006/01/25/business/25disney.html (accessed March 24, 2009).

IBM. (1956). "650 RAMAC announcement." IBM press release, at http://www-03.ibm.com/ibm/history/exhibits/650/650_pr2.html (accessed March 24, 2009).

Jameson, Fredric. (1998). "Postmodernism and Consumer Society." In Fredric Jameson, *The Cultural Turn: Selected Writing on the Postmodern, 1983–1998* (pp. 1–20). London: Verso.

Karnitschnig, Matthew. (2006). "That's All Folks: After Years of Pushing Synergy, Time Warner Inc. Says Enough – Media Titan Is Selling Units, Downplaying Cooperation; Rivals Make Similar Moves – New Buzzword Is 'Adjacencies.'" *Wall Street Journal*, June 2, A1.

Kaufman, Anthony. (2002). "Ghost of the Machine: Mourning Has Risen for Independent Film." *Village Voice*, May 28.

King, Geoff. (2005). *American Independent Cinema*. London: I. B.Tauris.

Lahr, John. (2003). "Becoming the Hulk." *New Yorker*, June 30, 72–81.

LaPorte, Nicole. (2009). "DVD Sales Way Down; High Def Slow to Rescue." *The Wrap*, February 15, at http://www.thewrap.com/article/1404 (accessed March 24, 2009).

Macaulay, Scott. (2008). "Mark Gill in Paris, Indiefreude, and Third Way Distribution." *Filmmaker*, July 8, at http://www.filmmakermagazine.com/blog/2008/07/mark-gill-in-paris-indiefreude-and.php (accessed March 24, 2009).

Maltby, Richard. (1996). "'A Brief Romantic Interlude': Dick and Jane Go to $3^1/_2$ Seconds of the Classical Hollywood Cinema." In David Bordwell and Noël Carroll (eds), *Post-Theory: Reconstructing Film Studies* (pp. 434–459). Madison: University of Wisconsin Press.

The Onion. (2004). "Why No One Want Make *Hulk 2*?" *The Onion*, 40.28, July 14, at http://www.theonion.com/content/node/33980 (accessed March 24, 2009).

Onstad, Katrina. (2008). "Pixar Gambles on a Robot in Love." *New York Times*, June 22, at www.nytimes.com/2008/06/22/movies/22onst.html (accessed March 24, 2009).

Poland, David. (2008). "The Indie Thing." *Movie City News*, June 23, at http://www.mcn-blogs.com/thehotbutton/2008/06/the_indie_thing.html (accessed March 24, 2009).

Schamus, James. (2000). "IFP Rant." *Filmmaker*, Spring, at http://www.filmmakermagazine.com/spring2000/short_reports/ifp_rant.php (accessed March 24, 2009).

Schamus, James. (2003). "Sing to Us, Muse, of the Rage of the Hulk." *New York Times*, May 11, MT29.

Silberman, Steve. (2005). "Life after Darth." *Wired*, 13.5, May, 140ff.

Smith, Murray. (1998). "Theses on the Philosophy of Hollywood History." In Stephen Neale & Murray Smith (eds), *Contemporary Hollywood Cinema* (pp. 3–20). New York: Routledge.

Solomon, Charles. (2006). "Pixar Creative Chief to Seek to Restore the Disney Magic." *New York Times*, January 25, at http://www.nytimes.com/2006/01/25/business/media/25lasseter.html (accessed March 24, 2009).

Thompson, Anne. (2008). "LAFF: Mark Gill on Indie Crisis." *Variety* blog, June 21, at http://weblogs.variety.com/thompsononhollywood/2008/06/laff-mark-gill.html (accessed March 24, 2009).

Traister, Rebecca. (2003). "Crouching Budgets, Hidden Profits: James Schamus, Columbia Professor, Bets $137 Million on Ang Lee Epic." *New York Observer*, June 22, at http://www.observer.com/node/47728 (accessed March 24, 2009).

Weintraub, Steve. (2008). Interview with *WALL•E* director Andrew Stanton. *Collider*, November 17, at http://www.collider.com/entertainment/interviews/article.asp/aid/9881/tcid/1 (accessed March 24, 2009).

Whitwell, Tom. (2005). "Tiny Music Makers, Pt 4: The Mac Startup Sound." *MusicThing*, May 26, at http://musicthing.blogspot.com/2005/05/tiny-music-makers-pt-4-mac-startup.html (accessed March 24, 2009).

Wyatt, Justin. (1994). *High Concept: Movies and Marketing in Hollywood*. Austin: University of Texas Press.

Wyatt, Justin, & Vlesmas, Katherine. (1998). "The Drama of Recoupment: On the Mass Media Negotiation of *Titanic*." In Gaylyn Studlar & Kevin Sandler (eds), *Titanic: Anatomy of a Blockbuster* (pp. 29–45). New Brunswick, NJ: Rutgers University Press.

29

Writing American Film History

Robert Sklar
Late Professor Emeritus, New York University, United States

Robert Sklar surveys approaches to film history over the past century. He identifies the **teleological approach** of early historians like **Terry Ramsaye** and **Benjamin Hampton** who viewed changes in film technology, aesthetic forms, and business practices as inevitable steps on a path toward maturity. With movie-company records and film prints difficult, if not impossible, to obtain, these historians were denied resources essential to academic research. Insisting that a nation's psychological dispositions could be traced through its cinema, **Siegfried Kracauer**'s 1947 study of German cinema influenced American film historians by shifting focus from entrepreneurs and inventors to **cinema as "social agent."** It was not until the 1960s, however, that film history – energized by the **New Left** critique of earlier **"consensus paradigms"** – would gain recognition as a serious, independent discipline. Aided by the opening of studio archives and unprecedented accessibility of films on video (and more recently on DVD), a new generation of university-trained film historians in the 1970s and 1980s – crucially including **Robert Sklar**, himself – defined and elevated the status of the discipline. Devoted solely to **film historiography**, Sklar's essay informs all essays in the print volumes and online edition of this series.

Additional terms, names, and concepts: high and low culture, Paul Rotha, Lewis Jacobs, MoMA, "classical" Hollywood cinema

Writing the history of history writing. It could almost be a palindrome, but it's also a fundamental way that historians assess and advance their work. The technical term is historiography, which, as practiced predominantly among British and European philosophers, theorizes the principles and rhetoric of history writing. In the United States, however, with several prominent exceptions, historiography has largely taken the form of historians critiquing books and articles written by their peers and predecessors. American historiography emphasizes the biographical and genealogical, the careers of historians and the schools of thought that they may represent.

This kind of historiography involves judgment and appraisal, laying the ground for an inescapable aspect of history writing: It is always and inevitably being

American Film History: Selected Readings, 1960 to the Present, First Edition. Edited by Cynthia Lucia, Roy Grundmann, and Art Simon.

superseded. Why do historians rewrite the past that already has been written? The motive, it has been said, is to correct the errors of prior historians. If that appears too pinched a purpose, then the source that transforms history writing is time itself, bringing forth new contexts, and often, new data, that require rethinking how the past is understood.

Writing the history of writing American film history poses, it could be argued, almost unprecedented challenges in the realm of historiography. It's not that any one aspect of writing film history creates problems that the critique of history writing has not encountered before; it's the totality of circumstances, the range of relations among its several facets and in a comparative framework with other forms of history writing. Take the matter of professional training. For film history's first half century, its practitioners were publicists, businessmen, journalists, critics, or filmmakers. Not only were they not academic historians, they had little or no academic background at all. And even when film history began to be written within university settings and by academic norms, few writers were grounded in studies undertaken in existing history departments; their formation had more typically come from literature, philosophy, or the visual arts. Within nascent film studies programs, where a practice of writing film history began to be shaped, the effort coexisted with, or struggled against, such disparate frameworks as their own theoretical and critical imperatives, and the rhetorical conventions of film journalism and commercial movie exploitation. At best, there was only sporadic contact with historians outside the film field. Scholarly film history developed almost as a separate discipline.

Perhaps it was an unavoidable or even a necessary separation. Motion pictures were hybrid phenomena that had few if any models among prior subjects for history writing. They were a technology; a science; a business; an art. They were manufactured, distributed, and exhibited to the public, but they were also written, designed, directed, performed, photographed. They had relations with government at every level from municipality to nation. They created or shaped ancillary developments in the world of commerce, in entertainment, and in the wider culture, high and low. If one were to seek parallel histories for comparative purposes, say, of the automobile, or of photography, it seems clear that many elements are shared, but that neither example offers the full range of aspects that makes film history distinctive in its own right.

Moreover, the writing of film history, in its emergence, confronted impediments that brought, one might say, its status as adequate history into question. History writing gained professional status by developing commonly accepted procedures and standards: It required evidence, the document or trace, accurately identified and cited, location specified, so that others could verify the factual basis for a historian's assertion or interpretation. How could film history, for the first half of the twentieth century and even beyond, qualify as history by these norms? Its documents and traces were almost entirely proprietary, held within the vaults and files of film companies. Films were commercial products that quickly obsolesced; after their economic value was exhausted, they were variously discarded, recycled for their chemical properties, or, at best, stored away. Meanwhile, the archival troves of paper documents that historians mined in public archives had almost no counterpart for those who wished to write the history of motion pictures.

The difficulties of writing film history for much of the medium's existence may be impossible to grasp for historians born, so to speak, with the VCR/DVD remote close to hand. Up until, say, 1960, the vast majority of films made up to that time, particularly from the early decades of production, were lost, missing, out of circulation, unattainable. A few museums, historical societies, libraries, and archives were developing film collections based on donations, fortuitous purchases, and, in some cases, far-sighted acquisition policies. The Library of Congress, the nation's unsurpassed depository for copyright print materials, only belatedly was moving toward a comprehensive collection plan for copyrighted moving images. Private collectors, and companies that rented 16mm prints for nontheatrical viewing, were often the sources for films not otherwise available. Under almost all circumstances, historians lacked wide and easy access to films, as well as the capacity for in-depth study by stopping, slowing, rewinding, or reviewing images, that later technologies made possible. The concept of historian as detective could amply be illustrated by aspiring film historians of that era, hunting obscure venues, surveilling revival houses and college film societies, scrutinizing local television channel schedules, for screenings crucial to their research.

With the haphazard availability of films, and the nearly complete lack of archival print document collections, what constitutes the writing of film history, in its earliest attempts, appears to be something other than what an academic discipline would define as writing history. It encompasses legend, memoir, anecdotes, publicity, and promotion, in multiple combinations, as well as, in several instances, economic insight and critical acumen. Overall, its factual value may be more or less equivalent to accounts of King Arthur's court. But it still merits attention for all that.

Early Film Histories, 1926–1939

Nearly every work of history writing, no matter how strong an impression it makes in the era of its appearance, is destined to become outmoded, unread, an ignored object on a library shelf. This may be particularly true for the pre-professional era of writing American film history, a time of history writing without historians. Yet it would be a mistake to ignore these early histories. Their narratives and tropes may well have served to establish a groundwork, a base account that some later historians found need to challenge and correct, establishing a dialectic that kept their precepts in play, even as the original authors were forgotten. This essay is not meant as a guided tour of the landmarks of writing American film history, but it may be useful to visit some of those now more obscure sites, to see what issues and themes of those endeavors remain to be acknowledged, or contested.

The very first thing to remark is that disparaging one's predecessors, clearing the ground, appeared to be necessary even for a historian who, strictly speaking, had no predecessors. "Many, and perhaps most, of the facts presented in these pages will be found to be new or at variance with the generally accepted traditions and writings of the motion picture," states Terry Ramsaye in the opening paragraph of his 1926 tome, *A Million and One Nights: A History of the Motion Picture*, the initial history of the medium by an American author (v). Ramsaye had been a journalist and also worked in film production and exhibition before embarking on a series of articles for *Photoplay* magazine that he expanded for his nearly 900-page book.

What were the "generally accepted traditions" that Ramsaye sought to contest? Previous "annals," as he calls them – a term with the stamp of document or chronicle rather than researched and verified historical discourse – he asserts were "written to serve special interests within the industry or other partisan purposes" (v). He, however, claims he has no ax to grind. But of course he does. Although nowhere suggested by his subtitle or introductory matter, the work is overwhelmingly, one might say almost totally, devoted to the United States.

In that context, "special interests" and partisans appear to be those who uphold the significance of non-American contributions to the medium, particularly in invention and early technology. "There have been many efforts on the part of various patriotic writers of various nationalities to show other origins for the screen arts overseas and to attribute priorities to those who really followed upon and amplified the work of [Thomas] Edison and [W. K. L.] Dickson, rather than anticipating them," Ramsaye writes, a slightly convoluted way of describing what he elsewhere deems "propaganda" or "fictions" (147, 560, 561). No wonder Edison endorsed the book for its "unrelenting effort at exact fact" (n.p.).

Ramsaye's style is breezy, his narrative driven by personalities. Only rarely, as noted above, is his equanimity ruffled (deploring censorship, he sarcastically opines that "to satisfy the public and official mind of the day the naughty, naughty motion picture had to be spanked on the wrist") (479, 481). His dominant trope might be called popular-Darwinian; "evolve" is his most salient verb. "The motion picture industry," he writes in summary, "is controlled by entirely automatic forces of growth … This is not the especially conscious plan of any one man or group of men but the following of basic laws of structure … Everything that grows grows the same way. Nobody can do anything about it" (831). This is the prototype, perhaps the apogee, of the teleological view of the growth and transformation of motion pictures and their industry that later historians would take to task.

The title of Benjamin B. Hampton's 1931 *A History of the Movies* also geographically overreached; a 1970 paperbound edition more accurately went by the name *History of the American Film Industry: From Its Beginnings to 1931*. Hampton notes that Ramsaye's publication temporarily derailed his own. He almost completely cedes the first dozen or so years to his predecessor and launches his detailed account chronologically around 1908–1909. His is a drier, less colorful, yet more analytical story; he adopts the language of evolution, but understands its processes in terms of conflict and interaction, human behavior, and choice, rather than Ramsaye's notion of organic inevitability. He was there to experience contingency: An executive at the American Tobacco Company, around World War I, he took part in a failed venture to merge major movie companies (1931, 150ff). In perhaps a direct riposte to Ramsaye, he writes that the fall of the Motion Picture Patents and General Film companies, which occurred about the same time as his own unsuccessful efforts, "deserves to be remembered as a perfect illustration of the futility of laws that lack the support and sympathy of the populace" (125). (These efforts to monopolize film production and distribution appeared to deploy considerable power and influence, but their competitors embraced innovation and won over the public, as Hampton says, even before the federal government challenged them on antitrust grounds.)

Because of their dominance of world film markets after World War I, American movies featured prominently in the first European histories of the medium, which were more concerned than Ramsaye or Hampton with evaluating film styles and the work of filmmakers. Paul Rotha, in his early twenties, having lost a job working in a British film studio, set out to write an historical and theoretical overview, published in 1930 as *The Film Till Now: A Survey of Cinema.* It went through at least four more editions, into the 1960s, with substantial additional contributions from Richard Griffith, a film curator at the Museum of Modern Art, New York. Rotha himself went on to become a prominent nonfiction filmmaker and documentary theorist. In the 1930 first publication, Rotha's disdain for recent developments in the American film industry was not constrained. The emergence of a star system in the 1920s he found particularly abhorrent, as a debasement of the artistic potential exhibited during the 1910s, a "golden era," by filmmakers such as D. W. Griffith, Thomas Ince, and Mack Sennett (Rotha 1963, 129). "The film business of Hollywood was to become one big bluff," he writes.

> Obviously, those who bluffed hardest (and no nation in the world is so accomplished in the art of bluffing as the American) made the most money … The cinema lost a public who loved it for itself and what it meant to them … In the place of the old filmgoer there arose a new type of audience, a vacant-minded, empty-headed public, who flocked to sensations, who thrilled to sexual vulgarity, and who would go anywhere and pay anything to see indecent situations riskily handled on the screen. (Rotha 1963, 130)

For Rotha, almost uniquely, the American film industry's evolution invoked nostalgia for a past recalled (or imagined) as better.

Museum of Modern Art film curators were also instrumental in bringing to the United States a 1935 French work, *Histoire du cinéma*, translated and edited by MoMA's Iris Barry in 1938 as *The History of Motion Pictures*, with a brief foreword by John E. Abbott, director of the museum's recently founded Film Library. Its authors were Maurice Bardèche and Robert Brasillach, both of whom, like Rotha, were also in their twenties, and already prominent as writers advocating fascism in France. Brasillach's enthusiastic collaboration with the Nazi occupiers of France during World War II, which involved his support for the deportation of French Jews, ranked him as one of the most notorious fascist propagandists of the era. After the war he was put on trial, amid controversy over whether writers should be held accountable not for actions, but for ideas. Convicted, and refused clemency, he was executed by a firing squad.

Britain's Rotha became known in his later filmmaking career for a socialist perspective; although not explicitly acknowledged, perhaps it accounts for his scorn toward Hollywood's businessmen in *The Film Till Now.* What signs of fascist sympathy appear in the French film history? Utilizing the translated version available to US readers, and focusing on their viewpoint on American cinema, little is to be discerned (Barry points out in footnotes that their treatment of American subject matter is considerably drawn from Hampton's book). The authors value Ince over Griffith; they unequivocally admire Chaplin (while identifying his mother as Jewish) and give him extensive coverage for every period of his career into the 1930s; after World War I, Cecil B. DeMille is credited with introducing sex appeal and high society and launching "Purilia, the city of the movies" (1938, 204); they find most subsequent American films dull, except when enlivened by the work of foreigners like Erich von Stroheim.

Anti-Semitism, often but not always masked, frequently played a role when writers expressed their contempt for motion picture producers, many of whom, overseas as well as in the United States, were Jewish. Bardèche and Brasillach's anti-Semitism, a component of their fascist views, was, in their final chapter, bluntly stated. "Itinerant carpet vendors, strange men from Poland and Rumania, adventurers of every sort who had already gained partial control of the cinema," they write, "now made matters worse by methods which would have endangered the future of any industry and which orientated the whole of production, but particularly that of France, towards a permanent mediocrity." If film is a gradually evolving art form, they conclude, "it has so far been primarily an industry, and often the basest of them all" (374). MoMA's Abbott notes in his foreword that the translation was not abridged, so as to "retain the attitudes and opinions" of the authors, which do not "necessarily coincide" with those of the Film Library (xii).

Left, right, or neither; American, British, or French; celebratory or condemnatory: The early historians of the medium seemed mesmerized by the sheer scale of American cinema's "evolution," from Edison's workshop to worldwide suzerainty in little more than a generation. Their attention was drawn to entrepreneurship, the personalities and tactics of the businessmen who ran the movie companies. Even the filmmakers they tended to valorize – Griffith, Ince, Chaplin – functioned as entrepreneurs, independent studio heads as well as film artists. Wide swaths of what might have constituted a historical perspective on motion pictures were barely touched upon. Relations with political authority came up only in brief allusions to censorship. Audiences and spectatorship were skimpily treated, with condescending sketches laden with attitudes of social class superiority. As for the industrial structure that the businessmen built, how it operated in practice was scarcely explained, and least of all the products of their endeavors, the films themselves, received, with few exceptions, cursory coverage.

These were lacunae that Lewis Jacobs sought to overcome in his 1939 work *The Rise of the American Film: A Critical History*. Jacobs's formation was as a young cineaste in the Great Depression years. In 1930, he was a founder of a film journal, *Experimental Cinema*; he wrote articles about the Soviet filmmakers Sergei Eisenstein and Aleksandr Dovzhenko and published a pamphlet on screenwriting; he made short films in the city symphony vein, including *City Block* (1933). Later in his career he worked in Hollywood and became a pioneering teacher of university film courses. What prompted him to undertake a 500-page survey of American film history is not recounted in his book, but his endeavor marked a shift toward a more professional methodology.

The Museum of Modern Art Film Library, founded in 1935, became a site for him to study films, rather than having to recall them from memory or draw on others' descriptions of unavailable titles. An extensive bibliography of writings on film became available to him while still in preparation by the New York City Writers' Project, a subdivision of the Writers' Program of the federal Works Progress Administration, the massive government agency designed to give work to the unemployed during the Great Depression. How the Project's instigator and editor, Harold Leonard, persuaded New Deal bureaucrats that a comprehensive collation of writings on motion pictures deserved to be funded has not been made clear. But MoMA's Film Library stepped forward in 1941 to cosponsor a partial publication of the Project's compilations, *The Film Index: A Bibliography, Vol. 1: The Film as Art*. Nothing remotely comparable would appear in English until the 1960s, when it was also reprinted. Iris Barry, in her own way an entrepreneur, wrote both a foreword to *The Film Index* and a preface to Jacobs's history. She praises Jacobs's effort as a work of "immense" research and scholarship, "dispelling many strange beliefs and false traditions concerning both influences and events" (1968, xxiii).

In fact, Jacobs gives little attention to correcting the errors of his predecessors. He adopts their basic chronological template of growth and transformation – the "rise" of his title is a different way of saying "evolution" – and strives to expand its coverage, with, for example, discussion of a much wider range of film directors and references to individual films. But his major contribution is to develop a concept of motion pictures as a "social agency." Early movies, he writes, "more vividly than any other single agency … revealed the social topography of America to the immigrant, to the poor, and to the country folk" (1968, 12). At different historical conjunctures he assesses "the great potency of motion pictures as a social force" (155). Throughout he is attentive to "the moving picture" as "a subtle and complex social instrument so vast in range and powerful in effect that it has become one of the most influential agencies of modern times," both responding to the "time spirit" and "instill[ing] ideas and attitudes" (538–539). He amply identifies changes in the representation of social life and values in motion picture content over the decades; however, it's not his purpose to theorize about the mechanism or consequences of their effects.

From Kracauer to the 1960s

That lack was answered after World War II with a theory of cinema's "social agency" whose historical implications were profound, urgent, and controversial – and though its focus was on the films of a different nation, its relevance for writing American film history was explicitly stated. Siegfried Kracauer's *From Caligari to Hitler: A Psychological History of the German Film*, published in 1947, also bore the indispensable imprimatur of MoMA's Film Library. In his preface, Kracauer, a German Jewish émigré, formerly a journalist and cultural critic in his native country, credits Iris Barry with suggesting the topic of study (let us proclaim Barry as film culture's Clio, muse of historians). But it's unlikely that Barry foresaw the audacious scope of Kracauer's historical hypothesis.

Kracauer's aim, in few words, was to show that the Nazis' rise in Germany could be traced retrospectively by analyzing the nation's films made between 1918 and 1933, the year that Hitler seized power. Viewing those films revealed the "deep psychological dispositions" of the German people that made fascism possible. And it wasn't that Germany was unique in this regard; the method, he asserts, holds true in general. "The technique, the story content, and the evolution of the films of a nation," Kracauer writes in his introduction, "are fully understandable only in relation to the actual psychological pattern of this nation." This is the case for two reasons: First, films are collective endeavors, which suppress "individual peculiarities in favor of traits common to many people"; second, they are made for the multitude, and thus their "popular screen motifs" can be "supposed to satisfy existing mass desires" (1947, 5).

Psychological approaches to cinema were in vogue during the World War II years and after. A young writer, Barbara Deming, later a renowned feminist and peace activist, shared ideas with Kracauer while both utilized MoMA's Film Library; she was working on a Library of Congress-sponsored project to analyze contemporary American films, but publication of her book, *Running Away from Myself: A Dream Portrait of America Drawn from the Films of the Forties*, was delayed until 1969, at which point it might also have been considered a psychological history. Additional wartime and postwar studies applying the methods of psychoanalysis and cultural anthropology to the era's American films could also be cited. Yet the impulse for such work rapidly faded. Kracauer's thesis, for one thing, was based on the medium's mass appeal, but within a few years after the war, it was apparent that the popularity of movies was in decline, superseded by the growing ubiquity of television in the home. If searching media content for the "deep psychological dispositions" of the American people could be a viable endeavor, then that effort would have to shift toward study of a new medium.

The 1950s was an in-between time for writing American film history, as it might be said to have been for American cinema itself. With rapidly falling attendance at motion picture theaters, movies seemed to be losing status as "one of the most influential agencies of modern times," but they were only beginning – and mostly overseas, in France and Britain – to be objects of critical study as works of art. Academics in the social sciences, and writers on cultural trends, became overwhelmingly concerned with the influence and effects – mainly deleterious, most of them argued – of mass media broadly conceived, of which movies were simply one aspect, and not a major one, among best-selling books, comics, popular magazines, and the like, satellites to the new Goliath, TV.

From a different perspective, a small number of university film studies teachers began gathering in the late 1950s – under the auspices once again of MoMA's Film Library – and in 1959 founded a scholarly organization, the Society of Cinematologists, a name intended to fend off dilettantes and foreground the scientific rigor of their fledging discipline. Original officers included Robert Gessner of New York University, author in 1968 of *The Moving Image: A Guide to Cinematic Literacy*, and Hugh Gray of University of California, Los Angeles, notable as translator of several volumes of essays by French critic André Bazin. Fewer than three dozen members were involved in the early years. Although nearly all had been trained in other academic fields, in the prior absence of cinema studies graduate programs, or had work experience in allied arts, some in the group aimed at establishing, in the words of one, "the singularity of film, its special nature as an art form" (Ellis 2003, 111). A medium-specific film theory might well be an attainable goal; but how could film history be written without reference to cinema's relations with other arts and its economic, social, and cultural contexts? As film studies expanded and membership grew, the organization widened its purview and changed its name, first to Society for Cinema Studies, then to Society for Cinema and Media Studies.

During the 1960s, the impulses toward writing American film history sprang up well outside the boundaries established by the new scholarly society. General United States history writing in the postwar era had come to be dominated by a "consensus" paradigm, valorizing a narrative of shared "liberal" values, as compared to Europe's destructive history, that enabled the nation to avoid divisive struggles between social classes and competing ideologies. (The Civil War of 1861–1865 posed a conundrum for this viewpoint.) The growing militancy of the Civil Rights Movement during the course of the 1960s decade led historians to challenge the idea of past social harmony, however, and the marches and demonstrations opposing the Vietnam War destroyed any notion of general accord. Class and race were the issues that were first reenergized and debated, and soon after, in the wake of second-wave feminism, came gender.

If social class antagonism had been a relatively neglected subject during the postwar "consensus" era in American historiography, historians who were involved in, or identified with, the political conflicts of the 1960s brought it back to center stage. Social and labor histories became prime topics for historians of the "New Left" persuasion, and at the same time concepts of culture that related not only to high art but also to everyday life animated a new rubric, cultural history. Under these different categories, histories of African-American life and of race relations became part of the mainstream of United States historiography, followed by women's history as a new and significant subfield in the larger discipline.

These themes animated a new wave of writing about American film history that reached publication in the 1970s. As well as being impelled by pressing social concerns, writers of film history were buoyed by an unexpected surge in the cultural valence of movies themselves. Although the Hollywood industry was much reduced, indeed experiencing severe financial distress, cinema's aura proved to be enduring. If television represented the quotidian values of common life, films still held powers of "social agency" after all, taking on symbolic status as expressions of larger conflict and change. This persisting significance, in a time of social turmoil, lent urgency to writing film history, as a source of relevant background knowledge.

Journalists and critics were the first to weigh in, where academic historians, by and large wary of how the arts fit into their traditional social, economic, and political perspectives, initially felt themselves unsure. The earliest works in this historical cycle featured colorful titles and a concern with demeaning "images" of women and African-Americans over the course of US film history. On gender, there was Marjorie Rosen's 1973 *Popcorn Venus: Women, Movies and the American Dream* and Molly Haskell's 1974 *From Reverence to Rape: The Treatment of Women in the Movies*, and on race, Donald Bogle's 1973 *Toms, Coons, Mulattoes, Mammies, and Bucks: An Interpretative History of Blacks in American Films*. And as African-American historiography was advancing as a subject in university history departments, several historians applied that scholarly foundation to the subject of movies: Daniel J. Leab, in his 1975 *From Sambo to Superspade: The Black Experience in Motion Pictures* and Thomas Cripps, in the 1977 *Slow Fade to Black: The Negro in American Film, 1900–1942*.

Here it's perhaps relevant to interject a personal account from those years. As a scholar trained in interdisciplinary American studies, employed by a history department, my studies on American culture of the 1920s led to a realization that movies played a central role in the development of US society and culture in the twentieth century, and that, professionally speaking, I knew next to nothing about this aspect of their history. I set out to read the existing writings on the medium, including the prewar historics and the postwar psychological studies discussed earlier. My concerns were formulated in part in the framework of the new historiography of the 1960s, particularly its concern with social class conflict. The available documents and traces amply made clear how centrally class issues were involved with the medium – in the movies' rise in popularity during the nickelodeon era, in battles over censorship of film content, in attitudes toward the Jewish immigrants who became studio heads, in debates over how movies were influencing, for good or ill, American ideologies. These were among the themes that animated my research and writing of *Movie-Made America: A Cultural History of American Movies*, published in 1975. From similar impulses, but with a different perspective, Garth Jowett's 1976 *Film: The Democratic Art* brought the methods of a social historian to an account of American motion picture history.

The 1970s: Formative Years of Academic Film History

The mid-1970s marked a conjuncture that fundamentally transformed the writing of American film history. Many factors drove the change, and not all were propitious. Let's begin with those that were.

Noted earlier was the scarcity of records and traces for motion picture history that historians expect to utilize for breadth and depth in research and accuracy of reference and citation. By the 1970s, however, it was apparent that materials previously inaccessible or considered lost were becoming available. The most dramatic new cache was the Library of Congress Paper Print Collection, comprising some 3,000 films made from the 1890s through 1912, only a very small number of which had been available for viewing since their original release. At a time before the US Congress extended copyright law to cover motion pictures, film producers had sought to protect their products from copying and piracy by printing them on long rolls of photographic paper and submitting the rolls for copyright as photographs. These had remained in storage at the Library of Congress until around 1960, when, with federal funding, a project began to rephotograph the paper prints onto motion picture film and prepare new 16mm prints for archival and research purposes. The restored films – cataloged in Kemp R. Niver's 1967 *Motion Pictures from the Library of Congress Paper Print Collection 1894–1912* – which included extensive early titles by Edwin S. Porter and D. W. Griffith, provided a previously unimagined foundation for what was to become a far-reaching revisionary approach to early cinema.

Additionally, libraries, university archives, and museums acquired paper records and film materials from motion picture studios, several of which also began to provide access for researchers to holdings that they retained. The American Film Institute, founded in 1968 under the auspices of the National Endowment for the Arts, inaugurated a project to catalog the entire corpus of fiction feature films produced in the United States. The myths and legends of American cinema history would not go away, but they would no longer constitute the state of knowledge of movies' past. American film history could now be written with an accuracy and comprehensiveness common to the standards of any other historical subject.

Among the potential beneficiaries of these freshly available resources was a cohort of advanced graduate students studying to become film scholars in recently founded, or expanded, university cinema studies programs. As part of the paradox of a growing cultural and historical interest in cinema, at a time when movie companies were coping with their most severe financial losses since the Great Depression, academic film studies courses were flourishing. University colleagues in other departments did not uniformly regard them with enthusiasm. Where, it was asked, would the rigor come from that other disciplines required: the extensive reading lists, the theoretical and methodological sophistication, the scholarly standards? Foundations were built as a new wave of film specialists attained doctoral degrees and began to redefine the field. For a brief period in the mid-1970s three branches of film writing coexisted: journalists, critics, and others with nonacademic backgrounds; scholars from other disciplines, such as literature, philosophy, and art history, and a few cultural and social historians; and the rising generation of academics trained almost entirely in film studies itself. As with other growing academic disciplines, at least in scholarly terms, the logic of development lay with the latter.

How would the writing of American film history fare under these new circumstances? There was a heady feeling that a new, "revisionist" era of writing film history had dawned. In particular the decline in motion picture attendance and the film industry's difficulties put an end to the metaphors of upward evolution that undergirded the histories of Ramsaye, Hampton, and Jacobs; these were criticized as a form of teleological thinking, as if history were a foreordained process leading to the medium's maturation in the Hollywood production system and style. This stance was especially generative in recasting early cinema, prior to 1915, not as a rudimentary "primitive" version of what was later to be achieved, but as operating on distinct and different visual and narrative principles to be valued in their own right.

Yet in the emerging discipline of cinema studies, film history's status was initially much more tenuous than might have been anticipated. Historical research often involves large bodies of data and painstaking searches through voluminous archives, so its results in publication were slow in coming. As a new scholarly field, frequently competing with traditional departments for students and institutional support, film studies needed to build a more immediately visible and differentiated intellectual foundation than history writing could provide. It found the grounding it required in European, predominantly French, philosophical, linguistic, and social theories of the era.

What came to be called, retrospectively, "Seventies Theory" fostered scholarly impulses quite unlike those that emanated alongside the activism and protests of the 1960s. Indeed one could say that they sprang from the perceived failures of 1960s struggles, in particular of the May 1968 student and worker rebellion in France. At the risk of simplifying the considerable breadth and diversity of the theoretical landscape, one could say that cinema scholars predominantly took from it a view that film's "social agency" was authoritarian and repressive – that it represented state power and "bourgeois" ideology, forming and controlling spectators as subjects. Feminist film theory – perhaps the cinema studies scholarship most influential in other disciplines, as exemplified by Laura Mulvey's renowned 1975 essay, "Visual Pleasure and Narrative Cinema" – drew on contemporary French psychoanalytic viewpoints to emphasize themes of patriarchal domination of women through representation and the male gaze.

In addition, an attack, in the French context, on traditional academic history writing as excessively positivist – uncritical of its sources and methodology, insufficiently aware of the subjectivity of its rhetoric and ideological biases – was translated by some theoretically inclined practitioners of US cinema studies into doubts about the efficacy of film history. History dealt with time and change; in one influential theoretical formulation, the sway of ideology was timeless and unchanging (until, in revolution, it could be overthrown). History writing, from this perspective, was thus a subset of ideological hegemony, not a practice that itself could identify and foster sites of transformation. At best, it was held, historians could provide empirical data for theorists to interpret.

Debates and recriminations over conflicting viewpoints continued into the next decade, but perhaps inevitably they gave way to convergences and reconciliations. As the discipline strengthened, its growing pains eased, and over time, as historians understood, ideas and attitudes would alter. In the long view, the challenges film historians faced in the field's early days proved salutary. Historians of cinema by and large steered away from old-fashioned positivism; they grounded themselves in a rich vein of new theories about history writing and explored theoretical approaches beyond the confines of the dominant 1970s paradigms. One such, for example, was "reception theory," which focused on the perceptions and experiences of spectators and audiences. Historical reception studies led to a further redefinition of the concept of "social agency," in which agency – in the sense of making meaning – was diffused among producers, spectators, reviewers, and others involved with film as a communicating medium.

Major Film History Projects

The lengthy process of producing a corpus of new academic writing on American film history, begun with dissertations and other projects in the 1970s, began to reach fruition over a decade later. The most expansive undertaking was a 10-volume *History of the American Cinema*, under the general editorship of Charles Harpole. It launched in 1990 with the simultaneous publication of three volumes on the era of silent film: *The Emergence of Cinema: The American Screen to 1907*, by Charles Musser; *The Transformation of Cinema, 1907–1915*, by Eileen Bowser; and *An Evening's Entertainment: The Age of the Silent Feature Picture, 1915–1928*, by Richard Koszarski. Subsequent volumes appeared in nonchronological order until the series was completed in 2003. After the fourth, *The Talkies: American Cinema's Transition to Sound, 1926–1931*, by Donald Crafton, the six later titles each represented a single decade, from the 1930s through the 1980s, relinquishing the effort to signify important transformations through a more precise form of periodization, that was evident in the earlier volumes (is 1930–1939, for example, as effective a period-unit as one that carries the Great Depression era through to 1941, which marked a decisive chronological break point with the US entry into World War II?).

Another significant change as the series progressed involved multiple authorship. A single historian wrote each of the first four volumes. In later works additional contributors supplemented the primary authors, a sign of increased compartmentalization in film history and a decision to defer certain topics to specialists. From the 1930s volume on, every work in the series contained, at the least, separate chapters by experts on documentary and avant-garde films. Volume 6, *Boom and Bust: The American Cinema in the 1940s*, has seven chapters by the principal author, Thomas Schatz, and additional chapters contributed by seven other writers. One may perhaps regard this 50–50 division as an example of the fragmentation of historical writing and the diminution of a unitary overview provided by a single author.

One of the most influential works of the post-1970s era of writing American film history has multiple authors but definitely a unitary point of view. *The Classical Hollywood Cinema: Film Style and Mode of Production to 1960*, by David Bordwell, Janet Staiger, and Kristin Thompson, published in 1985, was not the first work to apply the concept of classicism to Hollywood cinema – André Bazin had previously done so in the 1950s – but it made the term ubiquitous in cinema studies scholarship. In delineating a "classical style" that the authors described as "standardized" and "stringently uniform," they emphasized not only aesthetic norms that shaped filmmaking practices but also "a specific economic mode of film production and consumption" (1985, 6).

The breadth and ambition of *The Classical Hollywood Cinema* made it an enduring touchstone of American film historiography. Like all historical writings, however, it entered into a flow of debate and critique, the means by which the practice of history renews itself. Was the classical model too static or narrowly conceived in its focus on the Hollywood industry to the overall exclusion of external cultural, social, and political relationships and conflicts that affected filmmakers? Could competing terms or rubrics equally or more effectively give a name to the phenomena of American film history represented by the commercial Hollywood industry?

One possibility historians suggested was to apply to American film the not uncontested category of "national cinema" and explore the implications of that idea for film style and content, in terms of the industry's relationship to national values and state policies; two studies by Richard Abel (1999, 2006), for example, offer detailed research on topics such as patriotism and the role of social communication in early cinema, returning to themes raised earlier in works by Lewis Jacobs and Garth Jowett, among others. Perhaps conversely, other historians have regarded Hollywood from its early years as an avatar of "global cinema," given its worldwide domination following World War I and its capacity continually to draw in filmmaking talent from other countries.

Another productive thesis, offered by Miriam Hansen (1999), proposed that American cinema could be seen as an exemplar of "vernacular modernism," a site of mingled artistic innovation and popular cultural expression. This is one approach that has continued to stimulate historical research on ethnic, racial, gender, and cultural identities in American film, building on and expanding beyond the 1970s studies on the "images" of women and African-Americans to encompass many other groups. In 1981 Vito Russo's *The Celluloid Closet: Homosexuality in the Movies* inaugurated the historical study of gay and lesbian representation that has broadened into a wide-ranging investigation on subjects such as sexuality and performance in American movies.

New Technologies, Awaiting New Paradigms

The growth of cinema studies brought new scholarly standards and a considerable expansion of knowledge to the writing of American film history, but it did not alter the circumstance of a thriving film history discourse in many other cultural domains outside universities. For most of the twentieth century the pursuit of viewing past films had been a coterie experience among a devoted band of cinephiles. The advent of videocassette recorders (VCRs) in the 1980s considerably widened the audience for older films, as stores sprang up in nearly every neighborhood to rent or sell movies on cassette for viewing at home. A controversy over colorizing original black-and-white films for video and television release was one of the factors that led to Congressional establishment of a National Film Registry to which the Librarian of Congress was authorized to select 25 titles every year, while advocating for film preservation and promoting greater knowledge of the diversity of American filmmaking beyond the Hollywood commercial mainstream. As cable delivery of television expanded, new channels such as American Movie Classics (AMC) – in its original incarnation – and Turner Classic Movies (TCM) programmed past films without commercial interruptions, cuts, or the previous practice of altering widescreen titles for the narrower television screen; they also publicized efforts to archive and restore older films.

At the beginning of a new century the development of digital videodiscs (DVDs), with their enormous expanded data capacity beyond that of the videocassette, created extraordinary new opportunities for public dissemination of film history materials. The movie studios and other companies that produced DVDs of older films often included "extras" on the disc to enhance consumer interest; these could include outtakes and deleted scenes, screen tests, trailers, publicity stills, documents, even multiple versions of films. Additionally, voiceover commentaries were added as options for viewers, sometimes from directors and other personnel involved in making a film, but also from critics and academic scholars – perhaps the principal way the latter disseminated their knowledge outside the classroom and the university press monograph. The internet further enlarged access to films and ancillary matter: Anyone interested in film history had unprecedented, indeed previously unimaginable, fingertip access both to films and to historical information.

Amid these vast technological changes, different approaches to the writing of American film history, largely although not exclusively an academic enterprise, coexisted in a relatively conflict-free period. "Normal" history reigned, in the sense that Thomas Kuhn defined "normal" science in his study, *The Structure of Scientific Revolutions*: historians functioning in broad agreement on principles and paradigms and productively expanding and filling in a varied narrative of film history in the United States. But historians are likely to be aware that nothing stands still or stays the same over time. In Kuhn's model, challenges eventually arise that lead to ruptures in "normal" ways of thinking and eventually generate new paradigms for scholarship. New paradigms will emerge for writing American film history, of that we can be certain, and it will be both stimulating and unsettling to encounter them.

References

Abel, Richard. (1999). *The Red Rooster Scare: Making Cinema American, 1900–1910*. Berkeley: University of California Press.

Abel, Richard. (2006). *Americanizing the Movies and "Movie-Mad" Audiences, 1910–1914*. Berkeley: University of California Press.

Bardèche, Maurice, & Brasillach, Robert. (1938). *The History of Motion Pictures*, trans. and ed. Iris Barry. New York: W. W. Norton. (Originally published as *Histoire du cinéma*, 1935.)

Bazin, André. (1967, 1971). *What Is Cinema?*, 2 vols, trans. Hugh Gray. Berkeley: University of California Press. (Originally published as *Qu'est-ce que le cinéma?*, 1958–1962.)

Bogle, Donald. (1973). *Toms, Coons, Mulattoes, Mammies, and Bucks: An Interpretative History of Blacks in American Films*. New York: Viking.

Bordwell, David, Staiger, Janet, & Thompson, Kristin. (1985). *The Classical Hollywood Cinema: Film Style and Mode of Production to 1960*. New York: Columbia University Press.

Bowser, Eileen. (1990). *The Transformation of Cinema, 1907–1915*. Vol. 2 of *History of the American Cinema*, ed. Charles Harpole. New York: Scribner's.

Crafton, Donald. (1997). *The Talkies: American Cinema's Transition to Sound, 1926–1931*. Vol. 4 of *History of the American Cinema*, ed. Charles Harpole. New York: Scribner's.

Cripps, Thomas. (1977). *Slow Fade to Black: The Negro in American Film, 1900–1942*. New York: Oxford University Press.

Deming, Barbara. (1969). *Running Away from Myself: A Dream Portrait of America Drawn from the Films of the Forties*. New York: Grossman.

Ellis, Jack C. (2003). "The Society for Cinema Studies: A Personal Recollection of the Early Days." *Cinema Journal*, 43.1, 105–112.

Gessner, Robert. (1968). *The Moving Image: A Guide to Cinematic Literacy*. New York: Dutton.

Hampton, Benjamin B. (1931). *A History of the Movies*. New York: Covici, Friede.

Hansen, Miriam. (1999). "The Mass Production of the Senses: Classical Cinema as Vernacular Modernism." *Modernism/Modernity*, 6.2, 59–77.

Haskell, Molly. (1974). *From Reverence to Rape: The Treatment of Women in the Movies*. New York: Holt, Rinehart & Winston.

Jacobs, Lewis. (1968). *The Rise of the American Film: A Critical History*. New York: Teachers College Press. (Originally published 1939.)

Jowett, Garth. (1976). *Film: The Democratic Art*. Boston: Little, Brown.

Koszarski, Richard. (1990). *An Evening's Entertainment: The Age of the Silent Feature Picture, 1915–1928*. Vol. 3 of *History of the American Cinema*, ed. Charles Harpole. New York: Scribner's.

Kracauer, Siegfried. (1947). *From Caligari to Hitler: A Psychological History of the German Film*. Princeton: Princeton University Press.

Kuhn, Thomas S. (1962). *The Structure of Scientific Revolutions*. Chicago: University of Chicago Press.

Leab, Daniel J. (1975). *From Sambo to Superspade: The Black Experience in Motion Pictures*. Boston: Houghton Mifflin.

Leonard, Harold (ed.). (1941). *The Film Index: A Bibliography. Vol. 1: The Film as Art*. New York: Museum of Modern Art and H. W. Wilson.

Mulvey, Laura. (1989). "Visual Pleasure and Narrative Cinema." In Laura Mulvey, *Visual and Other Pleasures* (pp. 14–26). Bloomington: Indiana University Press. (Originally published in *Screen*, Autumn 1975.)

Musser, Charles. (1990). *The Emergence of Cinema: The American Screen to 1907*. Vol. 1 of *History of the American Cinema*, ed. Charles Harpole. New York: Scribner's.

Niver, Kemp R. (1967). *Motion Pictures from the Library of Congress Paper Print Collection 1894–1912*. Berkeley: University of California Press.

Ramsaye, Terry. (1926). *A Million and One Nights: A History of the Motion Picture*. New York: Simon & Schuster.

Rosen, Marjorie. (1973). *Popcorn Venus: Women, Movies and the American Dream*. New York: Coward, McCann & Geoghegan.

Rotha, Paul. (1963). *The Film Till Now: A Survey of World Cinema*. New edn, revised and enlarged. London: Vision. (Originally published as *The Film Till Now: A Survey of Cinema*, 1930.)

Russo, Vito. (1981). *The Celluloid Closet: Homosexuality in the Movies*. New York: Harper & Row.

Schatz, Thomas. (1997). *Boom and Bust: The American Cinema in the 1940s*. Vol. 6 of *History of the American Cinema*, ed. Charles Harpole. New York: Scribner's.

Sklar, Robert. (1975). *Movie-Made America: A Cultural History of American Movies*. Revised and updated 1994. New York: Random House.

Index

Entries for film titles are in italics, followed by the date of release in brackets – e.g. *Across 110th Street* (1972). Page references for illustrations are also in italics.

American Film History: Selected Readings, 1960 to the Present, First Edition. Edited by Cynthia Lucia, Roy Grundmann, and Art Simon.